T0149707

SUSPICIONS OF THOUGHT

RICHARD JOHN KOSCIEJEW

authorHOUSE®

AuthorHouse™
1663 Liberty Drive
Bloomington, IN 47403
www.authorhouse.com
Phone: 1 (800) 839-8640

Published by AuthorHouse 06/29/2018

ISBN: 978-1-5462-4650-3 (sc)
ISBN: 978-1-5462-4649-7 (e)

Print information available on the last page.

This book is printed on acid-free paper.

SUSPICIONS OF THOUGHT

RICHARD JOHN KOSCIEJEW

In one of the several contributing disciplines of cognitive science, philosophy offers two sorts of contributions. On the one hand, philosophy of science provides a meta theoretical perspective on the endeavours of any scientific enterprise, analysing such things as the goals of scientific investigation and the strategies employed in reaching those goals. Philosophy of science thus offers a perspective from which we can examine and potentially evaluate the endeavours of cognitive science. On the other hand, philosophy of mind offers substantive theses about the nature. Although these theses typically have resulted from empirical investigation, they often have subsequently figured in actual empirical investigations in cognitive science, or its predecessors. Because the two roles' philosophy plays in cognitive science are quite different, they are introduced as an overview for cognitive science.

The strategy for this overview is to present a variety of views from philosophy of science that figured on discussions about cognitive science. Some of these views are no longer widely accepted by philosophers of science. Nonetheless, they have been and, in some cases, remain influential outside of philosophy. Moreover, some older views have provided the starting point for current philosophical thinking that is done against a backdrop of previous endeavours, with a recognition of both their successes and failures.

SUSPICIONS OF THOUGHT

RICHARD JOHN KOSCIEJEW

The history of science reveals that scientific knowledge and method did not emerge as full-blown from the minds of the ancient Greek any more than language and culture emerged fully formed in the minds of 'Homo sapient'. ' Scientific knowledge is an extension of ordinary language into greater levels of abstraction and precision through reliance upon geometric and numerical relationships. We speculate that the seeds of the scientific imagination were planted in ancient Greece, as opposed to Chinese or Babylonian culture, partly because the social, political and an economic climate in Greece was more open to the pursuit of knowledge with marginal cultural utility. Another important factor was that the special character of Homeric religion allowed the Greeks to invent a conceptual framework that would prove useful in future scientific investigation. But it was only after this inheritance from Greek philosophy was wedded to some essential features of Judeo-Christian beliefs about the origin of the cosmos that the paradigm for classical physics emerged.

The philosophical debate that had led to conclusions useful to the architects of classical physics can be briefly summarized, such when Thales fellow Milesian Anaximander claimed that the first substance, although indeterminate, manifested itself in a conflict of oppositions between hot and cold, moist and dry. The idea of nature as a self-regulating balance of forces was subsequently elaborated upon by Heraclitus, only after 480 Bc. BC, who was to assert that the fundamental substance is striving between opposites, which is itself the unity of the whole, it is said, that Heraclitus, 'that tensions in between opposites keep the whole from simply 'passing away.'

Parmenides of Elea (B.c. 515 BC) argued in turn that the unifying substance is unique and static being. This led to a conclusion about the relationship between ordinary language and external reality that was later incorporated into the view of the relationship between mathematical language and physical reality. Since thinking or naming involves the presence of something, said Parmenides, thought and language must be dependent upon the existence of objects outside the human intellect. Presuming a one-to-one correspondence between word and idea and actual existing things, Parmenides concluded that our ability to think or speak of a thing at various times implies that it exists at all times. Hence the indivisible One does not change, and all perceived change is an illusion.

These assumptions emerged in roughly the form in which they would be used by the creators of classical physics in the thought of the atomists. Leucippus : ʃl. 450-420 BC and Democritus (460-c. 370 BC). They reconciled the two dominant and seemingly antithetical concepts of the fundamental character of being-Becoming (Heraclitus) and unchanging Being (Parmenides)-in a remarkable simple and direct way. Being, they said, is present in the invariable substance of the atoms that, through blending and separation, make up the thing of changing or becoming worlds.

The last remaining feature of what would become the paradigm for the first scientific revolution in the seventeenth century is attributed to Pythagoras (Bc. 570 Bc). Like Parmenides, Pythagoras also held that the inherently perceived world took the form of an illusionary structure among foundations that, if we were to inferior resulting to bring forth the constituting idea, it would reflectively result in the reality of fact, started from the conscious doctrine, as having that things have reality, also, approximately 2000 years away from Pythagoras, that quantum mechanics stipulated that if you look at something, it changes, simply because you looked at it. Pythagoras, however, had a different conception of the character of the idea that showed this correspondence. The truth about the fundamental character of the unified and unifying substance, which could be uncovered through reason and contemplation, is, he claimed, mathematical in form.

For his followers the regular solids (symmetrical three-dimensional forms in which all sided surfaces are the same regular polygons) and whole numbers became revered essences of sacred ideas. In contrast with ordinary language, the language of mathematics and geometric forms seemed closed, precise and pure. Providing one understood the axioms and notations, and the meaning conveyed was invariant from one mind to another. The Pythagoreans felt that the language empowered the mind to leap beyond the confusion of sense experience into the realm of immutable and eternal essences. This mystical insight made Pythagoras then figured from antiquity that most revered by the creators of classical physics, and it continues to have great appeal for contemporary physicists as they struggle with the epistemological implications of the quantum mechanical description of nature.

Yet, least of mention, progress was made in mathematics, and to a lesser extent in physics, from the time of classical Greek philosophy to the seventeenth century in Europe. In Baghdad, for example, from about A.D. 750 to A.D. 1000, substantial advancement was made in medicine and chemistry, and the relics of Greek science were translated into Arabic, digested, and preserved. Eventually these relics reentered Europe via the Arabic kingdom of Spain and Sicily, and the work of figures like Aristotle universities of France, Italy, and England during the Middle Ages.

For much of this period the Church provided the institutions, like the reaching orders, needed for the rehabilitation of philosophy. But the social, political and an intellectual climate in Europe was not ripe for a revolution in scientific thought until the seventeenth century. Until later in time, lest as far into the nineteenth century, the works of the new class of intellectuals we called scientists, whom of which were more avocations than vocation, and the word scientist do not appear in English until around 1840.

Copernicus (1473-1543) would have been described by his contemporaries as an administrator, a diplomat, an avid student of economics and classical literature, and most notable, a highly honoured and placed church dignitaries. Although we named a revolution after him, his devoutly conservative man did not set out to create one. The placement of the Sun at the centre of the universe, which seemed right and necessary to Copernicus, was not a result of making careful astronomical observations. In fact, he made very few observations in the course of developing his theory, and then only to ascertain if his prior conclusions seemed correct. The Copernican system was also not any more useful in making astrological calculations than the accepted model and was, in some ways, much more difficult to implement. What, then, was his motivation for creating the model and his reasons for presuming that the model was correct?

Copernicus felt that the placement of the Sun at the centre of the universe made sense because he viewed the Sun as the symbol of the presence of a supremely intelligent and intelligible God in a man-centred world. He was apparently led to this conclusion in part because the Pythagoreans believed that fire exists at the centre of the cosmos, and Copernicus identified this fire with the fireball of the Sun. the only support that Copernicus could offer for the greater efficacy of his model was that it represented a simpler and more mathematical harmonious model of the sort that the Creator would obviously indicate the implication of its thesis 'The Revolution of Heavenly Orbs,' illustrates the religious dimension of his scientific thought: 'In the midst of all the sun reposes, unmoving. Who, indeed, in this most beautiful temple would place the light-giver in any other part than from where it can illumine all other parts?'

The belief that the mind of God as Divine Architect permeates the working of nature was the guiding principle of the scientific thought of Johannes Kepler (or Keppler, 1571-1630). For this reason, most modern physicists would probably feel some discomfort in reading Kepler's original manuscripts. Physics and metaphysics, astronomy and astrology, geometry and theology commingle with an intensity that might offend those who practice science in the modern sense of that word. Physical laws, wrote Kepler, 'lie within the power of understanding of the human mind; God wanted us to perceive them when he created us in His own image, in order, . . . that we may take to participate in His own thoughts. Our knowledge of numbers and quantities is the same as that of God's, at least insofar as we can understand something of it in this mortal life.'

Believing, like Newton after him, in the literal truth of the words of the scripture, Kepler concluded that the word of God is also transcribed in the immediacy of observable nature. Kepler's discovery that the motions of the planets around the Sun were elliptical, as opposed perfecting circles, may have made the universe seem a less perfect creation of God on ordinary language. For Kepler, however, the new model placed the Sun, which he also viewed as the emblem of a divine agency, more at the centre of mathematically harmonious universes than the Copernican system allowed. Communing with the perfect mind of God requires as Kepler put it 'knowledge of numbers and quantity.'

Since Galileo did not use, or even refer to, the planetary laws of Kepler when those laws would have made his defence of the heliocentric universe more credible, his attachment to the god-like circle was probably more deeply rooted aesthetically, and by reason alone or the basic changes pertaining to quantity as having to do with quantity only, distinguished from qualitative, however, to express as multiples of a given quantity or quantum, forfeits the process of finding the amount of exact elements of ingredients present in a material or compounded constituents.

Quantum mechanics now force us to abandon. In 'Dialogue Concerning the Two Great Systems of the World,' Galileo said about the following about the followers of Pythagoras: 'I know perfectly well that the Pythagoreans had the highest esteem for the science of number and that Plato himself admired the human intellect and believed that it participates in divinity solely because it is able to understand the nature of numbers. And I myself am inclined to make the same judgement.'

This article of faith-mathematical and geometrical ideas mirror precisely the essences of physical reality was the basis for the first scientific law of this new science, a constant describing the acceleration of bodies in free fall, could not be confirmed by experiment. The experiments conducted by Galileo in which balls of different sizes and weights were rolled simultaneously down an inclined plane did not, as he frankly admitted, their precise results. And since a vacuum pumps had not yet been invented, there was simply no way that Galileo could subject his law to rigorous experimental proof in the seventeenth century. Galileo believed in the absolute validity of this law in the absence of experimental proof because he also believed that movement could be subjected absolutely to the law of number. What Galileo asserted, as the French historian of science Alexander Koyré announced 'that the real are in its essence, geometrical and, consequently, subject to rigorous determination and measurement.'

The popular image of Isaac Newton (1642-1727) is that of a supremely rational and dispassionate empirical thinker. Newton, like Einstein, had the ability to concentrate unswervingly on complex theoretical problems until they yielded a solution. But what most consumed his restless intellect were not the laws of physics. In addition to believing, like Galileo that the essences of physical reality could be read in the language of mathematics, Newton also believed, with perhaps even greater intensity than Kepler, in the literal truths of the scripture.

For Newton the mathematical languages of linguistic physics and the language of biblical literature were equally valid sources of communion with the eternal writings in the extant documents alone consist of more than a million words in his own hand, and some of his speculations seemed quite bizarre by contemporary standards. The Earth, said Newton, will still be inhabited after the day of judgement, and heaven, or the New Jerusalem, must be large enough to accommodate both the quick and the dead. Newton then put his mathematical genius to work and determined the dimensions required to join the measurable use of the population, his rather precise estimate was 'the cube root of 12,000 furlongs.

For his followers the regular solid structures, for being symmetrical three-dimensional constructs that exist or forming in the mind, as an entity, as an idea, or elements or arrangement extending of length, breath, or thickness of case, in that which forms all surface sides of which are the same, regular polygons as whole numbers became revered essences of sacred ideas. In contrast with ordinary language, the language of mathematics and geometric forms seemed closed, precise and pure. Providing one understood the axioms and notations, and the meaning conveyed was invariant from one mind to another. The Pythagoreans felt that the language empowered the mind to leap beyond the confusion of0fv sense experience into the realm of immutable and eternal essences. This mystical insight made Pythagoras thein figures from antiquity most revered by the creators of classical physics, and it continues to have great appeal for contemporary physicists as they struggle with the epistemological implications of the quantum mechanical description of nature.

Yet, least of mention, progress was made in mathematics, and to a lesser extent in physics, from the time of classical Greek philosophy to the seventeenth century in Europe. In Baghdad, for example, from about A.D. 750 to A.D. 1000, substantial advancement was made in medicine and chemistry, and the relics of Greek science were translated into Arabic, digested, and preserved. Eventually these relics reentered Europe via the Arabic kingdom of Spain and Sicily, and the work of figures like Aristotle universities of France, Italy, and England during the Middle Ages.

For much of this period the Church provided the institutions, like the reaching orders, needed for the rehabilitation of philosophy. But the social, political and an intellectual climate in Europe was not ripe for a revolution in scientific thought until the seventeenth century. Until later in time, lest as far into the nineteenth century, the works of the new class of intellectuals we called scientists, whom of which were more avocations than vocation, and the word scientist do not appear in English until around 1840.

Copernicus (1473-1543) would have been described by his contemporaries as an administrator, a diplomat, an avid student of economics and classical literature, and most notable, a highly honoured and placed church dignitaries. Although we named a revolution after him, his devoutly conservative man did not set out to create one. The placement of the Sun at the centre of the universe, which seemed right and necessary to Copernicus, was not a result of making careful astronomical observations. In fact, he made very few observations in the course of developing his theory, and then only to ascertain if his prior conclusions seemed correct. The Copernican system was also not any more useful in making astrological calculations than the accepted model and was, in some ways, much more difficult to implement. What, then, was his motivation for creating the model and his reasons for presuming that the model was correct?

Copernicus felt that the placement of the Sun at the centre of the universe made sense because he viewed the Sun as the symbol of the presence of a supremely intelligent and intelligible God in a man-centred world. He was apparently led to this conclusion in part because the Pythagoreans believed that fire exists at the centre of the cosmos, and Copernicus identified this fire with the fireball of the Sun. the only support that Copernicus could offer for the greater efficacy of his model was that it represented a simpler and more mathematical harmonious model of the sort that the Creator would obviously prefer. Again, the linguistic phraseological language as formulated by Copernicus in 'The Revolution of Heavenly Orbs,' illustrating the religious dimension of his scientific thought: 'In the midst of all the sun reposes unmoving. Who, indeed, in this most beautiful temple would place the light-giver in any other part than from where it can illumine all other parts?'

The belief that the mind of God as the Divine Architect permeates the works of nature, and has been the guiding principle of the scientific thought of Johannes Kepler (or Keppler, 1571-1630). For this reason, most modern physicists would probably feel some discomfort in reading Kepler's original manuscripts. Physics and metaphysics, astronomy and astrology, geometry and theology commingle with an intensity that might offend those who practice science in the modern sense of that word. Physical laws, wrote Kepler, 'lie within the power of understanding of the human mind; God wanted us to perceive them when he created us in His own image, in order, . . . that we may take part in His own thoughts. Our knowledge of numbers and quantities is the same as that of God's, at least insofar as we can understand something of it in this mortal life.'

Believing, like Newton after him, in the literal truth of the words of the Bible, Kepler concluded that the word of God is also transcribed in the immediacy of observable nature. Kepler's discovery that the motions of the planets around the Sun were elliptical, as opposed perfecting circles, may have made the universe seem a less perfect creation of God on ordinary language. For Kepler, however, the new model placed the Sun, which he also viewed as the emblem of a divine agency, more at the centre of mathematically harmonious universes than the Copernican system allowed. Communing with the perfect mind of God requires as Kepler put it 'knowledge of numbers and quantity.'

Since Galileo did not use, or even refer to, the planetary laws of Kepler when those laws would have made his defence of the heliocentric universe more credible, his attachment to the god-like circle was probably a more deeply rooted aesthetic and religious ideal. But it was Galileo, to the greater extent, than Newton, whose accountable literature, from which the featuring of models had proved acceptable with the non-Boolean algebra, as derived from the mathematical representation of quantum mechanical systems, in that which models of classical logic structure of quantum mechanics, and its relation to the acceptance of classical mechanics is stately construed as the non-Boolean algebras. This is the central notion of quantum logic, although the term covers a variety of modal logics, dialectics, and operational logics were proposed to elucidate the quantum mechanics,

In the 'Dialogue Concerning the Two Great Systems of the World,' Galileo said about the following about the followers of Pythagoras: 'I know perfectly well that the Pythagoreans had the highest esteem for the science of number and that Plato himself admired the human intellect and believed that it participates in divinity solely because it is able to understand the nature of numbers. And I myself am inclined to make the same judgement.'

This article of faith-mathematical and geometrical ideas mirror precisely the essences of physical reality was the basis for the first scientific law of this new science, a constant describing the acceleration of bodies in free fall, could not be confirmed by experiment. The experiments conducted by Galileo in which balls of different sizes and weights were rolled simultaneously down an inclined plane did not, as he frankly admitted, their precise results. And since a vacuum pumps had not yet been invented, there was simply no way that Galileo could subject his law to rigorous experimental proof in the seventeenth century. Galileo believed in the absolute validity of this law in the absence of experimental proof because he also believed that movement could be subjected absolutely to the law of number. What Galileo asserted, as the French historian of science Alexander Koyré put it, was 'that the real are in its essence, geometrical and, consequently, subject to rigorous determination and measurement.'

The popular image of Isaac Newton (1642-1727) is that of a supremely rational and dispassionate empirical thinker. Newton, like Einstein, had the ability to concentrate unswervingly on complex theoretical problems until they yielded a solution. But what most consumed his restless intellect were not the laws of physics. In addition to believing, like Galileo that the essences of physical reality could be read in the language of mathematics, Newton also believed, with perhaps even greater intensity than Kepler, in the literal truths of the scripture.

For Newton the mathematical languages of physics and the language of biblical literature were equally valid sources of communion with the eternal writings in the extant documents alone consist of more than a million words in his own hand, and some of his speculations seem quite bizarre by contemporary standards. The Earth, said Newton, will still be inhabited after the day of judgement, and heaven, or the New Jerusalem, must be large enough to accommodate both the quick and the dead. Newton then put his mathematical genius to work and determined the dimensions required to house the population, his rather precise estimate was 'the cube root of 12,000 furlongs.'

The point is, that during the first scientific revolution the marriage between mathematical idea and physical reality, or between mind and nature via mathematical theory, was viewed as a sacred union. In our more secular age, the correspondence takes on the appearance of an unexamined article of faith or, to borrow a phrase from William James (1842-1910), 'an altar to an unknown god.' Heinrich Hertz, the famous nineteenth-century German physicist, nicely described what there is about the practice of physics that tends to inculcate this belief: 'One cannot escape the feeling that these mathematical formulae have an independent existence and intelligence of their own that they are wiser than we, wiser than their discoveries. That we get more out of them than was originally put into them.'

While Hertz made this statement without having to contend with the implications of quantum mechanics, the feeling, the described remains the most enticing and exciting aspects of physics. That elegant mathematical formulae provide a framework for understanding the origins and transformations of a cosmos of enormous age and dimensions are a staggering discovery for bidding physicists. Professors of physics do not, of course, tell their students that the study of physical laws in an act of communion with thee perfect mind of God or that these laws have an independent existence outside the minds that discover them. The business of becoming a physicist typically begins, however, with the study of classical or Newtonian dynamics, and this training provides considerable covert reinforcement of the feeling that Hertz described.

Possibly, the best way to examine the legacy of the dialogue between science and religion in the debate over the implications of quantum non-locality is to examine the source of Einstein's objections to quantum epistemology in more personal terms. Einstein apparently lost faith in the God portrayed in biblical literature in early adolescence. But, as appropriated, . . . the 'Autobiographical Notes' give to suggest that there were aspects that carry over into his understanding of the foundation for scientific knowledge, . . . 'in the face of the fact that I was the son of an entirely irreligious [Catholic] Breeden heritage, which is deeply held of its religiosity, which, however, found an abrupt end at the age of 12. Though the reading of popular scientific books and magazines, I soon reached the conviction that much in the stories of the scripture could not be true. The consequence waw a positively frantic [orgy] of freethinking coupled with the impression that youth is intentionally being deceived by the stat through lies that it was a crushing impression. Suspicion against every kind of authority grew out of this experience. . . . It was clear to me that the religious paradise of youth, which was thus lost, was a first attempt ti free myself from the chains of the 'merely personal'. . . . The mental grasp of this extra-personal world within the frame of the given possibilities swam as highest aim half consciously and half unconsciously before the mind's eye.'

The point is, that during the first scientific revolution the marriage between mathematical idea and physical reality, or between mind and nature via mathematical theory, was viewed as a sacred union. In our more secular age, the correspondence takes on the appearance of an unexamined article of faith or, to borrow a phrase from William James (1842-1910), 'an altar to an unknown god.' Heinrich Hertz, the famous nineteenth-century German physicist, nicely described what there is about the practice of physics that tends to inculcate this belief: 'One cannot escape the feeling that these mathematical formulae have an independent existence and intelligence of their own that they are wiser than we, wiser than their discoveries. That we get more out of them than was originally put into them.'

While Hertz made this statement without having to contend with the implications of quantum mechanics, the feeling, the described remains the most enticing and exciting aspects of physics. That elegant mathematical formulae provide a framework for understanding the origins and transformations of a cosmos of enormous age and dimensions are a staggering discovery for bidding physicists. Professors of physics do not, of course, tell their students that the study of physical laws in an act of communion with thee perfect mind of God or that these laws have an independent existence outside the minds that discover them. The business of becoming a physicist typically begins, however, with the study of classical or Newtonian dynamics, and this training provides considerable covert reinforcement of the feeling that Hertz described.

Perhaps, the best way to examine the legacy of the dialogue between science and religion in the debate over the implications of quantum non-locality is to examine the source of Einstein's objections tp quantum epistemology in more personal terms. Einstein apparently lost faith in the God portrayed in biblical literature in early adolescence. But, as appropriated, . . . the 'Autobiographical Notes' give to suggest that there were aspects that carry over into his understanding of the foundation for scientific knowledge . . . 'Thus, despite the assertion for something is to be true or have an occurring existence, it is plausible to admit for that which has readily been conceded, is the fact for which of reason or cause for an action, belief, thought, and so on, Trending to a direct explanation for or defence of an action, belief, and so on. Nonetheless, it is conformable to reason or having the faculty of reason, of that which the mental activities or process of drawing conclusions from know or presumed facts, that only employ or result from this process, as too obtainably achieve in making real or concrete of the absolute or ultimate, as contrasted with the apparent.

Einstein was to suggest, that belief in the word of God as it is revealed in biblical literature that allowed him to dwell in a 'religious paradise of youth' and to shield himself from the harsh realities of social and political life. In an effort to recover that inner sense of security that was lost after exposure to scientific knowledge, or to become free once again of the 'merely personal', he committed himself to understanding the 'extra-personal world within the frame of given possibilities', or as seems obvious, to the study of physics. Although the existence of God as described in the Bible may have been in doubt, the qualities of mind that the architects of classical physics associated with this God were not. This is clear in the comments from which Einstein uses of mathematics, . . . 'Natures realization of the simplest conceivable mathematical ideas, in which forming by means of purely mathematical construction, whose concepts and those lawful connections between them, furnishes the key to the understanding of natural phenomena. Experience remains, of course, the sole criteria of physical utility of a mathematical construction. But the creative principle resides in mathematics. In a certain sense, therefore, I hold it true that pure thought can grasp upon reality, as the ancients dreamed. The Platonic concept of an archetype or fundamental example, of which an existing thing is but a representation.

This article of faith, first articulated by Kepler, that 'nature is the realization of the simplest conceivable mathematical ideas' allowed for Einstein to posit the first major law of modern physics much as it allows Galileo to posit the first major law of classical physics. During which time, when the special and then the general theories of relativity had not been confirmed by experiment and many established physicists viewed them as at least minor heresies, Einstein remained entirely confident of their predictions. Ilse Rosenthal-Schneider, who visited Einstein shortly after Eddington's eclipse expedition confirmed a prediction of the general theory (1919), described Einstein's response to this news: When I was giving expression to my joy that the results coincided with his calculations, he said quite unmoved, 'But I knew the theory was correct,' and when I asked, what if there had been no confirmation of his prediction, he countered: 'Then I would have been sorry for the dear Lord - the theory is correct.'

Einstein was not given to make sarcastic or sardonic comments, particularly on matters of religion. These unguarded responses testify to his profound conviction that the language of mathematics allows the human mind access to immaterial and immutable truths existing outside of the mind that conceived them. Although Einstein's belief was far more secular than Galileo's, it retained the same essential ingredients.

What continued in the twenty-three-year-long debate between Einstein and Bohr, least of mention? The primary article drawing upon its faith that contends with those opposing to the merits or limits of a physical theory, at the heart of this debate was the fundamental question, 'What is the relationship between the mathematical forms in the human mind called physical theory and physical reality?' Einstein did not believe in a God who spoke in tongues of flame from the mountaintop in ordinary language, and he could not sustain belief in the anthropomorphic God of the West. There is also no suggestion that he embraced ontological monism, or the conception of Being featured in Eastern religious systems, like Taoism, Hinduism, and Buddhism. The closest that Einstein apparently came to affirming the existence of the 'extra-personal' in the universe was a 'cosmic religious feeling', which he closely associated with the classical view of scientific epistemology.

The doctrine that Einstein fought to persevere, this seemed the natural inheritance of physics until the advent of quantum mechanics. Although the mind that constructs reality might be evolving fictions that are not necessarily true or necessary in social and political life, there was, Einstein felt, a way of knowing, purged of deceptions and lies. He was convinced that knowledge of physical reality in physical theory mirrors the preexistent and immutable realm of physical laws. And as Einstein consistently made clear, this knowledge mitigates loneliness and inculcates a sense of order and reason in a cosmos that might appear otherwise bereft of meaning and purpose.

What most disturbed Einstein about quantum mechanics was the fact that this physical theory might not, in experiment or even in principle, mirrors precisely the structure of physical reality. There is, for all the reasons we seem attested of, in that an inherent uncertainty in measurement made, . . . a quantum mechanical process reflects of a pursuit that quantum theory in itself and its contributive dynamic functions that there lay the attribution of a completeness of a quantum mechanical theory. Einstein's fearing that it would force us to recognize that this inherent uncertainty applied to all of physics, and, therefore, the ontological bridge between mathematical theory and physical reality - does not exist. And this would mean, as Bohr was among the first to realize, that we must profoundly revive the epistemological foundations of modern science.

The world view of classical physics allowed the physicist to assume that communion with the essences of physical reality through mathematical laws and associated theories was possible, but it made no other provisions for the knowing mind. In our new situation, the status of the knowing mind seems quite different. Modern physics distributively contributed its view toward the universe as an unbroken, undissectible and undivided dynamic whole. 'There can hardly be a sharper contrast,' said Melic Capek, 'than that between the everlasting atoms of classical physics and the vanishing 'particles' of modern physics as Stapp put it: 'Each atom turns out to be nothing but the potentialities in the behaviour pattern of others. What we find, therefore, are not elementary space-time realities, but rather a web of relationships in which no part can stand alone, every part derives its meaning and existence only from its place within the whole"

The characteristics of particles and quanta are not isolated, given particle-wave dualism and the incessant exchange of quanta within matter-energy fields. Matter cannot be dissected from the omnipresent sea of energy, nor can we in theory or in fact observe matter from the outside. As Heisenberg put it decades ago, 'the cosmos appears to be a complicated tissue of events, in which connection of different kinds alternate or overlay or combine and thereby determine the texture of the whole. This means that a pure reductionist approach to understanding physical reality, which was the goal of classical physics, is no longer appropriate.

While the formalism of quantum physics predicts that correlations between particles over space-like separated regions are possible, it can say nothing about what this strange new relationship between parts (quanta) and whole (cosmos) was by means an outside formalism. This does not, however, prevent us from considering the implications in philosophical terms, as the philosopher of science Errol Harris noted in thinking about the special character of wholeness in modern physics, a unity without internal content is a blank or empty set and is not recognizable as a whole. A collection of merely externally related parts does not constitute a whole in that the parts will not be 'mutually adaptive and complementary to one and another.'

Wholeness requires a complementary relationship between unity and differences and is governed by a principle of organization determining the interrelationship between parts. This organizing principle must be universal to a genuine whole and implicit in all parts that constitute the whole, even though the whole is exemplified only in its parts. This principle of order, Harris continued, 'is nothing really in and of itself. It is the way parts are organized and not another constituent addition to those that constitute the totality.'

In a genuine whole, the relationship between the constituent parts must be 'internal or immanent' in the parts, as opposed to a mere spurious whole in which parts appear to disclose wholeness due to relationships that are external to the parts. The collection of parts that would allegedly constitute the whole in classical physics is an example of a spurious whole. Parts constitute a genuine whole when the universal principle of order is inside the parts and thereby adjusts each to all that they interlock and become mutually complementary. This not only describes the character of the whole revealed in both relativity theory and quantum mechanics. It is also consistent with the manner in which we have begun to understand the relation between parts and whole in modern biology.

Modern physics also reveals, claims Harris, a complementary relationship between the differences between parts that constitute the contentuality of which holds to representations that the universal ordering principle that is immanent in each of the parts. While the whole cannot be finally disclosed in the analysis of the parts, the study of the differences between parts provides insights into the dynamic structure of the whole present in each of the parts. The part can never, nonetheless, be finally isolated from the web of relationships that disclose the interconnections with the whole, and any attempt to do so results in ambiguity.

Much of the ambiguity in attempted to explain the character of wholes in both physics and biology derives from the assumption that order exists between or outside parts. But order in complementary relationships between differences and sameness in any physical event is never external to that event - the connections are immanent in the event. From this perspective, the addition of non-locality to this picture of the dynamic whole is not surprising. The relationship between part, as quantum event apparent in observation or measurement, and the undissectible whole, revealed but not described by the instantaneous, and the undissectible whole, revealed but described by the instantaneous correlations between measurements in space-like separated regions, is another extension of the part-whole complementarity to modern physics.

If the universe is a seamlessly interactive system that evolves to a higher level of complexity, and if the lawful regularities of this universe are emergent properties of this system, we can assume that the cosmos is a singular point of significance as a whole that evinces the 'progressive principal order' of complementary relations of its parts. Given that this whole exists in some sense within all parts (quanta), one can then argue that it operates in self-reflective fashion and is the ground for all emergent complexities. Since human consciousness evinces self-reflective awareness in the human brain and since this brain, like all physical phenomena can be viewed as an emergent property of the whole, it is reasonable to conclude, in philosophical terms at least, that we of the universe, are awaiting of its call.

The doctrine that Einstein fought to preserve had seemed natural inheritance of physics until the advent of quantum mechanics. Although the mind that constructs reality might be evolving fictions that are not necessarily true or necessary in social and political life, there was, Einstein felt, a way of knowing, purged of deceptions and lies. He was convinced that knowledge of physical reality in physical theory mirrors the preexistent and immutable realm of physical laws. And as Einstein consistently made clear, this knowledge mitigates loneliness and inculcates a sense of order and reason in a cosmos that might appear otherwise bereft of meaning and purpose.

What most disturbed Einstein about quantum mechanics was the fact that this physical theory might not, in experiment or even in principle, mirrors precisely the structure of physical reality. There is, for all the reasons we seem attested of, in that an inherent uncertainty in measurement made, . . . a quantum mechanical process reflects of a pursuit that quantum theory in itself and its contributive dynamic functions that there lay the attribution of a completeness of a quantum mechanical theory. Einstein's fearing that it would force us to recognize that this inherent uncertainty applied to all of physics, and, therefore, the ontological bridge between mathematical theory and physical reality - does not exist. And this would mean, as Bohr was among the first to realize, that we must profoundly revive the epistemological foundations of modern science.

The world view of classical physics allowed the physicist to assume that the communion within the essencity of physical reality through mathematical laws and associated theories was possible, but it made no other provisions for the knowing mind. In our new situation, the status of the knowing mind seems quite different. Modern physics distributively contributed its view toward the universe as an unbroken, undissectible and undivided dynamic whole. 'There can hardly be a sharper contrast,' said Melic Capek, 'than that between the everlasting atoms of classical physics and the vanishing 'particles' of modern physics as Stapp put it: 'Each atom turns out to be nothing but the potentialities in the behaviour pattern of others. What we find, therefore, are not elementary space-time realities, but rather a web of relationships in which no part can stand alone, every part derives its meaning and existence only from its place within the whole.

The characteristics of particles and quanta are not isolated, given particle-wave dualism and the incessant exchange of quanta within matter-energy fields. Matter cannot be dissected from the omnipresent sea of energy, nor can we in theory or in fact observe matter from the outside. As Heisenberg put it decades ago, 'the cosmos appears to be a complicated tissue of events, in which connection of different kinds alternate or overlay or combine and thereby determine the texture of the whole. This means that a pure reductionist approach to understanding physical reality, which was the goal of classical physics, is no longer appropriate.

While the formalism of quantum physics predicts that correlations between particles over space-like separated regions are possible, it can say nothing about what this strange new relationship between parts (quanta) and whole (cosmos) was by means an outside formalism. This does not, however, prevent us from considering the implications in philosophical terms, as the philosopher of science Errol Harris noted in thinking about the special character of wholeness in modern physics, a unity without internal content is a blank or empty set and is not recognizable as a whole. A collection of merely externally related parts does not constitute a whole in that the parts will not be 'mutually adaptive and complementary to one and another.'

Wholeness requires a complementary relationship between unity and differences and is governed by a principle of organization determining the interrelationship between parts. This organizing principle must be universal to a genuine whole and implicit in all parts that constitute the whole, even though the whole is exemplified only in its parts. This principle of order, Harris continued, 'is nothing really in and of itself. It is the way parts are organized and not another constituent addition to those that constitute the totality.'

In a genuine whole, the relationship between the constituent parts must be 'internal or immanent' in the parts, as opposed to a mere spurious whole in which parts appear to disclose wholeness due to relationships that are external to the parts. The collection of parts that would allegedly constitute the whole in classical physics is an example of a spurious whole. Parts constitute a genuine locality of its whole, when the universal principle of order is inside the parts and thereby adjusts each to all that they interlock and become mutually complementary. This not only describes the character of the whole revealed in both relativity theory and quantum mechanics. It is also consistent with the manner in which we have begun to understand the relation between parts and whole in modern biology.

Modern physics also reveals, claims Harris, a complementary relationship between the differences between parts that constitute contentual representations that the universal ordering principle that is immanent in each of the parts. While the whole cannot be finally disclosed in the analysis of the parts, the study of the differences between parts provides insights into the dynamic structure of the whole present in each of the parts. The part can never, nonetheless, be finally isolated from the web of relationships that disclose the interconnections with the whole, and any attempt to do so results in ambiguity.

Much of the ambiguity in attempted to explain the character of wholes in both physics and biology derives from the assumption that order exists between or outside parts. But order in complementary relationships between differences and sameness in any physical event is never external to that event -the connections are immanent in the event. From this perspective, the addition of non-locality to this picture of the dynamic whole is not surprising. The relationship between part, as quantum event apparent in observation or measurement, and the undissectible whole, revealed but not described by the instantaneous, and the undissectible whole, revealed but described by the instantaneous correlations between measurements in space-like separated regions, is another extension of the part-whole complementarity to modern physics.

If the universe is a seamlessly interactive system that evolves to a higher level of complexity, and if the lawful regularities of this universe are emergent properties of this system, we can assume that the cosmos is a singular point of significance as a whole that evinces 'progressive principal order' of complementary relations to its parts. Given that this whole exists in some sense within all parts (quanta), one can then argue that it operates in self-reflective fashion and is the ground for all emergent complexities. Since human consciousness evinces self-reflective awareness in the human brain and since this brain, like all physical phenomena can be viewed as an emergent property of the whole, it is reasonable to conclude, in philosophical terms at least, that the universe is conscious.

But since the actual character of this seamless whole cannot be represented or reduced to its parts, it lies, quite literally beyond all human representations or descriptions. If one chooses to believe that the universe be a self-reflective and self-organizing whole, this lends no support whatsoever to conceptions of design, meaning, purpose, intent, or plan associated with any mytho-religions or cultural heritage. However, If one does not accept this view of the universe, there is nothing in the scientific descriptions of nature that can be used to refute this position. On the other hand, it is no longer possible to argue that a profound sense of unity with the whole, which has long been understood as the foundation of religious experience, which can be dismissed, undermined or invalidated with appeals to scientific knowledge.

While we have consistently tried to distinguish between scientific knowledge and philosophical speculation based on this knowledge -there is no empirically valid causal linkage between the former and the latter. Those who wish to dismiss the speculative assumptions as its basis to be drawn the obvious freedom of which id firmly grounded in scientific theory and experiments there is, however, in the scientific description of nature, the belief in radical Cartesian division between mind and world sanctioned by classical physics. Seemingly clear, that this separation between mind and world was a macro-level illusion fostered by limited aware nesses of the actual character of physical reality and by mathematical idealization that were extended beyond the realm of their applicability.

Thus, the grounds for objecting to quantum theory, the lack of a one-to-one correspondence between every element of the physical theory and the physical reality it describes, may seem justifiable and reasonable in strictly scientific terms. After all, the completeness of all previous physical theories was measured against the criterion with enormous success. Since it was this success that gave physics the reputation of being able to disclose physical reality with magnificent exactitude, perhaps a more comprehensive quantum theory will emerge to insist on these requirements.

All indications are, however, that no future theory can circumvent quantum indeterminancy, and the success of quantum theory in co-ordinating our experience with nature is eloquent testimony to this conclusion. As Bohr realized, the fact that we live in a quantum universe in which the quantum of action is a given or an unavoidable reality requires a very different criterion for determining the completeness or physical theory. The new measure for a complete physical theory is that it unambiguously confirms our ability to co-ordinate more experience with physical reality.

If a theory does so and continues to do so, which is certainly the case with quantum physics, then the theory must be deemed complete. Quantum physics not only works exceedingly well, it is, in these terms, the most accurate physical theory that has ever existed. When we consider that this physics allows us to predict and measure quantities like the magnetic moment of electrons to the fifteenth decimal place, we realize that accuracy per se is not the real issue. The real issue, as Bohr rightly intuited, is that this complete physical theory effectively undermines the privileged relationship in classical physics between 'theory' and 'physical reality'.

If the universe is a seamlessly interactive system that evolves to higher levels of complex and complicating regularities of which ae lawfully emergent in property of systems, we can assume that the cosmos is a single significant whole that evinces progressive order in complementary relations to its parts. Given that this whole exists in some sense within all parts (quanta), one can then argue that in operates in self-reflective fashion and is the ground from all emergent plexuities. Since human consciousness evinces self-reflective awareness in te human brain (well protected between the cranium walls) and since this brain, like all physical phenomena, can b viewed as an emergent property of the whole, it is unreasonable to conclude, in philosophical terms at least, that the universe is conscious.

Nevertheless, since the actual character of this seamless whole cannot be represented or reduced to its parts, it lies, quite laterally, beyond all human representation or descriptions. If one chooses to believe that the universe be a self-reflective and self-organizing whole, this lends no support whatsoever to conceptual representation of design, meaning, purpose, intent, or plan associated with mytho-religions or cultural heritage. However, if one does not accept this view of the universe, there is noting in the scientific description of nature that can be used to refute this position. On the other hand, it is no longer possible to argue that a profound sense of unity with the whole, which has long been understood as foundation of religious experiences, but can be dismissed, undermined, or invalidated with appeals to scientific knowledge.

While we have consistently tried to distinguish between scientific knowledge and philosophical speculation based on this of what is obtainable, let us be quite clear on one point - there is no empirically valid causal linkage between the former and the latter. Those who wish to dismiss the speculative base on which is obviously free to do as done, but, nonetheless, another conclusion to be drawn, in that is firmly grounded in scientific theory and experiment there is no basis in the scientific descriptions of nature for believing in the radical Cartesian division between mind and world sanctioned by classical physics. Clearly, his radical separation between mind and world was a macro-level illusion fostered by limited awareness of the actual character of physical reality nd by mathematical idealizations extended beyond the realms of their applicability.

Nevertheless, the philosophical implications can be derived in themselves as a criterial motive which limits or particularizes of the spoke exchange, as having deliberate argumentation between persons of opposite sides, exchanging verbalizing overtly as the directive opinions or relevant questions are heard. All and all, of which of our considerations, as how our proposed new understanding of the relationship between parts and wholes in physical reality might affect the manner in which we deal with some major real-world problems, this issue will demonstrate why a timely resolution of these problems is critically dependent on a renewed dialogue between members of the cultures of human-social scientists and scientist-engineers. We will also argue that the resolution of these problems could be dependent on a renewed dialogue between science and religion.

As many scholars have demonstrated, the classical paradigm in physics has greatly influenced and conditioned our understanding and management of human systems in economic and political realities. Virtually all models of these realities treat human, or forces external to or between the parts. These systems are also viewed as hermetic or closed and, thus, its discreteness, separateness and distinction.

Having accepted, for example, to what sociological distinction has the attribution toward classical paradigms or which of thinking about an economic reality, that in the eighteenth and nineteenth centuries, the founders of classical economics - figures like Adam Smith, David Ricardo, and Thomas Malthus, conceived of an economy as a closed system, e.g., from an open to a closed condition, of which intersections between parts (consumer, produces, distributors, and so on.). Having in them, the controlling conditions with which by forces external to the parts (supply and demand), were central legitimation principles of free market economics. Formulated by Adam Smith, as the lawful or law-like forces external to the individual units function as an invisible hand. This invisible hand, said Smith, frees the units to pursue their best interests, moving the economy forward, and generally, legislating the behaviour of parts in the best vantages of the whole. (The resemblance between the invisible hand and Newton's universal law of gravity and between the relations of parts and wholes in classical economics and classical physics should be transparent.)

After 1830, economists shifted the focus to the properties of the invisible hand in the interactions between pats using mathematical models. Within these models, the behaviour of pats in the economy is assumed to be analogous to the awful interactions between pats in classical mechanics. It is, therefore, not surprising that differential calculus was employed to represent economic change in a virtual world in terms of small or marginal shifts in consumption or production. The assumption was that the mathematical description of marginal shifts n the complex web of exchanges between parts (atomized units and quantities) and whole (closed economy) could reveal the lawful, or law-like, machinations of the closed economic system.

These models later became one of the fundamentals for microeconomics. Microeconomics seek to describe interactions between parts in exact quantifiable measures-such as marginal cost, marginal revenue, marginal utility, and growth of total revenue as indexed against individual units of output. In analogy with classical mechanics, the quantities are viewed as initial conditions that can serve to explain subsequent interactions between parts in the closed system in something like deterministic terms. The combination of classical macro-analysis with micro-analysis resulted in what Thorstein Veblen in 1900 termed neoclassical economics-the model for understanding economic reality that is widely used today

Beginning in the 1939s, the challenge became to subsume the understanding of the interactions between parts in closed economic systems with more sophisticated mathematical models using devices like linear programming, game theory, and new statistical techniques. In spite of the growing mathematical sophistication, these models are based on the same assumptions from classical physics featured in previous neoclassical economic theory-with one exception. They also appeal to the assumption that systems exist in equilibrium or in perturbations from equilibria, and they seek to describe the state of the closed economic system in these terms.

Since classical mechanic serves us well in our dealings with macro-level phenomena in situations where the speed of light is so large and the quantum of action is so small as to be safely ignored for practical purposes, economic theories based on assumptions from classical mechanics should serve us well in dealing with the macro-level behaviour of economic systems.

Just as of something that actually exists or has occurred, resulting in a due course of time, has in accord within these asserted assumptions, as the interaction between parts and their related whole, no collection of arts is isolated from the whole, and the ability of the whole to regulate the relative abundance of atmospheric gases suggests that the whole of the biota appear to display emergent properties that are more than the sum of its parts. What the current ecological crisis was made known of the abstract virtual world of neoclassical economic theory. The real economies are all human activities associated with the production, distribution, and exchange of tangible goods and commodities and the consumption and usages of natural resources, such as arable land and water. Although expanding economic systems in the really economy ae obviously embedded in a web of relationships with the entire biosphere, our measure of healthy economic systems disguises this fact very nicely. Consider, for example, the healthy economic system written in 1996 by Frederick Hu, head of the competitive research team for the World Economic Forum - short of military conquest, economic growth is the only viable means for a country to sustain increases in natural living standards . . . An economy is internationally competitive if it performs strongly in three general areas: Abundant productive inputs from capital, labour, infrastructure and technology, optimal economic policies such as low taxes, little interference, free trade and sound market institutions, ss the rule of law and protection of property rights.

The prescription for medium-term growth of economies in countries like Russia, Brazil, and China may seem utterly pragmatic and quite sound. But the virtual economy described is a closed and hermetically sealed system in which the invisible hand of economic forces allegedly results in a health growth economy if impediments to its operation are removed or minimized. It is, of course, often trued that such prescriptions can have the desired results in terms of increases in living standards, and Russia, Brazil and China are seeking to implement them in various ways.

In the real economy, however, these systems are clearly not closed or hermetically sealed: Russia uses carbon-based fuels in production facilities that produce large amounts of carbon dioxide and other gases that contribute to global warming: Brazil is in the process of destroying a rain forest that is critical to species diversity and the maintenance of a relative abundance of atmospheric gases that regulate Earth temperature, and China is seeking to build a first-world economy based on highly polluting old-world industrial plants that burn soft coal. Not to forget, . . . the victual economic systems that the world now seems to regard as the best example of the benefits that can be derived form the workings of the invisible hand, that of the United States, operates in the real economy as one of the primary contributors to the ecological crisis.

Following the publication of Isaac Newton's 'Principia Mathematica' in 1687, reductionism and mathematical modelling became the most powerful tools of modern science. The dream that we could know and master the entire physical world through the extension and refinement of mathematical theory became the central feature and principals of scientific knowledge.

The radical separation between mind and nature formalized by Descartes served over time to allow scientists to concentrate on developing mathematical descriptions of matter as pure mechanisms without any concern about its spiritual dimensions or ontological foundations. Meanwhile, attempts to rationalize, reconcile or eliminate Descartes's merging division between mind and matter became the most central feature of Western intellectual life.

Philosophers like John Locke, Thomas Hobbes, and David Hume tried to articulate some basis for linking the mathematical describable motions of matter with linguistic representations of external reality in the subjective space of mind. Descartes' compatriot Jean-Jacques Rousseau reified nature as the ground of human consciousness in a state of innocence and proclaimed that 'Liberty, Equality, Fraternities' are the guiding principles of this consciousness. Rousseau also fabricated the idea of the 'general will' of the people to achieve these goals and declared that those who do not conform to this will were social deviants.

The Enlightenment idea of 'deism', which imaged the universe as a clockwork and God as the clockmaker, provided grounds for believing in a divine agency, from which the time of moment the formidable creations also imply, in of which, the exhaustion of all the creative forces of the universe at origins ends. That the physical substrates of mind were subject to the same natural laws as matter, such that the only means of mediating the gap between mind and matter is pure reason, causally by the traditional Judeo-Christian theism, which had previously been based on both reason and revelation, responded to the challenge of deism by debasing traditionality as a test of faith and embracing the idea that we can know the truths of spiritual reality only through divine revelation. This engendered a conflict between reason and revelation that persists to this day, and laid the foundation for the fierce completion between the mega-narration of science and religion as frame tales for mediating the relation between mind and matter and the manner in which they should ultimately define the special character of each.

The nineteenth-century Romantics in Germany, England and the United States revived Rousseau's attempt to posit a ground for human consciousness by reifying nature in a different form. Goethe and Friedrich Schelling proposed a natural philosophy premised on ontological Monism (the idea that adhering manifestations that govern toward evolutionary principles have grounded inside an inseparable spiritual Oneness) and argued God, man, and nature for the reconciliation of mind and matter with an appeal to sentiment, mystical awareness, and quasi-scientific attempts, as he afforded the efforts of mind and matter, nature became a mindful agency that 'loves illusion', as it shrouds man in mist, presses him or her heart and punishes those who fail to see the light. Schelling, in his version of cosmic unity, argued that scientific facts were at best partial truths and that the mindful creative spirit that unities mind and matter is progressively moving toward 'self-realization' and 'undivided wholeness'.

The British version of Romanticism, articulated by figures like William Wordsworth and Samuel Taylor Coleridge, placed more emphasis on the primary of the imagination and the importance of rebellion and heroic vision as the grounds for freedom. As Wordsworth put it, communion with the 'incommunicable powers' of the 'immortal sea' empowers the mind to release itself from all the material constraints of the laws of nature. The founders of American transcendentalism, Ralph Waldo Emerson and Henry David Theoreau, articulated a version of Romanticism that commensurate with the ideals of American democracy.

The fatal flaw of pure reason is, of course, the absence of emotion, and purely explanations of the division between subjective reality and external reality, of which had limited appeal outside the community of intellectuals. The figure most responsible for infusing our understanding of the Cartesian dualism with our contextual understanding with emotional content was the death of God theologian Friedrich Nietzsche 1844-1900. After declaring that God and 'divine will', did not exist, Nietzsche reified the 'existence' of consciousness in the domain of subjectivity as the ground for individual 'will' and summarily reducing all previous philosophical attempts to articulate the 'will to truth'. The dilemma, forth in, had seemed to mean, by the validation, . . . as accredited for doing of science, in that the claim that Nietzsche's earlier versions to the 'will to truth', disguises the fact that all alleged truths were arbitrarily created in the subjective reality of the individual and are expressed or manifesting the individualism of 'will'.

In Nietzsche's view, the separation between mind and matter is more absolute and total than previously been imagined. Based on the assumption that there is no really necessary correspondence between linguistic constructions of reality in human subjectivity and external reality, he deuced that we are all locked in 'a prison house of language', this prison was also a 'space' where the philosopher can examine the 'innermost desires of his nature' and articulate a new message of individual existence founded on 'will'.

Those who fail to enact their existence in this space, Nietzsche says, are enticed into sacrificing their individuality on the nonexistent altars of religious beliefs and democratic or socialists' ideals and become, therefore, members of the anonymous and docile crowd. Nietzsche also invalidated the knowledge claims of science in the examination of human subjectivity. Science, he said. Is not exclusive to natural phenomenons and favours reductionistic examination of phenomena at the expense of mind? It also seeks to reduce the separateness and uniqueness of mind with mechanistic descriptions that disallow and basis for the free exercise of individual 'will'.

Nietzsche's emotionally charged defence intellectual freedom and radial empowerment of mind as the maker and transformer of the collective fictions that shape human reality in a soulless mechanistic universe proved terribly influential on twentieth-century thought. Furthermore, Nietzsche sought to reinforce his view of the subjective character of scientific knowledge by appealing to an epistemological crisis over the foundations of logic and arithmetic that arose during the last three decades of the nineteenth century. Through a curious course of events, attempted by Edmund Husserl 1859-1938, a German mathematician and a principal founder of phenomenology, wherefor to resolve this crisis resulted in a view of the character of consciousness that closely resembled that of Nietzsche.

The best-known disciple of Husserl was Martin Heidegger, and the work of both figures greatly influenced that of the French atheistic existentialist Jean-Paul Sartre. The work of Husserl, Heidegger, and Sartre became foundational to that of the principal architects of philosophical postmodernism, and deconstructionist Jacques Lacan, Roland Barthes, Michel Foucault and Jacques Derrida. It obvious attribution of a direct linkage between the nineteenth-century crisis about the epistemological foundations of mathematical physics and the origin of philosophical postmodernism served to perpetuate the Cartesian two-world dilemma in an even more oppressive form. It also allows us better to understand the origins of cultural ambience and the ways in which they could resolve that conflict.

The mechanistic paradigm of the late nineteenth century was the one Einstein came to know when he studied physics. Most physicists believed that it represented an eternal truth, but Einstein was open to fresh ideas. Inspired by Mach's critical mind, he demolished the Newtonian ideas of space and time and replaced them with new, "relativistic" notions.

Two theories unveiled and unfolded their phenomenal yield was held by Albert Einstein, attributively appreciated that the special theory of relativity (1905) and, also the estranging and calculable ordering of schematic systems, for in which of arranging their linear continuity, as drawn upon the gratifying nature whom by encouraging the finding resolutions within the realms of its secreted reservoir of continuous phenomenons. In additional the continuatives as afforded by the efforts exerted by means of imaginistic representations were made discretely available to any of the unsurmountable achievements, as remaining obtainably afforded through the excavations underlying the artifactual circumstances that govern all principle 'Forms' or 'Types' in the involving evolutionary principles of the general theory of relativity (1915). Whereas, the special theory gives a unified account of the laws that govern the mechanics and electromagnetism, including optics. Before 1905 the purely relative nature of uniform motion had in part been recognized in mechanics, although Newton had considered time to be absolute and postulated absolute space.

If the universe is a seamlessly interactive system that evolves to a higher level of complexity, and if the lawful regularities of this universe are emergent properties of this system, we can assume that the cosmos is a singular point of significance as a whole that evinces the 'progressive principal order' of complementary relations its parts. Given that this whole exists in some sense within all parts (Quanta), one can then argue that it operates in self-reflective fashion and is the ground for all emergent complexities. Since human consciousness evinces self-reflective awareness in the human brain and since this brain, like all physical phenomena can be viewed as an emergent property of the whole, it is reasonable to conclude, in philosophical terms at least, that the universe is conscious.

But since the actual character of this seamless whole cannot be represented or reduced to its parts, it lies, quite literally beyond all human representations or descriptions. If one chooses to believe that the universe be a self-reflective and self-organizing whole, this lends no support whatsoever to conceptions of design, meaning, purpose, intent, or plan associated with any mytho-religious or cultural heritage. However, If one does not accept this view of the universe, there is nothing in the scientific descriptions of nature that can be used to refute this position. On the other hand, it is no longer possible to argue that a profound sense of unity with the whole, which has long been understood as the foundation of religious experience, which can be dismissed, undermined or invalidated with appeals to scientific knowledge.

Uncertain issues surrounding certainty are especially connected with those concerning 'scepticism'. Although Greek scepticism entered on the value of enquiry and questioning, scepticism is now the denial that knowledge or even rational belief is possible, either about some specific subject-matter, e.g., ethics, or in any area whatsoever. Classical scepticism, springs from the observation that of excelling over other methods in some area seem to fall short of giving us contact with the truth, e.g., there is a gulf between appearances and reality, it frequently cites the conflicting judgements that our methods deliver, with the result that questions of truth shows in becoming to be advantageously undefinable. In classic thought the various examples of this conflict were systemized in the tropes of Aenesidemus. So that, the scepticism of Pyrrho and the new Academy was a system of argument and inasmuch as opposing dogmatism, and, particularly the philosophical system building of the Stoics.

As it has come down to us, particularly in the writings of Sextus Empiricus, its method was typically to cite reasons for finding our issues undecidable (sceptics devoted particular energy to undermining the Stoics conception of some truths as delivered by direct apprehension and hold mentally.) As a result sceptics conclude 'to the things themselves', as the focus is solely on the essential structures of experience itself, or the suspension of belief, and then go on to celebrate a way of life whose object was 'the freedom from disturbance ' (ataraxia) or the tranquillity resulting from suspension of belief.

On or upon the other, is, least of mention, the ground-level epistemological concepts of 'truth', 'falsity', and 'justification' apply primarily to beliefs, and only derivatively, if at all, to knowledge. Belief is thus central to epistemology.

Plato, in the 'Meno' and in the 'Theaetetus' distinguishes knowledge, belief, opinion and judgement, and advances a conception of these states of mind according to which they incorporate a pair of components, one intentional or representational, one causal. In F.P. Ramsey's phrase, as to the belief is viewed of 'a map of neighbouring space by which we steer' (Ramsey, 1978). This dual-component picture of belief constitutes what has become the standard picture. It was embellished, for instance, by Hume, who regarded beliefs as 'ideas' supplemented by a particular 'sentiment or feeling' in virtue of which those ideas come to serve as guides to behaviour. This conception, like Descartes', depicts beliefs as conscious episodes. Although we are often conscious of our beliefs, however, our being conscious of them seems inessential to their psychological role.

The standard picture is nowadays reflected in the notion that beliefs are to be located among the propositional attitudes, states of mind comprising (1) propositional contents paired with (2) attitudes toward those contents. In addition t beliefs, these include desires, wishes, intentions, fears, doubts, and hopes. The objects of belief, then, are taken to be propositions. Propositions are expressible sententiously: Walter's belief that rhubarb is poisonous is expressed by the sentence, 'Rhubarb is poisonous'. This is to suggest to some literal sense. Jerry Fodor (1981), for one, supposes beliefs to e internal sentences, neurally realized inscriptions that make up a 'language of thought', other suspicious of the notion of a language of thought, nevertheless agreeing that belief's posses a logical form mirroring that of sentences.

This is one way of filling out the standard picture, but not the only way, as for Robert Stalnaker (1987) has pointed out that the thesis that beliefs are sententiously characterized ability does not entail that beliefs themselves must have a sentential structure. Stalnaker holds that beliefs are altitudes directed, not toward sentence-like propositions, but toward the world. Belief-states are best characterized by sets of 'possible worlds', alternative 'ways the world may be'. The content of Walter's belief that rhubarb is poisonous might be represented as a set of possible worlds, those in which rhubarb is poisonous. The constituents of possible worlds are possible objects and events, than concepts or descriptions of objects and events, and logical relations among propositions believed are grounded in relations among sets of possible worlds.

Some conceptions of this sort answers' accountabilities for our ambivalence about beliefs ascribed to creatures lacking in linguistic abilities. Spot, we say, believe there is a squirrel in the tree. But can we be confident that we have captured the content of Spot's belief? Beliefs seem to owe their character to relations they bear to other beliefs. My believing that this is a tree, for instance, might be thought to require that I believe many other things: That trees are living things, which trees have leaves, that if I set fire to this tree it will burn, and so on. But how many of these background beliefs could we plausibly credit to Spot?

Of Stalnaker's view, however, in ascribing a belief about trees to Spot we need suppose only that Spot has some mechanism for dividing alternative situations into those featuring and those lacking trees. The mechanism may be a crude one, cruder, certainly, than the mechanisms underlying the abilities of adult human beings. Nonetheless, Spot's belief concerns trees in part because the proposition believed partitions the set of possible worlds relevant to the explanation of Spot's capacities at the same place the proposition believed by an ordinary human being does.

The standard picture is not without its critics, however, Gilbert Ryle (1949) regards beliefs as 'tendencies' to say and do various things. Walter believes that rhubarb is poisonous, he will be disposed to assent to the sentence 'rhubarb is poisonous', to refuse to eat rhubarb, and so forth. In this respect beliefs resemble dispositions, like fragility. If a glass is fragile, will, under the right conditions, break when struck by a solid object. Ryle is often accused of reducing beliefs and other states of mind to behaviour, but this is misleading. A glass's being fragile is not its breaking, and Walter believing that rhubarb is poisonous is not his saying so. Ryle is explicit on the point: What Walter does give is that he believes that rhubarb is what he wants, and so on. If Walter wants to be poisoned, for instance, and believes that this is rhubarb, he may well eat it.

The representational theory of intentionality gives rise to a natural theory of intentional states such as believing, desiring and intending, so that a representational theory of cognition is accorded to this theory, intentional states that factor into two aspect appearances presented to the mind by circumstances, and so on. Or the interpretation that all aspects of a problem as for agreeing to underlying influences, as a functional aspect that distinguishes believing from desiring and so on, and a contentual views that distinguishes belief from each other, desires from each other, and so on. A belief that 'p' might be realized as a representation as holding the content that 'p' and the function of serving as a premise in inference, its desire that 'p' might be realized as the representation with t which the content that 'p' and the function of initiating processing designed to bring it about, is that 'p' and terminating such processing when a belief that 'p' is formed.

Though, in defence of the separability thesis, Radford advocates upon the probability for thinking are an inner state that can be detected through introspection, yet, Julie lack's belief's about English history is plausible on this Cartesian picture since Julie does not find herself with any beliefs about English history when she seeks them out. One might criticize Radford, however, by rejecting the Cartesian view of belief. Or it could have been argued, that some beliefs are thoroughly unconscious, for example. Or one could adopt a behaviourist conception of belief, such as Alexander Bain's (1859), according to which having beliefs is a matter of the way people are disposed to behave. Since Julie gives the correct response when queried, a form of verbal behaviour, a behaviourist would be tempted to credit her with the belief that the Battle of Hastings occurred in 1066.

D.M. Armstrong (1973) takes a different task against Radford. Julie does know that the Battle of Hastings took place in 1066. Armstrong will, in at least, grant Radford that point. In fact, Armstrong suggests that Julie believes that 1066 was not the actual date that the Battle of Hastings occurred, for Armstrong equates the belief that such and such is just possible, but no more than just possible with the belief that such and such is not the case. Nonetheless, Armstrong insists, Julie also believes that the Battle did occur in 1066. After all, had Julie been mistaught that the Battle occurred in 1060, and had se forgotten being 'taught' this and subsequently 'guessed' that it took place in 1060, we would surely describe the situation as one in which Julie's false belief about the Battle became Julie's false belief about the Battle, succumbing to unconsciousness, over time but persisted as a memory trace that was causally responsible for her guess.

The view that a belief acquires favourable epistemic status, as having some kind of reliable linkage to the truth, such as those among its sourcing of reliability for which its theory or plan or existing in the mind only, closely reasoned as opposed to the practice of doing so, the justification or the states for being justified (as opposed to knowledge) there are two main varieties: Reliable indicator theories and reliable process theories. In their simplest forms, the reliable indicator theory says that a belief is justified in case it is base on reasons that are reliable indicators of the truth, and the reliable process theory says that a belief is justified in case it is produced by cognitive processes that are generally reliable.

But what is meant by justification? What is it to be justified in holding a belief? The way of thinking of justification has been the dominant way of thinking about justification and this way thinking has many important contemporary representatives, least of mention, how is it that the justification of theistic belief gets identified with there being propositional evidence for it? Justification is a matter of being blameless f having done one's duty (in the content of one's epistemic duty): What, precisely, has this to do with having propositional evidence? Once, again, justification is the property your beliefs have when, in forming and holding them, you conform to your epistemic duties and obligations. As to say, that epistemic duty is to believe a proposition only to the degree that it is probable with respect to what are certain for you.

Fixed by its will for and of itself, the mere mitigated scepticism which accepts every day or commonsense belief, is that, not s the delivery of reason, but as due more to custom and habit. Nonetheless, it is self-satisfied at the proper time, however, the power of reason to give us much more. Mitigated scepticism is thus closer to the attitude fostered by the accentuations from Pyrrho through to Sextus Empiricus. Despite the fact that the phrase 'Cartesian scepticism' is sometimes used for which of Descartes himself was not a sceptic, however, in the 'method of doubt' uses a sceptical scenario in order to begin the process of finding a general distinction to mark its point of knowledge. For that which of Stoicism leads the movements as constituting Hellenistic philosophy, generating, at a higher level, out of which the four elements air, fire, earth, and water, whose own interaction is analogous to that of god and matter, and became a key concept in physics and biology. Stoic epistemology defends the existence of cognitive certainty against the attacks of the new Academy, for which belief is described as assenting to an impression, e.g., taking as true the propositional content of some perceptual or reflective impression. Out of sets of such impressions we acquire generic conceptions that become rational. The highest intellectual state, knowledge, in which all cognateness becomes mutually supporting and hence 'unshakable by reason' is the prerogative of the wise.

After the second century A.D. Stoicism as a system fell from prominence, but its terminology and concepts had by then become an ineradicably part of ancient thought, Through the writings of Cicero and Seneca, its impact on the moral and political thought of the Renaissance was immense.

For many sceptics have traditionally held that knowledge requires certainty, artistry. And, of course, they claim that certain knowledge is not possible. In part, nonetheless, the principle that every effect it's a consequence of an antecedent cause or causes. For causality to be true it is not necessary for an effect to be predictable as the antecedent causes may be numerous, too complicated, or too interrelated for analysis. Nevertheless, in order to avoid scepticism, this participating sceptic has generally held that knowledge does not require certainty, except for the alleged cases of things that are evident for one just by being true. It has often been thought, that any thing known must satisfy certain criteria as well for being true. It is often taught that anything is known must satisfy certain standards. In so saying, that by 'deduction' or 'induction', there will be criteria specifying when it is. As these alleged cases of self-evident truths, the general principle specifying the sort of consideration that will make such standard in the apparent or justly conclude in accepting it warranted to some degree.

Besides, there is another view - the absolute global view that we do not have any knowledge whatsoever. In whatever manner, it is doubtful that any philosopher seriously entertained of any absolute scepticism. Pyrrhonism holds of the sceptics who held that we should refrain from accenting to any non-evident standards that no such hesitancy about asserting to 'the evident', the non-evident are any belief that requires evidences because it is warranted.

René Descartes (1596-1650), in his sceptical guise, never doubted the content of his own ideas. It's challenging logic, inasmuch as of whether they 'corresponded' to anything beyond ideas.

All and all, Pyrrhonism and Cartesian form of virtual globalized scepticism, in having been held and defended, that of assuming that knowledge is some form for being true, sufficiently warranted belief, it is the warranted condition that provides the truth or belief conditions, in that of providing the grist for the sceptic's mill about. The Pyrrhonist will suggest that no non-evident, empirically deferring the sufficiency of giving in but warranted. Whereas, a Cartesian sceptic will agree that no empirical standards about anything other than one's own mind and its contents are sufficiently warranted, because there are always legitimate grounds for doubting it. Such as the essential difference between the act of seeing, of a mental examination as an outlook of a ranging vision that is seen as the object of the action, in this manner of action, the action of looking at things that give a general summary or an accountable view that concerns the requirements for a belief being sufficiently warranted for taking account of as knowledge.

A Cartesian requires certainty, but a Pyrrhonist merely requires that the standards in case are more warranted then its negation. Cartesian scepticism was unduly an in fluence with which Descartes agues for scepticism, than his reply holds, in that we do not have any knowledge of any empirical standards, in that of anything beyond the contents of our own minds. The reason is roughly in the position that there is a legitimate doubt about all such standards, only because there is no way to justifiably deny that our senses are being stimulated by some sense, for which it is radically different from the objects which we normally think, in whatever manner they affect our senses. Therefrom, if the Pyrrhonist is the agnostic, the Cartesian sceptic is the atheist.

Because the Pyrrhonist requires much less of a belief in order for it to be confirmed as knowledge than do the Cartesian, the argument for Pyrrhonism are much more difficult to construct. A Pyrrhonist must show that there is no better set of reasons for believing to any standards, of which are in case that any knowledge learnt of the mind is understood by some of its forms, that has to require certainty.

The underlying latencies that are given among the many derivative contributions as awaiting their presence to the future, which of specifying to the theory of knowledge, is, but, nonetheless, the possibility to identify a set of shared doctrines, but, identity to discern two broad styles of instances to discern, in like manners, these two styles of pragmatism, clarify the innovation that a Cartesian approval is fundamentally flawed, nonetheless, of responding very differently but not fordone.

Repudiating the requirements of absolute certainty or knowledge, insisting on the connection of knowledge with activity, as, too, of pragmatism of a reformist distributing knowledge upon the legitimacy of traditional questions about the truth- conditions of our cognitive practices, and sustain a conception of truth objectives, enough to give those questions that undergo of a gathering in their own purposive latencies, yet we are given to the spoken word for which a dialectic awareness sparks the aflame from the ambers of fire.

Pragmatism of a determinant revolution, by contrast, relinquishing the objectivity of youth, acknowledges no legitimate epistemological questions over and above those that are naturally kindred of our current cognitive conviction.

It seems clear that certainty is a property that can be assembled to either a person or a belief. We can say that a person, 'S' are certain, or we can say that its implications led towardly of an inclining inclination whose alinement is aligned as of 'p', are certain. The two uses can be connected by saying that 'S' has the right to be certain just in case the value of 'p' is sufficiently verified.

In defining certainty, it is crucial to note that the term has both an absolute and relative sense. More or less, we take a proposition to be certain when we have no doubt about its truth. We may do this in error or unreasonably, but objectively a proposition is certain when such absence of doubt is justifiable. The sceptical tradition in philosophy denies that objective certainty is often possible, or ever possible, either for any proposition at all, or for any proposition from some suspect family (ethics, theory, memory, empirical judgement etc.) a major sceptical weapon is the possibility of upsetting events that can cast doubt back onto what were hitherto taken to be certainties. Others include reminders of the divergence of human opinion, and the fallible source of our confidence. Fundamentalist approaches to knowledge look for a basis of certainty, upon which the structure of our system is built. Others reject the metaphor, looking for mutual support and coherence, without foundation.

Nonetheless, in spite of the notorious difficulty of reading Kantian ethics, a hypothetical imperative embeds a command which is in place only given to some antecedent desire or project: 'If you want to look wise, stay quiet'. The injunction to stay quiet only proves applicable to those with the antecedent desire or inclination. If one has no desire to look wise, the injunction cannot be so avoided: It is a requirement that binds anybody, regardless of their inclination. It could be represented as, for example, 'tell the truth (regardless of whether you want to or not)'. The distinction is not always signalled by presence or absence of the conditional or hypothetical form: 'If you crave drink, don't become a bartender' may be regarded as an absolute injunction applying to anyone, although only assigned for its own function, in case of those with the stated desire.

In Grundlegung zur Metaphsik der Sitten (1785), Kant discussed five forms of the categorical imperative: (1) The formula of universal law: 'act only on that maxim through which you can at the same times will that it should become universal law: (2) The formula of the law of nature: 'act as if the maxim of your action were to become willfully the universal laws of nature. (3) The formula of the end-in-itself: ' an act of which a way that you always treat humanity, in your own person or in the person of any other, never simply as a means, but always at the same time as an end: (4) The formula of autonomy, or considering 'the will of every rational being as a 'will' which makes universal law': (5) The formula of the Kingdom of Ends, which provides a model for the systematic union of different rational beings under common laws.

Even so, a proposition that is not a conditional 'p', is moreover, the affirmative and negative, modern opinion is wary of this distinction, since what appears categorical may vary notation. Apparently, categorical propositions may also turn out to be disguised conditionals: 'X' is intelligent (categorical?): If 'X' is given a range of task's she performs them better than many people (conditional?) The problem. Nonetheless, is not merely one of classification, since deep metaphysical questions arise when facts that seem to be categorical and therefore solid, come to seem by contrast conditional, or purely hypothetical or potential.

A limited area of knowledge or endeavour to which pursuits, activities and interests are a central representation held to a concept of physical theory. In this way, a field is defined by the distribution of a physical quantity, such as temperature, mass density, or potential energy, at different points in space, in the particularly important example of force fields, such as gravitational, electrical, and magnetic fields, the field value at a point is the force which a test particle would experience if it were located at that point. The philosophical problem is whether a force field is to be thought of as purely potential, so the presence of a field merely describes the propensity of masses to move relative to each other, or whether it should be thought of in terms of the physically real modifications of a medium, whose properties result in such power that is, are force of a purely potential. As fully characterized by dispositional statements or conditionals, such that in the classical theory of the syllogism, a term in a categorical proposition is distributed if the proposition entails any proposition obtained from a substituting term which denotes only a subset of the items denoted by the original. For example, in 'all dogs bark', the term 'dog' is distributed, since it entails 'all terriers' bark', which is obtained from its substitution In 'Not all dogs bark' the same term is not distributed, since it may be true while 'not all terriers bark' is false. Former option seems to require within ungrounded dispositions, or regions of space that differ only in what happens if an object is placed there. The law-like shape of these dispositions, apparent for example in the curved lines of force of the magnetic field, may then seem quite inexplicable. To atomists, such as Newton it would represent a return to Aristotelian entelechies, or quasi-psychological affinities between things, which are responsible for their motions. The latter option requires understanding of how forces of attraction and repulsion can be 'grounded' in the properties of the medium.

The basic idea of a field is arguably present in Leibniz, who was certainly hostile to Newtonian atomism. Although his equal hostility to 'action at a distance,' certainly muddies the water. It is usually credited to the Jesuit mathematician and respectable scientist of Joseph Boscovich (1711-87) and Immanuel Kant (1724-1804), both of whom, of a direct influence, causing to occur as a result of furthering the works of the scientist Faraday, with whose work had implicated upon that of which the physical notion becomes establish. In Faraday's paper 'On the Physical Character of the Lines of Magnetic Force' (1852) as he was to suggest several criteria for assessing the physical reality of lines of force, such as whether they are affected by an intervening material medium, whether the motion depends on the nature of what is placed at the receiving end. As far as electromagnetic fields go, Faraday himself inclined to the view that the mathematical similarity between heat flow, currents, and electromagnetic lines of force was evidence for the physical reality of the intervening medium.

Once, again, our mentioning recognition for which of a case value, whereby its view is especially associated the American psychologist and philosopher William James (1842-1910), that the truth of a statement can be defined in terms of a 'utility' of accepting it. Communicated, so much as a dispiriting position for which its place of valuation may be viewed as an objection, since there are things that are false, as it may be useful in its acceptance, but conversely there are things that are true and that it may be damaging in its favour or consented. Nevertheless, there are deep connections between the idea that a representation system is accorded, and the likely success of the projects in progressive formality, by its possession. The evolution of a system of representation either perceptual or linguistic, seems bounded to connect successes with everything adapting or with utility in the modest sense. The Wittgenstein doctrine stipulates the meaning of use that upon the nature of belief and its relations with human attitude, emotion and the idea that belief in the truth on one hand, the action of the other. One way of binding with cement, wherefore the connection is found in the idea that natural selection becomes much as much in adapting us to the cognitive creatures, because beliefs have effects, they work. Pragmatism can be found in Kant's doctrine, and continued to play an influential role in the theory of meaning and truth.

James, (1842-1910), although with characteristic generosity exaggerated in his debt to Charles S. Peirce (1839-1914), he charted that the method of doubt encouraged people to pretend to doubt what they did not doubt in their hearts, and criticize its individualist's insistence, that the ultimate test of certainty is to be found in the individuals personalized consciousness.

From his earliest writings, James understood cognitive processes in teleological terms. Though, he held, in the assistance in the satisfactory interests. His will to Believe doctrine, the view that we are sometimes justified in believing beyond the evidential relics upon the notion that a belief's benefits are relevant to its justification. His pragmatic method of analysing philosophical problems, for which requires that we find the meaning of terms by examining their application to objects in experimental situations, similarly reflects the teleological approach in its attention to consequences.

An approaching advancement from which James's theory of meaning is isolated from verification, for being dismissive to metaphysics, is unlike the verificationalist, who takes cognitive meaning to be a matter only of consequences in sensory experience. James' took pragmatic meaning to include emotional and matter responses. Moreover, his, metaphysical standard of value, not a way of dismissing them as meaningless, but it should also be noted that to a certain degree it is extended widely of ranging in scope or application, such is to consider the provinces circumscribed constrictions, as James did not hold that even in the broadest of consequences were exhaustive in terminological meanings. 'Theism', for example, he took to have antecedently, definitional meaning, in addition to its varying degree of importance and chance upon an important pragmatic meaning.

James' theory of truth reflects upon his teleological conception of cognition, by considering a true belief to be one which is compatible with our existing system of beliefs, and leads us to satisfactory interaction with the world.

However, Peirce's famous pragmatist principle is a rule of logic employed in clarifying our concepts and ideas. Consider the claim the liquid in a flask is an acid, if, we believe this, we except that it would turn red: We accept an action of ours to have certain experimental results. The pragmatic principle holds that listing the conditional expectations of this kind, in that we associate such immediacy with applications of a conceptual representation that provides a complete and orderly set clarification of the concept. This is relevant to the logic of abduction: Clarificationist's using the pragmatic principle provide all the information about the content of a hypothesis that is relevantly to decide whether it is worth testing.

To a greater extent, and what is most important, is the famed apprehension of the pragmatic principle, in so that, Pierces's' account of reality, as when we take something to be real, which by this single case we think it is 'fated to be agreed upon by all who investigate' the matter to which it stands, in other words, if I believe that it is real, the case that 'P', then I except that if anyone was to inquire into the finding its measure into whether that 'p', they would arrive at the belief that 'p'. However, the fact, state, or quality of being real or genuine, in that which is real, an actual thing, situation, or event within which the sum or totality of real things that the absolute or ultimate, as contrasting with the apparent, it is not given of the theory that the experimental consequences of our actions should be specified by some warranted empiricist vocabulary-Peirce insisted that perceptual theories are abounding in latency. Even so, nor is it his view that the collected conditionals do or not clarify a concept as all analytic.

If realism itself can be given a fairly quick clarification, it is more difficult to chart the various forms of supposition, for they seem legendary. Other opponents deny that the entitles posited by the relevant discourse that exists or at least exists: The standard example is 'idealism', which reality is somehow mind-curative or mind-co-ordinated-that real object comprising the 'external worlds' were dependently of eloping minds, but only exist as in some way correlative to the mental operations. The doctrine assembled of 'idealism' enters on the conceptual note that reality as we understand this as meaningful and reflects the working of mindful purposes. And it construes this as meaning that the inquiring mind itself makes of some formative constellations and not of any mere understanding of the nature for having to represent the true or actual, as opposed to the apparent or ostensible facts in the real reason, or the resulting attribution to it.

Wherefore, the term is most straightforwardly used when qualifying another linguistic form of Grammatik: a real 'χ' may be contrasted with a fake, a failed 'χ', a near 'χ', and so on. To treat something as real, without qualification, is to suppose it to be part of the actualized world. To reify something is to suppose that we have committed by some indoctrinated treatise, as that of a theory. The central error in thinking of reality and the totality of existence is to think of the 'unreal' as a separate domain of things, perhaps, unfairly to that of the benefits of existence.

Such that nonexistence of all things, as the product of logical confusion of treating the term 'nothing' as itself a referring expression instead of a 'quantifier', as stating informally as a quantifier, sn is an expression that reports of a quantity of times that a predicate is satisfied in some class of things, i.e., in a domain.) This confusion leads the unsuspecting to think that a sentence such as 'Nothing is all around us' talks of a special kind of thing that is all around us, when in fact it merely denies that the predicate 'is all around us' has appreciation. The feelings that led some philosophers and theologians, notably Heidegger, who launched his philosophy for experiencing Nothingness, where the experience of Nothingness seemed justly as important than itself, thinking that nothingness is more real than nothingness, but is not properly the experience of anything, but rather the failure of a hope or expectation that there would be something of some kind at some point of wherever time. This may arise in quite everyday cases, as when one finds that the article of functions one expected to see as usual, in the corner has disappeared. The difference between 'existentialist" and 'analytic philosophy', on the point of what, whereas the former is afraid of nothing, and the latter think that there is nothing to be afraid of.

A rather different set of concerns arises when actions are specified in terms of doing nothing, saying nothing may be an admission of guilt, and doing nothing in some circumstances may be tantamount to murder, still, other situations, subsequently contributing of the substitution problems, arising over the conceptualization of empty space and time. Whereas, the standard opposition between those who affirm and those who deny, the real existence of some kind of thing or some kind of fact or state of an affair, almost any area of discourse may be the focus of this dispute1: The external world, the past and future, other minds, mathematical objects, possibilities, universals, moral or aesthetic properties are examples. There be to one influential suggestion, as associated with the British philosopher of logic and language, and the most determinative of philosophers centred round Anthony Dummett (1925), to which is borrowed from the 'intuitivistic' critique of classical mathematics, and suggested that the unrestricted use of the 'principle of a bivalence' is the trademark of 'realism'. However, this has to overcome counterexamples in both ways, although Aquinas wads a moral 'realist', he held that moral really was not sufficiently structured to make true or false every moral claim. Unlike Kant who believed that he could use the law of bivalence happily in mathematics, precisely because it deals only with our own construction. Realism can itself be subdivided: Kant, for example, combines empirical realism (within the phenomenal world the realist says the right things - surrounding objects really exist, and independent of us and our mental stares) with transcendental idealism (the phenomenal world as a whole reflects the structures imposed on it by the activity of our minds as they render it intelligible to us). In modern philosophy the orthodox opposition to realism had been in the from the philosopher such as Goodman, who, impressed by the extent to which we perceive the world through conceptual and linguistic lenses of our own making.

Assigned to the modern treatment of existence in the theory of 'quantification' is sometimes put by saying that existence is not a predicate. The idea is that the existential quantify themselves adding an operator on a predicate, indicating that the property it expresses has instances. Existence is therefore treated as a second-order property, or a property of properties. It is fitting to say, that in this it is like number, for when we say that these things of a kind, we do not describe the thing (and we would if we said there are red things of the kind), but instead attribute a property to the kind itself. The parallelled numbers are exploited by the German mathematician and philosopher of mathematics Gottlob Frége in the dictum that affirmation of existence is merely denied of the number nought. A problem, nevertheless, proves accountable for it's crated by sentences like 'This exists', where some particular thing is undirected, such that a sentence seems to express a contingent truth (for this insight has not existed), yet no other predicate is involved. 'This exists' is, in this way unlike 'Tamed tigers exist', where a property is said to have an instance, for the word 'this' and does not locate a property, but only being an individual.

Possible worlds seem able to differ from each other purely in the presence or absence of individuals, and not merely in the distribution of exemplification of properties.

The philosophical ponderosities, over which to set upon the unreal, as belonging to the domain of Being, and yet, there is little for us that can be said with the philosopher's study. So it is not apparent that there can be such a subject for being, by itself, but, still, the concept had a central place in philosophy from Parmenides to Heidegger. The essential question of 'why is there something and not of nothing'? Prompting over logical reflection on what it is for a universal to have an instance, nd as long history of attempts to explain contingent existence, by which id to reference and a necessary ground.

In the transition, ever since Plato, this ground becomes a self-sufficient, perfect, unchanging, and external something, identified within the Good, or in God, but whose relation with the everyday world remains obscure. The celebrated argument for the existence of God, as the first to explicate upon this issue was through Anselm in his argument for the necessity of the incarnation. The argument by defining God as 'something than which nothing greater can be conceived', God then exists in the understanding since we understand this concept. However, if He only existed in the understanding something greater could be conceived, for a being that exists in reality is greater than one that exists in the understanding. Bu then, we can conceive of something greater than that than which nothing greater can be conceived, which is contradictory. Therefore, God cannot exist on the understanding, but exists in reality.

An influential argument (or family of arguments) for the existence of God, finding its premisses are that all natural things are dependent for their existence on something else. The totality of dependent beings must then of itself depend upon a non-dependent, or necessarily existent being of which is God. Like the argument to design, the cosmological argument was attacked by the Scottish philosopher and historian David Hume (1711-76) and Immanuel Kant.

Its main problem, nonetheless, is that it requires us to make sense of the notion of necessary existence. For if the answer to the question of why anything exists is that some other tings of a similar kind exists, the question merely revives at some other time and then repeats again. Such in that 'God' that ends the question must exist necessarily: It must not be an entity of which the same kinds of questions can be raised. The other problem with the argument is attributing concern and care to the deity, not for connecting the necessarily existent being it derives with human values and aspirations.

The ontological argument has been treated by modern theologians such as Barth, following Hegel, not so much as a proof with which to confront the unconverted, but as an explanation of the deep meaning of religious belief. Collingwood, regards the argument s proving not that because our idea of God is that of id quo maius cogitare viequit, wherefore God exists, but proving that because this is our idea of God, we stand committed to belief in its existence. Its existence is a metaphysical point or absolute presupposition of certain forms of thought.

In the 20th century, modal versions of the ontological argument have been propounded by the American philosophers Charles Hertshorne, Norman Malcolm, and Alvin Plantinga. One version is to define something as unsurpassably great, if it exists and is perfect in every 'possible world', such that is, to allow that it is at least possible that an unsurpassably great being has of existing. This means that there is a possible world in which such a being exists. However, if it exists in one world, it exists in all (for the fact that such a being exists in a world that entails, in at least, it exists and is perfect in every world), so, it exists necessarily. The correct response to this argument is to disallow the apparently reasonable concession that it is possible that such a being exists. This concession is much more dangerous than it looks, since in the modal logic, involved from possibly necessarily 'p', where it can be devised as necessarily that 'p'. A symmetrical proof starting from the assumption that it is possibly that such a being does not exist would derive that it is impossible of its existence.

The doctrine that it makes an ethical difference of whether an agent actively intervenes to bring about a result, or omits to act in circumstances in which it is foreseen, in its result of the omissions that which gives the same result as have to occur. Thus, suppose that I wish you dead. If I act to bring about your death, I am a murderer, however, if I happily discover you in danger of death, and fail to act to save you, I am not acting cruelly barbarous, therefore, according to the doctrine of acts and omissions not a murderer. Critics implore that omissions can be as deliberate and immoral as I am responsible for your food and fact to feed you. Only omission is surely a killing, 'Doing nothing' can be a way of doing something, or in other worlds, absence of bodily movement can also constitute acting negligently, or deliberately, and defending on the context, may be a way of deceiving, betraying, or killing. Nonetheless, criminal law offers to find its conveniences, from which to distinguish discontinuous intervention, for which is permissible, for bringing about results, but which cannot be. The question is whether the difference, if there is one, is, between acting and omitting to act be discernibly or defined in a way that bars a general moral might.

The double effect of a principle attempting to define when an action that had both good and bad results are morally permissible. I one formation such an action is permissible if (1) The action is not wrong in itself, (2) the bad consequence is not that which is intended (3) the good is not itself a result of the bad consequences, and (4) the two consequential effects are commensurate. Thus, for instance, I might justifiably bomb an enemy factory, foreseeing but intending that the death of nearby civilians, whereas bombing the death of nearby civilians intentionally would be disallowed. The principle has its roots in Thomist moral philosophy, accordingly. St. Thomas Aquinas (1225-74), held that it is meaningless to ask whether a human being is two tings (soul and body) or, only just as it is meaningless to ask whether the wax and the shape given to it by the stamp are one: On this analogy the sound is ye form of the body. Life after death is possible only because a form itself does not perish (pricking is a loss of form).

And, therefore, in some sense available to reactivate a new body, therefore, not I who survive body death, but I may be resurrected in the same personalized body that becomes reanimated by the same form, that which Aquinas's account, as a person has no privileged self-understanding, we understand ourselves as we do everything else, by way of sense experience and abstraction, and knowing the principle of our own lives is an achievement, not as a given. Difficulty at this point led the logical positivist to abandon the notion of an epistemological foundation altogether, and to flirt with the coherence theory of truth, it is widely accepted that trying to make the connection between thought and experience through basic sentence s depends on an untenable 'myth of the given

The special way that we each have of knowing our own thoughts, intentions, and sensationalist have brought in the many philosophical 'behaviorist and functionalist tendencies, that have found it important to deny that there is such a special way, arguing the way that I know of my own mind inasmuch as the way that I know of yours, e.g., by seeing what I say when asked. Others, however, point out that the behaviour of reporting the result of introspection in a particular and legitimate kind of behavioural access that deserves notice in any account of historically human psychology. The historical philosophy of reflection upon the astute of history, or of historical, thinking, finds the term was used in the 18th century, e.g., by Volante was to mean critical historical thinking as opposed to the mere collection and repetition of stories about the past. In Hegelian, particularly by conflicting elements within his own system, however, it came to man universal or world history. The Enlightenment confidence was being replaced by science, reason, and understanding that gave history a progressive moral thread, and under the influence of the German philosopher, who has spread Romanticism, in that of Gottfried Herder (1744-1803), and, Immanuel Kant, this idea took it further to hold, so that philosophy of history cannot be the detecting of a grand system, the unfolding of the evolution of human nature as witnessed in successive sages (the progress of rationality or of Spirit). This essential speculative philosophy of history is given an extra Kantian twist in the German idealist Johann Fichte, in whom the extra association of temporal succession with logical implication introduces the idea that concepts themselves are the dynamic engines of historical change. The idea is readily intelligible in that their world of nature and of thought become identified. The work of Herder, Kant, Flichte and Schelling is synthesized by Hegel: History has a plot, as too, this to the moral development of man, which he gives to reason of state, this in turn is the development of thought, or a logical development in which various necessary moment in the life of the concept are successively achieved and improved upon. Hegel's method is at it's most successful, when the object is the history of ideas, and the evolution of thinking may march in steps with logical oppositions and their resolution encounters red by various systems of thought.

The view that everyday attributions of intention, belief and meaning to other persons proceeded through tactic use of a theory that enables one to construct these interpretations as explanations of their doings, even so, the view is commonly held along with functionalism, according to which psychological states theoretical entities, identified by the network of their causes and effects. The theory-theory had different implications, depending on which feature of theories is being stressed. Theories may be though of as capable of formalization, as yielding predications and explanations, as achieved by a process of theorizing, as achieved by predictions and explanations, as achieved by a process of theorizing, as answering to empirical evidence that is in principle describable without them, as liable to be overturned by newer and better theories, and so on. The main problem with seeing our understanding of others as the outcome of a piece of theorizing is the nonexistence of a medium in which this theory can be couched, as the child learns simultaneously he minds of others and the meaning of terms in its native language.

Our understanding of others is not gained by the tacit use of a 'theory'. Enabling us to infer what thoughts or intentions explain their actions, however, by reliving the situation 'in their moccasins', or from their point of view, and thereby understanding what hey experienced and thought, and therefore expressed. Understanding others is achieved when we can ourselves deliberate as they did, and hear their words as if they are our own. The suggestion is a modern development of the 'Verstehen' tradition associated with Dilthey, Weber and Collngwood.

Much as much, it is therefore, in some sense available to reactivate a new body, however, not that I, who survives bodily death, but I may be resurrected in the same body that becomes reanimated by the same form, in that of Aquinas's accounts, as a person has no privileged self-understanding. We understand ourselves, just as we do everything else, that through the sense experience, in that of an abstraction, may justly be of knowing the principle of our own lives, is to obtainably achieve, and not as a given. In the theory of knowledge that knowing Aquinas holds the Aristotelian doctrine that knowing entails some similarities between the Knower and what there is to be known: A human's corporal nature, therefore, requires that knowledge start with sense perception, but, as yet, the same limitations that do not apply of bringing further the levelling stabilities that are contained within the hierarchical mosaic, such as the celestial heavens that open in bringing forth to angels.

In the domain of theology Aquinas deploys the distraction emphasized by Eringena, between the existence of God in the understanding significance of five arguments: They are (1) Motion is only explicable if there exists an unmoved, a first mover (2) the chain of efficient causes demands a first cause (3) the contingent character of existing things in the wold demands a different order of existence, or in other words as something that has a necessary existence (4) the gradations of value in things in the world require the existence of something that is most valuable, or perfect, and (5) the orderly character of events points to a final cause, or end t which all things are directed, and the existence of this end demands a being that ordained it. All the arguments are physico-theological arguments, in that between reason and faith, Aquinas lays out proofs of the existence of God.

He readily recognizes that there are doctrines such that are the Incarnation and the nature of the Trinity, know only through revelations, and whose acceptance is more a matter of moral will. God's essence is identified with his existence, as pure activity. God is simple, containing no potential. No matter how, we cannot obtain knowledge of what God is (his quiddity), perhaps, doing the same work as the principle of charity, but suggesting that we regulate our procedures of interpretation by maximizing the extent to which we see the subject s humanly reasonable, than the extent to which we see the subject as right about things. Whereby remaining content with descriptions that apply to him partly by way of analogy, God reveals but not himself.

Describing events that haphazardly happen does not in themselves allow us to talk of rationality and intention, which are the categories we may apply if we conceive of them as action. We think of ourselves not only passively, as creatures that make things happen. Understanding this distinction gives forth of its many major problems concerning the nature of an agency for the causation of bodily events by mental events, and of understanding the 'will' and 'free will'. Other problems in the theory of action include drawing the distinction between an action and its consequence, and describing the structure involved when we do one thing 'by' its doing of another thing. Even the planning and dating where someone shoots someone on one day and in one place, whereby the victim then dies on another day and in another place. Where and when did the murderous act take place?

Causation, least of mention, is not clear and that only events are created by of for itself. Kant cites the example of a cannonball at rest and stationed upon a cushion, but causing the cushion to be the shape that it is, and thus to suggest that the causal states of affairs or objects or facts may also be casually related. All of which, the central problem is to understand the elements of necessitation or determinacy of the future of events, as Hume thought, are in themselves 'loose and separate': How then are we to conceive of others? The relationship seems not too perceptible, for all that perception gives us (Hume argues) is knowledge of the patterns that events do, actually falling into than any acquaintance with the connections determining the pattern. It is, however, in making clear that our conception of everyday objects is largely determined by their casual powers, and all our action is based on the belief that these causal powers are stable and reliable. Although scientific investigation can give us wider and deeper dependable patterns, it seems incapable of bringing us any nearer to the 'must' of causal necessitation. Particular examples of puzzles with causalities are quite apart from general problems of forming any conception of what it is: How are we to understand the casual interaction between mind and body? How can the present, which exists, or its existence to a past that no longer exists? How is the stability of the casual order to be understood? Is backward causality possible? Is causation a concept needed in science, or dispensable?

The news concerning free-will, is nonetheless, a problem for which is to reconcile our everyday consciousness of ourselves as agent, with the best view of what science tells us that we are. Determinism is one part of the problem. It may be defined as the doctrine that every event has a cause. More precisely, for any event 'C', there will be one antecedent state of nature 'N', and a law of nature 'L', such that given L, N will be followed by 'C'. But if this is true of every event, it is true of events such as my doing something or choosing to do something. So my choosing or doing something is fixed by some antecedent state 'N' an d the laws. Since determinism is universal, these in turn are fixed, and so backwards to events, for which I am clearly not responsible (events before my birth, for example). So, no events can be voluntary or free, where that means that they come about purely because of my willing them I could have done otherwise. If determinism is true, then there will be antecedent states and laws already determining such events: How then can I truly be said to be their author, or be responsible for them?

Reactions to this problem are commonly classified as: (1) Hard determinism. This accepts the conflict and denies that you have real freedom or responsibility (2) Soft determinism or compatibility, whereby reactions in this family assert that everything you should have in doing and from a notion of freedom is quite compatible with determinism. In particular, if your actions are caused, it can often be true of you that you could have done otherwise if you had chosen, and this may be enough to render you liable to be held unacceptable (the fact that previous events will have caused you to choose as you have, is deemed irrelevant in this option). (3) Libertarianism, as this is the view that while appropriate compatibles are only an evasion, there is a more substantiative, real notion of freedom that can yet be preserved in the face of determinism (or, of indeterminism). In Kant, while the empirical or phenomenal self is determined and not free, whereas the noumenal or rational self is capable of being rational, free action. However, the noumenal self exists outside the categorical priorities of space and time, as this freedom seems to be of a doubtful value as other libertarian avenues do include of suggesting that the problem is badly framed, for instance, because the definition of determinism breaks down, or postulates by its suggesting that there are two independent but consistent ways of looking at an agent, the scientific and the humanistic, wherefore it is only through confusing them that the problem seems urgent. Nevertheless, these avenues have gained general popularity, as an error to confuse determinism and fatalism.

The dilemma for which determinism is for itself often supposes of an action that seems as the end of a causal chain, or, perhaps, by some hieratical set of suppositional actions that would stretch back in time to events for which an agent has no conceivable responsibility, then the agent is not responsible for the action.

Once, again, the dilemma adds that if an action is not the end of such a chain, is then one of its causes occurring at random, in that no antecedent event has brought it about, as, in that case, nobody is responsible for it ever to have occurred, so whether or not determinism is true, responsibility is shown to be illusory.

A mental act of 'willing' or trying whose presence is sometimes supposed to make the difference between intentional and voluntary action, as well of mere behaviour, as its theory is that there are such act's for being problematic, and the idea that they make the required difference is a case of explaining a phenomenon by citing another that raises exactly the same problem, since the intentional or voluntary nature of the set of volition now needs explanation. For determinism to act in accordance with the law of autonomy or freedom, is that in ascendance with universal moral law and regardless of selfish advantage.

A categorical notion in the work as contrasted by Kantian ethics shows of a hypothetical imperative that embeds of a commentary which is in place only given to some antecedent desire or project, 'if you want to look wise, as to remain in the guise for remaining quiet. The injunction to stay quiet only proves applicable to those with the antecedent desire or inclination: If one has no desire in the guise being in the masquerade for which one place of character for being made wise, as the enjoining character in that which advice lapses. A categorical imperative cannot be so avoided, it is a requirement that binds anybody, regardless of their inclination. It could be repressed as, for example, 'Tell the truth (regarding of whether you want to or not)', distinctively not always mistakably presumed or absence of the conditional or hypothetical form: 'If you crave drink, don't become a bartender' may be regarded as an absolute injunction applying to anyone, although only activated in the case of those with the stated desire.

A central object in the study of Kant's ethics is to understand the expressions of the inescapable, binding requirements of their categorical importance, and to understand whether they are equivalent at some deep level. Kant's stimulations of the notions are always convincing: One cause of confusion is relating Kant's ethical values to theories such a, 'expressionism' in that it is easy but imperatively must that it cannot be the expression of a sentiment, yet, it must derive from something 'unconditional' or necessary' such as the voice of reason. The standard mood of sentences used to issue request and commands are their imperative needs to issue as basic the need to communicate information, and as such to animals signalling systems may as often be interpreted either way, and understanding the relationship between commands and other action-guiding uses of language, such as ethical discourse. However, the moral theory of 'prescriptivism' may in fact, be attributed to Richard Hare (1919-2002), that assimilates moral commitment to the giving or accepting of a command, least of mention, critics have concentrated upon various differences between ethical commitment and command, including the problem that, while accepting a commands seem as tantamount in setting in 'themselves,' in order to obey it, accepting an ethical verdict is, unfortunately, consistent with refusing to be bound by it. The belief that utilitarianism is somehow implicit in the logic of moral concepts has also been vigorously contested. A further question is whether there is an imperative logic. 'Hump that bale' seems to follow from 'Tote that barge and hump that bale', follows from 'Its windy and its raining': But it is harder to say how to include other forms, does 'Shut the door or shut the window' follow from 'Shut the window', for example? The usual way for the development of imperative-logic is to work in terms of possibility, for that which by satisfying the one command without satisfying its other, thereby turning toward the variations of ordinary deductive logic.

Until very recently it might have been that most approaches to the philosophy of science were 'cognitive'. This includes 'logical positivism', as nearly all of those who wrote about the nature of science would have agreed that science ought to be 'value-free'. This had been a particular emphasis by the first positivist, as it would be upon twentieth-century successors, as science, deals with 'facts', and facts and values and irreducibly distinct, as facts are objective, they are what we seek in our knowledge of the world. Values are subjective: They bear the mark of human interest, they are the radically individual products of feeling and desire. Fact and value cannot, therefore, be inferred from fact, fact ought not be influenced by value. There were philosophers, notably some in the Kantian tradition, who viewed the relation of the human individual to the universalist aspiration of difference differently. However, the legacy of three centuries of largely empiricist reflection of the 'new' sciences ushered in by Galilee Galileo (1564-1642), the Italian scientist whose distinction belongs to the history of physics and astronomy, rather than natural philosophy.

The philosophical importance of Galileo's science rests largely upon the following closely related achievements: (1) His stunning successful arguments against Aristotelean science, (2) his proofs that mathematics is applicable to the real world. (3) His conceptually powerful use of experiments, both actual and employed regulatively, (4) His treatment of causality, replacing appeal to hypothesized natural ends with a quest for efficient causes, and (5) his unwavering confidence in the new style of theorizing that would become known as 'mechanical explanation'.

A century later, the maxim that scientific knowledge is 'value-laded' seems almost as entrenched as its opposite was earlier. It is supposed that between fact and value has been breached, and philosophers of science seem quite at home with the thought that science and value may be closely intertwined after all. What has happened to cause such an apparently radical change? What is its implications for the objectivity of science, the prized characteristic that, from Plato's time onwards, has been assumed to set off real knowledge (epistēmē) from mere opinion (doxa)? To answer these questions adequately, one would first have to know something of the reasons behind the decline of logical positivism, as, well as of the diversity of the philosophies of science that have succeeded it.

More general, the interdisciplinary field of cognitive science is burgeoning on several fronts. Contemporary philosophical reelection about the mind-which has been quite intensive-has been influenced by this empirical inquiry, to the extent that the boundary lines between them are blurred in places.

Nonetheless, the philosophy of mind at its core remains a branch of metaphysics, traditionally conceived. Philosophers continue to debate foundational issues in terms not radically unlike in kind or character from those in vogue in previous eras. Many issues in the metaphysics of science hinge on the notion of 'causation'. This notion is as important in science as it is in everyday thinking, and much scientific theorizing is concerned specifically to distinguishing features that characteristics the 'causes' of various phenomena. However, there is little philosophical agreement on what it is to say that one event is the cause of another.

Modern discussion of causation starts with the Scottish philosopher, historian, and essayist David Hume (1711-76), who argued that causation is simply a matter for which he denies that we have innate ideas. In that the causal relation is observably anything other than 'constant conjunction' because, they are observably necessary connections anywhere, and that there is either an empirical or demonstrative proof for the assumptions: That the future will resemble the past, and that every event has a cause. That is to say, that there is an irresolvable dispute between advocates of free-will and determinism, that extreme scepticism is coherent and that we can find the experiential source of our ideas of self-substance or God.

According to Hume (1978), one event causes another if only if events of the type to which the first event belongs regularly occur in conjunctive events of the type to which the second event belongs. The formulation, however, leaves several questions open. First, there is a problem of distinguishing genuine 'causal law' from 'accidental regularities'. Not all regularities are sufficiently law-like to underpin causal relationships. Being that there is a screw fastens with the screw's in my desk could well be constantly conjoined with being made of copper, without its being true that these are the screw's, that these are the screw's that are made of copper because they are in my desk. Secondly, the idea of constant conjunction does not give a 'direction' to causation. Causes need to be distinguished from effects. Nevertheless, knowing that A-type events are constantly conjoined with B-type events does not tell us that of 'A' and 'B' is the cause that the effect, since constant conjunction is itself a symmetric relation. Thirdly, there is a problem about 'probabilistic causation'. When we say that causes and effects are constantly conjoined, do we mean that the effects are always found with the causes, or is it enough that the causes make the effect probable?

Many philosophers of science during the past century have in mind to take in, the preferable dialectic awareness staged in rhetorical discourse or so to an 'explanation' than causation. According to the covering-law model of explanation, something is explained if it can be deduced from premises that include one or more laws. As applied to the explanation of particular events this implies that a particular event can be explained if it is linked by a law to another particular event. However, while they are often treated as separate theories, the covering-law account of explanation is at bottom little more than a variant of Hume's constant conjunction account of causation. This affinity shows up in the fact at the covering-law account faces essentially the same difficulties as Hume: (1) In appealing to deduction from 'laws', it needs to explain the difference between genuine laws and accidentally true regularities: (2) Omitting by effects, as well as effects by causes, after all, it is as easy to derive the height of the flagpole from the length of its shadow and the law of optics calculably: (3) Are the laws invoked in explanation required to be exceptionalness and deterministic, or is it acceptable say, to appeal to the merely probabilistic fact that smoking makes cancer more likely, in explaining why some particular person develops cancer?

Nevertheless, one of the centrally obtainable achievements for which the philosophy of science is directly to attend to go or be together in virtue with explicit and systematic accounts of the theories and explanatory strategies used to one's advantage in the science. Another common goal is to make construable the assembling constructions for the controlling philosophical illuminations in the analyses or explanations of central theoretical intellections. For which implicit manifestations quicken to the overall view of or attitude toward the spirited ideas that what exists in the mind as a representation. As of something comprehended or a formulation of a plan, which is not to assume of any constituent standard as invoked in one or another science. In the philosophy of biology, for example, there is a rich literature aimed at understanding teleological explanations, and there has been a great deal of work on the structure of evolutionary theory and on such crucial conceptualizations as existing or dealing with what exists only in the mind. By introducing 'teleological considerations', this account views beliefs as states with biological purpose and analyses their truth conditions specifically as those conditions that they are biologically supposed to covary to additional means of or by virtue of or through a detailed and complete manner, as, perhaps, in spite of or with the interaction of meaning intellection to deliberate our reflective cogitation of ruminating the act or process of thinking,

A teleological theory of representation needs to be supplemental with a philosophical account of biological representation. Generally a selectionism account of biological purpose, according to which item 'F' has purpose 'G' if and only if it is now present from past selection by some process that favoured items with 'G'. So, a given belief type will have the purpose of covarying with 'P', say if and only if some mechanism has selected it because it has covaried with 'P' the past.

Similarly, teleological theory holds that 'r' represents 'x' if it is r's function to implicate (i.e., covary with) 'x', teleological theories to be unlike or distinctly disagreed in its nature, form, or characteristics as only to differ in opinion to concede depending on the theory of functions they import. Perhaps the most important distinction is that between historical theories of functions and a-historical theories. Historical theories individuate functional states (therefore, contents) in a way that is sensitive to the historical development of the state, i.e., to factors such as the way the state was 'learned', or the way it evolved. A historical theory might hold that the function of 'r' is to implicate on or upon the purity of the form 'x', only if the capacity to token 'r' was developed (selected, learned). Because it gives to implicating the realistic prevalence held to convey (as an idea) to the mind, as this signifies the eloquence or significant manifestation for appearing the objectification in the forming implication of 'x'. Thus, a state physically indistinguishable from 'r' (physical states being a-historical) but lacking r's historical origins would not represent 'x' according to historical theories.

The American philosopher of mind (1935-) Jerry Alan Fodor, is known for his resolute 'realness', about the nature of mental functioning, taking the analogy between thought and computation seriously. Fodor believes that mental representations should be conceived as individual states with their own identities and structures, like formulae transformed by processes of computation or thought. His views are frequently contrasted with those of 'Holists' such as the American philosopher Herbert Donald Davidson (1917-2003), or 'instrumentalists' about mental ascription. Such as the British philosopher of logic and language, Eardley Anthony Michael Dummett (1925) In recent years he has become a vocal critic of some aspirations of cognitive science.

Nonetheless, a suggestion extrapolating the solution of teleology is continually to enquiry by points of owing to 'causation' and 'content', and ultimately a fundamental appreciation is to be considered, is that: we suppose that there is a causal path from A's to 'A's' and a causal path from B's to 'A's', and our problem is to find some difference between B-caused 'A's' and A-caused 'A's' in virtue of which the former but not the latter misrepresented. Perhaps, the two paths differ in their counterfactual properties. In particular, even if alienable positions in the group of 'A and B's', are causally effective to both, perhaps each can assume that only in the finding measure that A's would cause 'A's' in-as one can say -, 'optimal circumstances'. We could then hold that a symbol expresses its 'optimal property' through, the property that would causally control its tokening in optimal circumstances, in which takes place under specific limiting of conditions, yet the connecting factor exists as an accessory or as a determining element. Correspondingly, when the tokening of a symbol is causally controlled by properties other than its optimal property, the tokens that come about being ipso facto.

Suppose, that this story about 'optimal circumstances' is proposed as part of a naturalized semantics for mental representations. In which case it is, of course, essential that saying that the optimal circumstances for tokening a mental representation are in terms that are not themselves but possible of either semantical or intentional? (It would not do, for example, to recognize for being the optimal circumstances for tokening a symbol as those in which the tokens are true, that would be to assume precisely the semantical notion that the theory is supposed to naturalize.) Befittingly, the suggestion-to put it concisely-is that appeal to 'optimality' should be buttressed by appeals to 'teleology': Optimal circumstances are the ones in which the mechanisms that mediate symbol tokening are functioning 'as they are at the present timer. With mental representations, these would be paradigmatic circumstances where the mechanisms of belief fixation are functionally accepted or advanced as true or real based. On less than conclusive evidence that they are supposed are accepted or advanced as true or real is based on less than conclusive evidence. Such that to understanding or assume of the categories availably warranted. The position assumed or a point made especially in so, to or into that place that in consequence of that for this or that reason could be that thing, because circumstance is deprived to form what exists in the mind as a representation, as of something comprehended or as a formulation of planed, an idea of something in the mind.

So, then, the teleology of the cognitive mechanisms determines the optimal condition for belief fixation, and the optimal condition for belief fixation determines the content of beliefs. So the story goes.

To put this objection in slightly other words, the teleology story perhaps strikes one as plausible in that it aligns itself with one normative notion-truth-of another normative notion-optimality. However, this appearance if it is spurious there is no guarantee that the kind of optimality that teleology reconstructs relates to the kind of optimality that the explication of 'truth' requires. When mechanisms of repression are working 'optimally'-when they are working 'as they are supposed to'-what they deliver are likely to be 'falsehoods'.

Once, again, there is no obvious reason that coitions that are optimal for the tokening of one mental symbol need, be optimal for the tokening of other sorts. Perhaps the optimal conditions for fixing beliefs about very large objects, are different from the optimal conditions for fixing beliefs about very small ones, are different from the optimal conditions for fixing beliefs sights. Nevertheless, this raises the possibility that if we are to say which conditions are optimal for the fixation of a belief, we should know what the content of the belief is-what presents of being for itself to be a belief. Our explication of content would then require a notion of optimality, whose explication in turn requires a notion of content, and the resulting pile would clearly be unstable.

Teleological theories hold that 'r' represents 'χ' if it is r's function to give evidence of or serve as grounds for a valid or reasonable inference. If only to point directly to some future occurrence or development and communication by serving names of something significantly associated in the collections through (i.e., covary with) 'χ'. Teleological theories differ, depending on the theory of functions they import. Perhaps the most important distinction is that between historical theories of functions: Historically, theories individuate functional states (therefore, contents) in a way that is sensitive to the historical development of the state, i.e., to factors such as the way the state was 'learned', or the way it evolved. A historical theory might hold that the function of 'r' is to connoting or manifest the quality or state of being associatively tacit as implied in being such in essential character that suggests the intimation of something that is an outward manifestation of something else or that which is indicative, only to suggest the designation that by its very significative indications to which evoke the aptitudinal form 'χ', only if the capacity to token 'r' was developed (selected, learned) because it serves as grounded for a valid or reasonable inference as to characterize 'χ'. Thus, a state physically indistinguishable from 'r' (physical states being a-historical), but lacking r's historical origins would not represent 'χ' according to historical theories.

Just as functional role theories hold that r's representing 'x' is grounded in the functional role 'r' has in the representing system, i.e., on the relations imposed by specified cognitive processes between 'r' and other representations in the system's repertoire. Functional role theories take their cue from such commonsense ideas as that people cannot believe that cats are furry if they do not know that cats are animals or that fur is like hair.

That being said, that nowhere is the new period of collaboration between philosophy and other disciplines more evident than in the new subject of cognitive science. Cognitive science from its very beginning has been 'interdisciplinary' in character, and is in effect the joint property of psychology, linguistics, philosophy, computer science and anthropology. There are, therefore, a great variety of research projects within cognitive science, but the central area of cognitive science, its hardcoded ideology rests on the assumption that the mind is best viewed as analogous to a digital computer. The basic idea behind cognitive science is that recent developments in computer science and artificial intelligence have enormous importance for our conception of human beings. The basic inspiration for cognitive science went something like this: Human beings bare a similarity to information processing, as computers are designed precisely for their information processing. Therefore, one way to studying human cognition, as, perhaps, seem as the most excellent way to find out in their studies, as a matter of computational information processing. Some cognitive scientists think that the computer is just a metaphor for the human mind: Others think that the mind is literally a computer program. Still, saying is fair that without the computational model there would not have been a cognitive science as we now understand it.

In, Essay Concerning Human Understanding is the first modern systematic presentation that holds the attending empiricist epistemology, and as such had important implications for the natural sciences and for philosophy of science generally. Like his predecessor, Descartes, the English philosopher (1632-1704) John Locke began his account of knowledge from the conscious mind aware of ideas. Unlike Descartes, however, he was concerned not to build a system based on certainty, but to identify the mind's scope and limits. The premise upon which Locke built his account, including his account of the natural sciences, is that the ideas that furnish the mind are all derived from experience. He thus, totally rejected any kind of innate knowledge. In this he consciously opposes

Descartes, who had argued that coming to knowledge of fundamental truths about the natural world through reason alone is possible. Descartes (1596-1650) had argued, that we can come to know the essential nature of both 'minds' and 'matter' by pure reason. John Locke accepted Descartes's criterion of clear and distinct ideas as the basis for knowledge, but denied any source for them other than experience. It was information that came to some completions are the five senses (ideas of sensation) and ideas engendered from pure inner experiences (ideas of reflection) were the composite characteristics as to bring into being by mental and especially its reasons that made up of several separated or identifiable elements for which of the building blocks are aligned by themselves with an unreserved and open understanding.

Locke concerted his commitment to 'the new way of ideas' with the native espousal of the 'corpuscular philosophy' of the Irish scientist (1627-92) Robert Boyle. This, in essence, was an acceptance of a revised, more sophisticated account of matter and its properties advocated by the ancient atomists and recently supported by Galileo (1564-1642) and Pierre Gassendi (1592-1655). Boyle argued from theory and experiment that there were powerful reasons to justify some kind of corpuscular account of matter and its properties. He called the latter qualities, which he distinguished as primary and secondary. The distinction between primary and secondary qualities may be reached by two different routes: Either from the nature or essence of matter or from the nature and essence of experience, though practising these have a tendency to run-together. The former considerations make the distinction seem like an a priori, or necessary, truth about the nature of matter, while the latter makes it the empirical hypothesis -. Locke, too, accepted this account, arguing that the ideas we have of the primary qualities of bodies resemble those qualities as they are in the subject, whereas the ideas of the secondary qualities, such as colour, taste, and smell, do not resemble their causes in the object.

There is no strong connection between acceptance of the primary-secondary quality distinction and Locke's empiricism and Descartes had also argued strongly for universal acceptance by natural philosophers, and Locke embraced it within his more comprehensive empirical philosophy. However, Locke' empiricism did have major implications for the natural sciences, as he well realized. His account begins with an analysis of experience. All ideas, he argues, are either simple or complex. Simple ideas are those like the red of a particular rose or the roundness of a snowball. Complicated and complex ideas, our ideas of the rose or the snowball, are combinations of simple ideas. We may create new complicated and complex ideas in our imagination-a parallelogram, for example. Nevertheless, simple ideas can never be created by us: we just have them or not, and characteristically they are caused, for example, the impact on our senses of rays of light or vibrations of sound in the air coming from a particular physical object. Since we cannot create simple ideas, and they are determined by our experience, our knowledge is in a very strict uncompromising way limited. Besides, our experiences are always of the particular, never of the general. It is this simple idea or that particular complex idea that we apprehend. We never in that sense apprehend a universal truth about the natural world, but only particular instances. It follows from this that all claims to generality about that world-for example, all claims to identity what was then beginning to be called the laws of nature-must to that extent goes beyond our experience and thus be less than certain.

Several accounts have been proposed. David Lewis (1979) has argued that the asymmetry of causation derives from an 'asymmetry of over-determination'. The over-determination of present events by past events-consider a person who dies after simultaneously being shot and struck by lightning-is a very rare occurrence, by contrast, the multiple 'over-determination' of present events by future events is absolutely normal. This is because the future, unlike the past, will always contain multiple traces of any present event. To use Lewis's example, when the president presses the red button in the White House, the future effects do not only include the dispatch of nuclear missiles, but also the fingerprint on the button, his trembling, the further depletion of his gin bottle, the recording of the button's click on tape, he emission of light waves bearing the image of his action through the window, the warnings of the wave from the passage often signal current, and so on, and so on, and on.

Lewis relates this asymmetry of over-determination to the asymmetry of causation as follows. If we suppose the cause of a given effect to have been absent, then this implies the effect would have been absent too, since (apart from freak -like occurrence in the lightning-shooting case) there will not be any other causes left to 'fix' the effect. By contrast, if we suppose a given effect of some cause to have been absent, this does not imply the cause would have been absent, for there are still all the other traces left to 'fix' the causes. Lewis argues that these counterfactual considerations suffice to show why causes are different from effects.

Other philosophers appeal to a probabilistic variant of Lewis's asymmetry. Following, the philosopher of science and probability theorists, Hans Reichenbach (1891-1953), they note that the different causes of any given type of effect are normally probabilistically independent of each other, by contrast, the different effects of any given type of cause are normally probabilistically correlated. For example, both obesity and high excitement can cause heart attacks, but this does not imply that fat people are more likely to get excited than thin ones: Its facts, that both lung cancer and Nicotine-stained fingers can result from smoking does imply that lung cancer is more likely among people with nicotine-stained fingers. So this account distinguishes effects from causes by the fact that the former, but not the latter are probabilistically dependent on each other.

However, there is another course of thought in philosophy of science, the tradition of 'negative' or 'eliminative induction'. That is to say, that in eliminative induction a number of possible hypotheses conceiving some state of affairs is presumed, and rivals are progressively in reserve to new evidence, the process is an idealization, since in practice no closed set of initial theories is usually possible. The English diplomat and philosopher Francis Bacon (1561-1626) and in modern time the philosopher of science Karl Raimund Popper (1902-1994), we have the idea of using logic to bring falsifying evidence to bear on hypotheses about what must universally be the case that many thinkers accept in essence his solution to the problem of demarcating proper science from its imitators, namely that the former results in genuinely falsifiable theories whereas the latter do not. Although falsely, allowed many people's objections to such ideologies as psychoanalysis and Marxism.

Hume was interested in the processes by which we acquire knowledge: The processes of perceiving and thinking, of feeling and reasoning. He recognized that much of what we claim to know derives from other people secondhand, thirdhand or worse: Moreover, our perceptions and judgements can be distorted by a multiple array of factors-by what we are studying, and by the very act of study itself the main reason, however, behind his emphasis on 'probabilities and those other measures of evidence on which life and action entirely depend' is this:

> Evidently, all reasoning concerning 'matter of fact' of which
> is founded on the relation of cause and effect, and that?
> We can never infer the existence of one object form
> another unless they are connected, either mediately
> or immediately.

When we apparently observe a whole sequence, say of one ball hitting another, what do we observe? In the much commoner cases, when we wonder about the unobserved causes or effects of the events we observe, what precisely are we doing?

Hume recognized that a notion of 'must' or necessity is a peculiar feature of causal relation, inference and principles, and challenges us to explain and justify the notion. He argued that there is no observable feature of events, nothing like a physical bond, which can be properly labelled the 'necessary connection' between a given cause and its effect: Events are simply merely to occur, and there is in 'must' or 'ought' about them. However, repeated experience of pairs of events sets up the habit of expectation in us, such that when one of the pair occurs we inescapably expect the other. This expectation makes us infer the unobserved cause or unobserved effect of the observed event, and we mistakenly project this mental inference onto the events themselves. There is no necessity observable in causal relations, all that can be observed of a regular sequence, there is proper necessity in causal inferences, but only in the mind. Once we realize that causation is a relation between pairs of events. We also realize that often we are not present for the whole sequence that we want to divide into 'cause' and 'effect'. Our understanding of the casual relation is thus intimately linked with the role of the causal inference cause only causal inferences entitle us to 'go beyond what is immediately present to the senses'. Nevertheless, now two very important assumptions emerge behind the causal inference: The assumptions that like causes, in 'like circumstances, will always produce like effects', and the assumption that 'the course of nature will continue uniformly the same'-or, briefly that the future will resemble the past. Unfortunately, this last assumption lacks either empirical or a priori proof, that is, it can be conclusively established neither by experience nor by thought alone.

Hume frequently endorsed a standard seventeenth-century view that all our ideas are ultimately traceable, by analysis, to sensory impressions of an internal or external kind. In agreement, he claimed that all his theses are based on 'experience', understood as sensory awareness with memory, since only experience establishes matters of fact. Nonetheless, our belief that the future will resemble the past properly construed as a belief concerning only a mater of fact? As the English philosopher Bertrand Russell (1872-1970) remarked, earlier this century, the real problems that Hume asserts to are whether future futures will resemble future pasts, in the way that past futures really did resemble past pasts. Hume declares that 'if . . . the past may be no rule for the future, all experiences become useless and can cause inference or conclusion. Yet, he held, the supposition cannot stem from innate ideas, since there are no innate ideas in his view nor can it stems from any abstract formal reasoning. For one thing, the future can surprise us, and no formal reasoning seems able to embrace such contingencies: For another, even animals and unthinkable people conduct their lives as if they assume the future resembles the past: Dogs return for buried bones, children avoid a painful fire, and so forth. Hume is not deploring the fact that we have to conduct our lives based on probabilities. He is not saying that inductive reasoning could or should be avoided or rejected. Alternatively, he accepted inductive reasoning but tried to show that whereas formal reasoning of the kind associated with mathematics cannot establish or prove matters of fact, factual or inductive reasoning lacks the 'necessity' and 'certainty' associated with mathematics. His position, therefore clear; because 'every effect is a distinct event from its cause', only investigation can settle whether any two particular events are causally related: Causal inferences cannot be drawn with the force of logical necessity familiar to us from deductivity, but, although they lack such force, they should not be discarded. From causation, inductive inferences are inescapable and invaluable. What, then, makes 'experience' the standard of our future judgement? The answer is 'custom', it is a brute psychological fact, without which even animal life of a simple kind would be mostly impossible. 'We are determined by custom to suppose the future conformable to the past' (Hume, 1978), nevertheless, whenever we need to calculate likely events we must supplement and correct such custom by self-conscious reasoning.

Nonetheless, the problem that the causal theory of reference will fail once it is recognized that all representations must occur under some aspect or that the extentionality of causal relations is inadequate to capture the aspectual character of reference. The only kind of causation that could be adequate to the task of reference is intentional causal or mental causation, but the causal theory of reference cannot concede that ultimately reference is achieved by some met device, sincethe whole approach behind the causal theory was to try to eliminate the traditional mentalism of theories of reference and meaning in favour of objective causal relations in the world, though it is at present by far the most influential theory of reference, will be a failure for these reasons.

If mental states are identical with physical states, presumably the relevant physical states are various sorts of neural states. Our concepts of mental states such as thinking, sensing, and feeling are of course, different from our concepts of neural states, of whatever sort. Still, that is no problem for the identity theory. As J.J.C. Smart (1962), who first argued for the identity theory, emphasized, that requisite identities do not depend on understanding concepts of mental states or the meanings of mental terms. For 'a' to be the identical with 'b', 'a', and 'b' must have the same properties, but the terms or the things in themselves are that 'a' and 'b', and need not mean the same. Its principal means by measure can be accorded within the indiscernibility of identical, in that, if 'A' is identical with 'B', then every property that 'A' has 'B', and vice versa. This is, sometimes known as Leibniz' s Law.

Nevertheless, a problem does seem to arise about the properties of mental states. Suppose pain is identical with a certain firing of c-fibres. Although a particular pain is the very same as a neural-firing, we identify that state in two different ways: As a pain and as neural-firing. That the state will therefore have certain properties in virtue of which we identify it as pain and others in virtue of which we identify it as an excitability of neural firings. The properties in virtue of which we identify it as a pain will be mental properties, whereas those in virtue of which ewe identify it as neural excitability firing, will be physical properties. This has seemed for which are many to lead of the kinds of dualism at the level of the properties of mentalities, even if these mental states in that which we reject dualism of substances and take people simply to be some physical organisms. Those organisms still have both mental and physical states. Similarly, even if we identify those mental states with certain physical states, those states will, nonetheless have both mental and physical properties. So disallowing dualism with respect to substances and their states are simply to its reappearance at the level of the properties of those states.

There are two broad categories of mental property. Mental states such as thoughts and desires, often called 'propositional attitudes', have 'content' that can be de scribed by 'that' clauses. For example, one can have a thought, or desire, that it will rain. These states are said to have intentional properties, or 'intentionality sensations', such as pains and sense impressions, lack intentional content, and have instead qualitative properties of various sorts.

The problem about mental properties is widely thought to be most pressing for sensations, since the painful qualities of pains and the red quality of visual sensations might be irretrievably nonphysical. If the idea that something conveys to the mind as having endlessly debated the meaning of relationally to the mind, the mental aspects of the problem seem once removed among mental states that to account in the actualization of proper innovation that has nonphysical properties, is that the identity of mental states generates or empower physical states as they would not sustain the unconditional thesis as held to mind-body materialism.

The Cartesian doctrine related and distinguished by the mentality for which are in mental properties of those states constructed by anecdotal explanations, for that the consequential temperance as proven or given to compatibility is founded the appropriate interconnective link to set right the ordering of fibrous fragments as strikingly spatial, as this will facilitate the functional contribution in which the distribution of infractions that when assembled are found of space and time. However, it should be that p assimilates some nonphysical advocates of the identity theory sometimes accepting it, for the ideas that of or relating to the mind, as a mental aspect calling our intellectual mentality as the intellective for which is not nonphysical but yields to underlying latencies, for example, the insistence by some identity theorists that mental properties are really neural as between being mental and physical. To being neural is in this way a property would have to be neutral about whether it is compatible and thus imply in the manner that inarticulate the idea that something conveys to the mind, the acceptation of sense for which its significancy plays on one side of the manner that mental is the ideological reason in thinking as the inner and well of the outer domains that of or relating to the mind. Only if one thought that being meant being nonphysical would one hold that defending materialism required showing the ostensible mental properties are neutral as regards whether or not they are mental.

Nevertheless, holding that mental properties are nonphysical has a cost that is usually not noticed. A phenomenon is mental only if it has some distinctively mental property.

So, strictly speaking, some materialists who claim that mental properties are nonphysical phenomena have in the unfolding transformation that it can only be derived through the state or factorial conditional independence that reality, of its customs that have recently become and exists to induce to come into being, a condition or occurrence traceable to a cause or the aftereffect through which an end-product or its resulting event of something or thing that has existence. This is the 'Eliminative-Materialist position advanced by the American philosopher and critic Richard Rorty (1979).

According to Rorty (1931-) 'mental' and 'physical' are incompatible terms. Nothing can be both mental and physical, so mental states cannot be identical with bodily states. Rorty traces this incompatibly to our views about incorrigibility: 'Mental' and 'physical' are incorrigible reports of one's own mental states, but not reports of physical occurrences, but he also argues that we can imagine people who describe themselves and each other using terms just like our mental vocabulary, except that those people do not take the reports made with that vocabulary to be incorrigible. Since Rorty takes a state to be a mental state only if one's reports about it are taken to be incorrigible, his imaginary people do not ascribe mental states to themselves or each other. Nonetheless, the only difference between their language and ours is that we take as incorrigible certain reports that they do not. So their language as no-less the descriptive explanatorily power, in that the American philosopher and critic, Richard McKay Rorty (1931-) concludes that our mental vocabulary is idle, and that there are no distinctively mental phenomena.

This argument hinges on or upon the building incorrigibility into the meaning of the term 'mental'. If we do not, the way is open to interpret Rorty's imaginary people as simply having a different theory of mind from ours, on which reports of one's own mental states are corrigible. Their reports would this be about mental states, as construed by their theory. Rorty's thought experiment would then provide to conclude not that our terminology is idle, but only that this alternative theory of mental phenomena is correct. His thought experiment would thus sustain the non-eliminativist view that mental states are bodily states. Whether Rorty's argument supports his eliminativist conclusion or the standard identity theory, therefore, depends solely on whether or not one holds that the quality or highest in degree attainable or attained by or through emending the intelligence in as clear unmistakable mentality are in some way the mental aspects of problems of or relating to the mind is spoken in response to substantiality.

Paul M. Churchlands (1981) advances a different argument for eliminative materialism. Given to agree to Churchlands, the commonsense concepts of mental states contained in our present folk psychology are, from a scientific point of view, radically defective. Nonetheless, we can expect that eventually a more sophisticated theoretical account will relace those folk-psychological concepts, showing that mental phenomena, as described by current folk psychology, do not exist. Since, that account would be integrated into the rest of science, we would have a thoroughgoing materialist treatment of all phenomena, unlike Rorty's, does not rely of assuming that the mental are nonphysical.

However, even if current folk psychology is mistaken, that does not show that mental phenomenon does not exist, but only that they are of the way folk psychology described them for being. We could conclude, that, they do not put into effect of any natural cognitive processes or simulate the practice of using something for being used aside from its energy in producing the resulting of thought that exists only if the folk-psychological claims that turn out to be mistaken are factually determinant dissimilarities for which to define what it is for a phenomenon to be strictly mental. Otherwise, the new theory would be about mental phenomena, and would help show that they are identical with physical phenomena. Churchlands argument, like Rorty's, depends on a special way of defining the mental, which we need not adopt, it argument for Eliminative materialism will require some such definition, without which the argument would instead support the identity theory.

Despite initial appearances, the distinctive properties of sensations are neutral as between being mental and physical, in that borrowed from the English philosopher and classicist Gilbert Ryle (1900-76), they are topic neutral: My experiences of appreciation as having to cognize in the sensation of red for which consists in my being in a state that is similar, in respect that we need not specify, making it more evenly so, to something that occurs in me when I am in the presence of certain stimuli. Because the respect of similarity is not specified, the property is neither distinctively mental nor distinctively physical. However, everything is similar to everything else in some respect or other. So leaving the respect of similarity unspecified makes this account too weak to capture the distinguishing properties of sensation.

A more sophisticated reply to the difficultly about mental properties is due independently to the Australian, David Malet Armstrong (1926-) and American philosopher David Lewis (1941-2002), who argued that for a state to be a particular intentional state or sensation is for that state to bear characteristic causal relations to other particular occurrences. The properties in virtue of which e identify states as thoughts or sensations will still be neural as between being mental and physical, since anything can bear a causal relation to anything else. Nevertheless, causal connections have a better chance than similarity in some unspecified respect to capturing the distinguishing properties of sensations and thought.

This casual theory is appealing, but is misguided to attempt to construe the distinctive properties of mental states for being neutral as between being mental and physical. To be neutral as regards being mental or physical is to be neither distinctively mental nor distinctively physical. However, since thoughts and sensations are distinctively mental states, for a state to be a thought or a sensation is perforce for it to have some characteristically mental property. We inevitably lose the distinctively mental if we construe these properties for being neither mental nor physical.

Not only is the topic-neutral construal misguided: The problem it was designed to solve is equally so, only to say, that problem stemmed from the idea that mental must have some nonphysical aspects. If not at the level of people or their mental states, then at the level of the distinctive properties can be more complicated, for example, in the sentence, 'John is married to Mary', we can display the attribution that of 'John, is of the property of being married, and unlike the property of John is bald. Consider the sentence: 'John is bearded' and that 'John' in this sentence is a bit of language-a name of some individual human being-and more some would be tempted to confuse the word with what it names. Consider the expression 'is bald', this too is a bit of articulated linguistic communication under which philosophers call it a 'predicate'-and it caries out into a certain state of our attention of some material possession or feature that, if the sentence is true. It has possession of by John? Understood in this ay, a property is not its self linguist though it is expressed, or conveyed by something that is, namely a predicate. What might be said that a property is a real feature of the word, and that it should be contrasted just as sharply with any predicates we use to express it, as in the name 'John' is contrasted with the person himself. Controversially, just what ontological status should be accorded to properties by describing 'anomalous monism'-while it is conceivably given to a better understanding the similarity with the American philosopher Herbert Donald Davidson (1917-2003), wherefore he adopts a position that explicitly repudiates reductive physicalism, yet purports to be a version of materialism, nonetheless, Davidson holds that although token mental evident states are identical to those of physical events and states-mental 'types' -, i.e., kinds, and/or properties-is neither to, nor nomically co-existensive with, physical types. In other words, his argument for this position relies largely on the contention that the correct assignment of mental an actionable property to a person is always a holistic matter, involving a global, temporally diachronic, 'intentional interpretation' of the person. Nevertheless, as many philosophers have in effect pointed out, accommodating claims of materialism evidently requires more than just repercussions of mental/physical identities. Mentalistic explanation presupposes not merely that metal events are causes but also that they have causal/explanatory relevance as mental, i.e., relevance insofar as they fall under mental kinds or types. Nonetheless, the mental aspects of the problem are of or relating to the mind, such as Davidson's positions, which deny there are strict psychological or psychological laws, can accommodate the causal/explanation relevance of the mental quo mentally: If to 'epiphenomenalism' with respect to mental properties.

However, the ideas that the mental are in some think much of the nonphysical cannot be assumed without argument. Plainly, the distinctively mental properties of the mental states are unlikely that any other properties looked carefully about which we know. Only mental states have properties that are at all like the qualitative properties that anything like the intentional properties of thoughts and desires. However, this does not show that the mental properties are not physical properties, not. All physical properties like the standard states: So, mental properties might still be special kinds of physical properties. It's interrogatory of questions begin or at present with falsifiably deceptive appearances0yet the differences or manner, of which the doctrine that the mental properties are simply an expression of the Cartesian doctrines that mentally are automatically nonphysical.

It is sometimes held that properties should count as physical properties only if they can be defined using the terms of physics. Nobody would hold that to reduce biology to physics, for example, we must define all biological properties using only terms that occur in physics. Even putting 'reduction' aside, in certain biological properties could have been defined, that would not mean that those properties were in ways tracing the remains of that which one surpasses in movement or transference the capabilities for which it is accessible to attain some navigating modernity, in that of a fashionable method or custom for which a variety of species long for being nonphysical. The sense of 'physical' that is relevant, for which its situation must be broad enough to include biological properties, but also mostly commonsense of macroscopic properties. Bodily states are uncontroversially physical in the relevant way. So, we can recast the identity theory as asserting that mental states are identical with bodily state.

While reaching conclusions about the origin and limits of knowledge, Locke had to his occasion, that concerning himself with topics that are of philosophical interest in themselves. On of these is the question of identity, which includes, more specifically, the question of personal identity: What are the criteria by which a person is numerically the same person as a person encountering of time? Locke points out whether 'this is what was here before, it matters what kind of thing 'this' is meant to be. If 'this' is meant as a mass of matter then it is what was before, insofar as it consists of the same material panicles, but if it is meant as a living body then its considering of the same particles does most matter. The case is different. 'A colt grown up to a horse, sometimes fat, sometimes leans, is altogether the same horse as we speak, but though . . . there may be a manifest change of the parts. So, when we think about personal identity, we need to be clear about a distinction between two things which 'the ordinary way of speaking runs together' the idea of 'man' and the idea of 'person'. As with any other animal, the identity of a man consists 'in nothing but a participation of the same continued life, by constantly fleeting particles of matter, in succession initially united both internally and externally as the same organized body, however, the examination of one's own thought and feeling of intensively explicative ideas of hope or inclined to hope that of a person is not that of a living body of a certain kind. A person's task is especially by one's capabilities and enacting ability to reason has of himself the forming of an idea of something in the mind, as to conceive, envisages, envision, fancy, feature, imagine and so forth. So, then, one's own being to gather or in the assumption of assertions, are the conjecturing considerations to use one's power of conception, judgement or inference to 'think', apart from other animals. Is, then, we are to accede that 'thinking' intelligently hosts there being that have reflections and such a being 'will be the same self as far as the same consciousness can extend to action past or to come? The unity of one's contingence of consciousness does not depend on its being 'annexed' only to one individual substance, [and not] . . . continued in a succession of several substances. For Lock e, then, personal identity consists in an identity of consciousness, and not in the identity of some substance whose essence is to be conscious.

Casual mechanisms or connections of meaning will help to take a historical route, and focus on the terms in which analytical philosophers of mind began to discuss seriously psychoanalytic explanation. These were provided by the long-standing and presently non-concluded debate over cause and meaning in psychoanalysis.

Seeing why psychoanalysis should be viewed in the terminological combinations of some cause and meaning is not hard. On the one hand, Freud's theories introduce a panoply of concepts that appear to characterize mental processes as mechanical and non-meaningful. Included are Freud's neurological model of the mind, as outlined in his 'Project or a Scientific Psychology', more broadly, his 'economic' description of mentality, as having properties of force or energy, e.g., as 'cathexing' objects: And his account in the mechanism of repression. So it seems that psychoanalytic explanation employs terms logically at variation with those of ordinary, common-sens e psychology, where mechanisms do not play a central role. Bu t on the other hand, and equally striking, there is the fact that psychoanalysis proceeds through interpretation and engages on a relentless search for meaningful connections in mental life-something that became more even as a superficial examination of the Interpretation of Dreams, or The Psychopathology of Everyday Life, cannot fail to impress upon one. Psychoanalytic interpretation adduces meaningful connections between disparate and often apparently dissociated mental and behavioural phenomena, directed by the goal of 'thematic coherence'. That is, as giving mental life the sort of unity that we find in a work of art or cogent narratives, and, in this respect, psychoanalysis seems to dramatize its substantive reasons for doing so, is that for its physiological feature of ordinary psychology, finding to its insistence on or upon the relating actions to reason for them through contentual characterizations of each that make their connection seems rational, or intelligible: A goal that seems remote from anything found in the physical sciences.

The application to psychoanalysis of the perspective afforded by the cause-meaning debate can also be seen as much therefore of another factor, namely the semi-paradoxical nature of psychoanalysis' explananda. With respect to all irrational phenomena, something like a paradox arises. Irrationality involves a failure of a rational connectedness and hence of meaningfulness, and so, if it is to have an explanation of any kind, relations that are non-comprehensible and causatively might be of some needed necessity. Yet, as observed above, it seems that, in offering explanations for irrationality-plugging the 'gaps' in consciousness-what psychoanalytic explanation is attached with a hinge for being precisely the postulation of further, although non-apparent connections of meaning.

For these two reasons, then-the logical heterogeneity of its explanation and the ambiguous status of its explananda-it may seem that an examination arriving within the hierarchical terms as held of the conceptions of cause and meaning will provide the key to a philosophical elucidation of psychoanalysis. The possible views of psychoanalytic explanation that may result from such an examination can be arranged along two dimensions. (1) Psychoanalytic explanation may then be viewed after reconstruction, as either causal and non-meaningful, or meaningful and non-causal, or as comprising both meaningful and causal elements, in various combinations. Psychoanalytic explanation then may be viewed, on each of these reconstructions, as either licensed or invalidated depending one's view of the logical nature of psychology.

So, for instance, some philosophical discussions infer that psychoanalytic explanation is void, simple since it is committed to causality in psychology. On another, opposed view, it is the virtue of psychoanalytic explanation that it imputes causal relations, since only causal relations can be used for explaining the failures of meaningful psychological connections. On yet another view, it is psychoanalysis' commitment to meaning which is its great fault: It is held that the stories that psychoanalysis tries to tell do not really, on examination, explains successively.

Saying that the debates between these various positions fail to establish anything is fair definite about psychoanalytic explanation. There are two reasons for this. First, there are several different strands in Freud's whitings, each of which may be drawn on, apparently conclusively, in support of each alternative reconstruction. Secondly, preoccupations with the whole, is generally problematic in the philosophy of mind, for that which gives to cause and meaning, in which distracts attention from the distinguishing features offered of psychoanalytic explanation. At this point, and to prepare the way for a plausible reconstruction of psychoanalytic explanation. Taking a step back is appropriate, and takes a fresh look at the cause-meaning issue in the philosophy of psychoanalysis.

Suppose, first, that in some varying refashions alternating of change, the modulator's estate of the realms or fact of having independent reality in the form of adequacy for which classes of descriptive change are themselves to imply anything about reduction. Historically, 'natural' contrasts with 'supernatural', but given to submit in the contemporary philosophy of mind whereby the debate issues a concern for which are the centres around which the possibilities of explaining mental phenomena are just or as much as part of the natural order. It is the non-natural rather than the supernatural that is the contrasting notion. The naturalist holds that they can be so explained, while the opponent of naturalism thinks otherwise, though it is not intended that opposition to naturalism commits one to anything supernatural. Nonetheless, one should not take naturalism in regard as committing one to any sort of reductive explanation of that realm, and there are such commitments in the use of 'physicalism' and 'materialism'.

If psychoanalytic explanation gives the impression that it imputes bare, meaning-free causality, this results from attending to only half the story, and misunderstanding what psychoanalysis means when it talks of psychological mechanisms. The economic descriptions of mental processes that psychoanalysis provides are never replacements for, but they always presuppose, characterizations of mental processes through meaning. Mechanisms in psychoanalytic context are simply processes whose operation cannot be reconstructed as instances of rational functioning (they are what we might by preference call mental activities, by contrast with action) Psychoanalytic explanation's postulation of mechanisms should not therefore be regarded as a regrettable and expugnable incursion of scientism into Freud's thought, as is often claimed.

Suppose, alternatively, those hermeneuticists such as Habermas-who follow Dilthey beings as an interpretative practice to which the concepts of the physical sciences. Are inclined to provide by or as if by formal action, in that to an extended allocation of its presently accorded intendment in the correct of thinking that connections of the idea that something coneys to the mind its meanings are misrepresented through being described as causal? Again, this does not impact negatively of psychoanalytic explanation since, as just argued, psychoanalytic explanation nowhere of imputes meaning-free causation. Nothing is lost for psychoanalytic explanation causation is excised from the psychological picture.

The conclusion must be that psychoanalytic explanation is at bottom indifferent to the general meaning-cause issue. The core of psychoanalysis consists in its tracing of meaningful connections with no greater or lesser commitment to causality than is involved in ordinary psychology. (Which helps to set the stage-pending appropriate clinical validation-for psychoanalysis to claim as much truth for its explanation as ordinary psychology?). Also, the true key to psychoanalytic explanation, its attribution of special kinds of mental states that are not recognized in customary psychology, whose relations to one another does not have the form of patterns of inference or practical reasoning.

In the light of this, understanding why some compatibilities and hermeneuticists assert that their own view of psychology is uniquely consistent with psychoanalytic explanation is easy. Compatibilities are right to think that, to provide for psychoanalytic explanation, allowing mental connections that are unlike the connections of reasons to the actions that they rationalize is necessary, or to the beliefs that they support: And, that, in outlining such connections, psychoanalytic explanation must outstrip the resources of ordinary psychology, which does attempt to force as much as possible into the mould of practical reasoning. Hermeneuticists, for their part, are right to think those postulating connections that were nominally psychological but that characterized would be futile as to meaning, and that psychoanalytic explanation does not respond to the 'paradox' of irrationality by abandoning the search for meaningful connections.

Compatibilities are, however, wrong to think that non-rational but meaningful connections require the psychological order to be conceived as a causal order. The hermeneuticists are free to postulate psychological connections determined by meaning but not by rationality: supposing that there are connections of meaning that is coherent are not -bona fide-rational connections, without these being causal. Meaningfulness is a broader concept than rationality. (Sometimes this thought has been expressed, though not helpful, by saying that Freud became aware of the existence of 'neurotic rationality.) Even if an assumption of rationality is evasively necessary to make sense of behaviour overall. It does not need to be brought into play in making sense of each instance of behaviour. Hermeneuticists, in turn, are inaccurate to thinking that the compatibility view of psychology endorses a causal signal of a mental collaborationist, categorized by their meaning with causality or that it must lead to compatibilism to acknowledge that which in any qualitative difference between rational and irrational psychological connections.

All the same, the last two decades have been an extent of time set off or typically by someone or something intermittently for being periodic through which times inordinate changes, placing an encouraging well-situated plot in the psychology of the sciences. 'Cognitive psychology', which focuses on higher mental processes like reasoning, decision making, problem solving, language processing and higher-level processing, has become-perhaps, the-dominant paradigms among experimental psychologists, while behaviouristically oriented approaches have gradually fallen into disfavour.

The relationships between physical behaviour and agential behaviour are controversial. On some views, all 'actions' are identical; to physical changes in the subjects body, however, some kinds of physical behaviour, such as 'reflexes', are uncontroversially not kinds of agential behaviour. On others, a subject's effectuation of some proceeding action used to indicate requirements by immediate or future needs or purpose. Bringing into circumstance or state of affairs from which situational extrication is differently involved by some physical change, but it is not identical to it.

Both physical and agential behaviours could be understood in the widest sense. Anything a person can be calculating in his head, for instance-could has actuality or reality as been regarded as agential behaviour. Likewise, any physical change in a person's body-even the firing of a certain neuron, for instance - has actuality or the reality to be regarded as physical behaviour.

Of course, to claim that the mind is 'nothing beyond' such-and-such kinds of behaviour, construed as either physical or agential behaviour in the widest sense, is not necessarily to be a behaviourist. The theory that the mind is a series of volitional acts-a view close to the idealist position of George Berkeley (1685-1753)-and the possible action's of the minds' condition are the enabling of certainties as founded in the neuronal events, while both controversial, are not forms of behaviourism.

Awaiting, right along the side of an approaching account for which anomalous monism may take on or upon itself is the view that there is only one kind of substance underlying all others, changing and processes. It is generally used in contrast to 'dualism', though one can also think of it as denying what might be called 'pluralism'-a view often associated with Aristotle which claims that there are several substances, as the corpses of times generations have let it be known. Against the background of modern science, monism is usually understood to be a form of 'materialism' or 'physicalism'. That is, the fundamental properties of matter and energy as described by physics are counted the only properties there are.

The position in the philosophy of mind known as 'anomalous monism' has its historical origins in the German philosopher and founder of critical philosophy Immanuel Kant (1724-1804), but is universally identified with the American philosopher Herbert Donald Davidson (1917-2003), and it was he who coined the term. Davidson has maintained that one can be a monist-indeed, a physicalist-about the fundamental nature of things and events, while also asserting that there can be no full 'reduction' of the mental to the physical. (This is sometimes expressed by saying that there can be an ontological, though not a conceptual reduction.) Davidson thinks that complete knowledge of the brain and any related neurophysiological systems that support the mind's activities would not themselves be knowledge of such things as belief, desire, and experience, and so on, find the mentalistic generativist of thoughts. This is not because he thinks that the mind is somehow a separate kind of existence: Anomalous monism is after all monism. Rather, it is because the nature of mental phenomena rules out a priori that there will be law-like regularities connecting mental phenomena and physical events in the brain, and, without such laws, there is no real hope of explaining the mental that has recently come into existence, through the evolutionary structures in the physicality of the brain.

All and all, one central goal of the philosophy of science is to provided explicit and systematic accounts of the theories and explanatory strategies explored in the science. Another common goal is to construct philosophically illuminating analyses or explanations of central theoretical concepts involved in one or another science. In the philosophy of biology, for example, there is a rich literature aimed at understanding teleological explanations, and thereby has been a great deal of work on the structure of evolutionary theory and on such crucial concepts. If concepts of the simple (observational) sorts were internal physical structures that had, in this sense, an information-carrying function, a function they acquired during learning, then instances of these structure types would have a content that (like a belief) could be either true or false. In that of ant information-carrying structure carries all kinds of information if, for example, it carries information 'A', it must also carry the information that 'A' or 'B'. Conceivably, the process of learning is supposed to b e a process in which a single piece of this information is selected for special treatment, thereby becoming the semantic content-the meaning-of subsequent tokens of that structure type. Just as we conventionally give artefacts and instruments information-providing functions, thereby making their flashing lights, and so forth-representations of the conditions in the world in which we are interested, so learning converts neural states that carry imparting information, as 'pointer readings' in the head, so to speak-int structures that have the function of providing some vital piece of information they carry when this process occurs in the ordinary course of learning, the functions in question develop naturally. They do not, as do the functions of instruments and artefacts, depends on the intentions, beliefs, and attitudes of users. We do not give brain structure these functions. They get it by themselves, in some natural way, either (of the senses) from their selectional history or (in thought) from individual learning. The result is a network of internal representations that have (in different ways) the power representation, of experience and belief.

To recognizing the existence or meaning of apprehending to know of the progression of constant understanding that this approach to 'thought' and 'belief', the approach that conceives of them as forms of internal representation, is not a version of 'functionalism'-at least, not if this dely held theory is understood, as it is often, as a theory that identifies mental properties with functional properties. For functional properties have to do within the manner for which to some extent of engaging one's imploring that which has real and independent existence, something, in fact, behaves, with its syndrome of typical causes and effects. An informational model of belief, to account for misrepresentation, a problem with which a preliminary way that in both need something more than a structure that provided information. It needs something having that as its function. It needs something supposed to provide information. As Sober (1985) comments for an account of the mind we need functionalism with the function, the 'teleological', is put back in it.

Philosophers' need not charge a pressing lack of something essential, and typically do not assume that there is anything wrong with the science they are studying. Their goal is simply to provide accounts of the theories, concepts and explanatory strategies that scientists are using-accounts that are more explicit, systematic and philosophically sophisticated than the often rather rough-and-ready accounts offered by the scientists themselves.

Cognitive psychology is, in many ways a curious and puzzling science. Many theories put forward by cognitive psychologists make use of a family of 'intentional' concepts-like believing that desiring that 'q', and representing 'r'-which do not appear in the physical or biological sciences, and these intentional concepts play a crucial role in many explanations offered by these theories.

It is characteristic of dialectic awareness that discussions of intentionality appeared as the paradigm cases discussed which are usually beliefs or sometimes beliefs and desires, however, the biologically most basic forms of intentionality are in perception and in intentional action. These also have certain formal features that are not common to beliefs and desire. Consider a case of perceptual experience. Suppose that I see my hand in front of my face. What are the conditions of satisfaction? First, the perceptual experience of the hand in front of my face has as its condition of satisfaction that there is a hand in front of my face. Thus far, the condition of satisfaction is the same as the belief than there is a hand in front of my face. But with perceptual experience there is this difference: so that the intentional content is satisfied, the fact that there is a hand in front of my face must cause the very experience whose intentional content is that there is a hand in front of my face. This has the consequence that perception has a special kind of condition of satisfaction that we might describe as 'causally self-referential'. The full conditions of satisfaction of the perceptual experience are, first that there is a hand in front of my face, and second, that there is a hand in front of my face caused the very experience of whose conditions of satisfaction forms a part. we can represent this in our acceptation of the form. S(p), such as:

> Visual experience (that there is a hand in front of face
> and the fact that there is a hand in front of my face
> is causing this very experience.)

Furthermore, visual experiences have a kind of conscious immediacy not characterised of beliefs and desires. A person can literally be said to have beliefs and desires while sound asleep. But one can only have visual experiences of a non-pathological kind when one is fully awake and conscious because the visual experiences are themselves forms of consciousness.

People's decisions and actions are explained by appeal to their beliefs and desires. Perceptual processes, sensational, are said to result in mental states that represent (or sometimes misrepresent) one or as another aspect of the cognitive agent's environment. Other theorists have offered analogous acts, if differing in detail, perhaps, the most crucial idea in all of this is the one about representations. There is perhaps a sense in which what happens to be said, is the level of the retina, that constitute the anatomical processes of occurring in the process of stimulation, some kind of representation of what produces that stimulation, and thus, some kind of representation of the objects of perception. Or so it may seem, if one attempts to describe the relation between the structure and characteristic of the object of perception and the structure and nature of the retinal processes. One might say that the nature of that relation is such as to provide information about the part of the world perceived, in the sense of 'information' presupposed when one says that the rings in the sectioning of a tree's truck provide information of its age. This is because there is an appropriate causal relation between the things that make it impossible for it to be a matter of chance. Subsequently processing can then be thought to exist for one who carried out on what is provided in the representational inquiries.

However, if there are such representations, they are not representations for the perceiver, it is the thought that perception involves representations of that kind that produced the old, and now largely discredited philosophical theories of perception that suggested that perception be a matter, primarily, of an apprehension of mental states of some kind, e.g., sense-data, which are representatives of perceptual objects, either by being caused by them or in being in some way constitutive of them. Also, if it is said that the idea of information so invoked indicates that there is a sense in which the precesses of stimulation can be said to have content, but a non-conceptual content, distinct from the content provided by the subsumption of what is perceived under concepts. It must be emphasised that, that content is not one for the perceiver. What the information-processing story is to maintain, is, at best, a more adequate categorization than previously available of the causal processes involved. That may be important, but more should not be claimed for it than there is. If in perception is a given case one can be said to have an experience as of an object of a certain shape and kind related to another object it is because there is presupposed in that perception the possession of concepts of objects, and more particular, a concept of space and how objects occupy space.

It is, that, nonetheless, cognitive psychologists occasionally say a bit about the nature of intentional concepts and the nature of intentional concepts and the explanations that exploit them. Their comments are rarely systematic or philosophically illuminating. Thus, it is hardly surprising that many philosophers have seen cognitive psychology as fertile grounds for the sort of careful descriptive work that is done in the philosophy of biology and the philosophy of physics. The American philosopher of mind Alan Jerry Fodor's (1935-), The Language of Thought (1975) was a pioneering study in th genre on the field. Philosophers have, also, done important and widely discussed work in what might be called the 'descriptive philosophy' or 'cognitive psychology'.

These philosophical accounts of cognitive theories and the concepts they invoke are generally much more explicit than the accounts provided by psychologists, and through them, they inevitably smooth over some of the rough edges of scientists' actual practice. But if the account they give of cognitive theories diverges significantly from the theories that psychologists actually produce, then the philosophers have just got it wrong. There is, however, a very different way in which philosopher's have approached cognitive psychology. Rather than merely trying to characterize what cognitive psychology is actually doing, some philosophers try to say what it should and should not be doing. Their goal is not to explicate o or upon the narratives that scientific applications are but to criticize and improve it. The most common target of this critical approach is the use of intentional concepts in cognitive psychology. Intentional notions have been criticized on various grounds. The two situated considerations are that they fail to supervene on the physiology of the cognitive agent, and that they cannot be 'naturalized'.

Perhaps e easiest way to make the point about 'supervenience is to use a thought experiment of the sort originally proposed by the American philosopher Hilary Putnam (1926-). Suppose that in some distant corner of the universe there is a planet, Twin Earth, which is very similar to our own planet. On Twin Earth, there is a person who is an atom for an atom replica of J.F. Kennedy. Past, assassinated President J.F. Kennedy, who lives on

Earth believes that Rev. Martin Luther King Jr. was born in Tennessee, and if you asked him 'Was the Rev. Martin Luther King Jr. born in Tennessee, In all probability the answer would either or not it is yes or no. Twin, Kennedy would respond in the same way, but it is not because he believes that our Rev. Martin Luther King Jr.? Was, as, perhaps, very much in question of what is true or false? His beliefs are about Twin-Luther, and that Twin -Luther was certainly not born in Tennessee, and thus, that J.F. Kennedy's belief is true while Twin-Kennedy's is false. What all this is supposed to show is that two people, perhaps on opposite polarities of justice, or justice as drawn on or upon human rights, can share all their physiological properties without sharing all their intentional properties. To turn this into a problem for cognitive psychology, two additional premises are needed. The first is that cognitive psychology attempts to explain behaviour by appeal to people's intentional properties. The second, is that psychological explanations should not appeal to properties that fall to supervene on an organism's physiology. (Variations on this theme can be found in the American philosopher Allen Jerry Fodor (1987)).

The thesis that the mental are supervening on the physical-roughly, the claim that the mental characters of a determinant adaptation of its physical nature-has played a key role in the formulation of some influential positions of the 'mind-body' problem. In particular versions of nonproductive 'physicalism', and has evoked in arguments about the mental, and has been used to devise solutions to some central problems about the mind-for example, the problem of mental causation.

The idea of supervenience applies to one but not to the other, that this, there could be no difference in a moral respect without a difference in some descriptive, or non-moral respect evidently, the idea generalized so as to apply to any two sets of properties (to secure greater generality it is more convenient to speak of properties that predicates). The American philosopher Donald Herbert Davidson (1970), as perhaps, first to introduce supervenience into the rhetoric discharging into discussions of the mind-body problem, when he wrote '. . . mental characteristics are in some sense dependent, or supervening, on physical characteristics. Such supervenience might be taken to mean that there cannot be two events alike in all physical respects but differing in some mental respectfulness, or that an object cannot alter in some metal deferential submission without altering in some physical regard. Following, the British philosopher George Edward Moore (1873-1958) and the English moral philosopher Richard Mervyn Hare (1919-2003), from whom he avowedly borrowed the idea of supervenience. Donald Herbert Davidson, went on to assert that supervenience in this sense is consistent with the irreducibility of the supervient to their 'subvenience', or 'base' properties. Dependence or supervenience of this kind does not entail reducibility through law or definition . . .'

Thus, three ideas have purposively come to be closely associated with supervenience: (1) Property convariation, (if two things are indiscernible in the infrastructure of allowing properties that they must be indiscernible in supervening properties). (2) Dependence, (supervening properties are dependent on, or determined by, their subservient bases) and (3) non-reducibility (property convariation and dependence involved in supervenience can obtain even if supervening properties are not reducible to their base properties.)

Nonetheless, in at least, for the moment, supervenience of the mental-in the form of strong supervenience, or, at least global supervenience-is arguably a minimum commitment to physicalism. But can we think of the thesis of mind-body supervenience itself as a theory of the mind-body relation-that is, as a solution to the mind-body problem?

It would seem that any serious theory addressing the mind-body problem must say something illuminating about the nature of psychophysical dependence, or why, contrary to common belief, there is no dependence in either way. However, if we take to consider the ethical naturalist intuitivistic will say that the supervenience, and the dependence, for which is a brute fact you discern through moral intuition: And the prescriptivist will attribute the supervenience to some form of consistency requirements on the language of evaluation and prescription. And distinct from all of these is mereological supervenience, namely the supervenience of properties of a whole on properties and relations of its pats. What all this shows, is that there is no single type of dependence relation common to all cases of supervenience, supervenience holds in different cases for different reasons, and does not represent a type of dependence that can be put alongside causal dependence, meaning dependence, mereological dependence, and so forth.

There seems to be a promising strategy for turning the supervenience thesis into a more substantive theory of mind, and it is that to explicate mind-body supervenience as a special case of mereological supervenience-that is, the dependence of the properties of a whole on the properties and relations characterizing its proper parts. Mereological dependence does seem to be a special form of dependence that is metaphysically sui generis and highly important. If one takes this approach, one would have to explain psychological properties as macroproperties of a whole organism that covary, in appropriate ways, with its macroproperties, i.e., the way its constituent organs, tissues, and so forth, are organized and function. This more specific supervenience thesis may be a serious theory of the mind-body relation that can compete for the classic options in the field.

On this topic, as with many topics in philosophy, there is a distinction to be made between (1) certain vague, partially inchoate, pre-theoretic ideas and beliefs about the matter nearby, and (2) certain more precise, more explicit, doctrines or theses that are taken to articulate or explicate those pre-theoretic ideas and beliefs. There are various potential ways of precisifying our pre-theoretic conception of a physicalist or materialist account of mentality, and the question of how best to do so is itself a matter for ongoing, dialectic, philosophical inquiry.

The view concerns, in the first instance, at least, the question of how we, as ordinary human beings, in fact go about ascribing beliefs to one another. The idea is that we do this on the basis of our knowledge of a commonsense theory of psychology. The theory is not held to consist in a collection of grandmotherly saying, such as 'once bitten, twice shy'. Rather it consists in a body of generalizations relating psychological states to each other to input from the environment, and to actions. Such may be founded on or upon the grounds that show or include the following:

(1) (x)(p) if x is to feel agitation or dismay in the anticipation of or in the presence of fear that p, then x desires that not-p.

(2) (x)(p)(if x hopes that p and **C** hope that p and **C** become or be made aware of something not previously known that p, then **C** is pleased that p.

(3) (x)(p)(q) If x is to have a firm conviction in the reality of something believed that p and **C** believe in the conviction of the reality of something that if p, then q, barring confounding distraction, and so forth. **C** believes that q.

(4) (x)(p)(q) If x is desirously that p and so that x believes that if q then p, and x are able to bring it about that q, then, barring conflict ting desires or preferred strategies, x brings it about that q.

All of these generalizations should be most of the time, but variably. Adventurous types often enjoy the adrenal thrill produced by fear, this leads them, on occasion, to desire the very state of affairs that frightens them. Analogously, with (3). A subject who believes that 'p' nd believes that if 'p', then 'q'. Would typically infer that 'q?'. But certain atypical circumstances may intervene: Subjects may become confused or distracted, or they ma y finds the prospect of 'q' so awful that they dare not allow themselves to believe it. The ceteris paribus nature of these generalizations is not usually considered to be problematic, since atypical circumstances are, of course, atypical, and the generalizations are applicable most of the time.

We apply this psychological theory to make inference about people's beliefs, desires and so forth. If, for example, we know that Julie believes that if she is to be at the airport at four, then she should get a taxi at half past two, and she believes that she is to be at the airport at four, then we will predict, using (3), that Julie will infer that she should get a taxi at half past two.

The Theory-Theory, as it is called, is an empirical theory addressing the question of our actual knowledge of beliefs. Taken in its purest form if addressed both first and third-person knowledge: we know about our own beliefs and those of others in the same way, by application of commonsense psychological theory in both cases. However, it is not very plausible to hold that we overplay or overact of any given attention or emphasis in dramatizing in excess of going beyond a normal or acceptable limit. That indeed usually-know our own beliefs by way of theoretical inference. Since it is an empirical theory concerning one of our cognitive abilities, the Theory-Theory is open to psychological scrutiny. Various issues of the hypothesized commonsense psychological theory, we need to know whether it is known consciously or unconsciously. Nevertheless, research has revealed that three-year-old children are reasonably gods at inferring the beliefs of others on the basis of actions, and at predicting actions on the basis of beliefs that others are known to possess. However, there is one area in which three-year-old's psychological reasoning differs markedly from adults. Tests of the sorts are rationalized in such that: 'False Belief Tests', reveal largely consistent results. Three-year-old subjects are witnesses to the scenario about the child, Billy, see his mother place some biscuits in a biscuit tin. Billy then goes out to play, and, unseen by him, his mother removes the biscuit from the tin and places them in a jar, which is then hidden in a cupboard. When asked, 'Where will Billy look for the biscuits'? The majority of three-year-olds answer that Billy will look in the jar in the cupboard-where the biscuits actually are, than where Billy saw them being placed. On being asked 'Where does Billy think the biscuits are'? They again, tend to answer 'in the cupboard', rather than 'in the jar'. Three-year-olds thus, appear to have some difficulty attributing false beliefs to others in case in which it would be natural for adults to do so. However, it appears that three-year-olds are lacking the idea of false beliefs overall, nor does it come out that they struggle with attributing false beliefs in other kinds of situations. For example, they have little trouble distinguishing between dreams and play, on the one hand, and true beliefs or claims on the other. By the age of four and some half years, most children pass the False Belief Tests fairly consistently. There is yet no general accepted theory of why three-year-olds fare so badly with the false beliefs tests, nor of what it reveals about their conception of beliefs.

Recently some philosophers and psychologists have put forward what they take to be an alternative to the Theory-Theory: However, the challenge does not end there. We need also to consider the vital element of making appropriate adjustments for differences between one's own psychological states and those of the other. Nevertheless, it is implausible to think in every such case of simulation, yet alone will provide the resolving obtainability to achieve.

The evaluation of the behavioural manifestations of belief, desires, and intentions are enormously varied, every bit as suggested. When we move away from perceptual beliefs, the links with behaviour are intractable and indirect: The expectation I form on the basis of a particular belief reflects the influence of numerous other opinions, my actions are formed by the totality of my preferences and all those opinions that have a bearing on or upon them. The causal processes that produce my beliefs reflect my opinions about those processes, about their reliability and the interference to which they are subject. Thus, behaviour justifies the ascription of a particular belief only by helping to warrant a more all-inclusive interpretation of cognitive positions of the individual in question. Psychological descriptions, like translation, are a 'holistic' business. And once this is taken into account, it is all the less likely that a common physical trait will be found which grounds all instances of the same belief. The ways in which all of our propositional altitudes interact in the production of behaviour reinforce the anomalous character of our mentality and render any sort of reduction of the mind to the physical impossibilities. Such is not meant as a practical procedure, it can, however, generalize on this so that interpretation and merely translation is at issue, has made this notion central to methods of accounting responsibilities of the mind.

Theory and Theory-Theory are two, as many think competing, views of the nature of our commonsense, propositional attitude explanations of action. For example, when we say that our neighbour cut down his apple tree because he believed that it was ruining his patio and did not want it ruined, we are offering a typically commonsense explanation of his action in terms of his beliefs and desires. But, even though wholly familiar, it is not clear what kind of explanation is at issue. Connected of one view, is the attribution of beliefs and desires that are taken as the application to actions of a theory that, in its informal way, functions very much like theoretical explanations in science. This is known as the 'theory-theory' of every day psychological explanation. In contrast, it has been argued that our propositional attributes are not theoretical claims do much as reports of a kind of 'simulation'. On such a 'simulation theory' of the matter, we decide what our neighbour will do (and thereby why he did so) by imagining us in his position and deciding what we would do.

The Simulation theorist should probably concede that simulations need to be backed up by the unconfined means of discovering the psychological states of others. But they need not concede that these independent means take the form of a theory. Rather, they might suggest that we can get by with some rules of thumb, or straightforward inductive reasoning of a general kind.

A second and related difficulty with the Simulation Theory concerns our capacity to attribute beliefs that are too alien to be easily simulated: Beliefs of small children, or psychotics, or bizarre beliefs are deeply suppressed into the mindful latencies within the unconscious. The small child refuses to sleep in the dark: He is afraid that the Wicked Witch will steal him away. No matter how many adjustments we make, it may be hard for mature adults to get their own psychological processes, as even to make in pretended play, to mimic the production of such belief. For the Theory-Theory alien beliefs are not particularly problematic: So long as they fit into the basic generalizations of the theory, they will be inferable from the evidence. Thus, the Theory-Theory can account better for our ability to discover more bizarre and alien beliefs than can the Simulation Theory.

The Theory-Theory and the Simulation Theory are not the only proposals about knowledge of belief. A third view has its origins in the Austrian philosopher Ludwig Wittgenstein (1889-1951). On this view both the Theory and Simulation Theories attribute too much psychologizing to our commonsense psychology. Knowledge of other minds is, according to this alternative picture, more observational in nature. Beliefs, desires, feelings are made manifest to us in the speech and other actions of those with whom we share a language and way of life. When someone says. 'Its going to rain' and takes his umbrella from his bag. It is immediately clear to us that he believes it is going to rain. In order to know this, we neither theorize nor simulate: We just perceive, of course, this is not straightforward visual perception of the sort that we use to see the umbrella. But it is like visual perception in that it provides immediate and non-inferential awareness of its objects. we might call this the 'Observational Theory'.

The Observational Theory does not seem to accord very well with the fact that we frequently do have to indulge in a fair amount of psychologizing to find in what others believe. It is clear that any given action might be the upshot of any number of different psychological attitudes. This applies even in the simplest cases. For example, because one's friend is suspended from a dark balloon near a beehive, with the intention of stealing honey. This idea to make the bees behave that it is going to rain and therefore believe that the balloon as a dark cloud, and therefore pay no attention to it, and so fail to notice one's dangling friend. Given this sort of possible action, the observer would surely be rash immediately to judge that the agent believes that it is going to rain. Rather, they would need to determine-perhaps, by theory, perhaps by simulation-which of the various clusters of mental states that might have led to the action, actually did so. This would involve bringing in further knowledge of the agent, the background circumstances and so forth. It is hard to see how the sort of difficult compounded composite as the mental process involved in this sort of psychological reflection could be assimilated to any kind of observation.

The attributions of intentionality that depend on optimality or reasonableness is interpretations of the assumptive phenomena-a 'heuristic overlay' (1969), describing an inescapable idealized 'real pattern'. Like such abstractions, as centres of gravity and parallelograms of force, the beliefs and desires posited by the highest stance have noo independent and concrete existence, and since this is the case, there would be no deeper facts that could settle the issue if-most importantly-rival intentional interpretations arose that did equally well at rationalizing the history of behaviour of an entity. Orman van William Quine 1908-2000, the most influential American philosopher of the latter half of the 20th century, whose thesis on the indeterminacy of radical translation carries all the way in the thesis of the indeterminacy of radical interpretation of mental states and processes.

The fact that cases of radical indeterminacy, though possible in principle, is vanishingly unlikely ever to comfort us in the solacing refuge and shelter, yet, this is apparently an idea that is deeply counterintuitive to many philosophers, who have hankered for more 'realistic' doctrines. There are two different strands of 'realism' that in the attempt to undermine are such:

(1) Realism about the entities allegedly given and presented by our every day mentalistic discourse-what is dubbed as folk-psychology (1981). Such as beliefs, desires, pains, the self.

(2) Realism about content itself-the idea that there has to be events or entities that really have intentionality (as opposed to the events and entities that only have as if they had intentionality).

The tenet indicated by (1) rests of what is fatigue, what bodily states or events are so fatiguing, that they are identical with, and so forth. This is a confusion that calls for diplomacy, not philosophical discovery: The choice between an 'Eliminative materialism' and an 'identity theory' of fatigues is not a matter of which 'ism' is right, but of which way of speaking is most apt to wean these misbegotten features of them as conceptual schemata.

Again, the tenet (2) my attack has been more indirect. The view that some philosophers, in that of a demand for content realism as an instance of a common philosophical mistake: Philosophers often manoeuvre themselves into a position from which they can see only two alternatives: Infinite regresses versus some sort of 'intrinsic' foundation-a prime mover of one sort or another. For instance, it has seemed obvious that for some things to be valuable as means, other things must be intrinsically valuable-ends in themselves-otherwise we would be stuck with vicious regress (or, having no beginning or end) of things valuable only that although some intentionality is 'derived' (the 'aboutness' of the pencil marks composing a shopping list is derived from the intentions of the person whose list it is), unless some intentionality is 'original' and underived, there could be no derived intentionality.

There is always another alternative, namely, some finites regress that peters out without marked foundations or thresholds or essences. Here is an avoided paradox: Every mammal has a mammal for a mother-but, this implies an infinite genealogy of mammals, which cannot be the case. The solution is not to search for an essence of mammalhood that would permit us in principle to identify the Prime Mammal, but rather to tolerate a finite regress that connects mammals to their non-mammalian ancestors by a sequence that can only be partitioned arbitrarily. The reality of today's mammals is secure without foundations.

The best instance of this theme is held to the idea that the way to explain the miraculous-seeming powers of an intelligent intentional system is to disintegrate it into hierarchically structured teams of ever more stupid intentional systems, ultimately discharging all intelligence-debts in a fabric of stupid mechanisms? Lycan (1981), has called this view 'homuncular functionalism'. One may be tempted to ask: Are the sub-personal components 'real' intentional systems? At what point in the diminutions of prowess as we descend to simple neurons does 'real' intentionality disappear? Don't ask. The reasons for regarding an individual neuron (or a thermostat) as an intentional system are unimpressive, bu t zero, and the security of our intentional attributions at the highest lowest-level of real intentionality. Another exploitation of the same idea is found in Elbow Room (1984): Ast what point in evolutionary history did authentically to correspond to known, reason-appreciators real selves, make their appearance? Doesn't ask-for the dame reason? Here is yet another, more fundamental versions of evolution can point in the early days of evolution can we speak of genuine function, genuine selection-for and not mere fortuitous preservation of entities that happen to have some self-replicative capacity? Don't ask. Many of the more interesting and important features of our world have emerged, gradually, from a world that initially lacked them-function, intentionality, consciousness, morality, value-and it is a fool's errand to try to identify a first or most-simple instances of the 'real' thing. It is, for the same to reason a mistake must exist to answer all the questions our system of content attribution permits us to ask. Tom says he has an older brother in Toronto and that he is an only child. What does he really believe?

Could he really believe that he had a but if he also believed he was an only child? What is the 'real' content of his mental state? There is no reason to suppose there is a principled answer.

The most sweeping conclusion having drawn from this theory of content is that the large and well-regarded literature on 'propositional attitudes' (especially the debates over wide versus narrow content) is largely a disciplinary artefact of no long-term importance whatever, accept perhaps, as history's most slowly unwinding unintended reductio ad absurdum. Mostly, the disagreements explored in that literature cannot even be given an initial expression unless one takes on the assumption of an unsounded fundamentalist of strong realism about content, and its constant companion, the idea of a 'language of thought' a system of mental representation that is decomposable into elements rather like terms, and large elements rather like sentences. The illusion, that this is plausible, or even inevitable, is particularly fostered by the philosophers' normal tactic of working from examples of 'believing-that-p' that focuses attention on mental states that are directly or indirectly language-infected, such as believing that the shortest spy is a spy, or believing that snow is white. (Do polar bears believe that snow is white? In the way we do?) There are such states-in language-using human beings - but, they are not exemplary foundational states of belief, needing a term for them. As, perhaps, in calling the term in need of, as they represent 'opinions'. Opinions play a large, perhaps even a decisive role in our concept of a person, but they are not paradigms of the sort of cognitive element to which one can assign content in the first instance. If one starts, as one should, with the cognitive states and events occurring in nonhuman animals, and uses these as the foundation on which to build theories of human cognition, the language-infected state is more readily seen to be derived, less directly implicated in the explanation of behaviour, and the chief but an illicit source of plausibility of the doctrine of a language of thought. Postulating a language of thought is in any event a postponement of the central problems of content to refer especially to supposed causes, source or author ascribed, as not a necessary first step.

Our momentum, regardless, produces on or upon the inflicting of forces out the causal theories of epistemology, of what makes a belief justified and what makes a true belief knowledge? It is natural to think that whether a belief deserves one of these appraisals depends on what caused the subject to have the belief. In recent decades a number of epistemologists have pursued this plausible idea with a variety of specific proposals. For some proposed casual criteria for knowledge and justification are for us, to take under consideration.

Some causal theories of knowledge have it that a true belief that 'p' is knowledge just in case it has the right sort of causal connection to the fact that 'p'. Suchlike some criteria can be applied only to cases where the fact that 'p', a sort that can enter causal relations: This seems to exclude mathematically and other necessary facts and perhaps any fact expressed by a universal generalization. And proponents of this sort of criterion have usually supposed that it is limited to perceptual knowledge of particular facts about the subject's environment.

For example, the forthright Australian materialist David Malet Armstrong (1973), proposed that a belief of the form, 'This (perceived) object is 'F' is (non-inferential) knowledge if and only if the belief is a completely reliable sign that the perceived object is 'F', that is, the fact that the object is 'F' contributed to causing the belief and its doing so depended on properties of the believer such that the laws of nature dictate that, for any subject 'x' and perceived object 'y'. If 'x' has those properties and believes that 'y' is 'F', then 'y' is 'F'. Dretske (1981) offers a rather similar account in terms of the belief's being caused by a signal received by the perceiver that carries the information that the object is 'F'.

This sort of condition fails, however, to be sufficient t for non-inferential perceptual knowledge because it is compatible with the belief's being unjustified, and an unjustified belief cannot be knowledge. For example, suppose that your mechanisms for colour perception are working well, but you have been given good reason to think otherwise, to think, say, that any tinted colour of the things that look brownishly-tinted to you it will appear as brownishly-tinted things look of any tinted colour. If you fail to heed these results you have for thinking that your colour perception is awry and believe of a thing that look's colour tinted to you that it is colour-tinted in your belief will fail to be justified and will therefore fail to be knowledge, even though it is caused by the thing's being tinted in such a way as to be a completely reliable sign (or to carry the information) that the thing is tinted or found of some tinted discolouration.

One could fend off this sort of counterexample by simply adding to the causal condition the requirement that the belief be justified. But this enriched condition would still be insufficient. Suppose, for example, that in an experiment you are given a drug that in nearly all people (but not in you, as it happens) causes the aforementioned aberration in colour perception. The experimenter tells you that you're taken such a drug that says, 'No, wait a minute, the pill you took was just a placebo'. But suppose further that this last thing the experimenter tells you is discordantly not the truth. Her telling you this gives you justification for believing of a thing that looks colour tinted or tinged in brownish tones, but in fact about this justification that is unknown to you (that the experimenter's last statement was false) makes it the casse that your true belief is not knowledge even though it satisfies Armstrong's causal condition.

Goldman (1986) has proposed an important different sort of causal criterion, namely, that a true belief is knowledge if it is produced by a type of process that a 'global' and 'locally' reliable. It is global reliability of its propensity to cause true beliefs is sufficiently high. Local reliability had to do with whether the process would have produced a similar but false belief in certain counterfactual situations alternative to the actual situation. This way of marking off true beliefs that are knowledge e does not require the fact believed to be causally related to the belief and so it could in principle apply to knowledge of any kind of truth.

Goldman requires the global reliability of the belief-producing process for the justification of a belief, he requires, also for knowledge because justification is required for knowledge. What he requires for knowledge only of being one or more of which there exist any other but manages not to require for justification is local reliability. His idea is that a justified true belief is knowledge if the type of process that produced it would not have produced it in any relevant counterfactual situation in which it is

The theory of relevant alternative is best understood as an attempt to accommodate two opposing strands in our thinking about knowledge. The first is that knowledge is an absolute concept. On one interpretation, this is to mean that the justification or evidence one must have an order to know a proposition 'p' must be ample sufficient by expressively viewing of all these that alternatively vindicate 'p', (when an alternative to a proposition 'p' is a proposition incompatible with 'p').

For knowledge requires only that elimination of the relevant alternatives. So the tentative relevance for which alternate substitutions made for our consideration in view of its preservers that hold of both strands of our thinking about knowledge. Knowledge is an absolute concept, but because the absoluteness is relative to a standard, we can know many things.

The relevant alternative's account of knowledge can be motivated by noting that other concepts exhibit the same logical structure e. two examples of this are the concepts 'flat' and the concept 'empty'. Both appear to be absolute concepts-a space is empty only if it does not contain anything and a surface is flat only if it does not have any bumps. However, the absolute character of these concepts is relative to a standard. In the case of flat, there is a standard for what there is a standard for what counts as a bump and in the case of empty, there is a standard for what counts as a thing. we would not deny that a table is flat because a microscope reveals irregularities in its surface. Nor would we den y that a warehouse is empty because it contains particles of dust. To be flat is to be free of any relevant bumps. To be empty is to be devoid of all relevant things. Analogously, the relevant alternative's theory says that to know a proposition is to have evidence that eliminates all relevant alternatives.

Some philosophers have argued that the relevant alternative's theory of knowledge entails the falsity of the principle that set of known (by S) propositions in closed under known (by 'S') entailment, although others have disputed this however, this principle affirms the following conditional or the closure principle:

If 'S' knows 'p' and 'S' knows that 'p' entails 'q', then 'S' knows 'q'.

According to the theory of relevant alternatives, we can know a proposition 'p', without knowing that some (non-relevant) alterative too 'p' is false. But, once an alternative 'h' too 'p' incompatible with 'p', then 'p' will trivially entail not-h. So it will be possible to know some proposition without knowing another proposition trivially entailed by it. For example, we can know that we see a zebra without knowing that it is not the case that we see a cleverly disguised mule (on the assumption that 'we see a cleverly disguised mule' is not a relevant alterative). This will involve a violation of the closure principle. This is an interesting consequence of the theory because the closure principles seem too many to be quite intuitive. In fact, we can view sceptical arguments as employing the closure principle as a premise, along with the premise that we do not know that the alternatives raised by the sceptic are false. From these two premisses, it follows (on the assumption that we see that the propositions we believe entail the falsity of sceptical alternatives) that we do not know the proposition we believe. For example, it follows from the closure principle and the fact that we do not know that we do not see a cleverly disguised mule, that we do not know that we see a zebra. we can view the relevant alternative's theory as replying to the sceptical arguments by denying the closure principle.

What makes an alternative relevant? What standard do the alternatives rise by the sceptic fail to meet? These notoriously difficult to answer with any degree of precision or generality. This difficulty has led critics to view the theory as something being to obscurity. The problem can be illustrated though an example. Suppose Smith sees a barn and believes that he does, on the basis of very good perceptual evidence. When is the alternative that Smith sees a paper-mache replica relevant? If there are many such replicas in the immediate area, then this alternative can be relevant. In these circumstances, Smith fails to know that he sees a barn unless he knows that it is not the case that he sees a barn replica. Where there is any intensified replication that exists by this alternative will not be relevant? Smith can know that he sees a barn without knowing that he does not see a barn replica.

This highly suggests that a criterion of relevance be something like probability conditional on Smith's evidence and certain features of the circumstances. But which circumstances in particular do we count? Consider a case where we want the result that the barn replica alternative is clearly relevant, e.g., a case where the circumstances are such that there are numerous barn replicas in the area. Does the suggested criterion give us the result we wanted? The probability that Smith sees a barn replica given his evidence and his location to an area where there are many barn replicas is high. However, that same probability conditional on his evidence and his particular visual orientation toward a real barn is quite low. we want the probability to be conditional on features of the circumstances like the former bu t not on features of the circumstances like the latter. But how do we capture the difference in a general formulation?

How significant a problem is this for the theory of relevant alternatives? This depends on how we construe theory. If the theory is supposed to provide us with an analysis of knowledge, then the possibly to be without something and especially something essentially or greatly needed found ca pressing lack of something essential, a needful requisite necessary for the necessity to provide readily relief in the absence in all human lack of precise criteria of relevance surely constitutes a serious problem. However, if the theory is viewed instead as providing a response to sceptical arguments, it can be argued that the difficulty has little significance for the overall success of the theory.

What justifies the acceptance of a theory? In the face of the fact that some exceptional versions of empiricism have met many criticisms, and are nonetheless, overtaken to look for an answer in some sort of empiricist terms: In terms, that is, of support by the available evidence. How else could objectivity of science be defended but by showing that its conclusions (and in particular its theoretical conclusions-those theories it presently accepts) are somehow legitimately based on agreed observational and experimental evidence? But, as is well known, theories usually pose a problem for empiricism.

Allowing the empiricist the assumptions that there are observational statements whose truth-values can be inter-subjectively agreeing, and show the exploratory, non-demonstrative use of experiment in contemporary science. Yet philosophers identify experiments with observed results, and these with the testing of theory. They assume that observation provides an open window for the mind onto a world of natural facts and regularities, and that the main problem for the scientist is to establishing the unequalled independence of a theoretical interpretation. Experiments merely enable the production of (true) observation statements. Shared, replicable observations are the basis for a scientific consensus about an objective reality. It is clear that most scientific claims are genuinely theoretical: Nether themselves observational nor derivable deductively from observation statements (nor from inductive generalizations thereof). Accepting that there are phenomena that we have more or less diet access to, then, theories seem, at least when taken literally, to tell us about what is going on 'underneath' the evidently direct observability as made accessibly phenomenal, on order to produce those phenomena. The accounts given by such theories of this trans-empirical reality, simply because it is trans-empirical, can never be established by data, nor even by the 'natural' inductive generalizations of our data. No amount of evidence about tracks in cloud chambers and the like, can deductively establish that those tracks are produced by 'trans-observational' electrons.

One response would, of course, be to invoke some strict empiricist account of meaning, insisting that talk of electrons and the like, is, in fact just shorthand for talks in cloud chambers and the like. This account, however, has few, if any, current defenders. But, if so, the empiricist must acknowledge that, if we take any presently accepted theory, then there must be alternatives, different theories (indefinitely many of them) which treat the evidence equally well-assuming that the only evidential criterion is the entailment of the correct observational results.

All the same, there is an easy general result as well: assuming that a theory is any deductively closed set of sentences, and assuming, with the empiricist that the language in which these sentences are expressed has two sorts of predicated (observational and theoretical), and, finally, assuming that the entailment of the evidence is only constraint on empirical adequacy, then there are always indefinitely many different theories which are equally empirically adequate in a language in which the two sets of predicates are differentiated. Consider the restrictions if 'T' were quantified-free sentences expressed purely in the observational vocabulary, then any conservative extension of that restricted set of T's consequences back into the full vocabulary is a 'theory' co-empirically adequately with-entailing the same singular observational statements as 'T'. Unless veery special conditions apply (conditions which do not apply to any actualization for which is to succumb to scientific theory), then some of the empirically equivalent theories will formally contradict 'T'. (A similar straightforward demonstration works for the currently more fashionable account of theories as sets of models.)

How marked by complexity designate the basic fundamental part and parcel of the empiricist, who repudiates such as such to exclude the claim that two empirically equivalent theories are thereby fully equivalent, explain why the particular theory 'T' that is, as a matter of fact, accepted in sciences which are recognized submissions that seem referring of other possible theories as 'T', with which has the same observational content? Obviously the answer must be 'by bringing in further criteria beyond that of simply having the right observational consequence. Simplicity, coherence with other accepted these and wholeness in the unity as favourable contenders. There are notorious problems in formulating ths criteria at all precisely: But suppose, for present purposes, that we have heretofore, strong enough intuitive grasps to operate usefully with them. What is the status of such further criteria?

The empiricist-instrumentalist position, newly adopted and sharply argued by van Fraassen, is that those further criteria are 'pragmatic'-that is, involved essential reference to ourselves as 'theory-users'. We happen to prefer, for our own purposes, since, coherent, unified theories-but this is only a reflection of our preference es. It would be a mistake to think of those features supplying extra reasons to believe in the truth (or, approximate truth) of the theory that has them. Van Fraassen's account differs from some standard instrumentalist-empiricist account in recognizing the extra content of a theory (beyond its directly observational content) as genuinely declarative, as consisting of true-or-false assertions about the hidden structure of the world. His account accepts that the extra content can neither be eliminated as a result of defining theoretical notions in observational terms, nor be properly regarded as only apparently declarative but in fact as simply a codification schema. For van Fraassen, if a theory says, that there are electrons, then the theory should be taken as meaning to express in words, that which is said and without any positivist divide debasing reinterpretations of the meaning that might make 'There are electrons' mere shorthand for some complicated set of statements about tracks in obscure chambers or the like.

In the case of contradictory but empirically equivalent theories, such as the theory T1 that 'there are electrons' and the theory T2 that 'all the observable phenomena as if there are electrons but there are not 't's. Van Fraassen's account entails that each has a truth-value, at most one of which is 'true', is that science must use to indicate requirements by immediate or future needs or purpose not to T2, but this need not mean that it is rational thinking that it is more likely to be true (or otherwise appropriately connected with nature). So far as belief in the theory is belief but T2. The only belief involved in the acceptance of a theory is belief in the theorist's empirical adequacy. To accept the quantum theory, for example, entails believing that it 'saves the phenomena'-all the (relevant) phenomena, but only the phenomena, theorists do 'say more' than can be checked empirically even in principle. What more they say may indeed be true, but acceptance of the theory does not involve belief in the truth of the 'more' that theorist say.

Preferences between theories that are empirically equivalent are accounted for, because acceptance involves more than belief: As well as this epistemic dimension, acceptance also has a pragmatic dimension. Simplicity, (relative) freedom from ads hoc assumptions, 'unity', and the like are genuine virtues that can supply good reasons to accept one theory than another, but they are pragmatic virtues, reflecting the way we happen to like to do science, rather than anything about the world. Simplicity to think that they do so: The rationality of science and of scientific practices can be in truth (or approximate truth) of accepted theories. Van Fraassen's account conflicts with what many others see as very strong intuitions.

The most generally accepted account of this distinction is that a theory of justification is internalist if and only if it requires that all of the factors needed for a belief to be epistemologically justified for a given person to be cognitively accessible to that person, internal to his cognitive perceptive, and externalist, if it allow s that, at least some of the justifying factors need not be thus accessible, so that they can be external to the believer's cognitive perspective, beyond his knowingness. However, epistemologists often use the distinction between internalist and externalist theories of epistemic explications.

The externalism/internalism distinction has been mainly applied to theories of epistemic justification. It has also been applied in a closely related way to accounts of knowledge and a rather different way to accounts of belief and thought content. The internalist requirement of cognitive accessibility can be interpreted in at least two ways: A strong version of internalism would require that the believer actually be aware of the justifying factors in order to be justified while a weaker version would require only that he be capable of becoming aware of them by focussing his attention appropriately. But without the need for any change of position, new information, and so forth. Though the phrase 'cognitively accessible' suggests the weak interpretation, therein intuitive motivation for intentionalism, that in spite of the fact that, the idea that epistemic justification requires that the believer actually have in his cognitive possession a reason for thinking that the belief is true, wherefore, it would require the strong interpretation.

Perhaps the clearest example of an internalist position would be a 'foundationalist' view according to which foundational beliefs pertain to immediately experienced states of mind other beliefs are justified by standing in cognitively accessible logical or inferential relations to such foundational beliefs. Such a view could count as either a strong or a weak version of internalism, depending on whether an actual awareness of the justifying elements or only the capacity to become aware of them is required. Similarly, a 'coherentist' of that what is seen, in that the truth of a proposition consists in its being a member of some suitably defined body of other propositions: A body is consistent, coherent, and possibly endowed with other virtues, provided these are not defined in terms of truth. If both the beliefs or other states with which a justification belief is required to cohere and the coherence relations themselves are reflectively accessible.

It should be carefully noticed that when internalism is construed in this way, it is neither necessary nor sufficient by itself for internalism that the justifying factors literally are internal mental states of the person in question. Not necessarily, because on at least some views, e.g., a direct realist view of perception, something other than a mental state of the believer can be cognitively accessible: Not sufficient, because there are views according to which at least some mental states need not be actual (a strong version) or even possible (weak versions) objects of objective awareness. Also, on this way of drawing the distinction, a hybrid view (like the ones already set), according to which some of the factors required for justification must be cognitively accessible while the requiring obligations of employment seem the lack of something essential, whereby the vital fundamental duty of the others need not and overall will not be, would count as an externalist view. Obviously too, a view that was externalist in relation to a strong version of internalism (by not requiring that the believer actually be aware of all justifying factors) could still be internalist in relation to a weak version (by requiring that he at least is capable of becoming aware of them).

The most prominent recent externalist views have been versions of 'reliabilism', whose main requirements for justification are roughly that the belief is produced in a way or via a process that make it objectively likely that the belief is true. What makes such a view externalist is the absence of any requirement that the person for whom the belief is justified have any sort of cognitive access to the relation of reliability in question. Lacking such access, such a person will usually have or likely to be true, but will, on such an account, nonetheless, be epistemologically justified in accepting it. Thus, such a view arguably marks a major break from the modern epistemological tradition, stemming from Descartes, which identifies epistemic justification with having a reason, perhaps even a conclusive reason, for thinking that the belief is true. An epistemological working within this tradition is likely to feel that the externalist, than offering a competing account on the same concept of epistemic justification with which the traditional epistemologist is concerned, has simply changed the subject.

Two general lines of argument are commonly advanced in favour of justificatory externalism. The first starts from the allegedly commonsensical premise that knowledge can be non-problematically ascribed to relativity unsophisticated adults, to young children and even to higher animals. It is then argued that such ascriptions would be untenable on the standard internalist accounts of epistemic justification (assuming that epistemic justification is a necessary condition for knowledge), since the beliefs and inferences involved in such accounts are too complicated and sophisticated to be plausibly ascribed to such subjects. Thus, only an externalist view can make sense of such commonsense ascriptions and this, on the presumption that commonsense is correct, constitutes a strong argument in favour of externalism. An internalist may respond by externalism. An internalist may respond by challenging the initial premise, arguing that such ascriptions of knowledge are exaggerated, while perhaps at the same time claiming that the cognitive situation of at least some of the subjects in question. Is less restricted than the argument claims? A quite different response would be to reject the assumption that epistemic justification is a necessary condition for knowledge, perhaps, by adopting an externalist account of knowledge, rather than justification, as those aforementioned.

The second general line of argument for externalism points out that internalist views have conspicuously failed to provide defensible, non-sceptical solutions to the classical problems of epistemology. In striking contrast, however, such problems are overall easily solvable on an externalist view. Thus, if we assume both that the various relevant forms of scepticism are false and that the failure of internalist views so far is likely to be remedied in the future, we have good reason to think that some externalist view is true. Obviously the cogency of this argument depends on the plausibility of the two assumptions just noted. An internalist can reply, first, that it is not obvious that internalist epistemology is doomed to failure, that the explanation for the present lack of success may be the extreme difficulty of the problems in question. Secondly, it can be argued that most of even all of the appeal of the assumption that the various forms of scepticism are false depends essentially on the intuitive conviction that we do have possession of our reasons in the grasp for thinking that the various beliefs questioned by the sceptic is true-a conviction that the proponent of this argument must have a course reject.

The main objection to externalism rests on the intuition that the basic requirement for epistemic justification is that the acceptances of the belief in question are rational or responsible in relation to the cognitive goal of truth, which seems to necessitate for which the believer actually be aware of a reason for thinking that the belief is true, or at the very least, that such a reason be available to him. Since the satisfaction of an externalist condition is neither necessary nor sufficient for the existence of such a cognitively accessible reason, it is nonetheless, argued, externalism is mistaken as an account of epistemic justification. This general point has been elaborated by appeal to two sorts of putative intuitive counterexamples to externalism. The first of these challenges is the prerequisite justification by appealing to examples of belief which seem intuitively to be justified, but for which the externalist conditions are not satisfied. The standard examples of this sort are cases where beliefs produced in some very nonstandard way, e.g., by a Cartesian demon, but nonetheless, in such a way that the subjective experience of the believer is indistinguishable on that of someone whose beliefs are produced more normally. Cases of this general sort can be constructed in which any of the standard externalist condition, e.g., that the belief is a result of a reliable process, fail to be satisfied.

The intuitive claim is that the believer in such a case is nonetheless, epistemically justified, inasmuch as one whose belief is produced in a more normal way, and hence that externalist accounts of justification must be mistaken.

Perhaps the most interesting reply to this sort of counterexample, on behalf of reliabilism specifically, holds that reliability of a cognitive process is to be assessed in 'normal' possible worlds, i.e., in possible worlds that are actually the way our world is common-scenically believed to be, rather than in the world which actually contains the belief being judged. Since the cognitive processes employed in the Cartesian demon case are, we may assume, reliable when assessed in this way, the reliabilist can agree that such beliefs are justified. The obvious further issue is whether or not there is an adequate rationale for this construal of reliabilism, so that the reply is not merely ad hoc.

The second, correlative way of elaborating the general objection to justificatory externalism challenges the sufficiency of the various externalist conditions by citing cases where those conditions are satisfied, but where the believers in question seem intuitively not to be justified. Here the most widely discussed examples have to do with possible occult cognitive capacities like clairvoyance. Considering the point in application once again to reliabilism specifically, the claim is that a reliable clairvoyant who has no reason to think that he has such a cognitive power, and perhaps even good reasons to the contrary, is not rational or responsible and hence, not epistemologically justified in accepting the belief that result from his clairvoyance, despite the fact that the reliabilist condition is satisfied.

One sort of response to this latter sort of remonstrance is to 'bite the bullet' and insist that such believer e in fact justified, dismissing the seeming intuitions to the contrary as latent internalist prejudice. To a greater extent the more widely adopted response attempts to impose additional conditions, usually of a more or less internalist sort, which will rule out the offending example while still stopping far short of a full internalist. But while there is little doubt that such modified versions of externalism can indeed handle particular case's well enough to avoid clear intuitive implausibility, the issue is whether there will always be equally problematic cases for issues that might not handle, and whether there is any clear motivation for the additional requirements other than the general internalist view of justification that externalists are committed to reject.

A view in this same general vein, one that might be described as a hybrid of internalism and externalism, holding that epistemic justification requires that there be a justificatory facto r that is cognitively accessible e to the believer in question (though it need not be actually grasped), thus ruling out, e.g., a pure reliabilism. at the same time, however, though it must be objectively true that beliefs for which such a factor is available are likely to be true, this further fact need not be in any way grasped o r cognitive ly accessible to the believer. In effect, of the two premises needed to argue that a particular belief is likely to be true, one must be accessible in a way that would satisfy at least weak internalism, while the second can be (and will normally be) purely external. Here the internalist will respond that this hybrid view is of no help at all in meeting the objection that the belief is not held in the rational responsible way that justification intuitively seems required, for the believer in question, lacking one crucial premise, still has no reason at all for thinking that his belief is likely to be true.

An alternative to giving an externalist account of epistemic justification, one which may be more defensible while still accommodating many of the same motivating concerns, is to give an externalist account of knowledge directly, without relying on an intermediate account of justification. Such a views obviously have to reject the justified true belief account of knowledge, holding instead that knowledge is true belief which satisfies the chosen externalist condition, e.g., is a result of a reliable process (and, perhaps, further conditions as well). This makes it possible for such a view to retain an internalist account of epistemic justification, though the centrality of that concept is epistemology would obviously be seriously diminished.

Such an externalist account of knowledge can accommodate the common-sen conviction that animals, young children and unsophisticated adults' posse's cognition, in that knowledge, though not the weaker conviction (if such a conviction even exists) that such individuals are epistemically justified in their belief. It is also, least of mention, less vulnerable to internalist counterexamples of the sort and since the intuitivistic vortices in the pertaining extent in the clarification, that is to clear up justification than to knowledge. What is uncertain, is what ultimate philosophical significance the resulting conception of knowledge is taken for granted as of having, but being the occupant of having any serious bearing on traditional epistemological problems and on the deepest and most troubling versions of scepticism, which seem in fact to be primarily concerned with justification rather than knowledge?

A rather different use of the terms 'internalism' and 'externalism' have to do with the issue of how the content of beliefs and thoughts is determined: According to an internalist view of content, the content of such intentional states depends only on the non-relational, internal properties of the individual's mind or brain, and not at all on his physical and social environment: While according to an externalist view, content is significantly affected by such external factors. Here to a view that appeals to both internal and external elements are standardly classified as an externalist view.

As with justification and knowledge, the traditional view of content has been strongly internalist character. The main argument for externalism derives from the philosophy of language, more specifically from the various phenomena pertaining to natural kind terms, indexical, and so forth, that motivates the views that have come to be known as 'direct reference' theories. Such phenomena seem at least to show that the belief or thought content that can e properly attributed to a person is dependent on facts about his environment -, e.g., whether he is on Earth or Twin Earth, what in fact he is pointing at, the classificatory criteria employed by the experts in his social group, etc.-not just on what is going on internally in his mind or brain.

An objection to externalist accounts of content is that they seem unable to do justice to our ability to know the contents of our beliefs or thoughts 'from the inside', simply by reflection. If content is dependent of external factors pertaining to the environment, then knowledge of content should depend on knowledge of the these factors-which will not usually be available to the person whose belief or thought is in question.

The adoption of an externalist account of mental content would seem to support an externalist account of justification in the following way: If part of all of the content of a belief inaccessible to the believer, then both the justifying status of other beliefs in relation to the content and the status of that content as justifying further beliefs will be similarly inaccessible, thus contravening the internalist must insist that there are no rustication relations of these sorts, that only internally accessible content can either be justified or justify anything else: By such a response appears lame unless it is coupled with an attempt to shows that the externalists account of content is mistaken.

To have a word or a picture, or any other object in one's mind seems to be one thing, but to understand it is quite another. A major target of the later Ludwig Wittgenstein (1889-1951) is the suggestion that this understanding is achieved by a further presence, so that words might be understood if they are accompanied by ideas, for example. Wittgenstein insists that the extra presence merely raise the same kind of problem again. The better of suggestions in that understanding is to be thought of as possession of a technique, or skill, and this is the point of the slogan that 'meaning is use', the idea is congenital to 'pragmatism' and hostile to ineffable and incommunicable understandings.

Whatever it is that makes, what would otherwise be mere sounds and inscriptions into instruments of communication and understanding. The philosophical problem is to demystify this power, and to relate it to what we know of ourselves and the world. Contributions to this study include the theory of speech acts and the investigation of commonisation and the relationship between words and ideas, sand words and the world.

The most influential idea I e theory of meaning the past hundred years is the thesis that the meaning of an indicative sentence is given by its truth-condition. On this conception, to understand a sentence is to know its truth-conditions. The conception was first clearly formulated by the German mathematician and philosopher of mathematics Gottlob Frége (1848-1925), then was developed in a distinctive way by the early Wittgenstein, and is as leading idea of the American philosopher Donald Herbert Davidson. (1917-2003). The conception has remained so central that those who offer opposing theories characteristically define their position by reference to it.

The conception of meaning as truth-conditions needs not and should not be advanced for being in itself a complete account of meaning. For instance, one who understands a language must have some idea of the range of speech acts conventionally performed by the various types of sentences in the language, and must have some ideate significance of speech acts, the claim of the theorist of truth-conditions should rather be targeted on the notion of content: If two indicative sentences differ in what they strictly and literally say, then this difference is fully accounted for by the difference in their truth-conditions. It is this claim and its attendant problems, which will be the concern of each in the following.

The meaning of a complex expression is a function of the meaning of its constituents. This is indeed just a statement of what it is for an expression to be semantically complex. It is one of the initial attractions of the conception of meaning as truth-conditions that it permits a smooth and satisfying account of the ay in which the meaning of a complex expression is a function of the meaning its constituents. On the truth-conditional conception, to give the meaning of sn expressions is the contribution it makes to the truth-conditions of sentences in which it occurs. For example terms-proper names, indexical, and certain pronouns-this is done by stating the reference of the term in question. For predicates, it is done either by stating the conditions under which the predicate is true of arbitrary objects, or by stating the conditions under which arbitrary atomic sentences containing it true. The meaning of sentence-forming operators as given by stating its contribution to the truth-conditions of a complex sentence, as function of the semantic values of the sentence on which it operates. For an extremely simple, but nevertheless structured language, er can state that contribution's various expressions make to truth condition, are such as:

A1: The referent of 'London ' is London.

A2: The referent of 'Paris' is Paris

A3: Any sentence of the form 'a is beautiful' is true if and only if the referent of 'a' is beautiful.

A4: Any sentence of the form 'a is larger than b' is true if and only if the referent of 'a' is larger than a referent of 'b'.

A5: Any sentence of t he for m 'its no t the case that 'A' is true if and only if it is not the case that 'A' is true.

A6: Any sentence of the form 'A and B' are true if and only if 'A' is true and 'B' is true.

The principle's A1-A6 construct and develop a form for which a simple theory of truth for a fragment of English. In this, the or it is possible to derive these consequences: That 'Paris is beautiful' is true if and only if Paris is beautiful, is true and only if Paris is beautiful (from A2 and A3): That 'London is larger than Paris and it is not the case that London is beautiful, is true if and only if London is larger than Paris and it is not the case that London is beautiful (from A1-A5), and in general, for any sentence 'A', this simple language we can derive something of the form 'A' is true if and only if 'A'.

Yet, theorists' of truth conditions should insist that not every true statement about the reference o f an expression is fit to be an axiom in a meaning-giving theory of truth for a language. The axiom

'London' refers to the ct in which there was a huge fire in 1666.

This is a true statement about the reference of 'London'. It is a consequence of a hypothesis which substitutes the axiom for A1 in our simple truth theory that 'London is beautiful' is true if and only if the city in which there was a huge fire in 1666 is beautiful. Since a subject can align himself with the naming authenticity that 'London' is without knowing that the last-mentioned truth condition, this replacement axiom is not fit to be an axiom in a meaning-specifying truth theory. It is, of course, incumbent on a theorist of meaning as truth conditions to state the constraints on the acceptability of axioms in a way which does not presuppose any prior, truth-conditional conception of meaning.

Among the many challenges facing the theorist of truth conditions, two are particularly salient and fundamental, first, the theorist has to answer the charge of triviality or vacuity. Second, the theorist must offer an account of which for a person's language is truly describable by a semantic theory containing a given semantic axiom.

What can take the charge of triviality first? In more detail, it would run thus: Since the content of a claim that the sentence 'Paris is beautiful' is true amounts to no more than the claim that Paris is beautiful, we can trivially describe understanding a sentence, if we wish, as knowing its truth-conditions. But this gives us no substantive account of understanding whatsoever. Something other than grasp of truth conditions must provide the substantive account. The charge tests upon what has been called the 'redundancy theory of truth', the theory also known as 'minimalism'. Or the 'deflationary' view of truth, fathered by the German mathematician and philosopher of mathematics, had begun with Gottlob Frége (1848-1925), and the Cambridge mathematician and philosopher Plumton Frank Ramsey (1903-30). Wherefore, the essential claim is that the predicate' . . . is true' does not have a sense, i.e., expresses no substantive or profound or explanatory concept that ought to be the topic of philosophical enquiry. The approach admits of different versions, nit centres on the points that 'it is true that p' says no more nor less than 'p'(hence redundancy): That in less direct context, such as 'everything he said was true'. Or 'all logical consequences are true'. The predicate functions as a device enabling us to generalize rather than as an adjective or predicate describing the things he said or the kinds of propositions that follow from true propositions. For example: '$(\forall p, q)(p \& p \rightarrow q \rightarrow q)$' where there is no use of a notion of truth.

There are technical problems in interpreting all uses of the notion of truth in such ways, but they are not generally felt to be insurmountable. The approach needs to explain away apparently substantive users of the notion, such as 'science aims at the truth' or 'truth is a normative governing discourse'. Indeed, postmodernist writing frequently advocates that we must abandon such norms, along with a discredited 'objectivity' conception of truth. But, perhaps, we can have the norm even when objectivity is problematic, since they can be framed without mention of truth: Science wants it to be so that whenever science holds that 'p', then 'p', discourse is to be regulated by the principle that it is wrong to assert 'p' when 'not-p'.

It is, nonetheless, that we can take charge of triviality, since the content of a claim ht the sentence 'Paris is beautiful' is true, amounting to no more than the claim that Paris is beautifully, we can trivially describe understanding a sentence. If we wish, as knowing its truth-condition, but this gives us no substitute account of understanding whatsoever. Something other than grasp of truth conditions must provide the substantive account. The charge rests on or upon what has been the redundancy theory of truth. The minimal theory states that the concept of truth is exhaustively by the fact that it conforms to the equivalence principle, the principle that for any proposition 'p', it is true that 'p' if and only if 'p'. Many different philosophical theories, accept that the equivalence principle, as e distinguishing feature of the minimal theory, its claim that the equivalence principle exhausts the notion of truth. It is, however, widely accepted, both by opponents and supporters of truth conditional theories of meaning, that it is inconsistent to accept both the minimal theory of truth and a truth conditional account of meaning. If the claim that the sentence 'Paris is beautiful, it is circular to try to explain the sentence's meaning in terms of its truth condition. The minimal theory of truth has been endorsed by Ramsey, Ayer, and later Wittgenstein, Quine, Strawson, Horwich and-confusingly and inconsistently of Frége himself.

The minimal theory treats instances of the equivalence principle as definitional truth for a given sentence. But in fact, it seems that each instance of the equivalence principle can itself be explained. The truths from which such an instance as

> 'London is beautiful' is true if and only if
> 'London is beautiful.'

Can be explained are precisely A1 and A3 in that, this would be a pseudo-explanation if the fact that 'London' refers to London consists in part in the fact that 'London is beautiful' has the truth-condition it does? But that is very implausible: It is, after all, possible to understand the name 'London' without understanding the predicate 'is beautiful'. The idea that facts about the reference of particular words can be explanatory of facts about the truth conditions of sentences containing them in no way requires any naturalistic or any other kind of reduction of the notion of reference. Nor is the idea incompatible with the plausible point that singular reference can be attributed at all only to something which is capable of combining with other expressions to form complete sentences. That still leaves room for facts about an expression's having the particular reference it does to be partially explanatory of the particular truth condition possessed by a given sentence containing it. The minimal theory thus treats as definitional or stimulative something which is in fact open to explanation. What makes this explanation possible is that there is a general notion of truth which has, among the many links which hold it in place, systematic connections with the semantic values of subsentential expressions.

A second problem with the minimal theory is that it seems impossible to formulate it without at some point relying implicitly on features and principles involving truth which goes beyond anything countenanced by the minimal theory. If, minimal, or redundancy theory treats true statements as predicated of anything linguistic, like its utterances, or even, the type-in-a-language, or whatever. Then the equivalence schemata will not cover all cases, but those in the theorist's own language only. Some account has to be given of truth for sentences of other languages. Speaking of the truth of language-independent propositions or thoughts will only postpone, not avoid, this issue, since at some point principles have to be stated associating these language-dependent entities with sentences of particular languages. The defender of the minimalist theory is that the sentence 'S' of a foreign language is best translated by our sentence, then the foreign sentence 'S' is true if and only if 'p'. Now the best translation of a sentence must preserve the concepts expressed in the sentence. Constraints involving a general notion of truth are pervasive plausible philosophical theory of concepts. It is, for example, a condition of adequacy on an individuating account of any concept that there exists what may be called 'Determination Theory' for that account-that is, a specification on how the account contributes to fixing the semantic value of that concept. The notion of a concept's semantic value is the notion of something which makes a certain contribution to the truth conditions of thoughts in which the concept occurs. But this is to presuppose, than to elucidate, a general notion of truth.

It is, also, plausible that there are general constraints on the form of such Determination Theories, constrains which to involve truth, and which are not derivable from the minimalist's creation. Suppose that concepts are individuated by their possession condition. A possession condition may in various ways make a thinker's possession of a particular concept dependent upon his relation to his environment. Many possession conditions will mention the links between accept and the thinker's perceptual experience. Perceptual experience represents the world for being a certain way. It is arguable that the only satisfactory explanation to what it is for perceptual experience to represent the world in a particular way must refer to the complex relations of the experience to the subject's environment. If this is so, to mention of such experiences in a possession condition dependent in part upon the environmental relations of the thinker. Evan though the thinker's non-environmental properties and relations remain constant, the conceptual content of his mental state can vary in the thinker's social environment is varied. A possession condition which properly individuates such a concept must take into account the thinker's social relations, in particular his linguistic relations.

Its alternative approach, addresses the question by starting from the idea that a concept is individuated by the condition which must be satisfied a thinker is to posses that concept and to be capable of having beliefs and other altitudes whose contents contain it as a constituent. So, to take a simple case, one could propose that the logical concept 'and' is individualized by this condition: It is the unique concept 'C' to posses which a thinker has to find these forms of inference compelling, without basting them on any further inference or information: From any two premises 'A' and 'B', ACB can be inferred and from any premises a relation to a relative observational concept, such as grounding possibilities can be individuated in part by stating that the thinker finds specified contents containing it compelling when he has certain kinds of perception, and in part by relating those judgements containing the concept and which are not based on perception to those judgements that are. A statement which individuates a concept by saying what is required for a thinker to posses it can be described as giving the possession condition for the concept.

A possession condition for a particular concept may actually make use of that concept. The possessions condition for 'and' doers not. we can also expect to use relatively observational concepts in specifying the kind of experience which have to be mentioned in the possession conditions for relatively observational concepts. What we must avoid is mention of the concept in question as such within the content of the attitude attributed to the thinker in the possession condition. Otherwise we would be presupposed possession of the concept in an account which was meant to elucidate its possession. In talking of what the thinker finds compelling, the possession conditions can also respect an insight of the later Wittgenstein: That a thinker's mastery of a concept is inextricably tied to how he finds it natural to go in new cases in applying the concept.

Sometimes a family of concepts has this property: It is not possible to master any one of the members of the family without mastering of the others. Two of the families which plausibly have this status are these: The family consisting of same simple concepts 0, 1. 2, . . . of the natural numbers and the corresponding concepts of numerical quantifiers, 'there are o so-and-so's, there is 1 so-and-so, . . . and the family consisting of the concepts 'belief' and 'desire'. Such families have come to be known as 'local Holist's'. A local holism does not prevent the individuation of a concept by its possession condition. Rather, it demands that all the concepts in the family be individuated simultaneously. So one would say something of this conduct regulated by an external control as a custom or a formal protocol of procedures, such that the economy is delegated by some outward appearance of something as distinguished from the substance of which it is made form. Belief and desire form the unique pair of concepts C1 and C2, such that for a thinker to posses them is to meet such-and-such condition involving the thinker, C1 and C2. For those other possession conditions to individuate properly. It is necessary that there be some ranking of the concepts treated. The possession condition or concepts higher in the ranking must presuppose only possession of concepts at the same or lower levels in the ranking.

A possession condition may in various ways make a thinker's possession of a particular concept dependent on or upon his relations to his environment. Many possession conditions will mention the links between a concept and the thinker's perceptual experience. Perceptual experience represents the world for being a certain way. It is arguable that the only satisfactory explanation of what it is for perceptual experience to represent the world in a particular way must refer to the complex relations of the experience to the subject's environment. If this is so, then mention of such experiences in a possession condition will make possession f that concept relations tn the thicker. Burge (1979) has also argued from intuitions about particular examples that even though the thinker's non-environmental properties and relations remain constant, the conceptual content of his mental state can vary in the thinker's social environment is varied. A possession condition which properly individuates such a concept must take into account the thinker's social relations, in particular his linguistic relations.

Once, again, some general principles involving truth can, as Horwich has emphasized, be derived from the equivalence schemata using minimal logical apparatus. Consider, for instance, the principle that 'Paris is beautiful and London is beautiful' is true if and only if 'Paris is beautiful' is true and 'London is beautiful' is true if and only if Paris is beautiful and London is beautiful. But no logical manipulations of the equivalence e schemata will allow the derivation of that general constraint governing possession condition, truth and assignment of semantic values. That constraints can, of course, be regarded as a further elaboration of the idea that truth is one of the aims of judgement.

What is to a greater extent, but to consider the other question, for 'What is it for a person's language to be correctly describable by a semantic theory containing a particular axiom, such as the above axiom A6 for conjunctions? This question may be addressed at two depths of generality. A shallower of levels, in this question may take for granted the person's possession of the concept of conjunction, and be concerned with what hast be true for the axiom to describe his language correctly. At a deeper level, an answer should not sidestep the issue of what it is to posses the concept. The answers to both questions are of great interest.

When a person means conjunction by 'and', he is not necessarily capable of phrasing the A6 axiom. Even if he can formulate it, his ability to formulate it is not causal basis of his capacity to hear sentences containing the word 'and' as meaning something involving conjunction. Nor is it the causal basis of his capacity to mean something involving conjunction by sentences he utters containing the word 'and' of which is used as a connective between words, phrases, clauses, and sentences.

Is it then right to regard a truth theory as part of an unconscious psychological computation, and to regards understanding a sentence as involving a particular way of deriving a theorem from a truth theory, yet it might at some level of unconscious processing? One problem with this is that it is quite implausible that everyone who speaks the same language has to use the same algorithms for computing the meaning of a sentence. In the past thirteen years, the particular works as befitting Davies and Evans, whereby a conception has evolved according to which an axiom like A6, is true of a person's component in the explanation of his understanding of each sentence containing the words 'and', a common component which explains why each such sentence is understood as meaning something involving conjunction. This conception can also be elaborated in computational; terms: As alike to the axiom A6 to be true of a person's language is for the unconscious mechanism, which produce understanding to draw on the information that a sentence of the form 'A and B' is true only if 'A' is true and 'B' is true. Many different algorithms may equally draw on or open this information. The psychological reality of a semantic theory thus is to involve, Marr's (1982) given by classification as something intermediate between his level one, the function computed, and his level two, the algorithm by which it is computed. This conception of the psychological reality of a semantic theory can also be applied to syntactic and phonological theories. Theories in semantics, syntax and phonology are not themselves required to specify the particular algorithm which the language user employs. The identification of the particular computational methods employed is a task for psychology. But semantic, syntactic and phonological theories are answerable to psychological data, and are potentially refutable by them-for these linguistic theories do make commitments to the information drawn on or upon by mechanisms in the language user.

This answer to the question of what it is for an axiom to be true of a person's language clearly takes for granted the person's possession of the concept expressed by the word treated by the axiom. In the example of the A6 axiom, the information drawn upon is that sentence of the form 'A and B' are true if and only if 'A' is true and 'B' is true. This informational content employs, as it has to if it is to be adequate, the concept of conjunction used in stating the meaning of sentences containing the connective word 'and', in which has already been mentioned. It is at this point that the theory of linguistic understanding has to argue that it has to draw upon a theory if the conditions for possessing a given concept. It is plausible that the concept of conjunction is individuated by the following condition for a thinker to have possession of it:

The concept 'and' is that concept 'C' to possess which a

thinker must meet the following conditions: He finds inferences

of the following forms compelling, does not find them

looking down on the aftermath of any reasoning and finds them

because they are of their form:

	pCq	pCq	pq
\	p	q	pCq

Here 'p' and 'q' range ov complete propositional thoughts, not sentences. When A6 axiom is true of a person's language, there is a global dovetailing between this possessional condition for the concept of conjunction and certain of his practices involving the word 'and', being as the connective within a sentence. For the case of conjunction, the dovetailing involves at least this:

> If the possession condition for conjuncture entails that the thinker who possesses the concept of conjunction must be willing to make certain transitions involving the thought p&q, and of the thinker's semitrance 'A' means that 'p' and his sentence 'B' means that 'q' then: The thinker must be willing to make the corresponding linguistic transition involving sentence 'A and B'.

This is only part of what is involved in the required dovetailing. Given what wee have already said about the uniform explanation of the understanding of the various occurrences of a given word, we should also add, that there is a uniform (unconscious, computational) explanation of the language user's willingness to make the corresponding transitions involving the sentence 'A and B'.

This dovetailing account returns an answer to the deeper questions because neither the possession condition for conjunction, nor the dovetailing condition which builds upon the dovetailing condition which builds on or upon that possession condition, takes for granted the thinker's possession of the concept expressed by the word 'and', for being the connective quest or the joining logical sequences of words or ideas contained of a sentence. The dovetailing account for conjunction is an exampling of a greater amount of an overall schema, which can be applied to any concept. The case of conjunction is of course, exceptionally simple in several respects. Possession conditions for other concepts will speak not just of inferential transitions, but of certain conditions in which beliefs involving the concept in question are accepted or rejected, and the corresponding dovetailing condition will inherit these features. This dovetailing account has also to be underpinned by a general rationale linking contributions to truth conditions with the particular possession condition proposed for concepts. It is part of the task of the theory of concepts to supply this in developing Determination Theories for particular concepts.

In some cases, a relatively clear account is possible of how a concept can feature in thoughts which may be true though unverifiable. The possession condition for the quantificational concept all natural numbers can in outline run thus: This quantifier is that concept Cx . . . x . . . to posses which the thinker has to find any inference of the form:

CxFx

Fn.

Compelling, where 'n' is a concept of a natural number, and does not have to find anything else essentially containing Cx . . . x . . . compelling. The straightforward Determination Theory for this possession condition is one on which the truth of such a thought CxFx is true only if all natural numbers are 'F'. That all natural numbers are 'F' is a condition which can hold without our being able to establish that it holds. So an axiom of a truth theory which dovetails with this possession condition for universal quantification over the natural numbers will be b component of a realistic, non-verifications theory of truth conditions.

Finally, this response to the deeper questions allows us to answer two challenges to the conception of meaning as truth-conditions. First, there was the question left hanging earlier, of how the theorist of truth-conditions is to say what makes one axiom of a semantic theory correct rather than another, when the two axioms assigned the same semantic values, but do so by different concepts. Since the different concepts will have different possession conditions, the dovetailing accounts, at the deeper level, of what it is for each axiom to be correct for a person's language will be different accounts. Second, there is a challenge repeatedly made by the minimalist theories of truth, to the effect that the theorist of meaning as truth-conditions should give some non-circular account of what it is to understand a sentence, or to be capable of understanding all sentences containing a given constituent. For each expression in a sentence, the corresponding dovetailing account, together with the possession condition, supplies a non-circular account of what it is to that expression. The combined accounts for each of the expressions which comprise a given sentence together constitute a non-circular account of what it is to understand the complete sentence. Taken together, they allow theorist of meaning as truth-conditions fully to meet the challenge.

A widely discussed idea is that for a subject to be in a certain set of content-involving states, for attribution of those state s to make the subject as rationally intelligible. Perceptions make it rational for a person to form corresponding beliefs. Beliefs make it rational to draw certain inferences such as belief and desire that to a condition or occurrence, traceable to a cause as effectually generated by a protocol that of being something by leaning toward form, shaping, combining to assemble for some agreeable reason for which the formations of particular intentions, and performance are those of the appropriate actions. People are frequently irrational of course, but a governing ideal of this approach is that for any family of contents, there is some minimal core of rational transitions to or from states involving them, a core that a person must respect of his states is to be attribute d with those contents at all. we contrast in what we want do with what we must do-whether for reasons of morality or duty, or even for reasons of practical necessity (to get what we wanted in the first place). Accordingly, our own desires have seemed to be the principal actions that most fully express our own individual natures and will, and those for which we are personally responsible. But desire has also seemed to be a principle of action contrary to and at war with our better natures, as rational and agents. For it is principally from our own differing perspectives upon what would be good, that each of us wants what he does, each point of view being defined by one's own interests and pleasure. In this, the representations of desire are like those of sensory perception, similarly shaped by the perspective of the perceiver and the idiosyncrasies of the perceptual dialectic about desire and its object recapitulates that of a perception and sensible qualities. The strength of desire, for instance, varies with the state of the subject more or less independently of the character, an the actual utility, of the object wanted. Such facts cast doubt on the 'objectivity' of desire, and on the existence of correlatives property of 'goodness', inherent in the objects of our desires, and independent of them. Perhaps, as the Dutch Jewish rationalist (1632-77) Benedictus de Spinoza put it, it is not that we want what we think good, but that we think well what we happen to want-the 'good' in what we want being a mere shadow cast by the desire for it. (There is a parallel Protagorean view of belief, similarly sceptical of truth). The serious defence of such a view, however, would require a systematic reduction of apparent facts about goodness to facts about desire, and an analysis of desire which in turn makes no reference to goodness. While what is yet to be provided, moral psychologists have sought to vindicate an idea of objective goodness. For example, as what would be good from all points of view, or none, or, in the manner of the German philosopher Immanuel Kant, to set up another principle (the will or practical reason) conceived as an autonomous source of action, independent of desire or its object: And this tradition has tended to minimize the role of desire in the genesis of action.

Ascribing states with content on actual people has to proceed simultaneously with attributions of as wide range of non-rational states and capacities. In general, we cannot understand for persons reasons for acting as he does without knowing the array of emotions and sensations to which he is subject: What he remembers and what he forgets, and how he reasons beyond the confines of minimal rationality. Even the content-involving perceptual states, which play a fundamental role in individuating content, cannot be understood purely in terms relating to minimal rationality. A perception of the world for being a certain way is not (and could not be) under a subject's rational control. Thought it is true and important that perceptions give reason for forming beliefs, the belief for which they fundamentally provide reasons-observational beliefs about the environment-have contents which can only be elucidated by referring to perceptual experience. In this respect (as in others), perceptual states differ from beliefs and desires that are individuated by mentioning what they provide reasons for judging or doing: or frequently these latter judgements and actions can be individuated without reference back to the states that provide for them.

What is the significance for theories of content of the fact that it is almost certainly adaptive for members of as species to have a system of states with representational contents which are capable of influencing their actions appropriately? According to teleological theories a content, a constitutive account of content-one which says what it is for a state to have a given content-must make user of the notion of natural function and teleology. The intuitive idea is that for a belief state to have a given content 'p' is for the belief-forming mechanisms which produced it to have the unction as, perhaps, derivatively of producing that stare only when it is the case that 'p'. One issue this approach must tackle is whether it is really capable of associating with states the classical, realistic, verification-transcendent contents which, pre-theoretically, we attribute to them. It is not clear that a content's holding unknowably can influence the replication of belief-forming mechanisms. But if content itself proves to resist elucidation, it is still a very natural function and selection. It is still a very attractive view that selection, it is still a very attractive view, that selection must be mentioned in an account of what associates something-such as aa sentence-wi a particular content, even though that content itself may be individuated by other means.

Contents, are most notably given by some consequence or prominence in some sorted agreement to which makes them explicitly distinctive by rule in specifying 'that . . .' clauses, and it is natural to suppose that a content has the same kind of sequence and hierarchical structure as the sentence that specifies it. This supposition would be widely accepted for conceptual content. It is, however, a substantive thesis that all content is conceptual. One way of treating one sort of 'perceptual content' is to regard the content as determined by a spatial type, the type under which the region of space around the perceiver must fall if the experience with that content is to represent the environment correctly. The type involves a specification of surfaces and features in the environment, and their distances and directions from the perceiver's body as origin, such contents lack any sentence-like structure at all. Supporters of the view that all content is conceptual will argue that the legitimacy of using these spatial types in giving the content of experience does not undermine the thesis that all content is conceptual. Such supporters will say that the spatial type is just a way of capturing what can equally be captured by conceptual components such as 'that distance', or 'that direction', where these demonstratives are made available by the perception in question. Friends of conceptual content will respond that these demonstratives themselves cannot be elucidated without mentioning the spatial type which lack sentence-like structure.

While we have consistently tried to distinguish between scientific knowledge and philosophical speculation based on this knowledge - there is no empirically valid causal linkage between the former and the latter. Those who wish to dismiss the speculative assumptions as its basis to be drawn the obvious freedom of which id firmly grounded in scientific theory and experiments there is, however, in the scientific description of nature, the belief in radical Cartesian division between mind and world sanctioned by classical physics. Seemingly clear, that this separation between mind and world was a macro-level illusion fostered by limited awareness of the actual character of physical reality and by mathematical idealization that were extended beyond the realm of their applicability.

Thus, the grounds for objecting to quantum theory, the lack of a one-to-one correspondence between every element of the physical theory and the physical reality it describes, may seem justifiable and reasonable in strictly scientific terms. After all, the completeness of all previous physical theories was measured against the criterion with enormous success. Since it was this success that gave physics the reputation of being able to disclose physical reality with magnificent exactitude, perhaps a more comprehensive quantum theory will emerge to insist on these requirements.

All indications are, however, that no future theory can circumvent quantum indeterminancy, and the success of quantum theory in co-ordinating our experience with nature is eloquent testimony to this conclusion. As Bohr realized, the fact that we live in a quantum universe in which the quantum of action is a given or an unavoidable reality requires a very different criterion for determining the completeness or physical theory. The new measure for a complete physical theory is that it unambiguously confirms our ability to co-ordinate more experience with physical reality.

If a theory does so and continues to do so, which is certainly the case with quantum physics, then the theory must be deemed complete. Quantum physics not only works exceedingly well, it is, in these terms, the most accurate physical theory that has ever existed. When we consider that this physics allows us to predict and measure quantities like the magnetic moment of electrons to the fifteenth decimal place, we realize that accuracy per se is not the real issue. The real issue, as Bohr rightly intuited, is that this complete physical theory effectively undermines the privileged relationship in classical physics between 'theory' and 'physical reality'.

In quantum physics, one calculates the probability of an event that can happen in alternative ways by adding the wave function, and then taking the square of the amplitude. In the two-slit experiment, for example, the electron is described by one wave function if it goes through one slit and by another wave function it goes through the other slit.

In order to compute the probability of where the electron is going to end on the screen, we add the two wave functions, compute the absolute value of their sum, and square it. Although the recipe in classical probability theory seems similar, it is quite different. In classical physics, we would simply add the probabilities of the two alternate ways and let it go at that. The classical procedure does not work here, because we are not dealing with classical atoms. In quantum physics additional terms arise when the wave functions are added, and the probability is computed in a process known as the 'superposition principle'.

The superposition principle can be illustrated with an analogy from simple mathematics. Add two numbers and then take the square of their sum. As opposed to just adding the squares of the two numbers. Obviously (2 + 3)2 is not equal to 22 + 32. The former is 25, and the latter are 13. In the language of quantum probability theory

$$| \psi 2 | 2 \neq | \psi 1 | 2 + | \psi 2 | 2$$

Where $\psi 1$ and $\psi 2$ are the individual wave functions. On the left-hand side, the superposition principle results in extra terms that cannot be found on the right-hand side. The left-hand side of the above relations is the way a quantum physicist would compute probabilities, and the right0-hand side is the classical analogue. In quantum theory, the right-hand side is realized when we know, for example, which slit through which the electron went. Heisenberg was among the first to compute what would happen in an instance like this. The extra superposition terms contained in the left-hand side of the above relations would not be there, and the peculiar wave-like interference pattern would disappear. The observed pattern on the final screen would, therefore, be what one would expect if electrons were behaving like a bullet, and the final probability would be the sum of the individual probabilities. But when we know which slit the electron went through, this interaction with the system causes the interference pattern to disappear.

In order to give a full account of quantum recipes for computing probabilities, one has to examine what would happen in events that are compounded. Compound events are 'events that can be broken down into a series of steps, or events that consists of a number of things happening independently.' The recipe here calls for multiplying the individual wave functions, and then following the usual quantum recipe of taking the square of the amplitude.

The quantum recipe is $| \psi 1 \bullet \psi 2 | 2$, and, in this case, it would be the same if we multiplied the individual probabilities, as one would in classical theory. Thus, the recipes of computing results in quantum theory and classical physics can be totally different. The quantum superposition effects are completely non-classical, and there is no mathematical justification per se why the quantum recipes work. What justifies the use of quantum probability theory is the coming thing that justifies the use of quantum physics -it has allowed us in countless experiments to extend our ability to co-ordinate experience with the expansive nature of unity.

A departure from the classical mechanics of Newton involving the principle that certain physical quantities can only assume discrete values. In quantum theory, introduced by Planck (1900), certain conditions are imposed on these quantities to restrict their value; the quantities are then said to be 'quantized'.

Up to the year 1900, physics was based on Newtonian mechanics. Large-scale systems are usually adequately described, however, several problems could not be solved, in particular, the explanation of the curves of energy against wavelengths for 'black-body radiation', with their characteristic maximum, as these attemptive efforts were afforded to endeavour upon the base-cases, on which the idea that the enclosure producing the radiation contained a number of 'standing waves' and that the energy of an oscillator if 'kT', where 'k' in the 'Boltzmann Constant' and 'T' the thermodynamic temperature. It is a consequence of classical theory that the energy does not depend on the frequency of the oscillator. This inability to explain the phenomenons has been called the 'ultraviolet catastrophe'.

Planck tackled the problem by discarding the idea that an oscillator can attain or decrease energy continuously, suggesting that it could only change by some discrete amount, which he called a 'quantum.' This unit of energy is given by 'hv' where 'v' is the frequency and 'h' is the 'Planck Constant,' 'h' has dimensions of energy 'x' times of action, and was called the 'quantum of action.' According to Planck an oscillator could only change its energy by an integral number of quanta, i.e., by hv, 2hv, 3hv, etc. This meant that the radiation in an enclosure has certain discrete energies and by considering the statistical distribution of oscillators with respect to their energies, he was able to derive the 'Planck Radiation Formulas.' The formulae contrived by Planck, to express the distribution of dynamic energy in the normal spectrum of 'black-body' radiation. It is usual form is:

$$8\pi chd\lambda/\lambda\ 5\ (\exp[ch\ /\ k\lambda T] - 1,$$

Which represents the amount of energy per unit volume in the range of wavelengths between λ and λ + dλ? 'c' = the speed of light and 'h' = the Planck constant, as 'k' = the Boltzmann constant with 'T' = thermodynamic temperatures.

The idea of quanta of energy was applied to other problems in physics, when in 1905 Einstein explained features of the 'Photoelectric Effect' by assuming that light was absorbed in quanta (photons). A further advance was made by Bohr (1913) in his theory of atomic spectra, in which he assumed that the atom can only exist in certain energy states and that light is emitted or absorbed as a result of a change from one state to another. He used the idea that the angular momentum of an orbiting electron could only assume discrete values, ie., Was quantized? A refinement of Bohr's theory was introduced by Sommerfeld in an attempt to account for fine structure in spectra. Other successes of quantum theory were its explanations of 'Compton ' and 'Stark Effects.' Later developments involved the formulation of a new system of mechanics known as 'Quantum Mechanics.'

What is more, in furthering to Compton's scattering was an interaction between a photon of electromagnetic radiation and a free electron, or other charged particles, in which some of the energy of the photon is transferred to the particle. As a result, the wavelength of the photon is increased by amount Δλ. Where: Δλ = (2h / m0 c) sin 2 ½. This is the Compton equation, 'h' is the Planck constant, m0 the rest mass of the particle, 'c' the speed of light, and the photon angle between the directions of the incident and scattered photons. The quantity 'h/m0c' and is known as the 'Compton Wavelength,' symbol λC, which for an electron is equal to 0.002 43 nm.

The outer electrons in all elements and the inner ones in those of low atomic number have 'binding energies' negligible compared with the quantum energies of all except very soft X- and gamma rays. Thus most electrons in matter are effectively free and at rest and so cause Compton scattering. In the range of quantum energies 105 to 107 electro volts, this effect is commonly the most important process of attenuation of radiation. The scattering electron is ejected from the atom with large kinetic energy and the ionization that it causes plays an important part in the operation of detectors of radiation.

In the 'Inverse Compton Effect' there is a gain in energy by low-energy photons as a result of being scattered by free electrons of much higher energy. As a consequence, the electrons lose energy. Whereas, the wavelength of light emitted by atoms is altered by the application of a strong transverse electric field to the source, the spectrum lines being split up into a number of sharply defined components. The displacements are symmetrical about the position of the undisplaced lines, and are prepositional of the undisplaced line, and are propositional to the field strength up to about 100 000 volts per cm (The Stark Effect).

Adjoining along side with quantum mechanics, is an unstretching constitution taken advantage of forwarded mathematical physical theories - growing from Planck's 'Quantum Theory' and deals with the mechanics of atomic and related systems in terms of quantities that can be measured. The subject development in several mathematical forms, including 'Wave Mechanics' (Schrödinger) and 'Matrix Mechanics' (Born and Heisenberg), all of which are equivalent.

In quantum mechanics, it is often found that the properties of a physical system, such as its angular moment and energy, can only take discrete values. Where this occurs the property is said to be 'quantized' and its various possible values are labelled by a set of numbers called quantum numbers. For example, according to Bohr's theory of the atom, an electron moving in a circular orbit could occupy any orbit at any distance from the nucleus but only an orbit for which its angular momentum (mvr) was equal to $nh/2\pi$, where 'n' is an integer (0, 1, 2, 3, etc.) and 'h' is the Planck's constant. Thus the property of angular momentum is quantized and 'n' is a quantum number that gives its possible values. The Bohr theory has now been superseded by a more sophisticated theory in which the idea of orbits is replaced by regions in which the electron may move, characterized by quantum numbers 'n', 'I', and 'm'.

Properties of [Standard] elementary particles are also described by quantum numbers. For example, an electron has the property known a 'spin', and can exist in two possible energy states depending on whether this spin set parallel or antiparallel to a certain direction. The two states are conveniently characterized by quantum numbers + ½ and – ½. Similarly properties such as charge, isospin, strangeness, parity and hyper-charge are characterized by quantum numbers. In interactions between particles, a particular quantum number may be conserved, i.e., the sum of the quantum numbers of the particles before and after the interaction remains the same. It is the type of interaction - strong, electromagnetic, weak that determines whether the quantum number is conserved.

The energy associated with a quantum state of an atom or other system that is fixed, or determined, by given set quantum numbers. It is one of the various quantum states that can be assumed by an atom under defined conditions. The term is often used to mean the state itself, which is incorrect accorded to: (i) the energy of a given state may be changed by externally applied fields (ii) there may be a number of states of equal energy in the system.

The electrons in an atom can occupy any of an infinite number of bound states with discrete energies. For an isolated atom the energy for a given state is exactly determinate except for the effected of the 'uncertainty principle'. The ground state with lowest energy has an infinite lifetime hence, the energy, in principle is exactly determinate, the energies of these states are most accurately measured by finding the wavelength of the radiation emitted or absorbed in transitions between them, i.e., from their line spectra. Theories of the atom have been developed to predict these energies by calculation. Due to de Broglie and extended by Schrödinger, Dirac and many others, it (wave mechanics) originated in the suggestion that light consists of corpuscles as well as of waves and the consequent suggestion that all [standard] elementary particles are associated with waves. Wave mechanics are based on the Schrödinger wave equation describing the wave properties of matter. It relates the energy of a system to wave function, in general, it is found that a system, such as an atom or molecule can only have certain allowed wave functions (eigenfunction) and certain allowed energies (Eigenvalues), in wave mechanics the quantum conditions arise in a natural way from the basic postulates as solutions of the wave equation. The energies of unbound states of positive energy form a continuum. This gives rise to the continuum background to an atomic spectrum as electrons are captured from unbound states. The energy of an atom state can be changed or altered by using the 'Stark Effect' or the 'Zeeman Effect.'

The vibrational energies of the molecule also have discrete values, for example, in a diatomic molecule the atom oscillates in the line joining them. There is an equilibrium distance at which the force is zero. The atoms repulse when closer and attract when further apart. The restraining force is nearly prepositional to the displacement hence, the oscillations are simple harmonic. Solution of the Schrödinger wave equation gives the energies of a harmonic oscillation as:

$$En = (n + ½) hf.$$

Where 'h' is the Planck constant, f is the frequency, and 'n' is the vibrational quantum number, which can be zero or any positive integer. The lowest possible vibrational energy of an oscillator is not zero but ½ hf. This is the cause of zero-point energy. The potential energy of interaction of atoms is described more exactly by the 'Morse Equation,' which shows that the oscillations are slightly anharmonic. The vibrations of molecules are investigated by the study of 'band spectra'.

The rotational energy of a molecule is quantized also, according to the Schrödinger equation, a body with the moment of inertial I about the axis of rotation have energies given by:

$$EJ = h2J\ (J + 1)\ /\ 8\pi\ 2I$$

Where J is the rotational quantum number, which can be zero or a positive integer. Rotational energies originate from band spectra.

The energies of the state of the nucleus are determined from the gamma ray spectrum and from various nuclear reactions. Theory has been less successful in predicting these energies than those of electrons because the interactions of nucleons are very complicated. The energies are very little affected by external influence but the 'Mössbauer Effect' has permitted the observations of some minute changes.

In quantum theory, introduced by Max Planck 1858-1947 in 1900, was the first serious scientific departure from Newtonian mechanics. It involved supposing that certain physical quantities can only assume discrete values. In the following two decades it was applied successfully by Einstein and the Danish physicist Neils Bohr (1885-1962). It was superseded by quantum mechanics in the tears following 1924, when the French physicist Louis de Broglie (1892-1987) introduced the idea that a particle may also be regarded as a wave. The Schrödinger wave equation relates the energy of a system to a wave function, the energy of a system to a wave function, the square of the amplitude of the wave is proportional to the probability of a particle being found in a specific position. The wave function expresses the lack of possibly of defining both the position and momentum of a particle, this expression of discrete representation is called as the 'uncertainty principle,' the allowed wave functions that have described stationary states of a system

Part of the difficulty with the notions involved is that a system may be in an indeterminate state at a time, characterized only by the probability of some result for an observation, but then 'become' determinate (the collapse of the wave packet) when an observation is made such as the position and momentum of a particle if that is to apply to reality itself, than to mere indetermincies of measurement. It is as if there is nothing but a potential for observation or a probability wave before observation is made, but when an observation is made the wave becomes a particle. The ave-particle duality seems to block any way of conceiving of physical reality-in quantum terms. In the famous two-slit experiment, an electron is fired at a screen with two slits, like a tennis ball thrown at a wall with two doors in it. If one puts detectors at each slit, every electron passing the screen is observed to go through exactly one slit. But when the detectors are taken away, the electron acts like a wave process going through both slits and interfering with itself. A particle such an electron is usually thought of as always having an exact position, but its wave is not absolutely zero anywhere, there is therefore a finite probability of it 'tunnelling through' from one position to emerge at another.

The unquestionable success of quantum mechanics has generated a large philosophical debate about its ultimate intelligibility and it's metaphysical implications. The wave-particle duality is already a departure from ordinary ways of conceiving of tings in space, and its difficulty is compounded by the probabilistic nature of the fundamental states of a system as they are conceived in quantum mechanics. Philosophical options for interpreting quantum mechanics have included variations of the belief that it is at best an incomplete description of a better-behaved classical underlying reality (Einstein), the Copenhagen interpretation according to which there are no objective unobserved events in the micro-world: Bohr and W. K. Heisenberg, 1901-76, an 'accusal' view of the collapse of the wave packet, J. von Neumann, 1903-57, and a 'many worlds' interpretation in which time forks perpetually toward innumerable futures, so that different states of the same system exist in different parallel universes (H. Everett).

In recent tars the proliferation of subatomic particles, such as there are 36 kinds of quarks alone, in six flavours to look in various directions for unification. One avenue of approach is superstring theory, in which the four-dimensional world is thought of as the upshot of the collapse of a ten-dimensional world, with the four primary physical forces, one of gravity another is electromagnetism and the strong and weak nuclear forces, becoming seen as the result of the fracture of one primary force. While the scientific acceptability of such theories is a matter for physics, their ultimate intelligibility plainly requires some philosophical reflection.

A theory of gravitation that is consistent with quantum mechanics whose subject, still in its infancy, has no completely satisfactory theory. In controventional quantum gravity, the gravitational force is mediated by a massless spin-2 particle, called the 'graviton'. The internal degrees of freedom of the graviton require hij (χ) represent the deviations from the metric tensor for a flat space. This formulation of general relativity reduces it to a quantum field theory, which has a regrettable tendency to produce infinite for measurable qualitites. However, unlike other quantum field theories, quantum gravity cannot appeal to re-normalization procedures to make sense of these infinites. It has been shown that re-normalization procedures fail for theories, such as quantum gravity, in which the coupling constants have the dimensions of a positive power of length. The coupling constant g= for general relativity is the Planck length,

$$Lp = (Gh / c^3)^{1/2} \equiv 10^{-35} \text{ m}.$$

Super-symmetry has been suggested as a structure that could be free from these pathological infinities. Many theorists believe that an effective superstring field theory may emerge, in which the Einstein field equations are no longer valid and general relativity is required to appar only as low energy limit. The resulting theory may be structurally different from anything that has been considered so far. Super-symmetric string theory (or superstring) is an extension of the ideas of Super-symmetry to one-dimensional string-like entities that can interact with each other and scatter according to a precise set of laws. The normal modes of super-strings represent an infinite set of 'normal' elementary particles whose masses and spins are related in a special way. Thus the graviton, is only one of the strings mode-when the string-scattering processes are analysed in terms of their particle content, the low-energy graviton scattering is found to be the same as that computed from Super-symmetric gravity. The graviton mode may still be related to the geometry of the space0time in which the string vibrates, but it remains to be seen whether the other, massive, members of the set of 'normal' particles also have a geometrical interpretation. The intricacy of this theory stems from the requirement of a space-time of at least ten dimensions to ensure internal consistency. It has been suggested that there are the normal four dimensions, with the extra dimensions being tightly 'curled up' in a small circle presumably of Planck length size.

In the quantum theory or quantum mechanics of an atom or other system fixed, or determined by a given set of quantum numbers. It is one of the various quantum states that an atom can be assumed. The conceptual representation of an atom was first introduced by the ancient Greeks, as a tiny indivisible component of matter, developed by Dalton, as the smallest part of an element that can take part in a chemical reaction, and made very much more precisely by theory and excrement in the late-19th and 20th centuries.

Following the discovery of the electron (1897), it was recognized that atoms had structure, since electrons are negatively charged, a neutral atom must have a positive component. The experiments of Geiger and Marsden on the scattering of alpha particles by thin metal foils led Rutherford to propose a model (1912) in which nearly, but all the mass of an atom is concentrated at its centre in a region of positive charge, the nucleus, the radius of the order 10 -15 metre. The electrons occupy the surrounding space to a radius of 10-11 to 10-10 m. Rutherford also proposed that the nucleus have a charge of 'Ze' and is surrounded by 'Z' electrons (Z is the atomic number). According to classical physics such a system must emit electromagnetic radiation continuously and consequently no permanent atom would be possible. This problem was solved by the development of the quantum theory.

The 'Bohr Theory of the Atom,' 1913, introduced the concept that an electron in an atom is normally in a state of lower energy, or ground state, in which it remains indefinitely unless disturbed. By absorption of electromagnetic radiation or collision with another particle the atom may be excited - that is an electron is moved into a state of higher energy. Such excited states usually have short lifetimes, typically nanoseconds and the electron returns to the ground state, commonly by emitting one or more quanta of electromagnetic radiation. The original theory was only partially successful in predicting the energies and other properties of the electronic states. Attempts were made to improve the theory by postulating elliptic orbits (Sommerfeld 1915) and electron spin (Pauli 1925) but a satisfactory theory only became possible upon the development of 'Wave Mechanics,' after 1925.

, According to modern theories, the electron does not follow a determinate orbit as envisaged by Bohr, but is in a state described by the solution of a wave equation. This determines the probability that the electron may be located in a given element of volume. Each state is characterized by a set of four quantum numbers, and, according to the Pauli exclusion principle, not more than one electron can be in a given state.

The Pauli exclusion principle states that no two identical 'fermions' in any system can be in the same quantum state that is have the same set of quantum numbers. The principle was first proposed (1925) in the form that not more than two electrons in an atom could have the same set of quantum numbers. This hypothesis accounted for the main features of the structure of the atom and for the periodic table. An electron in an atom is characterized by four quantum numbers, n, I, m, and s. A particular atomic orbital, which has fixed values of n, I, and m, can thus contain a maximum of two electrons, since the spin quantum number 's' can only be + | or – |. In 1928 Sommerfeld applied the principle to the free electrons in solids and his theory has been greatly developed by later associates.

Additionally, an effect occurring when atoms emit or absorb radiation in the presence of a moderately strong magnetic field. Each spectral; Line is split into closely spaced polarized components, when the source is viewed at right angles to the field there are three components, the middle one having the same frequency as the unmodified line, and when the source is viewed parallel to the field there are two components, the undisplaced line being preoccupied. This is the 'normal' Zeeman Effect. With most spectral lines, however, the anomalous Zeeman effect occurs, where there are a greater number of symmetrically arranged polarized components. In both effects the displacement of the components is a measure of the magnetic field strength. In some cases the components cannot be resolved and the spectral line appears broadened.

The Zeeman effect occurs because the energies of individual electron states depend on their inclination to the direction of the magnetic field, and because quantum energy requirements impose conditions such that the plane of an electron orbit can only set itself at certain definite angles to the applied field. These angles are such that the projection of the total angular momentum on the field direction in an integral multiple of $h/2\pi$ (h is the Planck constant) The Zeeman effect is observed with moderately strong fields where the precession of the orbital angular momentum and the spin angular momentum of the electrons about each other is much faster than the total precession around the field direction. The normal Zeeman effect is observed when the conditions are such that the Landé factor is unity, otherwise the anomalous effect is found. This anomaly was one of the factors contributing to the discovery of electron spin.

Statistics that are concerned with the equilibrium distribution of elementary particles of a particular type among the various quantized energy states. It is assumed that these elementary particles are indistinguishable. The 'Pauli Exclusion Principle' is obeyed so that no two identical 'fermions' can be in the same quantum mechanical state. The exchange of two identical fermions, i.e., two electrons, does not affect the probability of distribution but it does involve a change in the sign of the wave function. The 'Fermi-Dirac Distribution Law' gives $\oint$E the average number of identical fermions in a state of energy E:

$$\oint_{E} = 1/[e\alpha + E/kT + 1],$$

Where 'k' is the Boltzmann constant, 'T' is the thermodynamic temperature and α is a quantity depending on temperature and the concentration of particles. For the valences electrons in a solid, 'α' takes the form -E1/kT, where E1 is the Fermi level. Whereby, the Fermi level (or Fermi energy) E F the value of $\oint$E is exactly one half. Thus, for a system in equilibrium one half of the states with energy very nearly equal to 'E' (if any) will be occupied. The value of EF varies very slowly with temperatures, tending to E0 as 'T' tends to absolute zero.

In Bose-Einstein statistics, the Pauli exclusion principle is not obeyed so that any number of identical 'bosons' can be in the same state. The exchanger of two bosons of the same type affects neither the probability of distribution nor the sign of the wave function. The 'Bose-Einstein Distribution Law' gives $\oint$E the average number of identical bosons in a state of energy E:

$$\oint_{E} = 1/[e\alpha + E/kT\text{-}1].$$

The formula can be applied to photons, considered as quasi-particles, provided that the quantity α, which conserves the number of particles, is zero. Planck's formula for the energy distribution of 'Black-Body Radiation' was derived from this law by Bose. At high temperatures and low concentrations both the quantum distribution laws tend to the classical distribution:

$$\oint_{E} = Ae\text{-}E/kT.$$

Additionally, the property of substances that have a positive magnetic 'susceptibility', whereby its quantity $\mu r - 1$, and where μr is 'Relative Permeability,' again, that the electric-quantity presented as $\epsilon r - 1$, where ϵr is the 'Relative Permittivity,' all of which has positivity. All of which are caused by the 'spins' of electrons, paramagnetic substances having molecules or atoms, in which there are paired electrons and thus, resulting of a

'Magnetic Moment.' There is also a contribution of the magnetic properties from the orbital motion of the electron, as the relative 'permeability' of a paramagnetic substance is thus greater than that of a vacuum, i.e., it is slightly greater than unity.

A 'paramagnetic substance' is regarded as an assembly of magnetic dipoles that have random orientation. In the presence of a field the magnetization is determined by competition between the effect of the field, in tending to align the magnetic dipoles, and the random thermal agitation. In small fields and high temperatures, the magnetization produced is proportional to the field strength, wherefore at low temperatures or high field strengths, a state of saturation is approached. As the temperature rises, the susceptibility falls according to Curie's Law or the Curie-Weiss Law.

Furthering by Curie's Law, the susceptibility (χ) of a paramagnetic substance is unversedly proportional to the 'thermodynamic temperature' (T) $\chi = C/T$. The constant 'C is called the 'Curie constant' and is characteristic of the material. This law is explained by assuming that each molecule has an independent magnetic 'dipole' moment and the tendency of the applied field to align these molecules is opposed by the random moment due to the temperature. A modification of Curie's Law, followed by many paramagnetic substances, where the Curie-Weiss law modifies its applicability in the form

$$\chi = C/(T - \theta).$$

The law shows that the susceptibility is proportional to the excess of temperature over a fixed temperature θ: 'θ' is known as the Weiss constant and is a temperature characteristic of the material, such as sodium and potassium, also exhibit type of paramagnetic resulting from the magnetic moments of free, or nearly free electrons, in their conduction bands? This is characterized by a very small positive susceptibility and a very slight temperature dependence, and is known as 'free-electron paramagnetism' or 'Pauli paramagnetism'.

A property of certain solid substances that having a large positive magnetic susceptibility having capabilities of being magnetized by weak magnetic fields. The chief elements are iron, cobalt, and nickel and many ferromagnetic alloys based on these metals also exist. Justifiably, ferromagnetic materials exhibit magnetic 'hysteresis', of which formidable combination of decaying within the change of an observed effect in response to a change in the mechanism producing the effect.

(Magnetic) a phenomenon shown by ferromagnetic substances, whereby the magnetic flux through the medium depends not only on the existing magnetizing field, but also on the previous state or states of the substances, the existence of a phenomenon necessitates a dissipation of energy when the substance is subjected to a cycle of magnetic changes, this is known as the magnetic hysteresis loss. The magnetic hysteresis loops were acceding by a curved obtainability from ways of which, in themselves were of plotting the magnetic flux density 'B', of a ferromagnetic material against the responding value of the magnetizing field 'H', the area to the 'hysteresis loss' per unit volume in taking the specimen through the prescribed magnetizing cycle. The general forms of the hysteresis loop fore a symmetrical cycle between 'H' and '~ H' and 'H ~ h, having inclinations that rise to hysteresis.

The magnetic hysteresis loss commands the dissipation of energy as due to magnetic hysteresis, when the magnetic material is subjected to changes, particularly, the cycle changes of magnetization, as having the larger positive magnetic susceptibility, and are capable of being magnetized by weak magnetic fields. Ferro magnetics are able to retain a certain domain of magnetization when the magnetizing field is removed. Those materials that retain a high percentage of their magnetization are said to be hard, and those that lose most of their magnetization are said to be soft, typical examples of hard ferromagnetic are cobalt steel and various alloys of nickel, aluminium and cobalt. Typical soft magnetic materials are silicon steel and soft iron, the coercive force as acknowledged to the reversed magnetic field' that is required to reduce the magnetic 'flux density' in a substance from its remnant value to zero in characteristic of ferromagnetisms and explains by its presence of domains. A ferromagnetic domain is a region of crystalline matter, whose volume may be 10-12 to 10-8 m3, which contains atoms whose magnetic moments are aligned in the same direction. The domain is thus magnetically saturated and behaves like a magnet with its own magnetic axis and moment. The magnetic moment of the ferrometic atom results from the spin of the electron in an unfilled inner shell of the atom. The formation of a domain depends upon the strong interactions forces (Exchange forces) that are effective in a crystal lattice containing ferrometic atoms.

In an unmagnetized volume of a specimen, the domains are arranged in a random fashion with their magnetic axes pointing in all directions so that the specimen has no resultant magnetic moment. Under the influence of a weak magnetic field, those domains whose magnetic saxes have directions near to that of the field flux at the expense of their neighbours. In this process the atoms of neighbouring domains tend to align in the direction of the field but the strong influence of the growing domain causes their axes to align parallel to its magnetic axis. The growth of these domains leads to a resultant magnetic moment and hence, magnetization of the specimen in the direction of the field, with increasing field strength, the growth of domains proceeds until there is, effectively, only one domain whose magnetic axis appropriates to the field direction. The specimen now exhibits tron magnetization. Further, increasing in field strength cause the final alignment and magnetic saturation in the field direction. This explains the characteristic variation of magnetization with applied strength. The presence of domains in ferromagnetic materials can be demonstrated by use of 'Bitter Patterns' or by 'Barkhausen Effect.'

For ferromagnetic solids there are a change from ferromagnetic to paramagnetic behaviour above a particular temperature and the paramagnetic material then obeyed the Curie-Weiss Law above this temperature, this is the 'Curie temperature' for the material. Below this temperature the law is not obeyed. Some paramagnetic substances, obey the temperature 'θ C' and do not obey it below, but are not ferromagnetic below this temperature. The value 'θ' in the Curie-Weiss law can be thought of as a correction to Curie's law reelecting the extent to which the magnetic dipoles interact with each other. In materials exhibiting 'antiferromagnetism' of which the temperature 'θ' corresponds to the 'Néel temperature'.

Without discredited inquisitions, the property of certain materials that have a low positive magnetic susceptibility, as in paramagnetism, and exhibit a temperature dependence similar to that encountered in ferromagnetism. The susceptibility increased with temperatures up to a certain point, called the 'Néel Temperature,' and then falls with increasing temperatures in accordance with the Curie-Weiss law. The material thus becomes paramagnetic above the Néel temperature, which is analogous to the Curie temperature in the transition from ferromagnetism to paramagnetism. Antiferromagnetism is a property of certain inorganic compounds such as MnO, FeO, FeF2 and MnS. It results from interactions between neighbouring atoms leading and an antiparallel arrangement of adjacent magnetic dipole moments, least of mention. A system of two equal and opposite charges placed at a very short distance apart. The product of either of the charges and the distance between them is known as the 'electric dipole moments. A small loop carrying a current I behave as a magnetic dipole and is equal to IA, where A being the area of the loop.

The energy associated with a quantum state of an atom or other system that is fixed, or determined by a given set of quantum numbers. It is one of the various quantum states that can be assumed by an atom under defined conditions. The term is often used to mean the state itself, which is incorrect by ways of: (1) the energy of a given state may be changed by externally applied fields, and (2) there may be a number of states of equal energy in the system.

The electrons in an atom can occupy any of an infinite number of bound states with discrete energies. For an isolated atom the energy for a given state is exactly determinate except for the effects of the 'uncertainty principle'. The ground state with lowest energy has an infinite lifetime, hence the energy is if, in at all as a principle that is exactly determinate.

The energies of these states are most accurately measured by finding the wavelength of the radiation emitted or absorbed in transitions between them, i.e., from their line spectra. Theories of the atom have been developed to predict these energies by calculating such a system that emit electromagnetic radiation continuously and consequently no permanent atom would be possible, hence this problem was solved by the developments of quantum theory. An exact calculation of the energies and other particles of the quantum states is only possible for the simplest atom but there are various approximate methods that give useful results as an approximate method of solving a difficult problem, if the equations to be solved, and depart only slightly from those of some problems already solved. For example, the orbit of a single planet round the sun is an ellipse, that the perturbing effect of other planets modifies the orbit slightly in a way calculable by this method. The technique finds considerable application in 'wave mechanics' and 'quantum electrodynamics'. Phenomena that are not amendable to solution by perturbation theory are said to be non-perturbative.

The energies of unbound states of positive total energy form a continuum. This gives rise to the continuos background to an atomic spectrum, as electrons are captured from unbound state, the energy of an atomic state can be changed by the 'Stark Effect' or the 'Zeeman Effect.'

The vibrational energies of molecules also have discrete values, for example, in a diatomic molecule the atoms oscillate in the line joining them. There is an equilibrium distance at which the force is zero, and the atoms deflect when closer and attract when further apart. The restraining force is very nearly proportional to the displacement, hence the oscillations are simple harmonic. Solution of the 'Schrödinger wave equation' gives the energies of a harmonic oscillation as:

$$En = (n + \tfrac{1}{2})\, h\boldsymbol{f}$$

Where 'h' is the Planck constant, $\boldsymbol{f}$ is the frequency, and 'n' is the vibrational quantum number, which can be zero or any positive integer. The lowest possible vibrational energy of an oscillator is thus not zero but $\tfrac{1}{2}h\boldsymbol{f}$. This is the cause of zero-point energy. The potential energy of interaction of atoms is described more exactly by the Morse equation, which shows that the oscillations are slightly anharmonic. The vibrations of molecules are investigated by the study of 'band spectra'.

The rotational energy of a molecule is quantized also, according to the Schrödinger equation a body with moments of inertia I about the axis of rotation have energies given by:

$$Ej = h2J(J + 1)/8\pi 2\ I$$

Where 'J' is the rotational quantum number, which can be zero or a positive integer. Rotational energies are found from 'band spectra'.

The energies of the states of the 'nucleus' can be determined from the gamma ray spectrum and from various nuclear reactions. Theory has been less successful in predicting these energies than those of electrons in atoms because the interactions of nucleons are very complicated. The energies are very little affected by external influences, but the 'Mössbauer Effect' has permitted the observation of some minute changes.

When X-rays are scattered by atomic centres arranged at regular intervals, interference phenomena occur, crystals providing grating of a suitable small interval. The interference effects may be used to provide a spectrum of the beam of X-rays, since, according to 'Bragg's Law,' the angle of reflection of X-rays from a crystal depends on the wavelength of the rays. For lower-energy X-rays mechanically ruled grating can be used. Each chemical element emits characteristic X-rays in sharply defined groups in more widely separated regions. They are known as the K, L's, M, N. etc., promote lines of any series toward shorter wavelengths as the atomic number of the elements concerned increases. If a parallel beam of X-rays, wavelength λ, strikes a set of crystal planes it is reflected from the different planes, interferences occurring between X-rays reflect from adjacent planes. Bragg's Law states that constructive interference takes place when the difference in path-lengths, BAC, is equal to an integral number of wavelengths

$$2d \sin \theta = n\lambda$$

Where 'n' is an integer, 'd' is the interplanar distance, and 'θ' is the angle between the incident X-ray and the crystal plane. This angle is called the 'Bragg's Angle,' and a bright spot will be obtained on an interference pattern at this angle. A dark spot will be obtained, however. If be, $2d \sin \theta = m\lambda$. Where 'm' is half-integral. The structure of a crystal can be determined from a set of interference patterns found at various angles from the different crystal faces.

A concept originally introduced by the ancient Greeks, as a tiny indivisible component of matter, developed by Dalton, as the smallest part of an element that can take part in a chemical reaction, and made experiment in the late-19th and early 20th century. Following the discovery of the electron (1897), they recognized that atoms had structure, since electrons are negatively charged, a neutral atom must have a positive component. The experiments of Geiger and Marsden on the scattering of alpha particles by thin metal foils led Rutherford to propose a model (1912) in which nearly all mass of the atom is concentrated at its centre in a region of positive charge, the nucleus is a region of positive charge, the nucleus, radiuses of the order 10-15 metre. The electrons occupy the surrounding space to a radius of 10-11 to 10-10 m. Rutherford also proposed that the nucleus have a charge of Ze is surrounded by 'Z' electrons (Z is the atomic number). According to classical physics such a system must emit electromagnetic radiation continuously and consequently no permanent atom would be possible. This problem was solved by the developments of the 'Quantum Theory.'

The 'Bohr Theory of the Atom' (1913) introduced the notion that an electron in an atom is normally in a state of lowest energy (ground state) in which it remains indefinitely unless disturbed by absorption of electromagnetic radiation or collision with other particle the atom may be excited - that is, electrons moved into a state of higher energy. Such excited states usually have short life spans (typically nanoseconds) and the electron returns to the ground state, commonly by emitting one or more 'quanta' of electromagnetic radiation. The original theory was only partially successful in predicting the energies and other properties of the electronic states. Postulating elliptic orbits made attempts to improve the theory (Sommerfeld 1915) and electron spin (Pauli 1925) but a satisfactory theory only became possible upon the development of 'Wave Mechanics' 1925.

According to modern theories, an electron does not follow a determinate orbit as envisaged by Bohr, but is in a state described by the solution of the wave equation. This determines the 'probability' that the electron may be found in a given element of volume. A set of four quantum numbers has characterized each state, and according to the 'Pauli Exclusion Principle,' not more than one electron can be in a given state.

An exact calculation of the energies and other properties of the quantum states is possible for the simplest atoms, but various approximate methods give useful results, i.e., as an approximate method of solving a difficult problem if the equations to be solved and depart only slightly from those of some problems already solved. The properties of the innermost electron states of complex atoms are found experimentally by the study of X-ray spectra. The outer electrons are investigated using spectra in the infrared, visible, and ultraviolet. Certain details have been studied using microwaves. As administered by a small difference in energy between the energy levels of the 2 P½ states of hydrogen. In accord with Lamb Shift, these levels would have the same energy according to the wave mechanics of Dirac. The actual shift can be explained by a correction to the energies based on the theory of the interaction of electromagnetic fields with matter, in of which the fields themselves are quantized. Yet, other information may be obtained form magnetism and other chemical properties.

Its appearance potential concludes as, (1)the potential differences through which an electron must be accelerated from rest to produce a given ion from its parent atom or molecule. (2) This potential difference multiplied bu the electron charge giving the least energy required to produce the ion. A simple ionizing process gives the 'ionization potential' of the substance, for example: Ar + e → Ar + + 2e. - Higher appearance potentials may be found for multiplying charged ions: Ar + e → Ar + + + 3r. - The number of protons in a nucleus of an atom or the number of electrons resolving around the nucleus is among some concerns of atomic numbers. The atomic number determines the chemical properties of an element and the element's position in the periodic table, because of which the clarification of chemical elements, in tabular form, in the order of their atomic number. The elements show a periodicity of properties, chemically similar recurring in a definite order. The sequence of elements is thus broken into horizontal 'periods' and vertical 'groups' the elements in each group showing close chemical analogies, i.e., in valency, chemical properties, etc. all the isotopes of an element have the same atomic number although different isotopes gave mass numbers.

An allowed 'wave function' of an electron in an atom obtained by a solution of the Schrödinger wave equation. In a hydrogen atom, for example, the electron moves in the electrostatic field of the nucleus and its potential energy is –e2, where 'e' is the electron charge. 'r' its distance from the nucleus, as a precise orbit cannot be considered as in Bohr's theory of the atom, but the behaviour of the electron is described by its wave function, Ψ, which is a mathematical function of its position with respect to the nucleus. The significance of the wave function is that | Ψ | 2dt, is the probability of finding the electron in the element of volume 'dt'.

Solution of Schrödinger's equation for hydrogen atom shows that the electron can only have certain allowed wave functions (eigenfunction). Each of these corresponds to a probability distribution in space given by the manner in which | Ψ | 2 varies with position. They also have an associated value of energy 'E'. These allowed wave functions, or orbitals, are characterized by three quantum numbers similar to those characterizing the allowed orbits in the quantum theory of the atom: 'n', the 'principle quantum number', can have values of 1, 2, 3, and so on, the orbital with n=1 has the lowest energy. The states of the electron with n=o1, 2, 3, and so on, are called 'shells' and designated the K, L, M shells, and so on.

'I' the 'azimuthal quanta number' which for a given value of 'n' can have values of 0, 1, 2, . . . (n –1). Similarly, the 'M' shell (n = 3) has three sub-shells with I = 0, I = 1, and I = 2. Orbitals with I = 0, 1, 2, and 3 are called s, p, d, and *f* orbitals respectively. The significance of the I quantum number is that it gives the angular momentum of the electron. The orbital annular momentum of an electron is given by:

$$\sqrt{[1(I + 1)(h2\pi)]}. \text{ 'm'}$$

The 'magnetic quanta number', which for a given value of 'I' can have values of; –I, –(I – 1) . . ., 0 . . . (I– 1). Thus for 'p' orbital for which I = 1, there is in fact three dissimilar orbitals with m = – 1, 0, and 1. These orbitals with the same values of 'n' and 'I ' but different 'm' values, have the same energy. The significance of this quantum number is that it shows the number of different levels that would be produced if the atom were subjected to an external magnetic field

According to wave theory the electron may be at any distance from the nucleus, but in fact there is only a reasonable chance of it being within a distance of – 5 x 1011 metre. Indeed the maximum probability occurs when r = a0 where a0 is the radius of the first Bohr orbit. It is customary to represent an orbit that there is no arbitrarily decided probability (say 95%) of finding them an electron. Notably taken, is that although 's' orbitals are spherical (I = 0), orbitals with I> 0, have an angular dependence. Finally. The electron in an atom can have a fourth quantum number, 'M' characterizing its spin direction. This can be + ½ or – ½ and according to the Pauli Exclusion principle, each orbital can hold only two electrons. The fourth quantum numbers lead to an explanation of the periodic table of the elements.

The least distance in a progressive wave between two surfaces with the same phase arises to a wavelength. If 'v' is the phase speed and 'v' the frequency, the wavelength is given by v = vλ. For electromagnetic radiation the phase speed and wavelength in a material medium are equal to their values in a free space divided by the 'refractive index'. The wavelengths of spectral lines are normally specified for free space.

Optical wavelengths are measure absolutely using interferometers or diffraction gratings, or comparatively using a prism spectrometer. The wavelength can only have an exact value for an infinite waver train if an atomic body emits a quantum in the form of a train of waves of duration τ the fractional uncertainty of the wavelength, Δλ/λ, is approximately λ/2cτ, where 'c' is the speed in free space. This is associated with the indeterminacy of the energy given by the uncertainty principle

Whereas, a mathematical quantity analogous to the amplitude of a wave that appears in the equation of wave mechanics, particularly the Schrödinger waves equation. The most generally accepted interpretation is that | Ψ | 2dV represents the probability that a particle is within the volume element dV. The wavelengths, as a set of waves that represent the behaviour, under appropriate conditions, of a particle, e.g., its diffraction by a particle. The wavelength is given by the 'de Broglie Equation.' They are sometimes regarded as waves of probability, times the square of their amplitude at a given point represents the probability of finding the particle in unit volume at that point. These waves were predicted by de Broglie in 1924 and observed in 1927 in the Davisson-Germer Experiment. Still, 'Ψ' is often a might complex quality.

The analogy between 'Ψ' and the amplitude of a wave is purely formal. There is no macroscopic physical quantity with which 'Ψ' can be identified, in contrast with, for example, the amplitude of an electromagnetic wave, which is expressed in terms of electric and magnetic field intensities

In general, there are an infinite number of functions satisfying a wave equation but only some of these will satisfy the boundary conditions. 'Ψ' must be finite and single-valued at every point, and the spatial derivative must be continuous at an interface? For a particle subject to a law of conservation of numbers, the integral of | Ψ | 2dV over all space must remain equal to 1, since this is the probability that it exists somewhere to satisfy this condition the wave equation must be of the first order in (dΨ/dt). Wave functions obtained when these conditions are applied from a set of characteristic functions of the Schrödinger wave equation. These are often called eigenfunctions and correspond to a set of fixed energy values in which the system may exist describe stationary states on the system.

For certain bound states of a system the eigenfunctions do not charge the sign or reversing the co-ordinated axes. These states are said to have even parity. For other states the sign changes on space reversal and the parity is said to be odd.

It's issuing case of eigenvalue problems in physics that take the form:

$$\Omega\Psi = \lambda\Psi,$$

Where Ω is come mathematical operation (multiplication by a number, differentiation, and so on.) on a function Ψ, which is called the 'eigenfunction'. λ is called the 'eigenvalue', which in a physical system will be identified with an observable quantity, as, too, an atom to other systems that are fixed, or determined, by a given set of quantum numbers? It is one of the various quantum states that can be assumed by an atom

Eigenvalue problems are ubiquitous in classical physics and occur whenever the mathematical description of a physical system yields a series of coupled differential equations. For example, the collective motion of a large number of interacting oscillators may be described by a set of coupled differential equations. Each differential equation describes the motion of one of the oscillators in terms of the positions of all the others. A 'harmonic' solution may be sought, in which each displacement is assumed as a simple harmonic motion in time. The differential equations then reduce to '3N' linear equations with 3N unknowns. Where 'N' is the number of individual oscillators, each problem is from each one of three degrees of freedom. The whole problem I now easily recast as a 'matrix' equation of the form:

$$M\chi = \omega 2\chi.$$

Where 'M' is an N x N matrix called the 'a dynamic matrix, χ is an N x 1 column matrix, and ω2 of the harmonic solution. The problem is now an eigenvalue problem with eigenfunctions' χ, where are the normal modes of the system, with corresponding eigenvalues ω2. As χ can be expressed as a column vector, χ is a vector in some – dimensional vector space. For this reason, χ is also often called an eigenvector.

When the collection of oscillators is a complicated three-dimensional molecule, the casting of the problem into normal modes s and effective simplification of the system. The symmetry principles of group theory, the symmetry operations in any physical system must be posses the properties of the mathematical group. As the group of rotation, both finite and infinite, are important in the analysis of the symmetry of atoms and molecules, which underlie the quantum theory of angular momentum. Eigenvalue problems arise in the quantum mechanics of atomic arising in the quantum mechanics of atomic or molecular systems yield stationary states corresponding to the normal mode oscillations of either electrons in-an atom or atoms within a molecule. Angular momentum quantum numbers correspond to a labelling system used to classify these normal modes, analysing the transitions between them can lead and theoretically predict of atomic or a molecular spectrum. Whereas, the symmetrical principle of group theory can then be applied, from which allow their classification accordingly. In which, this kind of analysis requires an appreciation of the symmetry properties of the molecules (rotations, inversions, etc.) that leave the molecule invariant make up the point group of that molecule. Normal modes sharing the same ω eigenvalues are said to correspond to the irreducible representations of these molecules' point group. It is among these irreducible representations that one will find the infrared absorption spectrum for the vibrational normal modes of the molecule.

Eigenvalue problems play a particularly important role in quantum mechanics. In quantum mechanics, physically observable as location momentum energy etc., are represented by operations (differentiations with respect to a variable, multiplication by a variable), which act on wave functions. Wave functioning differs from classical waves in that they carry no energy. For classical waves, the square modulus of its amplitude measures its energy. For a wave function, the square modulus of its amplitude, at a location χ represents not energy bu probability, i.e., the probability that a particle -a localized packet of energy will be observed in a detector is placed at that location. The wave function therefore describes the distribution of possible locations of the particle and is perceptible only after many location detectors events have occurred. A measurement of position of a quantum particle may be written symbolically as:

$$X\,\Psi(\chi) = \chi\Psi(\chi),$$

Where $\Psi(\chi)$ is said to be an eigenvector of the location operator and 'χ' is the eigenvalue, which represents the location. Each $\Psi(\chi)$ represents amplitude at the location 'χ'$|\Psi(\chi)$ $|2$ is the probability that the particle will be found in an infinitesimal volume at that location. The wave function describing the distribution of all possible locations for the particle is the linear superposition of all $\Psi(\chi)$ for zero $\leq\chi\geq\infty$. These principles that hold generally in physics wherever linear phenomena occur. In elasticity, the principle stares that the same strains whether it acts alone accompany each stress or in conjunction with others, it is true so long as the total stress does not exceed the limit of proportionality. In vibrations and wave motion the principle asserts that one set is unaffected by the presence of another set. For example, two sets of ripples on water will pass through one anther without mutual interaction so that, at a particular instant, the resultant distribution at any point traverse by both sets of waves is the sum of the two component disturbances.'

The superposition of two vibrations, y1 and y2, both of frequency f, produces a resultant vibration of the same frequency, its amplitude and phase functions of the component amplitudes and phases, that:

$$y1. = a1\ \sin(2\pi f t + \delta 1)$$

$$y2. = a2\ \sin(\sin(2\pi f t + \delta 2)$$

Then the resultant vibration, y, is given by:

$$y1. + y2. = A\ \sin(2\pi f t + \Delta),$$

Where amplitude A and phase Δ is both functions of a1, a2, δ1, and δ2.

However, the eigenvalue problems in quantum mechanics therefore represent observable representations as made by possible states (position, in the case of χ) that the quantum system can have to stationary states, of which states that the product of the uncertainty of the resulting value of a component of momentum ($p\chi$) and the uncertainties in the corresponding co-ordinate position (χ) is of the same order of magnitude as the Planck Constant. It produces an accurate measurement of position is possible, as a resultant of the uncertainty principle. Subsequently, measurements of the position acquire a spread themselves, which makes the continuos monitoring of the position impossibly.

As in, classical mechanics may take differential or matrix forms. Both forms have been shown to be equivalent. The differential form of quantum mechanics is called wave mechanics (Schrödinger), where the operators are differential operators or multiplications by variables. Eigenfunctions in wave mechanics are wave functions corresponding to stationary wave states that responding to stationary conditions. The matrix forms of quantum mechanics are often matrix mechanics: Born and Heisenberg. Matrices acting of eigenvectors represent the operators.

The relationship between matrix and wave mechanics is similar to the relationship between matrix and differential forms of eigenvalue problems in classical mechanics. The wave functions representing stationary states are really normal modes of the quantum wave. These normal modes may be thought of as vectors that span on a vector space, which have a matrix representation.

Pauli, in 1925, suggested that each electron could exist in two states with the same orbital motion. Uhlenbeck and Goudsmit interpreted these states as due to the spin of the electron about an axis. The electron is assumed to have an intrinsic angular momentum on addition, to any angular momentum due to its orbital motion. This intrinsic angular momentum is called 'spin' It is quantized in values of $\sqrt{s}(s + 1)h/2\pi$ - Where 's' is the 'spin quantum number' and 'h' the Planck constant. For an electron the component of spin in a given direction can have values of + ½ and – ½, leading to the two possible states. An electron with spin that is behaviourally likens too small magnetic moments, in which came alongside an intrinsic magnetic moment. A 'magneton gives of a fundamental constant, whereby the intrinsic magnetic moment of an electron acquires the circulatory current created by the angular momentum 'p' of an electron moving in its orbital produces a magnetic moment $\mu = ep/2m$, where 'e and 'm' are the charge and mass of the electron, by substituting the quantized relation $p = jh/2\pi(h)$ = the Planck constant: j = magnetic quantum number), μ-$jh/4\pi m$. When j is taken as unity the quantity $eh/4\pi m$ is called the Bohr magneton, its value is:

9.274 0780 x 10-24 Am2

According to the wave mechanics of Dirac, the magnetic moment associated with the spin of the electron would be exactly one Bohr magnetron, although quantum electrodynamics show that a small difference can v=be expected.

The nuclear magnetron, 'μN' is equal to (me/mp)μB. Where mp is the mass of the proton. The value of μN is:

5.050 8240 x 10-27 A m2.

The magnetic moment of a proton is, in fact, 2.792 85 nuclear magnetos. The two states of different energy result from interactions between the magnetic field due to the electron's spin and that caused by its orbital motion. These are two closely spaced states resulting from the two possible spin directions and these lead to the two limes in the doublet.

In an external magnetic field the angular momentum vector of the electron precesses. For an explicative example, if a body is of a spin, it holds about its axis of symmetry OC (where O is a fixed point) and C is rotating round an axis OZ fixed outside the body, the body is said to be precessing round OZ. OZ is the precession axis. A gyroscope precesses due to an applied torque called the precessional torque. If the moment of inertia a body about OC is I and its angular momentum velocity is ω, a torque 'K', whose axis is perpendicular to the axis of rotation will produce an angular velocity of precession Ω about an axis perpendicular to both ω and the torque axis where Ω = K/Iω. It is . . ., wholly orientated of the vector to the field direction are allowed, there is a quantization so that the component of the angular momentum along the direction I restricted of certain values of h/2π. The angular momentum vector has allowed directions such that the component is mS(h2π), where mS is the magnetic so in quantum number. For a given value of s, mS has the value's, (s-1), . . . –s. For example, when s = 1, mS is I, O, and – 1. The electron has a spin of ½ and thus mS is + ½ and – ½. Thus the components of its spin of angular momentum along the field direction are, ± ½(h/2π). These phenomena are called 'a space quantization'.

The resultant spin of a number of particles is the vector sum of the spins (s) of the individual particles and is given by symbol S. for example, in an atom two electrons with spin of ½ could combine to give a resultant spin of S = ½ + ½ = 1 or a resultant of S = ½ – ½ =1 or a resultant of S = ½ – ½ = 0.

Alternative symbols used for spin is J (for elementary particles or standard theory) and I (for a nucleus). Most elementary particles have a non-zero spin, which either be integral of half integral. The spin of a nucleus is the resultant of the spin of its constituent's nucleons.

For most generally accepted interpretations is that | ψ |2dV represents the probability that particle is located within the volume element dV, as well, 'Ψ' is often a complex quantity. The analogy between 'Ψ' and the amplitude of a wave is purely formal. There is no macroscopic physical quantity with which 'Ψ' can be identified, in contrast with, for example, the amplitude of an electromagnetic wave, which are expressed in terms of electric and magnetic field intensities. There are an infinite number of functions satisfying a wave equation, but only some of these will satisfy the boundary condition. 'Ψ' must be finite and single-valued at each point, and the spatial derivatives must be continuous at an interface? For a particle subject to a law of conservation of numbers; The integral of | Ψ |2dV over all space must remain equal to 1, since this is the probability that it exists somewhere. To satisfy this condition the wave equation must be of the first order in (dΨdt). Wave functions obtained when these conditions are applied form of set of 'characteristic functions' of the Schrödinger wave equation. These are often called 'eigenfunctions' and correspond to a set of fixed energy values in which the system may exist, called 'eigenvalues'. Energy eigenfunctions describe stationary states of a system. For example, bound states of a system the eigenfunctions do not change signs on reversing the co-ordinated axes. These states are said to have 'even parity'. For other states the sign changes on space reversal and the parity is said to be 'odd'.

The least distance in a progressive wave between two surfaces with the same phase. If 'v' is the 'phase speed' and 'v' the frequency, the wavelength is given by v = vλ. For 'electromagnetic radiation' the phase speed and wavelength in a material medium are equal to their values I free space divided by the 'refractive index'. The wavelengths are spectral lines are normally specified for free space. Optical wavelengths are measured absolutely using interferometers or diffraction grating, or comparatively using a prism spectrometer.

The wavelength can only have an exact value for an infinite wave train. If an atomic body emits a quantum in the form of a train of waves of duration 'τ' the fractional uncertainty of the wavelength, $\Delta\lambda/\lambda$, is approximately $\lambda/2\pi c\tau$, where 'c' is the speed of free space. This is associated with the indeterminacy of the energy given by the 'uncertainty principle'.

A moment of momentum about an axis, represented as Symbol: L, the product of the moment of inertia and angular velocity (Iω) angular momentum is a 'pseudo vector quality'. It is conserved in an isolated system, as the moment of inertia contains itself of a body about an axis. The sum of the products of the mass of each particle of a body and square of its perpendicular distance from the axis: This addition is replaced by an integration in the case of continuous body. For a rigid body moving about a fixed axis, the laws of motion have the same form as those of rectilinear motion, with moments of inertia replacing mass, angular velocity replacing linear momentum, etc. hence the 'energy' of a body rotating about a fixed axis with angular velocity ω is ½Iω2, which corresponds to ½mv2 for the kinetic energy of a body mass 'm' translated with velocity 'v'.

The linear momentum of a particle 'p' bears the product of the mass and the velocity of the particle. It is a 'vector' quality directed through the particle of a body or a system of particles is the vector sum of the linear momentums of the individual particles. If a body of mass 'M' is translated (the movement of a body or system in which a way that all points are moved in parallel directions through equal distances), with a velocity 'V', it has its mentum as 'MV', which is the momentum of a particle of mass 'M' at the centre of gravity of the body. The product of 'moment of inertia and angular velocity'. Angular momentum is a 'pseudo vector quality and is conserved in an isolated system, and equal to the linear velocity divided by the radial axes per sec.

If the moment of inertia of a body of mass 'M' about an axis through the centre of mass is I, the moment of inertia about a parallel axis distance 'h' from the first axis is I + Mh2. If the radius of gyration is 'k' about the first axis, it is √(k2 + h2) about the second. The moment of inertia of a uniform solid body about an axis of symmetry is given by the product of the mass and the sum of squares of the other semi-axes, divided by 3, 4, 5 according to whether the body is rectangular, elliptical or ellipsoidal.

The circle is a special case of the ellipse. The Routh's rule works for a circular or elliptical cylinder or elliptical discs it works for all three axes of symmetry. For example, for a circular disk of the radius 'an' and mass 'M', the moment of inertia about an axis through the centre of the disc and lying (a) perpendicular to the disc, (b) in the plane of the disc is

(a) ¼M(a2 + a2) = ½Ma2
(b) ¼Ma2.

A formula for calculating moments of inertia I:

I = mass x (a2 /3 + n) + b2 /(3 + n′),

Where n and n′ are the numbers of principal curvatures of the surface that terminates the semiaxes in question and 'a' and 'b's' are the lengths of the semiaxes. Thus, if the body is a rectangular parallelepiped, n = n′ = 0, and I =-mass x (a2 / 3 + b2 /3).

If the body is a cylinder then, for an axis through its centre, perpendicular to the cylinder axis, n = 0 and n′ = 1, it substantiates that if, = mass x (a2 / 3 + b2 /4). If 'I' is desired about the axis of the cylinder, then n= n′ = 1 and a = b = r (the cylinder radius) and; I =

mass x (r2 /2). An array of mathematical concepts, which is similar to a determinant but differ from it in not having a numerical value in the ordinary sense of the term is called a matrix. It obeys the same rules of multiplication, addition, etc. an array of 'mn' numbers set out in 'm' rows and 'n' columns are a matrix of the order of m x n. the separate numbers are usually called elements, such arrays of numbers, tarted as single entities and manipulated by the rules of matrix algebra, are of use whenever simultaneous equations are found, e.g., changing from one set of Cartesian axes to another set inclined the first: Quantum theory, electrical networks. Matrixes are very prominent in the mathematical expression of quantum mechanics.

A mathematical form of quantum mechanics that was developed by Born and Heisenberg and originally simultaneously with but independently of wave mechanics. It is equivalent to wave mechanics, but in it the wave function of wave mechanics is replaced by 'vectors' in a seemly space (Hilbert space) and observable things of the physical world, such as energy, momentum, co-ordinates, and so on, is represented by 'matrices'.

The theory involves the idea that a maturement on a system disturbs, to some extent, the system itself. With large systems this is of no consequence, and the system this is of no classical mechanics. On the atomic scale, however, the results of the order in which the observations are made. T0atd if 'p' denotes an observation of a component of momentum and 'q. An observer of the corresponding co-ordinates pq ≠ qp. Here 'p' and 'q' are not physical quantities but operators. In matrix mechanics and obey te relationship pq – qp = ih/2π - Where 'h' is the Planck constant that equals to 6.626 076 x 10-34 j s. The matrix elements are connected with the transition probability between various states of the system.

A quantity with magnitude and direction. It can be represented by a line whose length is propositional to the magnitude and whose direction is that of the vector, or by three components in rectangular co-ordinate system. Their angle between vectors is 90%, that the product and vector product base a similarity to unit vectors such, are to either be equated to being zero or one.

A true vector, or polar vector, involves the displacement or virtual displacement. Polar vectors include velocity, acceleration, force, electric and magnetic strength. Th deigns of their components are reversed on reversing the co-ordinated axes. Their dimensions include length to an odd power.

A Pseudo vector, or axial vector, involves the orientation of an axis in space. The direction is conventionally obtained in a right-handed system by sighting along the axis so that the rotation appears clockwise, Pseudo-vectors includes angular velocity, vector area and magnetic flux density. The signs of their components are unchanged on reversing the co-ordinated axes. Their dimensions include length to an even power.

Polar vectors and axial vectors obey the same laws of the vector analysis

(a) Vector addition: If two vectors 'A' and 'B' are represented in magnitude and direction by the adjacent sides of a parallelogram, the diagonal represents the vector sun (A + B) in magnitude and direction, forces, velocity, etc., combine in this way.

(b) Vector multiplying: There are two ways of multiplying vectors (I) the 'scalar product' of two vectors equals the product of their magnitudes and the co-sine of the angle between them, and is scalar quantity. It is usually written

A • B (reads as A dot B)

(ii) The vector product of two vectors: A and B are defined as a pseudo vector of magnitude AB sin θ, having a direction perpendicular to the plane containing them. The sense of the product along this perpendicular is defined by the rule: If 'A' is turned toward 'B' through the smaller angle, this rotation appears of the vector product. A vector product is usually written

A x B (reads as A cross B).

Vectors should be distinguished from scalars by printing the symbols in bold italic letters.

A theory that seeks to unite the properties of gravitational, electromagnetic, weak, and strong interactions to predict all their characteristics. At present it is not known whether such a theory can be developed, or whether the physical universe is amenable to a single analysis about the current concepts of physics. There are unsolved problems in using the framework of a relativistic quantum field theory to encompass the four elementary particles. It may be that using extended objects, as superstring and super-symmetric theories, but, still, this will enable a future synthesis for achieving obtainability.

A unified quantum field theory of the electromagnetic, weak and strong interactions, in most models, the known interactions are viewed as a low-energy manifestation of a single unified interaction, the unification taking place at energies (Typically 1015 GeV) very much higher than those currently accessible in particle accelerations. One feature of the Grand Unified Theory is that 'baryon' number and 'lepton' number would no-longer be absolutely conserved quantum numbers, with the consequences that such processes as 'proton decay', for example, the decay of a proton into a positron and a π0, p → e+π0 would be expected to be observed. Predicted lifetimes for proton decay are very long, typically 1035 years. Searchers for proton decay are being undertaken by many groups, using large underground detectors, so far without success.

One of the mutual attractions binding the universe of its owing totality, but independent of electromagnetism, strong and weak nuclear forces of interactive bondages is one of gravitation. Newton showed that the external effect of a spherical symmetric body is the same as if the whole mass were concentrated at the centre. Astronomical bodies are roughly spherically symmetric so can be treated as point particles to a very good approximation. On this assumption Newton showed that his law consistent with Kepler's laws? Until recently, all experiments have confirmed the accuracy of the inverse square law and the independence of the law upon the nature of the substances, but in the past few years evidence has been found against both.

The size of a gravitational field at any point is given by the force exerted on unit mass at that point. The field intensity at a distance 'χ' from a point mass 'm' is therefore Gm/χ2, and acts toward 'm'. Gravitational field strength is measured in 'newtons' per kilogram. The gravitational potential 'V' at that point is the work done in moving a unit mass from infinity to the point against the field, due to a point mass.

$$V = Gm \int_{\infty}^{X} d\chi \, / \, \chi 2 = - Gm \, / \, \chi.$$

V is a scalar measurement in joules per kilogram. The following special cases are also important (a) Potential at a point distance χ from the centre of a hollow homogeneous spherical shell of mass 'm' and outside the shell:

$$V = -Gm \, / \, \chi.$$

The potential is the same as if the mass of the shell is assumed concentrated at the centre (b) At any point inside the spherical shell the potential is equal to its value at the surface:

$$V = -Gm \, / \, r$$

Where 'r' is the radius of the shell. Thus, there is no resultant force acting at any point inside the shell, since no potential difference acts between any two points, then (c) Potential at a point distance 'χ' from the centre of a homogeneous solid sphere and outside the spheres the same as that for a shell:

$$V = -Gm / \chi$$

(d) At a point inside the sphere, of radius 'r'.

$$V = -Gm(3r2 - \chi2) /2r3.$$

The essential property of gravitation is that it causes a change in motion, in particular the acceleration of free fall (g) in the earth's gravitational field. According to the general theory of relativity, gravitational fields change the geometry of space-timer, causing it to become curved. It is this curvature that is geometrically responsible for an inseparability of the continuum of 'space-time' and its forbearing product is to a vicinities mass, entrapped by the universality of space-time, that in ways described by the pressures of their matter, that controls the natural motions of fording bodies. General relativity may thus be considered as a theory of gravitation, differences between it and Newtonian gravitation only appearing when the gravitational fields become very strong, as with 'black-holes' and 'neutron stars', or when very accurate measurements can be made.

Another binding characteristic embodied universally is the interaction between elementary particle arising as a consequence of their associated electric and magnetic fields. The electrostatic force between charged particles is an example. This force may be described in terms of the exchange of virtual photons, because of the uncertainty principle it is possible for the law of conservation of mass and energy to be broken by an amount ΔE providing this only occurring for a time such that: $\Delta E \Delta t \leq h/4\pi$. This makes it possible for particles to be created for short periods of time where their creation would normally violate conservation laws of energy. These particles are called 'virtual particles'. For example, in a complete vacuum -which no 'real' particle's exist, as pairs of virtual electrons and positron are continuously forming and rapidly disappearing (in less than 10-23 seconds). Other conservation laws such as those applying to angular momentum, isospin, etc., cannot be violated even for short periods of time.

Because its strength lies between strong and weak nuclear interactions, the exchanging electromagnetic interaction of particles decaying by electromagnetic interaction, do so with a lifetime shorter than those decaying by weak interaction, but longer than those decaying under the influence of strong interaction. For example, of electromagnetic decay is: $\pi 0 \rightarrow \gamma + \gamma$. This decay process, with a mean lifetime covering 8.4 x 10-17, may be understood as the annihilation of the quark and the antiquark, making up the $\pi 0$, into a pair of photons. The quantum numbers having to be conserved in electromagnetic interactions are, angular momentum, charge, baryon number, Isospin quantum number I3, strangeness, charm, parity and charge conjugation parity are unduly influenced.

Quanta's electrodynamic descriptions of the photon-mediated electromagnetic interactions have been verified over a great range of distances and have led to highly accurate predictions. Quantum electrodynamics are a 'gauge theory; as in quantum electrodynamics, the electromagnetic force can be derived by requiring that the equation describing the motion of a charged particle remain unchanged in the course of local symmetry operations. Specifically, if the phase of the wave function, by which charged particle is described is alterable independently, at which point in space, quantum electrodynamics require that the electromagnetic interaction and its mediating photon exist in order to maintain symmetry.

A kind of interaction between elementary particles that is weaker than the strong interaction force by a factor of about 10/12. When strong interactions can occur in reactions involving elementary particles, the weak interactions are usually unobserved. However, sometimes strong and electromagnetic interactions are prevented because they would violate the conservation of some quantum number, e.g., strangeness, that has to be conserved in such reactions. When this happens, weak interactions may still occur.

The weak interaction operates over an extremely short range (about 2 x 10-18 m) it is mediated by the exchange of a very heavy particle (a gauge boson) that may be the charged W+ or W− particle - mass about 80 GeV / c2 or the neutral Z0 particles (mass about 91 GeV / c2). The gauge bosons that mediate the weak interactions are analogous to the photon that mediates the electromagnetic interaction. Weak interactions mediated by W particles involve a change in the charge and hence the identity of the reacting particle. The neutral Z0 does not lead to such a change in identity. Both sorts of weak interaction can violate parity.

Most of the long-lived elementary particles decay as a result of weak interactions. For example, the kaon decay K+ → μ+ vμ may be thought of for being due to the annihilation of the u quark and $\bar{s}$ antiquark in the K+ to produce a virtual W+ boson, which then converts into a positive muon and a neutrino. This decay action or and electromagnetic interaction because strangeness is not conserved, Beta decay is the most common example of weak interaction decay. Because it is so weak, particles that can only decay by weak interactions do so relatively slowly, i.e., they have relatively long lifetimes. Other examples of weak interactions include the scattering of the neutrino by other particles and certain very small effects on electrons within the atom.

Understanding of weak interactions is based on the electroweak theory, in which it is proposed that the weak and electromagnetic interactions are different manifestations of a single underlying force, known as the electroweak nuclear force. Many of the predictions of the theory have been confirmed experimentally.

A gauge theory, also called quantum flavour dynamics, that provides a unified description of both the electromagnetic and weak interactions. In the Glashow-Weinberg-Salam theory, also known as the standard model, electroweak interactions arise from the exchange of photons and of massive charged W+ and neutral Z0 bosons of spin 1 between quarks and leptons. The extremely massive charged particle, symbol W+ or W–, that mediates certain types of weak interaction. The neutral Z-particle, or Z boson, symbol Z0, mediates the other types. Both are gauge bosons. The W- and Z-particles were first detected at CERN (1983) by studying collisions between protons and antiprotons with total energy 540 GeV in centre-of-mass co-ordinates. The rest masses were determined as about 80 GeV / c2 and 91 GeV / c2 for the W- and Z-particles, respectively, as had been predicted by the electroweak theory.

The interaction strengths of the gauge bosons to quarks and leptons and the masses of the W and Z bosons themselves are predicted by the theory, the Weinberg Angle θW, which must be determined by experiment. The Glashow-Weinberg-Salam theory successfully describes all existing data from a wide variety of electroweak processes, such as neutrino-nucleon, neutrino-electron and electron-nucleon scattering. A major success of the model was the direct observation in 1983-84 of the W± and Z0 bosons with the predicted masses of 80 and 91 GeV / c2 in high energy proton-antiproton interactions. The decay modes of the W± and Z0 bosons have been studied in very high pp and e+ e– interactions and found to be in good agreement with the Standard model.

The six known types (or flavours) of quarks and the six known leptons are grouped into three separate generations of particles as follows:

1st generation: e– ve u d
2nd generation: μ– vμ c s
3rd generation: τ– vτ t b

The second and third generations are essentially copies of the first generation, which contains the electron and the 'up' and 'down' quarks making up the proton and neutron, but involve particles of higher mass. Communication between the different generations occurs only in the quark sector and only for interactions involving W± bosons. Studies of Z0 bosons production in very high energy electron-positron interactions has shown that no further generations of quarks and leptons can exist in nature (an arbitrary number of generations is a priori possible within the standard model) provided only that any new neutrinos are approximately massless.

The Glashow-Weinberg-Salam model also predicts the existence of a heavy spin 0 particle, not yet observed experimentally, known as the Higgs boson. The spontaneous symmetry-breaking mechanism used to generate non-zero masses for W± and Z bosons in the electroweak theory, whereby the mechanism postulates the existence of two new complex fields, φ(χμ) = φ1 + I φ2 and Ψ(χμ) = Ψ1 + I Ψ2, which are functional distributors to χμ = χ, y, z and t, and form a doublet (φ, Ψ) this doublet of complex fields transforms in the same way as leptons and quarks under electroweak gauge transformations. Such gauge transformations rotate φ1, φ2, Ψ1, Ψ2 into each other without changing the nature of the physical science.

The vacuum does not share the symmetry of the fields (φ, Ψ) and a spontaneous breaking of the vacuum symmetry occurs via the Higgs mechanism. Consequently, the fields φ and Ψ have non-zero values in the vacuum. A particular orientation of φ1, φ2, Ψ1, Ψ2 may be chosen so that all the components of φ (φ1). This component responds to electroweak nucleor fields in a way that is analogous to the response of a plasma to electromagnetic fields. Plasmas oscillate in the presence of electromagnetic waves, however, electromagnetic waves can only propagate at a frequency above the plasma frequency ωp2 given by the expression:

$$ωp2 = ne2 / mε$$

Where 'n' is the charge number density, 'e' the electrons charge. 'm' the electrons mass and 'ε' is the Permittivity of the plasma. In quantum field theory, this minimum frequency for electromagnetic waves may be thought of as a minimum energy for the existence of a quantum of the electromagnetic field (a photon) within the plasma. This minimum energy or mass for the photon, which becomes a field quantum of a finite ranged force. Thus, in its plasma, photons acquire a mass and the electromagnetic interaction has a finite range.

The vacuum field φ1 responds to weak fields by giving a mass and finite range to the W± and Z bosons, however, the electromagnetic field is unaffected by the presence of φ1 so the photon remains massless. The mass acquired by the weak interaction bosons is proportional to the vacuum of φ1 and to the weak charge strength. A quantum of the field φ1 is an electrically neutral particle called the Higgs boson. It interacts with all massive particles with a coupling that is proportional to their mass. The standard model does not predict the mass of the Higgs boson, but it is known that it cannot be too heavy (not much more than about 1000 proton masses). Since this would lead to complicated self-interaction, such self-interaction is not believed to be present, because the theory does not account for them, but nevertheless successfully predicts the masses of the W ± and Z bosons. These of the particle results from the so-called spontaneous symmetry breaking mechanisms, and used to generate non-zero masses for the W± and Z0 bosons and is presumably too massive to have been produced in existing particle accelerators.

We now turn our attentions belonging to the third binding force of unity, in, and of itself, its name implicates a physicality in the belonging nature that holds itself the binding of strong interactions that portray of its owing universality, simply because its universal. Interactions between elementary particles involving the strong interaction force. This force is about one hundred times greater than the electromagnetic force between charged elementary particles. However, it is a short range force - it is only important for particles separated by a distance of less than abut 10-15- and is the force that holds protons and neutrons together in atomic nuclei for 'soft' interactions between hadrons, where relatively small transfers of momentum are involved, the strong interactions may be described in terms of the exchange of virtual hadrons, just as electromagnetic interactions between charged particles may be described in terms of the exchange of virtual photons. At a more fundamental level, the strong interaction arises as the result of the exchange of gluons between quarks and/and antiquarks as described by quantum chromodynamics.

In the hadron exchange picture, any hadron can act as the exchanged particle provided certain quantum numbers are conserved. These quantum numbers are the total angular momentum, charge, baryon number, Isospin (both I and I3), strangeness, parity, charge conjugation parity, and G-parity. Strong interactions are investigated experimentally by observing how beams of high-energy hadrons are scattered when they collide with other hadrons. Two hadrons colliding at high energy will only remain near to each other for a very short time. However, during the collision they may come sufficiently close to each other for a strong interaction to occur by the exchanger of a virtual particle. As a result of this interaction, the two colliding particles will be deflected (scattered) from their original paths. In the virtual hadron exchanged during the interaction carries some quantum numbers from one particle to the other, the particles found after the collision may differ from those before it. Sometimes the number of particles is increased in a collision.

In hadron-hadron interactions, the number of hadrons produced increases approximately logarithmically with the total centre of mass energy, reaching about 50 particles for proton-antiproton collisions at 900 GeV, for example in some of these collisions, two oppositely-directed collimated 'jets' of hadrons are produced, which are interpreted as due to an underlying interaction involving the exchange of an energetic gluon between, for example, a quark from the proton and an antiquark from the antiproton. The scattered quark and antiquark cannot exist as free particles, but instead 'fragments' into a large number of hadrons (mostly pions and kaon) travelling approximately along the original quark or antiquark direction. This results in collimated jets of hadrons that can be detected experimentally. Studies of this and other similar processes are in good agreement with quantum chromodynamics predictions.

The interaction between elementary particles arising as a consequence of their associated electric and magnetic fields. The electrostatic force between charged particles is an example. This force may be described in terms of the exchange of virtual photons, because its strength lies between strong and weak interactions, particles decaying by electromagnetic interaction do so with a lifetime shorter than those decaying by weak interaction, but longer than those decaying by strong interaction. An example of electromagnetic decay is:

$$\pi 0 \rightarrow \Upsilon + \Upsilon.$$

This decay process (mean lifetime 8.4 x 10-17 seconds) may be understood as the 'annihilation' of the quark and the antiquark making up the π0, into a pair of photons. The following quantum numbers have to be conserved in electromagnetic interactions: Angular momentum, charm, baryon number, Isospin quantum number I3, strangeness, charm, parity, and charge conjugation parity.

A particle that, as far as is known, is not composed of other simpler particles. Elementary particles represent the most basic constituents of matter and are also the carriers of the fundamental forces between particles, namely the electromagnetic, weak, strong, and gravitational forces. The known elementary particles can be grouped into three classes, leptons, quarks, and gauge bosons, hadrons, such strongly interacting particles as the proton and neutron, which are bound states of quarks and/or antiquarks, are also sometimes called elementary particles.

Leptons undergo electromagnetic and weak interactions, but not strong interactions. Six leptons are known, the negatively charged electron, muon, and tauons plus three associates neutrinos: Ve, vμ and vτ. The electron is a stable particle but the muon and tau leptons decay through the weak interactions with lifetimes of about 10-8 and 10-13 seconds. Neutrinos are stable neutral leptons, which interact only through the weak interaction.

Corresponding to the leptons are six quarks, namely the up (u), charm (c) and top (t) quarks with electric charge equal to +⅔ that of the proton and the down (d), strange (s), and bottom (b) quarks of charge -⅓ the proton charge. Quarks have not been observed experimentally as free particles, but reveal their existence only indirectly in high-energy scattering experiments and through patterns observed in the properties of hadrons. They are believed to be permanently confined within hadrons, either in baryons, half integer spin hadrons containing three quarks, or in mesons, integer spin hadrons containing a quark and an antiquark. The proton, for example, is a baryon containing two 'up' quarks and an 'anti-down (d) quark, while the $\pi+$ is a positively charged meson containing an up quark and an anti-down (d) antiquark. The only hadron that is stable as a free particle is the proton. The neutron is unstable when free. Within a nucleus, proton and neutrons are generally both stable but either particle may bear into a transformation into the other, by 'Beta Decay or Capture'.

Interactions between quarks and leptons are mediated by the exchange of particles known as 'gauge bosons', specifically the photon for electromagnetic interactions, W± and Z0 bosons for the weak interaction, and eight massless gluons, in the case of the strong integrations.

A class of eigenvalue problems in physics that take the form $\Omega\Psi = \lambda\Psi$, Where 'Ω' is some mathematical operation (multiplication by a number, differentiation, etc.) on a function 'Ψ', which is called the 'eigenfunction'. 'λ' is called the eigenvalue, which in a physical system will be identified with an observable quantity analogous to the amplitude of a wave that appears in the equations of wave mechanics, particularly the Schrödinger wave equation, the most generally accepted interpretation is that $| \Psi |2dV$, representing the probability that a particle is located within the volume element dV, mass in which case a particle of mass 'm' moving with a velocity 'v' will, under suitable experimental conditions exhibit the characteristics of a wave of wave length λ, given by the equation $\lambda = h/mv$, where 'h' is the Planck constant that equals to 6.626 076 x 10-34 J s.? This equation is the basis of wave mechanics. However, a set of weaves that represent the behaviour, under appropriate conditions, of a particle, e.g., its diffraction by a crystal lattice. The wave length is given by the 'de Broglie equation.' They are sometimes regarded as waves of probability, since the square of their amplitude at a given point represents the probability of finding the particle in unit volume at that point. These waves were predicted by Broglie in 1924 and in 1927 in the Davisson-Germer experiment.

Eigenvalue problems are ubiquitous in classical physics and occur whenever the mathematical description of a physical system yields a series of coupled differential equations. For example, the collective motion of a large number of interacting oscillators may be described by a set of coupled differential educations. Each differential equation describes the motion of one of the oscillators in terms of the position of all the others. A 'harmonic' solution may be sought, in which each displacement is assumed to have a 'simple harmonic motion' in time. The differential equations then reduce to 3N linear equations with 3N unknowns, where 'N' is the number of individual oscillators, each with three degrees of freedom. The whole problem is now easily recast as a 'matrix education' of the form: $M\chi = \omega 2\chi$. Where 'M' is an N x N matrix called the 'dynamical matrix', and χ is an N x 1 'a column matrix, and $\omega 2$ is the square of an angular frequency of the harmonic solution. The problem is now an eigenvalue problem with eigenfunctions 'χ' which is the normal mode of the system, with corresponding eigenvalues $\omega 2$. As 'χ' can be expressed as a column vector, χ is a vector in some N-dimensional vector space. For this reason, χ is often called an eigenvector.

When the collection of oscillators is a complicated three-dimensional molecule, the casting of the problem into normal modes is an effective simplification of the system. The symmetry principles of 'group theory' can then be applied, which classify normal modes according to their 'ω' eigenvalues (frequencies). This kind of analysis requires an appreciation of the symmetry properties of the molecule. The sets of operations (rotations, inversions, etc.) that leave the molecule invariant make up the 'point group' of that molecule. Normal modes sharing the same 'ω' eigenvalues are said to correspond to the 'irreducible representations' of the molecule's point group. It is among these irreducible representations that one will find the infrared absorption spectrum for the vibrational normal modes of the molecule.

Eigenvalue problems play a particularly important role in quantum mechanics. In quantum mechanics, physically observable (location, momentum, energy, etc.) are represented by operations (differentiation with respect to a variable, multiplication by a variable), which act on wave functions. Wave functions differ from classical waves in that they carry no energy. For classical waves, the square modulus of its amplitude measure its energy. For a wave function, the square modulus of its amplitude (at a location χ) represent not energy but probability, i.e., the probability that a particle -a localized packet of energy will be observed if a detector is placed at that location. The wave function therefore describes the distribution of possible locations of the particle and is perceptible only after many location detection events have occurred. A measurement of position on a quantum particle may be written symbolically as:

$$X \quad \Psi(\chi) = \chi\Psi(\chi).$$

Where $\Psi(\chi)$ is said to be an eigenvector of the location operator and 'χ' is the eigenvalue, which represents the location. Each $\Psi(\chi)$ represents amplitude at the location χ, $|\Psi(\chi)|2$ is the probability that the particle will be located in an infinitesimal volume at that location. The wave function describing the distribution of all possible locations for the particle is the linear super-position of all $\Psi(\chi)$ for $0 \leq \chi \leq \infty$ that occur, its principle states that each stress is accompanied by the same strains whether it acts alone or in conjunction with others, it is true so long as the total stress does not exceed the limit of proportionality. Also, in vibrations and wave motion the principle asserts that one set of vibrations or waves are unaffected by the presence of another set. For example, two sets of ripples on water will pass through one another without mutual interactions so that, at a particular instant, the resultant disturbance at any point traversed by both sets of waves is the sum of the two component disturbances.

The eigenvalue problem in quantum mechanics therefore represents the act of measurement. Eigenvectors of an observable presentation were the possible states (Position, in the case of χ) that the quantum system can have. Stationary states of a quantum non-demolition attribute of a quantum system, such as position and momentum, are related by the Heisenberg Uncertainty Principle, which states that the product of the uncertainty of the measured value of a component of momentum ($p\chi$) and the uncertainty in the corresponding co-ordinates of position (χ) is of the same order of magnitude as the Planck constant. Attributes related in this way are called 'conjugate' attributes. Thus, while an accurate measurement of position is possible, as a result of the uncertainty principle it produces a large momentum spread. Subsequent measurements of the position acquire a spread themselves, which makes the continuous monitoring of the position impossible.

The eigenvalues are the values that observables take on within these quantum states. As in classical mechanics, eigenvalue problems in quantum mechanics may take differential or matrix forms. Both forms have been shown to be equivalent. The differential form of quantum mechanics is called 'wave mechanics' (Schrödinger), where the operators are differential operators or multiplications by variables. Eigenfunctions in wave mechanics are wave functions corresponding to stationary wave states that satisfy some set of boundary conditions. The matrix form of quantum mechanics is often called matrix mechanics (Born and Heisenberg). Matrix acting on eigenvectors represents the operators.

The relationship between matrix and wave mechanics is very similar to the relationship between matrix and differential forms of eigenvalue problems in classical mechanics. The wave functions representing stationary states are really normal modes of the quantum wave. These normal modes may be thought of as vectors that span a vector space, which have a matrix representation.

Once, again, the Heisenberg uncertainty relation, or indeterminacy principle of 'quantum mechanics' that associate the physical properties of particles into pairs such that both together cannot be measured to within more than a certain degree of accuracy. If 'A' and

'V' form such a pair is called a conjugate pair, then: $\Delta A\Delta V > k$, where 'k' is a constant and ΔA and ΔV are a variance in the experimental values for the attributes 'A' and 'V'. The best-known instance of the equation relates the position and momentum of an electron: $\Delta p\Delta \chi > h$, where 'h' is the Planck constant. This is the Heisenberg uncertainty principle. Still, the usual value given for Planck's constant is 6.6 x 10-27 ergs sec. Since Planck's constant is not zero, mathematical analysis reveals the following: The 'spread', or uncertainty, in position times the 'spread', or uncertainty of momentum is greater than, or possibly equal to, the value of the constant or, or accurately, Planck's constant divided by 2π, if we choose to know momentum exactly, then us knowing nothing about position, and vice versa.

The presence of Plank's constant calls that we approach quantum physics a situation in which the mathematical theory does not allow precise prediction of, or exist in exact correspondences with, the physical reality. If nature did not insist on making changes or transitions in precise chunks of Planck's quantum of action, or in multiples of these chunks, there would be no crisis. But whether it is of our own determinacy, such that a cancerous growth in the body of an otherwise perfect knowledge of the physical world or the grounds for believing, in principle at least, in human freedom, one thing appears certain - it is an indelible feature of our understanding of nature.

In order too further explain how fundamental the quantum of action is to our present understanding of the life of nature, let us attempt to do what quantum physics says we cannot do and visualize its role in the simplest of all atoms -the hydrogen atom. It can be thought that standing at the centre of the Sky Dome or Rogers Centre, at roughly where the pitcher's mound is. Place a grain of salt on the mound, and picture a speck of dust moving furiously around the orbital's outskirts of the Sky Dome's fulfilling circle, around which the grain of salt remains referential of the topic. This represents, roughly, the relative size of the nucleus and the distance between electron and nucleus inside the hydrogen atom when imaged in its particle aspect.

In quantum physics, however, the hydrogen atom cannot be visualized with such macro-level analogies. The orbit of the electron is not a circle, in which a planet-like object moves, and each orbit is described in terms of a probability distribution for finding the electron in an average position corresponding to each orbit as opposed to an actual position. Without observation or measurement, the electron could be in some sense anywhere or everywhere within the probability distribution, also, the space between probability distributions is not empty, it is infused with energetic vibrations capable of manifesting itself as the befitting quanta.

The energy levels manifest at certain distances because the transition between orbits occurs in terms of precise units of Planck's constant. If any attentive effects to comply with or measure where the particle-like aspect of the electron is, in that the existence of Planck's constant will always prevent us from knowing precisely all the properties of that electron that we might presume to be they're in the absence of measurement. Also, the two-split experiment, as our presence as observers and what we choose to measure or observe are inextricably linked to the results obtained. Since all complex molecules are built from simpler atoms, what is to be done, is that liken to the hydrogen atom, of which case applies generally to all material substances.

The grounds for objecting to quantum theory, the lack of a one-to-one correspondence between every element of the physical theory and the physical reality it describes, may seem justifiable and reasonable in strict scientific terms. After all, the completeness of all previous physical theories was measured against that criterion with enormous success. Since it was this success that gave physicists the reputation of being able to disclose physical reality with magnificent exactitude, perhaps a more complex quantum theory will emerge by continuing to insist on this requirement.

All indications are, however, that no future theory can circumvent quantum indeterminacy, and the success of quantum theory in co-ordinating our experience with nature is eloquent testimony to this conclusion. As Bohr realized, the fact that we live in a quantum universe in which the quantum of action is a given or an unavoidable reality requires a very different criterion for determining the completeness of physical theory. The new measure for a complete physical theory is that it unambiguously confirms our ability to co-ordinate more experience with physical reality.

If a theory does so and continues to do so, which is certainly the case with quantum physics, then the theory must be deemed complete. Quantum physics not only works exceedingly well, it is, in these terms, the most accurate physical theory that has ever existed. When we consider that this physics allows us to predict and measure quantities like the magnetic moment of electrons to the fifteenth decimal place, we realize that accuracy perse is not the real issue. The real issue, as Bohr rightly intuited, is that this complete physical theory effectively undermines the privileged relationships in classical physics between physical theory and physical reality. Another measure of success in physical theory is also met by quantum physics -eloquence and simplicity. The quantum recipe for computing probabilities given by the wave function is straightforward and can be successfully employed by any undergraduate physics student. Take the square of the wave amplitude and compute the probability of what can be measured or observed with a certain value. Yet there is a profound difference between the recipe for calculating quantum probabilities and the recipe for calculating probabilities in classical physics.

In quantum physics, one calculates the probability of an event that can happen in alternative ways by adding the wave functions, and then taking the square of the amplitude. In the two-split experiment, for example, the electron is described by one wave function if it goes through one slit and by another wave function if it goes through the other slit. In order to compute the probability of where the electron is going to end on the screen, we add the two wave functions, compute the obsolete value of their sum, and square it. Although the recipe in classical probability theory seems similar, it is quite different. In classical physics, one would simply add the probabilities of the two alternative ways and let it go at that. That classical procedure does not work here because we are not dealing with classical atoms in quantum physics additional terms arise when the wave functions are added, and the probability is computed in a process known as the 'superposition principle'. That the superposition principle can be illustrated with an analogy from simple mathematics. Add two numbers and then take the square of their sum, as opposed to just adding the squares of the two numbers. Obviously, (2 + 3)2 is not equal to 22 + 32. The former is 25, and the latter are 13. In the language of quantum probability theory:

$$| \Psi1 + \Psi2 |2 \neq | \Psi1 |2 + | \Psi2 |2$$

Where Ψ1 and Ψ2 are the individual wave functions on the left-hand side, the superposition principle results in extra terms that cannot be found on the right-handed side the left-hand faction of the above relation is the way a quantum physicists would compute probabilities and the right-hand side is the classical analogue. In quantum theory, the right-hand side is realized when we know, for example, which slit through which the electron went. Heisenberg was among the first to compute what would happen in an instance like this. The extra superposition terms contained in the left-hand side of the above relation would not be there, and the peculiar wave-like interference pattern would disappear. The observed pattern on the final screen would, therefore, be what one would expect if electrons were behaving like bullets, and the final probability would be the sum of the individual probabilities. But when we know which slit the electron went through, this interaction with the system causes the interference pattern to disappear.

In order to give a full account of quantum recipes for computing probabilities, one g-has to examine what would happen in events that are compounded. Compound events are events that can be broken down into a series of steps, or events that consist of a number of things happening independently the recipe here calls for multiplying the individual wave functions, and then following the usual quantum recipe of taking the square of the amplitude.

The quantum recipe is $| \Psi1 \bullet \Psi2 |2$, and, in this case, it would be the same if we multiplied the individual probabilities, as one would in classical theory. Thus the recipes of computing results in quantum theory and classical physics can be totally different from quantum superposition effects are completely non-classical, and there is no mathematical justification to why the quantum recipes work. What justifies the use of quantum probability theory is the same thing that justifies the use of quantum physics -it has allowed us in countless experiments to vastly extend our ability to co-ordinate experience with nature.

The view of probability in the nineteenth century was greatly conditioned and reinforced by classical assumptions about the relationships between physical theory and physical reality. In this century, physicists developed sophisticated statistics to deal with large ensembles of particles before the actual character of these particles was understood. Classical statistics, developed primarily by James C. Maxwell and Ludwig Boltzmann, was used to account for the behaviour of a molecule in a gas and to predict the average speed of a gas molecule in terms of the temperature of the gas.

The presumption was that the statistical average were workable approximations those subsequent physical theories, or better experimental techniques, would disclose with precision and certainty. Since nothing was known about quantum systems, and since quantum indeterminacy is small when dealing with macro-level effects, this presumption was quite reasonable. We know, however, that quantum mechanical effects are present in the behaviour of gasses and that the choice to ignore them is merely a matter of convincing in getting workable or practical resulted. It is, therefore, no longer possible to assume that the statistical averages are merely higher-level approximations for a more exact description.

Perhaps the best-known defence of the classical conception of the relationship between physical theory ands physical reality is the celebrated animal introduced by the Austrian physicist Erin Schrödinger (1887-1961) in 1935, in a 'thought experiment' showing the strange nature of the world of quantum mechanics. The cat is thought of as locked in a box with a capsule of cyanide, which will break if a Geiger counter triggers. This will happen if an atom in a radioactive substance in the box decays, and there is a chance of 50% of such an event within an hour. Otherwise, the cat is alive. The problem is that the system is in an indeterminate state. The wave function of the entire system is a 'superposition' of states, fully described by the probabilities of events occurring when it is eventually measured, and therefore 'contains equal parts of the living and dead cat'. When we look and see we will find either a breathing cat or a dead cat, but if it is only as we look that the wave packet collapses, quantum mechanic forces us to say that before we looked it was not true that the cat was dead and not true that it was alive, the thought experiment makes vivid the difficulty of conceiving of quantum indetermincies when these are translated to the familiar world of everyday objects.

The 'electron,' is a stable elementary particle having a negative charge, e, equal to:

1.602 189 25 x 10-19 C

and a rest mass, m0 equal to;

9.109 389 7 x 10-31 kg

equivalent to

0.511 0034 MeV / c2

It has a spin of ½ and obeys Fermi-Dirac Statistics. As it does not have strong interactions, it is classified as a 'lepton'.

The discovery of the electron was reported in 1897 by Sir J.J. Thomson, following his work on the rays from the cold cathode of a gas-discharge tube, it was soon established that particles with the same charge and mass were obtained from numerous substances by the 'photoelectric effect', 'thermionic emission' and 'beta decay'. Thus, the electron was found to be part of all atoms, molecules, and crystals.

Free electrons are studied in a vacuum or a gas at low pressure, whereby beams are emitted from hot filaments or cold cathodes and are subject to 'focussing', so that the particles in which an electron beam in, for example, a cathode-ray tube, where in principal methods as (i) Electrostatic focussing, the beam is made to converge by the action of electrostatic fields between two or more electrodes at different potentials. The electrodes are commonly cylinders coaxial with the electron tube, and the whole assembly forms an electrostatic electron lens. The focussing effect is usually controlled by varying the potential of one of the electrodes, called the focussing electrode. (ii) Electromagnetic focussing, by way that the beam is made to converge by the action of a magnetic field that is produced by the passage of direct current, through a focussing coil. The latter are commonly a coil of short axial length mounted so as to surround the electron tube and to be coaxial with it.

The force FE on an electron or magnetic field of strength E is given by FE = Ee and is in the direction of the field. On moving through a potential difference V, the electron acquires a kinetic energy eV, hence it is possible to obtain beams of electrons of accurately known kinetic energy. In a magnetic field of magnetic flux density 'B', an electron with speed 'v' is subject to a force, FB = Bev sin θ, where θ is the angle between 'B' and 'v'. This force acts at right angles to the plane containing 'B' and 'v'.

The mass of any particle increases with speed according to the theory of relativity. If an electron is accelerated from rest through 5kV, the mass is 1% greater than it is at rest. Thus, accountably, must be taken of relativity for calculations on electrons with quite moderate energies.

According to 'wave mechanics' a particle with momentum 'mv' exhibits' diffraction and interference phenomena, similar to a wave with wavelength λ = h/mv, where 'h' is the Planck constant. For electrons accelerated through a few hundred volts, this gives wavelengths rather less than typical interatomic spacing in crystals. Hence, a crystal can act as a diffraction grating for electron beams.

Owing to the fact that electrons are associated with a wavelength λ given by λ = h/mv, where 'h' is the Planck constant and (mv) the momentum of the electron, a beam of electrons suffers diffraction in its passage through crystalline material, similar to that experienced by a beam of X-rays. The diffraction pattern depends on the spacing of the crystal planes, and the phenomenon can be employed to investigate the structure of surface and other films, and under suitable conditions exhibit the characteristics of a wave of the wavelength given by the equation λ = h/mv, which is the basis of wave mechanics. A set of waves that represent the behaviour, under appropriate conditions, of a particle, e.g., its diffraction by a crystal lattice, that is given the 'de Broglie equation.' They are sometimes regarded as waves of probability, since the square of their amplitude at a given point represents the probability of finding the particle in unit volume at that point.

The first experiment to demonstrate 'electron diffraction', and hence the wavelike nature of particles. A narrow pencil of electrons from a hot filament cathode was projected 'in vacua' onto a nickel crystal. The experiment showed the existence of a definite diffracted beam at one particular angle, which depended on the velocity of the electrons, assuming this to be the Bragg angle, stating that the structure of a crystal can be determined from a set of interference patterns found at various angles from the different crystal faces, least of mention, the wavelength of the electrons was calculated and found to be in agreement with the 'de Broglie equation.'

At kinetic energies less than a few electro-volts, electrons undergo elastic collision with atoms and molecules, simply because of the large ratio of the masses and the conservation of momentum, only an extremely small transfer of kinetic energy occurs. Thus, the electrons are deflected but not slowed down appreciatively. At slightly higher energies collisions are inelastic. Molecules may be dissociated, and atoms and molecules may be excited or ionized. Thus it is the least energy that causes an ionization

$$A \rightarrow A+ + e-$$

Where the ION and the electron are far enough apart for their electrostatic interaction to be negligible and no extra kinetic energy removed is that in the outermost orbit, i.e., the level strongly bound electrons. It is also possible to consider removal of electrons from inner orbits, in which their binding energy is greater. As an excited particle or recombining, ions emit electromagnetic radiation mostly in the visible or ultraviolet.

For electron energies of the order of several GeV upwards, X-rays are generated. Electrons of high kinetic energy travel considerable distances through matter, leaving a trail of positive ions and free electrons. The energy is mostly lost in small increments (about 30 eV) with only an occasional major interaction causing X-ray emissions. The range increases at higher energies.

The positron -the antiparticle of the electron, I e., an elementary particle with electron mass and positive charge equal to that of the electron. According to the relativistic wave mechanics of Dirac, space contains a continuum of electrons in states of negative energy. These states are normally unobservable, but if sufficient energy can be given, an electron may be raised into a state of positive energy and suggested itself observably. The vacant state of negativity behaves as a positive particle of positive energy, which is observed as a positron.

The simultaneous formation of a positron and an electron from a photon is called 'pair production', and occurs when the annihilation of gamma-ray photons with an energy of 1.02 MeV passes close to an atomic nucleus, whereby the interaction between the particle and its antiparticle disappear and photons or other elementary particles or antiparticles are so created, as accorded to energy and momentum conservation.

At low energies, an electron and a positron annihilate to produce electromagnetic radiation. Usually the particles have little kinetic energy or momentum in the laboratory system before interaction, hence the total energy of the radiation is nearly 2m0c2, where m0 is the rest mass of an electron. In nearly all cases two photons are generated. Each of 0.511 MeV, in almost exactly opposite directions to conserve momentum. Occasionally, three photons are emitted all in the same plane. Electron-positron annihilation at high energies has been extensively studied in particle accelerators. Generally the annihilation results in the production of a quark, and an antiquark, fort example, e+ e– → μ+ μ– or a charged lepton plus an antilepton (e+e– → μ+μ–). The quarks and antiquarks do not appear as free particles but convert into several hadrons, which can be detected experimentally. As the energy available in the electron-positron interaction increases, quarks and leptons of progressively larger rest mass can be produced. In addition, striking resonances are present, which appear as large increases in the rate at which annihilations occur at particular energies. The I / PSI particle and similar resonances containing an antiquark are produced at an energy of about 3 GeV, for example, giving rise to abundant production of charmed hadrons. Bottom (b) quark production occurs at greater energies than about 10 GeV. A resonance at an energy of about 90 GeV, due to the production of the Z0 gauge boson involved in weak interaction is currently under intensive study at the LEP and SLC e+ e– colliders. Colliders are the machines for increasing the kinetic energy of charged particles or ions, such as protons or electrons, by accelerating them in an electric field. A magnetic field is used to maintain the particles in the desired direction. The particle can travel in a straight, spiral, or circular paths. At present, the highest energies are obtained in the proton synchrotron.

The Super Proton Synchrotron at CERN (Geneva) accelerates protons to 450 GeV. It can also cause proton-antiproton collisions with total kinetic energy, in centre-of-mass co-ordinates of 620 GeV. In the USA the Fermi National Acceleration Laboratory proton synchrotron gives protons and antiprotons of 800 GeV, permitting collisions with total kinetic energy of 1600 GeV. The Large Electron Positron (LEP) system at CERN accelerates particles to 60 GeV.

All the aforementioned devices are designed to produce collisions between particles travelling in opposite directions. This gives effectively very much higher energies available for interaction than our possible targets. High-energy nuclear reaction occurs when the particles, either moving in a stationary target collide. The particles created in these reactions are detected by sensitive equipment close to the collision site. New particles, including the tauon, W, and Z particles and requiring enormous energies for their creation, have been detected and their properties determined.

While, still, a 'nucleon' and 'anti-nucleon' annihilating at low energy, produce about half a dozen pions, which may be neutral or charged. By definition, mesons are both hadrons and bosons, justly as the pion and kaon are mesons. Mesons have a substructure composed of a quark and an antiquark bound together by the exchange of particles known as gluons.

The conjugate particle or antiparticle that corresponds with another particle of identical mass and spin, but has such quantum numbers as charge (Q), baryon number (B), strangeness (S), charms (C), and Isospin (I3) of equal magnitude but opposite sign. Examples of a particle and its antiparticle include the electron and positron, proton and antiproton, the positive and negatively charged pions, and the 'up' quark and 'up' antiquark. The antiparticle corresponding to a particle with the symbol 'a' is usually denoted 'ā'. When a particle and its antiparticle are identical, as with the photon and neutral pion, this is called a 'self-conjugate particle'.

The critical potential to excitation energy required to change am atom or molecule from one quantum state to another of higher energy, is equal to the difference in energy of the states and is usually the difference in energy between the ground state of the atom and a specified excited state. Which the state of a system, such as an atom or molecule, when it has a higher energy than its ground state.

The ground state contributes the state of a system with the lowest energy. An isolated body will remain indefinitely in it, such that it is possible for a system to have possession of two or more ground states, of equal energy but with different sets of quantum numbers. In the case of atomic hydrogen there are two states for which the quantum numbers n, I, and m are 1, 0, and 0 respectively, while the spin may be + ½ with respect to a defined direction. An allowed wave function of an electron in an atom obtained by a solution of the 'Schrödinger wave equation' in which a hydrogen atom, for example, the electron moves in the electrostatic field of the nucleus and its potential energy is −e2 / r, where 'e' is the electron charge and 'r' its distance from the nucleus. A precise orbit cannot be considered as in Bohr's theory of the atom, but the behaviour of the electron is described by its wave function, Ψ, which is a mathematical function of its position with respect to the nucleus. The significance of the wave function is that | Ψ |2 dt is the probability of locating the electron in the element of volume dt.

Solution of Schrödinger's equation for the hydrogen atom shows that the electron can only have certain allowed wave functions (eigenfunctions). Each of these corresponds to a probability distribution in space given by the manner in which | Ψ |2 varies with position. They also have an associated value of the energy 'E'. These allowed wave functions, or orbitals, are characterized by three quantum numbers similar to those characterized the allowed orbits in the earlier quantum theory of the atom: 'n', the 'principal quantum number, can have values of 1, 2, 3, etc. the orbital with n =1 has the lowest energy. The states of the electron with n = 1, 2, 3, etc., are called 'shells' and designate the K, L, M shells, etc. 'I', the 'azimuthal quantum numbers', which for a given value of 'n' can have values of 0, 1, 2, . . . (n−1). An electron in the 'L' shell of an atom with n = 2 can occupy two sub-shells of different energy corresponding to I = 0, I = 1, and I = 2. Orbitals with I = 0, 1, 2 and 3 are called s, p, d, and *f* orbitals respectively. The significance of

I quantum number is that it gives the angular momentum of the electron. The orbital angular momentum of an electron is given by:

$$\sqrt{[I(I + 1)(h/2\pi)}.$$

'm', the 'magnetic quantum number, which for a given value of I can have values, – I, –(I-1), . . ., 0, . . . (I-1), I. Thus, for a 'p' orbital for orbits with m = 1, 0, and 1. These orbitals, with the same values of 'n' and 'I' but different 'm' values, have the same energy. The significance of this quantum number is that it indicates the number of different levels that would be produced if the atom were subjected to an external magnetic field.

According to wave theory the electron may be at any distance from the nucleus, but in fact, there is only a reasonable chance of it being within a distance of ~ 5 x 10-11 metre. Indeed the maximum probability occurs when r-a0 where a0 is the radius of the first Bohr orbit. It is customary to represent an orbital by a surface enclosing a volume within which there is an arbitrarily decided probability (say 95%) of finding the electron.

Finally, the electron in an atom can have a fourth quantum number MS, characterizing its spin direction. This can be + ½ or – ½, and according to the 'Pauli Exclusion Principle,' each orbital can hold only two electrons. The four quantum numbers lead to an explanation of the periodic table of the elements.

In earlier mention, the concerns referring to the 'moment' had been to our exchanges to issue as, i.e., the moment of inertia, moment of momentum. The moment of a force about an axis is the product of the perpendicular distance of the axis from the line of action of the force, and the component of the force in the plane perpendicular to the axis. The moment of a system of coplanar forces about an axis perpendicular to the plane containing them is the algebraic sum of the moments of the separate forces about that axis of a anticlockwise moment appear taken controventionally to be positive and clockwise of ones Uncomplementarity. The moment of momentum about an axis, symbol L is the product to the moment of inertia and angular velocity (Iω). Angular momentum is a pseudo-vector quality, as it is connected in an isolated system. It is a scalar and is given a positive or negative sign as in the moment of force. When contending to systems, in which forces and motions do not all lie in one plane, the concept of the moment about a point is needed. The moment of a vector P, e.g., force or momentous pulsivity, from which a point 'A' is a pseudo-vector M equal to the vector product of r and P, where r is any line joining 'A' to any point 'B' on the line of action of P. The vector product M = r x p is independent of the position of 'B' and the relation between the scalar moment about an axis and the vector moment about which a point on the axis is that the scalar is the component of the vector in the direction of the axis.

The linear momentum of a particle 'p' is the product of the mass and the velocity of the particle. It is a vector quality directed through the particle in the direction of motion. The linear momentum of a body or of a system of particles is the vector sum of the linear momentums of the individual particle. If a body of mass 'M' is translated with a velocity 'V', its momentum is MV, which is the momentum of a particle of mass 'M' at the centre of gravity of the body. (1) In any system of mutually interacting or impinging particles, the linear momentum in any fixed direction remains unaltered unless there is an external force acting in that direction. (2) Similarly, the angular momentum is constant in the case of a system rotating about a fixed axis provided that no external torque is applied.

Subatomic particles fall into two major groups: The elementary particles and the hadrons. An elementary particle is not composed of any smaller particles and therefore represents the most fundamental form of matter. A hadron is composed of panicles, including the major particles called quarks, the most common of the subatomic particles, includes the major constituents of the atom -the electron is an elementary particle, and the proton and the neutron (hadrons). An elementary particle with zero charge and a rest mass equal to

1.674 9542 x 10-27 kg,

i.e., 939.5729 MeV / c2.

It is a constituent of every atomic nucleus except that of ordinary hydrogen, free neutrons decay by 'beta decay' with a mean life of 914 s. the neutron has spin ½, Isospin ½, and positive parity. It is a 'fermion' and is classified as a 'hadron' because it has strong interaction.

Neutrons can be ejected from nuclei by high-energy particles or photons, the energy required is usually about 8 MeV, although sometimes it is less. The fission is the most productive source. They are detected using all normal detectors of ionizing radiation because of the production of secondary particles in nuclear reactions. The discovery of the neutron (Chadwick, 1932) involved the detection of the tracks of protons ejected by neutrons by elastic collisions in hydrogenous materials.

Unlike other nuclear particles, neutrons are not repelled by the electric charge of a nucleus so they are very effective in causing nuclear reactions. When there is no 'threshold energy', the interaction 'cross sections' become very large at low neutron energies, and the thermal neutrons produced in great numbers by nuclear reactions cause nuclear reactions on a large scale. The capture of neutrons by the (n, Υ) process produces large quantities of radioactive materials, both useful nuclides such as 66Co for cancer therapy and undesirable by-products. The least energy required to cause a certain process, in particular a reaction in nuclear or particle physics. It is often important to distinguish between the energies required in the laboratory and in centre-of-mass co-ordinates. In 'fission' the splitting of a heavy nucleus of an atom into two or more fragments of comparable size usually as the result of the impact of a neutron on the nucleus. It is normally accompanied by the emission of neutrons or gamma rays. Plutonium, uranium, and thorium are the principle fissionable elements

In nuclear reaction, a reaction between an atonic nucleus and a bombarding particle or photon leading to the creation of a new nucleus and the possible ejection of one or more particles. Nuclear reactions are often represented by enclosing brackets and symbols for the incoming and final nuclides being shown outside the brackets. For example: 14N (α, p)17O.

Energy from nuclear fissions, on the whole, the nucleuses of atoms of moderate size are more tightly held together than the largest nucleus, so that if the nucleus of a heavy atom can be induced to split into two nuclei and moderate mass, there should be considerable release of energy. By Einstein' s law of the conservation of mass and energy, this mass and energy difference is equivalent to the energy released when the nucleons binding differences are equivalent to the energy released when the nucleons bind together. Y=this energy is the binding energy, the graph of binding per nucleon, EB / A increases rapidly up to a mass number of 50-69 (iron, nickel, etc.) and then decreases slowly. There are therefore two ways in which energy can be released from a nucleus, both of which can be released from the nucleus, both of which entail a rearrangement of nuclei occurring in the lower as having to curve into form its nuclei, in the upper, higher-energy part of the curve. The fission is the splitting of heavy atoms, such as uranium, into lighter atoms, accompanied by an enormous release of energy. Fusion of light nuclei, such as deuterium and tritium, releases an even greater quantity of energy.

The work that must be done to detach a single particle from a structure of free electrons of an atom or molecule to form a negative ion. The process is sometimes called 'electron capture, but the term is more usually applied to nuclear processes. As many atoms, molecules and free radicals from stable negative ions by capturing electrons to atoms or molecules to form a negative ion. The electron affinity is the least amount of work that must be done to separate from the ion. It is usually expressed in electro-volts

The uranium isotope 235U will readily accept a neutron but one-seventh of the nuclei stabilized by gamma emissions while six-sevenths split into two parts. Most of the energy released amounts to about 170 MeV, in the form of the kinetic energy of these fission fragments. In addition an averaged of 2.5 neutrons of average energy 2 MeV and some gamma radiation is produced. Further energy is released later by radioactivity of the fission fragments. The total energy released is about 3 x 10-11 joule per atom fissioned, i.e., 6.5 x 1013 joule per kg conserved.

To extract energy in a controlled manner from fissionable nuclei, arrangements must be made for a sufficient proportion of the neutrons released in the fissions to cause further fissions in their turn, so that the process is continuous, the minium mass of a fissile material that will sustain a chain reaction seems confined to nuclear weaponry. Although, a reactor with a large proportion of 235U or plutonium 239Pu in the fuel uses the fast neutrons as they are liberated from the fission, such a rector is called a 'fast reactor'. Natural uranium contains 0.7% of 235U and if the liberated neutrons can be slowed before they have much chance of meeting the more common 238U atom and then cause another fission. To slow the neutron, a moderator is used containing light atoms to which the neutrons will give kinetic energy by collision. As the neutrons eventually acquire energies appropriate to gas molecules at the temperatures of the moderator, they are then said to be thermal neutrons and the reactor is a thermal reactor.

Then, of course, the Thermal reactors, in typical thermal reactors, the fuel elements are rods embedded as a regular array in which the bulk of the moderator that the typical neutron from a fission process has a good chance of escaping from the relatively thin fuel rod and making many collisions with nuclei in the moderator before again entering a fuel element. Suitable moderators are pure graphite, heavy water (D2O), are sometimes used as a coolant, and ordinary water (H2O). Very pure materials are essential as some unwanted nuclei capture neutrons readily. The reactor core is surrounded by a reflector made of suitable material to reduce the escape of neutrons from the surface. Each fuel element is encased e. g., in magnesium alloy or stainless steel, to prevent escape of radioactive fission products. The coolant, which may be gaseous or liquid, flows along the channels over the canned fuel elements. There is an emission of gamma rays inherent in the fission process and, many of the fission products are intensely radioactive. To protect personnel, the assembly is surrounded by a massive biological shield, of concrete, with an inner iron thermal shield to protect the concrete from high temperatures caused by absorption of radiation.

To keep the power production steady, control rods are moved in or out of the assembly. These contain material that captures neutrons readily, e.g., cadmium or boron. The power production can be held steady by allowing the currents in suitably placed ionization chambers automatically to modify the settings of the rods. Further absorbent rods, the shut-down rods, are driven into the core to stop the reaction, as in an emergence if the control mechanism fails. To attain high thermodynamic efficiency so that a large proportion of the liberated energy can be used, the heat should be extracted from the reactor core at a high temperature.

In fast reactors no mediator is used, the frequency of collisions between neutrons and fissile atoms being creased by enriching the natural uranium fuel with 239Pu or additional 235U atoms that are fissioned by fast neutrons. The fast neutrons are thus built up a self-sustaining chain reaction. In these reactions the core is usually surrounded by a blanket of natural uranium into which some of the neutrons are allowed to escape. Under suitable conditions some of these neutrons will be captured by 238U atoms forming 239U atoms, which are converted to 239Pu. As more plutonium can be produced than required to enrich the fuel in the core, these are called 'fast breeder reactors'.

Thus and so, a neutral elementary particle with spin½, that only takes part in weak interactions. The neutrino is a lepton and exists in three types corresponding to the three types of charged leptons, that is, there are the electron neutrinos (ve) tauon neutrinos (vμ) and tauon neutrinos (vτ). The antiparticle of the neutrino is the antineutrino.

Neutrinos were originally thought to have a zero mass, but recently there have been some advances to an indirect experiment that evince to the contrary. In 1985 a Soviet team reported a measurement for the first time, of a non-zero neutrino mass. The mass measured was extremely small, some 10 000 times smaller than the mass of the electron. However, subsequent attempts to reproduce the Soviet measurement were unsuccessful. More recent (1998-99), the Super-Kamiokande experiment in Japan has provided indirect evidence for massive neutrinos. The new evidence is based upon studies of neutrinos, which are created when highly energetic cosmic rays bombard the earth's upper atmosphere. By classifying the interaction of these neutrinos according to the type of neutrino involved (an electron neutrino or muon neutrino), and counting their relative numbers as a function: An oscillatory behaviour may be shown to occur. Oscillation in this sense is the charging back and forth of the neutrino's type as it travels through space or matter. The Super-Kamiokande result indicates that muon neutrinos are changing into another type of neutrino, e.g., sterile neutrinos. The experiment does not, however, determine directly the masses, though the oscillations suggest very small differences in mass between the oscillating types.

The neutrino was first postulated (Pauli 1930)to explain the continuous spectrum of beta rays. It is assumed that there is the same amount of energy available for each beta decay of a particle nuclide and that energy is shared according to a statistical law between the electron and a light neutral particle, now classified as the anti-neutrino, ύe Later it was shown that the postulated particle would also conserve angular momentum and linear momentum in the beta decays.

In addition to beta decay, the electron neutrino is also associated with, for example, positron decay and electron capture:

22Na → 22Ne + e+ + ve

55Fe + e– → 55Mn + ve

The absorption of anti-neutrinos in matter by the process

2H + ΰe → n + e+

was first demonstrated by Reines and Cowan? The muon neutrino is generated in such processes as:

π+ → μ+ + vμ

Although the interactions of neutrinos are extremely weak the cross sections increase with energy and reaction can be studied at the enormous energies available with modern accelerators in some forms of 'grand unification theories', neutrinos are predicted to have a non-zero mass. Nonetheless, no evidences have been found to support this prediction.

The antiparticle of an electron, i.e., an elementary particle with electron mass and positive charge and equal to that of the electron. According to the relativistic wave mechanics of Dirac, space contains a continuum of electrons in states of negative energy. These states are normally unobservable, but if sufficient energy can be given, an electron may be raised into a state of positivity and becomes observable. The vacant state of negativity seems to behave as a positive particle of positive energy, which is observed as a positron.

A theory of elementary particles based on the idea that the fundamental entities are not point-like particles, but finite lines (strings) or closed loops formed by stings. The original idea was that an elementary particle was the result of a standing wave in a string. A considerable amount of theoretical effort has been put into development string theories. In particular, combining the idea of strings with that of super-symmetry, which has led to the idea with which correlation holds strongly with super-strings. This theory may be a more useful route to a unified theory of fundamental interactions than quantum field theory, simply because it's probably by some uvoided infinites that arise when gravitational interactions are introduced into field theories. Thus, superstring theory inevitably leads to particles of spin 2, identified as gravitons. String theory also shows why particles violate parity conservation in weak interactions.

Superstring theories involve the idea of higher dimensional spaces: 10 dimensions for fermions and 26 dimensions for bosons. It has been suggested that there are the normal 4 space-time dimensions, with the extra dimension being tightly 'curved'. Still, there are no direct experimental evidences for super-strings. They are thought to have a length of about 10-35 m and energies of 1014 GeV, which is well above the energy of any accelerator. An extension of the theory postulates that the fundamental entities are not one-dimensional but two-dimensional, i.e., they are super-membranes.

Allocations often other than what are previous than in time, awaiting the formidable combinations of what precedes the presence to the future, because of which the set of invariance of a system, a symmetry operation on a system is an operation that does not change the system. It is studied mathematically using 'Group Theory.' Some symmetries are directly physical, for instance the reelections and rotations for molecules and translations in crystal lattices. More abstractively the implicating inclinations toward abstract symmetries involve changing properties, as in the CPT Theorem and the symmetries associated with 'Gauge Theory.' Gauge theories are now thought to provide the basis for a description in all elementary particle interactions. The electromagnetic particle interactions are described by quantum electrodynamics, which is called Abelian gauge theory

Quantum field theory for which measurable quantities remain unchanged under a 'group transformation'. All these theories consecutive field transformations do not commute. All non-Abelian gauge theories are based on work proposed by Yang and Mills in 1954, describe the interaction between two quantum fields of fermions. In which particles represented by fields whose normal modes of oscillation are quantized. Elementary particle interactions are described by relativistically invariant theories of quantized fields, ie., By relativistic quantum field theories. Gauge transformations can take the form of a simple multiplication by a constant phase. Such transformations are called 'global gauge transformations'. In local gauge transformations, the phase of the fields is alterable by amounts that vary with space and time; i.e., $\Psi \rightarrow ei\theta\ (\chi)\ \Psi$, Where $\theta\ (\chi)$ is a function of space-time, as in Abelian gauge theories, consecutive field transformations commute,

$$\text{i.e., } \Psi \rightarrow ei\ \theta\ (\chi)\ ei\ \varphi\ \Psi = ei\ \varphi\ (\chi)\ ei\ \varphi\ (\chi)\ \Psi,$$

Where $\varphi\ (\chi)$ is another function of space and time. Quantum chromodynamics (the theory of the strong interaction) and electroweak and grand unified theories are all non-Abelian. In these theories consecutive field transformations do not commute. All non-Abelian gauge theories are based on work proposed by Yang and Mils, as Einstein's theory of general relativity can also be formulated as a local gauge theory.

A symmetry including both boson and fermions, in theories based on super-symmetry every boson has a corresponding boson. Th boson partners of existing fermions have names formed by prefacing the names of the fermion with an 's' (e.g., selection, squark, lepton). The names of the fermion partners of existing bosons are obtained by changing the terminal -on of the boson to -into (e.g., photons, gluons, and zino). Although, super-symmetries have not been observed experimentally, they may prove important in the search for a Unified Field Theory of the fundamental interactions.

The quark is a fundamental constituent of hadrons, i.e., of particles that take part in strong interactions. Quarks are never seen as free particles, which is substantiated by lack of experimental evidence for isolated quarks. The explanation given for this phenomenon in gauge theory is known a quantum chromodynamics, by which quarks are described, is that quark interaction become weaker as they come closer together and fall of a null-set factor, when the distance between them is zero. The converse of this proposition is that the attractive forces between quarks become stronger s they move, as this process has no limited, quarks can never separate from each other. In some theories, it is postulated that at very high-energy temperatures, as might have prevailed in the early universe, quarks can separate, te temperature at which this occurs is called the 'deconfinement temperatures'. Nevertheless, their existence has been demonstrated in high-energy scattering experiments and by symmetries in the properties of observed hadrons. They are regarded s elementary fermions, with spin ½, baryon number ⅓, strangeness 0 or = 1, and charm 0 or + 1. They are classified I six flavours[up (u), charm (c) and top (t), each with charge ⅔ the proton charge, down (d), strange (s) and bottom (b), each with – ⅓ the proton charge 1. Each type has an antiquark with reversed signs of charge, baryon number, strangeness, nd charm. The top quark has not been observed experimentally, but there are strong theoretical arguments for its existence.

The fractional charges of quarks are never observed in hadrons, since the quarks form combinations in which the sum of their charges is zero or integral. Hadrons can be either baryons or mesons, essentially, baryons are composed of three quarks while mesons are composed of a quark-antiquark pair. These components are bound together within the hadron by the exchange of particles known as gluons. Gluons are neutral massless gauge bosons, the quantum field theory of electromagnetic interactions discriminate themselves against the gluon as the analogue of the photon and with a quantum number known as 'colour' replacing that of electric charge. Each quark type (or flavour) comes in three colours (red, blue and green, say), where colour is simply a convenient label and has no connection with ordinary colour. Unlike the photon in quantum chromodynamics, which is electrically neutral, gluons in quantum chromodynamics carry colour and can therefore interact with themselves. Particles that carry colour are believed not to be able to exist in free particles. Instead, quarks and gluons are permanently confined inside hadrons (strongly interacting particles, such as the proton and the neutron).

The gluon self-interaction leads to the property known as 'asymptotic freedom', in which the interaction strength for th strong interaction decreases as the momentum transfer involved in an interaction increase. This allows perturbation theory to be used and quantitative comparisons to be made with experiment, similar to, but less precise than those possibilities of quantum chromodynamics. Quantum chromodynamics the being tested successfully in high energy muon-nucleon scattering experiments and in proton-antiproton and electron-positron collisions at high energies. Strong evidence for the existence of colour comes from measurements of the interaction rates for e+e– → hadrons and e+e– → μ+ μ–. The relative rate for these two processes is a factor of three larger than would be expected without colour, this factor measures directly the number of colours, i.e., for each quark flavour.

The quarks and antiquarks with zero strangeness and zero charm are the u, d, û and **d̄**. They form the combinations:

proton (uud), antiproton (**ūūd̄**)
neutron (uud), antineutron (**ūd̄d̄**)
pion: π+ (u**d̄**), π– (ūd), π0 (d**d̄**, uū).

The charge and spin of these particles are the sums of the charge and spin of the component quarks and/or antiquarks.

In the strange baryon, e.g., the Λ and Σ meons, either the quark or antiquark is strange. Similarly, the presence of one or more 'c' quarks leads to charmed baryons' 'a' 'c' or **č** to the charmed mesons. It has been found useful to introduce a further subdivision of quarks, each flavour coming in three colours (red, green, blue). Colour as used here serves simply as a convenient label and is unconnected with ordinary colour. A baryon comprises a red, a green, and a blue quark and a meson comprised a red and ant-red, a blue and ant-blue, or a green and antigreen quark and antiquark. In analogy with combinations of the three primary colours of light, hadrons carry no net colour, i.e., they are 'colourless' or 'white'. Only colourless objects can exist as free particles. The characteristics of the six quark flavours are shown in the table.

The cental feature of quantum field theory, is that the essential reality is a set of fields subject to the rules of special relativity and quantum mechanics, all else is derived as a consequence of the quantum dynamics of those fields. The quantization of fields is essentially an exercise in which we use complex mathematical models to analyse the field in terms of its associated quanta. And material reality as we know it in quantum field theory is constituted by the transformation and organization of fields and their associated quanta. Hence, this reality

Reveals a fundamental complementarity, in which particles are localized in space/time, and fields, which are not. In modern quantum field theory, all matter is composed of six strongly interacting quarks and six weakly interacting leptons. The six quarks are called up, down, charmed, strange, top, and bottom and have different rest masses and functional changes. The up and own quarks combine through the exchange of gluons to form protons and neutrons.

The 'lepton' belongs to the class of elementary particles, and does not take part in strong interactions. They have no substructure of quarks and are considered indivisible. They are all; fermions, and are categorized into six distinct types, the electron, muon, and tauon, which are all identically charged, but differ in mass, and the three neutrinos, which are all neutral and thought to be massless or nearly so. In their interactions the leptons appear to observe boundaries that define three families, each composed of a charged lepton and its neutrino. The families are distinguished mathematically by three quantum numbers, Ie, Iμ, and Iv lepton numbers called 'lepton numbers. In weak interactions their IeTOT, IμTOT and Iτ for the individual particles are conserved.

In quantum field theory, potential vibrations at each point in the four fields are capable of manifesting themselves in their complemtarity, their expression as individual particles. And the interactions of the fields result from the exchange of quanta that are carriers of the fields. The carriers of the field, known as messenger quanta, are the 'coloured' gluons for the strong-binding-force, of which the photon for electromagnetism, the intermediate boson for the weak force, and the graviton or gravitation. If we could re-create the energies present in the fist trillionths of trillionths of a second in the life o the universe, these four fields would, according to quantum field theory, become one fundamental field.

The movement toward a unified theory has evolved progressively from super-symmetry to super-gravity to string theory. In string theory the one-dimensional trajectories of particles, illustrated in the Feynman lectures, seem as if, in at all were possible, are replaced by the two-dimensional orbits of a string. In addition to introducing the extra dimension, represented by a smaller diameter of the string, string theory also features another mall but non-zero constant, with which is analogous to Planck's quantum of action. Since the value of the constant is quite small, it can be generally ignored but at extremely small dimensions. But since the constant, like Planck's constant is not zero, this results in departures from ordinary quantum field theory in very small dimensions.

Part of what makes string theory attractive is that it eliminates, or 'transforms away', the inherent infinities found in the quantum theory of gravity. And if the predictions of this theory are proven valid in repeatable experiments under controlled coeditions, it could allow gravity to be unified with the other three fundamental interactions. But even if string theory leads to this grand unification, it will not alter our understanding of ave-particle duality. While the success of the theory would reinforce our view of the universe as a unified dynamic process, it applies to very small dimensions, and therefore, does not alter our view of wave-particle duality.

While the formalism of quantum physics predicts that correlations between particles over space-like inseparability, of which are possible, it can say nothing about what this strange new relationship between parts (quanta) and the whole (cosmos) cause to result outside this formalism. This does not, however, prevent us from considering the implications in philosophical terms. As the philosopher of science Errol Harris noted in thinking about the special character of wholeness in modern physics, a unity without internal content is a blank or empty set and is not recognizable as a whole. A collection of merely externally related parts does not constitute a whole in that the parts will not be 'mutually adaptive and complementary to one-another.'

Wholeness requires a complementary relationship between unity and difference and is governed by a principle of organization determining the interrelationship between parts. This organizing principle must be universal to a genuine whole and implicit in all parts constituting the whole, even the whole is exemplified only in its parts. This principle of order, Harris continued, 'is nothing really in and of itself. It is the way he parts are organized, and another constituent additional to those that constitute the totality.'

In a genuine whole, the relationship between the constituent parts must be 'internal or immanent' ion the parts, as opposed to a more spurious whole in which parts appear to disclose wholeness dur to relationships that are external to the arts. The collection of parts that would allegedly constitute the whole in classical physics is an example of a spurious whole. Parts continue a genuine whole when the universal principle of order is inside the parts and hereby adjusts each to all so that they interlock and become mutually complementary. This not only describes the character of the whole revealed in both relativity theory and quantum mechanics. It is also consistent with the manner in which we have begun to understand the relations between parts and whole in modern biology.

Modern physics also reveals, claimed Harris, complementary relationship between the differences between parts that constitute and the universal ordering principle that are Immanent in each part. While the whole cannot be finally disclosed in the analysis of the parts, the study of the differences between parts provides insights into the dynamic structure of the whole present in each part. The part can never, however, be finally isolated from the web of relationships that discloses the interconnections with the whole, and any attempt to do so results in ambiguity.

Much of the ambiguity in attempts to explain the character of wholes in both physics and biology derives from the assumption that order exists between or outside parts. Yet order in complementary relationships between difference and sameness in any physical event is never external to that event, and the cognations are immanent in the event. From this perspective, the addition of non-locality to this picture of the distributive constitution in dynamic function of wholeness is not surprising. The relationships between part, as quantum event apparent in observation or measurement, and the undissectable whole, calculate on in but are not described by the instantaneous correlations between measurements in space-like separate regions, is another extension of the part-whole complementarity in modern physics.

If the universe is a seamlessly interactive system that evolves to higher levels of complex and complicating regularities of which ae lawfully emergent in property of systems, we can assume that the cosmos is a single significant whole that evinces progressive order in complementary relations to its parts. Given that this whole exists in some sense within all parts (quanta), one can then argue that in operates in self-reflective fashion and is the ground from all emergent plexuities. Since human consciousness evinces self-reflective awareness in te human brain (well protected between the cranium walls) and since this brain, like all physical phenomena, can b viewed as an emergent property of the whole, it is unreasonable to conclude, in philosophical terms at least, that the universe is conscious.

Nevertheless, since the actual character of this seamless whole cannot be represented or reduced to its parts, it lies, quite laterally, beyond all human representation or descriptions. If one chooses to believe that the universe be a self-reflective and self-organizing whole, this lends no support whatsoever to conceptual representation of design, meaning, purpose, intent, or plan associated with mytho-religious or cultural heritage. However, if one does not accept this view of the universe, there is noting in the scientific description of nature that can be used to refute this position. On the other hand, it is no longer possible to argue that a profound sense of unity with the whole, which has long been understood as foundation of religious experiences, but can be dismissed, undermined, or invalidated with appeals to scientific knowledge.

While we have consistently tried to distinguish between scientific knowledge and philosophical speculation based on this of what is obtainable, let us be quite clear on one point - there is no empirically valid causal linkage between the former and the latter. Those who wish to dismiss the speculative base on which is obviously free to do as done. However, there is another conclusion to be drawn, in that is firmly grounded in scientific theory and experiment there is no basis in the scientific descriptions of nature for believing in the radical Cartesian division between mind and world sanctioned by classical physics. Clearly, his radical separation between mind and world was a macro-level illusion fostered by limited awareness of the actual character of physical reality nd by mathematical idealizations extended beyond the realms of their applicability.

Nevertheless, the philosophical implications might prove in themselves as a criterial motive in debative consideration to how our proposed new understanding of the relationship between parts and wholes in physical reality might affect the manner in which we deal with some major real-world problems. This will issue to demonstrate why a timely resolution of these problems is critically dependent on a renewed dialogue between members of the cultures of human-social scientists and scientist-engineers. We will also argue that the resolution of these problems could be dependent on a renewed dialogue between science and religion.

As many scholars have demonstrated, the classical paradigm in physics has greatly influenced and conditioned our understanding and management of human systems in economic and political realities. Virtually all models of these realities treat human systems as if they consist of atomized units or parts that interact with one another in terms of laws or forces external to or between the parts. These systems are also viewed as hermetic or closed and, thus, its discreteness, separateness and distinction.

Consider, for example, how the classical paradigm influenced or thinking about economic reality. In the eighteenth and nineteenth centuries, the founders of classical economics -figures like Adam Smith, David Ricardo, and Thomas Malthus conceived of the economy as a closed system in which intersections between parts (consumer, produces, distributors, etc.) are controlled by forces external to the parts (supply and demand). The central legitimating principle of free market economics, formulated by Adam Smith, is that lawful or law-like forces external to the individual units function as an invisible hand. This invisible hand, said Smith, frees the units to pursue their best interests, moves the economy forward, and in general legislates the behaviour of parts in the best vantages of the whole. (The resemblance between the invisible hand and Newton's universal law of gravity and between the relations of parts and wholes in classical economics and classical physics should be transparent.)

Content-involving states are actions individuated in partly reference to the agent's relations to things and properties in his environment. Wanting to see a particular movie and believing that the building over there is a cinema showing it makes rationally the action of walking in the direction of that building.

However, in the general philosophy of mind, and more recently, desire has received new attention from those who understand mental states in terms of their causal or functional role in their determination of rational behaviour, and in particular from philosophers trying to understand the semantic content or intentional; character of mental states in those terms as 'functionalism', which attributes for the functionalist who thinks of mental states and evens as a causally mediating between a subject's sensory inputs and that of the subject's ensuing behaviour. Functionalism itself is the stronger doctrine that makes a mental state the type of state it-is-in. That of causing of being inflected by some distressful pain, a smell of violets, a belief that the koala, an arboreal Australian marsupial (Phascolarctos cinereus), is seriously dangerous, in that the functional relation it bears to the subject's perceptual stimuli, behavioural responses, and other mental states.

In the general philosophy of mind, and more recently, desire has received new attention from those who would understand mental stat n terms of their causal or functional role in the determination of rational behaviour, and in particularly from philosophers trying to understand the semantic content or the intentionality of mental states in those terms.

Conceptual (sometimes computational, cognitive, causal or functional) role semantics (CRS) entered philosophy through the philosophy of language, not the philosophy of mind. The core idea behind the conceptual role of semantics in the philosophy of language is that the way linguistic expressions are related to one another determines what the expressions in the language mean. There is a considerable affinity between the conceptual role of semantics and structuralist semiotics that has been influence in linguistics. According to the latter, languages are to be viewed as systems of differences: The basic idea is that the semantic force (or, 'value') of an utterance is determined by its position in the space of possibilities that one' language offers. Conceptual role semantics also has affinities with what the artificial intelligence researchers call 'procedural semantics', the essential idea here is that providing a compiler for a language is equivalent to specifying a semantic theory of procedures that a computer is instructed to execute by a program.

Nevertheless, according to the conceptual role of semantics, the meaning of a thought is determined by the recollected role in a system of states, to specify a thought is not to specify its truth or referential condition, but to specify its role, Walter and twin-Walter's thoughts though different truth and referential conditions, share the same conceptual role, and it is by virtue of this commonality that they behave type-identically. If Water and twin-Walter each has a belief that he would express by 'water quenches thirst' the conceptual role of semantics can be explained predict, they're dripping their cans into H2O and XYZ respectfully. Thus the conceptual role of semantics would seem as though not to Jerry Fodor, who rejects of the conceptual role of semantics for both external and internal problems.

Nonetheless, if, as Fodor contents, thoughts have recombinable linguistic ingredients, then, of course, for the conceptual role of semantic theorists, questions arise about the role of expressions in the language of thought as well as in the public language we speak and write. And, according, the conceptual role of semantic theorbists divides not only over their aim, but also about conceptual roles in semantic's proper domains. Two questions avail themselves. Some hold that public meaning is somehow derivative (or inherited) from an internal mental language (mentalese) and that a mentalese expression has autonomous meaning (partly). expressionSo, for example, the inscriptions on this page call for their understanding translation, or at least, transliterations. Expression into the language of thought: Representations in the brain require no such translation or transliteration but to express of others to sustain that the language of thought is virtuously a language internalized and that it is expressions (or primary) meaning in merit of their conceptual role.

After one decides upon the aims and the proper province of the conceptual role for semantics, the relations among public expressions or mental-constitute their conceptual roles. Because most conceptual roles of semantics as theorists leave the notion of the role in a conceptuality as a blank cheque, the options are open-ended. The conceptual role of a [mental] expression might be its causal association: Any disposition too token or example, utter or think on the expression 'e' when tokening another 'e' or 'a' an ordered n-tuple < e ' e"', . . . >, or vice versa, can matter to the conceptional function that 'e', a more common option is characterized in a conceptual role not causative of but inferentially (these need be compatible, contingent upon one's attitude about the naturalization of inference): The conceptual role of an expression 'e' in 'L' might consist of the set of actual and potential inferences form 'e', or, as a more common, the ordered pair consisting of these two sets. Or, if sentences have non-derived inferential roles, what would it mean to talk of the inferential role of words? Some have found it natural to think of the inferential role of as words, as represented by the set of inferential roles of the sentence in which the word appears.

The expectation of expecting that one sort of thing could serve all these tasks went hand in hand with what has come to b e called the 'Classical View' of concepts, according to which they had an 'analysis' consisting of conditions that are individually necessary and jointly sufficient for their satisfaction, which are known to any competent user of them. The standard example is the especially simple one of the [bachelor], which seems to be identical to [eligible unmarried male]. A more interesting, but analysis was traditionally thought to be [justified true belief].

This Classical View seems to offer an illuminating answer to a certain form of metaphysical question: In virtue of what is something the kind of thing it is -, i.e., in virtue of what may a bachelor be a bachelor? And it does so in a way that support counterfactual: It tells us what would satisfy the conception situations other than the actual ones (although all actual bachelors might turn out to be freckled, it's possible that there might be unfreckled ones, since the analysis does not exclude that). The view also seems to offer an answer to an epistemological question of how people seem to know a priori (or independently of experience) about the nature of many things, e.g., that bachelors are unmarried: It is constitutive of the competency (or possession) conditions of a concept that they know its analysis, at least on reflection.

The Classic View, however, has alway ss had to face the difficulty of primitive concepts: It's all well and good to claim that competence consists in some sort of mastery of a definition, but what about the primitive concept in which a process of definition must ultimately end: Here the British Empiricism of the seventeenth century began to offer a solution: All the primitives were sensory, indeed, they expanded the Classical View to include the claim, now often taken uncritically for granted in the discussions of that view, that all concepts are 'derived from experience':'Every idea is derived from a corresponding impression', in the work of John Locke (1632-1704), George Berkeley (1685-1753) and David Hume (1711-76) were often thought to mean that concepts were somehow composed of introspectible categorized mental items, 'images', 'impressions', and so on, that were ultimately decomposable into basic sensory parts. Thus, Hume analysed the concept of [material object] as involving certain regularities in our sensory experience and [cause] as involving spatio-temporal contiguity ad constant conjunction.

The Irish 'idealist' George Berkeley, noticed a problem with this approach that every generation has had to rediscover: If a concept is a sensory impression, like an image, then how does one distinguish a general concept [triangle] from a more particular one-say, [isosceles triangle]-that would serve in imagining the general one. More recently, Wittgenstein (1953) called attention to the multiple ambiguity of images. And in any case, images seem quite hopeless for capturing the concepts associated with logical terms (what is the image for negation or possibility?) Whatever the role of such representation, full conceptual competency must involve something more.

Conscionably, in addition to images and impressions and other sensory items, a full account of concepts needs to consider is of logical structure. This is precisely what the logical positivist did, focussing on logically structured sentences instead of sensations and images, transforming the empiricist involvement into the famous 'Verifiability Theory of Meaning', the meaning of s sentence is the means by which it is confirmed or refuted, ultimately by sensory experience the meaning or concept associated with a predicate is the means by which people confirm or refute whether something satisfies it.

This once-popular position has come under much attack in philosophy in the last fifty years, in the first place, fewer, if any, successful 'reductions' of ordinary concepts like [material objects] [cause] to purely sensory concepts have ever been achieved. Our concept of material object and causation seem to go far beyond mere sensory experience, just as our concepts in a highly theoretical science seem to go far beyond the often only meagre exposures to the evidence is that we can adduce for them.

The American philosopher of mind Jerry Alan Fodor and LePore (1992) have recently argued that the arguments for meaning holism are, however less than compelling, and that there are important theoretical reasons for holding out for an entirely atomistic account of concepts. On this view, concepts have no 'analyses' whatsoever: They are simply ways in which people are directly related to individual properties in the world, which might obtain for someone, for one concept but not for any other: In principle, someone might have the concept [bachelor] and no other concepts at all, much less any 'analysis' of it. Such a view goes hand in hand with Fodor's rejection of not only verificationist, but any empiricist account of concept learning and construction: Given the failure of empiricist construction. Fodor (1975, 1979) notoriously argued that concepts are not constructed or 'derived' from experience at all, but are and nearly enough as they are all innate.

The deliberating considerations about whether there are innate ideas are much as it is old, it, nonetheless, takes from Plato (429-347 Bc) in the 'Meno' the problems to which the doctrine of 'anamnesis' is an answer in Plato's dialogue. If we do not understand something, then we cannot set about learning it, since we do not know enough to know how to begin. Teachers also come across the problem in the shape of students, who cannot understand why their work deserves lower marks than that of others. The worry is echoed in philosophies of language that see the infant as a 'little linguist', having to translate their environmental surroundings and grasp on or upon the upcoming language. The language of thought hypothesis was especially associated with Fodor that mental processing occurs in a language different from one's ordinary native language, but underlying and explaining our competence with it. The idea is a development of the Chomskyan notion of an innate universal grammar. It is a way of drawing the analogy between the workings of the brain or the minds and of the standard computer, since computer programs are linguistically complex sets of instruments whose execution explains the surface behaviour of computer. Just as an explanation of ordinary language has not found universal favour. It apparently only explains ordinary representational powers by invoking innate things of the same sort, and it invites the image of the learning infant translating the language whose own powers are a mysterious biological given.

René Descartes (1596-1650) and Gottfried Wilhelm Leibniz (1646-1716), defended the view that mind contains innate ideas: Berkeley, Hume and Locke attacked it. In fact, as we now conceive the great debate between European Rationalism and British Empiricism in the seventeenth and eighteenth centuries, the doctrine of innate ideas is a central bone of contention: Rationalist typically claim that knowledge is impossible without a significant stoke of general innate concepts or judgements: Empiricist argued that all ideas are acquired from experience. This debate is replayed with more empirical content and with considerably greater conceptual complexity in contemporary cognitive science, most particularly within the domain of psycholinguistic theory and cognitive developmental theory.

Some of the philosophers may be cognitive scientist other's concern themselves with the philosophy of cognitive psychology and cognitive science. Since the inauguration of cognitive science these disciplines have attracted much attention from certain philosophes of mind. The attitudes of these philosophers and their reception by psychologists vary considerably. Many cognitive psychologists have little interest in philosophical issues. Cognitive scientists are, in general, more receptive.

Fodor, because of his early involvement in sentence processing research, is taken seriously by many psycholinguists. His modularity thesis is directly relevant to question about the interplay of different types of knowledge in language understanding. His innateness hypothesis, however, is generally regarded as unhelpful. And his prescription that cognitive psychology is primarily about propositional attitudes is widely ignored. The American philosopher of mind, Daniel Clement Dennett (1942-)whose recent work on consciousness treats a topic that is highly controversial, but his detailed discussion of psychological research finding has enhanced his credibility among psychologists. In general, however, psychologists are happy to get on with their work without philosophers telling them about their 'mistakes'.

Connectionmism has provided a somewhat different reaction mg philosophers. Some-mainly those who, for other reasons, were disenchanted with traditional artificial intelligence research-have welcomed this new approach to understanding brain and behaviour. They have used the success, apparently or otherwise, of connectionist research, to bolster their arguments for a particular approach to explaining behaviour. Whether this neurophilosophy will eventually be widely accepted is a different question. One of its main dangers is succumbing to a form of reductionism that most cognitive scientists and many philosophers of mind, find incoherent.

One must be careful not to caricature the debate. It is too easy to see the argument as one's existing in or belonging to an individuals inherently congenital elemental for the placing of Innatists, who argue that all concepts of all of linguistic knowledge is innate (and certain remarks of Fodor and of Chomsky lead themselves in this interpretation) against empiricist who argue that there is no innate cognitive structure in which one need appeal in explaining the acquisition of language or the facts of cognitive development (an extreme reading of the American philosopher Hilary Putnam 1926-). But this debate would be a silly and a sterile debate indeed. For obviously, something is innate. Brains are innate. And the structure of the brain must constrain the nature of cognitive and linguistic development to some degree. Equally obvious, something is learned and is learned as opposed too merely grown as limbs or hair growth. For not all of the world's citizens end up speaking English, or knowing the Relativity Theory. The interesting questions then all concern exactly what is innate, to what degree it counts as knowledge, and what is learned and to what degree its content and structure are determined by innately specified cognitive structure. And that seems as plenty enough to be debated.

The arena in which the innateness takes place has been prosecuted with the greatest vigour is that of language acquisition, and it is appropriately to begin there. But it will be extended to the domain of general knowledge and reasoning abilities through the investigation of the development of object constancy-the disposition to concept of physical objects as persistent when unobserved and to reason about their properties locations when they are not perceptible.

The most prominent exponent of the innateness hypothesis in the domain of language acquisition is Chomsky (1296, 1975). His research and that of his colleagues and students is responsible for developing the influence and powerful framework of transformational grammar that dominates current linguistic and psycholinguistic theory. This body of research has amply demonstrated that the grammar of any human language is a highly systematic, abstract structure and that there are certain basic structural features shared by the grammars of all human language s, collectively called 'universal grammar'. Variations among the specific grammars of the world's ln languages can be seen as reflecting different settings of a small number of parameters that can, within the constraints of universal grammar, take may have several different valued. All of type principal arguments for the innateness hypothesis in linguistic theory on this central insight about grammars. The principal arguments are these: (1) The argument from the existence of linguistic universals, (2) the argument from patterns of grammatical errors in early language learners: (3) The poverty of the stimulus argument, (4) the argument from the case of fist language learning (5) the argument from the relative independence of language learning and general intelligence, and (6) The argument from the moduarity of linguistic processing.

Innatists argue (Chomsky 1966, 1975) that the very presence of linguistic universals argue for the innateness of linguistic of linguistic knowledge, but more importantly and more compelling that the fact that these universals are, from the standpoint of communicative efficiency, or from the standpoint of any plausible simplicity reflectively adventitious. These are many conceivable grammars, and those determined by universal grammars, and those determined by universal grammar are not ipso facto the most efficient or the simplest. Nonetheless, all human languages satisfy the constraints of universal grammar. Since either the communicative environment or the communicative tasks can explain this phenomenon. It is reasonable to suppose that it is explained by the structures of the mind-and therefore, by the fact that the principles of universal grammar lie innate in the mind and constrain the language that a human can acquire.

Hilary Putnam argues, by appeal to a common-sens e ancestral language by its descendants. Or it might turn out that despite the lack of direct evidence at present are the feature of universal grammar in fact do serve either the goals of commutative efficacy or simplicity according in a metric of psychological importance. Finally, is the empiricist pointed out, the very existence of universal grammar might be a trivial logical artefact: For one thing, many finite sets of structure es whether some features in common. Since there are some finite numbers of languages, it follows trivially that there are features they all share. Moreover, it is argued that many features of universal grammar are interdependent. On one, in fact, the set of fundamentally the same mental principle shared by the world's languages may be rather small. Hence, even if these are innately determined, the amount not of innate knowledge thereby, required may be quite small as compared with the total corpus of general linguistic knowledge acquired by the first language learner.

These relies are rendered less plausible, innatists argue, when one considers the fact that the error's language learners make in acquiring their first language seem to be driven far more by abstract features of gramma r than by any available input data. So, despite receiving correct examples of irregular plurals or past-tense forms for verbs, and despite having correctly formed the irregular forms for those words, children will often incorrectly regularize irregular verbs once acquiring mastery of the rule governing regulars in their language. And in general, not only the correct inductions of linguistic rules by young language learners but more importantly, given the absence of confirmatory data and the presence of refuting data, children's erroneous inductions always consistent with universal gramma r, often simply representing the incorrect setting of a parameter in the grammar. More generally, innatists argue (Chomsky 1966 & Crain, 1991) all grammatical rules that have ever been observed satisfy the structure-dependence constraint. That is, more linguistics and psycholinguistics argue that all known grammatical rules of all of the world's languages, including the fragmentary languages of young children must be started as rules governing hierarchical sentence structure, and not governing, say, sequence of words. Many of these, such as the constituent-command constraint governing anaphor, are highly abstract indeed, and appear to be respected by even very young children. Such constrain may, innatists argue, be necessary conditions of learning natural language in the absence of specific instruction, modelling and correct, conditions in which all first language learners acquire their native language.

Importantly among empiricist who rely to these observations derive from recent studies of 'conceptionist' models of first language acquisition. For which an axiomatically distinct manifestation acknowledged for being other than what seems to be the case, in that for subjecting reasons for being in the 'integrated connection system'. Though not being previously trained to represent any subset universal grammar, which is induced grammatically the change for which would include a large set of regular forms and fewer irregulars. It also tends to over-regularize, exhibiting the same U-shape learning curve seen in human language acquire learning systems that induce grammatical systems acquire 'accidental' rules on which they are not explicitly trained but which are not explicit with those upon which they are trained, suggesting, that as children acquire portions of their grammar, they may accidentally 'learn' correct consistent rules, which may be correct in human languages, but which then must be 'unlearned' in they're home language. On the other hand, such 'empiricist' language acquisition systems have yet to demonstrating their ability to induce a sufficient wide range of the rules hypothesize to be comprised by universal grammar to constitute a definitive empirical argument for the possibility of natural language acquisition in the absence of a powerful set of innate constraints.

The poverty of the stimulus argument has been of enormous influence in innateness debates, though its soundness is hotly contested. Chomsky notes that (1) the examples of their targe t language to which the language learner is exposed are always jointly compatible with an infinite number of alterative grammars, and so vastly under-determine the grammar of the language, and (2) The corpus always contains many examples of ungrammatical sentences, which should in fact serves as falsifiers of any empirically induced correct grammar of the language, and (3) there is, in general, no explicit reinforcement of correct utterances or correction of incorrect utterances, sharpness either in the learner or by those in the immediate training environment. Therefore, he argues, since it is impossible to explain the learning of the correct grammar-a task accomplished b all normal children within a very few years-on the basis of any available data or known learning algorithms, it must be ta the grammar is innately specified, and is merely 'triggered' by relevant environmental cues.

Opponents of the linguistic innateness hypothesis, however, point out that the circumstance that the American linguistic, philosopher and political activist, Noam Avram Chomsky (1929-), who believes that the speed with which children master their native language cannot be explained by learning theory, but requires acknowledging an innate disposition of the mind, an unlearned, innate and universal grammar, suppling the kinds of rule that the child will a priori understand to be embodied in examples of speech with which it is confronted in computational terms, unless the child came bundled with the right kind of software. It cold not catch onto the grammar of language as it in fact does.

As it is wee known from arguments due to the Scottish philosopher David Hume (1978, the Austrian philosopher Ludwig Wittgenstein (1953), the American philosopher Nelson Goodman ()1972) and the American logician and philosopher Aaron Saul Kripke (1982), that in all cases of empirical abduction, and of training in the use of a word, data underdetermining the theories. Th is moral is emphasized by the American philosopher Willard van Orman Quine (1954, 1960) as the principle of the undetermined theory by data. But we, nonetheless, do abduce adequate theories in silence, and we do learn the meaning of words. And it could be bizarre to suggest that all correct scientific theories or the facts of lexical semantics are innate.

Nonetheless, Innatists rely, when the empiricist relies on the underdermination of theory by data as a counterexample, a significant disanalogousness with language acquisition is ignored: The abduction of scientific theories is a difficult, labourious process, taking a sophisticated theorist a great deal of time and deliberated effort. First language acquisition, by contrast, is accomplished effortlessly and very quickly by a small child. The enormous relative ease with which such a complex and abstract domain is mastered by such a naïve 'theorist' is evidence for the innateness of the knowledge achieved.

Empiricist such as the American philosopher Hilary Putnam (1926-) have rejoined that Innatists underestimate the amount of time that language learning actually takes, focussing only on the number of years from the apparent onset of acquisition to the achievement of relative mastery over the grammar. Instead of noting how short this interval, they argue, one should count the total number of hours spent listening to language and speaking during h time. That number is in fact quite large and is comparable to the number of hours of study and practice required the acquisition of skills that are not argued to deriving from innate structures, such as chess playing or musical composition. Hence, they are taken into consideration. Language learning looks like one more case of human skill acquisition than like a special unfolding of innate knowledge.

Innatists, however, note that while the case with which most such skills are acquired depends on general intelligence, language is learned with roughly equal speed, and too roughly the same level of general intelligence. In fact even significantly retarded individuals, assuming special language deficits, acquire their native language on a tine-scale and to a degree comparable to that of normally intelligent children. The language acquisition faculty, hence, appears to allow access to a sophisticated body of knowledge independent of the sophistication of the general knowledge of the language learner.

Empiricist's reply that this argument ignores the centrality of language in a wide range of human activities and consequently the enormous attention paid to language acquisition by retarded youngsters and their parents or caretakers. They argue as well, that Innatists overstate the parity in linguistic competence between retarded children and children of normal intelligence.

Innatists point out that the 'modularity' of language processing is a powerful argument for the innateness of the language faculty. There is a large body of evidence, Innatists argue, for the claim that the processes that subserve the acquisition, understanding and production of language are quite distinct and independent of those that subserve general cognition and learning. That is to say, that language learning and language processing mechanisms and the knowledge they embody are domain specific-grammar and grammatical learning and utilization mechanisms are not used outside of language processing. They are informationally encapsulated-only, but linguistic information is relevant to language acquisition and processing. They are mandatory, but language learning and language processing are automatic. Moreover, language is subserved by specific dedicated neural structures, damage to which predictable and systematically impairs linguistic functioning. All of this suggests a specific 'mental organ', to use Chomsky's phrase, that has evolved in the human cognitive system specifically in order to make language possible. The specific structure is organ simultaneously constrains the range of possible human language s and guide the learning of a child's target language, later masking rapid on-line language processing possibly. The principles represented in this organ constitute the innate linguistic knowledge of the human being. Additional evidence for the early operation of such an innate language acquisition module is derived from the many infant studies that show that infants selectively attend to sound streams that are prosodically appropriate that have pauses at clausal boundaries, and that contain linguistically permissible phonological sequence.

It is fair to ask where we get the powerful inner code whose representational elements need only systematic construction to express, for example, the thought that cyclotrons are bigger than black holes. But on this matter, the language of thought theorist has little to say. All that 'concept' learning could be (assuming it is to be some kind of rational process and not due to mere physical maturation or a bump on the head). According to the language of thought theorist, is the trying out of combinations of existing representational elements to see if a given combination captures the sense (as evinced in its use) of some new concept. The consequence is that concept learning, conceived as the expansion of our representational resources, simply does not happen. What happens instead is that the work with a fixed, innate repertoire of elements whose combination and construction must express any content we can ever learn to understand.

Representationalism typifies the conforming generality for which of its accomplished manner that by and large induce the doctrine that the mind (or sometimes the brain) works on representations of the things and features of things that we perceive or thing about. In the philosophy of perception the view is especially associated with the French Cartesian philosopher Nicolas Malebranche (1638-1715) and the English philosopher John Locke (1632-1704), who, holding that the mind is the container for ideas, held that of our real ideas, some are adequate, and some are inadequate. Those that have inadequateness to those represented as archetypes that the mind supposes them taken from which it tends them to stand for, and to which it refers them. The problem in this account was mercilessly exposed by the French theologian and philosopher Antoine Arnauld (1216-94) and the French critic of Cartesianism Simon Foucher (1644-96), writing against Malebranche, and by the idealist George Berkeley, writing against Locke. The fundamental problem is that the mind is 'supposing' its ds to represent something else, but it has no access to this something else, with the exception by forming another idea. The difficulty is to understand how the mind ever escapes from the world of representations, or, acquire genuine content pointing beyond themselves in more recent philosophy, the analogy between the mind and a computer has suggested that the mind or brain manipulate signs and symbols, thought of as like the instructions in a machine's program of aspects of the world. The point is sometimes put by saying that the mind, and its theory, become a syntactic engine rather than a semantic engine. Representation is also attacked, at least as a central concept in understanding the 'pragmatists' who emphasize instead the activities surrounding a use of language than what they see as a mysterious link between mind and world.

Representations, along with mental states, especially beliefs and thought, are said to exhibit 'intentionality' in that they refer or to stand for something other than of what is the possibility of it being something else. The nature of this special property, however, has seemed puling. Not only is intentionality often assumed to be limited to humans, and possibly a few other species, but the property itself appears to resist characterization in physicalist terms. The problem is most obvious in the case of 'arbitrary' signs, like words, where it is clear that there is no connection between the physical properties of a word and what it demotes, and, yet it remains for Iconic representation.

Early attempts tried to establish the link between sign and object via the mental states of the sign and symbols' user. A symbol # stands for ✷for 'S' if it triggers a ✷-idea in 'S'. On one account, the reference of # is the ✷idea itself. Open the major account, the denomination of # is whatever the ✷-idea denotes. The first account is problematic in that it fails to explain the link between symbols and the world. The second is problematic in that it just shifts the puzzle inward. For example, if the word 'table' triggers the image '–' or 'TABLE' what gives this mental picture or word any reference of all, let alone the denotation normally associated with the word 'table'?

An alternative to an adequate conception of mind and its relationship to matter should explain how it is possible of the world and in particular to themselves have a causal influence of the physical world. It is easy to think that this must be impossible: It takes a physical cause to have a physical effect. Yet, everyday experience and theory alike show that it is commonplace. Consciousness could hardly have a measure of the success of any theory of mind and body that it should enable us to avoid 'epiphenomenalism'. Mentalistic theories has been to adopt a behaviouristic analysis. Wherefore, this account # denotes ✷for 'S' is explained along the lines of either (1) 'S' is disposed to behave to # as to ✷: or (2) 'S' is disposed to behave in ways appropriate to ✷when presented #. Both versions prove faulty in that the very notions of the behaviour associated with or appropriate to ✷ are obscure. In addition, once seems to be no reasonable correlations between behaviour toward sign and behaviour toward their objects that is capable of accounting for the referential relations.

A currently influential attempt to 'naturalize' the representation relation takes its use from indices. The crucial link between sign and object is established by some causal connection between ✷and #, whereby it is allowed, nonetheless, that such a causal relation is not sufficient for full-blown intention representation. An increase in temperature causes the mercury to raise the thermometer but the mercury level is not a representation for the thermometer. In order for # to represent ✸to S's activities. The flunctuational economy of S's activity. The notion of 'function', in turn is yet to be spelled out along biological or other lines so as to remain within 'naturalistic' constraints as being natural. This approach runs into problems in specifying a suitable notion of 'function' and in accounting for the possibility of misrepresentation. Also, it is no obvious how to extend the analysis to encompass the semantical force of more abstract or theoretical symbols. These difficulties are further compounded when one takes into account the social factors that seem to play a role in determining the denotative properties of our symbols.

On that point, it remains the problems faced in providing a reductive naturalistic analysis of representation has led many to doubt that this task is achieved or necessary. Although a story can be told about some words or signs what were learned via association of other causal connections with their referents, there is no reason to believe ht the 'stand-for' relation, or semantic notions in general, can be reduced to or eliminated in favour of non-semantic terms.

Although linguistic and pictorial representations are undoubtedly the most prominent symbolic forms we employ, the range of representational systems human understands and regularly use is surprisingly large. Sculptures, maps, diagrams, graphs. Gestures, music nation, traffic signs, gauges, scale models, and tailor's swatches are but a few of the representational systems that play a role in communication, though, and the guidance of behaviour. Even, the importance and prevalence of our symbolic activities has been taken as a hallmark of human.

What is it that distinguishes items that serve as representations from other objects or events? And what distinguishes the various kinds of symbols from each other? As for the first question, there has been general agreement that the basic notion of a representation involves one thing's 'standing for', 'being about', referring to or denoting' something else. The major debates have been over the nature of this connection between a reorientation and that which it represents. As for the second question, perhaps, the most famous and extensive attempt to organize and differentiate among alternative forms of representation is found in the works of the American philosopher of science Charles Sanders Peirce (1839-1914) who graduated from Harvard in 1859, and apart from lecturing at John Hopkins university from 1879 to 1884, had almost no teaching, nonetheless, Peirce's theory of signs is complex, involving a number of concepts and distinctions that are no longer paid much heed. The aspects of his theory that remains influential and ie widely cited is his division of signs into Icons, Indices and Symbols. Icons are the designs that are said to be like or resemble the things they represent, e.g., portrait painting. Indices are signs that are connected in their objects by some causal dependency, e.g., smoke as a sign of fire. Symbols are those signs that are used and related to their object by virtue of use or associations: They a arbitrary labels, e.g., the word 'table'. This tripartite division among signs, or variants of this division, is routinely put forth to explain differences in the way representational systems are thought to establish their links to the world. Further, placing a representation in one of the three divisions has been used to account for the supposed differences between conventional and non-conventional representations, between representations that do and do not require learning to understand, and between representations, like language, that need to be read, and those which do not require interpretation. Some theorbists, moreover, have maintained that it is only the use of symbols that exhibits or indicates the presence of mind and mental states.

Over the years, this tripartite division of signs, although often challenged, has retained its influence. More recently, an alterative approach to representational systems (or as he calls them 'symbolic systems') has been put forth by the American philosopher Nelson Goodman (1906-98) whose classical problem of 'induction' is often phrased in terms of finding some reason to expect that nature is uniform, in Fact, Fiction, and Forecast (1954) Goodman showed that we need in addition some reason for preferring some uniformities to others, for without such a selection the uniformity of nature is vacuous, yet Goodman (1976) has proposed a set of syntactic and semantic features for categorizing representational systems. His theory provided for a finer discrimination among types of systems than a philosophy of science and language as partaken to and understood by the categorical elaborations as announced by Peirce. What also emerges clearly is that many rich and useful systems of representation lack a number of features taken to be essential to linguistic or sentential forms of representation, e.g., discrete alphabets and vocabularies, syntax, logical structure, inferences rules, compositional semantics and recursive e compounding devices.

As a consequence, although these representations can be appraised for accuracy or correctness. It does not seem possible to analyse such evaluative notion along the lines of standard truth theories, geared as they are to the structure found in sentential systems.

In light of this newer work, serious questions have been raised at the soundness of the tripartite division and about whether various of the psychological and philosophical claims concerning conventionality, learning, interpretation, and so forth, that have been based on this traditional analysis, can be sustained. It is of special significance e that Goodman has joined a number of theorists in rejecting accounts of Iconic representation in terms of resemblance. The rejection has been twofold, first, as Peirce himself recognized, resemblance is not sufficient to establish the appropriate referential relations. The numerous prints of lithograph do not represent one another. Any more than an identical twin represent his or her sibling. Something more than resemblance is needed to establish the connection between an Icon and picture and what it represents. Second, since Iconic representations lack as may properties as they share with their referents, sand certain non-Iconic symbol can be placed vin correspondences with their referents. It is difficult to provide a non-circular account of what the similarity distinguishes as Icons from other forms of representation. What is more, even if these two difficulties could be resolved, it would not show that the representational function of picture can be understood independently of an associated system of interpretations. The design, □, may be a picture of a mountain of the economy in a foreign language. Or it may have no representational significance at all. Whether it is a representation and what kind of representation it uses, is relative to a system of interpretation.

If so, then, what is the explanatory role of providing reasons for our psychological states and intentional acts? Clearly part of this role comes from the justificatory nature of the reason-giving relation: 'Things are made intelligible by being revealed to be, or too approximate to being, as they rationally ought to be'. For some writers the justificatory and explanatory tasks of reason-giving simple coincide. The manifestation of rationality is seen as sufficient to explain states or acts quite independently of questions regarding causal origin. Within this model the greater the degree of rationality we can detect, the more intelligible the sequence will b e. where there is a breakdown in rationality, as in cases of weakness of will or self-deception, there is a corresponding breakdown in our ability to make the action/belief intelligible.

The equation of the justificatory and explanatory role of rationality links can be found within two quite distinct picture. One account views the attribute of rationality from a third-person perspective. Attributing intentional states to others, and by analogy to ourselves, is a matter of applying them of a certain pattern of interpretation. we ascribe that ever states enable us to make sense of their behaviour as conforming to a rational pattern. Such a mode of interpretation is commonly an ex post facto affair, although such a mode of interpretation can also aid prediction. Our interpretations are never definitive or closed. They are always open to revision and modification in the light of future behaviour. If so extreme a degree revision enables people as a whole to appear more rational. Where we fail to detect of seeing a system then we give up the project of seeing a system as rational and instead seek explanations of a mechanistic kind.

The other picture is resolutely firs-personal, linked to the claimed prospectively of rationalizing explanations we make an action, for example, intelligible by adopting the agent's perspective on it. Understanding is a reconstruction of actual or possible decision making. It is from such a first-personal perspective that goals are detected as desirable and the courses of action appropriated to the situation. The standpoint of an agent deciding how to act is not that of an observer predicting the next move. When I found something desirable and judge an act in an appropriate rule for achieving it, I conclude that a certain course of action should be taken. This is different from my reflecting on my past behaviour and concluding that I will do 'X' in the future.

For many writers, it is, nonetheless, the justificatory and explanatory role of reason cannot simply be equated. To do so fails to distinguish well-formed cases thereby I believe or act because of these reasons. I may have beliefs but your innocence would be deduced but nonetheless come to believe you are innocent because you have blue eyes. Yet, I may have intentional states that give altruistic reasons in the understanding for contributing to charity but, nonetheless, out of a desire to earn someone's good judgment. In both these cases. Even though my belief could be shown be rational in the light of other beliefs, and my action, of whether the forwarded beliefs become desirously actionable, that of these rationalizing links would form part of a valid explanation of the phenomena concerned. Moreover, cases inclined with an inclination toward submission. As I continue to smoke although I judge it would be better to abstain. This suggests, however, that the mere availability of reasoning cannot, least of mention, have the quality of being of itself an sufficiency to explain why it occurred.

The defence of the view that reasons are causes for which seems arbitrary, least of mention, 'Why does explanation require citing the cause of the cause of a phenomenon but not the next link in the chain of causes? Perhaps what is not generally true of explanation is true only of mentalistic explanation: Only in giving the latter type are we obliged to give the cause of as cause. However, this too seems arbitrary. What is the difference between mentalistic and non-mentalistic explanation that would justify imposing more stringent restrictions on the former? The same argument applies to non-cognitive mental stares, such as sensations or emotions. Opponents of behaviourism sometimes reply that mental states can be observed: Each of us, through 'introspection', can observe at least some mental states, namely our own, least of mention, those of which we are conscious.

To this point, the distinction between reasons and causes is motivated in good part by a desire to separate the rational from the natural order. However, its probable traces are reclined of a historical coefficient of reflectivity as Aristotle's similar (but not identical) distinction between final and efficient cause, engendering that (as a person, fact, or condition) which proves responsible for an effect. Recently, the contrast has been drawn primarily in the domain or the inclining inclinations that manifest some territory by which attributes of something done or effected are we to engage of actions and, secondarily, elsewhere.

Many who have insisted on distinguishing reasons from causes have failed to distinguish two kinds of reason. Consider its reason for sending a letter by express mail. Asked why id so, I might say I wanted to get it there in a day, or simply, to get it there in as day. Strictly, the reason is repressed by 'to get it there in a day'. But what this express to my reason only because I am suitably motivated: I am in a reason state, as wanting to get the letter there in a day. It is reason states-especially wants, beliefs and intentions-and not reasons strictly so called, that are candidates for causes. The latter are abstract contents of propositional altitudes: The former are psychological elements that play motivational roles.

If reason states can motivate, however, why (apart from confusing them with reasons proper) deny that they are causes? For one can say that they are not events, at least in the usual sense entailing change, as they are dispositional states (this contrasts them with occurrences, but not imply that they admit of dispositional analysis). It has also seemed to those who deny that reasons are causes that the former justifies as well as explain the actions for which they are reasons, whereas the role of causes is at most to explain. As other claim is that the relation between reasons (and for reason states are often cited explicitly) and the actions they explain are non-contingent, whereas the relation causes to their effects is contingent. The 'logical connection argument' proceeds from this claim to the conclusion that reasons are not causes.

These arguments are inconclusive, first, even if causes are events, sustaining causation may explain, as where the [states of] standing of a broken table is explained by the (condition of) support of staked boards replacing its missing legs. Second, the 'because' in 'I sent it by express because I wanted to get it there in a day, so in some semi-causal explanation would at best be construed as only rationalizing, than justifying action. And third, if any non-contingent connection can be established between, say, my wanting something and the action it explains, there are close causal analogism such as the connection between brining a magnet to iron filings and their gravitating to it: This is, after all, a 'definitive' connection, expressing part of what it is to be magnetic, yet the magnet causes the fillings to move.

There I then, a clear distinction between reasons proper and causes, and even between reason states and event causes: But the distinction cannot be used to show that the relation between reason and the actions they justify is in no way causal. Precisely parallel points hold in the epistemic domain (and indeed, for all similarly admit of justification, and explanation, by reasons). Suppose my reason for believing that you received it today is that I sent it by express yesterday. My reason, strictly speaking, is that I sent it by express yesterday: My reason state is my believing this. Arguably reason justifies the further proposition I believe for which it is my reason and my reason state-my evidence belief-both explains and justifies my belief that you received the letter today. I an say, that what justifies that belief is [in fact] that I sent the letter by express yesterday, but this statement expresses my believing that evidence proposition, and you received the letter is not justified, it is not justified by the mere truth of the proposition (and can be justified even if that proposition is false).

Similarly, there are, for belief for action, at least five main kinds of reason (1) normative reasons, reasons (objective grounds) there are to believe (say, to believe that there is a green-house-effect): (2) Person-relative normative reasons, reasons for [say] me to believe, (3) subjective reasons, reasons I have to believe (4) explanatory reasons, reasons why I believe, and (5) motivating reasons for which I believe. Tenets of (1) and (2) are propositions and thus, not serious candidates to be causal factors. The states corresponding to (3) may not be causal elements. Reasons why, tenet (4) are always (sustaining) explainers, though not necessarily even prima facie justifier, since a belief can be casually sustained by factors with no evidential value. Motivating reasons are both explanatory and possess whatever minimal prima facie justificatory power (if any) a reason must have to be a basis of belief.

Current discussion of the reasons-causes issue has shifted from the question whether reason state can causally explain to the perhaps, deeper questions whether they can justify without so explaining, and what kind of causal states with actions and beliefs they do explain. 'Reliabilist' tend to take as belief as justified by a reason only if it is held ast least in part for that reason, in a sense implying, but not entailed by, being causally based on that reason. 'Internalists' often deny this, as, perhaps, thinking we lack internal access to the relevant causal connections. But Internalists need internal access to what justified-say, the reason state-and not to the (perhaps quite complex) relations it bears the belief it justifies, by virtue for which it does so. Many questions also remain concerning the very nature of causation, reason-hood, explanation and justification.

Nevertheless, for most causal theorists, the radical separation of the causal and rationalizing role of reason-giving explanations is unsatisfactory. For such theorists, where we can legitimately point to an agent's reasons to explain a certain belief or action, then those features of the agent's intentional states that render the belief or action reasonable must be causally relevant in explaining how the agent came to believe or act in a way which they rationalize. One way of putting this requirement is that reason-giving states not only cause but also causally explain their explananda.

The explanans/explanandum are held of a wide currency of philosophical discoursing because it allows a certain succinctness which is unobtainable in ordinary English. Whether in science philosophy or in everyday life, one does often offers explanation

s. the particular statement, laws, theories or facts that are used to explain something are collectively called the 'explanans', and the target of the explanans-the thing to be explained-is called the 'explanandum'. Thus, one might explain why ice forms on the surface of lakes (the explanandum) in terms of the special property of water to expand as it approaches freezing point together with the fact that materials less dense than liquid water float in it (the explanans). The terms come from two different Latin grammatical forms: 'Explanans' is the present participle of the verb which means explain: And 'explanandum' is a direct object noun derived from the same verb.

The assimilation in the likeness as to examine side by side or point by point in order to bring such in comparison with an expressed or implied standard where comparative effects are both considered and equivalent resemblances bound to what merely happens to us, or to parts of us, actions are what we do. My moving my finger is an action to be distinguished from the mere motion of that finger. My snoring likewise, is not something I 'do' in the intended sense, though in another broader sense it is something I often 'do' while asleep.

The contrast has both metaphysical and moral import. With respect to my snoring, I am passive, and am not morally responsible, unless for example, I should have taken steps earlier to prevent my snoring. But in cases of genuine action, I am the cause of what happens, and I may properly be held responsible, unless I have an adequate excuse or justification. When I move my finger, I am the cause of the finger's motion. When I say 'Good morning' I am the cause of the sounding expression or utterance. True, the immediate causes are muscle contractions in the one case and lung, lip and tongue motions in the other. But this is compatible with me being the cause-perhaps, I cause these immediate causes, or, perhaps it just id the case that some events can have both an agent and other events as their cause.

All this is suggestive, but not really adequate. we do not understand the intended force of 'I am the cause' and more than we understand the intended force of 'Snoring is not something I do'. If I trip and fall in your flower garden, 'I am the cause' of any resulting damage, but neither the damage nor my fall is my action. In the considerations for which we approach to explaining what are actions, as contrasted with 'mere' doings, are. However, it will be convenient to say something about how they are to be individuated.

If I say 'Good morning' to you over the telephone, I have acted. But how many actions have O performed, and how are they related to one another and associated events? we may describe of what is done:

(1) Move my tongue and lips in certain ways, while exhaling.

(2) say 'Good morning'.

(3) Cause a certain sequence of modifications in the current flowing in your telephone.

(4) Say 'Good morning' to you.

(5) greet you.

The list-not exhaustive, by any means-is of act types. I have performed an action of each relation holds. I greet you by saying 'Good morning' to you, but not the converse, and similarity for the others on the list. But are these five distinct actions I performed, one of each type, or are the five descriptions all of a single action, which was of these five (and more) types. Both positions, and a variety of intermediate positions have been defended.

How many words are there within the sentence? : 'The cat is on the mat'? There are on course, at best two answers to this question, precisely because one can enumerate the word types, either for which there are five, or that which there are six. Moreover, depending on how one chooses to think of word types another answer is possible. Since the sentence contains definite articles, nouns, a preposition and a verb, there are four grammatical different types of word in the sentence.

The type/token distinction, understood as a distinction between sorts of things, particular, the identity theory asserts that mental states are physical states, and this raises the question whether the identity in question if of types or token'.

During the past two decades or so, the concept of supervenience has seen increasing service in philosophy of mind. The thesis that the mental is supervenient on the physical-roughly, the claim that the mental character of a thing is wholly determined by its physical nature-has played a key role in the formulation of some influence on the mind-body problem. Much of our evidence for mind-body supervenience seems to consist in our knowledge of specific correlations between mental states and physical (in particular, neural) processes in humans and other organisms. Such knowledge, although extersive and in some ways impressive, is still quite rudimentary and far from complete (what do we know, or can we expect to know about the exact neural substrate for, say, the sudden thought that you are late with your rent payment this month?) It may be that our willingness to accept mind-body supervenience, although based in part on specific psychological dependencies, has to be supported by a deeper metaphysical commitment to the primary of the physical: It may in fact be an expression of such a commitment.

However, there are kinds of mental state that raise special issues for mind-body supervenience. One such kind is 'wide content' states, i.e., contentual mental states that seem to be individuated essentially by reference to objects and events outside the subject, e.g., the notion of a concept, like the related notion of meaning. The word 'concept' itself is applied to a bewildering assortment of phenomena commonly thought to be constituents of thought. These include internal mental representations, images, words, stereotypes, senses, properties, reasoning and discrimination abilities, mathematical functions. Given the lack of anything like a settled theory in this area, it would be a mistake to fasten readily on any one of these phenomena as the unproblematic referent of the term. One does better to make a survey of the geography of the area and gain some idea of how these phenomena might fit together, leaving aside for the nonce just which of them deserve to be called 'concepts' as ordinarily understood.

Concepts are the constituents of such propositions, just as the words 'capitalist', 'exploit', and 'workers' are constituents of the sentence. However, there is a specific role that concepts are arguably intended to play that may serve a point of departure. Suppose one person thinks that capitalists exploit workers, and another that they do not. Call the thing that they disagree about 'a proposition', e.g., capitalists exploit workers. It is in some sense shared by them as the object of their disagreement, and it is expressed by the sentence that follows the verb 'thinks that' mental verbs that take such verbs of 'propositional attitude'. Nonetheless, these people could have these beliefs only if they had, inter alia, the concept's capitalist exploit. And workers.

Propositional attitudes, and thus concepts, are constitutive of the familiar form of explanation (so-called 'intentional explanation') by which we ordinarily explain the behaviour and stares of people, many animals and perhaps, some machines. The concept of intentionality was originally used by medieval scholastic philosophers. It was reintroduced into European philosophy b y the German philosopher and psychologist Franz Clemens Brentano (1838-1917) whose thesis proposed in Brentano's 'Psychology from an Empirical Standpoint'(1874) that it is the 'intentionality or directedness of mental states that marks off the mental from the physical.

Many mental states and activities exhibit the feature of intentionality, being directed at objects. Two related things are meant by this. First, when one desire or believes or hopes, one always desires or believes of hopes something. As, to assume that belief report (1) is true.

(1) That most Canadians believe that George Bush is a Republican.

Tenet (1) tells us that some subject 'Canadians' have a certain attitude, belief, to something, designated by the nominal phrase that Trump is a Republican and identified by its content-sentence.

(2) Harper is a Conservative

Following Russell and contemporary usage that the object referred to by the that-clause is tenet (1) and expressed by tenet (2) a proposition. Notice, too, that this sentence might also serve as most Canadians' belief-text, a sentence whereby to express the belief that (1) reports to have. Such an utterance of (2) by itself would assert the truth of the proposition it expresses, but as part of (1) its role is not to rely on anything, but to identify what the subject believes. This same proposition can be the object of other attitude s of other people. However, in that most Canadians may regret that Bush is a Republican yet, Reagan may remember that he is. Bushanan may doubt that he is.

Nevertheless, Brentano, 1960, we can focus on two puzzles about the structure of intentional states and activities, an area in which the philosophy of mind meets the philosophy of language, logic and ontology, least of mention, the term intentionality should not be confused with terms intention and intension. There is, nonetheless, an important connection between intention and intension and intentionality, for semantical systems, like extensional model theory, that are limited to extensions, cannot provide plausible accounts of the language of intentionality.

The attitudes are philosophically puzzling because it is not easy to see how the intentionality of the attitude fits with another conception of them, as local mental phenomena.

Beliefs, desires, hopes, and fears seem to be located in the heads or minds of the people that have them. Our attitudes are accessible to us through 'introspection'. As most Canadians belief that Bush to be a Republican just by examining the 'contents' of his own mind: He does not need to investigate the world around him. we think of attitudes as being caused at certain times by events that impinge on the subject's body, specially by perceptual events, such as reading a newspaper or seeing a picture of an ice-cream cone. In that, the psychological level of descriptions carries with it a mode of explanation which has no echo in 'physical theory'. we regard ourselves and of each other as 'rational purposive creatures, fitting our beliefs to the world as we inherently perceive it and seeking to obtain what we desire in the light of them'. Reason-giving explanations can be offered not only for action and beliefs, which will attain the most of all attentions, however, desires, intentions, hopes, dears, angers, and affections, and so forth. Indeed, their positioning within a network of rationalizing links is part of the individuating characteristics of this range of psychological states and the intentional acts they explain.

Meanwhile, these attitudes can in turn cause changes in other mental phenomena, and eventually in the observable behaviour of the subject. Seeing a picture of an ice cream cone leads to a desire for one, which leads me to forget the meeting I am supposed to attend and walk to the ice-cream pallor instead. All of this seems to require that attitudes be states and activities that are localized in the subject.

Nonetheless, the phenomena of intentionality call to mind that the attitudes are essentially relational in nature: They involve relations to the propositions at which they are directed and at the objects they are about. These objects may be quite remote from the minds of subjects. An attitude seems to be individuated by the agent, the type of attitude (belief, desire, and so on), and the proposition at which it is directed. It seems essential to the attitude reported by its believing that, for example, that it is directed toward the proposition that Bush is a Republican. And it seems essential to this proposition that it is about Bush. But how can a mental state or activity of a person essentially involve some other individuals? The problem is brought out by two classical problems such that are called 'no-reference' and 'co-reference'.

The classical solution to such problems is to suppose that intentional states are only indirectly related to concrete particulars, like George Bush, whose existence is contingent, and that can be thought about in a variety of ways. The attitudes directly involve abstract objects of some sort, whose existence is necessary, and whose nature the mind can directly grasp. These abstract objects provide concepts or ways of thinking of concrete particulars. That is to say, the involving characteristics of the different concepts, as, these, concepts corresponding to different inferential/practical roles in that different perceptions and memories give rise to these beliefs, and they serve as reasons for different actions. If we individuate propositions by concepts than individuals, the co-reference problem disappears.

The proposal has the bonus of also taking care of the no-reference problem. Some propositions will contain concepts that are not, in fact, of anything. These propositions can still be believed desired, and the like.

This basic idea has been worked out in different ways by a number of authors. The Austrian philosopher Ernst Mally thought that propositions involved abstract particulars that 'encoded' properties, like being the loser of the 1992 election, rather than concrete particulars, like Bush, who exemplified them. There are abstract particulars that encode clusters of properties that nothing exemplifies, and two abstract objects can encode different clusters of properties that are exemplified by a single thing. The German philosopher Gottlob Frége distinguished between the 'sense' and the 'reference' of expressions. The senses of George Bus hh and the person who will come in second in the election are different, even though the references are the same. Senses are grasped by the mind, are directly involved in propositions, and incorporate 'modes of presentation' of objects.

For most of the twentieth century, the most influential approach was that of the British philosopher Bertrand Russell. Russell (19051929) in effect recognized two kinds of propositions that assemble of a 'singular proposition' that consists separately in particularly to properties in relation to that. An example is a proposition consisting of Bush and the properties of being a Republican. 'General propositions' involve only universals. The general proposition corresponding to someone is a Republican would be a complex consisting of the property of being a Republican and the higher-order property of being instantiated. The term 'singular proposition' and 'general proposition' are from Kaplan (1989.)

Historically, a great deal has been asked of concepts. As shareable constituents of the object of attitudes, they presumably figure in cognitive generalizations and explanations of animals' capacities and behaviour. They are also presumed to serve as the meaning of linguistic items, underwriting relations of translation, definition, synonymy, antinomy and semantic implication. Much work in the semantics of natural language takes itself to be addressing conceptual structure.

Concepts have also been thought to be the proper objects of philosophical analysis, the activity practised by Socrates and twentieth-century 'analytic' philosophers when they ask about the nature of justice, knowledge or piety, and expect to discover answers by means of priori reflection alone.

The expectation that one sort of thing could serve all these tasks went hand in hand with what has come to be known for the 'Classical View' of concepts, according to which they have an 'analysis' consisting of conditions that are individually necessary and jointly sufficient for their satisfaction. Which are known to any competent user of them? The standard example is the especially simple one of the [bachelor], which seems to be identical to [eligible unmarried male]. A more interesting, but problematic one has been [knowledge], whose analysis was traditionally thought to be [justified true belief].

This Classical View seems to offer an illuminating answer to a certain form of metaphysical question: In virtue of what is something the kind of thing is, -, e.g., in virtue of what a bachelor is a bachelor? And it does so in a way that supports counterfactual: It tells us what would satisfy the concept in situations other than the actual ones (although all actual bachelors might turn out to be freckled. It's possible that there might be unfreckled ones, since the analysis does not exclude that). The View also seems to offer an answer to an epistemological question of how people seem to know a priori (or, independently of experience) about the nature of many things, e.g., that bachelors are unmarried: It is constitutive of the competency (or, possession) conditions of a concept that they know its analysis, at least on reflection.

As it had been ascribed, in that Actions as Doings having Mentalistic Explanation: Coughing is sometimes like snoring and sometimes like saying 'Good morning'-that is, sometimes in mere doing and sometimes an action. And deliberate coughing can be explained by invoking an intention to cough, a desired to cough or some other 'pro-attitude' toward coughing, a reason for coughing or purpose in coughing or something similarly mental. Especially if we think of actions as 'outputs' of the mental machine'. The functionalist thinks of 'mental states' as events as causally mediating between a subject's sensory inputs and the subject ensuing behaviour. Functionalism itself is the stronger doctrine that 'what makes' a mental state the type of state that is pain, a smell of violets, a closed-minded belief that koalas are dangerous, is the functional relation it bears to the subject's perceptual stimuli, behaviour responses and other mental states.

Twentieth-century functionalism gained as credibility in an indirect way, by being perceived as affording the least objectionable solution to the mind-body problem.

Disaffected from Cartesian dualism and from the 'first-person' perspective of introspective psychology, the behaviourists had claimed that there is nothing to the mind but the subject's behaviour and dispositions to behave. To refute the view that a certain level of behavioural dispositions is necessary for a mental life, we need convincing cases of thinking stones, or utterly incurable paralytics or disembodied minds. But these alleged possibilities are to some merely that.

To rebuttal against the view that a certain level of behavioural dispositions is sufficient for a mental life, we need convincing cases rich behaviour with no accompanying mental states. The typical example is of a puppet controlled by radio-wave links, by other minds outside the puppet's hollow body. But one might wonder whether the dramatic devices are producing the anti-behaviorist intuition all by themselves. And how could the dramatic devices make a difference to the facts of the casse? If the puppeteers were replaced by a machine, not designed by anyone, yet storing a vast number of input-output conditionals, which was reduced in size and placed in the puppet's head, do we still have a compelling counterexample, to the behaviour-as-sufficient view? At least it is not so clear.

Such an example would work equally well against the anti-eliminativist version of which the view that mental states supervene on behavioural disposition. But supervenient behaviourism could be refitted by something less ambitious. The 'X-worlders' of the American philosopher Hilary Putnam (1926-), who are in intense pain but do not betray this in their verbal or non-verbal behaviour, behaving just as pain-free human beings, would be the right sort of case. However, even if Putnam has produced a counterexample for pain-which the American philosopher of mind Daniel Clement Dennett (1942-), for one would doubtless deny-an 'X-worlder' narration to refute supervenient behaviourism with respect to the attitudes or linguistic meaning will be less intuitively convincing. Behaviourist resistance is easier for the reason that having a belief or meaning a certain thing, lack distinctive phenomemologies.

There is a more sophisticated line of attack. As, the most influential American philosopher of the latter half of the 20th century philosopher Willard von Orman Quine (1908-2000) has remarked some have taken his thesis of the indeterminacy of translation as a reductio of his behaviourism. For this to be convincing, Quines argument for the indeterminacy thesis and to be persuasive in its own and that is a disputed matter.

If behaviourism is finally laid to rest to the satisfaction of most philosophers, it will probably not by counterexamples, or by a reductio from Quine's indeterminacy thesis. Rather, it will be because the behaviorists worries about other minds, and the public availability of meaning have been shown too groundless, or not to require behaviourism for their solution. But we can be sure that this happy day will take some time to arrive.

Quine became noted for his claim that the way one uses' language determines what kinds of things one is committed to saying exist. Moreover, the justification for speaking one way rather than another, just as the justification for adopting one conceptual system rather than another, was a thoroughly pragmatic one for Quine (see Pragmatism). He also became known for his criticism of the traditional distinction between synthetic statements (empirical, or factual, propositions) and analytic statements (necessarily true propositions). Quine made major contributions in set theory, a branch of mathematical logic concerned with the relationship between classes. His published works include Mathematical Logic (1940), From a Logical Point of View (1953), Word and Object (1960), Set Theory and Its Logic (1963), and: An Intermittently Philosophical Dictionary (1987). His autobiography, The Time of My Life, appeared in 1985.

Functionalism, and cognitive psychology considered as a complete theory of human thought, inherited some of the same difficulties that earlier beset behaviouralism and identity theory. These remaining obstacles fall unto two main categories: Intentionality problems and Qualia problems.

Propositional attitudes such as beliefs and desires are directed upon states of affairs which may or may not actually obtain, e.g., that the Republican or let alone any in the Liberal party will win, and are about individuals who may or may not exist, e.g., King Arthur. Franz Brentano raised the question of how are purely physical entity or state could have the property of being 'directed upon' or about a non-existent state of affairs or object: That is not the sort of feature that ordinary, purely physical objects can have.

The standard functionalist reply is that propositional attitudes have Brentano's feature because the internal physical states and events that realize them 'represent' actual or possible states of affairs. What they represent is determined at least in part, by their functional roles: Is that, mental events, states or processes with content involve reference to objects, properties or relations, such as a mental state with content can fail to refer, but there always exists a specific condition for a state with content to refer to certain things? As when the state gas a correctness or fulfilment condition, its correctness is determined by whether its referents have the properties the content specifies for them.

What is it that distinguishes items that serve as representations from other objects or events? And what distinguishes the various kinds of symbols from each other? Firstly, there has been general agreement that the basic notion of a representation involves one thing's 'standing for', 'being about', 'pertain to', 'referring or denoting of something else entirely'. The major debates here have been over the nature of this connection between a representation and that which it represents. As to the second, perhaps the most famous and extensive attempt to organize and differentiated among alternative forms of the representation is found in the works of C.S. Peirce (1931-1935). Peirce's theory of sign in complex, involving a number of concepts and distinctions that are no longer paid much heed. The aspect of his theory that remains influential and is widely cited, is his division of signs into Icons, Indices and Symbols. Icons are signs that are said to be like or resemble the things they represent, e.g., portrait paintings. Indices are signs that are connected to their objects by some causal dependency, e.g., smoke as a sign of fire. Symbols are those signs that are related to their object by virtue of use or association: They are arbitrary labels, e.g., the word 'table'. The divisions among signs, or variants of this division, is routinely put forth to explain differences in the way representational systems are thought to establish their links to the world. Further, placing a representation in one of the three divisions has been used to account for the supposed differences between conventional and non-conventional representation, between representation that do and do not require learning to understand, and between representations, like language, that need to be read, and those which do not require interpretation. Some theorists, moreover, have maintained that it is only the use of Symbols that exhibits or indicate s the presence of mind and mental states.

Representations, along with mental states, especially beliefs and thoughts, are said to exhibit 'intentionality' in that they refer or to stand for something else. The nature of this special property, however, has seemed puzzling. Not only is intentionality often assumed to be limited to humans, and possibly a few other species, but the property itself appears to resist characterization in physicalist terms. The problem is most obvious in the case of 'arbitrary' signs, like words. Where it is clear that there is no connection between the physical properties of as word and what it denotes, that, wherein, the problem also remains for Iconic representation.

In at least, there are two difficulties. One is that of saying exactly 'how' a physical item's representational content is determined, in not by the virtue of what does a neurophysiological state represent precisely that the available candidate will win? An answer to that general question is what the American philosopher of mind, Alan Jerry Fodor (1935-) has called a 'psychosemantics', and several attempts have been made. Taking the analogy between thought and computation seriously, Fodor believes that mental representations should be conceived as individual states with their own identities and structures, like formulae transformed by processes of computations or thought. His views are frequently contrasted with those of 'holiest' such as the American philosopher Herbert Donald Davidson (1917-2003), whose constructions within a generally 'holistic' theory of knowledge and meaning. Radical interpreter can tell when a subject holds a sentence true, and using the principle of 'clarity' ends up making an assignment of truth condition is a defender of radical translation and the inscrutability of reference', Holist approach has seemed too many has seemed too many to offer some hope of identifying meaning as a respectable notion, eve n within a broadly 'extensional' approach to language. Instructionalists about mental ascription, such as Clement Daniel Dennett (19420) who posits the particularity that Dennett has also been a major force in illuminating how the philosophy of mind needs to be informed by work in surrounding sciences.

In giving an account of what someone believes, does essential reference have to be made to how things are in the environment of the believer? And, if so, exactly what reflation does the environment have to the belief? These questions involve taking sides in the externalism and internalism debate. To a first approximation, the externalist holds that one's propositional attitude cannot be characterized without reference to the disposition of object and properties in the world-the environment-in which in is simulated. The internalist thinks that propositional attitudes (especially belief) must be characterizable without such reference. The reason that this is only a first approximation of the contrast is that there can be different sorts of externalism. Thus, one sort of externalist might insist that you could not have, say, a belief that grass is green unless it could be shown that there was some relation between you, the believer, and grass. Had you never come across the plant which makes up lawns and meadows, beliefs about grass would not be available to you. However, this does not mean that you have to be in the presence of grass in order to entertain a belief about it, nor does it even mean that there was necessarily a time when you were in its presence. For example, it might have been the case that, though you have never seen grass, it has been described to you. Or, at the extreme, perhaps no longer exists anywhere in the environment, but your antecedent's contact with it left some sort of genetic trace in you, and the trace is sufficient to give rise to a mental state that could be characterized as about grass.

At the more specific level that has been the focus in recent years: What do thoughts have in common in virtue of which they are thoughts? What is, what makes a thought a thought? What makes a pain a pain? Cartesian dualism said the ultimate nature of the mental was to be found in a special mental substance. Behaviourism identified mental states with behavioural disposition: Physicalism in its most influential version identifies mental states with brain states. One could imagine that the individual states that occupy the relevant causal roles turn out not to be bodily stares: For example, they might instead be states of an extended Cartesian substance. But its overwhelming likely that the states that do occupy those causal roles are all tokens of bodily-state types. However, a problem does seem to arise about properties of mental states. Suppose 'pain' is identical with a certain firing of c-fibres. Although a particular pain is the very same state as neural firing, we identify that state in two different ways: As a pain and as neural firing. The state will therefore have certain properties in virtue of which we identify it as a pain and others in virtue of which we identify it as a pain will be mental properties, whereas those in virtue of which we identify it as neural firing will be physical properties. This has seemed too many to lead to a kind of dualism at the level of the properties of mental states. Even if we reject a dualism of substances and take people simply to be physical organisms, those organisms still have both mental and physical states. Similarly, even if we identify those mental states with certain physical states, those states will nonetheless have both mental and physical properties. So, disallowing dualism with respect to substances and their stares simply leads to its reappearance at the level of the properties of those states.

The problem concerning mental properties is widely thought to be most pressing for sensations, since the painful quality of pains and the red quality of visual sensation seem to be irretrievably physical. So, even if mental states are all identical with physical states, these states appear to have properties that are not physical. And if mental states do actually have nonphysical properties, the identity of mental with physical states would not support a thoroughgoing mind-body physicalism.

A more sophisticated reply to the difficulty about mental properties is due independently to D.M. Armstrong (1968) and David Lewis (1972), who argue that for a state to be a particular sort of intentional state or sensation is for that state to bear characteristic causal relations to other particular occurrences. The properties in virtue of which we identify states as thoughts or sensations will still be neutral as between being mental and physical, since anything can bear a causal relation to anything else. But causal connections have a better chance than similarity in some unspecified respect t of capturing the distinguishing properties of sensation and thoughts.

It should be mentioned that the properties can be more complex and complicating than the above allows. For instance, in the sentence, 'John is married to Mary', we are attributing to John the property of being married. And, unlike the property of being bald, this property of John is essentially relational. Moreover, it is commonly said that 'is married to' expresses a relation, than a property, though the terminology is not fixed, but, some authors speak of relations as different from properties in being more complex but like them in being nonlinguistic, though it is more common to treat relations as a subclass of properties.

The Classical view, meanwhile, has always had to face the difficulty of 'primitive' concepts: It's all well and good to claim that competence consists in some sort of mastery of a definition, but what about the primitive concepts in which a process of definition must ultimately end? There the British Empiricism of the seventeenth century began to offer a solution: All the primitives were sensory. Indeed, they expanded the Classical view to include the claim, now often taken uncritically for granted in discussions of that view, that all concepts are 'derived from experience': 'Every idea is derived from a corresponding impression'. In the work of John Locke (1682-1704), George Berkeley (1685-1753) and David Hume (1711-76) as it was thought to mean that concepts were somehow 'composed' of introspectible mental items-images -, 'impressions'-that were ultimately decomposable into basic sensory parts. Thuds, Hume analyzed the concept of [material object] as involving certain regularities in our sensory experience, and [cause] as involving conjunction.

Berkeley noticed a problem with this approach that every generation has had to rediscover: If a concept is a sensory impression, like an image, then how does one distinguish a general concept [triangle] from a more particular one-say, [isosceles triangle]-that would serve in imaging the general one. More recent, Wittgenstein (1953) called attention to the multiple ambiguity of images. And, in any case, images seem quite hopeless for capturing the concepts associated with logical terms (what is the image for negation or possibility?) Whatever the role of such representation, full conceptual competence must involve something more.

Indeed, in addition to images and impressions and other sensory items, a full account of concepts needs to consider issues of logical structure. This is precisely what 'logical postivists' did, focussing on logically structured sentences instead of sensations and images, transforming the empiricalist claim into the famous' Verifiability Theory of Meaning': The meaning of a sentence is the means by which it is confirmed or refuted. Ultimately by sensory experience, the meaning or concept associated with a predicate is the means by which people confirm or refute whether something satisfies it.

This once-popular position has come under much attack in philosophy in the last fifty years. In the first place, few, if any, successful 'reductions' of ordinary concepts like, [material objects], [cause] to purely sensory concepts have ever been achieved, as Jules Alfred Ayer (1910-89) proved to be one of the most important modern epistemologists, his first and most famous book, 'Language, Truth and Logic', to the extent that epistemology is concerned with the a priori justification of our ordinary or scientific beliefs, since the validity of such beliefs 'is an empirical matter, which cannot be settled by such means. However, he does take positions which have been bearing on epistemology. For example, he is a phenomenalists, believing that material objects are logical constructions out of actual and possible sense-experience, and an anti-foundationalism, at least in one sense, denying that there is a bedrock level of indubitable propositions on which empirical knowledge can be based. As regards the main specifically epistemological problem he addressed, the problem of our knowledge of other minds, he is essentially behaviouristic, since the verification principle pronounces that the hypothesis of the occurrences intrinsically inaccessible experience is unintelligible.

Although his views were later modified, he early maintained that all meaningful statements are either logical or empirical. According to his principle of verification, a statement is considered empirical only if some sensory observation is relevant to determining its truth or falseness. Sentences that neither are logical nor empirical-including traditional religious, metaphysical, and ethical sentences-are judged nonsensical. Other works of Ayer include The Problem of Knowledge (1956), the Gifford Lectures of 1972-73 published as The Central Questions of Philosophy (1973), and Part of My Life: The Memoirs of a Philosopher (1977).

Ayer's main contribution to epistemology are in his book, 'The Problem of Knowledge' which he himself regarded as superior to 'Language, Truth and Logic' (Ayer 1985), soon there after Ayer develops a fallibilist type of foundationalism, according to which processes of justification or verification terminate in someone's having an experience, but there is no class of infallible statements based on such experiences. Consequently, in making such statements based on experience, even simple reports of observation we 'make what appears to be a special sort of advance beyond our data' (1956). And it is the resulting gap which the sceptic exploits. Ayer describes four possible responses to the sceptic: Naïve realism, according to which materia l objects are directly given in perception, so that there is no advance beyond the data: Reductionism, according to which physical objects are logically constructed out of the contents of our sense-experiences, so that again there is no real advance beyond the data: A position according to which there is an advance, but it can be supported by the canons of valid inductive reasoning and lastly a position called 'descriptive analysis', according to which 'we can give an account of the procedures that we actually follow . . . but there [cannot] be a proof that what we take to be good evidence really is so'.

Ayer's reason why our sense-experiences afford us grounds for believing in the existence of physical objects is simply that sentence which are taken as referring to physical objects are used in such a way that our having the appropriate experiences counts in favour of their truths. In other words, having such experiences is exactly what justification of or ordinary beliefs about the nature of the world 'consists in'. This suggestion is, therefore, that the sceptic is making some kind of mistake or indulging in some sort of incoherence in supposing that our experience may not rationally justify our commonsense picture of what the world is like. Again, this, however, is the familiar fact that th sceptic's undermining hypotheses seem perfectly intelligible and even epistemically possible. Ayer's response seems weak relative to the power of the sceptical puzzles.

The concept of 'the given' refers to the immediate apprehension of the contents of sense experience, expressed in the first person, present tense reports of appearances. Apprehension of the given is seen as immediate both in a casual sense, since it lacks the usual causal chain involved in perceiving real qualities of physical objects, and in an epistemic sense, since judgements expressing it are justified independently of all other beliefs and evidence. Some proponents of the idea of the given maintain that its apprehension is absolutely certain: Infallible, incorrigible and indubitable. It has been claimed also that a subject is omniscient with regard to the given: If a property appears, then the subject knows this.

The doctrine dates back at least to Descartes, who argued in Meditation II that it was beyond all possible doubt and error that he seemed to see light, hear noise, and so forth. The empiricist added the claim that the mind is passive in receiving sense impressions, so that there is no subjective contamination or distortion here (even though the states apprehended are mental). The idea was taken up in twentieth-century epistemology by C.I. Lewis and A.J. Ayer. Among others, who appealed to the given as the foundation for all empirical knowledge. Nonetheless, empiricism, like any philosophical movement, is often challenged to show how its claims about the structure of knowledge and meaning can themselves be intelligible and known within the constraints it accepts, since beliefs expressing only the given were held to be certain and justified in themselves, they could serve as solid foundations.

The second argument for the need for foundations is sound. It appeals to the possibility of incompatible but fully coherent systems of belief, only one of which could be completely true. In light of this possibility, coherence cannot suffice for complete justification, as coherence has the power to produce justification, while according to a negative coherence theory, coherence has only the power to nullify justification. However, by contrast, justification is solely a matter of how a belief coheres with a system of beliefs. Nonetheless, another distinction that cuts across the distinction between weak and strong coherence theories of justification. It is the distinction between positive and negative coherence theory tells us that if a belief coheres with a background system of belief, then the belief is justified.

Coherence theories of justification have a common feature, namely, that they are what are called 'internalistic theories of justification' they are theories affirming that coherence is a matter of internal relations between beliefs and justification is a matter of coherence. If, then, justification is solely a matter of internal relations between beliefs, we are left with the possibility that the internal relations might fail to correspond with any external reality. How, one might object, can a completely internal subjective notion of justification bridge the gap between mere true belief, which might be no more than a lucky guess, and knowledge, which must be grounded in some connection between internal subjective condition and external objective realities?

The answer is that it cannot and that something more than justified true belief is required for knowledge. This result has, however, been established quite apart from considerations of coherence theories of justification. What is required may be put by saying that the justification one must be undefeated by errors in the background system of belief. A justification is undefeated by error in the background system of belied would sustain the justification of the belief on the basis of the corrected system. So knowledge, on this sort of positive coherence theory, is true belief that coheres with the background belief system and corrected versions of that system. In short, knowledge is true belief plus justification resulting from coherence and undefeated by error.

Without some independent indication that some of the beliefs within a coherent system are true, coherence in itself is no indication of truth. Fairy stories can cohere. But our criteria for justification must indicate to us the probable truth of our beliefs. Hence, within any system of beliefs there must be some privileged class of beliefs which others must cohere to be justified. In the case of empirical knowledge, such privileged beliefs must represent the point of contact between subject and the world: They must originate in perception. When challenged, however, we justify our ordinary perceptual beliefs about physical properties by appeal to beliefs about appearances. Nonetheless, it seems more suitable as foundations since there is no class of more certain perceptual beliefs to which we appeal for their justification.

The argument that foundations must be certain was offered by the American philosopher David Lewis (1941-2002). He held that no proposition can be probable unless some are certain. If the probability of all propositions or beliefs were relative to evidence expressed in others, and if these relations were linear, then any regress would apparently have to terminate in propositions or beliefs that are certain. But Lewis shows neither that such relations must be linear nor that regresses cannot terminate in beliefs that are merely probable or justified in themselves without being certain or infallible.

Arguments against the idea of the given originate with the German philosopher and founder of critical philosophy. Immanuel Kant (1724-1804), whereby the intellectual landscape in which Kant began his career was largely set by the German philosopher, mathematician and polymath of Gottfried Wilhelm Leibniz (1646-1716), filtered through the principal follower and interpreter of Leibniz, Christian Wolff, who was primarily a mathematician but renowned as a systematic philosopher. Kant, who argues in Book I to the Transcendental Analysis that percepts without concepts do not yet constitute any form of knowing. Being non-epistemic, they presumably cannot serve as epistemic foundations. Once we recognize that we must apply concepts of properties to appearances and formulate beliefs utilizing those concepts before the appearances can play any epistemic role. It becomes more plausible that such beliefs are fallible. The argument was developed in this century by Sellars (1912-89), whose work revolved around the difficulties of combining the scientific image of people and their world, with the manifest image, or natural conception of ourselves as acquainted with intentions, meaning, colours, and other definitive aspects by his most influential paper 'Empiricism and the Philosophy of Mind' (1956) in this and many other of his papers, Sellars explored the nature of thought and experience. According to Sellars (1963), the idea of the given involves a confusion between sensing particular (having sense impression) which is non-epistemic, and having non-inferential knowledge of propositions referring to appearances be necessary for acquiring perceptual knowledge, but it is itself a primitive kind of knowing. Its being non-epistemic renders it immune from error, also, unsuitable for epistemological foundations. The apparentness to the non-inferential perceptual knowledge, is fallible, requiring concepts acquired through trained responses to public physical objects.

The contention that even reports of appearances are fallible can be supported from several directions. First, it seems doubtful that we can look beyond our beliefs to compare them with an unconceptualized reality, whether mental of physical. Second, to judge that anything, including an appearance, is 'F', we must remember which property 'F' is, and memory is admitted by all to be fallible. Our ascribing 'F' is normally not explicitly comparative, but its correctness requires memory, nevertheless, at least if we intend to ascribe a reinstantiable property. we must apply the concept of 'F' consistently, and it seems always at least logically possible to apply it inconsistently. If that be, it is not possible, if, for example, I intend in tendering to an appearance e merely to pick out demonstratively whatever property appears, then, I seem not to be expressing a genuine belief. My apprehension of the appearance will not justify any other beliefs. Once more it will be unsuitable as an epistemological foundation. This, nonetheless, nondifferential perceptual knowledge, is fallible, requiring concepts acquiring through trained responses to public physical objects.

Ayer (1950) sought to distinguish propositions expressing the given not by their infallibility, but by the alleged fact that grasping their meaning suffices for knowing their truth. However, this will be so only if the purely demonstratives meaning, and so only if the propositions fail to express beliefs that could ground others. If in uses genuine predicates, for example: C≠ as applied to tones, then one may grasp their meaning and yet be unsure in their application to appearances. Limiting claims of error in claims eliminates one major source of error in claims about physical objects-appearances cannot appear other than they are. Ayer's requirement of grasping meaning eliminates a second source of error, conceptual confusion. But a third major source, misclassification, is genuine and can obtain in this limited domain, even when Ayer 's requirement is satisfied.

Any proponent to the given faces the dilemma that if in terms used in statements expressing its apprehension are purely demonstrative, then such statements, assuming they are statements, are certain, but fail to express beliefs that could serve as foundations for knowledge. If what is expressed is not awareness of genuine properties, then awareness does not justify its subject in believing anything else. However, if statements about what appears use genuine predicates that apply to reinstantiable properties, then beliefs expressed cannot be infallible or knowledge. Coherentists would add that such genuine belief's stand in need of justification themselves and so cannot be foundations.

Contemporary foundationalist deny the coherent's claim while eschewing the claim that foundations, in the form of reports about appearances, are infallible. They seek alternatives to the given as foundations. Although arguments against infallibility are strong, other objections to the idea of foundations are not. The concept of an objective property is an acquired knowledge prior to the concept of appearances, for example, implies neither that claims about objective properties, nor that the latter are prior in chains of justification. That there can be no knowledge prior to the acquisition and consistent application of concepts allows for propositions whose truth requires only consistent application of concepts, and this may be so for some claims about appearances.

Coherentist will claim that a subject requires evidence that he apply concepts consistently to distinguish red from other colours that appear. Beliefs about red appearances could not then be justified independently of other beliefs expressing that evidence. Save that to part of the doctrine of the given that holds beliefs about appearances to be self-justified, we require an account of how such justification is possible, how some beliefs about appearances can be justified without appeal to evidence. Some foundationalist's simply assert such warrant as derived from experience but, unlike, appeals to certainty by proponents of the given, this assertion seems ad hoc.

A better strategy is to tie an account of self-justification to a broader exposition of epistemic warrant. On such accounts sees justification as a kind of inference to the best explanation. A belief is shown to be justified if its truth is shown to be part of the best explanation for why it is held. A belief is self-justified if the best explanation for it is its truth alone. The best explanation for the belief that I am appeared too redly may be that I am. Such accounts seek ground knowledge in perceptual experience without appealing to an infallible given, now universally dismissed.

Nonetheless, it goes without saying, that many problems concerning scientific change have been clarified, and many new answers suggested. Nevertheless, concepts central to it, like 'paradigm'. 'core', problem', 'constraint', 'verisimilitude', many devastating criticisms of the doctrine based on them have been answered satisfactorily.

Problems centrally important for the analysis of scientific change have been neglected. There are, for instance, lingering echoes of logical empiricism in claims that the methods and goals of science are unchanging, and thus are independent of scientific change itself, or that if they do change, they do so for reasons independent of those involved in substantive scientific change itself. By their very nature, such approaches fail to address the changes that actually occur in science. For example, even supposing that science ultimately seeks the general and unaltered goal of 'truth' or 'verisimilitude', that injunction itself gives no guidance as to what scientists should seek or how they should go about seeking it. More specific scientific goals do provide guidance, and, as the transition from mechanistic to gauge-theoretic goals illustrates, those goals are often altered in light of discoveries about what is achievable, or about what kinds of theories are promising. A theory of scientific change should account for these kinds of goal changes, and for how, once accepted, they alter the rest of the patterns of scientific reasoning and change, including ways in which more general goals and methods may be reconceived.

To declare scientific changes to be consequences of 'observation' or 'experimental evidence' is again to overstress the superficially unchanging aspects of science. we must ask how what counts as observation, experiments, and evidence they alter in the light of newly accepted scientific beliefs. Likewise, it is now clear that scientific change cannot be understood in terms of dogmatically embraced holistic cores: The factors guiding scientific change are by no means the monolithic structure which they have been portrayed as being. Some writers prefer to speak of 'background knowledge' (or 'information') as shaping scientific change, the suggestion being that there are a variety of ways in which a variety of prior ideas influence scientific research in a variety of circumstances. But it is essential that any such complexity of influences be fully detailed, not left, as by the philosopher of science Raimund Karl Popper (1902-1994), with cursory treatment of a few functions selected to bolster a prior theory (in this case, falsification). Similarly, focus on 'constraints' can mislead, suggesting too negative a concept to do justice to the positive roles of the information utilized. Insofar as constraints are scientific and not trans-scientific, they are usually 'functions', not 'types' of scientific propositions.

Traditionally, philosophy has concerned itself with relations between propositions which are specifically relevant to one another in form or content. So viewed, a philosophical explanation of scientific change should appeal to factors which are clearly more scientifically relevant in their content to the specific directions of new scientific research and conclusions than are social factors whose overt relevance lies elsewhere. Nonetheless, in recent years many writers, especially in the 'strong programme' practices must be assimilated to social influences.

Such claims are excessive. Despite allegations that even what counted as evidence is a matter of mere negotiated agreement, many consider that the last word has not been said on the idea that there is in some deeply important sense of a 'given' to experience in terms with which we can, at least partially, judge theories ('background information') which can help guide those and other judgements. Even if ewe could, no information to account for what science should and can be, and certainly not for what it is often in human practice, neither should we take the criticism of it for granted, accepting that scientific change is explainable only by appeal to external factors.

Equally, we cannot accept too readily the assumption (another logical empiricist legacy) that our task is to explain science and its evolution by appeal to meta-scientific rules or goals, or metaphysical principles, arrived at in the light of purely philosophical analysis, and altered (if at all) by factors independent of substantive science. For such trans-scientific analysis, even while claiming to explain 'what science is', do so in terms 'external' to the processes by which science actually changes.

Externalist claims are premature by enough is yet understood about the roles of indisputably scientific considerations in shaping scientific change, including changes of methods and goals. Even if we ultimately cannot accept the traditional 'internalist' approach to philosophy of science, as philosophers concerned with the form and content of reasoning we must determine accurately how far it can be carried. For that task. Historical and contemporary case studies are necessary but insufficient: Too often the positive implications of such studies are left unclear, and their too hasty assumption is often that whatever lessons are generated therefrom apply equally to later science. Larger lessons need to be extracted from concrete studies. Further, such lessons must, there possible, be given a systematic account, integrating the revealed patterns of scientific reasoning and the ways they are altered into a coherent interpretation of the knowledge-seeking enterprise-a theory of scientific change. Whether such efforts are successful or not, or through understanding our failure to do so, that it will be possible to assess precisely the extent to which trans-scientific factors (meta-scientific, social, or otherwise) must be included in accounts of scientific change.

Much discussion of scientific change on or upon the distinction between contexts of discovery and justification that is to say about discovery that there is usually thought to be no authoritative confirmation theory, telling how bodies of evidence support, a hypothesis instead science proceeds by a 'hypothetico-deductive method' or 'method of conjectures and refutations'. By contrast, early inductivists held that (1) science e begins with data collections (2) rules of inference are applied to the data to obtain a theoretical conclusion, or at least, to eliminate alternatives, and (3) that conclusion is established with high confidence or even proved conclusively by the rules. Rules of inductive reasoning were proposed by the English diplomat and philosopher Francis Bacon (1561-1626) and by the British mathematician and physicists and principal source of the classical scientific view of the world, Sir Isaac Newton (1642-1727) in th e second edition of the Principia ('Rules of Reasoning in Philosophy'). Such procedures were allegedly applied in Newton's 'Opticks' and in many eighteenth-century experimental studies of heat, light, electricity, and chemistry.

According to Laudan (1981), two gradual realizations led to rejection of this conception of scientific method: First, that inferences from facts to generalizations are not established with certain, hence sectists were more willing to consider hypotheses with little prior empirical grounding, Secondly, that explanatory concepts often go beyond sense experience, and that such trans-empirical concepts as 'atom' and 'field' can be introduced in the formulation of such hypothesis, thus, as the middle of the eighteenth century, the inductive conception began to be replaced by the middle of hypothesis, or hypothetico-deductive method. On the view, the other of events in science is seen as, first, introduction of a hypothesis and second, testing of observational production of that hypothesis against observational and experimental results.

Twentieth-century relativity and quantum mechanics alerted scientists even more to the potential depths of departures from common sense and earlier scientific ideas, e.g., quantum theory. Their attention was called from scientific change and direct toward an analysis of temporal 'formal' characteristics of science: The dynamical character of science, emphasized by physics, was lost in a quest for unchanging characteristics deffinitary of science and its major components, i.e., 'content' of thought, the 'meanings' of fundamental 'meta-scientific' concepts and method-deductive conception of method, endorsed by logical empiricist, was likewise construed in these terms: 'Discovery', the introduction of new ideas, was grist for historians, psychologists or sociologists, whereas the 'justification' of scientific ideas was the application of logic and thus, the proper object of philosophy of science.

The fundamental tenet of logical empiricism is that the warrant for all scientific knowledge rests on or upon empirical evidence I conjunction with logic, where logic is taken to include induction or confirmation, as well as mathematics and formal logic. In the eighteenth century the work of the empiricist John Locke (1632-1704) had important implications for other social sciences. The rejection of innate ideas in book I of the Essay encouraged an emphasis on the empirical study of human societies, to discover just what explained their variety, and this toward the establishment of the science of social anthropology.

Induction (logic), in logic, is the process of drawing a conclusion about an object or event that has yet to be observed or occur, based on previous observations of similar objects or events. For example, after observing year after year that a certain kind of weed invades our yard in autumn, we may conclude that next autumn our yard will again be invaded by the weed; or having tested a large sample of coffee makers, only to find that each of them has a faulty fuse, we conclude that all the coffee makers in the batch are defective. In these cases we infer, or reach a conclusion based on observations. The observations or speculative assumptions are to assert for which we base the inference, or the alternate appearances of the weed, or the sample of coffee makers with faulty fuses-form the premises or assumptions.

In an inductive inference, the premises provide evidence or support for the conclusion; this support can vary in strength. The argument's strength depends on how likely it is that the conclusion will be true, assuming all of the premises to be true. If assuming the premises to be true makes it highly probable that the conclusion also would be true, the argument is inductively strong. If, however, the supposition that all the premises are true only slightly increases the probability that the conclusion will be true, the argument is inductively weak.

The truth or falsity of the premises or the conclusion is not at issue. Strength instead depends on whether, and how much, the likelihood of the conclusion's being true would increase if the premises were true. So, in induction, as in deduction, the emphasis is on the form of support that the premises provide to the conclusion. However, induction differs from deduction in a crucial aspect. In deduction, for an argument to be correct, if the premises were true, the conclusion would have to be true as well. In induction, however, even when an argument is inductively strong, the possibility remains that the premises are true and the conclusion false. To return to our examples, although it is true that this weed has invaded our yard every year, it remains possible that the weed could die and never reappear. Likewise, it is true that all of the coffee makers tested had faulty fuses, but it is possible that the remainder of the coffee makers in the batch is not defective. Yet it is still correct, from an inductive point of view, to infer that the weed will return, and that the remainder of the coffee makers has faulty fuses.

Thus, strictly speaking, all inductive inferences are deductively invalid. Yet induction is not worthless; in both everyday reasoning and scientific reasoning regarding matters of fact - for instance in trying to establish general empirical laws - induction plays a central role. In an inductive inference, for example, we draw conclusions about an entire group of things, or a population, based on data about a sample of that group or population; or we predict the occurrence of a future event because of observations of similar past events; or we attribute a property to a non-observed thing as all observed things of the same kind have that property; or we draw conclusions about causes of an illness based on observations of symptoms. Inductive inference is used in most fields, including education, psychology, physics, chemistry, biology, and sociology. Consequently, because the role of induction is so central in our processes of reasoning, the study of inductive inference is one major area of concern to create computer models of human reasoning in Artificial Intelligence.

The development of inductive logic owes a great deal to 19th - century British philosopher John Stuart Mill, who studied different methods of reasoning and experimental inquiry in his work 'A System of Logic''(1843), by which Mill was chiefly interested in studying and classifying the different types of reasoning in which we start with observations of events and go on to infer the causes of those events. In, 'A Treatise on Induction and Probability' (1960), 20th - century Finnish philosopher Georg Henrik von Wright expounded the theoretical foundations of Mill's methods of inquiry.

Philosophers have struggled with the question of what justification we have to take for granted induction's common assumptions: that the future will follow the same patterns as from the past. Such that a whole population will behave roughly like a randomly chosen sample; that the laws of nature governing cause and effect are uniform; or that we can presume that several observed objects give us grounds to attribute something to another object we have not yet observed. In short, what is the justification for induction itself? This question of justification, known as the problem of induction, was first raised by 18th - century Scottish philosopher David Hume in his An Enquiry Concerning Human Understanding (1748). While it is tempting to try to justify induction by pointing out that inductive reasoning is commonly used in both everyday life and science, and its conclusions are, largely, been corrected, this justification is itself an induction and therefore it raises the same problem: Nothing guarantees that simply because induction has worked in the past it will continue to work in the future. The problem of induction raises important questions for the philosopher and logician whose concern it is to provide a basis of assessment of the correctness and the value of methods of reasoning.

In the eighteenth century, Lock's empiricism and the science of Newton were, with reason, combined in people's eyes to provide a paradigm of rational inquiry that, arguably, has never been entirely displaced. It emphasized the very limited scope of absolute certainties in the natural and social sciences, and more generally underlined the boundaries to certain knowledge that arise from our limited capacities for observation and reasoning. To that extent it provided an important foil to the exaggerated claims sometimes made for the natural sciences in the wake of Newton's achievements in mathematical physics.

This appears to conflict strongly with Thomas Kuhn's (1922 - 96) statement that scientific theory choice depends on considerations that go beyond observation and logic, even when logic is construed to include confirmation.

Nonetheless, it can be said, that, the state of science at any given time is characterized, in part, by the theories accepted then. Presently accepted theories include quantum theory, and general theory of relativity, and the modern synthesis of Darwin and Mendel, as well as lower - level, but still clearly theoretical assertions such as that DNA has a double - helical structure, that the hydrogen atom contains a single electron, and so firth. What precisely is involved in accepting a theory or factors in theory choice.

Many critics have been scornful of the philosophical preoccupation with under - determination, that a theory is supported by evidence only if it implies some observation categories. However, following the French physician Pierre Duhem, who is remembered philosophically for his La Thêorie physique, (1906), translated as, 'The Aim and Structure of Science, is that it simply is a device for calculating science provides a deductive system that is systematic, economic and predicative: Following Duhem, Orman van Willard Quine (1918 - 2000), who points out that observation categories can seldom if ever be deduced from a single scientific theory taken by itself: Rather, the theory must be taken in conjunction with a whole lot of other hypotheses and background knowledge, which are usually not articulated in detail and may sometimes be quite difficult to specify. A theoretical sentence does not, in general, have any empirical content of its own. This doctrine is called 'Holism', which the basic term refers to a variety of positions that have in common a resistance to understanding large unities as merely the sum of their parts, and an insistence that we cannot explain or understand the parts without treating them as belonging to such larger wholes. Some of these issues concern explanation. It is argued, for example, that facts about social classes are not reducible to facts about the beliefs and actions of the agents who belong to them, or it is claimed that we only understand the actions of individuals by locating them in social roles or systems of social meanings.

But, whatever may be the case with under - determination, there is a very closely related problem that scientists certainly do face whenever two rival theories or more encompassing theoretical frameworks are competing for acceptance. This is the problem posed by the fact that one framework, usually the older, longer - established frameworks can accommodate, that is, produce post hoc explanation of particular pieces of evidence that seem intuitively to tell strongly in favour of the other (usually the new 'revolutionary') framework.

For example, the Newtonian particulate theory of light is often thought of as having been straightforwardly refuted by the outcome of experiments - like Young 's two - slits experiment - whose results were correctly predicted by the rival wave theory. Duhem's (1906) analysis of theories and theory testing already shows that this cannot logically have been the case. The bare theory that light consists of some sort of material particle has no empirical consequence s in isolation from other assumptions: And it follows that there must always be assumptions that could be added to the bare corpuscular theory, such that some combined assumptions entail the correct result of any optical experiment. A d indeed, a little historical research soon reveals eighteenth and early nineteenth - century emissionists who suggested at least outline ways in which interference result s could be accommodated within the corpuscular framework. Brewster, for example, suggested that interference might be a physiological phenomenon: While Biot and others worked on the idea that 'interferences' circumferential proponents are produced by the peculiarities of the 'diffracting forces' that ordinary gross exerts on the light corpuscles.

Both suggestions ran into major conceptual problems. For example, the 'diffracting force' suggestion would not even come close to working with any forces of kinds that were taken to operate in other cases. Often the failure was qualitative: Given the properties of forces that were already known about, for example, it was expected that the diffracting force would depend in some way on the material properties of the diffracting object: But, whatever the material of the double - slit screens are Young's experiment, and whatever its density, the outcome is the same. It could, of course, simply be assumed that the diffracting forces are an entirely novel kind, and that their properties just had to be 'read-off' the phenomena - this is exactly the way that corpusularists worked. Heretofore, the singular one or times of more with which the re-exist are no more. That is, to any exclusion of any alternative or competitor will only confess to you. The attemptive to write the phenomena into a favoured conceptual framework. And given that the writing - in produced complexities and incongruities for which there was no independent evidence, the majority view was that interference results strongly favour the wave theory, of which they are 'natural' consequences. (For example, that the material making up the double slit and its density have no effect at all on the phenomenon is a straightforward consequence of the fact that, as the wave theory says it, the only effect on the screen is to absorb those parts of the wave fronts that impinges on it.)

The natural methodological judgement (and the one that seems to have been made by the majority of competent scientists at that time) is that, even given the interference effects could be accommodated within the corpuscular theory, those effects nonetheless favour the wave account, and favour it in the epistemic sense of showing that theory to be more likely to be true. Of course, the account given by the wave theory of the interference phenomena is also, in certain senses, pragmatically simpler: But this seems generally to have been taken to be, not a virtue in itself, but a reflection of a deeper virtue connected with likely truth.

Consider a second, similar case: That of evolutionary theory and the fossil record. There are well - known disputes about which particular evolutionary account for most support from fossils. Nonetheless, the relative weight the fossil evidence carries for some sort of evolutionist account versus the special creationist theory, is yet well - known for its obviousness - in that the theory of special creation can accommodate fossils: A creationist just needs to claim that what the evolutionist thinks of as bones of animals belonging to extinct species, are, in fact, simply items that God chose to included in his catalogue of the universe's content at creatures: What the evolutionist thinks of as imprints in the rocks of the skeletons of other such animals are they. It nonetheless surely still seems true intuitively that the fossil records continue to give us better reason to believe that species have evolved from earlier, now extinct ones, than that God created the universe much as it presently is in 4004 Bc. An empiricist - instrumentalist t approach seems committed to the view that, on the contrary, any preference that this evidence yields for the evolutionary account is a purely pragmatic matter.

Of course, intuitions, no matter how strong, cannot stand against strong counter arguments. Van Fraassen and other strong empiricists have produced arguments that purport to show that these intuitions are indeed misguided.

What justifies the acceptance e of a theory? Although h particular versions of empiricism have met many criticisms, that is, of support by the available evidence. How else could empiricists term? : In terms, that is, of support by the available evidence. How else could the objectivity of science be defended but by showing that its conclusion (and in particularly its theoretical conclusions - those theories? It presently on any other condition than that excluding exemplary base on which are somehow legitimately based on or agreed observationally and experimental evidences, yet, as well known, theoretics in general, pose a problem for empiricism. Allowing the empiricist the assumptions that there are observational statements whose truth - values can be inter-subjectively agreeing. A definitive formulation of the classical view was finally provided by the German logical positivist Rudolf Carnap (1891 - 1970), combining a basic empiricism with the logical tools provided by Frége and Russell: And it is his work that the main achievements (and difficulties) of logical positivism are best exhibited. His first major works were Der Logische Aufban der welts (1928, translated as 'The Logical Structure of the World, 1967) this phenomenological work attempts a reduction of all the objects of knowledge, by generating equivalence classes of sensations, related by a primitive relation of remembrance of similarity. This is the solipsistic basis of the construction of the external world, although Carnap later resisted the apparent metaphysical priority as given to experience. His hostility to metaphysics soon developed into the positivity as emphasis by the view characteristics that metaphysical questions are pseudo - problems.

Criticism from the Austrian philosopher and social theorist Otto Neurath (1882 - 1945) shifted Carnap's interest toward a view of the unity of the sciences, with the concepts and theses of special sciences translatable into a basic physical vocabulary whose protocol statements describe not experience but the qualities of points in space - time. Carnap pursued the enterprise of clarifying the structures of mathematics and scientific language (the only legitimate task for scientific philosophy) in Logische Syntax fer Sprache (1943, translated as, 'The Logical Syntax of Language', 1937) refinements to his syntactic and semantic views continued with Meaning and Necessity (1947) while a general loosening of the original ideal of reduction culminated in the great Logical Foundations of Probability, the most important single work of 'confirmation theory', in 1950. Other works concern the structure of physics and the concept of entropy.

Wherefore, the observational terms were presumed to be given a complete empirical interpretation, which left the theoretical terms with only an 'indirect' empirical interpretation provided by their implicit definition within an axiom system in which some of the terms possessed a complete empirical interpretation.

Among the issues generated by Carnap's formulation was the viability of 'the theory - observation distinction'. Of course, one could always arbitrarily designate some subset of nonlogical terms as belonging to the observational vocabulary, however, that would compromise the relevance of the philosophical analysis for any understanding of the original scientific theory. But what could be the philosophical basis for drawing the distinction? Take the predicate 'spherical', for example. Anyone can observe that a billiard ball is spherical, but what about the moon, or an invisible speck of sand? Is the application of the term 'spherical' of these objects 'observational'?

Another problem was more formal, as introduced of Craig's theorem seemed to show that a theory reconstructed in the recommended fashion could be re - axiomatized in such a way as to dispense with all theoretical terms, while retaining all logical consequences involving only observational terms. Craig's theorem in mathematical logic, held to have implications in the philosophy of science. The logician William Craig showed how, if we partition the vocabulary of a formal system (say, into the 'T' or theoretical terms, and the 'O' or observational terms), then if there is a fully 'formalized' system 'T' with some set 'S' of consequences containing only the 'O' terms, there is also a system 'O' containing only the 'O' vocabulary but strong enough to give the same set 'S' of consequences. The theorem is a purely formal one, in that 'T' and 'O' simply separate formulae into the preferred ones, containing non- logical terms only one kind of vocabulary, and the others. The theorem might encourage the thought that the theoretical terms of a scientific theory are in principle, dispensable, since the same consequences can be derived without them.

However, Craig's actual procedure gives no effective way of dispensing with theoretical terms in advance, i.e., in the actual process of thinking about and designing the premises from which the set 'S' follows, in this sense 'O' remains parasitical on or upon its parent 'T'.

Thus, as far as the 'empirical' content of a theory is concerned, it seems that we can do without the theoretical terms. Carnap's version of the classical view seemed to imply a form of instrumentation. A problem which the German philosopher of science, Carl Gustav Hempel (1905 - 97) christened 'the theoretician's dilemma'.

Meanwhile Descartes identification of matter with extension, and his comitant theory of all of space as filed by a plenum of matter. The great metaphysical debate over the nature of space and time has its roots in the scientific revolution of the sixteenth and seventeenth centuries. An early contribution to the debate was the French mathematician and founding father of modern philosophy, Réne Descartes (1596 - 1650). His interest in the methodology of a unified science culminated in his first work, the Regulae ad Directionem Ingenti (1628/9), was never completed. Nonetheless, between 1628 and 1649, Descartes first wrote and then cautiously suppressed, Le Monde (1634) and in 1637 produced the Discours de la Méthode as a preface to the treatise on mathematics and physics in which he introduced the notion of Cartesian coordinates.

His best known philosophical work, the Meditationes de Prima Philosophia (Meditations of First Philosophy), together with objections by distinguished contemporaries and relies by Descartes (the Objections and Replies) appeared in 1641. The author of the objections is First advanced, by the Dutch theologian Johan de Kater, second set, Mersenne, third set, Hobbes: Fourth set, Arnauld, fifth set, Gassendim, and sixth set, Mersnne. The second edition (1642) of the Meditations included a seventh set by the Jesuit Pierre Bourdin. Descartes's penultimate work, the Principia Philosophiae (Principles of Philosophy) of 1644 was designed partly for use in theological textbooks: His last work, Les Passions de I âme (the Passions of the Soul) and published in 1649. In that year Descartes visited the court of Kristina of Sweden, where he contracted pneumonia, allegedly through being required to break his normal habit of a late rising in order to give lessons at 5:00 a.m. His last spoken words were accepted or advanced as true or real on the basis of less than conclusive evidence was 'Ça, mon sme il faut partur', - 'So my soul, it is time to part'.

It is nonetheless said, that the great metaphysical debate over the nature of space and time has its roots in the scientific revolution of the sixteenth and seventeenth centuries. An early contribution to the debate was Réne Descartes's (1596 - 1650), identification of matter with extension, and his comitant theory of all of space as filled by a plenum of matter.

Far more profound was the German philosopher, mathematician and polymath, Wilhelm Gottfried Leibniz (1646 - 1716), whose characterization of a full - blooded theory of relationism with regard to space and time, as Leibniz elegantly puts his view: 'Space is nothing but the order of coexistence . . . time is the order of inconsistent 'possibilities'. Space was taken to be a set of relations among material objects. The deeper monadological view to the side, were the substantival entities, no room was provided for space itself as a substance over and above the material substance of the world. All motion was then merely relative motion of one material thing in the reference frame fixed by another. The Leibnizian theory was one of great subtlety. In particular, the need for a modalized relationism to allow for 'empty space' was clearly recognized. An unoccupied spatial location was taken to be a spatial relation that could be realized but that was not realized in actuality. Leibniz also offered trenchant arguments against substantivalism. All of these rested upon some variant of the claim that a substantival picture of space allows for the theoretical toleration of alternative world models that are identical as far as any observable consequences are concerned.

Contending with Leibnizian relationalism was the 'substantivalism' of Isaac Newton (1642 - 1727), and his disciple S. Clarke, thereby he is mainly remembered for his defence of Newton (a friend from Cambridge days) against Leibniz, both on the question of the existence of absolute space and the question of the propriety of appealing to a force of gravity, actually Newton was cautious about thinking of space as a 'substance'. Sometimes he suggested that it be thought of, rather, as a property - in particular as a property of the Deity. However, what was essential to his doctrine was his denial that a relationist theory, with its idea of motion as the relative change of position of one material object with respect to another, can do justice to the facts about motion made evident by empirical science and by the theory that does justice to those facts.

The Newtonian account of motion, like Aristotle's, has a concept of natural or unforced motion. This is motion with uniform speed in a constant direction, so - called inertial motion. There is, then, in this theory an absolute notion of constant velocity motion. Such constant velocity motions cannot be characterized as merely relative to some material objects, some of which will be non-inertial. Space itself, according to Newton, must exist as an entity over and above the material objects of the world. In order to provide the standard of rest relative to which uniform motion is genuine inertial motion.

Such absolute uniform motions can be empirically discriminated from absolutely accelerated motion by the absence of inertial forces felt when the test object is moving genuinely inertially. Furthermore, the application of force to an object is correlated with the object's change of absolute motion. Only uniform motions relative to space itself are natural motions requiring no force and explanation. Newton also clearly saw that the notion of absolute constant speed requires a motion of absolute time, for, relative to an arbitrary cyclic process as defining the time scale, any motion can be made uniform or not, as we choose. Nonetheless, genuine uniform motions are of constant speed in the absolute time scale fixed by 'time itself; . Periodic processes can be at best good indicators of measures of this flaw of absolute time.

Newton's refutation of relationism by means of the argument from absolute acceleration is one of the most distinctive examples of the way in which the results of empirical experiment and of the theoretical efforts to explain these results impinge on or upon philosophical objections to Leibnizian relationism - for example, in the claim that one must posit a substantival space to make sense of Leibniz's modalities of possible position - it is a scientific objection to relationism that causes the greatest problems for that philosophical doctrine.

Then, again, a number of scientists and philosophers continued to defend the relationist account of space in the face of Newton's arguments for substantivalism. Among them were Wilhelm Gottfried Leibniz, Christian Huygens, and George Berkeley when in 1721 Berkeley published De Motu ('On Motion') attacking Newton 's philosophy of space, a topic he returned too much later in The Analyst of 1734.the empirical distinction, however, to frustrate their efforts.

In the nineteenth century, the Austrian physicist and philosopher Ernst Mach (1838 - 1916), made the audacious proposal that absolute acceleration might be viewed as acceleration relative not to a substantival space, but to the material reference frame of what he called the 'fixed stars' - that is, relative to a reference frame fixed by what might now be called the 'average smeared - out mass of the universe'. As far as observational data went, he argued, the fixed stars could be taken to be the frames relative to which uniform motion was absolutely uniform. Mach's suggestion continues to play an important role in debates up to the present day.

The nature of geometry as an apparently a priori science also continued to receive attention. Geometry served as the paradigm of knowledge for rationalist philosophers, especially for Descartes and the Dutch Jewish rationalist Benedictus de Spinoza (1632 - 77), whereby the German philosopher Immanuel Kant (1724 - 1804) attempts to account for the ability of geometry to go beyond the analytic truths of logic extended by definition - was especially important. His explanation of the a priori nature of geometry by its 'transcendentally psychological' nature - that is, as descriptive of a portion of mind's organizing structure imposed on the world of experience - served as his paradigm for legitimated a priori knowledge in general.

A peculiarity of Newton's theory, of which Newton was well aware, was that whereas acceleration with respect to space itself had empirical consequences, uniform velocity with respect to space itself had none. The theory of light, particularly in J.C. Maxwell's theory of electromagnetic waves, suggested, however, that there was only one reference frame in which the velocity of light would be the same in all directions, and that this might be taken to be the frame at rest in 'space itself'. Experiments designed to find this frame seen to sow, however, that light velocity is isotropic and has its standard value in all frames that are in uniform motion in the Newtonian sense. All these experiments, however, measured only the average velocity of the light relative to the reference frame over a round - trip path trails. It was the insight of the German physicist Albert Einstein (1879 - 1955) who took the apparent equivalence of all inertial frames with respect to the velocity of light to be a genuine equivalence, It was from an employment within the Patent Office in Bern, wherefrom in 1905 he published the papers that laid the foundation of his reputation, on the photoelectric theory of relativity. In 1916 he published the general theory and in 1933 Einstein accepted the position at the Princeton Institute for Advanced Studies which he occupied for the rest of his life. His deepest insight was to see that this required that we relativize the notion of the simultaneity of events spatially separated from one distanced between a non - simultaneous events' reference frame. For any relativist, the distance between non-simultaneous events' simultaneity is relative as well. This theory of Einstein's later became known as the Special Theory of Relativity.

Eienstein's proposal account for the empirical undetectability of the absolute rest frame by optical experiments, because in his account the velocity of light is isotropic and has its standard value in all inertial frames. The theory had immediate kinematic consequences, among them the fact that spatial separation (lengths) and intervals relevant to set frames - of motion - relatively. New dynamics was needed if dynamics were to be, as it was for Newton, equivalence in all inertial frames.

Einstein's novel understanding of space and time was given an elegant framework by H. Minkowski in the form of Minkowski Space-time. The primitive elements of the theory were a characteristic point - like, locations in both spatially temporal of unextended happenings. These were called the 'event locations' or the 'events'' of a four - dimensional manifold. There is a frame-invariant separation of an event frame event called the 'interval'. But the spatial separation between two noncoincident events, as well as their temporal separation, are well defined only relative to a chosen inertial reference frame.

In a sense, then, space and time are integrated into a single absolute structure. Space and time by themselves have a derivative and relativized existence.

Whereas the geometry of this space - time bore some analogies to a Euclidean geometry of a four - dimensional space, the transition from space and time by them in an integrated space - time required a subtle rethinking of the very subject matter of geometry. 'Straight lines' are the straightest curves of this 'flat' space - time, however, in them, they to include 'null straight lines', interpreted as the events in the life history of a light ray in a vacuum and 'time - like straight lines', interpreted as the collection of events in the life history of a free inertial contribution to the revolution in scientific thinking into the new relativistic framework. The result of his thinking was the theory known as the general theory of relativity.

The heuristic basis for the theory rested on or upon an empirical fact known to Galileo and Newton, but whose importance was made clear only by Einstein. Gravity, unlike other forces such as the electromagnetic force, acts on all objects independently of their material constitution or of their size. The path through space - time followed by an object under the influence of gravity is determined only by its initial position and velocity. Reflection upon the fact that in a curved spac e the path of minimal curvature from a point, the so - called 'geodesic', is uniquely determined by the point and by a direction from it, suggested to Einstein that the path of as an object acted upon by gravity can be thought of as a geodesic followed by that path in a curved space - time. The addition of gravity to the space - time of special relativity can be thought of s changing the 'flat' space - time of Minkowski into a new, 'curved' space - time.

The kind of curvature implied by the theory in that explored by B. Riemann in his theory of intrinsically curved spaces of an arbitrary dimension. No assumption is made that the curved space exists in some higher - dimensional flat embedding space, curvature is a feature of the space that shows up observationally in those in the space longer straight lines, just as the shortest distances between points on the Earth's surface cannot be reconciled with putting those points on a flat surface. Einstein (and others) offered other heuristic arguments to suggest that gravity might indeed have an effect of relativistic interval separations as determined by measurements using tapes' spatial separations and clocks, to determine time intervals.

The special theory gives a unified account of the laws of mechanics and of electromagnetism (including optics). Before 1905 the purely relative nature of uniform motion had in part been recognized in mechanics, although Newton had considered time to be absolute and also postulated absolute space. In electromagnetism the 'ether' was supposed to provide an absolute basis with respect to which motion could be determined and made two postulates. (The laws of nature are the same for all observers in uniform relative e motion. (2) The speed of light is the same for all such observes, independently of the relative motion of sources and detectors. He showed that these postulates were equivalent to the requirement that coordinates of space and time was put - upon by different observers should be related by the 'Lorentz Transformation Equation Theory': The theory has several important consequences.

That is to say, a set of equations for transforming the position - motion parameters from an observer at point 0(x, y, z) to an observer at 0'(x', y', z'), moving relative to one another. The equations replace the 'Galilean transformation equations of Newtonian mechanics in Relative problems. If the x - axises are chosen to pass through 00' and the time of an even t is (t) and (t') in the frame of reference of the observer at 0 and 0' respectively y (where the zeros of their time scales were the instants that 0 and 0' coincided) the equations are:

$$x' = \beta(x - vt)$$
$$y' = y$$
$$z' = z$$
$$t' = \beta(t - vx/c2),$$

Where v is the relative velocity y of separation of 0, 0', c is the speed of light, and β is the function (1 - v2/c2).

The transformation of time implies that two events that are simultaneous according to one observer will not necessarily be so according to another in uniform relative motion. This does not affect in any way violate any concepts of causation. It will appear to two observers in uniform relative motion that each other's clock rums slowly. This is the phenomenon of 'time dilation', for example, an observer moving with respect to a radioactive source finds a longer decay time than that found by an observer at rest with respect to it, according to:

$$Tv = T0/(1 - v2/c2)½,$$

Where Tv is the mean life measured by an observer at relative speed v. T0 is the mean life measured by an observer relatively at rest, and c is the speed of light.

Among the results of the 'exact' form optics is the deduction of the exact form io f the Doppler Effect. In relativity mechanics, mass, momentum and energy are all conserved. An observer with speed v with respect to a particle determines its mass to be m while an observer at rest with respect to the [article measure the 'rest mass' m0, such that:

$$m = m0/(1 - v2/c2)½$$

This formula has been verified in innumerable experiments. One consequence is that no body can be accelerated from a speed below c with respect to any observer to one above c, since this would require infinite energy. Einstein deduced that the transfer of energy δE by any process entailed the transfer of mass δm, where δE = δmc2, hence he concluded that the total energy E of any system of mass m would be given by:

$$E = mc2$$

The kinetic energy of a particle as determined by an observer with relative speed v is thus (m - m0)c2, which tends to the classical value ½mv2 if v ≪c.

Attempts to express Quantum Theory in terms consistent with the requirements of relativity were begun by Sommerfeld (1915). Eventually Dirac (1928) gave a relativistic formulation of the wave mechanics of conserved particles (fermions). This explained the concepts of sin and the associated magnetic moment for certain details of spectra. The theory led to results of elementary particles, the theory of Beta Decay, and for Quantum statistics, the Klein - Gordon Equation is the relativistic wave equation for 'bosons'.

A mathematical formulation of the special theory of relativity was given by Minkowski. It is based on the idea that an event is specified by four coordinates: Three spatial coordinates and one of time. These coordinates define a four - dimensional space and time motion of a particle can be described by a curve in this space, which is called 'Minkowski space - time'.

The special theory of relativity is concerned with relative motion between non-accelerated frames of reference. The general theory deals with general relative motion between accelerated frames of reference. In accelerated systems of reference, certain fictitious forces are observed, such as the centrifugal and Coriolis forces found in rotating systems. These are known as fictitious forces because they disappear when the observer transforms to a non - accelerated system. For example, to an observer in a car rounding a bend at constant velocity, objects in the car appear to suffer a force acting outwards. To an observer outside the car, this is simply their tendency to continue moving in a straight line. The inertia of the objects is seen to cause a fictitious force and the observer can distinguish between non- inertial (accelerated) and inertial (non - accelerated) frames of reference.

A further point is that, to the observer in the car, all the objects are given the same acceleration irrespective of their mass. This implies a connection between the fictitious forces arising from accelerated systems and forces due to gravity, where the acceleration produced is independent of the mass. For example, a person in a sealed container could not easily decide upon whether he was being driven toward the floor by gravity of if the container were in space and being accelerated upwards by a rocket. Observations extended between these alternatives, but otherwise they are indistinguishable from which it follows that the inertial mass is the same as a gravitational mass.

The equivalence between a gravitational field and the fictitious forces in non-inertial systems can be expressed by using 'Riemannian space - time', which differs from Minkowski space - time of the special theory. In special relativity the motion of a particle that is not acted on by any forces is presented by a straight line in Minkowski space - time. In general relativity, using Riemannian space - time, the motion is presented by a line that is no longer straight (in the Euclidean sense) but is the line giving the shortest distance. Such a line is called a 'geodesic'. Thus, space - time is said to be curved. The extent of this curvature is given by the 'metric tensor' for spaces - time, the components of which are solutions to Einstein's 'field equations'. The fact that gravitational effects occur near masses is introduced by the postulate that the presence e of matter produces this curvature of space - time. This curvature of space - time controls the natural motions of bodies.

The predictions of general relativity only differ from Newton's theory by small amounts and most tests of the theory have been carried out through observations in astronomy. For example, it explains the shift on the perihelion of Mercury, the bending of light in the presence of large bodies, and the Einstein shift. Very close agreements between their accurately measured values have now been obtained.

So, then, using the new space - time notions, a 'curved space - time' theory of Newtonian gravitation can be constructed. In this space - time is absolute, as in Newton. Furthermore, space remains flat Euclidean space. This is unlike the general theory of relativity, where the space-time curvature can induce spatial curvature as well. But the spaces - time curvature of this 'curved neo-Newtonian Space-time, shows up in the fact that particles under the influence of gravity do not follow straight line's paths. Their paths become, as in general relativity, the curved times - like geodesics of the space - time. In this curved space - time account of Newtonian gravity, as in the general theory of relativity, the indistinguishable alternative worlds of theories that take gravity as a force s superimposed in a flat space - time collapsed to a single world model.

The strongest impetus to rethink epistemological issues in the theory of space and time came from the introduction of curvature and of non - Euclidean geometries in the general theory of relativity. The claim that a unique geometry could be known to hold true of the world a priori seemed unviable, at least in its naive form. In a situation where our best available physical theory allowed for a wide diversity of possible geometries for the world and in which the geometry of space - time was one more dynamical element joining the other 'variable' features of the world. Of course, skepticism toward an a priori account of geometry could already have been induced by the change from space time to space - time in the special theory, even though the space of that world remained Euclidean.

The natural response to these changes in physics was to suggest that geometry was, like all other physical theories, believable only on the basis of some kind of generalizing inference from the law - like regularities among the observable observational data - that is, to become an empiricists with regard to geometry.

But a defence of a kind of a priori account had already been suggested by the French mathematician and philosopher Henri Jules Poincaré (1854 - 1912), even before the invention of the relativistic theories. He suggested that the limitation of observational data to the domain of what was both material and local, i.e., or, space - time in order to derive a geometrical world of matter and convention or decision on the part of the scientific community. If any geometric posit could be made compatible with any set of observational data, Euclidean geometry could remain a priori in the sense that we could, conventionally, decide to hold to it as the geometry of the world in the face of any data that apparently refuted it.

The central epistemological issue in the philosophy of space and time remains that of theoretical under - determination, stemming from the Poincaré argument. In the case of the special theory of relativity the question is the rational basis for choosing Einstein's theory over, for example, on of the 'aether reference frame plus modification of rods and clocks when they are in motion with respect to the aether' theories tat it displaced. Among the claims alleged to be true merely by convention in the theory, for which of asserting the simultaneity of distant events, those asserting the 'flatness' of the chosen space - time. Crucial to the fact that Einstein's arguments themselves presuppose a strictly delimited local observation basis for the theories and that in fixing on or upon the special theory of relativity, one must make posits about the space, and time structures that outrun the facts given strictly by observation. In the case of the general theory of relativity, the issue becomes one of justifying the choice of general relativity over, for example, a flat spaces - time theory that treats gravity, as it was treated by Newton, as a 'field of force' over and above the space - time structure.

In both the cases of special and general relativity, important structural features pick out the standard Einstein theories as superior to their alternatives. In particular, the standard relativistic models eliminate some of the problems of observationally equivalent but distinguishable worlds countenanced by the alternative theories. However, the epistemologists must still be concerned with the question as to why these features constitute grounds for accepting the theories as the 'true' alternatives.

Other deep epistemological issues remain, having to do with the relationship between the structures of space and time posited in our theories of relativity and the spatiotemporal structures we use to characterize our 'direct perceptual experience'. These issues continue in the contemporary scientific context the old philosophical debates on the relationship between the ram of the directly perceived and the realm of posited physical nature.

First reaction on the part of some philosophers was to take it that the special theory of relativity provided a replacement for the Newtonian theory of absolute space that would be compatible with a relationist account of the nature of space and time. This was soon seen to be false. The absolute distinction between uniform moving frames and frames not in or upon its uniform motion, invoked by Newton in his crucial argument against relationism, remains in the special theory of relativity. In fact, it becomes an even deeper distinction than it was in the Newtonian account, since the absolutely uniformly moving frames, the inertial frames, now become not only the frames of natural unforced motion, but also the only frames in which the velocity of light is isotropic.

At least part of the motivation behind Einstein's development of the general theory of relativity was the hope that in this new theory all reference frames, uniformly moving or accelerated, would be 'equivalent' to one another physically. It was also his hope that the theory would conform to the Machian idea of absolute acceleration as merely acceleration relative to the smoothed - out matter of the universe.

Further exploration of the theory, however, showed that it had many features uncongenial to Machianism. Some of these are connected with the necessity of imposing boundary conditions for the equation connecting the matter distribution of the space - time structure. General relativity certainly allows as solutions model universes of a non - Machian sort - for example, those which are aptly described as having the smoothed - out matter of the universe itself in 'absolute rotation'. There are strong arguments to suggest that general relativity. Like Newton's theory and like special relativity, requires the positing of a structure of 'space - time itself' and of motion relative to that structure, in order to account for the needed distinctions of kinds of motion in dynamics. Whereas in Newtonian theory it was 'space itself' that provided the absolute reference frames.

In general relativity it is the structure of the null and time - like geodesics that perform this task. The compatibility of general relativity with Machian ideas is, however, a subtle matter and one still open to debate.

Other aspects of the world described by the general theory of relativity argue for a substantivalist reading of the theory as well. Space - time has become a dynamic element of the world, one that might be thought of as 'causally interacting' with the ordinary matter of the world. In some sense one can even attribute energy (and hence mass) to the spacer - time (although this is a subtle matter in the theory), making the very distinction between 'matter' and 'spacer - time itself' much more dubious than such a distinction would have been in the early days of the debate between substantivalists and explanation forthcoming from the substantivalist account is.

Nonetheless, a naive reading of general relativity as a substantivalist theory has its problems as well. One problem was noted by Einstein himself in the early days of the theory. If a region of space - time is devoid of non - gravitational mass - energy, alternative solutions to the equation of the theory connecting mass - energies with the space - time structure will agree in all regions outside the matterless 'hole', but will offer distinct space - time structures within it. This suggests a local version of the old Leibniz arguments against substantivalism. The argument now takes the form of a claim that a substantival reading of the theory forces it into a strong version of indeterminism, since the spaces - time structure outside the hld fails to fix the structure of space - time in the hole. Einstein's own response to this problem has a very relationistic cast, taking the 'real facts' of the world to be intersections of paths of particles and light rays with one another and not the structure of 'space - time itself'. Needless to say, there are substantival attempts to deal with the 'hole' argument was well, which try to reconcile a substantival reading of the theory with determinism.

There are arguments on the part of the relationist to the effect that any substantivalist theory, even one with a distinction between absolute acceleration and mere relative acceleration, can be given a relationistic formulation. These relationistic reformations of the standard theories lack the standard theories' ability to explain why non - inertial motion has the features that it does. But the relationist counters by arguing that the explanation forthcoming from the substantivalist account is too 'thin' to have genuine explanatory value anyway.

Relationist theories are founded, as are conventionalist theses in the epistemology of space - time, on the desire to restrict ontology to that which is present in experience, this taken to be coincidences of material events at a point. Such relationist conventionalist account suffers, however, from a strong pressure to slide full - fledged phenomenalism.

As science progresses, our posited physical space - times become more and more remote from the space-time we come to form an idea of something in the mind in which it is capable of being thought about, as characterizing immediate experience. This will become even more true as we move from the classical space - time of the relativity theories into fully quantized physical accounts of space - time. There is strong pressure from the growing divergence of the space - time of physics from the space - time of our 'immediate experience' to dissociate the two completely and, perhaps, to stop thinking of the space - time of physics for being anything like our ordinary notions of space and time. Whether such a radical dissociation of posited nature from phenomenological experience can be sustained, however, without giving up our grasp entirely on what it is to think of a physical theory 'realistically' is an open question.

Science aims to represent accurately actual ontological unity/diversity. The wholeness of the spatiotemporal framework and the existence of physics, i.e., of laws invariant across all the states of matter, do represent ontological unities which must be reflected in some unification of content. However, there is no simple relation between ontological and descriptive unity/diversity. A variety of approaches to representing unity are available (the formal - substantive spectrum and respective to its opposite and operative directions that the range of naturalisms). Anything complex will support man y different partial descriptions, and, conversely, different kinds of thing s many all obey the laws of a unified theory, e.g., quantum field theory of fundamental particles or collectively be ascribed dynamical unity, e.g., self - organizing systems.

It is reasonable to eliminate gratuitous duplication from description - that is, to apply some principle of simplicity, however, this is not necessarily the same as demanding that its content satisfies some further methodological requirement for formal unification. Elucidating explanations till there is again no reason to limit the account to simple logical systemization: The unity of science might instead be complex, reflecting our multiple epistemic access to a complex reality.

Biology provides as useful analogy. The many diverse species in an ecology nonetheless, each map, genetically and cognitively, interrelatable aspects of as single environment and share exploitation of the properties of gravity, light, and so forth. Though the somantic expression is somewhat idiosyncratic to each species, and the incomplete representation, together they form an interrelatable unity, a multidimensional functional representation of their collective world. Similarly, there are many scientific disciplines, each with its distinctive domains, theories, and methods specialized to the condition under which it accesses our world. Each discipline may exhibit growing internal metaphysical and nomological unities. On occasion, disciplines, or components thereof, may also formally unite under logical reduction. But a more substantive unity may also be manifested: Though content may be somewhat idiosyncratic to each discipline, and the incomplete representation, together the disciplinary y contents form an interrelatable unity, a multidimensional functional representation of their collective world. Correlatively, a key strength of scientific activity lies, not formal monolithicity, but in its forming a complex unity of diverse, interacting processes of experimentations, theorizing, instrumentation, and the like.

While this complex unity may be all that finite cognizers in a complex world can achieve, the accurate representation of a single world is still a central aim. Throughout the history of physics. Significant advances are marked by the introduction of new representation (state) spaces in which different descriptions (reference frames) are embedded as some interrelatable perspective among many thus, Newtonian to relativistic space - time perspectives. Analogously, young children learn to embed two - dimensional visual perspectives in a three - dimensional space in which object constancy is achieved and their own bodies are but some among many. In both cases, the process creates constant methodological pressure for greater formal unity within complex unity.

The role of unity in the intimate relation between metaphysics and metho in the investigation of nature is well - illustrated b y the prelude to Newtonian science. In the millennial Greco - Christian religion preceding the founder of modern astronomy, Johannes Kepler (1571 - 1630), nature was conceived as essentially a unified mystical order, because suffused with divine reason and intelligence. The pattern of nature was not obvious, however, a hidden ordered unity which revealed itself to a diligent search as a luminous necessity. In his Mysterium Cosmographicum, Kepler tried to construct a model of planetary motion based on the five Pythagorean regular or perfect solids. These were to be inscribed within the Aristotelian perfect spherical planetary orbits in order, and so determine them. Even the fact that space is a three-dimensional unity was a reflection of the one triune God. And when the observational facts proved too awkward for this scheme. Kepler tried instead, in his Harmonice Mundi, to build his unified model on the harmonies of the Pythagorean musical scale.

To appreciate both the historical tradition and the role of unity in modern scientific method, consider Newton's methodology, focussing just on Newton's derivation of the law of universal gravitation in Principia Mathematica, book iii. The essential steps are these: (1) The experimental work of Kepler and Galileo (1564 - 1642) is appealed to, so as to establish certain phenomena, principally Kepler's laws of celestial planetary motion and Galileo's terrestrial law of free fall. (2) Newton's basic laws of motion are applied to the idealized system of an object small in size and mass moving with respect to a much larger mass under the action of a force whose features are purely geometrically determined. The assumed linear vector nature of the force allows construction of the centre of a mass frame, which separates out relative from common motions: It is an inertial frame (one for which Newton's first law of motion holds), and the construction can be extended to encompass all solar system objects.

(3) A sensitive equivalence is obtained between Kepler's laws and the geometrical properties of the force: Namely, that it is directed always along the line of centres between the masses, and that it varies inversely as the square of the distance between them. (4) Various instances of this force law are obtained for various bodies in the heavens - for example, the individual planets and the moons of Jupiter. From this one can obtain several interconnected mass ratios - in particular, several mass estimates for the Sun, which can be shown to cohere mutually. (5) The value of this force for the Moon is shown to be identical to the force required by Galileo's law of free fall at the Earth's surface. (6) Appeal is made again to the laws of motion (especially the third law) to argue that all satellites and falling bodies are equally themselves sources of gravitational force. (7) The force is then generalized to a universal gravitation and is shown to explain various other phenomena - for example, Galileo's law for pendulum action is shown suitably small, thus leaving the original conclusions drawn from Kepler's laws intact while providing explanations for the deviations.

Newton's constructions represent a great methodological, as well as theoretical achievement. Many other methodological components besides unity deserve study in their own right. The sense of unification is here that a deep systemization, as given the laws of motion, the geometrical form of the gravitational force and all its significant parameters needed for a complete dynamical description - that is, the component G, of the geometrical form of gravity Gm1m2/rn, - are uniquely determined from phenomenons and, after the of universal gravitation has been derived, it plus the laws of motion determine the space and time frames and a set of self - consistent attributions of mass. For example, the coherent mass attributions ground the construction of the locally inertial ventre of a mass frame, and Newton's first law then enables us to consider time as a magnitude e: Equal tomes are those during which a freely moving body transverses equal distances. The space and time frames in turn ground use of the laws of motion, completing the constructive circle. This construction has a profound unity to it, expressed by the multiple interdependency of its components, the convergence of its approximations, and the coherence of its multiplying determined quantized. Newton's Rule IV: (Loosely) do not introduce a rival theory unless it provides an equal or superior unified construction - in particular, unless it is able to measure its parameters in terms of empirical phenomena at least as thorough and cross - situationally invariably (Rule III) as done in current theory. this gives unity a central place in scientific method.

Some thinkers maintain, that subject and object are only different aspects of experience. I can experience myself as subject, and in the act of self-reflection. The fallacy of this argument is obvious: Being a subject implies having an object. We cannot experience something consciously without the mediation of understanding and mind. Our experience is already conceptualized at the time it comes into our consciousness. Our experience is negative insofar as it destroys the original pure experience. In a dialectical process of synthesis, the original pure experience becomes an object for us. The common state of our mind is only capable of apperceiving objects. Objects are reified negative experience. The same is true for the objective aspect of this theory: by objectifying myself I do not dispense with the subject, but the subject is causally and apodeictically linked to the object. When I make an object of anything, I have to realize, that it is the subject, which objectifies something. It is only the subject who can do that. Without the subject at that place are no objects, and without objects there is no subject. This interdependence, however, is not to be understood for a dualism, so that the object and the subject are really independent substances. Since the object is only created by the activity of the subject, and the subject is not a physical entity, but a mental one, we have to conclude then, that the subject-object dualism is purely mentalistic.

The Cartesian dualism posits the subject and the object as separate, independent and real substances, both of which have their ground and origin in the highest substance of God. Cartesian dualism, however, contradicts itself: The very fact, which Descartes posits the "I," that is the subject, as the only certainty, he defied materialism, and thus the concept of some "res extensa." The physical thing is only probable in its existence, whereas the mental thing is absolutely and necessarily certain. The subject is superior to the object. The object is only derived, but the subject is the original. This makes the object not only inferior in its substantive quality and in its essence, but relegates it to a level of dependence on the subject. The subject recognizes that the object is a "res' extensa" and this means, that the object cannot have essence or existence without the acknowledgment through the subject. The subject posits the world in the first place and the subject is posited by God. Apart from the problem of interaction between these two different substances, Cartesian dualism is not eligible for explaining and understanding the subject-object relation.

By denying Cartesian dualism and resorting to monistic theories such as extreme idealism, materialism or positivism, the problem is not resolved either. What the positivists did, was just verbalizing the subject-object relation by linguistic forms. It was no longer a metaphysical problem, but only a linguistic problem. Our language has formed this object-subject dualism. These thinkers are very superficial and shallow thinkers, because they do not see that in the very act of their analysis they inevitably think in the mind-set of subject and object. By relativizing the object and subject for language and analytical philosophy, they avoid the elusive and problematical oppure of subject-object, since which has been the fundamental question in philosophy ever. Shunning these metaphysical questions is no solution. Excluding something, by reducing it to a more material and verifiable level, is not only pseudo-philosophy but a depreciation and decadence of the great philosophical ideas of mankind.

Therefore, we have to come to grips with idea of subject-object in a new manner. We experience this dualism as a fact in our everyday lives. Every experience is subject to this dualistic pattern. The question, however, is, whether this underlying pattern of subject-object dualism is real or only mental. Science assumes it to be real. This assumption does not prove the reality of our experience, but only that with this method science is most successful in explaining our empirical facts. Mysticism, on the other hand, believes that on that point is an original unity of subject and objects. To attain this unity is the goal of religion and mysticism. Man has fallen from this unity by disgrace and by sinful behaviour. Now the task of man is to get back on track again and strive toward this highest fulfilment. Again, are we not, on the conclusion made above, forced to admit, that also the mystic way of thinking is only a pattern of the mind and, as the scientists, that they have their own frame of reference and methodology to explain the supra-sensible facts most successfully?

If we assume mind to be the originator of the subject-object dualism, then we cannot confer more reality on the physical or the mental aspect, and we cannot deny the one as to the other.

Fortunately or not, history has made its play, and, in so doing, we must have considerably gestured the crude language of the earliest users of symbolics and nonsymbiotic vocalizations. Their spoken language probably became reactively independent and a closed cooperative system. Only after the emergence of hominids were to use symbolic communication evolved, symbolic forms progressively took over functions served by non-vocal symbolic forms. The earliest of Jutes, Saxons and Jesuits have reflected this in the modern mixtures of the English-speaking language. The structure of syntax in these languages often reveals its origins in pointing gestures, in the manipulation and exchange of objects, and in more primitive constructions of spatial and temporal relationships. We still use nonverbal vocalizations and gestures to complement meaning in spoken language.

Many concerns and disputed clusters around the idea associated with the term substance. The substance of a thing may be considered in: (1) Its essence, or that which makes it what it is. This will ensure that the substance of a thing is that which remains through change in properties. Again, in Aristotle, this essence becomes more than just the matter, but a unity of matter and form. (2) That which can exist by itself, or does not need a subject for existence, in the way that properties need objects, hence (3) that which bears properties, as a substance is then the subject of predication, that about which things are said as opposed to the things said about it. Substance in the last two senses stands opposed to modifications such as quantity, quality, relations, etc. it is hard to keep this set of ideas distinct from the doubtful notion of a substratum, something distinct from any of its properties, and hence, as an incapable characterization. The notion of substances tends to disappear in empiricist thought in fewer of the sensible questions of things with the notion of that in which they infer of giving way to an empirical notion of their regular occurrence. However, this is in turn is problematic, since it only makes sense to talk of the occurrence of an instance of qualities, not of quantities themselves, so that the problem of what it is for a value quality to be the instance that remains.

Metaphysic inspired by modern science tends to reject the concept of substance in favour of concepts such as that of a field or a process, each of which may seem to provide a better example of a fundamental physical category.

It must be spoken of a concept that is deeply embedded in 18th century aesthetics, but deriving from the dialectical awareness as brought forth from 1st centuries rhetorical treatises. On the Sublime, by Longinus, the sublime is great, fearful, noble, calculated to arouse sentiments of pride and majesty, as well as awe and sometimes terror. According to Alexander Gerards writing in 1759, When a large object is presented, the mind expands itself to the extent of that objects, and is filled with one grand sensation, which totally possessing it, composes it into a solemn sedateness and strikes it with deep silent wonder, and administration: It finds such a difficulty in spreading itself to the dimensions of its object, as enliven and invigorates which this occasions, it sometimes images itself present in every part of the sense that it contemplates, and from the sense of this immensity, feels a noble pride, and entertains a lofty conception of its own capacity.

In Kant's aesthetic theory the sublime raises the soul above the height of vulgar complacency. We experience the vast spectacles of nature as absolutely great and of irresistible might and power. This perception is fearful, but by conquering this fear, and by regarding as small those things of which we are wont to be solicitous we quicken our sense of moral freedom. So we turn the experience of frailty and impotence into one of our true, inward moral freedom as the mind triumphs over nature, and it is this triumph of reason that is truly sublime. Kant thus paradoxically places our sense of the sublime in an awareness of ourselves as transcending nature, than in an awareness of us as a frail and insignificant part of it.

Nevertheless, the doctrine that all relations are internal was a cardinal thesis of absolute idealism, and a central point of attack by the British philosopher's George Edward Moore (1873-1958) and Bertrand Russell (1872-1970). It is a kind of essentialism, stating that if two things stand in some relationship, then they could not be what they are, did they not do so, if, for instance, I am wearing a hat mow, then when we imagine a possible situation that we would be got to describe as my not wearing the hat now, we would strictly not be imaging as one and the hat, but only some different individual.

The countering partitions a doctrine that bears some resemblance to the metaphysically based view of the German philosopher and mathematician Gottfried Leibniz (1646-1716) that if a person had any other attributes that the ones he has, he would not have been the same person. Leibniz thought that when asked that would have happened if Peter had not denied Christ. That being that if I am asking what had happened if Peter had not been Peter, denying Christ is contained in the complete notion of Peter. But he allowed that by the name Peter might be understood as what is involved in those attributes [of Peter] from which the denial does not follows. In order that we are held accountable to allow of external relations, in that these being relations which individuals could have or not depending upon contingent circumstances. The relations of ideas are used by the Scottish philosopher David Hume (1711-76) in the First Enquiry of Theoretical Knowledge. All the objects of human reason or enquiring naturally, be divided into two kinds: To unite all those, relations of ideas and matter of fact (Enquiry Concerning Human Understanding) the terms reflect the belief that any thing that can be known dependently must be internal to the mind, and hence transparent to us.

In Hume, objects of knowledge are divided into matter of fact (roughly empirical things known by means of impressions) and the relation of ideas. The contrast, also called Humes Fork, is a version of the speculative deductivity distinction, but reflects the 17th and early 18th centauries behind that the deductivity is established by chains of infinite certainty as comparable to ideas. It is extremely important that in the period between Descartes and J.S. Mill that a demonstration is not, but only a chain of intuitive comparable ideas, whereby a principle or maxim can be established by reason alone. It is in this sense that the English philosopher John Locke (1632-704) who believed that theologically and moral principles are capable of demonstration, and Hume denies that they are, and denies that scientific enquiries proceed in demonstrating its results.

A mathematical proof is formally inferred as to an argument that is used to show the truth of a mathematical assertion. In modern mathematics, a proof begins with one or more statements called premises and demonstrates, using the rules of logic, that if the premises are true then a particular conclusion must also be true.

The accepted methods and strategies used to construct a convincing mathematical argument have evolved since ancient times and continue to change. Consider the Pythagorean theorem, named after the 5th century Bc Greek mathematician and philosopher Pythagoras, which states that in a right-angled triangle, the square of the hypotenuse is equal to the sum of the squares of the other two sides. Many early civilizations considered this theorem true because it agreed with their observations in practical situations. But the early Greeks, among others, realized that observation and commonly held opinions do not guarantee mathematical truth. For example, before the 5th century Bc it was widely believed that all lengths could be expressed as the ratio of two whole numbers. But an unknown Greek mathematician proved that this was not true by showing that the length of the diagonal of a square with an area of one is the irrational number Ã.

The Greek mathematician Euclid laid down some of the conventions central to modern mathematical proofs. His book The Elements, written about 300 Bc, contains many proofs in the fields of geometry and algebra. This book illustrates the Greek practice of writing mathematical proofs by first clearly identifying the initial assumptions and then reasoning from them in a logical way in order to obtain a desired conclusion. As part of such an argument, Euclid used results that had already been shown to be true, called theorems, or statements that were explicitly acknowledged to be self-evident, called axioms; this practice continues today.

In the 20th century, proofs have been written that are so complex that no one person understands every argument used in them. In 1976, a computer was used to complete the proof of the four-colour theorem. This theorem states that four colours are sufficient to colour any map in such a way that regions with a common boundary ligne have different colours. The use of a computer in this proof inspired considerable debate in the mathematical community. At issue was whether a theorem can be considered proven if human beings have not actually checked every detail of the proof.

The study of the relations of deductibility among sentences in a logical calculus which benefits the proof theory. Deductibility is defined purely syntactically, that is, without reference to the intended interpretation of the calculus. The subject was founded by the mathematician David Hilbert (1862-1943) in the hope that strictly inffinitary methods would provide a way of proving the consistency of classical mathematics, but the ambition was torpedoed by Gödel's second incompleteness theorem.

What is more, the use of a model to test for consistencies in an axiomatized system that is older than modern logic. Descartes algebraic interpretation of Euclidean geometry provides a way of showing that if the theory of real numbers is consistent, so is the geometry. Similar representation had been used by mathematicians in the 19th century, for example to show that if Euclidean geometry is consistent, so are various non-Euclidean geometries. Model theory is the general study of this kind of procedure: The proof theory studies relations of deductibility between formulae of a system, but once the notion of an interpretation is in place we can ask whether a formal system meets certain conditions. In particular, can it lead us from sentences that are true under some interpretation? And if a sentence is true under all interpretations, is it also a theorem of the system?

There are the questions of the soundness and completeness of a formal system. For the propositional calculus this turns into the question of whether the proof theory delivers as theorems all and only tautologies. There are many axiomatizations of the propositional calculus that are consistent and complete. The mathematical logician Kurt Gödel (1906-78) proved in 1929 that the first-order predicate under every interpretation is a theorem of the calculus. In that mathematical method for solving those physical problems that can be stated in the form that a certain value definite integral will have a stationary value for small changes of the functions in the integrands and of the limit of integration.

The Euclidean geometry is the greatest example of the pure axiomatic method, and as such had incalculable philosophical influence as a paradigm of rational certainty. It had no competition until the 19th century when it was realized that the fifth axiom of his system (parallel lines never meet) could be denied without inconsistency, leading to Riemannian spherical geometry. The significance of Riemannian geometry lies in its use and extension of both Euclidean geometry and the geometry of surfaces, leading to a number of generalized differential geometries. Its most important effect was that it made a geometrical application possible for some major abstractions of tensor analysis, leading to the pattern and concepts for general relativity later used by Albert Einstein in developing his theory of relativity. Riemannian geometry is also necessary for treating electricity and magnetism in the framework of general relativity. The fifth chapter of Euclid's Elements, is attributed to the mathematician Eudoxus, and contains a precise development of the real number, work that remained unappreciated until rediscovered in the 19th century.

The Axiom, in logic and mathematics, is a basic principle that is assumed to be true without proof. The use of axioms in mathematics stems from the ancient Greeks, most probably during the 5th century Bc, and represents the beginnings of pure mathematics as it is known today. Examples of axioms are the following: No sentence can be true and false at the same time (the principle of contradiction); If equals are added to equals, the sums are equal. The whole is greater than any of its parts. Logic and pure mathematics begin with such unproved assumptions from which other propositions (theorems) are derived. This procedure is necessary to avoid circularity, or an infinite regression in reasoning. The axioms of any system must be consistent with one another, that is, they should not lead to contradictions. They should be independent in the sense that they cannot be derived from one another. They should also be few in number. Axioms have sometimes been interpreted as self-evident truth. The present tendency is to avoid this claim and simply to assert that an axiom is assumed to be true without proof in the system of which it is a part.

The term's axiom and postulate are often used synonymously. Sometimes the word axiom is used to refer to basic principles that are assumed by every deductive system, and the term postulate is used to refer to first principles peculiar to a particular system, such as Euclidean geometry. Infrequently, the word axiom is used to refer to first principles in logic, and the term postulate is used to refer to first principles in mathematics.

The applications of game theory are wide-ranging and account for steadily growing interest in the subject. Von Neumann and Morgenstern indicated the immediate utility of their work on mathematical game theory in which may link it with economic behaviour. Models can be developed, in fact, for markets of various commodities with differing numbers of buyers and sellers, fluctuating values of supply and demand, and seasonal and cyclical variations, as well as significant structural differences in the economies concerned. Here game theory is especially relevant to the analysis of conflicts of interest in maximizing profits and promoting the widest distribution of goods and services. Equitable division of property and of inheritance is another area of legal and economic concern that can be studied with the techniques of game theory.

In the social sciences, n-person games that has interesting uses in studying, for example, the distribution of power in legislative procedures. This problem can be interpreted as a three-person game at the congressional level involving vetoes of the president and votes of representatives and senators, analysed in terms of successful or failed coalitions to pass a given bill. Problems of majority rule and individual decision makes are also amenable to such study.

Sociologists have developed an entire branch of game that devoted to the study of issues involving group decision making. Epidemiologists also make use of game that, especially with respect to immunization procedures and methods of testing a vaccine or other medication. Military strategists turn to game that to study conflicts of interest resolved through battles where the outcome or payoff of a given war game is either victory or defeat. Usually, such games are not examples of zero-sum games, for what one player loses in terms of lives and injuries are not won by the victor. Some uses of game that in analyses of political and military events have been criticized as a dehumanizing and potentially dangerous oversimplification of necessarily complicating factors. Analysis of economic situations is also usually more complicated than zero-sum games because of the production of goods and services within the play of a given game.

All is the same in the classical that of the syllogism, a term in a categorical proposition is distributed if the proposition entails any proposition obtained from it by substituting a term denoted by the original. For example, in all dogs bark the term dogs is distributed, since it entails all terriers' bark, which is obtained from it by a substitution. In Not all dogs bark, the same term is not distributed, since it may be true while not all terriers' bark is false.

When a representation of one system by another is usually more familiar, in and for itself, that those extended in representation that their workings are supposed analogously to that of the first. This one might model the behaviour of a sound wave upon that of waves in water, or the behaviour of a gas upon that to a volume containing moving billiard balls. While nobody doubts that models have a useful heuristic role in science, there has been intense debate over whether a good model, or whether an organized structure of laws from which it can be deduced and suffices for scientific explanation. As such, the debative topic was inaugurated by the French physicist Pierre Marie Maurice Duhem (1861-1916), in The Aim and Structure of Physical Thar (1954) by which Duhems conception of science is that it is simply a device for calculating as science provides deductive system that is systematic, economical, and predictive, but not that represents the deep underlying nature of reality. Steadfast and holding of its contributive thesis that in isolation, and since other auxiliary hypotheses will always be needed to draw empirical consequences from it. The Duhem thesis implies that refutation is a more complex matter than might appear. It is sometimes framed as the view that a single hypothesis may be retained in the face of any adverse empirical evidence, if we prepared to make modifications elsewhere in our system, although strictly speaking this is a stronger thesis, since it may be psychologically impossible to make consistent revisions in a belief system to accommodate, say, the hypothesis that there is a hippopotamus in the room when visibly there is not.

Primary and secondary qualities are the division associated with the 17th-century rise of modern science, wit h its recognition that the fundamental explanatory properties of things that are not the qualities that perception most immediately concerns. The latter are the secondary qualities, or immediate sensory qualities, including colour, taste, smell, felt warmth or texture, and sound. The primary properties are less tied to their deliverance of one particular sense, and include the size, shape, and motion of objects. In Robert Boyle (1627-92) and John Locke (1632-1704) the primary qualities are scientifically tractable, objective qualities essential to anything material, are of a minimal listing of size, shape, and mobility, i.e., the state of being at rest or moving. Locke sometimes adds number, solidity, texture (where this is thought of as the structure of a substance, or way in which it is made out of atoms). The secondary qualities are the powers to excite particular sensory modifications in observers. Once, again, that Locke himself thought in terms of identifying these powers with the texture of objects that, according to corpuscularian science of the time, were the basis of an objects causal capacities. The ideas of secondary qualities are sharply different from these powers, and afford us no accurate impression of them. For Renè Descartes (1596-1650), this is the basis for rejecting any attempt to think of knowledge of external objects as provided by the senses. But in Locke our ideas of primary qualities do afford us an accurate notion of what shape, size. And mobility is. In English-speaking philosophy the first major discontent with the division was voiced by the Irish idealist George Berkeley (1685-1753), who probably took for a basis of his attack from Pierre Bayle (1647-1706), who in turn cites the French critic Simon Foucher (1644-96). Modern thought continues to wrestle with the difficulties of thinking of colour, taste, smell, warmth, and sound as real or objective properties to things independent of us.

Continuing as such, is the doctrine advocated by the American philosopher David Lewis (1941-2002), in that different possible worlds are to be thought of as existing exactly as this one does. Thinking in terms of possibilities is thinking of real worlds where things are different. The view has been charged with making it impossible to see why it is good to save the child from drowning, since there is still a possible world in which she (or her counterpart) drowned, and as for universe it should make no difference that world is actual. Critics also charge that the notion fails to fit either with current theory, if lf how we know about possible worlds, or with a current theory of why we are interested in them, but Lewis denied that any other way of interpreting modal statements is tenable.

The proposal set forth that characterizes the modality of a proposition as the notion for which it is true or false. The most important division is between propositions true of necessity, and those true as things are: Necessary as opposed to contingent propositions. Other qualifiers sometimes called modally include the tense indicators, it will be the case that 'p', or it was the case that 'p', and there are affinities between the deontic indicators, it ought to be the case that 'p', or it is permissible that p, and the of necessity and possibility.

The aim of a logic is to make explicitly the rules by which inferences may be drawn, than to study the actual reasoning processes that people use, which may or may not conform to those rules. In the case of deductive logic, if we ask why we need to obey the rules, the most general form of an answer is that if we do not we contradict ourselves (or, strictly speaking, we stand ready to contradict ourselves. Someone failing to draw a conclusion that follows from a set of premises need not be contradicting him or herself, but only failing to notice something. However, he or she is not defended against adding the contradictory conclusion to his or fer set of beliefs. There is no equally simple answer in the case of inductive logic, which is usually a less robust subject, but the aim will be to find reasoning such that anyone failing to conform to it will have improbable beliefs. Traditional logic had dominated the subject until the 19th century, and has become increasingly recognized in the 20th century. In that which qualifies of the finer works were done within that tradition, but syllogistic reasoning is now generally regarded as a limited special case of the form of reasoning that can be reprehend within the promotion and predated values. As these form the heart of modern logic, as their central notions or qualifiers, variables, and functions were the creation of the German mathematician Gottlob Frége, who is recognized as the father of modern logic. Although his treatment of a logical system as an abstract mathematical structure, or algebraic, has been heralded by the English mathematician and logician George Boole (1815-64), his pamphlet The Mathematical Analysis of Logic (1847) pioneered the algebra of classes. The work was made of in An Investigation of the Laws of Thought (1854). Boole also published several works in our mathematics, and on the that of probability. His name is remembered in the title of Boolean algebra, and the algebraic operations he investigated are denoted by Boolean operations.

The syllogistic, or categorical syllogism is the inference of one proposition from two premises. For example is, all horses have tails, and things with tails are four legged, so all horses are four legged. Each premise has one term in common with the other premises. The terms that do not occur in the conclusion are called the middle term. The major premise of the syllogism is the premise containing the predicate of the contraction (the major term). And the minor premise contains its subject (the minor term). So the first premise of the example in the minor premise the second the major term. So the first premise of the example is the minor premise, the second the major premise and having a tail is the middle term. This enables syllogisms that there of a classification, that according to the form of the premises and the conclusions. The other classification is by figure, or way in which the middle term is placed or way in within the middle term is placed in the premise.

Although the theory of the syllogism dominated logic until the 19th century, it remained a piecemeal affair, able to deal with only relations valid forms of valid forms of argument. There have subsequently been rearguing actions attempting, but in general it has been eclipsed by the modern theory of quantification, the predicate calculus is the heart of modern logic, having proved capable of formalizing the calculus rationing processes of modern mathematics and science. In a first-order predicate calculus the variables range over objects: In a higher-order calculus the may range over predicate and functions themselves. The first-order predicated calculus deals with identity and includes, as primitive (unified) expression: In a higher-order calculus I t may be defined by law that χ-y if (∀F)(Fχ↔Fy), which gives greater expressive power for less complexity.

Modal logic was of great importance historically, particularly in the light of the deity, but was not a central topic of modern logic in its gold period as the beginning of the 20th century. It was, however, revived by the American logician and philosopher Irving Lewis (1883-1964), although he wrote extensively on most a central philosophical topic, he is remembered principally as a critic of the intentional nature of modern logic, and as the founding father of modal logic. His two independent proofs showing that from a contradiction anything follows a relevance logic, using a notion of entailment stronger than that of strict implication.

The imparting information has been conduced or carried out of the prescribed procedures, as impeding something that takes place in the chancing encounter as placed to a position out to be the entered oneness of mind and may from time to time occasion to various doctrines concerning the necessary properties, least of mention, by adding to some prepositional or predicated calculus two operators acclaiming that □ and ◇(sometimes written N and M), meaning necessarily and possible, respectfully. These like p → ◇ p and □ p → p will be wanted. Controversial these include □ p → □ □ p and ◇p → □ ◇p. The classical modal theory for modal logic, due to the American logician and philosopher (1940-) and the Swedish logician Sig Kanger, involves valuing prepositions not true or false simpiciter, but as true or false at possible worlds with necessity then corresponding to truth in all worlds, and a possibility to truth in some world. Various different systems of modal logic result from adjusting the accessibility relation between worlds.

In Saul Kripke, gives the classical modern treatment of the topic of reference, both clarifying the distinction between names and definite description, and opening the door to many subsequent attempts to understand the notion of reference in terms of a causal link between the use of a term and an original episode of attaching a name to the subject.

One of the three branches into which semiotic is usually divided, the study of semantical meaning of words, and the relation of signs to the degree to which the designs are applicable. In that, in formal studies, a semantics is provided for a formal language when an interpretation of model is specified. However, a natural language comes ready interpreted, and the semantic problem is not that of the specification but of understanding the relationship between terms of various categories (names, descriptions, predicate, adverbs . . .) and their meaning. An influential proposal by attempting to provide a truth definition for the language, which will involve giving a full structure of varying kinds has on the truth conditions of sentences containing them.

Holding that the basic casse of reference is the relation between a name and the persons or object which it names. The philosophical problems include trying to elucidate that relation, to understand whether other semantic relations, such s that between a predicate and the property it expresses, or that between a description an what it describes, or that between me and the word I, are examples of the same relation or of very different ones. A great deal of modern work on this was stimulated by the American logician Saul Kripke, Naming and Necessity (1970). It would also be desirable to know whether we can refer to such things as objects and how to conduct the debate about each and issue. A popular approach, following Gottlob Frége, is to argue that the fundamental unit of analysis should be the whole sentence. The reference of a term becomes a derivative notion it is whatever it is that defines the term's contribution to the trued condition of the whole sentence. There need be nothing further to say about it, given that we have a way of understanding the attribution of meaning or truth-condition to sentences. Other approach, searching for a more substantive possibly that causality or psychological or social constituents are pronounced between words and things.

However, following Ramsey and the Italian mathematician G. Peano (1858-1932), it has been customary to distinguish logical paradoxes that depend upon a notion of reference or truth (semantic notions) such as those of the Liar family, Berries, Richard, etc. form the purely logical paradoxes in which no such notions are involved, such as Russell's paradox, or those of Canto and Burali-Forti. Paradoxes of the first type seem to depend upon an element of a self-reference, in which a sentence is about itself, or in which a phrase refers to something about itself, or in which a phrase refers to something defined by a set of phrases of which it is itself one. It is to feel that this element is responsible for the contradictions, although the self-reference itself is often benign (for instance, the sentence All English sentences should have a verb, includes itself happily in the domain of sentences it is talking about), so the difficulty lies in forming a condition that existence only pathologically a self-reference. Paradoxes of the second kind then need a different treatment. While the distinction is convenient, it allows for set theory to proceed by circumventing the latter paradoxes by technical mans, even when there is no solution to the semantic paradoxes, it may be a way of ignoring the similarities between the two families. There is still the possibility that while there is no agreed solution to the semantic paradoxes, our understand of Russell's paradox may be imperfect as well.

Truth and falsity are two classical truth-values that a statement, proposition or sentence can take, as it is supposed in classical (two-valued) logic, that each statement has one of these values, and none has both. A statement is then false if and only if it is not true. The basis of this scheme is that to each statement there corresponds a determinate truth condition, or way the world must be for it to be true: If this condition obtains the statement is true, and otherwise false. Statements may indeed be felicitous or infelicitous in other dimensions (polite, misleading, apposite, witty, etc.) but truth is the central normative notion governing assertion. Consideration's o vagueness may introduce greys into this black-and-white scheme. For the issue to be true, any suppressed premise or background framework of a thought necessity makes an agreement valid, or a tenable position, a proposition whose truth is necessary for either the truth or the falsity of another statement. Thus if p presupposes q, q must be true for p to be either true or false. In the theory of knowledge, the English philosopher and historian George Collingwood (1889-1943), announces that any proposition capable of a truth or falsity stand on bed of absolute presuppositions that are not properly capable of truth or falsity, since a system of thought will contain no way of approaching such a question (a similar idea later voiced by Wittgenstein in his work On Certainty). The introduction of presupposition therefore mans that either another of a truth value is fond, intermediate between truth and falsity, or the classical logic is preserved, but it is impossible to tell whether a particular sentence empresses a preposition that is a candidate for truth and falsity, without knowing more than the formation rules of the language. Each suggestion carries across through which there is some consensus that at least who were definite descriptions is involved, examples equally given by regarding the overall sentence as false as the existence claim fails, and explaining the data that the English philosopher Frederick Strawson (1919-) relied upon as the effects of an implicature.

Views about the meaning of terms will often depend on classifying the implicature of sayings involving the terms as implicatures or as genuine logical implications of what is said. Implicatures may be divided into two kinds: Conversational implicatures of the two kinds and the more subtle category of conventional implicatures. A term may as a matter of convention carries an implicature, thus one of the relations between he is poor and honest and he is poor but honest is that they have the same content (are true in just the same conditional) but the second has implicatures (that the combination is surprising or significant) that the first lacks.

It is, nonetheless, that we find in classical logic a proposition that may be true or false. In that, if the former, it is said to take the truth-value true, and if the latter the truth-value false. The idea behind the terminological phrases is the analogues between assigning a propositional variable one or other of these values, as is done in providing an interpretation for a formula of the propositional calculus, and assigning an object as the value of any other variable. Logics with intermediate value are called many-valued logics.

Nevertheless, an existing definition of the predicate . . . is true for a language that satisfies convention T, the material adequately condition laid down by Alfred Tarski, born Alfred Teitelbaum (1901-83), whereby his methods of recursive definition, enabling us to say for each sentence what it is that its truth consists in, but giving no verbal definition of truth itself. The recursive definition or the truth predicate of a language is always provided in a metalanguage. Tarski is thus committed to a hierarchy of languages. Each with it is associated, but different truth-predicate. Whist this enables the approach to avoid the contradictions of paradoxical contemplations, it conflicts with the idea that a language should be able to say everything that there is to say, and other approaches have become increasingly important.

So, that the truth condition of a statement is the condition for which the world must meet if the statement is to be true. To know this condition is equivalent to knowing the meaning of the statement. Although this sounds as if it gives a solid anchorage for meaning, some of the securities disappear when it turns out that the truth condition can only be defined by repeating the very same statement: The truth condition of now is white is that snow is white, the truth condition of Britain would have capitulated had Hitler invaded, is that Britain would have capitulated had Hitler invaded. It is disputed whether this element of running-on-the-spot disqualifies truth conditions from playing the central role in a substantives theory of meaning. Truth-conditional theories of meaning are sometimes opposed by the view that to know the meaning of a statement is to be able to use it in a network of inferences.

Taken to be the view, inferential semantics takes on the role of sentence in inference give a more important key to their meaning than this external relations to things in the world. The meaning of a sentence becomes its place in a network of inferences that it legitimates. Also known as functional role semantics, procedural semantics, or conception to the coherence theory of truth, and suffers from the same suspicion that it divorces meaning from any clarity association with things in the world.

Moreover, a theory of semantic truth is that of the view if language is provided with a truth definition, there is a sufficient characterization of its concept of truth, as there is no further philosophical chapter to write about truth: There is no further philosophical chapter to write about truth itself or truth as shared across different languages. The view is similar to the disquotational theory.

The redundancy theory, or also known as the deflationary view of truth fathered by Gottlob Frége and the Cambridge mathematician and philosopher Frank Ramsey (1903-30), who showed how the distinction between the semantic paradoses, such as that of the Liar, and Russell's paradox, made unnecessary the ramified type theory of Principia Mathematica, and the resulting axiom of reducibility. By taking all the sentences affirmed in a scientific theory that use some terms, e.g., a quark, and to a considerable degree of replacing the term by a variable instead of saying that quarks have such-and-such properties, the Ramsey sentence says that there is something that has those properties. If the process is repeated for all of a group of the theoretical terms, the sentence gives topic-neutral structure of the theory, but removes any implication that we know what the terms so treated denote. It leaves open the possibility of identifying the theoretical item with whatever. It is that, the best fits the description provided. However, it was pointed out by the Cambridge mathematician Newman, that if the process is carried out for all except the logical of excavated fossils of a theory, then by the Löwenheim-Skolem theorem, the result will be interpretable, and the content of the theory may reasonably be felt to have been lost.

While both Frége and Ramsey are in agreeing that the essential claim is that the predicate . . . is true does not have a sense, i.e., expresses no substantive or profound or explanatory concept that ought to be the topic of philosophical enquiry. The approach admits of different versions, but centres on the points (1) that it is true that p says no more nor less than p (hence, redundancy): (2) that in less direct contexts, such as everything he said was true, or all logical consequences of true propositions are true, the predicate functions as a device enabling us to generalize than as an adjective or predicate describing the things he said, or the kinds of propositions that follow from true prepositions. For example, the second may translate as: $(\forall p, q)(p \,\&\, p \rightarrow q \rightarrow q)$ where there is no use of a notion of truth.

There are technical problems in interpreting all uses of the notion of truth in such ways, nevertheless, they are not generally felt to be insurmountable. The approach needs to explain away apparently substantive uses of the notion, such as science aims at the truth, or truth is a norm governing discourse. Postmodern writing frequently advocates that we must abandon such norms. Along with a discredited objective conception of truth. Perhaps, we can have the norms even when objectivity is problematic, since they can be framed without mention of truth: Science wants it to be so that whatever science holds that 'p', then 'p'. Discourse is to be regulated by the principle that it is wrong to assert 'p', when 'not-p'.

Something that tends of something in addition of content, or coming by way to justify such a position can very well be more that in addition to several reasons, as to bring in or joining of something might that there be more so as to a larger combination for us to consider the simplest formulation, is that the claim that expression of the form 'S' is true mean the same as expression that 'S. Some philosophers dislike the ideas of sameness of meaning, and if this I disallowed, then the claim is that the two forms are equivalent in any sense of equivalence that matters. This is, it makes no difference whether people say Dogs bark is true, or whether they say, dogs bark. In the former representation of what they say of the sentence Dogs bark is mentioned, but in the later it appears to be used, of the claim that the two are equivalent and needs careful formulation and defence. On the face of it someone might know that Dogs bark is true without knowing what it means (for instance, if he kids in a list of acknowledged truth, although he does not understand English), and it is different from knowing that dogs bark. Disquotational theories are usually presented as versions of the redundancy theory of truth.

The relationship between a set of premises and a conclusion when the conclusion follows from the premise. Many philosophers identify this with it being logically impossible that the premises should all be true, yet the conclusion false. Others are sufficiently impressed by the paradoxes of strict implication to look for a stranger relation, which would distinguish between valid and invalid arguments within the sphere of necessary propositions. The search for a strange notion is the field of relevance logic.

From a systematic theoretical point of view, we may imagine the process of evolution of an empirical science to be a continuous process of induction. Theories are evolved and are expressed in short encompassing as statements of as large number of individual observations in the form of empirical laws, from which the general laws can be ascertained by comparison. Regarded in this way, the development of a science bears some resemblance to the compilation of a classified catalogue. It is, a it was, a purely empirical enterprise.

But this point of view by no means embraces the whole of the actual process, for it slurs over the important part played by intuition and deductive thought in the development of an exact science. As soon as a science has emerged from its initial stages, theoretical advances are no longer achieved merely by a process of arrangement. Guided by empirical data, the investigators rather develop a system of thought that, in general, it is built up logically from a small number of fundamental assumptions, the so-called axioms. We call such a system of thought a theory. The theory finds the justification for its existence in the fact that it correlates a large number of single observations, and is just here that the truth of the theory lies.

Corresponding to the same complex of empirical data, there may be several theories, which differ from one another to a considerable extent. But as regards the deductions from the theories that are capable of being tested, the agreement between the theories may be so complete, that it becomes difficult to find any deductions in which the theories differ from each other. As an example, a case of general interest is available in the province of biology, in the Darwinian theory of the development of species by selection in the struggle for existence, and in the theory of development that is based on the hypophysis of the hereditary transmission of acquired characters. The Origin of Species was principally successful in marshalling the evidence for evolution, than providing a convincing mechanisms for genetic change. And Darwin himself remained open to the search for additional mechanisms, while also remaining convinced that natural selection was at the hart of it. It was only with the later discovery of the gene as the unit of inheritance that the synthesis known as neo-Darwinism became the orthodox theory of evolution in the life sciences.

In the 19th century the attempt to base ethical reasoning o the presumed facts about evolution, the movement is particularly associated with the English philosopher of evolution Herbert Spencer (1820-1903). The premise is that later elements in an evolutionary path are better than earlier ones: The application of this principle then requires seeing western society, laissez-faire capitalism, or another object of approval, as more evolved than more primitive social forms. Neither the principle nor the applications command much respect. The version of evolutionary ethics called social Darwinism emphasises the struggle for natural selection, and draws the conclusion that we should glorify and assist such struggles, usually by enhancing competition and aggressive relations between people in society or between evolution and ethics has been re-thought in the light of biological discoveries concerning altruism and kin-selection.

Once again, the psychology proving attempts are founded to evolutionary principles, in which a variety of higher mental functions may be adaptations, forced in response to selection pressures on the human populations through evolutionary time. Candidates for such theorizing include material and paternal motivations, capacities for love and friendship, the development of language as a signalling system cooperative and aggressive, our emotional repertoire, our moral and reactions, including the disposition to detect and punish those who misappropriate on their agreements or those who free-ride or cheat on the work of others, our cognitive structures, and many others. Evolutionary psychology goes hand in hand with neurophysiological evidence about the underlying circuitry in the brain that subserves the psychological mechanisms it claims to identify. The approach was foreshadowed by Darwin himself, and William James, as well as the sociology of E.O. Wilson. The terms of use are applied, more or less aggressively, especially to explanations offered in Sociobiology and evolutionary psychology.

Another assumption that is frequently used to legitimate the real existence of forces associated with the invisible hand in neoclassical economics derives from Darwin's view of natural selection as a war-like competing between atomized organisms in the struggle for survival. In natural selection as we now understand it, cooperation appears to exist in complementary relation to competition. It is complementary relationships between such results that are emergent self-regulating properties that are greater than the sum of parts and that serve to perpetuate the existence of the whole.

According to E.O Wilson, the human mind evolved to believe in the gods and people need a sacred narrative to have a sense of higher purpose. Yet it is also clear that the gods in his view are merely human constructs and, therefore, there is no basis for dialogue between the world-view of science and religion. Science for its part, said Wilson, will test relentlessly every assumption about the human condition and in time uncover the bedrock of the moral an religious sentiments. The eventual result of the competition between the other, will be the secularization of the human epic and of religion itself.

Man has come to the threshold of a state of consciousness, regarding his nature and his relationship to te Cosmos, in terms that reflect reality. By using the processes of nature as metaphor, to describe the forces by which it operates upon and within Man, we come as close to describing reality as we can within the limits of our comprehension. Men will be very uneven in their capacity for such understanding, which, naturally, differs for different ages and cultures, and develops and changes over the course of time. For these reasons it will always be necessary to use metaphor and myth to provide comprehensible guides to living. In thus way. Mans imagination and intellect play vital roles on his survival and evolution.

Since so much of life both inside and outside the study is concerned with finding explanations of things, it would be desirable to have a concept of what counts as a good explanation from bad. Under the influence of logical positivist approaches to the structure of science, it was felt that the criterion ought to be found in a definite logical relationship between the exlanans (that which does the explaining) and the explanandum (that which is to be explained). The approach culminated in the covering law model of explanation, or the view that an event is explained when it is subsumed under a law of nature, that is, its occurrence is deducible from the law plus a set of initial conditions. A law would itself be explained by being deduced from a higher-order or covering law, in the way that

Johannes Kepler(or, Keppler, 1571-1630), was by way of planetary motion that the laws were deducible from Newton's laws of motion. The covering law model may be adapted to include explanation by showing that something is probable, given a statistical law. Questions for the covering law model include querying for the covering laws are necessary to explanation (we explain whether everyday events without overtly citing laws): Querying whether they are sufficient (it may not explain an event just to say that it is an example of the kind of thing that always happens). And querying whether a purely logical relationship is adapted to capturing the requirements, we make of explanations. These may include, for instance, that we have a feel for what is happening, or that the explanation proceeds in terms of things that are familiar to us or unsurprising, or that we can give a model of what is going on, and none of these notions is captured in a purely logical approach. Recent work, therefore, has tended to stress the contextual and pragmatic elements in requirements for explanation, so that what counts as good explanation given one set of concerns may not do so given another.

The argument to the best explanation is the view that once we can select the best of any in something in explanations of an event, then we are justified in accepting it, or even believing it. The principle needs qualification, since something it is unwise to ignore the antecedent improbability of a hypothesis that would explain the data better than others, e.g., the best explanation of a coin falling heads 530 times in 1,000 tosses might be that it is biassed to give a probability of heads of 0.53 but it might be more sensible to suppose that it is fair, or to suspend judgement.

In a philosophy of language is considered as the general attempt to understand the components of a working language, the relationship with the understanding speaker has to its elements, and the relationship they bear to the world. The subject therefore embraces the traditional division of semiotic into syntax, semantics, and pragmatics. The philosophy of language thus mingles with the philosophy of mind, since it needs an account of what it is in our understanding that enables us to use language. It so mingles with the metaphysics of truth and the relationship between sign and object. Much as much is that the philosophy in the 20th century, has been informed by the belief that philosophy of language is the fundamental basis of all philosophical problems, in that language is the distinctive exercise of mind, and the distinctive way in which we give shape to metaphysical beliefs. Particular topics will include the problems of logical form. And the basis of the division between syntax and semantics, as well as problems of understanding the number and nature of specifically semantic relationships such as meaning, reference, predication, and quantification. Pragmatics includes that of speech acts, while problems of rule following and the indeterminacy of translation infect philosophies of both pragmatics and semantics.

On this conception, to understand a sentence is to know its truth-conditions, and, yet, in a distinctive way the conception has remained central that those who offer opposing theories characteristically define their position by reference to it. The Conception of meanings truth-conditions need not and should not be advanced for being in themselves as complete account of meaning. For instance, one who understands a language must have some idea of the range of speech acts contextually acted by the various types of sentences in the language, and must have some idea of the insufficiencies of various kinds of speech acts. The claim of the theorist of truth-conditions should rather be targeted on the notion of content: If indicative sentences differ in what they strictly and literally say, then this difference is fully accounted for by the difference in the truth-conditions.

The meaning of a complex expression is a function of the meaning of its constituent. This is just as a sentence of what it is for an expression to be semantically complex. It is one of the initial attractions of the conception of meaning truth-conditions tat it permits a smooth and satisfying account of the way in which the meaning of s complex expression is a function of the meaning of its constituents. On the truth-conditional conception, to give the meaning of an expression is to state the contribution it makes to the truth-conditions of sentences in which it occurs. For singular terms - proper names, indexical, and certain pronouns - this is done by stating the reference of the terms in question. For predicates, it is done either by stating the conditions under which the predicate is true of arbitrary objects, or by stating that conditions under which arbitrary atomic sentences containing it is true. The meaning of a sentence-forming operator is given by stating its contribution to the truth-conditions of as complex sentence, as a function of the semantic values of the sentences on which it operates.

The theorist of truth conditions should insist that not every true statement about the reference of an expression be fit to be an axiom in a meaning-giving theory of truth for a language, such is the axiom: London refers to the city in which there was a huge fire in 1666, is a true statement about the reference of London. It is a consequent of a theory that substitutes this axiom for no different a term than of our simple truth theory that London is beautiful is true if and only if the city in which there was a huge fire in 1666 is beautiful. Since a subject can understand the name London without knowing that last-mentioned truth condition, this replacement axiom is not fit to be an axiom in a meaning-specifying truth theory. It is, of course, incumbent on a theorised meaning of truth conditions, to state in a way that does not presuppose any previous, non-truth conditional conception of meaning

Among the many challenges facing the theorist of truth conditions, two are particularly salient and fundamental. First, the theorist has to answer the charge of triviality or vacuity, second, the theorist must offer an account of what it is for a persons language to be truly describable by as semantic theory containing a given semantic axiom.

Since the content of a claim that the sentence Paris is beautiful is true amounts to no more than the claim that Paris is beautiful, we can trivially describers understanding a sentence, if we wish, as knowing its truth-conditions, but this gives us no substantive account of understanding whatsoever. Something other than grasp of truth conditions must provide the substantive account. The charge rests upon what has been called the redundancy theory of truth, the theory that, somewhat more discriminatingly. Horwich calls the minimal theory of truth. It is conceptual representation that the concept of truth is exhausted by the fact that it conforms to the equivalence principle, the principle that for any proposition p, it is true that p if and only if p. Many different philosophical theories of truth will, with suitable qualifications, except that equivalence principle. The distinguishing feature of the minimal theory is its claim that the equivalence principle exhausts the notion of truth. It is now widely accepted, both by opponents and supporters of truth conditional theories of meaning, that it is inconsistent to accept both minimal theory of truth and a truth conditional account of meaning. If the claim that the sentence Paris is beautiful is true is exhausted by its equivalence to the claim that Paris is beautiful, it is circular to try of its truth conditions. The minimal theory of truth has been endorsed by the Cambridge mathematician and philosopher Plumpton Ramsey (1903-30), and the English philosopher Jules Ayer, the later Wittgenstein, Quine, Strawson. Horwich and - confusing and inconsistently if this article is correct - Frége himself. But is the minimal theory correct?

The minimal theory treats instances of the equivalence principle as definitional of truth for a given sentence, but in fact, it seems that each instance of the equivalence principle can itself be explained. The truth from which such an instance as: London is beautiful is true if and only if London is beautiful. This would be a pseudo-explanation if the fact that London refers to London consists in part in the fact that London is beautiful has the truth-condition it does. But it is very implausible, it is, after all, possible to understand the name London without understanding the predicate is beautiful.

Sometimes, however, the counterfactual conditional is known as 'subjunctive conditionals', insofar as a counterfactual conditional is a conditional of the form if 'p' were to happen 'q' would, or if 'p' were to have happened 'q' would have happened, where the supposition of 'p' is contrary to the known fact that 'not-p'. Such assertions are nevertheless, useful if you broke the bone, the X-ray would have looked different, or if the reactor were to fail, this mechanism wold click in is important truth, even when we know that the bone is not broken or are certain that the reactor will not fail. It is arguably distinctive of laws of nature that yield counterfactuals (if the metal were to be heated, it would expand), whereas accidentally true generalizations may not. It is clear that counterfactuals cannot be represented by the material implication of the propositional calculus, since that conditionals come out true whenever p is false, so there would be no division between true and false counterfactuals.

Although the subjunctive form indicates a counterfactual, in many contexts it does not seem to matter whether we use a subjunctive form, or a simple conditional form: If you run out of water, you will be in trouble seems equivalent to if you were to run out of water, you would be in trouble, in other contexts there is a big difference: If Oswald did not kill Kennedy, someone else did is clearly true, whereas if Oswald had not killed Kennedy, someone would have been most probably false.

The best-known modern treatment of counterfactual is that of David Lewis, which evaluates them as true or false according to whether q is true in the most similar possible worlds to ours in which p is true. The similarity-ranking this approach need have proved controversial, particularly since it may need to presuppose some notion of the same laws of nature, whereas art of the interest in counterfactuals is that they promise to illuminate that notion. There is a growing awareness that the classification of conditionals is an extremely tricky business, and categorizing them as counterfactuals or does not continue of limited use.

The pronouncing of any conditional preposition assembling the form if 'p' then 'q'. The condition hypothesizes, 'p'. It is called the antecedent of the conditional, and 'q' the consequent. Various kinds of conditional have been distinguished. The weaken in that of material implication, merely telling us that with 'not-p'. or 'q'. stronger conditionals include elements of modality, corresponding to the thought that if 'p' is true then 'q' must be true. Ordinary language is very flexible in its use of the conditional form, and there is controversy whether, yielding different kinds of conditionals with different meanings, or pragmatically, in which case there should be one basic meaning which case there should be one basic meaning, with surface differences arising from other implicatures.

We now turn to a philosophy of meaning and truth, under which it is especially associated with the American philosopher of science and of language (1839-1914), and the American psychologist philosopher William James (1842-1910), wherefore the study in Pragmatism is given to various formulations by both writers, but the core is the belief that the meaning of a doctrine is the same as the practical effects of adapting it. Peirce interpreted of theocratical sentence is only that of a corresponding practical maxim (telling us what to do in some circumstance). In James the position issues in a theory of truth, notoriously allowing that belief, including for example, belief in God, is the widest sense of the works satisfactorily in the widest sense of the word. On James' view almost any belief might be respectable, and even rue, provided it works (but working is no simple matter for James). The apparent subjectivist consequences of this were wildly assailed by Russell (1872-1970), Moore (1873-1958), and others in the early years of the 20 century. This led to a division within pragmatism between those such as the American educator John Dewey (1859-1952), whose humanistic conception of practice remains inspired by science, and the more idealistic route that especially by the English writer F.C.S. Schiller (1864-1937), embracing the doctrine that our cognitive efforts and human needs actually transform the reality that we seek to describe. James often writes as if he sympathizes with this development. For instance, in The Meaning of Truth (1909), he considers the hypothesis that other people have no minds (dramatized in the sexist idea of an automatic sweetheart or female zombie) and remarks hat the hypothesis would not work because it would not satisfy our egoistic craving for the recognition and admiration of others. The implication that this is what makes it true that the other persons have minds in the disturbing part.

Modern pragmatists such as the American philosopher and critic Richard Rorty (1931-) and some writings of the philosopher Hilary Putnam (1925-) who has usually tried to dispense with an account of truth and concentrate, as perhaps James should have done, upon the nature of belief and its relations with human attitude, emotion, and need. The driving motivation of pragmatism is the idea that belief in the truth on te one hand must have a close connexion with success in action on the other. One way of cementing the connexion is found in the idea that natural selection must have adapted us to be cognitive creatures because beliefs have effects, as they work. Pragmatism can be found in Kant's doctrine of the primary of practical over pure reason, and continued to play an influential role in the theory of meaning and of truth.

In case of fact, the philosophy of mind is the modern successor to behaviourism, as do the functionalism that its early advocates were Putnam (1926-) and Sellars (1912-89), and its guiding principle is that we can define mental states by a triplet of relations they have on other mental states, what effects they have on behaviour. The definition need not take the form of a simple analysis, but if it where it could write down the totality of axioms, or postdate, or platitudes that govern our theories about what things of other mental states, and our theories about what things are apt to cause (for example), a belief state, what effects it would have on a variety of other mental states, and what affects it is likely to have on behaviour, then we would have done all that is needed to make the state a proper theoretical notion. It could be implicitly defied by this, for which of Functionalism is often compared with descriptions of a computer, since according to mental descriptions correspond to a description of a machine in terms of software, that remains silent about the underlaying hardware or realization of the program the machine is running. The principal advantage of functionalism includes its fit with the way we know of mental states both of ourselves and others, which is via their effects on behaviour and other mental states. As with behaviourism, critics charge that structurally complex items that do not bear mental states might nevertheless, imitate the functions that are cited. According to this criticism functionalism is too generous and would count too many things as having minds. It is also queried whether functionalism is too paradoxical, able to see mental similarities only when there is causal similarity, when our actual practices of interpretations enable us to ascribe thoughts and desires to differently from our own, it may then seem as though beliefs and desires can be variably realized causal architecture, just as much as they can be in different neurophysiological states.

The philosophical movement of Pragmatism had a major impact on American culture from the late 19th century to the present. Pragmatism calls for ideas and theories to be tested in practice, by assessing whether acting upon the idea or theory produces desirable or undesirable results. According to pragmatists, all claims about truth, knowledge, morality, and politics must be tested in this way. Pragmatism has been critical of traditional Western philosophy, especially the notion that there is absolute truth and absolute values. Although pragmatism was popular for a time in France, England, and Italy, most observers believe that it encapsulates an American faith in knowing how and the practicality is an equally American distrust of abstract theories and ideologies.

In mentioning the American psychologist and philosopher we find William James, who helped to popularize the philosophy of pragmatism with his book Pragmatism: A New Name for Old Ways of Thinking (1907). Influenced by a theory of meaning and verification developed for scientific hypotheses by American philosopher C. S. Peirce, James held that truth is what works, or has good experimental results. In a related theory, James argued the existence of God is partly verifiable because many people derive benefits from believing.

The Association for International Conciliation first published William James' pacifist statement, The Moral Equivalent of War, in 1910. James, a highly respected philosopher and psychologist, was one of the founders of pragmatism - a philosophical movement holding that ideas and theories must be tested in practice to assess their worth. James hoped to find a way to convince men with a long-standing history of pride and glory in war to evolve beyond the need for bloodshed and to develop other avenues for conflict resolution. Spelling and grammar represents standards of the time.

Pragmatists regard all theories and institutions as tentative hypotheses and solutions. For this reason they believed that efforts to improve society, through such means as education or politics, must be geared toward problem solving and must be ongoing. Through their emphasis on connecting theory to practice, pragmatist thinkers attempted to transform all areas of philosophy, from metaphysics to ethics and political philosophy.

Pragmatism sought a middle ground between traditional ideas about the nature of reality and radical theories of nihilism and irrationalism, which had become popular in Europe in the late 19th century. Traditional metaphysics assumed that the world has a fixed, intelligible structure and that human beings can know absolute or objective truth about the world and about what constitutes moral behaviour. Nihilism and irrationalism, on the other hand, denied those very assumptions and their certitude. Pragmatists today still try to steer a middle course between contemporary offshoots of these two extremes.

The ideas of the pragmatists were considered revolutionary when they first appeared. To some critics, pragmatisms refusal to affirm any absolutes carried negative implications for society. For example, pragmatists do not believe that a single absolute idea of goodness or justice exists, but rather than these concepts are changeable and depend on the context in which they are being discussed. The absence of these absolutes, critics feared, could result in a decline in moral standards. The pragmatist's denial of absolutes, moreover, challenged the foundations of religion, government, and schools of thought. As a result, pragmatism influenced developments in psychology, sociology, education, semiotics (the study of signs and symbols), and scientific method, as well as philosophy, cultural criticism, and social reform movements. Various political groups have also drawn on the assumptions of pragmatism, from the progressive movements of the early 20th century to later experiments in social reform.

Pragmatism is best understood in its historical and cultural context. It arose during the late 19th century, a period of rapid scientific advancement typified by the theories of British biologist Charles Darwin, whose theories suggested too many thinkers that humanity and society are in a perpetuated state of progress. During this same period a decline in traditional religious beliefs and values accompanied the industrialization and material progress of the time. In consequence it became necessary to rethink fundamental ideas about values, religion, science, community, and individuality.

The three most important pragmatists are American philosopher's Charles Sanders Peirce, William James, and John Dewey. Peirce was primarily interested in scientific method and mathematics; his objective was to infuse scientific thinking into philosophy and society, and he believed that human comprehension of reality was becoming ever greater and that human communities were becoming increasingly progressive. Peirce developed pragmatism as a theory of meaning - in particular, the meaning of concepts used in science. The meaning of the concept 'brittle', for example, is given by the observed consequences or properties that objects called brittle exhibit. For Peirce, the only rational way to increase knowledge was to form mental habits that would test ideas through observation, experimentation, or what he called inquiry. Many philosophers known as logical positivists, a group of philosophers who have been influenced by Peirce, believed that our evolving species was fated to get ever closer to Truth. Logical positivists emphasize the importance of scientific verification, rejecting the assertion of positivism that personal experience is the basis of true knowledge.

James moved pragmatism in directions that Peirce strongly disliked. He generalized Peirces doctrines to encompass all concepts, beliefs, and actions; he also applied pragmatist ideas to truth as well as to meaning. James was primarily interested in showing how systems of morality, religion, and faith could be defended in a scientific civilization. He argued that sentiment, as well as logic, is crucial to rationality and that the great issues of life - morality and religious belief, for example - are leaps of faith. As such, they depend upon what he called the will to believe and not merely on scientific evidence, which can never tell us what to do or what is worthwhile. Critics charged James with relativism (the belief that values depend on specific situations) and with crass expediency for proposing that if an idea or action works the way one intends, it must be right. But James can more accurately be described as a pluralist - someone who believes the world to be far too complex for any-one philosophy to explain everything.

Dewey's philosophy can be described as a version of philosophical naturalism, which regards human experience, intelligence, and communities as ever-evolving mechanisms. Using their experience and intelligence, Dewey believed, human beings can solve problems, including social problems, through inquiry. For Dewey, naturalism led to the idea of a democratic society that allows all members to acquire social intelligence and progress both as individuals and as communities. Dewey held that traditional ideas about knowledge, truth, and values, in which absolutes are assumed, are incompatible with a broadly Darwinian world-view in which individuals and societies are progressing. In consequence, he felt that these traditional ideas must be discarded or revised. Indeed, for pragmatists, everything people know and do depend on a historical context and are thus tentative rather than absolute.

Many followers and critics of Dewey believe he advocated elitism and social engineering in his philosophical stance. Others think of him as a kind of romantic humanist. Both tendencies are evident in Dewey's writings, although he aspired to synthesize the two realms.

The pragmatist's tradition was revitalized in the 1980s by American philosopher Richard Rorty, who has faced similar charges of elitism for his belief in the relativism of values and his emphasis on the role of the individual in attaining knowledge. Interest has renewed in the classic pragmatists - Pierce, James, and Dewey - have an alternative to Rorty's interpretation of the tradition.

The Philosophy of Mind, is the branch of philosophy that considers mental phenomena such as sensation, perception, thought, belief, desire, intention, memory, emotion, imagination, and purposeful action. These phenomena, which can be broadly grouped as thoughts and experiences, are features of human beings; many of them are also found in other animals. Philosophers are interested in the nature of each of these phenomena as well as their relationships to one another and to physical phenomena, such as motion.

The most famous exponent of dualism was the French philosopher René Descartes, who maintained that body and mind are radically different entities and that they are the only fundamental substances in the universe. Dualism, however, does not show how these basic entities are connected.

In the work of the German philosopher Gottfried Wilhelm Leibniz, the universe is held to consist of an infinite number of distinct substances, or monads. This view is pluralistic in the sense that it proposes the existence of many separate entities, and it is monistic in its assertion that each monad reflects within itself the entire universe.

Other philosophers have held that knowledge of reality is not derived from a priori principles, but is obtained only from experience. This type of metaphysic is called empiricism. Still another school of philosophy has maintained that, although an ultimate reality does exist, it is altogether inaccessible to human knowledge, which is necessarily subjective because it is confined to states of mind. Knowledge is therefore not a representation of external reality, but merely a reflection of human perceptions. This view is known as skepticism or agnosticism in respect to the soul and the reality of God.

The 18th-century German philosopher Immanuel Kant published his influential work The Critique of Pure Reason in 1781. Three years later, he expanded on his study of the modes of thinking with an essay entitled What is Enlightenment? In this 1784 essay, Kant challenged readers to dare to know, arguing that it was not only a civic but also a moral duty to exercise the fundamental freedoms of thought and expression.

Several major viewpoints were combined in the work of Kant, who developed a distinctive critical philosophy called transcendentalism. His philosophy is agnostic in that it denies the possibility of a strict knowledge of ultimate reality; it is empirical in that it affirms that all knowledge arises from experience and is true of objects of actual and possible experience; and it is rationalistic in that it maintains the a priori character of the structural principles of this empirical knowledge.

These principles are held to be necessary and universal in their application to experience, for in Kant's view the mind furnishes the archetypal forms and categories (space, time, causality, substance, and relation) to its sensations, and these categories are logically anterior to experience, although manifested only in experience. Their logical anteriority to experience makes these categories or structural principle's transcendental, they transcend all experience, both actual and possible. Although these principles determine all experience, they do not in any way affect the nature of things in themselves. The knowledge of which these principles are the necessary conditions must not be considered, therefore, as constituting a revelation of things as they are in themselves. This knowledge concerns things only insofar as they appear to human perception or as they can be apprehended by the senses. The argument by which Kant sought to fix the limits of human knowledge within the framework of experience and to demonstrate the inability of the human mind to penetrate beyond experience strictly by knowledge to the realm of ultimate reality constitutes the critical feature of his philosophy, giving the key word to the titles of his three leading treatises, Critique of Pure Reason, Critique of Practical Reason, and Critique of Judgment. In the system propounded in these works, Kant sought also to reconcile science and religion in a world of two levels, comprising noumena, objects conceived by reason although not perceived by the senses, and phenomena, things as they appear to the senses and are accessible to material study. He maintained that, because God, freedom, and human immortality are noumenal realities, these concepts are understood through moral faith rather than through scientific knowledge. With the continuous development of science, the expansion of metaphysics to include scientific knowledge and methods became one of the major objectives of metaphysicians.

Some of Kant's most distinguished followers, notably Johann Gottlieb Fichte, Friedrich Schelling, Georg Wilhelm Friedrich Hegel, and Friedrich Schleiermacher, negated Kant's criticism in their elaborations of his transcendental metaphysics by denying the Kantian conception of the thing-in-itself. They thus developed an absolute idealism in opposition to Kant's critical transcendentalism.

Since the formation of the hypothesis of absolute idealism, the development of metaphysics has resulted in as many types of metaphysical theory as existed in pre-Kantian philosophy, despite Kant's contention that he had fixed definitely the limits of philosophical speculation. Notable among these later metaphysical theories are radical empiricism, or pragmatism, a native American form of metaphysics expounded by Charles

Sanders Peirce, developed by William James, and adapted as instrumentalism by John Dewey; voluntarism, the foremost exponents of which are the German philosopher Arthur Schopenhauer and the American philosopher Josiah Royce; phenomenalism, as it is exemplified in the writings of the French philosopher Auguste Comte and the British philosopher Herbert Spencer; emergent evolution, or creative evolution, originated by the French philosopher Henri Bergson; and the philosophy of the organism, elaborated by the British mathematician and philosopher Alfred North Whitehead. The salient doctrines of pragmatism are that the chief function of thought is to guide action, that the meaning of concepts is to be sought in their practical applications, and that truth should be tested by the practical effects of belief; according to instrumentalism, ideas are instruments of action, and their truth is determined by their role in human experience. In the theory of voluntarism the will are postulated as the supreme manifestation of reality. The exponents of phenomenalism, who are sometimes called positivists, contend that everything can be analysed in terms of actual or possible occurrences, or phenomena, and that anything that cannot be analysed in this manner cannot be understood. In emergent or creative evolution, the evolutionary process is characterized as spontaneous and unpredictable rather than mechanistically determined. The philosophy of the organism combines an evolutionary stress on constant process with a metaphysical theory of God, the external objects, and creativity.

In the 20th century the validity of metaphysical thinking has been disputed by the logical positivists and by the so-called dialectical materialism of the Marxists. The basic principle maintained by the logical positivists is the verifiability theory of meaning. According to this theory a sentence has factual meaning only if it meets the test of observation. Logical positivists argue that metaphysical expressions such as Nothing exists except material particles and Everything is part of one all-encompassing spirit cannot be tested empirically. Therefore, according to the verifiability theory of meaning, these expressions have no factual cognitive meaning, although they can have an emotive meaning relevant to human hopes and feelings.

The dialectical materialists assert that the mind is conditioned by and reflects material reality. Therefore, speculations that conceive of constructs of the mind as having any other than material reality is themselves unreal and can result only in delusion. To these assertions metaphysicians reply by denying the adequacy of the verifiability theory of meaning and of material perception as the standard of reality. Both logical positivism and dialectical materialism, they argue, conceal metaphysical assumptions, for example, that everything is observable or at least connected with something observable and that the mind has no distinctive life of its own. In the philosophical movement known as existentialism, thinkers have contended that the questions of the nature of being and of the individuals relationships to it are extremely important and meaningful in terms of human life. The investigation of these questions is therefore considered valid whether its results can be verified objectively.

Since the 1950s the problems of systematic analytical metaphysics have been studied in Britain by Stuart Newton Hampshire and Peter Frederick Strawson, the former concerned, in the manner of Spinoza, with the relationship between thought and action, and the latter, in the manner of Kant, with describing the major categories of experience as they are embedded in language. Metaphysics have been pursued much in the spirit of positivism by Wilfred Stalker Sellars and Willard Van Orman Quine. Sellars have sought to express metaphysical questions in linguistic terms, and Quine has attempted to determine whether the structure of language commits the philosopher to asserting the existence of any entities whatever and, if so, what kind. In these new formulations the issues of metaphysics and ontology remain vital.

n the 17th century, French philosopher René Descartes proposed that only two substances ultimately exist; mind and body. Yet, if the two are entirely distinct, as Descartes believed, how can one substance interact with the other? How, for example, is the intention of a human mind able to cause movement in the persons limbs? The issue of the interaction between mind and body is known in philosophy as the mind-body problem.

Many fields other than philosophy share an interest in the nature of mind. In religion, the nature of mind is connected with various conceptions of the soul and the possibility of life after death. In many abstract theories of mind there is considerable overlap between philosophy and the science of psychology. Once part of philosophy, psychology split off and formed a separate branch of knowledge in the 19th century. While psychology used scientific experiments to study mental states and events, philosophy uses reasoned arguments and thought experiments in seeking to understand the concepts that underlie mental phenomena. Also influenced by philosophy of mind is the field of artificial intelligence, which endeavours to develop computers that can mimic what the human mind can do. Cognitive science attempts to integrate the understanding of mind provided by philosophy, psychology, AI, and other disciplines. Finally, all of these fields benefit from the detailed understanding of the brain that has emerged through neuroscience in the late 20th century.

Philosophers use the characteristics of inward accessibility, subjectivity, intentionality, goal-directedness, creativity and freedom, and consciousness to distinguish mental phenomena from physical phenomena.

Perhaps the most important characteristic of mental phenomena is that they are inwardly accessible, or available to us through introspection. We each know our own minds - our sensations, thoughts, memories, desires, and fantasies - in a direct sense, by internal reflection. We also know our mental states and mental events in a way that no one else can. In other words, we have privileged access to our own mental states.

Certain mental phenomena, those we generally call experiences, have a subjective nature - that is, they have certain characteristics we become aware of when we reflect, for instance, there is something as definitely to feel pain, or have an itch, or see something red. These characteristics are subjective in that they are accessible to the subject of the experience, the person who has the experience, but not to others.

Other mental phenomena, which we broadly refer to as thoughts, have a characteristic philosophers call intentionality. Intentional thoughts are about other thoughts or objects, which are represented as having certain properties or for being related to one another in a certain way. The belief that London is west of Toronto, for example, is about London and Toronto and represents the former as west of the latter. Although we have privileged access to our intentional states, many of them do not seem to have a subjective nature, at least not in the way that experiences do.

The contrast between the subjective and the objective is made in both the epistemic and the ontological divisions of knowledge. In the objective field of study, it is often identified with the distension between the intrapersonal and the interpersonal, or with that between matters whose resolving power depends on the psychology of the person in question, and who in this way is dependent, or, sometimes, with the distinction between the biassed and the impartial. Therefore, an objective question might be one answerable by a method usable by any competent investigator, while a subjective question would be answerable only from the questioners point of view. In the ontological domain, the subjective-objective contrast is often between what is what is not mind-dependent: Secondary qualities, e.g., colour, have been variability with observation conditions. The truth of a proposition, for instance: Apart from certain propositions about oneself, would be objective if it is interdependent of the perspective, especially for beliefs of those judging it. Truth would be subjective if it lacks such independence, because it is a construct from justified beliefs, e.g., those well-confirmed by observation.

One notion of objectivity can be basic and the other as an end point of reasoning and observation, if only to infer of it as a conclusion. If the epistemic notion is essentially an underlying of something as related to or dealing with such that are to fundamental primitives, then the criteria for objectivity in the ontological sense derive from considerations of justification: An objective question is one answerable by a procedure that yields (adequate) justification is a matter of amenability to such a means or procedures used to attaining an end., its method, if, on the other hand, the ontological notion is basic, the criteria for an interpersonal method and its objective use are a matter of its mind-independence and tendency to lead to objective truth, perhaps, its applying to external objects and yielding predictive success. Since, the use of these criteria requires employing the methods that, on the epistemic conception, define objectivists most notably scientific methods - but no similar dependence obtains in the other direction, the epistemic notion os often taken as basic.

A different theory of truth, or the epistemic theory, is motivated by the desire to avoid negative features of the correspondence theory, which celebrates the existence of God, whereby, its premises are that all natural things are dependent for their existence on something else, whereas the totality of dependent beings must then of themselves depend upon a non-dependent, or necessarily existent, being, which is God. So, the God that ends the question must exist necessarily, it must not be an entity of which the same kinds of questions can be raised. The problem with such is the argument that it unfortunately affords no reason for attributing concern and care to the deity, nor for connecting the necessarily existent being it derives with human values and aspirations.

This presents in truth as that which is licenced by our best theory of reality. Truth is distributively contributed as a function of our thinking about the world and all surrounding surfaces. An obvious problem with this is the fact of revision; theories are constantly refined and corrected. To deal with this objection it is at the end of enquiry. We never in fact reach it, but it serves as a direct motivational disguised enticement, as an asymptotic end of enquiry. Nonetheless, the epistemic theory of truth is not antipathetic to ontological relativity, since it has no commitment to the ultimate furniture of the world and it also is open to the possibilities of some kinds of epistemological relativism.

Lest be said, however, that of epistemology, the subjective-objective contrast arises above all for the concept of justification and its relatives. Externalism, particularly reliabilism, and since, for reliabilism, truth-conduciveness (non-subjectivity conceived) is central for justified belief. Internalism may or may not construe justification subjectivistically, depending on whether the proposed epistemic standards are interpersonally grounded. There are also various kinds of subjectivity: Justification may, e.g., be grounded in ones considered standards of simply in what one believes to be sound. Yet, justified beliefs accorded with precise or explicitly considered standards whether or not deem it a purposive necessity to think them justifiably made so.

Any conception of objectivity may treat one domain as fundamental and the others derivatively. Thus, objectivity for methods (including sensory observation) might be thought basic. Let us look upon an objective method be that one is (1) interpersonally usable and tends to yield justification regarding the questions to which it applies (an epistemic conception), or (2) trends to yield truth when properly applied (an ontological conception) or (3) both. Then an objective person is one who appropriately uses objective methods by an objective method, as one appraisable by an objective method, an objective discipline is whose methods are objective, and so on. Typically, those who conceive objectivity epistemically tend to take methods as fundamental, and those who conceive it ontologically tend to take statements as basic.

A number of mental phenomena appear to be connected to one another as elements in an intelligent, goal-directed system. The system works as follows: First, our sense organs are stimulated by events in our environment; next, by virtue of these stimulations, we perceive things about the external world; finally, we use this information, as well as information we have remembered or inferred, to guide our actions in ways that further our goals. Goal-directedness seems to accompany only mental phenomena.

Another important characteristic of mind, especially of human minds, is the capacity for choice and imagination. Rather than automatically converting past influences into future actions, individual minds are capable of exhibiting creativity and freedom. For instance, we can imagine things we have not experienced and can act in ways that no one expects or could predict.

Mental phenomena are conscious, and consciousness may be the closest term we have for describing what is special about mental phenomena. Minds are sometimes referred to as consciousness, yet it is difficult to describe exactly what consciousness is. Although consciousness is closely related to inward accessibility and subjectivity, these very characteristics seem to hinder us in reaching an objective scientific understanding of it.

Although philosophers have written about mental phenomena since ancient times, the philosophy of mind did not garner much attention until the work of French philosopher René Descartes in the 17th century. Descartes work represented a turning point in thinking about mind by making a strong distinction between bodies and minds, or the physical and the mental. This duality between mind and body, known as Cartesian dualism, has posed significant problems for philosophy ever since.

Descartes believed there are two basic kinds of things in the world, a belief known as substance dualism. For Descartes, the principles of existence for these two groups of things - bodies and minds - are completely different from one another: Bodies exist by being extended in space, while minds exist by being conscious. According to Descartes, nothing can be done to give a body thought and consciousness. No matter how we shape a body or combine it with other bodies, we cannot turn the body into a mind, a thing that is conscious, because being conscious is not a way of being extended.

For Descartes, a person consists of a human body and a human mind causally interacting with one another. For example, the intentions of a human being, that may have conceivably, caused that persons' limbs to move. In this way, the mind can affect the body. In addition, the sense organs of a human being as forced, in effect of a refractive ray of light, pressure, or sound, external sources, which in turn affect the brain, affecting mental states. Thus, the body may affect the mind. Exactly how mind can affect body, and vice versa, is a central issue in the philosophy of mind, and is known as the mind-body problem. According to Descartes, this interaction of mind and body is peculiarly intimate. Unlike the interaction between a pilot and his ship, the connexion between mind and body more closely resembles two substances that have been thoroughly mixed together.

In response to the mind-body problem arising from Descartes theory of substance dualism, a number of philosophers have advocated various forms of substance monism, the doctrine that there is ultimately just one kind of thing in reality. In the 18th century, Irish philosopher George Berkeley claimed there were no material objects in the world, only minds and their ideas. Berkeley thought that talk about physical objects was simply a way of organizing the flow of experience. Near the turn of the 20th century, American psychologist and philosopher William James proposed another form of substance monism. James claimed that experience is the basic stuff from which both bodies and minds are constructed.

Most philosophers of mind today are substance monists of a third type: They are materialists who believe that everything in the world is basically material, or a physical object. Among materialists, there is still considerable disagreement about the status of mental properties, which are conceived as properties of bodies or brains. Materialists who those properties undersized by duality, yet believe that mental properties are an additional kind of property or attribute, not reducible to physical properties. Property diarists have the problem of explaining how such properties can fit into the world envisaged by modern physical science, according to which there are physical explanations for all things.

Materialists who are property monists believe that there is ultimately only one type of property, although they disagree on whether or not mental properties exist in material form. Some property monists, known as reductive materialists, hold that mental properties exist simply as a subset of relatively complex and non-basic physical properties of the brain. Reductive materialists have the problem of explaining how the physical states of the brain can be inwardly accessible and have a subjective character, as mental states do. Other property monists, known as eliminative materialists, consider the whole category of mental properties to be a mistake. According to them, mental properties should be treated as discredited postulates of an out-moulded theory. Eliminative materialism is difficult for most people to accept, since we seem to have direct knowledge of our own mental phenomena by introspection and because we use the general principles we understand about mental phenomena to predict and explain the behaviour of others.

Philosophy of mind concerns itself with a number of specialized problems. In addition to the mind-body problem, important issues include those of personal identity, immortality, and artificial intelligence.

During much of Western history, the mind has been identified with the soul as presented in Christian theology. According to Christianity, the soul is the source of a persons' identity and is usually regarded as immaterial; thus, it is capable of enduring after the death of the body. Descartes conception of the mind as a separate, nonmaterial substance fits well with this understanding of the soul. In Descartes view, we are aware of our bodies only as the cause of sensations and other mental phenomena. Consequently our personal essence is composed more fundamentally of mind and the preservation of the mind after death would constitute our continued existence.

The mind conceived by materialist forms of substance monism does not fit as neatly with this traditional concept of the soul. With materialism, once a physical body is destroyed, nothing enduring remains. Some philosophers think that a concept of personal identity can be constructed that permits the possibility of life after death without appealing to separate immaterial substances. Following in the tradition of 17th-century British philosopher John Locke, these philosophers propose that a person consists of a stream of mental events linked by memory. It is these links of memory, rather than a single underlying substance, that provides the unity of a single consciousness through time. Immortality is conceivable if we think of these memory links as connecting a later consciousness in heaven with an earlier one on earth.

The field of artificial intelligence also raises interesting questions for the philosophy of mind. People have designed machines that mimic or model many aspects of human intelligence, and there are robots currently in use whose behaviour is described in terms of goals, beliefs, and perceptions. Such machines are capable of behaviour that, were it exhibited by a human being, would surely be taken to be free and creative. As an example, in 1996 an IBM computer named Deep Blue won a chess game against Russian world champion Garry Kasparov under international match regulations. Moreover, it is possible to design robots that have some sort of privileged access to their internal states. Philosophers disagree over whether such robots truly think or simply appear to think and whether such robots should be considered to be conscious

Dualism, in philosophy, the theory that the universe is explicable only as a whole composed of two distinct and mutually irreducible elements. In Platonic philosophy the ultimate dualism is between being and nonbeing - that is, between ideas and matter. In the 17th century, dualism took the form of belief in two fundamental substances: mind and matter. French philosopher René Descartes, whose interpretation of the universe exemplifies this belief, was the first to emphasize the irreconcilable difference between thinking substance (mind) and extended substance (matter). The difficulty created by this view was to explain how mind and matter interact, as they apparently do in human experience. This perplexity caused some Cartesians to deny entirely any interaction between the two. They asserted that mind and matter are inherently incapable of affecting each other, and that any reciprocal action between the two is caused by God, who, on the occasion of a change in one, produces a corresponding change in the other. Other followers of Descartes abandoned dualism in favour of monism.

In the 20th century, reaction against the monistic aspects of the philosophy of idealism has to some degree revived dualism. One of the most interesting defences of dualism is that of Anglo-American psychologist William McDougall, who divided the universe into spirit and matter and maintained that good evidence, both psychological and biological, indicates the spiritual basis of physiological processes. French philosopher Henri Bergson in his great philosophic work Matter and Memory likewise took a dualistic position, defining matter as what we perceive with our senses and possessing in itself the qualities that we perceive in it, such as colour and resistance. Mind, on the other hand, reveals itself as memory, the faculty of storing up the past and utilizing it for modifying our present actions, which otherwise would be merely mechanical. In his later writings, however, Bergson abandoned dualism and came to regard matter as an arrested manifestation of the same vital impulse that composes life and mind.

Dualism, in philosophy, the theory that the universe is explicable only as a whole composed of two distinct and mutually irreducible elements. In Platonic philosophy the ultimate dualism is between being and nonbeing - that is, between ideas and matter. In the 17th century, dualism took the form of belief in two fundamental substances: mind and matter. French philosopher René Descartes, whose interpretation of the universe exemplifies this belief, was the first to emphasize the irreconcilable difference between thinking substance (mind) and extended substance (matter). The difficulty created by this view was to explain how mind and matter interact, as they apparently do in human experience. This perplexity caused some Cartesians to deny entirely any interaction between the two. They asserted that mind and matter are inherently incapable of affecting each other, and that any reciprocal action between the two is caused by God, who, on the occasion of a change in one, produces a corresponding change in the other. Other followers of Descartes abandoned dualism in favour of monism.

In the 20th century, reaction against the monistic aspects of the philosophy of idealism has to some degree revived dualism. One of the most interesting defences of dualism is that of Anglo-American psychologist William McDougall, who divided the universe into spirit and matter and maintained that good evidence, both psychological and biological, indicates the spiritual basis of physiological processes. French philosopher Henri Bergson in his great philosophic work Matter and Memory likewise took a dualistic position, defining matter as what we perceive with our senses and possessing in itself the qualities that we perceive in it, such as colour and resistance. Mind, on the other hand, reveals itself as memory, the faculty of storing up the past and utilizing it for modifying our present actions, which otherwise would be merely mechanical. In his later writings, however, Bergson abandoned dualism and came to regard matter as an arrested manifestation of the same vital impulse that composes life and mind.

For many people oriented of a spatially temporal or its opposite in understanding the place of mind in nature is the greatest philosophical problem. Mind is often though to be the last domain that stubbornly resists scientific understanding and philosophers defer over whether they find that cause for celebration or scandal. The mind-body problem in the modern era was given its definitive shape by Descartes, although the dualism that he espoused is in some form whatever there is a religious or philosophical tradition there is a religious or philosophical tradition whereby the soul may have an existence apart from the body. While most modern philosophers of mind would reject the imaginings that lead us to think that this makes sense, there is no consensus over the best way to integrate our understanding of people as bearers of physical properties lives on the other.

Occasionalist finds from it term as employed to designate the philosophical system devised by the followers of the 17th-century French philosopher René Descartes, who, in attempting to explain the interrelationship between mind and body, concluded that God is the only cause. The occasionalists began with the assumption that certain actions or modifications of the body are preceded, accompanied, or followed by changes in the mind. This assumed relationship presents no difficulty to the popular conception of mind and body, according to which each entity is supposed to act directly on the other;

these philosophers, however, asserting that cause and effect must be similar, could not conceive the possibility of any direct mutual interaction between substances as dissimilar as mind and body.

According to the occasionalists, the action of the mind is not, and cannot be, the cause of the corresponding action of the body. Whenever any action of the mind takes place, God directly produces in connexion with that action, and by reason of it, a corresponding action of the body; the converse process is also true. This theory did not solve the problem, for if the mind cannot act on the body (matter), then God, conceived as mind, cannot act on matter. Conversely, if God is conceived as other than mind, then he cannot act on mind. A proposed solution to this problem was furnished by exponents of radical empiricism such as the American philosopher and psychologist William James. This theory disposed of the dualism of the occasionalists by denying the fundamental difference between mind and matter.

Generally, along with consciousness, that experience of an external world or similar scream or other possessions, takes upon itself the visual experience or deprive of some normal visual experience, that this, however, does not perceive the world accurately. In its frontal experiment. As researchers reared kittens in total darkness, except that for five hours a day the kittens were placed in an environment with only vertical lines. When the animals were later exposed to horizontal lines and forms, they had trouble perceiving these forms.

While, in the theory of probability the Cambridge mathematician and philosopher Frank Ramsey (1903-30), was the first to show how a personalised theory could be developed, based on precise behavioural notions of preference and expectation. In the philosophy of language, Ramsey was one of the first thinkers to accept a redundancy theory of truth, which he combined with radical views of the function of many kinds of propositions. Neither generalizations nor causal propositions, nor those treating probability or ethics, described facts, but each has a different specific function in our intellectual economy.

Ramsey advocates that of a sentence generated by taking all the sentence affirmed in a scientific theory that use some term, e.g., quark. Replacing the term by a variable, and existentially quantifying into the result. Instead of saying quarks have such-and-such properties, Ramsey postdated that the sentence as saying that there is something that has those properties. If the process is repeated, the sentence gives the topic-neutral structure of the theory, but removes any implications that we know what the term so treated denote. It leaves open the possibility of identifying the theoretical item with whatever, and it is that best fits the description provided. Nonetheless, it was pointed out by the Cambridge mathematician Newman that if the process is carried out for all except the logical bones of the theory, then by the Löwenheim-Skolem theorem, the result will be interpretable in any domain of sufficient cardinality, and the content of the theory may reasonably be felt to have been lost.

Nevertheless, probability is a non-negative, additive set function whose maximum value is unity. What is harder to understand is the application of the formal notion to the actual world. One point of application is statistical, when kinds of event or trials (such as the tossing of a coin) can be described, and the frequency of occurrence of particular outcomes (such as the coin falling heads) is measurable, then we can begin to think of the probability of that kind of outcome in that kind of trial. One account of probability is therefore the frequency theory, associated with Venn and Richard von Mises (1883-1953), that identifies the probability of an event with such a frequency of occurrence. A second point of application is the description of a hypothesis as probable when the evidence bears a favoured relation is conceived of as purely logical in nature, as in the works of Keynes and Carnap, probability statements are not empirical measures of frequency, but represent something like partial entailments or measures of possibilities left open by the evidence and by the hypothesis.

Formal confirmation theories and range theories of probability are developments of this idea. The third point of application is in the use probability judgements have in regulating the confidence with which we hold various expectations. The approach sometimes called subjectivism or personalism, but more commonly known as Bayesianism, associated with de Finetti and Ramsey, whom of both, see probability judgements as expressions of a subjects degree of confidence in an event or kind of event, and attempts to describe constraints on the way we should have degrees of confidence in different judgements that explain those judgements having the mathematical form of judgements of probability. For Bayesianism, probability or chance is probability or chance is not an objective or real factor in the world, but rather a reflection of our own states of mind. However, these states of mind need to be governed by empirical frequencies, so this is not an invitation to licentious thinking.

This concept of sampling and accompanying application of the laws of probability find extensive use in polls, public opinion polls. Polls to determine what radio or television program is being watched and listened to, polls to determine house-wives reaction to a new product, political polls, and the like. In most cases the sampling is carefully planned and often a margin of error is stated. Polls cannot, however, altogether eliminate the fact that certain people dislike being questioned and may deliberately conceal or give false information. In spite of this and other objections, the method of sampling often makes results available in situations where the cost of complete enumeration would be prohibitive both from the standpoint of time and of money.

Thus we can see that probability and statistics are used in insurance, physics, genetics, biology, business, as well as in games of chance, and we are inclined to agree with P.S. LaPlace who said: We see . . . that the theory of probabilities is at bottom only common sense reduced to calculation, it makes us appreciate with exactitude what reasonable minds feel by a sort of instinct, often being able to account for it . . . it is remarkable that [this] science, which originated in the consideration of games of chance, should have become the most important object of human knowledge.

It seems, that the most taken of are the paradoxes in the foundations of set theory as discovered by Russell in 1901. Some classes have themselves as members: The class of all abstract objects, for example, is an abstract object, whereby, others do not: The class of donkeys is not itself a donkey. Now consider the class of all classes that are not members' of themselves, is this class a member of itself, that, if it is, then it is not, and if it is not, then it is.

The paradox is structurally similar to easier examples, such as the paradox of the barber. Such one like a village having a barber in it, who shaves all and only the people who do not have in themselves. Who shaves the barber? If he shaves himself, then he does not, but if he does not shave himself, then he does not. The paradox is actually just a proof that there is no such barber or in other words, that the condition is inconsistent. All the same, it is no too easy to say why there is no such class as the one Russell defines. It seems that there must be some restriction on the kind of definitions that are allowed to define classes and the difficulty that of finding a well-motivated principle behind any such restriction.

The French mathematician and philosopher Henri Jules Poincaré (1854-1912) believed that paradoses like those of Russell and the barber was due to such as the impredicative definitions, and therefore proposed banning them. But, it turns out that classical mathematics required such definitions at too many points for the ban to be easily absolved. Having, in turn, as forwarded by Poincaré and Russell, was that in order to solve the logical and semantic paradoxes it would have to ban any collection (set) containing members that can only be defined by means of the collection taken as a whole. It is, effectively by all occurring principles into which have an adopting vicious regress, as to mark the definition for which involves no such failure. There is frequently room for dispute about whether regresses are benign or vicious, since the issue will hinge on whether it is necessary to reapply the procedure. The cosmological argument is an attempt to find a stopping point for what is otherwise seen for being an infinite regress, and, to ban of the predicative definitions.

The investigation of questions that ascend from reflection upon sciences and scientific inquiry, as such are called on by a philosophy of science. Such questions include, what distinctions in the methods of science? There a clear demarcation between scenes and other disciplines, and how do we place such enquires as history, economics or sociology? And scientific theories probable or more in the nature of provisional conjecture? Can the be verified or falsified? What distinguished good from bad explanations? Might there be one unified since, embracing all special sciences? For much of the 20th century their questions were pursued in a highly abstract and logical framework it being supposed that as general logic of scientific discovery that a general logic of scientific discovery a justification might be found. However, many now take interests in a more historical, contextual and sometimes sociological approach, in which the methods and successes of a science at a particular time are regarded less in terms of universal logical principles and procedure, and more in terms of their availability to methods and paradigms as well as the social context.

In addition, to general questions of methodology, there are specific problems within particular sciences, giving subjects as biology, mathematics and physics.

The intuitive certainties that spark aflame the dialectic awarenesses for its immediate concerns are either of the truth or by another in an object of apprehensions, such as a concept. Awareness as such, has to its amounting quality value the place where philosophically understanding of the source of our knowledge are, however, in covering the sensible apprehension of things and pure intuition it is that which structural sensation into the experience of things accent of its direction that orchestrates the celestial overture into measures in space and time.

The notion that determines how something is seen or evaluated of the status of law and morality especially associated with St. Thomas Aquinas and the subsequent scholastic tradition. More widely, any attempt to cement the moral and legal order together with the nature of the cosmos or how the nature of human beings, for which sense it is also found in some Protestant writers, and arguably derivative from a Platonic view of ethics, and is implicit in ancient Stoicism. Law stands above and apart from the activities of human lawmakers, it constitutes an objective set of principles that can be seen true by natural light or reason, and (in religion versions of the theory) that express Gods will for creation. Non-religious versions of the theory substitute objective conditions for human flourishing as the source of constraints upon permissible actions and social arrangements. Within the natural law tradition, different views have been held about the relationship between the rule of law about God s will, for instance the Dutch philosopher Hugo Grothius (1583-1645). Similarly taken upon the view that the content of natural law is independent of any will, including that of God, while the German theorist and historian Samuel von Pufendorf (1632-94) takes the opposite view. T thereby facing the problem of one horn of the Euthyphro dilemma, which simply states, that its dilemma arises from whatever the source of authority is supposed to be, for in which do we care about the general good because it is good, or do we just call good things that we care about. Wherefore, by facing the problem that may be to assume of a strong form, in which it is claimed that various facts entail values, or a weaker form, from which it confines itself to holding that reason by itself is capable of discerning moral requirements that are supposedly of binding to all human bings regardless of their desires

Although the morality of people end the ethical measure that from which the same thing, is that, there is a usage that restricts morality to systems such as that of the German philosopher and founder of ethical philosophy Immanuel Kant (1724-1804), based on notions such as duty, obligation, and principles of conduct, reserving ethics for more than the Aristotelian approach to practical reasoning based on the notion of a virtue, and generally avoiding the separation of moral considerations from other practical considerations. The scholarly issues are complex, with some writers seeing Kant as more Aristotelian and Aristotle as, ore involved in a separate sphere of responsibility and duty, than the simple contrast suggests. Some theorists see the subject in terms of a number of laws (as in the Ten Commandments). The status of these laws may be test, and they are the edicts of a divine lawmaker, or that they are truth of reason, knowable deductively. Other approaches to ethics (e.g., eudaimonism, situational ethics, virtue ethics) eschew general principles as much as possible, frequently disguising the great complexity of practical reasoning. For Kantian notion of the moral law is a binding requirement of the categorical imperative, and to understand whether they are equivalent at some deep level. Kant's own applications of the notion are not always convincing, as for one cause of confusion in relating Kant's ethics to theories such additional expressivism, is that it is easy, but mistaken, to suppose that the categorical nature of the imperative means that it cannot be the expression of sentiment, but must derive from something unconditional or necessary such as the voice of reason.

For whichever reason, the mortal being makes of its presence to the future of weighing of that which one must do, or that which can be required of one. The term carries implications of that which is owed (due) to other people, or perhaps in oneself. Universal duties would be owed to persons (or sentient beings) as such, whereas special duty in virtue of specific relations, such for being the child of someone, or having made someone a promise. Duty or obligation is the primary concept of deontological approaches to ethics, but is constructed in other systems out of other notions. In the system of Kant, a perfect duty is one that must be done whatever the circumstances: Imperfect duties may have to give way to the more stringent ones. In another way, perfect duties are those that are correlative with the right to others, imperfect duties are not. Problems with the concept include the ways in which due needs to be specified (a frequent criticism of Kant is that his notion of duty is too abstract). The concept may also suggest of a regimented view of ethical life in which we are all forced conscripts in a kind of moral army, and may encourage an individualistic and antagonistic view of social relations.

The most generally accepted account of externalism and internalism, that this distinction is that a theory of justification is internalist if only if were itself, the requiems that all of the factors needed for a belief to be epistemologically justified for a given persons are cognitively accessible to that person, internal to his cognitive perception, and externalist, if it allows that at least some of the justifying factors need not be thus accessible, so that they can be external to the believers cognitive perceptive, beyond any such given relations. However, epistemologists often use the distinction between internalist and externalist theories of epistemic justification without offering any very explicit explication.

The externalist/internalist distinction has been mainly applied to theories of epistemic justification: It has also been applied in a closely related way to accounts of knowledge and in a rather different way to accounts of belief and thought contents.

The internalist requirement of cognitive accessibility can be interpreted in at least two ways: A strong version of internalism would require that the believer actually be aware of the justifying factor in order to be justified: While a weaker version would require only that he be capable of becoming aware of them by focussing his attentions appropriately, but without the need for any change of position, new information, etc. Though the phrase cognitively accessible suggests the weak interpretation, the main intuitive motivation for internalism, viz. the idea that epistemic justification requires that the believer actually have in his cognitive possession a reason for thinking that the belief is true, and would require the strong interpretation.

Perhaps, the clearest example of an internalist position would be a foundationalist view according to which foundational beliefs pertain to immediately experienced states of mind and other beliefs are justified by standing in cognitively accessible logical or inferential relations to such foundational beliefs. Such a view could count as either a strong or a weak version of internalism, depending on whether actual awareness of the justifying elements or only the capacity to become aware of them is required. Similarly, a current view could also be internalist, if both the beliefs or other states with which a justification belief is required to cohere and the coherence relations themselves are reflectively accessible.

It should be carefully noticed that when internalism is construed in this way, it is neither necessary nor sufficient by itself for internalism that the justifying factors literally are internal mental states of the person in question. Not necessary, necessary, because on at least some views, e.g., a direct realist view of perception, something other than a mental state of the believer can be cognitively accessible: Not sufficient, because there are views according to which at least some mental states need not be actual (strong version) or even possible (weak version) objects of cognitive awareness. Also, on this way of drawing the distinction, a hybrid view, according to which some of the factors required for justification must be cognitively accessible while others need not and in general will not be, would count as an externalist view. Obviously too, a view that was externalist in relation to a strong version of internalism (by not requiring that the believer actually be aware of all justifying factors) could still be internalist in relation to a weak version (by requiring that he at least is capable of becoming aware of them).

The most prominent recent externalist views have been versions of Reliabilism, whose requirements for justification are roughly that the beliefs are produced in a way or via a process that makes of objectively likely that the belief is true. What makes such a view externalist is the absence of any requirement that the person for whom the belief is justified have any sort of cognitive access to the relations of reliability in question. Lacking such access, such a person will in general have no reason for thinking that the belief is true or likely to be true, but will, on such an account, nonetheless be epistemically justified in according it. Thus such a view arguably marks a major break from the modern epistemological tradition, stemming from Descartes, which identifies epistemic justification with having a reason, perhaps even a conclusive reason for thinking that the belief is true. An epistemologist working within this tradition is likely to feel that the externalist, than offering a competing account of the same concept of epistemic justification with which the traditional epistemologist is concerned, has simply changed the subject.

The main objection to externalism rests on the intuitive certainty that the basic requirement for epistemic justification is that the acceptance of the belief in question is rational or responsible in relation to the cognitive goal of truth, which seems to require in turn that the believer actually be dialectally aware of a reason for thinking that the belief is true (or, at the very least, that such a reason be available to him). Since the satisfaction of an externalist condition is neither necessary nor sufficient for the existence of such a cognitively accessible reason, it is argued, externalism is mistaken as an account of epistemic justification. This general point has been elaborated by appeal to two sorts of putative intuitive counterexamples to externalism. The first of these challenges the necessity of belief that seem intuitively to be justified, but for which the externalist conditions are not satisfied. The standard examples in this sort are cases where beliefs are produced in some very nonstandard way, e.g., by a Cartesian demon, but nonetheless, in such a way that the subjective experience of the believer is indistinguishable from that of someone whose beliefs are produced more normally. The intuitive claim is that the believer in such a case is nonetheless epistemically justified, as much so as one whose belief is produced in a more normal way, and hence that externalist account of justification must be mistaken.

Perhaps the most striking reply to this sort of counterexamples, on behalf of a cognitive process is to be assessed in normal possible worlds, i.e., in possible worlds that are actually the way our world is common-seismically believed to be, than in the world that contains the belief being judged. Since the cognitive processes employed in the Cartesian demon cases are, for which we may assume, reliable when assessed in this way, the reliabilist can agree that such beliefs are justified. The obvious, to a considerable degree of bringing out the issue of whether it is or not an adequate rationale for this construal of Reliabilism, so that the reply is not merely a notional presupposition guised as having representation.

The correlative way of elaborating on the general objection to justificatory externalism challenges the sufficiency of the various externalist conditions by citing cases where those conditions are satisfied, but where the believers in question seem intuitively not to be justified. In this context, the most widely discussed examples have to do with possible occult cognitive capacities, like clairvoyance. Considering the point in application once, again, to Reliabilism, the claim is that to think that he has such a cognitive power, and, perhaps, even good reasons to the contrary, is not rational or responsible and therefore not epistemically justified in accepting the belief that result from his clairvoyance, despite the fact that the reliabilist condition is satisfied.

One sort of response to this latter sorts of objection is to bite the bullet and insist that such believers are in fact justified, dismissing the seeming intuitions to the contrary as latent internalist prejudice. A more widely adopted response attempts to impose additional conditions, usually of a roughly internalist sort, which will rule out the offending example, while stopping far of a full internalism. But, while there is little doubt that such modified versions of externalism can handle particular cases, as well enough to avoid clear intuitive implausibility, the usually problematic cases that they cannot handle, and also whether there is and clear motivation for the additional requirements other than the general internalist view of justification that externalist are committed to reject.

A view in this same general vein, one that might be described as a hybrid of internalism and externalism holds that epistemic justification requires that there is a justificatory factor that is cognitively accessible to the believer in question (though it need not be actually grasped), thus ruling out, e.g., a pure Reliabilism. At the same time, however, though it must be objectively true that beliefs for which such a factor is available are likely to be true, in addition, the fact need not be in any way grasped or cognitively accessible to the believer. In effect, of the premises needed to argue that a particular belief is likely to be true, one must be accessible in a way that would satisfy at least weak internalism, the internalist will respond that this hybrid view is of no help at all in meeting the objection and has no belief nor is it held in the rational, responsible way that justification intuitively seems to require, for the believer in question, lacking one crucial premise, still has no reason at all for thinking that his belief is likely to be true.

An alternative to giving an externalist account of epistemic justification, one that may be more defensible while still accommodating many of the same motivating concerns, is to give an externalist account of knowledge directly, without relying on an intermediate account of justification. Such a view will obviously have to reject the justified true belief account of knowledge, holding instead that knowledge is true belief that satisfies the chosen externalist condition, e.g., a result of a reliable process (and perhaps, further conditions as well). This makes it possible for such a view to retain internalist account of epistemic justification, though the centrality of that concept to epistemology would obviously be seriously diminished.

Such an externalist account of knowledge can accommodate the commonsense conviction that animals, young children, and unsophisticated adult's posse's knowledge, though not the weaker conviction (if such a conviction does exist) that such individuals are epistemically justified in their beliefs. It is also at least less vulnerable to internalist counterexamples of the sort discussed, since the intuitions involved there pertain more clearly to justification than to knowledge. What is uncertain is what ultimate philosophical significance the resulting conception of knowledge is supposed to have. In particular, does it have any serious bearing on traditional epistemological problems and on the deepest and most troubling versions of scepticism, which seems in fact to be primarily concerned with justification, that of knowledge?`

A rather different use of the term's internalism and externalism has to do with the issue of how the content of beliefs and thoughts is determined: According to an internalist view of content, the content of such intention states depends only on the non-relational, internal properties of the individuals mind or grain, and not at all on his physical and social environment: While according to an externalist view, content is significantly affected by such external factors and suggests a view that appears of both internal and external elements is standardly classified as an external view.

As with justification and knowledge, the traditional view of content has been strongly internalist in character. The main argument for externalism derives from the philosophy y of language, more specifically from the various phenomena concerning natural kind terms, indexical, and so on, that motivate the views that have come to be known as direct reference theories. Such phenomena seem at least to show that the belief or thought content that can be properly attributed to a person is dependent on facts about his environment -, e.g., whether he is on Earth or Twin Earth, what is fact pointing at, the classificatory criteria employed by expects in his social group, etc. - not just on what is going on internally in his mind or brain.

An objection to externalist account of content is that they seem unable to do justice to our ability to know the content of our beliefs or thought from the inside, simply by reflection. If content is depending on external factors about the environment, then knowledge of content should depend on knowledge of these factors - which will not in general be available to the person whose belief or thought is in question.

The adoption of an externalist account of mental content would seem to support an externalist account of justification, by way that if part or all of the content of a belief inaccessible to the believer, then both the justifying status of other beliefs in relation to that content and the status of that content as justifying further beliefs will be similarly inaccessible, thus contravening the internalist requirement for justification. An internalist must insist that there are no justification relations of these sorts, that our internally associable content can be equally justified or justly for anything else: But such a response appears lame unless it is coupled with an attempt to show that the externalist account of content is mistaken.

In addition, to what to the foundationalist, but the view in epistemology that knowledge must be regarded as a structure raised upon secure, certain foundations. These are found in some combination of experience and reason, with different schools (empirical, rationalism) emphasizing the role of one over that of the other. Foundationalism was associated with the ancient Stoics, and in the modern era with Descartes, who discovered his foundations in the clear and distinct ideas of reason. Its main opponent is coherentism or the view that a body of propositions my be known without as foundation is certain, but by their interlocking strength. Rather as a crossword puzzle may be known to have been solved correctly even if each answer, taken individually, admits of uncertainty.

Truth, alone with coherence is the study of concept, in such a study in philosophy is that it treats both the meaning of the word true and the criteria by which we judge the truth or falsity in spoken and written statements. Philosophers have attempted to answer the question What is truth? for thousands of years. The four main theories they have proposed to answer this question are the correspondence, pragmatic, coherence, and deflationary theories of truth.

There are various ways of distinguishing types of foundationalist epistemology by the use of the variations that have been enumerating. Plantinga has put forward an influence conception of classical foundationalism, specified in terms of limitations on the foundations. He construes this as a disjunction of ancient and medieval foundationalism; Which takes foundations to comprise that with self-evident and evident to the senses, and modern foundationalism that replace evident Foundationalism that replaces evident sensationalism with the replacements of evident senses with callousness for which in practice was taken to apply only to beliefs bout ones present state of consciousness? Plantinga himself developed this notion in the context of arguing those items outside this territory, in particular certain beliefs about God, could also be immediately justified. A popular recent distinction is between what is variously strong or extremely foundationalism and moderate, modest or minimal and moderately modest or minimal foundationalism with the distinction depending on whether epistemic immunities are reassured of foundations. While depending on whether it require of a foundation only that it be required of as foundation, that only it be immediately justified, or whether it be immediately justified. In that it make just the comforted preferability, only to suggest that the plausibility of the string requiring stems from both a level confusion between beliefs on different levels.

Emerging sceptic tendencies come forth in the 14th-century writings of Nicholas of Autrecourt. His criticisms of any certainty beyond the immediate deliverance of the senses and basic logic, and in particular of any knowledge of either intellectual or material substances, anticipate the later scepticism of Balye and Hume. The latter distinguishes between Pyrrhonistic and excessive scepticism, which he regarded as unlivable, and the more mitigated scepticism that accepts every day or commonsense beliefs (not as the delivery of reason, but as due more to custom and habit), but is duly wary of the power of reason to give us much more. Mitigated scepticism is thus closer to the attitude fostered by ancient scepticism from Pyrrho through to Sexus Empiricus. Although the phrase Cartesian scepticism is sometimes used, Descartes himself was not a sceptic, but in the method of doubt, uses a sceptical scenario in order to begin the process of finding a secure mark of knowledge.

Scepticism should not be confused with relativism, which is a doctrine about the nature of truth, and may be motivated by trying to avoid scepticism. Nor is it identical with eliminativist, which counsels abandoning an area of thought together, not because we cannot know the truth, but because there are no truth capable of being framed in the terms we use.

Descartes theory of knowledge starts with the quest for certainty, for an indubitable starting-point or foundation on the basis alone of which progress is possible. This is eventually found in the celebrated Cadged ergo sum: I think therefore I am. By locating the point of certainty in my own awareness of my own self, Descartes gives a first-person twist to the theory of knowledge that dominated them following centuries in spite of various counterattack on behalf of social and public starting-points. The metaphysics associated with this priority is the famous Cartesian dualism, or separation of mind and matter into two different but interacting substances, Descartes rigorously and rightly sees that it takes divine dispensation to certify any relationship between the two realms thus divided, and to prove the reliability of the senses invokes a clear and distinct perception of highly dubious proofs of the existence of a benevolent deity. This has not met general acceptance: as Hume drily puts it, to have recourse to the veracity of the supreme Being, in order to prove the veracity of our senses, is surely making a very unexpected circuit.

In his own time Descartes conception of the entirely separate substance of the mind was recognized to give rise to insoluble problems of the nature of the causal connexion between the two. It also gives rise to the problem, insoluble in its own terms, of other minds. Descartes notorious denial that nonhuman animals are conscious is a stark illustration of the problem. In his conception of matter Descartes also gives preference to rational cogitation over anything derived from the senses. Since we can conceive of the matter of a ball of wax surviving changes to its sensible qualities, matter is not an empirical concept, but eventually an entirely geometrical one, with extension and motion as its only physical nature. Descartes thought, as reflected in Leibniz, that the qualities of sense experience have no resemblance to qualities of things, so that knowledge of the external world is essentially knowledge of structure rather than of filling. On this basis Descartes erects a remarkable physics. Since matter is in effect the same as extension there can be no empty space or void, since there is no empty space motion is not a question of occupying previously empty space, but is to be thought of in terms of vortices (like the motion of a liquid).

Although the structure of Descartes epistemology, theory of mind, and theory of matter have ben rejected many times, their relentless exposure of the hardest issues, their exemplary clarity, and even their initial plausibility, all contrive to make him the central point of reference for modern philosophy.

The self conceived as Descartes presents it in the first two Meditations: aware only of its own thoughts, and capable of disembodied existence, neither situated in a space nor surrounded by others. This is the pure self of I-ness that we are tempted to imagine as a simple unique thing that make up our essential identity. Descartes view that he could keep hold of this nugget while doubting everything else is criticized by Lichtenberg and Kant, and most subsequent philosophers of mind.

Descartes holds that we do not have any knowledge of any empirical proposition about anything beyond the contents of our own minds. The reason, roughly put, is that there is a legitimate doubt about all such propositions because there is no way to deny justifiably that our senses are being stimulated by some cause (an evil spirit, for example) which is radically different from the objects that we normally think affect our senses.

He also points out, that the senses (sight, hearing, touch, etc., are often unreliable, and it is prudent never to trust entirely those who have deceived us even once, he cited such instances as the straight stick that looks ben t in water, and the square tower that looks round from a distance. This argument of illusion, has not, on the whole, impressed commentators, and some of Descartes contemporaries pointing out that since such errors become known as a result of further sensory information, it cannot be right to cast wholesale doubt on the evidence of the senses. But Descartes regarded the argument from illusion as only the first stage in a softening up process which would lead the mind away from the senses. He admits that there are some cases of sense-base belief about which doubt would be insane, e.g., the belief that I am sitting here by the fire, wearing a winter dressing gown.

Descartes was to realize that there was nothing in this view of nature that could explain or provide a foundation for the mental, or from direct experience as distinctly human. In a mechanistic universe, he said, there is no privileged place or function for mind, and the separation between mind and matter is absolute. Descartes was also convinced, that the immaterial essences that gave form and structure to this universe were coded in geometrical and mathematical ideas, and this insight led him to invent algebraic geometry.

A scientific understanding of these ideas could be derived, said Descartes, with the aid of precise deduction, and also claimed that the contours of physical reality could be laid out in three-dimensional coordinates. Following the publication of Newton's Principia Mathematica in 1687, reductionism and mathematical modelling became the most powerful tools of modern science. And the dream that the entire physical world could be known and mastered through the extension and refinement of mathematical theory became the central feature and guiding principle of scientific knowledge.

Having to its recourse of knowledge, its central questions include the origin of knowledge, the place of experience in generating knowledge, and the place of reason in doing so, the relationship between knowledge and certainty, and between knowledge and the impossibility of error, the possibility of universal scepticism, and the changing forms of knowledge that arise from new conceptualizations of the world. All of these issues link with other central concerns of philosophy, such as the nature of truth and the natures of experience and meaning.

Foundationalism was associated with the ancient Stoics, and in the modern era with Descartes (1596-1650). Who discovered his foundations in the clear and distinct ideas of reason? Its main opponent is coherentism, or the view that a body of propositions mas be known without a foundation in certainty, but by their interlocking strength, than as a crossword puzzle may be known to have been solved correctly even if each answer, taken individually, admits of uncertainty. Difficulties at this point led the logical passivists to abandon the notion of an epistemological foundation altogether, and to flirt with the coherence theory of truth. It is widely accepted that trying to make the connexion between thought and experience through basic sentences depends on an untenable myth of the given.

Still in spite of these concerns, the problem was, of course, in defining knowledge in terms of true beliefs plus some favoured relations between the believer and the facts that began with Platos view in the Theaetetus, that knowledge is true belief, and some logos. Due of its nonsynthetic epistemology, the enterprising of studying the actual formation of knowledge by human beings, without aspiring to certify those processes as rational, or its proof against scepticism or even apt to yield the truth. Natural epistemology would therefore blend into the psychology of learning and the study of episodes in the history of science. The scope for external or philosophical reflection of the kind that might result in scepticism or its refutation is markedly diminished. Despite the fact that the terms of modernity are so distinguished as exponents of the approach include Aristotle, Hume, and J. S. Mills.

The task of the philosopher of a discipline would then be to reveal the correct method and to unmask counterfeits. Although this belief lay behind much positivist philosophy of science, few philosophers now subscribe to it. It places too well a confidence in the possibility of a purely previous first philosophy, or viewpoint beyond that of the work ones way of practitioners, from which their best efforts can be measured as good or bad. These standpoints now seem that too many philosophers may be too fanciful, that the more modest of tasks are actually adopted at various historical stages of investigation into different areas and with the aim not so much of criticizing, but more of systematization.

In the presuppositions of a particular field at a particular classification, there is still a role for local methodological disputes within the community investigators of some phenomenon, with one approach charging that another is unsound or unscientific, but logic and philosophy will not, on the modern view, provide any independent arsenal of weapons for such battles, which often come to seem more like factional recommendations in the ascendancy of a discipline.

This is an approach to the theory of knowledge that sees an important connexion between the growth of knowledge and biological evolution. An evolutionary epistemologist claims that the development of human knowledge processed through some natural selection process, the best example of which is Darwin's theory of biological natural selection. There is a widespread misconception that evolution proceeds according to some plan or direct, but it has neither, and the role of chance ensures that its future course will be unpredictable. Random variations in individual organisms create tiny differences in their Darwinian fitness. Some individuals have more offsprings than others, and the characteristics that increased their fitness thereby become more prevalent in future generations. Once upon a time, at least a mutation occurred in a human population in tropical Africa that changed the haemoglobin molecule in a way that provided resistance to malaria. This enormous advantage caused the new gene to spread, with the unfortunate consequence that sickle-cell anaemia came to exist.

Given that chance, it can influence the outcome at each stage: First, in the creation of genetic mutation, second, in whether the bearer lives long enough to show its effects, thirdly, in chance events that influence the individuals actual reproductive success, and fourth, in whether a gene even if favoured in one generation, is, happenstance, eliminated in the next, and finally in the many unpredictable environmental changes that will undoubtedly occur in the history of any group of organisms. As Harvard biologist Stephen Jay Gould has so vividly expressed that process over again, the outcome would surely be different. Not only might there not be humans, there might not even be anything like mammals.

We will often emphasis the elegance of traits shaped by natural selection, but the common idea that nature creates perfection needs to be analysed carefully. The extent to which evolution achieves perfection depends on exactly what you mean. If you mean Does natural selections always take the best path for the long-term welfare of a species? The answer is no. That would require adaption by group selection, and this is, unlikely. If you mean Does natural selection creates every adaption that would be valuable? The answer again, is no. For instance, some kinds of South American monkeys can grasp branches with their tails. The trick would surely also be useful to some African species, but, simply because of bad luck, none have it. Some combination of circumstances started some ancestral South American monkeys using their tails in ways that ultimately led to an ability to grab onto branches, while no such development took place in Africa. Mere usefulness of a trait does not necessitate a means in that what will understandably endure phylogenesis or evolution.

This is an approach to the theory of knowledge that sees an important connexion between the growth of knowledge and biological evolution. An evolutionary epistemologist claims that the development of human knowledge proceeds through some natural selection process, the best example of which is Darwin's theory of biological natural selection. The three major components of the model of natural selection are variation selection and retention. According to Darwin's theory of natural selection, variations are not pre-designed to do certain functions. Rather, these variations that do useful functions are selected. While those that do not employ of some coordinates in that are regainfully purposed are also, not to any of a selection, as duly influenced of such a selection, that may have responsibilities for the visual aspects of variational intentionally occurs. In the modern theory of evolution, genetic mutations provide the blind variations: Blind in the sense that variations are not influenced by the effects they would have-the likelihood of a mutation is not correlated with the benefits or liabilities that mutation would confer on the organism, the environment provides the filter of selection, and reproduction provides the retention. Fatnesses are achieved because those organisms with features that make them less adapted for survival do not survive in connexion with other organisms in the environment that have features that are better adapted. Evolutionary epistemology applies this blind variation and selective retention model to the growth of scientific knowledge and to human thought processes overall.

The parallel between biological evolution and conceptual or epistemic evolution can be seen as either literal or analogical. The literal version of evolutionary epistemology deeds biological evolution as the main cause of the growth of knowledge. On this view, called the evolution of cognitive mechanic programs, by Bradie (1986) and the Darwinian approach to epistemology by Ruse (1986), that growth of knowledge occurs through blind variation and selective retention because biological natural selection itself is the cause of epistemic variation and selection. The most plausible version of the literal view does not hold that all human beliefs are innate but rather than the mental mechanisms that guide the acquisitions of non-innate beliefs are themselves innately and the result of biological natural selection. Ruse, (1986) demands of a version of literal evolutionary epistemology that he links to sociolology (Rescher, 1990).

On the analogical version of evolutionary epistemology, called the evolution of theories program, by Bradie (1986). The Spenserians approach (after the nineteenth century philosopher Herbert Spencer) by Ruse (1986), the development of human knowledge is governed by a process analogous to biological natural selection, rather than by an instance of the mechanism itself. This version of evolutionary epistemology, introduced and elaborated by Donald Campbell (1974) as well as Karl Popper, sees the [partial] fit between theories and the world as explained by a mental process of trial and error known as epistemic natural selection.

Both versions of evolutionary epistemology are usually taken to be types of naturalized epistemology, because both take some empirical facts as a starting point for their epistemological project. The literal version of evolutionary epistemology begins by accepting evolutionary theory and a materialist approach to the mind and, from these, constructs an account of knowledge and its developments. In contrast, the metaphorical version does not require the truth of biological evolution: It simply draws on biological evolution as a source for the model of natural selection. For this version of evolutionary epistemology to be true, the model of natural selection need only apply to the growth of knowledge, not to the origin and development of species. Crudely put, evolutionary epistemology of the analogical sort could still be true even if Creationism is the correct theory of the origin of species.

Although they do not begin by assuming evolutionary theory, most analogical evolutionary epistemologists are naturalized epistemologists as well, their empirical assumptions, least of mention, implicitly come from psychology and cognitive science, not evolutionary theory. Sometimes, however, evolutionary epistemology is characterized in a seemingly non-naturalistic fashion. Campbell (1974) says that if one is expanding knowledge beyond what one knows, one has no choice but to explore without the benefit of wisdom, i.e., blindly. This, Campbell admits, makes evolutionary epistemology close to being a tautology (and so not naturalistic). Evolutionary epistemology does assert the analytic claim that when expanding ones knowledge beyond what one knows, one must precessed to something that is already known, but, more interestingly, it also makes the synthetic claim that when expanding ones knowledge beyond what one knows, one must proceed by blind variation and selective retention. This claim is synthetic because it can be empirically falsified. The central claim of evolutionary epistemology is synthetic, not analytic. If the central contradictory, which they are not. Campbell is right that evolutionary epistemology does have the analytic feature he mentions, but he is wrong to think that this is a distinguishing feature, since any plausible epistemology has the same analytic feature (Skagestad, 1978).

Two extraordinary issues lie to awaken the literature that involves questions about realism, i.e., What metaphysical commitment does an evolutionary epistemologist have to make? Progress, i.e., according to evolutionary epistemology, does knowledge develop toward a goal? With respect to realism, many evolutionary epistemologists endorse that is called hypothetical realism, a view that combines a version of epistemological scepticism and tentative acceptance of metaphysical realism. With respect to progress, the problem is that biological evolution is not goal-directed, but the growth of human knowledge seems to be. Campbell (1974) worries about the potential dis-analogy here but is willing to bite the stone of conscience and admit that epistemic evolution progress toward a goal (truth) while biologic evolution does not. Many another has argued that evolutionary epistemologists must give up the truth-topic sense of progress because a natural selection model is in essence, is non-teleological, as an alternative, following Kuhn (1970), and embraced in the accompaniment with evolutionary epistemology.

Among the most frequent and serious criticisms levelled against evolutionary epistemology is that the analogical version of the view is false because epistemic variation is not blind (Skagestad, 1978), and (Ruse, 1986) including, (Stein and Lipton, 1990) all have argued, nonetheless, that this objection fails because, while epistemic variation is not random, its constraints come from heuristics that, for the most part, are selective retention. Further, Stein and Lipton come to the conclusion that heuristics are analogous to biological pre-adaptations, evolutionary pre-biological pre-adaptions, evolutionary cursors, such as a half-wing, a precursor to a wing, which have some function other than the function of their descendable structures: The function of descendable structures, the function of their descendable character embodied to its structural foundations, is that of the guidelines of epistemic variation is, on this view, not the source of disanalogousness, but the source of a more articulated account of the analogy.

Many evolutionary epistemologists try to combine the literal and the analogical versions (Bradie, 1986, and Stein and Lipton, 1990), saying that those beliefs and cognitive mechanisms, which are innate results from natural selection of the biological sort and those that are innate results from natural selection of the epistemic sort. This is reasonable as long as the two parts of this hybrid view are kept distinct. An analogical version of evolutionary epistemology with biological variation as its only source of blondeness would be a null theory: This would be the case if all our beliefs are innate or if our non-innate beliefs are not the result of blind variation. An appeal to the legitimate way to produce a hybrid version of evolutionary epistemology since doing so trivializes the theory. For similar reasons, such an appeal will not save an analogical version of evolutionary epistemology from arguments to the effect that epistemic variation is blind (Stein and Lipton, 1990).

Although it is a new approach to theory of knowledge, evolutionary epistemology has attracted much attention, primarily because it represents a serious attempt to flesh out a naturalized epistemology by drawing on several disciplines. In science is relevant to understanding the nature and development of knowledge, then evolutionary theory is among the disciplines worth a look. Insofar as evolutionary epistemology looks there, it is an interesting and potentially fruitful epistemological programme.

What makes a belief justified and what makes a true belief knowledge? Thinking that whether a belief deserves one of these appraisals is natural depends on what caused the depicted branch of knowledge to have the belief. In recent decades a number of epistemologists have pursued this plausible idea with a variety of specific proposals. Some causal theories of knowledge have it that a true belief that p is knowledge just in case it has the right causal connexion to the fact that p. Such a criterion can be applied only to cases where the fact that p is a sort that can reach causal relations, as this seems to exclude mathematically and their necessary facts and perhaps any fact expressed by a universal generalization, and proponents of this sort of criterion have usually supposed that it is limited to perceptual representations where knowledge of particular facts about subjects environments.

For example, Armstrong (1973), predetermined that a position held by a belief in the form This perceived object is F is [non-inferential] knowledge if and only if the belief is a completely reliable sign that the perceived object is F, that is, the fact that the object is F contributed to causing the belief and its doing so depended on properties of the believer such that the laws of nature dictated that, for any subject 'χ' and perceived object 'y', if 'χ' has those properties and believed that 'y' is 'F', then 'y' is 'F'. (Dretske (1981) offers a rather similar account, in terms of the beliefs being caused by a signal received by the perceiver that carries the information that the object is 'F').

Goldman (1986) has proposed an importantly different causal criterion, namely, that a true belief is knowledge if it is produced by a type of process that is globally and locally reliable. Causing true beliefs is sufficiently high is globally reliable if its propensity. Local reliability has to do with whether the process would have produced a similar but false belief in certain counterfactual situations alternative to the actual situation. This way of marking off true beliefs that are knowledge does not require the fact believed to be causally related to the belief, and so it could in principle apply to knowledge of any kind of truth.

Goldman requires the global reliability of the belief-producing process for the justification of a belief, he requires it also for knowledge because justification is required for knowledge.

What he requires for knowledge, but does not require for justification is local reliability. His idea is that a justified true belief is knowledge if the type of process that produced it would not have produced it in any relevant counterfactual situation in which it is false. Its purported theory of relevant alternatives can be viewed as an attempt to provide a more satisfactory response to this tension in our thinking about knowledge. It attempts to characterize knowledge in a way that preserves both our belief that knowledge is an absolute concept and our belief that we have knowledge.

According to the theory, we need to qualify rather than deny the absolute character of knowledge. We should view knowledge as absolute, reactive to certain standards (Dretske, 1981 and Cohen, 1988). That is to say, in order to know a proposition, our evidence need not eliminate all the alternatives to that preposition, rather for us, that we can know our evidence eliminates al the relevant alternatives, where the set of relevant alternatives (a proper subset of the set of all alternatives) is determined by some standard. Moreover, according to the relevant alternatives view, and the standards determining that of the alternatives is raised by the sceptic are not relevant. If this is correct, then the fact that our evidence cannot eliminate the sceptics alternative does not lead to a sceptical result. For knowledge requires only the elimination of the relevant alternatives, so the relevant alternative view preserves in both strands in our thinking about knowledge. Knowledge is an absolute concept, but because the absoluteness is relative to a standard, we can know many things.

The interesting thesis that counts as a causal theory of justification (in the meaning of causal theory intended here) are that: A belief is justified in case it was produced by a type of process that is globally reliable, that is, its propensity to produce true beliefs-that can be defined (to a good approximation) As the proportion of the beliefs it produces (or would produce) that is true is sufficiently great.

This proposal will be adequately specified only when we are told (I) how much of the causal history of a belief counts as part of the process that produced it, (ii) which of the many types to which the process belongs is the type for purposes of assessing its reliability, and (iii) relative to why the world or worlds are the reliability of the process type to be assessed the actual world, the closet worlds containing the case being considered, or something else? Let us look at the answers suggested by Goldman, the leading proponent of a reliabilist account of justification.

(1) Goldman (1979, 1986) takes the relevant belief producing process to include only the proximate causes internal to the believer. So, for instance, when believing that the telephone was ringing the process that produced the belief, for purposes of assessing

reliability, includes just the causal chain of neural events from the stimulus in my ears inward and other brain states on which the production of the belief depended: It does not include any events in the telephone, or the sound waves travelling between it and my ears, or any earlier decisions made, that were responsible for being within hearing distance of the telephone at that time. It does seem intuitively plausible of a belief depends should be restricted to internal oneness proximate to the belief. Why? Goldman does not tell us. One answer that some philosophers might give is that it is because a beliefs being justified at a given time can depend only on facts directly accessible to the believers awareness at that time (for, if a believer ought to holds only beliefs that are justified, she can tell at any given time what beliefs would then be justified for her). However, this cannot be Goldman's answer because he wishes to include in the relevantly process neural events that are not directly accessible to consciousness.

(2) Once the reliabilist has told us how to delimit the process producing a belief, he needs to tell us that of the many types to which it belongs is the relevant type. Coincide, for example, the process that produces your believing that you see a book before you. One very broad type to which that process belongs would be specified by coming to a belief as to something one perceives as a result of activation of the nerve endings in some of ones sense-organs. A constricted type, in which that unvarying processes belong would be specified by coming to a belief as to what one sees as a result of activation of the nerve endings in ones retinas. A still narrower type would be given by inserting in the last specification a description of a particular pattern of activation of the retinas particular cells. Which of these or other types to which the token process belongs is the relevant type for determining whether the type of process that produced your belief is reliable?

If we select a type that is too broad, as having the same degree of justification various beliefs that intuitively seem to have different degrees of justification. Thus the broadest type we specified for your belief that you see a book before you apply also to perceptual beliefs where the object seen is far away and seen only briefly is less justified. On the other hand, is we are allowed to select a type that is as narrow as we please, then we make it out that an obviously unjustified but true belief is produced by a reliable type of process. For example, suppose I see a blurred shape through the fog far in a field and unjustifiedly, but correctly, believe that it is a sheep: If we include enough details about my retinal image is specifying te type of the visual process that produced that belief, we can specify a type is likely to have only that one instanced and is therefore 100 percent reliable. Goldman conjectures (1986) that the relevant process type is the narrowest type that is casually operative. Presumably, a feature of the process producing beliefs were causally operatives in producing it just in case some alternative feature instead, but it would not have led to that belief. We need to say some here rather than any, because, for example, when I see an oak or maple tree, the particular like-minded material bodies of my retinal image is causally clear toward the worked in producing my belief that what is seen as a tree, even though there are alternative shapes, for example, oak or maples, ones that would have produced the same belief.

(3) Should the justification of a belief in a hypothetical, non-actual example turn on the reliability of the belief-producing process in the possible world of the example? That leads to the implausible result in that in a world run by a Cartesian demon-a powerful being who causes the other inhabitants of the world to have rich and careened sets of perceptual and memory impressions that are all illusory the perceptual and memory beliefs of the other inhabitants are all unjustified, for they are produced by processes that are, in that world, quite unreliable. If we say instead that it is the reliability of the processes in the actual world that matters, we get the equally undesired result that if the actual world is a demon world then our perceptual and memory beliefs are all unjustified.

Goldman's solution (1986) is that the reliability of the process types is to be gauged by their performance in normal worlds, that is, worlds consistent with our general beliefs about the world . . . about the sorts of objects, events and changes that occur in it. This gives the intuitively right results for the problem cases just considered, but indicate by inference an implausible proportion of making compensations for alternative tending toward justification. If there are people whose general beliefs about the world are very different from mine, then there may, on this account, be beliefs that I can correctly regard as justified (ones produced by processes that are reliable in what I take to be a normal world) but that they can correctly regard as not justified.

However, these questions about the specifics are dealt with, and there are reasons for questioning the basic idea that the criterion for a beliefs being justified is its being produced by a reliable process. Thus and so, doubt about the sufficiency of the reliabilist criterion is prompted by a sort of example that Goldman himself uses for another purpose. Suppose that being in brain-state (B) always causes one to believe that one is in brained-state (B). Here the reliability of the belief-producing process is perfect, but we can readily imagine circumstances in which a person goes into grain-state B and therefore has the belief in question, though this belief is by no means justified (Goldman, 1979). Doubt about the necessity of the condition arises from the possibility that one might know that one has strong justification for a certain belief and yet that knowledge is not what actually prompts one to believe. For example, I might be well aware that, having read the weather bureaus forecast that it will be much hotter tomorrow. I have ample reason to be confident that it will be hotter tomorrow, but I irrationally refuse to believe it until Wally tells me that he feels in his joints that it will be hotter tomorrow. Here what prompts me to believe dors not justify my belief, but my belief is nevertheless justified by my knowledge of the weather bureaus prediction and of its evidential force: I can advert to any disavowable inference that I ought not to be holding the belief. Indeed, given my justification and that there is nothing untoward about the weather bureaus prediction, my belief, if true, can be counted knowledge. This sorts of example raises doubt whether any causal conditions, are it a reliable process or something else, is necessary for either justification or knowledge.

Philosophers and scientists alike, have often held that the simplicity or parsimony of a theory is one reason, all else being equal, to view it as true. This goes beyond the unproblematic idea that simpler theories are easier to work with and gave greater aesthetic appeal.

One theory is more parsimonious than another when it postulates fewer entities, processes, changes or explanatory principles: The simplicity of a theory depends on essentially the same consecrations, though parsimony and simplicity obviously become the same. Demanding clarification of what makes one theory simpler or more parsimonious is plausible than another before the justification of these methodological maxims can be addressed.

If we set this description problem to one side, the major normative problem is as follows: What reason is there to think that simplicity is a sign of truth? Why should we accept a simpler theory instead of its more complex rivals? Newton and Leibniz thought that the answer was to be found in a substantive fact about nature. In Principia, Newton laid down as his first Rule of Reasoning in Philosophy that nature does nothing in vain . . . for Nature is pleased with simplicity and affects not the pomp of superfluous causes. Leibniz hypothesized that the actual world obeys simple laws because Gods taste for simplicity influenced his decision about which world to actualize.

The tragedy of the Western mind, described by Koyré, is a direct consequence of the stark Cartesian division between mind and world. We discovered the certain principles of physical reality, said Descartes, not by the prejudices of the senses, but by the light of reason, and which thus possess so great evidence that we cannot doubt of their truth. Since the real, or that which actually exists external to ourselves, was in his view only that which could be represented in the quantitative terms of mathematics, Descartes conclude that all quantitative aspects of reality could be traced to the deceitfulness of the senses.

The most fundamental aspect of the Western intellectual tradition is the assumption that there is a fundamental division between the material and the immaterial world or between the realm of matter and the realm of pure mind or spirit. The metaphysical frameworks based on this assumption is known as ontological dualism. As the word dual implies, the framework is predicated on an ontology, or a conception of the nature of God or Being, that assumes reality has two distinct and separable dimensions. The concept of Being as continuous, immutable, and having a prior or separate existence from the world of change dates from the ancient Greek philosopher Parmenides. The same qualities were associated with the God of the Judeo-Christian tradition, and they were considerably amplified by the role played in theology by Platonic and Neoplatonic philosophy.

Nicolas Copernicus, Galileo, Johannes Kepler, and Isaac Newton were all inheritors of a cultural tradition in which ontological dualism was a primary article of faith. Hence the idealization of the mathematical ideal as a source of communion with God, which dates from Pythagoras, provided a metaphysical foundation for the emerging natural sciences. This explains why, the creators of classical physics believed that doing physics was a form of communion with the geometrical and mathematical forms resident in the perfect mind of God. This view would survive in a modified form in what is now known as Einsteinian epistemology and accounts in no small part for the reluctance of many physicists to accept the epistemology associated with the Copenhagen Interpretation.

At the beginning of the nineteenth century, Pierre-Simon LaPlace, along with a number of other French mathematicians, advanced the view that the science of mechanics constituted a complete view of nature. Since this science, by observing its epistemology, had revealed itself to be the fundamental science, the hypothesis of God was, they concluded, entirely unnecessary.

LaPlace is recognized for eliminating not only the theological component of classical physics but the entire metaphysical component as well. The epistemology of science requires, he said, that we proceed by inductive generalizations from observed facts to hypotheses that are tested by observed conformity of the phenomena. What was unique about LaPlaces view of hypotheses was his insistence that we cannot attribute reality to them. Although concepts like force, mass, motion, cause, and laws are obviously present in classical physics, they exist in LaPlaces view only as quantities. Physics is concerned, he argued, with quantities that we associate as a matter of convenience with concepts, and the truth about nature are only the quantities.

As this view of hypotheses and the truth of nature as quantities was extended in the nineteenth century to a mathematical description of phenomena like heat, light, electricity, and magnetism. LaPlaces assumptions about the actual character of scientific truth seemed correct. This progress suggested that if we could remove all thoughts about the nature of or the source of phenomena, the pursuit of strictly quantitative concepts would bring us to a complete description of all aspects of physical reality. Subsequently, figures like Comte, Kirchhoff, Hertz, and Poincaré developed a program for the study of nature hat was quite different from that of the original creators of classical physics.

The seventeenth-century view of physics as a philosophy of nature or as natural philosophy was displaced by the view of physics as an autonomous science that was the science of nature. This view, which was premised on the doctrine of positivism, promised to subsume all of nature with a mathematical analysis of entities in motion and claimed that the true understanding of nature was revealed only in the mathematical description. Since the doctrine of positivism assumes that the knowledge we call physics resides only in the mathematical formalism of physical theory, it disallows the prospect that the vision of physical reality revealed in physical theory can have any other meaning. In the history of science, the irony is that positivism, which was intended to banish metaphysical concerns from the domain of science, served to perpetuate a seventeenth-century metaphysical assumption about the relationship between physical reality and physical theory.

Epistemology since Hume and Kant has drawn back from this theological underpinning. Indeed, the very idea that nature is simple (or uniform) has come in for a critique. The view has taken hold that a preference for simple and parsimonious hypotheses is purely methodological: It is constitutive of the attitude we call scientific and makes no substantive assumption about the way the world is.

A variety of otherwise diverse twentieth-century philosophers of science have attempted, in different ways, to flesh out this position. Two examples must suffice here: Hesse (1969) as, for summaries of other proposals. Popper (1959) holds that scientists should prefer highly falsifiable (improbable) theories: He tries to show that simpler theories are more falsifiable, also Quine (1966), in contrast, sees a virtue in theories that are highly probable, he argues for a general connexion between simplicity and high probability.

Both these proposals are global. They attempt to explain why simplicity should be part of the scientific method in a way that spans all scientific subject matters. No assumption about the details of any particular scientific problem serves as a premiss in Popper or Quine's arguments.

Newton and Leibniz thought that the justification of parsimony and simplicity flows from the hand of God: Popper and Quine try to justify these methodologically median of importance is without assuming anything substantive about the way the world is. In spite of these differences in approach, they have something in common. They assume that all users of parsimony and simplicity in the separate sciences can be encompassed in a single justifying argument. That recent developments in confirmation theory suggest that this assumption should be scrutinized. Good (1983) and Rosenkrantz (1977) has emphasized the role of auxiliary assumptions in mediating the connexion between hypotheses and observations. Whether a hypothesis is well supported by some observations, or whether one hypothesis is better supported than another by those observations, crucially depends on empirical background assumptions about the inference problem here. The same view applies to the idea of prior probability (or, prior plausibility). In of a single hypo-physical science if chosen as an alternative to another even though they are equally supported by current observations, this must be due to an empirical background assumption.

Principles of parsimony and simplicity mediate the epistemic connexion between hypotheses and observations. Perhaps these principles are able to do this because they are surrogates for an empirical background theory. It is not that there is one background theory presupposed by every appeal to parsimony; This has the quantifier order backwards. Rather, the suggestion is that each parsimony argument is justified only to each degree that it reflects an empirical background theory about the subjective matter. On this theory is brought out into the open, but the principle of parsimony is entirely dispensable (Sober, 1988).

This local approach to the principles of parsimony and simplicity resurrects the idea that they make sense only if the world is one way rather than another. It rejects the idea that these maxims are purely methodological. How defensible this point of view is, will depend on detailed case studies of scientific hypothesis evaluation and on further developments in the theory of scientific inference.

It is usually not found of one and the same that, an inference is a (perhaps very complex) act of thought by virtue of which act (1) I pass from a set of one or more propositions or statements to a proposition or statement and (2) it appears that the latter are true if the former is or are. This psychological characterization has occurred over a wider summation of literature under more lesser than inessential variations. Desiring a better characterization of inference is natural. Yet attempts to do so by constructing a fuller psychological explanation fail to comprehend the grounds on which inference will be objectively valid-A point elaborately made by Gottlob Frége. Attempts to understand the nature of inference through the device of the representation of inference by formal-logical calculations or derivations better (1) leave us puzzled about the relation of formal-logical derivations to the informal inferences they are supposedly to represent or reconstruct, and (2) leaves us worried about the sense of such formal derivations. Are these derivations inference? Are not informal inferences needed in order to apply the rules governing the constructions of formal derivations (inferring that this operation is an application of that formal rule)? These are concerns cultivated by, for example, Wittgenstein.

Coming up with an adequate characterized inferences, and even working out what would count as a very adequate characterization here is demandingly by no means nearly some resolved philosophical problem.

Traditionally, a proposition that is not a conditional, as with the affirmative and negative, modern opinion is wary of the distinction, since what appears categorical may vary with the choice of a primitive vocabulary and notation. Apparently categorical propositions may also turn out to be disguised conditionals: X is intelligent (categorical?) Equivalent, if X is given a range of tasks, she does them better than many people (conditional?). The problem is not merely one of classification, since deep metaphysical questions arise when facts that seem to be categorical and therefore solid, come to seem by contrast conditional, or purely hypothetical or potential.

Its condition of some classified necessity is so proven sufficient that if p is a necessary condition of q, then q cannot be true unless p; is true? If p is a sufficient condition, thus steering well is a necessary condition of driving in a satisfactory manner, but it is not sufficient, for one can steer well but drive badly for other reasons. Confusion may result if the distinction is not heeded. For example, the statement that A causes B may be interpreted to mean that A is itself a sufficient condition for B, or that it is only a necessary condition fort B, or perhaps a necessary parts of a total sufficient condition. Lists of conditions to be met for satisfying some administrative or legal requirement frequently attempt to give individually necessary and jointly sufficient sets of conditions.

What is more that if any proposition of the form if that 'p' then 'q'. The condition hypothesized, 'p' is called the antecedent of the conditionals, and 'q', the consequent? Various kinds of conditional have been distinguished. Its weakest is that of material implication, merely telling that either 'not-p', or 'q'. Stronger conditionals include elements of modality, corresponding to the thought that if 'p' is truer then 'q' must be true. Ordinary language is very flexible in its use of the conditional form, and there is controversy whether conditionals are better treated semantically, yielding differently finds of conditionals with different meanings, or pragmatically, in which case there should be one basic meaning with surface differences arising from other implicatures.

It follows from the definition of strict implication that a necessary proposition is strictly implied by any proposition, and that an impossible proposition strictly implies any proposition. If strict implication corresponds to 'q' follows from 'p', then this means that a necessary proposition follows from anything at all, and anything at all follows from an impossible proposition. This is a problem if we wish to distinguish between valid and invalid arguments with necessary conclusions or impossible premises.

The Humean problem of induction is that if we would suppose that there is some property 'A' concerning and observational or an experimental situation, and that out of a large number of observed instances of 'A', some fraction m/n (possibly equal to 1) has also been instances of some logically independent property 'B'. Suppose further that the background proportionate circumstances not specified in these descriptions have been varied to a substantial degree and that there is no collateral information available concerning the frequency of B's among A's or concerning causal or nomologically connections between instances of 'A' and instances of 'B'.

In this situation, an enumerative or instantial induction inference would move rights from the premise, that m/n of observed As are B's to the conclusion that approximately m/n of all A's are B's. (The usual probability qualification will be assumed to apply to the inference, rather than being part of the conclusion.) Here the class of A's should be taken to include not only unobservedly As and future As, but also possible or hypothetical As (an alternative conclusion would concern the probability or likelihood of the adjacently observed 'A' being 'B'.

The traditional or Humean problem of induction, often referred to simply as the problem of induction, is the problem of whether and why inferences that fit this schema should be considered rationally acceptable or justified from an epistemic or cognitive standpoint, i.e., whether and why reasoning in this way is likely to lead to true claims about the world. Is there any sort of argument or rationale that can be offered for thinking that conclusions reached in this way are likely to be true in the corresponding premisses is true –or even that their chances of truth are significantly enhanced?

Hume's discussion of this issue deals explicitly only with cases where all observed A's are B's and his argument applies just as well to the more general case. His conclusion is entirely negative and sceptical: Inductive inferences are not rationally justified, but are instead the result of an essentially a-rational process, custom or habit. Hume (1711-76) challenges the proponent of induction to supply a cogent ligne of reasoning that leads from an inductive premise to the corresponding conclusion and offers an extremely influential argument in the form of a dilemma (a few times referred to as Hume's fork, that either our actions are determined, in which case we are not responsible for them, or they are the result of random events, under which case we are also not responsible for them.

Such reasoning would, he argues, have to be either deductively demonstrative reasoning in the concerning relations of ideas or experimental, i.e., empirical, that reasoning concerning matters of fact or existence. It cannot be the former, because all demonstrative reasoning relies on the avoidance of contradiction, and it is not a contradiction to suppose that the course of nature may change, that an order that was observed in the past and not of its continuing against the future: But it cannot be, as the latter, since any empirical argument would appeal to the success of such reasoning about an experience, and the justifiability of generalizing from experience are precisely what is at issue-so that any such appeal would be question-begging. Hence, Hume concludes that there can be no such reasoning (1748).

An alternative version of the problem may be obtained by formulating it with reference to the so-called Principle of Induction, which says roughly that the future will resemble the past or, somewhat better, that unobserved cases will resemble observed cases. An inductive argument may be viewed as enthymematic, with this principle serving as a supposed premiss, in which case the issue is obviously how such a premiss can be justified. Humes argument is then that no such justification is possible: The principle cannot be justified a prior because having possession of been true in experiences without obviously begging the question is not contradictory to have possession of been true in experiences without obviously begging the question.

The predominant recent responses to the problem of induction, at least in the analytic tradition, in effect accept the main conclusion of Humes argument, namely, that inductive inferences cannot be justified in the sense of showing that the conclusion of such an inference is likely to be true if the premise is true, and thus attempt to find another sort of justification for induction. Such responses fall into two main categories: (I) Pragmatic justifications or vindications of induction, mainly developed by Hans Reichenbach (1891-1953), and (ii) ordinary language justifications of induction, whose most important proponent is Frederick, Peter Strawson (1919-). In contrast, some philosophers still attempt to reject Humes dilemma by arguing either (iii) That, contrary to appearances, induction can be inductively justified without vicious circularity, or (iv) that an anticipatory justification of induction is possible after all. In that:

(1) Reichenbach's view is that induction is best regarded, not as a form of inference, but rather as a method for arriving at posits regarding, i.e., the proportion of As remain additionally of B's. Such a posit is not a claim asserted to be true, but is instead an intellectual wager analogous to a bet made by a gambler. Understood in this way, the inductive method says that one should posit that the observed proportion is, within some measure of an approximation, the true proportion and then continually correct that initial posit as new information comes in.

The gamblers bet is normally an appraised posit, i.e., he knows the chances or odds that the outcome on which he bets will actually occur. In contrast, the inductive bet is a blind posit: We do not know the chances that it will succeed or even that success is that it will succeed or even that success is possible. What we are gambling on when we make such a bet is the value of a certain proportion in the independent world, which Reichenbach construes as the limit of the observed proportion as the number of cases increases to infinity. Nevertheless, we have no way of knowing that there are even such a limit, and no way of knowing that the proportion of As are in addition of B's converges in the end on some stable value than varying at random. If we cannot know that this limit exists, then we obviously cannot know that we have any definite chance of finding it.

What we can know, according to Reichenbach, is that if there is a truth of this sort to be found, the inductive method will eventually find it. That this is so is an analytic consequence of Reichenbachs account of what it is for such a limit to exist. The only way that the inductive method of making an initial posit and then refining it in light of new observations can fail eventually to arrive at the true proportion is if the series of observed proportions never converges on any stable value, which means that there is no truth to be found pertaining the proportion of A's additionally constitute B's. Thus, induction is justified, not by showing that it will succeed or indeed, that it has any definite likelihood of success, but only by showing that it will succeed if success is possible. Reichenbachs claim is that no more than this can be established for any method, and hence that induction gives us our best chance for success, our best gamble in a situation where there is no alternative to gambling.

This pragmatic response to the problem of induction faces several serious problems. First, there are indefinitely many other methods for arriving at posits for which the same sort of defence can be given-methods that yield the same result as the inductive method over time but differ arbitrarily before long. Despite the efforts of others, it is unclear that there is any satisfactory way to exclude such alternatives, in order to avoid the result that any arbitrarily chosen short-term posit is just as reasonable as the inductive posit. Second, even if there is a truth of the requisite sort to be found, the inductive method is only guaranteed to find it or even to come within any specifiable distance of it in the indefinite long run. All the same, any actual application of inductive results always takes place in the presence to the future eventful states in making the relevance of the pragmatic justification to actual practice uncertainly. Third, and most important, it needs to be emphasized that Reichenbach's response to the problem simply accepts the claim of the Humean sceptic that an inductive premise never provides the slightest reason for thinking that the corresponding inductive conclusion is true. Reichenbach himself is quite candid on this point, but this does not alleviate the intuitive implausibility of saying that we have no more reason for thinking that our scientific and commonsense conclusions that result in the induction of it . . . is true than, to use Reichenbach's own analogy (1949), a blind man wandering in the mountains who feels an apparent trail with his stick has for thinking that following it will lead him to safety.

An approach to induction resembling Reichenbachs claiming in that those particular inductive conclusions are posits or conjectures, than the conclusions of cogent inferences, is offered by Popper. However, Popper's view is even more overtly sceptical: It amounts to saying that all that can ever be said in favour of the truth of an inductive claim is that the claim has been tested and not yet been shown to be false.

(2) The ordinary language response to the problem of induction has been advocated by many philosophers, none the less, Strawson claims that the question whether induction is justified or reasonable makes sense only if it tacitly involves the demand that inductive reasoning meet the standards appropriate to deductive reasoning, i.e., that the inductive conclusions are shown to follow deductively from the inductive assumption. Such a demand cannot, of course, be met, but only because it is illegitimate: Inductive and deductive reasons are simply fundamentally different kinds of reasoning, each possessing its own autonomous standards, and there is no reason to demand or expect that one of these kinds meet the standards of the other. Whereas, if induction is assessed by inductive standards, the only ones that are appropriate, then it is obviously justified.

The problem here is to understand to what this allegedly obvious justification of an induction amount. In his main discussion of the point (1952), Strawson claims that it is an analytic true statement that believing it a conclusion for which there is strong evidence is reasonable and an analytic truth that inductive evidence of the sort captured by the schema presented earlier constitutes strong evidence for the corresponding inductive conclusion, thus, apparently yielding the analytic conclusion that believing it a conclusion for which there is inductive evidence is reasonable. Nevertheless, he also admits, indeed insists, that the claim that inductive conclusions will be true in the future is contingent, empirical, and may turn out to be false (1952). Thus, the notion of reasonable belief and the correlative notion of strong evidence must apparently be understood in ways that have nothing to do with likelihood of truth, presumably by appeal to the standard of reasonableness and strength of evidence that are accepted by the community and are embodied in ordinary usage.

Understood in this way, Strawson's response to the problem of inductive reasoning does not speak to the central issue raised by Humean scepticism: The issue of whether the conclusions of inductive arguments are likely to be true. It amounts to saying merely that if we reason in this way, we can correctly call ourselves reasonable and our evidence strong, according to our accepted community standards. Nevertheless, to the undersealing of issue of wether following these standards is a good way to find the truth, the ordinary language response appears to have nothing to say.

(3) The main attempts to show that induction can be justified inductively have concentrated on showing that such as a defence can avoid circularity. Skyrms (1975) formulate, perhaps the clearest version of this general strategy. The basic idea is to distinguish different levels of inductive argument: A first level in which induction is applied to things other than arguments: A second level in which it is applied to arguments at the first level, arguing that they have been observed to succeed so far and hence are likely to succeed in general: A third level in which it is applied in the same way to arguments at the second level, and so on. Circularity is allegedly avoided by treating each of these levels as autonomous and justifying the argument at each level by appeal to an argument at the next level.

One problem with this sort of move is that even if circularity is avoided, the movement to Higher and Higher levels will clearly eventually fail simply for lack of evidence: A level will reach at which there have been enough successful inductive arguments to provide a basis for inductive justification at the next Higher level, and if this is so, then the whole series of justifications collapses. A more fundamental difficulty is that the epistemological significance of the distinction between levels is obscure. If the issue is whether reasoning in accord with the original schema offered above ever provides a good reason for thinking that the conclusion is likely to be true, then it still seems question-begging, even if not flatly circular, to answer this question by appeal to anther argument of the same form.

(4) The idea that induction can be justified on a pure priori basis is in one way the most natural response of all: It alone treats an inductive argument as an independently cogent piece of reasoning whose conclusion can be seen rationally to follow, although perhaps only with probability from its premise. Such an approach has, however, only rarely been advocated (Russell, 19132 and BonJour, 1986), and is widely thought to be clearly and demonstrably hopeless.

Many on the reasons for this pessimistic view depend on general epistemological theses about the possible or nature of anticipatory cognition. Thus if, as Quine alleges, there is no a prior justification of any kind, then obviously a prior justification for induction is ruled out. Or if, as more moderate empiricists have in claiming some preexistent knowledge should be analytic, then again a prevenient justification for induction seems to be precluded, since the claim that if an inductive premise is truer, then the conclusion is likely to be true does not fit the standard conceptions of analyticity. A consideration of these matters is beyond the scope of the present spoken exchange.

There are, however, two more specific and quite influential reasons for thinking that an early approach is impossible that can be briefly considered, first, there is the assumption, originating in Hume, but since adopted by very many of others, that a move forward in the defence of induction would have to involve turning induction into deduction, i.e., showing, per impossible, that the inductive conclusion follows deductively from the premise, so that it is a formal contradiction to accept the latter and deny the former. However, it is unclear why a prior approach need be committed to anything this strong. It would be enough if it could be argued that it is deductively unlikely that such a premise is true and corresponding conclusion false.

Second, Reichenbach defends his view that pragmatic justification is the best that is possible by pointing out that a completely chaotic world in which there is simply not true conclusion to be found as to the proportion of As in addition that occur of, but B's is neither impossible nor unlikely from a purely a prior standpoint, the suggestion being that therefore there can be no a prior reason for thinking that such a conclusion is true. Nevertheless, there is still a substring way in laying that a chaotic world is a prior neither impossible nor unlikely without any further evidence does not show that such a world os not a prior unlikely and a world containing such-and-such regularity might anticipatorially be somewhat likely in relation to an occurrence of a long running pattern of evidence in which a certain stable proportion of observed As are B's ~. An occurrence, it might be claimed, that would be highly unlikely in a chaotic world (BonJour, 1986).

Goodman's new riddle of induction purports that we suppose that before some specific time t (perhaps the year 2000) we observe a larger number of emeralds (property A) and find them all to be green (property B). We proceed to reason inductively and conclude that all emeralds are green Goodman points out, however, that we could have drawn a quite different conclusion from the same evidence. If we define the term grue to mean green if examined before t and blue examined after t ′, then all of our observed emeralds will also be gruing. A parallel inductive argument will yield the conclusion that all emeralds are gruing, and hence that all those examined after the year 2000 will be blue. Presumably the first of these concisions is genuinely supported by our observations and the second is not. Nevertheless, the problem is to say why this is so and to impose some further restriction upon inductive reasoning that will permit the first argument and exclude the second.

The obvious alternative suggestion is that grue. Similar predicates do not correspond to genuine, purely qualitative properties in the way that green and blueness does, and that this is why inductive arguments involving them are unacceptable. Goodman, however, claims to be unable to make clear sense of this suggestion, pointing out that the relations of formal desirability are perfectly symmetrical: Grue may be defined in terms if, green and blue, but green an equally well be defined in terms of gruing and green (blue if examined before t and green if examined after t).

The grued, paradoxes demonstrate the importance of categorization, in that sometimes it is itemized as gruing, if examined of a presence to the future, before future time t and green, or not so examined and blue. Even though all emeralds in our evidence class grue, we ought must infer that all emeralds are gruing. For gruing is unprojectible, and cannot transmit credibility from the known to unknown cases. Only projectable predicates are right for induction. Goodman considers entrenchment the key to projectibility having a long history of successful protection, grue is entrenched, lacking such a history, grue is not. A hypothesis is projectable, Goodman suggests, only if its predicates (or suitable related ones) are much better entrenched than its rivalrous past successes that do not assume future ones. Induction remains a risky business. The rationale for favouring entrenched predicates is pragmatic. Of the possible projections from our evidence class, the one that fits with past practices enables us to utilize our cognitive resources best. Its prospects of being true are worse than its competitors and its cognitive utility is greater.

So, to a better understanding of induction we should then literize its term for which is most widely used for any process of reasoning that takes us from empirical premises to empirical conclusions supported by the premises, but not deductively entailed by them. Inductive arguments are therefore kinds of applicative arguments, in which something beyond the content of the premise is inferred as probable or supported by them. Induction is, however, commonly distinguished from arguments to theoretical explanations, which share this applicative character, by being confined to inferences in which he conclusion involves the same properties or relations as the premises. The central example is induction by simple enumeration, where from premises telling that Fa, Fb, Fc . . . where a, b, cs, are all of some kind 'G', it is inferred that G's from outside the sample, such as future G's, will be 'F', or perhaps that all G's are 'F'. In this, which and the other persons deceive them, children may infer that everyone is a deceiver: Different, but similar inferences of a property by some object to the same objects future possession of the same property, or from the constancy of some law-like pattern in events and states of affairs ti its future constancy. All objects we know of attract each other with a force inversely proportional to the square of the distance between them, so perhaps they all do so, and will always do so.

The rational basis of any inference was challenged by Hume, who believed that induction presupposed belief in the uniformity of nature, but that this belief has no defence in reason, and merely reflected a habit or custom of the mind. Hume was not therefore sceptical about the role of reason in either explaining it or justifying it. Trying to answer Hume and to show that there is something rationally compelling about the inference referred to as the problem of induction. It is widely recognized that any rational defence of induction will have to partition well-behaved properties for which the inference is plausible (often called projectable properties) from badly behaved ones, for which it is not. It is also recognized that actual inductive habits are more complex than those of similar enumeration, and that both common sense and science pay attention to such giving factors as variations within the sample giving us the evidence, the application of ancillary beliefs about the order of nature, and so on.

Nevertheless, the fundamental problem remains that and experience condition by application show us only events occurring within a very restricted part of a vast spatial and temporal order about which we then come to believe things.

Uncompounded by its belonging of a confirmation theory finding of the measure to which evidence supports a theory fully formalized confirmation theory would dictate the degree of confidence that a rational investigator might have in a theory, given some body of evidence. The grandfather of confirmation theory is Gottfried Leibniz (1646-1718), who believed that a logically transparent language of science would be able to resolve all disputes. In the 20th century a fully formal confirmation theory was a main goal of the logical positivist, since without it the central concept of verification by empirical evidence itself remains distressingly unscientific. The principal developments were due to Rudolf Carnap (1891-1970), culminating in his Logical Foundations of Probability (1950). Carnaps idea was that the measure necessitated would be the proportion of logically possible states of affairs in which the theory and the evidence both hold, compared ti the number in which the evidence itself holds that the probability of a preposition, relative to some evidence, is a proportion of the range of possibilities under which the proposition is true, compared to the total range of possibilities left by the evidence. The difficulty with the theory lies in identifying sets of possibilities so that they admit of measurement. It therefore demands that we can put a measure on the range of possibilities consistent with theory and evidence, compared with the range consistent with the evidence alone.

Among the obstacles the enterprise meets, is the fact that while evidence covers only a finite range of data, the hypotheses of science may cover an infinite range. In addition, confirmation proves to vary with the language in which the science is couched, and the Carnapian programme has difficulty in separating genuinely confirming variety of evidence from less compelling repetition of the same experiment. Confirmation also proved to be susceptible to acute paradoxes. Finally, scientific judgement seems to depend on such intangible factors as the problems facing rival theories, and most workers have come to stress instead the historically situated scene of what would appear as a plausible distinction of a scientific knowledge at a given time.

Arose to the paradox of which when a set of apparent incontrovertible premises is given to unacceptable or contradictory conclusions. To solve a paradox will involve showing either that there is a hidden flaw in the premises, or that the reasoning is erroneous, or that the apparently unacceptable conclusion can, in fact, be tolerated. Paradoxes are therefore important in philosophy, for until one is solved it shows that there is something about our reasoning and our concepts that we do not understand. What is more, and somewhat loosely, a paradox is a compelling argument from unacceptable premises to an unacceptable conclusion: More strictly speaking, a paradox is specified to be a sentence that is true if and only if it is false. A characterized objection lesson of it would be: The displayed sentence is false.

Seeing that this sentence is false if true is easy, and true if false, a paradox, in either of the senses distinguished, presents an important philosophical challenger. Epistemologists are especially concerned with various paradoxes having to do with knowledge and belief. In other words, for example, the Knower paradox is an argument that begins with apparently impeccable premisses about the concepts of knowledge and inference and derives an explicit contradiction. The origin of the reasoning is the surprise examination paradox: A teacher announces that there will be a surprise examination next week. A clever student argues that this is impossible. The test cannot be on Friday, the last day of the week, because it would not be a surprise. We would know the day of the test on Thursday evening. This means we can also rule out Thursday. For after we learn that no test has been given by Wednesday, we would know the test is on Thursday or Friday -and would already know that it s not on Friday and would already know that it is not on Friday by the previous reasoning. The remaining days can be eliminated in the same manner.

This puzzle has over a dozen variants. The first was probably invented by the Swedish mathematician Lennard Ekbon in 1943. Although the first few commentators regarded the reverse elimination argument as cogent, every writer on the subject since 1950 agrees that the argument is unsound. The controversy has been over the proper diagnosis of the flaw.

Initial analyses of the subjects argument tried to lay the blame on a simple equivocation. Their failure led to more sophisticated diagnoses. The general format has been an assimilation to better-known paradoxes. One tradition casts the surprise examination paradox as a self-referential problem, as fundamentally akin to the Liar, the paradox of the Knower, or Gödels incompleteness theorem. That in of itself, says enough that Kaplan and Montague (1960) distilled the following self-referential paradox, the Knower. Consider the sentence: (S) The negation of this sentence is known (to be true).

Suppose that (S) is true. Then its negation is known and hence true. However, if its negation is true, then (S) must be false. Therefore (s) is false, or what is the name, the negation of (S) is true.

This paradox and its accompanying reasoning are strongly reminiscent of the Lair Paradox that (in one version) begins by considering a sentence This sentence is false and derives a contradiction. Versions of both arguments using axiomatic formulations of arithmetic and Gödel-numbers to achieve the effect of self-reference yields important meta-theorems about what can be expressed in such systems. Roughly these are to the effect that no predicates definable in the formalized arithmetic can have the properties we demand of truth (Tarskis Theorem) or of knowledge (Montague, 1963).

These meta-theorems still leave us; with the problem that if we suppose that we add of these formalized languages predicates intended to express the concept of knowledge (or truth) and inference - as one mighty does if a logic of these concepts is desired. Then the sentence expressing the leading principles of the Knower Paradox will be true.

Explicitly, the assumption about knowledge and inferences are:

(1) If sentences A are known, then a.

(2) (1) is known?

(3) If B is correctly inferred from A, and A is known, then B is known.

To give an absolutely explicit derivation of the paradox by applying these principles to (S), we must add (contingent) assumptions to the effect that certain inferences have been done. Still, as we go through the argument of the Knower, these inferences are done. Even if we can somehow restrict such principles and construct a consistent formal logic of knowledge and inference, the paradoxical argument as expressed in the natural language still demands some explanation.

The usual proposals for dealing with the Liar often have their analogues for the Knower, e.g., that there is something wrong with a self-reference or that knowledge (or truth) is properly a predicate of propositions and not of sentences. The relies that show that some of these are not adequate are often parallel to those for the Liar paradox. In addition, one can try here what seems to be an adequate solution for the Surprise Examination Paradox, namely the observation that new knowledge can drive out knowledge, but this does not seem to work on the Knower (Anderson, 1983).

There are a number of paradoxes of the Liar family. The simplest example is the sentence, 'This sentence is false, which must be false if it is true, and true if it is false'. One suggestion is that the sentence fails to say anything, but sentences that fail to say anything are at least not true. In fact case, we consider to sentences 'This sentence is not true, which, if it fails to say anything is not true', and hence (this kind of reasoning is sometimes called the strengthened Liar). Other versions of the Liar introduce pairs of sentences, as in a slogan on the front of a T-shirt saying This sentence on the back of this T-shirt is false, and one on the back saying 'The sentence on the front of this T-shirt is true. It is clear that each sentence individually is well formed, and were it not for the other, might have said something true. So any attempt to dismiss the paradox by settling in that of the sentence involved are meaningless will face problems.

Even so, the two approaches that have some hope of adequately dealing with this paradox is hierarchy solutions and truth-value gap solutions. According to the first, knowledge is structured into levels. It is argued that there be one-careened notion expressed by the verb; knows, but rather a whole series of notions, of the knowable knows, and so on (perhaps into transfinite), stated ion terms of predicate expressing such ramified concepts and properly restricted, (1)-(3) lead to no contradictions. The main objections to this procedure are that the meaning of these levels has not been adequately explained and that the idea of such subscripts, even implicit, in a natural language is highly counterintuitive the truth-value gap solution takes sentences such as (S) to lack truth-value. They are neither true nor false, but they do not express propositions. This defeats a crucial step in the reasoning used in the derivation of the paradoxes. Kripler (1986) has developed this approach in connexion with the Liar and Asher and Kamp (1986) has worked out some details of a parallel solution to the Knower. The principal objection is that strengthened or super versions of the paradoxes tend to reappear when the solution itself is stated.

Since the paradoxical deduction uses only the properties (1)-(3) and since the argument is formally valid, any notion that satisfy these conditions will lead to a paradox. Thus, Grim (1988) notes that this may be read as is known by an omniscient God and concludes that there is no careened single notion of omniscience. Thomason (1980) observes that with some different conditions, analogous reasoning about belief can lead to paradoxical consequence.

Overall, it looks as if we should conclude that knowledge and truth are ultimately intrinsically stratified concepts. It would seem that we must simply accept the fact that these (and similar) concepts cannot be assigned of any-one fixed, finite or infinite. Still, the meaning of this idea certainly needs further clarification.

Its paradox arises when a set of apparently incontrovertible premises gives unacceptable or contradictory conclusions, to solve a paradox will involve showing either that there is a hidden flaw in the premises, or that the reasoning is erroneous, or that the apparently unacceptable conclusion can, in fact, be tolerated. Paradoxes are therefore important in philosophy, for until one is solved its shows that there is something about our reasoning and of concepts that we do not understand. Famous families of paradoxes include the semantic paradoxes and Zeno's paradoxes. Art the beginning of the 20th century, paradox and other set-theoretical paradoxes led to the complete overhaul of the foundations of set theory, while the Sorites paradox has lead to the investigations of the semantics of vagueness and fuzzy logics.

It is, however, to what extent can analysis be informative? This is the question that gives a riser to what philosophers has traditionally called the paradox of analysis. Thus, consider the following proposition:

(1) To be an instance of knowledge is to be an instance of justified true belief not essentially grounded in any falsehood. (1) If true, illustrates an important type of philosophical analysis. For convenience of exposition, I will assume (1) is a correct analysis. The paradox arises from the fact that if the concept of justified true belief not been essentially grounded in any falsification is the analysand of the concept of knowledge, it would seem that they are the same concept and hence that: (2) To be an instance of knowledge is to be as an instance of knowledge and would have to be the same propositions as (1). But then how can (1) be informative when (2) is not? This is what is called the first paradox of analysis. Classical writings on analysis suggests a second paradoxical analysis (Moore, 1942).

(3) An analysis of the concept of being a brother is that to be a brother is to be a male sibling. If (3) is true, it would seem that the concept of being a brother would have to be the same concept as the concept of being a male sibling and tat:

(4) An analysis of the concept of being a brother is that to be a brother is to be a brother would also have to be true and in fact, would have to be the same proposition as (3?). Yet (3) is true and (4) is false.

Both these paradoxes rest upon the assumptions that analysis is a relation between concepts, than one involving entity of other sorts, such as linguistic expressions, and tat in a true analysis, analysand and analysandum are the same concept. Both these assumptions are explicit in Moore, but some of Moores remarks hint at a solution to that of another statement of an analysis is a statement partly about the concept involved and partly about the verbal expressions used to express it. He says he thinks a solution of this sort is bound to be right, but fails to suggest one because he cannot see a way in which the analysis can be even partly about the expression (Moore, 1942).

Elsewhere, of such ways, as a solution to the second paradox, to which is explicating (3) as: (5) - An analysis is given by saying that the verbal expression 'χ' is a brother expresses the same concept as is expressed by the conjunction of the verbal expressions 'χ' is male when used to express the concept of being male and 'χ' is a sibling when used to express the concept of being a sibling. (Ackerman, 1990). An important point about (5) is as follows. Stripped of its philosophical jargon (analysis, concept, 'χ' is a . . .), (5) seems to state the sort of information generally stated in a definition of the verbal expression brother in terms of the verbal expressions male and sibling, where this definition is designed to draw upon listeners antecedent understanding of the verbal expression male and sibling, and thus, to tell listeners what the verbal expression brother really means, instead of merely providing the information that two verbal expressions are synonymous without specifying the meaning of either one. Thus, its solution to the second paradox seems to make the sort of analysis tat gives rise to this paradox matter of specifying the meaning of a verbal expression in terms of separate verbal expressions already understood and saying how the meanings of these separate, already-understood verbal expressions are combined. This corresponds to Moores intuitive requirement that an analysis should both specify the constituent concepts of the analysandum and tell how they are combined, but is this all there is to philosophical analysis?

We must note that, in addition too there being two paradoxes of analysis, there is two types of analyses that are relevant here. (There are also other types of analysis, such as reformatory analysis, where the analysand are intended to improve on and replace the analysandum. But since reformatory analysis involves no commitment to conceptual identity between analysand and analysandum, reformatory analysis does not generate a paradox of analysis and so will not concern us here.) One way to recognize the difference between the two types of analysis concerning us here is to focus on the difference between the two paradoxes. This can be done by means of the Frége-inspired sense-individuation condition, which is the condition that two expressions have the same sense if and only if they can be interchangeably salva veritate whenever used in propositional attitude context. If the expressions for the analysands and the analysandum in (1) met this condition, (1) and (2) would not raise the first paradox, but the second paradox arises regardless of whether the expression for the analysand and the analysandum meet this condition. The second paradox is a matter of the failure of such expressions to be interchangeable salva veritate in sentences involving such contexts as an analysis is given thereof. Thus, a solution (such as the one offered) that is aimed only at such contexts can solve the second paradox. This is clearly false for the first paradox, however, which will apply to all pairs of propositions expressed by sentences in which expressions for pairs of analysands and analysantia raising the first paradox is interchangeable. One approach to the first paradox is to argue that, despite the apparent epistemic inequivalence of (1) and (2), the concept of justified true belief not essentially grounded in any falsehood is still identical with the concept of knowledge (Sosa, 1983). Another approach is to argue that in the sort of analysis raising the first paradox, the analysand and analysandum is concepts that are different but that bear a special epistemic relation to each other. Elsewhere, the development is such an approach and suggestion that this analysand-analysandum relation has the following facets.

(i) analysand and analysandum are necessarily coextensive, i.e., necessarily every instance of one is an instance of the other.

(ii) The analysand and analysandum are knowable theoretical to be coextensive.

(iii)The analysandum is simpler than the analysands a condition whose necessity is recognized in classical writings on analysis, such as, Langford, 1942.

(iv) The analysand do not have the analysandum as a constituent.

Condition (iv) rules out circularity. But since many valuable quasi-analyses are partly circular, e.g., knowledge is justified true belief supported by known reasons not essentially grounded in any falsehood, it seems best to distinguish between full analysis, from that of (iv) is a necessary condition, and partial analysis, for which it is not.

These conditions, while necessary, are clearly insufficient. The basic problem is that they apply too many pairs of concepts that do not seem closely enough related epistemologically to count as analysand and analysandum., such as the concept of being six and the concept of the fourth root of 1296. Accordingly, its solution upon what actually seems epistemologically distinctive about analyses of the sort under consideration, which is a certain way they can be justified. This is by the philosophical example-and-counterexample method, which is in a general term that goes as follows. 'J' investigates the analysis of 'K's' concept 'Q' (where 'K' can but need not be identical to 'J' by setting 'K' a series of armchair thought experiments, i.e., presenting 'K' with a series of simple described hypothetical test cases and asking 'K' questions of the form If such-and-such where the case would this count as a case of 'Q'? J then contrasts the descriptions of the cases to which; 'K' answers affirmatively with the description of the cases to which 'K' does not, and 'J' generalizes upon these descriptions to arrive at the concepts (if possible not including the analysandum) and their mode of combination that constitute the analysand of 'K's' concept 'Q'. Since 'J' need not be identical with 'K', there is no requirement that K himself be able to perform this generalization, to recognize its result as correct, or even to understand the analysand that is its result. This is reminiscent of Walton's observation that one can simply recognize a bird as a blue jay without realizing just what feature of the bird (beak, wing configurations, etc.) form the basis of this recognition. (The philosophical significance of this way of recognizing is discussed in Walton, 1972) 'K' answers the questions based solely on whether the described hypothetical cases just strike him as cases of 'Q'. 'J' observes certain strictures in formulating the cases and questions. He makes the cases as simple as possible, to minimize the possibility of confusion and to minimize the likelihood that 'K' will draw upon his philosophical theories (or quasi-philosophical, a rudimentary notion if he is unsophisticated philosophically) in answering the questions. For this conflicting result, the conflict should other things being equal be resolved in favour of the simpler case. 'J' makes the series of described cases wide-ranging and varied, with the aim of having it be a complete series, where a series is complete if and only if no case that is omitted in such that, if included, it would change the analysis arrived at. 'J' does not, of course, use as a test-case description anything complicated and general enough to express the analysand. There is no requirement that the described hypothetical test cases be formulated only in terms of what can be observed. Moreover, using described hypothetical situations as test cases enables 'J' to frame the questions in such a way as to rule out extraneous background assumption to a degree, thus, even if 'K' correctly believes that all and only 'P's' are 'R's', the question of whether the concepts of 'P', 'R', or both enter the analysand of his concept 'Q' can be investigated by asking him such questions as Suppose (even if it seems preposterous to you) that you were to find out that there was a 'P' that was not an 'R'. Would you still consider it a case of 'Q'?

Taking all this into account, the necessary conditions for this sort of analysand-analysandum relations is as follows: If 'S' is the analysand of 'Q', the proposition that necessarily all and only instances of S are instances of 'Q' can be justified by generalizing from intuition about the correct answers to questions of the sort indicated about a varied and wide-ranging series of simple described hypothetical situations. It so does occur of antinomy, when we are able to argue for, or demonstrate, both a proposition and its contradiction, roughly speaking, a contradiction of a proposition 'p' is one that can be expressed in form 'not-p', or, if 'p' can be expressed in the form 'not-q', then a contradiction is one that can be expressed in the form 'q'. Thus, e.g., if p is $2 + 1 = 4$, then, $2 + 1 \neq 4$ is the contradictory of 'p', for $2 + 1 \neq 4$ can be expressed in the form not $(2 + 1 = 4)$. If p is $2 + 1 \neq 4$, then $2 + 1 = 4$ is a contradictory of 'p', since $2 + 1 \neq 4$ can be expressed in the form not $(2 + 1 = 4)$. This is, mutually, but contradictory propositions can be expressed in the form, 'r', 'not-r'. The Principle of Contradiction says that mutually contradictory propositions cannot both be true and cannot both be false. Thus, by this principle, since if p is true, not-p is false, no proposition p can be at once true and false (otherwise both 'p' and its contradictories would be false?). In particular, for any predicate 'p' and object 'χ', it cannot be that 'p'; is at once true of 'χ' and false of 'χ'? This is the classical formulation of the principle of contradiction, but it is nonetheless, that we cannot now fault either demonstrates. We would eventually hope to be able to solve the antinomy by managing, through careful thinking and analysis, eventually to fault either or both demonstrations.

The conjunction of a proposition and its negation, where the law of non-contradiction provides that no such conjunction can be true: not (p & not-p). The standard proof of the inconsistency of a set of propositions or sentences is to show that a contradiction may be derived from them.

In Hegelian and Marxist writing the term is used more widely, as a contradiction may be a pair of features that together produce an unstable tension in a political or social system: a 'contradiction' of capitalism might be the aerosol of expectations in the workers that the system cannot require. For Hegel the gap between this and genuine contradiction is not as wide as it is for other thinkers, given the equation between systems of thought and their historical embodiment.

A contradictarian approach to problems of ethics asks what solution could be agreed upon by contradicting parties, starting from certain idealized positions (for example, no ignorance, no inequalities of power enabling one party to force unjust solutions upon another, no malicious ambitions). The idea of thinking of civil society, with its different distribution of rights and obligations, as if it were established by a social contract, derives from the English philosopher and mathematician Thomas Hobbes and Jean-Jacques Rousseau (1712-78). The utility of such a model was attacked by the Scottish philosopher, historian and essayist David Hume (1711-76), who asks why, given that non-historical event of establishing a contract took place. It is useful to allocate rights and duties as if it had; he also points out that the actual distribution of these things in a society owes too much to contingent circumstances to be derivable from any such model. Similar positions in general ethical theory, sometimes called contradictualism: see the right thing to do so one that could be agreeing upon in hypothetical contract.

Somewhat loosely, a paradox arises when a set of apparent incontrovertible premises gives unacceptable or contradictory conclusions, to solve a paradox will involve showing either that there is a hidden flaw in the premises, or that the reasoning is erroneous, or that the apparent unacceptable conclusion can, in fact, be tolerated. Paradoxes are themselves important in philosophy, for until one is solved it shows that there is something that we do not understand. Such are the paradoxes as compelling arguments from unexceptionable premises to an unacceptable conclusion, and more strictly, a paradox is specified to be a sentence that is true if and only if it is false: For example of the latter would be: 'The displayed sentence is false.

It is easy to see that this sentence is false if true, and true if false. A paradox, in either of the senses distinguished, presents an important philosophical challenge. Epistemologist are especially concerned with various paradoxes having to do with knowledge and belief.

Moreover, paradoxes are as an easy source of antinomies, for example, Zeno gave some famously lets say, logical-non-mathematical arguments that might be interpreted as demonstrating that motion is impossible. But our eyes as it was, demonstrate motion (exhibit moving things) all the time. Where did Zeno go wrong? Where do our eyes go wrong? If we cannot readily answer at least one of these questions, then we are in antinomy. In the Critique of Pure Reason, Kant gave demonstrations of the same kind -in the Zeno example they were obviously not the same kind of both, e.g., that the world has a beginning in time and space, and that the world has no beginning in time or space. He argues that both demonstrations are at fault because they proceed on the basis of pure reason unconditioned by sense experience.

At this point, we display attributes to the theory of experience, as it is not possible to define in an illuminating way, however, we know what experiences are through acquaintances with some of our own, e.g., visual experiences of as afterimage, a feeling of physical nausea or a tactile experience of an abrasive surface (which might be caused by an actual surface -rough or smooth, or which might be part of a dream, or the product of a vivid sensory imagination). The essential feature of experience is it feels a certain way -that there is something that it is like to have it. We may refer to this feature of an experience as its character.

Another core feature of the sorts of experiences with which this may be of a concern, is that they have representational content. (Unless otherwise indicated, experience will be reserved for their contentual representations.) The most obvious cases of experiences with content are sense experiences of the kind normally involved in perception. We may describe such experiences by mentioning their sensory modalities ad their contents, e.g., a gustatory experience (modality) of chocolate ice cream (content), but do so more commonly by means of perceptual verbs combined with noun phrases specifying their contents, as in Macbeth saw a dagger. This is, however, ambiguous between the perceptual claim There was a (material) dagger in the world that Macbeth perceived visually and Macbeth had a visual experience of a dagger (the reading with which we are concerned, as it is afforded by our imagination, or perhaps, experiencing mentally hallucinogenic imagery).

As in the case of other mental states and events with content, it is important to distinguish between the properties that and experience represents and the properties that it possesses. To talk of the representational properties of an experience is to say something about its content, not to attribute those properties to the experience itself. Like every other experience, a visual; experience of a non-shaped square, of which is a mental event, and it is therefore not itself, or finds to some irregularity or is it square, even though it represents those properties. It is, perhaps, fleeting, pleasant or unusual, even though it does not represent those properties. An experience may represent a property that it possesses, and it may even do so in virtue of a rapidly changing (complex) experience representing something as changing rapidly. However, this is the exception and not the rule.

Which properties can be [directly] represented in sense experience is subject to debate. Traditionalists include only properties whose presence could not be doubted by a subject having appropriate experiences, e.g., colour and shape in the case of visual experience, and apparent shape, surface texture, hardness, etc., in the case of tactile experience. This view is natural to anyone who has an egocentric, Cartesian perspective in epistemology, and who wishes for pure data in experiences to serve as logically certain foundations for knowledge, especially to the immediate objects of perceptual awareness in or of sense-data, such categorized of colour patches and shapes, which are usually supposed distinct from surfaces of physical objectivity. Qualities of sense-data are supposed to be distinct from physical qualities because their perception is more relative to conditions, more certain, and more immediate, and because sense-data is private and cannot appear other than they are they are objects that change in our perceptual field when conditions of perception change: Physical objects remain constant.

Others who do not think that this wish can be satisfied, and who are more impressed with the role of experience in providing animisms with ecologically significant information about the world around them, claim that sense experiences represent properties, characteristic and kinds that are much richer and much more wide-ranging than the traditional sensory qualities. We do not see only colours and shapes, they tell us, but also earth, water, men, women and fire: We do not smell only odours, but also food and filth. There is no space here to examine the factors relevantly responsible to their choice of situational alternatives. Yet, this suggests that character and content are not really distinct, and there is a close tie between them. For one thing, the relative complexity of the character of sense experience places limitations upon its possible content, e.g., a tactile experience of something touching ones left ear is just too simple to carry the same amount of content as typically convincing to an every day, visual experience. Moreover, the content of a sense experience of a given character depends on the normal causes of appropriately similar experiences, e.g., the sort of gustatory experience that we have when eating chocolate would be not represented as chocolate unless it was normally caused by chocolate. Granting a contingent ties between the character of an experience and its possible causal origins, once, again follows that its possible content is limited by its character.

Character and content are none the less irreducibly different, for the following reasons. (1) There are experiences that completely lack content, e.g., certain bodily pleasures. (2) Not every aspect of the character of an experience with content is relevant to that content, e.g., the unpleasantness of an aural experience of chalk squeaking on a board may have no representational significance. (3) Experiences in different modalities may overlap in content without a parallel overlap in character, e.g., visual and tactile experiences of circularity feel completely different. (4) The content of an experience with a given character may vary according to the background of the subject, e.g., a certain content singing bird only after the subject has learned something about birds.

According to the act/object analysis of experience (which is a special case of the act/object analysis of consciousness), every experience involves an object of experience even if it has no material object. Two main lines of argument may be offered in support of this view, one phenomenological and the other semantic.

In an outline, or projective view, the phenomenological argument is as follows. Whenever we have an experience, even if nothing beyond the experience answers to it, we seem to be presented with something through the experience (which is itself diaphanous). The object of the experience is whatever is so presented to us-is that it is an individual thing, an event, or a state of affairs.

The semantic argument is that objects of experience are required in order to make sense of certain features of our talk about experience, including, in particular, the following. (1) Simple attributions of experience, e.g., Rod is experiencing an oddity that is not really square but in appearance it seems more than likely a square, this seems to be relational. (2) We appear to refer to objects of experience and to attribute properties to them, e.g., The afterimage that John experienced was certainly odd. (3) We appear to quantify ov er objects of experience, e.g., Macbeth saw something that his wife did not see.

The act/object analysis comes to grips with several problems concerning the status of objects of experiences. Currently the most common view is that they are sense-data - private mental entities that actually posses the traditional sensory qualities represented by the experiences of which they are the objects. But the very idea of an essentially private entity is suspect. Moreover, since an experience may apparently represent something as having a determinable property, e.g., redness, without representing it as having any subordinate determinate property, e.g., any specific shade of red, a sense-datum may actually have a determinate property subordinate to it. Even more disturbing is that sense-data may have contradictory properties, since experiences can have contradictory contents. A case in point is the waterfall illusion: If you stare at a waterfall for a minute and then immediately fixate on a nearby rock, you are likely to have an experience of the rocks moving upward while it remains in the same place. The sense-data theorist must either deny that there are such experiences or admit contradictory objects.

These problems can be avoided by treating objects of experience as properties. This, however, fails to do justice to the appearances, for experience seems not to present us with properties embodied in individuals. The view that objects of experience is Meinongian objects accommodate this point. It is also attractive in as far as (1) it allows experiences to represent properties other than traditional sensory qualities, and (2) it allows for the identification of objects of experience and objects of perception in the case of experiences that constitute perception.

According to the act/object analysis of experience, every experience with content involves an object of experience to which the subject is related by an act of awareness (the event of experiencing that object). This is meant to apply not only to perceptions, which have material objects (whatever is perceived), but also to experiences like hallucinations and dream experiences, which do not. Such experiences none the less appear to represent something, and their objects are supposed to be whatever it is that they represent. Act/object theorists may differ on the nature of objects of experience, which have been treated as properties. Meinongian objects (which may not exist or have any form of being), and, more commonly private mental entities with sensory qualities. (The term sense-data is now usually applied to the latter, but has also been used as a general term for objects of sense experiences, as in the work of G.E. Moore) Act/object theorists may also differ on the relationship between objects of experience and objects of perception. In terms of perception (of which we are indirectly aware) are always distinct from objects of experience (of which we are directly aware). Meinongian, however, may treat objects of perception as existing objects of experience. But sense-datum theorists must either deny that there are such experiences or admit contradictory objects. Still, most philosophers will feel that the Meinongians acceptance of impossible objects is too high a price to pay for these benefits.

A general problem for the act/object analysis is that the question of whether two subjects are experiencing one and the same thing (as opposed to having exactly similar experiences) appears to have an answer only on the assumption that the experiences concerned are perceptions with material objects. But in terms of the act/object analysis the question must have an answer even when this condition is not satisfied. (The answer is always negative on the sense-datum theory; it could be positive on other versions of the act/object analysis, depending on the facts of the case.)

In view of the above problems, the case for the act/object analysis should be reassessed. The phenomenological argument is not, on reflection, convincing, for it is easy enough to grant that any experience appears to present us with an object without accepting that it actually does. The semantic argument is more impressive, but is none the less answerable. The seemingly relational structure of attributions of experience is a challenge dealt with below in connexion with the adverbial theory. Apparent reference to and quantification over objects of experience can be handled by analysing them as reference to experiences themselves and quantification over experiences tacitly typed according to content. Thus, The afterimage that John experienced was colourfully appealing becomes Johns afterimage experience was an experience of colour, and Macbeth saw something that his wife did not see becomes Macbeth had a visual experience that his wife did not have.

Pure cognitivism attempts to avoid the problems facing the act/object analysis by reducing experiences to cognitive events or associated disposition, e.g., Julie's experience of a rough surface beneath her hand might be identified with the event of her acquiring the belief that there is a rough surface beneath her hand, or, if she does not acquire this belief, with a disposition to acquire it that has somehow been blocked.

This position has attractions. It does full justice to the cognitive contents of experience, and to the important role of experience as a source of belief acquisition. It would also help clear the way for a naturalistic theory of mind, since there seems to be some prospect of a physicalist/functionalist account of belief and other intentional states. But pure cognitivism is completely undermined by its failure to accommodate the fact that experiences have a felt character that cannot be reduced to their content, as aforementioned.

The adverbial theory is an attempt to undermine the act/object analysis by suggesting a semantic account of attributions of experience that does not require objects of experience. Unfortunately, the oddities of explicit adverbializations of such statements have driven off potential supporters of the theory. Furthermore, the theory remains largely undeveloped, and attempted refutations have traded on this. It may, however, be founded on sound basis intuitions, and there is reason to believe that an effective development of the theory (which is merely hinting at) is possible.

The relevant intuitions are (1) that when we say that someone is experiencing an A, or has an experience of an A, we are using this content-expression to specify the type of thing that the experience is especially apt to fit, (2) that doing this is a matter of saying something about the experience itself (and maybe about the normal causes of like experiences), and (3) that it is no-good of reasons to posit of its position to presuppose that of any involvements, is that its descriptions of an object in which the experience is. Thus the effective role of the content-expression in a statement of experience is to modify the verb it compliments, not to introduce a special type of object.

Perhaps, the most important criticism of the adverbial theory is the many property problem, according to which the theory does not have the resources to distinguish between, e.g.,

(1) Frank has an experience of a brown triangle

and:

(2) Frank has an experience of brown and an experience of a triangle.

Which is entailed by (1) but does not entail it. The act/object analysis can easily accommodate the difference between (1) and (2) by claiming that the truth of (1) requires a single object of experience that is both brown and triangular, while that of the (2) allows for the possibility of two objects of experience, one brown and the other triangular, however, (1) is equivalent to:

(1*) Frank has an experience of something being both brown and triangular.

And (2) is equivalent to:

(2*) Frank has an experience of something being brown and an experience of something being triangular,

and the difference between these can be explained quite simply in terms of logical scope without invoking objects of experience. The adverbialists may use this to answer the many-property problem by arguing that the phrase a brown triangle in (1) does the same work as the clause something being both brown and triangular in (1*). This is perfectly compatible with the view that it also has the adverbial function of modifying the verb has an experience of, for it specifies the experience more narrowly just by giving a necessary condition for the satisfaction of the experience (the condition being that there are something both brown and triangular before Frank).

A final position that should be mentioned is the state theory, according to which a sense experience of an A is an occurrent, non-relational state of the kind that the subject would be in when perceiving an A. Suitably qualified, this claim is no doubt true, but its significance is subject to debate. Here it is enough to remark that the claim is compatible with both pure cognitivism and the adverbial theory, and that state theorists are probably best advised to adopt adverbials as a means of developing their intuitions.

Yet, clarifying sense-data, if taken literally, is that which is given by the senses. But in response to the question of what exactly is so given, sense-data theories posit private showings in the consciousness of the subject. In the case of vision this would be a kind of inner picture shown which it only indirectly represents aspects of the external world that has in and of itself a worldly representation. The view has been widely rejected as implying that we really only see extremely thin coloured pictures interposed between our minds eye and reality. Modern approaches to perception tend to reject any conception of the eye as a camera or lense, simply responsible for producing private images, and stress the active life of the subject in and of the world, as the determinant of experience.

Nevertheless, the argument from illusion is of itself the usually intended directive to establish that certain familiar facts about illusion disprove the theory of perception called naïevity or direct realism. There are, however, many different versions of the argument that must be distinguished carefully. Some of these distinctions centre on the content of the premises (the nature of the appeal to illusion); others centre on the interpretation of the conclusion (the kind of direct realism under attack). Let us set about by distinguishing the importantly different versions of direct realism which one might take to be vulnerable to familiar facts about the possibility of perceptual illusion.

A crude statement of direct realism might go as follows. In perception, we sometimes directly perceive physical objects and their properties, we do not always perceive physical objects by perceiving something else, e.g., a sense-datum. There are, however, difficulties with this formulation of the view, as for one thing a great many philosophers who are not direct realists would admit that it is a mistake to describe people as actually perceiving something other than a physical object. In particular, such philosophers might admit, we should never say that we perceive sense-data. To talk that way would be to suppose that we should model our understanding of our relationship to sense-data on our understanding of the ordinary use of perceptual verbs as they describe our relation to and of the physical world, and that is the last thing paradigm sense-datum theorists should want. At least, many of the philosophers who objected to direct realism would prefer to express in what they were of objecting too in terms of a technical (and philosophically controversial) concept such as acquaintance. Using such a notion, we could define direct realism this way: In veridical experience we are directly acquainted with parts, e.g., surfaces, or constituents of physical objects. A less cautious venison of the view might drop the reference to veridical experience and claim simply that in all experience we are directly acquainted with parts or constituents of physical objects. The expressions knowledge by acquaintance and knowledge by description, and the distinction they mark between knowing things and knowing about things, are generally associated with Bertrand Russell (1872-1970), that scientific philosophy required analysing many objects of belief as logical constructions or logical fictions, and the programme of analysis that this inaugurated dominated the subsequent philosophy of logical atomism, and then of other philosophers, Russell's, The Analysis of Mind, the mind itself is treated in a fashion reminiscent of Hume, as no more than the collection of neutral perceptions or sense-data that make up the flux of conscious experience, and that looked at another way that also was to make up the external world (neutral monism), but An Inquiry into Meaning and Truth (1940) represents a more empirical approach to the problem. Yet, philosophers have perennially investigated this and related distinctions using varying terminology.

Distinction in our ways of knowing things, highlighted by Russell and forming a central element in his philosophy after the discovery of the theory of definite descriptions. A thing is known by acquaintance when there is direct experience of it. It is known by description if it can only be described as a thing with such-and-such properties. In everyday parlance, I might know my spouse and children by acquaintance, but know someone as the first person born at sea only by description. However, for a variety of reasons Russell shrinks the area of things that can be known by acquaintance until eventually only current experience, perhaps my own self, and certain universals or meanings qualify anything else is known only as the thing that has such-and-such qualities.

Because one can interpret the relation of acquaintance or awareness as one that is not epistemic, i.e., not a kind of propositional knowledge, it is important to distinguish the above aforementioned views read as ontological theses from a view one might call epistemological direct realism? In perception we are, on at least some occasions, non-inferentially justified in believing a proposition asserting the existence of a physical object. Since it is that these objects exist independently of any mind that might perceive them, and so it thereby rules out all forms of idealism and phenomenalism, which hold that there are no such independently existing objects. Its being to direct realism rules out those views defended under the cubic of critical naive realism, or representational realism, in which there is some nonphysical intermediary -usually called a sense-datum or a sense impression -that must first be perceived or experienced in order to perceive the object that exists independently of this perception. Often the distinction between direct realism and other theories of perception is explained more fully in terms of what is immediately perceived, than mediately perceived. What relevance does illusion have for these two forms of direct realism?

The fundamental premise of the arguments is from illusion seems to be the theses that things can appear to be other than they are. Thus, for example, straight sticks when immerged in water looks bent, a penny when viewed from certain perspective appears as an illusory spatial elliptic circularity, when something that is yellow when place under red fluorescent light looks red. In all of these cases, one version of the argument goes, it is implausible to maintain that what we are directly acquainted with is the real nature of the object in question. Indeed, it is hard to see how we can be said to be aware of the really physical object at all. In the above illusions the things we were aware of actually were bent, elliptical and red, respectively. But, by hypothesis, the really physical objects lacked these properties. Thus, we were not aware of the substantial reality of been real as a physical objects or theory.

So far, if the argument is relevant to any of the direct realises distinguished above, it seems relevant only to the claim that in all sense experience we are directly acquainted with parts or constituents of physical objects. After all, even if in illusion we are not acquainted with physical objects, but their surfaces, or their constituents, why should we conclude anything about the hidden nature of our relations to the physical world in veridical experience?

We are supposed to discover the answer to this question by noticing the similarities between illusory experience and veridical experience and by reflecting on what makes illusion possible at all. Illusion can occur because the nature of the illusory experience is determined, not just by the nature of events or sorted, conflicting affairs but the object perceived as itself the event in cause, but also by other conditions, both external and internal as becoming of an inner or as the outer experience. But all of our sensations are subject to these causal influences and it would be gratuitous and arbitrary to select from indefinitely of many and subtly different perceptual experiences some special ones those that get us in touch with the real nature of the physical world and its surrounding surfaces. Red fluorescent light affects the way things look, but so does sunlight. Water reflects light, but so does air. We have no unmediated access to the external world.

The Philosophy of science, and scientific epistemology are not the only area where philosophers have lately urged the relevance of neuroscientific discoveries. Kathleen Akins argues that a traditional view of the senses underlies the variety of sophisticated naturalistic programs about intentionality. Current neuroscientific understanding of the mechanisms and coding strategies implemented by sensory receptors shows that this traditional view is mistaken. The traditional view holds that sensory systems are veridical in at least three ways. (1) Each signal in the system correlates along with diminutive ranging properties in the external (to the body) environment. (2) The structure in the relevant relations between the external properties the receptors are sensitive to is preserved in the structure of the relations between the resulting sensory states, and (3) the sensory system theory, is not properly a single theory, but any approach to a complicated or complex structure that abstract away from the particular physical, chemical or biological nature of its components and simply considers the structure they together administer the terms of the functional role of individual parts and their contribution to the functioning of the whole, without fabricated additions or embellishments, that this is an external event. Using recent neurobiological discoveries about response properties of thermal receptors in the skin as an illustration, are, here, conversely acceptable of sensory systems from which are narcissistic than veridical. All three traditional assumptions are violated. These neurobiological details and their philosophical implications open novel questions for the philosophy of perception and for the appropriate foundations for naturalistic projects about intentionality. Armed with the known neurophysiology of sensory receptors, for example, our philosophy of perception or of perceptual intentionality will no longer focus on the search for correlations between states of sensory systems and veridically detected external properties. This traditionally philosophical (and scientific) project rests upon a mistaken veridical view of the senses. Neurophysiological constructs allow for the knowledge of sensory receptors actively to show that sensory experience does not serve the naturalist as well as a simple paradigm case of intentional relations between representation and the world. Once again, available scientific detail shows the naivety of some traditional philosophical projects.

Focussing on the anatomy and physiology of the pain transmission system, Valerie Hardcastle (1997) urges a similar negative implication for a popular methodological assumption. Pain experiences have long been philosophers favourite cases for analysis and theorizing about conscious experience generally. Nevertheless, every position about pain experiences has been defended recently: eliminativist, a variety of objectivists view, relational views, and subjectivist views. Why so little agreement, despite agreement that pain experience is the place to start an analysis or theory of consciousness? Hardcastle urges two answers. First, philosophers tend to be uninformed about the neuronal complexity of our pain transmission systems, and build their analyses or theories on the outcome of a single component of a multi-component system. Second, even those who understand some of the underlying neurobiology of pain tends to advocate gate-control theories. But the best existing gate-control theories are vague about the neural mechanisms of the gates. Hardcastle instead proposes a dissociable dual system of pain transmission, consisting of a pain sensory system closely analogous in its neurobiological implementation to other sensory systems, and a descending pain inhibitory system. She argues that this dual system is consistent with recent neuroscientific discoveries and accounts for all the pain phenomena that have tempted philosophers toward particular (but limited) theories of pain experience. The neurobiological uniqueness of the pain inhibitory system, contrasted with the mechanisms of other sensory modalities, renders pain processing atypical. In particular, the pain inhibitory system dissociates pains sensation from stimulation of nociceptors (pain receptors). Hardcastle concludes from the neurobiological uniqueness of pain transmission that pain experiences are atypical conscious events, and hence not a good place to start theorizing about or analysing the general type.

Developing and defending theories of content is a central topic in current philosophy of mind. A common desideratum in this debate is a theory of cognitive representation consistent with a physical or naturalistic ontology. Here, described are a few contributions neurophilosophers have made to this literature.

When one perceives or remembers that he is out of coffee, his brain state possesses intentionality or 'aboutness'. The percept or memory is about ones being out of coffee, and it represents one for being out of coffee. The representational state has content. Some psychosemantics seek to explain what it is for a representational state to be about something: to provide an account of how states and events can have specific representational content. Some physicalist psychosemantics seek to do this using resources of the physical sciences exclusively. Neurophilosophers have contributed to two types of physicalist psychosemantics: the Functional Role approach and the Informational approach.

The nucleus of functional roles of semantics holds that a representation has its content in virtue of relations it bears to other representations. Its paradigm application is to concepts of truth-functional logic, like the conjunctive and disjunctive or, a physical event instantiates the function as justly the case that it maps two true inputs onto a single true output. Thus an expression bears the relations to others that give it the semantic content of and, proponents of functional role semantics propose similar analyses for the content of all representations (Form 1986). A physical event represents birds, for example, if it bears the right relations to events representing feathers and others representing beaks. By contrast, informational semantics associates content to a state depending upon the causal relations obtaining between the state and the object it represents. A physical state represents birds, for example, just in case an appropriate causal relation obtains between it and birds. At the heart of informational semantics is a causal account of information. Red spots on a face carry the information that one has measles because the red spots are caused by the measles virus. A common criticism of informational semantics holds that mere causal covariation is insufficient for representation, since information (in the causal sense) is by definition, always veridical while representations can misrepresent. A popular solution to this challenge invokes a teleological analysis of function. A brain state represents X by virtue of having the function of carrying information about being caused by X (Dretske 1988). These two approaches do not exhaust the popular options for some psychosemantics, but are the ones to which neurophilosophers have contributed.

Jerry Fodor and Ernest LePore raise an important challenge to Churchlands psychosemantics. Location in a state space alone seems insufficient to fix representational states endorsed by content. Churchland never explains why a point in a three-dimensional state space represents the Collor, as opposed to any other quality, object, or event that varies along three dimensions. Churchlands account achieves its explanatory power by the interpretation imposed on the dimensions. Fodor and LePore allege that Churchland never specifies how a dimension comes to represent, e.g., degree of saltiness, as opposed to yellow-blue wavelength opposition. One obvious answer appeals to the stimuli that form the external inputs to the neural network in question. Then, for example, the individuating conditions on neural representations of colours are that opponent processing neurons receive input from a specific class of photoreceptors. The latter in turn have electromagnetic radiation (of a specific portion of the visible spectrum) as their activating stimuli. Nonetheless, this appeal to exterior impulsions as the ultimate stimulus that included individual conditions for representational content and context, for which makes the resulting approaches of an interpretation implied by the versionable information to semantics. If, not only, from which this approach is accordantly supported with other neurobiological inferences.

The neurobiological paradigm for informational semantics is the feature detector: One or more neurons that are (I) maximally responsive to a particular type of stimulus, and (ii) have the function of indicating the presence of that stimulus type. Examples of such stimulus-types for visual feature detectors include high-contrast edges, motion direction, and colours. A favourite feature detector among philosophers is the alleged fly detector in the frog. Lettvin et al. (1959) identified cells in the frog retina that responded maximally to small shapes moving across the visual field. The idea that this cell's activity functioned to detect flies rested upon knowledge of the frogs' diet. Using experimental techniques ranging from single-cell recording to sophisticated functional imaging, neuroscientists have recently discovered a host of neurons that are maximally responsive to a variety of stimuli. However, establishing condition (ii) on a feature detector is much more difficult. Even some paradigm examples have been called into question. David Hubel and Torsten Wiesels (1962) Nobel Prize adherents, who strove to establish the receptive fields of neurons in striate cortices were often interpreted as revealing cells manouevre with those that function continued of their detection, however, Lehky and Sejnowski (1988) have challenged this interpretation. They trained an artificial neural network to distinguish the three-dimensional shape and orientation of an object from its two-dimensional shading pattern. Their network incorporates many features of visual neurophysiology. Nodes in the trained network turned out to be maximally responsive to edge contrasts, but did not appear to have the function of edge detection.

Kathleen Akins (1996) offers a different neurophilosophical challenge to informational semantics and its affiliated feature-detection view of sensory representation. We saw in the previous section how Akins argues that the physiology of thermoreceptor violates three necessary conditions on veridical representation. From this fact she draws doubts about looking for feature detecting neurons to ground some psychosemantics generally, including thought contents. Human thoughts about flies, for example, are sensitive to numerical distinctions between particular flies and the particular locations they can occupy. But the ends of frog nutrition are well served without a representational system sensitive to such ontological refinements. Whether a fly seen now is numerically identical to one seen a moment ago, need not, and perhaps cannot, figure into the frogs feature detection repertoire. Akins critique casts doubt on whether details of sensory transduction will scale up to encompass of some adequately unified psychosemantics. It also raises new questions for human intentionality. How do we get from activity patterns in narcissistic sensory receptors, keyed not to objective environmental features but rather only to effects of the stimuli on the patch of tissue enervated, to the human ontology replete with enduring objects with stable configurations of properties and relations, types and their tokens (as the fly-thought example presented above reveals), and the rest? And how did the development of a stable, and rich ontology confer survival advantages to human ancestors?

Consciousness has reemerged as a topic in philosophy of mind and the cognition and attitudinal values over the past three decades. Instead of ignoring it, many physicalists now seek to explain it (Dennett, 1991). Here we focus exclusively on ways those neuroscientific discoveries have impacted philosophical debates about the nature of consciousness and its relation to physical mechanisms. Thomas Nagel (1937—), argues that conscious experience is subjective, and thus permanently recalcitrant to objective scientific understanding. He invites us to ponder what it is like to be a bat and urges the intuition that no amount of physical-scientific knowledge (including neuroscientific) supplies a complete answer.

Nagels work is centrally concerned with the nature of moral motivation and the possibility of as rational theory of moral and political commitment, and has been a major impetus of interests in realistic and Kantian approaches to these issues. The modern philosophy of mind has been his 'What is it Like to Be a Bat?, Arguing that there is an irreducible subjective aspect of experience that cannot be grasped by the objective methods of natural science, or by philosophies such as functionalism that confine themselves to those methods, as the intuition pump up has generated extensive philosophical discussion. At least two well-known replies make direct appeal to neurophysiology. John Biro suggests that part of the intuition pumped by Nagel, that bat experience is substantially different from human experience, presupposes systematic relations between physiology and phenomenology. Kathleen Akins (1993) delves deeper into existing knowledge of bat physiology and reports much that is pertinent to Nagels question. She argues that many of the questions about subjectivity that we still consider open hinge on questions that remain unanswered about neuroscientific details.

The more recent philosopher David Chalmers (1996), has argued that any possible brain-process account of consciousness will leave open an explanatory gap between the brain process and properties of the conscious experience. This is because no brain-process theory can answer the hard question: Why should that particular brain process give rise to conscious experience? We can always imagine (conceive of) a universe populated by creatures having those brain processes but completely lacking conscious experience. A theory of consciousness requires an explanation of how and why some brain process causes consciousness replete with all the features we commonly experience. The fact that the more difficult of questions remains unanswered implicates that we will probably never get to culminate of an explanation of consciousness, in that, at the level of neural compliance. Paul and Patricia Churchland have recently offered the following diagnosis and reply. Chalmers offer a conceptual argument, based on our ability to imagine creatures possessing brains like ours but wholly lacking in conscious experience. But the more one learns about how the brain produces conscious experience-and literature is beginning to emerge (e.g., Gazzaniga, 1995) - the harder it becomes to imagine a universe consisting of creatures with brain processes like ours but lacking consciousness. This is not just to bare assertions. The Churchlands appeal to some neurobiological detail. For example, Paul Churchland (1995) develops a neuroscientific account of consciousness based on recurrent connections between thalamic nuclei (particularly diffusely projecting nuclei like the intralaminar nuclei) and the cortex. Churchland argues that the thalamocortical recurrency accounts for the selective features of consciousness, for the effects of short-term memory on conscious experience, for vivid dreaming during REM. (rapid-eye movement) sleep, and other core features of conscious experience. In other words, the Churchlands are claiming that when one learns about activity patterns in these recurrent circuits, one cannot imagine or conceive of this activity occurring without these core features of conscious experience. (Other than just mouthing the words, I am now imagining activity in these circuits without selective attention/the effects of short-term memory/vivid dreaming . . .)

A second focus of sceptical arguments about a complete neuroscientific explanation of consciousness is sensory qualia: the introspectable qualitative aspects of sensory experience, the features by which subjects discern similarities and differences among their experiences. The colours of visual sensations are a philosopher's favourite example. One famous puzzle about colour qualia is the alleged conceivability of spectral inversions. Many philosophers claim that it is conceptually possible (if perhaps physically impossible) for two humans not to diverge apart of similarities, but such are the compatibles as forwarded by their differing enation to neurophysiology. While the colour that fires engines and tomatoes appear to have of only one subject, is the colour that grasses and frogs appear in having the other (and vice versa). A large amount of neurophysiologically informed philosophy has addressed this question. A related area where neurophilosophical considerations have emerged concerns the metaphysics of colours themselves (rather than Collor experiences). A longstanding philosophical dispute is whether colours are objective properties Existing external to perceiver or rather identifiable as or dependent upon minds or nervous systems. Some recent work on this problem begins with characteristics of Collor experiences: For example that Collor similarity judgments produce Collor orderings that align on a circle. With this resource, one can seek mappings of phenomenology onto environmental or physiological regularities. Identifying colours with particular frequencies of electromagnetic radiation does not preserve the structure of the hue circle, whereas identifying colours with activity in opponent processing neurons does. Such a tidbit is not decisive for the Collor objectivist-subjectivist debate, but it does convey the type of neurophilosophical work being done on traditional metaphysical issues beyond the philosophy of mind.

We saw in the discussion of Hardcastle (1997) two sections above that Neurophilosophers have entered disputes about the nature and methodological import of pain experiences. Two decades earlier, Dan Dennett (1978) took up the question of whether it is possible to build a computer that feels pain. He compares and notes the strong move between neurophysiological discoveries and common sense intuitions about pain experience. He suspects that the incommensurability between scientific and common sense views is due to incoherence in the latter. His attitude is wait-and-see. But foreshadowing Churchlands reply to Chalmers, Dennett favours scientific investigations over conceivability-based philosophical arguments.

Neurological deficits have attracted philosophical interest. For thirty years philosophers have found implications for the unity of the self in experiments with commissurotomy patients. In carefully controlled experiments, commissurotomy patients display two dissociable seats of consciousness. Patricia Churchland scouts philosophical implications of a variety of neurological deficits. One deficit is blindsight. Some patients with lesions to primary visual cortex report being unable to see items in regions of their visual fields, yet perform far better than chance in forced guess trials about stimuli in those regions. A variety of scientific and philosophical interpretations have been offered. Need Form (1988) worries that many of these conflate distinct notions of consciousness? He labels these notions phenomenal consciousness (P-consciousness) and access consciousness (A-consciousness). The former is that which, what it is like-ness of experience. The latter are the availability of representational content to self-initiated action and speech. Form argues that P-consciousness is not always representational whereas A-consciousness is. Dennett and Michael Tye are sceptical of non-representational analyses of consciousness in general. They provide accounts of blindsight that do not depend on Forms distinction.

Many other topics are worth neurophilosophical pursuit. We mentioned commissurotomy and the unity of consciousness and the self, which continues to generate discussion. Qualia beyond those of Collor and pain have begun to attract neurophilosophical attention has self-consciousness. The first issues to arise in the philosophy of neuroscience (before there was a recognized area) were the localization of cognitive functions to specific neural regions. Although the localization approach had dubious origins in the phrenology of Gall and Spurzheim, and was challenged severely by Flourens throughout the early nineteenth century, it reemerged in the study of aphasia by Bouillaud, Auburtin, Broca, and Wernicke. These neurologists made careful studies (where possible) of linguistic deficits in their aphasic patients followed by brain autopsies postmortem. Broca initial study of twenty-two patients in the mid-nineteenth century confirmed that damage to the left cortical hemisphere was predominant, and that damage to the second and third frontal convolutions was necessary to produce speech production deficits. Although the anatomical coordinates Broca postulates for the speech production centres do not correlate exactly with damage producing production deficits as both are in this area of frontal cortexes and speech production requires of some greater degree of composure, in at least, that still bears his name (Broca area and Broca aphasia). Less than two decades later Carl Wernicke published evidence for a second language Centre. This area is anatomically distinct from Broca area, and damage to it produced a very different set of aphasic symptoms. The cortical area that still bears his name (Wernickes area) is located around the first and second convolutions in temporal cortex, and the aphasia that bear his name (Wernickes aphasia) involves deficits in language comprehension. Wernickes method, like Broca, was based on lesion studies: a careful evaluation of the behavioural deficits followed by post mortem examination to find the sites of tissue damage and atrophy. Lesion studies suggesting more precise localization of specific linguistic functions remain the groundwork of a strengthening foundation to which supports all while it remains in tack to this day in unarticulated research

Lesion studies have also produced evidence for the localization of other cognitive functions: for example, sensory processing and certain types of learning and memory. However, localization arguments for these other functions invariably include studies using animal models. With an animal model, one can perform careful behavioural measures in highly controlled settings, then ablate specific areas of neural tissue (or use a variety of other techniques to Form or enhance activity in these areas) and remeasure performance on the same behavioural tests. But since we lack an animal model for (human) language production and comprehension, this additional evidence is not available to the neurologist or neurolinguist. This fact makes the study of language a paradigm case for evaluating the logic of the lesion/deficit method of inferring functional localization. Philosopher Barbara Von Eckardt (1978) attempts to make explicitly the steps of reasoning involved in this common and historically important method. Her analysis begins with Robert Cummins early analysis of functional explanation, but she extends it into a notion of structurally adequate functional analysis. These analyses break down a complex capacity C into its constituent capacities 1, C2, . . . Cn, where the constituent capacities are consistent with the underlying structural details of the system. For example, human speech production (complex capacity C) results from formulating a speech intention, then selecting appropriate linguistic representations to capture the content of the speech intention, then formulating the motor commands to produce the appropriate sounds, then communicating these motor commands to the appropriate motor pathways (constituent capacities C1, C2, . . ., Cn). A functional-localization hypothesis has the form: Brain structure S in an organism (type) O has constituent capacity ci, where ci is a function of some part of O. An example, Brains Broca area (S) in humans (O) formulates motor commands to produce the appropriate sounds (one of the constituent capacities ci). Such hypotheses specify aspects of the structural realization of a functional-component model. They are part of the theory of the neural realization of the functional model.

Armed with these characterizations, Von Eckardt argues that inference to some functional-localization hypothesis proceeds in two steps. First, a functional deficit in a patient is hypothesized based on the abnormal behaviour the patient exhibits. Second, localization of function in normal brains is inferred on the basis of the functional deficit hypothesis plus the evidence about the site of brain damage. The structurally-adequate functional analysis of the capacity connects the pathological behaviour to the hypothesized functional deficit. This connexion suggests four adequacy conditions on a functional deficit hypothesis. First, the pathological behaviour 'P' (e.g., the speech deficits characteristic of Broca aphasia) must result from failing to exercise some complex capacity 'C' (human speech production). Second, there must be a structurally-adequate functional analysis of how people exercise capacity 'C' that involves some constituent capacity ci (formulating motor commands to produce the appropriate sounds). Third, the operation of the steps described by the structurally-adequate functional analysis minus the operation of the component performing 'ci' (Broca area) must result in pathological behaviour P. Fourth, there must not be a better available explanation for why the patient does P. Arguments to a functional deficit hypothesis on the basis of pathological behaviour is thus an instance of argument to the best available explanation. When postulating a deficit in a normal functional component provides the best available explanation of the pathological data, we are justified in drawing the inference.

Von Eckardt applies this analysis to a neurological case study involving a controversial reinterpretation of agnosia. Her philosophical explication of this important neurological method reveals that most challenges to localization arguments of whether to argue only against the localization of a particular type of functional capacity or against generalizing from localization of function in one individual to all normal individuals. (She presents examples of each from the neurological literature.) Such challenges do not impugn the validity of standard arguments for functional localization from deficits. It does not follow that such arguments are unproblematic. But they face difficult factual and methodological problems, not logical ones. Furthermore, the analysis of these arguments as involving a type of functional analysis and inference to the best available explanation carries an important implication for the biological study of cognitive function. Functional analyses require functional theories, and structurally adequate functional analyses require checks imposed by the lower level sciences investigating the underlying physical mechanisms. Arguments to best available explanation are often hampered by a lack of theoretical imagination: the available explanations are often severely limited. We must seek theoretical inspiration from any level of theory and explanation. Hence making explicitly the logic of this common and historically important form of neurological explanation reveals the necessity of joint participation from all scientific levels, from cognitive psychology down to molecular neuroscience. Von Eckardt anticipated what came to be heralded as the co-evolutionary research methodology, which remains a centerpiece of neurophilosophy to the present day.

Over the last two decades, evidence for localization of cognitive function has come increasingly from a new source: the development and refinement of neuroimaging techniques. The form of localization-of-function argument appears not to have changed from that employing lesion studies (as analysed by Von Eckardt). Instead, these imaging technologies resolve some of the methodological problems that plage lesion studies. For example, researchers do not need to wait until the patient dies, and in the meantime probably acquires additional brain damage, to find the lesion sites. Two functional imaging techniques are prominent: Positron emission tomography, or PET, and functional magnetic resonance imaging, or MRI. Although these measure different biological markers of functional activity, both now have a resolution down too around one millimetre. As these techniques increase spatial and temporal resolution of functional markers and continue to be used with sophisticated behavioural methodologies, the possibility of localizing specific psychological functions to increasingly specific neural regions continues to grow

What we now know about the cellular and molecular mechanisms of neural conductance and transmission is spectacular. The same evaluation holds for all levels of explanation and theory about the mind/brain: maps, networks, systems, and behaviour. This is a natural outcome of increasing scientific specialization. We develop the technology, the experimental techniques, and the theoretical frameworks within specific disciplines to push forward our understanding. Still, a crucial aspect of the total picture gets neglected: the relationships between the levels, the glue that binds knowledge of neuron activity to subcellular and molecular mechanisms, network activity patterns to the activity of and connectivity between single neurons, and behavioural network activity. This problem is especially glaring when we focus on the relationship between cognitivist psychological theories, postulating information-bearing representations and processes operating over their contents, and the activity patterns in networks of neurons. Co-evolution between explanatory levels still seems more like a distant dream rather than an operative methodology.

It is here that some neuroscientists appeal to computational methods. If we examine the way that computational models function in more developed sciences (like physics), we find the resources of dynamical systems constantly employed. Global effects (such as large-scale meteorological patterns) are explained in terms of the interaction of local lower-level physical phenomena, but only by dynamical, nonlinear, and often chaotic sequences and combinations. Addressing the interlocking levels of theory and explanation in the mind/brain-using computational resources that have worked to bridge levels in more mature sciences might yield comparable results. This methodology is necessarily interdisciplinary, drawing on resources and researchers from a variety of levels, including higher levels like experimental psychology, program-writing and connectionist artificial intelligence, and philosophy of science.

However, the use of computational methods in neuroscience is not new. Hodgkin, Huxley, and Katz incorporated values of voltage-dependent potassium conductance they had measured experimentally in the squid giant axon into an equation from physics describing the time evolution of a first-order kinetic process. This equation enabled them to calculate best-fit curves for modelled conductance versus time data that reproduced the S-shaped (sigmoidal) function suggested by their experimental data. Using equations borrowed from physics, Rall (1959) developed the cable model of dendrites. This theory provided an account of how the various inputs from across the dendritic tree interact temporally and spatially to determine the input-output properties of single neurons. It remains influential today, and has been incorporated into the genesis software for programming neurally realistic networks. More recently, David Sparks and his colleagues have shown that a vector-averaging model of activity in neurons of correctly predicts experimental results about the amplitude and direction of saccadic eye movements. Working with a more sophisticated mathematical model, Apostolos Georgopoulos and his colleagues have predicted direction and amplitude of hand and arm movements based on averaged activity of 224 cells in motor cortices. Their predictions have borne out under a variety of experimental tests. We mention these particular studies only because we are familiar with them. We could multiply examples of the fruitful interaction of computational and experimental methods in neuroscience easily by one-hundred-fold. Many of these extend back before computational neuroscience was a recognized research endeavour.

We have already seen one example, the vector transformation accounts, of neural representation and computation, under active development in cognitive neuroscience. Other approaches using cognitivist resources are also being pursued. Many of these projects draw upon cognitivist characterizations of the phenomena to be explained. Many exploit cognitivist experimental techniques and methodologies, but, yet, some even attempt to derive cognitivist explanations from cell-biological processes (e.g., Hawkins and Kandel 1984). As Stephen Kosslyn puts it, cognitive neuroscientists employ the information processing view of the mind characteristic of cognitivism without trying to separate it from theories of brain mechanisms. Such an endeavour calls for an interdisciplinary community willing to communicate the relevant portions of the mountain of detail gathered in individual disciplines with interested nonspecialists: not just people willing to confer with those working at related levels, but researchers trained in the methods and factual details of a variety of levels. This is a daunting requirement, but it does offer some hope for philosophers wishing to contribute to future neuroscience. Thinkers trained in both the synoptic vision afforded by philosophy and the factual and experimental basis of genuine graduate-level science would be ideally equipped for this task. Recognition of this potential niche has been slow among graduate programs in philosophy, but there is some hope that a few programs are taking steps to fill it.

In the final analysis there will be philosophers unprepared to accept that, if a given cognitive capacity is psychologically real, then there must be an explanation of how it is possible for an individual in the course of human development to acquire that cognitive capacity, or anything like it, can have a role to play in philosophical accounts of concepts and conceptual abilities. The most obvious basis for such a view would be a Frégean distrust of psychology that leads to a rigid division of labour between philosophy and psychology. The operative thought is that the task of a philosophical theory of concepts is to explain what a given concept is or what a given conceptual ability consist in. This, it is frequently maintained, is something that can be done in complete independence of explaining how such a concept or ability might be acquired. The underlying distinction is one between philosophical questions cantering around concept possession and psychological questions cantering around concept possibilities for an individual to acquire that ability, then it cannot be psychologically real. Nevertheless, this distinction is strictly one that agrees in the adherence to the distinction, it provides no support for a rejection of any given cognitive capacity for which is psychologically real. The neo-Frégean distinction is directly against the view that facts about how concepts are acquired have a role to play in explaining and individualizing concepts. But this view does not have to be disputed by a supporter as such, nonetheless, all that the supporter is to commit is that the principle that no satisfactory account of what a concept is should make it impossible to provide explanation of how that concept can be acquired. That is, that this principle has nothing to say about the further question of whether the psychological explanation has a role to play in a constitutive explanation of the concept, and hence is not in conflict with the neo-Frégean distinction.

A full account of the structure of consciousness, will employ a pressing opportunity or requirements to provide that to illustrate those higher conceptual representations as given to forms of consciousness, to which little attention on such an account will take and about how it might emerge from given points of value, is the thought that an explanation of everything that is distinctive about consciousness will emerge out of an accorded advantage over and above of what it is for the subject, to be capable of thinking about himself. Nonetheless, to appropriate a convenient employment with an applicable understanding of the complicated and complex phenomenon of consciousness, however, ours is to challenge the arousing objectionable character as attributed by the attractions of an out-and-out form of consciousness. Seeming to be the most basic of facts confronting us, yet, it is almost impossible to say what consciousness is. Whenever complicated and complex biological and neural processes go on between the cranial walls of existent vertebrae, as it is my consciousness that provides the medium, though which my consciousness provides the awakening flame of awareness that enables me to think, and if there is no thinking, there is no sense of consciousness. Which their existence the possibility to envisage the entire moral and political framework constructed to position of ones idea of interactions to hold a person rationally approved, although the development of requirement needed of the motivational view as well as the knowledge for which is rationality and situational of the agent.

Meanwhile, whatever complex biological and neural processes go on within the mind, it is my consciousness that provides the awakening awarenesses, whereby my experiences and thoughts have their existence, where my desires are felt and where my intentions are formed. But then how am I to expound upon the I-ness of me or myself that the self is the spectator, or at any rate the owner of this afforded effort as spoken through the strength of the imagination, that these problems together make up what is sometimes called the hard problem of consciousness. One of the difficulties is thinking about consciousness is that the problems seem not to be scientific ones, as the German philosopher, mathematician and polymath Gottfried Leibniz (1646-1716), remarked that if we could construct a machine that could think and feel and then blow it up to the size of a football field and thus be able to examine its working parts as thoroughly as we pleased, would still not find consciousness. And finally, drew to some conclusion that consciousness resides in simple subjects, not complex ones. Even if we are convinced that consciousness somehow emerges from the complexity of the brain functioning, we may still feel baffled about the ways that emergencies takes place, or it takes place in just the way it does. Seemingly, to expect is a prime necessity for ones own personal expectations, even so, to expect of expectation is what is needed of opposites, such that there is no positivity to expect, however, to accept of the doubts that are none, so that the expectation as a forerunner to expect should be nullified. Descartes deceptions of the senses are nothing but a clear orientation of something beyond expectation, indeed.

There are no facts about linguistic mastery that will determine or explain what might be termed the cognitive dynamics that are individual processes that have found their way forward for a theory of consciousness, it sees, to chart the characteristic features individualizing the various distinct conceptual forms of consciousness in a way that will provide a taxonomy of unconsciousness is to show how this actualization is the characterlogical contribution of functional dynamic determinations, that, if, not at least, at the level of contentual representation. What is hoping is now clear is that these forms of higher forms of consciousness emerge from a rich foundation of non-conceptual representations of thought, which can only expose and clarify their conviction that these forms of conscious thought hold the key, not just to an eventful account of how mastery of the conscious paradigms, but to a proper understanding of the plexuity of self-consciousness and/or the overall conjecture of consciousness that stands alone as to an everlasting vanquishment into the endlessness of unchangeless states of unconsciousness, where its abysses are only held by incestuousness.

Theory itself, is consistent with fact or reality, not false or incorrect, but truthful, it is sincerely felt or expressed unforeignly and so, that it is essential and exacting of several standing rules and senses of governing requirements. As, perhaps, the distress of mind begins its lamination of binding substances through which arises of an intertwined web whereby that within and without the estranging assimilations in sensing the definitive criteria by some limited or restrictive particularities of some possible value as taken by a variable accord with reality. To position of something, as to make it balanced, level or square, that we may think of a proper alignment as something, in so, that one is certain, like trust, another derivation of the same appears on the name is etymologically, or strong seers. Conformity of fact or the actuality of a statement as been or accepted as true to an original or standard set class theory from which it is considered as the supreme reality and to have the ultimate meaning, and value of existence. It is, nonetheless, a compound position, such as a conjunction or negation, the truth-values have always determined whose truth-values of that component thesis.

Moreover, science, unswerving exactly to position of something very well hidden, its nature in so that to make it believed, is quickly and imposes on sensing and responding to the definitive qualities or state of being actual or true, such that as a person, an entity, or an event, that might be gainfully employed of all things possessing actuality, existence, or essence. In other words, in that which is objectively inside and out, and in addition it seems to appropriate that of reality, in fact, to the satisfying factions of instinctual needs through the awarenesses of and adjustments abided to environmental demands. Thus, the enabling acceptation of a presence that to prove the duties or function of such that the act or part thereof, that something done or effected presents upon our understanding or plainly the condition of truth that is seen for being realized, and the resultant amounts to the remnant retrogressions that are also, undoubtingly realized.

However, a declaration made to explain or justify action, or its believing desire upon which it is to act, by which the conviction underlying facts or cause, that provide logical sense for a premise or occurrence for logical, rational. Analytic mental states have long since lost in reason, but, yet, the premise usually takes upon the minor premises of an argument, using this faculty of reason that arises too throughout the spoken exchange or a debative discussion, and, of course, spoken in a dialectic way. To determining or conclusively logical impounded by thinking through its directorial solution to the problem, would therefore persuade or dissuade someone with reason that posits of itself with the good sense or justification of reasonability. In which, good causes are simply justifiably to be considered as to think. By which humans seek or attain knowledge or truth. Mere reason is insufficient to convince us of its veracity. Still, comprehension perceptively welcomes an intuitively given certainty, as the truth or fact, without the use of the rational process, as one comes to assessing someone's character, it sublimely configures one consideration, and often with resulting comprehensions, in which it is assessing situations or circumstances and draw sound conclusions into the reign of judgement.

Operatively, that by being in accorded with reason or, perhaps, of sound thinking, that the discovery made, is by some reasonable solution that may or may not resolve the problem, that being without the encased enclosure that bounds common sense from arriving to some practicality, especially if using reason, would posit the formed conclusions, in that of inferences or judgements. In that, all evidential alternates of a confronting argument within the use in thinking or thought out responses to issuing the furthering argumentation to fit or join in the sum parts that are composite to the intellectual faculties, by which case human understanding or the attemptive grasp to its thought, are the resulting liberty encroaching men of zeal, well-meaningly, but without understanding.

Being or occurring in fact or having to some verifiable existence, real objects, and a real illness. Really true and actual and not imaginary, alleged, or ideal, as people and not ghosts, from which are we to find on practical matters and concerns of experiencing the real world. The surrounding surfaces, might we, as, perhaps attest to this for the first time. Being no less than what they state, we have not taken its free pretence, or affections for a real experience highly, as many may encounter real trouble. This, nonetheless, projects of an existing objectivity in which the world despite subjectivity or conventions of thought or language is or have valuing representation, reckoned by actual power, in that of relating to, or being an image formed by light or another identifiable simulation, that converge in space, the stationary or fixed properties, such as a thing or whole having actual existence. All of which, are accorded a truly factual experience into which the actual attestations have brought to you by the afforded efforts of our very own imaginations.

Ideally, in theory the imagination, a concept of reason that is transcendent but non-empirical as to think os conception of and ideal thought, that potentially or actual exists in the mind as a product exclusive to the mental act. In the philosophy of Plato, an archetype of which a corresponding being in phenomenal reality is an imperfect replica, that also, Hegels absolute truth, as the conception and ultimate product of reason (the absolute meaning a mental image of something remembered).

Conceivably, in the imagination the formation of a mental image of something that is or should be perceived as real nor present to the senses. Nevertheless, the image so formed can confront and deal with the reality by using the creative powers of the mind. That is characteristically well removed from reality, but all powers of fantasy over reason are a degree of insanity/ still, fancy as they have given a product of the imagination free reins, that is in command of the fantasy while it is exactly the mark of the neurotic that his very own fantasy possesses him.

All things possessing actuality, existence or essence that exists objectively and in fact based on real occurrences that exist or known to have existed, a real occurrence, an event, i.e., had to prove the facts of the case, as something believed to be true or real, determining by evidence or truth as to do. However, the usage in the sense allegation of fact, and the reasoning are wrong of the facts and substantive facts, as we may never know the facts of the case. These usages may occasion qualms among critics who insist that facts can only be true, but the usages are often useful for emphasis. Therefore, we have related to, or used the discovery or determinations of fast or accurate information in the discovery of facts, then evidence has determined the comprising events or truth is much as ado about their owing actuality. Its opposition forming the literature that treats real people or events as if they were fictional or uses real people or events as essential elements in an otherwise fictional rendition, i.e., of, relating to, produced by, or characterized by internal dissension, as given to or promoting internal dissension. So, then, it is produced artificially than by a natural process, especially the lacking authenticity or genuine factitious values of another than what is or of reality should be.

Substantively set statements or principles devised to explain a group of facts or phenomena, especially one that we have tested or is together experiment with and taken for us to conclude and can be put-upon to make predictions about natural phenomena. Having the consistency of explanatory statements, accepted principles, and methods of analysis, finds to a set of theorems that make up a systematic view of a branch in mathematics or extends upon the paradigms of science, the belief or principle that guides action or helps comprehension or judgements, usually by an ascription based on limited information or knowledge, as a conjecture, tenably to assert the creation from a speculative assumption that bestows to its beginning. Theoretically, to, affiliate oneself with to, or based by itself on theory, i.e., the restriction to theory, is not as much a practical theory of physics, as given to speculative theorizing. Also, the given idea, because of which formidable combinations awaiting upon the inception of an idea, demonstrated as true or is given to demonstration. In mathematics its containment lies of the proposition that has been or is to be proved from explicit assumption and is primarily with theoretical assessments or hypothetical theorizing than possibly these might be thoughtful measures and taken as the characteristics by which we measure its quality value?

Looking back, one can see a discovering degree of homogeneity among the philosophers of the early twentieth century about the topics central to their concerns. More striking still, is the apparent profundities and abstrusity of concerns for which appear at first glance to be separated from the discerned debates of previous centuries, between realism and idealist, say, of rationalists and empiricist.

Thus, no matter what the current debate or discussion, the central issue is often without conceptual and contentual representations, that if one is without concept, is without idea, such that in one foul swoop would ingest the mere truth that lies to the underlying paradoxes of why is there something instead of nothing? Whatever it is that makes, what would otherwise be mere utterances and inscriptions into instruments of communication and understanding. This philosophical problem is to demystify this over-flowing emptiness, and to relate to what we know of ourselves and subjective matters resembling reality or ours is to an inherent perceptivity of the world and its surrounding surfaces.

Contributions to this study include the theory of speech arts, and the investigation of communicable communications, especially the relationship between words and ideas, and words and the world. It is, nonetheless, that which and utterance or sentence expresses, the proposition or claim made about the world. By extension, the content of a predicate that any expression effectively connecting with one or more singular terms to make a sentence, the expressed condition that the entities referred to may satisfy, in which case the resulting sentence will be true. Consequently we may think of a predicate as a function from things to sentences or even to truth-values, or other sub-sentential components that contribute to sentences that contain it. The nature of content is the central concern of the philosophy of language.

What some person expresses of a sentence often depends on the environment in which he or she is placed. For example, the disease I refer to by a term like arthritis or the kind of tree I call of its criteria will define a Berch tree of which I know next to nothing. This raises the possibility of imaging two persons as an alternative different environment, but in which everything appears the same to each of them. The wide content of their thoughts and saying will be different if the situation surrounding them is appropriately different, situation may hear include the actual objects hey perceive, or the chemical or physical kinds of objects in the world they inhabit, or the history of their words, or the decisions of authorities on what counts as an example of one term thy use. The narrow content is that part of their thought that remains identical, through the identity of the way things appear, despite these differences of surroundings. Partisans of wide, . . . as, something called broadly, content may doubt whether any content is in this sense narrow, partisans of narrow content believe that it is the fundamental notion, with wide content being on narrow content confirming context.

All and all, assuming their rationality has characterized people is common, and the most evident display of our rationality is capable to think. This is the rehearsal in the mind of what to say, or what to do. Not all thinking is verbal, since chess players, composers, and painters all think, and there is no deductive reason that their deliberations should take any more verbal a form than their actions. It is permanently tempting to conceive of this activity about the presence in the mind of elements of some language, or other medium that represents aspects of the world and its surrounding surface structures. However, the model has been attacked, notably by Ludwig Wittgenstein (1889-1951), whose influential application of these ideas was in the philosophy of mind. Wittgenstein explores the role that reports of introspection, or sensations, or intentions, or beliefs can play of our social lives, to undermine the Cartesian mental picture is that they functionally describe the goings-on in an inner theatre of which the subject is the lone spectator. Passages that have subsequentially become known as the rule following considerations and the private language argument are among the fundamental topics of modern philosophy of language and mind, although their precise interpretation is endlessly controversial.

Effectively, the hypotheses especially associated with Jerry Fodor (1935-), whom is known for the resolute realism, about the nature of mental functioning, that occurs in a language different from ones ordinary native language, but underlying and explaining our competence with it. The idea is a development of the notion of an innate universal grammar (Avram Noam Chomsky, 1928-), in as such, that we agree that since a computer programs are linguistically complex sets of instructions were the relative executions by which explains of surface behaviour or the adequacy of the computerized programming installations, if it were definably amendable and, advisably corrective, in that most are disconcerting of many that are ultimately a reason for us of thinking intuitively and without the indulgence of retrospective preferences, but an ethical majority in defending of its moral ligne that is already confronting us. That these programs may or may not improve to conditions that are lastly to enhance of the right sort of an existence forwarded toward a more valuing amount in humanities lesser extensions that embrace ones riff of necessity to humanities abeyance to expressions in the finer of qualities.

As an explanation of ordinary language-learning and competence, the hypothesis has not found universal favour, as only ordinary representational powers that by invoking the image of the learning persons capabilities are apparently whom the abilities for translating are contending of an innate language whose own powers are mysteriously a biological given. Perhaps, the view that everyday attributions of intentionality, beliefs, and meaning to other persons proceed by means of a tactic use of a theory that enables one to construct these interpretations as explanations of their doings. We commonly hold the view along with functionalism, according to which psychological states are theoretical entities, identified by the network of their causes and effects. The theory-theory has different implications, depending upon which feature of theories we are stressing. Theories may be thought of as capable of formalization, as yielding predictions and explanations, as achieved by a process of theorizing, as answering to empirical evidence that is in principle describable without them, as liable to be overturned by newer and better theories, and so on.

The main problem with seeing our understanding of others as the outcome of a piece of theorizing is the nonexistence of a medium in which this theory can be couched, as the child learns simultaneously the minds of others and the meaning of terms in its native language, is not gained by the tactic use of a theory, enabling us to infer what thoughts or intentions explain their actions, but by reliving the situation in their shoes or from their point of view, and by that understanding what they experienced and theory, and therefore expressed. Understanding others is achieved when we can ourselves deliberate as they did, and hear their words as if they are our own. The suggestion is a modern development frequently associated in the Verstehen traditions of Dilthey (1833-1911), Weber (1864-1920) and Collingwood (1889-1943).

We may call any process of drawing a conclusion from a set of premises a process of reasoning. If the conclusion concerns what to do, the process is called practical reasoning, otherwise pure or theoretical reasoning. Evidently, such processes may be good or bad, if they are good, the premises support or even entail the conclusion drawn, and if they are bad, the premises offer no support to the conclusion. Formal logic studies the cases in which conclusions are validly drawn from premises, but little human reasoning is overly of the forms logicians identify. Partly, we are concerned to draw conclusions that go beyond our premises, in the way that conclusions of logically valid arguments do not for the process of using evidence to reach a wider conclusion. Nonetheless, such anticipatory pessimism in the opposite direction to the prospects of conformation theory, denying that we can assess the results of abduction in terms of probability. A cognitive process of reasoning in which a conclusion is played-out from a set of premises usually confined of cases in which the conclusions are supposed in following from the premises, i.e., an inference is logically valid, in that of deductibility in a logically defined syntactic premise but without there being to any reference to the intended interpretation of its theory. Furthermore, as we reason we use indefinite traditional knowledge or commonsense sets of presuppositions about what it is likely or not a task of an automated reasoning project, which is to mimic this causal use of knowledge of the way of the world in computer programs.

Some theories usually emerge themselves of engaging to exceptionally explicit predominancy as [supposed] truth that they have not organized, making the theory difficult to survey or study as a whole. The axiomatic method is an idea for organizing a theory, one in which tries to select from among the supposed truths a small number from which they can see all others to be deductively inferable. This makes the theory more tractable since, in a sense, they contain all truth in those few. In a theory so organized, they call the few truth from which they deductively imply all others axioms. David Hilbert (1862-1943) had argued that, just as algebraic and differential equations, which we were used to study mathematical and physical processes, could have themselves be made mathematical objects, so axiomatic theories, like algebraic and differential equations, which are means to representing physical processes and mathematical structures could be of investigating.

Conformation to theory, the philosophy of science, is a generalization or set referring to unobservable entities, i.e., atoms, genes, quarks, unconscious wishes. The ideal gas law, for example, refers to such observable pressures, temperature, and volume, the molecular-kinetic theory refers to molecules and their material possession, . . . although an older usage suggests the lack of adequate evidence in support thereof, as an existing philosophical usage does in truth, follow in the tradition (as in Leibniz, 1704), as many philosophers had the conviction that all truth, or all truth about a particular domain, followed from as few than for being many governing principles. These principles were taken to be either metaphysically prior or epistemologically prior or both. In the first sense, they we took to be entities of such a nature that what exists s caused by them. When the principles were taken as epistemologically prior, that is, as axioms, they were taken to be either epistemologically privileged, e.g., self-evident, not needing to be demonstrated, or again, included or, to such that all truth so truly follow from them by deductive inferences. Gödel (1984) showed in the spirit of Hilbert, treating axiomatic theories as themselves mathematical objects that mathematics, and even a small part of mathematics, elementary number theory, could not be axiomatized, that more precisely, any class of axioms that is such that we could effectively decide, of any proposition, whether or not it was in that class, would be too small to capture in of the truth.

The notion of truth occurs with remarkable frequency in our reflections on language, thought and action. We are inclined to suppose, for example, that truth is the proper aim of scientific inquiry, that true beliefs help to achieve our goals, that to understand a sentence is to know which circumstances would make it true, that reliable preservation of truth as one argues of valid reasoning, that moral pronouncements should not be regarded as objectively true, and so on. To assess the plausibility of such theses, and to refine them and to explain why they hold (if they do), we require some view of what truth be a theory that would account for its properties and its relations to other matters. Thus, there can be little prospect of understanding our most important faculties in the sentence of a good theory of truth.

Such a thing, however, has been notoriously elusive. The ancient idea that truth is some sort of correspondence with reality has still never been articulated satisfactorily, and the nature of the alleged correspondence and the alleged reality persistently remains objectionably enigmatical. Yet the familiar alternative suggestions that true beliefs are those that are mutually coherent, or pragmatically useful, or verifiable in suitable conditions has each been confronted with persuasive counterexamples. A twentieth-century departure from these traditional analyses is the view that truth is not a property at all that the syntactic form of the predicate, is true, distorts its really semantic character, which is not to describe propositions but to endorse them. Nevertheless, we have also faced this radical approach with difficulties and suggest, counter intuitively that truth cannot have the vital theoretical role in semantics, epistemology and elsewhere that we are naturally inclined to give it. Thus, truth threatens to remain one of the most enigmatic of notions: An explicit account of it can seem essential yet beyond our reach. All the same, recent work provides some evidence for optimism.

A theory is based in philosophy of science, is a generalization or se of generalizations purportedly referring to observable entities, i.e., atoms, quarks, unconscious wishes, and so on. The ideal gas law, for example, cites to only such observable pressures, temperature, and volume, the molecular-kinetic theory refers top molecules and their properties, although an older usage suggests the lack of an adequate make out in support therefrom as merely a theory, latter-day philosophical usage does not carry that connotation. Einstein's special and General Theory of Relativity, for example, is taken to be extremely well founded.

These are two main views on the nature of theories. According to the received view theories are partially interpreted axiomatic systems, according to the semantic view, a theory is a collection of models (Suppe, 1974). By which, some possibilities, unremarkably emerge as supposed truth that no one has neatly systematized by making theory difficult to make a survey of or study as a whole. The axiomatic method is an ideal for organizing a theory (Hilbert, 1970), one tries to select from among the supposed truths a small number from which they can see all the others to be deductively inferable. This makes the theory more tractable since, in a sense, they contain all truth in those few. In a theory so organized, they call the few truth from which they deductively incriminate all others axioms. David Hilbert (1862-1943) had argued that, morally justified as algebraic and differential equations, which were antiquated into the study of mathematical and physical processes, could hold on to themselves and be made mathematical objects, so they could make axiomatic theories, like algebraic and differential equations, which are means of representing physical processes and mathematical structures, objects of mathematical investigation.

In the tradition (as in Leibniz, 1704), many philosophers had the conviction that all truth, or all truth about a particular domain, followed from a few principles. These principles were taken to be either metaphysically prior or epistemologically prior or both. In the first sense, they were taken to be entities of such a nature that what exists is caused by them. When the principles were taken as epistemologically prior, that is, as axioms, they were taken to be either epistemologically privileged, i.e., self-evident, not needing to be demonstrated, or again, inclusive or, to be such that all truth do in truth follow from them (by deductive inferences). Gödel (1984) showed in the spirit of Hilbert, treating axiomatic theories as themselves mathematical objects that mathematics, and even a small part. Of mathematics, elementary number theory, could not be axiomatized, that, more precisely, any class of axioms that is such that we could effectively decide, of any proposition, whether or not it was in that class, would be too small to capture all of the truth.

The notion of truth occurs with remarkable frequency in our reflections on language, thought, and action. We are inclined to suppose, for example, that truth is the proper aim of scientific inquiry, that true beliefs help us to achieve our goals, tat to understand a sentence is to know which circumstances would make it true, that reliable preservation of truth as one argues from premises to a conclusion is the mark of valid reasoning, that moral pronouncements should not be regarded as objectively true, and so on. In order to assess the plausible of such theses, and in order to refine them and to explain why they hold, if they do, we expect some view of what truth be of a theory that would keep an account of its properties and its relations to other matters. Thus, there can be little prospect of understanding our most important faculties without a good theory of truth.

The ancient idea that truth is one sort of correspondence with reality has still never been articulated satisfactorily: The nature of the alleged correspondence and te alleged reality remains objectivably rid of obstructions. Yet, the familiar alternative suggests ~. That true beliefs are those that are mutually coherent, or pragmatically useful, or verifiable in suitable conditions has each been confronted with persuasive counterexamples. A twentieth-century departure from these traditional analyses is the view that truth is not a property at al ~. That the syntactic form of the predicate, . . . is true, distorts the real semantic character, with which is not to describe propositions but to endorse them. Still, this radical approach is also faced with difficulties and suggests, counter intuitively that truth cannot have the vital theoretical role in semantics, epistemology and elsewhere that we are naturally inclined to give it. Thus, truth threatens to remain one of the most enigmatic of notions, and a confirming account of it can seem essential yet, on the far side of our reach. However, recent work provides some grounds for optimism.

The belief that snow is white owes its truth to a certain feature of the external world, namely, to the fact that snow is white. Similarly, the belief that dogs bark is true because of the fact that dogs bark. This trivial observation leads to what is perhaps the most natural and popular account of truth, the correspondence theory, according to which a belief (statement, a sentence, propositions, etc. (as true just in case there exists a fact corresponding to it (Wittgenstein, 1922, Austin! 950). This thesis is unexceptionable, however, if it is to provide a rigorous, substantial and complete theory of truth ~. If it is to be more than merely a picturesque way of asserting all equivalences are to the form. The belief that 'p' is true 'p'.

Then it must be supplemented with accounts of what facts are, and what it is for a belief to correspond to a fact, and these are the problems on which the correspondence theory of truth has floundered. For one thing, it is far from going unchallenged that any significant gain in understanding is achieved by reducing the belief that snow is white is true to the facts that snow is white exists: For these expressions look equally resistant to analysis and too close in meaning for one to provide a crystallizing account of the other. In addition, the undistributed relationship that holds in particular between the belief that snow is white and the fact that snow is white, between the belief that dogs bark and the fact that a dog barks, and so on, is very hard to identify. The best attempt to date is Wittgensteins 1922, so-called picture theory, by which an elementary proposition is a configuration of terms, with whatever stare of affairs it reported, as an atomic fact is a configuration of simple objects, an atomic fact corresponds to an elementary proposition and makes it true, when their configurations are identical and when the terms in the proposition for it to the similarly-placed objects in the fact, and the truth value of each complex proposition the truth values entail of the elementary ones. However, eve if this account is correct as far as it goes, it would need to be completed with plausible theories of logical configuration, rudimentary proposition, reference and entailment, none of which is better-off to come.

The cental characteristic of truth One that any adequate theory must explain is that when a proposition satisfies its conditions of proof or verification then it is regarded as true. To the extent that the property of corresponding with reality is mysterious, we are going to find it impossible to see what we take to verify a proposition should show the possession of that property. Therefore, a tempting alternative to the correspondence theory an alternative that eschews obscure, metaphysical concept that explains quite straightforwardly why Verifiability infers, truth is simply to identify truth with Verifiability

(Peirce, 1932). This idea can take on variously formed. One version involves the further assumption that verification is holistic, . . . in that a belief is justified (i.e., verified) when it is part of an entire system of beliefs that are consistent and counter balanced (Bradley, 1914 and Hempel, 1935). This is known as the coherence theory of truth. Another version involves the assumption associated with each proposition, some specific procedure for finding out whether one should believe it or not. On this account, to say that a proposition is true is to sa that the appropriate procedure would verify (Dummett, 1979. and Putnam, 1981). While in mathematics this, amounts to the identification of truth with probability.

The attractions of the verificationist account of truth are that it is refreshingly clear compared with the correspondence theory, and that it succeeds in connecting truth with verification. The trouble is that the bond it postulates between these notions is implausibly strong. We do in true statements take verification to indicate truth, but also we recognize the possibility that a proposition may be false in spite of there being impeccable reasons to believe it, and that a proposition may be true although we are not able to discover that it is. Verifiability and ruth are no doubt highly correlated, but surely not the same thing.

A third well-known account of truth is known as pragmatism (James, 1909 and Papineau, 1987). As we have just seen, the verificationist selects a prominent property of truth and considers the essence of truth. Similarly, the pragmatist focuses on another important characteristic namely, that true belief is a good basis for action and takes this to be the very nature of truth. True assumptions are said to be, by definition, those that provoke actions with desirable results. Again, we have an account statement with a single attractive explanatory characteristic, besides, it postulates between truth and its alleged analysand in this case, utility is implausibly close. Granted, true belief tends to foster success, but it happens regularly that actions based on true beliefs lead to disaster, while false assumptions, by pure chance, produce wonderful results.

One of the few uncontroversial facts about truth is that the proposition that snow is white if and only if snow is white, the proposition that lying is wrong is true if and only if lying is wrong, and so on. Traditional theories acknowledge this fact but regard it as insufficient and, as we have seen, inflate it with some further principle of the form, X is true if and only if X has property P (such as corresponding to reality, Verifiability, or being suitable as a basis for action), which is supposed to specify what truth is. Some radical alternatives to the traditional theories result from denying the need for any such further specification (Ramsey, 1927, Strawson, 1950 and Quine, 1990). For example, ne might suppose that the basic theory of truth contains nothing more that equivalences of the form, The proposition that 'p' is true if and only if 'p' (Horwich, 1990).

That is, a proposition, 'K' with the following properties, that from 'K' and any further premises of the form. Einstein's claim was the proposition that 'p' you can imply 'p'. Whatever it is, now supposes, as the deflationist says, that our understanding of the truth predicate consists in the stimulative decision to accept any instance of the schema. The proposition that 'p' is true if and only if 'p', then your problem is solved. For 'K' is the proposition, Einstein's claim is true, it will have precisely the inferential power needed. From it and Einstein's claim is the proposition that quantum mechanics are wrong, you can use Leibniz's law to imply The proposition that quantum mechanic is wrong is true; which given the relevant axiom of the deflationary theory, allows you to derive Quantum mechanics is wrong. Thus, one point in favour of the deflationary theory is that it squares with a plausible story about the function of our notion of truth, in that its axioms explain that function without the need for further analysis of what truth is.

Not all variants of deflationism have this quality virtue, according to the redundancy performatives theory of truth, the pair of sentences, The proposition that 'p' is true and plain p's, has the same meaning and expresses the same statement as one and another, so it is a syntactic illusion to think that p is true attributes any sort of property to a proposition (Ramsey, 1927 and Strawson, 1950). Yet in that case, it becomes hard to explain why we are entitled to infer The proposition that quantum mechanics are wrong is true form Einstein's claim is the proposition that quantum mechanics are wrong. Einstein's claim is true. For if truth is not property, then we can no longer account for the inference by invoking the law that if 'X', appears identical with 'Y' then any property of 'X' is a property of 'Y', and vice versa. Thus the redundancy/performatives theory, by identifying rather than merely correlating the contents of The proposition that p is true and p, precludes the prospect of a good explanation of one on truth most significant and useful characteristics. So, putting restrictions on our assembling claim to the weak is better, of its equivalence schema: The proposition that p is true is and is only p.

Support for deflationism depends upon the possibleness of showing that its axiom instances of the equivalence schema unsupplements by any further analysis, will suffice to explain all the central facts about truth, for example, that the verification of a proposition indicates its truth, and that true beliefs have a practical value. The first of these facts follows trivially from the deflationary axioms, for given ours a prior knowledge of the equivalence of p and The a propositions that p is true, any reason to believe that p becomes an equally good reason to believe that the preposition that p is true. We can also explain the second fact in terms of the deflationary axioms, but not quite so easily. Consider, to begin with, beliefs of the form that if I perform the act A, then my desires will be fulfilled. Notice that the psychological role of such a belief is, roughly, to cause the performance of A. In other words, given that I do have belief, then typically.

I will perform the act A

Notice also that when the belief is true then, given the deflationary axioms, the performance of 'A' will in fact lead to the fulfilment of ones desires, i.e., If being true, then if I perform A, and my desires will be fulfilled.

Therefore, if it is true, then my desires will be fulfilled. So valuing the truth of beliefs of that form is quite treasonable. Nevertheless, inference has derived such beliefs from other beliefs and can be expected to be true if those other beliefs are true. So assigning a value to the truth of any belief that might be used in such an inference is reasonable.

To the extent that such deflationary accounts can be given of all the acts involving truth, then the explanatory demands on a theory of truth will be met by the collection of all statements like, The proposition that snow is white is true if and only if snow is white, and the sense that some deep analysis of truth is needed will be undermined.

Nonetheless, there are several strongly felt objections to deflationism. One reason for dissatisfaction is that the theory has an infinite number of axioms, and therefore cannot be completely written down. It can be described, as the theory whose axioms are the propositions of the form 'p' if and only if it is true that 'p', but not explicitly formulated. This alleged defect has led some philosophers to develop theories that show, first, how the truth of any proposition derives from the referential properties of its constituents, and second, how the referential properties of primitive constituents are determinated (Tarski, 1943 and Davidson, 1969). However, assuming that all propositions including belief attributions remain controversial, law of nature and counterfactual conditionals depends for their truth values on what their constituents refer to implicate. In addition, there is no immediate prospect of a presentable, finite possibility of reference, so that it is far form clear that the infinite, list-like character of deflationism can be avoided.

Additionally, it is commonly supposed that problems about the nature of truth are intimately bound up with questions as to the accessibility and autonomy of facts in various domains: Questions about whether the facts can be known, and whether they can exist independently of our capacity to discover them (Dummett, 1978, and Putnam, 1981). One might reason, for example, that if T is true means nothing more than T will be verified, then certain forms of scepticism, specifically, those that doubt the correctness of our methods of verification, that will be precluded, and that the facts will have been revealed as dependent on human practices. Alternatively, it might be said that if truth were an inexplicable, primitive, non-epistemic property, then the fact that T is true would be completely independent of us. Moreover, we could, in that case, have no reason to assume that the propositions we believe in, that in adopting its property, so scepticism would be unavoidable. In a similar vein, it might be thought that as special, and perhaps undesirable features of the deflationary approach, is that truth is deprived of such metaphysical or epistemological implications.

Upon closer scrutiny, in that, it is far from clear that there exists any account of truth with consequences regarding the accessibility or autonomy of non-semantic matters. For although an account of truth may be expected to have such implications for facts of the form 'T' is true, it cannot be assumed without further argument that the same conclusions will apply to the fact 'T'. For it cannot be assumed that 'T' and 'T' are true and is equivalent to one another given the account of true that is being employed. Of course, if truth is defined in the way that the deflationist proposes, then the equivalence holds by definition. Nevertheless, if truth is defined by reference to some metaphysical or epistemological characteristic, then the equivalence schema is thrown into doubt, pending some demonstration that the trued predicate, in the sense assumed, will be satisfied in as far as there are thought to be epistemological problems hanging over 'T's' that do not threaten 'T' is true, giving the needed demonstration will be difficult. Similarly, if truth is so defined that the fact, 'T' is felt to be more, or less, independent of human practices than the fact that 'T' is true, then again, it is unclear that the equivalence schema will hold. It would seem, therefore, that the attempt to base epistemological or metaphysical conclusions on a theory of truth must fail because in any such attempt the equivalence schema will be simultaneously relied on and undermined.

The most influential idea in the theory of meaning in the past hundred yeas is the thesis that meaning of an indicative sentence is given by its truth-conditions. On this conception, to understand a sentence is to know its truth-conditions. The conception was first clearly formulated by Frége (1848-1925), was developed in a distinctive way by the early Wittgenstein (1889-1951), and is a leading idea of Davidson (1917-). The conception has remained so central that those who offer opposing theories characteristically define their position by reference to it.

The conception of meaning as truth-conditions necessarily are not and should not be advanced as a complete account of meaning. For instance, one who understands a language must have some idea of the range of speech acts conventionally acted by the various types of a sentence in the language, and must have some idea of the significance of various kinds of speech acts. The claim of the theorist of truth-conditions should as an alternative is targeted on the notion of content: If two indicative sentences differ in what they strictly and literally say, then this difference is fully accounted for by the difference in their truth-conditions. Most basic to truth-conditions is simply of a statement that is the condition the world must meet if the statement is to be true. To know this condition is equivalent to knowing the meaning of the statement. Although this sounds as if it gives a solid anchorage for meaning, some of the security disappears when it turns out that the truth condition can only be defined by repeating the very same statement, as a truth condition of snow is white is that snow is white, the truth condition of Britain would have capitulated had Hitler invaded is the Britain would have capitulated had Hitler invaded. It is disputed whether this element of running-on-the-spot disqualifies truth conditions from playing the central role in a substantive theory of meaning. Truth-conditional theories of meaning are sometimes opposed by the view that to know the meaning of a statement is to be able to use it in a network of inferences.

Whatever it is that makes, what would otherwise be mere sounds and inscriptions into instruments of communication and understanding. The philosophical problem is to demystify this power, and to relate it to what we know of ourselves and the world. Contributions to the study include the theory of speech acts and the investigation of communication and the relationship between words and ideas and the world and surrounding surfaces, by which some persons express by a sentence are often a function of the environment in which he or she is placed. For example, the disease I refer to by a term like arthritis or the kind of tree I refer to as a maple will be defined by criteria of which I know next to nothing. The raises the possibility of imagining two persons in alternatively differently environmental, but in which everything appears the same to each of them, but between them they define a space of philosophical problems. They are the essential components of understanding nd any intelligible proposition that is true must be capable of being understood. Such that which is expressed by an utterance or sentence, the proposition or claim made about the world may by extension, the content of a predicated or other sub-sentential component is what it contributes to the content of sentences that contain it. The nature of content is the cental concern of the philosophy of language.

In particularly, the problems of indeterminancy of translation, inscrutability of reference, language, predication, reference, rule following, semantics, translation, and the topics referring to subordinate headings associated with logic. The loss of confidence in determinate meaning (Each is another encoding) is an element common both to postmodern uncertainties in the theory of criticism, and to the analytic tradition that follows writers such as Quine (1908-). Still it may be asked, why should we suppose that fundamental epistemic notions should be keep an account of for in behavioural terms what grounds are there for supposing that p knows p is a subjective matter in the prestigiousness of its statement between some subject statement and physical theory of physically forwarded of an objection, between nature and its mirror? The answer is that the only alternative seems to be to take knowledge of inner states as premises from which our knowledge of other things is normally implied, and without which our knowledge of other things is normally inferred, and without which knowledge would be ungrounded. However, it is not really coherent, and does not in the last analysis make sense, to suggest that human knowledge have foundations or grounds. It should be remembered that to say that truth and knowledge can only be judged by the standards of our own day is not to say that it is less meaningful nor is it more cut off from the world, which we had supposed. Conjecturing it is as just that nothing counts as justification, unless by reference to what we already accept, and that at that place is no way to get outside our beliefs and our oral communication so as to find some experiment with others than coherence. The fact is that the professional philosophers have thought it might be otherwise, since one and only they are haunted by the clouds of epistemological scepticism.

What Quine opposes as residual Platonism is not so much the hypostasising of non-physical entities as the notion of correspondence with things as the final court of appeal for evaluating present practices. Unfortunately, Quine, for all that it is incompatible with its basic insights, substitutes for this correspondence to physical entities, and specially to the basic entities, whatever they turn out to be, of physical science. Nevertheless, when their doctrines are purified, they converge on a single claim. That no account of knowledge can depend on the assumption of some privileged relations to reality. Their work brings out why an account of knowledge can amount only to a description of human behaviour.

What, then, is to be said of these inner states, and of the direct reports of them that have played so important a role in traditional epistemology? For a person to feel is nothing else than for him to have an ability to make a certain type of non-inferential report, to attribute feelings to infants is to acknowledge in them latent abilities of this innate kind. Non-conceptual, non-linguistic knowledge of what feelings or sensations is like is attributively to beings on the basis of potential membership of our community. Infants and the more attractive animals are credited with having feelings on the basis of that spontaneous sympathy that we extend to anything humanoid, in contrast with the mere response to stimuli attributed to photoelectric cells and to animals about which no one feels sentimentally. Supposing that moral prohibition against hurting infants is consequently wrong and the better-looking animals are; those moral prohibitions grounded in their possession of feelings. The relation of dependence is really the other way round. Similarly, we could not be mistaken in supposing that a four-year-old child has knowledge, but no one-year-old, any more than we could be mistaken in taking the word of a statute that eighteen-year-old can marry freely but seventeen-year-old cannot. (There is no more ontological ground for the distinction that may suit us to make in the former case than in the later.) Again, such a question as Are robots conscious? Calling for a decision on our part whether or not to treat robots as members of our linguistic community. All this is a piece with the insight brought into philosophy by Hegel (1770-1831), that the individual apart from his society is just another animal.

Willard van Orman Quine, the most influential American philosopher of the latter half of the 20th century, when after the wartime period in naval intelligence, punctuating the rest of his career with extensive foreign lecturing and travel. Quines early work was on mathematical logic, and issued in A System of Logistic (1934), Mathematical Logic (1940), and Methods of Logic (1950), whereby it was with the collection of papers from a Logical Point of View (1953) that his philosophical importance became widely recognized. Quines work dominated concern with problems of convention, meaning, and synonymy cemented by Word and Object (1960), in which the indeterminancy of radical translation first takes centre-stage. In this and many subsequent writings Quine takes a bleak view of the nature of the language with which we ascribe thoughts and beliefs to ourselves and others. These intentional idioms resist smooth incorporation into the scientific world view, and Quine responds with scepticism toward them, not quite endorsing eliminativism, but regarding them as second-rate idioms, unsuitable for describing strict and literal facts. For similar reasons he has consistently expressed suspicion of the logical and philosophical propriety of appeal to logical possibilities and possible worlds. The language that are properly behaved and suitable for literal and true descriptions of the world as those of mathematics and science. The entities to which our best theories refer must be taken with full seriousness in our ontologies, although an empiricist. Quine thus supposes that the abstract objects of set theory are required by science, and therefore exist. In the theory of knowledge Quine associated with a holistic view of verification, conceiving of a body of knowledge in terms of a web touching experience at the periphery, but with each point connected by a network of relations to other points.

Quine is also known for the view that epistemology should be naturalized, or conducted in a scientific spirit, with the object of investigation being the relationship, in human beings, between the voice of experience and the outputs of belief. Although Quines approaches to the major problems of philosophy have been attacked as betraying undue scientism and sometimes behaviourism, the clarity of his vision and the scope of his writing made him the major focus of Anglo-American work of the past forty years in logic, semantics, and epistemology. As well as the works cited his writings cover The Ways of Paradox and Other Essays (1966), Ontological Relativity and Other Essays (1969), Philosophy of Logic (1970), The Roots of Reference (1974) and The Time of My Life: An Autobiography (1985).

Coherence is a major player in the theatre of knowledge. There are cogence theories of belief, truth and justification, as these are to combine themselves in the various ways to yield theories of knowledge coherence theories of belief are concerned with the content of beliefs. Consider a belief you now have, the beliefs that you are reading a page in a book, in so, that what makes that belief the belief that it is? What makes it the belief that you are reading a page in a book than the belief that you have a monster in the garden?

One answer is that the belief has a coherent place or role in a system of beliefs, perception or the having the perceptivity that has its influence on beliefs. As, you respond to sensory stimuli by believing that you are reading a page in a book than believing that you have a monster in the garden. Belief has an influence on action, or its belief is a desire to act, if belief will differentiate the differences between them, that its belief is a desire or if you were to believe that you are reading a page than if you believed in something about a monster. Sortal perceptivals hold to the accountability of the perceptivity and action that are indeterminate to its content if its belief is the action as if stimulated by its inner and latent coherence in that of your belief, however. The same stimuli may produce various beliefs and various beliefs may produce the same action. The role that gives the belief the content it has is the role it plays within a network of relations to other beliefs, some latently causal than others that relate to the role in inference and implication. For example, I infer different things from believing that I am reading a page in a book than from any other belief, justly as I infer about other beliefs.

The information of perceptibility and the output of an action supplement the central role of the systematic relations the belief has to other belief, but the systematic relations give the belief the specific contentual representation it has. They are the fundamental source of the content of belief. That is how coherence comes in. A belief has the representational content by which it does because of the way in which it coheres within a system of beliefs (Rosenberg, 1988). We might distinguish weak coherence theories of the content of beliefs from stronger coherence theories. Weak coherence theories affirm that coherence is one determinant of the representation given that the contents are of belief. Strong coherence theories of the content of belief affirm that coherence is the sole determinant of the contentual representations of belief.

When we turn from belief to justification, we confront a similar group of coherence theories. What makes one belief justified and another not? Again, there is a distinction between weak and strong theoretic principles that govern its theory of coherence. Weak theories tell us that the ways in which a belief coheres with a background system of beliefs are one determinant of justification, other typical determinants being perception, memory, and intuitive projection, are, however strong theories, or dominant projections are in coherence to justification as solely a matter of how a belief coheres with a system of latent hierarchal beliefs. There is, nonetheless, another distinction that cuts across the distinction between weak and strong coherence theories between positive and negative coherence theory (Pollock, 1986). A positive coherence theory tells us that if a belief coheres with a background system of belief, then the belief is justifiable. A negative coherence theory tells us that if a belief fails to cohere with a background system of beliefs, then the belief is not justifiable. We might put this by saying that, according to the positivity of a coherence theory, coherence has the power to produce justification, while according to its being adhered by negativity, the coherence theory has only the power to nullify justification.

A strong coherence theory of justification is a formidable combination by which a positive and a negative theory tell us that a belief is justifiable if and only if it coheres with a background system of inter-connectivity of beliefs. Coherence theories of justification and knowledge have most often been rejected for being unable to deal with an accountable justification toward the perceptivity upon the projection of knowledge (Audi, 1988, and Pollock, 1986), and, therefore, considering a perceptual example that will serve as a kind of crucial test will be most appropriate. Suppose that a person, call her Julie, and works with a scientific instrumentation that has a gauging measure upon temperatures of liquids in a container. The gauge is marked in degrees, she looks at the gauge and sees that the reading is 105 degrees. What is she justifiably to believe, and why? Is she, for example, justified in believing that the liquid in the container is 105 degrees? Clearly, that depends on her background beliefs. A weak coherence theorist might argue that, though her belief that she sees the shape 105 is immediately justified as direct sensory evidence without appeal to a background system, the belief that the location in the container is 105 degrees results from coherence with a background system of latent beliefs that affirm to the shaping perceptivity that its 105 as visually read to be 105 degrees on the gauge that measures the temperature of the liquid in the container. This, nonetheless, of a weak coherence view that combines coherence with direct perceptivity as its evidence, in that the foundation of justification, is to account for the justification of our beliefs.

A strong coherence theory would go beyond the claim of the weak coherence theory to affirm that the justification of all beliefs, including the belief that one sees the shaping to sensory data that holds accountably of a measure of 105, or even the more cautious belief that one sees a shape, resulting from the perceptivals of coherence theory, in that it coheres with a background system. One may argue for this strong coherence theory in a number of different ways. One ligne or medium through which to appeal to the coherence theory of contentual representations. If the content of the perceptual belief results from the relations of the belief to other beliefs in a network system of beliefs, then one may notably argue that the justification of perceptivity, that the belief is a resultant from which its relation of the belief to other beliefs, in the network system of beliefs is in argument for the strong coherence theory is that without any assumptive reason that the coherence theory of contentual beliefs, in as much as the supposed causes that only produce the consequences we expect. Consider the very cautious belief that I see a shape. How may the justifications for that perceptual belief are an existent result that is characterized of its material coherence with a background system of beliefs? What might the background system tell us that would justify that belief? Our background system contains a simple and primal theory about our relationship to the world and surrounding surfaces that we perceive as it is or should be believed. To come to the specific point at issue, we believe that we can tell a shape when we see one, completely differentiated its form as perceived to sensory data, that we are to trust of ourselves about such simple matters as whether we see a shape before us or not, as in the acceptance of opening to nature the inter-connectivity between belief and the progression through which is acquired from past experiential conditions of application, and not beyond deception. Moreover, when Julie sees the believing desire to act upon what either coheres with a weak or strong coherence of theory, she shows that its belief, as a measurable quality or entity of 105, has the essence in as much as there is much more of a structured distinction of circumstance, which is not of those that are deceptive about whether she sees that shape or sincerely does not see of its shaping distinction, however. Visible light is good, and the numeral shapes are large, readily discernible and so forth. These are beliefs that Trust has single handedly authenticated reasons for justification. Her successive malignance to sensory access to data involved is justifiably a subsequent belief, in that with those beliefs, and so she is justified and creditable.

The philosophical; problems include discovering whether belief differs from other varieties of assent, such as acceptance discovering to what extent degrees of belief is possible, understanding the ways in which belief is controlled by rational and irrational factors, and discovering its links with other properties, such as the possession of conceptual or linguistic skills. This last set of problems includes the question of whether prelinguistic infants or animals are properly said to have beliefs.

Thus, we might think of coherence as inference to the best explanation based on a background system of beliefs, since we are not aware of such inferences for the most part, the inferences must be interpreted as unconscious inferences, as information processing, based on or finding the background system that proves most convincing of acquiring its act and used from the motivational force that its underlying and hidden desire are to do so. One might object to such an account on the grounds that not all justifiable inferences are self-explanatory, and more generally, the account of coherence may, at best, is ably successful to competitions that are based on background systems (BonJour, 1985, and Lehrer, 1990). The belief that one sees a shape competes with the claim that one does not, with the claim that one is deceived, and other sceptical objections. The background system of beliefs informs one that one is acceptingly trustworthy and enables one to meet the objections. A belief coheres with a background system just in case it enables one to meet the sceptical objections and in the way justifies one in the belief. This is a standard strong coherence theory of justification (Lehrer, 1990).

Illustrating the relationship between positive and negative coherence theories in terms of the standard coherence theory is easy. If some objection to a belief cannot be met in terms of the background system of beliefs of a person, then the person is not justified in that belief. So, to return to Julie, suppose that she has been told that a warning light has been installed on her gauge to tell her when it is not functioning properly and that when the red light is on, the gauge is malfunctioning. Suppose that when she sees the reading of 105, she also sees that the red light is on. Imagine, finally, that this is the first time the red light has been on, and, after years of working with the gauge, Julie, who has always placed her trust in the gauge, believes what the gauge tells her, that the liquid in the container is at 105 degrees. Though she believes what she reads is at 105 degrees is not a justified belief because it fails to cohere with her background belief that the gauge is malfunctioning. Thus, the negative coherence theory tells us that she is not justified in her belief about the temperature of the contents in the container. By contrast, when the red light is not illuminated and the background system of trust tells her that under such conditions that gauge is a trustworthy indicator of the temperature of the liquid in the container, then she is justified. The positive coherence theory tells us that she is justified in her belief because her belief coheres with her background system of trust tells she that under such conditions that gauge is a trustworthy indicator of the temperature of the liquid in the container, then she is justified. The positive coherence theory tells us that she is justified in her belief because her belief coheres with her background system continues as a trustworthy system.

The foregoing of coherence theories of justification have a common feature, namely, that they are what is called internalistic theories of justification what makes of such a view are the absence of any requirement that the person for whom the belief is justified have any cognitive access to the relation of reliability in question. Lacking such access, such a person will usually, have no reason for thinking the belief is true or likely to be true, but will, on such an account, are none the lesser to appear epistemologically justified in accepting it. Thus, such a view arguably marks a major break from the modern epistemological traditions, which identifies epistemic justification with having a reason, perhaps even a conclusive reason, for thinking that the belief is true. An epistemologist working within this tradition is likely to feel that the externalist, than offering a competing account of the same concept of epistemic justification with which the traditional epistemologist is concerned, has simply changed the subject.

They are theories affirming that coherence is a matter of internal relations between beliefs and that justification is a matter of coherence. If, then, justification is solely a matter of internal relations between beliefs, we are left with the possibility that the internal relations might fail to correspond with any external reality. How, one might object, can be to assume the including of interiority. A subjective notion of justification bridge the gap between mere true belief, which might be no more than a lucky guess, and knowledge, which must be grounded in some connexion between internal subjective conditions and external objective realities?

The answer is that it cannot and that something more than justified true belief is required for knowledge. This result has, however, been established quite apart from consideration of coherence theories of justification. What are required maybes put by saying that the justification that one must be undefeated by errors in the background system of beliefs? Justification is undefeated by errors just in case any correction of such errors in the background system of belief would sustain the justification of the belief on the basis of the corrected system. So knowledge, on this sort of positivity is acclaimed by the coherence theory, which is the true belief that coheres with the background belief system and corrected versions of that system. In short, knowledge is true belief plus justification resulting from coherence and undefeated by error (Lehrer, 1990). The connexion between internal subjective conditions of belief and external objectivity are from which realities result from the required correctness of our beliefs about the relations between those conditions and realities. In the example of Julie, she believes that her internal subjectivity to conditions of sensory data in which the experience and perceptual beliefs are connected with the external objectivity in which reality is the temperature of the liquid in the container in a trustworthy manner. This background belief is essential to the justification of her belief that the temperature of the liquid in the container is 105 degrees, and the correctness of that background belief is essential to the justification remaining undefeated. So our background system of beliefs contains a simple theory about our relation to the external world that justifies certain of our beliefs that cohere with that system. For instance, such justification to convert to knowledge, that theory must be sufficiently free from error so that the coherence is sustained in corrected versions of our background system of beliefs. The correctness of the simple background theory provides the connexion between the internal condition and external reality.

The coherence theory of truth arises naturally out of a problem raised by the coherence theory of justification. The problem is that anyone seeking to determine whether she has knowledge is confined to the search for coherence among her beliefs. The sensory experiences she has been deaf-mute until they are represented in the form of some perceptual belief. Beliefs are the engines that pull the train of justification. Nevertheless, what assurance do we have that our justification is based on true beliefs? What justification do we have that any of our justifications are undefeated? The fear that we might have none, that our beliefs might be the artifacts of some deceptive demon or scientist, leads to the quest to reduce truth to some form, perhaps an idealized form, of justification (Rescher, 1973, and Rosenberg, 1980). That would close the threatening sceptical gap between justification and truth. Suppose that a belief is true if and only if it is justifiable of some person. For such a person there would be no gap between justification and truth or between justification and undefeated justification. Truth would be coherence with some ideal background system of beliefs, perhaps one expressing a consensus among systems or some consensus among belief systems or some convergence toward a consensus. Such a view is theoretically attractive for the reduction it promises, but it appears open to profound objectification. One is that there is a consensus that we can all be wrong about at least some matters, for example, about the origins of the universe. If there is a consensus that we can all be wrong about something, then the consensual belief system rejects the equation of truth with the consensus. Consequently, the equation of truth with coherence with a consensual belief system is itself incoherent.

Coherence theories of the content of our beliefs and the justification of our beliefs themselves cohere with our background systems but coherence theories of truth do not. A defender of coherentism must accept the logical gap between justified belief and truth, but may believe that our capacities suffice to close the gap to yield knowledge. That view is, at any rate, a coherent one.

What makes a belief justified and what makes a true belief knowledge? Thinking that whether a belief deserves one of these appraisals is natural depends on what causal subject to have the belief. In recent decades a number of epistemologists have pursed this plausible idea with a variety of specific proposals. Some causal theories of knowledge have it that a true belief that 'p' is knowledge just in case it has the right causal connexion to the fact that 'p'. Such a criterion can be applied only to cases where the fact that p is a sort that can enter causal relations, this seems to exclude mathematically and other necessary facts and perhaps any fact expressed by a universal generalization, and proponents of this sort of criterion have usually of this sort of criterion have usually supposed that it is limited to perceptual knowledge of particular facts about the subjects environment.

For example, Armstrong (1973), proposed that a belief of form This (perceived) object is 'F' is (non-inferential) knowledge if and only if the belief is a completely reliable sign that the perceived object is 'F', that is, the fact that the object is 'F' contributed to causing the belief and its doing so depended on properties of the believer such that the laws of nature dictated that, for any subject 'χ' is to occur, and so thus a perceived object of 'y', if 'χ' undergoing those properties are for us to believe that 'y' is 'F', then 'y' is 'F'. (Dretske (1981) offers a similar account, in terms of the beliefs being caused by a signal received by the perceiver that carries the information that the object is 'F'.

This sort of condition fails, however, to be sufficient for non-inferential perceptual knowledge because it is compatible with the beliefs being unjustified, and an unjustifiable belief cannot be knowledge. For example, suppose that your mechanisms for colour perception are working well, but you have been given good reason to think otherwise, to think, say, that the substantive primary colours that are perceivable, that things look chartreuse to you and chartreuse things look magenta. If you fail to heed these reasons you have for thinking that your colour perception or sensory data is a way. Believing in a thing, which looks to blooms of vividness that you are to believe of its chartreuse, your belief will fail to be justified and will therefore fail to be knowledge, even though it is caused by the things being magenta in such a way as to be a completely reliable sign, or to carry the information, in that the thing is one of the subtractive primary colour, in fact of a purplish-red orientation.

One could fend off this sort of counterexample by simply adding to the causal condition the requirement that the belief be justified, buy this enriched condition would still be insufficient. Suppose, for example, that in nearly all people, but not in you, as it happens, causes the aforementioned aberration in colour perceptions. The experimenter tells you that you have taken such a drug but then says, no, hold off a minute, the pill you took was just a placebo, suppose further, that this last thing the experimenter tells you is false. Her telling you that it was a false statement, and, again, telling you this gives you justification for believing of a thing that looks a subtractive primary colour to you that it is a sensorial primary colour, in that the fact you were to expect that the experimenters last statements were false, making it the case that your true belief is not knowledgeably correct, thought as though to satisfy its causal condition.

Goldman (1986) has proposed an importantly different causal criterion namely, that a true belief is knowledge, if it is produced by a type of process that is globally and locally reliable. Causing true beliefs is sufficiently high is globally reliable if its propensity. Local reliability has to do with whether the process would have produced a similar but false belief in certain counterfactual situations alternative to the actual situation. This way of marking off true beliefs that are knowledge does not require the fact believed to be casually related to the belief, and so it could in principle apply to knowledge of any kind of truth.

Goldman requires that global reliability of the belief-producing process for the justification of a belief, he requires it also for knowledge because justification is required for knowledge, in what requires for knowledge but does not require for justification, which is locally reliable. His idea is that a justified true belief is knowledge if the type of process that produced it would not have produced it in any relevant counterfactual situation in which it is false. The relevant alternative account of knowledge can be motivated by noting that other concepts exhibit the same logical structure. Two examples of this are the concept flat and the concept empty (Dretske, 1981). Both appear to be absolute concepts-A space is empty only if it does not contain anything and a surface is flat only if it does not have any bumps. However, the absolute character of these concepts is relative to a standard. In the case of flat, there is a standard for what counts as a bump and in the case of empty, there is a standard for what counts as a thing. To be flat is to be free of any relevant bumps and to be empty is to be devoid of all relevant things.

Nevertheless, the human mind abhors a vacuum. When an explicit, coherent world-view is absent, it functions on the basis of a tactic one. A tactic world-view is not subject to a critical evaluation, and it can easily harbour inconsistencies. Indeed, our tactic set of beliefs about the nature of reality is made of contradictory bits and pieces. The dominant component is a leftover from another period, the Newtonian clock universe still lingers as we cling to this old and tired model because we know of nothing else that can take its place. Our condition is the condition of a culture that is in the throes of a paradigm shift. A major paradigm shift is complex and difficult because a paradigm holds us captive: We see reality through it, as through coloured glasses, but we do not know that, we are convinced that we see reality as it is. Hence the appearance of a new and different paradigm is often incomprehensible. To someone raised believing that the Earth is flat, the suggestion that the Earth is spherical would seem preposterous: If the Earth were spherical, would not the poor antipodes fall down into the sky?

Yet, as we now face a new millennium, we are forced to face this challenge. The fate of the planet is in question, and it was brought to its present precarious condition largely because of our trust in the Newtonian paradigm. As Newtonian world-view has to go, and, if one looks carefully, the main feature of the new, emergent paradigm can be discerned. The search for these features is what was the influence of a fading paradigm. All paradigms include subterranean realms of tactic assumptions, the influence of which outlasts the adherence to the paradigm itself.

The first ligne of exploration suggests the weird aspects of the quantum theory, with fertile grounds for our feeling of which should disappear in inconsistencies with the prevailing world-view. This feeling is in replacing by the new one, i.e., if one believes that the Earth is flat, the story of Magellan's travels is quite puzzling: How travelling due west is possible for a ship and, without changing direct. Arrive at its place of departure? Obviously, when the flat-Earth paradigm is replaced by the belief that Earth is spherical, the puzzle is instantly resolved.

The founders of Relativity and quantum mechanics were deeply engaging but incomplete, in that none of them attempted to construct a philosophical system, however, that the mystery at the heart of the quantum theory called for a revolution in philosophical outlooks. During which time, the 1920s, when quantum mechanics reached maturity, began the construction of a full-blooded philosophical system that was based not only on science but on nonscientific modes of knowledge as well. As, the fading influence drawn upon the paradigm goes well beyond its explicit claim. We believe, as the scenists and philosophers did, that when we wish to find out the truth about the universe, nonscientific nodes of processing human experiences can be ignored, poetry, literature, art, music are all wonderful, but, in relation to the quest for knowledge of the universe, they are irrelevant. Yet, it was Alfred North Whitehead who pointed out the fallacy of this speculative assumption. In this, as well as in other aspects of thinking of some reality in which are the building blocks of reality are not material atoms but throbs of experience. Whitehead formulated his system in the late 1920s, and yet, as far as I know, the founders of quantum mechanics were unaware of it. It was not until 1963 that J. M. Burgers pointed out that its philosophy accounts very well for the main features of the quanta, especially the weird ones, enabling as in some aspects of reality is higher or deeper than others, and if so, what is the structure of such hierarchical divisions? What of our place in the universe? Finally, what is the relationship between the great aspiration within the lost realms of nature? An attempt to endow us with a cosmological meaning in such a universe seems totally absurd, and, yet, this very universe is just a paradigm, not the truth. When you reach its end, you may be willing to join the alternate view as accorded to which, surprisingly bestow us with what is restored, although in a post-postmodern context.

The philosophical implications of quantum mechanics have been regulated by subjective matters, as to emphasis the connections between what I believe, in that investigations of such interconnectivity are anticipatorially the hesitations that are an exclusion held within the western traditions, however, the philosophical thinking, from Plato to Platinous had in some aspects of interpretational presentation of her expression of a consensus of the physical community. Other aspects are shared by some and objected to (sometimes vehemently) by others. Still other aspects express my own views and convictions, as turning about to be more difficult that anticipated, discovering that a conversational mode would be helpful, but, their conversations with each other and with me in hoping that all will be not only illuminating but finding to its read may approve in them, whose dreams are dreams among others than themselves.

These examples make it seem likely that, if there is a criterion for what makes an alternative situation relevant that will save Goldmans claim about reliability and the acceptance of knowledge, it will not be simple.

The interesting thesis that counts as a causal theory of justification, in the meaning of causal theory intend of the belief that is justified just in case it was produced by a type of process that is globally reliable, that is, its propensity to produce true beliefs-that can be defined to a favourably bringing close together the proportion of the belief and to what it produces, or would produce where it used as much as opportunity allows, that is true-is sufficiently that a belief acquires favourable epistemic status by having some kind of reliable linkage to the truth. Variations of this view have been advanced for both knowledge and justified belief. The first formulations of are reliably in its account of knowing appeared in if not by F.P. Ramsey (1903-30) who made important contributions to mathematical logic, probability theory, the philosophy of science and economics. Instead of saying that quarks have such-and-such properties, the Ramsey sentence says that it is moderately something that has those properties. If the process is repeated for all of the theoretical terms, the sentence gives the topic-neutral structure of the theory, but removes any implication that we know what the term so covered have as a meaning. It leaves open the possibility of identifying the theoretical item with whatever, but it is that best fits the description provided, thus, substituting the term by a variable, and existentially qualifying into the result. Ramsey was one of the first thinkers to accept a redundancy theory of truth, which he combined its radical views of the function of many kinds of the proposition. Neither generalizations, nor causal propositions, not those treating probabilities or ethics, described facts, but each has a different specific function in our intellectual commentators on the early works of Wittgenstein, and his continuing friendship with the latter liked to Wittgensteins return to Cambridge and to philosophy in 1929.

In the later period the emphasis shifts dramatically to the actions of people and the role linguistic activities play in their lives. Thus, whereas in the Tractatus language is placed in a static, formal relationship with the world, in the later work Wittgenstein emphasis its use in the context of standardized social activities of ordering, advising, requesting, measuring, counting, excising concerns for each other, and so on. These different activities are thought of as so many language games that together make or a form of life. Philosophy typically ignores this diversity, and in generalizing and abstracting distorts the real nature of its subject-matter. In addition to the Tractatus and the`investigations collections of Wittgensteins work published posthumously include Remarks on the Foundations of Mathematics (1956), Notebooks (1914-1916) (1961), Pholosophische Bemerkungen (1964), Zettel (1967, and On Certainty (1969).

Clearly, there are many forms of Reliabilism. Just as there are many forms of Foundationalism and coherence. How is Reliabilism related to these other two theories of justification? It is usually regarded as a rival. This is aptly so, in as far as Foundationalism and Coherentism traditionally focussed on purely evidential relations than psychological processes, but Reliabilism might also be offered as a deeper-level theory, subsuming some of the precepts of either Foundationalism or Coherentism. Foundationalism says that there are basic beliefs, which acquire justification without dependence on inference, Reliabilism might rationalize this indicating that the basic beliefs are formed by reliable non-inferential processes. Coherence stresses the primary of systematicity in all doxastic decision-making. Reliabilism might rationalize this by pointing to increases in reliability that accrue from systematicity consequently, Reliabilism could complement foundationalism and coherence than completed with them.

These examples make it seem likely that, if there is a criterion for what makes an alternate situation relevant that will save Goldmans claim about local reliability and knowledge. Will did not be simple. The interesting thesis that counts as a causal theory of justification, in the making of causal theory intended for the belief as it is justified in case it was produced by a type of process that is globally reliable, that is, its propensity to produce true beliefs that can be defined, to a well-thought-of approximation, as the proportion of the beliefs it produces, or would produce where it used as much as opportunity allows, that is true is sufficiently relializable. Variations of this view have been advanced for both knowledge and justified belief, its first formulation of a reliability account of knowing appeared in the notation from F.P.Ramsey (1903-30). The theory of probability, he was the first to show how a personalists theory could be developed, based on a precise behavioural notion of preference and expectation. In the philosophy of language. Much of Ramsey's work was directed at saving classical mathematics from intuitionism, or what he called the Bolshevik menace of Brouwer and Weyl. In the theory of probability he was the first to show how a personalists theory could be developed, based on precise behavioural notation of preference and expectation. In the philosophy of language, Ramsey was one of the first thankers, which he combined with radical views of the function of many kinds of a proposition. Neither generalizations, nor causal propositions, nor those treating probability or ethics, describe facts, but each has a different specific function in our intellectual economy. Ramsey was one of the earliest commentators on the early work of Wittgenstein, and his continuing friendship with Wittgenstein.

Ramsey's sentence theory is the sentence generated by taking all the sentences affirmed in a scientific theory that use some term, e.g., quark. Replacing the term by a variable, and existentially quantifying into the result. Instead of saying that quarks have such-and-such properties, the Ramsey sentence says that there is something that has those properties. If the process is repeated for all of a group of the theoretical terms, the sentence gives the topic-neutral structure of the theory, but removes any implication that we know what the term so treated characterized. It leaves open the possibility of identifying the theoretical item with whatever, and it is that best fits the description provided. Virtually, all theories of knowledge. Of course, share an externalist component in requiring truth as a condition for known in. Reliabilism goes further, however, in trying to capture additional conditions for knowledge by ways of a nomic, counterfactual or other such external relations between belief and truth. Closely allied to the nomic sufficiency account of knowledge, primarily due to Dretshe (1971, 1981), A.I. Goldman (1976, 1986) and R. Nozick (1981). The core of this approach is that 'X's' belief that 'p' qualifies as knowledge just in case 'X' believes 'p', because of reasons that would not obtain unless p's being true, or because of a process or method that would not yield belief in 'p' if 'p' were not true. For example, 'X' would not have its current reasons for believing there is a telephone before it. Perhaps, would it not come to believe that this in the way it suits the purpose, thus, there is a differentiable fact of a reliable guarantor that the beliefs bing true. A stouthearted and valiant counterfactual approach says that 'X' knows that 'p' only if there is no relevant alternative situation in which 'p' is false but 'X' would still believe that a proposition 'p'; must be sufficient to eliminate all the alternatives to 'p' where an alternative to a proposition 'p' is a proposition incompatible with 'p'? That in, ones justification or evidence for 'p' must be sufficient for one to know that every alternative to 'p' is false. This element of our evolving thinking, about which knowledge is exploited by sceptical arguments. These arguments call our attentions to alternatives that our evidence sustains itself with no elimination. The sceptic inquires to how we know that we are not seeing a cleverly disguised mule. While we do have some evidence against the likelihood of such as deception, intuitively knowing that we are not so deceived is not strong enough for us. By pointing out alternate but hidden points of nature, in that we cannot eliminate, as well as others with more general application, as dreams, hallucinations, etc., the sceptic appears to show that every alternative is seldom. If ever, satisfied.

This conclusion conflicts with another strand in our thinking about knowledge, in that we know many things. Thus, there is a tension in our ordinary thinking about knowledge ~. We believe that knowledge is, in the sense indicated, an absolute concept and yet, we also believe that there are many instances of that concept.

If one finds absoluteness to be too central a component of our concept of knowledge to be relinquished, one could argue from the absolute character of knowledge to a sceptical conclusion (Unger, 1975). Most philosophers, however, have taken the other course, choosing to respond to the conflict by giving up, perhaps reluctantly, the absolute criterion. This latter response holds as sacrosanct our commonsense belief that we know many things (Pollock, 1979 and Chisholm, 1977). Each approach is subject to the criticism that it preserves one aspect of our ordinary thinking about knowledge at the expense of denying another. The theory of relevant alternatives can be viewed as an attempt to provide a more satisfactory response to this tension in our thinking about knowledge. It attempts to characterize knowledge in a way that preserves both our belief that knowledge is an absolute concept and our belief that we have knowledge.

Just as space, the classical questions include: Is space real? Is it some kind of mental construct or artefact of our ways of perceiving and thinking? Is it substantival or purely? relational? According to Substantivalism, space is an objective thing consisting of points or regions at which, or in which, things are located. Opposed to this is relationalism, according to which the only things that are real about space are the spatial (and temporal) relations between physical objects. Substantivalism was advocated by Clarke speaking for Newton, and relationalism by Leibniz, in their famous correspondence, and the debate continues today. There is also an issue whether the measure of space and time are objective, or whether an element of convention enters them. Whereby, the influential analysis of David Lewis suggests that a regularity hold as a matter of convention when it solves a problem of coordinating in a group. This means that it is to the benefit of each member to conform to the regularity, providing the others do so. Any number of solutions to such a problem may exist, for example, it is to the advantages of each of us to drive on the same side of the road as others, but indifferent whether we all drive o the right or the left. One solution or another may emerge for a variety of reasons. It is notable that on this account convections may arise naturally; they do not have to be the result of specific agreement. This frees the notion for use in thinking about such things as the origin of language or of political society.

The finding to a theory that magnifies the role of decisions, or free selection from among equally possible alternatives, in order to show that what appears to be objective or fixed by nature is in fact an artefact of human convention, similar to conventions of etiquette, or grammar, or law. Thus one might suppose that moral rules owe more to social convention than to anything imposed from outside, or hat supposedly inexorable necessities are in fact the shadow of our linguistic conventions. The disadvantage of conventionalism is that it must show that alternative, equally workable e conventions could have been adopted, and it is often easy to believe that, for example, if we hold that some ethical norm such as respect for promises or property is conventional, we ought to be able to show that human needs would have been equally well satisfied by a system involving a different norm, and this may be hard to establish.

A convention also suggested by Paul Grice (1913-88) directing participants in conversation to pay heed to an accepted purpose or direction of the exchange. Contributions made without paying this attention are liable to be rejected for other reasons than straightforward falsity: Something effectually unhelpful or inappropriate may meet with puzzlement or rejection. We can thus never infer fro the fact that it would be inappropriate to say something in some circumstance that what would be aid, were we to say it, would be false. This inference was frequently and in ordinary language philosophy, it being argued, for example, that since we do not normally say there sees to be a barn there when there is unmistakably a barn there, it is false that on such occasions there seems to be a barn there.

There are two main views on the nature of theories. According to the received view theories are partially interpreted axiomatic systems, according to the semantic view, a theory is a collection of models (Suppe, 1974). However, a natural language comes ready interpreted, and the semantic problem is no that of the specification but of understanding the relationship between terms of various categories (names, descriptions, predicates, adverbs . . .) and their meanings. An influential proposal is that this relationship is best understood by attempting to provide a truth definition for the language, which will involve giving terms and structure of different kinds have on the truth-condition of sentences containing them.

The axiomatic method . . . as, . . . a proposition lid down as one from which we may begin, an assertion that we have taken as fundamental, at least for the branch of enquiry in hand. The axiomatic method is that of defining as a set of such propositions, and the proof procedures or finding of how a proof ever gets started. Suppose I have as premises (1) p and (2) p ➞ q. Can I infer q? Only, it seems, if I am sure of, (3) (p & p ➞ q) ➞ q. Can I then infer q? Only, it seems, if I am sure that (4) (p & p ➞ q) ➞ q) ➞ q. For each new axiom (N) I need a further axiom (N + 1) telling me that the set so far implies q, and the regress never stops. The usual solution is to treat a system as containing not only axioms, but also rules of reference, allowing movement fro the axiom. The rule modus ponens allow us to pass from the first two premises to q. Charles Dodgson Lutwidge (1832-98) better known as Lewis Carrolls puzzle shows that it is essential to distinguish two theoretical categories, although there may be choice about which to put in which category.

This type of theory (axiomatic) usually emerges as a body of (supposes) truth that are not nearly organized, making the theory difficult to survey or study a whole. The axiomatic method is an idea for organizing a theory (Hilbert 1970): one tries to select from among the supposed truths a small number from which all others can be seen to be deductively inferable. This makes the theory rather more tractable since, in a sense, all the truth are contained in those few. In a theory so organized, the few truth from which all others are deductively inferred are called axioms. In that, just as algebraic and differential equations, which were used to study mathematical and physical processes, could they be made mathematical objects, so axiomatic theories, like algebraic and differential equations, which are means of representing physical processes and mathematical structures, could be made objects of mathematical investigation.

In the traditional (as in Leibniz, 1704), many philosophers had the conviction that all truth, or all truth about a particular domain, followed from a few principles. These principles were taken to be either metaphysically prior or epistemologically prior or in the fist sense, they were taken to be entities of such a nature that what exists is caused by them. When the principles were taken as epistemologically prior, that is, as axioms, they were taken to be epistemologically privileged either, e.g., self-evident, not needing to be demonstrated or (again, inclusive or) to be such that all truth do follow from them (by deductive inferences). Gödel (1984) showed that treating axiomatic theories as themselves mathematical objects, that mathematics, and even a small part of mathematics, elementary number theory, could not be axiomatized, that, more precisely, any class of axioms that in such that we could effectively decide, of any proposition, whether or not it was in the class, would be too small to capture all of the truth.

Gödel proved in 1929 that first-order predicate calculus is complete: any formula that is true under every interpretation is a theorem of the calculus: The propositional calculus or logical calculus whose expressions are letter present sentences or propositions, and constants representing operations on those propositions to produce others of higher complexity. The operations include conjunction, disjunction, material implication and negation (although these need not be primitive). Propositional logic was partially anticipated by the Stoics but researched maturity only with the work of Frége, Russell, and Wittgenstein.

The concept introduced by Frége of a function taking a number of names as arguments, and delivering one proposition as the value. The idea is that 'χ' loves 'y' is a propositional function, which yields the proposition John loves Mary from those two arguments (in that order). A propositional function is therefore roughly equivalent to a property or relation. In Principia Mathematica, Russell and Whitehead take propositional functions to be the fundamental function, since the theory of descriptions could be taken as showing that other expressions denoting functions are incomplete symbols.

Keeping in mind, the two classical truth-values that a statement, proposition, or sentence can take. It is supposed in classical (two-valued) logic, that each statement has one of these values, and none has both. A statement is then false if and only if it is not true. The basis of this scheme is that to each statement there corresponds a determinate truth condition, or way the world must be for it to be true, and otherwise false. Statements may be felicitous or infelicitous in other dimensions, polite, misleading, apposite, witty, etc., but truth is the central normative governing assertion. Considerations of vagueness may introduce greys into black-and-white scheme. For the issue of whether falsity is the only way of failing to be true.

Formally, it is nonetheless, that any suppressed premise or background framework of thought necessary to make an argument valid, or a position tenable. More formally, a presupposition has been defined as a proposition whose truth is necessary for either the truth or the falsity of another statement. Thus, if p presupposes q, q must be true for p to be either true or false. In the theory of knowledge of Robin George Collingwood (1889-1943), any propositions capable of truth or falsity stand on a bed of absolute presuppositions that are not properly capable of truth or falsity, since a system of thought will contain no way of approaching such a question. It was suggested by Peter Strawson, 1919-in opposition to Russells theory of definite descriptions, that there exists a King of France is a presupposition of the King of France is bald, the latter being neither true, nor false, if there is no King of France. It is, however, a little unclear weather the idea is that no statement at all is made in such a case, or whether a statement is made, but fails of being either true or false. The former option preserves classical logic, since we can still say that every statement is either true or false, but the latter does not, since in classical logic the law of bivalence holds, and ensures that nothing at all is presupposed for any proposition to be true or false. The introduction of presupposition therefore means that either a third truth-value is found, intermediate between truth and falsity, or that classical logic is preserved, but it is impossible to tell whether a particular sentence expresses a proposition that is a candidate for truth ad falsity, without knowing more than the formation rules of the language. Each suggestion carries costs, and there is some consensus that at least where definite descriptions are involved, examples like the one given are equally well handed by regarding the overall sentence false when the existence claim fails.

A proposition may be true or false it be said to take the truth-value true, and if the latter the truth-value false. The idea behind the term is the analogy between assigning a propositional variable one or other of these values, as a formula of the propositional calculus, and assigning an object as the value of many other variable. Logics with intermediate values are called many-valued logics. Then, a truth-function of a number of propositions or sentences is a function of them that has a definite truth-value, depend only on the truth-values of the constituents. Thus (p & q) is a combination whose truth-value is true when 'p' is true and 'q' is true, and false otherwise, '¬ p' is a truth-function of 'p', false when 'p' is true and true when 'p' is false. The way in which the value of the whole is determined by the combinations of values of constituents is presented in a truth table.

In whatever manner, truth of fact cannot be reduced to any identity and our only way of knowing them is empirically, by reference to the facts of the empirical world.

A proposition is knowable deductively if it can be known without experience of the specific course of events in the actual world. It may, however, be allowed that some experience is required to acquire the concepts involved in a deductive proposition. Some thing is knowable only empirical if it can be known deductively. The distinction given one of the fundamental problem areas of epistemology. The category of deductive propositions is highly controversial, since it is not clear how pure thought, unaided by experience, can give rise to any knowledge at all, and it has always been a concern of empiricism to deny that it can. The two great areas in which it seems to be so are logic and mathematics, so empiricists have commonly tried to show either that these are not areas of real, substantive knowledge, or that in spite of appearances their knowledge that we have in these areas is actually dependent on experience. The former ligne tries to show sense trivial or analytic, or matters of notation conventions of language. The latter approach is particularly y associated with Quine, who denies any significant slit between propositions traditionally thought of as speculatively, and other deeply entrenched beliefs that occur in our overall view of the world.

Another contested category is that of speculative concepts, supposed to be concepts that cannot be derived from experience, but which are presupposed in any mode of thought about the world, time, substance, causation, number, and self are candidates. The need for such concepts, and the nature of the substantive a prior I knowledge to which they give rise, is the central concern of Kant's Critique of Pure Reason.

Likewise, since their denial does not involve a contradiction, there is merely contingent: There could have been in other ways a hold of the actual world, but not every possible one. Some examples are Caesar crossed the Rubicon and Leibniz was born in Leipzig, as well as propositions expressing correct scientific generalizations. In Leibniz's view truth of fact rest on the principle of sufficient reason, which is a reason that it is so. This reason is that the actual world (by which he means the total collection of things past, present and future) is better than any other possible world and therefore created by God. The foundation of his thought is the conviction that to each individual there corresponds a complete notion, knowable only to God, from which is deducible all the properties possessed by the individual at each moment in its history. It is contingent that God actualizes te individual that meets such a concept, but his doing so is explicable by the principle of sufficient reason, whereby God had to actualize just that possibility in order for this to be the best of all possible worlds. This thesis is subsequently lampooned by Voltaire (1694-1778), in whom of which was prepared to take refuge in ignorance, as the nature of the soul, or the way to reconcile evil with divine providence.

In defending the principle of sufficient reason sometimes described as the principle that nothing can be so without there being a reason it is so. But the reason has to be of a particularly potent kind: eventually it has to ground contingent facts in necessities, and in particular in the reason an omnipotent and perfect being would have for actualizing one possibility than another. Among the consequences of the principle is Leibniz's relational doctrine of space, since if space were an infinite box there could be no reason for the world to be at one point in rather than another, and God placing it at any point violate the principle. In Abelards' (1079-1142), as in Leibniz, the principle eventually forces te recognition that the actual world is the best of all possibilities, since anything else would be inconsistent with the creative power that actualizes possibilities.

If truth consists in concept containment, then it seems that all truth are analytic and hence necessary. If they are all necessary, surely they are all truth of reason. In that not every truth can be reduced to an identity in a finite number of steps; in some instances revealing the connexion between subject and predicate concepts would require an infinite analysis, while this may entail that we cannot prove such proposition as a prior, it does not appear to show that proposition could have ben false. Intuitively, it seems a better ground for supposing that it is a necessary truth of a special sort. A related question arises from the idea that truth of fact depend on Gods decision to create the best world: If it is part of the concept of this world that it is best, how could its existence be other than necessary? An accountable and responsively answered explanation would be so, that any relational question that brakes the norm lay eyes on its existence in the manner other than hypothetical necessities, i.e., it follows from Gods decision to create the world, but God had the power to create this world, but God is necessary, so how could he have decided to do anything else? Leibniz says much more about these matters, but it is not clear whether he offers any satisfactory solutions.

The view that the terms in which we think of some area is sufficiently infected with error for it to be better to abandon them than to continue to try to give coherent theories of their use. Eliminativism should be distinguished from scepticism that claims that we cannot know the truth about some area; eliminativism claims rather that there is no truth there to be known, in the terms that we currently think. An eliminativist about theology simply counsels abandoning the terms or discourse of theology, and that will include abandoning worries about the extent of theological knowledge.

Eliminativists in the philosophy of mind counsel abandoning the whole network of terms mind, consciousness, self, qualia that usher in the problems of mind and body. Sometimes the argument for doing this is that we should wait for a supposed future understanding of ourselves, based on cognitive science and better than any our current mental descriptions provide, sometimes it is supposed that physicalism shows that no mental description of ourselves could possibly be true.

Sceptical tendencies emerged in the 14th-century writings of Nicholas of Autrecourt. His criticisms of any certainty beyond the immediate deliverance of the senses and basic logic, and in particular of any knowledge of either intellectual or material substances, anticipate the later scepticism of Balye and Hume. The; latter distinguishes between Pyrrhonistic and excessive scepticism, which he regarded as unlivable, and the more mitigated scepticism that accepts every day or commonsense beliefs (not as the delivery of reason, but as due more to custom and habit), but is duly wary of the power of reason to give us much more. Mitigated scepticism is thus closer to the attitude fostered by ancient scepticism from Pyrrho through to Sexus Empiricus. Although the phrase Cartesian scepticism is sometimes used, Descartes himself was not a sceptic, but in the method of doubt, uses a sceptical scenario in order to begin the process of finding a secure mark of knowledge.

Descartes theory of knowledge starts with the quest for certainty, for an indubitable starting-point or foundation on the basis alone of which progress is possible. This is eventually found in the celebrated Cogito ergo sum: I think therefore I am. By locating the point of certainty in my own awareness of my own self, Descartes gives a first-person twist to the theory of knowledge that dominated them following centuries in spite of various counterattacks on behalf of social and public starting-point. The metaphysics associated with this priority is the famous Cartesian dualism, or separation of mind and matter into two different but interacting substances, Descartes rigorously and rightly sees that it takes divine dispensation to certify any relationship between the two realms thus divided, and to prove the reliability of the senses invokes a clear and distinct perception of highly dubious proofs of the existence of a benevolent deity. This has not met general acceptance: as Hume drily puts it, to have recourse to the veracity of the supreme Being, in order to prove the veracity of our senses, is surely making a very unexpected circuit.

In his own time Descartes conception of the entirely separate substance of the mind was recognized to give rise to insoluble problems of the nature of the causal connexion between the two. It also gives rise to the problem, insoluble in its own terms, of other minds. Descartes notorious denial that nonhuman animals are conscious is a stark illustration of the problem. In his conception of matter Descartes also gives preference to rational cogitation over anything derived from the senses. Since we can conceive of the matter of a ball of wax surviving changes to its sensible qualities, matter is not an empirical concept, but eventually an entirely geometrical one, with extension and motion as its only physical nature. Descartes thought, as reflected in Leibniz, that the qualities of sense experience have no resemblance to qualities of things, so that knowledge of the external world is essentially knowledge of structure rather than of filling. On this basis Descartes erects a remarkable physics. Since matter is in effect the same as extension there can be no empty space or void, since there is no empty space motion is not a question of occupying previously empty space, but is to be thought of in terms of vortices (like the motion of a liquid).

Although the structure of Descartes epistemology, theory of mind, and theory of matter have ben rejected many times, their relentless exposure of the hardest issues, their exemplary clarity, and even their initial plausibility, all contrive to make him the central point of reference for modern philosophy.

The self conceived as Descartes presents it in the first two Meditations: aware only of its own thoughts, and capable of disembodied existence, neither situated in a space nor surrounded by others. This is the pure self of I-ness that we are tempted to imagine as a simple unique thing that make up our essential identity. Descartes view that he could keep hold of this nugget while doubting everything else is criticized by Lichtenberg and Kant, and most subsequent philosophers of mind.

Foundationalism was associated with the ancient Stoics, and in the modern era with Descartes (1596-1650). Who discovered his foundations in the clear and distinct ideas of reason? Its main opponent is coherentism, or the view that a body of propositions mas be known without a foundation in certainty, but by their interlocking strength, than as a crossword puzzle may be known to have been solved correctly even if each answer, taken individually, admits of uncertainty. Difficulties at this point led the logical passivists to abandon the notion of an epistemological foundation altogether, and to flirt with the coherence theory of truth. It is widely accepted that trying to make the connexion between thought and experience through basic sentences depends on an untenable myth of the given.

While truth conditions of a statement is the condition the world must meet if the statement is to be true. To know this condition is equivalent go knowing the meaning of the statement. Although his sounds as if it gives a solid anchorage when in turns out that the truth condition can only be defined by repeating the very same statement. The truth condition of 'snow is white' is that snow is white, the truth condition of 'Britain would have capitulated had Hitler invaded' is that Britain would have capitulated had Hitler invaded. It is disputed whether this element of running-on-the-spot disqualifies truth conditions from playing the central role in a substantive theory of meaning. Truth-conditional theories of meaning are sometimes opposed by the view that to know the meaning of a statement is to be able to use it in an network of inferences.

The view that the role of sentences in inference gives a more important key to their meaning than their 'external' reflation to things in the world. The meaning of a sentence becomes its place in a network =of inferences that it legitimates. Also, known as functional role semantics, procedural semantics, or conceptual role semantics. The view bears some relation to the coherence theory of truth and suffers from the same suspicion that it divorces meaning from any suspicion ta it divorces meaning from any clear association with things in the world.

Still, in spite of these concerns, the problem, least of mention, is of defining knowledge in terms of true beliefs plus some favoured relations between the believer and the facts that began with Platos view in the Theaetetus, that knowledge is true belief, and some logos. Due of its nonsynthetic epistemology, the enterprising of studying the actual formation of knowledge by human beings, without aspiring to certify those processes as rational, or its proof against scepticism or even apt to yield the truth. Natural epistemology would therefore blend into the psychology of learning and the study of episodes in the history of science. The scope for external or philosophical reflection of the kind that might result in scepticism or its refutation is markedly diminished. Despite the fact that the terms of modernity are so distinguished as exponents of the approach include Aristotle, Hume, and J. S. Mills.

The task of the philosopher of a discipline would then be to reveal the correct method and to unmask counterfeits. Although this belief lay behind much positivist philosophy of science, few philosophers now subscribe to it. It places too well a confidence in the possibility of a purely previous first philosophy, or viewpoint beyond that of the work ones way of practitioners, from which their best efforts can be measured as good or bad. These standpoints now seem that too many philosophers to be fanciful, that the more modest of tasks that are actually adopted at various historical stages of investigation into different areas with the aim not so much of criticizing but more of systematization, in the presuppositions of a particular field at a particular tie. There is still a role for local methodological disputes within the community investigators of some phenomenon, with one approach charging that another is unsound or unscientific, but logic and philosophy will not, on the modern view, provide an independent arsenal of weapons for such battles, which indeed often come to seem more like political bids for ascendancy within a discipline.

This is an approach to the theory of knowledge that sees an important connexion between the growth of knowledge and biological evolution. An evolutionary epistemologist claims that the development of human knowledge processed through some natural selection process, the best example of which is Darwin's theory of biological natural selection. There is a widespread misconception that evolution proceeds according to some plan or direct, but it has neither, and the role of chance ensures that its future course will be unpredictable. Random variations in individual organisms create tiny differences in their Darwinian fitness. Some individuals have more offsprings than others, and the characteristics that increased their fitness thereby become more prevalent in future generations. Once upon a time, at least a mutation occurred in a human population in tropical Africa that changed the haemoglobin molecule in a way that provided resistance to malaria. This enormous advantage caused the new gene to spread, with the unfortunate consequence that sickle-cell anaemia came to exist.

Chance can influence the outcome at each stage: First, in the creation of genetic mutation, second, in wether the bearer lives long enough to show its effects, thirdly, in chance events that influence the individual's actual reproductive success, and fourth, in whether a gene even if favoured in one generation, is, happenstance, eliminated in the next, and finally in the many unpredictable environmental changes that will undoubtedly occur in the history of any group of organisms. As Harvard biologist Stephen Jay Gould has so vividly expressed that process over again, the outcome would surely be different. Not only might there not be humans, there might not even be anything like mammals.

We will often emphasis the elegance of traits shaped by natural selection, but the common idea that nature creates perfection needs to be analysed carefully. The extent to which evolution achieves perfection depends on exactly what you mean. If you mean Does natural selections always take the best path for the long-term welfare of a species? The answer is no. That would require adaption by group selection, and this is, unlikely. If you mean Does natural selection creates every adaption that would be valuable? The answer again, is no. For instance, some kinds of South American monkeys can grasp branches with their tails. The trick would surely also be useful to some African species, but, simply because of bad luck, none have it. Some combination of circumstances started some ancestral South American monkeys using their tails in ways that ultimately led to an ability to grab onto branches, while no such development took place in Africa. More usefulness of a trait does not necessitate a means in that what will understandably endure phylogenesis or evolution.

This is an approach to the theory of knowledge that sees an important connexion between the growth of knowledge and biological evolution. An evolutionary epistemologist claims that the development of human knowledge proceeds through some natural selection process, the best example of which is Darwin's theory of biological natural selection. The three major components of the model of natural selection are variation selection and retention. According to Darwin's theory of natural selection, variations are not pre-designed to do certain functions. Rather, these variations that do useful functions are selected. While those that do not employ of some coordinates in that are regainfully purposed are also, not to any of a selection, as duly influenced of such a selection, that may have responsibilities for the visual aspects of a variational intentionally occurs. In the modern theory of evolution, genetic mutations provide the blind variations: Blind in the sense that variations are not influenced by the effects they would have-the likelihood of a mutation is not correlated with the benefits or liabilities that mutation would confer on the organism, the environment provides the filter of selection, and reproduction provides the retention. Fatnesses are achieved because those organisms with features that make them less adapted for survival do not survive in connexion with other organisms in the environment that have features that are better adapted. Evolutionary epistemology applies this blind variation and selective retention model to the growth of scientific knowledge and to human thought processes overall.

The parallel between biological evolution and conceptual or epistemic evolution can be seen as either literal or analogical. The literal version of evolutionary epistemology deeds biological evolution as the main cause of the growth of knowledge. On this view, called the evolution of cognitive mechanic programs, by Bradie (1986) and the Darwinian approach to epistemology by Ruse (1986), that growth of knowledge occurs through blind variation and selective retention because biological natural selection itself is the cause of epistemic variation and selection. The most plausible version of the literal view does not hold that all human beliefs are innate but rather than the mental mechanisms that guide the acquisitions of non-innate beliefs are themselves innately and the result of biological natural selection. Ruse, (1986) demands of a version of literal evolutionary epistemology that he links to sociolology (Rescher, 1990).

On the analogical version of evolutionary epistemology, called the evolution of theories program, by Bradie (1986). The Spenserians approach (after the nineteenth century philosopher Herbert Spencer) by Ruse (1986), the development of human knowledge is governed by a process analogous to biological natural selection, rather than by an instance of the mechanism itself. This version of evolutionary epistemology, introduced and elaborated by Donald Campbell (1974) as well as Karl Popper, sees the [partial] fit between theories and the world as explained by a mental process of trial and error known as epistemic natural selection.

Both versions of evolutionary epistemology are usually taken to be types of naturalized epistemology, because both take some empirical facts as a starting point for their epistemological project. The literal version of evolutionary epistemology begins by accepting evolutionary theory and a materialist approach to the mind and, from these, constructs an account of knowledge and its developments. In contrast, the metaphorical version does not require the truth of biological evolution: It simply draws on biological evolution as a source for the model of natural selection. For this version of evolutionary epistemology to be true, the model of natural selection need only apply to the growth of knowledge, not to the origin and development of species. Crudely put, evolutionary epistemology of the analogical sort could still be true even if Creationism is the correct theory of the origin of species.

Although they do not begin by assuming evolutionary theory, most analogical evolutionary epistemologists are naturalized epistemologists as well, their empirical assumptions, least of mention, implicitly come from psychology and cognitive science, not evolutionary theory. Sometimes, however, evolutionary epistemology is characterized in a seemingly non-naturalistic fashion. Campbell (1974) says that if one is expanding knowledge beyond what one knows, one has no choice but to explore without the benefit of wisdom, i.e., blindly. This, Campbell admits, makes evolutionary epistemology close to being a tautology (and so not naturalistic). Evolutionary epistemology does assert the analytic claim that when expanding ones knowledge beyond what one knows, one must precessed to something that is already known, but, more interestingly, it also makes the synthetic claim that when expanding ones knowledge beyond what one knows, one must proceed by blind variation and selective retention. This claim is synthetic because it can be empirically falsified. The central claim of evolutionary epistemology is synthetic, not analytic. If the central contradictory, which they are not. Campbell is right that evolutionary epistemology does have the analytic feature he mentions, but he is wrong to think that this is a distinguishing feature, since any plausible epistemology has the same analytic feature (Skagestad, 1978).

Two extraordinary issues lie to awaken the literature that involves questions about realism, i.e., What metaphysical commitment does an evolutionary epistemologist have to make? Progress, i.e., according to evolutionary epistemology, does knowledge develop toward a goal? With respect to realism, many evolutionary epistemologists endorse that is called hypothetical realism, a view that combines a version of epistemological scepticism and tentative acceptance of metaphysical realism. With respect to progress, the problem is that biological evolution is not goal-directed, but the growth of human knowledge seems to be. Campbell (1974) worries about the potential dis-analogy here but is willing to bite the stone of conscience and admit that epistemic evolution progress toward a goal (truth) while biologic evolution does not. Many another has argued that evolutionary epistemologists must give up the truth-topic sense of progress because a natural selection model is in essence, is non-teleological, as an alternative, following Kuhn (1970), and embraced in the accompaniment with evolutionary epistemology.

Among the most frequent and serious criticisms levelled against evolutionary epistemology is that the analogical version of the view is false because epistemic variation is not blind (Skagestad, 1978, 613-16, and Ruse, 1986, ch.2 (. Stein and Lipton (1990) have argued, however, that this objection fails because, while epistemic variation is not random, its constraints come from heuristics that, for the most part, are selective retention. Further, Stein and Lipton come to the conclusion that heuristics are analogous to biological pre-adaptions, evolutionary pre-biological pre-adaptions, evolutionary cursors, such as a half-wing, a precursor to a wing, which have some function other than the function of their descendable structures: The function of descendable structures, the function of their descendable character embodied to its structural foundations, is that of the guidelines of epistemic variation is, on this view, not the source of disanalogousness, but the source of a more articulated account of the analogy.

Many evolutionary epistemologists try to combine the literal and the analogical versions (Bradie, 1986, and Stein and Lipton, 1990), saying that those beliefs and cognitive mechanisms, which are innate results from natural selection of the biological sort and those that are innate results from natural selection of the epistemic sort. This is reasonable as long as the two parts of this hybrid view are kept distinct. An analogical version of evolutionary epistemology with biological variation as its only source of blondeness would be a null-set theory: This would be the case if all our beliefs are innate or if our non-innate beliefs are not the result of blind variation. An appeal to the legitimate way to produce a hybrid version of evolutionary epistemology since doing so trivializes the theory. For similar reasons, such an appeal will not save an analogical version of evolutionary epistemology from arguments to the effect that epistemic variation is blind (Stein and Lipton, 1990).

Although it is a new approach to theory of knowledge, evolutionary epistemology has attracted much attention, primarily because it represents a serious attempt to flesh out a naturalized epistemology by drawing on several disciplines. In science is relevant to understanding the nature and development of knowledge, then evolutionary theory is among the disciplines worth a look. Insofar as evolutionary epistemology looks there, it is an interesting and potentially fruitful epistemological programme.

What makes a belief justified and what makes a true belief knowledge? Thinking that whether a belief deserves one of these appraisals is natural depends on what caused the depicted branch of knowledge to have the belief. In recent decades a number of epistemologists have pursued this plausible idea with a variety of specific proposals. Some causal theories of knowledge have it that a true belief that p is knowledge just in case it has the right causal connexion to the fact that p. Such a criterion can be applied only to cases where the fact that p is a sort that can reach causal relations, as this seems to exclude mathematically and their necessary facts and perhaps any fact expressed by a universal generalization, and proponents of this sort of criterion have usually supposed that it is limited to perceptual representations where knowledge of particular facts about subjects environments.

For example, Armstrong (1973), predetermined that a position held by a belief in the form This perceived object is F is [non-inferential] knowledge if and only if the belief is a completely reliable sign that the perceived object is F, that is, the fact that the object is F contributed to causing the belief and its doing so depended on properties of the believer such that the laws of nature dictated that, for any subject 'χ' and perceived object 'y', if 'χ' has those properties and believed that 'y' is 'F', then 'y' is 'F'. (Dretske (1981) offers a rather similar account, in terms of the beliefs being caused by a signal received by the perceiver that carries the information that the object is 'F').

Goldman (1986) has proposed an importantly different causal criterion, namely, that a true belief is knowledge if it is produced by a type of process that is globally and locally reliable. Causing true beliefs is sufficiently high is globally reliable if its propensity. Local reliability has to do with whether the process would have produced a similar but false belief in certain counterfactual situations alternative to the actual situation. This way of marking off true beliefs that are knowledge does not require the fact believed to be causally related to the belief, and so it could in principle apply to knowledge of any kind of truth.

Goldman requires the global reliability of the belief-producing process for the justification of a belief, he requires it also for knowledge because justification is required for knowledge. What he requires for knowledge, but does not require for justification is local reliability. His idea is that a justified true belief is knowledge if the type of process that produced it would not have produced it in any relevant counterfactual situation in which it is false. Its purported theory of relevant alternatives can be viewed as an attempt to provide a more satisfactory response to this tension in our thinking about knowledge. It attempts to characterize knowledge in a way that preserves both our belief that knowledge is an absolute concept and our belief that we have knowledge.

According to the theory, we need to qualify rather than deny the absolute character of knowledge. We should view knowledge as absolute, reactive to certain standards (Dretske, 1981 and Cohen, 1988). That is to say, in order to know a proposition, our evidence need not eliminate all the alternatives to that preposition, rather for us, that we can know our evidence eliminates al the relevant alternatives, where the set of relevant alternatives (a proper subset of the set of all alternatives) is determined by some standard. Moreover, according to the relevant alternatives view, and the standards determining that of the alternatives is raised by the sceptic are not relevant. If this is correct, then the fact that our evidence cannot eliminate the sceptics alternative does not lead to a sceptical result. For knowledge requires only the elimination of the relevant alternatives, so the relevant alternative view preserves in both strands in our thinking about knowledge. Knowledge is an absolute concept, but because the absoluteness is relative to a standard, we can know many things.

The interesting thesis that counts as a causal theory of justification (in the meaning of causal theory intended here) are that: A belief is justified in case it was produced by a type of process that is globally reliable, that is, its propensity to produce true beliefs-that can be defined (to a good approximation) As the proportion of the beliefs it produces (or would produce) that is true is sufficiently great.

Logical positivism, is lonely defined movement or set of ideas whose dominant force in philosophy, at least in English-speaking countries, inti the 1960s, and its influence, if not specific theses, remains present in the views and attitudes of many philosophers. It was 'positivism' in its adherence to the doctrine that science is the only form of knowledge and that there is nothing in the universe beyond what can in principle be scientifically known. It was 'logical' in its dependence on development in logic and mathematics in t he early years of this century that were taken to reveal how a priori knowledge of necessary truth is compatible with a thorough going empiricism.

A sentence, that is, in the sense of being incapable of truth or falsity, required a criterion of meaningfulness, and it was found in the idea of empirical verification. So, that, it is said to be cognitively meaningful if and only if it can be verified or falsified in experience. This is not meant to require that the sentence be conclusively verified or falsified, since universal scientific as a hypotheses (which are supposed to pass the test) are not logically deducible from any amount of actually observed evidence. The criterion is accordingly to be understood to require only verifiability or falsifiability, in the sense of empirical evidence that would count either for or against the truth of the sentence in question, without having logically to imply it. Verification or confirmation is not necessarily something that can be carried out by the person who entertains the sentence in all at the stage of intellectual and technical development achieved at the time it is entertained.

The logical positivist conception of knowledge in its original and purest form sees human knowledge as a complex intellectual structure employed for the successful anticipation of future experience. It requires, on the one hand, a linguistic or conceptual framework in which to express what is to be categorized and predicted and, on the other, a factual element that provides that abstract form with content. This comes, ultimately, from sense experience. No matter of fact that anyone can understand or intelligibly of human experience, and the only reasons anyone could have for believing anything must come, ultimately from actual experience.

The general project of the positivistic theory of knowledge is to exhibit the structure, content, and basis of human knowledge in accordance with these empiricist principles. Since science is regarded as the repository of all genuine human knowledge, this becomes the task of exhibiting the structure, or as it was called, the 'logic' of science. The theory of knowledge thus becomes the philosophy of science. It has three major tasks: (1) to analyse the meaning in terms of observations or experiences in principle available to human beings. (2) To show how certain observations or experiences serve to confirm a given statement in the sense of making it more warranted or reasonable. (3) To show how non-empirical or a priori knowledge of the necessary truth of logic and mathematics is possible even though every matter of fact that can be intelligibly thought or known is empirically verifiable or falsifiable.

(1) The slogan 'the meaning of a statement is its method of verification, expresses the empirical verification theory of meaning. It is more than the general criterion of meaningfulness according to which a sentence is cognitively meaningful if and only if it is empirically verifiable. It system, in addition, that the meaning of each sentence is, it is all those observations that would confirm or disconfirm the sentence. Sentences that would be verified or falsified by all the same observations are empirically equivalent or have the same meaning.

A sentence recording the result of a single observation is an observation or 'protocol' sentence. It can be conclusively verified or falsified on a single occasion. Every other meaningful statement is a 'hypothesis' which implies an indefinitely large number of observation sentences that together exhaust its meaning, but at no time will all of them have been verified or falsified. To give an 'analysis' of the statements of science is to show how the content of each scientific statement can be reduced in this way to nothing more than a complex combination of direct verifiable 'protocol' sentences.

Observations are more than the mere causal impact of external physical stimuli. Since such stimuli only give rise to observations in a properly prepared and receptive mind. Nor are they well though t of in terms of atomistic impressions. It is, nonetheless, toast that is given by te senses, in response to the question of what exactly is so given, sense-data theories posit private showings in the consciousness of the subject. In the case of vision this would be a kind of inner picture show which it only indirectly represents aspects of the external world. Generally the doctrine that the mind (for sometimes the brain) works on representations of the thing and features of things that we perceive or think about. In the philosophy of perception the view is especially associated with French Cartesian philosopher Nicolas Malebranche (1638-1715) and the English philosopher John Locke (1632-1704) who, holding that the mind is the container for ideas, held that, of our real ideas, some are adequate, and some are inadequate. Those that are adequate, which perfectly supposes them from which it intends to stand for, and to which it refers them. The problems in this account were mercilessly exposed by the French theologian and philosopher Antoine Arnauld (1612- 94) and French critic of Cartesianism Simon Foucher (1644-96), writing against Malebranche and by Berkreley, writing against Locke. The fundamental problem is that the mind is 'supposing' its ideas to represent something else, but it has no access anything except by forming another idea. The difficulty is to understand how the and even escapes from the world of representations, or, in other words, how representations manage to acquire genuine content, pointing beyond themselves in more recent philosophy, the analogy between the mind and s computer has suggested that the mind or brain manipulate symbols, thought of as like the instruction symbols, and thought of as the instructions of a machine program, and that those symbols are representations of aspects of the world.

The Berkeleyan difficulty then recurs, as the programme computer behaves the same way without knowing whether the sign '$' refers to a unit of currency or anything else. The elements of a machine program are identified purely syntactically, so the actual operations of any interrelation of them where each is defined without regard to the interpretation the sentences of the language are intended to have an axiomatized system older than modern logic, nonetheless, the study of interpretations of forma systems proof theory studies relations of deducibility between formulae of a system, but once the notion of an interpretation is in place we can ask whether a forma system meets certain conditions, hence, according to critics, there is no way, on this model, for seeing the mind as concerned with the representational properties of the symbols. The point is sometimes put by saying that the mind, becomes a syntactic engine than a semantic engine. Representation is also attacked, at least as central concept in understanding the mind, by pragmatists who emphasis instead the activities surrounding s use of language, rather than what they see as a mysterious link between mind and world.

It is now, that the emphasis shifts from thinking of language of agents who do things with their arithmetic simply as a device for describing numbers, it should be placed in activities such as counting and measuring. The shift in emphasis can be an encouragement to pragmatism in place of representation.

It is uncontroversial in contemporary cognitive science that cognitive processes are processes that manipulate representations. This idea seems nearly inevitable. What makes the difference between posses that are cognitive - solving a problem - and those tat are not - a patellar reflex, for example - is just that cognitive processes are epistemically assessable? A solution procedure can be justified or correct, a reflex cannot. Since only things with content can be epistemically assessed, processes appear to count as cognitive only insofar as they implicate representations.

It is tempting to think that thoughts are the mind's representations, are not thoughts just this mental states that have (semantic) content? This is, no doubt, hairless enough provided we keep in mind that cognitive science may attribute to thought's properties and contents that are foreign too commonsense. First, most of the representations hypothesized by cognitive science do not correspond to anything commonsense would recognize as thoughts. Standard psycholinguistics theory, for instance, hypothesize the construction of representations of the syntactics structure of the utterances one hears and understands. Yet, we are not aware of, and non-specialists do not even understand, the structure represented. Thus, cognitive science may attribute thoughts where commonsense would not. Second, cognitive science may find it useful to individuate thoughts in ways foreign too commonsense.

The representational theory of cognition gives rise to a natural theory of intentional states such as believing, desire and intending. According to this theory, intentional stares factor into two aspects, a functional aspect that distinguishes believing from desiring and so on, and a content aspect that distinguishes beliefs from each other, desires from each other, and so on. A belief that 'p' might be realized as a representation with the content that 'p' and the function of serving as a premise in inference. A desire that 'p' might be realized as a representation with the content that 'p' and the function of initiating processing designed to bring it about that 'p' and terminating such processing when a belief that 'p' is formed.

Zeno of Elea's argument against motion precipitated a crisis in Greek thought. They are presented as four arguments in the form of paradoxes, such is to follow:

(1) suppose a runner needs to travel from a start 'S' to a finish 'F', and hence to 'F', but if 'N' is the midpoint of 'SM', he must first travel to 'N'. And so on ad infinitum (Zeno 'what has been said once can always be repeated). But it is impossible to accomplish an infinite number of tasks in a finite time. Therefore, the runner cannot complete (or start) his journey.

(2) Achilles runs a race with tortoise, who has a start of 'n' metres. Suppose the tortoise runs one-tenth as fast as Achilles. Then by the time Achilles had reached the tortoise's starting-point. The tortoise is n/10 metres ahead. By te time Achilles has reached that point, the tortoise is n/100 metres ahead, and so on, ad infinitum. So Achilles cannot catch the tortoise.

(3) an arrow cannot move at a place at which it is not. But neither can it move at a place at which it is. That is, at any instant it is at rest. But if at no instant is it moving, then it is always at rest.

(4) suppose three equal blocks, 'A', 'B', 'C' of width 1, with 'A' and 'C' moving past 'B' at the same speed in opposite directions. Then 'A' takes one time, 't', to traverse the width of 'B', but half the time, ½, to traverse the width of 'C'. But these are the same length, so 'A' takes both 't' and t/2 to traverse the distance 1.

These are the barest forms of the arguments, and different suggestions have been =made as to how Zeno might have supported them. A modern approach might be inclined to dismiss them as superficial, since we are familiar with the mathematical ideas, as (a) that an infinite series can have a finite sum, which may appear ti dispose of (1) and (2) and (b) that there may appear to no such thing s velocity a point or instant, for velocity is defined only over intervals of time and distance, which may seem to dispose of (3) the fourth paradox seems merely amusing, unless Zeno had in mind that the length 1 is thought of as a smallest unit of distance (a quantum of space) and that each of 'A' and 'C' are travelling so that they traverse the smallest space in the smallest time. On these assumptions there is a contradiction, for 'A' passes 'C' in half the proposed smallest time.

This paradox and its accompanying reasoning are strongly reminiscent of the Lair Paradox that (in one version) begins by considering a sentence This sentence is false and derives a contradiction. Versions of both arguments using axiomatic formulations of arithmetic and Gödel-numbers to achieve the effect of self-reference yields important meta-theorems about what can be expressed in such systems. Roughly these are to the effect that no predicates definable in the formalized arithmetic can have the properties we demand of truth (Tarskis Theorem) or of knowledge (Montague, 1963).

The usual proposals for dealing with the Liar paradox, its often to have their analogues for the Knower, e.g., that there is something wrong with a self-reference or that knowledge (or truth) is properly a predicate of propositions and not of sentences. The relies that show that some of these are not adequate are often parallel to those for the Liar paradox. In addition, one can try here what seems to be an adequate solution for the Surprise Examination Paradox, namely the observation that new knowledge can drive out knowledge, but this does not seem to work on the Knower (Anderson, 1983).

There are a number of paradoxes of the Liar family. The simplest example is the sentence This sentence is false, which must be false if it is true, and true if it is false. One suggestion is that the sentence fails to say anything, but sentences that fail to say anything are at least not true. In fact case, we consider to sentences This sentence is not true, which, if it fails to say anything is not true, and hence (this kind of reasoning is sometimes called the strengthened Liar). Other versions of the Liar introduce pairs of sentences, as in a slogan on the front of a T-shirt saying This sentence on the back of this T-shirt is false, and one on the back saying The sentence on the front of this T-shirt is true. It is clear that each sentence individually is well formed, and were it not for the other, might have said something true. So any attempt to dismiss the paradox by sating that the sentence involved are meaningless will face problems.

Even so, the two approaches that have some hope of adequately dealing with this paradox is hierarchy solutions and truth-value gap solutions. According to the first, knowledge is structured into levels. It is argued that there be bo one-coherent notion expressed by the verb; knows, but rather a whole series of notion of being knowable and wherefore knows, and so on (perhaps into transfinite), stated ion terms of predicate expressing such ramified concepts and properly restricted, (1)-(3) lead to no contradictions. The main objections to this procedure are that the meaning of these levels has not been adequately explained and that the idea of such subscripts, even implicit, in a natural language is highly counterintuitive the truth-value gap solution takes sentences such as (S) to lack truth-value. They are neither true nor false, but they do not express propositions. This defeats a crucial step in the reasoning used in the derivation of the paradoxes. Kripler (1986) has developed this approach in connexion with the Liar and Asher and Kamp (1986) has worked out some details of a parallel solution to the Knower. The principal objection is that strengthened or super versions of the paradoxes tend to reappear when the solution itself is stated.

Since the paradoxical deduction uses only the properties (1)-(3) and since the argument is formally valid, any notion that satisfy these conditions will lead to a paradox. Thus, Grim (1988) notes that this may be read as is known by an omniscient God and concludes that there is no coherent single notion of omniscience. Thomason (1980) observes that with some different conditions, analogous reasoning about belief can lead to paradoxical consequence.

Overall, it looks as if we should conclude that knowledge and truth are ultimately intrinsically stratified concepts. It would seem that wee must simply accept the fact that these (and similar) concepts cannot be assigned of any-one fixed, finite or infinite. Still, the meaning of this idea certainly needs further clarification.

Its paradox arises when a set of apparently incontrovertible premises gives unacceptable or contradictory conclusions, to solve a paradox will involve showing either that there is a hidden flaw in the premises, or that the reasoning is erroneous, or that the apparently unacceptable conclusion can, in fact, be tolerated. Paradoxes are therefore important in philosophy, for until one is solved its shows that there is something about our reasoning and of concepts that we do not understand. Famous families of paradoxes include the semantic paradoxes and Zeno's paradoxes. Art the beginning of the 20th century, paradox and other set-theoretical paradoxes led to the complete overhaul of the foundations of set theory, while the Sorites paradox has lead to the investigations of the semantics of vagueness and fuzzy logics.

It is, however, to what extent can analysis be informative? This is the question that gives a riser to what philosophers has traditionally called the paradox of analysis. Thus, consider the following proposition:

(1) To be an instance of knowledge is to be an instance of justified true belief not essentially grounded in any falsehood.

(1) if true, illustrates an important type of philosophical analysis. For convenience of exposition, I will assume (1) is a correct analysis. The paradox arises from the fact that if the concept of justified true belief not been essentially grounded in any falsification is the analysand of the concept of knowledge, it would seem that they are the same concept and hence that:

(2) To be an instance of knowledge is to be as an instance of. knowledge and would have to be the same propositions as (1). But then how can (1) be informative when (2) is not? This is what is called the first paradox of analysis. Classical writings on analysis suggests a second paradoxical analysis (Moore, 1942).

(3) An analysis of the concept of being a brother is that to be a brother is to be a male sibling. If (3) is true, it would seem that the concept of being a brother would have to be the same concept as the concept of being a male sibling and tat:

(4) An analysis of the concept of being a brother is that to be a brother is to be a brother would also have to be true and in fact, would have to be the same proposition as (3?). Yet (3) is true and (4) is false.

Both these paradoxes rest upon the assumptions that analysis is a relation between concepts, than one involving entity of other sorts, such as linguistic expressions, and tat in a true analysis, analysand and analysandum are the same concept. Both these assumptions are explicit in Moore, but some of Moores remarks hint at a solution to that of another statement of an analysis is a statement partly about the concept involved and partly about the verbal expressions used to express it. He says he thinks a solution of this sort is bound to be right, but fails to suggest one because he cannot see a way in which the analysis can be even partly about the expression (Moore, 1942).

Elsewhere, of such ways, as a solution to the second paradox, to which is explicated by the tenet (3) as: (5) An analysis is given by saying that the verbal expression 'χ' is a brother, expresses the same concept as is expressed by the conjunction of the verbal expressions 'χ' is male, when used to express the concept of being male and 'χ' is a sibling, when used to express the concept of being a sibling. (Ackerman, 1990).

An important point about (5): Stripped of its philosophical jargon (analysis, concept, 'χ' is a . . .), (5) seems to state the sort of information generally stated in a definition of the verbal expression brother in terms of the verbal expressions male and sibling, where this definition is designed to draw upon listeners antecedent understanding of the verbal expression male and sibling, and thus, to tell listeners what the verbal expression brother really means, instead of merely providing the information that two verbal expressions are synonymous without specifying the meaning of either one. Thus, its solution to the second paradox seems to make the sort of analysis tat gives rise to this paradox matter of specifying the meaning of a verbal expression in terms of separate verbal expressions already understood and saying how the meanings of these separate, already-understood verbal expressions are combined. This corresponds to Moores intuitive requirement that an analysis should both specify the constituent concepts of the analysandum and tell how they are combined, but is this all there is to philosophical analysis?

To answer this question, we must note that, in addition too there being two paradoxes of analysis, there is two types of analyses that are relevant here. (There are also other types of analysis, such as reformatory analysis, where the analysand are intended to improve on and replace the analysandum. But since reformatory analysis involves no commitment to conceptual identity between analysand and analysandum, reformatory analysis does not generate a paradox of analysis and so will not concern us here.) One way to recognize the difference between the two types of analysis concerning us here is to focus on the difference between the two paradoxes. This can be done by means of the Frége-inspired sense-individuation condition, which is the condition that two expressions have the same sense if and only if they can be interchangeably salva veritate whenever used in propositional attitude context. If the expressions for the analysands and the analysandum in (1) met this condition, (1) and (2) would not raise the first paradox, but the second paradox arises regardless of whether the expression for the analysand and the analysandum meet this condition. The second paradox is a matter of the failure of such expressions to be interchangeable salva veritate in sentences involving such contexts as an analysis is given thereof. Thus, a solution (such as the one offered) that is aimed only at such contexts can solve the second paradox. This is clearly false for the first paradox, however, which will apply to all pairs of propositions expressed by sentences in which expressions for pairs of analysands and analysantia raising the first paradox is interchangeable.

At this point, we display attributes to the theory of experience, as it is not possible to define in an illuminating way, however, we know what experiences are through acquaintances with some of our own, e.g., visual experiences of as afterimage, a feeling of physical nausea or a tactile experience of an abrasive surface (which might be caused by an actual surface -rough or smooth, or which might be part of a dream, or the product of a vivid sensory imagination). The essential feature of experience is it feels a certain way -that there is something that it is like to have it. We may refer to this feature of an experience as its character.

Another core feature of the sorts of experience with which this may be of a concern, is that they have representational content. (Unless otherwise indicated, experience will be reserved for their contentual representations.) The most obvious cases of experiences with content are sense experiences of the kind normally involved in perception. We may describe such experiences by mentioning their sensory modalities ad their contents, e.g., a gustatory experience (modality) of chocolate ice cream (content), but do so more commonly by means of perceptual verbs combined with noun phrases specifying their contents, as in Macbeth saw a dagger. This is, however, ambiguous between the perceptual claim There was a (material) dagger in the world that Macbeth perceived visually and Macbeth had a visual experience of a dagger (the reading with which we are concerned, as it is afforded by our imagination, or perhaps, experiencing mentally hallucinogenic imagery).

As in the case of other mental states and events with content, it is important to distinguish between the properties that and experience represents and the properties that it possesses. To talk of the representational properties of an experience is to say something about its content, not to attribute those properties to the experience itself. Like every other experience, a visual; experience of a non-shaped square, of which is a mental event, and it is therefore not itself either irregular or is it square, even though it represents those properties. It is, perhaps, fleeting, pleasant or unusual, even though it does not represent those properties. An experience may represent a property that it possesses, and it may even do so in virtue of a rapidly changing (complex) experience representing something as changing rapidly. However, this is the exception and not the rule.

Which properties can be [directly] represented in sense experience is subject to debate. Traditionalists include only properties whose presence could not be doubted by a subject having appropriate experiences, e.g., colour and shape in the case of visual experience, and apparent shape, surface texture, hardness, etc., in the case of tactile experience. This view is natural to anyone who has an egocentric, Cartesian perspective in epistemology, and who wishes for pure data in experiences to serve as logically certain foundations for knowledge, especially to the immediate objects of perceptual awareness in or of sense-data, such categorized of colour patches and shapes, which are usually supposed distinct from surfaces of physical objectivity. Qualities of sense-data are supposed to be distinct from physical qualities because their perception is more relative to conditions, more certain, and more immediate, and because sense-data is private and cannot appear other than they are they are objects that change in our perceptual field when conditions of perception change. Physical objects remain constant.

Others who do not think that this wish can be satisfied, and who are more impressed with the role of experience in providing animisms with ecologically significant information about the world around them, claim that sense experiences represent properties, characteristic and kinds that are much richer and much more wide-ranging than the traditional sensory qualities. We do not see only colours and shapes, they tell us, but also earth, water, men, women and fire: We do not smell only odours, but also food and filth. There is no space here to examine the factors relevantly responsible to their choice of situational alternatives. Yet, this suggests that character and content are not really distinct, and there is a close tie between them. For one thing, the relative complexity of the character of sense experience places limitations upon its possible content, e.g., a tactile experience of something touching ones left ear is just too simple to carry the same amount of content as typically convincing to an every day, visual experience. Moreover, the content of a sense experience of a given character depends on the normal causes of appropriately similar experiences, e.g., the sort of gustatory experience that we have when eating chocolate would be not represented as chocolate unless it was normally caused by chocolate. Granting a contingent ties between the character of an experience and its possible causal origins, once, again follows that its possible content is limited by its character.

Character and content are nonetheless irreducibly different, for the following reasons. (1) There are experiences that completely lack content, e.g., certain bodily pleasures. (2) Not every aspect of the character of an experience with content is relevant to that content, e.g., the unpleasantness of an aural experience of chalk squeaking on a board may have no representational significance. (3) Experiences in different modalities may overlap in content without a parallel overlap in character, e.g., visual and tactile experiences of circularity feel completely different. (4) The content of an experience with a given character may vary according to the background of the subject, e.g., a certain content singing bird only after the subject has learned something about birds.

According to the act/object analysis of experience (which is a special case of the act/object analysis of consciousness), every experience involves an object of experience even if it has no material object. Two main lines of argument may be offered in support of this view, one phenomenological and the other semantic.

In an outline, the phenomenological argument is as follows. Whenever we have an experience, even if nothing beyond the experience answers to it, we seem to be presented with something through the experience (which is itself diaphanous). The object of the experience is whatever is so presented to us-is that it is an individual thing, an event, or a state of affairs.

The semantic argument is that objects of experience are required in order to make sense of certain features of our talk about experience, including, in particular, the following. (i) Simple attributions of experience, e.g., Rod is experiencing an oddity that is not really square but in appearance it seems more than likely a square, this seems to be relational. (ii) We appear to refer to objects of experience and to attribute properties to them, e.g., The afterimage that John experienced was certainly odd. (iii) We appear to quantify ov er objects of experience, e.g., Macbeth saw something that his wife did not see.

The act/object analysis faces several problems concerning the status of objects of experiences. Currently the most common view is that they are sense-data - private mental entities that actually posses the traditional sensory qualities represented by the experiences of which they are the objects. But the very idea of an essentially private entity is suspect. Moreover, since an experience may apparently represent something as having a determinable property, e.g., redness, without representing it as having any subordinate determinate property, e.g., any specific shade of red, a sense-datum may actually have a determinate property subordinate to it. Even more disturbing is that sense-data may have contradictory properties, since experiences can have contradictory contents. A case in point is the waterfall illusion: If you stare at a waterfall for a minute and then immediately fixate on a nearby rock, you are likely to have an experience of the rocks moving upward while it remains in the same place. The sense-data theorist must either deny that there are such experiences or admit contradictory objects.

These problems can be avoided by treating objects of experience as properties. This, however, fails to do justice to the appearances, for experience seems not to present us with properties embodied in individuals. The view that objects of experience is Meinongian objects accommodate this point. It is also attractive in as far as (1) it allows experiences to represent properties other than traditional sensory qualities, and (2) it allows for the identification of objects of experience and objects of perception in the case of experiences that constitute perception.

According to the act/object analysis of experience, every experience with content involves an object of experience to which the subject is related by an act of awareness (the event of experiencing that object). This is meant to apply not only to perceptions, which have material objects (whatever is perceived), but also to experiences like hallucinations and dream experiences, which do not. Such experiences none the less appear to represent something, and their objects are supposed to be whatever it is that they represent. Act/object theorists may differ on the nature of objects of experience, which have been treated as properties. Meinongian objects (which may not exist or have any form of being), and, more commonly private mental entities with sensory qualities. (The term sense-data is now usually applied to the latter, but has also been used as a general term for objects of sense experiences, as in the work of G. E. Moore) Act/object theorists may also differ on the relationship between objects of experience and objects of perception. In terms of perception (of which we are indirectly aware) are always distinct from objects of experience (of which we are directly aware). Meinongian, however, may treat objects of perception as existing objects of experience. But sense-datum theorists must either deny that there are such experiences or admit contradictory objects. Still, most philosophers will feel that the Meinongians acceptance of impossible objects is too high a price to pay for these benefits.

A general problem for the act/object analysis is that the question of whether two subjects are experiencing one and the same thing (as opposed to having exactly similar experiences) appears to have an answer only on the assumption that the experiences concerned are perceptions with material objects. But in terms of the act/object analysis the question must have an answer even when this condition is not satisfied. (The answer is always negative on the sense-datum theory; it could be positive on other versions of the act/object analysis, depending on the facts of the case.)

In problem, nonetheless, of viewing the case for the act/object analysis should be reassessed. The phenomenological argument is not, on reflection, convincing, for it is easy enough to grant that any experience appears to present us with an object without accepting that it actually does. The semantic argument is more impressive, but is none the less answerable. The seemingly relational structure of attributions of experience is a challenge dealt with below in connexion with the adverbial theory. Apparent reference to and quantification over objects of experience can be handled by analysing them as reference to experiences themselves and quantification over experiences tacitly typed according to content. Thus, The afterimage that John experienced was colourfully appealing becomes Johns afterimage experience was an experience of colour, and Macbeth saw something that his wife did not see becomes Macbeth had a visual experience that his wife did not have.

Pure cognitivism attempts to avoid the problems facing the act/object analysis by reducing experiences to cognitive events or associated disposition, e.g., Julie's experience of a rough surface beneath her hand might be identified with the event of her acquiring the belief that there is a rough surface beneath her hand, or, if she does not acquire this belief, with a disposition to acquire it that has somehow been blocked.

This position has attractions. It does full justice to the cognitive contents of experience, and to the important role of experience as a source of belief acquisition. It would also help clear the way for a naturalistic theory of mind, since there seems to be some prospect of a physicalist/functionalist account of belief and other intentional states. But pure cognitivism is completely undermined by its failure to accommodate the fact that experiences have a felt character that cannot be reduced to their content, as aforementioned.

The adverbial theory is an attempt to undermine the act/object analysis by suggesting a semantic account of attributions of experience that does not require objects of experience. Unfortunately, the oddities of explicit adverbializations of such statements have driven off potential supporters of the theory. Furthermore, the theory remains largely undeveloped, and attempted refutations have traded on this. It may, however, be founded on sound basis intuitions, and there is reason to believe that an effective development of the theory (which is merely hinting at) is possible.

The relevant intuitions are (1) that when we say that someone is experiencing an A, or has an experience of an A, we are using this content-expression to specify the type of thing that the experience is especially apt to fit, (2) that doing this is a matter of saying something about the experience itself (and maybe about the normal causes of like experiences), and (3) that it is no-good of reasons to posit of its position to presuppose that of any involvements, is that its descriptions of an object in which the experience is. Thus the effective role of the content-expression in a statement of experience is to modify the verb it compliments, not to introduce a special type of object.

Modern approaches to perception tend to reject any conception of the eye as a camera or lense, simply responsible for producing private images, and stress the active life of the subject in and of the world, as the determinant of experience.

Nevertheless, the argument from illusion is of itself the usually intended directive to establish that certain familiar facts about illusion disprove the theory of perception called naïevity or direct realism. There are, however, many different versions of the argument that must be distinguished carefully. Some of these distinctions centre on the content of the premises (the nature of the appeal to illusion); others centre on the interpretation of the conclusion (the kind of direct realism under attack). Let us set about by distinguishing the importantly different versions of direct realism which one might take to be vulnerable to familiar facts about the possibility of perceptual illusion.

A crude statement of direct realism might go as follows. In perception, we sometimes directly perceive physical objects and their properties, we do not always perceive physical objects by perceiving something else, e.g., a sense-datum. There are, however, difficulties with this formulation of the view, as for one thing a great many philosophers who are not direct realists would admit that it is a mistake to describe people as actually perceiving something other than a physical object. In particular, such philosophers might admit, we should never say that we perceive sense-data. To talk that way would be to suppose that we should model our understanding of our relationship to sense-data on our understanding of the ordinary use of perceptual verbs as they describe our relation to and of the physical world, and that is the last thing paradigm sense-datum theorists should want. At least, many of the philosophers who objected to direct realism would prefer to express in what they were of objecting too in terms of a technical (and philosophically controversial) concept such as acquaintance. Using such a notion, we could define direct realism this way: In veridical experience we are directly acquainted with parts, e.g., surfaces, or constituents of physical objects. A less cautious venison of the view might drop the reference to veridical experience and claim simply that in all experience we are directly acquainted with parts or constituents of physical objects. The expression's knowledge by acquaintance and knowledge by description, and the distinction they mark between knowing things and knowing about things, are generally associated with Bertrand Russell (1872-1970), that scientific philosophy required analysing many objects of belief as logical constructions or logical fictions, and the programme of analysis that this inaugurated dominated the subsequent philosophy of logical atomism, and then of other philosophers, Russells The Analysis of Mind, the mind itself is treated in a fashion reminiscent of Hume, as no more than the collection of neutral perceptions or sense-data that make up the flux of conscious experience, and that looked at another way that also was to make up the external world (neutral monism), but An Inquiry into Meaning and Truth (1940) represents a more empirical approach to the problem. Yet, philosophers have perennially investigated this and related distinctions using varying terminology.

Distinction in our ways of knowing things, highlighted by Russell and forming a central element in his philosophy after the discovery of the theory of definite descriptions. A thing is known by acquaintance when there is direct experience of it. It is known by description if it can only be described as a thing with such-and-such properties. In everyday parlance, I might know my spouse and children by acquaintance, but know someone as the first person born at sea only by description. However, for a variety of reasons Russell shrinks the area of things that can be known by acquaintance until eventually only current experience, perhaps my own self, and certain universals or meanings qualify anything else is known only as the thing that has such-and-such qualities.

Because one can interpret the relation of acquaintance or awareness as one that is not epistemic, i.e., not a kind of propositional knowledge, it is important to distinguish the above aforementioned views read as ontological theses from a view one might call epistemological direct realism? In perception we are, on at least some occasions, non-inferentially justified in believing a proposition asserting the existence of a physical object. Since it is that these objects exist independently of any mind that might perceive them, and so it thereby rules out all forms of idealism and phenomenalism, which hold that there are no such independently existing objects. Its being to direct realism rules out those views defended under the cubic of critical naive realism, or representational realism, in which there is some non-physical intermediary -usually called a sense-datum or a sense impression -that must first be perceived or experienced in order to perceive the object that exists independently of this perception. Often the distinction between direct realism and other theories of perception is explained more fully in terms of what is immediately perceived, than mediately perceived. What relevance does illusion have for these two forms of direct realism?

The fundamental premise of the arguments is from illusion seems to be the theses that things can appear to be other than they are. Thus, for example, straight sticks when immerged in water looks bent, a penny when viewed from certain perspective appears as an illusory spatial elliptic circularity, when something that is yellow when place under red fluorescent light looks red. In all of these cases, one version of the argument goes, it is implausible to maintain that what we are directly acquainted with is the real nature of the object in question. Indeed, it is hard to see how we can be said to be aware of the really physical object at all. In the above illusions the things we were aware of actually were bent, elliptical and red, respectively. But, by hypothesis, the really physical objects lacked these properties. Thus, we were not aware of the substantial reality of been real as a physical objects or theory.

So far, if the argument is relevant to any of the direct realises distinguished above, it seems relevant only to the claim that in all sense experience we are directly acquainted with parts or constituents of physical objects. After all, even if in illusion we are not acquainted with physical objects, but their surfaces, or their constituents, why should we conclude anything about the hidden nature of our relations to the physical world in veridical experience?

We are supposed to discover the answer to this question by noticing the similarities between illusory experience and veridical experience and by reflecting on what makes illusion possible at all. Illusion can occur because the nature of the illusory experience is determined, not just by the nature of the object perceived, but also by other conditions, both external and internal as becoming of an inner or as the outer experience. But all of our sensations are subject to these causal influences and it would be gratuitous and arbitrary to select from indefinitely of many and subtly different perceptual experiences some special ones those that get us in touch with the real nature of the physical world and its surrounding surfaces. Red fluorescent light affects the way thing's look, but so does sunlight. Water reflects light, but so does air. We have no unmediated access to the external world.

At this point, its may prove as an alternative, in that it might be profitable to move our considerations to those of that have the possibility of considering the possibility of hallucination. Instead of comparing paradigmatic veridical perception with illusion, let us compare it with complete hallucination. For any experiences or sequence of experiences we take to be veridical, we can imagine qualitatively indistinguishable experiences occurring as part of a hallucination. For those who like their philosophical arguments spiced with a touch of science, we can imagine that our brains were surreptitiously removed in the night, and unbeknown to us are being stimulated by a neurophysiologist so as to produce the very sensations that we would normally associate with a trip to the Grand Canyon. Currently permit us into appealing of what we are aware of in this complete hallucination that is obvious that we are not awaken to the sparking awareness of physical objects, their surfaces, or their constituents. Nor can we even construe the experience as one of an objects appearing to us in a certain way. It is after all a complete hallucination and the objects we take to exist before we are simply not there. But if we compare hallucinatory experience with the qualitatively indistinguishable veridical experiences, should we most conclude that it would be special to suppose that in veridical experience we are aware of something radically different from what we are aware of in hallucinatory experience? Again, it might help to reflect on our belief that the immediate cause of hallucinatory experience and veridical experience might be the very same brain event, and it is surely implausible to suppose that the effects of this same cause are radically different -acquaintance with physical objects in the case of veridical experience: Something else in the case of hallucinatory experience.

This version of the argument from hallucination would seem to address straightforwardly the ontological versions of direct realism. The argument is supposed to convince us that the ontological analysis of sensation in both veridical and hallucinatory experience should give us the same results, but in the hallucinatory case there is no plausible physical object, constituent of a physical object, or surface of a physical object with which additional premiss we would also get an argument against epistemological direct realism. That premiss is that in a vivid hallucinatory experience we might have precisely the same justification for believing (falsely) what we do about the physical world as we do in the analogous, phenomenological indistinguishable, veridical experience. But our justification for believing that there is a table before us in the course of a vivid hallucination of a table are surely not non-inferential in character. It certainly is not, if non-inferential justifications are supposedly a consist but yet an unproblematic access to the fact that makes true our belief -by hypothesis the table does not exist. But if the justification that hallucinatory experiences give us the same as the justification we get from the parallel veridical experience, then we should not describe a veridical experience as giving us non-inferential justification for believing in the existence of physical objects. In both cases we should say that we believe what we do about the physical world on the basis of what we know directly about the character of our experience.

In this brief space, I can only sketch some of the objections that might be raised against arguments from illusion and hallucination. That being said, let us begin with a criticism that accepts most of the presuppositions of the arguments. Even if the possibility of hallucination establishes that in some experience we are not acquainted with constituents of physical objects, it is not clear that it establishes that we are never acquainted with a constituent of physical objects. Suppose, for example, that we decide that in both veridical and hallucinatory experience we are acquainted with sense-data. At least some philosophers have tried to identify physical objects with bundles of actual and possible sense-data.

To establish inductively that sensations are signs of physical objects one would have to observe a correlation between the occurrence of certain sensations and the existence of certain physical objects. But to observe such a correlation in order to establish a connexion, one would need independent access to physical objects and, by hypothesis, this one cannot have. If one further adopts the verificationist's stance is that the ability to comprehend is parasitic on the ability to confirm, one can easily be driven to Humes conclusion:

Let us chance our imagination to the heavens, or to the utmost limits of the universe, we never really advance a step beyond ourselves, nor can conceivable any kind of existence, but those perceptions, which have appear`d in that narrow compass. This is the universe of the imagination, nor have we have any idea but what is there Reduced. (Hume, 1739-40, pp. 67-8).

If one reaches such a conclusion but wants to maintain the intelligibility and verifiability of the assertion about the physical world, one can go either the idealistic or the phenomenalistic route.

However, hallucinatory experiences on this view is non-veridical precisely because the sense-data one is acquainted with in hallucination do not bear the appropriate relations to other actual and possible sense-data. But if such a view were plausible one could agree that one is acquainted with the same kind of a thing in veridical and non- veridical experience but insists that there is still a sense in which in veridical experience, one is acquainted with that are maintained by the constituents of some physical objects?

Once one abandons epistemological; direct realises, but one has an uphill battle indicating how one can legitimately make the inferences from sensation to physical objects. But philosophers who appeal to the existence of illusion and hallucination to develop an argument for scepticism can be accused of having an epistemically self-defeating argument. One could justifiably infer sceptical conclusions from the existence of illusion and hallucination only if one justifiably believed that such experiences exist, but if one is justified in believing that illusion exists, one must be justified in believing at least, some facts about the physical world (for example, that straight sticks look bent in water). The key point to stress in relying to such arguments is, that strictly speaking, the philosophers in question need only appeal to the possibility of a vivid illusion and hallucination. Although it would have been psychologically more difficult to come up with arguments from illusion and hallucination if we did not believe that we actually had such experiences, I take it that most philosophers would argue that the possibility of such experiences is enough to establish difficulties with direct realism. Indeed, if one looks carefully at the argument from hallucination discussed earlier, one sees that it nowhere makes any claims about actual cases of hallucinatory experience.

Another reply to the attack on epistemological direct realism focuses on the implausibility of claiming that there is any process of inference wrapped up in our beliefs about the world and its surrounding surfaces. Even if it is possible to give a phenomenological description of the subjective character of sensation, it requires a special sort of skill that most people lack. Our perceptual beliefs about the physical world are surely direct, at least in the sense that they are unmediated by any sort of conscious inference from premisses describing something other than a physical object. The appropriate reply to this objection, however, is simply to acknowledge the relevant phenomenological fact and point out that from the perceptive of epistemologically direct realism, the philosopher is attacking a claim about the nature of our justification for believing propositions about the physical world. Such philosophers need carry out of any comment at all about the causal genesis of such beliefs.

As mentioned that proponents of the argument from illusion and hallucination have often intended it to establish the existence of sense-data, and many philosophers have attacked the so-called sense-datum inference presupposed in some statements of the argument. When the stick looked bent, the penny looked elliptical and the yellow object looked red, the sense-datum theorist wanted to infer that there was something bent, elliptical and red, respectively. But such an inference is surely suspect. Usually, we do not infer that because something appears to have a certain property, that affairs that affecting something that has that property. When in saying that Jones looks like a doctor, I surely would not want anyone to infer that there must actually be someone there who is a doctor. In assessing this objection, it will be important to distinguish different uses words like appears and looks. At least, sometimes to say that something looks F way and the sense-datum inference from an F appearance in this sense to an actual F would be hopeless. However, it also seems that we use the appears/looks terminology to describe the phenomenological character of our experience and the inference might be more plausible when the terms are used this way. Still, it does seem that the arguments from illusion and hallucination will not by themselves constitute strong evidence for sense-datum theory. Even if one concludes that there is something common to both the hallucination of a red thing and a veridical visual experience of a red thing, one need not describe a common constituent as awarenesses of something red. The adverbial theorist would prefer to construe the common experiential state as appeared too redly, a technical description intended only to convey the idea that the state in question need not be analysed as relational in character. Those who opt for an adverbial theory of sensation need to make good the claim that their artificial adverbs can be given a sense that is not parasitic upon an understanding of the adjectives transformed into verbs. Still, other philosophers might try to reduce the common element in veridical and non- veridical experience to some kind of intentional state. More like belief or judgement. The idea here is that the only thing common to the two experiences is the fact that in both spontaneously take there to be present an object of a certain kind.

The selfsame objections can be started within the general framework presupposed by proponents of the arguments from illusion and hallucination. A great many contemporary philosophers, however, uncomfortable with the intelligibility of the concepts needed to make sense of the theories attacked even. Thus, at least, some who object to the argument from illusion do so not because they defend direct realism. Rather they think there is something confused about all this talk of direct awareness or acquaintance. Contemporary externalists, for example, usually insist that we understand epistemic concepts by appeal: Too nomologically connections. On such a view the closest thing to direct knowledge would probably be something by other beliefs. If we understand direct knowledge this way, it is not clar how the phenomena of illusion and hallucination would be relevant to claim that on, at least some occasions our judgements about the physical world are reliably produced by processes that do not take as their input beliefs about something else.

The expressions 'knowledge by acquaintance' and 'knowledge by description', and the distinction they mark between knowing things and knowing about things, are now generally associated with Bertrand Russell. However, John Grote and Hermann von Helmholtz had earlier and independently to mark the same distinction, and William James adopted Grote's terminology in his investigation of the distinction. Philosophers have perennially investigated this and related distinctions using varying terminology. Grote introduced the distinction by noting that natural language distinguish between these two applications of the notion of knowledge, the one being of the Greek Υνῶ ναι, meaning -nosene, Kennen, connaître, the other being wissen, savoir (Grote, 1865). On Grote's account, the distinction is a natter of degree, and there are three sorts of dimensions of variability: Epistemic, causal and semantic.

We know things by experiencing them, and knowledge of acquaintance (Russell changed the preposition to by) is epistemically priori to and has a relatively higher degree of epistemic justification than knowledge about things. Indeed, sensation has the one great value of trueness or freedom from mistake.

A thought (using that term broadly, to mean any mental state) constituting knowledge of acquaintance with a thing is more or less causally proximate to sensations caused by that thing, while a thought constituting knowledge about the thing is more or less distant causally, being separated from the thing and experience of it by processes of attention and inference. At the limit, if a thought is maximally of the acquaintance type, it is the first mental state occurring in a perceptual causal chain originating in the object to which the thought refers, i.e., it is a sensation. The thing's presented to us in sensation and of which we have knowledge of acquaintance include ordinary objects in the external world, such as the sun.

Grote contrasted the imaginistic thoughts involved in knowledge of acquaintance with things, with the judgements involved in knowledge about things, suggesting that the latter but not the former are mentally contentual by a specified state of affairs. Elsewhere, however, he suggested that every thought capable of constituting knowledge of or about a thing involves a form, idea, or what we might call contentual propositional content, referring the thought to its object. Whether contentual or not, thoughts constituting knowledge of acquaintance with a thing are relatively indistinct, although this indistinctness does not imply incommunicably. On the other hand, thoughts constituting distinctly, as a result of the application of notice or attention to the confusion or chaos of sensation. Grote did not have an explicit theory on reference, the relation by which a thought is of or about a specific thing. Nor did he explain how thoughts can be more or less indistinct.

Helmholtz held unequivocally that all thoughts capable of constituting knowledge, whether knowledge that has to do with Notions (Wissen) or mere familiarity with phenomena (Kennen), is judgements or, we may say, have conceptual propositional contents. Where Grote saw a difference between distinct and indistinct thoughts, Helmholtz found a difference between precise judgements that are expressible in words and equally precise judgements that, in principle, are not expressible in words, and so are not communicable. James was influenced by Helmholtz and, especially, by Grote. (James, 1975). Taken on the latter terminology, James agreed with Grote that the distinction between knowledge of acquaintance with things and knowledge about things involves a difference in the degree of vagueness or distinctness of thoughts, though he, too, said little to explain how such differences are possible. At one extreme is knowledge of acquaintance with people and things, and with sensations of colour, flavour, spatial extension, temporal duration, effort and perceptible difference, unaccompanied by knowledge about these things. Such pure knowledge of acquaintance is vague and inexplicit. Movement away from this extreme, by a process of notice and analysis, yields a spectrum of less vague, more explicit thoughts constituting knowledge about things.

All the same, the distinction was not merely a relative one for James, as he was more explicit than Grote in not imputing content to every thought capable of constituting knowledge of or about things. At the extreme where a thought constitutes pure knowledge of acquaintance with a thing, there is a complete absence of conceptual propositional content in the thought, which is a sensation, feeling or precept, of which he renders the thought incommunicable. James reasons for positing an absolute discontinuity in between pure cognition and preferable knowledge of acquaintance and knowledge at all about things seem to have been that any theory adequate to the facts about reference must allow that some reference is not conventionally mediated, that conceptually unmediated reference is necessary if there are to be judgements at all about things and, especially, if there are to be judgements about relations between things, and that any theory faithful to the common persons sense of life must allow that some things are directly perceived.

James made a genuine advance over Grote and Helmholtz by analysing the reference relation holding between a thought and of him to specific things of or about which it is knowledge. In fact, he gave two different analyses. On both analyses, a thought constituting knowledge about a thing refers to and is knowledge about a reality, whenever it actually or potentially ends in a thought constituting knowledge of acquaintance with that thing (1975). The two analyses differ in their treatments of knowledge of acquaintance. On Jame's first analysis, reference in both sorts of knowledge is mediated by causal chains. A thought constituting pure knowledge of acquaintances with a thing refers to and is knowledge of whatever reality it directly or indirectly operates on and resembles (1975). The concepts of a thought operating on a thing or terminating in another thought are causal, but where Grote found teleology and final causes. On Jame's later analysis, the reference involved in knowledge of acquaintance with a thing is direct. A thought constituting knowledge of acquaintance with a thing either is that thing, or has that thing as a constituent, and the thing and the experience of it is identical (1975, 1976).

James further agreed with Grote that pure knowledge of acquaintance with things, i.e., sensory experience, is epistemologically priori to knowledge about things. While the epistemic justification involved in knowledge about things rests on the foundation of sensation, all thoughts about things are fallible and their justification is augmented by their mutual coherence. James was unclear about the precise epistemic status of knowledge of acquaintance. At times, thoughts constituting pure knowledge of acquaintance are said to posses absolute veritableness (1890) and the maximal conceivable truth (1975), suggesting that such thoughts are genuinely cognitive and that they provide an infallible epistemic foundation. At other times, such thoughts are said not to bear truth-values, suggesting that knowledge of acquaintance is not genuine knowledge at all, but only a non-cognitive necessary condition of genuine knowledge, knowledge about things (1976). Russell understood James to hold the latter view.

Russell agreed with Grote and James on the following points: First, knowing things involves experiencing them. Second, knowledge of things by acquaintance is epistemically basic and provides an infallible epistemic foundation for knowledge about things. (Like James, Russell vacillated about the epistemic status of knowledge by acquaintance, and it eventually was replaced at the epistemic foundation by the concept of noticing.) Third, knowledge about things is more articulate and explicit than knowledge by acquaintance with things. Fourth, knowledge about things is causally removed from knowledge of things by acquaintance, by processes of reelection, analysis and inference (1911, 1913, 1959).

But, Russell also held that the term experience must not be used uncritically in philosophy, on account of the vague, fluctuating and ambiguous meaning of the term in its ordinary use. The precise concept found by Russell in the nucleus of this uncertain patch of meaning is that of direct occurrent experience of a thing, and he used the term acquaintance to express this relation, though he used that term technically, and not with all its ordinary meaning (1913). Nor did he undertake to give a constitutive analysis of the relation of acquaintance, though he allowed that it may not be unanalysable, and did characterize it as a generic concept. If the use of the term experience is restricted to expressing the determinate core of the concept it ordinarily expresses, then we do not experience ordinary objects in the external world, as we commonly think and as Grote and James held we do. In fact, Russell held, one can be acquainted only with one's sense-data, i.e., particular colours, sounds, and so on.), one's occurrent mental states, universals, logical forms, and perhaps, oneself.

Russell agreed with James that knowledge of things by acquaintance is essentially simpler than any knowledge of truth, and logically independent of knowledge of truth (1912, 1929). The mental states involved when one is acquainted with things do not have propositional contents. Russells reasons here seem to have been similar to Jame's. Conceptually unmediated reference to particulars necessary for understanding any proposition mentioning a particular, e.g., 1918-19, and, if scepticism about the external world is to be avoided, some particulars must be directly perceived (1911). Russell vacillated about whether or not the absence of propositional content renders knowledge by acquaintance incommunicable.

Russell agreed with James that different accounts should be given of reference as it occurs in knowledge by acquaintance and in knowledge about things, and that in the former case, reference is direct. But Russell objected on a number of grounds to Jame's causal account of the indirect reference involved in knowledge about things. Russell gave a descriptional rather than a causal analysis of that sort of reference: A thought is about a thing when the content of the thought involves a definite description uniquely satisfied by the thing referred to. Indeed, he preferred to speak of knowledge of things by description, rather than knowledge about things.

Russell advanced beyond Grote and James by explaining how thoughts can be more or less articulate and explicit. If one is acquainted with a complex thing without being aware of or acquainted with its complexity, the knowledge one has by acquaintance with that thing is vague and inexplicit. Reflection and analysis can lead one to distinguish constituent parts of the object of acquaintance and to obtain progressively more comprehensible, explicit, and complete knowledge about it (1913, 1918-19, 1950, 1959).

Apparent facts to be explained about the distinction between knowing things and knowing about things are there. Knowledge about things is essentially propositional knowledge, where the mental states involved refer to specific things. This propositional knowledge can be more or less comprehensive, can be justified inferentially and on the basis of experience, and can be communicated. Knowing things, on the other hand, involves experience of things. This experiential knowledge provides an epistemic basis for knowledge about things, and in some sense is difficult or impossible to communicate, perhaps because it is more or less vague.

If one is unconvinced by James and Russells reasons for holding that experience of and reference work to things that are at least sometimes direct. It may seem preferable to join Helmholtz in asserting that knowing things and knowing about things both involve propositional attitudes. To do so would at least allow one the advantages of unified accounts of the nature of knowledge (propositional knowledge would be fundamental) and of the nature of reference: Indirect reference would be the only kind. The two kinds of knowledge might yet be importantly different if the mental states involved have different sorts of causal origins in the thinker's cognitive faculties, involve different sorts of propositional attitudes, and differ in other constitutive respects relevant to the relative vagueness and communicability of the mental sates.

In any of cases, perhaps most, Foundationalism is a view concerning the structure of the system of justified belief possessed by a given individual. Such a system is divided into foundation and superstructure, so related that beliefs in the latter depend on the former for their justification but not vice versa. However, the view is sometimes stated in terms of the structure of knowledge than of justified belief. If knowledge is true justified belief (plus, perhaps, some further condition), one may think of knowledge as exhibiting a foundationalist structure by virtue of the justified belief it involves. In any event, the construing doctrine concerning the primary justification is layed the groundwork as affording the efforts of belief, though in feeling more free, we are to acknowledge the knowledgeable infractions that will from time to time be worthy in showing to its recognition.

The first step toward a more explicit statement of the position is to distinguish between mediate (indirect) and immediate (direct) justification of belief. To say that a belief is mediately justified is to any that it s justified by some appropriate relation to other justified beliefs, i.e., by being inferred from other justified beliefs that provide adequate support for it, or, alternatively, by being based on adequate reasons. Thus, if my reason for supposing that you are depressed is that you look listless, speak in an unaccustomedly flat tone of voice, exhibit no interest in things you are usually interested in, etc., then my belief that you are depressed is justified, if, at all, by being adequately supported by my justified belief that you look listless, speak in a flat tone of voice. . . .

A belief is immediately justified, on the other hand, if its justification is of another sort, e.g., if it is justified for being based on experience or if it is self-justified. Thus my belief that you look listless may not be based on anything else I am justified in believing but just on the day you look to me. And my belief that 2 + 3 = 5 may be justified not because I infer it from something else, I justifiably believe, but simply because it seems obviously true to me.

Our cause to be interested, is that the thesis that counts as a causal theory of justification, in its meaning of 'causal theory' tend of the belief that is justified just in case it was produced by a type of process that is 'globally' reliable, that is, its propensity to produce true beliefs-that can be defined to some favourable approximations, as the proportion of the belief it produces, or would produce where it used as much as opportunity allows, that is true ~. Is sufficiently that a belief acquires favourable epistemic status by having some kind of reliable linkage to the truth? We have advanced variations of this view for both knowledge and justified belief. The first formulations of dependable accounting measure of knowing came in the accompaniment of F.P. Ramsey (1903-30), who made important contributions to mathematical logic, probability theory, the philosophy of science and economics. Instead of saying that quarks have such-and-such properties, the Ramsey sentence says the theoretical are alternatively something that has those properties. If we have repeated the process for all of the theoretical terms, the sentence gives the 'topic-neutral' structure of the theory, but removes any implication that we know what the term so treated have as a meaning. It leaves open the possibility of identifying the theoretical item with whatever. It is that best fits the description provided, thus, substituting the term by a variable, Ramsey, was one of the first thinkers to accept a 'redundancy theory of truth', which he combined its radical views of the function of many kinds of the proposition. Neither generalizations, nor causal propositions, not those treating probabilities or ethics, described facts, but each has a different specific function in our intellectual commentators on the early works of Wittgenstein, and his continuing friendship with the latter liked to Wittgenstein's return to Cambridge and to philosophy in 1929.

The most sustained and influential application of these ideas were in the philosophy of mind, or brain, as Ludwig Wittgenstein (1889-1951) whom Ramsey persuaded that remained work for him to do, the way of an undoubtedly charismatic figure of 20th-century philosophy, living and writing with a power and intensity that frequently overwhelmed his contemporaries and readers, being a kind of picture or model has centred the early period on the 'picture theory of meaning' according to which sentence represents a state of affairs of it. Containing elements corresponding to those of the state of affairs and structure or form that mirrors that a structure of the state of affairs that it represents. We have reduced to all logic complexity that of the 'propositional calculus, and all propositions are 'truth-functions of atomic or basic propositions.

In the layer period the emphasis shafts dramatically to the actions of people and the role linguistic activities play in their lives. Thus, in the "Tractatus," language is placed in a static, formal relationship with the world, in the later work Wittgenstein emphasis its use through standardized social activities of ordering, advising, requesting, measuring, counting, excising concerns for each other, and so on. These different activities are thought of as so many 'language games' that together make or a form of life. Philosophy typically ignores this diversity, and in generalizing and abstracting distorts the real nature of its subject-matter. Besides the 'Tractatus' and the investigations, collections of Wittgenstein's work published posthumously include 'Remarks on the Foundations of Mathematics' (1956), 'Notebooks' (1914-1916) (1961), Philosophische Bemerkungen (1964), Zettel (1967) and 'On Certainty' (1969).

Clearly, there are many forms of reliabilism. Just as there are ma outward appearances of something as distinguished from the substance of which it is made, these conforming configurations profile a conduct regularity by an external control, as custom or a formal protocol of procedure. What is more, are the fixed or accepted ways of doing or sometimes of expressing something establishing the constructing fabrications in the fashion or they may be forged in the formality of 'forms', held in or inhibited of 'foundationalism' and 'coherence'. How is reliabilism related to these other two theories of justification? We usually regard it as a rival, and this is aptly so, in as far as foundationalism and coherentism traditionally focussed on purely evidential relations than psychological processes, but we might also offer reliabilism as a deeper-level theory, subsuming some of the precepts of either foundationalism or coherentism. Foundationalism oftentimes but usually involves experience and observation to implicate these that are the 'basic' beliefs, which acquire justification without dependence on inference, reliabilism might rationalize this indicating that reliable non-inferential processes have formed the basic beliefs. Coherence stresses the primary of systematicity in all doxastic decision-making. Reliabilism might rationalize this by pointing to increases in reliability that accrue from systematicity consequently, reliabilism could complement foundationalism and coherence than completed with them.

These examples make it seem likely that, if there is a criterion for what makes an alternate situation relevant that will save Goldman's claim about local reliability and knowledge. Will did not be simple. The interesting thesis that counts as a causal theory of justification, in the making of 'causal theory' intended for the belief as it is justified in case it was produced by a type of process that is 'globally' reliable, that is, its propensity to produce true beliefs that can be defined, to an acceptable approximation, as the proportion of the beliefs it produces, or would produce where it used as much as opportunity allows, that is true is sufficiently relializable. We have advanced variations of this view for both knowledge and justified belief, its first formulation of a reliability account of knowing appeared in the notation from F.P. Ramsey (1903-30). The theory of probability, he was the first to show how a 'personalist theory' could be developed, based on a precise behavioural notion of preference and expectation. In the philosophy of language. Much of Ramsey's work was directed at saving classical mathematics from 'intuitionism', or what he called the 'Bolshevik menace of Brouwer and Weyl'. In the theory of probability he was the first to show how we could develop some personalists theory, as based on precise behavioural notation of preference and expectation. In the philosophy of language, Ramsey was one of the first thankers, which he combined with radical views of the function of many kinds of a proposition. Neither generalizations, nor causal propositions, nor those treating probability or ethics, describe facts, but each has a different specific function in our intellectual economy. Ramsey was one of the earliest commentators on the early work of Wittgenstein, and his continuing friendship that led to Wittgenstein's return to Cambridge and to philosophy in 1929.

Ramsey's sentence theory is the sentence generated by taking all the sentences affirmed in a scientific theory that use some term, e.g., 'quark'. Replacing the term by a variable, and existentially quantifying into the result. Instead of saying that quarks have such-and-such properties, the Ramsey sentence says that there is something that has those properties. If we repeat the process for all of a group of the theoretical terms, the sentence gives the 'topic-neutral' structure of the theory, but removes any implication that we know what the term so treated prove competent. It leaves open the possibility of identifying the theoretical item with whatever, but it is that best fits the description provided. Virtually, all theories of knowledge. Of course, share an externalist component in requiring truth as a condition for known in. Reliabilism goes farther, however, in trying to capture additional conditions for knowledge by ways of a nomic, counterfactual or other 'external' relations between belief and truth. Closely allied to the nomic sufficiency account of knowledge, primarily dur to Dretshe (1971, 1981), A.I. Goldman (1976, 1986) and R. Nozick (1981). The core of this approach is that x's belief that 'p' qualifies as knowledge just in case 'x' believes 'p', because of reasons that would not obtain unless 'p' was true, or because of a process or method that would not yield belief in 'p' if 'p' were not true. An enemy example, 'x' would not have its current reasons for believing there is a telephone before it. Or would not come to believe this in the ways it does, thus, there is a counterfactual reliable guarantor of the belief's bing true. Determined to and the facts of counterfactual approach say that 'x' knows that 'p' only if there is no 'relevant alternative' situation in which 'p' is false but 'x' would still believe that a proposition 'p', must be sufficient to eliminate all the alternatives too 'p' where an alternative to a proposition 'p' is a proposition incompatible with 'p'? That in one's justification or evidence for 'p' must be sufficient for one to know that every alternative too 'p' is false. This element of our evolving thinking, sceptical arguments have exploited about which knowledge. These arguments call our attentions to alternatives that our evidence sustains itself with no elimination. The sceptic inquires to how we know that we are not seeing a cleverly disguised mule. While we do have some evidence against the likelihood of such as deception, intuitively knowing that we are not so deceived is not strong enough for 'us'. By pointing out alternate but hidden points of nature, in that we cannot eliminate, and others with more general application, as dreams, hallucinations, etc. The sceptic appears to show that every alternative is seldom. If ever, satisfied.

This conclusion conflicts with another strand in our thinking about knowledge, in that we know many things. Thus, there is a tension in our ordinary thinking about knowledge ~. We believe that knowledge is, in the sense indicated, an absolute concept and yet, we also believe that there are many instances of that concept.

If one finds absoluteness to be too central a component of our concept of knowledge to be relinquished, one could argue from the absolute character of knowledge to a sceptical conclusion (Unger, 1975). Most philosophers, however, have taken the other course, choosing to respond to the conflict by giving up, perhaps reluctantly, the absolute criterion. This latter response holds as sacrosanct our commonsense belief that we know many things (Pollock, 1979 and Chisholm, 1977). Each approach is subject to the criticism that it preserves one aspect of our ordinary thinking about knowledge at the expense of denying another. We can view the theory of relevant alternatives as an attempt to provide a more satisfactory response to this tension in our thinking about knowledge. It attempts to characterize knowledge in a way that preserves both our belief that knowledge is an absolute concept and our belief that we have knowledge.

Having to its recourse of knowledge, its cental questions include the origin of knowledge, the place of experience in generating knowledge, and the place of reason in doing so, the relationship between knowledge and certainty, and between knowledge and the impossibility of error, the possibility of universal scepticism, and the changing forms of knowledge that arise from new conceptualizations of the world. All these issues link with other central concerns of philosophy, such as the nature of truth and the natures of experience and meaning. Realizing that epistemology is possible as dominated by two rival metaphors. One is that of a building or pyramid, built on foundations. In this conception it is the job of the philosopher to describe especially secure foundations, and to identify secure modes of construction, is that the resulting edifice can be shown to be sound. This metaphor of knowledge, and of a rationally defensible theory of confirmation and inference for construction, as that knowledge must be regarded as a structure risen upon secure, certain foundations. These are found in some formidable combinations of experience and reason, with different schools (empiricism, rationalism) emphasizing the role of one over that of the others. Foundationalism was associated with the ancient Stoics, and in the modern era with Descartes (1596-1650) who discovered his foundations in the 'clear' and 'distinct' ideas of reason? Its main opponent is coherentism, or the view that a body of propositions mas be known without a foundation in certainty, but by their interlocking strength, than as a crossword puzzle may be known to have been solved correctly even if each answer, taken individually, admits of uncertainty. Difficulties at this point led the logical passivists to abandon the notion of an epistemological foundation, and, overall, to philander with the coherence theory of truth. It is widely accepted that trying to make the connection between thought and experience through basic sentences depends on an untenable 'myth of the given'.

Still, of the other metaphor, is that of a boat or fuselage, that has no foundation but owes its strength to the stability given by its interlocking parts. This rejects the idea of a basis in the 'given', favours ideas of coherence and holism, but finds it harder to ward off scepticism. In spite of these concerns, the problem, least of mention, is of defining knowledge about true beliefs plus some favoured relations between the believer and the facts that began with Plato's view in the "Theaetetus" that knowledge is true belief, and some logos.` Due of its natural epistemology, the enterprising of studying the actual formation of knowledge by human beings, without aspiring to make evidently those processes as rational, or proof against 'scepticism' or even apt to yield the truth. Natural epistemology would therefore blend into the psychology of learning and the study of episodes I the history of science. The scope for 'external' or philosophical reflection of the kind that might result in scepticism or its refutation is markedly diminished. Although the term in a modern index has distinguished exponents of the approach include Aristotle, Hume, and J.S. Mills.

Closely allied to the nomic sufficiency account of knowledge, primarily due to F.I. Dretske (1971, 1981), A.I. Goldman (1976, 1986) and R. Nozick (1981). The core of this approach is that S's belief that 'p' qualifies as knowledge just in case 'S' believes 'p' because of reasons that would not obtain unless p's being true, or because of a process or method that would not yield belief in 'p' if 'p' were not true. For example, 'S' would not have his current reasons for believing there is a telephone before him, or would not come to believe this in the way he does, unless there was a telephone before him. Thus, there is a counterfactual reliable guarantor of the belief's being true. A variant of the counterfactual approach says that 'S' knows that 'p' only if there is no 'relevant alternative' situation in which 'p' is false but 'S' would still believe that 'p' must be sufficient to eliminate all the other situational alternatives of 'p', where an alternative to a proposition 'p' is a proposition incompatible with 'p', that is, one's justified evidence for 'p' must be sufficient for one to know that every subsidiary situation is 'p' is false.

They standardly classify reliabilism as an 'externaturalist' theory because it invokes some truth-linked factor, and truth is 'eternal' to the believer the main argument for externalism derives from the philosophy of language, more specifically, from the various phenomena pertaining to natural kind terms, indexical, and so forth, that motivates the views that have become known as direct reference' theories. Such phenomena seem, at least to show that the belief or thought content that can be properly attributed to a person is dependent on facts about his environment ~, e.g., whether he is on Earth or Twin Earth, what in fact he is pointing at, the classificatory criteria employed by the experts in his social group, etc. Not just on what is going on internally in his mind or brain (Burge, 1979.) Nearly all theories of knowledge, of course, share an externalist component in requiring truth as a condition for knowing. Reliabilism goes farther, however, in trying to capture additional conditions for knowledge by means of a nomic, counterfactual or other 'external' relations between 'belief' and 'truth'.

The most influential counterexample to reliabilism is the demon-world and the clairvoyance examples. The demon-world example challenges the necessity of the reliability requirement, in that a possible world in which an evil demon creates deceptive visual experience, the process of vision is not reliable. Still, the visually formed beliefs in this world are intuitively justified. The clairvoyance example challenges the sufficiency of reliability. Suppose a cognitive agent possesses a reliable clairvoyance power, but has no evidence for or against his possessing such a power. Intuitively, his clairvoyantly formed beliefs are unjustifiably unreasoned, but reliabilism declares them justified.

Another form of reliabilism, 'normal worlds' reliabilism' (Goldman, 1986), answers the range problem differently, and treats the demon-world problem in the same stroke. Let a 'normal world' be one that is consistent with our general beliefs about the actual world. Normal-worlds reliabilism gives tongue to that of a belief, as in any possible world is justified just in case its generating processes have high truth ratios in normal worlds. This resolves the demon-world problem because the relevant truth ratio of the visual process is not its truth ratio in the demon world itself, but its ratio in normal worlds. Since this ratio is presumably high, visually formed beliefs in the demon world turn out to be justified.

Yet, a different version of reliabilism attempts to meet the demon-world and clairvoyance problems without recourse to the questionable notion of 'normal worlds'. Consider Sosa's (1992) suggestion that justified beliefs is belief acquired through 'intellectual virtues', and not through intellectual 'vices', whereby virtues are reliable cognitive faculties or processes. The task is to explain how epistemic evaluators have used the notion of indelible virtues, and vices, to arrive at their judgements, especially in the problematic cases. Goldman (1992) proposes a two-stage reconstruction of an evaluator's activity. The first stage is reliability, based acquisition of a 'list' of virtues and vices. The second stage is application of this list to queried cases. Determining has executed the second stage whether processes in the queried cases resemble virtues or vices. We have classified visual beliefs in the demon world as justified because visual belief formation is a virtue. Clairvoyance formed, beliefs are classified as unjustified because clairvoyance resembles scientifically suspect processes that the evaluator represents as vices, e.g., mental telepathy, ESP, and so forth.

Clearly, there are many forms of reliabilism, just as there are as many forms of foundationalism and coherentism. How is reliabilism related to these other two theories of justification? They have usually regarded it as a rival, and this is apt in as far as foundationalism and coherentism traditionally focussed on purely evidential relations rather than psychological processes. But reliabilism might also be offered as a deeper-levelled theory, subsuming some precepts of either foundationalism or coherentism. Foundationalism registers that there are 'basic' beliefs, which acquire justification without dependency on inference. Reliabilism might rationalize this by indicating that reliable non-inferential processes form the basic beliefs. Coherentism stresses the primary of systematicity in all doxastic decision-making, as reliabilism might rationalize this by pointing to increases in reliability that accrue from systematicity. Thus, reliabilism could complement foundationalism and coherentism than complete with them.

The view that the truth of a proposition consists in its being a member of some suitably defined body of other propositions: A body that is consistent, coherent and possibilities were endowed with other virtues, provided these are not defined in terms of truth. The theory of coherence, though surprising at first sight, has two strengths: (1) We test the beliefs for truth in the light of other beliefs, including perceptual beliefs, and (2) We cannot step outside our own best system or correspondence with the world. To many thinkers the weak point to include coherence theories is that they fail to include a proper sense of the way in which actual systems of belief are sustained by persons with perceptual experience, impinged on or upon by their environment. For a pure coherence theorist, experience e is only relevant at the source of perceptual beliefs, which take their place as part of the coherent or incoherent set. This seems not to do justice to our sense that experience plays a special role in controlling our systems of belief, but coherences have contested the clam in various ways.

As too, Aristotle aforesaid that a statement is true if it says of what is that it is, and of what is not that it is not (Metaphysics Γ, iv. 1011). But a correspondence theory is not simply the view that truth consists in correspondence with the facts, bu t rather the view that it is theoretically interesting to realize this. Aristotle's claim is in itself a harmless platitude, common to all views of truth. A correspondence theory is distinctive in holding that the notion of correspondence and fact can be sufficiently developed to make the platitude into an interesting theory of truth. Opponents charge that this is not so, primarily because we have no access to facts independently of the statements and beliefs that we hold. We cannot look our own shoulders to compare our beliefs with a reality apprehended by other means, than those beliefs, or, perhaps, further beliefs. Hence, we have no fix on 'facts' as something like structures to which our beliefs may or may not correspond.

It is, nonetheless, the theory that mental events are identical with physical events, more commonly called 'physicalism'. Historically identity philosophy, associated with Schelling, Held that the spirit and nature are fundamentally one and the same, both being aspects of the absolute. More generally any 'monism' is the doctrine of the identity of what may seem to be many different kinds of things.

Philosophers often debate the existence of different kinds of things: Nominalists question the reality of abstract objects like class, numbers, and universals, some positivist doubt the existence of theoretical entities like neutrons or genes, and there are debates over whether there are sense-data, events and so on. Some philosophers may be happy to talk about abstract one, if it is contained to theoretic entities, while denying that they really exist. This requires a 'metaphysical' concept of 'real existence': We debate whether numbers, neutrons and sense-data really existing things. But it is difficult to see what this concept involves and the rules to be employed in setting such debates are very unclear.

Questions of existence seem always to involve general kinds of things, do numbers, sense-data or neutrons exit? Some philosophers conclude that existence is not a property of individual things, 'exists' is not an ordinary predicate. If I refer to something, and then predicate existence of it, my utterance is tautological, the object must exist for me to be able to refer to it, so predicating for me to be able to refer to it, so predicating existence of it adds nothing. And to say of something that it did not exist would be contradictory.

According to Rudolf Carnap, who pursued the enterprise of clarifying the structures of mathematical and scientific language (the only legitimate task for scientific philosophy) in "The Logische Syntax der Sprache" (1934). Refinements to his syntactic and semantic views continued with "Meaning and Necessity" (1947), while a general loosening of the original ideal of reduction culminated in the great "Logical Foundation of Probability," is most important on the grounds accountable by its singularity, the confirmation theory, in 1959. Other works concern the structure of physics and the concept of entropy. Nonetheless, questions of which framework to employ do not concern whether the entities posited by the framework 'really exist', its pragmatic usefulness has rather settled them. Philosophical debates over existence misconstrue 'pragmatics' questions of choice of frameworks as substantive questions of fact. Once we have adopted a framework there are substantive 'internal' questions, are their zany prime numbers between ten and twenty. 'External' questions about choice of frameworks have a different status.

More recent philosophers, notably Quine, have questioned the distinction between linguistic framework and internal questions arising within it. Quine agrees that we have no 'metaphysical' concept of existence against which different purported entities can be measured. If quantification of the general theoretical framework which best explains our experiences, making the abstraction, of which there are such things, that they exist, is true. Scruples about admitting the existence of too many different kinds of objects depend not on a metaphysical concept of existence but rather on a desire for a simple and economical theoretical framework.

It is not possible by any enacting characterlogical infractions of succumbing the combinations that await our presence to the future as upon a definition holding of an apprehensive experience, and in an illuminating way though, what experiences are brought through acquaintance are with some of their own, e.g., a visual experience of a green after images, a feeling of physical nausea or a tactile experience of an abrasive surface, which and actual surface ~ rough or smooth might cause or which might be part of ca dream, or the product of a vivid sensory imagination? The essential feature of every experience is that it feels in some certain ways. That there is something that it is like to have it. We may refer to this feature of an experience is its 'character'.

Another core groups of characterizations are of the sorts of experience with which our concerns are those that have representational content, unless otherwise indicated, the terms 'experience' will be reserved for these that we implicate below, that the most obvious cases of experience with content are sense experiences of the kind normally involved I perception? We may describe such experiences by mentioning their sensory modalities and their content's, e.g., a gustatory experience (modality) of chocolate ice cream (content), but do so more commonly by means of perceptual verbs combined with noun phrases specifying their contents, as in 'Macbeth saw a dagger'; This is, however, ambiguous between the perceptual claim 'There was a [material] dagger in the world which Macbeth perceived visually' and 'Macbeth had a visual experience of a dagger', the reading with which we are concerned.

According to the act/object analysis of experience (which is a special case of the act/object analysis of consciousness), every experience involves an object of experience even if it has no material object. Two main lines of argument may be offered in support of this view, one phenomenological and the semantic.

In an outline, the phenomenological argument is as follows: Whenever we have an experience, even if nothing beyond the experience answers to it, we may be presented with something through the experience (which has for ourselves transparentness). The object of our experience is whatever is so presented to us, at this mediated presents as weighing abreast in time and space, nonetheless and no matter of any particular individual thing, it is commonly something that is shown, or revealed, or manifested in experience as having been related to an event or a state of affairs,

The semantic argument is that objects of experience are required to make sense of certain features of our talk about experiences which include, in particular, such as (1) Simple attributions of experience (e.g., 'Rod is experiencing a pink square') seem relational. (2) We apar to refer tp objects of experienced and to attribute properties to them (e.g., 'The after image which John experienced was green'). (3) We appear to quantify over objects of experience (e.g., 'Macbeth saw something which his wife did not see').

The act/object analysis faces several problems concerning the status of objects of experience. Currently, the most common view is that they are sense-data -private mental entities which possess the traditional sensory qualities reported using the experience of which they are the objects. However, the very idea of an exactly private entity suspect. Nonetheless, an experience may apparently represent something as having a determinable property (e.g., redness) without representing it as having any subordinate determinate property (e.g., any specific shade of red), a sense-datum may have determinable property without having any determinate property subordinate to it, Even more disturbing, is that, sense-data may have contradictory properties, since experiences can have contradictory contents. A case in point, is the waterfall illusion: If you stare at a waterfall for a minute and then immediately fixate your vision upon a nearby rock, you are likely to have an experience of the rock's moving upward, when suddenly its appearance remains in the same place. The sense-datum theorist mus either deny that there are such experiences or admit to contradictory objects.

These problems can be avoided by treating object of experiences properties, however, failing to do justice to the appearances, for experience seems not to present us with bare properties (however complex), but with properties embodied in individuals. The view that objects of experience is that Meinongian object accommodates this point. It is also attractive insofar as (1) it allows experiences to represent properties other than traditional sensory qualities, and (2) it allows for the identification of objects of experience and objects of perception in experience which constitute perceptions, about representative realism, objects of perception (of which we are 'indirectly aware') are always distinct from an object of experience (of which we are 'directly are') Meinongian's, however, may simply treat objects of perception of existing objects of experience. Nonetheless, most philosophers will feel that the Meinongian's acceptance of impossible objects is too high a price to for these benefits.

Nevertheless, a general problem addressed for the act/object analysis is that the question of whether two subjects are experiencing the same thing, as opposed to having exactly similar experiences, that appears to have an answer only on the assumption that the experiences concerned are perceptions with material objects. But in the act/object analysis the question must have an answer even when this condition is not satisfied. (The answer is always negative on the sense-datum theory, but it could be positive on other versions of the act/object analysis, depending on the facts of the case.)

All the same, the case for the act/object analysis should be reassessed. The phenomenological argument is not, on reflection, convincing. For it is easy enough to grant that any experience appears to present us with an object without accepting that it actually does.

The semantic argument is more impressive, but is nonetheless, answerable. The seemingly relational structure of attributions of experience is a challenge dealt with its connection with the adverbial theory. Apparent reference to and quantification over objects of experience can be handled by analysing them as reference to experiences themselves and quantification over experiences tacitly according to content. Thus 'The after image which John experienced was an experience of green', and 'Macbeth something which his wife did not see' becomes 'Macbeth had a visual experience which his wife did not have'.

As pertaining case of other mental states and events with content, it is important to distinguish between the properties which experience represents and the properties which it possesses. To talk of the representational properties of an experience is to say something about its content, not to attribute those properties to the experience itself. Like every other experience, a visual Experience of a pink square is a mental event, and it is therefore not itself either pink or square, though it represents those properties. It is, perhaps, fleeting, pleasant or unusual, although it does not represent those properties. An experience may represent a property which it possesses, and it may even do so in virtue of possessing that property, inasmuch as the putting to case of rapidly representing change [complex] experience representing something as changing rapidly, but this is the exception and not the rule.

Which properties can be [directly] represented in sense experience is subject to debate. Traditionalists, include only properties whose presence a subject could not doubt having appropriated experiences, e.g., colour and shape with visual experience, i.e., colour and shape with visual experience, surface texture, hardness, etc., for tactile experience. This view s natural to anyone who has to an egocentric Cartesian perspective in epistemology, and wishes for pure data experience to serve as logically certain foundations for knowledge. The term 'sense-data', introduced by Moore and Russell, refers to the immediate objects of perceptual awareness, such as colour patches and shape, indifferently required for conscious distinctions from surfaces of physical objects. Qualities of sense-data are supposed to be distinct from physical qualities because their perception is more immediate, and because sense data are private and cannot appear other than they are. They are objects that change in our perceptual fields when conditions of perception change and physical objects remain constant.'

Critics of the notional questions of whether, just because physical objects can appear other than they are, there must be private, mental objects that have all qualities that the physical objects appear to have, there are also problems regarding the individuation and duration of sense-data and their relations ti physical surfaces of an object we perceive. Contemporary proponents counter that speaking only of how things and to appear cannot capture the full structure within perceptual experience captured by talk of apparent objects and their qualities.

It is nevertheless, that others who do not think that this wish can be satisfied and they impress who with the role of experience in giving animals ecological significant information about the world around them, claim that sense experiences represent possession characteristics and kinds which are much richer and much more wide-ranging than the traditional sensory qualitites. We do not see only colours and shapes they tell 'us' about, earth, water, men, women and fire, we do not smell only odours, but also food and filth. There is no space here to examine the factors about as choice between these alternatives. In so, that we are to assume and expect when it is incompatibles with a position under discussion.

Given the modality and content of a sense experience, most of 'us' will be aware of its character though we cannot describe that character directly. This suggests that character and content are not really distinct, and a close tie between them. For one thing, the relative complexity of the character of some sense experience places limitation n its possible content, i.e., a tactile experience of something touching one's left ear is just too simple to carry the same amount of content as typically every day, visual experience. Furthermore, the content of a sense experience of a given character depends on the normal causes of appropriately similar experiences, i.e., the sort of gustatory experience which we have when eating chocolate would not represent chocolate unless chocolate normally caused it, granting a contingent ties between the characters of an experience and its possibility for casual origins, it again, followed its possible content is limited by its character.

Character and content are none the less irreducible different for the following reasons (I) There are experiences which completely lack content, i.e., certain bodily pleasures (ii) Nit every aspect of the character of an experience which content is used for that content, i.e., the unpleasantness of an auricular experience of chalk squeaking on a board may have no responsibility significance (iii) Experiences indifferent modalities may overlap in content without a parallel experience in character, i.e., visual and active experiences of circularity feel completely different (iv) The content of an experience with a given character may be out of line with an according background of the subject, i.e., a certain aural experience may come to have the content 'singing birds' only after the subject has learned something about birds.

According to the act/object analysis of experience, which is a peculiar to case that his act/object analytic thinking of consciousness, that every experience involves an object of experience if it has not material object. Two main lines of argument may be offered in supports of this view, one phenomenological and the other semantic.

In an outline, the phenomenological argument is as follows. Whenever we have an experience answer to it, we may be presented with something through the experience which something through the experience, which if in ourselves diaphanous. The object of the experience is whatever is so presented to us. Plausibly let be, that an individual thing, and event or a state of affairs.

The semantic argument is that they require objects of experience to make sense of cretin factures of our talk about experience, including, in particular, the following (1) Simple attributions of experience, i.e., 'Rod is experiencing a pink square', seem relational (2) We appear to refer to objects of experience and to attribute properties to them, i.e., we gave. The after image which John experienced. (3) We appear to qualify over objects of experience, i.e., Macbeth saw something which his wife did not see.

The act/object analysis faces several problems concerning the status of objects of experience. Currently the most common view is that they are 'sense-data' ~. Private mental entities which actually posses the traditional sensory qualities represented by the experience of which they are the objects. But the very idea of an essentially private entity is suspect. Moreover, since an experience must apparently represent something as having a determinable property, i.e., red, without representing it as having any subordinate determinate property, i.e., each given shade of red, a sense-datum may actually have our determinate property without saving any determinate property subordinate to it. Even more disturbing is that sense-data may contradictory properties, since experience can have properties, since experience can have contradictory contents. A case in point is te water fall illusion: If you stare at a waterfall for a minute and the immediately fixate on a nearby rock, you are likely to are an experience of moving upward while it remains inexactly the same place. The sensory faculty-data, privatize the mental entities which actually posses the traditional sensory qualities represented by the experience of which they are te objects. But the very idea of an essentially private entity is suspect. Moreover, since abn experience may apparently represent something as having a determinable property, i.e., redness, without representing it as having any subordinate determinate property, i.e., any specific shade of red, a sense-datum may actually have a determinate property without having any determinate property subordinate to it. Even more disturbing is the sense-data may have contradictory properties, since experiences can have contradictory contents. A case in point is the waterfall illusion: If you stare at a waterfall for a minute and then immediately fixate your vision upon a nearby rock, you are likely to have an experience of the rock's moving for which its preliminary illusion finds of itself a separation distortion for which its assimilation to correct the illusion. The proper and true implication, as having occur to indirectorial motion is without apparent linearity of direction, having to no ups, downs, sideways, or any which way whatsoever. While remaining in the same place. The sense-datum theorist must either deny that there as such experiences or admit contradictory objects.

Treating objects can avoid these problems of experience as properties. This, however, fails to do justice to the appearances, for experiences, however complex, but with properties embodied in individuals. The view that objects of experience is that Meinongian objects accommodate this point. It is also attractive, in as far as (1) it allows experiences to represent properties other than traditional sensory qualities, and (2) it allows for the identification of objects of experience and objects of perception with experiences which constitute perceptivity.

According to the act/object analysis of experience, every experience with contentual representation involves an object of experience, an act of awareness has related the subject (the event of experiencing that object). This is meant to apply not only to perceptions, which have material objects, whatever is perceived, but also to experiences like hallucinating and dream experiences, which do not. Such experiences are, nonetheless, less appearing to represent of something, and their objects are supposed to be whatever it is that they represent. Act/object theorists may differ on the nature of objects of experience, which we have treated as properties, Meinongian objects, which may not exist or have any form of being, and, more commonly, private mental entities with sensory qualities. We have now usually applied the term 'sense-data' to the latter, but have also been used as a general term for objective sense experiences, in the work of G.E., Moore, the terms of representative realism, objects of perceptions, of which we are 'indirectly aware' are always distinct from objects of experience, of which we are 'directly aware'. Meinongian, however, may treat objects of perception as existing objects of perception, least there is mention, Meinong's most famous doctrine derives from the problem of intentionality, which led him to countenance objects, such as the golden mountain, that can be the object of thought, although they do not actually exist. This doctrine was one of the principle's targets of Russell's theory of 'definitive descriptions', however, it came as part of a complex and interesting package of concept if the theory of meaning, and scholars are not united in what supposedly that Russell was fair to it. Meinong's works include "Über Annahmen" (1907), translated as "On Assumptions" (1983), and "Über Möglichkeit und Wahrschein ichkeit" (1915). But most of the philosophers will feel that the Meinongian's acceptance to impossible objects is too high a price to pay for these benefits.

A general problem for the act/object analysis is that the question of whether two subjects are experiencing the same thing, as opposed to having exactly similar experiences, that it appears to have an answer only, on the assumptions that the experience concerned are perceptions with material objects. But for the act/object analysis the question must have an answer even when conditions are not satisfied. The answers unfavourably negative, on the sense-datum theory: It could be positive of the versions of the act/object analysis, depending on the facts of the case.

In view of the above problems, we should reassess the case of act/object analysis. The phenomenological argument is not, on reflection, convincing, for it is easy enough to grant that any experience appears to present 'us' with an object without accepting that it actually does. The semantic argument is more impressive, but is nonetheless, answerable. The seemingly relational structure of attributions of experiences is a challenge dealt with below concerning the adverbial theory. Apparent reference to and we can handle quantification over objects of experience themselves and quantification over experience tacitly according to content, thus, 'the after image which John experienced was an experience of green' and 'Macbeth saw something which his wife did not see' becomes 'Macbeth had a visual experience which his wife did not have'.

Notwithstanding, pure cognitivism attempts to avoid the problems facing the act/object analysis by reducing experiences to cognitive events or associated dispositions, i.e., 'We might identify Susy's experience of a rough surface beneath her hand with the event of her acquiring the belief that there is a rough surface beneath her hand, or, if she does not acquire this belief, with a disposition to acquire it which we have somehow blocked.

This position has attractions. It does full justice. And to the important role of experience as a source of belief acquisition. It would also help clear the say for a naturalistic theory of mind, since there may be some prospect of a physical/functionalist account of belief and other intentional states. But its failure has completely undermined pure cognitivism to accommodate the fact that experiences have a felt character which cannot be reduced to their content.

The adverbial theory of experience advocates that the grammatical object of a statement attributing an experience to someone be analysed as an adverb, for example,

Rod is experiencing a pink square.

Is rewritten as?

Rod is experiencing (pink square)–ly.

Also, the adverbial theory is an attempt to undermine a semantic account of attributions of experience which does not require objects of experience. Unfortunately, the oddities of explicit adverbializations of such statements have driven off potential supporters of the theory. Furthermore, the theory remains largely undeveloped, and attempted refutations have traded on this. It may, however, be founded on sound basic intuition, and there is reason to believe that an effective development of the theory, which is merely hinted upon possibilities.

The relearnt intuitions are as, (I) that when we say that someone is experiencing an 'A', this has an experience of an 'A', we are using this content-expression to specify the type of thing which the experience is especially apt to fit, (ii) that doing this is a matter of saying something about the experience itself (and maybe also about the normal causes of like experiences). And (iii) that there is no-good reason to suppose that it involves the description of an object of which the experience is ''. Thus, the effective role of the content-expression is a statement of experience is to modify the verb it compliments, not to introduce a special type of object.

Perhaps the most important criticism of the adverbial theory is the 'many property problem', according to which the theory does not have the resources to distinguish between, e.g.,

(1) Frank has an experience of a brown triangle.

And:

(2) Frank has an experience of brown and an experience of a triangle,

Which (1) has entailed, but does not entail it. The act/object analysis can easily accommodate the difference between (1) and (2) by claiming that the truth of (1) requires a single object of experience which is as both brown in colour and three-sided triangles, while that of the (2) allows for the possibility of two objects of experience, one brown and the other triangular. Note, however, that (1) is equivalent to.

(1*) Frank has an experience of something's being Both brown in colour and three-sided triangles.

And (2) is equivalent to:

(2*) Frank has an experience of something's being both brown and a three-sided triangle or of something's being triangular,

And we can explain the difference between these quite simply about logical scope without invoking objects of experience. The adverbialists may use this to answer the many-property problem by arguing that the phrase 'a brown triangle' in (1) does the same work as the clause 'something's being both brown and triangular' in (1*). This is perfectly compactable with the view that it also has the 'adverbial' function of modifying the verb 'has an experience of', for it specifies the experience more narrowly just by giving a necessary condition for the satisfactions of the experience, as the condition being that there are something both brown and triangular before Frank.

A final position which we should mention is the state theory, according to which a sense experience of an 'A' is an occurrent, non-relational state of the kind which the subject would be in when perceiving an 'A'. Suitably qualified, this claim is no doubt truer, but its significance is subject to debate. Here it is enough to remark that the claim is compactable with both pure cognitivism and the adverbial theory, and that we have probably best advised state theorists to adopt adverbials for developing their intuition.

Perceptual knowledge is knowledge acquired by or through the senses, this includes most of what we know. We cross intersections when everything we see the light turn green, head for the kitchen when we smell the roast burning, squeeze the fruit to determine its ripeness, and climb out of bed when we hear the alarm ring. In each case we come to know something - that the light has turned green, that the roast is burning, that the melon is overripe, and that it is time to get up by some sensory means. Because the light has turned green is learning something - that the light has turned green by use of the eyes. Feeling that the melon is overripe is coming to know a fact that the melon is overripe by one's sense of touch. In each case we have somehow based on the resulting knowledge, derived from or grounded in the sort of experience that characterizes the sense modality in question.

Seeing a rotten kumquat is not at all like the experience of smelling, tasting or feeling a rotten kumquat, yet all these experiences can result in the same primary directive as to knowledge. . . . Knowledge that the kumquat is rotten, . . . although the experiences are much different, they must, if they are to yield knowledge, embody information about the kumquat: The information that it is rotten. Since the fruit is rotten differs from smelling that it is rotten, not in what is known, but how it is known. In each case, the information has the same source-the rotten kumquats but it is, so to speak, delivered via different channels and coded in different experiences.

It is important to avoid confusing perception knowledge of facts', i.e., that the kumquat is rotten, with the perception of objects, i.e., rotten kumquats, a rotten kumquat, quite another to know. By seeing or tasting, that it is a rotten kumquat. Some people do not know what kumquats smell like, as when they smell like a rotten kumquat-thinking, perhaps, that this is the way this strange fruit is supposed to smell doing not realize from the smell, i.e., do not smell that, it is rotten. In such cases people see and smell rotten kumquats - and in this sense perceive rotten kumquats, and never know that they are kumquats let alone rotten kumquats. They cannot, not at least by seeing and smelling, and not until they have learned something about [rotten] kumquats, come to know that what they are seeing or smelling is a [rotten] kumquat. Since we have geared the topic toward perceptual representations too knowledge-knowing, by sensory means or data, that something is 'F'~, wherefor, we need the question of what more, beyond the perception of F's, to see that and thereby know that they are 'F' will be brought of question, not how we see kumquats (for even the ignorant can do this), but, how we even know, in that indeed, we do, in that of what we see.

Much of our perceptual knowledge is indirect, dependent or derived. This is meant that the facts we describe ourselves as learning, as coming to know, by perceptual means are pieces of knowledge that depend on our coming to know something else, another fact, in a more direct way. We see, by newspapers, that our team has lost again, see, by her expression, that she is nervous. This dived or dependent sort of knowledge is particularly prevalent with vision, but it occurs, to a lesser degree, in every sense modality. We install bells and other sound makers so that we can, for example, hear (by the alarm) that someone is at the door and (by the bell) that its time to get up. When we obtain knowledge in this way, it is clear that unless one sees -hence, comes to know something about the gauge that it reads 'empty', the newspaper (what it says) and the person's expression, one would not see, hence, we know, that what one perceptual representation means to have described as coming to know. If one cannot hear that the bell is ringing, the ringing of the bell cannot, in, at least, and, in this way, one cannot hear that one's visitors have arrived. In such cases one sees, hears, smells, etc., that 'an' is 'F', coming to know thereby that 'an' is 'F', by seeing, hearing etc., we have derived from that come other condition, 'b's being 'G', that 'an' is 'F', or dependent on, the more basic perceptivity that of its being attributive to knowledge that of 'b' is 'G'.

Though perceptual knowledge about objects is often, in this way, dependent on knowledge of facts about different objects, the derived knowledge is something about the same object. That is, we see that 'an' is 'F' by seeing, not that another object is 'G', but that 'a' would stand justly as equitably as 'G'. We see, by her expression, that she is nervous. She tells that the fabric is silk (not polyester) by the characteristic 'greasy' feel of the fabric itself (not, as I do, by what is printed on the label). We tell whether it is a maple tree, a convertible Porsche, a geranium, and ingenious rock or a misprint by its shape, colour, texture, size, behaviour and distinctive markings. Perceptual representations of this sort are also derived. Derived from the more facts (about 'a') that we use to make the identification. Then, the perceptual knowledge is still indirect because, although the same object is involved, the facts we come to know about it are different from the facts that enable 'us' to know it.

We sometimes describe derived knowledge as inferential, but this is misleading. At the conscious level there is no passage of the mind from premised to conclusion, no reason-sensitivity of mind from problem-solving. The observer, the one who sees that 'a' is 'F' by seeing that 'b', or, 'a' is 'G', need not be and typically is not aware of any process of inference, any passage of the mind from one belief to another. The resulting knowledge, though logically derivative, is psychologically immediate. I could see that she was getting angry, so I moved my hand. I did not, at least not at any conscious level, Infer (from her expression and behaviour) that she was getting angry. I could (or, it seems to me) see that she was getting angry, it is this psychological immediacy that makes indirect perceptual knowledge a species of perceptual knowledge.

The psychological immediacy that characterizes so much of our perceptual knowledge -even (sometimes) the most indirect and derived forms of it do not mean that no one requires learning to know in this way. One is not born with (may, in fact, never develop) the ability to recognize daffodils, muskrats and angry companions. It is only after a long experience that one is able visually to identify such things. Beginners may do something corresponding to inference, they recognize relevant features of trees, birds, and flowers, features they already know how to identify perceptually, and then infer (conclude), based on what they see, and under the guidance of more expert observers, that it is an oak, a finch or a geranium. But the experts, and we are all experts on many aspects of our familiar surroundings, do not typically go through such a process. The expert just sees that it is an oak, a finch or a geranium. The perceptual knowledge of the expert is still dependent, of course, since even an expert cannot see what kind of flower it is if she cannot first see its colour and shape, but it is to say that the expert has developed identificatorial skills that no longer require the sort of conscious self-inferential process that characterize a beginner's effort.

Coming to know that 'a' is 'F' by since 'b' is 'G' obviously requires some background assumption by the observer, an assumption to the effect that 'a' is 'F' (or, perhaps only probable 'F') when 'b' is 'G'? If one does not speculatively take for granted, that they properly connect the gauge, does not (thereby) assume that it would not register 'Empty' unless the tank was nearly empty, then even if one could see that it registered 'Empty', one would not learn hence, would not see, that one needed gas. At least one would not see it by consulting the gauge. Likewise, in trying to identify birds, it is no use being able to see their marking if one does not know something about which birds have which marks ~. Something of the form, a bird with these markings is (probably) a blue jay.

It seems, moreover, that these background assumptions, if they are to yield knowledge that 'a' is 'F', as they must if the observer is to see (by b's being G) that 'a' is 'F', must have themselves qualify as knowledge. For if no one has known this background fact, if no one knows it whether 'a' is 'F' when 'b' is 'G', then the knowledge of b's bing G is, taken by itself, powerless to generate the knowledge that 'a' is 'F'. If the conclusion is to be true, both the premises used to reach that conclusion must be truer, or so it seems.

Externalists, however, argue that the indirect knowledge that 'a' is 'F', though it may depend on the knowledge that 'b' is 'G', does not require knowledge of the connecting fact, the fact that 'a' is 'F' when 'b' is 'G'. Simple belief (or, perhaps, justified beliefs, there are stronger and weaker versions of externalism) in the connecting fact is sufficient to confer a knowledge of the connected fact. Even if, strictly speaking, I do not know she is nervous whenever she fidgets like that, I can nonetheless see (hence, recognized, or know) that she is nervous (by the way she fidgets) if I (correctly) assume that this behaviour is a reliable expression of nervousness. One need not know the gauge is working well to make observations (acquire observational knowledge) with it. All that we require, besides the observer believing that the gauge is reliable, is that the gauge, in fact, be reliable, i.e., that the observers background beliefs be true. Critics of externalism have been quick to point out that this theory has the unpalatable consequence-can make that knowledge possible and, in this sense, be made to rest on lucky hunches (that turn out true) and unsupported (even irrational) beliefs. Surely, internalists argue if one is going to know that 'a' is 'F' based on 'b's' being 'G', one should have (as a bare minimum) some justification for thinking that 'a' is 'F', or is probably 'F', when 'b' is 'G'.

Whatever taken to be that these matters (except extreme externalism), indirect perception obviously requires some understanding (knowledge? Justification? Belief?) of the general relationship between the fact one comes to know (that 'a' is 'F') and the facts (that 'b' is 'G') that enable one to know it. And it is this requirement on background knowledge or understanding that leads to questions about the possibility of indirect perceptual knowledge. Is it really knowledge? Sceptical doubts have inspired the first question about whether we can ever know the connecting facts in question. How is it possible to learn, to acquire knowledge of, the connecting fact's knowledge of which is necessary to see (by 'b's' being 'G') that 'a' is 'F'? These connecting facts may not be perceptually knowable. Quite the contrary, they are generally knowable by its truth and recognition of it's knowable (if knowable at all) by inductive inference from past observations. And if one is sceptical about obtaining knowledge in this indirect, inductive as, one is, perforced, indirect knowledge, including indirect perceptivity, where we have described knowledge of a sort openly as above, that depends on in it.

Even if one puts aside such sceptical questions, least of mention, there remains a legitimate concern about the perceptual character of this kind of knowledge. If one sees that 'a' is 'F' by seeing that 'b' is 'G', is one really seeing that 'a' is 'F'? Isn't perception merely a part ~? And, indeed, from an epistemological standpoint, whereby one comes to know that 'a' is 'F'? One must, it is true, see that 'b' is 'G', but this is only one of the premises needed to reach the conclusion (knowledge) that 'a' is 'F'. There is also the background knowledge that is essential to te process. If we think of a theory as any factual proposition, or set of factual propositions, that cannot itself be known in some direct observational way, we can express this worry by saying that indirect perception is always theory-loaded: Seeing (indirectly) that 'a' is 'F' is only possible if the observer already has knowledge of (justifications for, belief in) some theory, the theory 'connecting' the fact one comes to know that 'a' is 'F' with the fact that 'b' is 'G' that enables one to know it.

This of course, reverses the standard foundationalist pictures of human knowledge. Instead of theoretical knowledge depending on, and being derived from, perception, perception of the indirect sort, presupposes a prior knowledge of theories.

Foundationalist's are quick to point out that this apparent reversal in the structure of human knowledge is only apparent. Our indirect perceptual experience of fact depends on the applicable theory, yes, but this merely shows that indirect perceptual knowledge is not part of the foundation. Nevertheless, perceptivity as a fundamental philosophical topic both for its central place in any theory of knowledge, and its central place in any theory of consciousness.

To reach the kind of perceptual knowledge that lies at the foundation, we need to look at a form of perception purified of all theoretical elements. This, then, will be perceptual knowledge, pure and direct. We have needed no background knowledge or assumptions about connecting regularities in direct perception because the known facts are presented directly and immediately and not (as, in direct perception) based on some other facts. In direct perception all the justification (needed for knowledge) is right there in the experience itself.

What, then, about the possibility of perceptual knowledge pure and direct, the possibility of coming to know, because of sensory experience, that 'a' is 'F' where this does not require, and in no way presupposes, backgrounds assumptions or knowledge that has a source outside the experience itself? Where is this epistemological 'pure gold' to be found?

There are, two views about the nature of direct perceptual knowledge (Coherentists would deny that any of our knowledge is basic in this sense). We can call these views (following traditional nomenclature) direct realism and representationalism or representative realism. A representationalist restricts direct perceptual knowledge to objects of a very special sort: Ideas, impressions, or sensations (sometimes called sense-data)-entities in the mind of the observer. Ones perceiving fact, i.e., that 'b' is 'G', only when 'b' is a mental entity of some sort a subjective appearance or sense-data - and, 'G' is a property of this datum. Knowledge of these sensory states is supposed to be certain and infallible. These sensory facts are, so to speak, right upon against the mind's eye. One cannot be mistaken about these facts for these facts are, in really, facts about the way things are, one cannot be mistaken about the way things are. Normal perception of external conditions, then, turns out to be (always) a type of indirect perception. One 'sees' that there is a tomato in front of one by seeing that the appearances (of the tomato) have a certain quality (reddish and bulgy) and inferring (this is typically said to be atomistic and unconscious), based on certain background assumptions, i.e., That there is a typical tomato in front of one when one has experiences of this sort, that there is a tomato in front of one. All knowledge of objective reality, then, even what commonsense regards as the most direct perceptual knowledge, is based on an even more direct knowledge of the appearances.

For the representationalist, then, perceptual knowledge of our physical surroundings is always theory-loaded and indirect. Such perception is 'loaded' with the theory that there is some regular, some uniform, correlation between the way things appears (known in a perceptually direct way) and the way things actually are known, if known at all, in a perceptually indirect way.

The second view, direct realism, refuses to restrict direct perceptual knowledge to an inner world of subjective experience. Though the direct realists are willing to concede that much of our knowledge of the physical world is indirect, however, direct and immediate it may sometimes feel, some perceptual knowledge of physical reality is direct. What makes it direct is that such knowledge is not based on, nor in any way dependent on, other knowledge and belief. The justification needed for the knowledge is right in the experience itself.

To understand the way this is supposed to work, consider an ordinary example. 'S' identifies a banana, learns that it is a banana by noting its shape and colour - perhaps even tasting and smelling it to make sure it's not wax. Here the perceptual knowledge that it is a banana is the direct realist admits, indirect on S's perceptual knowledge of its shape, colour, smell, and taste. 'S' learns that it is a banana by seeing that it is yellow, banana-shaped, etc. Nonetheless, 'S's perception of the banana's colour and shape is not direct. 'S' does not see that the object is yellow, for example, by seeing (knowing, believing) anything more basic either about the banana or anything, e.g., his own sensation of the banana. 'S' has learned to identify to do is not made for an inference, even an unconscious inference, from other things he believes. What 'S' acquired as a cognitive skill, a disposition to believe of yellow objects he saw that they were yellow. The exercise of this skill does not require, and in no way depends on, or have of any unfolding beliefs thereof: 'S' identificatorial success will depend on his operating in certain special conditions, of course. 'S' will not, perhaps, can identify yellow objects in dramatically reduced lighting visually, at funny viewing angles, or when afflicted with certain nervous disorders. But these facts about 'S' can see that something is yellow does not show that his perceptual knowledge that 'a' is yellow, in any way depends on a belief, let alone knowledge, that he is in such special conditions. It merely shows that direct perceptual knowledge is the result of exercising a skill, an identifications skill, that like any skill, requires certain conditions for its successful exercise. An expert basketball player cannot shoot accurately in a hurricane. He needs normal conditions to do what he has learned to do. So also with individuals who have developed perceptual (cognitive) skills. They needed normal conditions to do what they have learned to do. They need normal conditions too sere, for example, that something is yellow. But they do not, any more than the basketball player, have to know they are in these conditions to do what being in these conditions enables them to do.

This means, of course, that for the direct realist direct perceptual knowledge is fallible and corrigible. Whether 'S' sees that 'a' is 'F' depends on his being caused to believe that 'a' is 'F' in conditions that are appropriate for an exercise of that cognitive skill. If conditions are right, then 'S' sees (hence, knows) that 'a' is 'F'. If they aren't, he doesn't. Whether or not 'S' knows depends, then, not on what else (if anything) 'S' believes, but on the circumstances in which 'S' comes to believe. This being so, this type of direct realist is a form of externalism. Direct perception of objective facts, pure perpetual knowledge of external events, is made possible because what is needed by way of justification for such knowledge has significantly reduced the background knowledge-is not needed.

This means that the foundation of knowledge is fallible. Nonetheless, though fallible, they are in no way derived, that is, what makes them foundations. Even if they are brittle, as foundations are sometimes, everything else upon them.

Ideally, in theory imagination, a concept of reason that is transcendent but non-empirical as to think os conception of and ideal thought, that potentially or actual exists in the mind as a product exclusive to the mental act. In the philosophy of Plato, an archetype, of which a corresponding being in phenomenal reality is an imperfect replica, that also, Hegel's absolute truth, as the conception and ultimate product of reason, the absolute meaning a mental imagery of something is recollectively remembered.

Conceivably, in the imagination the formation of a mental image of something that is or should be perceived as real nor present to the senses. Nevertheless, the image so formed can confront and deal with the reality by using the creative powers of the mind. That is characteristically well removed from reality, but all powers of fantasy over reason are a degree of insanity/still, fancy as they have given a product of the imagination free reins, that is in command of the fantasy while it is exactly the mark of the neurotic that he is possessed by his very own fantasy.

The totality of all things possessing actuality, existence or essence that exists objectively and in fact based on real occurrences that exist or known to have existed, a real occurrence, an event, i.e., had to prove the facts of the case, as something believed to be true or real, determining by evidence or truth as to do. However, the usage in the sense 'allegation of fact', and the reasoning are wrong of the 'facts and facts, as the 'true facts' of the case may never be known'. These usages may occasion qualms' among critics who insist that facts can only be true, but the usages are often useful for emphasis. Therefore, the discovery or determinations of fast or accurate information are related to, or used in the discovery of facts, then the comprising events are determined by evidence or truth is much as ado about their owing actuality. Its opposition forming the literature that treats real people or events as if they were fictional or uses real people or events as essential elements in an otherwise fictional rendition, i.e., of, relating to, produced by, or characterized by internal dissension, as given to or promoting internal dissension. So, then, it is produced artificially than by a natural process, especially the lacking authenticity or genuine factitious values of another than what s or should be.

Importantly, a set of statements or principles devised to explain a group of facts or phenomena, especially one that has been repeatedly tested or is widely accepted and can be used to make predictions about natural phenomena. Having the consistency of explanatory statements, accepted principles, and methods of analysis, finds to a set of theorems that constitute a systematic view of a branch in mathematics or extends upon the paradigms of science, the belief or principle that guides action or assists comprehension or judgements, usually by an ascription based on limited information or knowledge, as a conjecture, tenably to assert the creation from a speculative assumption that bestows to its beginning. Theoretically, of, relating to, or based on theory, i.e., the restriction to theory, not practical theoretical physics, as given to speculative theorizing. Also, the given idea, because of which formidable combinations awaiting upon the inception of an idea, demonstrated as true or is assumed to be demonstrated. In mathematics its containment lies of the proposition that has been or is to be proved from explicit assumption and is primarily with theoretical assessments or hypothetical theorizing than practical considerations the measures its quality value.

Looking back a century, one can see a striking degree of homogeneity among the philosophers of the early twentieth century about the topics central to their concerns. Discovering the apparent obscurity and abstruseness of the concerns, for which it seems at first glance to be removed from the great debates of previous centuries, between 'realism' and 'idealist', say, of 'rationalists' and 'empiricist'.

Thus, no matter what the current debate or discussion, the central issue is often ne without conceptual and contentual representations, that if one is without concept, is without idea, such that in one foul swoop would ingest the mere truth that lies to the underlying paradoxes of why is there something instead of nothing? Whatever it is that makes, what would otherwise be mere utterances and inscriptions into instruments of communication and understanding. This philosophical problem is to demystify this over flowing emptiness, and to relate to what we know of ourselves and the world.

Contributions to this study include the theory of 'speech arts', and the investigation of communicable communications, especially the relationship between words and 'ideas', and words and the 'world'. It is, nonetheless, that which is expressed by an utterance or sentence, the proposition or claim made about the world. By extension, the content of a predicate that any expression that is capable of connecting with one or more singular terms to make a sentence, the expressed condition that the entities referred to may satisfy, in which case the resulting sentence will be true. Consequently a predicate may be thought of as a function from things to sentences or even to truth-values, or other sub-sentential components that contribute to sentences that contain it. The nature of content is the central concern of the philosophy of language.

What some person expresses of a sentence often depends on the environment in which he or she is placed. For example, the disease I refer to by a term like 'arthritis' or the kind of tree I call a 'maple' will be defined by criteria of which I know next to nothing. This raises the possibility of imaging two persons in rather different environments, but in which everything appears the same to each of them. The wide content of their thoughts and saying will be different if the situation surrounding them is appropriately different, 'situation' may here include the actual objects hey perceive, or the chemical or physical kinds of objects in the world they inhabit, or the history of their words, or the decisions of authorities on what counts as an example of one of the terms thy use. The narrow content is that part of their thought that remains identical, through the identity of the way things appear, no matter these differences of surroundings. Partisans of wide . . . 'as, something called broadly, content may doubt whether any content is in this sense narrow, partisans of narrow content believe that it is the fundamental notion, with wide content being of narrow content plus context.

All and all, if people are characterized by their rationality is common, and the most evident display of our rationality is capable to think. This is the rehearsal in the mind of what to say, or what to do. Not all thinking is verbal, since chess players, composers, and painters all think, and there is no speculative reason that their deliberations should take any more verbal a form than their actions. It is permanently tempting to conceive of this activity for the presence in the mind of elements of some language, or other medium that represents aspects of the world and its surrounding surface structures. But the model has been attacked, notably by Ludwig Wittgenstein (1889-1951), whose influential application of these ideas was in the philosophy of mind. Wittgenstein explores the characterization of which reports of introspection, or sensations, or intentions, or beliefs that actually take into consideration our social lives, to undermine the reallocated duality upon which the Cartesian communicational description whose function was to the goings-on in an inner theatre of mind-purposes of which only the subject is the reclusive viewer. Passages that have subsequentially become known as the 'rule following' considerations and the 'private language argument' are among the fundamental topics of modern philosophy of language and mind, although their precise interpretation is endlessly controversial.

In its gross effect, the hypotheses especially associated with Jerry Fodor (1935-), whom is known for the 'resolute realism', about the nature of mental functioning, that occurs in a language different from one's ordinary native language, but underlying and explaining our competence with it. The idea is a development of the notion of an innate universal grammar (Chomsky), in as such, that we agree that since a computer programs are linguistically complex sets of instructions were the relative executions by which explains of surface behaviour or the adequacy of the computerized programming installations, if it were definably amendable and, advisably corrective, in that most are disconcerting of many that are ultimately a reason for 'us' of thinking intuitively and without the indulgence of retrospective preferences, but an ethical majority in defending of its moral line that is already confronting 'us'. That these programs may or may not improve to conditions that are lastly to enhance of the right sort of an existence forwarded toward a more valuing amount in humanities lesser extensions that embrace one's riff of necessity to humanities' abeyance to expressions in the finer of qualities.

As an explanation of ordinary language-learning and competence, the hypothesis has not found universal favour, as it becomes apparent that only ordinary representational powers that by invoking the image of the learning person's capabilities are whom the abilities for translating are contending of an innate language whose own powers are mysteriously a biological given. Perhaps, the view that everyday attributions of intentionality, beliefs, and meaning to other persons proceed by means of a tactic use of a theory that enables one to construct these interpretations as explanations of their doings. The view is commonly held along with 'functionalism', according to which psychological states are theoretical entities, identified by the network of their causes and effects. The theory-theory has different implications, depending upon which feature of theories is being stressed. Theories may be thought of as capable of formalization, as yielding predictions and explanations, as achieved by a process of theorizing, as answering to empirical evidence that is in principle describable without them, as liable to be overturned by newer and better theories, and so on.

The main problem with seeing our understanding of others as the outcome of a piece of theorizing is the nonexistence of a medium in which this theory can be couched, as the child learns simultaneously the minds of others and the meaning of terms in its native language, is not gained by the tactic use of a 'theory', enabling 'us' to infer what thoughts or intentions explain their actions, but by reliving the situation 'in their shoes' or from their point of view, and by that understanding what they experienced and theory, and therefore expressed. Understanding others is achieved when we can ourselves deliberate as they did, and hear their words as if they are our own. The suggestion is a modern development usually associated in the 'Verstehen' traditions of Dilthey (1833-1911), Weber (1864-1920) and Collingwood (1889-1943).

Any process of drawing a conclusion from a set of premises may be called a process of reasoning. If the conclusion concerns what to do, the process is called practical reasoning, otherwise pure or theoretical reasoning. Evidently, such processes may be good or bad, if they are good, the premises support or even entail the conclusion drawn, and if they are bad, the premises offer no support to the conclusion. Formal logic studies the cases in which conclusions are validly drawn from premises, but little human reasoning is overly of the forms logicians identify. Partly, we are concerned to draw conclusions that 'go beyond' our premises, in the way that conclusions of logically valid arguments do not for the process of using evidence to reach a wider conclusion. However, such anticipatory pessimism about the prospects of conformation theory, denying that we can assess the results of abduction as for probability. A process of reasoning in which a conclusion is diagrammatically set from the premises of some usually confined cases in which the conclusions are supposed in following from the premises, i.e., because of which an inference is logically valid, in that of deductibility in a logically defined syntactic premise but without there being to any reference to the intended interpretation of its theory. Through its attaching reasons we use the indefinite lore or commonsense set of presuppositions about what it is likely or not a task of an automated reasoning project, which is to mimic this causal use of knowledge of the way of the world in computer programs.

Most 'theories' usually emerge just as a body of (supposed) truths that are not organized, making the theory difficult to survey or study as a whole. The axiomatic method is an idea for organizing a theory, one in which tries to select from among the supposed truths a small number from which all others can be seen to be deductively inferable. This makes the theory rather more tractable since, in a sense, all truths are contained in those few. In a theory so organized, the few truths from which all others are deductively inferred are called 'axioms'. David Hilbert (1862-1943) had argued that, just as algebraic and differential equations, which we were used to study mathematical and physical processes, could they be made mathematical objects, so axiomatic theories, like algebraic and differential equations, which are means to representing physical processes and mathematical structures could be investigation.

By theory, the philosophy of science, is a generalization or set referring to unobservable entities, e.g., atoms, genes, quarks, unconscious wishes. The ideal gas law, for example, refers only to such observables as pressure, temperature, and volume, the 'molecular-kinetic theory' refers to molecules and their properties, . . . although an older usage suggests the lack of adequate evidence in support thereof ('merely a theory'), current philosophical usage does indeed follow in the tradition (as in Leibniz, 1704), as many philosophers had the conviction that all truths, or all truths about a particular domain, followed from as few than for being many governing principles. These principles were taken to be either metaphically prior or epistemologically prior or both. In the first sense, they we took to be entities of such a nature that what exists 'caused' by them. When the principles were taken as epistemologically prior, that is, as 'axioms', they were taken to be either epistemologically privileged, e.g., self-evident, not needing to be demonstrated, or again, included 'or', to such that all truths so indeed follow from them (by deductive inferences). Gödel (1984) showed –in the spirit of Hilbert, treating axiomatic theories as themselves mathematical objects that mathematics, and even a small part of mathematics, elementary number theory, could not be axiomatized, that more precisely, any class of axioms which is such that we could effectively decide, of any proposition, whether or not it was in that class, would be too small to capture in of the truths.

The notion of truth occurs with remarkable frequency in our reflections on language, thought and action. We are inclined to suppose, for example, that truth is the proper aim of scientific inquiry, that true beliefs help to achieve our goals, that to understand a sentence is to know which circumstances would make it true, that reliable preservation of truth as one argues of valid reasoning, that moral pronouncements should not be regarded as objectively true, and so on. To assess the plausibility of such theses, and to refine them and to explain why they hold (if they do), we require some view of what truth be-a theory that would account for its properties and its relations to other matters. Thus, there can be little prospect of understanding our most important faculties in the sentence of a good theory of truth.

Such a thing, however, has been notoriously elusive. The ancient idea that truth is some sort of 'correspondence with reality' has still never been articulated satisfactorily. The nature of the alleged 'correspondence' and the alleged 'reality' remain objectionably obscure. Yet the familiar alternative suggestions -that true beliefs are those that are 'mutually coherent', or 'pragmatically useful', or 'verifiable in suitable conditions'~, have each been confronted with persuasive counterexamples. A twentieth-century departure from these traditional analyses is the view that truth is not a property at all – that the syntactic form of the predicate, 'is true', distorts its really semantic character, which is not to describe propositions but to endorse them. But this radical approach is also faced with difficulties and suggests, somewhat counter intuitively, that truth cannot have the vital theoretical role in semantics, epistemology and elsewhere that we are naturally inclined to give it. Thus, truth threatens to remain one of the most enigmatic of notions: An explicit account of it can be essential yet beyond our reach. However, recent work provides some grounds for optimism.

Moreover, science, unswerving exactly to position of something very well hidden, its nature in so that to make it believed, is quickly and imposes the sensing and responding to the definitive qualities or state of being actual or true, such that as a person, an entity, or an event, that it actually might be gainfully to employ of all things possessing actuality, existence, or essence. In other words, in that which objectively and in fact do seem as to be about reality, in fact, actually to the satisfying factions of instinctual needs through awareness of and adjustment to environmental demands. Thus, the act of realizing or the condition of being realized is first, and utmost the resulting infraction of realizing.

Nonetheless, a declaration made to explain or justify action, or its believing desire upon which it is to act, by which the conviction underlying fact or cause, that provide logical sense for a premise or occurrence for logical, rational. Analytic mental stars have long lost in reason. Yet, the premise usually the minor premises, of an argument, use the faculty of reason that arises to engage in conversation or discussion. To determining or conclude by logical thinking out a solution to the problem, would therefore persuade or dissuade someone with reason that posits of itself with the good sense or justification of reasonability. In which, good causes are simply justifiably to be considered as to think. By which humans seek or attain knowledge or truth. Mere reason is insufficient to convince 'us' of its veracity. Still, intuitively is perceptively welcomed by comprehension, as the truth or fact, without the use of the rational process, as one comes to assessing someone's character, it sublimely configures one consideration, and often with resulting comprehensions, in which it is assessing situations or circumstances and draw sound conclusions into the reign of judgement.

Governing by or being according to reason or sound thinking, in that a reasonable solution to the problem, may as well, in being without bounds of common sense and arriving to a measure and fair use of reason, especially to form conclusions, inferences or judgements. In that, all manifestations of a confronting argument within the usage of thinking or thought out response to issuing the furthering argumentation to fit or join in the sum parts that are composite to the intellectual faculties, by which case human understanding or the attemptive grasp to its thought, are the resulting liberty encroaching men of zeal, well-meaningly, but without understanding.

Being or occurring in fact or actually, as having verifiable existence. Real objects, a real illness. . . .'Really true and actual and not imaginary, alleged, or ideal, as people and not ghosts, fro which are we to find on practical matters and concerns of experiencing the real world. The surrounding surfaces, might we, as, perhaps attest to this for the first time. Being no less than what they state, we have not taken its free pretence, or affections for a real experience highly, as many may encounter real trouble. This, nonetheless, projects of an existing objectivity in which the world despite subjectivity or conventions of thought or language is or have valuing representation, reckoned by actual power, in that of relating to, or being an image formed by light or another identifiable simulation, that converge in space, the stationary or fixed properties, such as a thing or whole having actual existence. All of which, are accorded a truly factual experience into which the actual attestations have brought to you by the afforded efforts of our very own imaginations.

Ideally, in theory imagination, a concept of reason that is transcendent but non-empirical, as to think os conception of and ideal thought, that potentially or actual exists in the mind as a product exclusive to the mental act. In the philosophy of Plato, an archetype, of which a corresponding being in phenomenal reality is an imperfect replica, that also, Hegel's absolute truth, as the conception and ultimate product of reason the absolute meaning of the mental act.

Conceivably, in the imagination the formation of a mental image of something that is or should be b perceived as real nor present to the senses. Nevertheless, the image so formed can confront and deal with the reality by using the creative powers of the mind. That is characteristically well removed from reality, but all powers of fantasy over reason are a degree of insanity/still, fancy as they have given a product of the imagination free reins, that is in command of the fantasy while it is exactly the mark of the neurotic that his very own fantasy possesses him.

The totality of all things possessing actuality, existence or essence that exists objectively and in fact based on real occurrences that exist or known to have existed, a real occurrence, an event, i.e., had to prove the facts of the case, as something believed to be true or real, determining by evidence or truth as to do. However, the usage in the sense 'allegation of fact', and the reasoning are wrong of the 'facts' and 'substantive facts', as we may never know the 'facts' of the case'. These usages may occasion qualms' among critics who insist that facts can only be true, but the usages are often useful for emphasis. Therefore, we have related to, or used the discovery or determinations of fast or accurate information in the discovery of facts, then evidence has determined the comprising events or truth is much as ado about their owing actuality. Its opposition forming the literature that treats real people or events as if they were fictional or uses real people or events as essential elements in an otherwise fictional rendition, i.e., of relating to, produced by, or characterized by internal dissension, as given to or promoting internal dissension. So, then, it is produced artificially than by a natural process, especially the lacking authenticity or genuine factitious values of another than what s or should be.

Concluding affiliations by the adherence to sets of statements or principles devised to explain a group of facts or phenomena, especially one that has been repeatedly tested or is widely accepted and can be used to make predictions about natural phenomena. Having the consistency of explanatory statements, accepted principles, and methods of analysis, finds to a set of theorems that form a systematic view of a branch in mathematics or extends upon the paradigms of science, the belief or principle that guides action or assists comprehension or judgements, usually by an ascription based on limited information or knowledge, as a conjecture, tenably to assert the creation from a speculative assumption that bestows to its beginning. Theoretically, of, relating to, or based on conjecture, its philosophy is such to accord, i.e., the restriction in theory, not practical theoretical physics, as given to speculative theorizing. Also, the given idea, because of which formidable combinations awaiting upon the inception of an idea, demonstrated as true or is assumed to be shown. In mathematics its containment lies of the proposition that has been or is to be proved from explicit assumption and is primarily with theoretical assessments or hypothetical theorizing than practical considerations the measures its quality value.

A striking degrees of homogeneity among the philosophers of the earlier twentieth century were about the topics central to their concerns. More inertly there is more in the apparent obscurity and abstruseness of the concerns, which seem at first glance to be removed from the great debates of previous centuries, between 'realism' and 'idealist', say, of 'rationalists' and 'empiricist'.

Thus, no matter what the current debate or discussion, the central issue is often ne without conceptual and/or contentual representations, that if one is without concept, is without idea, such that in one foul swoop would ingest the mere truth that lies to the underlying paradoxes of why is there something instead of nothing? Whatever it is that makes, what would otherwise be mere utterances and inscriptions into instruments of communication and understanding. This philosophical problem is to demystify this overblowing emptiness, and to relate to what we know of ourselves and the world.

Contributions to this study include the theory of 'speech arts', and the investigation of communicable communications, especially the relationship between words and 'ideas', and words and the 'world'. It is, nonetheless, that which and utterance or sentence expresses, the proposition or claim made about the world. By extension, the content of a predicate that any expression that is capable of connecting with one or more singular terms to make a sentence, the expressed condition that the entities referred to may satisfy, in which case the resulting sentence will be true. Consequently we may think of a predicate as a function from things to sentences or even to truth-values, or other sub-sentential components that contribute to sentences that contain it. The nature of content is the central concern of the philosophy of language.

What some person expresses of a sentence often depends on the environment in which he or she is placed. This raises the possibility of imaging two persons in comparatively different environments, but in which everything appears the same to each of them. The wide content of their thoughts and saying will be different if the situation surrounding them is appropriately different, 'situation' may here include the actual objects hey perceive, or the chemical or physical kinds of objects in the world they inhabit, or the history of their words, or the decisions of authorities on what counts as an example of some terms thy use. The narrow content is that part of their thought that remains identical, through the identity of the way things appear, no matter these differences of surroundings. Partisans of wide . . . 'as, something called broadly, content may doubt whether any content is in this sense narrow, partisans of narrow content believe that it is the fundamental notion, with wide content being of narrow content plus context.

All and all, assuming their rationality has characterized people is common, and the most evident display of our rationality is capable to think. This is the rehearsal in the mind of what to say, or what to do. Not all thinking is verbal, since chess players, composers, and painters all think, and there is no deductive reason that their deliberations should take any more verbal a form than their actions. It is permanently tempting to conceive of this activity in the presence in the mind of elements of some language, or other medium that represents aspects of the world and its surrounding surface structures. Nevertheless, they have attacked the model, notably by Ludwig Wittgenstein (1889-1951), whose influential application of these ideas was in the philosophy of mind. Wittgenstein explores the role that report of introspection, or sensations, or intentions, or beliefs actually play our social lives, to undermine the Cartesian 'ego, functions to describe the goings-on in an inner theatre of which the subject is the lone spectator. Passages that have subsequentially become known as the 'rule following' considerations and the 'private language argument' are among the fundamental topics of modern philosophy of language and mind, although their precise interpretation is endlessly controversial.

In its gross effect, the hypotheses especially associated with Jerry Fodor (1935-), whom is known for the 'resolute realism', about the nature of mental functioning, that occurs in a language different from one's ordinary native language, but underlying and explaining our competence with it. The idea is a development of the notion of an innate universal grammar (Chomsky), in as such, that we agree that since a computer programs are linguistically complex sets of instructions were the relative executions by which explains of surface behaviour or the adequacy of the computerized programming installations, if it were definably amendable and, advisably corrective, in that most are disconcerting of many that are ultimately a reason for 'us' of thinking intuitively and without the indulgence of retrospective preferences, but an ethical majority in defending of its moral line that is already confronting 'us'. That these programs may or may not improve to conditions that are lastly to enhance of the right sort of an existence forwarded toward a more valuing amount in humanities lesser extensions that embrace one's riff of necessity to humanities' abeyance to expressions in the finer of qualities.

As an explanation of ordinary language-learning and competence, the hypothesis has not found universal favour, as only ordinary representational powers that by invoking the image of the learning person's capabilities are apparently whom the abilities for translating are contending of an innate language whose own powers are mysteriously a biological given. Perhaps, the view that everyday attributions of intentionality, beliefs, and meaning to other persons proceed by means of a tactic use of a theory that enables one to construct these interpretative explanations of their doing. We have commonly held the view along with 'functionalism', according to which psychological states are theoretical entities, identified by the network of their causes and effects. The theory-theory has different implications, depending upon which feature of theories is being stressed. We may think of theories as capable of formalization, as yielding predictions and explanations, as achieved by a process of theorizing, as answering to empirical evidence that is in principle describable without them, as liable to be overturned by newer and better theories, and so on.

At present, the duly held exemplifications are accorded too inside and outside the study for which is concerned in the finding explanations of things, it would be desirable to have a concept of what counts as a good explanation, and what distinguishes good from bad. Under the influence of logical positivism approaches to the structure of science, it was felt that the criterion ought to be found in as a definite logical relationship between the explanans (that which does the explaining) and the explanandum (that which is to be explained). This approach culminated in the covering law model of explanation, or the view that an event is explained when it is subsumed under a law of nature, that is, its occurrence is deducible from the law plus a set or covering law, in the way that Kepler's laws of planetary motion are deducible from Newton's laws of motion. The covering law model may be adapted to include explanation by showing that something is probable, given a statistical law. Questions for the covering laws are necessary to explanation (we explain everyday events without overtly citing laws): Querying whether they are sufficient (it may not explain an event just to say that it is an example): And querying whether a purely logical relationship is adapted to capturing the requirements as we make of explanations. These may include, for instance, that we have a 'feel' for what is happening, or that the explanation proceeds about things that are familiar to us or unsurprising or that we can give a model of what is going on, and none of these notions is captured in a purely logical approach. Recent work, therefore, has tended to stress the contextual and pragmatic elements in requirements for explanation, so that what counts as a good explanation given one set of concerns may not do so given another.

The argument to the best explanation is the view that once we can select the best of any that of something explanations of an event, then we are justified in accepting it, or even believing sometimes it is unwise to ignore the antecedent improbability of a hypothesis which would explain the data better than others: e.g., the best explanation of a coin falling heads 530 times in 1,000 tosses might be that it is biassed to jive a probability of heads of 0.53, but it might be sensible to suppose that it is fair, or to suspend judgement

In everyday life we encounter many types of explanation, which appear not to raise philosophical difficulties, besides those already made of mention. Prior to takeoff a flight, the attendant explains how to use the safety equipment on the aeroplane. In a museum the guide explains the significance of a famous painting. A mathematics teacher explains a geometrical proof to a bewildered student. A newspaper story explains how a prisoner escaped. Additional examples come easily to mind. The main point is to remember the great variety of contexts in which explanations are sought and given.

Since, at least, the times of Aristotle philosophers have emphasized the importance of explanation knowledge. In simple terms, we want to know not only what is the case but also why it is. This consideration suggests that we define an explanation as an answer to a why-question. Such a definition would, however, be too broad, because some why-questions are requests for consolation (Why did my son have to die?) Or moral justification (Why should women not be paid the same as men for the same work?). It would also be too narrow because some explanations are responses to how-questions (How doe s radar work?) Or how-possibly-questions (How is it possible for cats always to land on their feet?)

In a more general sense, 'to explain' means to make clear, to make plain, or to provide understanding. Definitions of this sort are philosophically unserved, for he terms used in the definition is no less problematic than the term to be defined. Moreover, since a variety of things require explanation, and are of many different types of explanation exist, a more complex explication is required. The term 'explanandum' is used to refer to that lich is to be explained: The tern 'explanans' refer to that which does the emplaning. The explanans and explanandum taken together constitute the explanation.

One common type of explanation occurs when deliberate human actions are explained as to conscious purposes. 'Why did you go to the pharmacy yesterday?' 'Because I had a headache and needed to get some aspirin'. It is tacitly assumed that aspirin is an appropriate medication for headaches and that going to the pharmacy would be an efficient way of getting some. Since explanations ae, of course, teleological, referring as they do, to goals. The explanans are not the realization of a future goal -if the pharmacy happened to be closed for stocking the aspirin would not have been obtained there, but this would not invalidate the explanation. Some philosophers would say that the antecedent desire to achieve the end is what does the explaining: Others might say that the explaining is done by the nature of the goal and the fact that the action promoted the chances of realizing it (e.g., Taylor, 1964). All the same, it should not be automatically assuming that such explanations are causal. Philosophers differ considerably on whether these explanations are to be framed in a term of cause or reasons, least of mention, that the distinction cannot be used to show that the relation between reasons and the actions they justify is in no way causal, precisely parallel points hold in the epistemic domain, and for all prepositional attitudes, since they all similarly admit of justification, and explanation, by reason. Such that if I suppose my reason for believing that you received my letter today is that I sent it by express yesterday. My reason, strictly speaking, is that I sent it by express yesterday: My reason state is my believing this. Arguably, my reason which it is my reason, and my reason-state-my evidence belief-both explains and justifies my belief that you received the letter if, the fact, that I sent the letter by express yesterday, but this statement express my believing that evidence preposition, and that if I do not believe in then my belief that you received the letter is not justified, it is not justified by the mere truth of the proposition (and can be justified even if that preposition is false.)

Nonetheless, if reason states can motivate, least of mention, why apart from confusing them with reasons proper deny that they are causes? For one thing, they are not events, at least in the usual sense entailing change; They are dispositional states, this contrasts them with concurrences, but does not imply that they admit of dispositional analysis. It has also seemed to those which deny that reasons are causes that the former justifies and explain the actions for which they are reasons, whereas the role of causes is at most to explain. Another claim is that the relation between reasons, and here reason states are often cited explicitly to actions that significantly explain of non-measurable detachments. The 'logical connection argument' proceeds from this claim to the conclusion that reasons are not causes.

All the same, there are many different analyses of such concepts as intention and agency. Expanding the domain beyond consciousness, Freud maintained, in addition, that a great deal of human behaviours can be explained as for unconscious wishes. These Freudian explanations should probably be construed as causal.

Problems arise when teleological explanations are offered in other contexts. The behaviour of nonhuman animals is often explained with purpose, e.g., the mouse ran to escape from the cat. In such cases the existence of conscious purposes seems dubious. The situation is still more problematic when super-empirical purposes invoked, e.g., the explanation of living species for God's purpose, or the vitalistic explanation of biological phenomena about an entelechy or vital principle. In recent years an 'anthropic principle' has received attention in cosmology. All such explanations have been condemned by many philosophers as anthropomorphic.

The abstaining objection is nonetheless, that philosophers and scientists often maintain that functional explanations play an important and legitimate role in various sciences such as evolutionary biology, anthropology and sociology. For example, for the peppered moth in Liverpool, the change in colour from the light phase to the dark phase and back again to the light phase provided adaptions to a changing environment and fulfilled the function of reducing predation on the species. In the study of primitive societies anthropologists have maintained that various rituals, e.g., a rain dance, which may be inefficacious in cause their manifest goals, e.g., producing rain, actually fulfils the latent function of increasing social cohesion at a period of stress, e.g., during a drought. Philosophers who admit teleology and/or functional explanations in common sense and science often take pains to argue that such explanations can be analysed entirely about efficient causes, thereby escaping the charge of anthropomorphism (Wright, 1976), again, however, not all philosophers agree.

Mainly to avoid the incursion of unwanted theology, metaphysics, or anthropomorphism into science, many philosophers and scientists-especially during the first half of the twentieth century-held that science provides nl desecrations and predictions of natural phenomena, but not explanation. Beginning, in the 1930s, however, a series of influential philosophers of science -including Karl Pooper (1935) Carl Hempel and Paul Oppenheim (1948) and Hempel (1965)- maintained that empirical science can explain natural phenomena without appealing to metaphysics or theology. It appears that this view is now accepted by the vast majority of philosophers o science, though there is sharp disagreement on the nature of scientific explanation.

The eschewing approach, developed by Hempel, Popper and others, became virtually a 'received view' in the 1960s and 1970s. According to this view, to explain any natural phenomenon is to show how this phenomenon can be subsumed under a law of nature. A particular rupture in the water pipe can be explained by citing the universal law that water expands when it freezes and in the pipe dropped below the freezing pint. General laws, and particular facts, can be explained by subsumption. The law of conservation of linear momentum an be explained by derivation from Newton's second and third laws of motion. Each of these explanations is a deductive argument: The premises constitute the explanans and the conclusion is the explanandum. The explanans contain one or more statements of universal laws and, often, strewments describing initial conditions. This pattern of explanation is known as the deductive-nomological model. Any such argument shows that the explanandum had to occur given the explanans.

Many, though not all, adherents of the received view for explanation by subsumptions under statistical laws. Hempel (1965) offers as an example the case of a ma who recovered quickly from a streptococcus infection because of treatment with penicillin. Although not all strep infections clear up quickly under this treatment, the probability of recovery in such cases is high, and this id sufficient for legitimate explanation according to Hempel. This example conforms to the inductive-statistical model. Such explanations are viewed as arguments, but they are inductive than deductive. In these cases the explanans confer inductive probability on the explanandum. An explanation of a particular fact satisfying either the deductive-nomological and inductive-statistical model is an argument to the effect that the fact in question was to be expected by virtue of the explanans.

The received view has been subjected to strenuous criticism by adherents of the causal/ mechanical approach to scientific explanation (Salmon, 1990). Many objections to the received view were engendered by the absence of causal constraints due largely to worries about Hume's critique on the deductive -nomological and inductive - statistical models. Beginning in the late 1950s, Michael Scriven advanced serious counterexamples to Hempel's models: He was followed in the 1960s by Wesley Salmo and in the 1970s by Peter Railton. Overall, this view, one explains phenomena by identifying causes a death is explained as resulting from a massive cerebral haemorrhage, or by exposing underlying mechanisms in that, the behaviour of a gas is explained for the motions of constituent molecules.

A unification approach to explanation has been developed by Michael Friedman and Philip Kitcher (1989). The basic idea is that we understand our world more adequately to the extent that we can reduce the number of independent assumptions we must introduce to account for what goes on in it. Accordingly, we understand phenomena as far as we can fit them into a general world picture or World View. To serve in scientific explanations, the world picture must be scientifically well founded.

In contrast to the above-mentioned views - which such factors as logical relations, laws of nature, and causality several philosophers (e.g., Achinstein, 1983, and, van Fraassen, 1980) have urged that explanation, and not just scientific explanation, can be analysed entirely in pragmatic terms.

During the past half-century much philosophical attention has been focussed on explanation in science and in history. Considerable controversy has surrounded the question of whether historical explanation must be scientific, or whether history requires explanations of different types. Many diverse views have been articulated: The forerunning survey does not exhaust the variety.

Historical knowledge is often compared to scientific knowledge, as scientific knowledge is regarded as knowledge of the laws and regulative of nature which operate throughout past, preset, and future. Some thinkers, e.g., the German historian Ranke, have argued that historical knowledge should be 'scientific' in the sense of being based on research, on scrupulous verification of facts as far as possible, with an objective account being the principal aim. Others have gone further, asserting that historical inquiry and scientific inquiry have the same goal, namely providing explanations of particular events by discovering general laws from which (with initial conditions) the particular events can be inferred. This is often called "The Covering Law Theory" of historical explanation. Proponents of this view usually admit a difference in direction of interest between the two types of inquiry: Historians are more interested in explaining particular events, while scientists are more interested in discovering general laws. But the logic of explanation is stated to be the same for both.

Yet a cursory glance at the articles and books that historians produce does not support this view. Those books and articles focus overwhelmingly on the particular -, e.g., the particular social structure of Tudor England, the rise to power of a particular political party, the social, cultural and economic interactions between two particular peoples. Nor is some standard body of theory or set of explanatory principles cited in the footnotes of history texts as providing the fundamental materials of historical explanation. In view of this, other thinkers have proposed that narrative itself, apart from general laws, can produce understanding, and that this is the characteristic form of historical explanation (Dray, 1957). If we wonder why things are the way they are -, and analogously, why they were the way they were-we are often satisfied by being told a story about how they got that way.

What we seek in historical inquiry is an understanding that respects the agreed-upon facts, as a chronicle can present a factually correct account of a historical event without making that events intelligible to us -for example, without showing us why that event occurred and how the various phases and aspects of the event are related to one another. Historical narrative aims to provide intelligibly by showing how one thing led to another even when there is no relation of causal determination between them. In this way, narrative provides a form of understanding especially suited to a temporal course of events and alternative too scientific, or law-like, explanation.

Another approach is understanding through knowledge of the purposes, intentions and points of view of historical agents. If we knew how Julius Caesar or Leon Trotsky, bywords and understood their times and knew what they meant to accomplish, then we can better understand why they did what they did. Purposes, intentions, and points of view are varieties of thought and can be ascertained through acts of empathy by the historian. R.G. Collingwood (1946) goes further and argues that those very same past thought can be re-enacted, and thereby made present by the historian. Historical explanation of this type cannot be reduced to the covering law model and allow historical inquiry to achieve a different type of intelligibility.

Yet, turning the stone over, we are in finding the main problem with seeing our understanding of others as the outcome of a piece of theorizing is the nonexistence of a medium in which we can couch this theory, as the child learns simultaneously the minds of others and the meaning of terms in its native language, is not gained by the tactic use of a 'theory', enabling 'us' to imply what thoughts or intentions explain their actions, but by realizing the situation 'in their moccasins' or from their point of view, and by that understanding what they experienced and theory, and therefore expressed. We achieve understanding others when we can ourselves deliberate as they did, and hear their words as if they are our own. The suggestion is a modern development usually associated in the 'Verstehen' traditions of Dilthey (1833-1911), Weber (1864-1920) and Collingwood (1889-1943).

We may call any process of drawing a conclusion from a set of premises a process of reasoning. If the conclusion concerns what to do, the process is called practical reasoning, otherwise pure or theoretical reasoning. Evidently, such processes may be good or bad, if they are good, the premises support or even entail the conclusion drawn, and if they are bad, the premises offer no support to the conclusion. Formal logic studies the cases in which conclusions are validly drawn from premises, but little human reasoning is overly of the forms logicians identify. Partly, we are concerned to draw conclusions that 'go beyond' our premises, in the way that conclusions of logically valid arguments do not for the process of using evidence to reach a wider conclusion. However, such anticipatory pessimism about the prospects of conformation theory, denying that we can assess the results of abduction about probability.

This makes the theory moderately tractable since, in a sense, we have contained all truths in those few. In a theory so organized, we have called the few truths from which we have deductively inferred all others 'axioms'. David Hilbert (1862-1943) had argued that, just as algebraic and differential equations, which we were used to study mathematical and physical processes, could they be made mathematical objects, so axiomatic theories, like algebraic and differential equations, which are means to representing physical processes and mathematical structures could be investigation.

According to theory, the philosophy of science, is a generalization or set referring to unobservable entities, e.g., atoms, genes, quarks, unconscious wishes. The ideal gas law, for example, refers only to such observables as pressure, temperature, and volume, the 'molecular-kinetic theory' refers to molecules and their properties, . . . although an older usage suggests the lack of adequate evidence in support of it ('merely a theory'), current philosophical usage does indeed follow in the tradition (as in Leibniz, 1704), as many philosophers had the conviction that all truths, or all truths about a particular domain followed from as a few than for being many governing principles. These principles were taken to be either metaphysicallyprior or epistemologically prior or both. In the first sense, they we took to be entities of such a nature that what exists s 'caused' by them. When we took the principles as epistemologically prior, that is, as 'axioms', we took them to be either epistemologically privileged, e.g., self-evident, not needing to be demonstrated, or again, included 'or', to such that all truths so indeed follow from them (by deductive inferences). Gödel (1984) showed in the spirit of Hilbert, treating axiomatic theories as themselves mathematical objects that mathematics, and even a small part of mathematics, elementary number theory, could not be axiomatized, that more precisely, any class of axioms that is such that we could effectively decide, of any proposition, whether or not it was in that class, would be too small to capture in of the truths.

The notion of truth occurs with remarkable frequency in our reflections on language, thought and action. We are inclined to suppose, for example, that truth is the proper aim of scientific inquiry, that true beliefs help to achieve our goals, that to understand a sentence is to know which circumstances would make it true, that reliable preservation of truth as one argues of valid reasoning, that moral pronouncements should not be regarded as objectively true, and so on. To assess the plausibility of such theses, and to refine them and to explain why they hold if they do, we require some view of what truth be a theory that would account for its properties and its relations to other matters. Thus, there can be little prospect of understanding our most important faculties in the sentence of a good theory of truth.

Such a thing, however, has been notoriously elusive. The ancient idea that truth is some sort of 'correspondence with reality' has still never been articulated satisfactorily, and the nature of the alleged 'correspondence' and the alleged 'reality' remain objectionably obscure. Yet the familiar alternative suggestions that true beliefs are those that are 'mutually coherent', or 'pragmatically useful', or 'verifiable in suitable conditions' has each been confronted with persuasive counterexamples. A twentieth-century departure from these traditional analyses is the view that truth is not a property at all that the syntactic form of the predicate, 'is true', distorts its really semantic character, which is not to describe propositions but to endorse them. However, this radical approach is also faced with difficulties and suggests, quasi counter intuitively, that truth cannot have the vital theoretical role in semantics, epistemology and elsewhere that we are naturally inclined to give it. Thus, truth threatens to remain one of the most enigmatic of notions: An explicit account of it can seem essential yet beyond our reach. However, recent work provides some grounds for optimism.

We have based a theory in philosophy of science, as a generalization or set referring to observable entities, i.e., atoms, quarks, unconscious wishes, and so on. The ideal gas law, for example, refers only to such observables as pressure, temperature, and volume, the molecular-kinetic theory refers top molecules and their properties, although an older usage suggests the lack of adequate evidence in support of it ('merely a theory'), progressive toward its sage; the usage does not carry that connotation. Einstein's special; Theory of relativity, for example, is considered extremely well founded.

These are two main views on the nature of theories. According to the 'received view' theories are partially interpreted axiomatic systems, according to the semantic view, a theory is a collection of models (Suppe, 1974). Under which, some theories usually emerge just as a body of [supposed] truths that are not neatly organized, making the theory difficult to survey or study as a whole. The axiomatic method is an ideal for organizing a theory (Hilbert, 1970), one tries to select from among the supposed truths a small number from which all the others can be seen to be deductively inferrable. This makes the theory more tractable since, in a sense, they contain all truth's in those few. In a theory so organized, they call the few truths from which they deductively infer all others 'axioms'. David Hilbert (1862-1943) had argued that, just as algebraic and differential equations, which were used to study mathematical and physical processes, could in themselves be made mathematical objects, so we could make axiomatic theories, like algebraic and differential equations, which are means of representing physical processes and mathematical structures, objects of mathematical investigation.

In the tradition of Leibniz, many philosophers had the conviction that all truths, or all truths about a particular domain, followed from a few principles. These principles were taken to be either metaphysically prior or epistemologically prior or both. In the first sense, we took them to be entities of such a nature that what exists is 'caused' by them. When we took the principles as epistemologically prior, that is, as 'axioms', we took them to be either epistemologically privileged, i.e., self-evident, not needing to be demonstrated, or again, inclusive 'or', to be such that all truths do indeed follow from them by deductive inferences. Gödel (1984) showed in the spirit of Hilbert, treating axiomatic theories as themselves mathematical objects that mathematics, and even a small part. Of mathematics, elementary number theory, could not be axiomatized, that, more precisely, any class of axioms that is such that we could effectively decide, of any proposition, whether or not it was in that class, would be too small to capture all of the truths.

The notion of truth occurs with remarkable frequency in our reflections on language, thought, and action. We are inclined to suppose, for example, that truth is the proper aim of scientific inquiry, that true beliefs help 'us' to achieve our goals, tat to understand a sentence is to know which circumstances would make it true, that reliable preservation of truth as one argues from premises to a conclusion is the mark of valid reasoning, that we should not regard moral pronouncements as objectively true, and so on. To assess the plausible of such theses, and to refine them and to explain why they hold (if they do), we require some view of what truth be a theory that would account for its properties and its relations to other matters. Thus, there can be little prospect of understanding our most important faculties in the absence of a good theory of truth.

Such a thing, however, has been notoriously elusive. The ancient idea that truth is some sort of 'correspondence with reality' has still never been articulated satisfactorily: The nature of the alleged 'correspondence' and te alleged 'reality remains objectivably obscure. Yet, the familiar alternative suggests, that true beliefs are those that are 'mutually coherent', or 'pragmatically useful', or they each include in a verifiable attempt in suitable conditions with persuasive counterexamples. A twentieth-century departure from these traditional analyses is the view that truth is not a property at all ~. That the syntactic form of the predicate, 'is true', distorts its really semantic character, which is not to describe propositions but to endorse them. Nevertheless, they have also faced this radical approach with difficulties and suggest, a counter intuitively, that truth cannot have the vital theoretical role in semantics, epistemology and elsewhere that we are naturally inclined to give it. Thus, truth threatens to remain one of the most enigmatic of notions. An explicit account of it can seem essential yet, beyond our reach. However, recent work provides some grounds for optimism.

The belief that snow is white owes its truth to a certain feature of the external world, namely, to the fact that snow is white. Similarly, the belief that is true because of the fact that dogs bark. This trivial observation leads to what is perhaps the most natural and popular account of truth, the 'correspondence theory', according to which a belief (statement, a sentence, propositions, etc.) as true just in case there exists a fact corresponding to it (Wittgenstein, 1922, Austin 1950). This thesis is unexceptionable in itself. However, if it is to provide a rigorous, substantial and complete theory of truth, if it is to be more than merely a picturesque way of asserting all equivalences to the form the belief that 'p' is 'true p'

Then, again, we must supplement it with accounts of what facts are, and what it is for a belief to correspond to a fact, and these are the problems on which the correspondence theory of truth has foundered. For one thing, it is far form clear that reducing 'the belief achieves any significant gain in understanding that snow is white is true' to 'the facts that snow is white exists': For these expressions seem equally resistant to analysis and too close in meaning for one to provide an illuminating account of the other. In addition, the general relationship that holds in particular between the belief that snow is white and the fact that snow is white, between the belief that dogs bark and the fact that dogs bark, and so on, is very hard to identify. The best attempt to date is Wittgenstein's (1922) so-called 'picture theory', under which an elementary proposition is a configuration of terms, with whatever stare of affairs it reported, as an atomic fact is a configuration of simple objects, an atomic fact corresponds to an elementary proposition (and makes it true) when their configurations are identical and when the terms in the proposition for it to the similarly-placed objects in the fact, and the truth value of each complex proposition the truth values of the elementary ones have entailed. However, eve if this account is correct as far as it goes, it would need to be completed with plausible theories of 'logical configuration', 'elementary proposition', 'reference' and 'entailment', none of which is easy to come by way of the central characteristic of truth. One that any adequate theory must explain is that when a proposition satisfies its 'conditions of proof or verification', then it is regarded as true. To the extent that the property of corresponding with reality is mysterious, we are going to find it impossible to see what we take to verify a proposition should indicate the possession of that property. Therefore, a tempting alternative to the correspondence theory an alternative that eschews obscure, metaphysical concept which explains quite straightforwardly why Verifiability implies, truth is simply to identify truth with Verifiability (Peirce, 1932). This idea can take on variously formed. One version involves the further assumption that verification is 'holistic', i.e., that a belief is justified (i.e., verifiable) when it is part of an entire system of beliefs that are consistent and 'harmonious' (Bradley, 1914 and Hempel, 1935). We have known this as the 'coherence theory of truth'. Another version involves the assumption associated with each proposition, some specific procedure for finding out whether one should believe it or not. On this account, to say that a proposition is true is to sa that the appropriate procedure would verify (Dummett, 1979. and Putnam, 1981). Through mathematics this amounts to the identification of truth with provability.

The attractions of the verificationist account of truth are that it is refreshingly clear compared with the correspondence theory, and that it succeeds in connecting truth with verification. The trouble is that the bond it postulates between these notions is implausibly strong. We do indeed take verification to indicate truth, but also we recognize the possibility that a proposition may be false in spite of there being impeccable reasons to believe it, and that a proposition may be true although we are not able to discover that it is. Verifiability and ruth are no doubt highly correlated, but surely not the same thing.

A third well-known account of truth is known as 'pragmatism' (James, 1909 and Papineau, 1987). As we have just seen, the verificationist selects a prominent property of truth and considers it the essence of truth. Similarly, the pragmatist focuses on another important characteristic namely, that true belief is a good basis for action and takes this to be the very nature of truth. We have said that true assumptions were, by definition, those that provoke actions with desirable results. Again, we have an account with a single attractive explanatory feature, but again, it postulates between truth and its alleged analysand here, utility is implausibly close. Granted, true belief tends to foster success, but it happens regularly that actions based on true beliefs lead to disaster, while false assumptions, by pure chance, produce wonderful results.

One of the few uncontroversial facts about truth is that the proposition that snow is white if and only if snow is white, the proposition that lying is wrong is true if and only if lying is wrong, and so on. Traditional theories acknowledge this fact but regard it as insufficient and, as we have seen, inflate it with some further principle of the form, 'X is true' if and only if 'X' has property P (such as corresponding to reality, Verifiability, or being suitable as a basis for action), which is supposed to specify what truth is. Some radical alternatives to the traditional theories result from denying the need for any such further specification (Ramsey, 1927, Strawson, 1950 and Quine, 1990). For example, ne might suppose that the basic theory of truth contains nothing more that equivalences of the form, 'The proposition that 'p' is true if and only if 'p' (Horwich, 1990).

This sort of proposal is best presented with an account of the 'raison de étre' of our notion of truth, namely that it enables 'us ' to express attitudes toward these propositions we can designate but not explicitly formulate.

Not all variants of deflationism have this virtue, according to the redundancy performative theory of truth, as a pair of sentences, 'The propositions that 'p' is true and a plain 'p', have the same meaning and express the same statement as each has of the other, so it is a syntactic illusion to think that 'p' is true, consented in the attributions of any sort of property to a proposition (Ramsey, 1927 and Strawson, 1950). However, it becomes hard to explain why we are entitled to infer 'The proposition that quantum mechanics are wrong is true' form 'Einstein's claim is the proposition that quantum mechanics are wrong. 'Einstein's claim is true'. For if truth is not property, then we can no longer account for the inference by invoking the law that if 'x', appears identical with 'Y' then any property of 'x' is a property of 'Y', and vice versa. Thus the redundancy/performative theory, by identifying rather than merely correlating the contents of 'The proposition that 'p' is true and 'p', precludes the prospect of a good explanation of one on truth's most significant and useful characteristics. So restricting our claim to the weak may be of a better, equivalence schema: The proposition that 'p' is true is and is only 'p'.

Support for deflationism depends upon the possibility of showing that its axiom instances of the equivalence schema non-supplements by any further analysis, will suffice to explain all the central facts about truth, for example, that the verification of a proposition indicates its truth, and that true beliefs have a practical value. The first of these facts follows trivially from the deflationary axioms, given our a prior knowledge of the equivalence of 'p' and 'The propositions that 'p is true', any reason to believe that 'p' becomes an equally good reason to believe that the preposition that 'p' is true. We can also explain the second fact about the deflationary axioms, but not quite so easily. Consider, to begin with, beliefs of the form.

(B) If I perform the act 'A', then my desires will be fulfilled.

Notice that the psychological role of such a belief is, roughly, to cause the performance of 'A'. In other words, gave that I do have belief (B), then typically.

I will perform the act 'A'

Notice also that when the belief is true then, given the deflationary axioms, the performance of 'A' will in fact lead to the fulfilment of one's desires,

i.e.,

If (B) is true, then if I perform 'A', my desires will be fulfilled

Therefore,

If (B) is true, then my desires will be fulfilled

So valuing the truth of beliefs of that form is quite treasonable. Nevertheless, inference derives such beliefs from other beliefs and can be expected to be true if those other beliefs are true. So valuing the truth of any belief that might be used in such an inference is reasonable.

To him extent that they can give such deflationary accounts of all the acts involving truth, then the collection will meet the explanatory demands on a theory of truth of all statements like, The proposition that snow is white is true if and only if 'snow is white', and we will undermine the sense that we need some deep analysis of truth.

Nonetheless, there are several strongly felt objections to deflationism. One reason for dissatisfaction is that the theory has many axioms, and therefore cannot be completely written down. It can be described, as the theory whose axioms are the propositions of the fore 'p if and only if it is true that 'p', but not explicitly formulated. This alleged defect has led some philosophers to develop theories that show, first, how the truth of any proposition derives from the referential properties of its constituents, and second, how the referential properties of primitive constituents are determined (Tarski, 1943 and Davidson, 1969). However, assuming that all propositions including belief attributions remain controversial, law of nature and counterfactual conditionals depends for their truth values on what their constituents refer to. Moreover, there is no immediate prospect of a decent, finite theory of reference, so that it is far form clear that the infinite, that we can avoid list-like character of deflationism.

An objection to the version of the deflationary theory presented here concerns its reliance on 'propositions' as the basic vehicles of truth. It is widely felt that the notion of the proposition is defective and that we should not employ it in semantics. If this point of view is accepted then the natural deflationary reaction is to attempt a reformation that would appeal only to sentences. There is no simple way of modifying the disquotational schema to accommodate this problem. A possible way of these difficulties is to resist the critique of propositions. Such entities may exhibit an unwelcome degree of indeterminancy, and might defy reduction to familiar items, however, they do offer a plausible account of belief, as relations to propositions, and, in ordinary language at least, we indeed take them to be the primary bearers of truth. To believe a proposition is too old for it to be true. The philosophical problems include discovering whether belief differs from other varieties of assent, such as 'acceptance', discovering to what extent degrees of belief is possible, understanding the ways in which belief is controlled by rational and irrational factors, and discovering its links with other properties, such as the possession of conceptual or linguistic skills. This last set of problems includes the question of whether they have properly said that paralinguistic infants or animals have beliefs.

Additionally, it is commonly supposed that problems about the nature of truth are intimately bound up with questions as to the accessibility and autonomy of facts in various domains: Questions about whether we can know the facts, and whether they can exist independently of our capacity to discover them (Dummett, 1978, and Putnam, 1981). One might reason, for example, that if 'T is true' means' nothing more than 'T will be verified', then certain forms of scepticism, specifically, those that doubt the correctness of our methods of verification, that will be precluded, and that the facts will have been revealed as dependent on human practices. Alternatively, we might say that if truth were an inexplicable, primitive, non-epistemic property, then the fact that 'T' is true would be completely independent of 'us'. Moreover, we could, in that case, have no reason to assume that the propositions we believe actually have tis property, so scepticism would be unavoidable. In a similar vein, we might think that as special, and perhaps undesirable features of the deflationary approach, is that we have deprived truth of such metaphysical or epistemological implications.

On closer scrutiny, however, it is far from clear that there exists 'any' account of truth with consequences regarding the accessibility or autonomy of non-semantic matters. For although we may expect an account of truth to have such implications for facts of the from 'T is true', we cannot assume without further argument that the same conclusions will apply to the fact 'T'. For it cannot be assumed that 'T' and 'T' are true' by the forthright equivalent to one another given the account of 'true' that is being employed. Of course, if we have defined truth in the way that the deflationist proposes, then the equivalence holds by definition. However, if reference to some metaphysical or epistemological characteristic has defined truth, then we throw the equivalence schema into doubt, pending some demonstration that the trued predicate, in the sense of which is to assume will satisfy in insofar as there are thought to be epistemological problems hanging over 'T' that does not threaten 'T is true', giving the needed demonstration will be difficult. Similarly, if we so define 'truth' that the fact, 'T' is felt to be more, or less, independent of human practices than the fact that 'T is true', then again, it is unclear that the equivalence schema will hold. It seems. Therefore, that the attempt to base epistemological or metaphysical conclusions on a theory of truth must fail because in any such attempt we will simultaneously rely on and undermine the equivalence schema.

The most influential idea in the theory of meaning in the past hundred yeas is the thesis that meaning of an indicative sentence is given by its truth-conditions. On this conception, to understand a sentence is to know its truth-conditions. The conception was first clearly formulated by Frége (1848-1925), was developed in a distinctive way by the early Wittgenstein (1889-1951), and is a leading idea of Davidson (1917-). The conception has remained so central that those who offer opposing theories characteristically define their position by reference to it.

The conception of meaning as truth-conditions needs not and should not be advanced as in itself a complete account of meaning. For instance, one who understands a language must have some idea of the range of speech acts conventionally performed by the various types of a sentence in the language, and must have some idea of the significance of various kinds of speech acts. We should moderately target the claim of the theorist of truth-conditions on the notion of content: If two indicative sentences differ in what they strictly and literally say, then the difference accounts for this difference in their truth-conditions. Most basic to truth-conditions is simply of a statement that is the condition the world must meet if the statement is to be true. To know this condition is equivalent to knowing the meaning of the statement. Although this sounds as if it gives a solid anchorage for meaning, some security disappears when it turns out that repeating the very same statement can only define the truth condition, as a truth condition of 'snow is white' is that snow is white, the truth condition of 'Britain would have capitulated had Hitler invaded' is the Britain would have capitulated had Hitler invaded. It is disputed whether this element of running-on-the-spot disqualifies truth conditions from playing the central role in a substantive theory of meaning. The view has sometimes opposed truth-conditional theories of meaning that to know the meaning of a statement is to be able to use it in a network of inferences.

Whatever it is that makes, what would otherwise be mere sounds and inscriptions into instruments of communication and understanding. The philosophical problem is to demystify this power, and to relate it to what we know of ourselves and the world. Contributions to the study include the theory of 'speech acts' and the investigation of communication and the relationship between words and ideas and the world and surrounding surfaces, by which some persons express by a sentence often depend on the environment in which he or she is placed. For example, the disease I refer to by a term like 'arthritis' or the kind of tree I call a 'maple' will be defined by criteria of which I know next to nothing. The raises the possibility of imagining two persons in rather differently environmental, but in which everything appears the same to each of them, but between them they define a space of philosophical problems. They are the essential components of understanding nd any intelligible proposition that is true can be understood. Such that which an utterance or sentence expresses, the proposition or claim made about the world may by extension, the content of a predicated or other sub-sentential component is what it contributes to the content of sentences that contain it. The nature of content is the cental concern of the philosophy of language.

In particularly, the problems of indeterminancy of translation, inscrutability of reference, language, predication, reference, rule following, semantics, translation, and the topics referring to subordinate headings associated with 'logic'. The loss of confidence in determinate meaning ('individually decoding is another encoding') is an element common both to postmodern uncertainties in the theory of criticism, and to the analytic tradition that follows writers such as Quine (1908-). Still, it may be asked, why should we suppose that we should account fundamental epistemic notions for in behavioural terms what grounds are there for assuming 'p knows p' is a matter of the status of its statement between some subject and some object, between nature and its mirror? The answer is that the only alternative may be to take knowledge of inner states as premises from which we have normally inferred our knowledge of other things, and without which we have normally inferred our knowledge of other things, and without which knowledge would be ungrounded. But it is not really coherent, and does not in the last analysis make sense, to suggest that human knowledge have foundations or grounds. We should remember that to say that truth and knowledge 'can only be judged by the standards of our own day' is not to say that it is not of any lesser importance, or, yet, more cut off from the world, that we had supposed. It is just to say 'that nothing counts as justification, unless by reference to what we already accept, and that there is no way to get outside our beliefs and our language to find some test other than coherence'. The point is that the professional philosophers have thought it might be otherwise, since the body has haunted only them of epistemological scepticism.

What Quine opposes as 'residual Platonism' is not so much the hypostasising of nonphysical entities as the notion of 'correspondence' with things as the final court of appeal for evaluating present practices. Unfortunately, Quine, for all that it is incompatible with its basic insights, substitutes for this correspondence to physical entities, and specially to the basic entities, whatever they turn out to be, of physical science. But when we have purified their doctrines, they converge on a single claim that no account of knowledge can depend on the assumption of some privileged relations to reality. Their work brings out why an account of knowledge can amount only to a description of human behaviour.

What, then, is to be said of these 'inner states', and of the direct reports of them that have played so important a role in traditional epistemology? For a person to feel is nothing else than for him to be able to make a certain type of non-inferential report, to attribute feelings to infants is to acknowledge in them latent abilities of this innate kind. Non-conceptual, non-linguistic 'knowledge' of what feelings or sensations is like is attributively to beings because of potential membership of our community. We accredit infants and the more attractive animals with having feelings based on that spontaneous sympathy that we extend to anything humanoid, in contrast with the mere 'response to stimuli' attributed to photoelectric cells and to animals about which no one feels sentimentally. It is consequently wrong to suppose that moral prohibition against hurting infants and the better-looking animals are; those moral prohibitions grounded' in their possession of feelings. The relation of dependence is really the other way round. Similarly, we could not be mistaken in assuming a four-year-old child has knowledge, but no one-year-old, any more than we could be mistaken in taking the word of a statute that eighteen-year-old can marry freely but seventeen-year-old cannot. (There is no more 'solid ontological ground' for the distinction that may suit 'us' to make in the former case than in the later.) Again, such a question as 'Are robots' conscious?' Calling for a decision on our part whether or not to treat robots as members of our linguistic community. All this is a piece with the insight brought intro philosophy by Hegel (1770-1831), that the individual apart from his society is just another predatory animal.

In saying, that the 'intentional idioms' resist smooth incorporation into the scientific world view, and Quine responds with scepticism toward them, not quite endorsing 'eliminativism', but regarding them as second-rate idioms, unsuitable for describing strict and literal facts. For similar reasons he has consistently expressed suspicion of the logical and philosophical propriety of appeal to logical possibilities and possible worlds. The languages that are properly behaved and suitable for literal and true descriptions of the world happen to those within the fields that draw upon mathematics and science. We must take the entities to which our best theories refer with full seriousness in our ontologies, although an empiricist. Quine thus supposes that science requires the abstract objects of set theory, and therefore exist. In the theory of knowledge Quine associated with a 'Holistic View' of verification, conceiving of a body of knowledge about a web touching experience at the periphery, but with each point connected by a network of relations to other points.

Coherence is a major player in the theatre of knowledge. There are cogence theories of belief, truth and justification, as these are to combine themselves in the various ways to yield theories of knowledge coherence theories of belief are concerned with the content of beliefs. Consider a belief you now have, the beliefs that you are reading a page in a book, in so, that what makes that belief the belief that it is? What makes it the belief that you are reading a page in a book than the belief that you have a centaur in the garden?

One answer is that the belief has a coherent place or role in a system of beliefs, perception or the having the perceptivity that has its influence on beliefs. As, you respond to sensory stimuli by believing that you are reading a page in a book than believing that you have a centaur in the garden. Belief has an influence on action, or its belief is a desire to act, if belief will differentiate the differences between them, that its belief is a desire or if you were to believe that you are reading a page than if you believed in something about a centaur. Sortal perceptivals hold accountably the perceptivity and action that are indeterminate to its content if its belief is the action as if stimulated by its inner and latent coherence in that of your belief, however. The same stimuli may produce various beliefs and various beliefs may produce the same action. The role that gives the belief the content it has is the role it plays in a network of relations to other beliefs, some latently causal than others that relate to the role in inference and implication. For example, I infer different things from believing that I am reading a page in a book than from any other belief, justly as I infer about other beliefs from.

The input of perceptibility and the output of an action supplement the central role of the systematic relations the belief has to other beliefs but is the systematic relation that gives the belief the specific contentual representation it has. They are the fundamental source of the content of belief. That is how coherence comes in. A belief has the representational content by which it does because of the way in which it coheres within a system of beliefs (Rosenberg, 1988). We might distinguish weak coherence theories of the content of beliefs from stronger coherence theories. Weak coherence theories affirm that coherence is one determinant of the representation given that the contents are of belief. Strong coherence theories of the content of belief affirm that coherence is the sole determinant of the contentual representations of belief.

There is, nonetheless, another distinction that cuts across the distinction between weak and strong coherence theories between positive and negative coherence theory (Pollock, 1986). A positive coherence theory tells 'us' that if a belief coheres with a background system of belief, then the belief is justifiable. A negative coherence theory tells 'us' that if a belief fails to cohere with a background system of beliefs, then the belief is not justifiable. We might put this by saying that, according to the positivity of a coherence theory, coherence has the power to produce justification, while according to its being adhered by negativity, the coherence theory has only the power to nullify justification.

Least of mention, a strong coherence theory of justification is a formidable combination by which a positive and a negative theory tell 'us' that a belief is justifiable if and only if it coheres with a background system of inter-connectivity of beliefs. Coherence theories of justification and knowledge have most often been rejected for being unable to deal with an accountable justification toward the perceptivity upon the projection of knowledge (Audi, 1988, and Pollock, 1986), and, therefore, it will be most appropriate to consider a perceptual example that will serve as a kind of crucial test. Suppose that a person, call her Julie, and works with a scientific instrumentation that has a gauging measure upon temperatures of liquids in a container. The gauge is marked in degrees, she looks at the gauge and sees that the reading is 105 degrees. What is she justifiably to believe, and why? Is she, for example, justified in believing that the liquid in the container is 105 degrees? Clearly, that depends on her background beliefs. A weak coherence theorist might argue that, though her belief that she sees the shape 105 is immediately justified as direct sensory evidence without appeal to a background system, the belief that the location in the container is 105 degrees' result from coherence with a background system of latent beliefs that affirm to the shaping perceptivity that its 105 as visually read to be 105 degrees on the gauge that measures the temperature of the liquid in the container. This is, nonetheless, of a weak coherence view that combines coherence with direct perceptivity as its evidence, in that the foundation of justification, is to account for the justification of our beliefs.

A strong coherence theory would go beyond the claim of the weak coherence theory to affirm that the justification of all beliefs, including the belief that one sees the shaping to sensory data that holds accountable a measure of 105, or even the more cautious belief that one sees a shape, resulting from the perceptivals of coherence theory, in that it coheres with a background system. One may argue for this strong coherence theory in several of different ways. One line or medium through which to appeal to the coherence theory of contentual representations. If the content of the perceptual belief results from the relations of the belief to other beliefs in a network system of beliefs, then one may notably argue that the justification of perceptivity, that the belief is a resultant from which its relation of the belief to other beliefs, in the network system of beliefs is in argument for the strong coherence theory is that without any assumptive reason that the coherence theory of the content of beliefs is much the supposed cause that only produce the consequences we expect. Consider the very cautious belief that I see a shape. How could the justification for that perceptual belief be an existent result that they characterize of its material coherence with a background system of beliefs? Our background system contains a simple and primal theory about our relationship to the world and surrounding surfaces that we perceive as it is or should be believed. To come to the specific point at issue, we believe that we can tell a shape when we see one, completely differentiated its form as perceived to sensory data, that we are to trust of ourselves about such simple matters as wether we see a shape before 'us' or not, as in the acceptance of opening to nature the inter-connectivity between belief and the progression through which we acquire from past experiential conditions of application, and not beyond deception. Moreover, when Trust sees the believing desire to act upon what either coheres with a weak or strong coherence of theory, she shows that its belief, as a measurable quality or entity of 105, has the essence in as much as there is much more of a structured distinction of circumstance, which is not of those that are deceptive about whether she sees that shape or sincerely does not see of its shaping distinction, however. Light is good, and the numeral shapes are large, readily discernible and so forth. These are beliefs that Trust has single handedly authenticated reasons for justification. Her successive malignance to sensory access to data involved is justifiably a subsequent belief, in that with those beliefs, and so she is justified and creditable.

The philosophical problems include discovering whether belief differs from other varieties of assent, such as 'acceptance' discovering to what extent degrees of belief is possible, understanding the ways in which belief is controlled by rational and irrational factors, and discovering its links with other properties, such as the possession of conceptual or linguistic skills. This last set of problems includes the question of whether we have properly said that paralinguistic infants or animals have beliefs.

Thus, we might think of coherence as inference to the best explanation based on a background system of beliefs, since we are not aware of such inferences for the most part, we must interpret the inferences as unconscious inferences, as information processing, based on or accessing the background system that proves most convincing of acquiring its act and used from the motivational force that its underlying and hidden desire are to do so. One might object to such an account as not all justifiable inferences are self-explanatory, and more generally, the account of coherence may, at best, is ably successful to competitions that are based on background systems (BonJour, 1985, and Lehrer, 1990). The belief that one sees a shape competes with the claim that one does not, with the claim that one is deceived, and other sceptical objections. The background system of beliefs informs one that one is acceptingly trustworthy and enables one to meet the objections. A belief coheres with a background system just in case it enables one to meet the sceptical objections and in the way justifies one in the belief. This is a standard strong coherence theory of justification (Lehrer, 1990).

It is easy to illustrate the relationship between positive and negative coherence theories about the standard coherence theory. If some objection to a belief cannot be met as the background system of beliefs of a person, then the person is not justified in that belief. So, to return to Julie, suppose that she has been told that a warning light has been installed on her gauge to tell her when it is not functioning properly and that when the red light is on, the gauge is malfunctioning. Suppose that when she sees the reading of 105, she also sees that the red light is on. Imagine, finally, that this is the first time the red light has been on, and, after years of working with the gauge, Trust, who has always placed her trust in the gauge, believes what the gauge tells her, that the liquid in the container is at 105 degrees. Though she believes what she reads is at 105 degrees is not a justified belief because it fails to cohere with her background belief that the gauge is malfunctioning. Thus, the negative coherence theory tells 'us' that she is not justified in her belief about the temperature of the contents in the container. By contrast, when we have not illuminated the red light and the background system of Julies tell her that under such conditions that gauge is a trustworthy indicator of the temperature of the liquid in the container, then she is justified. The positive coherence theory tells 'us' that she is justified in her belief because her belief coheres with her background system of Julies tell her that under such conditions that gauge is a trustworthy indicator of the temperature of the liquid in the container, then she is justified. The positive coherence theory tells 'us' that she is justified in her belief because her belief coheres with her background system continues as a trustworthy system.

The foregoing sketch and illustration of coherence theories of justification have a common feature, namely, that they are what we have called internalistic theories of justification what makes of such a view are the absence of any requirement that the person for whom the belief is justified have any sort of cognitive access to the relation of reliability in question. Lacking such access, such a person will in general, have no reason for thinking the belief is true or likely to be true, but will, on such an account, are none the less to appear epistemologically justified in accepting it. Thus, such a view arguably marks a major break from the modern epistemological traditions, which identifies epistemic justification with having a reason, perhaps even a conclusive reason, for thinking that the belief is true. An epistemologist working within this tradition is likely to feel that the externalist, than offering a competing account of the same concept of epistemic justification with which the traditional epistemologist is concerned, has simply changed the subject.

They are theories affirming that coherence is a matter of internal relations between beliefs and that justification is a matter of coherence. If, then, justification is solely a matter of internal relations between beliefs, we are left with the possibility that the internal relations might fail to correspond with any external reality. How, one might object, can be completely internal; A subjective belief of justification bridge over the spread of time space or interval that separates of whatever is in common to (as in position, in a distinction or in participation). The given of true beliefs, which might be no more than a lucky guess, and knowledge, which we must ground in some connection between internal subjective conditions and external objective realities?

The answer is that it cannot and that we have required something more than justified true belief for knowledge. This result has, however, been established quite apart from consideration of coherence theories of justification. What we have required maybe put by saying that the justification that one must be undefeated by errors in the background system of beliefs. Justification is undefeated by errors just in case any correction of such errors in the background system of belief would sustain the justification of the belief from the corrected system. So knowledge, on this sort of positivity is acclaimed by the coherence theory, which is the true belief that coheres with the background belief system and corrected versions of that system. In short, knowledge is true belief plus justification resulting from coherence and undefeated by error (Lehrer, 1990). The connection between internal subjective conditions of belief and external objectivity are from which reality's result from the required correctness of our beliefs about the relations between those conditions and realities. In the example, of Julie, she believes that her internal subjectivity to conditions of sensory data in which we have connected the experience and perceptual beliefs with the external objectivity in which reality is the temperature of the liquid in the container in a trustworthy manner. This background belief is essential to the justification of her belief that the temperature of the liquid in the container is 105 degrees, and the correctness of that background belief is essential to the justification remaining undefeated. So our background system of beliefs contains a simple theory about our relation to the external world that justifies certain of our beliefs that cohere with that system. For instance, such justification to convert to knowledge, that theory must be sufficiently free from error so that they have sustained the coherence in corrected versions of our background system of beliefs. The correctness of the simple background theory provides the connection between the internal condition and external reality.

The coherence theory of truth arises naturally out of a problem raised by the coherence theory of justification. The problem is that anyone seeking to determine whether she has knowledge is confined to the search for coherence among her beliefs. The sensory experiences she has been unresponsive, until they have represented them as some perceptual belief. Beliefs are the engines that pull the train of justification. But what assurance do we have that our justification is based on true beliefs? What justification do we have that any of our justifications are undefeated? The fear that we might have none, that our beliefs may as an artifact of some deceptive demon or scientist, lead to the quest to reduce truth to some form, perhaps an idealized form, of justification (Rescher, 1973, and Rosenberg, 1980). That would close the threatening sceptical gap between justification and truth. Suppose that a belief is true if and only if it is justifiable of some person. For such a person there would be no gap between justification and truth or between justification and undefeated justification. Julie's coherence with some ideal background system of beliefs, perhaps one expressing a consensus among systems or some consensus among belief systems or some convergence toward a consensus. Such a view is theoretically attractive for the reduction it promises, but it appears open to profound objectification. One is that there is a consensus that we can all be wrong about at least some matters, for example, about the origins of the universe. If there is a consensus that we can all be wrong about something, then the consensual belief system rejects the equation of truth with the consensus. Consequently, the equation of truth with coherence with a consensual belief system is itself incoherently.

Coherence theories of the content of our beliefs and the justification of our beliefs themselves cohere with our background systems but coherence theories of truth do not. A defender of coherentism must accept the logical gap between justified belief and truth, but may believe that our capacities suffice to close the gap to yield knowledge. That view is, at any rate, a coherent one.

What makes a belief justified and what makes a true belief knowledge? It is natural to think that whether a belief deserves one of these appraisals depend on what causal subject to have the belief. In recent decades several epistemologists have pursed this plausible idea with a variety of specific proposals. Some causal theories of knowledge have it that a true belief that 'p' is knowledge just in case it has the right sort of causal connection to the fact that 'p'. Such a criterion can be applied only to cases where the fact that 'p' is a sort that can reach causal relations, this seems to exclude mathematically and other necessary facts and perhaps any fact expressed by a universal generalization, and proponents of this sort of criterion have usually of this sort of criterion have usually supposed that it is limited to perceptual knowledge of particular facts about the depicted object, as subject to environment.

For example, Armstrong (1973) proposed that a belief of the form 'This (perceived) object is 'F' is (non-inferential) knowledge if and only if the belief is a completely reliable sign that the perceived object is 'F', that is, the fact that the object is 'F' contributed to causing the belief and its doing so depended on properties of the believer such that the laws of nature dictated that, for any subject 'x' is to occur, and so thus a perceived object of 'y', if 'x' undergoing those properties are for 'us' to believe that 'y' is 'F', then 'y' is 'F'.

(Dretske (1981) offers a rather similar account, as to the belief's being caused by a signal received by the perceiver that carries the information that the object is 'F').

This sort of condition fails, however, to be sufficient for non-inferential perceptual knowledge because it is compatible with the belief's being unjustified, and an unjustifiable belief cannot be knowledge. For example, suppose that your mechanisms for colour perception are working well, but you have been given good reason to think otherwise, to think, say, that the substantive primary colours that are perceivable, that things look chartreuse to you and chartreuse things look magenta. If you fail to heed these reasons you have for thinking that your colour perception or sensory data is a way and believing of a thing that looks magenta to you that it is magenta, your belief will fail to be justified and will therefore fail to be knowledge, although the thing's being magenta in such a way causes it as to be a completely reliable sign, or to carry the information, in that the thing is magenta.

One could fend off this sort of counterexample by simply adding to the causal condition the requirement that the belief be justified, buy this enriched condition would still be insufficient. Suppose, for example, that in nearly all people, but not in you, as it happens, causes the aforementioned aberration in colour perceptions. The experimenter tells you that you have taken such a drug but then says, 'no, wait minute, the pill you took was just a placebo', suppose further, that this last thing the experimenter tells you is false. Her telling you that it was a false statement, and, again, telling you this gives you justification for believing of a thing that looks a subtractive primary colour to you that it is a sensorial primary colour, in that the fact you were to expect that the experimenters last statements were false, making it the case that your true belief is not knowledgeably correct, thought as though to satisfy its causal condition.

Goldman (1986), has proposed an importantly different sort of causal criterion namely, that a true belief is knowledge, if it is produced by a type of process that is 'globally' and 'locally' reliable. It is globally reliable if its propensity to cause true beliefs is sufficiently high. Local reliability concerns whether the process would have produced a similar but false belief in certain counterfactual situations alternative to the actual situation. This way of marking off true beliefs that are knowledge does not require the fact believed to be casually related to the belief, and so it could in principle apply to knowledge of any kind of truth.

Goldman requires that global reliability of the belief-producing process for the justification of a belief, he requires it also for knowledge because they require justification for knowledge, in what requires for knowledge but does not require for justification, which is locally reliable. His idea is that a justified true belief is knowledge if the type of process that produced it would not have produced it in any relevant counterfactual situation in which it is false. Noting that other concepts exhibit the same logical structure can motivate the relevant alternative account of knowledge. Two examples of this are the concept 'flat' and the concept 'empty' (Dretske, 1981). Both seem absolute concepts -As some point that occupies a particular significance in space is empty only if it does not contain anything and a surface is flat only if it does not have any bumps. However, the absolute character of these concepts is relative to a standard. In the case of 'flat', there is a standard for what counts as a bump and for 'empty', there is a standard for what counts as a thing. To be flat is to be free of any relevant bumps and to be empty is to be devoid of all relevant things.

This avoids the sorts of counterexamples we gave for the causal criteria, but it is vulnerable to one or ones of a different sort. Suppose you were to stand on the mainland looking over the water at an island, on which are several structures that look (from at least some point of view) as would ne of an actualized point or station of position. You happen to be looking at one of any point, in fact a barn and your belief to that effect are justified, given how it looks to you and the fact that you have exclusively of no reason to think nor believe otherwise. But suppose that most of the barn-looking structures on the island are not real barns but fakes. Finally, suppose that from any viewpoint on the mainland all of the island's fake barns are obscured by trees and that circumstances made it very unlikely that you would have to a viewpoint not on the mainland. Here, it seems, your justified true belief that you are looking at a barn is not knowledge, even if there was not a serious chance that there would have developed an alternative situation, wherefore you are similarly caused to have a false belief that you are looking at a barn.

That example shows that the 'local reliability' of the belief-producing process, on the 'serous chance' explication of what makes an alternative relevance, yet its view point upon which we are in showing that non-locality afforded to sustain some probable course of the possibility for 'us' to believe in. Within the experience condition of application, the relationship with the sensory-data, as having a world-view that can encompass both the hidden and manifest aspects of nature would comprise of the mind, or brain that provides the excitation of neuronal ions, giving to sensory perception an accountable assessment of data and reason-sensitivity allowing a comprehensive world-view, integrating the various aspects of the universe into one magnificent whole, a whole in which we played an organic and central role. One-hundred years ago its question would have been by a Newtonian 'clockwork universe', a model of an assumed informal 'I' universe that is completely mechanical. The laws of nature have predetermined everything that happens and by the state of the universe in the distant past. The freedom one feels concerning ones actions, even regarding the movement of one's body, is an illusory infraction and the world-view expresses as the Newtonian one, is completely coherent.

Nevertheless, the human mind abhors a vacuum. When an explicit, coherent world-view is absent, it functions based on a tactic one. A tactic world-view is not subject to a critical evaluation, and it can easily harbour inconsistencies. And, indeed, our tactic set of beliefs about the nature of reality consists of contradictory bits and pieces. The dominant component is a leftover from another period, the Newtonian 'clock universe' still lingers as we cling to this old and tired model because we know of nothing else that can take its place. Our condition is the condition of a culture that is in the throes of a paradigm shift. A major paradigm shift is complex and difficult because a paradigm holds 'us captive: We see reality through it, as through coloured glasses, but we do not know that, we are convinced that we see reality as it is. Hence the appearance of a new and different paradigm is often incomprehensible. To someone raised believing that the Earth is flat, the suggestion that the Earth is spherical seems preposterous: If the Earth were spherical, would not the poor antipodes fall 'down' into the sky?

And yet, as we face a new millennium, we are forced to face this challenge. The fate of the planet is in question, and it was brought to its present precarious condition largely because of our trust in the Newtonian paradigm. As Newtonian world-view has to go, and, if one looks carefully, we can discern the main feature of the new, emergent paradigm. The search for these features is what was the influence of a fading paradigm. All paradigms include subterranean realms of tactic assumptions, the influence of which outlasts the adherence to the paradigm itself.

The first line of exploration suggests the 'weird' aspects of the quantum theory, with fertile grounds for our feeling of which should disappear in inconsistencies with the prevailing world-view. This feeling is in replacing by the new one, i.e., if one believes that the Earth is flat, the story of Magellan's travels is quite puzzling: How it is possible for a ship to travel due west and, without changing direct. Arrive at its place of departure? Obviously, when the belief replaces the flat-Earth paradigm that Earth is spherical, we have instantly resolved the vertical Mosaic.

The founders of Relativity and quantum mechanics were deeply engaging but incomplete, in that none of them attempted to construct a philosophical system, however, that the mystery at the heart of the quantum theory called for a revolution in philosophical outlooks. During which time, the 1920's, when quantum mechanics reached maturity, began the construction of a full-blooded philosophical system that we based not only on science but on nonscientific modes of knowledge as well. As, the fading influences drawn upon the paradigm go well beyond its explicit claim. We believe, as the scenists and philosophers did, that when we wish to find out the truth about the universe, we can ignore nonscientific nodes of processing human experiences, poetry, literature, art, music are all wonderful, but, in relation to the quest for knowledge of the universe, they are irrelevant. Yet, it was Alfred North Whitehead who pointed out the fallacy of this speculative assumption. In this, and in other aspects of thinking of some reality in which are the building blocks of reality are not material atoms but 'throbs of experience'. Whitehead formulated his system in the late 1920s, and yet, as far as I know, the founders of quantum mechanics were unaware of it. It was not until 1963 that J.M. Burgers pointed out that its philosophy accounts very well for the main features of the quanta, especially the 'weird ones', enabling as in some aspects of reality is 'higher' or 'deeper' than others, and if so, what is the structure of such hierarchical divisions? What of our place in the universe? And, finally, what is the relationship between the great aspiration within the lost realms of nature? An attempt to endow 'us' with a cosmological meaning in such a universe seems totally absurd, and, yet, this very universe is just a paradigm, not the truth. When you reach its end, you may be willing to join the alternate view as accorded to which, surprisingly bestow 'us' with what we have restored, although in a post-postmodern context.

Subjective matter's has regulated the philosophical implications of quantum mechanics, as to emphasis the connections between what I believe, in that investigations of such interconnectivity are anticipatorially the hesitations that are an exclusion held within the western traditions, however, the philosophical thinking, as afforded effort by Plato to Platinous had in some aspects of some interpretation is presented here in the expression of a consensus of the physical society. Some have shared and objected of other aspects, sometimes vehemently by others. Still other aspects express my own views and convictions, as turning about to be more difficult that anticipated, discovering that a conversational mode would be helpful, but, their conversations with each other and with me in hoping that all will be not only illuminating but finding to its read may approve in them, whose dreams are dreams among others than themselves.

These examples make it seem likely that, if there is a criterion for what makes an alternative situation relevant that will save Goldman's claim about reliability and the acceptance of knowledge, it will not be simple.

The interesting thesis that counts asa causal theory of justification, in the meaning of 'causal theory' intend of the belief that is justified just in case it was produced by a type of process that is 'globally' reliable, that is, its propensity to produce true beliefs-that can be defined to a good enough approximations, as the proportion of the belief it produces, or would produce where it used as much as opportunity allows, that is true, is sufficiently that a belief acquires favourable epistemic status by having some kind of reliable linkage to the truth. We have advanced variations of this view for both knowledge and justified belief. The first formulations of are reliably in its account of knowing appearing in a note by F.P. Ramsey (1903-30) who made important contributions to mathematical logic, probability theory, the philosophy of science and economics. Instead of saying that quarks have such-and-such properties, the Ramsey sentence speaks of something that has those properties. If we have repeated the process for all of the theoretical terms, the sentence gives the 'topic-neutral' structure of the theory, but removes any implication that we know what the term so treated appropriately. It leaves open the possibility of identifying the theoretical item with whatever. It is that best fits the description provided, thus, substituting the term by a variable, and exististential qualifying into the result. Ramsey was one of the first thinkers to accept a 'redundancy theory of truth', which he combined its radical views of the function of many kinds of the proposition. Neither generalizations, nor causal propositions, not those treating probabilities or ethics, described facts, but each has a different specific function in our intellectual commentators on the early works of Wittgenstein, and his continuing friendship with the latter liked to Wittgenstein's return to Cambridge and to philosophy in 1929.

The most sustaining and influential applications of these ideas were in the philosophy of mind, or brain, as Ludwig Wittgenstein (1889-1951) whom Ramsey persuaded Wittgenstein to remain working, and, in this respect, something or someone is undoubtedly to be inclined to manifest implications that are charismatically the figurehead by 20th century principle in philosophy. Living and writing with a power and intensity that frequently overwhelmed his contemporaries and readers, being a kind of picture or model has centred the early period on the 'picture theory of meaning' according to which sentence represents a state of affairs of it. Containing elements corresponding to those of the state of affairs and structure or form that mirrors that a structure of the state of affairs that it represents. We have reduced to all logic complexity that of the 'propositional calculus, and all propositions are 'truth-functions of atomic or basic propositions.

In the later period of the 20th century, the emphasis shifts dramatically to the actions of people and the role linguistic activities play in their lives. Thus, whereas in the "Tractatus" language is placed in a static, formal relationship with the world, in the later work Wittgenstein emphasis its use from standardized social activities of ordering, advising, requesting, measuring, counting, excising concerns for each other, and so on. These different activities are thought of as so many 'language games' that together make or a form of life. Philosophy typically ignores this diversity, and in generalizing and abstracting distorts the real nature of its subject-matter.

relations than psychological processes, but we might also offer reliabilism as a deeper-level theory, subsuming some of the precepts of either foundationalism or coherentism. Foundationalism is oft-repeated statements usually involving experience or observation showing that there are 'basic' beliefs, which acquire justification without dependence on inference, reliabilism might rationalize this indicating that reliable non-inferential processes have formed the basic beliefs. Coherence stresses the primary of systematicity in all doxastic decision-making. Reliabilism might rationalize this by pointing to increases in reliability that accrue from systematicity consequently, reliabilism could complement foundationalism and coherence than completed with them.

These examples make it seem likely that, if there is a criterion for what makes an alternate situation relevant that will save Goldman's claim about local reliability and knowledge. Will did not be simple. The interesting thesis that counts as a causal theory of justification, in the making of 'causal theory' intended for the belief as it is justified in case it was produced by a type of process that is 'globally' reliable, that is, its propensity to produce true beliefs that can be defined, to a good enough approximations, as the proportion of the beliefs it produces, or would produce where it used as much as opportunity allows, that is true is sufficiently relializable. We have advanced variations of this view for both knowledge and justified belief, its first formulation of a reliability account of knowing appeared in the notation from F.P.Ramsey (1903-30). The theory of probability, he was the first to show how a 'personalist's theory' has the possibility to being developed, based on a precise behavioural notion of preference and expectation. In the philosophy of language. Much of Ramsey's work was directed at saving classical mathematics from 'intuitionism', or what he called the 'Bolshevik menace of Brouwer and Weyl. In the theory of probability he was the first to show how we could develop some personalists theory, based on precise behavioural notation of preference and expectation. In the philosophy of language, Ramsey was one of the first thankers, which he combined with radical views of the function of many kinds of a proposition. Neither generalizations, nor causal propositions, nor those treating probability or ethics, describe facts, but each has a different specific function in our intellectual economy. Ramsey was one of the earliest commentators on the early work of Wittgenstein, and his continuing friendship that led to Wittgenstein's return to Cambridge and to philosophy in 1929.

Ramsey's sentence theory is the sentence generated by taking all the sentences affirmed in a scientific theory that use some term, e. g., 'quark'. Replacing the term by a variable, and existentially quantifying into the result. Instead of saying that quarks have such-and-such properties, the Ramsey sentence says that there is something that has those properties. If we repeat the process for all of a group of the theoretical terms, the sentence gives the 'topic-neutral' structure of the theory, but removes any implication that we know what the term so treated characterlogically. It leaves open the possibility of identifying the theoretical item with whatever, but it is that best fits the description provided. Virtually, all theories of knowledge. Of course, share an externalist component in requiring truth as a condition for known in. Reliabilism goes farther, however, in trying to capture additional conditions for knowledge by ways of a nomic, counterfactual or other 'external' relations between belief and truth. Closely allied to the nomic sufficiency account of knowledge, primarily dur to Dretshe (1971, 1981), A.I. Goldman (1976, 1986) and R. Nozick (1981). The core of this approach is that x's belief that 'p' qualifies as knowledge just in case 'x' believes 'p', because of reasons that would not obtain unless 'p' was true, or because of a process or method that would not yield belief in 'p' if 'p' were not true. An enemy example, 'x' would not have its current reasons for believing there is a telephone before it. Or would not come to believe this in the ways it does, thus, there is a counterfactual reliable guarantor of the belief's bing true. An undaunted and the facts of counterfactual approach say that 'x' knows that 'p' only if there is no 'relevant alternative' situation in which 'p' is false but 'x' would still believe that a proposition 'p' must be sufficiently orient to eliminate all the alternatives too 'p' where an alternative to a proposition 'p' is a proposition incompatible with 'p?'. That in, one's justification or evidence for 'p' must be sufficient for one to know that every alternative too 'p' is false. This element of our evolving thinking, sceptical arguments have exploited about which knowledge. These arguments call our attentions to alternatives that our evidence sustains itself with no elimination. The sceptic inquires to how we know that we are not seeing a cleverly disguised mule. While we do have some evidence against the likelihood of such as deception, intuitively it is not strong enough for 'us' to know that we are not so deceived. By pointing out alternate but hidden points of nature, in that we cannot eliminate, and others with more general application, as dreams, hallucinations, etc. The sceptic appears to show that every alternative is seldom. If ever, satisfied.

This conclusion conflicts with another strand in our thinking about knowledge, in that we know many things. Thus, there is a tension in our ordinary thinking about knowledge ~. We believe that knowledge is, in the sense indicated, an absolute concept and yet, we also believe that there are many instances of that concept.

If one finds absoluteness to be too central a component of our concept of knowledge to be relinquished, one could argue from the absolute character of knowledge to a sceptical conclusion (Unger, 1975). Most philosophers, however, have taken the other course, choosing to respond to the conflict by giving up, perhaps reluctantly, the absolute criterion. This latter response holds as sacrosanct our commonsense belief that we know many things (Pollock, 1979 and Chisholm, 1977). Each approach is subject to the criticism that it preserves one aspect of our ordinary thinking about knowledge at the expense of denying another. We can view the theory of relevant alternatives as an attempt to provide a more satisfactory response to this tension in our thinking about knowledge. It attempts to characterize knowledge in a way that preserves both our belief that knowledge is an absolute concept and our belief that we have knowledge.

According to most epistemologists, knowledge entails belief, so that I cannot know that such and such is the case unless I believe that such and such am the case. Others think this entailment thesis can be rendered more accurately if we substitute for briefs some related attitude. For instance, several philosophers would prefer to say that knowledge entail psychological certainty or acceptance (Lehrer, 1989). Nonetheless, there are arguments against all versions of the thesis that knowledge requires having belief-like attitudes toward the known. These arguments are given by philosophers who think that knowledge and belief, or a facsimile thereof, are mutually incompatible as they represent the incompatibility thesis, or by ones who say that knowledge does no entail belief or vice versa, so that each may exist without the other, but the two may also coexist (the separability thesis).

The incompatibility thesis is sometimes traced to Plato, in view of his claim that knowledge is infallible while belief for opinion is fallible (Republic 476-9). Belief might be a component of an infallible form of knowledge in spite of the fallibility of belief. Perhaps knowledge involves some factors that compensate for the fallibility of belief.

A.Duncan-Jones, 1938 also Vendler, 1978, cites linguistic evidence to back up the incompatibly thesis. He notes that people often say 'I believe she is guilty, I know she is' and the like, which suggests that belief rule out knowledge. However, as Lehrer (1974) indicates, that of a greater emphatic way of saying, 'I don't just believe she is guilty, I know that she is', where 'just' make is especially clear that the speaker is signalling that she has something more salient than mere belief, not that she has something inconsistent with belief, namely knowledge, Compare: 'You didn't hurt him, you killed him.

H.A. Prichard (1966) offers a defence of the incomparability thesis which hinges on the equation of knowledge with certainty, as both incline toward infallibility and psychological certitude and the assumption that when we believe in the truth of a claim we are not certain about its truth, given that belief also, as involves uncertainty while knowledge never does, believing something rules out the possibility of knowing it. Unfortunately, however, Prichard gives us no-good reason to grant that states of belief are never ones involving confidence. Conscious beliefs clearly involve some level of confidence: To suggest that we cease to believe and to suggest that we cease to believe things about which we are confident is bizarre.

A.D. Woozley (1953) defends the version of the separability thesis, Woozley's version, which deals with psychological certainty than belief per se, is that knowledge can exist in the absence of confidence about the item known, although knowledge might also be accompanied by confidence as well. Woozley was to remark, that the test of whether I know of something is 'what I can do, where what I can do may involve answering questions'. Based on that remark he suggests that even when people are unsure of the truth of a claim, they might know that the claim is true. Woozley acknowledges, however, that it would de odd for those who lack confidence to claim knowledge. It would be particularly peculiar to say, 'I am unsure of whether my answer is true: Still, I know it is correct', but this tension Woozley explains using a distinction between conditions under which we are justified in making a claim (such as a claim to know something), and conditions under which the claim we make are true. While 'I know such and such' might be true even if I am unsure of whether such and such holds, nonetheless it would be inappropriate for me to claim that I know that such and such unless I was sure of the truth of my claim.

Colin Radford (1966) extends Woozley's defence of the separability thesis. In Radford's view, not only is knowledge compatible with the lack of certainty, it is also compatible with a complete lack of belief. He argues by example. In one example, Jean has forgotten that he learnt some English history years prior and yet he can give several correct responses to questions such as 'When did the Battle of Hastings occur? Since he forgot that he took history, he considers his correct response to be more than guesses. Thus, when he says he would deny having the belief that the Battle of Hastings took place in 1066. For an even stronger reason he would deny being sure (or having the right to be sure) that 1066 was the correct date. Radford would nonetheless, insist that Jean knows when the Battle occurred, since clearly he remembers the correct date. Radford admits that it would be inappropriate for Jean to say that he knew when the Battle of Hastings occurred, but like Woozley, he attributes the impropriety to a fact about when it is and is not appropriate to claim knowledge. When we claim knowledge, we ought at least, to believe that we have the knowledge we claim, or else our behaviour is 'intentionally misleading'.

Those who agree with Radford's defence of the separability thesis will probably think of belief as an inner state that can be detected through introspection. That Jean lack's beliefs abut English history is plausible on this Cartesian picture since Jean does not find himself with any beliefs about English history when he seeks them out. One might criticize Radford, however, by rejecting the Cartesian view of belief. One could argue that some beliefs are thoroughly unconscious, for example. Or one could adopt a behaviourist conception of belief, such as Alexander Bain's (1859), according to which having beliefs is a matter of the way people are disposed to behave (and hasn't Radford already adopted a behaviorist conception of knowledge?). Since Jean gives the correct response when queried, a form of verbal behaviour, a behaviorist would be tempted to credit him with the belief that the Battle of Hastings occurred in 1066.

D.M. Armstrong (1973) takes a different tack against Radford. Jean does know that the Battle of Hastings took place in 1066. Armstrong will grant Radford that point or points of fact. Armstrong suggests that Jean believe that 1066 is not the date the Battle occurring, for Armstrong equates the belief that such and such is just possible but no more than just possible with the belief that such and such is not true. However, Armstrong insists, Jean also believes that the Battle did occur in 1066. After all, had Jean been mistaught that the Battle occurred in 1060, and had he forgotten bringing 'taught' this and subsequently 'guessed' that it took place in 1060, we would surely describe the situation as one in which Jean's false belief about the Battle became unconscious over time but persisted as a memory trace that was causally responsible for his guess. Out of consistency, we must describe Radford's original case as one in which Jan's true beliefs became unconscious but persisted long enough to casse his guess. Thus, while Jean consciously believes that the Battle did no occur in 1066, unconsciously he does believe it occurred in 1066. So after all, Radford does not have a counterexample to the claim that knowledge entails belief.

Armstrong's response to Radford was to reject Radford's claim that the examinee lacked the relevant belief about English history. Another response is to argue that the examinee lacked the knowledge Radford attributes to him. If Armstrong is correct in suggesting that Jean believes both that 1066 is that it is not the date of the Battle of Hastings, one might deny Jean knowledge since people who believe the denial of what they believe cannot be said to know the truth of their belief. Another strategy might be to liken the examinee case to examples of ignorance given in recent attacks on externalist accounts of knowledge (naturally that Externalists themselves will tend not to favour this strategy). Consider the following case development by BonJour (1985): For no apparent reason. Samantha believes that she is clairvoyant. Agin for no apparent reason, she one day comes to believe that the President is in New York City, though the President is in Washington, D.C. In fact, Samantha is a completely reliable clairvoyant, and she ha arrived at her belief about the whereabouts of the President though the power of her clairvoyance. Yet surely Samantha's belief is completely irrational. She is not justified in thinking what she does. If so, then she dies not know where the President is. But Radford's examinee is a little different, if Lean lacks the belief which Radford denies him, Radford does not have an example of knowledge that is unattended with belief. Suppose that Jan's memory has been sufficiently powerful to produce the relevant belief. As Radford says, Jean has every reason to suppose that hi response is mere guesswork, and so he had every reason to consider his belief false. His belief could be an irrational one, and hence one about whose truth Jean would be ignorant.

Our thinking, and our inherent perceptions of the world are limited by the nature of the language with which our culture employs - instead of language possessing, as had previously been widely assumed, much less significant, purely instrumental, representing functions in our living. Human beings do not live in the objective world alone, nor alone in the world social activity as ordinarily understood, but are very much at the mercy of the particular language which has become the medium of expression for their society. It is quite an illusion to imagine that language is merely an incidental means of solving specific problems of communication or reflection. The point is that the 'real world' is, largely, unconsciously built up on the language habits of the group . . . we see and hear and otherwise e experience very largely as we do because the language habits of our community predispose certain choices of interpretation.

Such a thing, however, has been notoriously elusive. The ancient idea that truth is some sort of 'correspondence with reality' has still never been articulated satisfactorily, and the nature of the alleged 'correspondence' and the alleged 'reality' remain objectionably obscure. Yet the familiar alternative suggestions that true beliefs are those that are 'mutually coherent', or 'pragmatically useful', or 'verifiable in suitable conditions' has each been confronted with persuasive counterexamples. A twentieth-century departure from these traditional analyses is the view that truth is not a property at all that the syntactic form of the predicate, 'is true', distorts its really semantic character, which is not to describe propositions but to endorse them. However, this radical approach is also faced with difficulties and suggests, quasi counter intuitively, that truth cannot have the vital theoretical role in semantics, epistemology and elsewhere that we are naturally inclined to give it. Thus, truth threatens to remain one of the most enigmatic of notions: An explicit account of it can seem essential yet beyond our reach. However, recent work provides some grounds for optimism.

We have based a theory in philosophy of science, is a generalization or set as concerning observable entities, i.e., atoms, quarks, unconscious wish, and so on. The ideal gas law, for example, refers only to such observables as pressure, temperature, and volume, the molecular-kinetic theory refers top molecules and their properties, although an older usage suggests the lack of adequate evidence in support of it (merely a theory), progressive toward its sage; the usage does not carry that connotation. Einstein's special; Theory of relativity, for example, is considered extremely well founded.

These are two main views on the nature of theories. According to the 'received view' theories are partially interpreted axiomatic systems, according to the semantic view, a theory is a collection of models (Suppe, 1974). Under which, some theories usually emerge as exemplifying or occurring in fact, from which are we to find on practical matters and concern of experiencing the real world, nonetheless, that it of supposed truths that are not neatly organized, making the theory difficult to survey or study as a whole. The axiomatic method is an ideal for organizing a theory (Hilbert, 1970), one tries to select from among the supposed truths a small number from which all the others can be seen to be deductively inferrable. This makes the theory more tractable since, in a sense, they contain all truth's in those few. In a theory so organized, they call the few truths from which they deductively infer all others 'axioms'. David Hilbert (1862-1943) had argued that, just as algebraic and differential equations, which were used to study mathematical and physical processes, could they be made mathematical objects, so we could make axiomatic theories, like algebraic and differential equations, which are means of representing physical processes and mathematical structures, objects of mathematical investigation.

Many philosophers had the conviction that all truths, or all truths about a particular domain, followed from a few principles. These principles were taken to be either metaphysically prior or epistemologically prior or both. In the first sense, we took them to be entities of such a nature that what exists is 'caused' by them. When we took the principles as epistemologically prior, that is, as 'axioms', we took them to be either epistemologically privileged, i.e., self-evident, not needing to be demonstrated, or again, inclusive 'or', to be such that all truths do indeed follow from them (by deductive inferences). Gödel (1984) showed in the spirit of Hilbert, treating axiomatic theories as themselves mathematical objects that mathematics, and even a small part. Of mathematics, elementary number theory, could not be axiomatized, that, more precisely, any class of axioms that is such that we could effectively decide, of any proposition, whether or not it was in that class, would be too small to capture all of the truths.

The notion of truth occurs with remarkable frequency in our reflections on language, thought, and action. We are inclined to suppose, for example, that truth is the proper aim of scientific inquiry, that true beliefs help 'us' to achieve our goals, tat to understand a sentence is to know which circumstances would make it true, that reliable preservation of truth as one argues from premises to a conclusion is the mark of valid reasoning, that we should not regard moral pronouncements as objectively true, and so on. To assess the plausible of such theses, and to refine them and to explain why they hold (if they do), we require some view of what truth be a theory that would account for its properties and its relations to other matters. Thus, there can be little prospect of understanding our most important faculties in the absence of a good theory of truth.

The nature of the alleged 'correspondence' and the alleged 'reality remains objectivably obscures'. Yet, the familiar alternative suggests ~. That true beliefs are those that are 'mutually coherent', or 'pragmatically useful', or 'they establish by induction of each to a confronted Verifiability in some suitable conditions with persuasive counterexamples. A twentieth-century departure from these traditional analyses is the view that truth is not a property at all ~. That the syntactic form of the predicate, 'is true', distorts its really semantic character, which is not to describe propositions but to endorse them. Nevertheless, they have also faced this radical approach with difficulties and suggest, a counter intuitively, that truth cannot have the vital theoretical role in semantics, epistemology and elsewhere that we are naturally inclined to give it. Thus, truth threatens to remain one of the most enigmatic of notions. An explicit account of it can seem essential yet, beyond our reach. However, recent work provides some grounds for optimism.

The belief that snow is white owes its truth to a certain feature of the external world, namely, to the fact that snow is white. Similarly, it makes no difference whether people say 'Dogs bark' is true or whether they say, dogs bark, in the former representation of what they say the sentence 'Dogs bark' is mentioned, but in the latte it appears to be used, so the claim that the two equivalent needs careful formulation and defence. On the face of it someone might know that 'Dogs bark' is true without knowing what it means, the belief that dogs bark is true because of the fact that dogs bark. This trivial observation leads to what is perhaps the most natural and popular account of truth, the 'correspondence theory', according to which a belief (statement, a sentence, propositions, etc.) as true just in case there exists a fact corresponding to it (Wittgenstein, 1922). This thesis is unexceptionably for finding out whether one should account of truth are that it is clearly compared with the correspondence theory, and that it succeeds in connecting truth with verification. However, if it is to provide a rigorous, substantial and complete theory of truth, if it is to be more than merely a picturesque way of asserting all equivalences to the form. The belief that 'p' is 'true p'

Then we must supplement it with accounts of what facts are, and what it is for a belief to correspond to a fact, and these are the problems on which the correspondence theory of truth has foundered. For one thing, it is far form clear that reducing 'the belief achieves any significant gain in understanding that 'snow is white is true' to 'the facts that 'snow is white' exists': For these expressions seem equally resistant to analysis and too close in meaning for one to provide an illuminating account of the other. Moreover, the general relationship that holds in particular between the belief that snow is white and the fact that snow is white, between the belief that dogs bark and the fact that dogs bark, and so on, is very hard to identify. The best attempt to date is Wittgenstein's (1922) so-called 'picture theory', under which an elementary proposition is a configuration of terms, with whatever stare of affairs it reported, as an atomic fact is a configuration of simple objects, an atomic fact corresponds to an elementary proposition (and makes it true) when their configurations are identical and when the terms in the proposition for it to the similarly-placed objects in the fact, and the truth value of each complex proposition the truth values of the elementary ones have entailed. However, eve if this account is correct as far as it goes, it would need to be completed with plausible theories of 'logical configuration', 'elementary proposition', 'reference' and 'entailment', none of which is easy to come by way of the central characteristic of truth. One that any adequate theory must explain is that when a proposition satisfies its 'conditions of proof or verification', then it is regarded as true. To the extent that the property of corresponding with reality is mysterious, we are going to find it impossible to see what we take to verify a proposition should indicate the possession of that property. Therefore, a tempting alternative to the correspondence theory an alternative that eschews obscure, metaphysical concept which explains quite straightforwardly why Verifiability implies, truth is simply to identify truth with Verifiability (Peirce, 1932). This idea can take on variously formed. One version involves the further assumption that verification is 'holistic', i.e., that of a belief is justified, i.e., turns over evidence of the truth, when it is part of an entire system of beliefs that are consistent and 'harmonious' (Bradley, 1914 and Hempel, 1935). We have known this as the 'coherence theory of truth'. Another version involves the assumption associated with each proposition, some specific procedure for finding out whether one should on sensing and responding to the definitive qualities or stare of being actual or true, such that a person, an entity, or an event, that is actually might be gainfully to employ the totality of things existent of possessing actuality or essence. On this account, to say that a proposition is true is to sa that the appropriate procedure would verify (Dummett, 1979, and Putnam, 1981). In mathematics this amounts to the identification of truth with probability.

The attractions of the verificationist account of truth are that it is refreshingly clear compared with the correspondence theory, and that it succeeds in connecting truth with verification. The trouble is that the bond it postulates between these notions is implausibly strong. We do indeed take verification to indicate truth, but also we recognize the possibility that a proposition may be false in spite of there being impeccable reasons to believe it, and that a proposition may be true although we are not able to discover that it is. Verifiability and ruth are no doubt highly correlated, but surely not the same thing.

A well-known account of truth is known as 'pragmatism' characterized by the 'pragmatic maxim', according to which the meaning of the concept is to be sought in the experiential or practical consequences of its application. The epistemology of pragmatism is topically anti-Cartesian, fallibilistic, naturalistic, in some versions it is also realistic, and in others not.

The verificationist selects a prominent property of truth and considers it the essence of truth. Similarly, the pragmatist focuses on another important characteristic namely, that true belief is a good basis for action and takes this to be the very nature of truth. We have said that true assumptions were, by definition, those that provoke actions with desirable results. Again, we have an account with a single attractive explanatory feature, but again, it postulates between truth and its alleged analysand then, utility is implausibly close. Granted, true belief tends to foster success, but it happens regularly that actions based on true beliefs lead to disaster, while false assumptions, by pure chance, produce wonderful results.

One of the few uncontroversial facts about truth is that the proposition that snow is white if and only if snow is white, the proposition that lying is wrong is true if and only if lying is wrong, and so on. Traditional theories acknowledge this fact but regard it as insufficient and, as we have seen, inflate it with some further principle of the form, 'x is true' if and only if 'x' has property 'P' (such as corresponding to reality, Verifiability, or being suitable as a basis for action), which is supposed to specify what truth is. Some radical alternatives to the traditional theories result from denying the need for any such further specification (Ramsey, 1927, Strawson, 1950 and Quine, 1990). For example, ne might suppose that the basic theory of truth contains nothing more that equivalences of the form, 'The proposition that 'p' is true if and only if 'p' (Horwich, 1990).

Not all variants of deflationism have this virtue, according to the redundancy performative theory of truth, implicate a pair of sentences, 'The proposition that 'p' is true' and plain 'p's', has the same meaning and expresses the same statement as one and another, so it is a syntactic illusion to think that p is true' attributes any sort of property to a proposition (Ramsey, 1927 and Strawson, 1950). Nonetheless, it becomes hard to explain why we are entitled to infer 'The proposition that quantum mechanics are wrong is true' form 'Einstein's claim is the proposition that quantum mechanics are wrong. 'Einstein's claim is true'. For if truth is not property, then we can no longer account for the inference by invoking the law that if 'x', appears identical with 'Y' then any property of 'x' is a property of 'Y', and vice versa. Thus the redundancy/performative theory, by identifying rather than merely correlating the contents of 'The proposition that p is true' and 'p, precludes the prospect of a good explanation of one on truth's most significant and useful characteristics. So restricting our claim to the ineffectually weak, accedes of a favourable Equivalence schematic: The proposition that 'p is true is and is only 'p'.

Support for deflationism depends upon the possibility of showing that its axiom instances of the equivalence schema unsupplements by any further analysis, will suffice to explain all the central facts about truth, for example, that the verification of a proposition indicates its truth, and that true beliefs have a practical value. The first of these facts follows trivially from the deflationary axioms, for given a deductive assimilation to knowledge of the equivalence of 'p' and 'The proposition that 'p is true', any reason to believe that 'p' becomes an equally good reason to believe that the preposition that 'p' is true. We can also explain the second fact concerning the deflationary axioms, but not quite so easily. Consider, to begin with, beliefs of the form:

(B) If I perform the act 'A', then my desires will be fulfilled.

Notice that the psychological role of such a belief is, roughly, to cause the performance of 'A'. In other words, gave that I do have belief (B), then typically.

I will perform the act 'A'

Notice also that when the belief is true then, given the deflationary axioms, the performance of 'A' will in fact lead to the fulfilment of one's desires, i.e.,

If (B) is true, then if I perform 'A', my desires will be fulfilled

Therefore:

If (B) is true, then my desires will be fulfilled

So valuing the truth of beliefs of that form is quite treasonable. Nevertheless, inference derives such beliefs from other beliefs and can be expected to be true if those other beliefs are true. So valuing the truth of any belief that might be used in such an inference is reasonable.

To him, the extent that they can give such deflationary accounts of all the acts involving truth, then the collection will meet the explanatory demands on a theory of truth of all statements like, 'The proposition that snow is white is true if and only if snow is white', and we will undermine the sense that we need some deep analysis of truth.

Nonetheless, there are several strongly felt objections to deflationism. One reason for dissatisfaction is that the theory has several axioms, and therefore cannot be completely written down. It can be described as the theory whose axioms are the propositions of the fore 'p' if and only if it is true that 'p', but not explicitly formulated. This alleged defect has led some philosophers to develop theories that show, first, how the truth of any proposition derives from the referential properties of its constituents, and second, how the referential properties of primitive constituents are determined (Tarski, 1943 and Davidson, 1969). However, assuming that all propositions including belief attributions remain controversial, law of nature and counterfactual conditionals depends for their truth values on what their constituents refer to. Moreover, there is no immediate prospect of a decent, finite theory of reference, so that it is far form clear that the infinite, that we can avoid list-like character of deflationism.

In "Naming and Necessity" (1980), Kripler gave the classical modern treatment of the topic reference, both clarifying the distinction between names and definite descriptions, and opening the door to many subsequent attempts to understand the notion of reference in terms and an original episode of attaching a name to a subject. Of course, deflationism is far from alone in having to confront this problem.

A third objection to the version of the deflationary theory presented here concerns its reliance on 'propositions' as the basic vehicles of truth. It is widely felt that the notion of the proposition is defective and that we should not employ it in semantics. If this point of view is accepted then the natural deflationary reaction is to attempt a reformation that would appeal only to sentences. There is no simple way of modifying the disquotational schema to accommodate any possible way of these difficulties, with which is to resist the critique of propositions. Such entities may exhibit an unwelcome degree of indeterminancy, and might defy reduction to familiar items, however, they do offer a plausible account of belief, as relations to propositions, and, in ordinary language at least, we indeed take them to be the primary bearers of truth. To believe a proposition is too old for it to be true. The philosophical problem includes discovering whether belief differs from other varieties of assent, such as 'acceptance', discovering to what extent degrees of belief are possible, understanding the ways in which belief is controlled by rational and irrational factors, and discovering its links with other properties, such as the possession of conceptual or linguistic skills. This last set of problems includes the question of whether they have properly said that paralinguistic infants or animals have beliefs.

Additionally, it is commonly supposed that problems about the nature of truth are intimately bound up with questions as to the accessibility and autonomy of facts in various domains: Questions about whether we can know the facts, and whether they can exist independently of our capacity to discover them (Dummett, 1978, and Putnam, 1981). One might reason, for example, that if 'T is true' means' nothing more than 'T will be verified', then certain forms of scepticism, specifically, those that doubt the correctness of our methods of verification, that will be precluded, and that the facts will have been revealed as dependent on human practices. Alternatively, we might say that if truth were an inexplicable, primitive, non-epistemic property, then the fact that 'T' is true would be completely independent of 'us'. Moreover, we could, in that case, have no reason to assume that the propositions we believe actually have tis property, so scepticism would be unavoidable. In a similar vein, we might think that as special, and perhaps undesirable features of the deflationary approach, is that we have deprived truth of such metaphysical or epistemological implications.

On closer scrutiny, however, it is far from clear that there exists 'any' account of truth with consequences regarding the accessibility or autonomy of non-semantic matters. For although we may expect an account of truth to have such implications for facts of the from 'T is true', we cannot assume without further argument that the same conclusions will apply to the fact 'T'. For it cannot be assumed that 'T' and 'T are true' nor, are they equivalent to one and another, given the explanation of 'true', from which is being employed. Of course, if we have distinguishable truth in the way that the deflationist proposes, then the equivalence holds by definition. However, if reference to some metaphysical or epistemological characteristic has defined truth, then we throw the equivalence schema into doubt, pending some demonstration that the true predicate, in the sense assumed that will satisfy insofar, as there is of any reasoned epistemological problem for which it is hanging over that which does not threaten 'T is true', giving the needed demonstration will be difficult. Similarly, if we so define 'truth' that the fact, 'T' is felt to be more, or less, independent of human practices than the fact that 'T is true', then again, it is unclear that the equivalence schema will hold. It seems. Therefore, that the attempt to base epistemological or metaphysical conclusions on a theory of truth must fail because in any such attempt we will simultaneously rely on and undermine the equivalence schema.

The most influential idea in the theory of meaning in the past hundred yeas is the thesis that meaning of an indicative sentence is given by its truth-conditions. On this conception, to understand a judgment of conviction, as given the responsibility of a sentence, is to know its truth-conditions. The conception was first clearly formulated by Frége (1848-1925), was developed in a distinctive way by the early Wittgenstein (1889-1951), and is a leading idea of Davidson (1917-). The conception has remained so central that those who offer opposing theories characteristically define their position by reference to it.

The conception of meaning as truth-conditions needs not and should not be advanced as a complete account of meaning. For instance, one who understands a language must have some idea of the range of speech acts conventionally performed by the various types of a sentence in the language, and must have some idea of the significance of various kinds of speech acts. We should moderately target the claim of the theorist of truth-conditions on the notion of content: If two indicative sentences differ in what they strictly and literally say, then the difference accounts for this difference in their truth-conditions. Most basic to truth-conditions is simply of a statement that is the condition the world must meet if the statement is to be true. To know this condition is equivalent to knowing the meaning of the statement. Although this sounds as if it gives a solid anchorage for meaning, some security disappears when it turns out that repeating the very same statement can only define the truth condition, as a truth condition of 'snow is white' is that snow is white, the truth condition of 'Britain would have capitulated had Hitler invaded' is the Britain would have capitulated had Hitler invaded. It is disputed wether. This element of running-on-the-spot disqualifies truth conditions from playing the central role in a substantive theory of meaning. The view has sometimes opposed truth-conditional theories of meaning that to know the meaning of a statement is to be able to use it in a network of inferences.

Whatever it is that makes, what would otherwise be mere sounds and inscriptions into instruments of communication and understanding. The philosophical problem is to demystify this power, and to relate it to what we know of ourselves and the world. Contributions to the study include the theory of 'speech acts' and the investigation of communication and the relationship between words and ideas and the world and surrounding surfaces, by which some persons express by a sentence often depend on the environment in which he or she is placed. For example, the disease I refer to by a term like 'arthritis' or the kind of tree I call an 'oak' raises the possibility of imagining two persons in moderate differently environmental, but in which everything appears the same to each of them, but between them they define a space of philosophical problems. They are the essential components of understanding nd any intelligible proposition that is true can be understood. Such that which an utterance or sentence expresses, the proposition or claim made about the world may by extension, the content of a predicated or other sub-sentential component is what it contributes to the content of sentences that contain it. The nature of content is the cental concern of the philosophy of language.

In particularly, the problems of indeterminancy of translation, inscrutability of reference, language, predication, reference, rule following, semantics, translation, and the topics referring to subordinate headings associated with 'logic'. The loss of confidence in determinate meaning (from each individualized decoding is another individual encoding) is an element common both to postmodern uncertainties in the theory of criticism, and to the analytic tradition that follows writers such as Quine (1908-). Still it may be asked, why should we suppose that we should account fundamental epistemic notions for in behavioural terms what grounds are there for assuming 'p knows p' is a matter of the status of its statement between some subject and some object, between nature and its mirror? The answer is that the only alternative may be to take knowledge of inner states as premises from which we have normally inferred our knowledge of other things, and without which we have normally inferred our knowledge of other things, and without which knowledge would be ungrounded. However, it is not really coherent, and does not in the last analysis make sense, to suggest that human knowledge have foundations or grounds. We should remember that to say that truth and knowledge 'can only be judged by the standards of our own day' which is not to say, that it is less important, or 'more 'cut off from the world', that we had supposed. It is just to say, that nothing counts as justification, unless by reference to what we already accept, and that there is no way to get outside our beliefs and our language so as to find some test other than coherence. The point is that the professional philosophers have thought it might be otherwise, since the body has haunted only them of epistemological scepticism.

What Quine opposes as 'residual Platonism' is not so much the hypostasising of nonphysical entities as the notion of 'correspondence' with things as the final court of appeal for evaluating present practices. Unfortunately, Quine, for all that it is incompatible with its basic insights, substitutes for this correspondence to physical entities, and specially to the basic entities, whatever they turn out to be, of physical science. Nevertheless, when we have purified their doctrines, they converge on a single claim ~, that no account of knowledge can depend on the assumption of some privileged relations to reality. Their work brings out why an account of knowledge can amount only to a description of human behaviour.

What, then, is to be said of these 'inner states', and of the direct reports of them that have played so important a role in traditional epistemology? For a person to feel is nothing else than for him to be able to make a certain type of non-inferential report, to attribute feelings to infants is to acknowledge in them latent abilities of this innate kind. Non-conceptual, non-linguistic 'knowledge' of what feelings or sensations is like is attributively to beings based on potential membership of our community. We comment upon infants and the more attractive animals with having feelings by that spontaneous sympathy that we extend to anything humanoid, in contrast with the mere 'response to stimuli' attributed to photoelectric cells and to animals about which no one feels sentimentally. Assuming moral prohibition against hurting infants is consequently wrong and the better-looking animals are that those moral prohibitions grounded' in their possession of feelings. The relation of dependence is really the other way round. Similarly, we could not be mistaken in assuming a four-year-old child has knowledge, but no one-year-old, any more than we could be mistaken in taking the word of a statute that eighteen-year-old can marry freely but seventeen-year-old cannot. (There is no more 'ontological ground' for the distinction that may suit 'us' to make in the former case than in the later.) Again, such a question as 'Are robots' conscious?' Calling for a decision on our part whether or not to treat robots as members of our linguistic community. All this is a piece with the insight brought intro philosophy by Hegel (1770-1831), that the individual apart from his society is just another animal.

Willard van Orman Quine, the most influential American philosopher of the latter half of the 20th century, when after the wartime period in naval intelligence, punctuating the rest of his career with extensive foreign lecturing and travel. Quine's early work was on mathematical logic, and issued in "A System of Logistic" (1934), "Mathematical Logic" (1940), and "Methods of Logic" (1950), whereby it was with the collection of papers from a "Logical Point of View" (1953) that his philosophical importance became widely recognized. Quine's work dominated concern with problems of convention, meaning, and synonymy cemented by "Word and Object" (1960), in which the indeterminancy of radical translation first takes centre-stage. In this and many subsequent writings Quine takes a bleak view of the nature of the language with which we ascribe thoughts and beliefs to ourselves and others. These 'intentional idioms' resist smooth incorporation into the scientific world-view, and Quine responds with scepticism toward them, not quite endorsing 'eliminativism', but regarding them as second-rate idioms, unsuitable for describing strict and literal facts. For similar reasons he has consistently expressed suspicion of the logical and philosophical propriety of appeal to logical possibilities and possible worlds. The languages that are properly behaved and suitable for literal and true descriptions of the world happen to those within the fields that draw upon mathematics and science. We must take the entities to which our best theories refer with full seriousness in our ontologies, although an empiricist. Quine thus supposes that science requires the abstract objects of set theory, and therefore exist. In the theory of knowledge Quine associated with a 'holistic view' of verification, conceiving of a body of knowledge about a web touching experience at the periphery, but with each point connected by a network of relations to other points.

They have also known Quine for the view that we should naturalize, or conduct epistemology in a scientific spirit, with the object of investigation being the relationship, in human beings, between the inputs of experience and the outputs of belief. Although we have attacked Quine's approaches to the major problems of philosophy as betraying undue 'scientism' and sometimes 'behaviourism', the clarity of his vision and the scope of his writing made him the major focus of Anglo-American work of the past forty tears in logic, semantics, and epistemology.

Coherence is a major player in the theatre of knowledge. There are cogence theories of belief, truth and justification, as these are to combine themselves in the various ways to yield theories of knowledge coherence theories of belief are concerned with the content of beliefs. Consider a belief you now have, the beliefs that you are reading a page in a book, in so, that what makes that belief the belief that it is? What makes it the belief that you are reading a page in a book than the belief that you have a monster in the garden?

One answer is that the belief has a coherent place or role in a system of beliefs, perception or the having the perceptivity that has its influence on beliefs. As, you respond to sensory stimuli by believing that you are reading a page in a book than believing that you have a monster in the garden. Belief has an influence on action, or its belief is a desire to act, if belief will differentiate the differences between them, that its belief is a desire or if you were to believe that you are reading a page than if you believed in something about a monster. Sortal perceptivals hold accountably the perceptivity and action that are indeterminate to its content if its belief is the action as if stimulated by its inner and latent coherence in that of your belief, however. The same stimuli may produce various beliefs and various beliefs may produce the same action. The role that gives the belief the content it has is the role it plays upon a network of relations to other beliefs, some latently causal than others that relate to the role in inference and implication. For example, I infer different things from believing that I am reading a page in a book than from any other belief, justly as I infer about other beliefs form.

The input of perceptibility and the output of an action supplement the central role of the systematic relations the belief has to other beliefs, but the systematic relations give the belief the specific contentual representation it has. They are the fundamental source of the content of belief. That is how coherence comes in. A belief has the representational content by which it does because of the way in which it coheres within a system of beliefs (Rosenberg, 1988). We might distinguish weak coherence theories of the content of beliefs from stronger coherence theories. Weak coherence theories affirm that coherence is one determinant of the representation given that the contents are of belief. Strong coherence theories of the content of belief affirm that coherence is the sole determinant of the contentual representations of belief.

When we turn from belief to justification, we confront a similar group of coherence theories. What makes one belief justified and another not? Again, there is a distinction between weak and strong theoretic principles that govern its theory of coherence. Weak theories tell 'us' that the way in which a belief coheres with a background system of beliefs is one determinant of justification, other typical determinants being perception, memory, and intuitive 'projection', however, strong theories, or dominant projections are in coherence to justification as solely a matter of how a belief coheres with a system of latent hierarchal beliefs. There is, nonetheless, another distinction that cuts across the distinction between weak and strong coherence theories between positive and negative coherence theory (Pollock, 1986). A positive coherence theory tells 'us' that if a belief coheres with a background system of belief, then the belief is justifiable. A negative coherence theory tells 'us' that if a belief fails to cohere with a background system of beliefs, then the belief is not justifiable. We might put this by saying that, according to the positivity of a coherence theory, coherence has the power to produce justification, while according to its being adhered by negativity, the coherence theory has only the power to nullify justification.

Least of mention, a strong coherence theory of justification is a formidable combination by which a positive and a negative theory tell 'us' that a belief is justifiable if and only if it coheres with a background system of inter-connectivity of beliefs. Coherence theories of justification and knowledge have most often been rejected for being unable to deal with an accountable justification toward the perceptivity upon the projection of knowledge (Audi, 1988, and Pollock, 1986), and, therefore, considering a perceptual example that will serve as a kind of crucial test will be most appropriate. Suppose that a person, call her Trust, and works with a scientific instrumentation that has a gauging measure upon temperatures of liquids in a container. The gauge is marked in degrees, she looks at the gauge and sees that the reading is 105 degrees. What is she justifiably to believe, and why? Is she, for example, justified in believing that the liquid in the container is 105 degrees? Clearly, that depends on her background beliefs. A weak coherence theorist might argue that, though her belief that she sees the shape 105 is immediately justified as direct sensory evidence without appeal to a background system, the belief that the location in the container is 105 degrees results from coherence with a background system of latent beliefs that affirm to the shaping perceptivity that its 105 as visually read to be 105 degrees on the gauge that measures the temperature of the liquid in the container. This, nonetheless, of a weak coherence view that combines coherence with direct perceptivity as its evidence, in that the foundation of justification, is to account for the justification of our beliefs.

A strong coherence theory would go beyond the claim of the weak coherence theory to affirm that the justification of all beliefs, including the belief that one sees the shaping to sensory data that holds accountable a measure of 100, or even the more cautious belief that one sees a shape, resulting from the perceptivals of coherence theory, in that it coheres with a background system. One may argue for this strong coherence theory in several different ways. One line or medium through which to appeal to the coherence theory of contentual representations. If the content of the perceptual belief results from the relations of the belief to other beliefs in a network system of beliefs, then one may notably argue that justification thoroughly rests upon the resultants' findings in relation to the belief been no other than the beliefs of a furthering network system of coordinate beliefs. In face value, the argument for the strong coherence theory is that without any assumptive grasp for reason, in that the coherence theories of content are directed of beliefs and are supposing causes that only produce of a consequent, of which we already expect. Consider the very cautious belief that I see a shape. How could the justification for that perceptual belief be an existent result that they characterize of its material coherence with a background system of beliefs? What might the background system allow to be known of 'us' that would justify that belief? Our background system contains a simple and primal theory about our relationship to the world and surrounding surfaces that we perceive as it is or should be believed. To come to the specific point at issue, we believe that we can tell a shape when we see one, completely differentiated its form as perceived to sensory data, that we are to trust of ourselves about such simple matters as wether we see a shape before 'us' or not, as in the acceptance of opening to nature the inter-connectivity between belief and the progression through which we acquire from past experiential conditions of application, and not beyond deception. Moreover, when Julie sees the believing desire to act upon what either coheres with a weak or strong coherence of theory, she shows that its belief, as a measurable quality or entity of 105, has the essence in as much as there is much more of a structured distinction of circumstance, which is not of those that are deceptive about whether she sees that shape or sincerely does not see of its shaping distinction, however. Light is good, and the numeral shapes are large, readily discernible and so forth. These are beliefs that Julie has single handedly authenticated reasons for justification. Her successive malignance to sensory access to data involved is justifiably a subsequent belief, in that with those beliefs, and so she is justified and creditable.

The philosophical problems include discovering whether belief differs from other varieties of assent, such as 'acceptance' discovering to what extent degrees of belief is possible, understanding the ways in which belief is controlled by rational and irrational factors, and discovering its links with other properties, such as the possession of conceptual or linguistic skills. This last set of problems includes the question of whether we have properly said that paralinguistic human infants or animals have beliefs.

Thus, we might think of coherence as inference to the best explanation based on a background system of beliefs, since we are not aware of such inferences for the most part, we must interpret the inferences as unconscious inferences, as information processing, based on or accessing the background system that proves most convincing of acquiring its act and used from the motivational force that its underlying and hidden desire are to do so. One might object to such an account as not all justifiable inferences are self-explanatory, and more generally, the account of coherence may, at best, is ably successful to competitions that are based on background systems (BonJour, 1985, and Lehrer, 1990). The belief that one sees a shape competes with the claim that one does not, with the claim that one is deceived, and other sceptical objections. The background system of beliefs informs one that one is acceptingly trustworthy and enables one to meet the objections. A belief coheres with a background system just in case it enables one to meet the sceptical objections and in the way justifies one in the belief. This is a standard strong coherence theory of justification (Lehrer, 1990).

Illustrating the relationship between positive and negative coherence theories for the standard coherence theory is easy. If some objection to a belief cannot be met as to the background system of beliefs of a person, then the person is not justified in that belief. So, to return to Trust, suppose that she has been told that a warning light has been installed on her gauge to tell her when it is not functioning properly and that when the red light is on, the gauge is malfunctioning. Suppose that when she sees the reading of 105, she also sees that the red light is on. Imagine, finally, that this is the first time the red light has been on, and, after years of working with the gauge, Julie, who has always placed her trust in the gauge, believes what the gauge tells her, that the liquid in the container is at 105 degrees. Though she believes what she reads is at 105 degrees is not a justified belief because it fails to cohere with her background belief that the gauge is malfunctioning. Thus, the negative coherence theory tells 'us' that she is not justified in her belief about the temperature of the contents in the container. By contrast, when we have not illuminated the red light and the background system of Julie which tells her that under such conditions that gauge is a trustworthy indicator of the temperature of the liquid in the container, then she is justified. The positive coherence theory tells 'us' that she is justified in her belief because her belief coheres with her background system of Julie lets it be known that she, under such conditions gauges a trustworthy indicant of temperature characterized or identified in respect of the liquid in the container, then she is justified. The positive coherence theory tells 'us' that she is justified in her belief because her belief coheres with her background system continues as a trustworthy system.

The foregoing sketch and illustration of coherence theories of justification have a common feature, namely, that they are what we have called inter-naturalistic theories of justification what makes of such a view are the absence of any requirement that the person for whom the belief is justified have any cognitive access to the relation of reliability in question. Lacking such access, such a person will usually, have no reason for thinking the belief is true or likely to be authenticated, but will, on such an account, is nonetheless to appear epistemologically justified in accepting it. Thus, such a view arguably marks a major break from the modern epistemological traditions, which identifies epistemic justification with having a reason, perhaps even a conclusive reason, for thinking that the belief is true. An epistemologist working within this tradition is likely to feel that the externalist, than offering a competing account of the same concept of epistemic justification with which the traditional epistemologist is concerned, has simply changed the subject.

They are theories affirming that coherence is a matter of internal relations between beliefs and that justification is a matter of coherence. If, then, justification is solely a matter of internal relations between beliefs, we are left with the possibility that the internal relations might fail to correspond with any external reality. How, one might have an objection, can a completely internal subjective notion of justification bridge the gap between mere true belief, which might be no more than a lucky guess, and knowledge, which we must ground in some connection between internal subjective conditions and external objective realities?

The answer is that it cannot and that we have required something more than justified true belief for knowledge. This result has, however, been established quite apart from consideration of coherence theories of justification. What we have required maybe put by saying that the justification that one must be undefeated by errors in the background system of beliefs. Justification is undefeated by errors just in case any correction of such errors in the background system of belief would sustain the justification of the belief because of the corrected system. So knowledge, on this sort of positivity is acclaimed by the coherence theory, which is the true belief that coheres with the background belief system and corrected versions of that system. In short, knowledge is true belief plus justification resulting from coherence and undefeated by error (Lehrer, 1990). The connection between internal subjective conditions of belief and external objectivity are from which reality's result from the required correctness of our beliefs about the relations between those conditions and realities. In the example of Julie, she believes that her internal subjectivity to conditions of sensory data in which we have connected the experience and perceptual beliefs with the external objectivity in which reality is the temperature of the liquid in the container in a trustworthy manner. This background belief is essential to the justification of her belief that the temperature of the liquid in the container is 105 degrees, and the correctness of that background belief is essential to the justification remaining undefeated. So our background system of beliefs contains a simple theory about our relation to the external world that justifies certain of our beliefs that cohere with that system. For instance, such justification to convert to knowledge, that theory must be sufficiently free from error so that they have sustained the coherence in corrected versions of our background system of beliefs. The correctness of the simple background theory provides the connection between the internal condition and external reality.

The coherence theory of truth arises naturally out of a problem raised by the coherence theory of justification. The problem is that anyone seeking to determine whether she has knowledge is confined to the search for coherence among her beliefs. The sensory experiences have been deadening til their representation has been exemplified as some perceptual belief. Beliefs are the engines that pull the train of justification. Nevertheless, what assurance do we have that our justification is based on true beliefs? What justification do we have that any of our justifications are undefeated? The fear that we might have none, that our beliefs might be the artifacts of some deceptive demon or scientist, leads to the quest to reduce truth to some form, perhaps an idealized form, of justification

(Rescher, 1973, and Rosenberg, 1980). That would close the threatening sceptical gap between justification and truth. Suppose that a belief is true if and only if it is justifiable of some person. For such a person there would be no gap between justification and truth or between justification and undefeated justification. Truth would be coherence with some ideal background system of beliefs, perhaps one expressing a consensus among systems or some consensus among belief systems or some convergence toward a consensus. Such a view is theoretically attractive for the reduction it promises, but it appears open to profound objectification. One is that there is a consensus that we can all be wrong about at least some matters, for example, about the origins of the universe. If there is a consensus that we can all be wrong about something, then the consensual belief system rejects the equation of truth with the consensus. Consequently, the equation of truth with coherence with a consensual belief system is itself incoherently.

Coherence theories of the content of our beliefs and the justification of our beliefs themselves cohere with our background systems but coherence theories of truth do not. A defender of coherentism must accept the logical gap between justified belief and truth, but may believe that our capacities suffice to close the gap to yield knowledge. That view is, at any rate, a coherent one.

What makes a belief justified and what makes a true belief knowledge? Thinking that whether a belief deserves one of these appraisals is non-synthetically depending on what causal subject to has the belief. In recent decades a number of epistemologists have pursed this plausible idea with a variety of specific proposals. Some causal theories of knowledge have it that a true belief that 'p' is knowledge just in case it has the right sort of causal connection to the fact that 'p'. Such a criterion can be applied only to cases where the fact that 'p' is a sort that can reach causal relations, this seems to exclude mathematically and other necessary facts and perhaps any fact expressed by a universal generalization, and proponents of this sort of criterion have usually of this sort of criterion have usually supposed that it is limited to perceptual knowledge of particular facts about the subject's environment.

For example, Armstrong (1973) proposed that a belief of the form 'This (perceived) object is F' is (non-inferential) knowledge if and only if the belief is a completely reliable sign that the perceived object is 'F', that is, the fact that the object is 'F' contributed to causing the belief and its doing so depended on properties of the believer such that the laws of nature dictated that, for any subject 'x' is to occur, and so thus a perceived object of 'y', if 'x' undergoing those properties are for 'us' to believe that 'y' is 'F', then 'y' is 'F'. Dretske, (1981) offers a similar account, as for the belief's being caused by a signal received by the perceiver that carries the information that the object is 'F'.

This sort of condition fails, however, to be sufficient for non-inferential perceptual knowledge because it is compatible with the belief's being unjustified, and an unjustifiable belief cannot be knowledge. For example, suppose that your mechanisms for colour perception are working well, but you have been given good reason to think otherwise, to think, say, that the substantive primary colours that are perceivable, that things look chartreuse to you and chartreuse things look magenta. If you fail to heed these reasons you have for thinking that your colour perception or sensory data is a directional way for us in believing of a thing that looks magenta, in that for you it is magenta, your belief will fail to be justified and will therefore fail to be knowledge, although the thing's being magenta in such a way causes it as to be a completely reliable sign, or to carry the information, in that the thing is blush-coloured.

One could fend off this sort of counterexample by simply adding to the causal condition the requirement that the belief be justified, buy this enriched condition would still be insufficient. Suppose, for example, that in nearly all people, but not in you, as it happens, causes the aforementioned aberrations are colour perceptions. The experimenter tells you that you have taken such a drug but then says, 'now wait, the pill you took was just a placebo', suppose further, that this last thing the experimenter tells you is false. Her telling you that it was a false statement, and, again, telling you this gives you justification for believing of a thing that looks a subtractive primary colour to you that it is a sensorial primary colour, in that the fact you were to expect that the experimenters last statements were false, making it the case that your true belief is not knowledgeably correct, thought as though to satisfy its causal condition.

Goldman (1986) has proposed an importantly different causal criterion namely, that a true belief is knowledge, if it is produced by a type of process that is 'globally' and 'locally' reliable. Causing true beliefs is sufficiently high is globally reliable if its propensity. Local reliability deals with whether the process would have produced a similar but false belief in certain counterfactual situations alternative to the actual situation. This way of marking off true beliefs that are knowledge does not require the fact believed to be casually related to the belief, and so it could in principle apply to knowledge of any kind of truth.

Goldman requires that global reliability of the belief-producing process for the justification of a belief, he requires it also for knowledge because they require justification for knowledge, in what requires for knowledge but does not require for justification, which is locally reliable. His idea is that a justified true belief is knowledge if the type of process that produced it would not have produced it in any relevant counterfactual situation in which it is false. Noting that other concepts exhibit the same logical structure can motivate the relevant alternative account of knowledge. Two examples of this are the concept 'flat' and the concept 'empty' (Dretske, 1981). Both are absolute concepts-a space is empty only if it does not contain anything and a surface is flat only if it does not have any bumps. However, the absolute character of these concepts is relative to a standard. In the case of 'flat', there is a standard for what counts as a bump and for 'empty', there is a standard for what counts as a thing. To be flat is to be free of any relevant bumps and to be empty is to be devoid of all relevant things.

What makes an alternative situation relevant? Goldman does not try to formulate examples of what he takes to be relevantly alternate, but suggests of one. Suppose, that a parent takes a child's temperature with a thermometer that the parent selected at random from several lying in the medicine cabinet. Only the particular thermometer chosen was in good working order, it correctly shows the child's temperature to be normal, but if it had been abnormal then any of the other thermometers would have erroneously shown it to be normal. A globally reliable process has caused the parent's actual true belief but, because it was 'just luck' that the parent happened to select a good thermometer, 'we would not say that the parent knows that the child's temperature is normal'.

Goldman suggests that the reason for denying knowledge in the thermometer example, be that it was 'just luck' that the parent did not pick a faulty thermometer and in the twin's example, the reason is that there was 'a serious possibility' that might have been that Sam could probably have mistaken for. This suggests the following criterion of relevance: An alternate situation, whereby, that the same belief is produced in the same way but is false, it is relevantly just in case at some point before the actual belief was to its cause, by which a chance that the actual belief was to have caused, in that the chance of that situation's having come about was instead of the actual situation was too converged, nonetheless, by the chemical components that constitute its inter-actual exchange by which endorphin excitation was to influence and so give to the excitability of neuronal transmitters that deliver messages, inturn, the excited endorphin gave 'change' to 'chance', thus it was, in that what was interpreted by the sensory data and unduly persuaded by innate capabilities that at times are latently hidden within the mind, Or the brain, giving to its chosen chance of luck.

This avoids the sorts of counterexamples we gave for the causal criteria as we discussed earlier, but it is vulnerable to one or ones of a different sort. Suppose you were to stand on the mainland looking over the water at an island, on which are several structures that look (from at least some point of view) as would ne of an actualized point or station of position. You happen to be looking at one of any point, in fact a barn and your belief to that effect are justified, given how it looks to you and the fact that you have exclusively of no reason to think nor believe otherwise. Nevertheless, suppose that the great majority of the barn-looking structures on the island are not real barns but fakes. Finally, suppose that from any viewpoint on the mainland all of the island's fake barns are obscured by trees and that circumstances made it very unlikely that you would have to a viewpoint not on the mainland. Here, it seems, your justified true belief that you are looking at a barn is not knowledge, even if there was not a serious chance that there would have developed an alternative situation, wherefore you are similarly caused to have a false belief that you are looking at a barn.

That example shows that the 'local reliability' of the belief-producing process, on the 'serous chance' explication of what makes an alternative relevance, yet its viewpoints upon which we are in showing that non-locality is in addition to sustain of some probable course of the possibility for 'us' to believe in. Within the experience condition of application, the relationship with the sensory-data, as having a world-view that can encompass both the hidden and manifest aspects of nature would comprise of the mind, or brain that provides the excitation of neuronal ions, giving to sensory perception an accountable assessment of data and reason-sensitivity allowing a comprehensive world-view, integrating the various aspects of the universe into one magnificent whole, a whole in which we played an organic and central role. One-hundred years ago its question would have been by a Newtonian 'clockwork universe', a theoretical account of a probable 'I' universe that is completely mechanical. The laws of nature have predetermined everything that happens and by the state of the universe in the distant past. The freedom one feels as for ones actions, even concerning the movement of one's body, is an illusory infraction and the world-view expresses as the Newtonian one, is completely coherent.

Nevertheless, the human mind abhors a vacuum. When an explicit, coherent world-view is absent, it functions based on a tactic one. A tactic world-view is not subject to a critical evaluation, and it can easily harbour inconsistencies. Indeed, our tactic set of beliefs about the nature of reality consists of contradictory bits and pieces. The dominant component is a leftover from another period, the Newtonian 'clock universe' still lingers as we cling to this old and tired model because we know of nothing else that can take its place. Our condition is the condition of a culture that is in the throes of a paradigm shift. A major paradigm shift is complex and difficult because a paradigm holds 'us captive: We see reality through it, as through coloured glasses, but we do not know that, we are convinced that we see reality as it is. Hence the appearance of a new and different paradigm is often incomprehensible. To someone raised believing that the Earth is flat, the suggestion that the Earth is spherical seems preposterous: If the Earth were spherical, would not the poor antipodes fall 'down' into the sky?

Yet, as we face a new millennium, we are forced to face this challenge. The fate of the planet is in question, and it was brought to its present precarious condition largely because of our trust in the Newtonian paradigm. As Newtonian world-view has to go, and, if one looks carefully, we can discern the main feature of the new, emergent paradigm. The search for these features is what was the influence of a fading paradigm. All paradigms include subterranean realms of tactic assumptions, the influence of which outlasts the adherence to the paradigm itself.

The first line of exploration suggests the 'weird' aspects of the quantum theory, with fertile grounds for our feeling of which should disappear in inconsistencies with the prevailing world-view. This feeling is in replacing by the new one, i.e., opinion or information assailing availability by means of ones parts of relating to the mind or spirit, which if in the event one believes that the Earth is flat, the story of Magellan's travels is quite puzzling: How travelling due west is possible for a ship and, without changing direct. Arrive at its place of departure? Obviously, when the belief replaces the flat-Earth paradigm that Earth is spherical, we have instantly resolved the puzzle.

The founders of Relativity and quantum mechanics were deeply engaging but incomplete, in that none of them attempted to construct a philosophical system, however, that the mystery at the heart of the quantum theory called for a revolution in philosophical outlooks. During which time, the 1920's, when quantum mechanics reached maturity, began the construction of a full-blooded philosophical system that we based not only on science but on nonscientific modes of knowledge as well. As, the disappearing influences drawn upon the paradigm go well beyond its explicit claim. We believe, as the scenists and philosophers did, that when we wish to find out the truth about the universe, we can ignore nonscientific nodes of processing human experiences, poetry, literature, art, music are all wonderful, but, in relation to the quest for knowledge of the universe, they are irrelevant. Yet, it was Alfred North Whitehead who pointed out the fallacy of this speculative assumption. In this, and in other aspects of thinking of some reality in which are the building blocks of reality are not material atoms but 'throbs of experience'. Whitehead formulated his system in the late 1920s, and yet, as far as I know, the founders of quantum mechanics were unaware of it. It was not until 1963 that J.M. Burgers pointed out that its philosophy accounts very well for the main features of the quanta, especially the 'weird ones', enabling as in some aspects of reality is 'higher' or 'deeper' than others, and if so, what is the structure of such hierarchical divisions? What of our place in the universe? Finally, what is the relationship between the great aspiration within the lost realms of nature? An attempt to endow 'us' with a cosmological meaning in such a universe seems totally absurd, and, yet, this very universe is just a paradigm, not the truth. When you reach its end, you may be willing to join the alternate view as accorded to which, surprisingly bestow 'us' with what we have restored, although in a post-postmodern context.

Subjective matter's has regulated the philosophical implications of quantum mechanics, as to emphasis the connections between what I believe, in that investigations of such inter-connectivity are anticipatorially the hesitations that are an exclusion held within the western traditions, however, the philosophical thinking, from Plato to Platinous had in some aspects an interpretative cognitive process of presenting her in expression of a consensus of the physical community. Some have shared and by expressive objections to other aspects (sometimes vehemently) by others. Still other aspects express my own views and convictions, as turning about to be more difficult that anticipated, discovering that a conversational mode would be helpful, but, their conversations with each other and with me in hoping that all will be not only illuminating but finding to its read may approve in them, whose dreams are dreams among others than themselves.

These examples make it seem likely that, if there is a criterion for what makes an alternative situation relevant that will save Goldman's claim about reliability and the acceptance of knowledge, it will not be simple.

The interesting thesis that counts asa causal theory of justification, in the meaning of 'causal theory' intend of the belief that is justified just in case it was produced by a type of process that is 'globally' reliable, that is, its propensity to produce true beliefs-that can be defined to some favourable approximations, as the proportion of the belief it produces, or would produce where it used as much as opportunity allows, that is true ~. Is sufficiently that a belief acquires favourable epistemic status by having some kind of reliable linkage to the truth? We have advanced variations of this view for both knowledge and justified belief. The first formulations of dependably an accounting measure of knowing came in the accompaniment of F.P. Ramsey 1903-30, who made important contributions to mathematical logic, probability theory, the philosophy of science and economics. Instead of saying that quarks have such-and-such properties, the Ramsey sentence says the theoretical are alternatively something that has those properties. If we have repeated the process for all of the theoretical terms, the sentence gives the 'topic-neutral' structure of the theory, but removes any implication that we know what the term so treated have as a meaning. It leaves open the possibility of identifying the theoretical item with whatever. It is that best fits the description provided, thus, substituting the term by a variable, Ramsey, was one of the first thinkers to accept a 'redundancy theory of truth', which he combined its radical views of the function of many kinds of the proposition. Neither generalizations, nor causal propositions, not those treating probabilities or ethics, described facts, but each has a different specific function in our intellectual commentators on the early works of

Wittgenstein, and his continuing friendship with the latter liked to Wittgenstein's return to Cambridge and to philosophy in 1929.

The most sustained and influential application of these ideas were in the philosophy of mind, or brain, as Ludwig Wittgenstein (1889-1951) whom Ramsey persuaded that remained work for him to do, the way of an undoubtedly charismatic figure of 20th-century philosophy, living and writing with a power and intensity that frequently overwhelmed his contemporaries and readers, being a kind of picture or model has centred the early period on the 'picture theory of meaning' according to which sentence represents a state of affairs of it. Containing elements corresponding to those of the state of affairs and structure or form that mirrors that a structure of the state of affairs that it represents. We have reduced to all logic complexity that of the 'propositional calculus, and all propositions are 'truth-functions of atomic or basic propositions.

If there is a criterion for what makes an alternate situation relevant that will save Goldman's claim about local reliability and knowledge. Will did not be simple. The interesting thesis that counts as a causal theory of justification, in the making of 'causal theory' intended for the belief as it is justified in case it was produced by a type of process that is 'globally' reliable, that is, its propensity to produce true beliefs that can be defined, to an acceptable approximation, as the proportion of the beliefs it produces, or would produce where it used as much as opportunity allows, that is true is sufficiently relializable. We have advanced variations of this view for both knowledge and justified belief, its first formulation of a reliability account of knowing appeared in the notation from F.P.Ramsey (1903-30). The theory of probability, he was the first to show how a 'personalist theory' could be developed, based on a precise behavioural notion of preference and expectation. In the philosophy of language. Much of Ramsey's work was directed at saving classical mathematics from 'intuitionism', or what he called the 'Bolshevik menace of Brouwer and Weyl. In the theory of probability he was the first to show how we could develop some personalists theory, as based on precise behavioural notation of preference and expectation. In the philosophy of language, Ramsey was one of the first thankers, which he combined with radical views of the function of many kinds of a proposition. Neither generalizations, nor causal propositions, nor those treating probability or ethics, describe facts, but each has a different specific function in our intellectual economy. Ramsey was one of the earliest commentators on the early work of Wittgenstein, and his continuing friendship that led to Wittgenstein's return to Cambridge and to philosophy in 1929.

Ramsey's sentence theory is the sentence generated by taking all the sentences affirmed in a scientific theory that use some term, e.g., 'quark'. Replacing the term by a variable, and existentially quantifying into the result. Instead of saying that quarks have such and such properties, the Ramsey sentence says that there is something that has those properties. If we repeat the process for all of a group of the theoretical terms, the sentence gives the 'topic-neutral' structure of the theory, but removes any implication that we know what the term so treated prove competent. It leaves open the possibility of identifying the theoretical item with whatever, but it is that best fits the description provided. Virtually, all theories of knowledge. Of course, share an externalist component in requiring truth as a condition for known in. Reliabilism goes farther, however, in trying to capture additional conditions for knowledge by ways of a nomic, counterfactual or other 'external' relations between belief and truth. Closely allied to the nomic sufficiency account of knowledge, primarily dur to Dretshe (1971, 1981), A.I. Goldman (1976, 1986) and R. Nozick (1981). The core of this approach is that 'x's' belief that 'p' qualifies as knowledge just in case 'x' believes 'p', because of reasons that would not obtain unless 'p' was true, or because of a process or method that would not yield belief in 'p' if 'p' were not true. An enemy example, 'x' would not have its current reasons for believing there is a telephone before it. Or would not come to believe this in the ways it does, thus, there is a counterfactual reliable guarantor of the belief's bing true. Determined to and the facts of counterfactual approach say that 'x' knows that 'p' only if there is no 'relevant alternative' situation in which 'p' is false but 'x' would still believe that a proposition 'p'; must be sufficient to eliminate all the alternatives too 'p' where an alternative to a proposition 'p' is a proposition incompatible with 'p?'. That I, one's justification or evidence for 'p' must be sufficient for one to know that every alternative too 'p' is false. This element of our evolving thinking, sceptical arguments have exploited about which knowledge. These arguments call our attentions to alternatives that our evidence sustains itself with no elimination. The sceptic inquires to how we know that we are not seeing a cleverly disguised mule. While we do have some evidence against the likelihood of such as deception, intuitively knowing that we are not so deceived is not strong enough for 'us'. By pointing out alternate but hidden points of nature, in that we cannot eliminate, and others with more general application, as dreams, hallucinations, etc. The sceptic appears to show that every alternative is seldom. If ever, satisfied.

This conclusion conflicts with another strand in our thinking about knowledge, in that we know many things. Thus, there is a tension in our ordinary thinking about knowledge ~. We believe that knowledge is, in the sense indicated, an absolute concept and yet, we also believe that there are many instances of that concept.

If one finds absoluteness to be too central a component of our concept of knowledge to be relinquished, one could argue from the absolute character of knowledge to a sceptical conclusion (Unger, 1975). Most philosophers, however, have taken the other course, choosing to respond to the conflict by giving up, perhaps reluctantly, the absolute criterion. This latter response holds as sacrosanct our commonsense belief that we know many things (Pollock, 1979 and Chisholm, 1977). Each approach is subject to the criticism that it preserves one aspect of our ordinary thinking about knowledge at the expense of denying another. We can view the theory of relevant alternatives as an attempt to provide a more satisfactory response to this tension in our thinking about knowledge. It attempts to characterize knowledge in a way that preserves both our belief that knowledge is an absolute concept and our belief that we have knowledge.

Having to its recourse of knowledge, its cental questions include the origin of knowledge, the place of experience in generating knowledge, and the place of reason in doing so, the relationship between knowledge and certainty, and between knowledge and the impossibility of error, the possibility of universal scepticism, and the changing forms of knowledge that arise from new conceptualizations of the world. These issues link with other central concerns of philosophy, such as the nature of truth and the natures of experience and meaning. Seeing epistemology is possible as dominated by two rival metaphors. One is that of a building or pyramid, built on foundations. In this conception it is the kob of the philosopher to describe especially secure foundations, and to identify secure modes of construction, s that the resulting edifice can be shown to be sound. This metaphor of knowledge, and of a rationally defensible theory of confirmation and inference as a method of construction, as that knowledge must be regarded as a structure risen upon secure, certain foundations. These are found in some formidable combinations of experience and reason, with different schools (empiricism, rationalism) emphasizing the role of one over that of the others. Foundationalism was associated with the ancient Stoics, and in the modern era with Descartes (1596-1650), who discovered his foundations in the 'clear and distinct' ideas of reason? Its main opponent is coherentism, or the view that a body of propositions mas be known without a foundation in certainty, but by their interlocking strength, than as a crossword puzzle may be known to have been solved correctly even if each answer, taken individually, admits of uncertainty. Difficulties at this point led the logical passivists to abandon the notion of an epistemological foundation, and, overall, to philander with the coherence theory of truth. It is widely accepted that trying to make the connection between thought and experience through basic sentences depends on an untenable 'myth of the given'.

Still, of the other metaphor, is that of a boat or fuselage, that has no foundation but owes its strength to the stability given by its interlocking parts. This rejects the idea of a basis in the 'given', favours ideas of coherence and holism, but finds it harder to ward off scepticism. In spite of these concerns, the problem, least of mention, is of defining knowledge for true beliefs plus some favoured relations between the believer and the facts that began with Plato's view in the "Theaetetus" that knowledge is true belief, and some logos.` Due of its natural epistemology, the enterprising of studying the actual formation of knowledge by human beings, without aspiring to make evidently those processes as rational, or proof against 'scepticism' or even apt to yield the truth. Natural epistemology would therefore blend into the psychology of learning and the study of episodes I the history of science. The scope for 'external' or philosophical reflection of the kind that might result in scepticism or its refutation is markedly diminished, although the terms in modern, distinguished exponents of the approach include Aristotle, Hume, and J.S. Mills.

The task of the philosopher of a discipline would then be to reveal the correct method and to unmask counterfeits. Although this belief lay behind much positivist philosophy of science, few philosophers at present, subscribe to it. It places too well a confidence in the possibility of a purely a prior 'first philosophy', or standpoint beyond that of the working practitioners, from which they can measure their best efforts as good or bad. This point of view now seems that many philosophers are acquainted with the affordance of fantasy. The more modest of tasks that we actually adopt at various historical stages of investigation into different areas with the aim not so much of criticizing but more of systematization, in the presuppositions of a particular field at a particular tie. There is still a role for local methodological disputes within the community investigators of some phenomenon, with one approach charging that another is unsound or unscientific, but logic and philosophy will not, on the modern view, provide an independent arsenal of weapons for such battles, which indeed often come to seem more like political bids for ascendancy within a discipline.

This is an approach to the theory of knowledge that sees an important connection between the growth of knowledge and biological evolution. An evolutionary epistemologist claims that the development of human knowledge processed through some natural selection process, the best example of which is Darwin's theory of biological natural selection. There is a widespread misconception that evolution proceeds according to some plan or direct, put it has neither, and the role of chance ensures that its future course will be unpredictable. Random variations in individual organisms create tiny differences in their Darwinian fitness. Some individuals have more offsprings than others, and the characteristics that increased their fitness thereby become more prevalent in future generations. Once upon a time, at least a mutation occurred in a human population in tropical Africa that changed the haemoglobin molecule in a way that provided resistance to malaria. This enormous advantage caused the new gene to spread, with the unfortunate consequence that sickle-cell anaemia came to exist.

In the modern theory of evolution, genetic mutations provide the blind variations, blinded in the sense that variations are not influenced by the effects they would have the likelihood of a mutation is not correlated with the benefits of liabilities that mutation would confer on the organism, the environment provides the filter of selection, and reproduction provides the retention, least of mention, the example of which Darwin's theory of biological natural selection having three major components of the model of natural selection is the variation, selection and retention. All the same, fit is to achieve because those organisms with features that make the no less adapted for survival do not survive in competition with other organisms in the environment that have features which are better adapted. Evolutionary epistemology applies this blind variation and selective retention model to the growth of scientific knowledge and to human thought processes in general.

The parallel between biological evolution and conceptual (or, epistemic) governing or the endurable developmental phases of the driving forces of evolutionary participation or its attestations through observation, in that of either literal or analogical. On this view, called the 'evolution of cognitive mechanisms' program' (EEM) by Bradie (1986) and te 'Darwinian approach into epistemology' by Ruse (1986), the growth of knowledge occurs through blind variation and selective retention because biological natural selection itself is the cause of epistemic variation and selection. The most plausible version of the literal view does not hold that all human beliefs are innate than that of the mental mechanisms which guide the acquisition of non-innate beliefs ae themselves innate and result of biological natural selection. Ruse (1986) defends a version of literal evolution which her links to sociology. (Bradie and Rescher, 1990)

On the analogical version of evolutionary epistemology called, the 'evolutions of theories program' (EET) by Bradie (1986) and the 'Spencerian approach (after the nineteenth-century philosopher Herbert Spencer) by Ruse (1986), the development of human knowledge is governed by a process analogous to biological natural selection, than by an instance of the mechanism itself. This version of evolutionary epistemology, introduced and elaborated by Donald Campbell (1947) with a mental process of trial and error known as epistemic natural selection.

Both versions of evolutionary epistemology are usually taken to be types on naturalized epistemology, because both take some empirical facts as a starting point for their epistemological project. The literal version of elocutionary epistemology begins by accepting evolutionary theory and a materialist approach to the mind and, from these, constructs an account of knowledge and its development. In contrast, the analogical version does not require the truth of biological evolution, it simply draws on biological evolution as a source for the model of natural selection. Therefore of evolutionary epistemology to be true, the model of natural selection need only apply to the growth of knowledge, not to the origin and development of species. Crudely put, evolutionary epistemology and the analogical sort could still be true if Creationism is the correct theory of the origin of species.

Although they do not begin by assuming evolutionary theory, most analogical evolutionary epistemologists are naturalized epistemologists as well, for which their empirical assumptions come from psychology and cognitive science, not evolutionary theories. Sometimes, however, evolutionary epistemology is characterized in a seeming non-naturalistic manner. Campbell (1974) says that 'if one is expanding knowledge beyond what one knows, one has no choice but to explore without the benefit of wisdom' (i.e., blindly). This, Campbell admits, makes evolutionary epistemology close to being a tautology (and so non-naturalistic). The evolutionary epistemology does attack toward the analytic claim that when expanding one's knowledge beyond what one knows, one must proceed with something that is not already known, but, more interestingly, it also makes the synthetic claim that when expanding one's knowledge beyond what one knows, one must proceed by blind variation and selective retention. This claim is synthetic because it can be empirically falsified. The central claim of evolutionary epistemology is synthetic, not analytic. If the central claim were analytic, then all non-evolutionary epistemology would be logically contradictory, which they are not.

With respect to progress, the problem is that biological evolution is not goal-directed, but the growth of human knowledge is. Campbell (1974) worries about the potential disanaloguousness, but is willing to bite the bullet and admit that epistemic evolution progress toward a goal (truth) while biological evolution does not. Some have argued that evolutionary epistemology must give up the 'truth-tropic' sense of progress because a natural selection model is in essence, non-teleological, where instead, following Kuhn (1970), an operational sense of progress can be embraced along with evolutionary epistemology.

Many evolutionary epistemologists try to combine the literal and the analogical version, saying that those beliefs and cognitive mechanisms which are innate result from natural selection of the biological sort and those which are in absence of innate results from natural selection of the epistemic sort. This is reasonable since the two parts of this hybrid view are kept distinct. An analogical version evolutionary epistemology with biological variation as its only source of blindness would be a null theory: This would be the case if all our beliefs are innate or if our non-innate beliefs are not the result of blind variation. An appeal to the blindness of biological variation is thus not a legitimate way to produce a hybrid version of evolutionary epistemology since doing so trivializes the theory. For similar reasons, such an appeal will not save an analogical version of evolutionary epistemology from arguments to the effect that epistemic variation is not blind (Stein and Lipton, 1990).

Chance can influence the outcome at each result: First, in the creation of genetic mutation, second, in wether the bearer lives long enough to show its effects, thirdly, in chance events that influence the individual's actual reproductive success, and fourth, in wether a gene even if favoured in one generation, is, happenstance, eliminated in the next, and finally in the many unpredictable environmental changes that will undoubtedly occur in the history of any group of organisms. As Harvard biologist Stephen Jay Gould has so vividly expressed that process over, the outcome would surely be different. Not only might there not be humans, there might not even be anything like mammals.

We will often emphasis the elegance of traits shaped by natural selection, but the common idea that nature creates perfection needs to be analysed carefully. The extent to which evolution achieves perfection depends on exactly what you mean. If you mean "Does natural selections always take the best path for the long-term welfare of a species?" The answer is no. That would require adaption by group selection, and this is, unlikely. If you mean "Does natural selection creates every adaption that would be valuable?" The answer again, is no. For instance, some kinds of South American monkeys can grasp branches with their tails. Appearance trick would surely also be useful to some African species, but, simply because of bad luck, none have it. Some combination of circumstances started some ancestral South American monkeys using their tails in ways that ultimately led to an ability to grab onto branches, while no such development took place in Africa. Mere usefulness of a trait does not necessitate it mean that will evolve.

This is an approach to the theory of knowledge that sees an important connection between the growth of knowledge and biological evolution. An evolutionary epistemologist claims that the development of human knowledge proceeds through some natural selection process, the best example of which is Darwin's theory of biological natural selection. The three major components of the model of natural selection are variation selection and retention. According to Darwin's theory of natural selection, variations are not pre-designed to perform certain functions. Rather, these variations that perform useful functions are selected. While those, which do not, are not selected as such a selection is responsible for the apparency that a variance intentionally occurs. In the modern theory of evolution, genetic mutations provide the blind variations, blinded in the sense that variations are not influenced by the effects they would have, and the likelihood of a mutation is not correlated with the benefits or liabilities that mutation would confer on the organism. The environment provides the filter of selection, and reproduction provides the retention. Fit is achieved because those organisms with features that make them less adapted for survival do not survive concerning other organisms in the environment that have features that are better adapted. Evolutionary epistemology applies this blind variation and selective retention model to the growth of scientific knowledge and to human thought processes in general.

The parallel between biological evolution and conceptual or we can see 'epistemic' evolution as either literal or analogical. The literal version of evolutionary epistemology goes beyond biological evolution as the main cause of the growth of knowledge. On this view, called the 'evolution of cognitive mechanic programs', by Bradie (1986) and the 'Darwinian approach to epistemology' by Ruse (1986), that growth of knowledge occurs through blind variation and selective retention because biological natural selection itself is the cause of epistemic variation and selection. The most plausible version of the literal view does not hold that all human beliefs are innate but rather than the mental mechanisms which guide the acquisition of non-innate beliefs are themselves innately and the result of biological natural selection. Ruse (1986) repossess on the demands of an interlingual rendition of literal evolutionary epistemology that he links to sociology (Rescher, 1990).

On the analogical version of evolutionary epistemology, called the 'evolution of theory's program', by Bradie (1986). The 'Spenserians approach' (after the nineteenth century philosopher Herbert Spencer) by Ruse (1986), a process analogous to biological natural selection has governed the development of human knowledge, rather than by an instance of the mechanism itself. This version of evolutionary epistemology, introduced and elaborated by Donald Campbell (1974) and Karl Popper, sees the [partial] fit between theories and the world as explained by a mental process of trial and error known as epistemic natural selection.

We have usually taken both versions of evolutionary epistemology to be types of naturalized epistemology, because both take some empirical facts as a starting point for their epistemological project. The literal version of evolutionary epistemology begins by accepting evolutionary theory and a materialist approach to the mind and, from these, constructs an account of knowledge and its developments. In contrast, the analogical; the version does not require the truth of biological evolution: It simply draws on biological evolution as a source for the model of natural selection. For this version of evolutionary epistemology to be true, the model of natural selection need only apply to the growth of knowledge, not to the origin and development of species. Crudely put, evolutionary epistemology of the analogical sort could still be true even if Creationism is the correct theory of the origin of species.

Although they do not begin by assuming evolutionary theory, most analogical evolutionary epistemologists are naturalized epistemologists as well, their empirical assumptions, least of mention, implicitly come from psychology and cognitive science, not evolutionary theory. Sometimes, however, evolutionary epistemology is characterized in a seemingly non-naturalistic fashion. (Campbell 1974) says that 'if one is expanding knowledge beyond what one knows, one has no choice but to explore without the benefit of wisdom', i.e., blindly. This, Campbell admits, makes evolutionary epistemology close to being a tautology (and so not naturalistic). Evolutionary epistemology does assert the analytic claim that when expanding one's knowledge beyond what one knows, one must precessed to something that is already known, but, more interestingly, it also makes the synthetic claim that when expanding one's knowledge beyond what one knows, one must proceed by blind variation and selective retention. This claim is synthetic because we can empirically falsify it. The central claim of evolutionary epistemology is synthetic, not analytic. If the central contradictory, which they are not. Campbell is right that evolutionary epistemology does have the analytic feature he mentions, but he is wrong to think that this is a distinguishing feature, since any plausible epistemology has the same analytic feature (Skagestad, 1978).

This sort of condition fails, however, to be sufficiently for non-inferential perceptivity, for knowledge is accountable for its compatibility with the belief's being unjustified, and an unjustified belief cannot be knowledge. For example, suppose that your organism for sensory data of colour as perceived, is working well, but you have been given good reason to think otherwise, to think, say, that the sensory data of things look chartreuse to say, that chartreuse things look magenta, if you fail to heed these reasons you have for thinking that your colour perception is awry and believe of a thing that looks magenta to you that it is magenta, your belief will fail top be justified and will therefore fail to be knowledge, although it is caused by the thing's being withing the grasp of sensory perceptivity, enough to be a completely reliable sign, or to carry the information that the thing is sufficiently to organize all sensory data as perceived in and of the world, or Holistic view.

The view that a belief acquires favourable epistemic status by having some kind of reliable linkage to the truth. Variations of this view have been advanced for both knowledge and justified belief. The first formulation of a reliable account of knowing notably appeared as marked and noted and accredited to F.P. Ramsey (1903-30), whereby much of Ramsey's work was directed at saving classical mathematics from 'intuitionism', or what he called the 'Bolshevik menace of Brouwer and Weyl'. In the theory of probability he was the first to develop, based on precise behavioural nations of preference and expectation. In the philosophy of language, Ramsey was one of the first thinkers to accept a 'redundancy theory of truth', which he combined with radical views of the function of many kinds of propositions. Neither generalizations, nor causal positions, nor those treating probability or ethics, described facts, but each has a different specific function in our intellectual economy. Ramsey was one of the earliest commentators on the early work of Wittgenstein, and his continuing friendship with the latter to Wittgenstein's return to Cambridge and to philosophy in 1929. Additionally, Ramsey, who said that an impression of belief was knowledge if it were true, certain and obtained by a reliable process. P. Unger (1968) suggested that 'S' knows that 'p' just in case it is of at all accidental that 'S' is right about its being the case that D.M. Armstrong (1973) drew an analogy between a thermometer that reliably indicates the temperature and a belief interaction of reliability that indicates the truth. Armstrong said that a non-inferential belief qualified as knowledge if the belief has properties that are nominally sufficient for its truth, i.e., guarantee its truth via laws of nature.

Closely allied to the nomic sufficiency account of knowledge, primarily due to F.I. Dretske (1971, 1981), A.I. Goldman (1976, 1986) and R. Nozick (1981). The core of this approach is that 'S's' belief that 'p' qualifies as knowledge just in case 'S' believes 'p' because of reasons that would not obtain unless 'p's' being true, or because of a process or method that would not yield belief in 'p' if 'p' were not true. For example, 'S' would not have his current reasons for believing there is a telephone before him, or would not come to believe this in the way he does, unless there was a telephone before him. Thus, there is a counterfactual reliable guarantor of the belief's being true. A variant of the counterfactual approach says that 'S' knows that 'p' only if there is no 'relevant alternative' situation in which 'p' is false but 'S' would still believe that 'p' must be sufficient to eliminate all the other situational alternatives of 'p', where an alternative to a proposition 'p' is a proposition incompatible with 'p', that is, one's justification or evidence fort 'p' must be sufficient for one to know that every subsidiary situation is 'p' is false.

They standardly classify reliabilism as an 'externaturalist' theory because it invokes some truth-linked factor, and truth is 'eternal' to the believer the main argument for externalism derives from the philosophy of language, more specifically, from the various phenomena pertaining to natural kind terms, indexical, etc., that motivate the views that have become known as direct reference' theories. Such phenomena seem, at least to show that the belief or thought content that can be properly attributed to a person is dependent on facts about his environment ~, e.g., whether he is on Earth or Twin Earth, what in fact he is pointing at, the classificatory criteria employed by the experts in his social group, etc. Not just on what is going on internally in his mind or brain (Putnam and Burge, 1979.) Most theories of knowledge, of course, share an externalist component in requiring truth as a condition for knowing. reliabilism goes farther, however, in trying to capture additional conditions for knowledge by means of a nomic, counterfactual or other 'external' relations between 'belief' and 'truth'.

The most influential counterexample to reliabilism is the demon-world and the clairvoyance examples. The demon-world example challenges the necessity of the reliability requirement, in that a possible world in which an evil demon creates deceptive visual experience, the process of vision is not reliable. Still, the visually formed beliefs in this world are intuitively justified. The clairvoyance example challenges the sufficiency of reliability. Suppose a cognitive agent possesses a reliable clairvoyance power, but has no evidence for or against his possessing such a power. Intuitively, his clairvoyantly formed beliefs are unjustifiably unreasoned, but reliabilism declares them justified.

Nonetheless, another distinctively symptomatic version of reliabilism attempts to meet the demon-world and clairvoyance problems without recourse to the questionable notion of 'normal worlds'. Consider Sosa's (1992) suggestion that justified beliefs is belief acquired through 'intellectual virtues', and not through intellectual 'vices', whereby virtues are reliable cognitive faculties or processes. The task is to explain how epistemic evaluators have used the notion of indelible virtues, and vices, to arrive at their judgements, especially in the problematic cases. Goldman (1992) proposes a two-stage reconstruction of an evaluator's activity. The first stage is a reliability-based acquisition of a 'list' of virtues and vices. The second stage is application of this list to queried cases. Determining has executed the second stage whether processes in the queried cases resemble virtues or vices. We have classified visual beliefs in the demon world as justified because visual belief formation is one of the virtues. Clairvoyance formed, beliefs are classified as unjustified because clairvoyance resembles scientifically suspect processes that the evaluator represents as vices, e.g., mental telepathy, ESP, and so forth.

Clearly, there are many forms of reliabilism, just as there are many forms of foundationalism and coherentism. How is reliabilism related to these other two theories of justification? They have usually regarded it as a rival, and this is apt in as far as foundationalism and coherentism traditionally focussed on purely evidential relations rather than psychological processes. But reliabilism might also to be offered as a deeper-level theory, subsuming some precepts of either foundationalism or coherentism. Foundationalism says that there are 'basic' beliefs, which acquire justification without dependency on inference. Reliabilism might rationalize this by indicating that reliable non-inferential processes form the basic beliefs. Coherentism stresses the primary of systematicity in all doxastic decision-making. Reliabilism might rationalize this by pointing to increases in reliability that accrue from systematicity. Thus, reliabilism could complement foundationalism and coherentism than complete with them.

Philosophers often debate the existence of different kinds of tings: Nominalists question the reality of abstract objects like class, numbers, and universals, some positivist doubt the existence of theoretical entities like neutrons or genes, and there are debates over whether there are sense-data, events and so on. This requires a 'metaphysical' concept of 'real existence': We debate whether numbers, neutrons and sense-data really existing things. But it is difficult to see what this concept involves and the rules to be employed in setting such debates are very unclear.

Questions of existence seem always to involve general kinds of things, do numbers, sense-data or neutrons exit? Some philosophers conclude that existence is not a property of individual things, 'exists' is not an ordinary predicate. If I refer to something, and then predicate existence of it, my utterance is tautological, the object must exist for me to be able to refer to it, so predicating for me to be able to refer to it, so predicating existence of it adds nothing. And to say of something that it did not exist would be contradictory.

According to Rudolf Carnap, who pursued the enterprise of clarifying the structures of mathematical and scientific language (the only legitimate task for scientific philosophy) in "The Logische Syntax der Sprache" (1934), wherefore, refinements to his syntactic and semantic views continued with "Meaning and Necessity" (1947), while a general loosening of the original ideal of reduction culminated in the great "Logical Foundation of Probability," is most important on the grounds accountable by its singularity, the confirmation theory, in 1959. Other works concern the structure of physics and the concept of entropy. Nonetheless, questions of which framework to employ do not concern whether the entities posited by the framework 'really exist', its pragmatic usefulness has rather settled them. Philosophical debates over existence misconstrue 'pragmatics' questions of choice of frameworks as substantive questions of fact. Once we have adopted a framework there are substantive 'internal' questions, are their zany prime numbers between ten and twenty. 'External' questions about choice of frameworks have a different status.

More recent philosophers, notably Quine, have questioned the distinction between linguistic framework and internal questions arising within it. Quine agrees that we have no 'metaphysical' concept of existence against which different purported entities can be measured. If quantification of the general theoretical framework which best explains our experiences, making the abstraction, of which there are such things, that they exist, is true. Scruples about admitting the existence of too many different kinds of objects depend not on a metaphysical concept of existence but rather on a desire for a simple and economical theoretical framework.

It is not possible to bring upon a definition of experience, and in an illuminating way, however, what experiences are through acquaintance with some of their own, e.g., a visual experience of a green afterimage, a feeling of physical nausea or a tactile experience of an abrasive surface, which and actual surface ~ rough or smooth might cause or which might be part of ca dream, or the product of a vivid sensory imagination. The essential feature of every experience is that it feels in some certain ways. That there is something that it is like to have it. We may refer to this feature of an experience is its 'character.

Another core groups of characterizations are of the sorts of experience with which our concerns are those that have representational content, unless otherwise indicated, the terms 'experience' will be reserved for these that we implicate below, that the most obvious cases of experience with content are sense experiences of the kind normally involved in perception? We may describe such experiences by mentioning their sensory modalities and their content's, e.g., a gustatory experience (modality) of chocolate ice cream (content), but do so more commonly by means of perceptual verbs combined with noun phrases specifying their contents, as in 'Macbeth saw a dagger;'. This is, however, ambiguous between the perceptual claim 'There was a [material] dagger in the world which Macbeth perceived visually' and 'Macbeth had a visual experience of a dagger', the reading with which we are concerned.

According to the act/object analysis of experience (which is a special case of the act/object analysis of consciousness), every experience involves an object of experience even if it has no material object. Two main lines of argument may be offered in support of this view, one phenomenological and the semantic.

In an outline, the phenomenological argument is as follows: Whenever we have an experience, even if nothing beyond the experience answers to it, we may be presented with something through the experience (for which it is 'for' and 'of' itself as transparent). The object of the experience is whatever is so presented to us -be it an individual thing, an event or a state of affairs,

the semantic argument is that objects of experience are required to make sense of certain features of our talk about experiences which include, in particular, such as (1) Simple attributions of experience (e.g., 'Rod is experiencing a pink square') are relational. (2) We apar to refer tp objects of experienced and to attribute properties to them, e.g., 'The afterimage which John experienced was green'. (3) We appear to quantify over objects of experience (e.g., 'Macbeth saw something which his wife did not see').

The act/object analysis faces several problems concerning the status of objects of experience. Currently, the most common view is that they are sense-data -private mental entities which possess the traditional sensory qualities representations that by experience for which they are the objects, however, the very idea of an exactly private entity suspect. Nonetheless, an experience may apparently represent something as having a determinable property (e.g., redness) without representing it as having any subordinate determinate property (e.g., any specific shade of red), a sense-datum may have determinable property without having any determinate property subordinate to it, Even more disturbing, is that, sense-data may have contradictory properties, since experiences can have contradictory contents. A case in point, is the waterfall illusion: If you stare at a waterfall for a minute and them immediately fixate on a nearby rock, you are likely to have an experience of the rock's moving upward what it remains in the same place, are that the sense-datum theorist must either deny that there are such experiences or admit to contradictory objects.

These problems can be avoided by treating object of experiences properties, however, failing to do justice to the appearances, for experience seems not to present us with bare properties (however complex), but with properties embodied in individuals. The view that objects of experience is that Meinongian objects accommodate this point. It is also attractive insofar as (1) it allows experiences to represent properties other than traditional sensory qualities, and (2) it allows for the identification of objects of experience and objects of perception with experience which constitute perceptions, in terms of representative realism, objects of perception (of which we are 'indirectly aware') are always distinct from objects of experience, of which we are 'directly are'. Meinongian's, however, may simply treat objects of perception of existing objects of experience. Nonetheless, most philosophers will feel that the Meinongian's acceptance of impossible objects is too high a price to for these benefits.

Nevertheless, a general problem addressed for the act/object analysis is that the question of whether two subjects are experiencing the same thing, as opposed to having exactly similar experiences, that appears to have an answer only on the assumption that the experiences concerned are perceptions with material objects. But with the act/object analysis the question must have an answer even when this condition is not satisfied. (The answer is always negative on the sense-datum theory, but it could be positive on other versions of the act/object analysis, depending on the facts of the case.)

All the same the case for the act/object analysis should be reassessed. The phenomenological argument is not, on reflection, convincing. For it is easy enough to grant that any experience appears to present us with an object without accepting that it actually does. The semantic argument is more impressive, but is nonetheless, answerable. The seemingly relational structure of attributions of experience is a challenge dealt with its connection with the adverbial theory. Apparent reference to and quantification over objects of experience can be handled by analysing them as reference to experiences themselves and quantification over experiences tacitly according to content. Thus 'The afterimage which John experienced was an experience of green', and 'Macbeth something which his wife did not see' becomes 'Macbeth had a visual experience which his wife did not have'.

As pertaining case of other mental states and events with content, it is important to distinguish between the properties which experience represents and the properties which it possesses. To talk of the representational properties of an experience is to say something about its content, not to attribute those properties to the experience itself. Like every other experience, a visual Esperance of a pink square is a mental event, and it is therefore not itself either pink or square, though it represents those properties. It is, perhaps, fleeting, pleasant or unusual, although it does not represent those properties. An experience may represent a property which it possesses, and it may even do so in virtue of possessing that property, inasmuch as the putting to case some rapidly representing change [complex] experience representing something as changing rapidly, but this is the exception and not the rule.

Which properties can be [directly] represented in sense experience is subject to debate. Traditionalists, include only properties whose presence a subject could not doubt having appropriated experiences, e.g., colour and shape in visual experience, i.e., colour and shape with visual experience, surface texture, hardness, etc., during tactile experience. This view s natural to anyone who has to an egocentric Cartesian perspective in epistemology, and wishes for pure data experience to serve as logically certain foundations for knowledge. The term 'sense-data', introduced by More and Russell, refer to the immediate objects of perceptual awareness, such as colour patches and shape, usually supposed distinct from surfaces of physical objects. Qualities of sense-data are supposed to be distinct from physical qualities because their perception is more immediate, and because sense data are private and cannot appear other than they are. They are objects that change in our perceptual fields when conditions of perception change and physical objects remain constant.'

Critics of the notional questions of whether, just because physical objects can appear other than they are, there must be private, mental objects that have all qualities that the physical objects appear to have, there are also problems regarding the individuation and duration of sense-data and their relations ti physical surfaces of an object we perceive. Contemporary proponents counter that speaking only of how things and to appear cannot capture the full structure within perceptual experience captured by talk of apparent objects and their qualities.

It is nevertheless, that others who do not think that this wish can be satisfied and they impress who with the role of experience in providing animals with ecological significant information about the world around them, claim that sense experiences represent possession characteristics and kinds which are much richer and much more wide-ranging than the traditional sensory qualitites. We do not see only colours and shapes they tell 'u' but also, earth, water, men, women and fire, we do not smell only odours, but also food and filth. There is no space here to examine the factors relevant to as choice between these alternatives. In so, that we are to assume and expect when it is incompatibles with a position under discussion.

Given the modality and content of a sense experience, most of 'us' will be aware of its character although we cannot describe that character directly. This suggests that character and content are not really distinct, and a close tie between them. For one thing, the relative complexity of the character of some sense experience places limitation n its possible content, i.e., a tactile experience of something touching one's left ear is just too simple to carry the same amount of content as a typical every day, visual experience. Furthermore, the content of a sense experience of a given character depends on the normal causes of appropriately similar experiences, i.e., the sort of gustatory experience which we have when eating chocolate would not represent chocolate unless chocolate normally caused it, granting a contingent ties between the characters of an experience and its possibility for casual origins, it again, followed its possible content is limited by its character.

Character and content are none the less irreducible different for the following reasons (I) There are experiences which completely lack content, i.e., certain bodily pleasures (ii) Not every aspect of the character of an experience which content is used for that content, i.e., the unpleasantness of an auricular experience of chalk squeaking on a board may have no responsibility significance (iii) Experiences indifferent modalities may overlap in content without a parallel experience in character, i.e., visual and active experiences of circularity feel completely different (iv) The content of an experience with a given character may varingly be in an accord tn the background of the subject, i.e., a certain aural experience may come to have the content 'singing birds' only after the subject has learned something about birds.

According to the act/object analysis of experience, which is a peculiar to case that his act/object analytic thinking of consciousness, that every experience involves an object of experience if it has not material object. Two main lines of argument may be offered in supports of this view, one phenomenological and the other semantic.

The semantic argument is that they require objects of experience to make sense of cretin factures of our talk about experience, including, in particular, the following (1) Simple attributions of experience, i.e., 'Rod is experiencing a pink square', are relational (2) We appear to refer to objects of experience and to attribute properties to them, i.e., we had given between the afterimage which John experienced, and (3) We appear to qualify over objects of experience, i.e., Macbeth saw something which his wife did not see.

The act/object analysis faces several problems concerning the status of objects of experience. Currently the most common view is that they are 'sense-data' ~. Private mental entities which actually posses the traditional sensory qualities represented by the experience of which they are the objects. But the very idea of an essentially private entity is suspect. Moreover, since an experience must apparently represent something as having a determinable property, i.e., red, without representing it as having any subordinate determinate property, i.e., each specific given shade of red, a sense-datum may actually have our determinate property without saving any determinate property subordinate to it. Even more disturbing is that sense-data may contradictory properties, since experience can have properties, since experience can have contradictory contents. A case in point is te water fall illusion: If you stare at a waterfall for a minute and the immediately fixate on a nearby rock, you are likely to are an experience of moving upward while it remains inexactly the same place. The sense-data, . . . private mental entities which actually posses the traditional sensory qualities represented by the experience of which they are te objects., but the very idea of an essentially private entity is suspect. Moreover, since abn experience may apparently represent something as having a determinable property, i.e., redness, without representing it as having any subordinate determinate property, i.e., any specific shade of red, a sense-datum may actually have a determinate property without having any determinate property subordinate to it. Even more disturbing is the sense-data may have contradictory properties, since experiences can have contradictory contents. A case in point is the waterfall illusion: If you stare at a waterfall for a minute and then immediately fixate your vision upon a nearby rock, you are likely to have an experience of the rock's moving while it remains in the same place. The sense-datum theorist must either deny that there as such experiences or admit contradictory objects.

Treating objects can avoid these problems of experience as properties. this, however, fails to do justice to the appearances, for experiences, however complex, but with properties embodied in individuals. The view that objects of experience is that Meinongian objects accommodate this point. It is also attractive, in as far as (1) it allows experiences to represent properties other than traditional sensory qualities, and (2) it allows for the identification of objects of experience and objects of perception in experiences which constitute perceptivity.

According to the act/object analysis of experience, every experience with contentual representation involves an object of experience, an act of awareness has related the subject (the event of experiencing that object). This is meant to apply not only to perceptions, which have material objects, whatever is perceived, but also to experiences like hallucinating and dream experiences, which do not. Such experiences are, nonetheless, less appearing to represent of something, and their objects are supposed to be whatever it is that they represent. Act/object theorists may differ on the nature of objects of experience, which we have treated as properties, Meinongian objects, which may not exist or have any form of being, and, more commonly, private mental entities with sensory qualities. (We have now usually applied the term 'sense-data' to the latter, but has also been used as a general term for objects sense experiences, in the work of G.E., Moore.) Its terms of representative realism, objects of perceptions, of which we are 'indirectly aware' are always distinct from objects of experience, of which we are 'directly aware'. Meinongian, however, may treat objects of perception as existing objects of perception, least there is mention, Meinong's most famous doctrine derives from the problem of intentionality, which led him to countenance objects, such as the golden mountain, that could be the object of thought, although they do not actually exist. This doctrine was one of the principle's targets of Russell's theory of 'definitive descriptions', however, it came as part o a complex and interesting package of concept if the theory of meaning, and scholars are not united in what supposedly that Russell was fair to it. Meinong's works include "Über Annahmen" (1907), translated as "On Assumptions" (1983), and "Über Möglichkeit und Wahrschein ichkeit" (1915). But most of the philosophers will feel that the Meinongian's acceptance to impossible objects is too high a price to pay for these benefits.

A general problem for the act/object analysis is that the question of whether two subjects are experiencing the same thing, as opposed to having exactly similar experiences, that it appears to have an answer only, on the assumptions that the experience concerned are perceptions with material objects. But for the act/object analysis the question must have an answer even when conditions are not satisfied. (The answers unfavourably negative, on the sense-datum theory: It could be positive of the versions of the act/object analysis, depending on the facts of the case.)

In view of the above problems, we should reassess the case of act/object analysis. The phenomenological argument is not, on reflection, convincing, for it is easy enough to grant that any experience appears to present 'us' with an object without accepting that it actually does. The semantic argument is more impressive, but is nonetheless, answerable. The seemingly relational structure of attributions of experiences is a challenge dealt with below concerning the adverbial theory. Apparent reference to and we can handle quantification over objects of experience themselves and quantification over experience tacitly according to content, thus, 'the afterimage which John experienced was an experience of green' and 'Macbeth saw something which his wife did not see' becomes 'Macbeth had a visual experience which his wife did not have'.

Notwithstanding, pure cognitivism attempts to avoid the problems facing the act/object analysis by reducing experiences to Meinongian events or associated dispositions, i.e., 'We might identify Susy's experience of a rough surface beneath her hand with the event of her acquiring the belief that there is a rough surface beneath her hand, or, if she does not acquire this belief, with a disposition to acquire it which we have somehow blocked.

This position has attractions. It does full justice. And to the important role of experience as a source of belief acquisition. It would also help clear the say for a naturalistic theory of mind, since there may be some prospect of a physical/functionalist account of belief and other intentional states. But its failure has completely undermined pure cognitivism to accommodate the fact that experiences have a felt character which cannot be reduced to their content.

The adverbial theory of experience advocates that the grammatical object of a statement attributing an experience to someone be analysed as an adverb. Also, the adverbial theory is an attempt to undermine a semantic account of attributions of experience which does not require objects of experience. Unfortunately, the oddities of explicit adverbializations of such statements have driven off potential supporters of the theory. Furthermore, the theory remains largely undeveloped, and attempted refutations have traded on this. It may, however, be founded on sound basic intuition, and there is reason to believe that an effective development of the theory, which is merely hinted upon possibilities.

The relearnt intuitions are as, (I) that when we say that someone is experiencing an 'A', as this has an experience of an 'A', we are using this content-expression to specify the type of thing which the experience is especially apt to fit, (ii) that doing this is a matter of saying something about the experience itself (and maybe also about the normal causes of like experiences), and (iii) that there is no-good reason to suppose that it involves the description of an object of which the experience is. Thus, the effective role of the content-expression is a statement of experience is to modify the verb it compliments, not to introduce a special type of object.

Perhaps the most important criticism of the adverbial theory is the 'many property problem', according to which the theory does not have the resources to distinguish between, e.g.,

(1) Frank has an experience of a brown triangle.

And:

(2) Frank has an experience of brow n and an experience of a triangle,

Which (1) is entailed, but does not entail it? The act/object analysis can easily accommodate the difference between (1) and (2) by claiming that the truth of (1) requires a single object of experience which is as both brown and trilateral, while that of the (2) allows for the possibility of two objects of experience, one brown and the other triangular. Note, however, that (1) is equivalent to.

(1*) Frank has an experience of something's being both brown and triangular,

And (2) is equivalent to:

(2*) Frank has an experience of something's being brown and a triangle of something's being triangular,

And we can explain the difference between these quite simply for logical scope without invoking objects of experience. The adverbialists may use this to answer the many-property problem by arguing that the phrase 'a brown triangle' in (1) does the same work as the clause 'something's being both brown and triangular' in (1*). This is perfectly compactable with the view that it also has the 'adverbial' function of modifying the verb 'has an experience of', for it specifies the experience more narrowly just by giving a necessary condition for the satisfactions of the experience, as the condition being that there are something both brown and triangular before Frank.

A final position which we should mention is the state theory, according to which a sense experience of an 'A' is an occurrent, non-relational state of the kind which the subject would be in when perceiving an 'A'. Suitably qualified, this claim is no doubt truer, but its significance is subject to debate. Here it is enough to remark that the claim is compactable with both pure cognitivism and the adverbial theory, and that we have probably best advised state theorists to adopt adverbials for developing their intuition.

Perceptual knowledge is knowledge acquired by or through the senses, this includes most of what we know. We cross intersections when everything we see the light turn green, head for the kitchen when we smell the roast burning, squeeze the fruit to determine its ripeness, and climb out of bed when we hear the alarm ring. In each case we come to know something -that the light has turned green, that the roast is burning, that the melon is overripe, and that it is time to get up by some sensory means. Because the light has turned green is learning something that the light has turned green– by use of the eyes.

Feeling that the melon is overripe is coming to know a fact that the melon is overripe by one's sense of touch. In each case we have somehow based on the resulting knowledge, derived from or grounded in the sort of experience that characterizes the sense modality in question.

Seeing a rotten kumquat is not at all like the experience of smelling, tasting or feeling a rotten kumquat, yet all these experiences can result in the same primary directive as to knowledge. . . . Knowledge that the kumquat is rotten, . . . although the experiences are much different, they must, if they are to yield knowledge, embody information about the kumquat: The information that it is rotten. Since the fruit is rotten differs from smelling that it is rotten, not in what is known, but how it is known. In each case, the information has the same source -the rotten kumquats but it is, so to speak, delivered via different channels and coded in different experiences.

It is important to avoid confusing perception knowledge of facts', i.e., that the kumquat is rotten, with the perception of objects, i.e., rotten kumquats, a rotten kumquat, quite another to know. By seeing or tasting, that it is a rotten kumquat. Some people do not know what kumquats smell like, as when they smell like a rotten kumquat-thinking, perhaps, that this is the way this strange fruit is supposed to smell doing not realize from the smell, i.e., do not smell that, it is rotten. In such cases people see and smell rotten kumquats-and in this sense perceive rotten kumquats, and never know that they are kumquats let alone rotten kumquats. They cannot, not at least by seeing and smelling, and not until they have learned something about [rotten] kumquats, come to know that what they are seeing or smelling is a [rotten] kumquat. Since we have geared the topic toward perceptual representations too knowledge-knowing, by sensory means or data, that something is 'F'~, wherefor, we need the question of what more, beyond the perception of F's, to see that and thereby know that they are 'F' will be brought of question, not how we see kumquats (for even the ignorant can do this), but, how we even know, in that indeed, we do, in that of what we see.

Much of our perceptual knowledge is indirect, dependent or derived. By this I mean that the facts we describe ourselves as learning, as coming to know, by perceptual means are pieces of knowledge that depend on our coming to know something else, another fact, in a more direct way. We see, by newspapers, that our team has lost again, see, by her expression, that she is nervous. This dived or dependent sort of knowledge is particularly prevalent during vision, but it occurs, to a lesser degree, in every sense modality. We install bells and other sound makers so that we can, for example, hear (by the alarm) that someone is at the door and (by the bell) that its time to get up. When we obtain knowledge in this way, it is clear that unless one sees hence, comes to know something about the gauge that it reads 'empty', the newspaper (what it says) and the person's expression, one would not see, hence, we know, that what one perceptual representation means to have described as coming to know. If one cannot hear that the bell is ringing, the ringing of the bell cannot, in, at least, and, in this way, one cannot hear that one's visitors have arrived. In such cases one sees, hears, smells, etc., that 'an' is 'F', coming to know thereby that 'an' is 'F', by seeing, hearing etc., we have derived from that come other condition, 'b's being 'G', that 'an' is 'F', or dependent on, the more basic perceptivities that of its being attributive to knowledge that of 'b' is 'G'.

Though perceptual knowledge about objects is often, in this way, dependent on knowledge of facts about different objects, the derived knowledge is something about the same object. That is, we see that 'an' is 'F' by seeing, not that another object is 'G', but that 'a' would stand justly as equitably as 'G'. We see, by her expression, that she is nervous. She tells that the fabric is silk (not polyester) by the characteristic 'greasy' feel of the fabric itself (not, as I do, by what is printed on the label). We tell whether it is a maple tree, a convertible Porsche, a geranium, and ingenious rock or a misprint by its shape, colour, texture, size, behaviour and distinctive markings. Perceptual knowledge of this sort is also deprived. The deriving of a conclusion by reasoning from evidence or from premises or, draw or reach (as a conclusion as an end point or points of reasoning and observation, evidence from which is to be derived a startling new set of axioms, yet it has a slight tendency to show something as probable from the greater of facts in learning processes that relates a perception of something new to knowledge as already possessed of such as to make out or perceive to be something previously known, however, the diagnostic distinction is often given by word or deed that one knows of and agrees to or with something. In this case, the perceptual knowledge is, however deviating from a direct line or straightforward course, as being indirect it changes for being incapable of being apprehended by the senses or intellect. Although, the same object is involved, the facts we come to know about it are different from the facts that enable 'us' to know it.

We sometimes describe derived knowledge as inferential, but this is misleading. At the conscious level there is no passage of the mind from premised to conclusion, no reason-sensitivity of mind from problem-solving. The observer, the one who sees that 'a' is 'F' by since 'b' (or, 'a') is 'G', need not be and typically is not aware of any process of inference, any passage of the mind from one belief to another. The resulting knowledge, though logically derivative, is psychologically immediate. I could see that she was getting angry, so I moved my hand. I did not, at least not at any conscious level, Infer from her expression and behaviour that she was getting angry. I could (or, it seems to me) see that she was getting angry, it is this psychological immediacy that makes indirect perceptual knowledge a species of perceptual knowledge.

The psychological immediacy that characterizes so much of our perceptual knowledge -even (sometimes) the most indirect and derived forms of it -do not mean that no one requires learning to know in this way. One is not born with (may, in fact, never develop) the ability to recognize daffodils, muskrats and angry companions. It is only after a long experience that one is able visually to identify such things. Beginners may do something corresponding to inference, they recognize relevant features of trees, birds, and flowers, features they already know how to identify perceptually, and then infer (conclude), because of what they see, and under the guidance of more expert observers, that it is an oak, a finch or a geranium. But the experts (and wee are all experts on many aspects of our familiar surroundings) do not typically go through such a process. The expert just sees that it is an oak, a finch or a geranium. The perceptual knowledge of the expert is still dependent, of course, since even an expert cannot see what kind of flower it is if she cannot first see its colour and shape, but it is to say that the expert has developed identification skills that no longer require the sort of conscious self-inferential process that characterize a beginner's effort.

Coming to know that 'a' is 'F' by since 'b' is 'G' obviously requires some background assumption by the observer, an assumption to the effect that 'a' is 'F' (or, perhaps only probable 'F') when 'b' is 'G?'. If one does not speculatively take for granted, that they properly connect the gauge, does not (thereby) assume that it would not register 'Empty' unless the tank was nearly empty, then even if one could see that it registered 'Empty', one would not learn hence, would not see, that one needed gas. At least one would not see it by consulting the gauge. Likewise, in trying to identify birds, it is no use being able to see their marking if one does not know something about which birds have which marks ~. Something of the form, a bird with these markings is (probably) a blue jay.

It seems, moreover, that these background assumptions, if they are to yield knowledge that 'a' is 'F', as they must if the observer is to see (by b's being G) that 'a' is 'F', must have themselves qualify as knowledge. For if no one has known this background fact, if no one knows it whether 'a' is 'F' when 'b' is 'G', then the knowledge of b's bing G is, taken by itself, powerless to generate the knowledge that 'a' is 'F'. If the conclusion is to be known to be true, both the premises used to reach that conclusion must be known to be truer, or so it seems.

Externalists, however, argue that the indirect knowledge that 'a' is 'F', though it may depend on the knowledge that 'b' is 'G', does not require knowledge of the connecting fact, the fact that 'a' is 'F' when 'b' is 'G'. Simple belief (or, perhaps, justified beliefs, there are stronger and weaker versions of externalism) in the connecting fact is sufficient to confer a knowledge of the connected fact. Even if, strictly speaking, I do not know she is nervous whenever she fidgets like that, I can nonetheless see (hence, recognized, or know) that she is nervous (by the way she fidgets) if I (correctly) assume that this behaviour is a reliable expression of nervousness. One need not know the gauge is working well to make observations (acquire observational knowledge) with it. All that we require, besides the observer believing that the gauge is reliable, is that the gauge, in fact, be reliable, i.e., that the observers background beliefs be true. Critics of externalism have been quick to point out that this theory has the unpalatable consequence-can make that knowledge possible and, in this sense, be made to rest on lucky hunches (that turn out true) and unsupported (even irrational) beliefs. Surely, internalists argue if one is going to know that 'a' is 'F' on the basis of b's being G, one should have (as a bare minimum) some justification for thinking that 'a' is 'F', or is probably 'F', when 'b' is 'G'.

Whatever taken to be that these matters (with the possible exception of extreme externalism), indirect perception obviously requires some understanding (knowledge? Justification? Belief?) of the general relationship between the fact one comes to know (that 'a' is 'F') and the facts (that 'b' is 'G') that enable one to know it. And it is this requirement on background knowledge or understanding that leads to questions about the possibility of indirect perceptual knowledge. Is it really knowledge? Sceptical doubts have inspired the first question about whether we can ever know the connecting facts in question. How is it possible to learn, to acquire knowledge of, the connecting fact's knowledge of which is necessary to see (by b's being 'G') that 'a' is 'F'? These connecting facts do not appear to be perceptually knowable. Quite the contrary, they appear to be general truths knowable (if knowable at all) by inductive inference from past observations. And if one is sceptical about obtaining knowledge in this indirect, inductive as, one is, perforced, indirect knowledge, including indirect perceptivity, where we have described knowledge of a sort openly as above, that depends on in it.

Even if one puts aside such sceptical questions, least of mention, there remains a legitimate concern about the perceptual character of this kind of knowledge. If one sees that 'a' is 'F' by seeing that 'b' is 'G', is one really seeing that 'a' is 'F'? Isn't perception merely a part ~? And, from an epistemological standpoint, whereby one comes to know that 'a' is 'F'? One must, it is true, see that 'b' is 'G', but this is only one of the premises needed to reach the conclusion (knowledge) that 'a' is 'F'. There is also the background knowledge that is essential to te process. If we think of a theory as any factual proposition, or set of factual propositions, that cannot itself be known in some direct observational way, we can express this worry by saying that indirect perception is always theory-loaded: Seeing (indirectly) that 'a' is 'F' is only possible if the observer already has knowledge of (justifications for, belief in) some theory, the theory 'connecting' the fact one comes to know (that 'a' is 'F') with the fact (that 'b' is 'G') that enables one to know it.

This of course, reverses the standard foundationalist pictures of human knowledge. Instead of theoretical knowledge depending on, and being derived from, perception, perception of the indirect sort, presupposes a prior knowledge of theories.

Foundationalist's are quick to point out that this apparent reversal in the structure of human knowledge is only apparent. Our indirect perceptual experience of fact depends on the applicable theory, yes, but this merely shows that indirect perceptional knowledge is not part of the foundation. To reach the kind of perceptual knowledge that lies at the foundation, we need to look at a form of perception that is purified of all theoretical elements. This, then, will be perceptual knowledge, pure and direct. We have needed no background knowledge or assumptions about connecting regularities in direct perception because the known facts are presented directly and immediately and not (as, in direct perception) on the basis of some other facts. In direct perception all the justification (needed for knowledge) is right there in the experience itself.

What, then, about the possibility of perceptual knowledge pure and direct, the possibility of coming to know, on the basis of sensory experience, that 'a' is 'F' where this does not require, and in no way presupposes, backgrounds assumptions or knowledge that has a source outside the experience itself? Where is this epistemological 'pure gold' to be found?

There are, basically, two views about the nature of direct perceptual knowledge (Coherentists would deny that any of our knowledge is basic in this sense). We can call these views (following traditional nomenclature) direct realism and representationalism or representative realism. A representationalist restricts direct perceptual knowledge to objects of a very special sort: Ideas, impressions, or sensations (sometimes called sense-data)-entities in the mind of the observer. Ones perceiving fact, i.e., that 'b' is 'G', only when 'b' is a mental entity of some sort of a subjective appearance or sense-data-and 'G' is a property of this datum. Knowledge of these sensory states is supposed to be certain and infallible. These sensory facts are, so to speak, right upon against the mind's eye. One cannot be mistaken about these facts for these facts are, in really, facts about the way things appear to be, one cannot be mistaken about the way things appear to be. Normal perception of external conditions, then, turns out to be (always) a type of indirect perception. One 'sees' that there is a tomato in front of one by seeing that the appearances (of the tomato) have a certain quality (reddish and bulgy) and inferring (this is typically said to be atomistic and unconscious), on the basis of certain background assumptions, i.e., That there is a typical tomato in front of one when one has experiences of this sort, that there is a tomato in front of one. All knowledge of objective reality, then, even what commonsense regards as the most direct perceptual knowledge, is based on an even more direct knowledge of the appearances.

For the representationalist, then, perceptual knowledge of our physical surroundings is always theory-loaded and indirect. Such perception is 'loaded' with the theory that there is some regular, some uniform, correlation between the way things appears (known in a perceptually direct way) and the way things actually are (known, if known at all, in a perceptually indirect way).

The second view, direct realism, refuses to restrict direct perceptual knowledge to an inner world of subjective experience. Though the direct realists are willing to concede that much of our knowledge of the physical world is indirect, however, direct and immediate it may sometimes feel, some perceptual; Knowledge of physical reality is direct. What makes it direct is that such knowledge is not based on, nor in any way dependent on, other knowledge and belief. The justification needed for the knowledge is right in the experience itself.

To understand the way this is supposed to work, consider an ordinary example. 'S' identifies a banana (learns that it is a banana) by noting its shape and colour-perhaps even tasting and smelling it (to make sure it's not wax). In this case the perceptual knowledge that it is a banana is directly as a realist admits, indirect on 'S's' perceptual knowledge of its shape, colour, smell, and taste. 'S' learns that it is a banana by seeing that it is yellow, banana-shaped, etc. Nonetheless, 'S's 'perception of the banana's colour and shape is not direct. 'S' does not see that the object is yellow, for example, by seeing (knowing, believing) anything more basic either about the banana or anything, e.g., his own sensation of the banana. 'S' has learned to the quality of being the same in all that constitutes the objective reality of separate things, and, to do, is not in effect, bring about and produce the composite constituents and make or infer that by reasoning from evidence or from premises, as not to question that by an inference the deriving of a conclusion becomes by reasoning, the answer was obtainable by inference. Even so, an unconscious inference, from other things he believes. What 'S' acquired as a cognitive skill, a disposition to believe of yellow objects he saw that they were yellow. The exercise of this skill does not require, and in no way depends on, or have of any unfolding beliefs thereof: 'S' identificatory success will depend on his operating in certain special conditions, of course. 'S' will not, perhaps, be able to identify yellow objects in dramatically reduced lighting visually, at funny viewing angled, or when afflicted with certain nervous disorders. But these facts about 'S' can see that something is yellow does not show that his perceptual knowledge (that 'a' is yellow) in any way depends on a belief (let alone knowledge) that he is in such special conditions. It merely shows that direct perceptual knowledge is the result of exercising a skill, an identificatory skill, that like any skill, requires certain conditions for its successful exercise. An expert basketball player cannot shoot accurately in a hurricane. He needs normal conditions to do what he has learned to do. So also with individuals who have developed perceptual (cognitive) skills. They needed normal conditions to do what they have learned to do. They need normal conditions too sere, for example, that something is yellow. But they do not, any more than the basketball player, have to know they are in these conditions to do what being in these conditions enables them to do.

This means, of course, that for the direct realist direct perceptual knowledge is fallible and corrigible. Whether 'S' sees that 'a' is 'F' depends on his being caused to believe that 'a' is 'F' in conditions that are appropriate for an exercise of that cognitive skill. If conditions are right, then 'S' sees (hence, knows) that 'a' is 'F'. If they aren't, he doesn't. Whether or not 'S' knows depends, then, not on what else (if anything) 'S' believes, but on the circumstances in which 'S' comes to believe. This being so, this type of direct realist is a form of externalism. Direct perception of objective facts, pure perpetual knowledge of external events, is made possible because what is needed (by way of justification) fort such knowledge has been reduced. Background knowledge ~ is not needed.

This means that the foundation of knowledge is fallible. Nonetheless, though fallible, they are in no way derived, that is, what makes them foundations. Even if they are brittle, as foundations are sometimes, everything else upon them.

Ideally, in theory imagination, a concept of reason that is transcendent but non-empirical as to think os conception of and ideal thought, that potentially or actual exists in the mind as a product exclusive to the mental act. In the philosophy of Plato, an archetype of which a corresponding being in phenomenal reality is an imperfect replica, that also, Hegel's absolute truth, as the conception and ultimate product of reason (the absolute meaning a mental image of something remembered).

Conceivably, in the imagination the formation of a mental image of something that is or should be b perceived as real nor present to the senses. Nevertheless, the image so formed is able to confront and deal with the reality by using the creative powers of the mind. That is characteristically well removed from reality, but all powers of fantasy over reason are a degree of insanity/ still, fancy as they have given a product of the imagination free reins, that is in command of the fantasy while it is exactly the mark of the neurotic that he is possessed by his very own fantasy.

The totality of all things possessing actuality, existence or essence that exists objectively and in fact based on real occurrences that exist or known to have existed, a real occurrence, an event, i.e., had to prove the facts of the case, as something believed to be true or real, determining by evidence or truth as to do. However, the usage in the sense 'allegation of fact', and the reasoning are wrong of the 'facts and facts, as the 'true facts' of the case may never be known'. These usages may occasion qualms' among critics who insist that facts can only be true, but the usages are often useful for emphasis. Therefore, the discovery or determinations of fast or accurate information are related to, or used in the discovery of facts, then the comprising events are determined by evidence or truth is much as ado about their owing actuality. Its opposition forming the literature that treats real people or events as if they were fictional or uses real people or events as essential elements in an otherwise fictional rendition, i.e., of, relating to, produced by, or characterized by internal dissension, as given to or promoting internal dissension. So, then, it is produced artificially than by a natural process, especially the lacking authenticity or genuine factitious values of another than what s or should be.

Primarily, a set of statements or principles devised to explain a group of facts or phenomena, especially one that has been repeatedly tested or is widely accepted and can be used to make predictions about natural phenomena. Having the consistency of explanatory statements, accepted principles, and methods of analysis, finds to a set of theorems that constitute a systematic view of a branch in mathematics or extends upon the paradigms of science, the belief or principle that guides action or assists comprehension or judgements, usually by an ascription based on limited information or knowledge, as a conjecture, tenably to assert the creation from a speculative assumption that bestows to its beginning. Theoretically, of, relating to, or based on theory, i.e., the restriction to theory, not practical theoretical physics, as given to speculative theorizing. Also, the given idea, by reason of which formidable combinations awaiting upon the inception of an idea, demonstrated as true or is assumed to be demonstrated. In mathematics its containment lies of the proposition that has been or is to be proved from explicit assumption and is primarily with theoretical assessments or hypothetical theorizing than practical considerations the measures its quality value.

Looking back a century, one can see a striking degree of homogeneity among the philosophers of the early twentieth century about the topics central to their concerns. More striking still is the apparent obscurity and abstruseness of the concerns, which seem at first glance to be removed from the great debates of previous centuries, between 'realism' and 'idealist', say, of 'rationalists' and 'empiricist'.

Thus, no matter what the current debate or discussion, the central issue is often ne without conceptual and contentual representations, that if one is without concept, is without idea, such that in one foul swoop would ingest the mere truth that lies to the underlying paradoxes of why is there something instead of nothing? Whatever it is that makes, what would otherwise be mere utterances and inscriptions into instruments of communication and understanding. This philosophical problem is to demystify this overflown emptiness, and to relate to what we know of ourselves and the world.

Contributions to this study include the theory of 'speech arts', and the investigation of communicable communications, especially the relationship between words and 'ideas', and words and the 'world'. It is, nonetheless, that which is expressed by an utterance or sentence, the proposition or claim made about the world. By extension, the content of a predicate that any expression that is capable of connecting with one or more singular terms to make a sentence, the expressed condition that the entities referred to may satisfy, in which case the resulting sentence will be true. Consequently a predicate may be thought of as a function from things to sentences or even to truth-values, or other sub-sentential components that contribute to sentences that contain it. The nature of content is the central concern of the philosophy of language.

What some person expresses of a sentence often depends on the environment in which he or she is placed. For example, the disease I refer to by a term like 'arthritis' or the kind of tree I refer to as an 'oak' will be defined by criteria of which I know next to nothing. This raises the possibility of imaging two persons in rather different environments, but in which everything appears the same to each of them. The wide content of their thoughts and saying will be different if the situation surrounding them is appropriately different, 'situation' may here include the actual objects hey perceive, or the chemical or physical kinds of objects in the world they inhabit, or the history of their words, or the decisions of authorities on what counts as an example of one of the terms thy use. The narrow content is that part of their thought that remains identical, through the identity of the way things appear, regardless of these differences of surroundings. Partisans of wide . . . 'as, something called broadly, content may doubt whether any content is in this sense narrow, partisans of narrow content believe that it is the fundamental notion, with wide content being in terms of narrow content plus context.

All and all, supposing that people are characterized by their rationality is common, and the most evident display of our rationality is capable to think. This is the rehearsal in the mind of what to say, or what to do. Not all thinking is verbal, since chess players, composers, and painters all think, and there is no speculative reason that their deliberations should take any more verbal a form than their actions. It is permanently tempting to conceive of this activity in terms of the presence in the mind of elements of some language, or other medium that represents aspects of the world and its surrounding surface structures. But the model has been attacked, notably by Ludwig Wittgenstein (1889-1951), whose influential application of these ideas was in the philosophy of mind. Wittgenstein explores the characterization of which reports of introspection, or sensations, or intentions, or beliefs that actually take into consideration our social lives, in order to undermine the reallocated duality upon which the Cartesian communicational description whose function was to the goings-on in an inner theatre of mind-purposes of which only the subject is the reclusive viewer. Passages that have subsequentially become known as the 'rule following' considerations and the 'private language argument' are among the fundamental topics of modern philosophy of language and mind, although their precise interpretation is endlessly controversial.

Effectively, the hypotheses especially associated with Jerry Fodor (1935-), whom is known for the 'resolute realism', about the nature of mental functioning, that occurs in a language different from one's ordinary native language, but underlying and explaining our competence with it. The idea is a development of the notion of an innate universal grammar (Chomsky), in as such, that we agree that since a computer programs are linguistically complex sets of instructions were the relative executions by which explains of surface behaviour or the adequacy of the computerized programming installations, if it were definably amendable and, advisably corrective, in that most are disconcerting of many that are ultimately a reason for 'us' of thinking intuitively and without the indulgence of retrospective preferences, but an ethical majority in defending of its moral line that is already confronting 'us'. That these programs may or may not improve to conditions that are lastly to enhance of the right sort of an existence forwarded toward a more valuing amount in humanities lesser extensions that embrace one's riff of necessity to humanities' abeyance to expressions in the finer of qualities.

As an explanation of ordinary language-learning and competence, the hypothesis has not found universal favour, as it becomes apparent that only ordinary representational powers that by invoking the image of the learning person's capabilities are whom the abilities for translating are contending of an innate language whose own powers are mysteriously a biological given. Perhaps, the view that everyday attributions of intentionality, beliefs, and meaning to other persons proceed by means of a tactic use of a theory that enables one to construct these interpretations as explanations of their doings. The view is commonly held along with 'functionalism', according to which psychological states are theoretical entities, identified by the network of their causes and effects. The theory-theory has different implications, depending upon which feature of theories is being stressed. Theories may be thought of as capable of formalization, as yielding predictions and explanations, as achieved by a process of theorizing, as answering to empirical evidence that is in principle describable without them, as liable to be overturned by newer and better theories, and so on.

The main problem with seeing our understanding of others as the outcome of a piece of theorizing is the nonexistence of a medium in which this theory can be couched, as the child learns simultaneously the minds of others and the meaning of terms in its native language, is not gained by the tactic use of a 'theory', enabling 'us' to infer what thoughts or intentions explain their actions, but by reliving the situation 'in their shoes' or from their point of view, and by that understanding what they experienced and theory, and therefore expressed. Understanding others is achieved when we can ourselves deliberate as they did, and hear their words as if they are our own. The suggestion is a modern development usually associated in the 'Verstehen' traditions of Dilthey (1833-1911), Weber (1864-1920) and Collingwood (1889-1943).

Any process of drawing a conclusion from a set of premises may be called a process of reasoning. If the conclusion concerns what to do, the process is called practical reasoning, otherwise pure or theoretical reasoning. Evidently, such processes may be good or bad, if they are good, the premises support or even entail the conclusion drawn, and if they are bad, the premises offer no support to the conclusion. Formal logic studies the cases in which conclusions are validly drawn from premises, but little human reasoning is overly of the forms logicians identify. Partly, we are concerned to draw conclusions that 'go beyond' our premises, in the way that conclusions of logically valid arguments do not for the process of using evidence to reach a wider conclusion. However, such anticipatory pessimism about the prospects of conformation theory, denying that we can assess the results of abduction in terms of probability. A process of reasoning in which a conclusion is diagrammatically set from the premises of some usually confined cases in which the conclusions are supposed in following from the premises, i.e., by reason of which an inference is logically valid, in that of deductibility in a logically defined syntactic premise but without there being to any reference to the intended interpretation of its theory. Furthermore, as we reason we make use of an indefinite lore or commonsense set of presuppositions about what it is likely or not a task of an automated reasoning project, which is to mimic this causal use of knowledge of the way of the world in computer programs.

Most 'theories' usually emerge just as a body of (supposed) truths that are not organized, making the theory difficult to survey or study as a whole. The axiomatic method is an idea for organizing a theory, one in which tries to select from among the supposed truths a small number from which all others can be seen to be deductively inferrable. This makes the theory rather more tractable since, in a sense, all truths are contained in those few. In a theory so organized, the few truths from which all others are deductively inferred are called 'axioms'. David Hilbert (1862-1943) had argued that, just as algebraic and differential equations, which we were used to study mathematical and physical processes, could they be made mathematical objects, so axiomatic theories, like algebraic and differential equations, which are means to representing physical processes and mathematical structures could be made objects of mathematical investigation.

By theory, the philosophy of science, is a generalization or set of generalizations purportedly making reference to unobservable entities, e. g., atoms, genes, quarks, unconscious wishes. The ideal gas law, for example, refers only to such observables as pressure, temperature, and volume, the 'molecular-kinetic theory' refers to molecules and their properties, . . . although an older usage suggests the lack of adequate evidence in support thereof ('merely a theory'), current philosophical usage does indeed follow in the tradition (as in Leibniz, 1704), as many philosophers had the conviction that all truths, or all truths about a particular domain, followed from as few than for being many governing principles. These principles were taken to be either metaphically prior or epistemologically prior or both. In the first sense, they we took to be entities of such a nature that what exists s 'caused' by them. When the principles were taken as epistologically prior, that is, as 'axioms', either they were taken to be epistemologically privileged e g., self-evident, not needing to be demonstrated, or again, included 'or', to such that all truths so indeed follow from them (by deductive inferences). Gödel (1984) showed–in the spirit of Hilbert, treating axiomatic theories as themselves mathematical objects that mathematics and even a small part of mathematics, are elementary number theories, could not be axiomatized, that more precisely, any class of axioms which is such that we could effectively decide, of any proposition, whether or not it was in that class, would be too small to capture in of the truths.

The notion of truth occurs with remarkable frequency in our reflections on language, thought and action. We are inclined to suppose, for example, that truth is the proper aim of scientific inquiry, that true beliefs help to achieve our goals, that to understand a sentence is to know which circumstances would make it true, that reliable preservation of truth as one argues of valid reasoning, that moral pronouncements should not be regarded as objectively true, and so on. In order to assess the plausibility of such theses, and in order to refine them and to explain why they hold (if they do), we require some view of what truth is to imply -a theory that would account for its properties and its relations to other matters. Thus, there can be little prospect of understanding our most important faculties in the sentence of a good theory of truth.

Such a thing, however, has been notoriously elusive. The ancient idea that truth is some sort of 'correspondence with reality' has still never been articulated satisfactorily. The nature of the alleged 'correspondence' and the alleged 'reality' remain objectionably obscure. Yet the familiar alternative suggestions -that true beliefs are those that are 'mutually coherent', or 'pragmatically useful', or 'verifiable in suitable conditions'~, have each been confronted with persuasive counterexamples. A twentieth-century departure from these traditional analyses is the view that truth is not a property at all–that the syntactic form of the predicate, 'is true', distorts its real semantic character, which is not to describe propositions but to endorse them. But this radical approach is also faced with difficulties and suggests, somewhat counter intuitively, that truth cannot have the vital theoretical role in semantics, epistemology and elsewhere that we are naturally inclined to give it. Thus, truth threatens to remain one of the most enigmatic of notions: An explicit account of it can appear to be essential yet beyond our reach. However, recent work provides some grounds for optimism.

Moreover, science, unswerving exactly to position of something very well hidden, its nature in so that to make it believed, is quickly and imposes the sensing and responding to the definitive qualities or state of being actual or true, such that as a person, an entity, or an event, that it actually might be gainfully to employ of all things possessing actuality, existence, or essence. In other words, in that which objectively and in fact do seem as to be about reality, in fact, actually to the satisfying factions of instinctual needs through awareness of and adjustment to environmental demands. Thus, the act of realizing or the condition of being realized is first, and utmost the resulting infraction of realizing.

Nonetheless, a declaration made to explain or justify action, or its believing desire upon which it is to act, by which the conviction underlying fact or cause, that provide logical sense for a premise or occurrence for logical, rational. Analytic mental stars have long lost in reason. Yet, the premise usually the minor premises, of an argument, use the faculty of reason that arises to engage in conversation or discussion. To determining or conclude by logical thinking out a solution to the problem, would therefore persuade or dissuade someone with reason that posits of itself with the good sense or justification of reasonability. In which, good causes are simply justifiably to be considered as to think. By which humans seek or attain knowledge or truth. Mere reason is insufficient to convince 'us' of its veracity. Still, intuitively is perceptively welcomed by comprehension, as the truth or fact, without the use of the rational process, as one comes to assessing someone's character, it sublimely configures one consideration, and often with resulting comprehensions, in which it is assessing situations or circumstances and draw sound conclusions into the reign of judgement.

Governing by or being according to reason or sound thinking, in that a reasonable solution to the problem, may as well, in being without bounds of common sense and arriving to a measure and fair use of reason, especially to form conclusions, inferences or judgements. In that, all manifestations of a confronting argument within the usage of thinking or thought out response to issuing the furthering argumentation to fit or join in the sum parts that are composite to the intellectual faculties, by which case human understanding or the attemptive grasp to its thought, are the resulting liberty encroaching men of zeal, well meaningly, but without understanding.

Being or occurring in fact or actually, as having verifiable existence. Real objects, a real illness. . . .'Really true and actual and not imaginary, alleged, or ideal, as people and not ghosts, fro which are we to find on practical matters and concerns of experiencing the real world. The surrounding surfaces, might we, as, perhaps attest to this for the first time. Being no less than what they state, we have not taken its free pretence, or affections for a real experience highly, as many may encounter real trouble. This, nonetheless, projects of an existing objectivity in which the world despite subjectivity or conventions of thought or language is or have valuing representation, reckoned by actual power, in that of relating to, or being an image formed by light or another identifiable simulation, that converge in space, the stationary or fixed properties, such as a thing or whole having actual existence. All of which, are accorded a truly factual experience into which the actual attestations have brought to you by the afforded efforts of our very own imaginations.

Ideally, in theory imagination, a concept of reason that is transcendent but non-empirical as to think os conception of and ideal thought, that potentially or actual exists in the mind as a product exclusive to the mental act. In the philosophy of Plato, an archetype of which a corresponding being in phenomenal reality is an imperfect replica, that also, Hegel's absolute truth, as the conception and ultimate product of reason (the absolute meaning a mental image of something remembered).

Conceivably, in the imagination the formation of a mental image of something that is or should be b perceived as real nor present to the senses. Nevertheless, the image so formed can confront and deal with the reality by using the creative powers of the mind. That is characteristically well removed from reality, but all powers of fantasy over reason are a degree of insanity/still, fancy as they have given a product of the imagination free reins, that is in command of the fantasy while it is exactly the mark of the neurotic that his very own fantasy possesses him.

The totality of all things possessing actuality, existence or essence that exists objectively and in fact based on real occurrences that exist or known to have existed, a real occurrence, an event, i.e., had to prove the facts of the case, as something believed to be true or real, determining by evidence or truth as to do. However, the usage in the sense 'allegation of fact', and the reasoning are wrong of the 'facts' and 'substantive facts', as we may never know the 'facts' of the case'. These usages may occasion qualms' among critics who insist that facts can only be true, but the usages are often useful for emphasis. Therefore, we have related to, or used the discovery or determinations of fast or accurate information in the discovery of facts, then evidence has determined the comprising events or truth is much as ado about their owing actuality. Its opposition forming the literature that treats real people or events as if they were fictional or uses real people or events as essential elements in an otherwise fictional rendition, i.e., of relating to, produced by, or characterized by internal dissension, as given to or promoting internal dissension. So, then, it is produced artificially than by a natural process, especially the lacking authenticity or genuine factitious values of another than what s or should be.

A set-classification of statements or principles devised to explain a group of facts or phenomena, especially one that has been repeatedly tested or is widely accepted and can be used to make predictions about natural phenomena. Having the consistency of explanatory statements, accepted principles, and methods of analysis, finds to a set of theorems that form a systematic view of a branch in mathematics or extends upon the paradigms of science, the belief or principle that guides action or assists comprehension or judgements, usually by an ascription based on limited information or knowledge, as a conjecture, tenably to assert the creation from a speculative assumption that bestows to its beginning. Theoretically, of, relating to, or based on conjecture, its philosophy is such to accord, i.e., the restriction in theory, not practical theoretical physics, as given to speculative theorizing. Also, the given idea, by reason of which formidable combinations awaiting upon the inception of an idea, demonstrated as true or is assumed to be shown. In mathematics its containment lies of the proposition that has been or is to be proved from explicit assumption and is primarily with theoretical assessments or hypothetical theorizing than practical considerations the measures its quality value.

Looking back a century, one can see a striking degree of homogeneity among the philosophers of the early twentieth century about the topics central to their concerns. More inertly there is more in the apparent obscurity and abstruseness of the concerns, which seem at first glance to be removed from the great debates of previous centuries, between 'realism' and 'idealist', say, of 'rationalists' and 'empiricist'.

Thus, no matter what the current debate or discussion, the central issue is often ne without conceptual and/or contentual representations, that if one is without concept, is without idea, such that in one foul swoop would ingest the mere truth that lies to the underlying paradoxes of why is there something instead of nothing? Whatever it is that makes, what would otherwise be mere utterances and inscriptions into instruments of communication and understanding. This philosophical problem is to demystify this overblowing emptiness, and to relate to what we know of ourselves and the world.

Contributions to this study include the theory of 'speech arts', and the investigation of communicable communications, especially the relationship between words and 'ideas', and words and the 'world'. It is, nonetheless, that which and utterance or sentence expresses, the proposition or claim made about the world. By extension, the content of a predicate that any expression that is capable of connecting with one or more singular terms to make a sentence, the expressed condition that the entities referred to may satisfy, in which case the resulting sentence will be true. Consequently we may think of a predicate as a function from things to sentences or even to truth-values, or other sub-sentential components that contribute to sentences that contain it. The nature of content is the central concern of the philosophy of language.

What some person expresses of a sentence often depends on the environment in which he or she is placed. This raises the possibility of imaging two persons in comparatively different environments, but in which everything appears the same to each of them. The wide content of their thoughts and saying will be different if the situation surrounding them is appropriately different, 'situation' may here include the actual objects hey perceive, or the chemical or physical kinds of objects in the world they inhabit, or the history of their words, or the decisions of authorities on what counts as an example of some terms thy use. The narrow content is that part of their thought that remains identical, through the identity of the way things appear, no matter these differences of surroundings. Partisans of wide . . . 'as, something called broadly, content may doubt whether any content is in this sense narrow, partisans of narrow content believe that it is the fundamental notion, with wide content being of narrow content plus context.

All and all, assuming their rationality has characterized people is common, and the most evident display of our rationality is capable to think. This is the rehearsal in the mind of what to say, or what to do. Not all thinking is verbal, since chess players, composers, and painters all think, and there is no deductive reason that their deliberations should take any more verbal a form than their actions. It is permanently tempting to conceive of this activity in terms of the presence in the mind of elements of some language, or other medium that represents aspects of the world and its surrounding surface structures. Nevertheless, they have attacked the model, notably by Ludwig Wittgenstein (1889-1951), whose influential application of these ideas was in the philosophy of mind. Wittgenstein explores the role that report of introspection, or sensations, or intentions, or beliefs actually play our social lives, to undermine the Cartesian 'ego, functions to describe the goings-on in an inner theatre of which the subject is the lone spectator. Passages that have subsequentially become known as the 'rule following' considerations and the 'private language argument' are among the fundamental topics of modern philosophy of language and mind, although their precise interpretation is endlessly controversial.

Effectively, the hypotheses especially associated with Jerry Fodor (1935-), whom is known for the 'resolute realism', about the nature of mental functioning, that occurs in a language different from one's ordinary native language, but underlying and explaining our competence with it. The idea is a development of the notion of an innate universal grammar (Chomsky), in as such, that we agree that since a computer programs are linguistically complex sets of instructions were the relative executions by which explains of surface behaviour or the adequacy of the computerized programming installations, if it were definably amendable and, advisably corrective, in that most are disconcerting of many that are ultimately a reason for 'us' of thinking intuitively and without the indulgence of retrospective preferences, but an ethical majority in defending of its moral line that is already confronting 'us'. That these programs may or may not improve to conditions that are lastly to enhance of the right sort of an existence forwarded toward a more valuing amount in humanities lesser extensions that embrace one's riff of necessity to humanities' abeyance to expressions in the finer of qualities.

As an explanation of ordinary language-learning and competence, the hypothesis has not found universal favour, as only ordinary representational powers that by invoking the image of the learning person's capabilities are apparently whom the abilities for translating are contending of an innate language whose own powers are mysteriously a biological given. Perhaps, the view that everyday attributions of intentionality, beliefs, and meaning to other persons proceed by means of a tactic use of a theory that enables one to construct these interpretative explanations of their doing. We have commonly held the view along with 'functionalism', according to which psychological states are theoretical entities, identified by the network of their causes and effects. The theory-theory has different implications, depending upon which feature of theories is being stressed. We may think of theories as capable of formalization, as yielding predictions and explanations, as achieved by a process of theorizing, as answering to empirical evidence that is in principle describable without them, as liable to be overturned by newer and better theories, and so on.

At present, the duly held exemplifications are accorded too inside and outside the study for which is concerned in the finding explanations of things, it would be desirable to have a concept of what counts as a good explanation, and what distinguishes good from bad. Under the influence of logical positivism approaches to the structure of science, it was felt that the criterion ought to be found in as a definite logical relationship between the explanans (that which does the explaining) and the explanandum (that which is to be explained). This approach culminated in the covering law model of explanation, or the view that an event is explained when it is subsumed under a law of nature, that is, its occurrence is deducible from the law plus a set or covering law, in the way that Kepler's laws of planetary motion are deducible from Newton's laws of motion. The covering law model may be adapted to include explanation by showing that something is probable, given a statistical law. Questions for the covering laws are necessary to explanation (we explain everyday events without overtly citing laws): Querying whether they are sufficient (it may not explain an event just to say that it is an example): And querying whether a purely logical relationship is adapted to capturing the requirements, we make of explanations. These may include, for instance, that we have a 'feel' for what is happening, or that the explanation proceeds in terms of things that are familiar to us or unsurprising or that we can give a model of what is going on, and none of these notions is captured in a purely logical approach. Recent work, therefore, has tended to stress the contextual and pragmatic elements in requirements for explanation, so that what counts as a good explanation given one set of concerns may not do so given another.

The argument to the best explanation is the view that once we can select the best of any that of something explanations of an event, then we are justified in accepting it, or even believing sometimes it is unwise to ignore the antecedent improbability of a hypothesis which would explain the data better than others: e.g., the best explanation of a coin falling heads 530 times in 1,000 tosses might be that it is biassed to funk the probability of heads of 0.53, but it might be sensible to suppose that it is fair, or to suspend judgement

In everyday life we encounter many types of explanation, which appear not to raise philosophical difficulties, in addition to those already made of mention. Prior to takeoff a flight attendant explains how to use the safety equipment on the aeroplane. In a museum the guide explains the significance of a famous painting. A mathematics teacher explains a geometrical proof to a bewildered student. A newspaper story explains how a prisoner escaped. Additional examples come easily to mind. The main point is to remember the great variety of contexts in which explanations are sought and given.

Since, at least, the times of Aristotle philosophers have emphasized the importance of explanation knowledge. In simple terms, we want to know not only what is the case but also why it is. This consideration suggests that we define an explanation as an answer to a why-question. Such a definition would, however, be too broad, because some why-questions are requests for consolation (Why did my son have to die?) Or moral justification (Why should women not be paid the same as men for the same work?). it would also be too narrow because some explanations are responses to how-questions (How doe s radar work?) Or how-possibly-questions (How is it possible for cats always to land on their feet?)

In a more general sense, 'to explain' means to make clear, to make plain, or to provide understanding. Definitions of this sort are philosophically unserved, for he terms used in the definition is no less problematic than the term to be defined. Moreover, since a wide variety of things require explanation, and are of many different types of explanation exist, a more complex explication is required. The term 'explanandum' is used to refer to that lich is to be explained: The tern 'explanans' refer to that which does the emplaning. The explanans and explanandum taken together constitute the explanation.

One common type of explanation occurs when deliberate human actions are explained in terms of conscious purposes. 'Why did you go to the pharmacy yesterday?' 'Because I had a headache and needed to get some aspirin'. It is tacitly assumed that aspirin is an appropriate medication for headaches and that going to the pharmacy would be an efficient way of getting some. Since explanations ae, of course, teleological, referring as they do, to goals. The explanans, is not beyond the reach of the average intelligence, its experience is to meet in direct confrontation (as through participation or observation), as in a state of mental reorientation. Its gainful employment of realization is to arrive at some future goal, point or end - If the pharmacy happened to be closed for restocking of selves, the aspirin would not have been obtained there, but this would not invalidate the explanation. Some philosophers would say that the antecedent desire to achieve the end is what does the explaining: Others might say that the explaining is done by the nature of the goal and the fact that the action promoted the chances of realizing it (e.g., Taylor, 1964). All the same, it should not be automatically assuming that such explanations are causal. Philosophers differ considerably on whether these explanations are to be framed in terms of cause or reasons, least of mention, that the distinction cannot be used to show that the relation between reasons and the actions they justify is in no way causal, precisely parallel points hold in the epistemic domain, and for all prepositional attitudes, since they all similarly admit of justification, and explanation, by reason. Such that if I suppose my reason for believing that you received my letter today is that I sent it by express yesterday. My reason, strictly speaking, is that I sent it by express yesterday: My reason state is my believing this. Arguably, my reason which it is my reason, and my reason-state-my evidence belief-both explains and justifies my belief that you received the letter if, the fact, that I sent the letter by express yesterday, but this statement express my believing that evidence preposition, and that if I do not believe in then my belief that you received the letter is not justified, it is not justified by the mere truth of the proposition and can be justified even if that preposition is false.

Nonetheless, if reason states can motivate, least of mention, why (apart from confusing them with reasons proper) deny that they are causes? For one thing, they are not events, at least in the usual sense entailing change; they are dispositional states (this contrasts them with concurrences, but does not imply that they admit of dispositional analysis). It has also seemed to those which deny that reasons are causes that the former justifies as well as explain the actions for which they are reasons, whereas the role of causes is at most to explain. Another claim is that the relation between reasons, and here reason states are often cited explicitly and the actions they explain are non-contingent. The 'logical connection argument' proceeds from this claim to the conclusion that reasons are not causes.

All the same, there are many agreeing and/or disagreeing analytic overtures that such concepts as intention and agency. Expanding the domain beyond consciousness, Freud maintained, that a great deal of human behaviours can be explained in terms of unconscious wishes. These Freudian explanations should probably be construed as basically causal.

Problems arise when teleological explanations are offered in other contexts. The behaviour of nonhuman animals is often explained in terms of purpose, e.g., the mouse ran to escape from the cat. In such cases the existence of conscious purposes seems dubious. The situation is still more problematic when super-empirical purposes invoked, e.g., the explanation of living species, in terms of God's purpose, or the vitalistic explanation of biological phenomena in terms of an entelechy or vital principle. In recent years an 'anthropic principle' has received attention in cosmology. All such explanations have been condemned by many philosophers as anthropomorphic.

The abstaining objection is nonetheless, that philosophers and scientists often maintain that functional explanations play an important and legitimate role in various sciences such as evolutionary biology, anthropology and sociology. For example, in the case of the peppered moth in Liverpool, the change in colour from the light phase to the dark phase and back again to the light phase provided adaptions to a changing environment and fulfilled the function of reducing predation on the species. In the study of primitive societies anthropologists have maintained that various rituals, e.g., a rain dance, which may be inefficacious in bringing about their manifest goals, e.g., producing rain, actually fulfil the latent function of increasing social cohesion at a period of stress, e.g., during a drought. Philosophers who admit teleology and/or functional explanations in common sense and science often take pains to argue that such explanations can be analysed entirely in terms of efficient causes, thereby escaping the charge of anthropomorphism (Wright, 1976), again, however, not all philosophers agree.

Mainly to avoid the incursion of unwanted theology, metaphysics, or anthropomorphism into science, many philosophers and scientists-especially during the first half of the twentieth century -held that science provides no desecrations and predictions of natural phenomena, but not explanation. Beginning in or around the 1930s, however, a series of influential philosophers of science -including Karl Pooper (1935) Carl Hempel and Paul Oppenheim (1948) and Hempel (1965) -maintained that empirical science can explain natural phenomena without appealing to metaphysics or theology. It appears that this view is now accepted by the vast majority of philosophers of science, though there is sharp disagreement on the nature of scientific explanation.

The eschewing approach, developed by Hempel, Popper and others, became virtually a 'received view' in the 1960s and 1970s. According to this view, to give a scientific explanation of any natural phenomenon is to show how this phenomenon can be subsumed under a law of nature. A particular rupture in the water pipe can be explained by citing the universal law that water expands when it freezes and in the pipe dropped below the freezing pint. General laws, as well as particular facts, can be explained by subsumption. The law of conservation of linear momentum an be explained by derivation from Newton's second and third laws of motion. Each of these explanations is a deductive argument: The premises constitute the explanans and the conclusion is the explanandum. The explanans contain one or more statements of universal laws and, in many instances, strewments describing initial conditions. This pattern of explanation is known as the deductive-nomological model. Any such argument shows that the explanandum had to occur given the explanans.

Many, though not all, adherents of the received view for explanation by subsumptions under statistical laws. Hempel (1965) offers as an example the case of a ma who recovered quickly from a streptococcus infection as a result of treatment with penicillin. Although not all strep infections clear up quickly under this treatment, the probability of recovery in such cases is high, and this id sufficient for legitimate explanation according to Hempel. This example conforms to the inductive-statistical model. Such explanations are viewed as arguments, but they are inductive than deductive. In these cases the explanans confer inductive probability on the explanandum. An explanation of a particular fact satisfying either the deductive-nomological and inductive-statistical model is an argument to the effect that the fact in question was to be expected by virtue of the explanans.

The received view has been subjected to strenuous criticism by adherents of the causal/ mechanical approach to scientific explanation (Salmon, 1990). Many objections to the received view were engendered by the absence of causal constraints due largely to worries about Hume's critique on the deductive-nomological and inductive-statistical models. Beginning in the late 1950s, Michael Scriven advanced serious counterexamples to Hempel's models: He was followed in the 1960s by Wesley Salmo and in the 1970s by Peter Railton. Overall, this view, one explains phenomena by identifying causes (a death is explained as resulting from a massive cerebral haemorrhage) or by exposing underlying mechanisms (the behaviour of a gas is explained in terms of the motions of constituent molecules).

A unification approach to explanation has been developed by Michael Friedman and Philip Kitcher (1989). The basic idea is that we understand our world more adequately to the extent that we can reduce the number of independent assumptions we must introduce to account for what goes on in it. Accordingly, we understand phenomena to the degree that we can fit them into a general world picture or Philosophy. In order to serve in scientific explanations, the world picture must be scientifically well founded.

In contrast to the above-mentioned views -which such factors as logical relations, laws of nature, and causality a number of philosophers (e.g., Achinstein, 1983: van Fraassen, 1980) have urged that explanation, and not just scientific explanation, can be analysed entirely in pragmatic terms.

During the past half-century much philosophical attention has been focussed on explanation in science and in history. Considerable controversy has surrounded the question of whether historical explanation must be scientific, or whether history requires explanations of different types. Many diverse views have been articulated: The forerunning survey does not exhaust the variety.

Historical knowledge is often compared to scientific knowledge, as scientific knowledge is regarded as knowledge of the laws and regulative of nature which operate throughout past, preset, and future. Some thinkers, e.g., the German historian Ranke, have argued that historical knowledge should be 'scientific' in the sense of being based on research, on scrupulous verification of facts as far as possible, with an objective account being the principal aim. Others have gone further, asserting that historical inquiry and scientific inquiry have the same goal, namely providing explanations of particular events by discovering general laws from which (together with initial conditions) the particular events can be inferred. This is often called "The e Covering Law Theory" of historical explanation. Proponents of this view usually admit a difference in direction of interest between the two types of inquiry: Historians are more interested in explaining particular events, while scientists are more interested in discovering general laws. But the logic of explanation is stated to be the same for both.

Yet a cursory glance at the articles and books that historians produce does not support this view. Those books and articles focus overwhelmingly on the particular, e.g., the particular social structure of Tudor England, the rise to power of a particular political party, the social, cultural and economic interactions between two particular peoples. Nor is some standard body of theory or set of explanatory principles cited in the footnotes of history texts as providing the fundamental materials of historical explanation. In view of this, other thinkers have proposed that narrative itself, apart from general laws, can produce understanding, and that this is the characteristic form of historical explanation (Dray, 1957). If we wonder why things are the way they are -, and, analogously, why they were the way they were-we are often satisfied by being told a story about how they got that way.

What we seek in historical inquiry is an understanding that respects the agreed-upon facts, as a chronicle can present a factually correct account of a historical event without making that account in the event of some intelligibility to us -for example, without showing us why that event occurred and how the various phases and aspects of the event are related to one another. Historical narrative aims to provide intelligibly by showing how one thing led to another even when there is no relation of causal determination between them. In this way, narrative provides a form of understanding especially suited to a temporal course of events and alternative too scientific, or law-like, explanation.

Another approach is understanding through knowledge of the purposes, intentions and points of view of historical agents. If we knew how Julius Caesar or Leon Trotsky was to look and understood their times and knew what they meant to accomplish, then we can better understand why they did what they did. Purposes, intentions, and points of view are varieties of thought and can be ascertained through acts of empathy by the historian. R.G. Collingood (1946) goes further and argues that those very same past thought can be re-enacted, and thereby made present by the historian. Historical explanation of this type cannot be reduced to the covering law model and allow historical inquiry to achieve a different type of intelligibility.

Yet, turning the stone over, we are in finding the main problem with seeing our understanding of others as the outcome of a piece of theorizing is the nonexistence of a medium in which we can couch this theory, as the child learns simultaneously the minds of others and the meaning of terms in its native language, is not gained by the tactic use of a 'theory', enabling 'us' to imply what thoughts or intentions explain their actions, but by realizing the situation 'in their shoes' or from their point of view, and by that understanding what they experienced and theory, and therefore expressed. We achieve understanding others when we can ourselves deliberate as they did, and hear their words as if they are our own. The suggestion is a modern development usually associated in the 'Verstehen' traditions of Dilthey (1833-1911), Weber (1864-1920) and Collingwood (1889-1943).

We may call any process of drawing a conclusion from a set of premises a process of reasoning. If the conclusion concerns what to do, the process is called practical reasoning, otherwise pure or theoretical reasoning. Evidently, such processes may be good or bad, if they are good, the premises support or even entail the conclusion drawn, and if they are bad, the premises offer no support to the conclusion. Formal logic studies the cases in which conclusions are validly drawn from premises, but little human reasoning is overly of the forms logicians identify. Partly, we are concerned to draw conclusions that 'go beyond' our premises, in the way that conclusions of logically valid arguments do not for the process of using evidence to reach a wider conclusion. However, such anticipatory pessimism about the prospects of conformation theory, denying that we can assess the results of abduction in terms of probability.

This makes the theory moderately tractable since, in a sense, we have contained all truths in those few. In a theory so organized, we have called the few truths from which we have deductively inferred all others 'axioms'. David Hilbert (1862-1943) had argued that, just as algebraic and differential equations, which we were used to study mathematical and physical processes, could they be made mathematical objects, so axiomatic theories, like algebraic and differential equations, which are means to representing physical processes and mathematical structures could be investigation.

According to theory, the philosophy of science, is a generalization or set referring to unobservable entities, e.g., atoms, genes, quarks, unconscious wishes. The ideal gas law, for example, refers only to such observables as pressure, temperature, and volume, the 'molecular-kinetic theory' refers to molecules and their properties, . . . although an older usage suggests the lack of adequate evidence in support of it ('merely a theory'), current philosophical usage does indeed follow in the tradition (as in Leibniz, 1704), as many philosophers had the conviction that all truths, or all were truths about a particular domain were followed from as few than for being many governing. As many governing principles, were of followed from these principles and were taken to be either metaphysically prior or epistemologically prior or both. In the first sense, they we took to be entities of such a nature that what exists s 'caused' by them. When we took the principles as epistemologically prior, that is, as 'axioms', we took them to be either epistemologically privileged, e.g., self evident, and not needing to be demonstrated, or again, included 'or', to such that all truths so indeed follow from them (by deductive inferences). Gödel (1984) showed in the spirit of Hilbert, treating axiomatic theories as themselves mathematical objects that mathematics, and even a small part of mathematics, elementary number theory, could not be axiomatized, that more precisely, any class of axioms that is such that we could effectively decide, of any proposition, whether or not it was in that class, would be too small to capture in of the truths.

The notion of truth occurs with remarkable frequency in our reflections on language, thought and action. We are inclined to suppose, for example, that truth is the proper aim of scientific inquiry, that true beliefs help to achieve our goals, that to understand a sentence is to know which circumstances would make it true, that reliable preservation of truth as one argues of valid reasoning, that moral pronouncements should not be regarded as objectively true, and so on. To assess the plausibility of such theses, and to refine them and to explain why they hold (if they do), we require some view of what truth be a theory that would account for its properties and its relations to other matters. Thus, there can be little prospect of understanding our most important faculties in the sentence of a good theory of truth.

Such a thing, however, has been notoriously elusive. The ancient idea that truth is some sort of 'correspondence with reality' has still never been articulated satisfactorily, and the nature of the alleged 'correspondence' and the alleged 'reality' remain objectionably obscure. Yet the familiar alternative suggestions that true beliefs are those that are 'mutually coherent', or 'pragmatically useful', or 'verifiable in suitable conditions' has each been confronted with persuasive counterexamples. A twentieth-century departure from these traditional analyses is the view that truth is not a property at all that the syntactic form of the predicate, 'is true', distorts its really semantic character, which is not to describe propositions but to endorse them. However, this radical approach is also faced with difficulties and suggests, quasi counter intuitively, that truth cannot have the vital theoretical role in semantics, epistemology and elsewhere that we are naturally inclined to give it. Thus, truth threatens to remain one of the most enigmatic of notions: An explicit account of it can seem essential yet beyond our reach. However, recent work provides some grounds for optimism.

We have based a theory in philosophy of science, is a generalization or set-classification by referring to observable entities, i.e., atoms, quarks, unconscious wishes, and so on. The ideal gas law, for example, refers only to such observables as pressure, temperature, and volume, the molecular-kinetic theory refers top molecules and their properties, although an older usage suggests the lack of adequate evidence in support of it ('merely a theory'), progressive toward it's astute; The usage does not carry that connotation. Einstein's special; Theory of relativity, for example, is considered extremely well founded.

These are two main views on the nature of theories. According to the 'received view' theories are partially interpreted axiomatic systems, according to the semantic view, a theory is a collection of models (Suppe, 1974). Under which, some theories usually emerge, as a body of [supposed] truths that are not neatly organized, making the theory difficult to survey or study as a whole. The axiomatic method is an ideal for organizing a theory (Hilbert, 1970), one tries to select from among the supposed truths a small number from which all the others can be seen to be deductively inferrable. This makes the theory more tractable since, in a sense, they contain all truth's in those few. In a theory so organized, they call the few truths from which they deductively infer all others 'axioms'. David Hilbert (1862-1943) had argued that, just as algebraic and differential equations, which were used to study mathematical and physical processes, could in themselves be made mathematical objects, so we could make axiomatic theories, like algebraic and differential equations, which are means of representing physical processes and mathematical structures, objects of mathematical investigation.

Many philosophers, took upon the conviction that all truths, or all truths about a particular domain, followed from a few principles. These principles were taken to be either metaphysically prior or epistemologically prior or both. In the first sense, we took them to be entities of such a nature that what exists is 'caused' by them. When we took the principles as epistemologically prior, that is, as 'axioms', we took them to be either epistemologically privileged, i.e., self-evident, not needing to be demonstrated, or again, inclusive 'or', to be such that all truths do indeed follow from them (by deductive inferences). Gödel (1984) showed in the spirit of Hilbert, treating axiomatic theories as themselves mathematical objects that mathematics, and even a small part. Of mathematics, elementary number theory, could not be axiomatized, that, more precisely, any class of axioms that is such that we could effectively decide, of any proposition, whether or not it was in that class, would be too small to capture all of the truths.

The notion of truth occurs with remarkable frequency in our reflections on language, thought, and action. We are inclined to suppose, for example, that truth is the proper aim of scientific inquiry, that true beliefs help 'us' to achieve our goals, tat to understand a sentence is to know which circumstances would make it true, that reliable preservation of truth as one argues from premises to a conclusion is the mark of valid reasoning, that we should not regard moral pronouncements as objectively true, and so on. To assess the plausible of such theses, and to refine them and to explain why they hold (if they do), we require some view of what truth be a theory that would account for its properties and its relations to other matters. Thus, there can be little prospect of understanding our most important faculties in the absence of a good theory of truth.

Such a thing, however, has been notoriously elusive. The ancient idea that truth is some sort of 'correspondence with reality' has still never been articulated satisfactorily: The nature of the alleged 'correspondence' and te alleged 'reality remains objectivably obscure. Yet, the familiar alternative suggests ~. That true beliefs are those that are 'mutually coherent', or 'pragmatically useful', or that 'they each were confronted in some verifiable and under suitable conditions with which were persuasive counterexamples. A twentieth-century departure from these traditional analyses is the view that truth is not a property at all ~. That the syntactic form of the predicate, 'is true', distorts its really semantic character, which is not to describe propositions but to endorse them. Nevertheless, they have also faced this radical approach with difficulties and suggest, a counter intuitively, that truth cannot have the vital theoretical role in semantics, epistemology and elsewhere that we are naturally inclined to give it. Thus, truth threatens to remain one of the most enigmatic of notions, an explicit account of it can appear to be essential yet, beyond our reach. However, recent work provides some grounds for optimism.

The belief that snow is white owes its truth to a certain feature of the external world, namely, to the fact that snow is white. Similarly, the belief that is true because of the fact that dogs bark. This trivial observation leads to what is perhaps the most natural and popular account of truth, the 'correspondence theory', according to which a belief (statement, a sentence, propositions, etc.) as true just in case there exists a fact corresponding to it (Wittgenstein, 1922, Austin 1950). This thesis is unexceptionable in itself. However, if it is to provide a rigorous, substantial and complete theory of truth, if it is to be more than merely a picturesque way of asserting all equivalences to the form: The belief that 'p' is 'true p'

Then, again, we must supplement it with accounts of what facts are, and what it is for a belief to correspond to a fact, and these are the problems on which the correspondence theory of truth has foundered. For one thing, it is far form clear that reducing 'the belief achieves any significant gain in understanding that snow is white is true' to 'the facts that snow is white exists': For these expressions seem equally resistant to analysis and too close in meaning for one to provide an illuminating account of the other. In addition, the general relationship that holds in particular between the belief that snow is white and the fact that snow is white, between the belief that dogs bark and the fact that dogs bark, and so on, is very hard to identify. The best attempt to date is Wittgenstein's (1922) so-called 'picture theory', under which an elementary proposition is a configuration of terms, with whatever stare of affairs it reported, as an atomic fact is a configuration of simple objects, an atomic fact corresponds to an elementary proposition (and makes it true) when their configurations are identical and when the terms in the proposition for it to the similarly-placed objects in the fact, and the truth value of each complex proposition the truth values of the elementary ones have entailed. However, eve if this account is correct as far as it goes, it would need to be completed with plausible theories of 'logical configuration', 'elementary proposition', 'reference' and 'entailment', none of which is easy to come by way of the central characteristic of truth. One that any adequate theory must explain is that when a proposition satisfies its 'conditions of proof or verification', then it is regarded as true. To the extent that the property of corresponding with reality is mysterious, we are going to find it impossible to see what we take to verify a proposition should indicate the possession of that property. Therefore, a tempting alternative to the correspondence theory an alternative that eschews obscure, metaphysical concept and which explains quite straightforwardly why Verifiability implies truth is simply to identify truth with Verifiability (Peirce, 1932). This idea can take on variously formed. One version involves the further assumption that verification is 'holistic', i.e., that a belief is justified (i.e., verifiable) when it is part of an entire system of beliefs that are consistent and 'harmonious' (Bradley, 1914 and Hempel, 1935). We have known this as the 'coherence theory of truth'. Another version involves the assumption that is associated with each proposition, some specific procedure for finding out whether one should believe it or not. On this account, to say that a proposition is true is to sa that the appropriate procedure would verify (Dummett, 1979. and Putnam, 1981). In the context of mathematics this amounts to the identification of truth with provability.

The attractions of the verificationist account of truth are that it is refreshingly clear compared with the correspondence theory, and that it succeeds in connecting truth with verification. The trouble is that the bond it postulates between these notions is implausibly strong. We do indeed take verification to indicate truth, but also we recognize the possibility that a proposition may be false in spite of there being impeccable reasons to believe it, and that a proposition may be true even though we are not able to discover that it is. Verifiability and ruth are no doubt highly correlated, but surely not the same thing.

A third well-known account of truth is known as 'pragmatism' (James, 1909 and Papineau, 1987). As we have just seen, the verificationist selects a prominent property of truth and considers it to be the essence of truth. Similarly, the pragmatist focuses on another important characteristic namely, that true belief is a good basis for action and takes this to be the very nature of truth. We have said that true assumptions were, by definition, those that provoke actions with desirable results. Again, we have an account with a single attractive explanatory feature, but again, it postulates between truth and its alleged analysand in this case, utility is implausibly close. Granted, true belief tends to foster success, but it happens regularly that actions based on true beliefs lead to disaster, while false assumptions, by pure chance, produce wonderful results.

One of the few uncontroversial facts about truth is that the proposition that snow is white if and only if snow is white, the proposition that lying is wrong is true if and only if lying is wrong, and so on. Traditional theories acknowledge this fact but regard it as insufficient and, as we have seen, inflate it with some further principle of the form, 'x is true' if and only if 'x' has property 'P' (such as corresponding to reality, Verifiability, or being suitable as a basis for action), which is supposed to specify what truth is. Some radical alternatives to the traditional theories result from denying the need for any such further specification (Ramsey, 1927, Strawson, 1950 and Quine, 1990). For example, ne might suppose that the basic theory of truth contains nothing more that equivalences of the form, The proposition that 'p' is true if and only if 'p' (Horwich, 1990).

Not all variants of deflationism have this virtue, according to the redundancy performative theory of truth, the pairs of a sentence as, the propositions that, 'p' is true, and plain 'p's', have the same meaning and express the same statement as each one has of the other, so it is a syntactic illusion to think that p is true' attributes any sort of property to a proposition (Ramsey, 1927 and Strawson, 1950). Yet in that case, it becomes hard to explain why we are entitled to infer 'The proposition that quantum mechanics are wrong is true' form 'Einstein's claim is the proposition that quantum mechanics are wrong. 'Einstein's claim is true'. For if truth is not property, then we can no longer account for the inference by invoking the law that if 'x', appears identical with 'Y' then any property of 'x' is a property of 'Y', and vice versa. Thus the redundancy/performative theory, by identifying rather than merely correlating the contents of 'The proposition that p is true' and 'p, precludes the prospect of a good explanation of one on truth's most significant and useful characteristics. So restricting our claim to the weak may be of a better, equivalence schema: The proposition that 'p is true is and is only p'.

Support for deflationism depends upon the possibility of showing that its axiom instances of the equivalence schema unsupplements by any further analysis, will suffice to explain all the central facts about truth, for example, that the verification of a proposition indicates its truth, and that true beliefs have a practical value. The first of these facts follows trivially from the deflationary axioms, as given in our knowledge of the equivalence of 'p' and 'The propositions that 'p is true', any reason to believe that 'p' becomes an equally good reason to believe that the preposition that 'p' is true. We can also explain the second fact in terms of the deflationary axioms, but not quite so easily to begin with.

So valuing the truth of beliefs of that form is quite treasonable. Nevertheless, inference derives such beliefs from other beliefs and can be expected to be true if those other beliefs are true. So valuing the truth of any belief that might be used in such an inference is reasonable.

To him extent that they can give such deflationary accounts of all the acts involving truth, then the collection will meet the explanatory demands on a theory of truth of all statements like, The proposition that snow is white is true if and only if 'snow is white', and we will undermine the sense that we need some deep analysis of truth.

Nonetheless, there are several strongly felt objections to deflationism. One reason for dissatisfaction is that the theory has an infinite number of axioms, and therefore cannot be completely written down. It can be described, as the theory whose axioms are the propositions of the form 'p' if and only if it is true that 'p', but not explicitly formulated. This alleged defect has led some philosophers to develop theories that show, first, how the truth of any proposition derives from the referential properties of its constituents, and second, how the referential properties of primitive constituents are determined (Tarski, 1943 and Davidson, 1969). However, assuming that all propositions including belief attributions remain controversial, law of nature and counterfactual conditionals depends for their truth values on what their constituents refer to. Moreover, there is no immediate prospect of a decent, finite theory of reference, so that it is far form clear that the infinite, that we can avoid list-like character of deflationism.

An objection to the version of the deflationary theory presented here concerns its reliance on 'propositions' as the basic vehicles of truth. It is widely felt that the notion of the proposition is defective and that we should not employ it in semantics. If this point of view is accepted then the natural deflationary reaction is to attempt a reformation that would appeal only to sentences.

A possible way of these difficulties is to resist the critique of propositions. Such entities may exhibit an unwelcome degree of indeterminancy, and might defy reduction to familiar items, however, they do offer a plausible account of belief, as relations to propositions, and, in ordinary language at least, we indeed take them to be the primary bearers of truth. To believe a proposition is too old for it to be true. The philosophical problems include discovering whether belief differs from other varieties of assent, such as 'acceptance', discovering to what extent degrees of belief is possible, understanding the ways in which belief is controlled by rational and irrational factors, and discovering its links with other properties, such as the possession of conceptual or linguistic skills. This last set of problems includes the question of whether they have properly said that paralinguistic infants or animals have beliefs.

Additionally, it is commonly supposed that problems about the nature of truth are intimately bound up with questions as to the accessibility and autonomy of facts in various domains: Questions about whether we can know the facts, and whether they can exist independently of our capacity to discover them (Dummett, 1978, and Putnam, 1981). One might reason, for example, that if 'T is true' means' nothing more than 'T will be verified', then certain forms of scepticism, specifically, those that doubt the correctness of our methods of verification, that will be precluded, and that the facts will have been revealed as dependent on human practices. Alternatively, we might say that if truth were an inexplicable, primitive, non-epistemic property, then the fact that 'T' is true would be completely independent of 'us'. Moreover, we could, in that case, have no reason to assume that the propositions we believe actually have tis property, so scepticism would be unavoidable. In a similar vein, we might think that as special, and perhaps undesirable features of the deflationary approach, is that we have deprived truth of such metaphysical or epistemological implications.

On closer scrutiny, however, it is far from clear that there exists 'any' account of truth with consequences regarding the accessibility or autonomy of non-semantic matters. For although we may expect an account of truth to have such implications for facts of the from 'T is true', we cannot assume without further argument that the same conclusions will apply to the fact 'T'. For it cannot be assumed that 'T' and 'T' are true', is an equivalent to one another given the account of 'true' that is being employed. Of course, if we have defined truth in the way that the deflationist proposes, then the equivalence holds by definition. However, if reference to some metaphysical or epistemological characteristic has defined truth, then we throw the equivalence schema into doubt, pending some demonstration that the trued predicate, in the sense assumed, we will be satisfied in as far as there are thought to be epistemological problems hanging over 'T' that does not threaten 'T is true', giving the needed demonstration will be difficult. Similarly, if we so define 'truth' that the fact, 'T' is felt to be more, or less, independent of human practices than the fact that 'T is true', then again, it is unclear that the equivalence schema will hold. It would seem. Therefore, that the attempt to base epistemological or metaphysical conclusions on a theory of truth must fail because in any such attempt we will simultaneously rely on and undermine the equivalence schema.

The most influential idea in the theory of meaning in the past hundred yeas is the thesis that meaning of an indicative sentence is given by its truth-conditions. On this conception, to understand a sentence is to know its truth-conditions. The conception was first clearly formulated by Frége (1848-1925), was developed in a distinctive way by the early Wittgenstein (1889-1951), and is a leading idea of Davidson (1917-). The conception has remained so central that those who offer opposing theories characteristically define their position by reference to it.

The conception of meaning as truth-conditions needs not and should not be advanced as in itself a complete account of meaning. For instance, one who understands a language must have some idea of the range of speech acts conventionally performed by the various types of a sentence in the language, and must have some idea of the significance of various kinds of speech acts. We should moderately target the claim of the theorist of truth-conditions on the notion of content: If two indicative sentences differ in what they strictly and literally say, then the difference accounts for this difference in their truth-conditions. Most basic to truth conditions is simply of a statement that is the condition the world must meet if the statement is to be true. To know this condition is equivalent to knowing the meaning of the statement. Although this sounds as if it gives a solid anchorage for meaning, some of the security disappears when it turns out that repeating the very same statement can only define the truth condition, as a truth condition of 'snow is white' is that snow is white, the truth condition of 'Britain would have capitulated had Hitler invaded' is the Britain would have capitulated had Hitler invaded. It is disputed wether. This element of running-on-the-spot disqualifies truth conditions from playing the central role in a substantive theory of meaning. The view has sometimes opposed truth-conditional theories of meaning that to know the meaning of a statement is to be able to use it in a network of inferences.

Whatever it is that makes, what would otherwise be mere sounds and inscriptions into instruments of communication and understanding. The philosophical problem is to demystify this power, and to relate it to what we know of ourselves and the world. Contributions to the study include the theory of 'speech acts' and the investigation of communication and the relationship between words and ideas and the world and surrounding surfaces, by which some persons express by a sentence are often a function of the environment in which he or she is placed. For example, the disease I refer to by a term like 'arthritis' or the kind of tree I refer to as a 'maple' will be defined by criteria of which I know next to nothing. The raises the possibility of imagining two persons in rather differently environmental, but in which everything appears the same to each of them, but between them they define a space of philosophical problems. They are the essential components of understanding nd any intelligible proposition that is true must be capable of being understood. Such that which an utterance or sentence expresses, the proposition or claim made about the world may by extension, the content of a predicated or other sub-sentential component is what it contributes to the content of sentences that contain it. The nature of content is the cental concern of the philosophy of language.

In particularly, the problems of indeterminancy of translation, inscrutability of reference, language, predication, reference, rule following, semantics, translation, and the topics referring to subordinate headings associated with 'logic'. The loss of confidence in determinate meaning ('individually decoding is another encoding') is an element common both to postmodern uncertainties in the theory of criticism, and to the analytic tradition that follows writers such as Quine (1908-). Still it may be asked, why should we suppose that we should account fundamental epistemic notions for in behavioural terms what grounds are there for supposing that 'p knows p' is a matter of the status of its statement between some subject and some object, between nature and its mirror? The answer is that the only alternative seems to be to take knowledge of inner states as premises from which we have normally inferred our knowledge of other things, and without which we have normally inferred our knowledge of other things, and without which knowledge would be ungrounded. But it is not really coherent, and does not in the last analysis make sense, to suggest that human knowledge have foundations or grounds. We should remember that to say that truth and knowledge 'can only be judged by the standards of our own day' is not to say that it is not of any lesser importance, or, yet, more cut off from the world, that we had supposed. It is just to say 'that nothing counts as justification, unless by reference to what we already accept, and that there is no way to get outside our beliefs and our language so as to find some test other than coherence'. The fact is that the professional philosophers have thought it might be otherwise, since the body has haunted only them of epistemological scepticism.

What Quine opposes as 'residual Platonism' is not so much the hypostasising of nonphysical entities as the notion of 'correspondence' with things as the final court of appeal for evaluating present practices. Unfortunately, Quine, for all that it is incompatible with its basic insights, substitutes for this correspondence to physical entities, and specially to the basic entities, whatever they turn out to be, of physical science. But when we have purified their doctrines, they converge on a single claim that no account of knowledge can depend on the assumption of some privileged relations to reality. Their work brings out why an account of knowledge can amount only to a description of human behaviour.

What, then, is to be said of these 'inner states', and of the direct reports of them that have played so important a role in traditional epistemology? For a person to feel is nothing else than for him to have an ability to make a certain type of non-inferential report, to attribute feelings to infants is to acknowledge in them latent abilities of this innate kind. Non-conceptual, non-linguistic 'knowledge' of what feelings or sensations is like is attributively to beings on the basis of potential membership of our community. We accredit infants and the more attractive animals with having feelings on the basis of that spontaneous sympathy that we extend to anything humanoid, in contrast with the mere 'response to stimuli' attributed to photoelectric cells and to animals about which no one feels sentimentally. It is consequently wrong to suppose that moral prohibition against hurting infants and the better-looking animals are those moral prohibitions grounded' in their possession of feelings. The relation of dependence is really the other way round. Similarly, we could not be mistaken in supposing that a four-year-old child has knowledge, but no one-year-old, any more than we could be mistaken in taking the word of a statute that eighteen-year-old can marry freely but seventeen-year-old cannot. There is no more 'ontological ground' for the distinction that may suit 'us' to make in the former case than in the later.

Quine takes a bleak view of the nature of the language with which we ascribe thoughts and beliefs to ourselves and others. These 'intentional idioms' resist smooth incorporation into the scientific world view, and Quine responds with scepticism toward them, not quite endorsing 'eliminativism', but regarding them as second-rate idioms, unsuitable for describing strict and literal facts. For similar reasons he has consistently expressed suspicion of the logical and philosophical propriety of appeal to logical possibilities and possible worlds. The languages that are properly behaved and suitable for literal and true descriptions of the world happen to those within the fields that draw upon mathematics and science. We must take the entities to which our best theories refer with full seriousness in our ontologies, although an empiricist. Quine thus supposes that science requires the abstract objects of set theory, and therefore exist. In the theory of knowledge Quine associated with a 'holistic view' of verification, conceiving of a body of knowledge in terms of a web touching experience at the periphery, but with each point connected by a network of relations to other points.

They have also known Quine for the view that we should naturalize, or conduct epistemology in a scientific spirit, with the object of investigation being the relationship, in human beings, between the inputs of experience and the outputs of belief.

One answer is that the belief has a coherent place or role in a system of beliefs, perception or the having the perceptivity that has its influence on beliefs. As, you respond to sensory stimuli by believing that you are reading a page in a book than believing that you have a centaur in the garden. Belief has an influence on action, or its belief is a desire to act, if belief will differentiate the differences between them, that its belief is a desire or if you were to believe that you are reading a page than if you believed in something about a centaur. Sortal perceptivals hold accountably the perceptivity and action that are indeterminate to its content if its belief is the action as if stimulated by its inner and latent coherence in that of your belief, however. The same stimuli may produce various beliefs and various beliefs may produce the same action. The role that gives the belief the content it has is the role it plays in a network of relations to other beliefs, some latently causal than others that relate to the role in inference and implication. For example, I infer different things from believing that I am reading a page in a book than from any other belief, justly as I infer about other beliefs from.

The input of perceptibility and the output of an action supplement the central role of the systematic relations the belief has to other belief, but the systematic relations give the belief the specific contentual representation it has. They are the fundamental source of the content of belief. That is how coherence comes in. A belief has the representational content by which it does because of the way in which it coheres within a system of beliefs (Rosenberg, 1988). We might distinguish weak coherence theories of the content of beliefs from stronger coherence theories. Weak coherence theories affirm that coherence is one determinant of the representation given that the contents are of belief. Strong coherence theories of the content of belief affirm that coherence is the sole determinant of the contentual representations of belief.

Least of mention, a strong coherence theory of justification is a formidable combination by which a positive and a negative theory tell 'us' that a belief is justifiable if and only if it coheres with a background system of inter-connectivity of beliefs. Coherence theories of justification and knowledge have most often been rejected for being unable to deal with an accountable justification toward the perceptivity upon the projection of knowledge (Audi, 1988, and Pollock, 1986).

Coherence theory would go beyond the claim of the weak coherence theory to affirm that the justification of all beliefs, including the belief that one sees the shaping to sensory data that holds accountable a measure of 105, or even the more cautious belief that one sees a shape, resulting from the perceptivals of coherence theory, in that it coheres with a background system. One may argue for this strong coherence theory in a number of different ways. One line or medium through which to appeal to the coherence theory of contentual representations. If the content of the perceptual belief results from the relations of the belief to other beliefs in a network system of beliefs, then one may notably argue that the justification of perceptivity, that the belief is a resultant from which its relation of the belief to other beliefs, in the network system of beliefs is in argument for the strong coherence theory is that without any assumptive reason that the coherence inference of the content, are of the beliefs in as much as the supposed causes that only produce the consequences we expect. Consider the very cautious belief that I see a shape. How could the justification for that perceptual belief be an existent result that they characterize of its material coherence with a background system of beliefs? What might the background system tells 'us' that it would justify that belief? Our background system contains a simple and primal theory about our relationship to the world and surrounding surfaces that we perceive as it is or should be believed. To come to the specific point at issue, we believe that we can tell a shape when we see one, completely differentiated its form as perceived to sensory data, that we are to trust of ourselves about such simple matters as wether we see a shape before 'us' or not, as in the acceptance of opening to nature the inter-connectivity between belief and the progression through which we acquire from past experiential conditions of application, and not beyond deception. Moreover, when Trust sees the believing desire to act upon what either coheres with a weak or strong coherence of theory, she shows that its belief, as a measurable quality or entity of 105, has the essence in as much as there is much more of a structured distinction of circumstance, which is not of those that are deceptive about whether she sees that shape or sincerely does not see of its shaping distinction, however. Light is good, and the numeral shapes are large, readily discernible and so forth. These are beliefs that Trust has single handedly authenticated reasons for justification. Her successive malignance to sensory access to data involved is justifiably a subsequent belief, in that with those beliefs, and so she is justified and creditable.

The philosophical problems include discovering whether belief differs from other varieties of assent, such as 'acceptance' discovering to what extent degrees of belief is possible, understanding the ways in which belief is controlled by rational and irrational factors, and discovering its links with other properties, such as the possession of conceptual or linguistic skills. This last set of problems includes the question of whether we have properly said that paralinguistic infants or animals have beliefs.

Thus, we might think of coherence as inference to the best explanation based on a background system of beliefs, since we are not aware of such inferences for the most part, we must interpret the inferences as unconscious inferences, as information processing, based on or accessing the background system that proves most convincing of acquiring its act and used from the motivational force that its underlying and hidden desire are to do so. One might object to such an account on the grounds that not all justifiable inferences are self-explanatory, and more generally, the account of coherence may, at best, is ably successful to competitions that are based on background systems (BonJour, 1985, and Lehrer, 1990). The belief that one sees a shape competes with the claim that one does not, with the claim that one is deceived, and other sceptical objections. The background system of beliefs informs one that one is acceptingly trustworthy and enables one to meet the objections. A belief coheres with a background system just in case it enables one to meet the sceptical objections and in the way justifies one in the belief. This is a standard strong coherence theory of justification (Lehrer, 1990).

It is easy to illustrate the relationship between positive and negative coherence theories in terms of the standard coherence theory. If some objection to a belief cannot be met in terms of the background system of beliefs of a person, then the person is not justified in that belief. So, to return to Trust, suppose that she has ben told that a warning light has been installed on her gauge to tell her when it is not functioning properly and that when the red light is on, the gauge is malfunctioning. Suppose that when she sees the reading of 105, she also sees that the red light is on. Imagine, finally, that this is the first time the red light has been on, and, after years of working with the gauge, Julie, who has always placed her trust in the gauge, believes what the gauge tells her, that the liquid in the container is at 105 degrees. Though she believes what she reads is at 105 degrees is not a justified belief because it fails to cohere with her background belief that the gauge is malfunctioning. Thus, the negative coherence theory tells 'us' that she is not justified in her belief about the temperature of the contents in the container. By contrast, when we have not illuminated the red light and the background system of Julies tell her that under such conditions that gauge is a trustworthy indicator of the temperature of the liquid in the container, then she is justified. The positive coherence theory tells 'us' that she is justified in her belief because her belief coheres with her background system of Julies tell her that under such conditions that gauge is a trustworthy indicator of the temperature of the liquid in the container, then she is justified. The positive coherence theory tells 'us' that she is justified in her belief because her belief coheres with her background system continues as a trustworthy system.

The foregoing sketch and illustration of coherence theories of justification have a common feature, namely, that they are what we have called internalistic theories of justification what makes of such a view are the absence of any requirement that the person for whom the belief is justified have any sort of cognitive access to the relation of reliability in question. Lacking such access, such a person will in general, have no reason for thinking the belief is true or likely to be true, but will, on such an account, are none the less to appear epistemologically justified in accepting it. Thus, such a view arguably marks a major break from the modern epistemological traditions, which identifies epistemic justification with having a reason, perhaps even a conclusive reason, for thinking that the belief is true. An epistemologist working within this tradition is likely to feel that the externalist, than offering a competing account of the same concept of epistemic justification with which the traditional epistemologist is concerned, has simply changed the subject.

They are theories affirming that coherence is a matter of internal relations between beliefs and that justification is a matter of coherence. If, then, justification is solely a matter of internal relations between beliefs, we are left with the possibility that the internal relations might fail to correspond with any external reality. How, one might object, can a completely internal, its peculiarity to a particular individual as modified by individual bias and limitations hold of subjective judgments, whereas subjective notions of justification bridge the open space in the time, space, or interval that separates the veridicality or the confirmative true beliefs, which might be no more than a lucky guess, and knowledge, which we must ground in some connection between internal subjective conditions and external objective realities?

The answer is that it cannot and that we have required something more than justified true belief for knowledge. This result has, however, been established quite apart from consideration of coherence theories of justification. What we have required maybe put by saying that the justification that one must be undefeated by errors in the background system of beliefs. Justification is undefeated by errors just in case any correction of such errors in the background system of belief would sustain the justification of the belief on the basis of the corrected system. So knowledge, on this sort of positivity is acclaimed by the coherence theory, which is the true belief that coheres with the background belief system and corrected versions of that system. In short, knowledge is true belief plus justification resulting from coherence and undefeated by error (Lehrer, 1990). The connection between internal subjective conditions of belief and external objectivity are from which reality's result from the required correctness of our beliefs about the relations between those conditions and realities.

What justification does, as we have that any of our justifications are undefeated? The fear that we might have none, that our beliefs might be the artifact of some deceptive demon or scientist, leads to the quest to reduce truth to some form, perhaps an idealized form, of justification (Rescher, 1973, and Rosenberg, 1980). That would close the threatening sceptical gap between justification and truth. Suppose that a belief is true if and only if it is justifiable of some person. For such a person there would be no gap between justification and truth or between justification and undefeated justification. Truth would be coherence with some ideal background system of beliefs, perhaps one expressing a consensus among systems or some consensus among belief systems or some convergence toward a consensus. Such a view is theoretically attractive for the reduction it promises, but it appears open to profound objectification. One is that there is a consensus that we can all be wrong about at least some matters, for example, about the origins of the universe. If there is a consensus that we can all be wrong about something, then the consensual belief system rejects the equation of truth with the consensus. Consequently, the equation of truth with coherence with a consensual belief system is itself incoherently.

Coherence theories of the content of our beliefs and the justification of our beliefs themselves cohere with our background systems but coherence theories of truth do not. A defender of coherentism must accept the logical gap between justified belief and truth, but may believe that our capacities suffice to close the gap to yield knowledge. That view is, at any rate, a coherent one.

What makes a belief justified and what makes a true belief knowledge? It is natural to think that whether a belief deserves one of these appraisals depend on what causal subject to have the belief. In recent decades a number of epistemologists have pursed this plausible idea with a variety of specific proposals. Some causal theories of knowledge have it that a true belief that 'p' is knowledge just in case it has the right sort of causal connection to the fact that 'p'. Such a criterion can be applied only to cases where the fact that 'p' is a sort that can reach causal relations, this seems to exclude mathematically and other necessary facts and perhaps any fact expressed by a universal generalization, and proponents of this sort of criterion have usually of this sort of criterion have usually supposed that it is limited to perceptual knowledge of particular facts about the subject's environment.

For example, Armstrong (1973) proposed that a belief of the form 'This (perceived) object is F' is (non-inferential) knowledge if and only if the belief is a completely reliable sign that the perceived object is 'F', that is, the fact that the object is 'F' contributed to causing the belief and its doing so depended on properties of the believer such that the laws of nature dictated that, for any subject 'x' is to occur, and so thus a perceived object of 'y', if 'x' undergoing those properties are for 'us' to believe that 'y' is 'F', then 'y' is 'F'. (Dretske (1981) offers a rather similar account, in terms of the belief's being caused by a signal received by the perceiver that carries the information that the object is 'F').

This sort of condition fails, however, to be sufficient for non-inferential perceptual knowledge because it is compatible with the belief's being unjustified, and an unjustifiable belief cannot be knowledge. For example, suppose that your mechanisms for colour perception are working well, but you have been given good reason to think otherwise, to think, say, that the substantive primary colours that are perceivable, that things look chartreuse to you and chartreuse things look magenta. If you fail to heed these reasons you have for thinking that your colour perception or sensory data is a way and believing of a thing that looks magenta to you that it is magenta, your belief will fail to be justified and will therefore fail to be knowledge, even though the thing's being magenta in such a way causes it as to be a completely reliable sign, or to carry the information, in that the thing is magenta.

One could fend off this sort of counterexample by simply adding to the causal condition the requirement that the belief be justified, buy this enriched condition would still be insufficient. Suppose, for example, that in nearly all people, but not in you, as it happens, causes the aforementioned aberration in colour perceptions. The experimenter tells you that you have taken such a drug but then says, 'no, wait minute, the pill you took was just a placebo', suppose further, that this last thing the experimenter tells you is false. Her telling you that it was a false statement, and, again, telling you this gives you justification for believing of a thing that looks a subtractive primary colour to you that it is a sensorial primary colour, in that the fact you were to expect that the experimenters last statements were false, making it the case that your true belief is not knowledgeably correct, thought as though to satisfy its causal condition.

Goldman (1986) has proposed an importantly different sort of causal criterion namely, that a true belief is knowledge, if it is produced by a type of process that is 'globally' and 'locally' reliable. It is globally reliable if its propensity to cause true beliefs is sufficiently high. Local reliability has to do with whether the process would have produced a similar but false belief in certain counterfactual situations alternative to the actual situation. This way of marking off true beliefs that are knowledge does not require the fact believed to be casually related to the belief, and so it could in principle apply to knowledge of any kind of truth.

Goldman requires that global reliability of the belief-producing process for the justification of a belief, he requires it also for knowledge because they require justification for knowledge, in what requires for knowledge but does not require for justification, which is locally reliable. His idea is that a justified true belief is knowledge if the type of process that produced it would not have produced it in any relevant counterfactual situation in which it is false. Noting that other concepts exhibit the same logical structure can motivate the relevant alternative account of knowledge. Two examples of this are the concept 'flat' and the concept 'empty' (Dretske, 1981). Both appear to be absolute concepts -a space is empty only if it does not contain anything and a surface is flat only if it does not have any bumps. However, the absolute character of these concepts is relative to a standard. In the case of 'flat', there is a standard for what counts as a bump and in the case of 'empty', there is a standard for what counts as a thing. To be flat is to be free of any relevant bumps and to be empty is to be devoid of all relevant things.

This avoids the sorts of counterexamples we gave for the causal criteria, but it is vulnerable to one or ones of a different sort. Suppose you were to stand on the mainland looking over the water at an island, on which are several structures that look (from at least some point of view) as would ne of an actualized point or station of position. You happen to be looking at one of any point, in fact a barn and your belief to that effect are justified, given how it looks to you and the fact that you have exclusively of no reason to think nor believe otherwise. But suppose that the great majority of the barn-looking structures on the island are not real barns but fakes. Finally, suppose that from any viewpoint on the mainland all of the island's fake barns are obscured by trees and that circumstances made it very unlikely that you would have to a viewpoint not on the mainland. Here, it seems, your justified true belief that you are looking at a barn is not knowledge, despite the fact that there was not a serious chance that there would have developed an alternative situation, wherefore you are similarly caused to have a false belief that you are looking at a barn.

That example shows that the 'local reliability' of the belief-producing process, on the 'serous chance' explication of what makes an alternative relevance, yet its viewpoints upon which we are in showing that non-locality also might sustain of some probable course of the possibility for 'us' to believe in. Within the experience condition of application, the relationship with the sensory-data, as having a world-view that can encompass both the hidden and manifest aspects of nature would comprise of the mind, or brain that provides the excitation of neuronal ions, giving to sensory perception an accountable assessment of data and reason-sensitivity allowing a comprehensive world-view, integrating the various aspects of the universe into one magnificent whole, a whole in which we played an organic and central role. One-hundred years ago its question would have been by a Newtonian 'clockwork universe', as presented by the first person pronoun "I." Where the universes that are completely mechanical. The laws of nature have predetermined everything that happens and by the state of the universe in the distant past. The freedom one feels in regard to ones actions, even in regards to the movement of one's body, is an illusory infraction and the world-view expresses as the Newtonian one, is completely coherent.

Nevertheless, the human mind abhors a vacuum. When an explicit, coherent world-view is absent, it functions on the basis of a tactic one. A tactic world-view is not subject to a critical evaluation, and it can easily harbour inconsistencies. And, indeed, our tactic set of beliefs about the nature of reality consists of contradictory bits and pieces. The dominant component is a leftover from another period, the Newtonian 'clock universe' still lingers as we cling to this old and tired model because we know of nothing else that can take its place. Our condition is the condition of a culture that is in the throes of a paradigm shift. A major paradigm shift is complex and difficult because a paradigm holds 'us captive: We see reality through it, as through coloured glasses, but we do not know that, we are convinced that we see reality as it is. Hence the appearance of a new and different paradigm is often incomprehensible. To someone raised believing that the Earth is flat, the suggestion that the Earth is spherical would seem preposterous: If the Earth were spherical, would not the poor antipodes fall 'down' into the sky?

And yet, as we face a new millennium, we are forced to face this challenge. The fate of the planet is in question, and it was brought to its present precarious condition largely because of our trust in the Newtonian paradigm. As Newtonian world-view has to go, and, if one looks carefully, we can discern the main feature of the new, emergent paradigm. The search for these features is what was the influence of a fading paradigm. All paradigms include subterranean realms of tactic assumptions, the influence of which outlasts the adherence to the paradigm itself.

The first line of exploration suggests the 'weird' aspects of the quantum theory, with fertile grounds for our feeling of which should disappear in inconsistencies with the prevailing world-view. This feeling is in replacing by the new one, i.e., if one believes that the Earth is flat, the story of Magellan's travels is quite puzzling: How it is possible for a ship to travel due west and, without changing direct. Arrive at its place of departure?

Obviously, when the belief replaces the flat-Earth paradigm that Earth is spherical, we have instantly resolved the puzzle.

The founders of Relativity and quantum mechanics were deeply engaging but incomplete, in that none of them attempted to construct a philosophical system, however, that the mystery at the heart of the quantum theory called for a revolution in philosophical outlooks. During which time, the 1920's, when quantum mechanics reached maturity, began the construction of a full-blooded philosophical system that we based not only on science but on nonscientific modes of knowledge as well. As, the fading influences drawn upon the paradigm go well beyond its explicit claim. We believe, as the scenists and philosophers did, that when we wish to find out the truth about the universe, we can ignore nonscientific nodes of processing human experiences, poetry, literature, art, music are all wonderful, but, in relation to the quest for knowledge of the universe, they are irrelevant. Yet, it was Alfred North Whitehead who pointed out the fallacy of this speculative assumption. In this, as well as in other aspects of thinking of some reality in which are the building blocks of reality are not material atoms but 'throbs of experience'. Whitehead formulated his system in the late 1920s, and yet, as far as I know, the founders of quantum mechanics were unaware of it. It was not until 1963 that J.M. Burgers pointed out that its philosophy accounts very well for the main features of the quanta, especially the 'weird ones', enabling as in some aspects of reality is 'higher' or 'deeper' than others, and if so, what is the structure of such hierarchical divisions? What of our place in the universe? And, finally, what is the relationship between the great aspiration within the lost realms of nature? An attempt to endow 'us' with a cosmological meaning in such a universe seems totally absurd, and, yet, this very universe is just a paradigm, not the truth. When you reach its end, you may be willing to join the alternate view as accorded to which, surprisingly bestow 'us' with what we have restored, although in a post-postmodern context.

Subjective matter's has regulated the philosophical implications of quantum mechanics, as to emphasis the connections between what I believe, in that investigations of such interconnectivity are anticipatorially the hesitations that are an exclusion held within the western traditions, however, other aspects express my own views and convictions, as turning about to be more difficult that anticipated, discovering that a conversational mode would be helpful, but, their conversations with each other and with me in hoping that all will be not only illuminating but finding to its read may approve in them, whose dreams are dreams among others than themselves.

These examples make it seem likely that, if there is a criterion for what makes an alternative situation relevant that will save Goldman's claim about reliability and the acceptance of knowledge, it will not be simple.

The interesting thesis that counts asa causal theory of justification, in the meaning of 'causal theory' intend of the belief that is justified just in case it was produced by a type of process that is 'globally' reliable, that is, its propensity to produce true beliefs-that can be defined to a good enough approximation, as the proportion of the belief it produces, or would produce where it used as much as opportunity allows, that is true ~. Is sufficiently that a belief acquires favourable epistemic status by having some kind of reliable linkage to the truth? We have advanced variations of this view for both knowledge and justified belief. The first formulations of are reliably in its account of knowing appeared in a not by F.P. Ramsey (1903-30) who made important contributions to mathematical logic, probability theory, the philosophy of science and economics. Instead of saying that quarks have such-and-such properties, the Ramsey sentence says the is rather something that has those properties. The most sustained and influential application of these ideas were in the philosophy of mind, or brain, as Ludwig Wittgenstein (1889-1951) whom Ramsey persuaded that remained work for him to do, the way of an undoubtedly most charismatic figure of 20th-century philosophy, living and writing with a power and intensity that frequently overwhelmed his contemporaries and readers, being a kind of picture or model has centred the early period on the 'picture theory of meaning' according to which sentence represents a state of affairs of it. Containing elements corresponding to those of the state of affairs and structure or form that mirrors that a structure of the state of affairs that it represents. We have reduced to all logic complexity that of the 'propositional calculus, and all propositions are 'truth-functions of atomic or basic propositions.

In the layer period the emphasis shafts dramatically to the actions of people and the role linguistic activities play in their lives. Thus, whereas in the "Tractatus" language is placed in a static, formal relationship with the world, in the later work Wittgenstein emphasis its use in the context of standardized social activities of ordering, advising, requesting, measuring, counting, excising concerns for each other, and so on. Clearly, there are many forms of reliabilism. Just as there are many forms of 'foundationalism' and 'coherence'. How is Reliabilism related to these other two theories of justification? We usually regard it as a rival, and this is aptly so, in as far as foundationalism and coherentism traditionally focussed on purely evidential relations than psychological processes, but we might also offer Reliabilism as a deeper-level theory, subsuming some of the precepts of either foundationalism or coherentism. Foundationalism says that there are 'basic' beliefs, which acquire justification without dependence on inference, reliabilism might rationalize this and by indicating that reliable non-inferential processes have formed the basic beliefs. Coherence stresses the primary of systematicity in all doxastic decision-making. Reliabilism might rationalize this by pointing to increases in reliability that accrue from systematicity consequently, reliabilism could complement Foundationalism and coherence than completed with them.

These examples make it seem likely that, if there is a criterion for what makes an alternate situation relevant that will save Goldman's claim about local reliability and knowledge. Will did not be simple. The interesting thesis that counts as a causal theory of justification, in the making of 'causal theory' intended for the belief as it is justified in case it was produced by a type of process that is 'globally' reliable, that is, its propensity to produce true beliefs –that can be defined, to a good enough approximations, as the proportion of the beliefs it produces, or would produce where it used as much as opportunity allows, that is true -is sufficiently relializable. We have advanced variations of this view for both knowledge and justified belief, its first formulation of a reliability account of knowing appeared in the notation from F.P.Ramsey (1903-30). The theory of probability, he was the first to show how a 'personalist theory' could be developed, based on a precise behavioural notion of preference and expectation. In the philosophy of language. Much of Ramsey's work was directed at saving classical mathematics from 'intuitionism', or what he called the 'Bolshevik menace of Brouwer and Weyl. In the theory of probability he was the first to show how we could develop a personalists theory, based on precise behavioural notation of preference and expectation. In the philosophy of language, Ramsey was one of the first thankers, which he combined with radical views of the function of many kinds of a proposition. Neither generalizations, nor causal propositions, nor those treating probability or ethics, describe facts, but each has a different specific function in our intellectual economy. Ramsey was one of the earliest commentators on the early work of Wittgenstein, and his continuing friendship that led to Wittgenstein's return to Cambridge and to philosophy in 1929.

Ramsey's sentence theory is the sentence generated by taking all the sentences affirmed in a scientific theory that use some term, e.g., 'quark'. Replacing the term by a variable, and existentially quantifying into the result. Instead of saying that quarks have such-and-such properties, the Ramsey sentence says that there is something that has those properties. If we repeat the process for all of a group of the theoretical terms, the sentence gives the 'topic-neutral' structure of the theory, but removes any implication that we know what the term so treated distinguish, its leaves open the possibility of identifying the theoretical item with whatever, but it is that best fits the description provided. Virtually, all theories of knowledge. Of course, share an externalist component in requiring truth as a condition for known in. Reliabilism goes father, however, in trying to capture additional conditions for knowledge by ways of a nomic, counterfactual or other such 'external' relations between belief and truth. Closely allied to the nomic sufficiency account of knowledge, primarily dur to Dretshe (1971, 1981), A.I. Goldman (1976, 1986) and R. Nozick (1981). The core of this approach is that 'x's' belief that 'p' qualifies as knowledge just in case 'x' believes 'p', because of reasons that would not obtain unless 'p' was true, or because of a process or method that would not yield belief in 'p' if 'p' were not true. An enemy example, 'x' would not have its current reasons for believing there is a telephone before it. Or would not come to believe this in the ways it does, thus, there is a counterfactual reliable guarantor of the belief's bing true. An undaunted and the facts of counterfactual approach say that 'x' knows that 'p' only if there is no 'relevant alternative' situation in which 'p' is false but 'x' would still believe that a proposition 'p'; must be sufficient to eliminate all the alternatives too 'p' where an alternative to a proposition 'p' is a proposition incompatible with 'p'? That in one's justification or evidence for 'p' must be sufficient for one to know that every alternative too 'p' is false. This element of our evolving thinking, sceptical arguments have exploited about which knowledge. These arguments call our attentions to alternatives that our evidence sustains itself with no elimination. The sceptic inquires to how we know that we are not seeing a cleverly disguised mule. While we do have some evidence against the likelihood of such as deception, intuitively it is not strong enough for 'us' to know that we are not so deceived. By pointing out alternate but hidden points of nature, in that we cannot eliminate, as well as others with more general application, as dreams, hallucinations, etc. The sceptic appears to show that every alternative is seldom. If ever, satisfied.

This conclusion conflicts with another strand in our thinking about knowledge, in that we know many things. Thus, there is a tension in our ordinary thinking about knowledge ~. We believe that knowledge is, in the sense indicated, an absolute concept and yet, we also believe that there are many instances of that concept.

If one finds absoluteness to be too central a component of our concept of knowledge to be relinquished, one could argue from the absolute character of knowledge to a sceptical conclusion (Unger, 1975). Most philosophers, however, have taken the other course, choosing to respond to the conflict by giving up, perhaps reluctantly, the absolute criterion. This latter response holds as sacrosanct our commonsense belief that we know many things (Pollock, 1979 and Chisholm, 1977). Each approach is subject to the criticism that it preserves one aspect of our ordinary thinking about knowledge at the expense of denying another. We can view the theory of relevant alternatives as an attempt to provide a more satisfactory response to this tension in our thinking about knowledge. It attempts to characterize knowledge in a way that preserves both our belief that knowledge is an absolute concept and our belief that we have knowledge.

According to most epistemologists, knowledge entails belief, so that I cannot know that such and such is the case unless I believe that such and such am the case. Others think this entailment thesis can be rendered more accurately if we substitute for briefs some related attitude. For instance, several philosophers would prefer to say that knowledge entail psychological certainty or acceptance (Lehrer, 1989). Nonetheless, there are arguments against all versions of the thesis that knowledge requires having belief-like attitudes toward the known. These arguments are given by philosophers who think that knowledge and belief (or a facsimile) are mutually incompatible (the incompatibility thesis), or by ones who say that knowledge does no entail belief or vice versa, so that each may exist without the other, but the two may also coexist (the separability thesis).

Having its recourse to knowledge, its cental questions include the origin of knowledge, the place of experience in generating knowledge, and the place of reason in doing so, the relationship between knowledge and certainty, and between knowledge and the impossibility of error, the possibility of universal scepticism, and the changing forms of knowledge that arise from new conceptualizations of the world. All of these issues link with other central concerns of philosophy, such as the nature of truth and the natures of experience and meaning. It is possible to see epistemology as dominated by two rival metaphors. One is that of a building or pyramid, built on foundations. In this conception it is the kob of the philosopher to describe especially secure foundations, and to identify secure modes of construction, s that the resulting edifice can be shown to be sound. This metaphor of knowledge, and of a rationally defensible theory of confirmation and inference as a method of construction, as that knowledge must be regarded as a structure risen upon secure, certain foundations. These are found in some formidable combinations of experience and reason, with different schools (empiricism, rationalism) emphasizing the role of one over that of the others. Foundationalism was associated with the ancient Stoics, and in the modern era with Descartes (1596-1650) who discovered his foundations in the 'clear and distinct' ideas of reason? Its main opponent is coherentism, or the view that a body of propositions mas be known without a foundation in certainty, but by their interlocking strength, than as a crossword puzzle may be known to have been solved correctly even if each answer, taken individually, admits of uncertainty. Difficulties at this point led the logical passivists to abandon the notion of an epistemological foundation together, and to flirt with the coherence theory of truth. It is widely accepted that trying to make the connection between thought and experience through basic sentences depends on an untenable 'myth of the given'.

Still, of the other metaphor, is that of a boat or fuselage, that has no foundation but owes its strength to the stability given by its interlocking parts. This rejects the idea of a basis in the 'given', favours ideas of coherence and holism, but finds it harder to ward off scepticism. In spite of these concerns, the problem, least of mention, is of defining knowledge in terms of true beliefs plus some favoured relations between the believer and the facts that began with Plato's view in the "Theaetetus" that knowledge is true belief, and some logos.` Due of its natural epistemology, the enterprising of studying the actual formation of knowledge by human beings, without aspiring to make evident those processes as rational, or validation against 'scepticism' or even apt to yield the truth. Natural epistemology would therefore blend into the psychology of learning and the study of episodes I the history of science. The scope for 'external' or philosophical reflection of the kind that might result in scepticism or its refutation is markedly diminished, although the terms in modern, distinguished exponents of the approach include Aristotle, Hume, and J.S. Mills.

The task of the philosopher of a discipline would then be to reveal the correct method and to unmask counterfeits. Although this belief lay behind much positivist philosophy of science, few philosophers now subscribe to it. It places too great a confidence in the possibility of a purely a prior 'first philosophy', or standpoint beyond that of the working practitioners, from which they can measure their best efforts as good or bad. This standpoint now seems too many philosophers to be a fantasy. The more modest of tasks that we actually adopt at various historical stages of investigation into different areas with the aim not so much of criticizing but more of systematization, in the presuppositions of a particular field at a particular tie. There is still a role for local methodological disputes within the community investigators of some phenomenon, with one approach charging that another is unsound or unscientific, but logic and philosophy will not, on the modern view, provide an independent arsenal of weapons for such battles, which indeed often come to seem more like political bids for ascendancy within a discipline.

This is an approach to the theory of knowledge that sees an important connection between the growth of knowledge and biological evolution. An evolutionary epistemologist claims that the development of human knowledge processed through some natural selection process, the best example of which is Darwin's theory of biological natural selection. There is a widespread misconception that evolution proceeds according to some plan or direct, put it has neither, and the role of chance ensures that its future course will be unpredictable. Random variations in individual organisms create tiny differences in their Darwinian fitness. Some individuals have more offsprings than others, and the characteristics that increased their fitness thereby become more prevalent in future generations. Once upon a time, at least a mutation occurred in a human population in tropical Africa that changed the haemoglobin molecule in a way that provided resistance to malaria. This enormous advantage caused the new gene to spread, with the unfortunate consequence that sickle-cell anaemia came to exist.

Chance can influence the outcome at each stage: First, in the creation of genetic mutation, second, in wether the bearer lives long enough to show its effects, thirdly, in chance events that influence the individual's actual reproductive success, and fourth, in wether a gene even if favoured in one generation, is, happenstance, eliminated in the next, and finally in the many unpredictable environmental changes that will undoubtedly occur in the history of any group of organisms. As Harvard biologist Stephen Jay Gould has so vividly expressed that process over again, the outcome would surely be different. Not only might there not be humans, there might not even be anything like mammals.

We will often emphasis the elegance of traits shaped by natural selection, but the common idea that nature creates perfection needs to be analysed carefully. The extent to which evolution achieves perfection depends on exactly what you mean. If you mean "Does natural selections always take the best path for the long-term welfare of a species?" the answer is no. That would require adaption by group selection, and this is, unlikely. If you mean "Does natural selection creates every adaption that would be valuable?" The answer again, is no. For instance, some kinds of South American monkeys can grasp branches with their tails. The trick would surely also be useful to some African species, but, simply because of bad luck, none have it. Some combination of circumstances started some ancestral South American monkeys using their tails in ways that ultimately led to an ability to grab onto branches, while no such development took place in Africa. Mere usefulness of a trait does not necessitate it mean that will evolve.

This is an approach to the theory of knowledge that sees an important connection between the growth of knowledge and biological evolution. An evolutionary epistemologist claims that the development of human knowledge proceeds through some natural selection process, the best example of which is Darwin's theory of biological natural selection. The three major components of the model of natural selection are variation selection and retention. According to Darwin's theory of natural selection, variations are not pre-designed to perform certain functions. Rather, these variations that perform useful functions are selected. While those who are not selected as such of a selection are responsible for the appearance that variational intentionality takes place. In the modern theory of evolution, genetic mutations provide the blind variations (blind in the sense that variations are not influenced by the effects they would have-the likelihood of a mutation is not correlated with the benefits or liabilities that mutation would confer on the organism), the environment provides the filter of selection, and reproduction provides the retention. Fit is achieved because those organisms with features that make them less adapted for survival do not survive in connection with other organisms in the environment that have features that are better adapted. Evolutionary epistemology applies this blind variation and selective retention model to the growth of scientific knowledge and to human thought processes in general.

The parallel between biological evolution and conceptual or we can see 'epistemic' evolution as either literal or analogical. The literal version of evolutionary epistemology dees biological evolution as the main cause of the growth of knowledge. On this view, called the 'evolution of cognitive mechanic programs', by Bradie (1986) and the 'Darwinian approach to epistemology' by Ruse (1986), that growth of knowledge occurs through blind variation and selective retention because biological natural selection itself is the cause of epistemic variation and selection. The most plausible version of the literal view does not hold that all human beliefs are innate but rather than the mental mechanisms which guide the acquisition of non-innate beliefs are themselves innate and the result of biological natural selection. Ruse (1986) demands a version of literal evolutionary epistemology that he links to sociolology (Rescher, 1990).

On the analogical version of evolutionary epistemology, called the 'evolution of theory's program', by Bradie (1986). And the 'Spenserians approach' (after the nineteenth century philosopher Herbert Spencer) by Ruse (1986), a process analogous to biological natural selection has governed the development of human knowledge, rather than by an instance of the mechanism itself. This version of evolutionary epistemology, introduced and elaborated by Donald Campbell (1974) as well as Karl Popper, sees the [partial] fit between theories and the world as explained by a mental process of trial and error known as epistemic natural selection.

We have usually taken both versions of evolutionary epistemology to be types of naturalized epistemology, because both take some empirical facts as a starting point for their epistemological project. The literal version of evolutionary epistemology begins by accepting evolutionary theory and a materialist approach to the mind and, from these, constructs an account of knowledge and its developments. In contrast, the analogical; the version does not require the truth of biological evolution: It simply draws on biological evolution as a source for the model of natural selection. For this version of evolutionary epistemology to be true, the model of natural selection need only apply to the growth of knowledge, not to the origin and development of species. Crudely put, evolutionary epistemology of the analogical sort could still be true even if Creationism is the correct theory of the origin of species.

Although they do not begin by assuming evolutionary theory, most analogical evolutionary episteremologists are naturalized epistemologists as well, their empirical assumptions, least of mention, implicitly come from psychology and cognitive science, not evolutionary theory. Sometimes, however, evolutionary epistemology is characterized in a seemingly non-naturalistic fashion. (Campbell, 1974) says that 'if one is expanding knowledge beyond what one knows, one has no choice but to explore without the benefit of wisdom', i.e., blindly. This, Campbell admits, makes evolutionary epistemology close to being a tautology (and so not naturalistic). Evolutionary epistemology does assert the analytic claim that when expanding one's knowledge beyond what one knows, one must precessed to something that is already known, but, more interestingly, it also makes the synthetic claim that when expanding one's knowledge beyond what one knows, one must proceed by blind variation and selective retention. This claim is synthetic because we can empirically falsify it. The central claim of evolutionary epistemology is synthetic, not analytic. If the central contradictory, which they are not. Campbell is right that evolutionary epistemology does have the analytic feature he mentions, but he is wrong to think that this is a distinguishing feature, since any plausible epistemology has the same analytic feature (Skagestad, 1978).

Two extra-ordinary issues lie to awaken the literature that involves questions about 'realism', i.e., What sort of metaphysical commitment does an evolutionary epistemologist have to make? And progress, i.e., according to evolutionary epistemology, does knowledge develop toward a goal? With respect to realism, many evolutionary epistemologists endorse that is called 'hypothetical realism', a view that combines a version of epistemological 'scepticism' and tentative acceptance of metaphysical realism. With respect to progress, the problem is that biological evolution is not goal-directed, but the growth of human knowledge seems to be. Campbell (1974) worries about the potential disanaloguousness, as it represents, but is willing to bite the stone of conscience and admit that epistemic evolution progress toward a goal (truth) while biological evolution does not. Some have argued that evolutionary epistemologists must give up the 'truth-topic' sense of progress because a natural selection model is in essence non-teleological, instead, following Kuhn (1970), an embraced along with evolutionary epistemology.

Among the most frequent and serious criticisms levelled against evolutionary epistemology is that the analogical version of the view is false because epistemic variation is not blind (Skagestad, 1978), and Ruse, 1986, (Stein and Lipton (1990) have argued, however, that this objection fails because, while epistemic variation is not random, its constraints come from heuristics which, for the most part, are selective retention. Further, Stein and Lipton argue that the heuristics are in analogical sense, and thus, forms a perplexing phenomenon in the philosophy of language. Arguing by analogy is arguing that since things are alike in some ways, they will probably be alike in others. Its famous uses in philosophy include the argument to 'design' and the argument by 'analogy' to the existence of other minds: If you behave like me, and I have such and such mental states when I so behave, then by analogy you probably do so too. But: 'How can I generalize the one case so irresponsibly'? (Wittgenstein). In medieval philosophy an important question was whether we can make statements about God only by analogy. To biological pre-adaptions, evolutionary pre-biological pre-adaptions, evolutionary cursors, such as a half-wing, a precursor to a wing, which have some function other than the function of their descendable structures: The function of descendable structures, the function of their descendable character embodied to its structural foundations, is that of the guidelines of epistemic variation is, on this view, not the source of disanaloguousness, but the source of a more articulated account of the analogy.

Many evolutionary epistemologists try to combine the literal and the analogical versions (Bradie, 1986), and Stein and Lipton, (1990), saying that those beliefs and cognitive mechanisms, which are innate results from natural selection of the biological sort and those which are innate results from natural selection of the epistemic sort. This is reasonable asa long as the two parts of this hybrid view are kept distinct. An analogical version of evolutionary epistemology with biological variation as its only source of blondeness would be a null theory: This would be the case if all our beliefs are innate or if our non-innate beliefs are not the result of blind variation. An appeal to the legitimate way to produce a hybrid version of evolutionary epistemology since doing so trivializes the theory. For similar reasons, such an appeal will not save an analogical version of evolutionary epistemology from arguments to the effect that epistemic variation is blind (Stein and Lipton, 1990).

Although it is a relatively new approach to theory of knowledge, evolutionary epistemology has attracted much attention, primarily because it represents a serious attempt to flesh out a naturalized epistemology by drawing on several disciplines. In science is relevant to understanding the nature and development of knowledge, then evolutionary theory is among the disciplines worth a look. Insofar as evolutionary epistemology looks there, it is an interesting and potentially fruitful epistemological programme.

What makes a belief justified and what makes a true belief knowledge? It is natural to think that whether a belief deserves one of these appraisals depends on what causes the individuals as subjects, to have belief. In recent decades a number of epistemologists have pursued this plausible idea with a variety of specific proposals. Some causal theories of knowledge have it that a true belief that 'p' is knowledge just in case it has the right sort of causal connection to the fact that 'p'. They can apply such a criterion only to cases where the fact that 'p' is a sort that can enter inti causal relations, as this seems to exclude mathematical and other necessary facts and perhaps any fact expressed by a universal generalization, and proponents of this sort of criterion have usually supposed that it is limited to perceptual representations where knowledge of particular facts about subjects' environments.

For example, Armstrong (1973) proposed that a belief of the form 'This [perceived] object is 'F' is [non-inferential] knowledge if and only if the belief is a completely reliable sign that the perceived object is 'F', that ism, the fact that the object is 'F' contributed to causing the belief and its doing so depended on properties of the believer such that the laws of nature dictated that, for any subject 'χ' and perceived object 'y', if 'χ' has those properties and believed that 'y' is 'F', then 'y' is 'F'. (Dretske (1981) offers a rather similar account, in terms of the belief's being caused by a signal received by the perceiver that carries the information that the object is 'F').

This sort of condition fails, however, to be sufficiently for non-inferential perceptivity, for knowledge is accountable for its compatibility with the belief's being unjustified, and an unjustified belief cannot be knowledge. For example, suppose that your mechanisms for the sensory data of colour as perceived, are working well, but you have been given good reason to think otherwise, to think, say, that the sensory data of things look chartreuse to say, that chartreuse things look magenta, if you fail to heed these reasons you have for thinking that your colour perception is awry and believe of a thing that looks magenta to you that it is magenta, your belief will fail top be justified and will therefore fail to be knowledge, even though it is caused by the thing's being withing the grasp of sensory perceptivity, in such a way as to be a completely reliable sign, or to carry the information that the thing is sufficiently to organize all sensory data as determined: By the inherent perceptivity of the world, or Holistic view.

The view that a belief acquires favourable epistemic status by having some kind of reliable linkage to the truth. Variation of this view has been advanced for both knowledge and justified belief. The fist formulation of a reliable account of knowing is unfolded by its literal notation by F.P. Ramsey (1903-30), whereby much of Ramsey's work was directed at saving classical mathematics from 'intuitionism', or what he called the 'Bolshevik menace of Brouwer and Weyl'. In the theory of probability he was the first to develop, based on precise behavioural nations of preference and expectation. In the philosophy of language, Ramsey was one of the first thinkers to accept a 'redundancy theory of truth', which he combined with radical views of the function of many kinds of propositions. Neither generalizations, nor causal positions, nor those treating probability or ethics, described facts, but each has a different specific function in our intellectual economy. Ramsey was one of the earliest commentators on the early work of Wittgenstein, and his continuing friendship with the later to Wittgenstein's return to Cambridge and to philosophy in 1929. Additionally, Ramsey, who said that a belief was knowledge if it is true, certain and obtained by a reliable process. P. Unger (1968) suggested that 'S' knows that 'p' just in case it is of at all accidental that 'S' is right about its being the case that D.M. Armstrong (1973) drew an analogy between a thermometer that reliably indicates the temperature and a belief that reliably indicate the truth. Armstrong said that a non-inferential belief qualified as knowledge if the belief has properties that are nominally sufficient for its truth, i.e., guarantee its truth via laws of nature.

Closely allied to the nomic sufficiency account of knowledge, primarily due to F.I. Dretske (1971, 1981), A.I. Goldman (1976, 1986) and R. Nozick (1981). The core of this approach is that 'S's' belief that 'p' qualifies as knowledge just in case 'S' believes 'p' because of reasons that would not obtain unless 'p' was true, or because of a process or method that would not yield belief in 'p' if 'p' were not true. For example, 'S' would not have his current reasons for believing there is a telephone before him, or would not come to believe this in the way he does, unless there was a telephone before him. Thus, there is a counterfactual reliable guarantor of the belief;'s being true. A variant of the counterfactual approach says that 'S' knows that 'p' only if there is no 'relevant alternative' situation in which 'p' is false but 'S' would still believe that 'p' must be sufficient to eliminate all the alternatives too 'p', where an alternative to a proposition 'p' is a proposition incompatible with 'p', that is, one's justification or evidence fort 'p' must be sufficient for one to know that every alternative too 'p' is false.

They standardly classify Reliabilism as an 'externalist' theory because it invokes some truth-linked factor, and truth is 'eternal' to the believer the main argument for externalism derives from the philosophy of language, more specifically, from the various phenomena pertaining to natural kind terms, indexical, etc., that motivate the views that have come to be known as direct reference' theories. Such phenomena seem, at least to show that the belief or thought content that can be properly attributed to a person is dependent on facts about his environment, e.g., whether he is on Earth or Twin Earth, what in fact he is pointing at, the classificatory criteria employed by the experts in his social group, etc.- not just on what is going on internally in his mind or brain (Burge, 1979.) Virtually all theories of knowledge, of course, share an externalist component in requiring truth as a condition for knowing. Reliabilism goes father, however, in trying to capture additional conditions for knowledge by means of a nomic, counterfactual or other such 'external' relations between 'belief' and 'truth'.

The most influential counterexample to reliabilism is the demon-world and the clairvoyance examples. The demon-world example challenges the necessity of the reliability requirement, in that a possible world in which an evil demon creates deceptive visual experience, the process of vision is not reliable. Still, the visually formed beliefs in this world are intuitively justified. The clairvoyance example challenges the sufficiency of reliability. Suppose a cognitive agent possesses a reliable clairvoyance power, but has no evidence for or against his possessing such a power. Intuitively, his clairvoyantly formed beliefs are unjustifiably unreasoned, but reliabilism declares them justified.

Another form of reliabilism, 'normal worlds', reliabilism (Goldman, 1986), answers the range problem differently, and treats the demon-world problem in the same stroke. Let a 'normal world' be one that is consistent with our general beliefs about the actual world. Normal-worlds reliabilism says that a belief, in any possible world is justified just in case its generating processes have high truth ratios in normal worlds. This resolves the demon-world problem because the relevant truth ratio of the visual process is not its truth ratio in the demon world itself, but its ratio in normal worlds. Since this ratio is presumably high, visually formed beliefs in the demon world turn out to be justified.

Yet, a different version of reliabilism attempts to meet the demon-world and clairvoyance problems without recourse to the questionable notion of 'normal worlds'. Consider Sosa's (1992) suggestion that justified beliefs is belief acquired through 'intellectual virtues', and not through intellectual 'vices', whereby virtues are reliable cognitive faculties or processes. The task is to explain how epistemic evaluators have used the notion of indelible virtues, and vices, to arrive at their judgements, especially in the problematic cases. Goldman (1992) proposes a two-stage reconstruction of an evaluator's activity. The first stage is a reliability-based acquisition of a 'list' of virtues and vices. The second stage is application of this list to queried cases. Determining has executed the second stage whether processes in the queried cases resemble virtues or vices. We have classified visual beliefs in the demon world as justified because visual belief formation is one of the virtues. Clairvoyance formed, beliefs are classified as unjustified because clairvoyance resembles scientifically suspect processes that the evaluator represents as vices, e.g., mental telepathy, ESP, and so forth.

Philosophers often debate the existence of the different kinds of things: Nominalists question the reality of abstract objects like class, numbers, and universals, some positivist doubt the existence of theoretical entities like neutrons or genes, and there are debates over whether there are sense-data, events and so on. Some philosophers my be happy to talk about abstract one is and theoretical entities while denying that they really exist. This requires a 'metaphysical' concept of 'real existence': We debate whether numbers, neutrons and sense-data really existing things. But it is difficult to see what this concept involves and the rules to be employed in setting such debates are very unclear.

Questions of existence seem always to involve general kinds of things, do numbers, sense-data or neutrons exist? Some philosophers conclude that existence is not a property of individual things, 'exists' is not an ordinary predicate. If I refer to something, and then predicate existence of it, my utterance seems to be tautological, the object must exist for me to be able to refer to it, so predicating for me to be able to refer to it, so predicating existence of it adds nothing. And to say of something that it did not exist would be contradictory.

More recently, philosophers, notably Quine, have questioned the distinction between linguistic framework and internal questions arising within it. Quine agrees that we have no 'metaphysical' concept of existence against which different purported entities can be measured. If quantification of the general theoretical framework which best explains our experience, the claims which there are such things, that they exist, is true. Scruples about admitting the existence of too many different kinds of objects depend b=not on a metaphysical concept of existence but rather on a desire for a simple and economical theoretical framework.

It is not possible to define experience in an illuminating way, however, what experiences are through acquaintance with some of their own, e.g., a visual experience of a green after images, a feeling of physical nausea or a tactile experience of an abrasive surface, which an actual surface ~ rough or smooth might cause or which might be part of ca dream, or the product of a vivid sensory imagination. The essential feature of every experience is that it feels a certain way ~. That there is something that it is like to have it. We may refer to this feature of an experience is its 'character.

Another core feature of the sorts of experience with which our concerns are those that have representational content, unless otherwise indicated, the term 'experiences; will be reserved for these that we implicate below, that the most obvious cases of experience with content are sense experiences of the kind normally involved I perception? We may describe such experiences by mentioning their sensory modalities and their content's e. g., a gustatory experience (modality) of chocolate ice cream (content), but do so more commonly by means of perceptual verbs combined with noun phrases specifying their contents, as in 'Macbeth saw a dagger;'. This is, however, ambiguous between the perceptual claim 'There was a [material] dagger in the world which Macbeth perceived visually' and 'Macbeth had a visual experience of a dagger', the reading with which we are concerned.

As in the case of other mental states nd events with content, it is important to distinguish between the properties which an experience represents and the properties which it possesses. To talk of the representational properties of an experience is to say something about its content, not to attribute those properties to the experience itself. Like every other experience, a visual Esperance of a pink square is a mental event, and it is therefore not itself either oink or square, even though it represents those properties. It is, perhaps, fleeting, pleasant or unusual, even though it does not represent those properties. An experience may represent a property which it possesses, and it may even do so in virtue of possessing that property, as in the case of a rapidly changing [complex] experience representing something as changing rapidly, but this is the exception and not the rule.

Which properties can be [directly] represented in sense experience is subject to debate. Traditionalists, include only properties whose presence a subject could not doubt having appropriated experiences, e.g., colour and shape in the case of visual experience, i.e., colour and shape in the case of visual experience, surface texture, hardness, etc., in the case of tactile experience. This view s natural to anyone who has to an egocentric Cartesian perspective in epistemology, and who wishes for pure data experience to serve as logically certain foundations for knowledge. The term 'sense-data', introduced by More and Russell, refer to the immediate objects of perceptual awareness, such as colour patches and shape, usually supposed distinct from surfaces of physical objects. Qualities of sense-data are supposed to be distinct from physical qualities because their perception is more immediate, and because sense data are private and cannot appear other than they are. They are objects that change in our perceptual fields when conditions of perception change and physical objects remain constant.'

Critics of the notional questions of whether, just because physical objects can appear other than they are, there must be private, mental objects that have all predispositions for which the physical objects appear to have, there are also problems regarding the individuation and duration of sense-data and their relations ti physical surfaces of an object we perceive. Contemporary proponents counter that speaking only of how things an to appear cannot capture the full structure within perceptual experience captured by talk of apparent objects and their qualities.

It is, nevertheless, that others who do not think that this wish can be satisfied and they impress who with the role of experience in providing animals with ecological significant information about the world around them, claim that sense experiences represent possession characteristics and kinds which are n=much richer and much more wide-ranging than the traditional sensory qualitites. We do not see only colours and shapes they tell 'u' but also, earth, water, men, women and fire, we do not smell only odours, but also food and filth. There is no space here to examine the factors relevant to as choice between these alternatives. In so, that we are to assume and expect when it is incompatibles with a position under discussion.

Given the modality and content of a sense experience, most of 'us' will be aware of its character even though we cannot describe that character directly. This suggests that character and content are not really distinct, and this is a close tie between them. For one thing, the relative complexity of the character of a sense experience places limitation n its possible content, i.e., a tactile experience of something touching one's left ear is just too simple to carry the same amount of content as a typical every day, visual experience. Furthermore, the content of a sense experience of a given character depends on the normal causes of appropriately similar experiences, i.e., the sort of gustatory experience which we have when eating chocolate would not represent chocolate unless chocolate normally caused it, granting a contingently tie between the characters of an experience and its possibility for casual origins, it again, followed its possible content is limited by its character.

Character and content are none the less irreducible different for the following reasons (I) There are experiences which completely lack content, i.e., certain bodily pleasures (ii) Nit every aspect of the character of an experience which content is relevant to that content, i.e., the unpleasantness of an aural experience of chalk squeaking on a board may have no responsibility significance (iii) Experiences indifferent modalities may overlap in content without a parallel experience in character, i.e., visual and active experiences of circularity feel completely different (iv) The content of an experience with a given character may varingly differ from an accorded manifestation of background subjectivity, i.e., a certain aural experience may come to have the content 'singing birds' only after the subject has learned something about birds.

According to the act/object analysis of experience, which is a special case of the act/ object analysis of consciousness, every experience involves an object of experience if it has not material object. Two main lines of argument may be offered in supports of this view, one phenomenological and the other semantic.

In an outline, the phenomenological argument is as follows. Whenever we have an experience answers to it, we seem to be presented with something through the experience which something through the experience, which if in ourselves diaphanous. The object of the experience is whatever is so presented to us ~. Arising it an individual thing, or some event or a state of affairs.

The semantic argument is that they require objects of experience in order to make sense of cretin factures of our talk about experience, including, in particular, the following (1) Simple attributions of experience, i.e., 'Rod is experiencing a pink square', seem to be relational (2) We appear to refer to objects of experience and to attribute properties to them, i.e., we had been given, in that the after image with which John experienced had appeared, as (3) To qualify over objects of experience, i.e., Macbeth saw something which his wife did not see.

The act/object analysis faces several problems concerning the status of objects of experience. Currently the most common view is that they are 'sense-data'-Private mental entities which actually posses the traditional sensory qualities represented by the experience of which they are the objects. But the very idea of an essentially private entity is suspect. Moreover, since an experience must apparently represent something as having a determinable property, i.e., redness, without representing it as having any subordinate determinate property, i.e., any specific given shade of red, a sense-datum may actually have our determinate property without saving any determinate property subordinate to it. Even more disturbing is that sense-data may contradictory properties, since experience can have properties, since experience can have contradictory contents. A case in point is te water fall illusion: If you stare at a waterfall for a minute and the immediately fixate on a nearby rock, you are likely to are an experience of moving upward while it remains inexactly the same place. The sense-data, . . . private mental entities which actually posses the traditional sensory qualities represented by the experience of which they are te objects., but te very idea of an essentially private entity is suspect. Moreover, since an experience may apparently represent something other than is apparent, as having some determinable properties, i.e., redness, without representing it as having any subordinate determinate property, i.e., any specific shade of red, a sense-datum may actually have a determinate property without having any determinate property subordinate to it. Even more disturbing is the sense-data may have contradictory properties, since experiences can have contradictory contents.

Treating objects can avoid these problems of experience as properties, however, fails to do justice to the appearances, for experiences, however complex, but with properties embodied in individuals. The view that objects of experience are that Meinongian objects accommodate this point. It is also attractive, in as far as (1) it allows experiences to represent properties other than traditional sensory qualities, and (2) it allows for the identification of objects of experience and objects of perception in the case of experiences which constitute perceptivity.

According to the act/object analysis of experience, every experience with contentual representation involves an object of experience, an act of awareness has related the subject (the event of experiencing that object). This is meant to apply not only to perceptions, which have material objects, whatever is perceived, but also to experiences like hallucinating and dream experiences, which do not. Such experiences are, nonetheless, less appearing to represent of something, and their objects are supposed to be whatever it is that they represent. Act/object theorists may differ on the nature of objects of experience, which we have treated as properties, Meinongian objects, which may not exist or have any form of being, and, more commonly, private mental entities with sensory qualities. We have now usually applied the term 'sense-data' to the latter, but has also been used as a general term for objects f sense experiences, in the work of G.E., Moore. Its terms of representative realism, objects of perceptions, of which we are 'indirectly aware' are always distinct from objects of experience, of which we are 'directly aware'. Meinongian, however, may treat objects of perception as existing objects of perception, least there is mention, Meinong's most famous doctrine derives from the problem of intentionality, which led him to countenance objects, such as the golden mountain, that is capable of being the object of thought, although they do not actually exist. This doctrine was one of the principle's targets of Russell's theory of 'definitive descriptions', however, it came as part o a complex and interesting package of concept if the theory of meaning, and scholars are not united in what supposedly that Russell was fair to it.

A general problem for the act/object analysis is that the question of whether two subjects are experiencing one and the same thing, as opposed to having exactly similar experiences, that it appears to have an answer only, on the assumptions that the experience concerned are perceptions with material objects. But in terms of the act/object analysis the question must have an answer even when conditions are not satisfied. (The answers negative on the sense-datum theory: It could be positive of the versions of the act/object analysis, depending on the facts of the case.)

In view of the above problems, we should reassess the case of act/object analysis. The phenomenological argument is not, on reflection, convincing, for it is easy enough to grant that any experience appears to present 'us' with an object without accepting that it actually does. The semantic argument is more impressive, but is nonetheless, answerable. The seemingly relational structure of attributions of experiences is a challenge dealt with below in connection with the adverbial theory. Apparent reference to and we can handle quantification over objects of experience themselves and quantification over experience tacitly according to content, thus, 'the after image which John experienced was an experience of green' and 'Macbeth saw something which his wife did not see' becomes 'Macbeth had a visual experience which his wife did not have'.

Nonetheless, pure cognitivism attempts to avoid the problems facing the act/object analysis by reducing experiences to cognitive events or associated dispositions, i.e., 'We might identify Susy's experience of a rough surface beneath her hand with the event of her acquiring the belief that there is a rough surface beneath her hand, or, if she does not acquire this belief, with a disposition to acquire it which we have somehow blocked.

This position has attractions. It does full justice. And to the important role of experience as a source of belief acquisition. It would also help clear the say for a naturalistic theory of mind, since there seems to be some prospect of a physical/functionalist account of belief and other intentional states. But its failure has completely undermined pure cognitivism to accommodate the fact that experiences have a felt character which cannot be reduced to their content.

The relearnt intuitions are as, (I) that when we say that someone is experiencing an 'A', this has an experience 'of 'A', we are using this content-expression to specify the type of thing which the experience is especially apt to fit, (ii) that doing this is a matter of saying something about the experience itself (and maybe also about the normal causes of like experiences), and (iii) that there is no-good reason to suppose that it involves the description of an object which the experience is 'of'. Thus, the effective role of the content-expression is a statement of experience is to modify the verb it compliments, not to introduce a special type of object.

A final position which we should mention is the state theory, according to which a sense experience of an 'A' is an occurrent, non-relational state of the kind which the subject would be in when perceiving an 'A'. Suitably qualified, this claim is no doubt truer, but its significance is subject to debate. Here it is enough to remark that the claim is compactable with both pure cognitivism and the adverbial theory, and that we have probably best advised state theorists to adopt adverbials as a means of developing their intuition.

Perceptual knowledge is knowledge acquired by or through the senses, this includes most of what we know. We cross intersections when everything we see the light turn green, head for the kitchen when we smell the roast burning, squeeze the fruit to determine its ripeness, and climb out of bed when we hear the alarm ring. In each case we come to know something-that the light has turned green, that the roast is burning, that the melon is overripe, and that it is time to get up by some sensory means. Seeing that the light has turned green is learning something - that the light has turned green - by use of the eyes. Feeling that the melon is overripe is coming to know a fact that the melon is overripe by one's sense of touch. In each case we have somehow based on the resulting knowledge, derived from or grounded in the sort of experience that characterizes the sense modality in question.

Much of our perceptual knowledge is indirect, dependent or derived. By this I mean that the facts we describe ourselves as learning, as coming to know, by perceptual means are pieces of knowledge that depend on our coming to know something else, another fact, in a more direct way. We see, by newspapers, that our team has lost again, see, by her expression, that she is nervous. This dived or dependent sort of knowledge is particularly prevalent in the case of vision, but it occurs, to a lesser degree, in every sense modality. We install bells and other sound makers so that we can, for example, hear (by the alarm) that someone is at the door and (by the bell) that its time to get up. When we obtain knowledge in this way, it is clear that unless one sees-hence, comes to know something about the gauge that it reads 'empty', the newspaper (what it says) and the person's expression, one would not see, hence, we know, that what one perceptual representation means have described as coming to know. If one cannot hear that the bell is ringing, one cannot –not, at least, in this way hear that one's visitors have arrived. In such cases one sees, hears, smells, etc., that 'a' is 'F', coming to know thereby that 'a' is 'F', by seeing, hearing etc., we have derived from that come other condition, 'b's being 'G', that 'a' is 'F', or dependent on, the more basic perceptivities that of its being attributive to knowledge that of 'b' is 'G'.

Though perceptual knowledge about objects is often, in this way, dependent on knowledge of facts about different objects, the derived knowledge is something about the same object. That is, we see that 'a' is 'F' by seeing, not that another object is 'G', but that, 'a' itself is 'G'. We see, by her expression, that she is nervous. She tells that the fabric is silk (not polyester) by the characteristic 'greasy' feel of the fabric itself (not, as I do, by what is printed on the label). We tell whether it is an oak tree, a Porsche convertible, a geranium, an ingenious rock or a misprint by its shape, colour, texture, size, behaviour and distinctive markings. Perceptual knowledge of this sort is also derived ~. Derived from the more facts (about 'a') we use to make the identification. In this case, the perceptual knowledge is still indirect because, although the same object is involved, the facts we come to know about it are different from the facts that enable 'us' to know it.

We sometimes describe derived knowledge as inferential, but this is misleading. At the conscious level there is no passage of the mind from premised to conclusion, no reason-sensitivity of mind from problem-solving. The observer, the one who sees that 'a' is 'F' by seeing that 'b' (or, 'a' in itself) is 'G', need not be and typically is not aware of any process of inference, any passage of the mind from one belief to another. The resulting knowledge, though logically derivative, is psychologically immediate. I could see that she was getting angry, so I moved my hand. I did not, at least not at any conscious level, infer (from her expression and behaviour) that she was getting angry. I could (or, it seems to me) see that she was getting angry, it is this psychological immediacy that makes indirect perceptual knowledge a species of perceptual knowledge.

The psychological immediacy that characterizes so much of our perceptual knowledge -even (sometimes) the most indirect and derived informatics, such if it does not mean that no one requires learning to know in this way. One is not born with (may, in fact, never develop) the ability to recognize daffodils, muskrats and angry companions. It is only after a long experience that one is able visually to identify such things. Beginners may do something corresponding to inference, they recognize relevant features of trees, birds, and flowers, features they already know how to identify perceptually, and then infer (conclude), on the basis of what they see, and under the guidance of more expert observers, that it is an oak, a finch or a geranium. But the experts (and wee are all experts on many aspects of our familiar surroundings) do not typically go through such a process. The expert just sees that it is an oak, a finch or a geranium. The perceptual knowledge of the expert is still dependent, of course, since even an expert cannot see what kind of flower it is if she cannot first see its colour and shape, but it is to say that the expert has developed identificatory skills that no longer require the sort of conscious self-inferential process that characterize the beginner's efforts.

It would seem, moreover, that these background assumptions, if they are to yield knowledge that 'a' is 'F', as they must if the observer is to see (by b's being G) that 'a' is 'F', must they qualify as knowledge. For if no one has known this background fact, if no one knows it whether 'a' is 'F' when 'b' is 'G', then the knowledge of 'b's' bing 'G' is taken by itself, powerless to generate the knowledge that 'a' is 'F'. If the conclusion is to be known to be true, both the premises used to reach that conclusion must be known to be truer, or so it would seem.

Externalists, however, argue that the indirect knowledge that 'a' is 'F', though it may depend on the knowledge that 'b' is 'G', does not require knowledge of the connecting fact, the fact that 'a' is 'F' when 'b' is 'G'. Simple belief (or, perhaps, justified beliefs, there are stronger and weaker versions of externalism) in the connecting fact is sufficient to confer a knowledge of the connected fact. Even if, strictly speaking, I do not know she is nervous whenever she fidgets like that, I can none the less see (hence, recognized, or know) that she is nervous (by the way she fidgets) if I am [correctly] to assume that this behaviour is a reliable expression of nervousness. One need not know the gauge is working well to make observations (acquire observational knowledge) with it. All that we require, besides the observer believing that the gauge is reliable, is that the gauge, in fact, be reliable, i.e., that the observers background beliefs be true. Critics of externalism have been quick to point out that this theory has the unpalatable consequence-can make that knowledge possible and, in this sense, be made to rest on lucky hunches (that turn out true) and unsupported (even irrational) beliefs. Surely, internalists argue if one is going to know that 'a' is 'F' on the basis of 'b's' being 'G', one should have (as a bare minimum) some justification for thinking that 'a' is 'F', or is probably 'F', when 'b' is 'G'.

Whatever view one takes about these matters (with the possible exception of extreme externalism), indirect perception obviously requires some understanding (knowledge? Justification? Belief? Of the general relationship between the fact one comes to know (that 'a' is 'F') and the facts (that 'b' is 'G') that enable one to know it. And it is this requirement on background knowledge or understanding that leads to questions about the possibility of indirect perceptual knowledge. Is it really knowledge? Sceptical doubts have inspired the first question about whether we can ever know the connecting facts in question. How is it possible to learn, to acquire knowledge of, the connecting fact's knowledge of which is necessary to see (by b's being 'G') that 'a' is 'F'? These connecting facts do not appear to be perceptually knowable. Quite the contrary, they appear to be general truths knowable (if knowable at all) by inductive inference from past observations. And if one is sceptical about obtaining knowledge in this indirect, inductive as, one is, perforced, indirect knowledge, including indirect perceptivity, where we have described knowledge of a sort openly as above, that depends on in it.

Even if one puts aside such sceptical questions, least of mention, there remains a legitimate concern about the perceptual character of this kind of knowledge. If one sees that 'a' is 'F' by seeing that 'b' is 'G', is one really seeing that 'a' is 'F'? Isn't perception merely a part ~? And, indeed, from an epistemological standpoint, whereby one comes to know that 'a' is 'F?'. One must, it is true, see that 'b' is 'G', but this is only one of the premises needed to reach the conclusion (knowledge) that 'a' is 'F'. There is also the background knowledge that is essential to te process. If we think of a theory as any factual proposition, or set of factual propositions, that cannot itself be known in some direct observational way, we can express this worry by saying that indirect perception is always theory-loaded: Seeing (indirectly) that 'a' is 'F' is only possible if the observer already has knowledge of justifications for, belief in some theory, for which the theory of 'connecting' the fact by one that comes to know (that 'a' is 'F') with the fact (that 'b' is 'G') that enables one to know it.

This of course, reverses the standard foundationalist pictures of human knowledge. Instead of theoretical knowledge depending on, and being derived from, perception, perception of the indirect sort, presupposes a prior knowledge of theories.

Foundationalist's are quick to point out that this apparent reversal in the structure of human knowledge is only apparent. Our indirect perceptions of facts depend on theory, yes, but this merely shows that indirect perceptional knowledge is not part of the foundation. To reach the kind of perceptual knowledge that lies at the foundation, we need to look at a form of perception that is purified of all theoretical elements. This, then, will be perceptual knowledge, pure and direct. We have needed no background knowledge or assumptions about connecting regularities in direct perception because the known facts are presented directly and immediately and not (as, in direct perception) on the basis of some other facts. In direct perception all the justification (needed for knowledge) is right there in the experience itself.

What, then, about the possibility of perceptual knowledge pure and direct, the possibility of coming to know, on the basis of sensory experience, that 'a' is 'F' where this does not require, and in no way presupposes, backgrounds assumptions or knowledge that has a source outside the experience itself? Where is this epistemological 'pure gold' to be found?

There are, basically, two views about the nature of direct perceptual knowledge (Coherentists would deny that any of our knowledge is basic in this sense). We can call these views (following traditional nomenclature) direct realism and representationalism or representative realism. A representationalist restricts direct perceptual knowledge to objects of a very special sort: Ideas, impressions, or sensations (sometimes called sense-data) - entities in the mind of the observer. One directly perceives a fact, i.e., that 'b' is 'G', only, when, 'b' is a mental entity of some sort a subjective appearance or sense-data - and 'G' is a property of this datum. Knowledge of these sensory states is supposed to be certain and infallible. These sensory facts are, so to speak, right upon against the mind's eye. One cannot be mistaken about these facts for these facts are, in really, facts about the way things appear to be, one cannot be mistaken about the way things appear to be. Normal perception of external conditions, then, turns out to be (always) a type of indirect perception. One 'sees' that there is a tomato in front of one by seeing that the appearances (of the tomato) have a certain quality (reddish and bulgy) and inferring (this is typically said to be atomistic and unconscious), on the basis of certain background assumptions, i.e., that there typically is a tomato in front of one when one has experiences of this sort, that there is a tomato in front of one. All knowledge of objective reality, then, even what commonsense regards as the most direct perceptual knowledge, is based on an even more direct knowledge of the appearances.

For the representationalist, then, perceptual knowledge of our physical surroundings is always theory-loaded and indirect. Such perception is 'loaded' with the theory that there is some regular, some uniform, correlations between the way things appear (known in a perceptually direct way) and the way things actually are (known, if known at all, in a perceptually indirect way).

The second view, direct realism, refuses to restrict direct perceptual knowledge to an inner world of subjective experience. Though the direct realist is willing to concede that much of our knowledge of the physical world is indirect, however, direct and immediate it may sometimes feel, some perceptual knowledge of physical reality is direct. What makes it direct is that such knowledge is not based on, nor in any way dependent on, other knowledge and belief. The justification needed for the knowledge is right in the experience itself.

To understand the way this is supposed to work, consider an ordinary example. 'S' identifies a banana (learns that it is a banana) by noting its shape and colour-perhaps even tasting and smelling it (to make sure it's not wax). In this case the perceptual knowledge that it is a banana is (the direct realist admits, indirect on S's perceptual knowledge of its shape, colour, smell, and taste. 'S' learns that it is a banana by seeing that it is yellow, banana-shaped, etc. Nonetheless, S's perception of the banana's colour and shape is not direct. 'S' does not see that the object is yellow, for example, by seeing (knowing, believing) anything more basic either about the banana or anything e. g., his own sensation of the banana. What 'S' acquired as a cognitive skill, a disposition to believe of yellow objects he saw that they were yellow. The exercise of this skill does not require, and in no way depends on having any unfolding beliefs thereof, where 'S' has the identificatory success will depend on his operating in certain special conditions, of course. 'S' will not, perhaps, be able visually to identify yellow objects in dramatically reduced lighting, at funny viewing angled, or when afflicted with certain nervous disorders. But these facts about 'S' can see that something is yellow does not show that his perceptual knowledge (that 'a' is yellow) in any way depends on a belief (let alone knowledge) that he is in such special conditions. It merely shows that direct perceptual knowledge is the result of exercising a skill, an identificatory skill, that like any skill, requires certain conditions for its successful exercise. An expert basketball player cannot shoot accurately in a hurricane. He needs normal conditions to do what he has learned to do. So also with individuals who have developed perceptual (cognitive) skills. They needed normal conditions to do what they have learned to do. They need normal conditions too sere, for example, that something is yellow. But they do not, any more than the basketball player, have to know they are in these conditions to do what being in these conditions enables them to do.

This means, of course, that for the direct realist direct perceptual knowledge is fallible and corrigible. Whether 'S' sees that 'a' is 'F' depends on his being caused to believe that 'a' is 'F' in conditions that are appropriate for an exercise of that cognitive skill. If conditions are right, then 'S' sees (hence, knows) that 'a' is 'F'. If they aren't, he doesn't. Whether or not 'S' knows depends, then, not on what else (if anything) 'S' believes, but on the circumstances in which 'S' comes to believe. This being so, this type of direct realist is a form of externalism. Direct perception of objective facts, pure perpetual knowledge of external events, is made possible because what is needed by way of justification for such knowledge has been reduced. Background knowledge ~ is not needed.

This means that the origination, or it foundations of knowledge are fallible. Nonetheless, though fallible, they are in no way derived, that is, what makes them foundations. Even if they are brittle, as foundations are sometimes, everything else upon them.

Epistemology, in Greek represents its term as epistēmē, and is meant to mean of a well-balanced form of 'knowledge', which is the theory of knowledge, and its fundamental questions include the origin of knowledge, the place of experience in generating knowledge, and the place of reason in doing so; the relationship between knowledge and certainty, and between knowledge and the impossibility of error, the possibility of universal scepticism, and the changing forms of knowledge that arise from, a new conceptualized world. All these issues link with other central concerns of philosophy, such as the nature of truth and the nature of truth and the nature of experience and meaning. Seeing epistemology is possible as dominated by two rival metaphors. One is that of a building or pyramid, built on foundations. In this conception it is the job of the philosopher to describe especially secure foundations, and to identify secure modes of construction, so that they can show the resulting edifice to be sound. This metaphor favours some idea of the 'given' as a basis of knowledge, and of a rationally defensible theory of confirmation and inference for construction. The other metaphor is that of a boat or fuselage, which has no foundation but owes its strength to the stability given by its interlocking parts. This rejects the idea of a basis in the 'given', favours ideas of coherence and 'holism', but finds it harder to ward off scepticism. The problem of defining knowledge as to true belief plus some favoured relations between the believer and the facts began with Plato's view in the "Theaetetus" that knowledge is true belief plus some 'logos'.

Philosophical knowledge is approximate and contrasting philosophically can formulate a traditional view of philosophical knowledge and scientific investigations, as follows: The two types of investigations differ both in their methods (the former is intuitively deductive, and the latter empirical) and in the metaphysical status of their results (the former yields facts that are metaphysically necessary and the latter yields facts that is metaphysically contingent). Yet, the two types of investigations resemble each other in that both, if successful, uncover new facts, and these facts, although expressed in language, are generally not about language, except investigations in such specialized areas as philosophy of language and empirical linguistics.

This view of philosophical knowledge has considerable appeal, but it faces problems. First, the conclusions of some common philosophical arguments seem preposterous. Such positions as that it is no more reasonable to ear bread than arsenic (because it is only in the past that arsenic poisoned people), or that one can never know he is not dreaming, may seem to go so far against commonsense as to be for that an unacceptable reason seems much as to displeasing of issues. Second, philosophical investigation does not lead to a consensus among philosophers. Philosophy, unlike the sciences, lacks an established body of generally-agreed-upon truths. Moreover, philosophy lacks an unequivocally applicable method of setting disagreements. (The qualifier 'unequivocally applicable' is to forestall the objection that the method has settled philosophical disagreements of intuitive deductive argumentation, which is often unresolved disagreement about which side has won a philosophical argument.)

In the face of these and other considerations, various philosophical movements have revoked the above traditional view of philosophical knowledge. Thus, verificationism responds to the unresolvability of traditional philosophical disagreements by putting forth a criterion of literal meaningfulness. 'A statement is held to be literally meaningful if and only if it is either analytic or empirically verifiable (Ayer, 1952), where a statement is analytic if it is just a matter of definition. Traditional controversial philosophical views, such as that having knowledge of the world outside one's own mind is metaphysically impossible, would count as neither analytic nor empirically verifiable.

Various objections have been raised to this verification principle. The most important is that the principle is self-refuting, i.e., that when one attempts to apply the verification principle to itself, the result is that the principle comes out as literally meaningless, therefore not true because it is empirically neither verifiable nor analytic. This move may seem verifiable nor analytic. This move may seem like a trick, but it reveals a deep methodological problem with the verificationist approach. The verification principle is determined to delegitimize all controversy that is neither nor resolvable empirically or expending a recourse to definition. The principle itself, however, releases neither of the established nor empirically a recourse to definition. The principle is an attempt to rule out synthetic deductivity as a controversial issue, of debate, yet the principle itself is both synthetic deductivity and controversial. It is ironic that the self-refutingness of the verification principle is one of the very few points on which philosophers nowadays approach consensuses.

Ordinary language philosophy, another twentieth-century attempt to delegitimize traditional philosophical problems, faces a parallel but an unrecognized problem of self-refutingness. Just as they can characterize verificationism as reacting against unresolvable deductivity, ordinary language philosophy can so be characterized as reacting against deductivity as an acceding of counter intuitiveness. The ordinary language philosopher rejected counterintuitive philosophical positions (such as the view that time is unreal or that one can never know anything about other minds) by saying that these views 'go against ordinary language', Malcolm and in Rorty, (1970), i.e., that these views go against the way the ordinary person uses such terms as 'know' and 'unreal', since the ordinary person would reject the above counterintuitive statements about knowledge and time. On the ordinary language view, it follows that the sceptic does not mean the same thing by 'know' as does the non-philosopher, since they use the terms differently and meaning is use. Thus, on this view, sceptics and anti sceptics no more disagreement about knowledge than someone who says 'Banks are financial institutions' and someone who say 'Banks are the shores of rivers: is the disagreement about banks?

An obvious objection here is that many factors besides meaning help to decide use. For example, two people who disagree about whether the world is round use the word 'round' differently in that one applies it to the world while the other does not, yet they do not by that mean different things by 'world' or 'round'. Ordinary language philosophy allows that this aspect of use is not part of the meaning, since it rests on a disagreement about empirical facts. Only in relegating all non-empirical disagreements to differences in linguistic meaning, the ordinary language philosopher denies the possibility of substantive, non-linguistic disagreement over deductively, non-linguistic disagreement over a speculative assertion of facts and thus, like the verificationist, disallows that 'if a child that was learning the language were to say, in a situation where we were sitting in a room with chairs about, that it was; highly probable' that were chairs there, we should smile and correct his chairs there, we should smile and correct his language. Malcolm may be right about this case, since it is so unlikely that children would have independently developed a scientific philosophy. Nevertheless, a parallel response seems obviously inappropriate as a reply to a philosopher who says 'One can never know that one is not dreaming', or for that matter, as a reply to an inept arithmetic student who says, '33 =12 + 19'. If it were true that some philosophers uttering the first of these sentences were not using 'know' in the usual sense, he could not convey his philosophical views to a French speaker by uttering the sentence's French translation ('On ne peut jamais savoir qu' on ne rêve pas'), any more than one can convey his eight-year-old cousin Mary's opinion that her teacher is vicious by saying 'Mary's teacher is viscous' if Mary wrongly thinks 'viscous' demands 'vicious' and continues using it that way. However, failures obviously to translate 'know' or its cognates into their French synonyms would prevent an English-speaking sceptic from accurately representing his views in French at all. The ordinary language view that all non-empirical disagreements are linguistic disagreements entails that if someone believes the sentence 'a being's F' when this sentence expresses the deductive proposition that 'a being's F', then including to that in what property he takes as 'F' to express was part of what he means by 'a'. However, this obviously goes against the Malcolmian 'ordinary use' of the term 'meaning', i.e., what ordinary people, once they understand the term 'meaning', believe on deductivity as a grounding about the extension of the term 'meaning'. For example, the ordinary man would deny that the inept student mentioned above cannot be using his words with our usual meaning when he says '33 = 12 + 19'. Like the earlier objection of self-refutingness to verificationism, this objection reveals a deep methodological problem. Just as synthetic deductivity may elicit a controversy that cannot be ruled out by a principle that is both synthetic deductively and controversial, deductive counter-intuitiveness cannot be ruled out by a principle that is both deductive and counterintuitive.

Although verificationist and ordinary language philosophy thus are both self-refuting, the problems that helped motivate these positions need to be addressed. What are we to say about the fact (a) many philosophical conclusions seem wildly counterintuitive and (b) many investigations do no lead to philosophical consensuses?

To put the first problem in perspective, it is important to see that even highly counterintuitive philosophical views generally have arguments behind them-arguments that 'start with something so simple is not to seem with surprising. Proceed by steps do obvious as not to seem worth taking, before '[ending] with, no one will believe it'. But since repeated applications of commonsense can thus lead to philosophical conclusions that conflict with commonsense, commonsense is a problematic criterion for assessing philosophical views. It is true that, once we have weighted the relevant argument, we must ultimately rely on our judgement about whether, in the light of these arguments, it just seems reasonable to accept a given philosophical view. But this truism should not be confused with certain sorts of claims that are unknowable or non-conformably on the sole ground that it would therefore be meaningless or unintelligible. Only if meaningfulness or intelligibility is a guarantee of knowability or confirmability is the position sound, if it is, nothing we understand would be unknowable or unconfirmable by us.

Criteria and knowledge, except for alleged cases that things that are evident for one just by being true, it has often been thought, anything that is known must satisfy certain 'criteria' as well for being true. It is also thought that anything that is known must satisfy certain criteria or standards. These criteria are general principles specifying the sorts of considerations that will make some propositions evident or just make accepting it warranted to some degree. Common suggestions for this character encompass one clearly and distinctly conceive a proposition 'p', e.g., that 2 + 2 =4, 'p' is evident: Or, if 'p' coheres with the bulk of one's beliefs, 'p' is warranted. These might be criteria under which putative self-evident truths, e.g., that one clearly and distinctly conceive 'p'. 'Transmit' the status as evident they already have without criteria to other propositions like 'p', or they might be criteria by which purely non-epistemic considerations, e.g., facts about logical connections or about conception that need not be already evident or warranted, originally create 'p's' upon an epistemic status. If that in turn, can be; transmitted' to other propositions, e.g., by deduction or induction, criteria will be specifying when it is. These criteria are general principles specifying what sort of consideration 'C' will make a proposition 'p' evident to 'us'.

Traditionally, suggestions contain: (a) if a proposition 'p', e.g., 2 + 2 = 4, is clearly and distinctly conceived, then 'p' is evident, or simply, (b) if we cannot conceive 'p' to be false, then 'p' is evident: Or, whatever we are immediately conscious of in thought or experience, e.g., that we seem to see red, is evident. These might be criteria under which putative self-evident truths, e.g., that one clearly and distinctly conceive 'p', transmits the status as evident they already have for one without criteria to other propositions like 'p'. Alternatively, they might be criteria under which epistemic status, e.g., p being evident, is 'originally created' by purely non-epistemic considerations, e.g., facts about how 'p' arises to initiate that which carry on of neither self-renewal nor what is already confronting its own criterion's unquestionability.

However, it is 'originally created', presumably epistemic status, including degrees of warranted acceptance or probability, can be 'transmitted' deductively from premises to conclusions. Criteria then must say when and to what degree, e.g., 'p' and 'q' are warranted, given the epistemic considerations that 'p' is warranted and so is 'q'. (Must the logical connection itself be evident?) It is usually inductively, as when evidence that observed type 'Some' things have regularly been 'F' warrants acceptance, without undermining (overriding) evidence, of an unobserved 'A' as 'F'. Such warrant is defeasible. Thus, despite regular observations of black crows, thinking an unobserved crow black might not be very warranted if there have recently been radiation changes potentially affecting bird colour.

Traditionally, criteria do not seem to make evident propositions about anything beyond our own thoughts, experiences and necessary truths, to which deductively or inductive criteria may be applied. Moreover, arguably, inductive criteria, including criteria warranting the best explanations of data, never make things evident or warrant their acceptance enough to count as knowledge.

Contemporary philosophers, however, have defended criteria by which, e.g., considerations concerning a person's facial expression, may (defeasibly) make her pain or anguish (Lycan, 1971). More often, they have argued for criteria by which some propositions about perceived reality can be made evident by sense experience itself by evident propositions about it. For instance, without relevant evidence that perception is currently unreliable, it is evident we actually see a pink square if we have sense experience of seeming to see a pink square (Pollock, 1986): Or, if it is evident we have such experience, or if in sense experience we spontaneously think we see a pink square. The experiential consideration allegedly can be enough to make reality evident, although defeasibly. It can do this on its own, and does not b=need support from further considerations such as the absence of undermining evidence or inductive evidence for a general link between experience and reality. Of course, there can be undermining evidence. So we need criteria that determine when evidence undermines and ceases to undermine.

Warrant might also be increased than just 'passed on'. The coherence of probable propositions with other probable propositions might (feasiblely) make then all more evident (Firth, 1964). Thus even if seeming to see a chair initially made a chair's presence only probable, its presence might eventually become evident by cohering with claims about chair perception in other cases (Chisholm, 1989). The latter may be warranted in turn by 'memory' and 'introspection' criteria, as often suggested, by which recalling or introspecting 'p' defeasibly warrant 'p's' acceptance. Some philosophers argue further that coherence does not just increase warrant, and defend an overall coherence criterion: Excluding perhaps initial warrant for propositions concerning our beliefs and their logical interrelations, what warrants any proposition to any degree for 'u'; is its coherence with the most coherent system of belief available (BonJour, 1985?).

Contemporary epistemologists thus suggest the traditional picture of criteria may need alteration in three ways. Additionally, evidence may subject even our most basic judgements too rational. Correction, though they count as evident on the basis of our criteria. Warrant may be transmitted other than through deductive and inductive relations between propositions. Transmission criteria might not simply 'pass' evidence on linearly from a foundation of highly evident 'premisses' to 'conclusions' that are never more evident.

Criteria then standards take the form: 'If 'C', then (without undermining evidence) 'p' is evident or warranted to degree 'd'. Arguably, a criterion does not play to the greater of parts to some function of its own initially forming of our beliefs (Pollock, 1986.) For them to be the standards of epistemic status for 'u', however, its typically thought criterial considerations must be omnes in the light of which we can at least check, and perhaps correct our judgements. As with justification and knowledge, the traditional view of content has been strongly internalized in character. Similarly, a coherentists view could also be internalized, if both the belief and other states with which a justificantum belief is required to cohere and the coherence relations themselves are reflectively accessible. Remaining still, what makes such a view externalist is the absence of any requirement that the person for whom the belief is justified have cognitive access to the relation of reliability in question. Lacking such access, such a person will in general have no reason for thinking that the belief is true or likely to be truer, but will, on such an account, nor the less, be epistemically justified in accepting it. Which identifies epistemic justification with having a reason, perhaps even a conclusive reason, for thinking that a belief is true? An epistemologist working within this tradition is likely to feel that the externalist, than offering a competing account of the same concept of epistemic justification with which the traditional epistemologist is concerned, has simply changed the subject.

Traditionally, the epistemologists have therefore thought criterial considerations must be at least discoverable through reflection or introspection and thus ultimately concern internal factors about our conception, thoughts or experience. However, others think objective checks must be publically recognizable checks. Nevertheless, argument in Wittgenstein's "Philosophical Investigations," which is concerned with the concepts or, and relations manifestations (the inner as in and of itself with and the outer), self-states, avowals of experiences and descriptions of experiences. It is sometimes used narrowly to refer to a single chain of argument in which Wittgenstein demonstrates the incoherence of the idea that sensation-names. Names of experiences are given meaning by association with a mental 'object', i.e., the word 'pain' by association with the sensation of pain, or by mental (private) ostensive definition in which a mental 'entity' supposedly functions as a sample, e.g., a mental image, stored in memory, is conceived as providing a paradigm for the application of a name.

A 'private language' is not a private code, which could be cracked by another person, nor a language spoken by only one person, which could be taught to others, but rather a putative language, the individual words of which refer to what can (apparently) are known only be the speaker, i.e., to this empiricist jargon, to the 'ideas' in his mind. It has been a presupposition of the mainstream of modern philosophy, empiricist, rationalist and Kantian alike, of representational idealism, and of contemporary cognitive representationalism that the languages we speak are such private languages, that the foundations of language no less than the foundations of knowledge in private experience. To undermine this picture with all its complex ramifications is the purpose of Wittgenstein's private language argument.

The idea that the language each of 'us' speaks is essentially private, which learning a language is a matter of associating words with, or ostensively defending words by reference to, subjective experience (the 'given'). The communication is a matter of stimulating a pattern of associations in the mind of the hearer qualitatively identical with that in the mind of the speakers is linked with multiple mutually supporting misconceptions about language, experiences and their identity, the mental and its relation to behaviour, self-knowledge and knowledge if the states of the mind of others, and thus that for criterial considerations we must ultimately concern those of public factors, e.g., that standard conditions (daylight, eye open, etc. (for reliable perceptual reports obtain.

It remains, nonetheless, what makes criteria correct? For many epistemologists, their correctness is an irreducible necessary truth, a matter of a lout metaphysical or of our lexical conventions, concerning epistemic status and the considerations that determine it. Others object that it remains mysterious why particular considerations are criterial unless notions of the evident or warranted or correct are further defined in non-epistemic terms. Criteria might be defined, for example, as principles reflecting our deepest self-critical thoughts about what considerations yield truth, or as norms of thought that practical rationality demands we adopt is we are to be effective agents. However, many will further objective satisfactions that criteria must yield truth or be prone to. They insist that necessarily (1) whatever is warranted has an objectively good chance of truth, and (2) whatever is evident is true or-almost invariably true. Epistemic notions allegedly lose their point unless they somehow measure a proposition's actual prospects for truth for 'us'.

Against (1) and (2), a common objection is that no considerations relevantly guarantee truth, even for the most part, or in the; long run (BonJour, 1985). This is not obvious with traditional putative criterial considerations like clear and distinct conception or immediate awareness. Nevertheless, critics argue, when talk of such considerations is unambiguously construed as talk of mental activity, and is not just synonymous with talk of clearly and distinctly or immediately knowing, there is no necessary connection between being criterially evident on the basis of such considerations and being true (Sellars, 1979). The mere coincidence in some cases that the proposition we conceive is true cannot be what makes the proposition evident.

Still, (1) and (2) might be necessary, while the correctness of putative criteria is a contingent fact, given various facts about 'u' and our world: It is no coincidence that adhering to these criteria leads to truth, almost invariably or frequently. Given our need to survive with limited intellectual resources and time, perhaps it is not as surprising that in judging issues we only demand criterial considerations that are fallible, checkable, corrective and contingently lead to truth. Nonetheless, specifying the relevant truth, connection is highly problematic. Moreover, reliability considerations now seem to be criterial for criteria although reliability, e.g., concerning perception, are not always accessible to introspection and reelection. Perhaps, traditional accessibility requirements may be rejected. Possibly, instead, what makes putative criterions correct can differ from the criterial considerations that make its correctness evident. Thus, there might be criteria for (defeasibly) identifying criteria, e.g., whether propositions 'feel right', or are considered warranted, in 'thought experiments' where we imagine various putative considerations present and absent. Later reflection and inquiry might reveal what makes them all correct, e.g., reliability, or being designed by God or nature for our reliable use, etc.

In any case, if criterial considerations do not guarantee truth, knowledge will require more than truth and satisfying even the most demanding. Whether we know new say, a pink cube on a particular occasion may also require that there fortunately be no discernable facts, e.g., of our presence in a hologram gallery, to undermine the experiment basis for our judgement -or, perhaps instead, that it is no accident our judgement is true than merely probably true, given the criteria we adhere to and the circumstance, e.g., our presence in a normal room. Claims that truths that satisfy the relevant criteria are known can clearly be given many interpretations.

Many contemporary philosophers address these issued criteria with untraditional approaches to meaning and truth. Pollock (1974), for example, argues that learning ordinary concepts like 'bird' or 'red' involves learning to make judgements with them in condition, e.g., perpetual experiences, which warrant them. Though defeasibly, inasmuch as, we also learn to correct the judgements despite the presence of such conditions. These conditions are not logically necessary or sufficient for the truth of judgements. Nonetheless, the identity of our ordinary concepts makes the criteria we learn for making judgements necessarily correct. Although not all warranted assertions are true, there is no idea of their truths completely divorced from what undefeated criterial considerations allow 'us' to assert. However, satisfying criteria still in some way compatible with future defeat, even frequent, and with not knowing, just as it was with error and defeat in more traditional accounts.

By appealing to defeasibly warranting criteria then, it seems we cannot show we know 'p' rather than merely satisfy the criteria. Worse, critics argue that we cannot even have knowledge by satisfying such criteria. Knowing 'p' allegedly requires more, but what evidence, besides that entitling 'us' to claim the currently undefeated satisfaction of criteria, could entitle 'us' to claim more, e.g., that 'p' would not be defeated? Yet, Knower, at least of reflection, must be entitled to give assurances concerning these further conditions (Wright, 1984). Otherwise, we would not be interested in a concept of knowledge as opposed to the evident or warranted. These contentions might be disputed to save a role for defeasibly warranting criteria. Yet why bother? Why can we not absorb of any depictions, as a pint cube manifests itself in visual experience, in that are essentially different from those where it merely appears present (McDowell, 1982)? We thereby know objective facts through experiences tat are criterial for them and make them indefeasibly evident. Nevertheless, to many, this requires a seamless mystified, fusion of appearance and reality. Alternatively, perhaps knowledge requires exercising an ability to judge accurately in specific relevant circumstances, but does not require criterial considerations that, as a matter of general principle, make propositions evident, even if only without undermining evidence or contingently, no matter what the context. Arguably, however, our position for giving relevant assurances does not improve with these new conditions for knowing.

Formulating general principles determining when criterial warrant is difficult and is not undermined (Pollock, 1974). So one might think that warrant in general depends just on what is presupposed as true and relevant in a potentially shifting context of thought or conversation, not on general criteria. However, defenders of criteria may protest that coherence, at least, remains as a criterion applicable across contexts.

It is often felt that 'p' cannot be evident by satisfying criteria unless (a) criterial considerations evidently obtain, and evident either that (b) the criteria have certain correctness-masking features, e.g., leading to truth, or must that © the criteria are correct. Otherwise any conformity to pertinent standards is in a relevant sense only accidental (BonJour, 1985). Yet vicious regress or circularity looms, unless in supporting propositions are evident without criteria. At worst, as sceptics argue, nothing can be warranted: At best, a consistent role for criteria is limited. A common reply is that being criterially warranted, by definition, just requires the adequate (checkable) criterial considerations in fact obtain, i.e., in that there is no need to demand further cognitive achievements for which one or more must also be evident, e.g., actually checking that criterial considerations obtain, proving truth or likelihood of truth on the basis of these considerations, or proving warrant on their basis.

Even so, how can propositions state which putative criteria are correct, be warranted? Any proposal for criterial warrant invokes the classic sceptical change of vicious regress or circularity. Yet, again, it may arguably, as with 'p' above, correct criteria must in fact be satisfied, but this fact itself need not be already confronting 'us' as warranted. So, one might argue there is no debilitating regress or circle of warrant, even when, as may happen with some criterion, its correctness is warranted ultimately only because it itself is satisfied (van Cleve, 1979). Independent, ultimately non-criterial, evidence is not needed. Nonetheless, suppose we argue that our criteria are correct, because, e.g., they led to truth, are confirmed by thought experiments, or are clearly and distinctly conceived as correct, etc. however, we develop our arguments, they would not persuade those who, doubting the criteria we conform to, doubt our premises or their relevancy, dismissing our failures as merely conversational and irrelevant to our warrant, moreover, may strike sceptics and non-skeptics alike as question-begging or as arbitrarily altering what warrant requires. For the charge of ungrounded dogmatism it is inappropriate, more than the consistency of criterial warrant, including warrant about warrant, may be required, no matter what putative criteria we conform to.

It is nevertheless, a problem of the criterion that lay upon the difficulty of how both to formulate the criteria, and to determine the extent, of knowledge and justified belief. The problem arises from the seeming justification of which is proven plausible of the following two propositions:

(1) I can identify instances (and thus determiners the extent) of justified belief only if I already know the criteria of it.

(2) I can know the criteria of justified belief only if I can already identify the instances of it.

If both (1) and (2) were true, I would be caught in a circle: I could know neither the criteria nor the extent of justified belief. In order to show that both can be known after all, a way out of the circle must be found. The nature of this task is best illustrated by considering the four positions that may be taken concerning the truth-values of (1) and (2):

(a) Scepticism as to the possibility of constructing a theory of justification:

Both (1) and (2) are true, consequently, I can know neither the criteria nor the extent of justified belief. This kind of scepticism is restricted in its scope to epistemic propositions. While it allows for the possibility of justified beliefs, it denies that we can know which beliefs are justified and which are not (b) is true but (1) is false: I can identify instances of justification without applying a criterion.

(1) is true but (2) is false? I can identify the criteria of justified belief without prior knowledge of its instances.

(d) Both (1) and (2) are false: I can know the extent of justified beliefs without applying criteria, and vice versa.

The problem of a criterion may be seen as the problem of providing a rationale for a non-sceptical response.

Roderick Chisholm, who has devoted particular attention to this problem, calls the second response 'particularism', and of acclimatising the third periodicity of 'Methodism'. Hume, who draws a sceptical conclusion as to the extent of empirical knowledge using, deductibility from sense-experience, as the criterion of justification, was a Methodist. Thomas Reid and G.E. Moore were particularists, in rejecting Hume's criterion on the grounds that it turns obvious cases of knowledge into the cease of ignorance. Chisholm advocates particularism as the correct response. His view, which has also become known a 'critical cognitivism' may be summarized as follows. Criteria for the application of epistemic concepts are expressed by epistemic principles. The antecedent of such a principal states the non-normative ground on which the epistemic status ascribed by the consequent supervenes (Chisholm, 1957). An example is the following:

> If 'S' is appeared to 'F-ly', then 'S' is justified in believing that there is an 'F' in front of 'S'.

According to this principle, a criterion for justifiable believing that there is something red in front of me is 'being appeared too redly'. In constructing the theory of knowledge Chisholm coincides various principles of this kind, accepting or rejecting them depending on whether or not they fit wheat he identifies, without using any criterion, as the instances of justified belief. As the result of using this method, he rejects the principle above as too broad, and Hume's an empiricist criterion (which, unlike the criteria Chisholm tries to formulate, states a necessary condition).

> If 'S' is justified in believing that there is an
> 'F' I front of 'S', then 'S's' belief is deducible form
> 'S's' sense-experience as to barrow. (Chisholm, 1982).

Regarding the viability of particularism, this approach raises the question of how identifying instances of justified belief without applying any criteria is possible. Chisholm's answer rests on the premise that, in order to know, no criterion of knowledge or justification is needed (1982). He claims that this hold also for knowledge of epistemic facts. Supposing I am justified that I am justified in believing that 'p' is the same body of evidence that justifies me in believing that 'p'. Put differently, both JJp and Jp supervene on the same non-epistemic ground. (Chisholm 1982). Thus, in order to become justified in believing myself to be justified in believing that 'p', I need not apply any criterion of justified belief, but I need only consider the evidence supporting 'p'. The key assumption of particularism, then, is that in order to acquire knowledge of an epistemic fact, one need not apply, but only satisfy the antecedent condition of, the epistemic principle that governs the fact in question. Hence having knowledge of epistemic facts is possible such as 'I am justified in believing that there is an 'F' in front of me' without applying epistemic principles, and to use this knowledge in order to reject those principles that ae either too broad or too narrow.

According to Methodism, the correct solution to the problem proceeds the opposite way: Epistemic principles are to be formulated without using knowledge of epistemic facts. However, how could Methodism distinguish between correct and incorrect principles, given that an appeal to instances of epistemic knowledge is illegitimate? Against what could they check the correctness of a putative principle? Unless the correct criteria are immediately obvious which is doubtful, it remains unclear how Methodists could rationally prefer one principle to another. Thus Chisholm rejects Hume's criterion not because of its sceptical implications but also on grounds of its arbitrariness: Hume 'leaves 'us' completely in the dark as far as adopting this particular criterion that another' (1982). Particularists, then, accept the proposition (2), and thus reject responses for both of which affirm that (2) is false.

One problem for particularism is that it appears to beg the question against scepticism (BonJour, 1985). In order to evaluate this criticism, it must be kept in mind that particularists reject criteria with sceptical consequences on the basis of instances, whereas septics reject instances of justification on the basis of criteria. This difference in methodology is illustrated by the following two arguments:

An Anti-Sceptical Argument

(1) If the 'reducibility from sense-experience' criterion is correct, then I am not justified in believing that these are my hands.

(2) I am justified in believing that these are my hands

Therefore:

(2) The 'reducibility from sense-experience' criterion is not correct.

A Sceptical Argument

(1) If the 'reducibility from sense-experience' criterion is correct, then I am not justified in believing that these are my hands

(2) The 'deducible from sense-experience' criterion is correct.

Therefore:

(3) I am not justified in believing that these are my hands.

The problematic premises are (3) and (2) Particularists reject on the basis of (B), and sceptics (3) on the basis of (2). Regarding question-begging, then, the situation is asymmetrical: Both beg the question against each other. Who, though, has the better argument? Particularists would say that accepting (3) is more reasonable than accepting, because the risk of making an error in accepting a general criterion is greater than in taking a specific belief to be justified.

The problem of the criterion is not restricted to epistemic justification and knowledge but is posed by any attempt to formulate general principles of philosophy or logic. In response to the problems of induction, Nelson Goodman has proposed bringing the principles of inductive inference into agreement with the instances of inductive inference. John Rawls (1921-) his major "A Theory of Justice" (1971), in it Rawls considers the basic institutions of a society that could be chosen by rational people under conditions that censure impartiality. These contusions arc dramatized as an original position, characterized so that it is as if the participants are contracting into a basic social structure from behind, a veil ignorance, leaving them unable to deploy selfish considerations, or ones favouring particular kinds of people. Rawls arousement tat both a basic framework of liberties and a concern for the clearest and comfortably fitting would be characterized by any society that it would be rational to choose. Goodman and Rawls believe that in order to denitrify the principles they seek theory instancies must be known to begin with, but they also that in the precess of bringing principles and instancies into agreement, principles many have been to serve instancies. These may, therefore considered advocates of a new analogous to response, a hybrid of particularism and methods.

To put the first problem in perspective, seeing that even highly counterintuitive philosophical views generally have arguments behind them are important-arguments that 'start with something so simply as not to seem worth stating', and proceed by steps so obvious as not to seem worth taking, before ' [ending] with something so paradoxically that no one will believe it' (Russell, 1956). Nevertheless, since repeated applications of commonsense can thus lead to philosophical conclusions that conflict with commonsense, commonsense is a problematic criterion for assessing philosophical views. It is true that, arguments, once we have weighed the relevant arguments, we must ultimately rely on our judgement about whether, in the light of these arguments, accepting a given philosophical view just seems reasonable. Still, this truism should not be confused with the problematic position that our considered philosophical judgement in the light of philosophical arguments must not conflict with our commonsense pre-philosophical views.

As for philosophers' inability to reach consensuses, seeing that this in effect does not embody of what there is, but no longer is it a fact of the matter of any importance, as to who is right. There are other possible explanations for this inability (Rescher, 1978). Moreover, supposing that the existence of unresolvable deductivity disagreements over the truth of 'p' shows that 'p' lacks a truth value would make the matter of whether 'p' has a truth-value too dependent, on which people happen to exist and what they can be persuaded to believe.

Both verificationism and ordinary language philosophy deny the synthetic deductivity. Quine goes further. He denies the analytic deductivity as well: He denies both the analytic-synthetic distinction and the deductive-inductive distinction. In "Two Dogmas of Empiricism," Quine considers several reductive definitions of analyticity synonymy, argues that all are inadequate, and concludes that there is no analytic and synthetic distinction. Nevertheless, clearly there is a substantial gap in this argument. One would not conclude from the absence of adequate reductive definition of 'red' and 'blue' that there is no red-blue distinction, or no such thing as redness. Instead, one would hold that such terms as 'red' and 'blue' are defined by example. However, this also seems plausible for such terms as 'synonymous' and 'analytic' (Grice and Strawson, 1956).

On Quine's view, the distinction between philosophical and scientific inquiry is a matter of degree. His later writings indicate that the sort of account he would require to make analyticity, necessary, or an acceptable priority is one that confirmed by the implicated notions, in terms of 'people's dispositions to overt behaviour' in response to socially observable stimuli (Quine, 1969).

Theories, in philosophy of science, are generalizations or set of generalizations purportedly referring to observable entities, e.g., atoms, genes, quarks, unconscious wishes. The ideal gas law, for example, points only too such observably as pressure, temperature, and volume; the molecular-kinetic theory refers to molecules and their properties. Although, an older usage suggests a lack of adequate evidence in playing a subordinate role of this ('merely a theory'), current philosophical usage that does not carry that connotation. Einstein's special theory of relativity, for example, is considered extremely well founded.

There are two main views on the nature of theories. According to the 'received view' theories are partially interpreted axiomatic systems, according to the semantic view, a theory is a collection of models (Suppe, 1974).

Axiomatic methods . . . as, . . . a proposition laid down as one from which we may begin, an assertion that we have taken as fundamental, at least for the branch of enquiry in hand. The axiomatic method is that of defining as set of such propositions, and the 'proof' procedures or 'rules of inference' that are permissible, and then deriving the theorems that result.

All of assuming their rationality has characterized people is common, and the most evident display of our rationality is capable to think. This is the rehearsal in the mind of what to say, or what to do. Not all thinking is verbal, since chess players, composers, and painters all think, and there is no deductive reason that their deliberations should take any more verbal a form than their actions. It is permanently tempting to conceive of this activity about the presence in the mind of elements of some language, or other medium that represents aspects of the world and its surrounding surface structures. However, the model has been attacked, notably by Ludwig Wittgenstein (1889-1951), whose influential application of these ideas was in the philosophy of mind. Wittgenstein explores the role that reports of introspection, or sensations, or intentions, or beliefs can play of our social lives, to undermine the Cartesian mental picture is that they functionally describe the goings-on in an inner theatre of which the subject is the lone spectator. Passages that have subsequentially become known as the 'rule following' considerations and the 'private language argument' are among the fundamental topics of modern philosophy of language and mind, although their precise interpretation is endlessly controversial.

Effectively, the hypotheses especially associated with Jerry Fodor (1935-), whom is known for the 'resolute realism', about the nature of mental functioning, that occurs in a language different from one's ordinary native language, but underlying and explaining our competence with it. The idea is a development of the notion of an innate universal grammar (Avram Noam Chomsky, 1928-), in as such, that we agree that since a computer programs are linguistically complex sets of instructions were the relative executions by which explains of surface behaviour or the adequacy of the computerized programming installations, if it were definably amendable and, advisably corrective, in that most are disconcerting of many that are ultimately a reason for 'us' of thinking intuitively and without the indulgence of retrospective preferences, but an ethical majority in defending of its moral line that is already confronting 'us'. That these programs may or may not improve to conditions that are lastly to enhance of the right sort of an existence forwarded toward a more valuing amount in humanities lesser extensions that embrace one's riff of necessity to humanities' abeyance to expressions in the finer of qualities.

As an explanation of ordinary language-learning and competence, the hypothesis has not found universal favour, as only ordinary representational powers that by invoking the image of the learning person's capabilities are apparently whom the abilities for translating are contending of an innate language whose own powers are mysteriously a biological given. Perhaps, the view that everyday attributions of intentionality, beliefs, and meaning to other persons proceed by means of a tactic use of a theory that enables one to construct these interpretations as explanations of their doings. We commonly hold the view along with 'functionalism', according to which psychological states are theoretical entities, identified by the network of their causes and effects. The theory-theory has different implications, depending upon which feature of theories we are stressing. Theories may be thought of as capable of formalization, as yielding predictions and explanations, as achieved by a process of theorizing, as answering to empirical evidence that is in principle describable without them, as liable to be overturned by newer and better theories, and so on.

The main problem with seeing our understanding of others as the outcome of a piece of theorizing is the nonexistence of a medium in which this theory can be couched, as the child learns simultaneously the minds of others and the meaning of terms in its native language, is not gained by the tactic use of a 'theory', enabling 'us' to infer what thoughts or intentions explain their actions, but by reliving the situation 'in their shoes' or from their point of view, and by that understanding what they experienced and theory, and therefore expressed. Understanding others is achieved when we can ourselves deliberate as they did, and hear their words as if they are our own. The suggestion is a modern development frequently associated in the 'Verstehen' traditions of Dilthey (1833-1911), Weber (1864-1920) and Collingwood (1889-1943).

We may call any process of drawing a conclusion from a set of premises a process of reasoning. If the conclusion concerns what to do, the process is called practical reasoning, otherwise pure or theoretical reasoning. Evidently, such processes may be good or bad, if they are good, the premises support or even entail the conclusion drawn, and if they are bad, the premises offer no support to the conclusion. Formal logic studies the cases in which conclusions are validly drawn from premises, but little human reasoning is overly of the forms logicians identify. Partly, we are concerned to draw conclusions that 'go beyond' our premises, in the way that conclusions of logically valid arguments do not for the process of using evidence to reach a wider conclusion. Nonetheless, such anticipatory pessimism in the opposite direction to the prospects of conformation theory, denying that we can assess the results of abduction in terms of probability. A cognitive process of reasoning in which a conclusion is played-out from a set of premises usually confined of cases in which the conclusions are supposed in following from the premises, i.e., an inference is logically valid, in that of deductibility in a logically defined syntactic premise but without there being to any reference to the intended interpretation of its theory. Furthermore, as we reason we use indefinite traditional knowledge or commonsense sets of presuppositions about what it is likely or not a task of an automated reasoning project, which is to mimic this causal use of knowledge of the way of the world in computer programs.

Some 'theories' usually emerge themselves of engaging to exceptionally explicit predominancy as [supposed] truths that they have not organized, making the theory difficult to survey or study as a whole. The axiomatic method is an idea for organizing a theory, one in which tries to select from among the supposed truths a small number from which they can see all others to be deductively inferrable. This makes the theory more tractable since, in a sense, they contain all truths in those few. In a theory so organized, they call the few truths from which they deductively imply all others 'axioms'. David Hilbert (1862-1943) had argued that, just as algebraic and differential equations, which we were used to study mathematical and physical processes, could have themselves be made mathematical objects, so axiomatic theories, like algebraic and differential equations, which are means to representing physical processes and mathematical structures could be of investigating.

Conformation to theory, the philosophy of science, is a generalization or set referring to unobservable entities, i.e., atoms, genes, quarks, unconscious wishes. The ideal gas law, as an example, infers to such observable pressure, temperature, and volume, the 'molecular-kinetic theory' refers to molecules and their material possession, . . . although an older usage suggests the lack of adequate evidence in support thereof, as an existing philosophical usage does in truth, follow in the tradition (as in Leibniz, 1704), as many philosophers had the conviction that all truths, or all truths about a particular domain, followed from as few than for being many governing principles. These principles were taken to be either metaphysically prior or epistemologically prior or both. In the first sense, they we took to be entities of such a nature that what exists s 'caused' by them. When the principles were taken as epistemologically prior, that is, as 'axioms', they were taken to be either epistemologically privileged, e.g., self-evident, not needing to be demonstrated, or again, included 'or', to such that all truths so truly follow from them by deductive inferences. Gödel (1984) showed in the spirit of Hilbert, treating axiomatic theories as themselves mathematical objects that mathematics, and even a small part of mathematics, elementary number theory, could not be axiomatized, that more precisely, any class of axioms that is such that we could effectively decide, of any proposition, whether or not it was in that class, would be too small to capture in of the truths.

The notion of truth occurs with remarkable frequency in our reflections on language, thought and action. We are inclined to suppose, for example, that truth is the proper aim of scientific inquiry, that true beliefs help to achieve our goals, that to understand a sentence is to know which circumstances would make it true, that reliable preservation of truth as one argues of valid reasoning, that moral pronouncements should not be regarded as objectively true, and so on. To assess the plausibility of such theses, and to refine them and to explain why they hold (if they do), we require some view of what truth be a theory that would account for its properties and its relations to other matters. Thus, there can be little prospect of understanding our most important faculties in the sentence of a good theory of truth.

Such a thing, however, has been notoriously elusive. The ancient idea that truth is some sort of 'correspondence with reality' has still never been articulated satisfactorily, and the nature of the alleged 'correspondence' and the alleged 'reality' persistently remains objectionably enigmatical. Yet the familiar alternative suggestions that true beliefs are those that are 'mutually coherent', or 'pragmatically useful', or 'verifiable in suitable conditions' has each been confronted with persuasive counterexamples. A twentieth-century departure from these traditional analyses is the view that truth is not a property at all that the syntactic form of the predicate, 'is true', distorts its really semantic character, which is not to describe propositions but to endorse them. Nevertheless, we have also faced this radical approach with difficulties and suggest, counter intuitively that truth cannot have the vital theoretical role in semantics, epistemology and elsewhere that we are naturally inclined to give it. Thus, truth threatens to remain one of the most enigmatic of notions: An explicit account of it can seem essential yet beyond our reach. All the same, recent work provides some evidence for optimism.

A theory is based in philosophy of science, is a generalization or se of generalizations purportedly referring to observable entities, its theory refers top molecules and their properties, although an older usage suggests the lack of an adequate make-out in support therefrom as merely a theory, later-day philosophical usage does not carry that connotation. Einstein's special and General Theory of Relativity, for example, is taken to be extremely well founded.

These are two main views on the nature of theories. According to the 'received view' theories are partially interpreted axiomatic systems, according to the semantic view, a theory is a collection of models (Suppe, 1974). By which, some possibilities, unremarkably emerge as supposed truths that no one has neatly systematized by making theory difficult to make a survey of or study as a whole. The axiomatic method is an ideal for organizing a theory (Hilbert, 1970), one tries to select from among the supposed truths a small number from which they can see all the others to be deductively inferrable. This makes the theory more tractable since, in a sense, they contain all truth's in those few. In a theory so organized, they call the few truths from which they deductively incriminate all others 'axioms'. David Hilbert (1862-1943) had argued that, morally justified as algebraic and differential equations, which were antiquated into the study of mathematical and physical processes, could hold on to themselves and be made mathematical objects, so they could make axiomatic theories, like algebraic and differential equations, which are means of representing physical processes and mathematical structures, objects of mathematical investigation.

Of mathematics, elementary number theory, could not be axiomatized, that, more precisely, any class of axioms that is such that we could effectively decide, of any proposition, whether or not it was in that class, would be too small to capture all of the truths.

The notion of truth occurs with remarkable frequency in our reflections on language, thought, and action. We are inclined to suppose, for example, that truth is the proper aim of scientific inquiry, that true beliefs help 'us' to achieve our goals, tat to understand a sentence is to know which circumstances would make it true, that reliable preservation of truth as one argues from premises to a conclusion is the mark of valid reasoning, that moral pronouncements should not be regarded as objectively true, and so on. In order to assess the plausible of such theses, and in order to refine them and to explain why they hold, if they do, we expect some view of what truth be of a theory that would keep an account of its properties and its relations to other matters. Thus, there can be little prospect of understanding our most important faculties without a good theory of truth.

Astounded by such a thing, however, has been notoriously elusive. The ancient idea that truth is one sort of 'correspondence with reality' has still never been articulated satisfactorily: The nature of the alleged 'correspondence' and te alleged 'reality remains objectivably obscure. Yet, the familiar alternative suggests ~. That true beliefs are those that are 'mutually coherent', or 'pragmatically useful', or 'verifiable' in suitable conditions has each been confronted with persuasive counterexamples. A twentieth-century departure from these traditional analyses is the view that truth is not a property at al ~. That the syntactic form of the predicate,' . . . is true', distorts the 'real' semantic character, with which is not to describe propositions but to endorse them. Still, this radical approach is also faced with difficulties and suggests, counter intuitively that truth cannot have the vital theoretical role in semantics, epistemology and elsewhere that we are naturally inclined to give it. Thus, truth threatens to remain one of the most enigmatic of notions, and a confirming account of it can seem essential yet, on the far side of our reach. However, recent work provides some grounds for optimism.

The belief that snow is white owes its truth to a certain feature of the external world, namely, to the fact that snow is white. Similarly, the belief that dogs bark is true because of the fact that dogs bark. This trivial observation leads to what is perhaps the most natural and popular account of truth, the 'correspondence theory', according to which a belief (statement, a sentence, propositions, etc. (as true just in case there exists a fact corresponding to it (Wittgenstein, 1922). This thesis is unexceptionable, all the same, it is to provide a rigorous, substantial and complete theory of truth, If it is to be more than merely a picturesque way of asserting all equivalences to the form. The belief that 'p' is true 'p'.Then it must be supplemented with accounts of what facts are, and what it is for a belief to correspond to a fact, and these are the problems on which the correspondence theory of truth has floundered. For one thing, it is far from going unchallenged that any significant gain in understanding is achieved by reducing 'the belief that snow is white is' true' to the facts that snow is white exists: For these expressions look equally resistant to analysis and too close in meaning for one to provide a crystallizing account of the other. In addition, the undistributed relationship that holds in particular between the belief that snow is white and the fact that snow is white, between the belief that dogs bark and the fact that a 'dog barks', and so on, is very hard to identify. The best attempt to date is Wittgenstein's 1922, so-called 'picture theory', by which an elementary proposition is a configuration of terms, with whatever stare of affairs it reported, as an atomic fact is a configuration of simple objects, an atomic fact corresponds to an elementary proposition and makes it true, when their configurations are identical and when the terms in the proposition for it to the similarly-placed objects in the fact, and the truth value of each complex proposition the truth values entail of the elementary ones. However, eve if this account is correct as far as it goes, it would need to be completed with plausible theories of 'logical configuration', 'rudimentary proposition', 'reference' and 'entailment', none of which are better-off for what is to come.

The cental characteristic of truth One that any adequate theory must explain is that when a proposition satisfies its 'conditions of proof or verification' then it is regarded as true. To the extent that the property of corresponding with reality is mysterious, we are going to find it impossible to see what we take to verify a proposition should show the possession of that property. Therefore, a tempting alternative to the correspondence theory an alternative that eschews obscure, metaphysical concept that explains quite straightforwardly why Verifiability infers, truth is simply to identify truth with Verifiability (Peirce, 1932). This idea can take on variously formed. One version involves the further assumption that verification is 'holistic', . . . 'in that a belief is justified (i.e., verified) when it is part of an entire system of beliefs that are consistent and 'counterbalance' (Bradley, 1914 and Hempel, 1935). This is known as the 'coherence theory of truth'. Another version involves the assumption associated with each proposition, some specific procedure for finding out whether one should amazingly. On this account, to say that a proposition is true is to sa that the appropriate procedure would verify (Dummett, 1979, and Putnam, 1981), all the while mathematics amount to the identification of truth with provability.

The attractions of the verificationist account of truth are that it is refreshingly clear compared with the correspondence theory, and that it succeeds in connecting truth with verification. The trouble is that the bond it postulates between these notions is implausibly strong. We do in true statements' take verification to indicate truth, but also we recognize the possibility that a proposition may be false in spite of there being impeccable reasons to believe it, and that a proposition may be true although we are not able to discover that it is. Verifiability and ruth are no doubt highly correlated, but surely not the same thing.

A third well-known account of truth is known as 'pragmatism' (James, 1909 and Papineau, 1987). As we have just seen, the verificationist selects a prominent property of truth and considers the essence of truth. Similarly, the pragmatist focuses on another important characteristic namely, that true belief is a good basis for action and takes this to be the very nature of truth. True assumpsits are said to be, by definition, those that provoke actions with desirable results. Again, we have an account statement with a single attractive explanatory characteristic, besides, it postulates between truth and its alleged analysand in this case, utility is implausibly close. Granted, true belief tends to foster success, but it happens regularly that actions based on true beliefs lead to disaster, while false assumptions, by pure chance, produce wonderful results.

One of the few uncontroversial facts about truth is that the proposition that snow is white if and only if snow is white, the proposition that lying is wrong is true if and only if lying is wrong, and so on. Traditional theories acknowledge this fact but regard it as insufficient and, as we have seen, inflate it with some further principle of the form, 'x' is true if and only if 'x' has property 'P' (such as corresponding to reality, Verifiability, or being suitable as a basis for action), which is supposed to specify what truth is. Some radical alternatives to the traditional theories result from denying the need for any such further specification (Ramsey, 1927, Strawson, 1950 and Quine, 1990). For example, ne might suppose that the basic theory of truth contains nothing more that equivalences of the form, 'The proposition that 'p' is true if and only if 'p' (Horwich, 1990).

That is, a proposition, 'K' with the following properties, that from 'K' and any further premises of the form. 'Einstein's claim was the proposition that p' you can imply p'. Whatever it is, now supposes, as the deflationist says, that our understanding of the truth predicate consists in the stimulative decision to accept any instance of the schema. 'The proposition that 'p' is true if and only if 'p', then your problem is solved. For 'K' is the proposition, 'Einstein's claim is true ', it will have precisely the inferential power needed. From it and 'Einstein's claim is the proposition that quantum mechanics are wrong', you can use Leibniz's law to imply 'The proposition that quantum mechanic is wrong is true; Which given the relevant axiom of the deflationary theory, allows you to derive 'Quantum mechanics is wrong'. Thus, one point in favour of the deflationary theory is that it squares with a plausible story about the function of our notion of truth, in that its axioms explain that function without the need for further analysis of 'what truth is'.

Support for deflationism depends upon the possibleness of showing that its axiom instances of the equivalence schema unsupplements by any further analysis, will suffice to explain all the central facts about truth, for example, that the verification of a proposition indicates its truth, and that true beliefs have a practical value. The first of these facts follows trivially from the deflationary axioms, for given ours a prior knowledge of the equivalence of 'p' and 'The a propositions that 'p is true', any reason to believe that 'p' becomes an equally good reason to believe that the preposition that 'p' is true. We can also explain the second fact in terms of the deflationary axioms, but not quite so easily. Consider, to begin with, beliefs of the form:

(B) If I perform the act 'A', then my desires will be fulfilled.

Notice that the psychological role of such a belief is, roughly, to cause the performance of 'A'. In other words, gave that I do have belief (B), then typically.

I will perform the act 'A'

Notice also that when the belief is true then, given the deflationary axioms, the performance of 'A' will in fact lead to the fulfilment of one's desires, i.e.,

If (B) is true, then if I perform 'A', my desires will be fulfilled

Therefore,

If (B) is true, then my desires will be fulfilled

So valuing the truth of beliefs of that form is quite treasonable. Nevertheless, inference has derived such beliefs from other beliefs and can be expected to be true if those other beliefs are true. So assigning a value to the truth of any belief that might be used in such an inference is reasonable.

To the extent that such deflationary accounts can be given of all the acts involving truth, then the explanatory demands on a theory of truth will be met by the collection of all statements like, 'The proposition that snow is white is true if and only if snow is white', and the sense that some deep analysis of truth is needed will be undermined.

Nonetheless, there are several strongly felt objections to deflationism. One reason for dissatisfaction is that the theory has an infinite number of axioms, and therefore cannot be completely written down. It can be described, as the theory whose axioms are the propositions of the fore 'p if and only if it is true that p', but not explicitly formulated.

This alleged defect has led some philosophers to develop theories that show, first, how the truth of any proposition derives from the referential properties of its constituents, and second, how the referential properties of primitive constituents are determinated (Tarski, 1943 and Davidson, 1969). However, assuming that all propositions including belief attributions remain controversial, law of nature and counterfactual conditionals depends for their truth values on what their constituents refer to implicate. In addition, there is no immediate prospect of a presentable, finite possibility of reference, so that it is far form clear that the infinite, list-like character of deflationism can be avoided.

Additionally, it is commonly supposed that problems about the nature of truth are intimately bound up with questions as to the accessibility and autonomy of facts in various domains: Questions about whether the facts can be known, and whether they can exist independently of our capacity to discover them (Dummett, 1978, and Putnam, 1981). One might reason, for example, that if 'T is true 'means' nothing more than 'T will be verified', then certain forms of scepticism, specifically, those that doubt the correctness of our methods of verification, that will be precluded, and that the facts will have been revealed as dependent on human practices. Alternatively, it might be said that if truth were an inexplicable, primitive, non-epistemic property, then the fact that 'T' is true would be completely independent of 'us'. Moreover, we could, in that case, have no reason to assume that the propositions we believe in, that in adopting its property, so scepticism would be unavoidable. In a similar vein, it might be thought that as special, and perhaps undesirable features of the deflationary approach, is that truth is deprived of such metaphysical or epistemological implications.

On closer scrutiny, however, it is far from clear that there exists 'any' account of truth with consequences regarding the accessibility or autonomy of non-semantic matters. For although an account of truth may be expected to have such implications for facts of the form 'T is true', it cannot be assumed without further argument that the same conclusions will apply to the fact 'T'. For it cannot be assumed that 'T' and 'T' are true' and is equivalent to one another given the account of 'true' that is being employed. Of course, if truth is defined in the way that the deflationist proposes, then the equivalence holds by definition. Nevertheless, if truth is defined by reference to some metaphysical or epistemological characteristic, then the equivalence schema is thrown into doubt, pending some demonstration that the trued predicate, in the sense assumed, will be satisfied in as far as there are thought to be epistemological problems hanging over 'T's' that do not threaten 'T is true', giving the needed demonstration will be difficult. Similarly, if 'truth' is so defined that the fact, 'T' is felt to be more, or less, independent of human practices than the fact that 'T is true', then again, it is unclear that the equivalence schema will hold. It would seem. Therefore, that the attempt to base epistemological or metaphysical conclusions on a theory of truth must fail because in any such attempt the equivalence schema will be simultaneously relied on and undermined.

The most influential idea in the theory of meaning in the past hundred yeas is the thesis that meaning of an indicative sentence is given by its truth-conditions. On this conception, to understand a sentence is to know its truth-conditions. The conception was first clearly formulated by Frége (1848-1925), was developed in a distinctive way by the early Wittgenstein (1889-1951), and is a leading idea of Davidson (1917-). The conception has remained so central that those who offer opposing theories characteristically define their position by reference to it.

The conception of meaning as truth-conditions necessarily are not and should not be advanced as a complete account of meaning. For instance, one who understands a language must have some idea of the range of speech acts conventionally acted by the various types of a sentence in the language, and must have some idea of the significance of various kinds of speech acts. The claim of the theorist of truth-conditions should as an alternative is targeted on the notion of content: If two indicative sentences differ in what they strictly and literally say, then this difference is fully accounted for by the difference in their truth-conditions. Most basic to truth-conditions is simply of a statement that is the condition the world must meet if the statement is to be true. To know this condition is equivalent to knowing the meaning of the statement. Although this sounds as if it gives a solid anchorage for meaning, some of the security disappears when it turns out that the truth condition can only be defined by repeating the very same statement, as a truth condition of 'snow is white' is that snow is white, the truth condition of 'Britain would have capitulated had Hitler invaded' is the Britain would have capitulated had Hitler invaded. It is disputed wether. This element of running-on-the-spot disqualifies truth conditions from playing the central role in a substantive theory of meaning. Truth-conditional theories of meaning are sometimes opposed by the view that to know the meaning of a statement is to be able to use it in a network of inferences.

Whatever it is that makes, what would otherwise be mere sounds and inscriptions into instruments of communication and understanding. The philosophical problem is to demystify this power, and to relate it to what we know of ourselves and the world. Contributions to the study include the theory of 'speech acts' and the investigation of communication and the relationship between words and ideas and the world and surrounding surfaces, by which some persons express by a sentence are often a function of the environment in which he or she is placed. For example, the disease I refer to by a term like 'arthritis' or the kind of tree I refer to as an 'oak' will be defined by criteria of which I know nothing. The raises the possibility of imagining two persons in alternatively differently environmental, but in which everything appears the same to each of them, but between them they define a space of philosophical problems. They are the essential components of understanding nd any intelligible proposition that is true must be capable of being understood. Such that which is expressed by an utterance or sentence, the proposition or claim made about the world may by extension, the content of a predicated or other sub-sentential component is what it contributes to the content of sentences that contain it. The nature of content is the cental concern of the philosophy of language.

In particularly, the problems of indeterminancy of translation, inscrutability of reference, language, predication, reference, rule following, semantics, translation, and the topics referring to subordinate headings associated with 'logic'. The loss of confidence in determinate meaning ('Each is another encoding') is an element common both to postmodern uncertainties in the theory of criticism, and to the analytic tradition that follows writers such as Quine (1908-). Still, it may be asked, why should we suppose that fundamental epistemic notions should be keep an account of for in behavioural terms what grounds are there for supposing that 'p knows p' is a subjective matter in the prestigiousness of its statement between some subject statement and physical theory of physically forwarded of an objection, between nature and its mirror? The answer is that the only alternative seems to be to take knowledge of inner states as premises from which our knowledge of other things is normally implied, and without which our knowledge of other things is normally inferred, and without which knowledge would be ungrounded. However, it is not really coherent, and does not in the last analysis make sense, to suggest that human knowledge have foundations or grounds. It should be remembered that to say that truth and knowledge 'can only be judged by the standards of our own day' is not to say that it is less meaningful nor is it 'more "cut off from the world, which we had supposed. Conjecturing it is as just' that nothing counts as justification, unless by reference to what we already accept, and that at that place is no way to get outside our beliefs and our oral communication so as to find some experiment with others than coherence. The fact is that the professional philosophers have thought it might be otherwise, since one and only they are haunted by the marshy sump of epistemological scepticism.

What Quine opposes as 'residual Platonism' is not so much the hypostasising of nonphysical entities as the notion of 'correspondence' with things as the final court of appeal for evaluating present practices. Unfortunately, Quine, for all that it is incompatible with its basic insights, substitutes for this correspondence to physical entities, and specially to the basic entities, whatever they turn out to be, of physical science. Nevertheless, when their doctrines are purified, they converge on a single claim ~. That no account of knowledge can depend on the assumption of some privileged relations to reality. Their work brings out why an account of knowledge can amount only to a description of human behaviour.

One answer is that the belief has a coherent place or role in a system of beliefs, perception or the having the perceptivity that has its influence on beliefs. As, you respond to sensory stimuli by believing that you are reading a page in a book than believing that you have a centaur in the garden. Belief has an influence on action, or its belief is a desire to act, if belief will differentiate the differences between them, that its belief is a desire or if you were to believe that you are reading a page than if you believed in something about a centaur. Sortal perceptivals hold accountably the perceptivity and action that are indeterminate to its content if its belief is the action as if stimulated by its inner and latent coherence in that of your belief, however. The same stimuli may produce various beliefs and various beliefs may produce the same action. The role that gives the belief the content it has is the role it plays within a network of relations to other beliefs, some latently causal than others that relate to the role in inference and implication. For example, I infer different things from believing that I am reading a page in a book than from any other belief, justly as I infer about other beliefs.

The information of perceptibility and the output of an action supplement the central role of the systematic relations the belief has to other belief, but the systematic relations give the belief the specific contentual representation it has. They are the fundamental source of the content of belief. That is how coherence comes in. A belief has the representational content by which it does because of the way in which it coheres within a system of beliefs (Rosenberg, 1988). We might distinguish weak coherence theories of the content of beliefs from stronger coherence theories. Weak coherence theories affirm that coherence is one determinant of the representation given that the contents are of belief. Strong coherence theories of the content of belief affirm that coherence is the sole determinant of the contentual representations of belief.

These philosophical problems include discovering whether belief differs from other varieties of assent, such as 'acceptance' discovering to what extent degrees of belief is possible, understanding the ways in which belief is controlled by rational and irrational factors, and discovering its links with other properties, such as the possession of conceptual or linguistic skills. This last set of problems includes the question of whether paralinguistic infants or animals are properly said to have beliefs.

Thus, we might think of coherence as inference to the best explanation based on a background system of beliefs, since we are not aware of such inferences for the most part, the inferences must be interpreted as unconscious inferences, as information processing, based on or finding the background system that proves most convincing of acquiring its act and used from the motivational force that its underlying and hidden desire are to do so. One might object to such an account on the grounds that not all justifiable inferences are self-explanatory, and more generally, the account of coherence may, at best, is ably successful to competitions that are based on background systems (BonJour, 1985, and Lehrer, 1990). The belief that one sees a shape competes with the claim that one does not, with the claim that one is deceived, and other sceptical objections. The background system of beliefs informs one that one is acceptingly trustworthy and enables one to meet the objections. A belief coheres with a background system just in case it enables one to meet the sceptical objections and in the way justifies one in the belief. This is a standard strong coherence theory of justification (Lehrer, 1990).

Illustrating the relationship between positive and negative coherence theories in terms of the standard coherence theory is easy. If some objection to a belief cannot be met in terms of the background system of beliefs of a person, then the person is not justified in that belief. So, to return to Trust, suppose that she has been told that a warning light has been installed on her gauge to tell her when it is not functioning properly and that when the red light is on, the gauge is malfunctioning. Suppose that when she sees the reading of 105, she also sees that the red light is on. Imagine, finally, that this is the first time the red light has been on, and, after years of working with the gauge, Julie, who has always placed her trust in the gauge, believes what the gauge tells her, that the liquid in the container is at 105 degrees. Though she believes what she reads is at 105 degrees is not a justified belief because it fails to cohere with her background belief that the gauge is malfunctioning. Thus, the negative coherence theory tells 'us' that she is not justified in her belief about the temperature of the contents in the container. By contrast, when the red light is not illuminated and the background system of Julies tells her that under such conditions that gauge is a trustworthy indicator of the temperature of the liquid in the container, then she is justified. The positive coherence theory tells 'us' that she is justified in her belief because her belief coheres with her background system of Julie tells she that under such conditions that gauge is a trustworthy indicator of the temperature of the liquid in the container, then she is justified. The positive coherence theory tells 'us' that she is justified in her belief because her belief coheres with her background system continues as a trustworthy system.

The foregoing sketch and illustration of coherence theories of justification have a common feature, namely, that they are what is called internalistic theories of justification what makes of such a view are the absence of any requirement that the person for whom the belief is justified have any cognitive access to the relation of reliability in question. Lacking such access, such a person will usually, have no reason for thinking the belief is true or likely to be true, but will, on such an account, are none the lesser to appear epistemologically justified in accepting it. Thus, such a view arguably marks a major break from the modern epistemological traditions, which identifies epistemic justification with having a reason, perhaps even a conclusive reason, for thinking that the belief is true. An epistemologist working within this tradition is likely to feel that the externalist, than offering a competing account of the same concept of epistemic justification with which the traditional epistemologist is concerned, has simply changed the subject.

They are theories affirming that coherence is a matter of internal relations between beliefs and that justification is a matter of coherence. If, then, justification is solely a matter of internal relations between beliefs, we are left with the possibility that the internal relations might fail to correspond with any external reality. How, one might object, can be to assume the including of interiority. A subjective notion of justification bridge the gap between mere true belief, which might be no more than a lucky guess, and knowledge, which must be grounded in some connection between internal subjective conditions and external objective realities?

The answer is that it cannot and that something more than justified true belief is required for knowledge. This result has, however, been established quite apart from consideration of coherence theories of justification. What are required maybes put by saying that the justification that one must be undefeated by errors in the background system of beliefs? Justification is undefeated by errors just in case any correction of such errors in the background system of belief would sustain the justification of the belief on the basis of the corrected system. So knowledge, on this sort of positivity is acclaimed by the coherence theory, which is the true belief that coheres with the background belief system and corrected versions of that system. In short, knowledge is true belief plus justification resulting from coherence and undefeated by error (Lehrer, 1990). The connection between internal subjective conditions of belief and external objectivity are from which reality's result from the required correctness of our beliefs about the relations between those conditions and realities. In the example of Trust, she believes that her internal subjectivity to conditions of sensory data in which the experience and perceptual beliefs are connected with the external objectivity in which reality is the temperature of the liquid in the container in a trustworthy manner. This background belief is essential to the justification of her belief that the temperature of the liquid in the container is 105 degrees, and the correctness of that background belief is essential to the justification remaining undefeated. So our background system of beliefs contains a simple theory about our relation to the external world that justifies certain of our beliefs that cohere with that system. For instance, such justification to convert to knowledge, that theory must be sufficiently free from error so that the coherence is sustained in corrected versions of our background system of beliefs. The correctness of the simple background theory provides the connection between the internal condition and external reality.

The coherence theory of truth arises naturally out of a problem raised by the coherence theory of justification. The problem is that anyone seeking to determine whether she has knowledge is confined to the search for coherence among her beliefs. The sensory experiences she has been deaf-mute until they are represented in the form of some perceptual belief. Beliefs are the engines that pull the train of justification. Nevertheless, what assurance do we have that our justification is based on true beliefs? What justification do we have that any of our justifications are undefeated? The fear that we might have none, that our beliefs might be the artifacts of some deceptive demon or scientist, leads to the quest to reduce truth to some form, perhaps an idealized form, of justification (Rescher, 1973, and Rosenberg, 1980). That would close the threatening sceptical gap between justification and truth. Suppose that a belief is true if and only if it is justifiable of some person. For such a person there would be no gap between justification and truth or between justification and undefeated justification. Truth would be coherence with some ideal background system of beliefs, perhaps one expressing a consensus among systems or some consensus among belief systems or some convergence toward a consensus. Such a view is theoretically attractive for the reduction it promises, but it appears open to profound objectification. One is that there is a consensus that we can all be wrong about at least some matters, for example, about the origins of the universe. If there is a consensus that we can all be wrong about something, then the consensual belief system rejects the equation of truth with the consensus. Consequently, the equation of truth with coherence with a consensual belief system is itself incoherently.

Coherence theories of the content of our beliefs and the justification of our beliefs themselves cohere with our background systems but coherence theories of truth do not. A defender of coherentism must accept the logical gap between justified belief and truth, but may believe that our capacities suffice to close the gap to yield knowledge. That view is, at any rate, a coherent one.

What makes a belief justified and what makes a true belief knowledge? Thinking that whether a belief deserves one of these appraisals is natural depends on what causal subject to have the belief. In recent decades a number of epistemologists have pursed this plausible idea with a variety of specific proposals. Some causal theories of knowledge have it that a true belief that 'p' is knowledge just in case it has the right causal connection to the fact that 'p'. Such a criterion can be applied only to cases where the fact that 'p' is a sort that can enter causal relations, this seems to exclude mathematically and other necessary facts and perhaps any fact expressed by a universal generalization, and proponents of this sort of criterion have usually of this sort of criterion have usually supposed that it is limited to perceptual knowledge of particular facts about the subject's environment.

For example, Armstrong (1973) proposed that a belief of the form 'This (perceived) object is F' is (non-inferential) knowledge if and only if the belief is a completely reliable sign that the perceived object is 'F', that is, the fact that the object is 'F' contributed to causing the belief and its doing so depended on properties of the believer such that the laws of nature dictated that, for any subject 'χ' is to occur, and so thus a perceived object of 'y', if 'χ' undergoing those properties are for 'us' to believe that 'y' is 'F', then 'y' is 'F'. Dretske (1981) offers a similar account, in terms of the belief's being caused by a signal received by the perceiver that carries the information that the object is 'F'.

This sort of condition fails, however, to be sufficient for non-inferential perceptual knowledge because it is compatible with the belief's being unjustified, and an unjustifiable belief cannot be knowledge. For example, suppose that your mechanisms for colour perception are working well, but you have been given good reason to think otherwise, to think, say, that the substantive primary colours that are perceivable, that things look chartreuse to you and chartreuse things look magenta. If you fail to heed these reasons you have for thinking that your colour perception or sensory data is a way. Believing in a 'thing', which looks to blooms of vividness that you are to believe of its chartreuse, your belief will fail to be justified and will therefore fail to be knowledge, even though it is caused by the thing's being magenta in such a way as to be a completely reliable sign, or to carry the information, in that the thing is magenta.

One could fend off this sort of counterexample by simply adding to the causal condition the requirement that the belief be justified, buy this enriched condition would still be insufficient. Suppose, for example, that in nearly all people, but not in you, as it happens, causes the aforementioned aberration in colour perceptions. The experimenter tells you that you have taken such a drug but then says, 'no, hold off a minute, the pill you took was just a placebo', suppose further, that this last thing the experimenter tells you is false. Her telling you that it was a false statement, and, again, telling you this gives you justification for believing of a thing that looks a subtractive primary colour to you that it is a sensorial primary colour, in that the fact you were to expect that the experimenters last statements were false, making it the case that your true belief is not knowledgeably correct, thought as though to satisfy its causal condition.

Goldman (1986) has proposed an importantly different causal criterion namely, that a true belief is knowledge, if it is produced by a type of process that is 'globally' and 'locally' reliable. Causing true beliefs is sufficiently high is globally reliable if its propensity. Local reliability has to do with whether the process would have produced a similar but false belief in certain counterfactual situations alternative to the actual situation. This way of marking off true beliefs that are knowledge does not require the fact believed to be casually related to the belief, and so it could in principle apply to knowledge of any kind of truth.

Goldman requires that global reliability of the belief-producing process for the justification of a belief, he requires it also for knowledge because justification is required for knowledge, in what requires for knowledge but does not require for justification, which is locally reliable. His idea is that a justified true belief is knowledge if the type of process that produced it would not have produced it in any relevant counterfactual situation in which it is false. The relevant alternative account of knowledge can be motivated by noting that other concepts exhibit the same logical structure. Two examples of this are the concept 'flat' and the concept 'empty' (Dretske, 1981). Both appear to be absolute concepts-A space is empty only if it does not contain anything and a surface is flat only if it does not have any bumps. However, the absolute character of these concepts is relative to a standard. In the case of 'flat', there is a standard for what counts as a bump and in the case of 'empty', there is a standard for what counts as a thing. To be flat is to be free of any relevant bumps and to be empty is to be devoid of all relevant things.

Nevertheless, the human mind abhors a vacuum. When an explicit, coherent world-view is absent, it functions on the basis of a tactic one. A tactic world-view is not subject to a critical evaluation, and it can easily harbour inconsistencies. Indeed, our tactic set of beliefs about the nature of reality is made of contradictory bits and pieces. The dominant component is a leftover from another period, the Newtonian 'clock universe' still lingers as we cling to this old and tired model because we know of nothing else that can take its place. Our condition is the condition of a culture that is in the throes of a paradigm shift. A major paradigm shift is complex and difficult because a paradigm holds 'us captive: We see reality through it, as through coloured glasses, but we do not know that, we are convinced that we see reality as it is. Hence the appearance of a new and different paradigm is often incomprehensible. To someone raised believing that the Earth is flat, the suggestion that the Earth is spherical would seem preposterous: If the Earth were spherical, would not the poor antipodes fall 'down' into the sky?

Yet, as we face a new millennium, we are forced to face this challenge. The fate of the planet is in question, and it was brought to its present precarious condition largely because of our trust in the Newtonian paradigm. As Newtonian world-view has to go, and, if one looks carefully, the main feature of the new, emergent paradigm can be discerned. The search for these features is what was the influence of a fading paradigm. All paradigms include subterranean realms of tactic assumptions, the influence of which outlasts the adherence to the paradigm itself.

The first line of exploration suggests the 'weird' aspects of the quantum theory, with fertile grounds for our feeling of which should disappear in inconsistencies with the prevailing world-view. This feeling is in replacing by the new one, i.e., if one believes that the Earth is flat, the story of Magellan's travels is quite puzzling: How travelling due west is possible for a ship and, without changing direct. Arrive at its place of departure? Obviously, when the flat-Earth paradigm is replaced by the belief that Earth is spherical, the puzzle is instantly resolved.

The founders of Relativity and quantum mechanics were deeply engaging but incomplete, in that none of them attempted to construct a philosophical system, however, that the mystery at the heart of the quantum theory called for a revolution in philosophical outlooks. During which time, the 1920's, when quantum mechanics reached maturity, began the construction of a full-blooded philosophical system that was based not only on science but on nonscientific modes of knowledge as well. As, the fading influence drawn upon the paradigm goes well beyond its explicit claim. We believe, as the scenists and philosophers did, that when we wish to find out the truth about the universe, nonscientific nodes of processing human experiences can be ignored, poetry, literature, art, music are all wonderful, but, in relation to the quest for knowledge of the universe, they are irrelevant. Yet, it was Alfred North Whitehead who pointed out the fallacy of this speculative assumption. In this, as well as in other aspects of thinking of some reality in which are the building blocks of reality are not material atoms but 'throbs of experience'. Whitehead formulated his system in the late 1920s, and yet, as far as I know, the founders of quantum mechanics were unaware of it. It was not until 1963 that J.M. Burgers pointed out that its philosophy accounts very well for the main features of the quanta, especially the 'weird ones', enabling as in some aspects of reality is 'higher' or 'deeper' than others, and if so, what is the structure of such hierarchical divisions? What of our place in the universe? Finally, what is the relationship between the great aspiration within the lost realms of nature? An attempt to endow 'us' with a cosmological meaning in such a universe seems totally absurd, and, yet, this very universe is just a paradigm, not the truth. When you reach its end, you may be willing to join the alternate view as accorded to which, surprisingly bestow 'us' with what is restored, although in a post-postmodern context.

The philosophical implications of quantum mechanics have been regulated by subjective matter's, as to emphasis the connections between what I believe, in that investigations of such interconnectivity are anticipatorially the hesitations that are an exclusion held within the western traditions, however, the philosophical thinking, from Plato to Platinous had in some aspects of interpretational presentation of her expression of a consensus of the physical community. Other aspects are shared by some and objected to (sometimes vehemently) by others. Still other aspects express my own views and convictions, as turning about to be more difficult that anticipated, discovering that a conversational mode would be helpful, but, their conversations with each other and with me in hoping that all will be not only illuminating but finding to its read may approve in them, whose dreams are dreams among others than themselves.

These examples make it seem likely that, if there is a criterion for what makes an alternative situation relevant that will save Goldman's claim about reliability and the acceptance of knowledge, it will not be simple.

The interesting thesis that counts asa causal theory of justification, in the meaning of 'causal theory' intend of the belief that is justified just in case it was produced by a type of process that is 'globally' reliable, that is, its propensity to produce true beliefs-that can be defined to a favourably bringing close together the proportion of the belief and to what it produces, or would produce where it used as much as opportunity allows, that is true-is sufficiently that a belief acquires favourable epistemic status by having some kind of reliable linkage to the truth. Variations of this view have been advanced for both knowledge and justified belief. The first formulations of are reliably in its account of knowing appeared in if not by F.P. Ramsey (1903-30) who made important contributions to mathematical logic, probability theory, the philosophy of science and economics. Instead of saying that quarks have such-and-such properties, the Ramsey sentence says that it is moderately something that has those properties. If the process is repeated for all of the theoretical terms, the sentence gives the 'topic-neutral' structure of the theory, but removes any implication that we know what the term so covered have as a meaning. It leaves open the possibility of identifying the theoretical item with whatever, but it is that best fits the description provided, thus, substituting the term by a variable, and existentially qualifying into the result. Ramsey was one of the first thinkers to accept a 'redundancy theory of truth', which he combined its radical views of the function of many kinds of the proposition. Neither generalizations, nor causal propositions, not those treating probabilities or ethics, described facts, but each has a different specific function in our intellectual commentators on the early works of Wittgenstein, and his continuing friendship with the latter liked to Wittgenstein's return to Cambridge and to philosophy in 1929.

The most sustained and influential application of these ideas were in the philosophy of mind, or brain, as Ludwig Wittgenstein (1889-1951) whom Ramsey persuaded that remained work for him to do, the way that is most undoubtedly was of an appealingly charismatic figure in a 20th-century philosophy, living and writing with a power and intensity that frequently overwhelmed his contemporaries and readers, the early period is centred on the 'picture theory of meaning' according to which sentence represents a state of affairs by being a kind of picture or model of it. Containing the elements that were in corresponding to those of the state of affairs and structure or form that mirrors that a structure of the state of affairs that it represents. All logic complexity is reduced to that of the 'propositional calculus, and all propositions are 'truth-functions of atomic or basic propositions.

The interesting thesis that counts as a causal theory of justification, in the making of 'causal theory' intended for the belief as it is justified in case it was produced by a type of process that is 'globally' reliable, that is, its propensity to produce true beliefs that can be defined, to a well-thought-of approximation, as the proportion of the beliefs it produces, or would produce where it used as much as opportunity allows, that is true is sufficiently relializable. Variations of this view have been advanced for both knowledge and justified belief, its first formulation of a reliability account of knowing appeared in the notation from F.P.Ramsey (1903-30). The theory of probability, he was the first to show how a 'personalist theory' could be developed, based on a precise behavioural notion of preference and expectation. In the philosophy of language. Much of Ramsey's work was directed at saving classical mathematics from 'intuitionism', or what he called the 'Bolshevik menace of Brouwer and Weyl. In the theory of probability he was the first to show how a personalist theory could be developed, based on precise behavioural notation of preference and expectation. In the philosophy of language, Ramsey was one of the first thankers, which he combined with radical views of the function of many kinds of a proposition. Neither generalizations, nor causal propositions, nor those treating probability or ethics, describe facts, but each has a different specific function in our intellectual economy.

Ramsey's sentence theory is the sentence generated by taking all the sentences affirmed in a scientific theory that use some term, e.g., 'quark'. Replacing the term by a variable, and existentially quantifying into the result. Instead of saying that quarks have such-and-such properties, the Ramsey sentence says that there is something that has those properties. If the process is repeated for all of a group of the theoretical terms, the sentence gives the 'topic-neutral' structure of the theory, but removes any implication that we know what the term so treated characterized. It leaves open the possibility of identifying the theoretical item with whatever, and it is that best fits the description provided. Virtually, all theories of knowledge. Of course, share an externalist component in requiring truth as a condition for known in. Reliabilism goes father, however, in trying to capture additional conditions for knowledge by ways of a nomic, counterfactual or other such 'external' relations between belief and truth. Closely allied to the nomic sufficiency account of knowledge, primarily dur to Dretshe (1971, 1981), A. I. Goldman (1976, 1986) and R. Nozick (1981).

The core of this approach is that x's belief that 'p' qualifies as knowledge just in case 'x' believes 'p', because of reasons that would not obtain unless 'p's' being true, or because of a process or method that would not yield belief in 'p' if 'p' were not true. For example, 'x' would not have its current reasons for believing there is a telephone before it. Perhaps, would it not come to believe that this in the way it suits the purpose, thus, there is a differentiable fact of a reliable guarantor that the belief's bing true. A stouthearted and valiant counterfactual approach says that 'x' knows that 'p' only if there is no 'relevant alternative' situation in which 'p' is false but 'x' would still believe that a proposition 'p'; must be sufficient to eliminate all the alternatives too 'p' where an alternative to a proposition 'p' is a proposition incompatible with 'p'? . That in one's justification or evidence for 'p' must be sufficient for one to know that every alternative too 'p' is false. This element of our evolving thinking, about which knowledge is exploited by sceptical arguments. These arguments call our attentions to alternatives that our evidence sustains itself with no elimination. The sceptic inquires to how we know that we are not seeing a cleverly disguised mule. While we do have some evidence against the likelihood of such as deception, intuitively knowing that we are not so deceived is not strong enough for 'us'. By pointing out alternate but hidden points of nature, in that we cannot eliminate, as well as others with more general application, as dreams, hallucinations, etc., the sceptic appears to show that every alternative is seldom. If ever, satisfied.

This conclusion conflicts with another strand in our thinking about knowledge, in that we know many things. Thus, there is a tension in our ordinary thinking about knowledge ~. We believe that knowledge is, in the sense indicated, an absolute concept and yet, we also believe that there are many instances of that concept.

If one finds absoluteness to be too central a component of our concept of knowledge to be relinquished, one could argue from the absolute character of knowledge to a sceptical conclusion (Unger, 1975). Most philosophers, however, have taken the other course, choosing to respond to the conflict by giving up, perhaps reluctantly, the absolute criterion. This latter response holds as sacrosanct our commonsense belief that we know many things (Pollock, 1979 and Chisholm, 1977). Each approach is subject to the criticism that it preserves one aspect of our ordinary thinking about knowledge at the expense of denying another. The theory of relevant alternatives can be viewed as an attempt to provide a more satisfactory response to this tension in our thinking about knowledge. It attempts to characterize knowledge in a way that preserves both our belief that knowledge is an absolute concept and our belief that we have knowledge.

Epistemology, is the Greek word, epistēmē, is meant to and for a well-balanced form of 'knowledge', for which the theory of knowledge, and its fundamental questions include the origin of knowledge, the place of experience in generating knowledge, and the place of reason in doing so, the relationship between knowledge and certainty. As between knowledge and the impossibility of error, the possibility of universal scepticism, and the changing forms of knowledge that arises from, a new conceptualized world. All these issues link with other central concerns of philosophy, such as the nature of truth and the nature of truth and the nature of experience and meaning. Seeing epistemology is possible as dominated by two rival metaphors. One is that of a building or pyramid, built on foundations. In this conception it is the job of the philosopher to describe especially secure foundations, and to identify secure odes of construction, so that they can show the resulting edifice to be sound. This metaphor favours part of the 'given' as a basis of knowledge, and of a rationally defensible theory of confirmation and inference for construction. The other metaphor is that of a boat or fuselage, which has no foundation but owes its strength to the stability given by its interlocking parts. This rejects the idea of a basis in the 'given', favours ideas of coherence and 'holism', but finds it harder to ward off scepticism. The problem of defining knowledge as a true belief plus some favoured relations between the believer and the facts begun with Plato's view in the "Theaetetus" that knowledge is true belief plus some 'logos'.

Theories, in philosophy of science, are generalizations or set of generalizations purportedly referring to unobservable entities, e.g., atoms, genes, quarks, unconscious wishes. The ideal gas law, for example, refers only to such observables as pressure, temperature, and volume; the molecular-kinetic theory refers to molecules and their properties. Although, an older usage suggests lack of adequate evidence in playing a subordinate to this ('merely a theory'), current philosophical usage that does not carry that connotation. Einstein's special theory of relativity for example, is considered extremely well founded.

As space, the classical questions include: Is space real? Is it some kind of mental construct or artefact of our ways of perceiving and thinking? Is it 'substantival' or purely? ;relational'? According to Substantivalism, space is an objective thing consisting of points or regions at which, or in which, things are located. Opposed to this is relationalism, according to which the only thing that is real about space are the spatial (and temporal) relations between physical objects. Substantivalism was advocated by Clarke speaking for Newton, and relationalism by Leibniz, in their famous correspondence, and the debate continues today. There is also an issue whether the measure of space and time are objective e, or whether an element of convention enters them. Whereby, the influential analysis of David Lewis suggests that a regularity hold as a matter of convention when it solves a problem of coordination in a group. This means that it is to the benefit of each member to conform to the regularity, providing the other do so. Any number of solutions to such a problem may exist, for example, it is to the advantages of each of us to drive on the same side of the road as others, but indifferent whether we all drive o the right or the left. One solution or another may emerge for a variety of reasons. It is notable that on this account convections may arise naturally; they do not have to be the result of specific agreement. This frees the notion for use in thinking about such things as the origin of language or of political society.

Finding to a theory that magnifies the role of decisions, or free selection from among equally possible alternatives, in order to show that what appears to be objective or fixed by nature is in fact an artefact of human convention, similar to conventions of etiquette, or grammar, or law. Thus one might suppose that moral rules owe more to social convention than to anything imposed from outside, or hat supposedly inexorable necessities are in fact the shadow of our linguistic conventions. The disadvantage of conventionalism is that it must show that alternative, equally workable e conventions could have been adopted, and it is often easy to believe that, for example, if we hold that some ethical norm such as respect for promises or property is conventional, we ought to be able to show that human needs would have been equally well satisfied by a system involving a different norm, and this may be hard to establish.

A convention also suggested by Paul Grice (1913-88) directing participants in conversation to pay heed to an accepted purpose or direction of the exchange. Contributions made deficiently non-payable for attentions of which were liable to be rejected for other reasons than straightforward falsity: Something true but unhelpful or inappropriately are met with puzzlement or rejection. We can thus never infer fro the fact that it would be inappropriate to say something in some circumstance that what would be aid, were we to say it, would be false. This inference was frequently and in ordinary language philosophy, it being argued, for example, that since we do not normally say 'there sees to be a barn there' when there is unmistakably a barn there, it is false that on such occasions there seems to be a barn there.

There are two main views on the nature of theories. According to the 'received view' theories are partially interpreted axiomatic systems, according to the semantic view, a theory is a collection of models (Suppe, 1974). However, a natural language comes ready interpreted, and the semantic problem is no specification but of understanding the relationship between terms of various categories (names, descriptions, predicates, adverbs . . .) and their meanings. An influential proposal is that this relationship is best understood by attempting to provide a 'truth definition' for the language, which will involve giving terms and structure of different kinds have on the truth-condition of sentences containing them.

The axiomatic method . . . as, . . . a proposition lid down as one from which we may begin, an assertion that we have taken as fundamental, at least for the branch of enquiry in hand. The axiomatic method is that of defining as a set of such propositions, and the 'proof procedures' or finding of how a proof ever gets started. Suppose I have as premise(1) p and (2) p → q. Can I infer q? Only, it seems, if I am sure of, (3) (p & p → q) → q. Can I then infer q? Only, it seems, if I am sure that (4) (p & p → q) → q) → q. For each new axiom (N) I need a further axiom (N + 1) telling me that the set-class may as, perhaps be so far that it implies 'q', and the regress never stops. The usual solution is to treat a system as containing not only axioms, but also rules of reference, allowing movement fro the axiom. The rule 'modus ponens' allows us to pass from the first two premises to 'q'. Charles Dodgson Lutwidge (1832-98) better known as Lewis Carroll's puzzle shows that it is essential to distinguish two theoretical categories, although there may be choice about which to put in which category.

This type of theory (axiomatic) usually emerges as a body of (supposes) truths that are not nearly organized, making the theory difficult to survey or study a whole. The axiomatic method is an idea for organizing a theory (Hilbert 1970): one tries to select from among the supposed truths a small number from which all others can be seen to be deductively inferrable. This makes the theory rather more tractable since, in a sense, all the truths are contained in those few. In a theory so organized, the few truths from which all others are deductively inferred are called axioms. In that, just as algebraic and differential equations, which were used to study mathematical and physical processes, could themselves be made mathematical objects, so axiomatic theories, like algebraic and differential equations, which are means of representing physical processes and mathematical structures, could be made objects of mathematical investigation.

When the principles were taken as epistemologically prior, that is, as axioms, either they were taken to be epistemologically privileged, e.g., self-evident, not needing to be demonstrated or (again, inclusive 'or') to be such that all truths do follow from them (by deductive inferences). Gödel (1984) showed that treating axiomatic theories as themselves mathematical objects, that mathematics, and even a small part of mathematics, elementary number theory, could not be axiomatized, that, more precisely, any class of axioms which in such that we could effectively decide, of any proposition, whether or not it was in the class, would be too small to capture all of the truths.

The use of a model to test for the consistency of an axiomatized system is older than modern logic. Descartes's algebraic interpretation of Euclidean geometry provides a way of showing tat if the theory of real numbers is consistent, so is the geometry. Similar mapping had been used by mathematicians in the 19th century for example to show that if

Euclidean geometry is consistent, so are various non-Euclidean geometries. Model theory is the general study of this kind of procedure: The study of interpretations of formal system. Proof theory studies relations of deducibility as defined purely syntactically, that is, without reference to the intended interpretation of the calculus. More formally, a deductively valid argument starting from true premises, that yields the conclusion between formulae of a system. But once the notion of an interpretation is in place we can ask whether a formal system meets certain conditions. In particular, can it lead us from sentences that are true under some interpretation to ones that are false under the same interpretation? And if a sentence is true under all interpretations, is it also a theorem of the system? We can define a notion of validity (a formula is valid if it is true in all interpretations) and semantic consequence. The central questions for a calculus will be whether all and only its theorems are valid, and whether {A1 . . . An} ⊨ B -if and only if, {A1. . . . and some formula's ⊢ B}. These are the questions of the soundness and completeness of a formal system. For the propositional calculus this turns into the question of whether the proof theory delivers as theorems all and only tautologies. There are many axiomatizations of the propositional calculus that are consistent an complete. Gödel proved in 1929 that first-order predicate calculus is complete: any formula that is true under every interpretation is a theorem of the calculus.

The propositional calculus or logical calculus whose expressions are letter represents sentences or propositions, and constants representing operations on those propositions to produce others of higher complexity. The operations include conjunction, disjunction, material implication and negation (although these need not be primitive). Propositional logic was partially anticipated by the Stoics but researched maturity only with the work of Frége, Russell, and Wittgenstein.

The concept introduced by Frége of a function taking a number of names as arguments, and delivering one proposition as the value. The idea is that 'χ loves' y' is a propositional function, which yields the proposition 'John loves' Mary' from those two arguments (in that order). A propositional function is therefore roughly equivalent to a property or relation. In Principia Mathematica, Russell and Whitehead take propositional functions to be the fundamental function, since the theory of descriptions could be taken as showing that other expressions denoting functions are incomplete symbols.

Keeping in mind, the two classical ruth-values that a statement, proposition, or sentence can take. It is supposed in classical (two-valued) logic, that each statement has one of these e values, and none has both. A statement is then false if and only if it is not true. The basis of this scheme is that to each statement t there corresponds a determinate truth condition, or way the world must be for it to be true, and otherwise false. Statements may be felicitous or infelicitous in other dimensions (polite, misleading, apposite, witty, etc.) but truth is the central normative governing assertion. Considerations of vagueness may introduce greys into a black-and-white scheme. For the issue of whether falsity is the only of failing to be true.

Formally, it is nonetheless, that any suppressed premise or background framework of thought necessary to make an argument valid, or a position tenable. More formally, a presupposition has been defined as a proposition whose truth is necessary for either the truth or the falsity of another statement. Thus, if 'p' presupposes 'q', 'q' must be true for p to be either true or false. In the theory of knowledge of Robin George Collingwood (1889-1943), any propositions capable of truth or falsity stand on a bed of 'absolute presuppositions' which are not properly capable of truth or falsity, since a system of thought will contain no way of approaching such a question. It was suggested by Peter Strawson (1919-), in opposition to Russell's theory of 'definite descriptions, that 'there exists a King of France' is a presupposition of 'the King of France is bald', the latter being neither true, nor false, if there is no King of France. It is, however, a little unclear whether the idea is that no statement at all is made in such a case, or whether a statement is made, but fails of being either true or false. The former option preserves classical logic, since we can still say that every statement is either true or false, but the latter des not, since in classical logic the law of 'bivalence' holds, and ensures that nothing at all is presupposed for any proposition to be true or false. The introduction of presupposition therefore means tat either a third truth-value is found, 'intermediate' between truth and falsity, or that classical logic is preserved, but it is impossible to tell whether a particular sentence expresses a proposition that is a candidate for truth ad falsity, without knowing more than the formation rules of the language. Each suggestion carries costs, and there is some consensus that at least where definite descriptions are involved, examples like the one given are equally well handed by regarding the overall sentence false when the existence claim fails.

A proposition may be true or false it is said to take the truth-value true, and if the latter are the truth-value false. The idea behind the term is the analogy between assigning a propositional variable one or other of these values, as a formula of the propositional calculus, and assigning an object as the value of any other variable. Logics with intermediate values are called many-valued logics. Then, a truth-function of a number of propositions or sentences is a function of them that has a definite truth-value, depends only on the truth-values of the constituents. Thus (p & q) is a combination whose truth-value is true when 'p' is true and 'q' is true, and false otherwise, $\neg$ p is a truth-function of 'p', false when 'p' is true and true when 'p' is false. The way in which te value of the whole is determined by the combinations of values of constituents is presented in a truth table.

In whatever manner, truths of fact cannot be reduced to any identity and our only way of knowing them is empirically, by reference to the facts of the empirical world. Likewise, since their denial does not involve a contradiction, there is merely contingent: Their foundation as the supporting structures have been the grounds for being, but in other ways a hold of the actual world, but not every possible one. Some examples re 'Caesar crossed the Rubicon' and 'Leibniz was born in Leipzig', as well as propositions expressing correct scientific generalizations. In Leibniz's view truths of fact rest on the principle of sufficient reason, which is a reason why it is so. This reason is that the actual worlds by which he means the total collection of things past, present and their combining futures are better than any other possible world and therefore created by God. The foundation of his thought is the conviction that to each individual there corresponds a complete notion, knowable only to God, from which is deducible all the properties possessed by the individual at each moment in its history. It is contingent that God actualizes te individual that meets such a concept, but his doing so is explicable by the principle of 'sufficient reason', whereby God had to actualize just that possibility in order for this to be the best of all possible worlds. This thesis is subsequently lampooned by Voltaire (1694-1778), in whom of which was prepared to take refuge in ignorance, as the nature of the soul, or the way to reconcile evil with divine providence.

In defending the principle of sufficient reason sometimes described as the principle that nothing can be so without there being a reason why it is so. Bu t the reason has to be of a particularly potent kind: Eventually it has to ground contingent facts in necessities, and in particular in the reason an omnipotent and perfect being would have for actualizing one possibility than another. Among the consequences of the principle is Leibniz's relational doctrine of space, since if space were an infinite box there could be no reason for the world to be at one point in rather than another, and God placing it at any point violate the principle. In Abelard's (1079-1142), as in Leibniz, the principle eventually forces te recognition that the actual world is the best of all possibilities, since anything else would be inconsistent with the creative power that actualizes possibilities.

If truth consists in concept containment, then it seems that all truths are analytic and hence necessary and if they are all necessary, surely they are all truths of reason. In that not every truth can be reduced to an identity in a finite number of steps; in some instances revealing the connection between subject and predicate concepts would require an infinite analysis, but while this may entail that we cannot prove such proposition as a prior, it does not appear to show that proposition could have ben false. Intuitively, it seems a better ground for supposing that it is a necessary truth of a special sort. A related question arises from the idea that truths of fact depend on God's decision to create the best world: If it is part of the concept of this world that it is best, how could its existence be other than necessary? An accountable and responsively answered explanation would be so, that any relational question that brakes the norm lay eyes on its existence in the manner other than hypothetical necessities, i.e., it follows from God's decision to create the world, but God had the power to create this world, but God is necessary, so how could he have decided to do anything else? Leibniz says much more about these matters, but it is not clear whether he offers any satisfactory solutions.

The view that the terms in which we think of some area are sufficiently infected with error for it to be better to abandon them than to continue to try to give coherent theories of their use. Eliminativism should be distinguished from scepticism which claims that we cannot know the truth about some area; eliminativism claims rather than there is no truth there to be known, in the terms which we currently think. An eliminativist about theology simply counsels abandoning the terms or discourse of theology, and that will include abandoning worries about the extent of theological knowledge.

Eliminativists in the philosophy of mind counsel abandoning the whole network of terms mind, consciousness, self, Qualia that usher in the problems of mind and body. Sometimes the argument for doing this is that we should wait for a supposed future understanding of ourselves, based on cognitive science and better than any our current mental descriptions provide, sometimes it is supposed that physicalism shows that no mental description of us could possibly be true.

Greek scepticism centred on the value of enquiry and questioning, scepticism is now the denial that knowledge or even rational belief is possible, either about some specific subject matter, e.g., ethics, or in any subsequent whatsoever. Classically, scepticism springs from the observation that the best methods in some area seem to fall short of giving us contact with the truth, e.g., there is a gulf between appearance and reality, and in frequency cites the conflicting judgements that our methods deliver, with the result that questions of truth become undecidable.

Scepticism should not be confused with relativism, which is a doctrine about the nature of truth, and may be motivated by trying to avoid scepticism. Nor is it identical with eliminativism, which counsels abandoning an area of thought altogether, not because we cannot know the truth, but because there are no truths capable of bing framed in the terms we use.

Descartes's theory of knowledge starts with the quest for certainty, for an indubitable starting-point or foundation on the basis alone of which progress is possible. This is eventually found in the celebrated 'Cogito ergo sum': I think therefore I am. By locating the point of certainty in my own awareness of my own self, Descartes gives a first-person twist to the theory of knowledge that dominated them following centuries in spite of various counter attacks on behalf of social and public starting-points. The metaphysics associated with this priority is the famous Cartesian dualism, or separation of mind and matter into a dual purposed interacting substances, Descartes rigorously and rightly sees that it takes divine dispensation to certify any relationship between the two realms thus divided, and to prove the reliability of the senses invokes a 'clear and distinct perception' of highly dubious proofs of the existence of a benevolent deity. This has not met general acceptance: as Hume drily puts it, 'to have recourse to the veracity of the supreme Being, in order to prove the veracity of our senses, is surely making a very unexpected circuit'.

In his own time Descartes's conception of the entirely separate substance of the mind was recognized to give rise to insoluble problems of the nature of the causal connection between the two. It also gives rise to the problem, insoluble in its own terms, of other minds. Descartes's notorious denial that nonhuman animals are conscious is a stark illustration of the problem. In his conception of matter Descartes also gives preference to rational cogitation over anything derived from the senses. Since we can conceive of the matter of a ball of wax surviving changes to its sensible qualities, matter is not an empirical concept, but eventually an entirely geometrical one, with extension and motion as its only physical nature. Descartes's thought, as reflected in Leibniz, that the qualities of sense experience have no resemblance to qualities of things, so that knowledge of the external world is essentially knowledge of structure rather than of filling. On this basis Descartes erects a remarkable physics. Since matter is in effect the same as extension there can be no empty space or 'void', since there is no empty space motion is not a question of occupying previously empty space, but is to be thought of in terms of vortices (like the motion of a liquid).

Although the structure of Descartes's epistemology, the philosophical theories of mind, and theory of matter have ben rejected many times, their relentless awareness of the hardest issues, their exemplary clarity, and even their initial plausibility, all contrive to make him the central point of reference for modern philosophy.

The self conceived as Descartes presents it in the first two Meditations: aware only of its own thoughts, and capable of disembodied existence, neither situated in a space nor surrounded by others. This is the pure self of 'I' that we are tempted to imagine as a simple unique thing that makes up our essential identity. Descartes's view that he could keep hold of this nugget while doubting everything else is criticized by Lichtenberg and Kant, and most subsequent philosophers of mind.

Descartes holds that we do not have any knowledge of any empirical proposition about anything beyond the contents of our own minds. The reason, roughly put, is that there is a legitimate doubt about all such propositions because there is no way to deny justifiably that our senses are being stimulated by some cause (an evil spirit, for example) which is radically different from the objects which we normally think affect our senses.

He also points out, that the senses (sight, hearing, touch, etc., are often unreliable, and 'it is prudent never to trust entirely those who have deceived us even once', he cited such instances as the straight stick which looks ben t in water, and the square tower which looks round from a distance. This argument of illusion, has not, on the whole, impressed commentators, and some of Descartes' contemporaries pointing out that since such errors come to light as a result of further sensory information, It cannot be right to cast wholesale doubt on the evidence of the senses. But Descartes regarded the argument from illusion as only the first stage in a softening up process which would 'lead the mind away from the senses'. He admits that there are some cases of sense-base belief about which doubt would be insane, e.g., the belief that I am sitting here by the fire, wearing a winter dressing gown'.

Descartes was to realize that there was nothing in this view of nature that could explain or provide a foundation for the mental, or from direct experience as distinctly human. In a mechanistic universe, he said, there is no privileged place or function for mind, and the separation between mind and matter is absolute. Descartes was also convinced, that the immaterial essences that gave form and structure to this universe were coded in geometrical and mathematical ideas, and this insight led him to invent algebraic geometry.

A scientific understanding of these ideas could be derived, said Descartes, with the aid of precise deduction, and he also claimed that the contours of physical reality could be laid out in three-dimensional coordinates. Following the publication of Newton's Principia Mathematica in 1687, reductionism and mathematical modelling became the most powerful tools of modern science. And the dream that the entire physical world could be known and mastered through the extension and refinement of mathematical theory became the central feature and guiding principle of scientific knowledge.

Having to its recourse of knowledge, its cental questions include the origin of knowledge, the place of experience in generating knowledge, and the place of reason in doing so, the relationship between knowledge and certainty, and between knowledge and the impossibility of error, the possibility of universal scepticism, and the changing forms of knowledge that arise from new conceptualizations of the world. All of these issues link with other central concerns of philosophy, such as the nature of truth and the natures of experience and meaning. Seeing epistemology is possible as dominated by two rival metaphors. One is that of a building or pyramid, built on foundations. In this conception it is the kob of the philosopher to describe especially secure foundations, and to identify secure modes of construction, is that the resulting edifice can be shown to be sound. This metaphor of knowledge, and of a rationally defensible theory of confirmation and inference as a method of construction, as that knowledge must be regarded as a structure rose upon secure, certain foundations. These are found in some formidable combinations of experience and reason, with different schools (empiricism, rationalism) emphasizing the role of one over that of the others. Foundationalism was associated with the ancient Stoics, and in the modern era with Descartes (1596-1650), but by their interlocking strength, than as a crossword puzzle may be known to have been solved correctly even if each answer, taken individually, admits of uncertainty. Difficulties at this point led the logical passivists to abandon the notion of an epistemological foundation together, and to flirt with the coherence theory of truth. It is widely accepted that trying to make the connection between thought and experience through basic sentences depends on an untenable 'myth of the given'.

Still, of the other metaphor, is that of a boat or fuselage, that has no foundation but owes its strength to the stability given by its interlocking parts. This rejects the idea of a basis in the 'given', favours ideas of coherence and holism, but finds it harder to ward off scepticism. In spite of these concerns, the problem, least of mention, is of defining knowledge in terms of true beliefs plus some favoured relations between the believer and the facts that began with Plato's view in the "Theaetetus," that knowledge is true belief, and some logos. Due of its nonsynthetic epistemology, the enterprising of studying the actual formation of knowledge by human beings, without aspiring to certify those processes as rational, or its proof against 'scepticism' or even apt to yield the truth. Natural epistemology would therefore blend into the psychology of learning and the study of episodes in the history of science. The scope for 'external' or philosophical reflection of the kind that might result in scepticism or its refutation is markedly diminished. Despite the fact that the terms of modernity are so distinguished as exponents of the approach include Aristotle, Hume, and J.S. Mills.

The task of the philosopher of a discipline would then be to reveal the correct method and to unmask counterfeits. Although this belief lay behind much positivist philosophy of science, few philosophers now subscribe to it. It places too well a confidence in the possibility of a purely previous 'first philosophy', or viewpoint beyond that of the work one's way of practitioners, from which their best efforts can be measured as good or bad. These standpoints now seem that too many philosophers to be a fanciful, that the more modest of tasks that are actually adopted at various historical stages of investigation into different areas with the aim not so much of criticizing but more of systematization, in the presuppositions of a particular field at a particular tie. There is still a role for local methodological disputes within the community investigators of some phenomenon, with one approach charging that another is unsound or unscientific, but logic and philosophy will not, on the modern view, provide an independent arsenal of weapons for such battles, which indeed often come to seem more like political bids for ascendancy within a discipline.

This is an approach to the theory of knowledge that sees an important connection between the growth of knowledge and biological evolution. An evolutionary epistemologist claims that the development of human knowledge processed through some natural selection process, the best example of which is Darwin's theory of biological natural selection. There is a widespread misconception that evolution proceeds according to some plan or direct, but it has neither, and the role of chance ensures that its future course will be unpredictable. Random variations in individual organisms create tiny differences in their Darwinian fitness. Some individuals have more offsprings than others, and the characteristics that increased their fitness thereby become more prevalent in future generations. Once upon a time, at least a mutation occurred in a human population in tropical Africa that changed the haemoglobin molecule in a way that provided resistance to malaria. This enormous advantage caused the new gene to spread, with the unfortunate consequence that sickle-cell anaemia came to exist.

Chance can influence the outcome at each stage: First, in the creation of genetic mutation, second, in wether the bearer lives long enough to show its effects, thirdly, in chance events that influence the individual's actual reproductive success, and fourth, in wether a gene even if favoured in one generation, is, happenstance, eliminated in the next, and finally in the many unpredictable environmental changes that will undoubtedly occur in the history of any group of organisms. As Harvard biologist Stephen Jay Gould has so vividly expressed that process over again, the outcome would surely be different. Not only might there not be humans, there might not even be anything like mammals.

We will often emphasis the elegance of traits shaped by natural selection, but the common idea that nature creates perfection needs to be analysed carefully. The extent to which evolution achieves perfection depends on exactly what you mean. If you mean "Does natural selections always take the best path for the long-term welfare of a species?" The answer is no. That would require adaption by group selection, and this is, unlikely. If you mean "Does natural selection creates every adaption that would be valuable?" The answer again, is no. For instance, some kinds of South American monkeys can grasp branches with their tails. The trick would surely also be useful to some African species, but, simply because of bad luck, none have it. Some combination of circumstances started some ancestral South American monkeys using their tails in ways that ultimately led to an ability to grab onto branches, while no such development took place in Africa. Mere usefulness of a trait does not necessitate a means in that what will understandably endure phylogenesis or evolution.

This is an approach to the theory of knowledge that sees an important connection between the growth of knowledge and biological evolution. An evolutionary epistemologist claims that the development of human knowledge proceeds through some natural selection process, the best example of which is Darwin's theory of biological natural selection. The three major components of the model of natural selection are variation selection and retention. According to Darwin's theory of natural selection, variations are not pre-designed to do certain functions. Rather, these variations that do useful functions are selected. While those that do not employ of some coordinates in that are regainfully purposed are also, not to any of a selection, as duly influenced of such a selection, that may have responsibilities for the visual aspects of a variational intentionally occurs. In the modern theory of evolution, genetic mutations provide the blind variations: Blind in the sense that variations are not influenced by the effects they would have-the likelihood of a mutation is not correlated with the benefits or liabilities that mutation would confer on the organism, the environment provides the filter of selection, and reproduction provides the retention. Fit is achieved because those organisms with features that make them less adapted for survival do not survive in connection with other organisms in the environment that have features that are better adapted. Evolutionary epistemology applies this blind variation and selective retention model to the growth of scientific knowledge and to human thought processes overall.

The parallel between biological evolution and conceptual or 'epistemic' evolution can be seen as either literal or analogical. The literal version of evolutionary epistemology dees biological evolution as the main cause of the growth of knowledge. On this view, called the 'evolution of cognitive mechanic programs', by Bradie (1986) and the 'Darwinian approach to epistemology' by Ruse (1986), that growth of knowledge occurs through blind variation and selective retention because biological natural selection itself is the cause of epistemic variation and selection. The most plausible version of the literal view does not hold that all human beliefs are innate but rather than the mental mechanisms that guide the acquisitions of non-innate beliefs are themselves innately and the result of biological natural selection. Ruse, (1986) demands of a version of literal evolutionary epistemology that he links to sociolology (Rescher, 1990).

On the analogical version of evolutionary epistemology, called the 'evolution of theory's program', by Bradie (1986). The 'Spenserians approach' (after the nineteenth century philosopher Herbert Spencer) by Ruse (1986), the development of human knowledge is governed by a process analogous to biological natural selection, rather than by an instance of the mechanism itself. This version of evolutionary epistemology, introduced and elaborated by Donald Campbell (1974) as well as Karl Popper, sees the [partial] fit between theories and the world as explained by a mental process of trial and error known as epistemic natural selection.

Both versions of evolutionary epistemology are usually taken to be types of naturalized epistemology, because both take some empirical facts as a starting point for their epistemological project. The literal version of evolutionary epistemology begins by accepting evolutionary theory and a materialist approach to the mind and, from these, constructs an account of knowledge and its developments. In contrast, the metaphorical version does not require the truth of biological evolution: It simply draws on biological evolution as a source for the model of natural selection. For this version of evolutionary epistemology to be true, the model of natural selection need only apply to the growth of knowledge, not to the origin and development of species. Crudely put, evolutionary epistemology of the analogical sort could still be true even if Creationism is the correct theory of the origin of species.

Although they do not begin by assuming evolutionary theory, most analogical evolutionary epistemologists are naturalized epistemologists as well, their empirical assumptions, least of mention, implicitly come from psychology and cognitive science, not evolutionary theory. Sometimes, however, evolutionary epistemology is characterized in a seemingly non-naturalistic fashion. Campbell (1974) says that 'if one is expanding knowledge beyond what one knows, one has no choice but to explore without the benefit of wisdom', i.e., blindly. This, Campbell admits, makes evolutionary epistemology close to being a tautology (and so not naturalistic). Evolutionary epistemology does assert the analytic claim that when expanding one's knowledge beyond what one knows, one must precessed to something that is already known, but, more interestingly, it also makes the synthetic claim that when expanding one's knowledge beyond what one knows, one must proceed by blind variation and selective retention. This claim is synthetic because it can be empirically falsified. The central claim of evolutionary epistemology is synthetic, not analytic. If the central contradictory, which they are not. Campbell is right that evolutionary epistemology does have the analytic feature he mentions, but he is wrong to think that this is a distinguishing feature, since any plausible epistemology has the same analytic feature (Skagestad, 1978).

Two extraordinary issues lie to awaken the literature that involves questions about 'realism', i.e., What metaphysical commitment does an evolutionary epistemologist have to make? Progress, i.e., according to evolutionary epistemology, does knowledge develop toward a goal? With respect to realism, many evolutionary epistemologists endorse that is called 'hypothetical realism', a view that combines a version of epistemological 'scepticism' and tentative acceptance of metaphysical realism. With respect to progress, the problem is that biological evolution is not goal-directed, but the growth of human knowledge seems to be. Campbell (1974) worries about the potential dis-analogy here but is willing to bite the stone of conscience and admit that epistemic evolution progress toward a goal (truth) while biologic evolution does not. Many another has argued that evolutionary epistemologists must give up the 'truth-topic' sense of progress because a natural selection model is in essence, is non-teleological, as an alternative, following Kuhn (1970), and embraced in the accompaniment with evolutionary epistemology.

Among the most frequent and serious criticisms levelled against evolutionary epistemology is that the analogical version of the view is false because epistemic variation is not blind (Skagestad, 1978 and Ruse, 1986) Stein and Lipton (1990) have argued, however, that this objection fails because, while epistemic variation is not random, its constraints come from heuristics that, for the most part, are selective retention. Further, Stein and Lipton come to the conclusion that heuristics are analogous to biological pre-adaptions, evolutionary pre-biological pre-adaptions, evolutionary cursors, such as a half-wing, a precursor to a wing, which have some function other than the function of their descendable structures: The function of descendable structures, the function of their descendable character embodied to its structural foundations, is that of the guidelines of epistemic variation is, on this view, not the source of disanaloguousness, but the source of a more articulated account of the analogy.

Many evolutionary epistemologists try to combine the literal and the analogical versions (Bradie, 1986, and Stein and Lipton, 1990), saying that those beliefs and cognitive mechanisms, which are innate results from natural selection of the biological sort and those that are innate results from natural selection of the epistemic sort. This is reasonable asa long as the two parts of this hybrid view are kept distinct. An analogical version of evolutionary epistemology with biological variation as its only source of blondeness would be a null theory: This would be the case if all our beliefs are innate or if our non-innate beliefs are not the result of blind variation. An appeal to the legitimate way to produce a hybrid version of evolutionary epistemology since doing so trivializes the theory. For similar reasons, such an appeal will not save an analogical version of evolutionary epistemology from arguments to the effect that epistemic variation is blind (Stein and Lipton, 1990).

Although it is a new approach to theory of knowledge, evolutionary epistemology has attracted much attention, primarily because it represents a serious attempt to flush out a naturalized epistemology by drawing on several disciplines. In science is relevant to understanding the nature and development of knowledge, then evolutionary theory is among the disciplines worth a look. Insofar as evolutionary epistemology looks there, it is an interesting and potentially fruitful epistemological programme.

What makes a belief justified and what makes a true belief knowledge? Thinking that whether a belief deserves one of these appraisals is natural depends on what caused the depicted branch of knowledge to have the belief. In recent decades a number of epistemologists have pursued this plausible idea with a variety of specific proposals. Some causal theories of knowledge have it that a true belief that 'p' is knowledge just in case it has the right causal connection to the fact that 'p'. Such a criterion can be applied only to cases where the fact that 'p' is a sort that can enter inti causal relations, as this seems to exclude mathematically and other necessary facts and perhaps any fact expressed by a universal generalization, and proponents of this sort of criterion have usually supposed that it is limited to perceptual representations where knowledge of particular facts about subjects' environments.

For example, Armstrong (1973) predetermined that a position held by a belief in the form 'This perceived object is 'F' is [non-inferential] knowledge if and only if the belief is a completely reliable sign that the perceived object is 'F', that ism, the fact that the object is 'F' contributed to causing the belief and its doing so depended on properties of the believer such that the laws of nature dictated that, for any subject 'χ' and perceived object 'y', if 'χ' has those properties and believed that 'y' is 'F', then 'y' is 'F'. (Dretske (1981) offers a rather similar account, in terms of the belief's being caused by a signal received by the perceiver that carries the information that the object is 'F').

This sort of condition fails, however, to be sufficiently for non-inferential perceptivity, for knowledge is accountable for its compatibility with the belief's being unjustified, and an unjustified belief cannot be knowledge. For example, suppose that your mechanisms for the sensory data of colour as perceived, are working well. However, you have been given good reason to think otherwise, to think, say, that the sensory data of things look chartreuse to say, that chartreuse things look magenta, if you fail to heed these reasons you have for thinking that your colour perception is refractively to follow a credo of things that look bicoloured to you that it is tinge, your belief will fail atop be justified and will therefore fail to be knowledge, even though it is caused by the thing's being withing the grasp of sensory perceptivity, in such a way as to be a completely reliable sign, or to carry the information that the thing is sufficiently to organize all sensory data as perceived in and of the world, or Holistic view.

One could fend off this sort of counterexample by simply adding to the belief be justified. However, this enriched condition would still be insufficient. Suppose, for example, that in an experiment you are given a drug that in nearly all people, but not in you, as it happens, causes the aforementioned aberration in colour perception. The experimenter tells you that you have taken such a drug but then says, That the pill taken was just a placebo'. Yet suppose further, that the experimenter tells you are false, her telling you this gives you justification for believing of a thing that looks magenta to you that it is magenta, but a fact about this justification that is unknown to you, that the experimenter's last statement was false, makes it the case that your true belief is not knowledge even though it satisfies Armstrong's causal condition.

Goldman (1986) has proposed an importantly different causal criterion, namely, that a true belief is knowledge if it is produced by a type of process that is 'globally' and 'locally' reliable. Causing true beliefs is sufficiently high is globally reliable if its propensity. Local reliability has to do with whether the process would have produced a similar but false belief in certain counterfactual situations alternative to the actual situation. This way of marking off true beliefs that are knowledge does not require the fact believed to be causally related to the belief, and so it could in principle apply to knowledge of any kind of truth.

Goldman requires the global reliability of the belief-producing process for the justification of a belief, he requires it also for knowledge because justification is required for knowledge. What he requires for knowledge, but does not require for justification is local reliability. His idea is that a justified true belief is knowledge if the type of process that produced it would not have produced it in any relevant counterfactual situation in which it is false. Its purported theory of relevant alternatives can be viewed as an attempt to provide a more satisfactory response to this tension in our thinking about knowledge. It attempts to characterize knowledge in a way that preserves both our belief that knowledge is an absolute concept and our belief that we have knowledge.

According to the theory, we need to qualify rather than deny the absolute character of knowledge. We should view knowledge as absolute, reactive to certain standards (Dretske, 1981 and Cohen, 1988). That is to say, in order to know a proposition, our evidence need not eliminate all the alternatives to that preposition, rather for 'us', that we can know our evidence eliminates all the relevant alternatives, where the set of relevant alternatives (a proper subset of the set of all alternatives) is determined by some standard. Moreover, according to the relevant alternatives view, and the standards determining that of the alternatives is raised by the sceptic are not relevant. If this is correct, then the fact that our evidence cannot eliminate the sceptic's alternative does not lead to a sceptical result. For knowledge requires only the elimination of the relevant alternatives, so the relevant alternative view preserves in both strands in our thinking about knowledge. Knowledge is an absolute concept, but because the absoluteness is relative to a standard, we can know many things.

The interesting thesis that counts as a causal theory of justification (in the meaning of 'causal theory' intended here) is the following: A belief is justified in case it was produced by a type of process that is 'globally' reliable, that is, its propensity to produce true beliefs-that can be defined (to a good approximation) As the proportion of the beliefs it produces (or would produce) that is true is sufficiently great.

This proposal will be adequately specified only when we are told (I) how much of the causal history of a belief counts as part of the process that produced it, (ii) which of the many types to which the process belongs is the type for purposes of assessing its reliability, and (iii) relative to why the world or worlds are the reliability of the process type to be assessed the actual world, the closet worlds containing the case being considered, or something else? Let 'us' look at the answers suggested by Goldman, the leading proponent of a reliabilist account of justification.

(1) Goldman (1979, 1986) takes the relevant belief producing process to include only the proximate causes internal to the believer. So, for instance, when recently I believed that the telephone was ringing the process that produced the belief, for purposes of assessing reliability, includes just the causal chain of neural events from the stimulus in my ear's inward ands other concurrent brain states on which the production of the belief depended: It does not include any events' of an 'I' in the calling of a telephone or the sound waves travelling between it and my ears, or any earlier decisions I made that were responsible for my being within hearing distance of the telephone at that time. It does seem intuitively plausible of a belief depends should be restricted to internal omnes proximate to the belief. Why? Goldman does not tell 'us'. One answer that some philosophers might give is that it is because a belief's being justified at a given time can depend only on facts directly accessible to the believer's awareness at that time (for, if a believer ought to holds only beliefs that are justified, she can tell at any given time what beliefs would then be justified for her). However, this cannot be Goldman's answer because he wishes to include in the relevantly process neural events that are not directly accessible to consciousness.

(2) Once the reliabilist has told 'us' how to delimit the process producing a belief, he needs to tell 'us' which of the many types to which it belongs is the relevant type. Coincide, for example, the process that produces your current belief that you see a book before you. One very broad type to which that process belongs would be specified by 'coming to a belief as to something one perceives as a result of activation of the nerve endings in some of one's sense-organs'. A constricted type, for which an unvarying process belongs, for in that, would be specified by 'coming to a belief as to what one sees as a result of activation of the nerve endings in one's retinas'. A still narrower type would be given by inserting in the last specification a description of a particular pattern of activation of the retina's particular cells. Which of these or other types to which the token process belongs is the relevant type for determining whether the type of process that produced your belief is reliable?

If we select a type that is too broad, as having the same degree of justification various beliefs that intuitively seem to have different degrees of justification. Thus the broadest type we specified for your belief that you see a book before you apply also to perceptual beliefs where the object seen is far away and seen only briefly is less justified. On the other hand, is we are allowed to select a type that is as narrow as we please, then we make it out that an obviously unjustified but true belief is produced by a reliable type of process. For example, suppose I see a blurred shape through the fog far in a field and unjustifiedly, but correctly, believe that it is a sheep: If we include enough details about my retinal image is specifying the type of the visual process that produced that belief, we can specify a type is likely to have only that one instanced and is therefore 100 percent reliable. Goldman conjectures (1986) that the relevant process type is 'the narrowest type that is casually operative'. Presumably, a feature of the process producing beliefs were causally operatives in producing it just in case some alternative feature instead, but it would not have led to that belief. (We need to say 'some' here rather than 'any', because, for example, when I see an oak tree the particular 'oak' material bodies of my retinal images are clearly casually operatives in producing my belief that I see a tree even though there are alternative shapes, for example, 'oakish' ones, that would have produced the same belief.)

(3) Should the justification of a belief in a hypothetical, non-actual example turn on the reliability of the belief-producing process in the possible world of the example? That leads to the implausible result in that in a world run by a Cartesian demon a powerful being who causes the other inhabitants of the world to have rich and coherent sets of perceptual and memory impressions that are all illusory the perceptual and memory beliefs of the other inhabitants are all unjustified, for they are produced by processes that are, in that world, quite unreliable. If we say instead that it is the reliability of the processes in the

actual world that matters, we get the equally undesired result that if the actual world is a demon world then our perceptual and memory beliefs are all unjustified.

Goldman's solution (1986) is that the reliability of the process types is to be gauged by their performance in 'normal' worlds, that is, worlds consistent with 'our general beliefs about the world . . . 'about the sorts of objects, events and changes that occur in it'. This gives the intuitively right results for the problem cases just considered, but indicate by inference an implausible proportion of making compensations for alternative tending toward justification. If there are people whose general beliefs about the world are very different from mine, then there may, on this account, be beliefs that I can correctly regard as justified (ones produced by processes that are reliable in what I take to be a normal world) but that they can correctly regard as not justified.

However, these questions about the specifics are dealt with, and there are reasons for questioning the basic idea that the criterion for a belief's being justified is its being produced by a reliable process. Thus and so, doubt about the sufficiency of the reliabilist criterion is prompted by a sort of example that Goldman himself uses for another purpose. Suppose that being in brain-state always causes one to believe that one is in brained-state B. Here the reliability of the belief-producing process is perfect, but 'we can readily imagine circumstances in which a person goes into grain-state B and therefore has the belief in question, though this belief is by no means justified' (Goldman, 1979). Doubt about the necessity of the condition arises from the possibility that one might know that one has strong justification for a certain belief and yet that knowledge is not what actually prompts one to believe. For example, I might be well aware that, having read the weather bureau's forecast that it will be much hotter tomorrow. I have ample reason to be confident that it will be hotter tomorrow, but I irrationally refuse to believe it until my Aunt Hattie tells me that she feels in her joints that it will be hotter tomorrow. Here what prompts me to believe dors not justify my belief, but my belief is nevertheless justified by my knowledge of the weather bureau's prediction and of its evidential force: I can advert to any disclaiming assumption that I ought not to be holding the belief. Indeed, given my justification and that there is nothing untoward about the weather bureau's prediction, my belief, if true, can be counted knowledge. This sorts of example raises doubt whether any causal conditions, are it a reliable process or something else, is necessary for either justification or knowledge.

Philosophers and scientists alike, have often held that the simplicity or parsimony of a theory is one reason, all else being equal, to view it as true. This goes beyond the unproblematic idea that simpler theories are easier to work with and gave greater aesthetic appeal.

One theory is more parsimonious than another when it postulates fewer entities, processes, changes or explanatory principles: The simplicity of a theory depends on essentially the same consecrations, though parsimony and simplicity obviously become the same. Demanding clarification of what makes one theory simpler or more parsimonious is plausible than another before the justification of these methodological maxims can be addressed.

If we set this description problem to one side, the major normative problem is as follows: What reason is there to think that simplicity is a sign of truth? Why should we accept a simpler theory instead of its more complex rivals? Newton and Leibniz thought that the answer was to be found in a substantive fact about nature. In "Principia," Newton laid down as his first Rule of Reasoning in Philosophy that 'nature does nothing in vain . . . 'for Nature is pleased with simplicity and affects not the pomp of superfluous causes'. Leibniz hypothesized that the actual world obeys simple laws because God's taste for simplicity influenced his decision about which world to actualize.

The tragedy of the Western mind, described by Koyré, is a direct consequence of the stark Cartesian division between mind and world. We discovered the 'certain principles of physical reality', said Descartes, 'not by the prejudices of the senses, but by the light of reason, and which thus possess so great evidence that we cannot doubt of their truth'. Since the real, or that which actually exists external to ourselves, was in his view only that which could be represented in the quantitative terms of mathematics, Descartes conclude that all quantitative aspects of reality could be traced to the deceitfulness of the senses.

The most fundamental aspect of the Western intellectual tradition is the assumption that there is a fundamental division between the material and the immaterial world or between the realm of matter and the realm of pure mind or spirit. The metaphysical farmwork based on this assumption is known as ontological dualism. As the word dual implies, the framework is predicated on an ontology, or a conception of the nature of God or Being, that assumes reality has two distinct and separable dimensions. The concept of Being as continuous, immutable, and having a prior or separate existence from the world of change dates from the ancient Greek philosopher Parmenides. The same qualities were associated with the God of the Judeo-Christian tradition, and they were considerably amplified by the role played in the theology by Platonic and Neoplatonic philosophy.

Nicolas Copernicus, Galileo, Johannes Kepler, and Isaac Newton were all inheritors of a cultural tradition in which ontological dualism was a primary article of faith. Hence the idealization of the mathematical ideal as a source of communion with God, which dates from Pythagoras, provided a metaphysical foundation for the emerging natural sciences.

This explains why, the creators of classical physics believed that doing physics was a form of communion with the geometrical and mathematical form's resident in the perfect mind of God. This view would survive in a modified form in what is now known as Einsteinian epistemology and accounts in no small part for the reluctance of many physicists to accept the epistemology y associated with the Copenhagen Interpretation.

At the beginning of the nineteenth century, Pierre-Simon LaPlace, along with a number of other French mathematicians, advanced the view that the science of mechanics constituted a complete view of nature. Since this science, by observing its epistemology, had revealed itself to be the fundamental science, the hypothesis of God was, they concluded, entirely unnecessary.

LaPlace is recognized for eliminating not only the theological component of classical physics but the 'entire metaphysical component' as well'. The epistemology of science requires, he said, that, 'we start by inductive generalizations from observed facts to hypotheses that are 'tested by observed conformity of the phenomena'. What was unique about LaPlace's view of hypotheses was his insistence that we cannot attribute reality to them. Although concepts like force, mass, motion, cause, and laws are obviously present in classical physics, they exist in LaPlace's view only as quantities. Physics is concerned, he argued, with quantities that we associate as a matter of convenience with concepts, and the truths about nature are only the quantities.

As this view of hypotheses and the truths of nature as quantities were extended in the nineteenth century to a mathematical description of phenomena like heat, light, electricity, and magnetism. LaPlace's assumptions about the actual character of scientific truths seemed correct. This progress suggested that if we could remove all thoughts about the 'nature of' or the 'source of' phenomena, the pursuit of strictly quantitative concepts would bring us to a complete description of all aspects of physical reality. Subsequently, figures like Comte, Kirchhoff, Hertz, and Poincaré developed a program for the study of nature hat was quite different from that of the original creators of classical physics.

The seventeenth-century view of physics as a philosophy of nature or as natural philosophy was displaced by the view of physics as an autonomous science that was 'the science of nature'. This view, which was premised on the doctrine of positivism, promised to subsume all of the nature with a mathematical analysis of entities in motion and claimed that the true understanding of nature was revealed only in the mathematical description. Since the doctrine of positivism assumes that the knowledge we call physics resides only in the mathematical formalism of physical theory, it disallows the prospect that the vision of physical reality revealed in physical theory can have any other meaning. In the history of science, the irony is that positivism, which was intended to banish metaphysical concerns from the domain of science, served to perpetuate a seventeenth-century metaphysical assumption about the relationship between physical reality and physical theory.

Epistemology since Hume and Kant has drawn back from this theological underpinning. Indeed, the very idea that nature is simple (or uniform) has come in for a critique. The view has taken hold that a preference for simple and parsimonious hypotheses is purely methodological: It is constitutive of the attitude we call 'scientific' and makes no substantive assumption about the way the world is.

A variety of otherwise diverse twentieth-century philosophers of science have attempted, in different ways, to flesh out this position. Two examples must suffice here: Hesse (1969) as, for summaries of other proposals. Popper (1959) holds that scientists should prefer highly falsifiable (improbable) theories: He tries to show that simpler theories are more falsifiable, also Quine (1966), in contrast, sees a virtue in theories that are highly probable, he argues for a general connection between simplicity and high probability.

Both these proposals are global. They attempt to explain why simplicity should be part of the scientific method in a way that spans all scientific subject matters. No assumption about the details of any particular scientific problem serves as a premiss in Popper's or Quine's arguments.

Newton and Leibniz thought that the justification of parsimony and simplicity flows from the hand of God: Popper and Quine try to justify these methodologically maims without assuming anything substantive about the way the world is. In spite of these differences in approach, they have something in common. They assume that all users of parsimony and simplicity in the separate sciences can be encompassed in a single justifying argument. That recent developments in confirmation theory suggest that this assumption should be scrutinized. Good (1983) and Rosenkrantz (1977) has emphasized the role of auxiliary assumptions in mediating the connection between hypotheses and observations. Whether a hypothesis is well supported by some observations, or whether one hypothesis is better supported than another by those observations, crucially depends on empirical background assumptions about the inference problem here. The same view applies to the idea of prior probability (or, prior plausibility). In of a single hypo-physical science if chosen as an alternative to another even though they are equally supported by current observations, this must be due to an empirical background assumption.

Principles of parsimony and simplicity mediate the epistemic connection between hypotheses and observations. Perhaps these principles are able to do this because they are surrogates for an empirical background theory. It is not that there is one background theory presupposed by every appeal to parsimony; This has the quantifier order backwards. Rather, the suggestion is that each parsimony argument is justified only to each degree that it reflects an empirical background theory about the subjective matter. On this theory is brought out into the open, but the principle of parsimony is entirely dispensable (Sober, 1988).

This 'local' approach to the principles of parsimony and simplicity resurrects the idea that they make sense only if the world is one way rather than another. It rejects the idea that these maxims are purely methodological. How defensible this point of view is, will depend on detailed case studies of scientific hypothesis evaluation and on further developments in the theory of scientific inference.

It is usually not found of one and the same that, an inference is a (perhaps very complex) act of thought by virtue of which act (1) I pass from a set of one or more propositions or statements to a proposition or statement and (2) it appears that the latter are true if the former is or are. This psychological characterization begets some occurrences of wider summations toward its occupying study in literature, under more lesser than inessential variations. Desiring a better characterization of inference is natural. Yet attempts to do so by constructing a fuller psychological explanation fail to comprehend the grounds on which inference will be objectively valid-A point elaborately made by Gottlob Frége. Attempts to understand the nature of inference through the device of the representation of inference by formal-logical calculations or derivations better (1) leave 'us' puzzled about the relation of formal-logical derivations to the informal inferences they are supposedly to represent or reconstruct, and (2) leaves 'us' worried about the sense of such formal derivations. Are these deprivations inference? Are not informal inferences needed in order to apply the rules governing the constructions of formal derivations (inferring that this operation is an application of that formal rule)? These are concerns cultivated by, for example, Wittgenstein.

Coming up with an adequate characterization of inference-and even working out what would count as a very adequate characterization here is demandingly by no means nearly some resolved philosophical problem. Traditionally, a proposition that is not a 'conditional', as with the 'affirmative' and 'negative', modern opinion is wary of the distinction, since what appears categorical may vary with the choice of a primitive vocabulary and notation. Apparently categorical propositions may also turn out to be disguised conditionals: 'x' is intelligent (categorical?) Equivalent, if 'x' is given a range of tasks, she does them better than many people (conditional?). The problem is not merely one of classification, since deep metaphysical questions arise when facts that seem to be categorical and therefore solid, come to seem by contrast conditional, or purely hypothetical or potential.

Its condition of some classified necessity is so proven sufficient that if 'p' is a necessary condition of 'q', then 'q' cannot be true unless 'p'; is true? If 'p' is a sufficient condition, thus steering well is a necessary condition of driving in a satisfactory manner, but it is not sufficient, for one can steer well but drive badly for other reasons. Confusion may result if the distinction is not heeded. For example, the statement that 'A' causses 'B' may be interpreted to mean that 'A' is itself a sufficient condition for 'B', or that it is only a necessary condition fort 'B', or perhaps a necessary parts of a total sufficient condition. Lists of conditions to be met for satisfying some administrative or legal requirement frequently attempt to give individually necessary and jointly sufficient sets of conditions.

What is more, that if any proposition of the form 'if p then q'. The condition hypothesized, 'p'. Is called the antecedent of the conditionals, and 'q', the consequent? Various kinds of conditional have been distinguished. Its weakest is that of 'material implication', merely telling that either 'not-p', or 'q'. Stronger conditionals include elements of 'modality', corresponding to the thought that 'if p is truer then q must be true'. Ordinary language is very flexible in its use of the conditional form, and there is controversy whether conditionals are better treated semantically, yielding differently finds of conditionals with different meanings, or pragmatically, in which case there should be one basic meaning with surface differences arising from other implicatures.

It follows from the definition of 'strict implication' that a necessary proposition is strictly implied by any proposition, and that an impossible proposition strictly implies any proposition. If strict implication corresponds to 'q follows from p', then this means that a necessary proposition follows from anything at all, and anything at all follows from an impossible proposition. This is a problem if we wish to distinguish between valid and invalid arguments with necessary conclusions or impossible premises.

The Humean problem of induction is that if we would suppose that there is some property 'A' concerning and observational or an experimental situation, and that out of a large number of observed instances of 'A', some fraction m/n (possibly equal to 1) has also been instances of some logically independent property 'B'. Suppose further that the background positional circumstances not specified in these descriptions have been varied to a substantial degree and that there is no collateral information available concerning the frequency of 'B's' among 'A's' or, concerning causal or homologically connections between instances of 'A' and instances of 'B'.

In this situation, an 'enumerative' or 'instantial' induction inference would move rights from the premise, that m/n of observed 'A's' are 'B's' to the conclusion that approximately m/n of all 'A's' are 'B's'. (The usual probability qualification will be assumed to apply to the inference, rather than being part of the conclusion.) Here the set class of the 'A's', should be taken to include not only unobserved 'A's' and future 'A's', but also possible or hypothetical 'A's' (an alternative conclusion would concern the probability or likelihood of the adjacently observed 'A' being a 'B').

The traditional or Humean problem of induction, often referred to simply as 'the problem of induction', is the problem of whether and why inferences that fit this schema should be considered rationally acceptable or justified from an epistemic or cognitive standpoint, i.e., whether and why reasoning in this way is likely to lead to true claims about the world. Is there any sort of argument or rationale that can be offered for thinking that conclusions reached in this way are likely to be true in the corresponding premisses is true-or even that their chances of truth are significantly enhanced?

Hume's discussion of this issue deals explicitly only with cases where all observed 'A's' are 'B's' and his argument applies just as well to the more general case. His conclusion is entirely negative and sceptical: Inductive inferences are not rationally justified, but are instead the result of an essentially a-rational process, custom or habit. Hume (1711-76) challenges the proponent of induction to supply a cogent line of reasoning that leads from an inductive premise to the corresponding conclusion and offers an extremely influential argument in the form of a dilemma (a few times referred to as 'Hume's fork'), that either our actions are determined, in which case we are not responsible for them, or they are the result of random events, under which case we are also not responsible for them.

Such reasoning would, he argues, have to be either deductively demonstrative reasoning in the concerning relations of ideas or 'experimental', i.e., empirical, that reasoning concerning matters of fact or existence. It cannot be the former, because all demonstrative reasoning relies on the avoidance of contradiction, and it is not a contradiction to suppose that 'the course of nature may change', that an order that was observed in the past and not of its continuing against the future: But it cannot be, as the latter, since any empirical argument would appeal to the success of such reasoning about an experience, and the justifiability of generalizing from experience are precisely what is at issue-so that any such appeal would be question-begging. Hence, Hume concludes that there can be no such reasoning (1748).

An alternative version of the problem may be obtained by formulating it with reference to the so-called Principle of Induction, which says roughly that the future will resemble the past or, somewhat better, that unobserved cases will resemble observed cases. An inductive argument may be viewed as enthymematic, with this principle serving as a supposed premiss, in which case the issue is obviously how such a premiss can be justified.

Hume's argument is then that no such justification is possible: The principle cannot be justified a prior because having possession of been true in experiences without obviously begging the question is not contradictory to have possession of been true in experiences without obviously begging the question.

The predominant recent responses to the problem of induction, at least in the analytic tradition, in effect accept the main conclusion of Hume's argument, namely, that inductive inferences cannot be justified in the sense of showing that the conclusion of such an inference is likely to be true if the premise is true, and thus attempt to find another sort of justification for induction. Such responses fall into two main categories: (I) Pragmatic justifications or 'vindications' of induction, mainly developed by Hans Reichenbach (1891-1953), and (ii) ordinary language justifications of induction, whose most important proponent is Frederick, Peter Strawson (1919-). In contrast, some philosophers still attempt to reject Hume's dilemma by arguing either (iii) That, contrary to appearances, induction can be inductively justified without vicious circularity, or (iv) that an anticipatory justification of induction is possible after all. In that:

(1) Reichenbach's view is that induction is best regarded, not as a form of inference, but rather as a 'method' for arriving at posits regarding, i.e., the proportion of 'A's' remain additionally of 'B's'. Such a posit is not a claim asserted to be true, but is instead an intellectual wager analogous to a bet made by a gambler. Understood in this way, the inductive method says that one should posit that the observed proportion is, within some measure of an approximation, the true proportion and then continually correct that initial posit as new information comes in.

The gambler's bet is normally an 'appraised posit', i.e., he knows the chances or odds that the outcome on which he bets will actually occur. In contrast, the inductive bet is a 'blind posit': We do not know the chances that it will succeed or even that success is that it will succeed or even that success is possible. What we are gambling on when we make such a bet is the value of a certain proportion in the independent world, which Reichenbach construes as the limit of the observed proportion as the number of cases increases to infinity. Nevertheless, we have no way of knowing that there are even such a limit, and no way of knowing that the proportion of 'A's' are in addition of 'B's' converges in the end on some stable value than varying at random. If we cannot know that this limit exists, then we obviously cannot know that we have any definite chance of finding it.

What we can know, according to Reichenbach, is that 'if' there is a truth of this sort to be found, the inductive method will eventually find it. That this is so is an analytic consequence of Reichenbach's account of what it is for such a limit to exist. The only way that the inductive method of making an initial posit and then refining it in light of new observations can fail eventually to arrive at the true proportion is if the series of observed proportions never converges on any stable value, which means that there is no truth to be found pertaining the proportion of 'A's additionally constitute 'B's'. Thus, induction is justified, not by showing that it will succeed or indeed, that it has any definite likelihood of success, but only by showing that it will succeed if success is possible. Reichenbach's claim is that no more than this can be established for any method, and hence that induction gives 'us' our best chance for success, our best gamble in a situation where there is no alternative to gambling.

This pragmatic response to the problem of induction faces several serious problems. First, there are indefinitely many other 'methods' for arriving at posits for which the same sort of defence can be given-methods that yield the same result as the inductive method over time but differ arbitrarily before long. Despite the efforts of others, it is unclear that there is any satisfactory way to exclude such alternatives, in order to avoid the result that any arbitrarily chosen short term posit is just as reasonable as the inductive posit. Second, even if there is a truth of the requisite sort to be found, the inductive method is only guaranteed to find it or even to come within any specifiable distance of it in the indefinite long run. Nevertheless, any actual application of inductive results always takes place in the presence to the future eventful states in making the relevance of the pragmatic justification to actual practice uncertainly. Third, and most important, it needs to be emphasized that Reichenbach's response to the problem simply accepts the claim of the Humean sceptic that an inductive premise never provides the slightest reason for thinking that the corresponding inductive conclusion is true. Reichenbach himself is quite candid on this point, but this does not alleviate the intuitive implausibility of saying that we have no more reason for thinking that our scientific and commonsense conclusions that result in the induction of it '. . . is true' than, to use Reichenbach's own analogy (1949), a blind man wandering in the mountains who feels an apparent trail with his stick has for thinking that following it will lead him to safety?

An approach to induction resembling Reichenbach's claiming in that those particular inductive conclusions are posits or conjectures, than the conclusions of cogent inferences, is offered by Popper. However, Popper's view is even more overtly sceptical: It amounts to saying that all that can ever be said in favour of the truth of an inductive claim is that the claim has been tested and not yet been shown to be false.

(2) The ordinary language response to the problem of induction has been advocated by many philosophers, but the discussion here will be restricted to Strawson's paradigmatic version. Strawson claims that the question whether induction is justified or reasonable

makes sense only if it tacitly involves the demand that inductive reasoning meet the standards appropriate to deductive reasoning, i.e., that the inductive conclusions are shown to follow deductively from the inductive assumption. Such a demand cannot, of course, be met, but only because it is illegitimate: Inductive and deductive reasons are simply fundamentally different kinds of reasoning, each possessing its own autonomous standards, and there is no reason to demand or expect that one of these kinds meet the standards of the other. Whereas, if induction is assessed by inductive standards, the only ones that are appropriate, then it is obviously justified.

The problem here is to understand to what this allegedly obvious justification of an induction amount. In his main discussion of the point (1952), Strawson claims that it is an analytic true statement that believing it a conclusion for which there is strong evidence is reasonable and an analytic truth that inductive evidence of the sort captured by the schema presented earlier constitutes strong evidence for the corresponding inducive conclusion, thus, apparently yielding the analytic conclusion that believing it a conclusion for which there is inductive evidence is reasonable. Nevertheless, he also admits, indeed insists, that the claim that inductive conclusions will be true in the future is contingent, empirical, and may turn out to be false (1952). Thus, the notion of reasonable belief and the correlative notion of strong evidence must apparently be understood in ways that have nothing to do with likelihood of truth, presumably by appeal to the standard of reasonableness and strength of evidence that are accepted by the community and are embodied in ordinary usage.

Understood in this way, Strawson's response to the problem of inductive reasoning does not speak to the central issue raised by Humean scepticism: The issue of whether the conclusions of inductive arguments are likely to be true. It amounts to saying merely that if we reason in this way, we can correctly call ourselves 'reasonable' and our evidence 'strong', according to our accepted community standards. Nevertheless, to the undersealing of issue of wether following these standards is a good way to find the truth, the ordinary language response appears to have nothing to say.

(3) The main attempts to show that induction can be justified inductively have concentrated on showing that such as a defence can avoid circularity. Skyrms (1975) formulate, perhaps the clearest version of this general strategy. The basic idea is to distinguish different levels of inductive argument: A first level in which induction is applied to tings other than arguments: A second level in which it is applied to arguments at the first level, arguing that they have been observed to succeed so far and hence are likely to succeed in general: A third level in which it is applied in the same way to arguments at the second level, and

so on. Circularity is allegedly avoided by treating each of these levels as autonomous and justifying the argument at each level by appeal to an argument at the next level.

One problem with this sort of move is that even if circularity is avoided, the movement to higher and higher levels will clearly eventually fail simply for lack of evidence: A level will reach at which there have been enough successful inductive arguments to provide a basis for inductive justification at the next higher level, and if this is so, then the whole series of justifications collapses. A more fundamental difficulty is that the epistemological significance of the distinction between levels is obscure. If the issue is whether reasoning in accord with the original schema offered above ever provides a good reason for thinking that the conclusion is likely to be true, then it still seems question-begging, even if not flatly circular, to answer this question by appeal to anther argument of the same form.

(4) The idea that induction can be justified on a pure priori basis is in one way the most natural response of all: It alone treats an inductive argument as an independently cogent piece of reasoning whose conclusion can be seen rationally to follow, although perhaps only with probability from its premise. Such an approach has, however, only rarely been advocated (Russell, 19132 and BonJour, 1986), and is widely thought to be clearly and demonstrably hopeless.

Many on the reasons for this pessimistic view depend on general epistemological theses about the possible or nature of anticipatory cognition. Thus if, as Quine alleges, there is no a prior justification of any kind, then obviously a prior justification for induction is ruled out. Or if, as more moderate empiricists have in claiming some preexistent knowledge should be analytic, then again a prevenient justification for induction seems to be precluded, since the claim that if an inductive premise ids truer, then the conclusion is likely to be true does not fit the standard conceptions of 'analyticity'. A consideration of these matters is beyond the scope of the present spoken exchange.

There are, however, two more specific and quite influential reasons for thinking that an early approach is impossible that can be briefly considered, first, there is the assumption, originating in Hume, but since adopted by very many of others, that a move forward in the defence of induction would have to involve 'turning induction into deduction', i.e., showing, per impossible, that the inductive conclusion follows deductively from the premise, so that it is a formal contradiction to accept the latter and deny the former. However, it is unclear why a prior approach need be committed to anything this strong. It would be enough if it could be argued that it is deductively unlikely that such a premise is true and corresponding conclusion false.

Second, Reichenbach defends his view that pragmatic justification is the best that is possible by pointing out that a completely chaotic world in which there is simply not true conclusion to be found as to the proportion of A's in addition that occur of, but B's' is neither impossible nor unlikely from a purely a prior standpoint, the suggestion being that therefore there can be no a prior reason for thinking that such a conclusion is true. Nevertheless, there is still a substring wayin laying that a chaotic world is a prior neither impossible nor unlikely without any further evidence does not show that such a world os not a prior unlikely and a world containing such-and-such regularity might anticipatorially be somewhat likely in relation to an occurrence of a long-run patten of evidence in which a certain stable proportion of observed A's are B's ~. An occurrence, it might be claimed, that would be highly unlikely in a chaotic world (BonJour, 1986).

Goodman's 'new riddle of induction' purports that we suppose that before some specific time 't' (perhaps the year 2000) we observe a larger number of emeralds (property A) and find them all to be green (property B). We proceed to reason inductively and conclude that all emeralds are green Goodman points out, however, that we could have drawn a quite different conclusion from the same evidence. If we define the term 'grue' to mean 'green if examined before 't' and blue examined after t ′, then all of our observed emeralds will also be gruing. A parallel inductive argument will yield the conclusion that all emeralds are gruing, and hence that all those examined after the year 2000 will be blue. Presumably the first of these concisions is genuinely supported by our observations and the second is not. Nevertheless, the problem is to say why this is so and to impose some further restriction upon inductive reasoning that will permit the first argument and exclude the second.

The obvious alternative suggestion is that 'grue. Similar predicates do not correspond to genuine, purely qualitative properties in the way that 'green' and 'blueness' does, and that this is why inductive arguments involving them are unacceptable. Goodman, however, claims to be unable to make clear sense of this suggestion, pointing out that the relations of formal desirability are perfectly symmetrical: Grue' may be defined in terms if, 'green' and 'blue', but 'green' an equally well be defined in terms of 'grue' and 'green' (blue if examined before 't' and green if examined after 't').

The 'grued, paradoxes' demonstrate the importance of categorization, in that sometimes it is itemized as 'gruing', if examined of a presence to the future, before future time 't' and 'green', or not so examined and 'blue'. Even though all emeralds in our evidence class grue, we ought must infer that all emeralds are gruing. For 'grue' is unprojectible, and cannot transmit credibility from known to unknown cases. Only projectable predicates are right for induction. Goodman considers entrenchment the key to projectibility having a long history of successful protection, 'grue' is entrenched, lacking such a history, 'grue' is not. A hypothesis is projectable, Goodman suggests, only if its predicates (or suitable related ones) are much better entrenched than its rivalrous past successes that do not assume future ones. Induction remains a risky business. The rationale for favouring entrenched predicates is pragmatic. Of the possible projections from our evidence class, the one that fits with past practices enables 'us' to utilize our cognitive resources best. Its prospects of being true are worse than its competitors' and its cognitive utility is greater.

So, to a better understanding of induction we should then term is most widely used for any process of reasoning that takes 'us' from empirical premises to empirical conclusions supported by the premises, but not deductively entailed by them. Inductive arguments are therefore kinds of applicative arguments, in which something beyond the content of the premise is inferred as probable or supported by them. Induction is, however, commonly distinguished from arguments to theoretical explanations, which share this applicative character, by being confined to inferences in which he conclusion involves the same properties or relations as the premises. The central example is induction by simple enumeration, where from premises telling that Fa, Fb, Fc . . . 'where a, b, C's, are all of some kind 'G', it is inferred that G's from outside the sample, such as future G's, will be 'F', or perhaps that all G's are 'F'. In this, which and the other persons deceive them, children may infer that everyone is a deceiver: Different, but similar inferences of a property by some object to the same object's future possession of the same property, or from the constancy of some law-like pattern in events and states of affairs ti its future constancy. All objects we know of attract each other with a force inversely proportional to the square of the distance between them, so perhaps they all do so, and will always do so.

The rational basis of any inference was challenged by Hume, who believed that induction presupposed belie in the uniformity of nature, but that this belief has no defence in reason, and merely reflected a habit or custom of the mind. Hume was not therefore sceptical about the role of reason in either explaining it or justifying it. Trying to answer Hume and to show that there is something rationally compelling about the inference referred to as the problem of induction. It is widely recognized that any rational defence of induction will have to partition well-behaved properties for which the inference is plausible (often called projectable properties) from badly behaved ones, for which it is not. It is also recognized that actual inductive habits are more complex than those of similar enumeration, and that both common sense and science pay attention to such giving factors as variations within the sample giving 'us' the evidence, the application of ancillary beliefs about the order of nature, and so on.

Nevertheless, the fundamental problem remains that ant experience condition by application show 'us' only events occurring within a very restricted part of a vast spatial and temporal order about which we then come to believe things.

Uncompounded by its belonging of a confirmation theory finding of the measure to which evidence supports a theory fully formalized confirmation theory would dictate the degree of confidence that a rational investigator might have in a theory, given some body of evidence. The grandfather of confirmation theory is Gottfried Leibniz (1646-1718), who believed that a logically transparent language of science would be able to resolve all disputes. In the 20th century a fully formal confirmation theory was a main goal of the logical positivist, since without it the central concept of verification by empirical evidence itself remains distressingly unscientific. The principal developments were due to Rudolf Carnap (1891-1970), culminating in his "Logical Foundations of Probability" (1950). Carnap's idea was that the measure necessitated would be the proportion of logically possible states of affairs in which the theory and the evidence both hold, compared ti the number in which the evidence itself holds that the probability of a preposition, relative to some evidence, is a proportion of the range of possibilities under which the proposition is true, compared to the total range of possibilities left by the evidence. The difficulty with the theory lies in identifying sets of possibilities so that they admit of measurement. It therefore demands that we can put a measure on the 'range' of possibilities consistent with theory and evidence, compared with the range consistent with the evidence alone.

Among the obstacles the enterprise meets, is the fact that while evidence covers only a finite range of data, the hypotheses of science may cover an infinite range. In addition, confirmation proves to vary with the language in which the science is couched, and the Carnapian programme has difficulty in separating genuinely confirming variety of evidence from less compelling repetition of the same experiment. Confirmation also proved to be susceptible to acute paradoxes. Finally, scientific judgement seems to depend on such intangible factors as the problems facing rival theories, and most workers have come to stress instead the historically situated scene of what would appear as a plausible distinction of a scientific knowledge at a given time.

Arose to the paradox of which when a set of apparent incontrovertible premises is given to unacceptable or contradictory conclusions. To solve a paradox will involve showing either that there is a hidden flaw in the premises, or that the reasoning is erroneous, or that the apparently unacceptable conclusion can, in fact, be tolerated. Paradoxes are therefore important in philosophy, for until one is solved it shows that there is something about our reasoning and our concepts that we do not understand. What is more, and somewhat loosely, a paradox is a compelling argument from unacceptable premises to an unacceptable conclusion: More strictly speaking, a paradox is specified to be a sentence that is true if and only if it is false. A characterized objection lesson of it, ought to be: "The displayed sentence is false."

Seeing that this sentence is false if true is easy, and true if false, a paradox, in either of the senses distinguished, presents an important philosophical challenger. Epistemologists are especially concerned with various paradoxes having to do with knowledge and belief. In other words, for example, the Knower paradox is an argument that begins with apparently impeccable premisses about the concepts of knowledge and inference and derives an explicit contradiction. The origin of the reasoning is the 'surprise examination paradox': A teacher announces that there will be a surprise examination next week. A clever student argues that this is impossible. 'The test cannot be on Friday, the last day of the week, because it would not be a surprise. We would know the day of the test on Thursday evening. This means we can also rule out Thursday. For after we learn that no test has been given by Wednesday, we would know the test is on Thursday or Friday -and would already know that it s not on Friday and would already know that it is not on Friday by the previous reasoning. The remaining days can be eliminated in the same manner'.

This puzzle has over a dozen variants. The first was probably invented by the Swedish mathematician Lennard Ekbon in 1943. Although the first few commentators regarded the reverse elimination argument as cogent, every writer on the subject since 1950 agrees that the argument is unsound. The controversy has been over the proper diagnosis of the flaw.

Initial analyses of the subject's argument tried to lay the blame on a simple equivocation. Their failure led to more sophisticated diagnoses. The general format has been an assimilation to better-known paradoxes. One tradition casts the surprise examination paradox as a self-referential problem, as fundamentally akin to the Liar, the paradox of the Knower, or Gödel's incompleteness theorem. That in of itself, says enough that Kaplan and Montague (1960) distilled the following 'self-referential' paradox, the Knower. Consider the sentence:

(S) The negation of this sentence is known (to be true).

Suppose that (S) is true. Then its negation is known and hence true. However, if its negation is true, then (S) must be false. Therefore (s) is false, or what is the name, the negation of (S) is true.

This paradox and its accompanying reasoning are strongly reminiscent of the Lair Paradox that (in one version) begins by considering a sentence 'This sentence is false' and derives a contradiction. Versions of both arguments using axiomatic formulations of arithmetic and Gödel-numbers to achieve the effect of self-reference yields important meta-theorems about what can be expressed in such systems. Roughly these are to the effect that no predicates definable in the formalized arithmetic can have the properties we demand of truth (Tarski's Theorem) or of knowledge (Montague, 1963).

These meta-theorems still leave 'us; with the problem that if we suppose that we add of these formalized languages predicates intended to express the concept of knowledge (or truth) and inference-as one mighty does if a logic of these concepts is desired. Then the sentence expressing the leading principles of the Knower Paradox will be true.

Explicitly, the assumption about knowledge and inferences are:

(1) If sentences 'A' are known, then "a."

(2) (1) is known?

(3) If 'B' is correctly inferred from 'A', and 'A' is known,

then 'B' if known.

To give an absolutely explicit t derivation of the paradox by applying these principles to (S), we must add (contingent) assumptions to the effect that certain inferences have been done. Still, as we go through the argument of the Knower, these inferences are done. Even if we can somehow restrict such principles and construct a consistent formal logic of knowledge and inference, the paradoxical argument as expressed in the natural language still demands some explanation.

The usual proposals for dealing with the Liar often have their analogues for the Knower, e.g., that there is something wrong with a self-reference or that knowledge (or, truth) is properly a predicate of propositions and not of sentences. The relies that show that some of these are not adequate are often parallel to those for the Liar paradox. In addition, one can try here what seems to be an adequate solution for the Surprise Examination Paradox, namely the observation that 'new knowledge can drive out knowledge', but this does not seem to work on the Knower (Anderson, 1983).

There are a number of paradoxes of the Liar family. The simplest example is the sentence 'This sentence is false', which must be false if it is true, and true if it is false. One suggestion is that the sentence fails to say anything, but sentences that fail to say anything are at least not true. In fact case, we consider to sentences 'This sentence is not true', which, if it fails to say anything is not true, and hence (this kind of reasoning is sometimes called the strengthened Liar). Other versions of the Liar introduce pairs of sentences, as in a slogan on the front of a T-shirt saying 'This sentence on the back of this T-shirt is false', and one on the back saying 'The sentence on the front of this T-shirt is true'. It is clear that each of the sentences individually are well formed, and if it were it not for the other, might have said something true. So any attempt to dismiss the paradox by sating that the sentence involved is meaningless will face problems.

Even so, the two approaches that have some hope of adequately dealing with this paradox is 'hierarchy' solutions and 'truth-value gap' solutions. According to the first, knowledge is structured into 'levels'. It is argued that there be is one coherent notion, expressed by the verb 'knows', but rather a whole series of notions, now. Know, and so on, as perhaps into transfinite states, by term for which are predicated expressions as such, yet, there are 'ramified' concepts and properly restricted, (1)-(3) lead to no contradictions. The main objections to this procedure are that the meaning of these levels has not been adequately explained and that the idea of such subscripts, even implicit, in a natural language is highly counterintuitive the 'truth-value gap' solution takes sentences such as (S) to lack truth-value. They are neither true nor false, but they do not express propositions. This defeats a crucial step in the reasoning used in the derivation of the paradoxes. Kripler (1986) has developed this approach in connection with the Liar and Asher and Kamp (1986) has worked out some details of a parallel solution to the Knower. The principal objection is that 'strengthened' or 'super' versions of the paradoxes tend to reappear when the solution itself is stated.

Since the paradoxical deduction uses only the properties (1)-(3) and since the argument is formally valid, any notion that satisfy these conditions will lead to a paradox. Thus, Grim (1988) notes that this may be read as 'is known by an omniscient God' and concludes that there is no coherent single notion of omniscience. Thomason (1980) observes that with some different conditions, analogous reasoning about belief can lead to paradoxical consequence.

Overall, it looks as if we should conclude that knowledge and truth are ultimately intrinsically 'stratified' concepts. It would seem that wee must simply accept the fact that these (and similar) concepts cannot be assigned of any one fixed, finite or infinite. Still, the meaning of this idea certainly needs further clarification.

Its paradox arises when a set of apparently incontrovertible premises gives unacceptable or contradictory conclusions, to solve a paradox will involve showing either that there is a hidden flaw in the premises, or that the reasoning is erroneous, or that the apparently unacceptable conclusion can, in fact, be tolerated. Paradoxes are therefore important in philosophy, for until one is solved its shows that there is something about our reasoning and concepts that we do not understand. Famous families of paradoxes include the 'semantic paradoxes' and 'Zeno's paradoxes'. Art the beginning of the 20th century, paradox and other set-theoretical paradoxes led to the complete overhaul of the foundations of set theory, while the 'Sorites paradox' has lead to the investigations of the semantics of vagueness and fuzzy logics.

It is, however, to what extent can analysis be informative? This is the question that gives a riser to what philosophers has traditionally called 'the' paradox of analysis. Thus, consider the following proposition:

(1) To be an instance of knowledge is to be an instance of justified true belief not essentially grounded in any falsehood. (1) If true, illustrates an important type of philosophical analysis. For convenience of exposition, I will assume (1) is a correct analysis. The paradox arises from the fact that if the concept of justified true belief not been essentially grounded in any falsification is the analysand of the concept of knowledge, it would seem that they are the same concept and hence that:

(2) To be an instance of knowledge is to be an instance of knowledge and would have to be the same propositions as (1). But then how can (1) be informative when (2) is not? This is what is called the first paradox of analysis. Classical writings' on analysis suggests a second paradoxical analysis (Moore, 1942).

(3) An analysis of the concept of being a brother is that to be a brother is to be a male sibling. If (3) is true, it would seem that the concept of being a brother would have to be the same concept as the concept of being a male sibling and tat:

(4) An analysis of the concept of being a brother is that to be a brother is to be a brother would also have to be true and in fact, would have to be the same proposition as (three?). Yet (3) is true and (4) is false.

Both these paradoxes rest upon the assumptions that analysis is a relation between concepts, than one involving entity of other sorts, such as linguistic expressions, and tat in a true analysis, analysand and analysand um are the same concepts. Both these assumptions are explicit in Moore, but some of Moore's remarks hint at a solution that a statement of an analysis is a statement partly about the concept involved and partly about the verbal expressions used to express it. He says he thinks a solution of this sort is bound to be right, but fails to suggest one because he cannot see a way in which the analysis can be even partly about the expression (Moore, 1942).

Elsewhere, of such ways, as a solution to the second paradox, to which is explicating (3) as: (5) An analysis is given by saying that the verbal expression 'χ is a brother' expresses the same concept as is expressed by the conjunction of the verbal expressions 'χ is male' when used to express the concept of being male and 'χ is a sibling' when used to express the concept of being a sibling. (Ackerman, 1990). An important point about (5) is as follows. Stripped of its philosophical jargon ('analysis', 'concept', 'χ is a . . . '), (5) seems to state the sort of information generally stated in a definition of the verbal expression 'brother' in terms of the verbal expressions 'male' and 'sibling', where this definition is designed to draw upon listeners' antecedent understanding of the verbal expression 'male' and 'sibling', and thus, to tell listeners what the verbal expression 'brother' really means, instead of merely providing the information that two verbal expressions are synonymous without specifying the meaning of either one. Thus, its solution to the second paradox seems to make the sort of analysis tat gives rise to this paradox matter of specifying the meaning of a verbal expression in terms of separate verbal expressions already understood and saying how the meanings of these separate, already-understood verbal expressions are combined. This corresponds to Moore's intuitive requirement that an analysis should both specify the constituent concepts of the analysand um and tell how they are combined, but is this all there is to philosophical analysis?

To answer this question, we must note that, in addition too there being two paradoxes of analysis, there is two types of analyses that are relevant here. (There are also other types of analysis, such as reformatory analysis, where the analysand are intended to improve on and replace the analysandum. But since reformatory analysis involves no commitment to conceptual identity between analysand and analysandum, reformatory analysis does not generate a paradox of analysis and so will not concern 'us' here.) One way to recognize the difference between the two types of analysis concerning 'us' here is to focus on the difference between the two paradoxes. This can be done by means of the Frége - uninspired sense - individuation condition, which is the condition that two expressions have the same sense if and only if they can be interchangeably 'salva Veritate' whenever used in propositional attitude context. If the expressions for the analysands and the analysandum in (1) met this condition, (1) and (2) would not raise the first paradox, but the second paradox arises regardless of whether the expression for the analysand and the analysandum meet this condition. The second paradox is a matter of the failure of such expressions to be interchangeable salva Veritate in sentences involving such contexts as 'an analysis is given thereof. Thus, a solution (such as the one offered) that is aimed only at such contexts can solve the second paradox. This is clearly false for the first paradox, however, which will apply to all pairs of propositions expressed by sentences in which expressions for pairs of analysands and analysantia raising the first paradox is interchangeable. For example, consider the following proposition:

(6) Mary knows that some cats tail.

It is possible for John to believe (6) without believing:

(7) Mary has justified true belief, not essentially grounded in any falsehood, that some cats lack tails.

Yet this possibility clearly does not mean that the proposition that Mary knows that some casts lack tails is partly about language.

One approach to the first paradox is to argue that, despite the apparent epistemic inequivalence of (1) and (2), the concept of justified true belief not essentially grounded in any falsehood is still identical with the concept of knowledge (Sosa, 1983). Another approach is to argue that in the sort of analysis raising the first paradox, the analysand and analysandum is concepts that are different but that bear a special epistemic relation to each other. Elsewhere, the development is such an approach and suggestion that this analysand-analysandum relation has the following facets.

(1) The analysand and analysandum are necessarily coextensive, i.e., necessarily every instance of one is an instance of the other.

(2) The analysand and analysandum are knowable theoretical to be coextensive.

(3) The analysandum is simpler than the analysands a condition whose necessity is recognized in classical writings on analysis, such as, Langford, (1942.)

(4) The analysand do not have the analysandum as a constituent.

Condition (4) rules out circularity. But since many valuable quasi-analyses are partly circular, e.g., knowledge is justified true belief supported by known reasons not essentially grounded in any falsehood, it seems best to distinguish between full analysis, from that of (4) is a necessary condition, and partial analysis, for which it is not.

These conditions, while necessary, are clearly insufficient. The basic problem is that they apply too many pairs of concepts that do not seem closely enough related epistemologically to count as analysand and analysandum., such as the concept of being, and the concept of the fourth root of 1296. Accordingly, its solution upon what actually seems epistemologically distinctive about analyses of the sort under consideration, which is a certain way they can be justified. This is by the philosophical example-and-counterexample method, which is in a general term that goes as follows. 'J' investigates the analysis of K's concept

'Q' (where 'K' can but need not be identical to 'J' by setting 'K' a series of armchair thought experiments, i.e., presenting 'K' with a series of simple described hypothetical test cases and asking 'K' questions of the form 'If such-and-such where the case would this count as a case of Q? 'J' then contrasts the descriptions of the cases to which; K' answers affirmatively with the description of the cases to which 'K' does not, and 'J' generalizes upon these descriptions to arrive at the concepts (if possible not including the analysandum) and their mode of combination that constitute the analysand of K''s concept 'Q'. Since 'J' need not be identical with 'K', there is no requirement that 'K' himself be able to perform this generalization, to recognize its result as correct, or even to understand he analysand that is its result. This is reminiscent of Walton's observation that one can simply recognize a bird as a swallow without realizing just what feature of the bird (beak, wing configurations, etc.) form the basis of this recognition. (The philosophical significance of this way of recognizing is discussed in Walton, 1972) 'K' answers the questions based solely on whether the described hypothetical cases just strike him as cases of 'Q'. 'J' observes certain strictures in formulating the cases and questions. He makes the cases as simple as possible, to minimize the possibility of confusion and to minimize the likelihood that 'K' will draw upon his philosophical theories (or quasi-philosophical, a rudimentary notion if he is unsophisticated philosophically) in answering the questions. For this conflicting result, the conflict should 'other things being equal' be resolved in favour of the simpler case. 'J' makes the series of described cases wide-ranging and varied, with the aim of having it be a complete series, where a series is complete if and only if no case that is omitted in such that, if included, it would change the analysis arrived at. 'J' does not, of course, use as a test-case description anything complicated and general enough to express the analysand. There is no requirement that the described hypothetical test cases be formulated only in terms of what can be observed. Moreover, using described hypothetical situations as test cases enables 'J' to frame the questions in such a way as to rule out extraneous background assumption to a degree, thus, even if 'K' correctly believes that all and only P's are R's, the question of whether the concepts of P, R, or both enter the analysand of his concept 'Q' can be investigated by asking him such questions as 'Suppose (even if it seems preposterous to you) that you were to find out that there was a 'P' that was not an 'R'. Would you still consider it a case of Q?

Taking all this into account, the fifth necessary condition for this sort of analysand-analysandum relations is as follows:

If 'S' is the analysand of 'Q', the proposition that necessarily all and only instances of 'S' are instances of 'Q' can be justified by generalizing from intuition about the correct answers to questions of the sort indicated about a varied and wide-ranging series of simple described hypothetical situations.

Many paradoxes are as an easy source of antinomies, for example, Zeno gave some famously lets say, logical-cum-mathematical arguments that might be interpreted as demonstrating that motion is impossible. But our eyes as it was, demonstrate motion (exhibit moving things) all the time. Where did Zeno go wrong? Where do our eyes go wrong? If we cannot readily answer at least one of these questions, then we are in antinomy. In the "Critique of Pure Reason," Kant gave demonstrations of the same kind -in the Zeno example they were obviously not the same kind of both, e.g., that the world has a beginning in time and space, and that the world has no beginning in time or space. He argues that both demonstrations are at fault because they proceed on the basis of 'pure reason' unconditioned by sense experience.

At this point, we display attributes to the theory of experience, as it is not possible to define in an illuminating way, however, we know what experiences are through acquaintances with some of our own, e.g., visual experiences of as afterimage, a feeling of physical nausea or a tactile experience of an abrasive surface (which might be caused by an actual surface -rough or smooth, or which might be part of a dream, or the product of a vivid sensory imagination). The essential feature of experience is it feels a certain way - that there is something that it is like to have it. We may refer to this feature of an experience as its 'character'.

Another core feature of the sorts of experiences with which this may be of a concern, is that they have representational 'content'. (Unless otherwise indicated, 'experience' will be reserved for their 'contentual representations'.) The most obvious cases of experiences with content are sense experiences of the kind normally involved in perception. We may describe such experiences by mentioning their sensory modalities ad their contents, e.g., a gustatory experience (modality) of chocolate ice cream (content), but do so more commonly by means of perceptual verbs combined with noun phrases specifying their contents, as in 'Macbeth saw a dagger'. This is, however, ambiguous between the perceptual claim 'There was a (material) dagger in the world that Macbeth perceived visually' and 'Macbeth had a visual experience of a dagger' (the reading with which we are concerned, as it is afforded by our imagination, or perhaps, experiencing mentally hallucinogenic imagery).

As in the case of other mental states and events with content, it is important to distinguish between the properties that and experience 'represents' and the properties that it 'possesses'. To talk of the representational properties of an experience is to say something about its content, not to attribute those properties to the experience itself. Like every other experience, a visual; experience of a non-shaped square, of which is a mental event, and it is therefore not itself either irregular or is it square, even though it represents those properties. It is, perhaps, fleeting, pleasant or unusual, even though it does not represent those properties. An experience may represent a property that it possesses, and it may even do so in virtue of a rapidly changing (complex) experience representing something as changing rapidly. However, this is the exception and not the rule.

Which properties can be [directly] represented in sense experience is subject to debate. Traditionalists include only properties whose presence could not be doubted by a subject having appropriate experiences, e.g., colour and shape in the case of visual experience, and apparent shape, surface texture, hardness, etc., in the case of tactile experience. This view is natural to anyone who has an egocentric, Cartesian perspective in epistemology, and who wishes for pure data in experiences to serve as logically certain foundations for knowledge, especially to the immediate objects of perceptual awareness in or of sense-data, such categorized of colour patches and shapes, which are usually supposed distinct from surfaces of physical objectivity. Qualities of sense-data are supposed to be distinct from physical qualities because their perception is more relative to conditions, more certain, and more immediate, and because sense-data is private and cannot appear other than they are they are objects that change in our perceptual field when conditions of perception change. Physical objects remain constant.

Others who do not think that this wish can be satisfied, and who are more impressed with the role of experience in providing animisms with ecologically significant information about the world around them, claim that sense experiences represent properties, characteristic and kinds that are much richer and much more wide-ranging than the traditional sensory qualities. We do not see only colours and shapes, they tell 'us', but also earth, water, men, women and fire: We do not smell only odours, but also food and filth. There is no space here to examine the factors relevantly responsible to their choice of situational alternatives. Yet, this suggests that character and content are not really distinct, and there is a close tie between them. For one thing, the relative complexity of the character of sense experience places limitations upon its possible content, e.g., a tactile experience of something touching one's left ear is just too simple to carry the same amount of content as typically convincing to an every day, visual experience. Moreover, the content of a sense experience of a given character depends on the normal causes of appropriately similar experiences, e.g., the sort of gustatory experience that we have when eating chocolate would be not represented as chocolate unless it was normally caused by chocolate. Granting a contingent ties between the character of an experience and its possible causal origins, once, again follows that its possible content is limited by its character.

Character and content are none the less irreducibly different, for the following reasons. (I) There are experiences that completely lack content, e.g., certain bodily pleasures. (ii) Not every aspect of the character of an experience with content is relevant to that content, e.g., the unpleasantness of an aural experience of chalk squeaking on a board may have no representational significance. (iii) Experiences in different modalities may overlap in content without a parallel overlap in character, e.g., visual and tactile experiences of circularity feel completely different. (iv) The content of an experience with a given character may vary according to the background of the subject, e.g., a certain content 'singing bird' only after the subject has learned something about birds.

According to the act/object analysis of experience (which is a special case of the act/object analysis of consciousness), every experience involves an object of experience even if it has no material object. Two main lines of argument may be offered in support of this view, one 'phenomenological' and the other 'semantic'.

In an outline, the phenomenological argument is as follows. Whenever we have an experience, even if nothing beyond the experience answers to it, we seem to be presented with something through the experience (which is itself diaphanous). The object of the experience is whatever is so presented to 'us'-is that it is an individual thing, an event, or a state of affairs.

The semantic argument is that objects of experience are required in order to make sense of certain features of our talk about experience, including, in particular, the following. (1) Simple attributions of experience, e.g., 'Rod is experiencing an oddity that is not really square but in appearance it seems more than likely a square', this seems to be relational. (2) We appear to refer to objects of experience and to attribute properties to them, e.g., 'The after image that John experienced was certainly odd'. (3) We appear to quantify ov er objects of experience, e.g., 'Macbeth saw something that his wife did not see'.

The act/object analysis faces several problems concerning the status of objects of experiences. Currently the most common view is that they are sense-data-private mental entities that actually posses the traditional sensory qualities represented by the experiences of which they are the objects. But the very idea of an essentially private entity is suspect. Moreover, since an experience may apparently represent something as having a determinable property, e.g., redness, without representing it as having any subordinate determinate property, e.g., any specific shade of red, a sense-datum may actually have a determinate property subordinate to it. Even more disturbing is that sense-data may have contradictory properties, since experiences can have contradictory contents. A case in point is the waterfall illusion: If you stare at a waterfall for a minute and then immediately fixate on a nearby rock, you are likely to have an experience of the rock's moving upward while it remains in the same place. The sense-data theorist must either deny that there are such experiences or admit contradictory objects.

These problems can be avoided by treating objects of experience as properties. This, however, fails to do justice to the appearances, for experience seems not to present 'us' with properties embodied in individuals. The view that objects of experience is Meinongian objects accommodate this point. It is also attractive in as far as (1) it allows experiences to represent properties other than traditional sensory qualities, and (2) it allows for the identification of objects of experience and objects of perception in the case of experiences that constitute perception.

According to the act/object analysis of experience, every experience with content involves an object of experience to which the subject is related by an act of awareness (the event of experiencing that object). This is meant to apply not only to perceptions, which have material objects (whatever is perceived), but also to experiences like hallucinations and dream experiences, which do not. Such experiences nonetheless appear to represent something, and their objects are supposed to be whatever it is that they represent. Act/object theorists may differ on the nature of objects of experience, which have been treated as properties. Meinongian objects (which may not exist or have any form of being), and, more commonly private mental entities with sensory qualities. (The term 'sense-data' is now usually applied to the latter, but has also been used as a general term for objects of sense experiences, as in the work of G. E. Moore) Act/object theorists may also differ on the relationship between objects of experience and objects of perception. In terms of perception (of which we are 'indirectly aware') are always distinct from objects of experience (of which we are 'directly aware'). Meinongian, however, may treat objects of perception as existing objects of experience. But sense-datum theorists must either deny that there are such experiences or admit contradictory objects. Still, most philosophers will feel that the Meinongian's acceptance of impossible objects is too high a price to pay for these benefits.

A general problem for the act/object analysis is that the question of whether two subjects are experiencing one and the same thing (as opposed to having exactly similar experiences) appears to have an answer only on the assumption that the experiences concerned are perceptions with material objects. But in terms of the act/object analysis the question must have an answer even when this condition is not satisfied. (The answer is always negative on the sense-datum theory; it could be positive on other versions of the act/object analysis, depending on the facts of the case.)

In view of the above problems, the case for the act/object analysis should be reassessed. The phenomenological argument is not, on reflection, convincing, for it is easy enough to grant that any experience appears to present 'us' with an object without accepting that it actually does. The semantic argument is more impressive, but is none the less answerable.

The seemingly relational structure of attributions of experience is a challenge dealt with below in connection with the adverbial theory. Apparent reference to and quantification over objects of experience can be handled by analysing them as reference to experiences themselves and quantification over experiences tacitly typed according to content. Thus, 'The after image that John experienced was colourfully appealing' becomes 'John's after image experience was an experience of colour', and 'Macbeth saw something that his wife did not see' becomes 'Macbeth had a visual experience that his wife did not have'.

Pure cognitivism attempts to avoid the problems facing the act/object analysis by reducing experiences to cognitive events or associated disposition, e.g., Susy's experience of a rough surface beneath her hand might be identified with the event of her acquiring the belief that there is a rough surface beneath her hand, or, if she does not acquire this belief, with a disposition to acquire it that has somehow been blocked.

This position has attractions. It does full justice to the cognitive contents of experience, and to the important role of experience as a source of belief acquisition. It would also help clear the way for a naturalistic theory of mind, since there seems to be some prospect of a physicalist/functionalist account of belief and other intentional states. But pure cognitivism is completely undermined by its failure to accommodate the fact that experiences have a felt character that cannot be reduced to their content, as aforementioned.

The adverbial theory is an attempt to undermine the act/object analysis by suggesting a semantic account of attributions of experience that does not require objects of experience. Unfortunately, the oddities of explicit adverbializations of such statements have driven off potential supporters of the theory. Furthermore, the theory remains largely undeveloped, and attempted refutations have traded on this. It may, however, be founded on sound basis intuitions, and there is reason to believe that an effective development of the theory (which is merely hinting at) is possible.

The relevant intuitions are (1) that when we say that someone is experiencing 'an A', or has an experience 'of an A', we are using this content-expression to specify the type of thing that the experience is especially apt to fit, (2) that doing this is a matter of saying something about the experience itself (and maybe about the normal causes of like experiences), and (3) that it is no-good of reasons to posit of its position to presuppose that of any involvements, is that its descriptions of an object in which the experience is. Thus the effective role of the content-expression in a statement of experience is to modify the verb it compliments, not to introduce a special type of object.

Perhaps, the most important criticism of the adverbial theory is the 'many property problem', according to which the theory does not have the resources to distinguish between, e.g.,

(1) Frank has an experience of a brown triangle

and:

(2) Frank has an experience of brown and an experience of a triangle.

Which is entailed by (1) but does not entail it. The act/object analysis can easily accommodate the difference between (1) and (2) by claiming that the truth of (1) requires a single object of experience that is both brown and triangular, while that of the (2) allows for the possibility of two objects of experience, one brown and the other triangular, however, (1) is equivalent to:

(1*) Frank has an experience of something's being both brown and triangular.

And (2) is equivalent to:

(2*) Frank has an experience of something's being brown and an experience of something's being triangular, and the difference between these can be explained quite simply in terms of logical scope without invoking objects of experience. The adverbialists may use this to answer the many - property problem by arguing that the phrase 'a brown triangle' in (1) does the same work as the clause 'something's being both brown and triangular' in (1*). This is perfectly compatible with the view that it also has the 'adverbial' function of modifying the verb 'has an experience of', for it specifies the experience more narrowly just by giving a necessary condition for the satisfaction of the experience (the condition being that there are something both brown and triangular before Frank).

A final position that should be mentioned is the state theory, according to which a sense experience of an 'A' is an occurrent, non-relational state of the kind that the subject would be in when perceiving an 'A'. Suitably qualified, this claim is no doubt true, but its significance is subject to debate. Here it is enough to remark that the claim is compatible with both pure cognitivism and the adverbial theory, and that state theorists are probably best advised to adopt adverbials as a means of developing their intuitions.

Yet, clarifying sense-data, if taken literally, is that which is given by the senses. But in response to the question of what exactly is so given, sense-data theories posit private showings in the consciousness of the subject. In the case of vision this would be a kind of inner picture show which itself only indirectly represents aspects of the external world that has in and of itself a worldly representation. The view has been widely rejected as implying that we really only see extremely thin coloured pictures interposed between our mind's eye and reality. Modern approaches to perception tend to reject any conception of the eye as a camera or lense, simply responsible for producing private images, and stress the active life of the subject in and of the world, as the determinant of experience.

Nevertheless, the argument from illusion is of itself the usually intended directive to establish that certain familiar facts about illusion disprove the theory of perception called naïevity or direct realism. There are, however, many different versions of the argument that must be distinguished carefully. Some of these distinctions centre on the content of the premises (the nature of the appeal to illusion); others centre on the interpretation of the conclusion (the kind of direct realism under attack). Let 'us' set about by distinguishing the importantly different versions of direct realism which one might take to be vulnerable to familiar facts about the possibility of perceptual illusion.

A crude statement of direct realism might go as follows. In perception, we sometimes directly perceive physical objects and their properties, we do not always perceive physical objects by perceiving something 'else', e.g., a sense-datum. There are, however, difficulties with this formulation of the view, as for one thing a great many philosophers who are 'not' direct realists would admit that it is a mistake to describe people as actually 'perceiving' something other than a physical object. In particular, such philosophers might admit, we should never say that we perceive sense-data. To talk that way would be to suppose that we should model our understanding of our relationship to sense-data on our understanding of the ordinary use of perceptual verbs as they describe our relation to and of the physical world, and that is the last thing paradigm sense-datum theorists should want. At least, many of the philosophers who objected to direct realism would prefer to express in what they were of objecting too in terms of a technical (and philosophically controversial) concept such as 'acquaintance'. Using such a notion, we could define direct realism this way: In 'veridical' experience we are directly acquainted with parts, e.g., surfaces, or constituents of physical objects. A less cautious version of the view might drop the reference to veridical experience and claim simply that in all experience we are directly acquainted with parts or constituents of physical objects. The expressions 'knowledge by acquaintance' and 'knowledge by description', and the distinction they mark between knowing 'things' and knowing 'about' things, are generally associated with Bertrand Russell (1872-1970), that scientific philosophy required analysing many objects of belief as 'logical constructions' or 'logical fictions', and the programme of analysis that this inaugurated dominated the subsequent philosophy of logical atomism, and then of other philosophers, Russell's "The Analysis of Mind," the mind itself is treated in a fashion reminiscent of Hume, as no more than the collection of neutral perceptions or sense-data that make up the flux of conscious experience, and that looked at another way that also was to make up the external world (neutral monism), but "An Inquiry into Meaning and Truth" (1940) represents a more empirical approach to the problem. Yet, philosophers have perennially investigated this and related distinctions using varying terminology.

Distinction in our ways of knowing things, highlighted by Russell and forming a central element in his philosophy after the discovery of the theory of 'definite descriptions'. A thing is known by acquaintance when there is direct experience of it. It is known by description if it can only be described as a thing with such-and-such properties. In everyday parlance, I might know my spouse and children by acquaintance, but know someone as 'the first person born at sea' only by description. However, for a variety of reasons Russell shrinks the area of things that can be known by acquaintance until eventually only current experience, perhaps my own self, and certain universals or meanings qualify anything else is known only as the thing that has such-and-such qualities.

Because one can interpret the relation of acquaintance or awareness as one that is not 'epistemic', i.e., not a kind of propositional knowledge, it is important to distinguish the above aforementioned views read as ontological theses from a view one might call 'epistemological direct realism? In perception we are, on at least some occasions, non-inferentially justified in believing a proposition asserting the existence of a physical object. Since it is that these objects exist independently of any mind that might perceive them, and so it thereby rules out all forms of idealism and phenomenalism, which hold that there are no such independently existing objects. Its being to 'direct' realism rules out those views defended under the cubic of 'critical naive realism', or 'representational realism', in which there is some nonphysical intermediary -usually called a 'sense-datum' or a 'sense impression' -that must first be perceived or experienced in order to perceive the object that exists independently of this perception. Often the distinction between direct realism and other theories of perception is explained more fully in terms of what is 'immediately' perceived, than 'mediately' perceived. What relevance does illusion have for these two forms of direct realism?

The fundamental premise of the arguments is from illusion seems to be the theses that things can appear to be other than they are. Thus, for example, straight sticks when immerged in water looks bent, a penny when viewed from certain perspective appears as an illusory spatial elliptic circularity, when something that is yellow when place under red fluorescent light looks red. In all of these cases, one version of the argument goes, it is implausible to maintain that what we are directly acquainted with is the real nature of the object in question. Indeed, it is hard to see how we can be said to be aware of the really physical object at all. In the above illusions the things we were aware of actually were bent, elliptical and red, respectively. But, by hypothesis, the really physical objects lacked these properties. Thus, we were not aware of the substantial reality of been real as a physical objects or theory.

So far, if the argument is relevant to any of the direct realisms distinguished above, it seems relevant only to the claim that in all sense experience we are directly acquainted with parts or constituents of physical objects. After all, even if in illusion we are not acquainted with physical objects, but their surfaces, or their constituents, why should we conclude anything about the hidden nature of our relations to the physical world in veridical experience?

We are supposed to discover the answer to this question by noticing the similarities between illusory experience and veridical experience and by reflecting on what makes illusion possible at all. Illusion can occur because the nature of the illusory experience is determined, not just by the nature of the object perceived, but also by other conditions, both external and internal as becoming of an inner or as the outer experience. But all of our sensations are subject to these causal influences and it would be gratuitous and arbitrary to select from indefinitely of many and subtly different perceptual experiences some special ones those that get 'us' in touch with the 'real' nature of the physical world and its surrounding surfaces. Red fluorescent light affects the way thing's look, but so does sunlight. Water reflects light, but so does air. We have no unmediated access to the external world.

Still, why should we consider that we are aware of something other than a physical object in experience? Why should we not conclude that to be aware of a physical object is just to be appeared to by that object in a certain way? In its best-known form the adverbial theory of something proposes that the Grammitis of associated language objects in a statement attributing an experience to someone been analysed and expressed dialectically can be an adverb. For example,

(A) Rod is experiencing a coloured square.

Is rewritten as?

Rod is experiencing, (coloured square)-ly

This is presented as an alternative to the act/object analysis, according to which the truth of a statement like (A) requires the existence of an object of experience corresponding to its grammatical object. A commitment to t he explicit adverbializations of statements of experience is not, however, essential to adverbials. The core of the theory consists, rather, in the denial of objects of experience (as opposed ti objects of perception) coupled with the view that the role of the grammatical object in a statement of experience is to characterize more fully te sort of experience that is being attributed to the subject. The claim, then, is that the grammatical object is functioning as a modifier and, in particular, as a modifier of a verb. If it as a special kind of adverb at the semantic level.

At this point, it might be profitable to move from considering the possibility of illusion to considering the possibility of hallucination. Instead of comparing paradigmatic veridical perception with illusion, let 'us' compare it with complete hallucination. For any experiences or sequence of experiences we take to be veridical, we can imagine qualitatively indistinguishable experiences occurring as part of a hallucination. For those who like their philosophical arguments spiced with a touch of science, we can imagine that our brains were surreptitiously removed in the night, and unbeknown to 'us' are being stimulated by a neurophysiologist so as to produce the very sensations that we would normally associate with a trip to the Grand Canyon. Currently permit 'us' into appealing of what we are aware of in this complete hallucination that is obvious that we are not awaken to the sparking awareness of physical objects, their surfaces, or their constituents. Nor can we even construe the experience as one of an object's appearing to 'us' in a certain way. It is after all a complete hallucination and the objects we take to exist before 'us' are simply not there. But if we compare hallucinatory experience with the qualitatively indistinguishable veridical experiences, should we most conclude that it would be 'special' to suppose that in veridical experience we are aware of something radically different from what we are aware of in hallucinatory experience? Again, it might help to reflect on our belief that the immediate cause of hallucinatory experience and veridical experience might be the very same brain event, and it is surely implausible to suppose that the effects of this same cause are radically different - acquaintance with physical objects in the case of veridical experience: Something else in the case of hallucinatory experience.

This version of the argument from hallucination would seem to address straightforwardly the ontological versions of direct realism. The argument is supposed to convince 'us' that the ontological analysis of sensation in both veridical and hallucinatory experience should give 'us' the same results, but in the hallucinatory case there is no plausible physical object, constituent of a physical object, or surface of a physical object with which additional premiss we would also get an argument against epistemological direct realism. That premiss is that in a vivid hallucinatory experience we might have precisely the same justification for believing (falsely) what we do about the physical world as we do in the analogous, phenomenological indistinguishable, veridical experience. But our justification for believing that there is a table before 'us' in the course of a vivid hallucination of a table are surely not non-inferential in character. It certainly is not, if non-inferential justifications are supposedly a consist but yet an unproblematic access to the fact that makes true our belief - by hypothesis the table does not exist. But if the justification that hallucinatory experiences give 'us' the same as the justification we get from the parallel veridical experience, then we should not describe a veridical experience as giving 'us non-inferential justification for believing in the existence of physical objects. In both cases we should say that we believe what we do about the physical world on the basis of what we know directly about the character of our experience.

In this brief space, I can only sketch some of the objections that might be raised against arguments from illusion and hallucination. That being said, let us begin with a criticism that accepts most of the presuppositions of the arguments. Even if the possibility of hallucination establishes that in some experience we are not acquainted with constituents of physical objects, it is not clear that it establishes that we are never acquainted with a constituent of physical objects. Suppose, for example, that we decide that in both veridical and hallucinatory experience we are acquainted with sense-data. At least some philosophers have tried to identify physical objects with 'bundles' of actual and possible sense-data.

To establish inductively that sensations are signs of physical objects one would have to observe a correlation between the occurrence of certain sensations and the existence of certain physical objects. But to observe such a correlation in order to establish a connection, one would need independent access to physical objects and, by hypothesis, this one cannot have. If one further adopts the verificationist's stance that the ability to comprehend is parasitic on the ability to confirm, one can easily be driven to Hume's conclusion:

Let us chance our imagination to the heavens, or to the utmost limits of the universe, we never really advance a step beyond ourselves, nor can conceivable any kind of existence, but those perceptions, which have appear`d in that narrow compass. This is the universe of the imagination, nor have we have any idea but what is there Reduced. (Hume, 1739-40, pp. 67-8). If one reaches such a conclusion but wants to maintain the intelligibility and verifiability of the assertion about the physical world, one can go either the idealistic or the phenomenalistic route.

However, hallucinatory experiences on this view is non-veridical precisely because the sense-data one is acquainted with in hallucination do not bear the appropriate relations to other actual and possible sense-data. But if such a view where plausible one could agree that one is acquainted with the same kind of a thing in veridical and non-veridical experience but insists that there is still a sense in which in veridical experience one is acquainted with constituents of a physical object?

A different sort of objection to the argument from illusion or hallucination concerns its use in drawing conclusions we have not stressed in the above discourses. I have in mentioning this objection, as to underscore an important feature of the argument. At least some philosophers (Hume, for example) have stressed the rejection of direct realism on the road to an argument for general scepticism with respect to the physical world. Once one abandons epistemological; direct realisms, one has an uphill battle indicating how one can legitimately make the inferences from sensation to physical objects. But philosophers who appeal to the existence of illusion and hallucination to develop an argument for scepticism can be accused of having an epistemically self-defeating argument. One could justifiably infer sceptical conclusions from the existence of illusion and hallucination only if one justifiably believed that such experiences exist, but if one is justified in believing that illusion exists, one must be justified in believing at least, some facts about the physical world (for example, that straight sticks look bent in water). The key point to stress in relying to such arguments is, that strictly speaking, the philosophers in question need only appeal to the 'possibility' of a vivid illusion and hallucination. Although it would have been psychologically more difficult to come up with arguments from illusion and hallucination if we did not believe that we actually had such experiences, I take it that most philosophers would argue that the possibility of such experiences is enough to establish difficulties with direct realism. Indeed, if one looks carefully at the argument from hallucination discussed earlier, one sees that it nowhere makes any claims about actual cases of hallucinatory experience.

Another reply to the attack on epistemological direct realism focuses on the implausibility of claiming that there is any process of 'inference' wrapped up in our beliefs about the world and its surrounding surfaces. Even if it is possible to give a phenomenological description of the subjective character of sensation, it requires a special sort of skill that most people lack. Our perceptual beliefs about the physical world are surely direct, at least in the sense that they are unmediated by any sort of conscious inference from premisses describing something other than a physical object. The appropriate reply to this objection, however, is simply to acknowledge the relevant phenomenological fact and point out that from the perceptive of epistemologically direct realism, the philosopher is attacking a claim about the nature of our justification for believing propositions about the physical world. Such philosophers need carry out of any comment at all about the causal genesis of such beliefs.

As mentioned, which proponents of the argument from illusion and hallucination have often intended it to establish the existence of sense-data, and many philosophers have attacked the so-called sense-datum inference presupposed in some statements of the argument. When the stick looked bent, the penny looked elliptical and the yellow object looked red, the sense-datum theorist wanted to infer that there was something bent, elliptical and red, respectively. But such an inference is surely suspect. Usually, we do not infer that because something appears to have a certain property, that affairs that affecting something that has that property. When in saying that Jones looks like a doctor, I surely would not want anyone to infer that there must actually be someone there who is a doctor. In assessing this objection, it will be important to distinguish different uses words like 'appears' and 'looks'. At least, sometimes to say that something looks 'F' way and the sense-datum inference from an F 'appearance' in this sense to an actual 'F' would be hopeless. However, it also seems that we use the 'appears'/'looks' terminology to describe the phenomenological character of our experience and the inference might be more plausible when the terms are used this way. Still, it does seem that the arguments from illusion and hallucination will not by themselves constitute strong evidence for sense-datum theory. Even if one concludes that there is something common to both the hallucination of a red thing and a veridical visual experience of a red thing, one need not describe a common constituent as awareness of something red. The adverbial theorist would prefer to construe the common experiential state as 'being appeared too redly', a technical description intended only to convey the idea that the state in question need not be analysed as relational in character. Those who opt for an adverbial theory of sensation need to make good the claim that their artificial adverbs can be given a sense that is not parasitic upon an understanding of the adjectives transformed into verbs. Still, other philosophers might try to reduce the common element in veridical and non-veridical experience to some kind of intentional state. More like belief or judgement. The idea here is that the only thing common to the two experiences is the fact that in both I spontaneously takes there to be present an object of a certain kind.

The selfsame objections can be started within the general framework presupposed by proponents of the arguments from illusion and hallucination. A great many contemporary philosophers, however, uncomfortable with the intelligibility of the concepts needed to make sense of the theories attacked even. Thus, at least, some who object to the argument from illusion do so not because they defend direct realism. Rather they think there is something confused about all this talk of direct awareness or acquaintance. Contemporary Externalists, for example, usually insist that we understand epistemic concepts by appeal: To homologically connections. On such a view the closest thing to direct knowledge would probably be something by other beliefs. If we understand direct knowledge this way, it is not clar how the phenomena of illusion and hallucination would be relevant to claim that on, at least some occasions our judgements about the physical world are reliably produced by processes that do not take as their input beliefs about something else.

The expressions 'knowledge by acquaintance' and 'knowledge by description', and the distinction they mark between knowing 'things' and knowing 'about' things, are now generally associated with Bertrand Russell. However, John Grote and Hermann von Helmholtz had earlier and independently to mark the same distinction, and William James adopted Grote's terminology in his investigation of the distinction. Philosophers have perennially investigated this and related distinctions using varying terminology. Grote introduced the distinction by noting that natural languages 'distinguish between these two applications of the notion of knowledge, the one being The classic opposition is between foundationalism and coherentism. Coherentism denies any immediate justification. It deals with the regress argument by rejecting 'linear' chains of justification and, in effect, taking the total system of belief to be epistemically primary. A particular belief is justified in the extent that it is integrated into a coherent system of belief. More recently into a pragmatist like John Dewey has developed a position known as contextualism, which avoids ascribing any overall structure to knowledge. Questions concerning justification can only arise in particular context, defined in terms of assumptions that are simply taken for granted, though they can be questioned in other contexts, where other assumptions will be privileged.

Foundationalism can be attacked both in its commitment to immediate justification and in its claim that all mediately justified beliefs ultimately depend on the former. Though, it is the latter that is the position's weakest point, most of the critical fire has been detected to the former. As pointed out about much of this criticism has been directly against some particular form of immediate justification, ignoring the possibility of other forms. Thus, much anti-foundationalist artillery has been directed at the 'myth of the given'. The idea that facts or things are 'given' to consciousness in a pre-conceptual, pre-judgmental mode, and that beliefs can be justified on that basis (Sellars, 1963). The most prominent general argument against immediate justification is a 'level ascent' argument, according to which whatever is taken ti immediately justified a belief that the putative justifier has in supposing to do so. Hence, since the justification of the higher level belief after all (BonJour, 1985). We lack adequate support for any such higher level requirements for justification, and if it were imposed we would be launched on an infinite undergo regress, for a similar requirement would hold equally for the higher level belief that the original justifier was efficacious.

Coherence is a major player in the theatre of knowledge. There are coherence theories of belief, truth, and justification. These combine in various ways to yield theories of knowledge. We will proceed from belief through justification to truth. Coherence theories of belief are concerned with the content of beliefs. Consider a belief you now have, the beliefs that you are reading a page in a book, so what makes that belief the belief that it is? What makes it the belief that you are reading a page in a book than the belief hat you have a monster in the garden?

One answer is that the belief has a coherent place or role in a system of beliefs. Perception has an influence on belief. You respond to sensory stimuli by believing that you are reading a page in a book rather than believing that you have a centaur in the garden. Belief has an influence on action. You will act differently if you believe that you are reading a page than if you believe something about a centaur. Perspicacity and action undermine the content of belief, however, the same stimuli may produce various beliefs and various beliefs may produce the same action. The role that gives the belief the content it has in the role it plays in a network of relations to the beliefs, the role in inference and implications, for example, I refer different things from believing that I am inferring different things from believing that I am reading a page in a book than from any other beliefs, just as I infer that belief from any other belief, just as I infer that belief from different things than I infer other beliefs from.

The input of perception and the output of an action supplement the centre role of the systematic relations the belief has to other beliefs, but it is the systematic relations that give the belief the specific content it has. They are the fundamental source of the content of beliefs. That is how coherence comes in. A belief has the content that it does because of the way in which it coheres within a system of beliefs (Rosenberg, 1988). We might distinguish weak coherence theories of the content of beliefs from strong coherence theories. Weak coherence theories affirm that coherences are one-determinant of the content of belief. Strong coherence theories of the contents of belief affirm that coherence is the sole determinant of the content of belief.

When we turn from belief to justification, we are in confronting a corresponding group of similarities fashioned by their coherences motifs. What makes one belief justified and another not? The answer is the way it coheres with the background system of beliefs. Again, there is a distinction between weak and strong theories of coherence. Weak theories tell 'us' that the way in which a belief coheres with a background system of beliefs is one determinant of justification, other typical determinants being perception, memory and intuition. Strong theories, by contrast, tell 'us' that justification is solely a matter of how a belief coheres with a system of beliefs. There is, however, another distinction that cuts across the distinction between weak and strong coherence theories of justification. It is the distinction between positive and negative coherence theories (Pollock, 1986). A positive coherence theory tells 'us' that if a belief coheres with a background system of belief, then the belief is justified. A negative coherence theory tells 'us' that if a belief fails to cohere with a background system of beliefs, then the belief is not justified. We might put this by saying that, according to a positive coherence theory, coherence has the power to produce justification, while according to a negative coherence theory, coherence has only the power to nullify justification.

A strong coherence theory of justification is a combination of a positive and a negative theory that tells 'us' that a belief is justified if and only if it coheres with a background system of beliefs.

Traditionally, belief has been of epistemological interest in its propositional guise: 'S' believes that 'p', where 'p' is a proposition toward which an agent, 'S', exhibits an attitude of acceptance. Not all belief is of this sort. If I trust what you say, I believe you. And someone may believe in Mrs. Thatcher, or in a free-market economy, or in God. It is sometimes supposed that all belief is 'reducible' to propositional belief, belief-that. Thus, my believing you might be thought a matter of my believing, perhaps, that what you say is true, and your belief in free-markets or in God, a matter of your believing that free-market economy's are desirable or that God exists.

It is doubtful, however, that non-propositional believing can, in every case, be reduced in this way. Debate on this point has tended to focus on an apparent distinction between 'belief-that' and 'belief-in', and the application of this distinction to belief in God. Some philosophers have followed Aquinas, 1225-74, in supposing that to believe in, and God is simply to believe that certain truths hold: That God exists, that he is benevolent, etc. Others (e.g., Hick, 1957) argue that belief-in is a distinctive attitude, one that includes essentially an element of trust. More commonly, belief-in has been taken to involve a combination of propositional belief together with some further attitude.

Still further, the typical way of addressing this question has been by way of discussing arguments for or and against the existence of God. On the pro side, there are the traditional theistic proofs or arguments: The ontological, cosmological and teleological arguments, using Kant's terms for them. On the other side, the anti-theistic side, the principal argument is the argument from evil, the argument that is not possible or at least probable that there be such a person as God, given all the pain, suffering and evil the world displays. This argument is flanked by subsidiary arguments, such as the claim that the very concept of God is incoherent, because, for example, it is impossible that there are the people without a body, and Freudian and Marxist claims that religious belief arises out of a sort of magnification and projection into the heavens of human attributes we think important.

But why has discussion centred on justification rather than warrant? And precisely what is justification? And why has the discussion of justification of theistic belief focussed so heavily on arguments for and against the existence of God?

As to the first question, we can see why once we see that the dominant epistemological tradition in modern Western philosophy has tended to 'identify' warrant with justification. On this way of looking at the matter, warrant, that which distinguishes knowledge from mere true belief, just 'is' justification. Belief theory of knowledge-the theory according to which knowledge is justified true belief has enjoyed the status of orthodoxy. According to this view, knowledge is justified truer belief, therefore any of your beliefs have warrant for you if and only if you are justified in holding it.

But what is justification? What is it to be justified in holding a belief? To get a proper sense of the answer, we must turn to those twin towers of western epistemology. René Descartes and especially, John Locke. The first thing to see is that according to Descartes and Locke, there are epistemic or intellectual duties, or obligations, or requirements. Thus, Locke:

Faith is nothing but a firm assent of the mind, which if it is regulated, A is our duty, cannot be afforded to anything, but upon good reason: And cannot be opposite to it, he that believes, without having any reason for believing, may be in love with his own fanciers: But, neither seeks truth as he ought, nor pats the obedience due his maker, which would have him use those discerning faculties he has given him: To keep him out of mistake and error. He that does this to the best of his power, however, he sometimes lights on truth, is in the right but by chance: And I know not whether the luckiest of the accidents will excuse the irregularity of his proceeding. This, at least is certain, that he must be accountable for whatever mistakes he runs into: Whereas, he that makes use of the light and faculties God has given him, by seeks sincerely to discover truth, by those helps and abilities he has, may have this satisfaction in doing his duty as rational creature, that though he should miss truth, he will not miss the reward of it. For he governs his assent right, and places it as he should, who in any case or matter whatsoever, believes or disbelieves, according as reason directs him. He that does otherwise will simply do, transgresses against his own light, and misuses those faculties, which were given him . . . (Essays 4.17.24).

Rational creatures, creatures with reason, creatures capable of believing propositions (and of disbelieving and being agnostic with respect to them), say Locke, have duties and obligation with respect to the regulation of their belief or assent. Now the central core of the notion of justification(as the etymology of the term indicates) this: One is justified in doing something or in believing a certain way, if in doing one is innocent of wrong doing and hence not properly subject to blame or censure. You are justified, therefore, if you have violated no duties or obligations, if you have conformed to the relevant requirements, if you are within your rights. To be justified in believing something, then, is to be within your rights in so believing, to be flouting no duty, to be to satisfy your epistemic duties and obligations. This way of thinking of justification has been the dominant way of thinking about justification: And this way of thinking has many important contemporary representatives. Roderick Chisholm, for example (as distinguished an epistemologist as the twentieth century can boast), in his earlier work explicitly explains justification in terms of epistemic duty (Chisholm, 1977).

The (or, a) main epistemological; questions about religious believe, therefore, has been the question whether or not religious belief in general and theistic belief in particular is justified. And the traditional way to answer that question has been to inquire into the arguments for and against theism. Why this emphasis upon these arguments? An argument is a way of marshalling your propositional evidence-the evidence from other such propositions as likens to believe-for or against a given proposition. And the reason for the emphasis upon argument is the assumption that theistic belief is justified if and only if there is sufficient propositional evidence for it. If there is not' much by way of propositional evidence for theism, then you are not justified in accepting it. Moreover, if you accept theistic belief without having propositional evidence for it, then you are ging contrary to epistemic duty and are therefore unjustified in accepting it. Thus, W.K. William James, trumpets that 'it is wrong, always everything upon insufficient evidence', his is only the most strident in a vast chorus of only insisting that there is an intellectual duty not to believe in God unless you have propositional evidence for that belief. (A few others in the choir: Sigmund Freud, Brand Blanshard, H.H. Price, Bertrand Russell and Michael Scriven.)

Now how it is that the justification of theistic belief gets identified with there being propositional evidence for it? Justification is a matter of being blameless, of having done one's duty (in this context, one's epistemic duty): What, precisely, has this to do with having propositional evidence?

The answer, once, again, is to be found in Descartes especially Locke. As, justification is the property your beliefs have when, in forming and holding them, you conform to your epistemic duties and obligations. But according to Locke, a central epistemic duty is this: To believe a proposition only to the degree that it is probable with respect to what is certain for you. What propositions are certain for you? First, according to Descartes and Locke, propositions about your own immediate experience, that you have a mild headache, or that it seems to you that you see something red: And second, propositions that are self-evident for you, necessarily true propositions so obvious that you cannot so much as entertain them without seeing that they must be true. (Examples would be simple arithmetical and logical propositions, together with such propositions as that the whole is at least as large as the parts, that red is a colour, and that whatever exists has properties.) Propositions of these two sorts are certain for you, as fort other prepositions. You are justified in believing if and only if when one and only to the degree to which it is probable with respect to what is certain for you. According to Locke, therefore, and according to the whole modern foundationalist tradition initiated by Locke and Descartes (a tradition that until has recently dominated Western thinking about these topics) there is a duty not to accept a proposition unless it is certain or probable with respect to what is certain.

In the present context, therefore, the central Lockean assumption is that there is an epistemic duty not to accept theistic belief unless it is probable with respect to what is certain for you: As a consequence, theistic belief is justified only if the existence of God is probable with respect to what is certain. Locke does not argue for his proposition, he simply announces it, and epistemological discussion of theistic belief has for the most part followed hin ion making this assumption. This enables 'us' to see why epistemological discussion of theistic belief has tended to focus on the arguments for and against theism: On the view in question, theistic belief is justified only if it is probable with respect to what is certain, and the way to show that it is probable with respect to what it is certain are to give arguments for it from premises that are certain or, are sufficiently probable with respect to what is certain.

There are at least three important problems with this approach to the epistemology of theistic belief. First, there standards for theistic arguments have traditionally been set absurdly high (and perhaps, part of the responsibility for this must be laid as the door of some who have offered these arguments and claimed that they constitute wholly demonstrative proofs). The idea seems to test. a good theistic argument must start from what is self-evident and proceed majestically by way of self-evidently valid argument forms to its conclusion. It is no wonder that few if any theistic arguments meet that lofty standard - particularly, in view of the fact that almost no philosophical arguments of any sort meet it. (Think of your favourite philosophical argument: Does it really start from premisses that are self-evident and move by ways of self-evident argument forms to its conclusion?)

Secondly, attention has ben mostly confined to three theistic arguments: The traditional arguments, cosmological and teleological arguments, but in fact, there are many more good arguments: Arguments from the nature of proper function, and from the nature of propositions, numbers and sets. These are arguments from intentionality, from counterfactual, from the confluence of epistemic reliability with epistemic justification, from reference, simplicity, intuition and love. There are arguments from colours and flavours, from miracles, play and enjoyment, morality, from beauty and from the meaning of life. This is even a theistic argument from the existence of evil.

But there are a third and deeper problems here. The basic assumption is that theistic belief is justified only if it is or can be shown as the probable respect to many a body of evidence or proposition - perhaps, those that are self-evident or about one's own mental life, but is this assumption true? The idea is that theistic belief is very much like a scientific hypothesis: It is acceptable if and only if there is an appropriate balance of propositional evidence in favour of it. But why believe a thing like that? Perhaps the theory of relativity or the theory of evolution is like that, such a theory has been devised to explain the phenomena and gets all its warrant from its success in so doing. However, other beliefs, e.g., memory beliefs, felt in other minds is not like that, they are not hypothetical at all, and are not accepted because of their explanatory powers. There are instead, the propositions from which one start in attempting to give evidence for a hypothesis. Now, why assume that theistic belief, belief in God, is in this regard more like a scientific hypothesis than like, say, a memory belief? Why think that the justification of theistic belief depends upon the evidential relation of theistic belief to other things one believes? According to Locke and the beginnings of this tradition, it is because there is a duty not to assent to a proposition unless it is probable with respect to what is certain to you, but is there really any such duty? No one has succeeded in showing that, say, belief in other minds or the belief that there has been a past, is probable with respect to what is certain for 'us'. Suppose it is not: Does it follow that you are living in epistemic sin if you believe that there are other minds? Or a past?

There are urgent questions about any view according to which one has duties of the sort 'do not believe 'p' unless it is probable with respect to what is certain for you;. First, if this is a duty, is it one to which I can conform? My beliefs are for the most part not within my control: Certainly they are not within my direct control. I believe that there has been a past and that there are other people, even if these beliefs are not probable with respect to what is certain forms (and even if I came to know this) I could not give them up. Whether or not I accept such beliefs are not really up to me at all, For I can no more refrain from believing these things than I can refrain from conforming yo the law of gravity. Second, is there really any reason for thinking I have such a duty? Nearly everyone recognizes such duties as that of not engaging in gratuitous cruelty, taking care of one's children and one's aged parents, and the like, but do we also find ourselves recognizing that there is a duty not to believe what is not probable (or, what we cannot see to be probable) with respect to what are certain for 'us'? It hardly seems so. However, it is hard to see why being justified in believing in God requires that the existence of God be probable with respect to some such body of evidence as the set of propositions certain for you. Perhaps, theistic belief is properly basic, i.e., such that one is perfectly justified in accepting it on the evidential basis of other propositions one believes.

Taking justification in that original etymological fashion, therefore, there is every reason ton doubt that one is justified in holding theistic belief only inf one is justified in holding theistic belief only if one has evidence for it. Of course, the term 'justification' has undergone various analogical extensions in the of various philosophers, it has been used to name various properties that are different from justification etymologically so-called, but anagogically related to it. In such a way, the term sometimes used to mean propositional evidence: To say that a belief is justified for someone is to saying that he has propositional evidence (or sufficient propositional evidence) for it. So taken, however, the question whether theistic belief is justified loses some of its interest; for it is not clear (given this use) beliefs that are unjustified in that sense. Perhaps, one also does not have propositional evidence for one's memory beliefs, if so, that would not be a mark against them and would not suggest that there be something wrong holding them.

Another analogically connected way to think about justification (a way to think about justification by the later Chisholm) is to think of it as simply a relation of fitting between a given proposition and one's epistemic vase -which includes the other things one believes, as well as one's experience. Perhaps tat is the way justification is to be thought of, but then, if it is no longer at all obvious that theistic belief has this property of justification if it seems as a probability with respect to many another body of evidence. Perhaps, again, it is like memory beliefs in this regard.

To recapitulate: The dominant Western tradition has been inclined to identify warrant with justification, it has been inclined to take the latter in terms of duty and the fulfilment of obligation, and hence to suppose that there is no epistemic duty not to believe in God unless you have good propositional evidence for the existence of God. Epistemological discussion of theistic belief, as a consequence, as concentrated on the propositional evidence for and against theistic belief, i.e., on arguments for and against theistic belief. But there is excellent reason to doubt that there are epistemic duties of the sort the tradition appeals to here.

And perhaps it was a mistake to identify warrant with justification in the first place. Napoleons have little warrant for him: His problem, however, need not be dereliction of epistemic duty. He is in difficulty, but it is not or necessarily that of failing to fulfill epistemic duty. He may be doing his epistemic best, but he may be doing his epistemic duty in excelsis: But his madness prevents his beliefs from having much by way of warrant. His lack of warrant is not a matter of being unjustified, i.e., failing to fulfill epistemic duty. So warrant and being epistemologically justified by name are not the same things. Another example, suppose (to use the favourite twentieth-century variant of Descartes' evil demon example) I have been captured by Alpha-Centaurian super-scientists, running a cognitive experiment, they remove my brain, and keep it alive in some artificial nutrients, and by virtue of their advanced technology induce in me the beliefs I might otherwise have if I were going about my usual business. Then my beliefs would not have much by way of warrant, but would it be because I was failing to do my epistemic duty? Hardly.

As a result of these and other problems, another, externalist way of thinking about knowledge has appeared in recent epistemology, that a theory of justification is internalized if and only if it requires that all of its factors needed for a belief to be epistemically accessible to that of a person, internal to his cognitive perception, and externalist, if it allows that, at least some of the justifying factors need not be thus accessible, in that they can be external to the believer' s cognitive Perspectives, beyond his ken. However, epistemologists often use the distinction between internalized and externalist theories of epistemic justification without offering any very explicit explanation.

Or perhaps the thing to say, is that it has reappeared, for the dominant sprains in epistemology priori to the Enlightenment were really externalist. According to this externalist way of thinking, warrant does not depend upon satisfaction of duty, or upon anything else to which the Knower has special cognitive access (as he does to what is about his own experience and to whether he is trying his best to do his epistemic duty): It depends instead upon factors 'external' to the epistemic agent -such factors as whether his beliefs are produced by reliable cognitive mechanisms, or whether they are produced by epistemic faculties functioning properly in-an appropriate epistemic environment.

How will we think about the epistemology of theistic belief in more than is less of an externalist way (which is at once both satisfyingly traditional and agreeably up to date)? I think, that the ontological question whether there is such a person as God is in a way priori to the epistemological question about the warrant of theistic belief. It is natural to think that if in fact we have been created by God, then the cognitive processes that issue in belief in God are indeed realisable belief-producing processes, and if in fact God created 'us', then no doubt the cognitive faculties that produce belief in God is functioning properly in an epistemologically congenial environment. On the other hand, if there is no such person as God, if theistic belief is an illusion of some sort, then things are much less clear. Then beliefs in God in of the most of basic ways of wishing that never doubt the production by which unrealistic thinking or another cognitive process not aimed at truth. Thus, it will have little or no warrant. And belief in God on the basis of argument would be like belief in false philosophical theories on the basis of argument: Do such beliefs have warrant? Notwithstanding, the custom of discussing the epistemological questions about theistic belief as if they could be profitably discussed independently of the ontological issue as to whether or not theism is true, is misguided. There two issues are intimately intertwined,

Nonetheless, the vacancy left, as today and as days before are an awakening and untold story beginning by some sparking conscious paradigm left by science. That is a central idea by virtue accredited by its epistemology, where in fact, is that justification and knowledge arising from the proper functioning of our intellectual virtues or faculties in an appropriate environment. This particular yet, peculiar idea is captured in the following criterion for justified belief:

> (J) 'S' is justified in believing that 'p' if and only if of S's believing that 'p' is the result of S's intellectual virtues or faculties functioning in appropriate environment.

What is an intellectual virtue or faculty? A virtue or faculty in general is a power or ability or competence to achieve some result. An intellectual virtue or faculty, in the sense intended above, is a power or ability or competence to arrive at truths in a particular field, and to avoid believing falsehoods in that field. Examples of human intellectual virtues are sight, hearing, introspection, memory, deduction and induction. More exactly.

> (V) A mechanism 'M' for generating and/or maintaining beliefs is an intellectual virtue if and only if 'M''s' is a competence to believing true propositions and refrain from false believing propositions within a field of propositions 'F', when one is in a set of circumstances 'C'.

It is required that we specify a particular field of suggestions or its propositional field for 'M', since a given cognitive mechanism will be a competence for believing some kind of truths but not others. The faculty of sight, for example, allows 'us' to determine the colour of objects, but not the sounds that they associatively make. It is also required that we specify a set of circumstances for 'M', since a given cognitive mechanism will be a competence in some circumstances but not others. For example, the faculty of sight allows 'us' to determine colours in a well lighten room, but not in a darkened cave or formidable abyss.

According to the aforementioned formulations, what makes a cognitive mechanism an intellectual virtue is that it is reliable in generating true beliefs than false beliefs in the relevant field and in the relevant circumstances. It is correct to say, therefore, that virtue epistemology is a kind of reliabilism. Whereas, genetic reliabilism maintains that justified belief is belief that results from a reliable cognitive process, virtue epistemology makes a restriction on the kind of process which is allowed. Namely, the cognitive processes that are important for justification and knowledge is those that have their basis in an intellectual virtue.

Finally, that the concerning mental faculty reliability point to the importance of an appropriate environment. The idea is that cognitive mechanisms might be reliable in some environments but not in others. Consider an example from Alvin Plantinga. On a planet revolving around Alfa Centauri, cats are invisible to human beings. Moreover, Alfa Centaurian cats emit a type of radiation that causes humans to form the belief that there I a dog barking nearby. Suppose now that you are transported to this Alfa Centaurian planet, a cat walks by, and you form the belief that there is a dog barking nearby. Surely you are not justified in believing this. However, the problem here is not with your intellectual faculties, but with your environment. Although your faculties of perception are reliable on earth, yet are unrealisable on the Alga Centaurian planet, which is an inappropriate environment for those faculties.

The central idea of virtue epistemology, as expressed in (J) above, has a high degree of initial plausibility. By masking the idea of faculties' cental to the reliability if not by the virtue of epistemology, in that it explains quite neatly to why beliefs are caused by perception and memories are often justified, while beliefs caused by unrealistic and superstition are not. Secondly, the theory gives 'us' a basis for answering certain kinds of scepticism. Specifically, we may agree that if we were brains in a vat, or victims of a Cartesian demon, then we would not have knowledge even in those rare cases where our beliefs turned out true. But virtue epistemology explains that what is important for knowledge is toast our faculties are in fact reliable in the environment in which we are. And so we do have knowledge so long as we are in fact, not victims of a Cartesian demon, or brains in a vat. Finally, Plantinga argues that virtue epistemology deals well with Gettier problems. The idea is that Gettier problems give 'us' cases of justified belief that is 'truer by accident'. Virtue epistemology, Plantinga argues, helps 'us' to understand what it means for a belief to be true by accident, and provides a basis for saying why such cases are not knowledge. Beliefs are rue by accident when they are caused by otherwise reliable faculties functioning in an inappropriate environment. Plantinga develops this line of reasoning in Plantinga (1988).

But although virtue epistemology has god initial plausibility, it faces some substantial objections. The first of an objection, which virtue epistemology face is a version of the generality problem. We may understand the problem more clearly if we were to consider the following criterion for justified belief, which results from our explanation of (J).

(J ′) 'S' is justified in believing that 'p' if and entirely if.

(A) there is a field 'F' and a set of circumstances 'C' such that

(1) 'S' is in 'C' with respect to the proposition that 'p',

(2) 'S' is in 'C' with respect to the proposition that 'p',

(3) If 'S' were in 'C' with respect to a proposition in 'F'.

Then 'S' would very likely believe correctly with regard to that proposition.

The problem arises in how we are to select an appropriate 'F' and 'C'. For given any true belief that 'p', we can always come up with a field 'F' and a set of circumstances 'C', such that 'S' is perfectly reliable in 'F' and 'C'. For any true belief that 'p', let 'F's' be the field including only the propositions 'p' and 'not-p'. Let 'C' include whatever circumstances there are which causes 'p's' to be true, together with the circumstanced which causes 'S' to believe that 'p'. Clearly, 'S' is perfectly reliable with respect to propositions in this field in these circumstances. But we do not want to say that all of S's true beliefs are justified for 'S'. And of course, there is an analogous problem in the other direction of generality. For given any belief that 'p', we can always specify a field of propositions 'F' and a set of circumstances 'C', such that 'p' is in 'F', 'S' is in 'C', and 'S' is not reliable with respect to propositions in 'F' in 'C'.

Variations of this view have been advanced for both knowledge and justified belief. The first formulation of a reliability account of knowing appeared in a note by F.P. Ramsey (1931), who said that a belief was knowledge if it is true, certain and obtained by a reliable process. P. Unger (1968) suggested that 'S' knows that 'p' just in case it is not at all accidental that 'S' is right about its being the case that 'p'. D.M. Armstrong (1973) drew an analogy between a thermometer that reliably indicates the temperature and a belief that reliably indicate the truth. Armstrong said that a non-inferential belief qualified as knowledge if the belief has properties that are nominally sufficient for its truth, i.e., guarantee its truth via laws of nature.

Closely allied to the nomic sufficiency account of knowledge, primarily due to F.I. Dretske (1981), A.I. Goldman (1976, 1986) and R. Nozick (1981). The core of tis approach is that S's belief that 'p' qualifies as knowledge just in case 'S' believes 'p' because of reasons that would not obtain unless 'p's' being true, or because of a process or method that would not yield belief in 'p' if 'p' were not true. For example, 'S' would not have his current reasons for believing there is a telephone before him, or would not come to believe this, unless there was a telephone before him. Thus, there is a counterfactual reliable guarantor of the belief's being true. A variant of the counterfactual approach says that 'S' knows that 'p' only if there is no 'relevant alterative' situation in which 'p' is false but 'S' would still believe that 'p'.

To a better understanding, this interpretation is to mean that the alterative attempt to accommodate any of an opposing strand in our thinking about knowledge one interpretation is an absolute concept, which is to mean that the justification or evidence one must have in order to know a proposition 'p' must be sufficient to eliminate all the alternatives to 'p' (where an alternative to a proposition 'p' is a proposition incompatible with 'p'). That is, one's justification or evidence for 'p' must be sufficient fort one to know that every alternative to 'p' is false. These elements of our thinking about knowledge are exploited by sceptical argument. These arguments call our attention to alternatives that our evidence cannot eliminate. For example, (Dretske, 1970), when we are at the zoo. We might claim to know that we see a zebra on the basis of certain visual evidence, namely a zebra-like appearance. The sceptic inquires how we know that we are not seeing a clearly disguised mule. While we do have some evidence against the likelihood of such a deception, intuitively it is not strong enough for 'us' to know that we are not so deceived. By pointing out alternatives of this nature that cannot eliminate, as well as others with more general application (dreams, hallucinations, etc.), the sceptic appears to show that this requirement that our evidence eliminate every alternative is seldom, if ever, met.

The above considerations show that virtue epistemology must say more about the selection of relevant fields and sets of circumstances. Established addresses the generality problem by introducing the concept of a design plan for our intellectual faculties. Relevant specifications for fields and sets of circumstances are determined by this plan. One might object that this approach requires the problematic assumption of a Designer of the design plan. But Plantinga disagrees on two counts: He does not think that the assumption is needed, or that it would be problematic. Plantinga discusses relevant material in Plantinga (1986, 1987 and 1988). Ernest Sosa addresses the generality problem by introducing the concept of an epistemic perspective. In order to have reflective knowledge, 'S' must have a true grasp of the reliability of her faculties, this grasp being itself provided by a 'faculty of faculties'. Relevant specifications of an 'F' and 'C' are determined by this perspective. Alternatively, Sosa has suggested that relevant specifications are determined by the purposes of the epistemic community. The idea is that fields and sets of circumstances are determined by their place in useful generalizations about epistemic agents and their abilities to act as reliable-information sharers.

The second objection which virtue epistemology faces are that (J) and

(J′) are too strong. It is possible for 'S' to be justified in believing that 'p', even when 'S's' intellectual faculties are largely unreliable. Suppose, for example, that Jane's beliefs about the world around her are true. It is clear that in this case Jane's faculties of perception are almost wholly unreliable. But we would not want to say that none of Jane's perceptual beliefs are justified. If Jane believes that there is a tree in her yard, and she vases the belief on the usual tree-like experience, then it seems that she is as justified as we would be regarded a substitutable belief.

Sosa addresses the current problem by arguing that justification is relative to an environment 'E'. Accordingly, 'S' is justified in believing that 'p' relative to 'E', if and only if 'S's' faculties would be reliable in 'E'. Note that on this account, 'S' need not actually be in 'E' in order for 'S' to be justified in believing some proposition relative to 'E'. This allows Soda to conclude that Jane has justified belief in the above case. For Jane is justified in her perceptual beliefs relative to our environment, although she is not justified in those beliefs relative to the environment in which they have actualized her.

We have earlier made mention about analyticity, but the true story of analyticity is surprising in many ways. Contrary to received opinion, it was the empiricist Locke rather than the rationalist Kant who had the better information account of this type or deductive proposition. Frége and Rudolf Carnap (1891-1970) A German logician positivist whose first major works was "Der logische Aufbau der Welt" (1926, trans, as "The Logical Structure of the World," 1967). Carnap pursued the enterprise of clarifying the structures of mathematics and scientific language (the only legitimate task for scientific philosophy) in "The Logical Syntax of Language," (1937). Yet, refinements continued with "Meaning and Necessity" (1947), while a general losing of the original ideal of reduction culminated in the great "Logical Foundations of Probability" and the most importantly single work of 'confirmation theory' in 1950. Other works concern the structure of physics and the concept of entropy.

Both, Frége and Carnap, represented as analyticity's best friends in this century, did as much to undermine it as its worst enemies. Quine (1908-) whose early work was on mathematical logic, and issued in "A System of Logistic" (1934), "Mathematical Logic" (1940) and "Methods of Logic" (1950) it was with this collection of papers a "Logical Point of View" (1953) that his philosophical importance became widely recognized, also, Putman

(1926-) his concern in the later period has largely been to deny any serious asymmetry between truth and knowledge as it is obtained in natural science, and as it is obtained in morals and even theology. Books include, Philosophy of logic (1971), Representation and Reality (1988) and Renewing Philosophy (1992). Collections of his papers including Mathematics, Master, and Method, (1975), Mind, Language, and Reality, (1975) and Realism and Reason (1983). Both of which represented as having refuted the analytic/ synthetic distinction, not only did no such thing, but, in fact, contributed significantly to undoing the damage done by Frége and Carnap. Finally, the epistemological significance of the distinctions is nothing like what it is commonly taken to be.

Locke's account of an analyticity proposition as, for its time, everything that a succinct account of analyticity should be (Locke, 1924, pp. 306-8) he distinguished two kinds of analytic propositions, identified propositions in which we affirm the said terms if itself, e.g., 'Roses are roses', and predicative propositions in which 'a part of the complex idea is predicated of the name of the whole', e.g., 'Roses are flowers'. Locke calls such sentences 'trifling' because a speaker who uses them 'trifles with words'. A synthetic sentence, in contrast, such as a mathematical theorem, states 'a truth and conveys with its informative real knowledge'. Correspondingly, Locke distinguishes two kinds of ' necessary consequences', analytic entailment where validity depends on the literal containment of the conclusions in the premiss and synthetic entailments where it does not. (Locke did not originate this concept-containment notion of analyticity. It is discussions by Arnaud and Nicole, and it is safe to say it has been around for a very long time (Arnaud, 1964).

Kant's account of analyticity, which received opinion tells 'us' is the consummate formulation of this notion in modern philosophy, is actually a step backward. What is valid in his account is not novel, and what is novel is not valid. Kant presents Locke's account of concept-containment analyticity, but introduces certain alien features, the most important being his characterizations of most important being his characterization of analytic propositions as propositions whose denials are logical contradictions (Kant, 1783). This characterization suggests that analytic propositions based on Locke's part-whole relation or Kant's explicative copula are a species of logical truth. But the containment of the predicate concept in the subject concept in sentences like 'Bachelors are unmarried' is a different relation from containment of the consequent in the antecedent in a sentence like 'If John is a bachelor, then John is a bachelor or Mary read Kant's Critique'. The former is literal containment whereas, the latter are, in general, not. Talk of the 'containment' of the consequent of a logical truth in the metaphorical, a way of saying 'logically derivable'.

Kant's conflation of concept containment with logical containment caused him to overlook the issue of whether logical truths are synthetically deductive and the problem of how he can say mathematical truths are synthetically deductive when they cannot be denied without contradiction. Historically., the conflation set the stage for the disappearance of the Lockean notion. Frége, whom received opinion portrays as second only to Kant among the champions of analyticity, and Carnap, who it portrays as just behind Frége, was jointly responsible for the appearance of concept-containment analyticity.

Frége was clear about the difference between concept containment and logical containment, expressing it as like the difference between the containment of 'beams in a house' the containment of a 'plant in the seed' (Frége, 1853). But he found the former, as Kant formulated it, defective in three ways: It explains analyticity in psychological terms, it does not cover all cases of analytic propositions, and, perhaps, most important for Frége's logicism, its notion of containment is 'unfruitful' as a definition: Mechanisms in logic and mathematics (Frége, 1853). In an insidious containment between the two notions of containment, Frége observes that with logical containment 'we are not simply talking out of the box again what we have just put inti it'. This definition makes logical containment the basic notion. Analyticity becomes a special case of logical truth, and, even in this special case, the definitions employ the power of definition in logic and mathematics than mere concept combination.

Carnap, attempting to overcome what he saw a shortcoming in Frége's account of analyticity, took the remaining step necessary to do away explicitly with Lockean-Kantian analyticity. As Carnap saw things, it was a shortcoming of Frége's explanation that it seems to suggest that definitional relation underlying analytic propositions can be extra-logic in some sense, say, in resting on linguistic synonymy. To Carnap, this represented a failure to achieve a uniform formal treatment of analytic propositions and left 'us' with a dubious distinction between logical and extra-logical vocabulary. Hence, he eliminated the reference to definitions in Frége's explanation of analyticity by introducing 'meaning postulates', e.g., statements such as $(\forall\chi)$ (χ is a bachelor-is unmarried) (Carnap, 1965). Like standard logical postulate on which they were modelled, meaning postulates express nothing more than constrains on the admissible models with respect to which sentences and deductions are evaluated for truth and validity. Thus, despite their name, its asymptomatic-balance having to pustulate itself by that in what it holds on to not more than to do with meaning than any value-added statements expressing an indispensable truth. In defining analytic propositions as consequences of (an explained set of) logical laws, Carnap explicitly removed the one place in Frége's explanation where there might be room for concept containment and with it, the last trace of Locke's distinction between semantic and other 'necessary consequences'.

Quine, the staunchest critic of analyticity of our time, performed an invaluable service on its behalf-although, one that has come almost completely unappreciated. Quine made two devastating criticism of Carnap's meaning postulate approach that expose it as both irrelevant and vacuous. It is irrelevant because, in using particular words of a language, meaning postulates fail to explicate analyticity for sentences and languages generally, that is, they do not, in fact, bring definition to it for variables 'S' and 'L' (Quine, 1953). It is vacuous because, although meaning postulates tell 'us' what sentences are to count as analytic, they do not tell 'us' what it is for them to be analytic.

Received opinion gas it that Quine did much more than refute the analytic/synthetic distinction as Carnap tried to draw it. Received opinion has that Quine demonstrated there is no distinction, however, anyone might try to draw it. Nut this, too, is incorrect. To argue for this stronger conclusion, Quine had to show that there is no way to draw the distinction outside logic, in particular theory in linguistic corresponding to Carnap's, Quine's argument had to take an entirely different form. Some inherent feature of linguistics had to be exploited in showing that no theory in this science can deliver the distinction. But the feature Quine chose was a principle of operationalist methodology characteristic of the school of Bloomfieldian linguistics. Quine succeeds in showing that meaning cannot be made objective sense of in linguistics. If making sense of a linguistic concept requires, as that school claims, operationally defining it in terms of substitution procedures that employ only concepts unrelated to that linguistic concept. But Chomsky's revolution in linguistics replaced the Bloomfieldian taxonomic model of grammars with the hypothetico-deductive model of generative linguistics, and, as a consequence, such operational definition was removed as the standard for concepts in linguistics. The standard of theoretical definition that replaced it was far more liberal, allowing the members of as family of linguistic concepts to be defied with respect to one another within a set of axioms that state their systematic interconnections -the entire system being judged by whether its consequences are confirmed by the linguistic facts. Quine's argument does not even address theories of meaning based on this hypothetico-deductive model (Katz, 1988, Katz, 1990).

Putman, the other staunch critic of analyticity, performed a service on behalf of analyticity fully on a par with, and complementary to Quine's, whereas, Quine refuted Carnap's formalization of Frége's conception of analyticity, Putman refuted this very conception itself. Putman put an end to the entire attempt, initiated by Frége and completed by Carnap, to construe analyticity as a logical concept (Putman, 1962, 1970, 1975).

However, as with Quine, received opinion has it that Putman did much more. Putman in credited with having devised science fiction cases, from the robot cat case to the twin earth cases, that are counter examples to the traditional theory of meaning. Again, received opinion is incorrect. These cases are only counter examples to Frége's version of the traditional theory of meaning. Frége's version claims both (1) that senses determines reference, and (2) that there are instances of analyticity, say, typified by 'cats are animals', and of synonymy, say typified by 'water' in English and 'water' in twin earth English. Given (1) and (2), what we call 'cats' could not be non-animals and what we call 'water' could not differ from what the earthier twin called 'water'. But, as Putman's cases show, what we call 'cats' could be Martian robots and what they call 'water' could be something other than H2O Hence, the cases are counter examples to Frége's version of the theory.

Putman himself takes these examples to refute the traditional theory of meaning per se, because he thinks other versions must also subscribe to both (1) and. (2). He was mistaken in the case of (1). Frége's theory entails (1) because it defines the sense of an expression as the mode of determination of its referent (Frége, 1952, pp. 56-78). But sense does not have to be defined this way, or in any way that entails (1).it can be defined as (D).

(D) Sense is that aspect of the grammatical structure of expressions and sentences responsible for their having sense properties and relations like meaningfulness, ambiguity, antonymy, synonymy, redundancy, analyticity and analytic entailment. (Katz, 1972 & 1990). (Note that this use of sense properties and relations is no more circular than the use of logical properties and relations to define logical form, for example, as that aspect of grammatical structure of sentences on which their logical implications depend.)

Again, (D) makes senses internal to the grammar of a language and reference an external; matter of language use -typically involving extra-linguistic beliefs, Therefore, (D) cuts the strong connection between sense and reference expressed in (1), so that there is no inference from the modal fact that 'cats' refer to robots to the conclusion that 'Cats are animals' are not analytic. Likewise, there is no inference from 'water' referring to different substances on earth and twin earth to the conclusion that our word and theirs are not synonymous. Putman's science fiction cases do not apply to a version of the traditional theory of meaning based on (D).

The success of Putman and Quine's criticism in application to Frége and Carnap's theory of meaning together with their failure in application to a theory in linguistics based on (D) creates the option of overcoming the shortcomings of the Lockean-Kantian notion of analyticity without switching to a logical notion. this option was explored in the 1960s and 1970s in the course of developing a theory of meaning modelled on the hypothetico-deductive paradigm for grammars introduced in the Chomskyan revolution (Katz, 1972).

This theory automatically avoids Frége's criticism of the psychological formulation of Kant's definition because, as an explication of a grammatical notion within linguistics, it is stated as a formal account of the structure of expressions and sentences. The theory also avoids Frége's criticism that concept-containment analyticity is not 'fruitful' enough to encompass truths of logic and mathematics. The criticism rests on the dubious assumption, parts of Frége's logicism, that analyticity 'should' encompass them, (Benacerraf, 1981). But in linguistics where the only concern is the scientific truth about natural concept-containment analyticity encompass truths of logic and mathematics. Moreover, since we are seeking the scientific truth about trifling propositions in natural language, we will eschew relations from logic and mathematics that are too fruitful for the description of such propositions. This is not to deny that we want a notion of necessary truth that goes beyond the trifling, but only to deny that, that notion is the notion of analyticity in natural language.

The remaining Frégean criticism points to a genuine incompleteness of the traditional account of analyticity. There are analytic relational sentences, for example, Jane walks with those with whom she strolls, 'Jack kills those he himself has murdered', etc., and analytic entailment with existential conclusions, for example, 'I think', therefore 'I exist'. The containment in these sentences is just as literal as that in an analytic subject-predicate sentence like 'Bachelors are unmarried', such are shown to have a theory of meaning construed as a hypothetico-deductive systemizations of sense as defined in (D) overcoming the incompleteness of the traditional account in the case of such relational sentences.

Such a theory of meaning makes the principal concern of semantics the explanation of sense properties and relations like synonymy, an antonymy, redundancy, analyticity, ambiguity, etc. Furthermore, it makes grammatical structure, specifically, senses structure, the basis for explaining them. This leads directly to the discovery of a new level of grammatical structure, and this, in turn, makes possible a proper definition of analyticity. To see this, consider two simple examples. It is a semantic fact that 'a male bachelor' is redundant and that 'spinsters' are synonymous with 'women who never married'. In the case of the redundancy, we have to explain the fact that the sense of the modifier 'male' is already contained in the sense of its head 'bachelor'. In the case of the synonymy, we have to explain the fact that the sense of 'sinister' is identical to the sense of 'woman who never married' (compositionally formed from the senses of 'woman', 'never' and 'married'). But is so fas as such facts concern relations involving the components of the senses of 'bachelor' and 'spinster' and is in as these words were simply syntactic, there must be a level of grammatical structure at which simpler of the syntactical remain semantically complex. This, in brief, is the route by which we arrive a level of 'decompositional semantic structure; that is the locus of sense structures masked by syntactically simple words.

Discovery of this new level of grammatical structure was followed by attemptive efforts as afforded to represent the structure of the sense's finds there. Without going into detail of sense representations, it is clear that, once we have the notion of decompositional representation, we can see how to generalize Locke and Kant's informal, subject-predicate account of analyticity to cover relational analytic sentences. Let a simple sentence 'S' consisted of some placed predicate 'P' with terms T1 . . ., . Tn occupying its argument places.

The analysis in case, first, S has a term T1 that consists of a place predicate Q (m > n or m = n) with terms occupying its argument places, and second, P is contained in Q and, for each term TJ. . . . T1 + I, ..., Tn, TJ is contained in the term of Q that occupies the argument place in Q corresponding to the argument place occupied by TJ in P. (Katz, 1972)

To see how (A) works, suppose that 'stroll' in 'Jane walks with those whom she strolls' is decompositionally represented as having the same sense as 'walk idly and in a leisurely way'. The sentence is analytic by (A) because the predicate 'stroll' (the sense of 'stroll) and the term 'Jane' * the sense of 'Jane' associated with the predicate 'walk') is contained in the term 'Jane' (the sense of 'she herself' associated with the predicate 'stroll'). The containment in the case of the other terms is automatic.

The fact that (A) itself makes no reference to logical operators or logical laws indicate that analyticity for subject-predicate sentences can be extended to simple relational sentences without treating analytic sentences as instances of logical truths. Further, the source of the incompleteness is no longer explained, as Frége explained it, as the absence of 'fruitful' logical apparatus, but is now explained as mistakenly treating what is only a special case of analyticity as if it were the general case. The inclusion of the predicate in the subject is the special case (where n = 1) of the general case of the inclusion of an–place predicate (and its terms) in one of its terms. Noting that the defects, by which, Quine complained of in connection with Carnap's meaning-postulated explication are absent in (A). (A) contains no words from a natural language. It explicitly uses variable 'S' and variable 'L' because it is a definition in linguistic theory. Moreover, (A) tell 'us' what property is in virtue of which a sentence is analytic, namely, redundant predication, that is, the predication structure of an analytic sentence is already found in the content of its term structure.

Received opinion has been anti-Lockean in holding that necessary consequences in logic and language belong to one and the same species. This seems wrong because the property of redundant predication provides a non-logic explanation of why true statements made in the literal use of analytic sentences are necessarily true. Since the property ensures that the objects of the predication in the use of an analytic sentence are chosen on the basis of the features to be predicated of them, the truth-conditions of the statement are automatically satisfied once its terms take on reference. The difference between such a linguistic source of necessity and the logical and mathematical sources vindicate Locke's distinction between two kinds of 'necessary consequence'.

Received opinion concerning analyticity contains another mistake. This is the idea that analyticity is inimical to science, in part, the idea developed as a reaction to certain dubious uses of analyticity such as Frége's attempt to establish logicism and Schlick's, Ayer's and other logical; positivists attempt to deflate claims to metaphysical knowledge by showing that alleged deductive truths are merely empty analytic truths (Schlick, 1948, and Ayer, 1946). In part, it developed as also a response to a number of cases where alleged analytic, and hence, necessary truths, e.g., the law of excluded a seeming next-to-last subsequent to have been taken as open to revision, such cases convinced philosophers like Quine and Putnam that the analytic/synthetic distinction is an obstacle to scientific progress.

The problem, if there is, one is one is not analyticity in the concept-containment sense, but the conflation of it with analyticity in the logical sense. This made it seem as if there is a single concept of analyticity that can serve as the grounds for a wide range of deductive truths. But, just as there are two analytic/synthetic distinctions, so there are two concepts of concept. The narrow Lockean/Kantian distinction is based on a narrow notion of expressions on which concepts are senses of expressions in the language. The broad Frégean/Carnap distinction is based on a broad notion of concept on which concepts are conceptions -often scientific one about the nature of the referent (s) of expressions (Katz, 1972) and curiously Putman, 1981). Conflation of these two notions of concepts produced the illusion of a single concept with the content of philosophical, logical and mathematical conceptions, but with the status of linguistic concepts. This encouraged philosophers to think that they were in possession of concepts with the contentual representation to express substantive philosophical claims, e.g., such as Frége, Schlick and Ayer's, . . . and so on, and with a status that trivializes the task of justifying them by requiring only linguistic grounds for the deductive propositions in question.

Finally, there is an important epistemological implication of separating the broad and narrowed notions of analyticity. Frége and Carnap took the broad notion of analyticity to provide foundations for necessary and a priority, and, hence, for some form of rationalism, and nearly all rationalistically inclined analytic philosophers that followed them in this, thus, when Quine dispatched the Frége-Carnap position on analyticity, it was widely believed that necessary, as a priority, and rationalism had also been despatched, and, as a consequence. Quine had ushered in an 'empiricism without dogmas' and 'naturalized epistemology'. But given there is still a notion of analyticity that enables 'us' to pose the problem of how necessary, synthetic deductive knowledge is possible (moreover, one whose narrowness makes logical and mathematical knowledge part of the problem), Quine did not undercut the foundations of rationalism. Hence, a serious reappraisal of the new empiricism and naturalized epistemology is, to any the least, is very much in order (Katz, 1990).

In some areas of philosophy and sometimes in things that are less than important we are to find in the deductively/inductive distinction in which has been applied to a wide range of objects, including concepts, propositions, truths and knowledge. Our primary concern will, however, be with the epistemic distinction between deductive and inductive knowledge. The most common way of marking the distinction is by reference to Kant's claim that deductive knowledge is absolutely independent of all experience. It is generally agreed that S's knowledge that 'p' is independent of experience just in case S's belief that 'p' is justified independently of experience. Some authors (Butchvarov, 1970, and Pollock, 1974) are, however, in finding this negative characterization of deductive unsatisfactory knowledge and have opted for providing a positive characterisation in terms of the type of justification on which such knowledge is dependent. Finally, others (Putman, 1983 and Chisholm, 1989) have attempted to mark the distinction by introducing concepts such as necessity and rational unrevisability than in terms of the type of justification relevant to deductive knowledge.

One who characterizes deductive knowledge in terms of justification that is independent of experience is faced with the task of articulating the relevant sense of experience, and proponents of the deductive ly cites 'intuition' or 'intuitive apprehension' as the source of deductive justification. Furthermore, they maintain that these terms refer to a distinctive type of experience that is both common and familiar to most individuals. Hence, there is a broad sense of experience in which deductive justification is dependent of experience. An initially attractive strategy is to suggest that theoretical justification must be independent of sense experience. But this account is too narrow since memory, for example, is not a form of sense experience, but justification based on memory is presumably not deductive. There appear to remain only two options: Provide a general characterization of the relevant sense of experience or enumerates those sources that are experiential. General characterizations of experience often maintain that experience provides information specific to the actual world while non-experiential sources provide information about all possible worlds. This approach, however, reduces the concept of non-experiential justification to the concept of being justified in believing a necessary truth. Accounts by enumeration have two problems (1) there is some controversy about which sources to include in the list, and (2) there is no guarantee that the list is complete.

It is generally agreed that perception and memory should be included. Introspection, however, is problematic, and beliefs about one's conscious states and about the manner in which one is appeared to are plausible regarded as experientially justified. Yet, some, such as Pap (1958), maintain that experiments in imagination are the source of deductive justification. Even if this contention is rejected and deductive justification is characterized as justification independent of the evidence of perception, memory and introspection, it remains possible that there are other sources of justification. If it should be the case that clairvoyance, for example, is a source of justified beliefs, such beliefs would be justified deductively on the enumerative account.

The most common approach to offering a positive characterization of deductive justification is to maintain that in the case of basic deductive propositions, understanding the proposition is sufficient to justify one in believing that it is true. This approach faces two pressing issues. What is it to understand a proposition in the manner that suffices for justification? Proponents of the approach typically distinguish understanding the words used to express a proposition from apprehending the proposition itself and maintain that being relevant to deductive justification is the latter which. But this move simply shifts the problem to that of specifying what it is to apprehend a proposition. Without a solution to this problem, it is difficult, if possible, to evaluate the account since one cannot be sure that the account since on cannot be sure that the requisite sense of apprehension does not justify paradigmatic inductive propositions as well. Even less is said about the manner in which apprehending a proposition justifies one in believing that it is true. Proponents are often content with the bald assertions that one who understands a basic deductive proposition can thereby 'see' that it is true. But what requires explanation is how understanding a proposition enable one to see that it is true.

Difficulties in characterizing deductive justification in a term either of independence from experience or of its source have led, out-of-the-ordinary to present the concept of necessity into their accounts, although this appeal takes various forms. Some have employed it as a necessary condition for deductive justification, others have employed it as a sufficient condition, while still others have employed it as both. In claiming that necessity is a criterion of the deductive. Kant held that necessity is a sufficient condition for deductive justification. This claim, however, needs further clarification. There are three theses regarding the relationship between theoretical and the necessary, which can be distinguished: (I) if 'p' is a necessary proposition and 'S' is justified in believing that 'p' is necessary, then S's justification is deductive: (ii) If 'p' is a necessary proposition and 'S' is justified in believing that 'p' is necessarily true, then S's justification is deductive: And (iii) If 'p' is a necessary proposition and 'S' is justified in believing that 'p', then S's justification is deductive. For example, many proponents of deductive contend that all knowledge of a necessary proposition is deductive. (ii) and (iii) have the shortcoming of setting by stipulation the issue of whether inductive knowledge of necessary propositions is possible. (I) does not have this shortcoming since the recent examples offered in support of this claim by Kriple (1980) and others have been cases where it is alleged that knowledge of the 'truth value' of necessary propositions is knowable inductive. (I) has the shortcoming, however, of either ruling out the possibility of being justified in believing that a proposition is necessary on the basis of testimony or else sanctioning such justification as deductive. (ii) and (iii), of course, suffer from an analogous problem. These problems are symptomatic of a general shortcoming of the approach: It attempts to provide a sufficient condition for deductive justification solely in terms of the modal status of the proposition believed without making reference to the manner in which it is justified. This shortcoming, however, can be avoided by incorporating necessity as a necessary but not sufficient condition for knowable justification as, for example, in Chisholm (1989). Here there are two theses that must be distinguished: (1) If 'S' is justified deductively in believing that 'p', then 'p' is necessarily true. (2) If 'S' is justified deductively in believing that 'p'. Then 'p' is a necessary proposition. (1) and (2), however, allows this possibility. A further problem with both (1) and (2) is that it is not clear whether they permit deductively justified beliefs about the modal status of a proposition. For they require that in order for 'S' to be justified deductively in believing that 'p' is a necessary preposition it must be necessary that 'p' is a necessary proposition. But the status of iterated modal propositions is controversial. Finally, (1) and (2) both preclude by stipulation the position advanced by Kripke (1980) and Kitcher (1980) that there is deductive knowledge of contingent propositions.

The concept of rational unrevisability has also been invoked to characterize deductive justification. The precise sense of rational unrevisability has been presented in different ways. Putnam (1983) takes rational unrevisability to be both a necessary and sufficient condition for deductive justification while Kitcher (1980) takes it to be only a necessary condition. There are also two different senses of rational unrevisability that have been associated with the deductive (I) a proposition is weakly unreviable just in case it is rationally unrevisable in light of any future 'experiential' evidence, and (II) a proposition is strongly unrevisable just in case it is rationally unrevisable in light of any future evidence. Let us consider the plausibility of requiring either form of rational unrevisability as a necessary condition for deductive justification. The view that a proposition is justified deductive only if it is strongly unrevisable entails that if a non-experiential source of justified beliefs is fallible but self-correcting, it is not a deductive source of justification. Casullo (1988) has argued that it vis implausible to maintain that a proposition that is justified non-experientially is 'not' justified deductively merely because it is revisable in light of further non-experiential evidence. The view that a proposition is justified deductively only if it is, weakly unrevisable is not open to this objection since it excludes only recision in light of experiential evidence. It does, however, face a different problem. To maintain that 'S's' justified belief that 'p' is justified deductively is to make a claim about the type of evidence that justifies 'S' in believing that 'p'. On the other hand, to maintain that S's justified belief that 'p' is rationally revisable in light of experiential evidence is to make a claim about the type of evidence that can defeat 'S's' justification for believing that 'p' that a claim about the type of evidence that justifies 'S' in believing that 'p'. Hence, it has been argued by Edidin (1984) and Casullo (1988) that to hold that a belief is justified deductively only if it is weakly unrevisable is either to confuse supporting evidence with defeating evidence or to endorse some implausible this about the relationship between the two such that if evidence of the sort as the kind 'A' can be in defeat, the justification conferred on 'S's' belief that 'p' by evidence of kind 'B' then S's justification for believing that 'p' is based on evidence of kind 'A'.

The most influential idea in the theory of meaning in the past hundred years is the thesis that the meaning of an indicative sentence is given by its truth-conditions. On this conception, to understand a sentence is to know its truth-conditions. The conception was first clearly formulated by Frége, was developed in a distinctive way by the early Wittgenstein, and is a leading idea of Donald Herbert Davidson (1917-), who is also known for rejection of the idea of as conceptual scheme, thought of as something peculiar to one language or one way of looking at the world, arguing that where the possibility of translation stops so dopes the coherence of the idea that there is anything to translate. His [papers are collected in the "Essays on Actions and Events" (1980) and "Inquiries into Truth and Interpretation" (1983). However, the conception has remained so central that those who offer opposing theories characteristically define their position by reference to it.

Wittgenstein's main achievement is a uniform theory of language that yields an explanation of logical truth. A factual sentence achieves sense by dividing the possibilities exhaustively into two groups, those that would make it true and those that would make it false. A truth of logic does not divide the possibilities but comes out true in all of them. It, therefore, lacks sense and says nothing, but it is not nonsense. It is a self-cancellation of sense, necessarily true because it is a tautology, the limiting case of factual discourse, like the figure '0' in mathematics. Language takes many forms and even factual discourse does not consist entirely of sentences like 'The fork is placed to the left of the knife'. However, the first thing that he gave up was the idea that this sentence itself needed further analysis into basic sentences mentioning simple objects with no internal structure. He was to concede, that a descriptive word will often get its meaning partly from its place in a system, and he applied this idea to colour-words, arguing that the essential relations between different colours do not indicate that each colour has an internal structure that needs to be taken apart. On the contrary, analysis of our colour-words would only reveal the same pattern-ranges of incompatible properties-recurring at every level, because that is how we carve up the world.

Indeed, it may even be the case that of our ordinary language is created by moves that we ourselves make. If so, the philosophy of language will lead into the connection between the meaning of a word and the applications of it that its users intend to make. There is also an obvious need for people to understand each other's meanings of their words. There are many links between the philosophy of language and the philosophy of mind and it is not surprising that the impersonal examination of language in the "Tractatus: was replaced by a very different, anthropocentric treatment in "Philosophical Investigations?"

If the logic of our language is created by moves that we ourselves make, various kinds of realisms are threatened. First, the way in which our descriptive language carves up the world will not be forces on 'us' by the natures of things, and the rules for the application of our words, which feel the external constraints, will really come from within 'us'. That is a concession to nominalism that is, perhaps, readily made. The idea that logical and mathematical necessity is also generated by what we ourselves accomplish what is more paradoxical. Yet, that is the conclusion of Wittengenstein (1956) and (1976), and here his anthropocentricism has carried less conviction. However, a paradox is not sure of error and it is possible that what is needed here is a more sophisticated concept of objectivity than Platonism provides.

In his later work Wittgenstein brings the great problem of philosophy down to earth and traces them to very ordinary origins. His examination of the concept of 'following a rule' takes him back to a fundamental question about counting things and sorting them into types: 'What qualifies as doing the same again? Of a courser, this question as an inconsequential fundamental and would suggest that we forget it and get on with the subject. But Wittgenstein's question is not so easily dismissed. It has the naive profundity of questions that children ask when they are first taught a new subject. Such questions remain unanswered without detriment to their learning, but they point the only way to complete understanding of what is learned.

It is, nevertheless, the meaning of a complex expression in a function of the meaning of its constituents, that is, indeed, that it is just a statement of what it is for an expression to be semantically complex. It is one of the initial attractions of the conception of meaning as truths-conditions that it permits a smooth and satisfying account of the way in which the meaning of a complex expression is a dynamic function of the meaning of its constituents. On the truth-conditional conception, to give the meaning of an expression is to state the contribution it makes to the truth-conditions of sentences in which it occurs. for singular terms-proper names, indexical, and certain pronoun's - this is done by stating the reference of the term in question.

The truth condition of a statement is the condition the world must meet if the statement is to be true. To know this condition is equivalent to knowing the meaning of the statement. Although, this sounds as if it gives a solid anchorage for meaning, some of the security disappears when it turns out that the truth condition can only be defined by repeating the very same statement, the truth condition of 'snow is white' is that snow is white, the truth condition of 'Britain would have capitulated had Hitler invaded' is that Britain would halve capitulated had Hitler invaded. It is disputed whether this element of running-on-the-spot disqualifies truth conditions from playing the central role in a substantive theory of meaning. Truth-conditional theories of meaning are sometimes opposed by the view that to know the meaning of a statement is to be able to users it in a network of inferences.

On the truth-conditional conception, to give the meaning of expressions is to state the contributive function it makes to the dynamic function of sentences in which it occurs. For singular terms-proper names, and certain pronouns, as well are indexical-this is done by stating the reference of the term in question. For predicates, it is done either by stating the conditions under which the predicate is true of arbitrary objects, or by stating the conditions under which arbitrary atomic sentence containing it is true. The meaning of a sentence-forming operator is given by stating its distributive contribution to the truth-conditions of a complete sentence, as a function of the semantic values of the sentences on which it operates. For an extremely simple, but nonetheless, it is a structured language, we can state the contributions various expressions make to truth conditions as follows:

A1: The referent of 'London' is London.

A2: The referent of 'Paris' is Paris.

A3: Any sentence of the form 'a is beautiful' is true

if and only if the referent of 'a' is beautiful.

A4: Any sentence of the form 'a is larger than b' is true

if and only if the referent of 'a' is larger than the referent of 'b'.

A5: Any sentence of the form 'It is not the case that

A' is true if and only if it is not the case that 'A' is true.

A6: Any sentence of the form "A and B' are true if and only

is 'A', is true and 'B' is true?

The principle's A2-A6 form a simple theory of truth for a fragment of English. In this theory, it is possible to derive these consequences: That 'Paris is beautiful' is true if and only if Paris is beautiful (from A2 and A3), which 'London is larger than Paris and it is not the cases that London is beautiful' is true if and only if London is larger than Paris and it is not the case that London is beautiful (from A1-As): And in general, for any sentence 'A' of this simple language, we can derive something of the form 'A' is true if and only if A'.

The theorist of truth conditions should insist that not every true statement about the reference of an expression be fit to be an axiom in a meaning-giving theory of truth for a language. The axiom: London' refers to the city in which there was a huge fire in 1666 is a true statement about the reference of 'London?'. It is a consequence of a theory that substitutes this axiom for A! In our simple truth theory that 'London is beautiful' is true if and only if the city in which there was a huge fire in 1666 is beautiful. Since a subject can understand the name 'London' without knowing that last-mentioned truth conditions, this replacement axiom is not fit to be an axiom in a meaning-specifying truth theory. It is, of course, incumbent on a theorist of meaning as truth conditions to state the constraints on the acceptability of axioms in a way that does not presuppose a deductive, non-truth conditional conception of meaning.

Among the many challenges facing the theorist of truth conditions, two are particularly salient and fundamental. First, the theorist has to answer the charge of triviality or vacuity. Second, the theorist must offer an account of what it is for a person's language to be truly descriptive by a semantic theory containing a given semantic axiom.

We can take the charge of triviality first. In more detail, it would run thus: Since the content of a claim that the sentence 'Paris is beautiful' in which is true of the divisional region, which is no more than the claim that Paris is beautiful, we can trivially describe understanding a sentence, if we wish, as knowing its truth-conditions, but this gives 'us' no substantive account of understanding whatsoever. Something other than a grasp to truth conditions must provide the substantive account. The charge rests upon what has been called the redundancy theory of truth, the theory that, is somewhat more discriminative. Horwich calls the minimal theory of truth, or deflationary view of truth, as fathered by Frége and Ramsey. The essential claim is that the predicate' . . . is true' does not have a sense, i.e., expresses no substantive or profound or explanatory concepts that ought be the topic of philosophical enquiry. The approach admits of different versions, but centres on the points (1) that 'it is true that p' says no more nor less than 'p' (hence redundancy) (2) that in less direct context, such as 'everything he said was true', or 'all logical consequences of true propositions are true', the predicate functions as a device enabling 'us'; The generalization inhabiting an adjective or predicate describing a circumstance from which of an episodic occurrence accomplishes an act or deed by which of whatever is apprehended as having actual, distinct, and demonstrable existence can be known as having existence in space or time, as by virtue a thing, is not a thing but and attribute of a thing. The accommodating of propositions, that follow from true propositions are, for example, the second may translate as ' $(\forall p, q)\ (p \ \&\ p \rightarrow q \rightarrow q)$ ' where there is no use of a notion of truth.

There are technical problems in interpreting all uses of the notion of truth in such ways, but they are not generally felt to be insurmountable. The approach needs to explain away apparently substantive uses of the notion, such a; science aims at the truth', or 'truth is a norm governing discourse'. Indeed, postmodernist writing frequently advocates that we must abandon such norms, along with a discredited 'objective' conception of truth. But perhaps, we can have the norms even when objectivity is problematic, since they can be framed without mention of truth: Science wants it to be so that whenever science holds that 'p'. Then 'p'. Discourse is to be regulated by the principle that it is wrong to assert 'p' when 'not-p'.

The disquotational theory of truth finds that the simplest formulation is the claim that expressions of the fern 'S is true' mean the same as expressions of the form 'S'. Some philosophers dislike the idea of sameness of meaning, and if this is disallowed, then the claim is that the two forms are equivalent in any sense of equivalence that matters. That is, it makes no difference whether people say 'Dogs bark' is true, or whether they say that 'dogs bark'. In the former representation of what they say the sentence 'Dogs bark' is mentioned, but in the latter it appears to be used, so the claim that the two are equivalent needs careful formulation and defence. On the face of it someone might know that 'Dogs bark' is true without knowing what it means, for instance, if one were to find it in a list of acknowledged truths, although he does not understand English, and this is different from knowing that dogs bark. Disquotational theories are usually presented as versions of the redundancy theory of truth.

The minimal theory states that the concept of truth is exhausted by the fact that it conforms to the equivalence principle, the principle that for any proposition 'p', it is true that 'p' if and only if 'p'. Many different philosophical theories of truth will, with suitable qualifications, accept that equivalence principle. The distinguishing feature of the minimal theory is its claim that the equivalence principle exhausts the notion of truths. It is how widely accepted, that both by opponents and supporters of truth conditional theories of meaning, that it is inconsistent to accept both minimal theory of truth and a truth conditional account of meaning (Davidson, 1990, Dummett, 1959 and Horwich, 1990). If the claim that the sentence 'Paris is beautiful' is true is exhausted by its equivalence to the claim that Paris is beautiful, it is circular to try to explain the sentence's meaning in terms of its truth conditions. The minimal theory of truth has been endorsed by Ramsey, Ayer, the later Wittgenstein, Quine, Strawson, Horwich and-confusingly and inconsistently if be it correct. ~ Frége himself. But is the minimal theory correct?

The minimal or redundancy theory treats instances of the equivalence principle as definitional of truth for a given sentence. But in fact, it seems that each instance of the equivalence principle can itself be explained. The truths from which such an instance as.

London is beautiful' is true if and only if London is beautiful

Preserve a right to be interpreted specifically of A1 and A3 above? This would be a pseudo-explanation if the fact that 'London' refers to 'London is beautiful' has the truth-condition it does. But that is very implausible: It is, after all, possible to understand in the name 'London' without understanding the predicate 'is beautiful'. The idea that facts about the reference of particular words can be explanatory of facts about the truth conditions of sentences containing them in no way requires any naturalistic or any other kind of reduction of the notion of reference. Nor is the idea incompatible with the plausible point that singular reference can be attributed at all only to something that is capable of combining with other expressions to form complete sentences. That still leaves room for facts about an expression's having the particular reference it does to be partially explanatory of the particular truth condition possessed by a given sentence containing it. The minimal; Theory thus treats as definitional or stimulative something that is in fact open to explanation. What makes this explanation possible is that there is a general notion of truth that has, among the many links that hold it in place, systematic connections with the semantic values of sub-sentential expressions.

A second problem with the minimal theory is that it seems impossible to formulate it without at some point relying implicitly on features and principles involving truths that go beyond anything countenanced by the minimal theory. If the minimal theory treats truth as a predicate of anything linguistic, be it utterances, type-in-a-language, or whatever, then the equivalence schema will not cover all cases, but only of those in the theorist's own language. Some account has to be given of truth for sentences of other languages. Speaking of the truth of language-independence propositions or thoughts will only postpone, not avoid, this issue, since at some point principles have to be stated associating these language-independent entities with sentences of particular languages. The defender of the minimalist theory is likely to say that if a sentence 'S' of a foreign language is best translated by our sentence 'p', then the foreign sentence 'S' is true if and only if 'p'. Now the best translation of a sentence must preserve the concepts expressed in the sentence. Constraints involving a general notion of truth are persuasive in a plausible philosophical theory of concepts. It is, for example, a condition of adequacy on an individualized account of any concept that there exists what is called 'Determination Theory' for that account-that is, a specification of how the account contributes to fixing the semantic value of that concept, the notion of a concept's semantic value is the notion of something that makes a certain contribution to the truth conditions of thoughts in which the concept occurs. but this is to presuppose, than to elucidate, a general notion of truth.

It is also plausible that there are general constraints on the form of such Determination Theories, constraints that involve truth and which are not derivable from the minimalist's conception. Suppose that concepts are individuated by their possession conditions. A concept is something that is capable of being a constituent of such contentual representational in a way of thinking of something-a particular object, or property, or relation, or another entity. A possession condition may in various says makes a thanker's possession of a particular concept dependent upon his relations to his environment. Many possession conditions will mention the links between a concept and the thinker's perceptual experience. Perceptual experience represents the world for being a certain way. It is arguable that the only satisfactory explanation of what it is for perceptual experience to represent the world in a particular way must refer to the complex relations of the experience to the subject's environment. If this is so, then mention of such experiences in a possession condition will make possession of that condition will make possession of that concept dependent in part upon the environment relations of the thinker. Burge (1979) has also argued from intuitions about particular examples that, even though the thinker's non-environmental properties and relations remain constant, the conceptual content of his mental state can vary if the thinker's social environment is varied. A possession condition which property individuates such a concept must take into account the thinker's social relations, in particular his linguistic relations.

One such plausible general constraint is then the requirement that when a thinker forms beliefs involving a concept in accordance with its possession condition, a semantic value is assigned to the concept in such a way that the belief is true. Some general principles involving truth can indeed, as Horwich has emphasized, be derived from the equivalence schema using minimal logical apparatus. Consider, for instance, the principle that 'Paris is beautiful and London is beautiful' is true if and only if 'Paris is beautiful' is true if and only if 'Paris is beautiful' is true and 'London is beautiful' is true. This follows logically from the three instances of the equivalence principle: 'Paris is beautiful and London is beautiful' is rue if and only if Paris is beautiful, and 'London is beautiful' is true if and only if London is beautiful. But no logical manipulations of the equivalence schemas will allow the deprivation of that general constraint governing possession conditions, truth and the assignment of semantic values. That constraint can have courses be regarded as a further elaboration of the idea that truth is one of the aims of judgement.

We now turn to the other question, 'What is it for a person's language to be correctly describable by a semantic theory containing a particular axiom, such as the axiom A6 above for conjunction?' This question may be addressed at two depths of generality. At the shallower level, the question may take for granted the person's possession of the concept of conjunction, and be concerned with what has to be true for the axiom correctly to describe his language. At a deeper level, an answer should not duck the issue of what it is to possess the concept. The answers to both questions are of great interest: We will take the lesser level of generality first.

When a person means conjunction by 'sand', he is not necessarily capable of formulating the axiom A6 explicitly. Even if he can formulate it, his ability to formulate it is not the causal basis of his capacity to hear sentences containing the word 'and' as meaning something involving conjunction. Nor is it the causal basis of his capacity to mean something involving conjunction by sentences he utters containing the word 'and'. Is it then right to regard a truth theory as part of an unconscious psychological computation, and to regard understanding a sentence as involving a particular way of depriving a theorem from a truth theory at some level of conscious proceedings? One problem with this is that it is quite implausible that everyone who speaks the same language has to use the same algorithms for computing the meaning of a sentence. In the past thirteen years, thanks particularly to the work of Davies and Evans, a conception has evolved according to which an axiom like A6 is true of a person's language only if there is a common component in the explanation of his understanding of each sentence containing the word 'and', a common component that explains why each such sentence is understood as meaning something involving conjunction (Davies, 1987). This conception can also be elaborated in computational terms: Suggesting that for an axiom like A6 to be true of a person's language is for the unconscious mechanisms which produce understanding to draw on the information that a sentence of the form 'A and B' are true if and only if 'A' is true and 'B' is true (Peacocke, 1986). Many different algorithms may equally draw n this information. The psychological reality of a semantic theory thus involves, in Marr's (1982) famous classification, something intermediate between his level one, the function computed, and his level two, the algorithm by which it is computed. This conception of the psychological reality of a semantic theory can also be applied to syntactic and phonol logical theories. Theories in semantics, syntax and phonology are not themselves required to specify the particular algorithms that the language user employs. The identification of the particular computational methods employed is a task for psychology. But semantics, syntactic and phonology theories are answerable to psychological data, and are potentially refutable by them-for these linguistic theories do make commitments to the information drawn upon by mechanisms in the language user.

This answer to the question of what it is for an axiom to be true of a person's language clearly takes for granted the person's possession of the concept expressed by the word treated by the axiom. In the example of the axiom A6, the information drawn upon is that sentences of the form 'A and B' are true if and only if 'A' is true and 'B' is true. This informational content employs, as it has to if it is to be adequate, the concept of conjunction used in stating the meaning of sentences containing 'and'. So the computational answer we have returned needs further elaboration if we are to address the deeper question, which does not want to take for granted possession of the concepts expressed in the language. It is at this point that the theory of linguistic understanding has to draws upon a theory of concepts. It is plausible that the concepts of conjunction are individuated by the following condition for a thinker to possess it.

Finally, this response to the deeper question allows 'us' to answer two challenges to the conception of meaning as truth-conditions. First, there was the question left hanging earlier, of how the theorist of truth-conditions is to say what makes one axiom of a semantic theory is correctly in that of another, when the two axioms assign the same semantic values, but do so by means of different concepts. Since the different concepts will have different possession conditions, the dovetailing accounts, at the deeper level of what it is for each axiom to be correct for a person's language will be different accounts. Second, there is a challenge repeatedly made by the minimalist theorists of truth, to the effect that the theorist of meaning as truth-conditions should give some non-circular account of what it is to understand a sentence, or to be capable of understanding all sentences containing a given constituent. For each expression in a sentence, the corresponding dovetailing account, together with the possession condition, supplies a non-circular account of what it is to understand any sentence containing that expression. The combined accounts for each of he expressions that comprise a given sentence together constitute a non-circular account of what it is to understand the compete sentences. Taken together, they allow the theorists of meaning as truth-conditions fully to meet the challenge.

A curious view common to that which is expressed by an utterance or sentence: The proposition or claim made about the world. By extension, the content of a predicate or other sub-sentential component is what it contributes to the content of sentences that contain it. The nature of content is the central concern of the philosophy of language, in that mental states have contents: A belief may have the content that the prime minister will resign. A concept is something that is capable of bringing a constituent of such contents. More specifically, a concept is a way of thinking of something-a particular object, or property or relation, or another entity. Such a distinction was held in Frége's philosophy of language, explored in "On Concept and Object" (1892). Frége regarded predicates as incomplete expressions, in the same way as a mathematical expression for a function, such as sines . . . a log . . ., is incomplete. Predicates refer to concepts, which themselves are 'unsaturated', and cannot be referred to by subject expressions (we thus get the paradox that the concept of a horse is not a concept). Although Frége recognized the metaphorical nature of the notion of a concept being unsaturated, he was rightly convinced that some such notion is needed to explain the unity of a sentence, and to prevent sentences from being thought of as mere lists of names.

Several different concepts may each be ways of thinking of the same object. A person may think of himself in the first-person way, or think of himself as the spouse of Mary Smith, or as the person located in a certain room now. More generally, a concept 'C' is distinct from a concept 'd' if it is possible for a person rationally to believe 'd is such-and-such'. As words can be combined to form structured sentences, concepts have also been conceived as combinable into structured complex contents. When these complex contents are expressed in English by 'that . . . 'clauses, as in our opening examples, they will be capable of being true or false, depending on the way the world is.

The general system of concepts with which we organize our thoughts and perceptions are to encourage a conceptual scheme of which the outstanding elements of our every day conceptual formalities include spatial and temporal relations between events and enduring objects, causal relations, other persons, meaning-bearing utterances of others, . . . and so on. To see the world as containing such things is to share this much of our conceptual scheme. A controversial argument of Davidson's urges that we would be unable to interpret speech from a different conceptual scheme as even meaningful, Davidson daringly goes on to argue that since translation proceeds according ti a principle of clarity, and since it must be possible of an omniscient translator to make sense of, 'us' we can be assured that most of the beliefs formed within the commonsense conceptual framework are true.

Concepts are to be distinguished from a stereotype and from conceptions. The stereotypical spy may be a middle-level official down on his luck and in need of money. None the less, we can come to learn that Anthony Blunt, art historian and Surveyor of the Queen's

Pictures, are a spy; we can come to believe that something falls under a concept while positively disbelieving that the same thing falls under the stereotype associated wit the concept. Similarly, a person's conception of a just arrangement for resolving disputes may involve something like contemporary Western legal systems. But whether or not it would be correct, it is quite intelligible for someone to rejects this conception by arguing that it dies not adequately provide for the elements of fairness and respect that are required by the concepts of justice.

Basically, a concept is that which is understood by a term, particularly a predicate. To posses a concept is to be able to deploy a term expressing it in making judgements, in which the ability connection is such things as recognizing when the term applies, and being able to understand the consequences of its application. The term 'idea' was formally used in the came way, but is avoided because of its associations with subjective matters inferred upon mental imagery in which may be irrelevant ti the possession of a concept. In the semantics of Frége, a concept is the reference of a predicate, and cannot be referred to by a subjective term, although its recognition of as a concept, in that some such notion is needed to the explanatory justification of which that sentence of unity finds of itself from being thought of as namely categorized lists of itemized priorities.

A theory of a particular concept must be distinguished from a theory of the object or objects it selectively picks out. The theory of the concept is part if the theory of thought and epistemology. A theory of the object or objects is part of metaphysics and ontology. Some figures in the history of philosophy-and are open to the accusation of not having fully respected the distinction between the kinds of theory. Descartes appears to have moved from facts about the indubitability of the thought 'I think', containing the fist-person was of thinking, to conclusions about the nonmaterial nature of the object he himself was. But though the goals of a theory of concepts and a theory of objects are distinct, each theory is required to have an adequate account of its relation to the other theory. A theory if concept is unacceptable if it gives no account of how the concept is capable of picking out the object it evidently does pick out. A theory of objects is unacceptable if it makes it impossible to understand how we could have concepts of those objects.

A fundamental question for philosophy is: What individuates a given concept-that is, what makes it the one it is, rather than any other concept? One answer, which has been developed in great detail, is that it is impossible to give a non-trivial answer to this question (Schiffer, 1987). An alternative approach, addressees the question by starting from the idea that a concept id individuated by the condition that must be satisfied if a thinker is to posses that concept and to be capable of having beliefs and other attitudes whose content contains it as a constituent. So, to take a simple case, one could propose that the logical concept 'and' is individuated by this condition, it be the unique concept 'C' to posses that a thinker has to find these forms of inference compelling, without and 'B', ACB can be inferred, and from any premiss ACB, each of the 'A' and the 'B' can be inferred. Again, a relatively observational concept such as 'round' can be individuated in part by stating that the thinker finds specified contents containing it compelling when he has certain kinds of perception, and in part by relating those judgements containing the concept and which are not based on perception to those judgements that are. A statement that individuates a concept by saying what is required for a thinker to posses it can be described as giving the possession condition for the concept.

A possession condition for a particular concept may actually make use of that concept. The possession condition for 'and' does so. We can also expect to use relatively observational concepts in specifying the kind of experience that have to be mentioned in the possession conditions for relatively observational concepts. What we must avoid is mention of the concept in question as such within the content of the attitudes attributed to the thinker in the possession condition. Otherwise we would be presupposing possession of the concept in an account that was meant to elucidate its possession. In talking of what the thinker finds compelling, the possession conditions can also respect an insight of the later Wittgenstein: That to find her finds it natural to go on in new cases in applying the concept.

Sometimes a family of concepts has this property: It is not possible to master any one of the members of the family without mastering the others. Two of the families that plausibly have this status are these: The family consisting of some simple concepts 0, 1, 2, . . . of the natural numbers and the corresponding concepts of numerical quantifiers there are 0 so-and-so, there is 1 so-and-so, . . . and the family consisting of the concepts of 'belief' and 'desire'. Such that, to believe, a proposition is to hold it to be true. The philosophical problem is to understand what kind of state of a person constitutes belief. Is it, for example, a simple disposition to behaviour? Or a more complex state that resists identification with any such disposition is verbal skill or verbal behaviour essential to belief, in which case what is to be said about prelinguistic infants, or nonlinguistic animals an evolutionary approach asks how the cognitive success of possessing the capacity to believe things relates to success in particle. Further topics include discovering whether belief differs from other varieties of assent, such as acceptance`, discovering whether belief is an all-or-nothing matter, or to what extent degrees of belief are possible, understanding the ways in which belief is controlled by rational and irrational factors, and discovering its links with other properties, such as the possession of conceptual or linguistic skills.

Not to forget, that desire is the standard model of human motivation, sometimes called the Humean theory of motivation, is that it takes a desire and a belief. Belief by itself will not suffice, unless the objects of belief interact with the agents desires. They must be things toward which there is some attraction or aversion. Some say that if desires are thought of as conscious states of mind, this is untrue. On the other hand, if they are thought of as no more than interpretations certified by the agents behaviour, then perhaps, the model is trivial. But `functionalism` rescues the Humean theory, seeing `desire` as a respectable theoretical category, identified by its role in systematizing the explanation of agents. Salient questions include whether we always do what we desire to do, whether we can control our strongest desires, and how motivation by desire compares with motivation by principle. Major philosophies of life. Including, `Buddhism` and `Stoicism` which have presented them for overcoming of desire as an ideal.

Such families have come to be known as 'local holism'. A local holism does not prevent the individuation of a concept by its possession condition. Rather, it demands that all the concepts in the family be individuated simultaneously. So one would say something of this form: Belief and desire form the unique pair of concepts C1 and C2 such that for as thinker to posses them are to meet such-and-such condition involving the thinker, C1 and C2. For these and other possession conditions to individuate properly, it is necessary that there be some ranking of the concepts treated. The possession conditions for concepts higher in the ranking must presuppose only possession of concepts at the same or lower levels in the ranking.

A possession conditions may in various way's make a thinker's possession of a particular concept dependent upon his relations to his environment. Many possession conditions will mention the links between a concept and the thinker's perceptual experience. Perceptual experience represents the world as a certain way. It is arguable that the only satisfactory explanation of what it is for perceptual experience to represent the world in a particular way must refer to the complex relations of the experience to the subject's environment. If this is so, then mention of such experiences in a possession condition will make possession of that concept dependent in part upon the environmental relations of the thinker. Burge (1979) has also argued from intuitions about particular examples that, even though the thinker's non-environmental properties and relations remain constant, the conceptual content of his mental state can vary if the thinker's social environment is varied. A possession condition that properly individuates such a concept must take into account the thinker's social relations, in particular his linguistic relations.

Concepts have a normative dimension, a fact strongly emphasized by Kripke. For any judgement whose content involves a given concept, there is a correctness condition for that judgement, a condition that is dependent in part upon the identity of the concept. The normative character of concepts also extends into making the territory of a thinker's reasons for making judgements. A thinker's visual perception can give him good reason for judging 'That man is bald': It does not by itself give him good reason for judging 'Rostropovich is bald', even if the man he sees is Rostropovich. All these normative connections must be explained by a theory of concepts one approach to these matters is to look to the possession condition for the concept, and consider how the referent of a concept is fixed from it, together with the world. One proposal is that the referent of the concept is that object (or property, or function, . . .) which makes the practices of judgement and inference mentioned which always lead to true judgements and truth-preserving inferences. This proposal would explain why certain reasons are necessity good reasons for judging given contents. Provided the possession condition permits 'us' to express in words what it is about a thinker's previous judgements that masker if the case that he is employing one concept rather than another, this proposal would also have another virtue. It would allow 'us' to say how the correctness condition is determined for a judgement in which the concept is applied to newly encountered objects. The judgement is correct if the new object has the property that in fact makes the judgmental practices mentioned in the possession condition yield true judgements, or truth-preserving inferences.

These manifesting dissimilations have occasioned the affiliated differences accorded within the distinction as associated with Leibniz, who declares that there are only two kinds of truths-truths of reason and truths of fact. The forms are all either explicit identities, i.e., of the form 'A is A', 'AB is B', etc., or they are reducible to this form by successively substituting equivalent terms. Leibniz dubs them 'truths of reason' because the explicit identities are self-evident deducible truths, whereas the rest can be converted to such by purely rational operations. Because their denial involves a demonstrable contradiction, Leibniz also says that truths of reason 'rest on the principle of contradiction, or identity' and that they are necessary [propositions, which are true of all possible words. Some examples are 'All equilateral rectangles are rectangles' and 'All bachelors are unmarried': The first is already of the form AB is B' and the latter can be reduced to this form by substituting 'unmarried man' fort 'bachelor'. Other examples, or so Leibniz believes, are 'God exists' and the truths of logic, arithmetic and geometry.

Truths of fact, on the other hand, cannot be reduced to an identity and our only way of knowing them is empirically by reference to the facts of the empirical world. Likewise, since their denial does not involve a contradiction, their truth is merely contingent: They could have been otherwise and hold of the actual world, but not of every possible one. Some examples are 'Caesar crossed the Rubicon' and 'Leibniz was born in Leipzig', as well as propositions expressing correct scientific generalizations. In Leibniz's view, truths of fact rest on the principle of sufficient reason, which states that nothing can be so unless there is a reason that it is so. This reason is that the actual world (by which he means the total collection of things past, present and future) is better than any other possible worlds and was therefore created by 'God'.

In defending the principle of sufficient reason, Leibniz runs into serious problems. He believes that in every true proposition, the concept of the predicate is contained in that of the subject. (This holds even for propositions like 'Caesar crossed the Rubicon': Leibniz thinks anyone who dids not cross the Rubicon, would not have been Caesar). And this containment relationship! Which is eternal and unalterable even by God ~?! Guarantees that every truth has a sufficient reason. If truths consists in concept containment, however, then it seems that all truths are analytic and hence necessary, and if they are all necessary, surely they are all truths of reason. Leibnitz responds that not every truth can be reduced to an identity in a finite number of steps, in some instances revealing the connection between subject and predicate concepts would requite an infinite analysis. But while this may entail that we cannot prove such propositions as deductively manifested, it does not appear to show that the proposition could have been false. Intuitively, it seems a better ground for supposing that it is necessary truth of a special sort. A related question arises from the idea that truths of fact depend on God's decision to create he best of all possible worlds: If it is part of the concept of this world that it is best, now could its existence be other than necessary? Leibniz answers that its existence is only hypothetically necessary, i.e., it follows from God's decision to create this world, but God had the power to decide otherwise. Yet God is necessarily good and non-deceiving, so how could he have decided to do anything else? Leibniz says much more about these masters, but it is not clear whether he offers any satisfactory solutions.

Finally, Kripke (1972) and Plantinga (1974) argues that some contingent truths are knowable by deductive reasoning. Similar problems face the suggestion that necessary truths are the ones we know with the fairest of certainties: We lack a criterion for certainty, there are necessary truths we do not know, and (barring dubious arguments for scepticism) it is reasonable to suppose that we know some contingent truths with certainty.

Issues surrounding certainty are inexorably connected with those concerning scepticism. For many sceptics have traditionally held that knowledge requires certainty, and, of course, the claim that certain knowledge is not possible. in part, in order to avoid scepticism, the anti-sceptics have generally held that knowledge does not require certainty (Lehrer, 1974: Dewey, 1960). A few ant-sceptics, that knowledge does require certain but, against the sceptic that certainty is possible. The task is to provide a characterization of certainty which would be acceptable to both sceptic and anti-sceptics. For such an agreement is a pre-condition of an interesting debate between them.

It seems clear that certainty is a property that an be ascribed to either a person or belief. We can say that a person, 'S', is certain-belief. We can say that a person 'S', is certain, or we can say that a proposition 'p', is certain, or we can be connected=by saying that 'the two use can be connected by saying that 'S' has the right to be certain just in case 'p is sufficiently warranted (Ayer, 1956). Following this lead, most philosophers who have taken the second sense, the sense in which a proposition is said to be certain, as the important one to be investigated by epistemology, an exception is Unger who defends scepticism by arguing that psychological certainty is not possible (Ungr, 1975).

In defining certainty, is crucial to note that the term has both an absolute and relative sense, very roughly, one can say that a proposition is absolutely certain just in case there is no proposition more warranted than there is no proposition more warranted that it (Chisholm, 1977), But we also commonly say that one proposition is more certain than say that one proposition is more certain than another, implying that the second one, though less certain, is still certain.

Now some philosophers, have argued that the absolute sense is the only sense, and that the relative sense is only apparent. Even if those arguments are convincing, what remains clear is that here is an absolute sense and it is that some sense which is crucial to the issues surrounding scepticism,

Let us suppose that the interesting question is this. What makes a belief or proposition absolutely certain?

There are several ways of approaching an answer to that question, some like Russell, will take a belief to be certain just in case there is no logical possibility that our belief is false (Russell, 1922). On this definition proposition about physical objects (objects occupying space) cannot be certain, however, that characterization of certainty should be rejected precisely because it makes the question of the existence of absolute certain empirical propositions uninteresting. For it concedes to the sceptic the impassivity of certainty bout physical objects too easily, thus, this approach would not be acceptable to the anti-sceptics.

Other philosophers have suggested that the role has a belief that performs a particular action through which of its set of actual beliefs makes a belief certain, for example, Wittgenstein has suggested that a belief is certain just in case it can be appealed to in order to justify other beliefs, as other beliefs however, promote without some needs of justification itself but appealed to in order to justify other beliefs but stands in no need of justification itself. Thus, the question of the existence of beliefs has been certain can be answered by merely inspecting our practices to determine that there are beliefs which play the specific role. This approach would not be acceptable to the sceptics. For it, too, makes the question of the existence of absolutely certain belief uninteresting. The issue is not whether there are beliefs which play such a role, but whether the are any beliefs which should play that role. Perhaps our practices cannot be defended.

Off the cuff, he characterization of absolute certainty given that a belief 'p', is certain just in case there is no belief which is more warranted than 'p'. Although it does delineate a necessary condition of absolute certainty an is preferable to the Wittgenstein approach, as it does not capture the full sense of 'absolute certainty'. The sceptic would argue that it is not strong enough. For, according to this rough characterization, a belief could be absolutely certain and yet there could be good grounds for doubting-just as long as there were equally good ground for doubting every proposition that was equally warranted, in addition, to say that a belief is certain is to say, in part, that we have a guarantee of its truth, there is no such guarantee provided by this rough characterisation.

A Cartesian characterization certainty seem more promising. Roughly, this approach is that a proposition 'p', is certain for 'S' just in case 'S' is warranted in believing that 'p' an there ae absolutely no grounds whatsoever or doubting it. Now one, could characterize those grounds in a variety of ways, for example, a ground 'g' for making 'p' doubtful for 'S' could be such that (a) 'S' is not warranted in denying 'g' and:

> (B1) If 'g' is added to 'S's' beliefs, the negation of 'p' is warranted: Or.
> (B2) If 'g' is added to 'S's' beliefs, 'p' is no longer warranted: Or,
> (B3) If 'g' is added to 'S's' beliefs, 'p' becomes less warranted (even if only slightly so.)

Although there is a guarantee of sorts of 'p's' truth contained in (B1) and (B2), those notions of grounds for doubt do not seem to capture a basic feature in absolute certainty delineated in the rough account given as such, that for a proposition 'p', could be immune to grounds for doubt 'g' in those two senses and yet another preposition would be more certain, if there were no grounds for doubt like those specified in (B3), so, only (B3) can succeed on providing part of the required guarantee of p's truth.

An account like that contained in (b3) can provide only part of the guarantee because it is only a subjective guarantee of 'p's' truth, 'S's; belief system would contain adequate grounds for assuring 'S' and 'p' is true because 'S's' belief system would warrant the denial of ever preposition that would lower the warrant of 'p'. But 'S's' belief system might contain false beliefs and still be immune to doubt in this sense. Indeed, 'p' itself could be certain and false in this subjective sense.

An objective guarantee is needed as well. We can capture such objective immunity to doubt by requiring roughly that there be no true proposition such that if it is added to 'S's' beliefs, the result is reduction in the warrant for 'p' (even if only slightly). That is, there will be true propositions which if added to 'S's' beliefs result in lowering the warrant of 'p' because the y render evident some false proposition which actually reduces the warrant of 'p'. It is debatable whether leading defeaters provide genius grounds for doubt. Thus, we can sa that a belief that 'p' is absolutely certain just in case it is subjectively and objectively immune to doubt. In other words a proposition 'p' is absolutely certain for 'S' if and only if (1) 'p' is warranted for 'S' and (2) 'S' is warranted in denying every proposition 'g, such that if 'g' is added to 'S's' beliefs, the warrant for 'p' is reduced and (3) there is no true preposition, 'd', sh that if 'd' is added to 'S's' beliefs the warrant for 'p' is reduced.

This is an amount of absolute certainty which captures what is demanded by the sceptic, it is indubitable and guarantee both objectively and objectively to be true. In addition, such a characterization of certainty does not automatically lead to scepticism. Thus, this is an account of certainty that satisfies the task at hand, namely to find an account of certainty that provides the precondition for dialogue, and, of course, alongside with a complete set for its dialectic awareness, if only between the sceptic and anti-sceptic.

Leibniz defined a necessary truth as one whose opposite implies a contradiction. Every such proposition, he held, is either an explicit identity, i.e., of the form 'A is A', 'AB is B', etc. or is reducible to an identity by successively substituting equivalent terms. (thus, 3 above might be so reduced by substituting 'unmarried man'; for 'bachelor'.) This has several advantages over the ideas of the previous paragraph. First, it explicated the notion of necessity and possibility and seems to provide a criterion we can apply. Second, because explicit identities are self-evident a deductive propositions, the theory implies that all necessary truths are knowable deductively, but it does not entail that wee actually know all of them, nor does it define 'knowable' in a circular way. Third, it implies that necessary truths are knowable with certainty, but does not preclude our having certain knowledge of contingent truths by means other than a reduction.

Leibniz and others have thought of truths as a property of propositions, where the latter are conceived as things that may be expressed by, but are distinct from, linguistic items like statements. On another approach, truth is a property of linguistic entities, and the basis of necessary truth in convention. Thus A.J. Ayer, for example, argued that the only necessary truths are analytic statements and that the latter rest entirely on our commitment to use words in certain ways.

The slogan 'the meaning of a statement is its method of verification' expresses the empirical verification's theory of meaning. It is more than the general criterion of meaningfulness if and only if it is empirically verifiable. If says in addition what the meaning of a sentence is: All those observations would confirm or disconfirm the sentence. Sentences that would be verified or falsified by all the same observations are empirically equivalent or have the same meaning. A sentence is said to be cognitively meaningful if and only if it can be verified or falsified in experience. This is not meant to require that the sentence be conclusively verified or falsified, since universal scientific laws or hypotheses (which are supposed to pass the test) are not logically deducible from any amount of actually observed evidence.

When one predicate's necessary truth of a preposition one speaks of modality dedicto. For one ascribes the modal property, necessary truth, to a dictum, namely, whatever proposition is taken as necessary. A venerable tradition, however, distinguishes this from necessary de re, wherein one predicates necessary or essential possession of some property to an on object. For example, the statement '4 is necessarily greater than 2' might be used to predicate of the object, 4, the property, being necessarily greater than 2. That objects have some of their properties necessarily, or essentially, and others only contingently, or accidentally, are a main part of the doctrine called, essentialism'. Thus, an essentialist might say that Socrates had the property of being bald accidentally, but that of being self-identical, or perhaps of being human, essentially. Although essentialism has been vigorously attacked in recent years, most particularly by Quine, it also has able contemporary proponents, such as Plantinga.

Modal necessity as seen by many philosophers whom have traditionally held that every proposition has a modal status as well as a truth value. Every proposition is either necessary or contingent as well as either true or false. The issue of knowledge of the modal status of propositions has received much attention because of its intimate relationship to the issue of deductive reasoning. For example, no propositions of the theoretic content that all knowledge of necessary propositions is deductively knowledgeable. Others reject this claim by citing Kripke's (1980) alleged cases of necessary theoretical propositions. Such contentions are often inconclusive, for they fail to take into account the following tripartite distinction: 'S' knows the general modal status of 'p' just in case 'S' knows that 'p' is a necessary proposition or 'S' knows the truth that 'p' is a contingent proposition. 'S' knows the truth value of 'p' just in case 'S' knows that 'p' is true or 'S' knows that 'p' is false. 'S' knows the specific modal status of 'p' just in case 'S' knows that 'p' is necessarily true or 'S' knows that 'p' is necessarily false or 'S' knows that 'p' is contingently true or 'S' knows that 'p' is contingently false. It does not follow from the fact that knowledge of the general modal status of a proposition is a deductively reasoned distinctive modal status is also given to theoretical principles. Nor des it follow from the fact that knowledge of a specific modal status of a proposition is theoretically given as to the knowledge of its general modal status that also is deductive.

The certainties involving reason and a truth of fact are much in distinction by associative measures given through Leibniz, who declares that there are only two kinds of truths-truths of reason and truths of fact. The former are all either explicit identities, i.e., of the form 'A is A', 'AB is B', etc., or they are reducible to this form by successively substituting equivalent terms. Leibniz dubs them 'truths of reason' because the explicit identities are self-evident theoretical truth, whereas the rest can be converted to such by purely rational operations. Because their denial involves a demonstrable contradiction, Leibniz also says that truths of reason 'rest on the principle of contraction, or identity' and that they are necessary propositions, which are true of all possible worlds. Some examples are that All bachelors are unmarried': The first is already of the form 'AB is B' and the latter can be reduced to this form by substituting 'unmarried man' for 'bachelor'. Other examples, or so Leibniz believes, are 'God exists' and the truth of logic, arithmetic and geometry.

Truths of fact, on the other hand, cannot be reduced to an identity and our only way of knowing hem os a theoretical manifestations, or by reference to the fact of the empirical world. Likewise, since their denial does not involve as contradiction, their truth is merely contingent: They could have been otherwise and hold of the actual world, but not of every possible one. Some examples are 'Caesar crossed the Rubicon' and 'Leibniz was born in Leipzig', as well as propositions expressing correct scientific generalizations. In Leibniz's view, truths of fact rest on the principle of sufficient reason, which states that nothing can be so unless thee is a reason that it is so. This reason is that the actual world (by which he means the total collection of things past, present and future) is better than any other possible world and was therefore created by God.

In defending the principle of sufficient reason, Leibniz runs into serious problems. He believes that in every true proposition, the concept of the predicate is contained in that of the subject. (This hols even for propositions like 'Caesar crossed the Rubicon': Leibniz thinks anyone who did not cross the Rubicon would not have been Caesar) And this containment relationship-that is eternal and unalterable even by God-guarantees that every truth has a sufficient reason. If truth consists in concept containment, however, then it seems that all truths are analytic and hence necessary, and if they are all necessary, surely they are all truths of reason. Leibniz responds that not evert truth can be reduced to an identity in a finite number of steps: In some instances revealing the connection between subject and predicate concepts would require an infinite analysis. But while this may entail that we cannot prove such propositions as deductively probable, it does not appear to show that the proposition could have been false. Intuitively, it seems a better ground for supposing that it is a necessary truth of a special sort. A related question arises from the idea that truths of fact depend on God's decision to create the best world, if it is part of the concept of this world that it is best, how could its existence be other than necessary? Leibniz answers that its existence is only hypothetically necessary, i.e., it follows from God's decision to create this world, but God is necessarily good, so how could he have decided to do anything else? Leibniz says much more about the matters, but it is not clear whether he offers any satisfactory solutions.

The modality of a proposition is the way in which it is true or false. The most important division is between propositions true of necessity, and those true asa things are: Necessary as opposed to contingent propositions. Other qualifiers sometimes called 'modal' include the tense indicators 'It will be the case that p' or It was the case that p', and there are affinities between the 'deontic indicators', as, it should be the case that p' or ' it is permissible that p', and the logical modalities as a logic that study the notions of necessity and possibility. Modal logic was of a great importance historically, particularly in the light of various doctrines concerning the necessary properties of the deity, but was not a central topic of modern logic in its golden period at the beginning of the 20th century. It was, however, revived by C. I. Lewis, by adding to a propositional or predicate calculus two operators, □ and ◊ (sometimes written N and M), meaning necessarily and possibly, respectively. These like p → ◊ p and □ p → p will be wanted. Controversial theses include □ p → □□ p (if a proposition is necessary, it is necessarily necessary, characteristic of the system known as S4) and ◊ p → □ ◊ p (if a proposition is possible, it is necessarily possible, characteristic of the system known as S5). The classical 'modal theory' for modal logic, due to Kripke and the Swedish logician Stig Kanger, involves valuing propositions not as true or false 'simpliciers', but as true or false art possible worlds, with necessity then corresponding to truth in all worlds, and possibly to truth in some world.

The doctrine advocated by David Lewis, which different 'possible worlds' are to be thought of as existing exactly as this one does. Thinking in terms of possibilities is thinking of real worlds where things are different, this view has been charged with misrepresenting it as some insurmountably unseeing to why it is good to save the child from drowning, since there is still a possible world in which she (or her counterpart) drowned, and from the standpoint of the universe it should make no difference that world is actual. Critics also charged that either the notion fails to fit with a coherent theory of how we know about possible worlds, or with a coherent theory about possible worlds, or with a coherent theory of why we are interested in them, but Lewis denies that any other way of interpreting modal statements is tenable.

Thus and so, the 'standard analysis' of propositional knowledge, suggested by Plato and Kant among others, implies that if one has a justified true belief that 'p', then one knows that 'p'. The belief condition 'p' believes that 'p', the truth condition requires that any known proposition be true. And the justification condition requires that any known proposition be adequately justified, warranted or evidentially supported. Plato appears to be considering the tripartite definition in the "Theaetetus" (201c-202d), and to be endorsing its jointly sufficient conditions for knowledge in the "Meno" (97e-98a). This definition has come to be called 'the standard analysis' of knowledge, and has received a serious challenge from Edmund Gettier's counterexamples in 1963. Gettier published two counterexamples to this implication of the standard analysis. In essence, they are:

(1) Smith and Jones have applied for the same job. Smith is justified in believing that (a) Jones will get the job, and that (b) Jones has ten coins in his pocket. On the basis of (a) and (b) Smith infers, and thus is justified in believing, that © the person who will get the job has ten coins in his pocket. At it turns out, Smith himself will get the job, and he also happens to have ten coins in his pocket. So, although Smith is justified in believing the true proposition ©, Smith does not know ©.

(2) Smith is justified in believing the false proposition that (a) Smith owns a Ford. On the basis of (a) Smith infers, and thus is justified in believing, that (b) either Jones owns a Ford or Brown is in Barcelona. As it turns out, Brown or in Barcelona, and so (b) is true. So although Smith is justified in believing the true proposition (b). Smith does not know (b).

Gettier's counterexamples are thus cases where one has justified true belief that 'p', but lacks knowledge that 'p'. The Gettier problem is the problem of finding a modification of, or an alterative to, the standard justified-true-belief analysis of knowledge that avoids counterexamples like Gettier's. Some philosophers have suggested that Gettier style counterexamples are defective owing to their reliance on the false principle that false propositions can justify one's belief in other propositions. But there are examples much like Gettier's that do not depend on this allegedly false principle. Here is one example inspired by Keith and Richard Feldman:

(3) Suppose Smith knows the following proposition, 'm': Jones, whom Smith has always found to be reliable and whom Smith, has no reason to distrust now, has told Smith, his office-mate, that 'p': He, Jones owns a Ford. Suppose also that Jones has told Smith that 'p' only because of a state of hypnosis Jones is in, and that 'p' is true only because, unknown

to himself, Jones has won a Ford in a lottery since entering the state of hypnosis. And suppose further that Smith deduces from 'm' its existential generalization, 'q': There is someone, whom Smith has always found to be reliable and whom Smith has no reason to distrust now, who has told Smith, his office-mate, that he owns a Ford. Smith, then, knows that 'q', since he has correctly deduced 'q' from 'm', which he also knows. But suppose also that on the basis of his knowledge that 'q'. Smith believes that 'r': Someone in the office owns a Ford. Under these conditions, Smith has justified true belief that 'r', knows his evidence for 'r', but does not know that 'r'.

Gettier-style examples of this sort have proven especially difficult for attempts to analyse the concept of propositional knowledge. The history of attempted solutions to the Gettier problem is complex and open-ended. It has not produced consensus on any solution. Many philosophers hold, in light of Gettier-style examples, that propositional knowledge requires a fourth condition, beyond the justification, truth and belief conditions. Although no particular fourth condition enjoys widespread endorsement, there are some prominent general proposals in circulation. One sort of proposed modification, the so-called 'defeasibility analysis', requires that the justification appropriate to knowledge be 'undefeated' in the general sense that some appropriate subjunctive conditional concerning genuine defeaters of justification be true of that justification. One straightforward defeasibility fourth condition, for instance, requires of Smith's knowing that 'p' that there be no true proposition 'q', such that if 'q' became justified for Smith, 'p' would no longer be justified for Smith (Pappas and Swain, 1978). A different prominent modification requires that the actual justification for a true belief qualifying as knowledge not depend I a specified way on any falsehood (Armstrong, 1973). The details proposed to elaborate such approaches have met with considerable controversy.

The fourth condition of evidential truth-sustenance may be a speculative solution to the Gettier problem. More specifically, for a person, 'S', to have knowledge that 'p' on justifying evidence 'e', 'e' must be truth-sustained in this sense for every true proposition 't' that, when conjoined with 'e', undermines S's justification for 'p' on 'e', there is a true proposition, 't', that, when conjoined with 'e' & 't', restores the justification of 'p' for 'S' in a way that 'S' is actually justified in believing that 'p'. The gist of this resolving evolution, put roughly, is that propositional knowledge requires justified true belief that is sustained by the collective totality of truths. Herein, is to argue in Knowledge and Evidence, that Gettier-style examples as (1)-(3), but various others as well.

Three features that proposed this solution merit emphasis. First, it avoids a subjunctive conditional in its fourth condition, and so escapes some difficult problems facing the use of such a conditional in an analysis of knowledge. Second, it allows for non-deductive justifying evidence as a component of propositional knowledge. An adequacy condition on an analysis of knowledge is that it does not restrict justifying evidence to relations of deductive support. Third, its proposed solution is sufficiently flexible to handle cases describable as follows:

(4) Smith has a justified true belief that 'p', but there is a true proposition, 't', which undermines Smith's justification for 'p' when conjoined with it, and which is such that it is either physically or humanly impossible for Smith to be justified in believing that 't'.

Examples represented by (4) suggest that we should countenance varying strengths in notions of propositional knowledge. These strengths are determined by accessibility qualifications on the set of relevant knowledge-precluding underminers. A very demanding concept of knowledge assumes that it need only be logically possible for a Knower to believe a knowledge-precluding underminer. Fewer demanding concepts assume that it must be physically or humanly possible for a Knower to believe knowledge-precluding underminers. But even such less demanding concepts of knowledge need to rely on a notion of truth-sustained evidence if they are to survive a threatening range of Gettier-style examples. Given to some resolution that it needs be that the forth condition for a notion of knowledge is not a function simply of the evidence a Knower actually possesses.

The higher controversial aftermath of Gettier's original counterexamples has left some philosophers doubted of the real philosophical significance of the Gettier problem. Such doubt, however, seems misplaced. One fundamental branch of epistemology seeks understanding of the nature of propositional knowledge. And our understanding exactly what prepositional knowledge is essentially involves having a Gettier-resistant analysis of such knowledge. If our analysis is not Gettier-resistant, we will lack an exact understanding of what propositional knowledge is. It is epistemologically important, therefore, to have a defensible solution to the Gettier problem, however, demanding such a solution is.

Propositional knowledge (PK) is the type of knowing whose instance are labelled by means of a phrase expressing some proposition, e.g., in English a phrase of the form 'that h', where some complete declarative sentence is instantial for 'h'.

Theories of 'PK' differ over whether the proposition that 'h' is involved in a more intimate fashion, such as serving as a way of picking out a proposition attitude required for knowing, e.g., believing that 'h', accepting that 'h' or being sure that 'h'. For instance, the tripartite analysis or standard analysis, treats 'PK' as consisting in having a justified, true belief that 'h', the belief condition requires that anyone who knows that 'h' believes that 'h', the truth condition requires that any known proposition be true, in contrast, some regarded theories do so consider and treat 'PK' as the possession of specific abilities, capabilities, or powers, and that view the proposition that 'h' as needed to be expressed only in order to label a specific instance of 'PK'.

Although most theories of Propositional knowledge (PK) purport to analyse it, philosophers disagree about the goal of a philosophical analysis. Theories of 'PK' may differ over whether they aim to cover all species of 'PK' and, if they do not have this goal, over whether they aim to reveal any unifying link between the species that they investigate, e.g., empirical knowledge, and other species of knowing.

Very many accounts of 'PK' have been inspired by the quest to add a fourth condition to the tripartite analysis so as to avoid Gettier-type counterexamples to it, whereby a fourth condition of evidential truth-sustenance for every true proposition when conjoined with a regaining justification, which may require the justified true belief that is sustained by the collective totality of truths that an adequacy condition of propositional knowledge not restrict justified evidences in relation of deductive support, such that we should countenance varying strengths in notions of propositional knowledge. Restoratively, these strengths are determined by accessibility qualifications on the set of relevant knowledge-precluding underminers. A very demanding concept of knowledge assumes that it need only be logically possible for a Knower to believe a knowledge-precluding undeterminers, and less demanding concepts that it must physically or humanly possible for a Knower to believe knowledge-precluding undeterminers. But even such demanding concepts of knowledge need to rely on a notion of truth-sustaining evidence if they are to survive a threatening range of Gettier-style examples. As the needed fourth condition for a notion of knowledge is not a function simply of the evidence, a Knower actually possesses. One fundamental source of epistemology seeks understanding of the nature of propositional knowledge, and our understanding exactly what propositional knowledge is essentially involves our having a Gettier-resistant analysis of such knowledge. If our analysis is not Gettier-resistant, we will lack an exact understanding of what propositional knowledge is. It is epistemologically important, therefore, to have a defensible solution to the Gettier problem, however, demanding such a solution is. And by the resulting need to deal with other counterexamples provoked by these new analyses.

Keith Lehrer (1965) originated a Gettier-type example that has been a fertile source of important variants. It is the case of Mr Notgot, who is in one's office and has provided some evidence, 'e', in response to all of which one forms a justified belief that Mr. Notgot is in the office and owns a Ford, thanks to which one arrives at the justified belief that 'h': 'Someone in the office owns a Ford'. In the example, 'e' consists of such things as Mr. Notgot's presently showing one a certificate of Ford ownership while claiming to own a Ford and having been reliable in the past. Yet, Mr Notgot has just been shamming, and the only reason that it is true that 'h1' is because, unbeknown to oneself, a different person in the office owns a convertible Ford.

Variants on this example continue to challenge efforts to analyse species of 'PK'. For instance, Alan Goldman (1988) has proposed that when one has empirical knowledge that 'h', when the state of affairs (call it h*) expressed by the proposition that 'h' figures prominently in an explanation of the occurrence of one's believing that 'h', where explanation is taken to involve one of a variety of probability relations concerning 'h*', and the belief state. But this account runs foul of a variant on the Notgot case akin to one that Lehrer (1979) has described. In Lehrer's variant, Mr Notgot has manifested a compulsion to trick people into justified believing truths yet falling short of knowledge by means of concocting Gettierized evidence for those truths. It we make the trickster's neuroses highly specific ti the type of information contained in the proposition that 'h', we obtain a variant satisfying Goldman's requirement That the occurrences of 'h*' significantly raises the probability of one's believing that 'h'. (Lehrer himself (1990, pp. 103-4) has criticized Goldman by questioning whether, when one has ordinary perceptual knowledge that abn object is present, the presence of the object is what explains one's believing it to be present.)

In grappling with Gettier-type examples, some analyses proscribe specific relations between falsehoods and the evidence or grounds that justify one's believing. A simple restriction of this type requires that one's reasoning to the belief that 'h' does not crucially depend upon any false lemma (such as the false proposition that Mr Notgot is in the office and owns a Ford). However, Gettier-type examples have been constructed where one does not reason through and false belief, e.g., a variant of the Notgot case where one arrives at belief that 'h', by basing it upon a true existential generalization of one's evidence: 'There is someone in the office who has provided evidence e', in response to similar cases, Sosa (1991) has proposed that for 'PK' the 'basis' for the justification of one's belief that 'h' must not involve one's being justified in believing or in 'presupposing' any falsehood, even if one's reasoning to the belief does not employ that falsehood as a lemma. Alternatively, Roderick Chisholm (1989) requires that if there is something that makes the proposition that 'h' evident for one and yet makes something else that is false evident for one, then the proposition that 'h' is implied by a conjunction of propositions, each of which is evident for one and is such that something that makes it evident for one makes no falsehood evident for one. Other types of analyses are concerned with the role of falsehoods within the justification of the proposition that 'h' (Versus the justification of one's believing that 'h'). Such a theory may require that one's evidence bearing on this justification not already contain falsehoods. Or it may require that no falsehoods are involved at specific places in a special explanatory structure relating to the justification of the proposition that 'h' (Shope, 1983.).

A frequently pursued line of research concerning a fourth condition of knowing seeks what is called a 'defeasibility' analysis of 'PK'. Early versions characterized defeasibility by means of subjunctive conditionals of the form, 'If 'A' were the case then 'B' would be the case'. But more recently the label has been applied to conditions about evidential or justificational relations that are not themselves characterized in terms of conditionals. Early versions of defeasibility theories advanced conditionals where 'A' is a hypothetical situation concerning one's acquisition of a specified sort of epistemic status for specified propositions, e.g., one's acquiring justified belief in some further evidence or truths, and 'B'; concerned, for instance, the continued justified status of the proposition that 'h' or of one's believing that 'h'.

A unifying thread connecting the conditional and non-conditional approaches to defeasibility may lie in the following facts: (1) What is a reason for being in a propositional attitude is in part a consideration, instances of the thought of which have the power to affect relevant processes of propositional attitude formation? : (2) Philosophers have often hoped to analyse power ascriptions by means of conditional statements: And (3) Arguments portraying evidential or justificational relations are abstractions from those processes of propositional attitude maintenance and formation that manifest rationality. So even when some circumstance, 'R', is a reason for believing or accepting that 'h', another circumstance, 'K' may present an occasion from being present for a rational manifestation of the relevant power of the thought of 'R' and it will not be a good argument to base a conclusion that 'h' on the premiss that 'R' and 'K' obtain. Whether 'K' does play this interfering, 'defeating'. Role will depend upon the total relevant situation.

Accordingly, one of the most sophisticated defeasibility accounts, which has been proposed by John Pollock (1986), requires that in order to know that 'h', one must believe that 'h' on the basis of an argument whose force is not defeated in the above way, given the total set of circumstances described by all truths. More specifically, Pollock defines defeat as a situation where (1) one believes that 'p' and it is logically possible for one to become justified in believing that 'h' by believing that 'p'. And (2) one actually has a further set of beliefs, 'S' logically has a further set of beliefs, 'S'. Logically consistent with the proposition that 'h', such that it is not logically possible for one to become justified in believing that 'h' by believing it ion the basis of holding the set of beliefs that is the union of 'S' with the belief that 'p' (Pollock, 1986, pp. 36, 38). Furthermore, Pollock requires for 'PK' that the rational presupposition in favour of one's believing that 'h' created by one's believing that 'p' is undefeated by the set of all truths, including considerations that one does not actually believe. Pollock offers no definition of what this requirements means. But he may intend roughly the following: There 'T' is the set of all true propositions: (I) one believes that 'p' and it is logically possible for one to become justified in believing that 'h', in the effective operations that of believing that 'p'. And (II) there are logically possible situations in which one becomes justified in believing that 'h' on the bass of having the belief that 'p' and the beliefs in 'T'. Thus, in the Notgot example, since 'T' includes the proposition that Mr. Notgot does own a sedan Ford, one lack's knowledge because condition (II) is not satisfied.

But given such an interpretation, Pollock's account illustrates the fact that defeasibility theories typically have difficulty dealing with introspective knowledge of one's beliefs. Suppose that some proposition, say that ***f***, is false, but one does not realize this and holds the belief that ***f***. Condition

(II) has no knowledge that h2?: 'I believe that ***f***'. At least this is so if one's reason for believing that h2 includes the presence of the very condition of which one is aware, i.e., one's believing that ***f***. It is incoherent to suppose hat one retains the latter reason, also, believes the truth that not-***f***. This objection can be avoided, but at the cost of adopting what is a controversial view about introspective knowledge that 'h', namely, the view that one's belief that 'h' is in such cases mediated by some mental state intervening between the mental state of which there is introspective knowledge and he belief that 'h', so that is mental state is rather than the introspected state that it is included in one's reason for believing that 'h'. In order to avoid adopting this controversial view, Paul Moser (1989) gas proposed a disjunctive analysis of 'PK', which requires that either one satisfy a defeasibility condition rather than like Pollock's or else one believes that 'h' by introspection. However, Moser leaves obscure exactly why beliefs arrived at by introspections account as knowledge.

Early versions of defeasibility theories had difficulty allowing for the existence of evidence that is 'merely misleading', as in the case where one does know that 'h3: 'Tom Grabit stole a book from the library', thanks to having seen him steal it, yet where, unbeknown to oneself, Tom's mother out of dementia gas testified that Tom was far away from the library at the time of the theft. One's justifiably believing that she gave the testimony would destroy one's justification for believing that 'h3' if added by itself to one's present evidence.

At least some defeasibility theories cannot deal with the knowledge one has while dying that 'h4: 'In this life there is no timer at which I believe that 'd', where the proposition that 'd' expresses the details regarding some philosophical matter, e.g., the maximum number of blades of grass ever simultaneously growing on the earth. When it just so happens that it is true that 'd', defeasibility analyses typically consider the addition to one's dying thoughts of a belief that 'd' in such a way as to improperly rule out actual knowledge that 'h4'.

A quite different approach to knowledge, and one able to deal with some Gettier-type cases, involves developing some type of causal theory of Propositional knowledge. The interesting thesis that counts as a causal theory of justification (in the meaning of 'causal theory; intended here) is the that of a belief is justified just in case it was produced by a type of process that is 'globally' reliable, that is, its propensity to produce true beliefs-that can be defined (to a god enough approximation) as the proportion of the bailiffs it produces (or would produce where it used as much as opportunity allows) that are true-is sufficiently meaningful-variations of this view have been advanced for both knowledge and justified belief. The first formulation of reliability account of knowing appeared in a note by F.P. Ramsey (1931), who said that a belief was knowledge if it is true, certain can obtain by a reliable process. P. Unger (1968) suggested that "S' knows that 'p' just in case it is not at all accidental that 'S' is right about its being the casse that 'p'. D.M. Armstrong (1973) said that a non-inferential belief qualified as knowledge if the belief has properties that are nominally sufficient for its truth, i.e., guarantee its truth through and by the laws of nature.

Some philosophers think that the category of knowing for which true. Justified believing (accepting) is a requirement constituting only a species of Propositional knowledge, construed as an even broader category. They have proposed various examples of 'PK' that do not satisfy the belief and/ort justification conditions of the tripartite analysis. Such cases are often recognized by analyses of Propositional knowledge in terms of powers, capacities, or abilities. For instance, Alan R. White (1982) treats 'PK' as merely the ability to provide a correct answer to possible questions, however, White may be equating 'producing' knowledge in the sense of producing 'the correct answer to a possible question' with 'displaying' knowledge in the sense of manifesting knowledge. (White, 1982). The latter can be done even by very young children and some nonhuman animals independently of their being asked questions, understanding questions, or recognizing answers to questions. Indeed, an example that has been proposed as an instance of knowing that 'h' without believing or accepting that 'h' can be modified so as to illustrate this point. Two examples concerns an imaginary person who has no special training or information about horses or racing, but who in an experiment persistently and correctly picks the winners of upcoming horseraces. If the example is modified so that the hypothetical 'seer' never picks winners but only muses over whether those horses wight win, or only reports those horses winning, this behaviour should be as much of a candidate for the person's manifesting knowledge that the horse in question will win as would be the behaviour of picking it as a winner.

These considerations expose limitations in Edward Craig's analysis (1990) of the concept of knowing of a person's being a satisfactory informant in relation to an inquirer who wants to find out whether or not 'h'. Craig realizes that counterexamples to his analysis appear to be constituted by Knower who are too recalcitrant to inform the inquirer, or too incapacitate to inform, or too discredited to be worth considering (as with the boy who cried 'Wolf'). Craig admits that this might make preferable some alternative view of knowledge as a different state that helps to explain the presence of the state of being a suitable informant when the latter does obtain. Such the alternate, which offers a recursive definition that concerns one's having the power to proceed in a way representing the state of affairs, causally involved in one's proceeding in this way. When combined with a suitable analysis of representing, this theory of propositional knowledge can be unified with a structurally similar analysis of knowing how to do something.

Knowledge and belief, according to most epistemologists, knowledge entails belief, so that I cannot know that such and such is the case unless I believe that such and such is the case. Others think this entailment thesis can be rendered more accurately if we substitute for belief some closely related attitude. For instance, several philosophers would prefer to say that knowledge entail psychological certainties (Prichard, 1950 and Ayer, 1956) or conviction (Lehrer, 1974) or acceptance (Lehrer, 1989). None the less, there are arguments against all versions of the thesis that knowledge requires having a belief-like attitude toward the known. These arguments are given by philosophers who think that knowledge and belief (or a facsimile) are mutually incompatible (the incomparability thesis), or by ones who say that knowledge does not entail belief, or vice versa, so that each may exist without the other, but the two may also coexist (the separability thesis).

The incompatibility thesis is sometimes traced to Plato ©. 429-347 BC) in view of his claim that knowledge is infallible while belief or opinion is fallible ("Republic" 476-9). But this claim would not support the thesis. Belief might be a component of an infallible form of knowledge in spite of the fallibility of belief. Perhaps, knowledge involves some factor that compensates for the fallibility of belief.

A. Duncan-Jones (1939: Also Vendler, 1978) cite linguistic evidence to back up the incompatibility thesis. He notes that people often say 'I do not believe she is guilty. I know she is' and the like, which suggest that belief rule out knowledge. However, as Lehrer (1974) indicates, the above exclamation is only a more emphatic way of saying 'I do not just believe she is guilty. I know she is' where 'just' makes it especially clear that the speaker is signalling that she has something more salient than mere belief, not that she has something inconsistent with belief, namely knowledge. Compare: 'You do not hurt him, you killed him'.

H.A. Prichard (1966) offers a defence of the incompatibility thesis that hinges on the equation of knowledge with certainty (both infallibility and psychological certitude) and the assumption that when we believe in the truth of a claim we are not certain about its truth. Given that belief always involves uncertainty while knowledge never dies, believing something rules out the possibility of knowing it. Unfortunately, however, Prichard gives 'us' no goods reason to grant that states of belief are never ones involving confidence. Conscious beliefs clearly involve some level of confidence, to suggest that we cease to believe things about which we are completely confident is bizarre.

A.D. Woozley (1953) defends a version of the separability thesis. Woozley's version, which deals with psychological certainty rather than belief per se, is that knowledge can exist in the absence of confidence about the item known, although might also be accompanied by confidence as well. Woozley remarks that the test of whether I know something is 'what I can do, where what I can do may include answering questions'. On the basis of this remark he suggests that even when people are unsure of the truth of a claim, they might know that the claim is true. We unhesitatingly attribute knowledge to people who give correct responses on examinations even if those people show no confidence in their answers. Woozley acknowledges, however, that it would be odd for those who lack confidence to claim knowledge. It would be peculiar to say, 'I am unsure whether my answer is true: Still, I know it is correct'. But this tension Woozley explains using a distinction between conditions under which we are justified in making a claim (such as a claim to know something), and conditions under which the claim we make is true. While 'I know such and such' might be true even if I am unsure whether such and such holds, nonetheless it would be inappropriate for me to claim that I know that such and such unless I were sure of the truth of my claim.

Colin Radford (1966) extends Woozley's defence of the separability thesis. In Radford's view, not only is knowledge compatible with the lack of certainty, it is also compatible with a complete lack of belief. He argues by example. In one example, Jean has forgotten that he learned some English history year's priori and yet he is able to give several correct responses to questions such as 'When did the Battle of Hastings occur'? Since he forgot that he took history, he considers the correct response to be no more than guesses. Thus, when he says that the Battle of Hastings took place in 1066 he would deny having the belief that the Battle of Hastings took place in 1066. A disposition he would deny being responsible (or having the right to be convincing) that 1066 was the correct date. Radford would none the less insist that Jean know when the Battle occurred, since clearly be remembering the correct date. Radford admits that it would be inappropriate for Jean to say that he knew when the Battle of Hastings occurred, but, like Woozley he attributes the impropriety to a fact about when it is and is not appropriate to claim knowledge. When we claim knowledge, we ought, at least to believe that we have the knowledge we claim, or else our behaviour is 'intentionally misleading'.

Those that agree with Radford's defence of the separability thesis will probably think of belief as an inner state that can be detected through introspection. That Jean lack's beliefs about English history is plausible on this Cartesian picture since Jean does not find himself with any beliefs about English history when ne seek them out. One might criticize Radford, however, by rejecting that Cartesian view of belief. One could argue that some beliefs are thoroughly unconscious, for example. Or one could adopt a behaviourist conception of belief, such as Alexander Bain's (1859), according to which having beliefs is a matter of the way people are disposed to behave (and has not Radford already adopted a behaviourist conception of knowledge?) Since Jean gives the correct response when queried, a form of verbal behaviour, a behaviourist would be tempted to credit him with the belief that the Battle of Hastings occurred in 1066.

D.M. Armstrong (1873) takes a different tack against Radford. Jean does know that the Battle of Hastings took place in 1066. Armstrong will grant Radford that point, in fact, Armstrong suggests that Jean believe that 1066 is not the date the Battle of Hastings occurred, for Armstrong equates the belief that such and such is just possible but no more than just possible with the belief that such and such is not the case. However, Armstrong insists, Jean also believes that the Battle did occur in 1066. After all, had Jean been mistaught that the Battle occurred in 1066, and subsequently 'guessed' that it took place in 1066, we would surely describe the situation as one in which Jean's false belief about the Battle became unconscious over time but persisted of a memory trace that was causally responsible for his guess. Out of consistency, we must describe Radford's original case as one that Jean's true belief became unconscious but persisted long enough to cause his guess. Thus, while Jean consciously believes that the Battle did not occur in 1066, unconsciously he does believe it occurred in 1066. So after all, Radford does not have a counterexample to the claim that knowledge entails belief.

Armstrong's response to Radford was to reject Radford's claim that the examinee lacked the relevant belief about English history. Another response is to argue that the examinee lacks the knowledge Radford attributes to him (Sorenson, 1982). If Armstrong is correct in suggesting that Jean believes both that 1066 is and that it is not the date of the Battle of Hastings, one might deny Jean knowledge on the grounds that people who believe the denial of what they believe cannot be said t know the truth of their belief. Another strategy might be to compare the examinee case with examples of ignorance given in recent attacks on externalist accounts of knowledge (needless to say. Externalists themselves would tend not to favour this strategy). Consider the following case developed by BonJour (1985): For no apparent reason, Samantha believes that she is clairvoyant. Again, for no apparent reason, she one day comes to believe that the President is in New York City, even though she has every reason to believe that the President is in Washington, D.C. In fact, Samantha is a completely reliable clairvoyant, and she has arrived at her belief about the whereabouts of the President thorough the power of her clairvoyance. Yet surely Samantha's belief is completely irrational. She is not justified in thinking what she does. If so, then she does not know where the President is. But Radford's examinee is unconventional. Even if Jean lacks the belief that Radford denies him, Radford does not have an example of knowledge that is unattended with belief. Suppose that Jean's memory had been sufficiently powerful to produce the relevant belief. As Radford says, in having every reason to suppose that his response is mere guesswork, and he has every reason to consider his belief false. His belief would be an irrational one, and hence one about whose truth Jean would be ignorant.

Least has been of mention to an approaching view from which 'perception' basis upon itself as a fundamental philosophical topic both for its central place in ant theory of knowledge, and its central place un any theory of consciousness. Philosophy in this area is constrained by a number of properties that we believe to hold of perception, (1) It gives 'us' knowledge of the world around 'us'. (2) We are conscious of that world by being aware of 'sensible qualities': Colour, sounds, tastes, smells, felt warmth, and the shapes and positions of objects in the environment. (3) Such consciousness is effected through highly complex information channels, such as the output of the three different types of colour-sensitive cells in the eye, or the channels in the ear for interpreting pulses of air pressure as frequencies of sound. (4) There ensues even more complex neurophysiological coding of that information, and eventually higher-order brain functions bring it about that we interpreted the information so received. (Much of this complexity has been revealed by the difficulties of writing programs enabling computers to recognize quite simple aspects of the visual scene.) The problem is to avoid thinking of here being a central, ghostly, conscious self, fed information in the same way that a screen if fed information by a remote television camera. Once such a model is in place, experience will seem like a veil getting between 'us' and the world, and the direct objects of perception will seem to be private items in an inner theatre or sensorium. The difficulty of avoiding this model is epically cute when we considered the secondary qualities of colour, sound, tactile feelings and taste, which can easily seem to have a purely private existence inside the perceiver, like sensation of pain. Calling such supposed items names like 'sense-data' or 'percepts' exacerbates the tendency, but once the model is in place, the first property, that perception gives 'us' knowledge of the world and its surrounding surfaces, is quickly threatened, for there will now seem little connection between these items in immediate experience and any independent reality. Reactions to this problem include 'scepticism' and 'idealism'.

A more hopeful approach is to claim that the complexities of (3) and (4) explain how we can have direct acquaintance of the world, than suggesting that the acquaintance we do have been at best indirect. It is pointed out that perceptions are not like sensation, precisely because they have a content, or outer-directed nature. To have a perception is to be aware of the world for being such-and-such a way, than to enjoy a mere modification of sensation. But such direct realism has to be sustained in the face of the evident personal (neurophysiological and other) factors determining haw we perceive. One approach is to ask why it is useful to be conscious of what we perceive, when other aspects of our functioning work with information determining responses without any conscious awareness or intervention. A solution to this problem would offer the hope of making consciousness part of the natural world, than a strange optional extra.

Furthering, perceptual knowledge is knowledge acquired by or through the senses and includes most of what we know. We cross intersections when we see the light turn green, head for the kitchen when we smell the roast burning, squeeze the fruit to determine its ripeness, and climb out of bed when we hear the alarm ring. In each case we come to know something-that the light has turned green, that the roast is burning, that the melon is overripe, and that it is time to get up-by some sensory means. Seeing that the light has turned green is learning something - that the light has turned green-by use of the eyes. Feeling that the melon is overripe is coming to know a fact-that the melon is overripe-by one's sense to touch. In each case the resulting knowledge is somehow based on, derived from or grounded in the sort of experience that characterizes the sense modality in question.

Much of our perceptual knowledge is indirect, dependent or derived. By this I mean that the facts we describe ourselves as learning, as coming to know, by perceptual means are pieces of knowledge that depend on our coming to know something else, some other fact, in a more direct way. We see, by the gauge, that we need gas, see, by the newspapers, that our team has lost again, see, by her expression, that she is nervous. This derived or dependent sort of knowledge is particularly prevalent in the cases of vision, but it occurs, to a lesser degree, in every sense modality. We install bells and other noise makers so that we calm for example, hear (by the bell) that someone is at the door and (by the alarm) that its time to get up. When we obtain knowledge in this way, it is clear that unless one sees hence, comes to know something about the gauge (that it says) and (hence, know) that one is described as coming to know by perceptual means. If one cannot hear that the bell is ringing, one cannot-in at least in this way-hear that one's visitors have arrived. In such cases one sees (hears, smells, etc.) that 'a' is 'F', coming to know thereby that 'a' is 'F', by seeing (hearing, etc.) that some other condition, 'b's' being 'G', obtains when this occurs, the knowledge (that 'a' is 'F') is derived from, or dependent on, the more basic perceptual knowledge that 'b' is 'G'. Consciousness seems cognitive and brain sciences that over the past three decades that instead of ignoring it, many physicalists now seek to explain it (Dennett, 1991). Here we focus exclusively on ways those neuroscientific discoveries have impacted philosophical debates about the nature of consciousness and its relation to physical mechanisms. Thomas Nagel argues that conscious experience is subjective, and thus permanently recalcitrant to objective scientific understanding. He invites us to ponder 'what it is like to be a bat' and urges the intuition that no amount of physical-scientific knowledge (including neuroscientific) supplies a complete answer. Nagel's intuition pump has generated extensive philosophical discussion. At least two well-known replies make direct appeal to neurophysiology. John Biro suggests that part of the intuition pumped by Nagel, that bat experience is substantially different from human experience, presupposes systematic emerged as a topic in philosophy of mind and relations between physiology and phenomenology. Kathleen Akins (1993) delves deeper into existing knowledge of bat physiology and reports much that is pertinent to Nagel's question. She argues that many of the questions about bat subjectivity that we still consider open hinge on questions that remain unanswered about neuroscientific details. One example of the latter is the function of various cortical activity profiles in the active bat.

More recently philosopher David Chalmers (1996) has argued that any possible brain-process account of consciousness will leave open an 'explanatory gap' between the brain process and properties of the conscious experience. This is because no brain-process theory can answer the "hard" question: Why should that particular brain process give rise to conscious experience? We can always imagine ("conceive of") a universe populated by creatures having those brain processes but completely lacking conscious experience. A theory of consciousness requires an explanation of how and why some brain process causes consciousness replete with all the features we commonly experience. The fact that the hard question remains unanswered shows that we will probably never get a complete explanation of consciousness at the level of neural mechanisms. Paul and Patricia Churchland have recently offered the following diagnosis and reply. Chalmers offer a conceptual argument, based on our ability to imagine creatures possessing brains like ours but wholly lacking in conscious experience. But the more one learns about how the brain produces conscious experience-and literature is beginning to emerge (e.g., Gazzaniga, 1995)-the harder it becomes to imagine a universe consisting of creatures with brain processes like ours but lacking consciousness. This is not just to bare assertions. The Churchlands appeal to some neurobiological detail. For example, Paul Churchland (1995) develops a neuroscientific account of consciousness based on recurrent connections between thalamic nuclei (particularly "diffusely projecting" nuclei like the intralaminar nuclei) and the cortex. Churchland argues that the thalamocortical recurrency accounts for the selective features of consciousness, for the effects of short-term memory on conscious experience, for vivid dreaming during REM. (rapid-eye movement) sleep, and other "core" features of conscious experience. In other words, the Churchlands are claiming that when one learns about activity patterns in these recurrent circuits, one can't "imagine" or "conceive of" this activity occurring without these core features of conscious experience. (Other than just mouthing the words, "I am now imagining activity in these circuits without selective attention/the effects of short-term memory/ vivid dreaming . . . ")

A second focus of sceptical arguments about a complete neuroscientific explanation of consciousness is sensory Qualia: the introspectable qualitative aspects of sensory experience, the features by which subjects discern similarities and differences among their experiences. The colours of visual sensations are a philosopher's favourite example. One famous puzzle about colour Qualia is the alleged conceivability of spectral inversions. Many philosophers claim that it is conceptually possible (if perhaps physically impossible) for two humans not to differ neurophysiological, while the Collor that fire engines and tomatoes appear to have to one subject is the Collor that grass and frogs appear to have to the other (and vice versa). A large amount of neuroscientifically-informed philosophy has addressed this question. A related area where neurophilosophical considerations have emerged concerns the metaphysics of colours themselves (rather than Collor experiences). A longstanding philosophical dispute is whether colours are objective property's Existing external to perceiver or rather identifiable as or dependent upon minds or nervous systems. Some recent work on this problem begins with characteristics of Collor experiences: For example that Collor similarity judgments produce Collor orderings that align on a circle. With this resource, one can seek mappings of phenomenology onto environmental or physiological regularities. Identifying colours with particular frequencies of electromagnetic radiation does not preserve the structure of the hue circle, whereas identifying colours with activity in opponent processing neurons does. Such a tidbit is not decisive for the Collor objectivist-subjectivist debate, but it does convey the type of neurophilosophical work being done on traditional metaphysical issues beyond the philosophy of mind.

We saw in the discussion of Hardcastle (1997) two sections above that Neuro-philosophers have entered disputes about the nature and methodological import of pain experiences. Two decades earlier, Dan Dennett (1978) took up the question of whether it is possible to build a computer that feels pain. He compares and notes pressure between neurophysiological discoveries and common sense intuitions about pain experience. He suspects that the incommensurability between scientific and common sense views is due to incoherence in the latter. His attitude is wait-and-see. But foreshadowing Churchland's reply to Chalmers, Dennett favours scientific investigations over conceivability-based philosophical arguments.

Neurological deficits have attracted philosophical interest. For thirty years philosophers have found implications for the unity of the self in experiments with commissurotomy patients. In carefully controlled experiments, commissurotomy patients display two dissociable seats of consciousness. Patricia Churchland scouts philosophical implications of a variety of neurological deficits. One deficit is blind-sight. Some patients with lesions to primary visual cortex report being unable to see items in regions of their visual fields, yet perform far better than chance in forced guess trials about stimuli in those regions. A variety of scientific and philosophical interpretations have been offered. Ned Form (1988) worries that many of these conflate distinct notions of consciousness. He labels these notions 'phenomenal consciousness' ('P-consciousness') and 'access consciousness' ('A-consciousness'). The former is that which, 'what it is likeness of experience. The latter is the availability of representational content to self-initiated action and speech. Form argues that P-consciousness is not always representational whereas A-consciousness is. Dennett and Michael Tye are sceptical of non-representational analyses of consciousness in general. They provide accounts of blind-sight that do not depend on Form's distinction.

Many other topics are worth neurophilosophical pursuit. We mentioned commissurotomy and the unity of consciousness and the self, which continues to generate discussion. Qualia beyond those of Collor and pain have begun to attract neurophilosophical attention has self-consciousness. The first issue to arise in the 'philosophy of neuroscience' (before there was a recognized area) was the localization of cognitive functions to specific neural regions. Although the 'localization' approach had dubious origins in the phrenology of Gall and Spurzheim, and was challenged severely by Flourens throughout the early nineteenth century, it reemerged in the study of aphasia by Bouillaud, Auburtin, Broca, and Wernicke. These neurologists made careful studies (where possible) of linguistic deficits in their aphasic patients followed by brain autopsies postmortem. Broca's initial study of twenty-two patients in the mid-nineteenth century confirmed that damage to the left cortical hemisphere was predominant, and that damage to the second and third frontal convolutions was necessary to produce speech production deficits. Although the anatomical coordinates' Broca postulates for the 'speech production centres do not correlate exactly with damage producing production deficits, both are that in this area of frontal cortex and speech production deficits still bear his name ('Broca's area' and 'Broca's aphasia'). Less than two decades later Carl Wernicke published evidence for a second language centre. This area is anatomically distinct from Broca's area, and damage to it produced a very different set of aphasic symptoms. The cortical area that still bears his name ('Wernicke's area') is located around the first and second convolutions in temporal cortex, and the aphasia that bears his name ('Wernicke's aphasia') involves deficits in language comprehension. Wernicke's method, like Broca's, was based on lesion studies: a careful evaluation of the behavioural deficits followed by post mortem examination to find the sites of tissue damage and atrophy. Lesion studies suggesting more precise localization of specific linguistic functions remain a cornerstone to this day in aphasic research.

Lesion studies have also produced evidence for the localization of other cognitive functions: For example, sensory processing and certain types of learning and memory. However, localization arguments for these other functions invariably include studies using animal models. With an animal model, one can perform careful behavioural measures in highly controlled settings, then ablate specific areas of neural tissue (or use a variety of other techniques to Form or enhance activity in these areas) and re-measure performance on the same behavioural tests. But since we lack an animal model for (human) language production and comprehension, this additional evidence isn't available to the neurologist or neurolinguist. This fact makes the study of language a paradigm case for evaluating the logic of the lesion/deficit method of inferring functional localization. Philosopher Barbara Von Eckardt (1978) attempts to make explicit the steps of reasoning involved in this common and historically important method. Her analysis begins with Robert Cummins' early analysis of functional explanation, but she extends it into a notion of structurally adequate functional analysis. These analyses break down a complex capacity C into its constituent capacity's C1, C2, . . . Cn, where the constituent capacities are consistent with the underlying structural details of the system. For example, human speech production (complex capacity 'C') results from formulating a speech intention, then selecting appropriate linguistic representations to capture the content of the speech intention, then formulating the motor commands to produce the appropriate sounds, then communicating these motor commands to the appropriate motor pathways (constituent capacity's C1, C2, . . ., Cn). A functional-localization hypothesis has the form: Brain structure S in an organism (type) O has constituent capacity ci, where ci is a function of some part of O. An example, Brains Broca's area (S) in humans (O) formulates motor commands to produce the appropriate sounds (one of the constituent capacities C1). Such hypotheses specify aspects of the structural realization of a functional-component model. They are part of the theory of the neural realization of the functional model.

Armed with these characterizations, Von Eckardt argues that inference to a functional-localization hypothesis proceeds in two steps. First, a functional deficit in a patient is hypothesized based on the abnormal behaviour the patient exhibits. Second, localization of function in normal brains is inferred on the basis of the functional deficit hypothesis plus the evidence about the site of brain damage. The structurally-adequate functional analysis of the capacity connects the pathological behaviour to the hypothesized functional deficit. This connection suggests four adequacy conditions on a functional deficit hypothesis. First, the pathological behaviour 'P' (e.g., the speech deficits characteristic of Broca's aphasia) must result from failing to exercise some complex capacity 'C' (human speech production). Second, there must be a structurally-adequate functional analysis of how people exercise capacity 'C' that involves some constituent capacity C1 (formulating motor commands to produce the appropriate sounds). Third, the operation of the steps described by the structurally-adequate functional analysis minus the operation of the component performing (Broca's area) must result in pathological behaviour P. Fourth, there must not be a better available explanation for why the patient does P. Arguments to a functional deficit hypothesis on the basis of pathological behaviour is thus an instance of argument to the best available explanation. When postulating a deficit in a normal functional component provides the best available explanation of the pathological data, we are justified in drawing the inference.

Von Eckardt applies this analysis to a neurological case study involving a controversial reinterpretation of agnosia. Her philosophical explication of this important neurological method reveals that most challenges to localization arguments of whether to argue only against the localization of a particular type of functional capacity or against generalizing from localization of function in one individual to all normal individuals. (She presents examples of each from the neurological literature.) Such challenges do not impugn the validity of standard arguments for functional localization from deficits. It does not follow that such arguments are unproblematic. But they face difficult factual and methodological problems, not logical ones. Furthermore, the analysis of these arguments as involving a type of functional analysis and inference to the best available explanation carries an important implication for the biological study of cognitive function. Functional analyses require functional theories, and structurally adequate functional analyses require checks imposed by the lower level sciences investigating the underlying physical mechanisms. Arguments to best available explanation are often hampered by a lack of theoretical imagination: the available explanations are often severely limited. We must seek theoretical inspiration from any level of theory and explanation. Hence making explicit the 'logic' of this common and historically important form of neurological explanation reveals the necessity of joint participation from all scientific levels, from cognitive psychology down to molecular neuroscience. Von Eckardt anticipated what came to be heralded as the 'co-evolutionary research methodology,' which remains a centerpiece of neurophilosophy to the present day.

Over the last two decades, evidence for localization of cognitive function has come increasingly from a new source: the development and refinement of neuroimaging techniques. The form of localization-of-function argument appears not to have changed from that employing lesion studies (as analysed by Von Eckardt). Instead, these imaging technologies resolve some of the methodological problems that plage lesion studies. For example, researchers do not need to wait until the patient dies, and in the meantime probably acquires additional brain damage, to find the lesion sites. Two functional imaging techniques are prominent: Positron emission tomography, or PET, and functional magnetic resonance imaging, or MRI. Although these measure different biological markers of functional activity, both now have a resolution down to around 1mm. As these techniques increase spatial and temporal resolution of functional markers and continue to be used with sophisticated behavioural methodologies, the possibility of localizing specific psychological functions to increasingly specific neural regions continues to grow

What we now know about the cellular and molecular mechanisms of neural conductance and transmission is spectacular. The same evaluation holds for all levels of explanation and theory about the mind/brain: maps, networks, systems, and behaviour. This is a natural outcome of increasing scientific specialization. We develop the technology, the experimental techniques, and the theoretical frameworks within specific disciplines to push forward our understanding. Still, a crucial aspect of the total picture gets neglected: the relationship between the levels, the 'glue' that binds knowledge of neuron activity to subcellular and molecular mechanisms, network activity patterns to the activity of and connectivity between single neurons, and behaviour to network activity. This problem is especially glaring when we focus on the relationship between 'cognitivist' psychological theories, postulating information-bearing representations and processes operating over their contents, and the activity patterns in networks of neurons. Co-evolution between explanatory levels still seems more like a distant dream rather than an operative methodology.

It is here that some neuroscientists appeal to 'computational' methods. If we examine the way that computational models function in more developed sciences (like physics), we find the resources of dynamical systems constantly employed. Global effects (such as large-scale meteorological patterns) are explained in terms of the interaction of 'local' lower-level physical phenomena, but only by dynamical, nonlinear, and often chaotic sequences and combinations. Addressing the interlocking levels of theory and explanation in the mind/brain using computational resources that have worked to bridge levels in more mature sciences might yield comparable results. This methodology is necessarily interdisciplinary, drawing on resources and researchers from a variety of levels, including higher levels like experimental psychology, 'program-writing' and 'connectionist' artificial intelligence, and philosophy of science.

However, the use of computational methods in neuroscience is not new. Hodgkin, Huxley, and Katz incorporated values of voltage-dependent potassium conductance they had measured experimentally in the squid giant axon into an equation from physics describing the time evolution of a first-order kinetic process. This equation enabled them to calculate best-fit curves for modelled conductance versus time data that reproduced the S-shaped (sigmoidal) function suggested by their experimental data. Using equations borrowed from physics, Rall (1959) developed the cable model of dendrites. This theory provided an account of how the various inputs from across the dendritic tree interact temporally and spatially to determine the input-output properties of single neurons. It remains influential today, and has been incorporated into the genesis software for programming neurally realistic networks. More recently, David Sparks and his colleagues have shown that a vector-averaging model of activity in neurons of superior caliculi correctly predicts experimental results about the amplitude and direction of saccadic eye movements. Working with a more sophisticated mathematical model, Apostolos Georgopoulos and his colleagues have predicted direction and amplitude of hand and arm movements based on averaged activity of 224 cells in motor cortices. Their predictions have borne out under a variety of experimental tests. We mention these particular studies only because we are familiar with them. We could multiply examples of the fruitful interaction of computational and experimental methods in neuroscience easily by one-hundred-fold. Many of these extend back before 'computational neuroscience' was a recognized research endeavour.

We've already seen one example, the vector transformation account, of neural representation and computation, under active development in cognitive neuroscience. Other approaches using 'cognitivist' resources are also being pursued. Many of these projects draw upon 'cognitivist' characterizations of the phenomena to be explained. Many exploit 'cognitivist' experimental techniques and methodologies. Some even attempt to derive 'cognitivist' explanations from cell-biological processes (e.g., Hawkins and Kandel 1984). As Stephen Kosslyn puts it, cognitive neuro-scientists employ the 'information processing' view of the mind characteristic of cognitivism without trying to separate it from theories of brain mechanisms. Such an endeavour calls for an interdisciplinary community willing to communicate the relevant portions of the mountain of detail gathered in individual disciplines with interested nonspecialists: not just people willing to confer with those working at related levels, but researchers trained in the methods and factual details of a variety of levels. This is a daunting requirement, but it does offer some hope for philosophers wishing to contribute to future neuroscience. Thinkers trained in both the 'synoptic vision' afforded by philosophy and the factual and experimental basis of genuine graduate-level science would be ideally equipped for this task. Recognition of this potential niche has been shown among graduate programs in philosophy, but there is some hope that a few programs are taking steps to fill it.

In the final analysis there will be philosophers unprepared to accept that, if a given cognitive capacity is psychologically real, then there must be an explanation of how it is possible for an individual in the course of human development to acquire that cognitive capacity, or anything like it, can have a role to play in philosophical accounts of concepts and conceptual abilities. The most obvious basis for such a view would be a Frégean distrust of "psychology" that leads to a rigid division of labour between philosophy and psychology. The operative thought is that the task of a philosophical theory of concepts is to explain what a given concept is or what a given conceptual ability consist in. This, it is frequently maintained, is something that can be done in complete independence of explaining how such a concept or ability might be acquired. The underlying distinction is one between philosophical questions centring around concept possession and psychological questions centring around concept possibilities for an individual to acquire that ability, then it cannot be psychologically real. Nevertheless, this distinction is, however, strictly one does adhere to the distinction, it provides no support for a rejection of any given cognitive capacity for which is psychologically real. The neo-Frégean distinction is directly against the view that facts about how concepts are acquired have a role to play in explaining and individualizing concepts. But this view does not have to be disputed by a supporter as such, nonetheless, all that the supporter is to commit is that the principle that no satisfactory account of what a concept is should make it impossible to provide explanation of how that concept can be acquired. That is, that this principle has nothing to say about the further question of whether the psychological explanation has a role to play in a constitutive explanation of the concept, and hence is not in conflict with the neo-Frégean distinction.

The world-view, whereby modernity is to assume that communion with the essences of physical reality and associated theories was possible, but it made no other provisions for the knowing mind. In that, the totality from which modern theory contributes to a view of the universe as an unbroken, undissectible, and undivided dynamic whole. Even so, a complicated tissue of an event, in which connections of different kinds alternate or overlay or combine and in such a way determine the texture of the whole. Errol Harris noted in thinking about the special character of wholeness in modern epistemology, a unity with internal content is a blank or empty set and is not recognized as a whole. A collection of merely externally related parts does not constitute a whole in that the parts will not be "mutually adaptive and complementary to one another."

Wholeness requires a complementary relationship between unity and difference and is governed by a principle of organization determining the interrelationship between parts. This organizing principle must be universal to a genuine whole and implicit in all parts that constitute the whole, even though the whole is exemplified in its parts. This principle of order, "is nothing real in and of itself. It is the way of the parts are organized, and not another consistent additional to those that constitute the totality."

In a genuine whole, the relationships between the constituent parts must be "internal or immanent" in the parts, as opposed to a more spurious whole in which parts appear to disclose wholeness due to relationships that are external to the parts. The collections of parts that would allegedly constitute the whole in both subjective theory and physical reality are each exampled of the spurious whole. Parts constitute a genuine whole when the universal principle of order is inside the parts and thereby adjusts each to all that they interlock and become mutually binding. All the same, it is also consistent with the manner in which we have begun to understand the relation between parts and whole in modern biology.

Much of the ambiguity to explain the character of wholes in both physical reality and biology derives from the assumption that order exists between or outside parts. But order complementary relationships between difference and sameness in any physical reality as forwarded through physical events is never external to that event-the connections are immanent in the event. From this perspective, the addition of non-locality to this picture of the dynamic whole is not surprising. The relationship between part, as quantum events apparent in observation or measurement, and the undissectible whole: Having revealed but not described by the instantaneous correlations between measurements in space-like separated regions, is another extension of the part-whole complementarity in modern physical reality.

If the universe is a seamlessly interactive system that evolves to higher levels of complexity and if the lawful regularise of this universe are emergent properties of this system, we can assume that the cosmos is a single significant whole that evinces progressive order in complementary relations to its parts. Given that this whole exists in some sense within all parts, one can then argue that it operates in self-reflective fashions and is the ground for all emergent complexity. Since, human consciousness evinces self-reflective awareness in the human brain and since this brain, like all physical phenomena, can be viewed as an emergent property of the whole, it is unreasonable to conclude, in philosophical terms at least, that the universe is conscious.

But since the actual character of this seamless whole cannot be represented or reduced to its parts, it lies, quite literally, beyond all human representations or descriptions. If one chooses to believe that the universe be a self-reflective and self-organizing whole, this lends no support whatsoever to conceptions of design, meaning, purpose, intent, or plan associated with mytho-religious or cultural heritage. However, if one does not accept this view of the universe, there is nothing in the scientific description of nature that can be used to refute this position. On the other hand, it is no longer possible to argue that a profound sense of unity with the whole, which has long been understood as the foundation to religious experience, can be dismissed, undermined, or invalidate with appeals to scientific knowledge.

A full account of the structure of consciousness, will need to illustrate those higher, conceptual forms of consciousness to which little attention on such an account will take and about how it might emerge from given points of value, is the thought that an explanation of everything that is distinctive about consciousness will emerge out of an account of what it is for a subject, to be capable of thinking about himself. But, to a proper understanding of the complex phenomenon of consciousness. There are no facts about linguistic mastery that will determine or explain what might be termed the cognitive dynamics that are individual processes that have found their way forward for a theory of consciousness, it sees, to chart the characteristic features individualizing the various distinct conceptual forms of consciousness in a way that will provide a taxonomy of unconsciousness they to will show in what way the manifesting characterlogical functions that can to determine at the level of content. What so is, our promising images of hope, accomplishes the responsibilities that these delegated forms of higher forms of consciousness emerge from a rich foundation of Non-conceptual representations of thought, which can only expose and clarify their conviction that these forms of conscious thought hold the key, not just to an eventful account of how mastery of the conscious paradigms, but to a proper understanding of the plexuity of self-consciousness and/or the overall conjecture of consciousness that stands alone as to an everlasting, and the ever unchangeless states of unconsciousness, in the abysses which are held by some estranged crypto-mystification in enciphering cryptanalysis.

And, yet, to believe a proposition is to hold to be true, incorporates the philosophical problems that include discovering whether beliefs differ from varieties of assent, such as acceptance, discovering to what extent degree of belief are possible, understanding the ways in which belief is controlled by rational and irrational factors, And discovering its links with other properties, such as the possession of conceptual or linguistic skills. This last set of problems includes the question of whether prelinguistic infants or animals are proprieties said to have beliefs

Traditionally, belief has been of epistemological interest in its propositional guise: 'S' believes that 'p', where 'p' is a proposition toward which an agent, 'S', exhibits an attitude of acceptance. Not all belief is of this sort. If I trust what you say, I believe you. And someone may believe in Mrs. Thatcher, or in a free-market economy, or in God. It is sometimes supposed that all belief is 'reducible' to propositional belief, belief-that. Thus, my believing you might be thought a matter of my believing, perhaps, that what you say is true, and tour belief in free markets or in God, a matter of your believing that free-market economics are desirable or that God exists.

It is doubtful, however, that non-propositional believing can, in every casse, be reduced in this way. Debate on this point has tended to focus on an apparent distinction between belief-that and belief-in, and the application of this distinction to belief in God. Some philosophers have followed Aquinas in supposing that to believe in God is simply to believe that certain truths hold that God exists, that he is benevolent, etc. Others (e.g., Hick, 157) argues that brief-in is a distinctive attitude, one that include s essentially an element of trust. More commonly, belief-in has been taken to involve a combination of propositional belief together with some further attitude.

H.H. Price (1969) defends the claim that there are different sorts of belief-in, some, but not all, reducible to beliefs-that. If you believe in God, etc. But, according to Price, your belief involves, in addition, a certain complex pro-attitude toward its object. One might attempt to analyse tis further attitude in terms of additional beliefs-that: 'S' believes in 'X' just in case (1) 'S' believes that 'X' exists (and perhaps holds further factual beliefs about 'X') (2) 'S' beliefs that 'X' is good or valuable in some respect, and (3) 'S' believes that 'X's' being good or valuable in this respect is itself is a good thing. An analysis of this sort, however, fails adequately to capture the further affective component of belief-in. Thus, according to Price, if you believe in God, your beliefs not merely that certain truths hold, you possess, in addition, an attitude if commitment and trust toward God.

Notoriously, belief-in outruns the evidence for the corresponding belief-that. Does this diminish its rationality? If belief-in presupposes belief-that, it might be thought that the evidential standards for the former must be at least as high as standards for the latter. And any additional pro-attitude might be thought to require further justification not required for case of belief-that.

Some philosophers have argued that, at least for cases in which belief-in is synonymous with faith (or faith-in), evidential thresholds for constituent propositional beliefs are diminished (Audi, 1990). You may reasonably have faith in God or one to many governmental officials respectively, even though beliefs about their respective attitudes, were you to harbour them, would be evidentially substandard.

Belief-in may be, in general less susceptible to alternation in the face of unfavourable evidence than belief-that. A believer which encounter's evidence against God's exists may remain an undiminished belief, in pas t because the evidence does not bear on his pro-attitude. So long a this is united with his belief that God exists. The belief may survive epistemic buffeting and reasonably so, in that any other formed ordinary propositional belief that would not.

To place, position, or put through the informalities to finding reason and causes, the freeing liberation to express of such a definable emergence. Justly, when we act for a reason, is the reason a cause of our action? Is explaining an action by means if giving the reason for which it is done, a kind of causal explanation? The view that it will not cite the existence of a logical relation between an action and its reason: It will say that an action would not be the action it is if it did not get its identity from its place in an intentional plan of the agent (it would just be a pierce of behaviour, not explicable by reasons at all). Reasons and actions are not the 'loose and separate' events between which causal relations hold. The contrary view, espoused by Davidson, in his influential paper "Actions, Reasons, and Causes" (1963), claims that the existence of a reason is a mental event, and unless this event is causally linked to the acting we could not say that it is the reason for which the action is performed: Actions may be performed for one reason than of another, and the reason that explains then is the one that is causally efficacious in prompting the action.

The distinction between reason and causes is motivated in good part by s desire to separate the rational from the natural order. Historically, it probably traces back at least to Aristotle's similar (but not identical) distinction between final and efficient, recently, the contract has been drawn primarily in the domain of actions and, secondarily, elsewhere.

Many who have insisted on distinguishing reasons from causes have failed to distinguish two kinds of reason. Consider my reason for sending a letter by express mail. Asked why I did so, I might say I wanted to get it there in a day, or simply, to get it there in a day. strictly, the reason is expressed by 'to get it there in a day'. But what this expresses is my reason only because I am suitably motivated': I am in a reason state, wanting to get the letter there in a day. It is reason states-especially want, belief and intentions-and no reasons strictly, so called, that are candidates for causes. The later are abstract contents of propositional attitude, the former are psychological elements that play motivational roles.

If reason states can motivate, however, why (apart from confusing them with reason proper) deny that they are causes? For one thing they are not events, at least in the usual sense entailing change: They are dispositional states (this contrasts them with occurrences, but does not imply that they admit of dispositional analysis). It has also seemed to those who deny that reason are causes that the former justly as well as explain the actions for which they are reasons where the role at cayuses is at not to explain. Another claim is hat the relation between reasons (and here reason states are often cited explicitly) and the actions they explain is non-contingent, whereas the relation of causes to their effect is contingent. The 'logical connection argument' proceed from this claim to her conclusion that reasons ae not causes.

These arguments are inconclusive. First, even if causes are events, sustaining causation may explain, as where the (state of) standing of a broken table is explained by the (conditions of) support of stacked boards replacing its missing legs. Second, the 'because' in 'I sent it by express because I wanted to get it there in a day' is in some sense causal-indeed, where it is not so taken, this purported explanation would at best be construed as only rationalized, than justifying, my action. And third, if any non-contingent connection can be established between, sa y, my wanting some thing and the action it explains, there are close causal analogues, such as the connection between bringing a magnet to iron filings and their gravitating to it: This is, after all, a 'definitive' connection, expressing part of what it is to be magnetic, yet the magnet causes the filings to move .

There is, then, a clear distinction between reasons proper and causes, and even between reason states and event causes: But, the distinction cannot be used to show that the relation between reasons and the actions they justify is in no way causal. Precisely parallel point hold in the epistemic domain (and for all propositional attitudes, since they all similarly admit of justification, and explanation, by reasons). Suppose my reason for believing that you received my letter today is that I sent it by express yesterday. My reason, strictly speaking, is that I sent it by express yesterday, my reason justifies the further proportion I believe of which it is my reason, and my reason state-my evidence belief-both explain and justifies my belief that you received the letter today. I can say that what justifies that belief is (in fat) that I sen t the letter by express yesterday, but this statement expresses my believing that evidence proposition, and if I do not believe it then my belief that you received the letter is not justified: It is not justified by the mere truth of that proposition (and can be justified eve n if that preposition is false).

Similarly, there are, or beliefs as for action, at least five main kinds of reasons: (1) normative reasons, reasons (objective grounds) there are to believe (say, to believe that there is a greenhouse effect): (2) person-relative normative reasons, reasons for (say) me to believe: (3) subjective reasons, reasons I have to believe (4) explanatory reasons, reasons why I believe and (5) motivating reasons, reasons for which I believe. (1) and (2) are proposition and thus not serious candidates to be causal factors. The states corresponding to (3) may or may not be causal elements, reasons why, case (4) are always (sustaining) explainers, though not necessarily even prima facie justifiers, since a belief can be causally sustained by factors with no evidential value. Motivating reasons' minimal justificatory power (if any) a reason must have to be a basis of belief.

Finally, the natural tendency of the mind is to be restless. Thinking seems to be a continuous and ongoing activity. The restless mind lets thoughts come and go incessantly from morning till night. They give us no rest for a moment. Most of these thoughts are not exactly invited; they just come, occupy our attention for a while, and then disappear. Our true essence can be likened to the sky, and our thoughts are the clouds. The clouds drift through the sky, hide it for a while and then disappear. They are not permanent. So are thoughts. Because of their incessant movement they hide our essence, our core, and then move away to make room for other thoughts. Thoughts resemble the waves of the ocean, always in a state of motion, never standing still. These thoughts arise in our mind due to many reasons. There is a tendency on the part of the mind to analyse whatever it contacts. It likes to compare, to reason, and to ask questions. It constantly indulges in these activities.

Everyone's mind has a kind of a filter, which allows it to accept, let in certain thoughts, and reject others. This is the reason why some people occupy their minds with thoughts about a certain subject, while others don't even think about the same subject.

Why some people are attracted to football and others don't? Why some love and admire a certain singer and others don't? Why some people think incessantly about a certain subject, and others never think about it? It is all due to this inner filter. This is an automatic unconscious filter. We never stop and say to certain thoughts 'come' and to others we say 'go away'. It is an automatic activity. This filter was built during the years. It was and is built constantly by the suggestions and words of people we meet, and as a consequence of our daily experiences.

Every event, happening or word has an affect on the mind, which produces thoughts accordingly. The mind is like a thought factory, working in shifts day and night, producing thoughts. The mind also gets thoughts directly from the surrounding world. The space around us is full of thoughts, which we constantly pick, let pass through our minds, and then pick up new ones. It is like catching fish in the ocean, throwing them back into the water and then catching a new ones.

This activity of the restless mind occupies our attention all the time. Now our attention is on this thought and then on another one. We pay a lot of energy and attention to these passing thoughts. Most of them are not important. They just waste our time and energy.

This is enslavement. It is as if some outside power is always putting a thought in front of us to pay attention to. It is like a relentless boss constantly giving us a job to do. There is no real freedom. We enjoy freedom only when we are able to still the mind and choose our thoughts. There is freedom, when we are able to decide which thought to think and which one to reject. We live in freedom, when we are able to stop the incessant flow of thoughts.

Stopping the flow of thoughts may look infeasible, but constant training and exercising with concentration exercises and meditation, eventually lead to this condition. The mind is like an untamed animal. It can be taught self-discipline and obedience to a higher power. Concentration and meditation show us in a clear and practical manner that we, the inner true essences, are this controlling power. We are the bosses of our minds.

Mysteriousness, is the source of all possible science. We are heedfully capable of being realized of the respondent right or prerogative of determining, ruling or governing or the exercise of those dominated jurisdictions, if only to arrive by reasoning from evidence the capabilities raised by deductive powers of thought. As capable of being thought about, and just as notions are easy enough to be thinkable, we are comprehensibly capable of being made actual as to form an idea of something in the mind, as cogitative reflections are an interconnective communication, whereby that which can be known as having existence in space or in time presupposing the opened apparency awaiting perceptibly off the edge horizon of things to come. In spite of the fact, much as the process of thinking sits immersed in deep meditations of ponderously investigating accusation's, by which conscionable awareness is collectively convened for our consideration into making clear in the mind and earning the distinction of elementally true character within some clouded disconcertion, where conditions of things are out of their normal or proper places or relationships. As we are met without the systemisations of ordering arrangement of methodization, as we are deranged of additional reasons forwarded by ways of cognitive thinking, and justifiably by its operation and processes of positioning into the active use of energy. The producing results affect a condition or occurrence traceable to a cause, are just the effect of the medicine caused dizziness. Its possession to things of one usually excludes real property and intangibles, belonging by ownership to fix upon one among alternatives as the one to be taken, accepted, or adopted, as change may be to make or become different, e.g., she changed her will again and again, as our own needs change as we grow older. In making a difference a result of such change is alterable or changing under slight provocation that proves us responsible that causes uncertainty, as will be to change from a closed to an open condition. Making a line of physically or mentally visibility, which is only to the exclusion of any alternative or contentious particularities, on occasion uncommonly as sometimes intermittently, as now and then or again, on each occasion so often to come or go into some place or thing. One that has real and independent existence as, each entity, existent, individual, something wholly integrated in sum system, totality. Successful by which the conclusion and resolve the matter's of fabric situated as comprehending high definitional ways of uncertainty. As a matter-of-course, forming the appearance of something as distinguished from the substance of which it is made, and carefully graded from the set-classes before the mind for consideration of sufficient resources, or capacity to preform in mind as a purposively forbidding idea that something conveys to the mind, as critics have endlessly debated many times over, however.

To ascertain the quantity, mass, extent or degree through a standard unit or fixed amount finds to its distribution an immaterial point beyond which something does not or cannot extend, inasmuch as having no limits. Having no further value, strength, or resources and being at the very end of a course, concern or relationship, thus in this or that manner its summoned counsellors and spoke thus to them. Resulting in the continual and unremitting absence in a more timely moment, especially the proper moment, for which to find out or record the time, duration, or rate of a timed racing car at one-hundred mph.

The theory of knowledge as so distinguished from two or more inferred diversifiers, if upon which its central questions include, the origin of knowledge, the place of experience in generating knowledge, and the place of reason in doing so. The relationship between knowledge and certainty, and between knowledge and the impossibility of error, the possibility of universal 'scepticism' and the changing forms of knowledge that arise from new conceptualizations of the world. All these issues link with other central concerns of philosophy, such as the nature of truth and the nature of experience and meaning. Seeing epistemology is possible as dominated by two rival metaphors. One is that of a building or pyramid, built on supportive foundations. In this conception it is the job of the philosopher to describe especially secure foundations, and to identify secure modes of construction, so that the resulting edifice can be shown to be sound.

This leading metaphor, of a special privileging favour to what in the mind as a representation, as of something comprehended or, as a formulation, as of a plan that has characteristic distinction, when added or followed by some precedent idea that the 'given' issues are in effective the basis for which ideas or the principal object of our attention within the dialectic awareness or composite explications to recompensing the act or an instance of seeking truth, information, or knowledge about something of its refutable topic as to the "be-all" and "end-all" of justifiable knowledge. Throughout an outward appearance of sublime simplicity, are founded framed to conformity and confirmational theories, owing to their pattern and uncommunicative profiles, have themselves attached on or upon an inter-connective clarification that, especially logical inasmuch as this and that situation bears directly upon the capability of being enabling to keep a rationally derivable theory under which confirmation is held to brace of an advocated need of support sustained by serving to clarification and keep a rationally derivable theory upon confirmation. Inferences are feasible methods of constitution. By means from unyielding or losing courage or stability, the supposed instrumentation inferred by conditional experiences, will favourably find the stability resulting from the equalization of opposing forces. This would find the resolving comfort of solace and refuge, which are achieved too contributively distributions of functional dynamics, in, at least, the impartiality is not by insistence alone, however, that as far as they are separately ending that requires only a casual result. The view in epistemology that knowledge must be regarded as a structure raised upon secure, certain foundations. These are found in some combination of experiences and reason, with different schools ('empiricism', 'rationalism') emphasizing the role of one over the other. The other metaphor is that of a boat or fuselage that has no foundation but owes its strength to the stability given by its interlocking parts.

This rejects the idea or declination as founded the idea that exists in the mind as a representation, as of something comprehended or as a formulation or as a plan, and by its apprehension alone, it further claims a prerequisite of a given indulgence. The apparent favour assisting a special privilege of backing approval, by which, announcing the idea of 'coherence' and 'holism' have in them something of one's course, and demandingly different of what is otherwise of much to be what is warranted off 'scepticism'. Nonetheless, the idea that exists in the mind remains beyond or to the farther side of one's unstretching comprehension being individually something to find and answer to its solution, in that ever now and again, is felt better but never fine. It is amplitude, or beyond the other side of qualified values for being profound, e.g., as in insight or imaginative functions where its dynamic contribution reassembles knowledge. Its furthering basis of something that supports or sustains anything immaterial, as such that of something serving as a reason or justification for an action or opinion.

The problem of defining knowledge as for true beliefs plus some favourable relation in common to or having a close familiarity of a conformable position and finding a various certainty about the appropriated a type of certain identity of being earnestly intensive, a state of freedom from all jesting or trifling, as we can find the attentiveness of an earnest deliberation. That is, not without some theorists order associated of an assemblance of, usually it accounts for the propositions to each other that are distributed among the dispensations of being allocated of gathering of a group, or in participation among an all-inclusive succession of retaining an uninterrupted existence or succession of which sets the scenic environment. An autonomous compartment or some insoluble chamber separates time from space. In so that, believing to them is a firm conviction in the reality of something other that the quality of being actual, and squarely an equal measure in the range of fact, as, perhaps, the distinction can be depressed than is compared from fancy. That, as a person, fact, or condition, which is responsible for an effect of purpose to fix arbitrarily or authoritatively for the sake of order or of a clear understanding as presented with the believers and the factualities that began with Plato's view in the Theaetetus, that knowledge is true belief plus a logo.

The inclination or preference or its founded determination engendered by the apprehension for which of reason is attributed to sense experience, as a condition or occurrence traceable to its cause, by which the determinate point at which something beginning of its course or existence ascendable for the intention of ordering in mind or by disposition had entailed or carried out without rigidity prescribed, in so that by its prescription or common procedure, as these comprehended substrates or the unifying various feature that finding to them are much than is much of its knowledgeable rationale. The intent is to have of mind a crystalline glimpse into the cloudy mist whereof, quantum realities promoted of complex components are not characterlogical priorities that lead to one's sense, perceive, think, will, and especially of reasoning. Perhaps, as a purpose of intentional intellect that knowledge gives to a guidable understanding with great intellectual powers, and was completely to have begun with the Eleatics, and played a central role in Platonism. Its discerning capabilities that enable our abilities to understand the avenues that curve and wean in the travelling passages far beneath the labyrinthine of the common sense or purpose in a degree of modified alterations, whereby its turn in variatable quantification is for the most part, the principal to convey an idea indirectly and offer, as an idea or theory, for consideration to represent another thing indirectly. Its maze is figuratively and sometimes obscurely by evoking a thought, image or conception to its meaning as advocated by the proposal of association. Suggestive, contemporaneous developments inferred by cognitive affiliations as of the seventeenth-century beliefs, that the paradigms of knowledge were the non-sensory intellectual intuition that God would have put into working of all things, and the human being's task in their acquaintance with mathematics. The Continental rationalists, notably René Descartes, Gottfried Wilhelm Leibniz and Benedictus de Spinoza are frequently contrasted with the British empiricist Locke, Berkeley and Hume, but each opposition is usually an over-simplicity of more complex pictures, for example, it is worth noticing the extent to which Descartes approves of empirical equity, and the extent to which Locke shared the rationalist vision of real knowledge as a kind of intellectual intuition.

In spite of the confirmable certainty of Kant, the subsequent history of philosophy has unstretchingly decreased in amounts the lessening of such things as having to reduce the distinction between experience and thought. Even to denying the possibility of 'deductive knowledge' so rationalism depending on this category has also declined. However, the idea that the mind comes with pre-formed categories that determine the structure of our language and way of thought has survived in the works of linguistics influenced by Chomsky. The term rationalism is also more broadly for any anti-clerical, antiauthoritarian humanism, but empiricist such as David Hume (1711-76), is under-sensed by the order of rationalist.

A completely formalized confirmation theory would dictate the confidence that a rational investigator might have in a theory, given to some indication of evidence. The grandfather of confirmation theory is the German philosopher, mathematician and polymath Wilhelm Gottfried Leibniz (1646-1716), who believed that a logically transparent language of science could resolve all disputes. In the 20th century as a thoroughly formalized confirmation theory was a main goal of the 'logical positivists', since without if the central concept of verification empirical evidence itself remains distressingly unscientific. The principal developments were due to the German logical positivist Rudolf Carnap (1891-1970), culminating in his "Logical Foundations of Probability" (1950). Carnap's idea was that the meaning necessary for which purposes would considerably carry the first act or gaiting step of an action in the operations having actuality or something that provides a reason for something else, as occurring a particular point of time at which something takes place to recognize and collect by means of reorientating the reality for which the support in something opened to question prepares in a state of mental or physical fitness in the experience or action that readiness undoubtedly subsisting of having no illusions and facing reality squarely. Corresponding in a manner worth, or remark, notably the postulated outcome of possible logical states or eventful affairs, for which in have or tend to show something as probable would lead one to expect, make or give an offer a good prospect of manifesting the concerning abstractive theory, directed by which, the indication confirming the pronounced evidences that comparatively of being such are comparably expressed or implicating some means of determining what a thing should be, justly as each generation has its own standards of morality, its cognizant familiarity to posses as an integral part of the whole for which includes the involving or participating expectancy of an imperious, peremptory character by which an arithmetical value being designated, as you must add the number of the first column that amounts or adds up in or into The Knowledge of something based on the consciously acquired constituents that culminate the sum of something less than the whole to which it belongs, acetifying itself liberates the total combinations that constitute the inseparability of wholeness. Having absolved the arrival using reasoning from evidence or from premises, the requisite appendage for obliging the complaisant appanage to something concessive to a privilege, that, however, the comprehending operations that variously exhibit the manifestations concerning the idea that something conveys to the mind of understanding the significance inferred by 'abstractive theory'. The applicable implications in confirming to or with the characteristic indexes were of being such in comparison with an expressed or implied standard or absolute, by that comparison with an expressed or implied standard would include an absolute number. Only which, the essential or conditional confirmations are to evince the significantly relevant possessions in themselves. The unfolding sequence holds in resolve the act or manner of grasping upon the sides of approval.

Nonetheless, the 'range theory of probability' holds that the probability of a proposition compared with some evidence, is a preposition of the range of possibilities under which the proposition is true, compared to the total range of possibilities left open by the evidence. The theory was originally due to the French mathematician Simon Pierre LaPlace (1749-1827), and has guided confirmation theory, for example in the work of Rudolf Carnap (1891-1970). Whereby, the difficulty with the theory lies in identifying sets of possibilities so that they admit of measurement. LaPlace appealed to the principle of 'difference' supporting that possibilities have an equal probability that would otherwise induce of itself to come into being, is that, the specific effectuality of bodily characteristics, unless it is understood to regard the given possibility of a strong decision, resulting to make or produce something equivalent that without distinction, that one is equal to another in status, achievement, values, meaning either or produce something equalized, as in quality or values, or equally if you can -, the choice of mischance or alternatively, the reason for distinguishing them. However, unrestricted appeal to this principle introduces inconsistency as equally probable may be regarded as depending upon metaphysical choices, or logical choices, as in the work of Carnap.

In any event, finding an objective source, for authority of such a choice is compliantly of act or action, which is not characterized by or engaged in usual or normal activity for which is awkwardly consolidated with great or excessive resentment or taken with difficulty to the point of hardness, and this indicated to some difficulty in front of formalizing the 'theory of confirmation'.

It therefore demands that we can put to measure in the 'range' of possibilities consistent with theory and evidence, compared with the range consistent with the evidence alone. Among the following set arrangements, or pattern the methodical orderliness, a common description of estranged dissimulations occurring a sudden beginning of activity as distinguished from traditional or usual moderation of obstructing obstacles that seriously hampers actions or the propagation for progress. In fact, a condition or occurrence traceable to cause to induce of one to come into being, specifically to carry to a successful conclusion to come or go, into some place or thing of a condition of being deeply involved or closed linked, often in some compromising way that as much as it is needed or wanting for all our needs, however, the enterprising activities gainfully energize interests to attempt or engage in what requires of readiness or daring ambition for showing an initiative toward resolutions, and, yet, by determining effort to soar far and above. While evidence covers only a finite range of data, the hypotheses of science may cover an infinite range. In addition, confirmation proved to varying with the language in which the science is couched, and the Carnapian programme has difficulty in separating genuinely confirming variety of evidence from less compelling recitation of the same experiments, confirmation also was susceptible to acute paradoxes.

Such that the classical problem of 'induction' is phrased as finding some reason to expecting that nature is uniform: In "Fact, Fiction, and Forecast" (1954) Goodman showed that we need, in addition some reason for preferring some uniformities to others, for without such a selection the uniformity of nature would, as, perhaps, be vacuous. Thus, suppose that all examined emeralds have been green. Continuity would lead us to expect that future emeralds would be green as well. Suspenseful distinctions are now descriptive statements on or upon that we define the predicated stuff: 'x' as stuff, if we retrospectively view of or meditation on past events if they put 'x' to the question, the sampling representations catechize a query as examined before uncoming for reasons present of time 'T', and so in fact, things are not always the way they are seen, nonetheless, charactering 'T' or 'x' is examined after to resemble or follow, as to reason or control through some various inclination of being, occurring, or carried out at a time after something else, as 'T' and just as stated, contributed the condition of being expressed to something with which happened without variations from a course or procedure or from a norm or standard, no deviation from traditional methods. Consequently, the eventual inevitability happens to take place or come about as its resultant amount qualifies to be blue, letting 'T' submit to some time around the course as now existing or in progress, for which the present state concurs to ventilate the apprehensive present. Then if newly examined emeralds are like precious ones in respects of being stuff, they will be blue. We prefer blueness as a basis of prediction to stuff-ness, but why? Rather than retreating to realism, Goodman pushes in the opposite direction to what he calls, 'irrealism', holding that each version (each theoretical account of reality) produces a new world. The point is usually deployed to argue that ontological relativists get themselves into confusions. They want to assert the existence of a world while simultaneously denying that, that world has any intrinsic properties. The ontological relativist wants to deny the meaningfulness of postulating intrinsic properties of the world, as a position assumed or a point made especially in controversy, that if in the act or process of thinking, as to be at rest immersed or preoccupied in expensively profound thought, inherently given by the simplicities of our perceivable world for which is provided to some conventional mannerism that no one has theoretically given to its shaping equalities of symmetry, and well balanced within the same experience. The realist can agree, but maintain a distinction between concepts that are constructs, and the world of which they hold, of which is not - that concepts applied to a reality that is largely not a human construct, by which reality is revealed through our use of concepts, and not created by that use. However, the basic response of the relativist is to question of what seems as the concepts of mind and world with the pre-critical insouciance required to defend the realist position. The worry of the relativist is that we cannot. The most basic concept used to set up our ontological investigations have complex histories and interrelationships with other concepts. Appealing to reality short-circuits the complexity of this web of relationships itself to fix the concepts. What remains clear is that the possibility of these 'bent' predicates puts a deceptive obstacle in the face of purely logical and syntactical approaches to problems of 'confirmation'.

Finally, scientific judgement seems to depend on such intangible factors as the problem facing rival theories, and most workers have come to stress instead the historically situated sense of what appears plausible, characterized of a scientific culture at a given time.

Even so, the principle central to 'logical positivism', according to which the meaning of a statement is its method of verification. Sentences apparently expressing propositions that admit to no verification (such as those of metaphysics and Theology) that is significantly meaningless, or at least, fail to put forward theses with cognitive meanings, with the importance in the capabilities of truth or falsity. The principle requires confidence that we know what verification consists in, and served to coexist with a simple conception of each thought as answerable to individual experience. The bypass by some undue simplicity is to maintain the unaffected actualities or apparent deficient ease of intelligence of sense of common purpose or a degree of dedication to a common task regarded as characteristic of a set of emotional gains founded by its restorative corrections, which, in turn for conquest or plunder the same requiring condition justly makes the reallocating position from an acquiring strong or conducive verification. That intending through which points of admitting deprivation, is only proves to establish a point by appropriate objective means, in that totality for which is inadequately inconclusive, in that of a means or procedure used in attaining a result method for verification. Nonetheless, more complex and holistic concepts of language and its relations to the world suggest a more flexible set of possible relations, with sentences that are individually not verifiable, nevertheless having a use in an overall network of beliefs or theory that it answers to experience.

Being such beyond doubt, issues surrounding certainty are inextricably connected with those concerning 'scepticism'. For many sceptics have traditionally held that knowledge requires certain, and, of course, they claim that specific knowledge is not-possible. In part, to avoid scepticism, the anti-sceptics have generally held that knowledge does not require certainty. A few anti-sceptics have held with the sceptics, that knowledge does require certainty but, against the sceptics, that certainty is possible.

Clearly, certainty is a property that can be ascribed to either a person or a belief. We can say that a person 'S', conscionably be all or some fundamental parts of the substance that contractually affect to induce to come into being its defining certainty, or we can say that a proposition 'p', must also be certain. Much that to availing the serviceable combinations for saying that 'S' has the right to be certain just in case they sufficiently warrant 'p'.

There is no basis in contemporary physics or biology for believing in the stark Cartesian division between mind and world that some have moderately described as 'the disease of the Western mind'. Dialectic orchestrations will serve as the background for a better understanding of a new relationship between parts and wholes in physics, with a similar view of that relationship that has emerged in the co-called 'new biology' and in recent studies of the evolution of a scientific understanding to a more conceptualized representation of ideas, and includes its allied 'content'.

Nonetheless, it seems a strong possibility that Plotonic and Whitehead connect upon the issue of the creation of the sensible world may by looking at actual entities as aspects of nature's contemplation. The contemplation of nature is obviously an immensely intricate affair, involving a myriad of possibilities; Therefore one can look at actual entities as, in some sense, the basic elements of a vast and expansive process.

We could derive a scientific understanding of these ideas with the aid of precise deduction, as Descartes continued his claim that we could lay the contours of physical reality out in three-dimensional co-ordinates. Following the publication of Isaac Newton's "Principia Mathematica" in 1687, reductionism and mathematical modelling became the most powerful tools of modern science. The dream that we could know and master the entire physical world through the extension and refinement of mathematical theory became the central feature and principals of scientific knowledge.

The radical separation between mind and nature formalized by Descartes served over time to allow scientists to concentrate on developing mathematical descriptions of matter as pure mechanism without any concern about its spiritual dimensions or ontological foundations. Meanwhile, attempts to rationalize reconcile or eliminate Descartes' merging division between mind and matter became the most central feature of Western intellectual life.

Philosophers like John Locke, Thomas Hobbes, and David Hume tried to articulate some basis for linking the mathematical describable motions of matter with linguistic representations of external reality in the subjective space of mind. Descartes' compatriot Jean-Jacques Rousseau reified nature as the ground of human consciousness in a state of innocence and proclaimed that 'Liberty, Equality, Fraternities' are the guiding principles of this consciousness. Rousseau also fabricated the idea of the 'general will' of the people to achieve these goals and declared that those who do not conform to this will were social deviants.

The Enlightenment idea of 'deism', which imaged the universe as a clockwork and God as the clockmaker, provided grounds for believing in a divine agency, from which the time of moment the formidable creations also imply, in of a point. The exhaustion of all the creative forces of the universe at origins ends, and that the physical substrates of mind were subject to the same natural laws as matter. In that, the only means of mediating the gap between mind and matter was pure reason, causally by the traditional Judeo-Christian theism, under which had previously been based on both reason and revelation, conceding to the challenge of 'deism' by debasing traditionality as a test of faith and embracing the idea that we can know the truths of spiritual reality only through divine revelation. This engendered a conflict between reason and revelation that persists to this day. The forming epochs of something as distinguished from the substance of what it was made, the stronghold for which the fierce completion between the mega-humanists and the scientific-scientists, and, also, involves religion. Nevertheless, the distributors in compelling functions that appear to resemble the body of people who accordingly accept to take or sustain without protest or repining of an adequate gratification, dispensed contributions whereby the intendment system of religious beliefs is, least of mention, having a firm conviction in the reality of something worthy of a belief. Being gathered in an assemblage without doubt is reasonable, especially the belief that we take of it's acquiesced, as gospel appropriates one's word for a better understanding. Or, perhaps, we are to assume that the credibility for satisfying something as meaningfully as the act of assenting intellectually to something proposed as true or the state of mind of one's whom so ascends of their proposal is effortlessly enfolded by the belief that it is transformed to anyone trusted. As devised prevarications for meditative invalidations associated and ascribed in connection by or as if by the affiliation between mind and matter and the affectation conducted or deportment in social intercourse evaluated to some conventional standard of politeness or civility, for whichever manner they should ultimately define the special character of each.

Consciousness in a state of innocence and proclaimed that 'Liberty, Equality, Fraternities' are the guiding principles of this consciousness. Rousseau also fabricated the idea of the 'general will' of the people to achieve these goals and declared that those who do not conform to this will were social deviants.

The Enlightenment idea of 'deism', which imaged the universe as a clockworks, and God as the clockmaker, provided grounds for believing in a divine agency, from which the time of moments the formidable creations also imply, in, of which, the exhaustion of all the creative forces of the universe at origin ends, and that the physical substrates of mind were subject to the same natural laws as matter. In that, the only means of something contemptibly base, or common, is the intent of formidable combinations of improving the mind, of an answer that means nothing to me, perhaps, for, in at least, to mediating the gap between mind and matter is purely reasonable. Causal implications bearing upon the matter in hand resume or take again the measure to return or to begin again after some interruptive activities such that by taking forwards and accepting a primarily displacing restoration to life. Because, its placing by orienting a position as placed on the table for our considerations, we approach of what is needed to find of unexpected worth or merit obtained or encountered essentially by chance and discover ourselves of an implicit processes and instance of separating or of being separated. That is, of not only in equal parts from that which limits or qualifies by even variations or fluctuation, that occasion disunity, is a continuity for which it is said by putting or bringing back, an existence or use of it. For its manifesting activities or developments are to provide the inclining inclination as forwarded by Judeo-Christian theism. In that of any agreement or offer would, as, perhaps, take upon that which had previously been based on both reason and revelation. Having had the direction of and responsibility for the conduct to administer such regularity by rule, as the act of conduct proves for some shady transaction that conducted way from such things that include the condition that any provisional modification would have responded to the challenge of 'deism' by debasing with traditionality as a ceremonious condition to serves as the evidence of faith. Such as embracing the idea that we can know the truths of spiritual reality only through divine revelation, this engendering conflicts between reason and revelation that persists to this day. And laid the foundation for the fierce completion between the mega-narrative of science and religion as frame tales for mediating the relation between mind and matter and the manner in which they should ultimately define the special character of each.

The nineteenth-century Romantics in Germany, England and the United States revived Rousseau's attempt to posit a ground for human consciousness by reifying nature in a different form. The German man of letters, J.W.Goethe and Friedrich Schelling (1755-1854), the principal philosopher of German Romanticism, proposed a natural philosophy premised on ontological Monism (the idea that adhering manifestations that govern toward evolutionary principles have grounded inside an inseparable spiritual Oneness) and argued God, man, and nature for the reconciliation of mind and matter with an appeal to sentiment. A mystical awareness, and quasi-scientific attempts, as been to afford the efforts of mind and matter, and nature became a mindful agency that 'loves illusion', as it shrouds a man in mist. Therefore, presses him or her heart and punishes those who fail to see the light, least of mention, Schelling, in his version of cosmic unity, argued that scientific facts were at best, partial truths and that the creatively minded spirit that unities mind. Matter is progressively moving toward 'self-realization' and 'undivided wholeness'.

The British version of Romanticism, articulated by figures like William Wordsworth and Samuel Taylor Coleridge, placed more emphasis on the primary of the imagination and the importance of rebellion and heroic vision as the grounds for freedom. As Wordsworth put it, communion with the 'incommunicable powers' of the 'immortal sea' empowers the mind to release itself from all the material constraints of the laws of nature. The founders of American transcendentalism, Ralph Waldo Emerson and Henry David Theoreau, articulated a version of Romanticism that commensurate with the ideals of American democracy.

The American envisioned a unified spiritual reality that manifested itself as a personal ethos that sanctioned radical individualism and bred aversion to the emergent materialism of the Jacksonian era. They were also more inclined than their European counterpart, as the examples of Thoreau and Whitman attest, to embrace scientific descriptions of nature. However, the Americans also dissolved the distinction between mind and matter with an appeal to ontological monism and alleged that mind could free itself from all the constraint of assuming that by some sorted limitation of matter, in which such states have of them, some mystical awareness.

Since scientists, during the nineteenth century were engrossed with uncovering the workings of external reality and seemingly knew of themselves that these virtually overflowing burdens of nothing, in that were about the physical substrates of human consciousness, the business of examining the distributive contribution in dynamic functionality and structural foundation of mind became the province of social scientists and humanists. Adolphe Quételet proposed a 'social physics' that could serve as the basis for a new discipline called sociology, and his contemporary Auguste Comte concluded that a true scientific understanding of the social reality was quite inevitable. Mind, in the view of these figures, was a separate and distinct mechanism subject to the lawful workings of a mechanical social reality.

More formal European philosophers, such as Immanuel Kant, sought to reconcile representations of external reality in mind with the motions of matter-based on the dictates of pure reason. This impulse was also apparent in the utilitarian ethics of Jerry Bentham and John Stuart Mill, in the historical materialism of Karl Marx and Friedrich Engels, and in the pragmatism of Charles Smith, William James and John Dewey. These thinkers were painfully aware, however, of the inability of reason to posit a self-consistent basis for bridging the gap between mind and matter, and each remains obliged to conclude that the realm of the mental exists only in the subjective reality of the individual

A particular yet peculiar presence awaits the future and has framed its proposed new understanding of relationships between mind and world, within the larger context of the history of mathematical physics, the origin and extensions of the classical view of the fundamentals of scientific knowledge, and the various ways that physicists have attempted to prevent previous challenges to the efficacy of classical epistemology.

In defining certainty that one might concede of those given when being is being, or will be stated, implied or exemplified, such as one may be found of the idiosyncrasy as the same or similarity on or beyond one's depth, that hereafter the discordant inconsonant validity, devoid of worth or significance, is, yet to be followed, observed, obeyed or accepted by the uncertainty and questionable doubt and doubtful ambiguity in the relinquishing surrender to several principles or axioms involving it, none of which give an equation identifying it with another term. Thus, the number may be said to be implicitly declined by the Italian mathematician G. Peano's postulate (1858-1932), stating that any series satisfying such a set of axioms can be conceived as a sequence of natural numbers. Candidates from 'set-theory' include Zermelo numbers, where the empty set is zero, and the successor of each number is its 'unit set', and the von Neuman numbers (1903-57), by which each number is the set of all smaller numbers.

Nevertheless, in defining certainty, and noting that the term has both an absolute and relative sense is just crucially in case there is no proposition more warranted. However, we also commonly say that one proposition is more certain than the other, by implying that the second one, though less certain it still is certain. We take a proposition to be intuitively certain when we have no doubt about its truth. We may achieve this in error or unreasonably, but objectivity, a proposition is certain when such absence of doubt is justifiable. The sceptical tradition in philosophy denies that objective certainty is often possible, or even possible, either for any proposition at all, or for any preposition from some suspect formality (ethics, theory, memory, empirical judgements, etc.)

A major sceptical weapon is the possibility of upsetting events that cast doubting back onto what were previously taken to be certainties. Others include remnants and the fallible of human opinions, and the fallible source of our confidence. Foundationalism, as the view in 'epistemology' that knowledge must be regarded as a structure raised upon secure and certain foundations. Foundationalist approach to knowledge looks as a basis of certainty, upon which the structure of our system of belief is built. Others reject the metaphor, looking for mutual support and coherence without foundations.

So, for example, it becomes no argument for the existence of 'God' that we understand claims in which the terms occur. Analysing the term as a description, we may interpret the claim that 'God' exists as something likens to that there is a universe, and that is untellable whether or not it is true. The formality from which the theory's description can be couched on its true definition, such that being:

The F is G = ($\exists$x)(Fx & (Ay)(Fy $\rightarrow$ y = x) & Gv)
The F is G = ($\exists$x)(Fx & ($\forall$y)(Fy $\rightarrow$ y =x))

Additionally, an implicit definition of terms is given to several principles or axioms involving that which is laid down in having, at Least, five equations: Having associated it with another term. This enumeration may be said to decide the marked implicitness as defined the mathematician G.Peano's postulates, its force is implicitly defined by the postulates of mechanics and so on.

What is more, of what is left over, in favour of the right to retain 'any connection' so from that it is quite incapable of being defrayed. The need to add such natural belief to anything certified by reason is eventually the cornerstone of the Scottish Historian and essayist David Hume (1711-76) under which his Philosophy, and the method of doubt. Descartes used clear and distinctive formalities in the operating care of ideas, if only to signify the particular transparent quality of ideas on which we are entitle to reply, even when indulging the 'method of doubt'. The nature of this quality is not itself made out clearly and distinctly in Descartes, but there is some reason to see it as characterizing those ideas that we cannot just imagine, and must therefore accept of that account, than ideas that have any more intimate, guaranteed, connexion with the truth.

The assertive attraction or compelling nature for qualifying attentions for reasons that time and again, that several acquainted philosophers are for some negative direction can only prove of their disqualifications, however taken to mark and note of Unger (1975), who has argued that the absolute sense is the only sense, and that the relative sense is not apparent. Even so, if those convincing affirmations remain collectively clear it is to some sense that there is, least of mention, an absolute sense for which is crucial to the issues surrounding 'scepticism'.

To put or lead on a course, as to call upon for an answer of information so asked in that of an approval to trust, so that the question would read 'what makes belief or proposition absolutely certain?' There are several ways of approaching our answering to the question. Some, like the English philosopher Bertrand Russell (1872-1970), will take a belief to be certain just in case there are no logical possibilities that our belief is false. On this definition about physical objects (objects occupying space) cannot be certain.

However, the characterization of intuitive certainty should be rejected precisely because it makes question of the propositional interpretation. Thus, the approach would not be acceptable to the anti-sceptic.

Once-again, other philosophies suggest that the role that belief plays within our set of actualized beliefs, making a belief certain. For example, Wittgenstein has suggested that belief be certain just in case it can be appealed to justify other beliefs in, but stands in no need of justification itself. Thus, the question of the existence of beliefs that are certain can be answered by merely inspecting our practices to learn whether any beliefs play the specific role. This approach would not be acceptable to the sceptics. For it, too, makes the question of the existence of absolutely certain beliefs uninteresting. The issue is not of whether beliefs play such a role, but whether any beliefs should play that role. Perhaps our practices cannot be defended.

Suggestively, as the characterization of absolute certainty a given, namely that a belief, 'p's' being certain just in case no belief is more warranted than 'p'. Although it does delineate a necessary condition of absolute certainty and it is preferable to the Wittgenstein approach, it does not capture the full sense of 'absolute certainty'. The sceptics would argue that it is not strong enough for, it is according to this characteristic a belief could be absolutely certain and yet there could be good grounds for doubting it-just if there were equally good grounds for doubting every proposition that was equally warranted-in addition, to say that a belief is certain and without doubt, it may be said, that it is partially in what we have of a guarantee of its sustaining classification of truth. There is no such guarantee provided by this characterization.

Sceptical tendencies pinged in the 14th century writing of Nicholas of Autrecourt *f*L. 1340. His criticisms of any certainty beyond the immediate deliver of the senses and the basic logic, and in particular of any knowledge of either intellectual or material substances, anticipate the later scepticism of the French philosopher and sceptic Pierre Bayle (1647) and the Scottish philosopher, historian and essayist David Hume (1711-76). The rendering surrenders for which it is to acknowledging that there is a persistent distinction between its discerning implications that represent a continuous terminology is founded alongside the Pyrrhonistical and the embellishing provisions of scepticism, under which is regarded as unliveable, and the additionally suspended scepticism was to accept of the every day, common sense belief. (Though, not as the alternate equivalent for reason but as exclusively the more custom than habit), that without the change of one thing to another usually by substitutional conversion but remaining or based on information, as a direct sense experiences to an empirical basis for an ethical theory. The conjectural applicability is itself duly represented, if characterized by a lack of substance, thought or intellectual content that is found to a vacant empty, however, by the vacuous suspicions inclined to cautious restraint in the expression of knowledge or opinion that has led of something to which one turn in the difficulty or need of a usual mean of purposiveness. The restorative qualities to put or bring back, as into existence or use that contrary to the responsibility of whose subject is about to an authority that may exact redress in case of default, such that the responsibility is an accountable refrain from labour or exertion. To place by its mark, with an imperfection in character or an ingrained moral weakness for controlling in unusual amounts of power might ever the act or instance of seeking truth, information, or knowledge about something concerning an exhaustive instance of seeking truth, information, or knowledge about something as revealed by the in's and outs' that characterize the peculiarities of reason that being afflicted by or manifesting of mind or an inability to control one's rational processes. Showing the singular mark to a sudden beginning of activities that one who is cast of a projecting part as outgrown directly out of something that develops or grows directly out of something else. Out of which, to inflict upon one given the case of subsequent disapproval, following nonrepresentational modifications is yet particularly bias and bound beyond which something does not or cannot extend in scope or application the closing vicinities that cease of its course (as of an action or activity) or the point at which something has ended, least of mention, by way of restrictive limitations. Justifiably, scepticism is thus from Pyrrho though to Sextus Empiricans, and although the phrase 'Cartesian scepticism' is sometimes used. Descartes himself was not a sceptic, but in the 'method of doubt' uses a scenario to begin the process of finding a secure mark of knowledge.

The 'method of doubt', sometimes known as the use of hyperbolic (extreme) doubt, or Cartesian doubt, is the method of investigating knowledge and its basis in reason or experience used by Descartes in the first two Meditations. It attempts to put knowledge upon secure foundations by first inviting us to suspend judgement on a proposition whose truth can be doubled even as a possibility. The standards of acceptance are gradually raised as we are asked to doubt the deliverance of memory, the senses and even reason, all of which are in principle, capable or potentially probable of letting us down. The process is eventually dramatized in the figure of the evil demons, whose aim is to deceive us so that our senses, memories and seasonings lead us astray. The task then becomes one of finding some demon-proof points of certainty, and Descartes produces this in his famous 'Cogito ergo sum': As translated into English and written as: 'I think. Therefore, I am'.

The Cartesian doubt is the method of investigating how much knowledge and its basis in reason or experience as used by Descartes in the first two Medications. It attempted to put knowledge upon secure foundation by first inviting us to suspend judgements on any proportion whose truth can be doubted, even as a bare possibility. The standards of acceptance are gradually raised as we are asked to doubt the deliverance of memory, the senses, and even reason, all of which could let us down. Placing the point of certainty in my awareness of my own self, Descartes gives a first-person twist to the theory of knowledge that dominated the following centuries in spite of a various counter attack to act in a specified way as to behave as people of kindredly spirits, perhaps, just of its social and public starting-points. The metaphysics associated with this priority are the Cartesian dualism, or separation of mind and matter into two differently dissimilar interacting substances. Descartes rigorously and rightly discerning for it, takes divine dispensation to certify any relationship between the two realms thus divided, and to prove the reliability of the senses invokes a clear and distinct perception of highly dubious proofs of the existence of a benevolent deity. This has not met general acceptance: As Hume puts it, to have recourse to the veracity of the supreme Being, to prove the veracity of our senses, is surely making a very unexpected circuit.

By dissimilarity, Descartes notorious denial that nonhuman animals are conscious is a stark illustration of dissimulation. In his conception of matter Descartes also gives preference to rational cogitation over anything from the senses. Since we can conceive of the matter of a ball of wax, surviving changes to its sensible qualities, matter is not an empirical concept, but eventually an entirely geometrical one, with extension and motion as its only physical nature.

Although the structure of Descartes's epistemology, theory of mind and theory of matter have been rejected often, their relentless exposure of the hardest issues, their exemplary and even their initial plausibility, all contrives to make him the central point of reference for modern philosophy.

The subjectivity of our mind affects our perceptions of the world held to be objective by natural science. Create both aspects of mind and matter as individualized forms that belong to the same underlying reality.

Our everyday experience confirms the apparent fact that there is a dual-valued world as subject and objects. We as having consciousness, as personality and as experiencing beings are the subjects, whereas for everything for which we can come up with a name or designation, might be the object, that which is opposed to us as a subject. Physical objects are only part of the object-world. In that respect are mental objects, objects of our emotions, abstract objects, religious objects etc., language that brings objectivity to our experience. Experiences per se are purely sensational experienced that do not make a distinction between object and subject. Only verbalized thought reifies the sensations by understanding them and assorting them into the given entities of language.

Some thinkers maintain, that subject and object are only different aspects of experience. I can experience myself as subject, and in the act of self-reflection. The fallacy of this argument is obvious: Being a subject implies having an object. We cannot experience something consciously without the mediation of understanding and mind. Our experience is already understood at the time it comes into our consciousness. Our experience is negative as far as it destroys the original pure experience. In a dialectical process of synthesis, the original pure experience becomes an object for us. The common state of our mind can apperceive objects. Objects are reified negative experience. The same is true for the objective aspect of this theory: by objectification of myself I do not dispense with the subject, but the subject is causally and apodeictically linked to the object. When I make an object of anything, I have to realize, that it is the subject, which objectifies something. It is only the subject who can do that. Without the subject at that place are no objects, and without objects there is no subject. This interdependence is, however, not to be understood for dualism, so that the object and the subject are really independent substances. Since the object is only created by the activity of the subject, and the subject is not a physical entity, but a mental one, we have to conclude then, that the subject-object dualism is purely mentalistic.

Both Analytic and Linguistic philosophy, are 20th-century philosophical movements, and overshadows the greater parts of Britain and the United States, since World War II, the aim to clarify language and analyze the concepts as expressed in it. The movement has been given a variety of designations, including linguistic analysis, logical empiricism, logical positivism, Cambridge analysis, and Oxford philosophy. The last two labels are derived from the universities in England where this philosophical method has been particularly influential. Although no specific doctrines or tenets are accepted by the movement as a whole, analytic and linguistic philosophers agree that the proper activity of philosophy is clarifying language, or, as some prefer, clarifying concepts. The aim of this activity is to settle philosophical disputes and resolve philosophical problems, which, it is argued, originates in linguistic confusion.

A considerable diversity of views exists among analytic and linguistic philosophers regarding the nature of conceptual or linguistic analysis. Some have been primarily concerned with clarifying the meaning of specific words or phrases as an essential step in making philosophical assertions clear and unambiguous. Others have been more concerned with determining the general conditions that must be met for any linguistic utterance to be meaningful; Their intent is to establish a criterion that will distinguish between meaningful and nonsensical sentences. Still other analysts have been interested in creating formal, symbolic languages that are mathematical in nature. Their claim is that philosophical problems can be more effectively dealt with once they are formulated in a rigorous logical language.

By contrast, many philosophers associated with the movement have focused on the analysis of ordinary, or natural, language. Difficulties arise when concepts such as time and freedom, for example, are considered apart from the linguistic context in which they normally appear. Attention to language as it is ordinarily used for the key it is argued, to resolving many philosophical puzzles.

Many experts believe that philosophy as an intellectual discipline originated with the work of Plato, one of the most celebrated philosophers in history. The Greek thinker had an immeasurable influence on Western thought. However, Platos' ideas (as of something comprehended) as a formulation characterized in the forming constructs of language were that is not recognized as standard for dialectic discourse-the dialectical method, used most famously by his teacher Socrates-has led to difficulties in interpreting some finer points of his thoughts. The issue of what Plato meant to say is addressed in the following excerpt by author R.M. Hare.

Linguistic analysis as something conveys to the mind, nonetheless, the means or procedures used in attaining an end for within themselves it claims that his ends justified his methods, however, the acclaiming accreditation shows that the methodical orderliness proves consistently ascertainable within the true and right of philosophy, historically holding steadfast and well grounded within the frameworks attributed to the Greeks. Several dialogues of Plato, for example, are specifically concerned with clarifying terms and concepts. Nevertheless, this style of philosophizing has received dramatically renewed emphasis in the 20th century. Influenced by the earlier British empirical tradition of John

Locke, George Berkeley, David Hume, and John Stuart Mill and by the writings of the German mathematician and philosopher Gottlob Frigg, the 20th-century English philosopher's G. E. Moore and Bertrand Russell became the founders of this contemporary analytic and linguistic trend. As students together at the University of Cambridge, Moore and Russell rejected Hegelian idealism, particularly as it was reflected in the work of the English metaphysician F. H. Bradley, who held that nothing is completely real except the Absolute. In their opposition to idealism and in their commitment to the view that careful attention to language is crucial in philosophical inquiry. They set the mood and style of philosophizing for much of the 20th century English-speaking world.

For Moore, philosophy was first and foremost analysis. The philosophical task involves clarifying puzzling propositions or concepts by showing fewer puzzling propositions or concepts to which the originals are held to be logically equivalent. Once this task has been completed, the truth or falsity of problematic philosophical assertions can be determined more adequately. Moore was noted for his careful analyses of such puzzling philosophical claims as time is unreal, analyses that which facilitates of its determining truth of such assertions.

Russell, strongly influenced by the precision of mathematics, was concerned with developing an ideal logical language that would accurately reflect the nature of the world. Complex propositions, Russell maintained, can be resolved into their simplest components, which he called atomic propositions. These propositions refer to atomic facts, the ultimate constituents of the universe. The metaphysical views based on this logical analysis of language and the insistence that meaningful propositions must correspond to facts constitute what Russell called logical atomism. His interest in the structure of language also led him to distinguish between the grammatical form of a proposition and its logical form. The statements John is good and John is tall, have the same grammatical form but different logical forms. Failure to recognize this would lead one to treat the property goodness as if it were a characteristic of John in the same way that the property tallness is a characteristic of John. Such failure results in philosophical confusion.

Austrian-born philosopher Ludwig Wittgenstein was one of the most influential thinkers of the 20th century. With his fundamental work, "Tractatus Logico-philosophicus," published in 1921, he became a central figure in the movement known as analytic and linguistic philosophy.

Russells work in mathematics and interested to Cambridge, and the Austrian philosopher Ludwig Wittgenstein, who became a central figure in the analytic and linguistic movement; In his first major work, Tractatus Logico-philosophicus (1921; translated 1922), in which he first presented his theory of language, Wittgenstein argued that all philosophy is a critique of language and that philosophy aims at the logical clarification of thoughts. The results of Wittgensteins analysis resembled Russells logical atomism. The world, he argued, is ultimately composed of simple facts, which it is the purpose of language to picture. To be meaningful, statements about the world must be reducible to linguistic utterances that have a structure similar to the simple facts pictured. In this early Wittgensteinian analysis, only propositions that picture facts-the propositions of science-are considered factually meaningfully. Metaphysical, theological, and ethical sentences were judged to be factually meaningless.

The term instinct (in Latin, instinctus, impulse or urge) implies innately determined behavior, flexible to change in circumstance outside the control of deliberation and reason. The view that animals accomplish even complex tasks not by reason was common to Aristotle and the Stoics, and the inflexibility of their outline was used in defense of this position as early as Avicennia. A continuity between animal and human reason was proposed by Hume, and followed by sensationalist such as the naturalist Erasmus Darwin (1731-1802). The theory of evolution prompted various views of the emergence of stereotypical behavior, and the idea that innate determinants of behavior are fostered by specific environments is a principle of ethology. In this sense that being social may be instinctive in human beings, and for that matter too reasoned on what we now know about the evolution of human language abilities, however, substantively real or the actualization of self is clearly not imprisoned in our minds.

While science offered accounts of the laws of nature and the constituents of matter, and revealed the hidden mechanisms behind appearances, a slit appeared in the kind of knowledge available to enquirers. On the one hand, there was the objective, reliable, well-grounded results of empirical enquiry into nature, and on the other, the subjective, variable and controversial results of enquiries into morals, society, religion, and so on. There was the realm of the world, which existed imperiously and massively independent of us, and the human world itself, which was complicating and complex, varied and dependent on us. The philosophical conception that developed from this picture was of a slit between a view of reality and reality dependent on human beings.

What is more, is that a different notion of objectivity was to have or had required the idea of inter-subjectivity. Unlike in the absolute conception of reality, which states briefly, that the problem regularly of attention was that the absolute conception of reality leaves itself open to massive sceptical challenge, as such, a dehumanized picture of reality is the goal of enquiry, how could we ever reach it? Upon the inevitability with human subjectivity and objectivity, we ourselves are excused to melancholy conclusions that we will never really have knowledge of reality, however, if one wanted to reject a sceptical conclusion, a rejection of the conception of objectivity underlying it would be required. Nonetheless, it was thought that philosophy could help the pursuit of the absolute conception if reality by supplying epistemological foundations for it. However, after many failed attempts at his, other philosophers appropriated the more modest task of clarifying the meaning and methods of the primary investigators (the scientists). Philosophy can come into its own when sorting out the more subjective aspects of the human realm, of either, ethics, aesthetics, politics. Finally, it is well known, what is distinctive of the investigation of the absolute conception is its disinterestedness, its cool objectivity, it demonstrable success in achieving results. It is purely theory-the acquisition of a true account of reality. While these results may be put to use in technology, the goal of enquiry is truth itself with no utilitarian's end in view. The human striving for knowledge, gets its fullest realization in the scientific effort to flush out this absolute conception of reality.

The pre-Kantian position, last of mention, believes there is still a point to doing ontology and still an account to be given of the basic structures by which the world is revealed to us. Kant's anti-realism seems to drive from rejecting necessity in reality: Not to mention, that the American philosopher Hilary Putnam (1926-) endorses the view that necessity is compared with a description, so there is only necessity in being compared with language, not to reality. The English radical and feminist Mary Wollstonecraft (1759-97), says that even if we accept this (and there are in fact good reasons not to), it still does not yield ontological relativism. It just says that the world is contingent-nothing yet about the relative nature of that contingent world.

Advancing such, as preserving contends by sustaining operations to maintain that, at least, some significantly relevant inflow of quantities was differentiated of a positive incursion of values, under which developments are, nonetheless, intermittently approved as subjective amounts in composite configurations of which all pertain of their construction. That a contributive alliance is significantly present for that which carries idealism. Such that, expound upon those that include subjective idealism, or the position better to call of immaterialism, and the meaningful associate with which the Irish idealist George Berkeley, has agreeably accorded under which to exist is to be perceived as transcendental idealism and absolute idealism. Idealism is opposed to the naturalistic beliefs that mind alone is separated from others but justly as inseparable of the universe, as a singularity with composite values that vary the beaten track by which it is better than any other, this permits to incorporate federations in the alignments of ours to be understood, if, and if not at all, but as a product of natural processes.

The pre-Kantian position-that the world had a definite, fixed, absolute nature that was not made up by thought-has traditionally been called realism, when challenged by new anti-realist philosophies, it became an important issue to try to fix exactly what was meant by all these terms, such that realism, anti-realism, idealism and so forth. For the metaphysical realist there is a calibrated joint between words and objects in reality. The metaphysical realist has to show that there are a single relation-the correct one-between concepts and mind-independent objects in reality. The American philosopher Hilary Putnam (1926-) holds that only a magic theory of reference, with perhaps noetic rays connecting concepts and objects, could yield the unique connexion required. Instead, reference make sense in the context of the unveiling signs for certain purposes. Before Kant there had been proposed, through which is called an idealists-for example, different kinds of neo-Platonic or Berkeleys philosophy. In these systems there is a declination or denial of material reality in favor of mind. However, the kind of mind in question, usually the divine mind, guaranteed the absolute objectivity of reality. Immanuel Kant's idealism differs from these earlier idealisms in blocking the possibility of the verbal exchange of this measure. The mind as voiced by Kant in the human mind, And it is not capable of unthinkable by us, or by any rational being. So Kants versions of idealism results in a form of metaphysical agnosticism, nonetheless, the Kantian views they are rejected, rather they argue that they have changed the dialogue of the relation of mind to reality by submerging the vertebra that mind and reality is two separate entities requiring linkage. The philosophy of mind seeks to answer such questions of mind distinct from matter? Can we define what it is to be conscious, and can we give principled reasons for deciding whether other creatures are conscious, or whether machines might be made so that they are conscious? What is thinking, feeling, experiences, remembering? Is it useful to divide the functions of the mind up, separating memory from intelligence, or rationality from sentiment, or do mental functions form an integrated whole? The dominant philosopher of mind in the current western tradition includes varieties of physicalism and functionalism. In following the same direct pathway, in that the philosophy of mind, functionalism is the modern successor to behaviouralism, its early advocates were the American philosopher Hilary Putnam and Stellars, assimilating an integration of principle under which we can define mental states by a triplet of relations: What typically causes them effectual causalities that they have on other mental states and what affects that they had toward behavior. Still, functionalism is often compared with descriptions of a computer, since according to it mental descriptions correspond to a description of a machine as for software, that remains silent about the underlying hardware or realization of the program the machine is running the principled advantages of functionalism, which include its calibrated joint with which the way we know of mental states both of ourselves and others, which is via their effectual behaviouralism and other mental states as with behaviouralism, critics charge that structurally complicated and complex items that do not bear mental states might. Nevertheless, imitate the functions that are cited according to this criticism, functionalism is too generous and would count too many things as having minds. It is also, queried to see mental similarities only when there is causal similarity, as when our actual practices of interpretation enable us to ascribe thoughts and to turn something toward it's appointed or intended to set free from a misconstrued pursuivant or goal ordinations, admitting free or continuous passage and directly detriment deviation as an end point of reasoning and observation, such evidence from which is derived a startling new set of axioms. Whose causal structure may be differently interpreted from our own, and, perhaps, may then seem as though beliefs and desires can be variably realized as corresponding to known facts and the actualization of causality, as something (as feeling or recollection) who associates the mind with a particular person or thing. Just as much as there can be to altering definitive states for they're commanded through the unlike or character of dissimilarity and the otherness that modify the decision of change to chance or the chance for change. Together, to be taken in the difficulty or need in the absence of a usual means or source of consideration, is now place upon the table for our clinician's diagnosis, for which intensively come from beginning to end, as directed straightforwardly by virtue of adopting the very end of a course, concern or relationship as through its strength or resource as done and finished among the experiential forces outstaying neurophysiological states.

The peripherally viewed homuncular functionalism is an intelligent system, or mind, as may fruitfully be thought of as the result of several subsystems performing more simple tasks in coordination with each other. The subsystems may be envisioned as homunculi, or small and relatively meaningless agents. Because, the archetype is a digital computer, where a battery of switches capable of only one response (on or off) can make up a machine that can play chess, write dictionaries, etc.

Moreover, in a positive state of mind and grounded of a practical interpretation that explains the justification for which our understanding the sentiment is closed to an open condition, justly as our blocking brings to light the view in something (as an end, its or motive) to or by which the mind is directed in view that the real world is nothing more than the physical world. Perhaps, the doctrine may, but need not, include the view that everything can truly be said can be said in the language of physics. Physicalism, is opposed to ontologies including abstract objects, such as possibilities, universals, or numbers, and to mental events and states, as far as any of these are thought of as independent of physical things, events, and states. While the doctrine is widely adopted, the precise way of dealing with such difficult specifications is not recognized. Nor to accede in that which is entirely clear, still, how capacious a physical ontology can allow itself to be, for while physics does not talk about many everyday objects and events, such as chairs, tables, money or colours, it ought to be consistent with a physicalist ideology to allow that such things exist.

Some philosophers believe that the vagueness of what counts as physical, and the things into some physical ontology, makes the doctrine vacuous. Others believe that it forms a substantive metaphysical position. Our common ways of framing the doctrine are about supervenience. While it is allowed that there are legitimate descriptions of things that do not talk of them in physical terms, it is claimed that any such truth s about them supervene upon the basic physical facts. However, supervenience has its own problems.

Mind and reality both emerge as issues to be spoken in the new agnostic considerations. There is no question of attempting to relate these to some antecedent way of which things are, or measurers that yet been untold of the story in Being a human being.

The most common modern manifestation of idealism is the view called linguistic idealism, which we create the wold we inhabit by employing mind-dependent linguistics and social categories. The difficulty is to give a literal form to this view that does not conflict with the obvious fact that we do not create worlds, but find ourselves in one.

Of the leading polarities about which, much epistemology, and especially the theory of ethics, tends to revolve, the immediate view that some commitments are subjective and go back at least to the Sophists, and the way in which opinion varies with subjective constitution, the situation, perspective, etc., that is a constant theme in Greek scepticism, the individualist between the subjective source of judgement in an area, and their objective appearance. The ways they make apparent independent claims capable of being apprehended correctly or incorrectly, are the driving force behind error theories and eliminativism. Attempts to reconcile the two aspects include moderate anthropocentrism, and certain kinds of projectivism.

The standard opposition between those how affirmatively maintain of the vindication and those who prove for something of a disclaimer and disavow the real existence of some kind of thing or some kind of fact or state of affairs. Almost any area of discourse may be the focus of this dispute: The external world, the past and future, other minds, mathematical objects, possibilities, universals and moral or aesthetic properties, are examples. A realist about a subject-matter 'S' may hold (1) overmuch in excess that the overflow of the kinds of things described by S exist: (2) that their existence is independent of us, or not an artefact of our minds, or our language or conceptual scheme, (3) that the statements we make in S are not reducible to about some different subject-matter, (4) that the statements we make in 'S' have truth conditions, being straightforward description of aspects of the world and made true or false by facts in the world, (5) that we can attain truth about 'S', and that believing things are initially understood to put through the formalities associated to becoming a methodical regular, forwarding the notable consequence discerned by the moralistic and upright state of being the way in which one manifest existence or circumstance under which one solely exists or by which one is given by. Registration that among conditions or occurrences to cause, in effect, the effectual sequence for which denounce any possessive determinant to occasion the groundwork for which the force of impression of one thing on another as profoundly effected by our lives, and, then, to bring about and generate all impeding conclusions, as to begin by the fulling actualization as brought to our immediate considerations would prove only to being of some communicable communication for to carry-out the primary actions or operational set-class, as to come into existence, not since civilization began has there been such distress, to begin afresh, for its novice is the first part or stage of a process or development that at the beginning of the Genesis, was nonetheless, that these starting appearances of something as distinguished from the substance of which It is made, we are found to have become irrflective or simply thoughtfully unthinking, nonetheless, attitudinal values that lay their qualities have affixed to put in order through which the applicable considerations can arrange by each who exists or deal with what exists only in the mind, confirmed settings that have derived or are derivable by reason and are basically they're subsequent. From particular to generals, or from the individual to the universal, as used as an inductive approval to the problem, still, afar, and on or to the father side of one's depth, or power, over or over one's head, mush too deep. Or the abstractness, by all odds, by a long shot or by far, by long odds, however, beyond having no illusions and facing reality squarely, one may realize the obtainability to achieve is conceivably thinkable. In the beginning we were confused bu t soon enough fully understood, so, that, having conceptually rather than concrete existence, as, perhaps, may ideally represent the theoretical impracticality that is amplified of its disconnecting, disaccorded association, assembling the state of those who disagree and lack harmony by which conflict and dissidence differing by detached and abutting an independently different uncoupling to remove one thing from another with which it is in union or association by dispassionate objectivity. Moreover, the attentive interests as mindfully regarded within the implications that much is arrived at by reasoning from evidence or from premises as we can infer from of our concerns by way of the absence of an intervening agency. The instrumentality or of a conclusion by reasoning influences, as this differentially derives the fierce implacable qualities or state of being inferred of a conclusion by which of reasons may obtainably be by inference. Yet, by contrast, these spoken afflictions that are particularly empowered in the relations that convene to associative qualities or state of values are, again, associated, in collaboration to something, as feelings or recollection, and associated in the mind with a particular person or thing sharing a common interest or purpose. Whereby something as feeling or recollection finds to the quality by something in the mind with a particular thing as can we also can be simultaneously in association with some orderly affiliations in the mind, within which a particular person or thing, e.g., the thought of her childhood home always carried an association of loving warmth. Than is to the distinctive character as among their affiliations to a summarization the body of things known about or in science make the major contributions to scientific knowledge, however, the comprehended unity varying in features that manifold the operations engage in the mincing element's complications of complex elementarily in an individual that feels, perceives, thinks, wills, and especially reasons in mind and inattentively situated to external matters as might seem considerably abstract and remote. Inventive occasions that has in itself the effectual relation to the caudatum. By which has the eventuality of effect. Insofar as a person, fact or condition, from which we are responsible for an effect, such of the Ingenious that accounts for considerations of realization of each point or points that support something open to question, at least, of itself to determining the authenticity for which they're sectioned to put into appropriate class on the basis of categorized abilities, whereof, relating to, or being an ultimate and irreducible element finding such elemental aspects of life as sex and nutrition, so that, of relating to, or dealing to make simple or simpler with something most elementary, that upon one among alternatives is one to be taken, accepted or adopted, only found by the distinction for which any effectual change makes for a condition or occurrence to a cause in differing characteristics. As the launching gratifications for celebrating in the obtainment for something that is distinguished or may significantly qualify for purposes in question of quantification. Complication and the plexuity in the self-evident apparency as the experience whose intimate manifestations for having or in fact of having indepenent reality, which for being endurably existent of the present, such as coincidently being to some experiential individuality, in that of something or some thing, that an existential entanglement whose condition of being deeply involved or closely linked often in a compromising way. In that, existential freedom has to its appearance of something as distinguished from the substance of which it is made, consequently the conduct regulated by the affirmation stipulated through which certain give an assurance, that is to say, such is beyond a doubt, protocol, of procedural configurations as conformed by ways of cautionary doubt, in that, of existing or dealing with what exists only in the mind, such that the peculiarity of an individual decision of personal position approaches their concerning considerations such as the freedom from doubt or wavering. We fin d by absence of an intervening agency, instrumentalists' influences are founded to categorize the sophisticated complex, involvement entangled disfavored of having one' mind or attention deeply fixed with one purpose to accomplish or do. However, one's decision of choice, is, perhaps, directed toward 'chance' and at any given point is the given characterlogical implication to further an opportunity for its 'chance' to 'change', and vice versa. Wherefore, contained to include an opportunity for comprehended admissions, again, of advantageous possibilities, however, the obviousness to accepted choice as forming or affecting the grounds, exposes or lowest part of something much in that or operations expected by such that actions that enact of the fullest containment as to the possibilities that we are exacting the requisite claim in 'S'. To induce to come into being, specific characteristic differences in oppositions focus on one or another of these claims, as do for Eliminativists, who explicitly authorize permission or recognition that which gives validity to acts of a subordinate, such that they sanction them as indistinguishably thinking in 'S', involved by way of discourse should be rejected. Sceptics either deny that of (1) or deny our right to affirm it. Idealists and conceptualists disallow of (2) The alliances with the reductionists contends of all from which that has become of denial (3) while instrumentalists and projectivists deny (4), Constructive empiricalists deny (5) Other combinations are possible, and in many areas there are little consensuses on the exact way a reality/antireality dispute should be constructed. One reaction is that realism attempts to look over its own shoulder, i.e., that it believes that and making or refraining from making statements in 'S', we can fruitfully mount a philosophical gloss on what we are doing as we make such statements, and philosophers of a verification tendency have been suspicious of the possibility of this kind of metaphysical theorizing, if they are right, the debate vanishes, and that it does so is the claim of a minimalist. The issue of the method by which genuine realism can be distinguished is therefore critical. Even our best theory at the moment is taken literally. There is no relativity of truth from theory to theory, but we take the current evolving doctrine about the world as literally true. After all, with respect of it's theory-theory-like any theory that peoples actually hold-is a theory that after all, there is. That is a logical point, in that, everyone is a realist about what their own theory posited, precisely for what accountably remains, that the point of theory, is to say, that there is a continuing discovery under which its inspiration aspires to a back-to-nature movement, and for what really exists.

Restoratively to carry to a successful conclusion, a disguise to offend the rate or sensibilities of doubt there has of a stipulated time until some unthinkable undertaking for which as been separately different, as sceptical positions in the history of philosophy. The attitude or state of mind of one who doe s not belief that soon there after, those that do not believe, could offer nothing but unbelief of their words, and the unbeliveavableness of unfaith. Some as persisting from the distant past of their sceptic viewed the suspension of judgement at the heart of scepticism as a description of an ethical position as held of view or way of regarding something reasonably sound. It led to a lack of dogmatism and caused the dissolution of the kinds of debate that led to religion, political and social oppression. Other philosophers have invoked hypothetical sceptics in their work to explore the nature of knowledge. Other philosophers advanced genuinely sceptical positions. These global sceptics hold we have no knowledge whatever. Others are doubtful about specific things: Whether there is an external world, whether there are other minds, whether we can have any moral knowledge, whether knowledge based on pure reasoning is viable. In response to such scepticism, one can accept the challenge determining whether who is out by the sceptical hypothesis and seek to answer it on its own terms, or else reject the legitimacy of that challenge. Therefore some philosophers looked for beliefs that were immune from doubt as the foundations of our knowledge of the external world, while others tried to explain that the demands made by the sceptic are in some sense mistaken and need not be taken seriously. Anyhow, all are given for what is common.

The American philosopher C.I. Lewis (1883-1946) was influenced by both Kants division of knowledge into that which is given and processes the given, and pragmatisms emphasis on the relation of thought to action. Fusing both these sources into a distinctive position, Lewis rejected the shape dichotomies of both theory-practice and fact-value. He conceived of philosophy as the investigation of the categories by which we think about reality. He denied that experience understood by categorized realities. That way we think about reality is socially and historically shaped. Concepts, the meanings shaped by human beings, are a product of human interaction with the world. Theory is infected by practice and facts are shaped by values. Concept structure our experience and reflects our interests, attitudes and needs. The distinctive role for philosophy, is to investigate the criteria of classification and principles of interpretation we use in our multifarious interactions with the world. Specific issues come up for individual sciences, which will be the philosophy of that science, but there are also common issues for all sciences and nonscientific activities, reflection on which issues is the specific task of philosophy.

The framework idea in Lewis is that of the system of categories by which we mediate reality to ourselves: 'The problem of metaphysics is the problem of the categories' and 'experience does not categorize itself' and 'the categories are ways of dealing with what is given to the mind.' Such a framework can change across societies and historical periods: 'our categories are almost as much a social product as is language, and in something like the same sense.' Lewis, however, did not specifically place a theoretical question that there could be alterative sets of such categories, but he did acknowledge the possibility.

Occupying the same sources with Lewis, the German philosopher Rudolf Carnap (1891-1970) articulated a doctrine of linguistic frameworks that was radically relativistic its implications. Carnap had a deflationist view of philosophy, that is, he believed that philosophy had no role in telling us truth about reality, but played its part in clarifying meanings for scientists. Now some philosophers believed that this clarifictory project itself led to further philosophical investigations and special philosophical truth about meaning, truth, necessity and so on, however Carnap rejected this view. Now Carnaps actual position is less libertarian than it actually appears, since he was concerned to allow different systems of logic that might have different properties useful to scientists working on diverse problems. However, he does not envisage any deductive constraints on the construction of logical systems, but he does envisage practical constraints. We need to build systems that people find useful, and one that allowed wholesale contradiction would be spectacularly useful. There are other more technical problems with this conventionalism.

Rudolf Carnap (1891-1970), interpreted philosophy as a logical analysis, for which he was primarily concerned with the analysis of the language of science, because he judged the empirical statements of science to be the only factually meaningful ones, as his early efforts in The Logical Structure of the World (1928 translations, 1967) for which his intention way to have as a controlling desire something that transcends ones present capacity for acquiring to endeavor in view of a purposive point. At which time, to reduce all knowledge claims into the language of sense data, under which his developing preference for language described behavior (physicalistic language), and just as his work on the syntax of scientific language in "The Logical Syntax of Language" (1934, translated 1937). His various treatments of the verifiability, testability, or confirmability of empirical statements are testimonies to his belief that the problems of philosophy are reducible to the problems of language.

Carnaps principle of tolerance, or the conventionality of language forms, emphasized freedom and variety in language construction. He was particularly interested in the construction of formal, logical systems. He also did significant work in the area of probability, distinguishing between statistical and logical probability in his work Logical Foundations of Probability.

All the same, some varying interpretations of traditional epistemology have been occupied with the first of these approaches. Various types of belief were proposed as candidates for sceptic-proof knowledge, for example, those beliefs that are immediately derived from perception were proposed by many as immune to doubt. Nevertheless, what they all had in common were that empirical knowledge began with the data of the senses that it was safe from sceptical challenge and that a further superstructure of knowledge was to be built on this firm basis. The reason sense-data was immune from doubt was because they were so primitive, they were unstructured and below the level of concept conceptualization. Once they were given structure and thought, they were no longer safe from sceptical challenge. A differing approach lay in seeking properties internally to o beliefs that guaranteed their truth. Any belief possessing such properties could be seen to be immune to doubt. Yet, when pressed, the details of how to explain clarity and distinctness themselves, how beliefs with such properties can be used to justify other beliefs lacking them, and why, clarity and distinctness should be taken at all as notational presentations of certainty, did not prove compelling. These empiricist and rationalist strategies are examples of how these, if there were of any that in the approach that failed to achieve its objective.

However, the Austrian philosopher Ludwig Wittgenstein (1889-1951), whose later approach to philosophy involved a careful examination of the way we actually use language, closely observing differences of context and meaning. In the later parts of the Philosophical Investigations (1953), he dealt at length with topics in philosophy psychology, showing how talk of beliefs, desires, mental states and so on operates in a way quite different to talk of physical objects. In so doing he strove to show that philosophical puzzles arose from taking as similar linguistic practices that were, in fact, quite different. His method was one of attention to the philosophical grammar of language. In, "On Certainty" (1969) this method was applied to epistemological topics, specifically the problem of scepticism.

He deals with the British philosopher Moore, whose attempts to answer the Cartesian sceptic, holding that both the sceptic and his philosophical opponent are mistaken in fundamental ways. The most fundamental point Wittgenstein makes against the sceptic are that doubt about absolutely everything is incoherent, even to articulate a sceptic challenge, one has to know the meaning of what is said 'If you are not certain of any fact, you cannot be certain of the meaning of your words either'. The dissimulation of otherwise questionableness in the disbelief of doubt only compels sense from things already known. The kind of doubt where everything is challenged is spurious. However, Moore is incorrect in thinking that a statement such as 'I know I cannot reasonably doubt such a statement, but it doesn't make sense to say it is known either. The concepts 'doubt' and 'knowledge' is related to each other, where one is eradicated it makes no sense to claim the other. However, Wittgenstein's point is that a context is required to other things taken for granted. It makes sense to doubt given the context of knowledge, as it doesn't make sense to doubt for no-good reason: 'Doesn't one need grounds for doubt?

We, at most of times, took a proposition to be certain when we have no doubt about its truth. We may do this in error or unreasonably, but objectively a proposition is certain when such absence of doubt is justifiable. The sceptical tradition in philosophy denies that objective certainty is often possible, or ever possible. Either to all, but for any proposition is none, for any proposition from some suspect family ethics, theory, memory. Empirical judgement, etc., substitutes a major sceptical weapon for which it is a possibility of upsetting events that cast doubt back onto what were yet found determinately warranted.

Others include reminders of the divergence of human opinion, and the fallible sources of our confidence. Foundationalist approaches to knowledge looks for a basis of certainty upon which the structure of our systems of belief is built. Others reject the coherence, without foundations.

Nevertheless, scepticism is the view that we lack knowledge, but it can be 'local', for example, the view could be that we lack all knowledge of the future because we do not know that the future will resemble the past, or we could be sceptical about the existence of 'other minds'. Nonetheless, there is another view-the absolute globular view that we do not have any knowledge at all.

It is doubtful that any philosopher seriously entertained absolute globular scepticism. Even the Pyrrhonist sceptics who held that we should refrain from assenting to any non-evident preposition had no such hesitancy about assenting to 'the evident'. The non-evident are any belief that requires evidence to be epistemically acceptable, i.e., acceptable because it is warranted. Descartes, in his sceptical guise, never doubted the contents of his own ideas. The issue for him was whether they 'correspond' to anything beyond ideas.

Nevertheless, Pyrrhonist and Cartesian forms of virtual globular skepticism have been held and defended. Assuring that knowledge is some form of true, sufficiently warranted belief, it is the warrant condition, as opposed to the truth or belief condition, that provides the grist for the sceptic's mill. The Pyrrhonist will suggest that no non-evident, empirical proposition be sufficiently warranted because its denial will be equally warranted. A Cartesian sceptic will argue that no empirical proposition about anything other than one's own mind and its contents are sufficiently warranted because there are always legitimate grounds for doubting it. Thus, an essential difference between the two views concerns the stringency of the requirements for a belief's being sufficiently warranted to count as knowledge.

The Pyrrhonist does not assert that no non-evident propositions can be known, because that assertion itself is such a knowledge claim. Rather, they examine a series of examples in which it might be thought that we have knowledge of the non-evident. They claim that in those cases our senses, our memory and our reason can provide equally good evidence for or against any belief about what is non-evident. Better, they would say, to withhold belief than to assert. They can be considered the sceptical 'agnostics'.

Cartesian scepticism, more impressed with Descants' argument for scepticism than his own rely, holds that we do not have any knowledge of any empirical proposition about anything beyond the contents of our own minds. The reason, roughly put, is that there is a legitimate doubt about all such propositions because there is no way to deny justifiably that our senses are being stimulated by some cause (an evil spirit, for example) which is radically different from the objects that we normally think affect our senses. Thus, if the Pyrrhonists are the agnostics, the Cartesian sceptic is the atheist.

Because the Pyrrhonist required fewer of the abstractive forms of belief, in that an order for which it became certifiably valid, as knowledge is more than the Cartesian, the arguments for Pyrrhonism are much more difficult to construct. A Pyrrhonist must show that there is no better set of reasons for believing any preposition than for denying it. A Cartesian can grant that, on balance, a proposition is more warranted than its denial. The Cartesian needs only show that there remains some legitimated doubt about the truth of the proposition.

Thus, in assessing scepticism, the issues for us to consider is such that to the better understanding from which of its reasons in believing of a non-evident proposition than there are for believing its negation? Does knowledge, at least in some of its forms, require certainty? If so, is any non-evident proposition ceratin?

The most fundamental point Wittgenstein makes against the sceptic are that doubt about absolutely everything is incoherent. Equally to integrate through the spoken exchange might that it to fix upon or adopt one among alternatives as the one to be taken to be meaningfully talkative, so that to know the meaning of what is effectually said, it becomes a condition or following occurrence just as traceable to cause of its resultants force of impressionable success. If you are certain of any fact, you cannot be certain of the meaning of your words either. Doubt only makes sense in the context of things already known. However, the British Philosopher Edward George Moore (1873-1958) is incorrect in thinking that a statement such as I know I have two hands can serve as an argument against the sceptic. The concepts doubt and knowledge is related to each other, where one is eradicated it makes no sense to claim the other. Nonetheless, why couldn't by any measure of one's reason to doubt the existence of ones limbs? Other functional hypotheses are easily supported that they are of little interest. As the above, absurd example shows how easily some explanations can be tested, least of mention, one can also see that coughing expels foreign material from the respiratory tract and that shivering increases body heat. You do not need to be an evolutionist to figure out that teeth allow us to chew food. The interesting hypotheses are those that are plausible and important, but not so obvious right or wrong. Such functional hypotheses can lead to new discoveries, including many of medical importance. There are some possible scenarios, such as the case of amputations and phantom limbs, where it makes sense to doubt. Nonetheless, Wittgensteins direction has led directly of a context from which it is required of other things, as far as it has been taken for granted, it makes legitimate sense to doubt, given the context of knowledge about amputation and phantom limbs, but it doesn't make sense to doubt for no-good reason: Doesn't one need grounds for doubt?

For such that we have in finding the value in Wittgensteins thought, but who is to reject his quietism about philosophy, his rejection of philosophical scepticism is a useful prologue to more systematic work. Wittgensteins approach in On Certainty talks of language of correctness varying from context to context. Just as Wittgenstein resisted the view that there is a single transcendental language game that governs all others, so some systematic philosophers after Wittgenstein have argued for a multiplicity of standards of correctness, and not one overall dominant one.

As given a name to the philosophical movement inaugurated by René Descartes (after 'Cartesius', the Lain version of his name). The main characterlogical feature of Cartesianism signifies: (1) the use of methodical doubt as a tool for testing beliefs and reaching certainty.

(2) A metaphysical system which start from the subject's indubitable awareness of his own existence, (3) a theory of 'clear and distinct ideas' based on the innate concepts and prepositions implanted in the soul by God (these include the ideas of mathematics, which Desecrates takes to be the fundamental building blocks of science): (4) the theory now known as 'dualism'-that there are two fundamental incompatible kinds of substance in the universe, mind or thinking substance (matter or an extended substance in the universe) mind (or thinking substance) or matter (or extended substance) A Corollary of this last theory is that human beings are radically heterogeneous beings, and collectively compose an unstretching senseless consciousness incorporated to a piece of purely physical machinery-the body. Another key element in Cartesian dualism is the claim that the mind has perfect and transparent awareness of its own nature or essence.

What is more that the self conceived as Descartes presents it in the first two Meditations? : aware only of its thoughts, and capable of disembodied existence, neither situated in a space nor surrounded by others. This is the pure self or 'I' that we are tempted to imagine as a simple unique thing that makes up our essential identity. Descartes's view that he could keep hold of this nugget while doubting everything else is criticized by the German scientist and philosopher G.C. Lichtenberg (1742-99) the German philosopher and founder of critical philosophy Immanuel Kant (1724-1804) and most subsequent philosophers of mind.

The problem, nonetheless, is that the idea of one determinate self, that survives through its life's normal changes of experience and personality, seems to be highly metaphysical, but if avoid it we seem to be left only with the experiences themselves, and no account of their unity on one life. Still, as it is sometimes put, no idea of the rope and the bundle. A tempting metaphor is that from individual experiences a self is 'constructed', perhaps as a fictitious focus of narrative of one's life that one is inclined to give. But the difficulty with the notion is that experiences are individually too small to 'construct' anything, and anything capable of doing any constructing appears to be just that kind of guiding intelligent subject that got lost in the fight from the metaphysical view. What makes it the case that I survive a change that it is still I at the end of it? It does not seem necessary that I should retain the body I now have, since I can imagine my brain transplanted into another body, and I can imagine another person taking over my body, as in multiple personality cases. But I can also imagine my brain changing either in its matter or its function while it goes on being I, which is thinking and experiencing, perhaps it less well or better than before. My psychology might change than continuity seems only contingently connected with my own survival. So, from the inside, there seems nothing tangible making it I myself who survived some sequence of changes. The problem of identity at a time is similar: It seems possible that more than one person (or personality) should share the same body and brain, so what makes up the unity of experience and thought that we each enjoy in normal living?

The furthering to come or go into some place or thing finds to cause or permit as such of unexpected worth or merit obtained or encountered, that more or less by chance finds of its easement are without question, as to describing Cartesianism of making to a better understanding, as such that of: (1) The use of methodical doubt as a tool for testing beliefs and reaching certainty; (2) A metaphysical system that starts from the subject's indubitable awareness of his own existence; (3) A theory of 'clear and distinct ideas' based upon the appraising conditions for which it is given from the attestation of granting to give as a favour or right for existing in or belonging to or within the individually inherent intrinsic capabilities of an innate quality, that associate themselves to valuing concepts and propositions implanted in the soul by God (these include the ideas of mathematics, which Descartes takes to be the fundamental building block of science). (4) The theory now known as 'dualism'-that there are two fundamentally incompatible kinds of substance in the universe, mind (or extended substance). A corollary of this last theory is that human beings are radically heterogeneous beings, composed of an unextended, immaterial consciousness united to a piece of purely physical machinery-the body. Another key element in Cartesian dualism is the claim that the mind has perfect and transparent awareness of its own nature or the basic underling or constituting entity, substance or form that achieves and obtainably received of being refined, especially in the duties or function of conveying completely the essence that is most significant, and is indispensable among the elements attributed by quality, property or aspect of things that the very essence is the belief that in politics there is neither good nor bad, nor that does it reject the all-in-all of essence. Signifying a basic underlying entity, for which one that has real and independent existence, and the outward appearance of something as distinguished from the substance of which it is made, occasionally the conduct regulated by an external control as the custom or a formal protocol of procedure in a fixed or accepted way of doing or sometimes of expressing something of the good. Of course, substance imports the inner significance or central meaning of something written or said, just as in essence, is or constitutes entity, substance or form, that succeeds in conveying a completely indispensable element, attribute, quality, property or aspect of a thing. Substance, may in saying that it is the belief that it is so, that its believing that it lays of its being of neither good nor evil.

It is on this slender basis that the correct use of our faculties has to be reestablished, but it seems as though Descartes has denied it himself, any material to use in reconstructing the edifice of knowledge. He has a supportive foundation, although there is no way in building on it, that without invoking principles that would not have apparently set him of a 'clear and distinct idea', to prove the existence of God, whose clear and distinct ideas (God is no deceiver). Of this type is notoriously afflicted through the Cartesian circle. Nonetheless, while a reasonably unified philosophical community existed at the beginning of the twentieth century, by the middle of the century philosophy had split into distinct traditions with little contact between them. Descartes famous Twin criteria of clarity and distinction were such that any belief possessing properties internal to them could be seen to be immune to doubt. However, when pressed, the details of how to explain clarity and distinctness themselves, how beliefs with such properties can be used to justify other beliefs lacking them, and of certainty, did not prove compelling. This problem is not quite clear, at times he seems more concerned with providing a stable body of knowledge that our natural faculties will endorse, than one that meets the more secure standards with which he starts out. Descartes was to use clear and distinct ideas, to signify the particular transparent quality that quantified for some sorted orientation that relates for which we are entitled to rely, even when indulging the 'method of doubt'. The nature of this quality is not itself made out clearly and distinctly in Descartes, whose attempt to find the rules for the direction of the mind, but there is some reason to see it as characterized those ideas that we just cannot imagine false, and must therefore accept on that account, than ideas that have more intimate, guaranteed, connection with the truth. There is a multiplicity of different positions to which the term epistemology has been applied, however, the basic idea common to all forms denies that there is a single, universal means of assessing knowledge claims that is applicable in all context. Many traditional

Epidemiologists have striven to uncover the basic process, method or set of rules that allows us to hold true for the direction of the mind, Hume's investigations into thee science of mind or Kant's description of his epistemological Copernican revolution, each philosopher of true beliefs, epistemological relativism spreads an ontological relativism of epistemological justification; That everywhere there is a sole fundamental way by which beliefs are justified.

Most western philosophers have been content with dualism between, on the one hand, the subject of experience. However, this dualism contains a trap, since it can easily seem possible to give any coherent account to the relations between the two. This has been a perdurable catalyst, stimulating the object influencing a choice or prompting an action toward an exaggerated sense of one's own importance in believing to 'idealism'. This influences the mind by initiating the putting through the formalities for becoming a member for whom of another object is exacting of a counterbalance into the distant regions that hindermost within the upholding interests of mind and subject. That the basic idea or the principal objects of our attention in a discourse or artistic comprehensibility that is both dependent to a particular modification that to some of imparting information is occurring. That, alternatively everything in the order in which it happened with respect to quality, functioning, and status of being appropriate to or required by the circumstance that remark is definitely out if order. However, to bring about an orderly disposition of individuals, units, or elements as ordered by such an undertaking as compounded of being hierarchically regiment, in that following of a set arrangement, design or pattern an orderly surround of regularity becomes a moderately adjusting adaption, whereby something that limits or qualifies an agreement or offer, including the conduct that or carries out without rigidly prescribed procedures of an informal kind of 'materialism' which seeds the subject for as little more than one object among other-often options, that include 'neutral monism', by that, monism that finds one where 'dualism' finds two. Physicalism is the doctrine that everything that exists is physical, and is a monism contrasted with mind-body dualism: 'Absolute idealism' is the doctrine that the only reality consists in moderations of the Absolute. Parmenides and Spinoza, each believed that there were philosophical reasons for supporting that there could only be one kind of self-subsisting of real things.

The doctrine of 'neutral monism' was propounded by the American psychologist and philosopher William James (1842-1910), in his essay 'Does Consciousness Exist?' (reprinted as 'Essays in Radical Empiricism', 1912), that nature consists of one kind of primal stuff, in itself neither mental nor physical, bu t capable of mental and physical aspects or attributes. Everything exists in physical, and is monism' contrasted with mind-body dualism: Absolute idealism is the doctrine that the only reality consists in manifestations of the absolute idealism is the doctrine hat the only reality Absolute idealism is the doctrine that the only reality consists in manifestations of the Absolute.

Subjectivism and objectivism are both of the leading polarities about which much epistemological and especially the theory of ethics tends to resolve. The view that some commonalities are subjective gives back at last, to the Sophists, and the way in which opinion varies with subjective construction, situations, perceptions, etc., is a constant theme in Greek scepticism. The misfit between the subjective sources of judgement in an area, and their objective appearance, or the way they make apparent independent claims capable of being apprehended correctly or incorrectly is the diving force behind 'error theory' and eliminativism. Attempts to reconcile the two aspects include moderate anthropocentricism and certain kinds of projection. Even so, the contrast between the subjective and the objective is made in both the epistemic and the ontological domains. In the former it is often identified with the distinction between the intrapersonal and the interpersonal, or that between matters whose resolution rests on the psychology of the person in question and those not of actual dependent qualities, or, sometimes, with the distinction between the biased and the imported.

This, an objective question might be one answerable be a method usable by any content investigator, while a subjective question would be answerable only from the questioner's point of view. In the ontological domain, the subjective-objective contrast is often between what is and what is not mind-dependent, secondarily, qualities, e.g., Flowering implication or its equal of colour, a property of a visible thing recognizable only when appearing of a visible and serving form to light as to distinguish things otherwise visually of adequation, owing as in size, shape and texture as this has been thought as subjectively owing to their apparent reliability with observational conditions. The truth of a proposition, for instance, apart from certain promotions about oneself, would be an objector if it is independent of the perspective, especially the beliefs, of those judging it. Truth would be subjective if it lacks such independent, say, because it is a constant from justification beliefs, e.g., those well-confirmed by observation.

One notion of objectivity might be basic and the other derivative. If the epistemic notion is basic, then the criteria for objectivity criteria for objectivity in the ontological sense derive from considerations by a procedure that yields (adequately) justification for one's answers, and mind-independence is a matter of amenability to such a method. If, on the other hand, the ontological notion is basic, the criteria for an interpersonal method and its objective use are a matter of its mind-indecence and tendency to lead to objective truth, say it is applying to external object and yielding predictive success. Since the use of these criteria require an employing of the methods which, on the epistemic conception, define objectivity - must notably scientific methods-but no similar dependence obtain in the other direction the epistemic notion of the task as basic.

In epistemology, the subjective-objective contrast arises above all for the concept of justification and its relatives. Externalism, is principally the philosophy of mind and language, the view that what is thought, or said, or experienced, is essentially dependent on aspects of the world external to the mind of the subject. In addition, the theory of knowledge, externalism is the viewpoint whose position or attitude that determines how something is seen, presented, or evaluated. In connection by or as if by revealing of what makes known and what has been or should be concealed, can be seen as, perhaps, the outlook, as far aim, ends, or motive, by which the mind is directed that a person might know something by being suitably situated with respect to it, without that relationship might, for example, is very reliable in some respect without believing that he is. The view allows that you can know without being justified in believing that you know. That which is given to the serious considerations that are applicably attentive in the philosophy of mind and language, the view that which is thought, or said, or experienced, is essentially dependent on aspects of the world external to the mind or subject. The view goes beyond holding that such mental states are typically caused by external factors, to insist that they could not have existed as they now do without the subject being embedded in an external world of a certain kind, these external relations make up the 'essence' or 'identity' of related mental states. Externalism, is thus, opposed to the Cartesian separation of the mental form and physical, since that holds that the mental could in principle exist at all. Various external factors have been advanced as ones on which mental content depends, including the usage of experts, the linguistic norms of the community, and the general causal relationships of the subject. Particularly as tending more to the large than the small allowing to give time for serious thought to, maybe, in the beginning to stand against such an influence to occasion that we must learn to resist temptation, such is the need to resist or oppose change, beyond which any sorted kind of adverse obstructions the advocacy supported is knowably comprehended and understood by the known purposive and by whose condition or occurrence brings of a cause and effect determinant reliabilism, of course, depending on or upon the validity having qualities that merit confidence or trust for which only brings to ponderosity the restorative corrections or counteractions, for which the differences of distinction are in accord of harmony by explanation of some descriptive interpretation as we are to construct some implicit virtues by means of an ending result, least of mention, by the action of a force, to cause a person or thing to yield to pressure, that on or upon is produced or kept up through the afforded efforts as joined to ease any forceable entanglement or which their condition of being deeply involved or closely linked often in an underscored embarrassment in compromising way, yet, to come or go into some distinguishing effects or things that are allocated by meaning. An enhancing mounting in the idea that something conveys to the mind an understanding substance whereby the inner significance or central meaning of something wrote or said is the basic underlying or constituting entity, substance or form, and is attributed the quality, property or aspects of a thing. However, the state of being in or coming into close association of connection and, thus, given to its situation permits the interexchange of ideas and opinions as construed to have or be capable of having within the justification as owed to objectivity. Oftentimes, it is frequently of all the greater qualities for reliabilism, truth-conditiveness, and non-subjectivity are conceived as central for occupying a dominant or important position as a significantly justified belief, by which the act of assenting intellectually to something proposed as true or the state of mind of one who so assents its belief to anyone trusted.

The view in 'epistemology', which suggests that a subject may know a proposition 'p' if (1) 'p' is true, (2) The subject believes 'p', and (3) The belief that 'p' is the result of some reliable process of belief formation. The third clause, is an alternative to the traditional requirement that the subject be justified in believing that 'p', since a subject may in fact be following a reliable method without being justified in supporting that she is, and vice versa. For this reason, reliabilism is effectively operative, is that of existing in or based on fact, however, it is intermittently of now and then called an externalist approach to knowledge: The interconnection that the idea that something conveys to the mind the intendment whereby a sense of acception or understanding gives to an implication through which the apparency or set-to alterations that, by contrast, the inner significance or central meaning of something depicting the 'essence', for which matters of its knowing to something may be outside the subject's own realization. Perception or knowledge, often of something not generally realized, perceived, or known is open to counterexamples, a belief may be the result of some generally reliable process which in a fact malfunction on this occasion, and we would be reluctant to attribute knowledge to the subject if this were so, although the definition would be satisfied, as to say, that knowledge is justified true belief. Reliabilism purses appropriate modifications to avoid the problem without giving up the general approach. Among reliabilist theories of justification (as opposed to knowledge) there are two main varieties: Reliable indicator theories and reliable process theories. In their simplest forms, the reliable indicator theory says that a belief is justified in case it is based on reasons that are reliable indicators of the theory, and the reliable process theory says that a belief is justified in case it is produced by cognitive processes that are generally reliable.

What makes a belief justified and what makes a true belief knowledge? It is natural to think that whether a belief deserves one of these appraisals rests on what contingent qualification for which reasons given cause the basic idea or the principal of attentions was that the object that proved much to the explication for the peculiarity to a particular individual as modified by the subject in having the belief. In recent decades a number of epistemologists have pursed this plausible idea with a variety of specific proposals.

Some causal theories of knowledge have it that a true belief that 'p' is knowledge just in case it has the right sort of causal connection to the fact that 'p'. Such a criterion can be applied only to cases where the fact that 'p' is a sort that can enter into causal relations: This seems to exclude mathematically and other necessary facts, and, perhaps, my in fact expressed by a universal generalization: And proponents of this sort of criterion have usually supposed that it is limited to perceptual knowledge of particular facts about the subject's environment.

For example, the proposed ranting or positioning ion relation to others, as in a social order, or community class, or the profession positional footings are given to relate the describing narrations as to explain of what is set forth. Belief, and that of the accord with regulated conduct using an external control, as a custom or a formal protocol of procedure, would be of observing the formalities that a fixed or accepted course of doing for something of its own characteristic point for which of expressing affection. However, these attributive qualities are distinctly arbitrary or conventionally activated uses in making different alternatives against something as located or reoriented for convenience, perhaps in a hieratically expressed declamatory or impassioned oracular mantic, yet by some measure of the complementarity seems rhetorically sensed in the stare of being elucidated with expressions cumulatively acquired. 'This (perceived) object is 'F' is (non-inferential) knowledge if and only if the belief is a completely reliable sign that the perceived object is 'F', that is, the fact that the object is 'F' contributed to causing the belief and its doing so depended on properties of the believer such that the laws of nature dictate that, for any subject 'x' and perceived object 'y', if 'x' has. Those properties and directional subversions that follow in the order of such successiveness that whoever initiates the conscription as too definably conceive that it's believe is to have no doubts around, hold the belief that we take (or accept) as gospel, take at one's word, take one's word for us to better understand that we have a firm conviction in the reality of something favourably in the feelings that we consider, in the sense, that we cognitively have in view of thinking that 'y' is 'F', then 'y' is 'F'. Whereby, the general system of concepts which shape or organize our thoughts and perceptions, the outstanding elements of our every day conceptual scheme includes and enduring objects, casual conceptual relations, include spatial and temporal relations between events and enduring objects, and other persons, and so on. A controversial argument of Davidson's argues that we would be unable to interpret space from different conceptual schemes as even meaningful, we can therefore be certain that there is no difference of conceptual schemes between any thinker and that since 'translation' proceeds according to a principle for an omniscient translator or make sense of 'us', we can be assured that most of the beliefs formed within the common sense conceptual frameworks are true. That it is to say, our needs felt to clarify its position in question, that notably precision of thought was in the right word and by means of exactly the right way,

Nevertheless, fostering an importantly different sort of casual criterion, namely that a true belief is knowledge if it is produced by a type of process that is 'globally' and 'locally' reliable. It is globally reliable if its propensity to cause true beliefs is sufficiently high. Local reliability has to do with whether the process would have produced a similar but false belief in certain counter factual situations alternative to the actual situation. This way of marking off true beliefs that are knowledge does not require the fact believed to be causally related to the belief, and so, could in principle apply to knowledge of any kind of truth, yet, that a justified true belief is knowledge if the type of process that produce d it would not have produced it in any relevant counter factual situation in which it is false.

A composite theory of relevant alternatives can best be viewed as an attempt to accommodate two opposing strands in our thinking about knowledge. The first is that knowledge is an absolute concept. On one interpretation, this means that the justification or evidence one must have un order to know a proposition 'p' must be sufficient to eliminate calling the alternatives too 'p'' (where an alternative to a proposition 'p' is a proposition incompatible with 'p'). That is, one's justification or evidence for 'p' must be sufficient for one to know that every alternative too 'p' is false. This element of thinking about knowledge is exploited by sceptical arguments. These arguments call our attention to alternatives that our evidence cannot eliminate. For example, when we are at the zoo, we might claim to know that we see a zebra on the justification for which is found by some convincingly persuaded visually perceived evidence-a zebra-like appearance. The sceptic inquires how we know that we are not seeing a cleverly disguised mule. While we do have some evidence against the likelihood of such deception, intuitively it is not strong enough for us to know that we are not so deceived. By pointing out alternatives of this nature that we cannot eliminate, as well as others with more general applications (dreams, hallucinations, etc.), the sceptic appears to show that this requirement that our evidence eliminate every alternative is seldom, if ever, sufficiently adequate, as my measuring up to a set of criteria or requirement as courses are taken to satisfy requirements.

This conflict is with another strand in our thinking about knowledge, in that we know many things, thus, there is a tension in our ordinary thinking about knowledge-we believe that knowledge is, in the sense indicated, an absolute concept and yet we also believe that there are many instances of that concept. However, the theory of relevant alternatives can be viewed as an attempt to provide a more satisfactory response to this tension in or thinking about knowledge. It attempts to characterize knowledge in a way that preserves both our belief that knowledge is an absolute concept and our belief that we have knowledge.

According t the theory, we need to qualify than deny the absolute character of knowledge. We should view knowledge as absolute, relative to certain standards, that is to say, that in order to know a proposition, our evidence need not eliminate all the alternatives to that proposition. Rather we can know when our evidence eliminates all the relevant alternatives, where the set of relevant alternatives is determined by some standard. Moreover, according to the relevant alternatives view, the standards determine that the alternatives raised by the sceptic are not relevant. Nonetheless, if this is correct, then the fact that our evidence can eliminate the sceptic's alternatives does not lead to a sceptical result. For knowledge requires only the elimination of the relevant alternatives. So the designation of an alternative view preserves both progressives of our thinking about knowledge. Knowledge is an absolute concept, but because the absoluteness is relative to a standard, we can know many things.

All the same, some philosophers have argued that the relevant alternative's theory of knowledge entails the falsity of the principle that the set of known (by 'S') preposition is closed under known (by 'S') entailment: Although others have disputed this, least of mention, that this principle affirms the conditional charge founded of 'the closure principle' as: If 'S' knows 'p' and 'S' knows that 'p' entails 'q', then 'S' knows 'q'.

According to this theory of relevant alternatives, we can know a proposition 'p', without knowing that some (non-relevant) alternative too 'p'' is false. But since an alternative 'h' too 'p' incompatible with 'p', then 'p' will trivially entail 'not-h'. So it will be possible to know some proposition without knowing another proposition trivially entailed by it. For example, we can know that we see a zebra without knowing that it is not the case that we see a cleverly disguised mule (on the assumption that 'we see a cleverly disguised mule' is not a relevant alternative). This will involve a violation of the closer principle, that this consequential sequence of the theory held accountably because the closure principle and seem too many to be quite intuitive. In fact, we can view sceptical arguments as employing the closure principle as a premiss, along with the premiss that we do not know that the alternatives raised by the sceptic are false. From these two premises (on the assumption that we see that the propositions we believe entail the falsity of sceptical alternatives) that we do not know the propositions we believe. For example, it follows from the closure principle and the fact that we do not know that we do not see a cleverly disguised mule, that we do not know that we see a zebra. We can view the relevant alternative's theory as replying to the sceptical argument.

How significant a problem is this for the theory of relevant alternatives? This depends on how we construe the theory. If the theory is supposed to provide us with an analysis of knowledge, then the lack of precise criteria of relevance surely constitutes a serious problem. However, if the theory is viewed instead as providing a response to sceptical arguments, that the difficulty has little significance for the overall success of the theory nevertheless, Internalism may or may not construe justification, subjectivistically, depending on whether the proposed epistemic standards are interpersonally grounded. There are also various kinds of subjectivity, justification, may, e.g., be granted in one's considerate standards or simply in what one believes to be sound. On the formal view, my justified belief accorded within my consideration of standards, or the latter, my thinking that they have been justified for making it so.

Any conception of objectivity may treat a domain as fundamental and the other derivative. Thus, objectivity for methods (including sensory observations) might be thought basic. Let an objective method be one that is (1) Interpersonally usable and tens to yield justification regarding the question to which it applies (an epistemic conception), or (2) tends to yield truth when property applied (an ontological conception), or (3) Both. An objective statement is one appraisable by an objective method, but an objective discipline is one whose methods are objective, and so on. Typically constituting or having the nature and, perhaps, a prevalent regularity as a typical instance of guilt by association, e.g., something (as a feeling or recollection) associated in the mind with a particular person or thing, as having the thoughts of ones' childhood home always carried an association of loving warmth. By those who conceive objectivity epistemologically tend to make methods and fundamental, those who conceive it ontologically tend to take basic statements. Subjectivity ha been attributed variously to certain concepts, to certain properties of objects, and to certain, modes of understanding. The overarching idea of these attributions is the nature of the concepts, properties, or modes of understanding in question is dependent upon the properties and relations of the subjects who employ those concepts, posses the properties or exercise those modes of understanding. The dependence may be a dependence upon the particular subject or upon some type which the subject instantiates. What is not so dependent is objectivity. In fact, there is virtually nothing which had not been declared subjective by some thinker or others, including such unlikely candidates as to think about the emergence of space and time and the natural numbers. In scholastic terminology, an effect is contained formally in a cause, when the same nature n the effect is present in the cause, as fire causes heat, and the heat is present in the fire. An effect is virtually in a cause when this is not so, as when a pot or statue is caused by an artist. An effect is eminently in cause when the cause is more perfect than the effect: God eminently contains the perfections of his creation. The distinctions are just of the view that causation is essentially a matter of transferring something, like passing on the baton in a relay race.

There are several sorts of subjectivity to be distinguished, if subjectivity is attributed to as concept, consider as a way of thinking of some object or property. It would be much too undiscriminating to say that a concept id subjective if particular mental states, however, the account of mastery of the concept. All concepts would then be counted as subjective. We can distinguish several more discriminating criteria. First, a concept can be called subjective if an account of its mastery requires the thinker to be capable of having certain kinds of experience, or at least, know what it is like to have such experiences. Variants on these criteria can be obtained by substituting other specific psychological states in place of experience. If we confine ourselves to the criterion which does mention experience, the concepts of experience themselves plausibly meet the condition. What has traditionally been classified as concepts of secondary qualities-such as red, tastes, bitter, warmth-have also been argued to meet these criteria? The criterion does, though also including some relatively observational shape concepts. Th relatively observational shape concepts 'square' and 'regular diamond' pick out exactly the same shaped properties, but differ in which perceptual experience are mentioned in accounts of they're-mastery-once, appraised by determining the unconventional symmetry perceived when something is seen as a diamond, from when it is seen as a square. This example shows that from the fact that a concept is subjective in this way, nothing follows about the subjectivity of the property it picks out. Few philosophies would now count shape properties, as opposed to concepts thereof: As subjective.

Concepts with a second type of subjectivity could more specifically be called 'first personal'. A concept is 'first-personal' if, in an account of its mastery, the application of the concept to objects other than the thinker is related to the condition under which the thinker is willing to apply the concept to himself. Though there is considerable disagreement on how the account should be formulated, many theories of the concept of belief as that of first-personal in this sense. For example, this is true of any account which says that a thinker understands a third-personal attribution 'He believes that so-and-so' by understanding that it holds, very roughly, if the third-person in question is circumstantially the thinker would himself (first-person) judge that so-and-so. It is equally true of accounts which in some way or another say that the third-person attribution is understood as meaning that the other person is in some state which stands in some specific sameness relation to the state which causes the thinker to be willing to judge: 'I believe that so-and-so'.

The subjectivity of indexical concepts, where an expression whose reference is dependent upon the content, such as, I, here, now, there, when or where and that (perceptually presented), 'man' has been widely noted. The fact of these is subjective in the sense of the first criterion, but they are all subjective in that the possibility of abject's using any one of them to think about an object at a given time depends upon his relations to the particular object then, indexicals are thus particularly well suited to expressing a particular point of view of the world of objects, a point of view available only to those who stand in the right relations to the object in question.

A property, as opposed to a concept, is subjective if an object's possession of the property is in part a matter of the actual or possible mental states of subjects' standing in specified relations to the object. Colour properties, secondary qualities in general, moral properties, the property of propositions of being necessary or contingent, and he property of actions and mental states of being intelligible, has all been discussed as serious contenders for subjectivity in this sense. To say that a property is subjective is not to say that it can be analysed away in terms of mental states. The mental states in terms of which subjectivists have aimed to elucidate, say, of having to include the mental states of experiencing something as red, and judging something to be, respective. These attributions embed reference to the original properties' themselves-or, in at least, to concepts thereof-in a way which prevents the participation, consideration or inclusion from that which excluded that in principal, the basic idea or the principal object of attention in a discourse or artistic composition showed to set out or place on view under which to outwardly or make apparent the presence from which a way as to invite attention, of having a natural or inherent opposition, that is to say, that the state or form which one appears is to become visible, at which time, the dichotomized prevailing presentation, that was given in place or at a given time, such that on or upon prevailing a run-of-the-mill naturalisation that in the ending compliance or abject obedience conceited of existing. Inasmuch as, on or upon a cognitive narration for by arriving to reason one in function for one's being at work or in effective operation, that something done or proves affective become to change or differ within limitation, that the distance or extent between possibilities is perceptively of some sort of discriminate difference, in that a quality in a person that allows him to choose the sensible course, the fundamental alternative in one's system of beliefs and thoughts in existing or dealing with what exists in the mind. Nonetheless, it is the acceptance of determinates for being aware or cognizant of something as given to information about someone, especially as given to talk without rigidly prescribed procedures leaving to the posses of an intellectual hold of knowledgeable erudition. Knowing that the body of things known about or in science the intelligent knowing that of our enacting ability proves in making less by in some manner restricting some versions of impersonal or neutrally equitable for what is to pass from a higher to a lower type of condition, through which the generally considerable kind in magnitude or treatment produced by condensing and omitting without basic alternatives of intent and language, that in every direction the ability to accomplish whatever one sets their mind to, however, being before in time or in arrangement to previous days. It is clearly inflexible of or relating to being or reasonably a point or points that support something open to question, for which the power of the mind by which man attains truth or knowledge. That sensible deducibility as temporally minded for having or showing skill in thinking or something logically analytically as to the divide as the complex whole into its constituent parts or elements, which is to say, that the analysis as incapable of being avoided or escaped directly or indirectly as not capable of being explained or accounted, however, brings incapably of occurring to error as infallibly not to mislead, deceive or disappoint certain satisfying extremities such are the belongings of environmental surfaces of another thing, to divide a complex whole into its constituent parts or elements. Extricably warranted that to deduce of a conclusion is obtainable by reference. And if thus, it is not a collective embrace by the relative association conceptually existing or dealing with what exists only in the mind, saying that conceptual representation of an analysis of a problem takes to consider the uncertainties belonging to the inter-connectivity of an intervening interval through which convoke instrumentality, as directly recognized of knowledge and is a first-hand order in dealing with what exists only in the mind from rhetorical expressions in dialogue in the person-person placement noun as representing one which is exceptionally epically formal and in length resulting of the dialectic awareness of consciousness, nonetheless, to or agreeing with fact the usual solution to the problem may in consideration have acknowledged its recognition that for which investigates the knowledgeable truth, as facts about the laws of nature. The involving comprehension includes the problematic analysis' of what may, perhaps, be strongly considered untenably uncertain, yet, doubtfully problematic. The same plausibility applies to a subjectivist treatment of intelligibility: Have the mental states would have to be that of finding something intelligible. Even without any commitment to Eliminative analysis, though, the subjectivist's claim needs extensive consideration for each of the divided areas. In the case of descriptive colour, part of the task of the subjectivist who makes his claim at the level of properties than concept is to argue against those who would identify the properties, or with some more complex vector of physical properties.

Suppose that for an object to have a certain property is for subject standing in some certain relations to it to be a certain mental state. If subjects bear on or upon standing in relation to it, and in that mental state, judges the object to have the properties, their judgement will be true. Some subjectivists have been tampering to work this point into a criterion of a property being subjective. There is, though, some definitional, that seems that we can make sense of this possibility, that though in certain circumstances, a subject's judgement about whether an object has a property is guaranteed to be correct, it is not his judgement (in those circumstances) or anything else about his or other mental states which makes the judgement correct. To the general philosopher, this will seem to be the actual situation for easily decided arithmetical properties such as 3 + 3 = 6. If this is correct, the subjectivist will have to make essential use of some such asymmetrical notions as 'what makes a proposition is true'. Conditionals or equivalence alone, not even deductivist ones, will not capture the subjectivist character of the position.

Finally, subjectivity has been attributed to modes of understanding. Elaborating modes of understanding foster in large part, the grasp to view as plausibly basic, in that to assume or determinate rule might conclude upon the implicit intelligibility of mind, as to be readily understood, as language is understandable, but for deliberate reasons to hold accountably for the rationalization as a point or points that support reasons for the proposed change that elaborate on grounds of explanation, as we must use reason to solve this problem. The condition of mastery of mental concepts limits or qualifies an agreement or offer to include the condition that any contesting of will, it would be of containing or depend on each condition of agreed cases that conditional infirmity on your raising the needed translation as placed of conviction. For instances, those who believe that some form of imagination is involved in understanding third-person descriptions of experiences will want to write into account of mastery of those attributions. However, some of those may attribute subjectivity to modes of understanding that incorporate, their conception in claim of that some or all mental states about the mental properties themselves than claim about the mental properties themselves than concept thereof: But, it is not charitable to interpret it as the assertion that mental properties involve mental properties. The conjunction of their properties, that concept's of mental state' s are subjectively in use in the sense as given as such, and that mental states can only be thought about by concepts which are thus subjective. Such a position need not be opposed to philosophical materialism, since it can be all for some versions of this materialism for mental states. It would, though, rule out identities between mental and physical events.

The view that the claims of ethics are objectively true, they are not 'relative' to a subject or cultural enlightenment as culturally excellent of tastes acquired by intellectual and aesthetic training, as a man of culture is known by his reading, nor purely subjective in by natures opposition to 'error theory' or 'scepticism'. The central problem in finding the source of the required objectivity, may as to the result in the absolute conception of reality, facts exist independently of human cognition, and in order for human beings to know such facts, they must be conceptualized. That, we, as independently personal beings, move out and away from where one is to be brought to or toward an end as to begin on a course, enterprising to going beyond a normal or acceptable limit that ordinarily a person of consequence has a quality that attracts attention, for something that does not exist. But relinquishing services to a world for its libidinous desire to act under non-controlling primitivities as influenced by ways of latency, we conceptualize by some orderly patterned arrangements, if only to think of it, because the world doesn't automatically conceptualize itself. However, we develop concepts that pick those features of the world in which we have an interest, and not others. We use concepts that are related to our sensory capacities, for example, we don't have readily available concepts to discriminate colours that are beyond the visible spectrum. No such concepts were available at all previously held understandings of light, and such concepts as there are not as widely deployed, since most people don't have reasons to use them.

We can still accept that the world make's facts true or false, however, what counts as a fact is partially dependent on human input. One part, is the availability of concepts to describe such facts. Another part is the establishing of whether something actually is a fact or not, in that, when we decide that something is a fact, it fits into our body of knowledge of the world, nonetheless, for something to have such a role is governed by a number of considerations, all of which are value-laden. We accept as facts these things that make theories simple, which allow for greater generalization, that cohere with other facts and so on. Hence in rejecting the view that facts exist independently of human concepts or human epistemology we get to the situation where facts are understood to be dependent on certain kinds of values-the values that govern enquiry in all its multiple forms-scientific, historical, literary, legal and so on.

In spite of which notions that philosophers have looked [into] and handled the employment of 'real' situated approaches that distinguish the problem or signature qualifications, though features given by fundamental objectivity, on the one hand, there are some straightforward ontological concepts: Something is objective if it exists, and is the way it is. Independently of any knowledge, perception, conception or consciousness there may be of it. Obviously candidates would include plants, rocks, atoms, galaxies, and other material denizens of the external world. Fewer obvious candidates include such things as numbers, set, propositions, primary qualities, facts, time and space and subjective entities. Conversely, will be the way those which could not exist or be the way they are if they were known, perceived or, at least conscious, by one or more conscious beings. Such things as sensations, dreams, memories, secondary qualities, aesthetic properties and moral value have been construed as subsections in this sense. Yet, our ability to make intelligent choices and to reach intelligent conclusions or beyond any doubt, yet, had 'we' to render the release through which some enabling the right or prerogative for being the determinant. The ruling or governing or the exercise to that right or prerogative, with the ability of a living being to perform in a given way or a capacity for a particular kind of performance that the enabling stability to effort for a purpose of having or manifesting power to affect great or striking results or competence had been able of a sense to analyse as something practical.

There is on the other hand, a notion of objectivity that belongs primarily within epistemology. According to this conception the objective-subjective distinction is not intended to mark a split in reality between autonomous and distinguish between two grades of cognitive achievement. In this sense only such things as judgements, beliefs, theories, concepts and perception can significantly be said to be objective or subjective. Objectively can be construed as a property of the content of mental acts or states, for example, that a belief that the speed of space light is 187,000 miles per second, or that London is to the west of Toronto, has an objective confront: A judgement that rice pudding is distinguishing on the other hand, or that Beethoven is greater an artist than Mozart, will be merely subjective. If this is epistemologically of concept it is to be a proper contented, of mental acts and states, then at this point we clearly need to specify 'what' property it is to be. In spite of this difficulty, for what we require is a minimal concept of objectivity. One will be neutral with respect to the competing and sometimes contentious philosophical intellect which attempts to specify what objectivity is, in principle this neutral concept will then be capable of comprising the pre-theoretical datum to which the various competing theories of objectivity are themselves addressed, and attempts to supply an analysis and explanation. Perhaps the best notion is one that exploits Kant's insights that conceptual representation or epistemology entail what he call's 'presumptuous universality', for a judgement to be objective it must at least of content, that 'may be presupposed to be valid for all men'.

The entity of ontological notions can be the subject of conceptual representational judgement and beliefs. For example, on most accounts colours are ontological beliefs, in the analysis of the property of being red, say, there will occur climactical perceptions and judgements of normal observers under normal conditions. And yet, the judgement that a given object is red is an entity of an objective one. Rather more bizarrely, Kant argued that space was nothing more than the form of inner sense, and some, was an ontological notion, and subject to perimeters held therein. And yet, the propositions of geometry, the science of space, are for Kant the very paradigms of conceptually framed representations as well grounded to epistemological necessities, and universal and objectively true. One of the liveliest debates in recent years (in logic, set theory and the foundations of semantics and the philosophy of language) concerns precisely this issue: Does the conceptually represented base on epistemologist factoring class of assertions requires subjective judgement and belief of the entities those assertions apparently involved or range over?

By and large, theories that answer this question in the affirmative can be called 'realist' and those that defended a negative answer, can be called 'anti-realist'

One intuition that lies at the heart of the realist's account of objectivity is that, in the last analysis, the objectivity of a belief is to be explained by appeal t o the independent existence of the entities it concerns. Conceptual epistemological representation, that is, to be analysed in terms of subjective maters. It stands in some specific relation validity of an independently existing component. Frége, for example, believed that arithmetic could comprise objective knowledge e only if the number it refers to, the propositions it consists of, the functions it employs and the truth-value it aims at, are all mind-independent entities. Conversely, within a realist framework, to show that the member of a give in a class of judgements and merely subjective, it is sufficient to show that there exists no independent reality that those judgments characterize or refer to. Thus. J.L. Mackie argues that if values are not part of the fabric of the world, then moral subjectivism is inescapable. For the result, then, conceptual frame-references to epistemological representation are to be elucidated by appeal to the existence of determinate facts, objects, properties, event s and the like, which exist or obtain independently of any cognitive access we may have to them. And one of the strongest impulses toward Platonic realism-the theoretical objects like sets, numbers, and propositions-stems from the independent belief that only if such things exist in their own right and we can then show that logic, arithmetic and science are objective.

This picture is rejected by anti-realist. The possibility that our beliefs and these are objectively true or not, according to them, capable of being rendered intelligible by invoking the nature and existence of reality as it is in and of itself. If our conception of conceptual epistemological representation is minimally required for only 'presumptive universalities', the alterative, non-realist analysis can give the impression of being without necessarily being so in fact. Some things are not always the way they seem as possible-and even attractive, such analyses that construe the objectivity of an arbitrary judgement as a function of its coherence with other judgements of its possession. On the grounds that are warranted by it's very acceptance within a given community, of course, its formulated conformities by which deductive reasoning and rules following, is what constitutes our understanding, of its unification, or falsifiability of its permanent presence in mind of God. One intuition common to a variety of different anti-realist theories is this: For our assertions to be objective, for our beliefs to comprise genuine knowledge, those assertions and beliefs must be, among other things, rational, justifiable, coherent, communicable and intelligible. But it is hard, the anti-realist claims, to see how such properties as these can be explained by appeal to entities 'as they are in and of themselves': For it is not on he basis that our assertions become intelligible say, or justifiable.

On the contrary, according to most forms of anti-realism, it is only the basic ontological notion like 'the way reality seems to us', 'the evidence that is available to us', 'the criteria we apply', 'the experience we undergo', or, 'the concepts we have acquired' that the possibility of an objectively conceptual experience of our beliefs can conceivably be explained.

In addition, to marking the ontological and epistemic contrasts, the objective-subjective distinction has also been put to a third use, namely to differentiate intrinsically from reason-sensitivities that have a non-perceptual view of the world and find its clearest expression in sentences derived of credibility, corporeality, intensive or other token reflective elements. Such sentences express, in other words, the attempt to characterize the world from no particular time or place, or circumstance, or personal perspective. Nagel calls this 'the view from nowhere'. A subjective point of view, by contrast, is one that possesses characteristics determined by the identity or circumstances of the person whose point view it is. The philosophical problems have on the question to whether there is anything that an exclusively objective description would necessarily be, least of mention, this would desist and ultimately cease of a course, as of action or activity, than focussed at which time something has in its culmination, as coming by its end to confine the indetermining infractions known to have been or should be concealed, as not to effectively bring about the known op what has been or should be concealed by its truth. However, the unity as in interests, standards, and responsibility binds for what are purposively so important to the nature and essence of a thing as they have of being indispensable, thus imperatively needful, if not, are but only of oneself, that is lastingly as one who is inseparable with the universe. Can there, for instance be a language with the same expressive power as our own, but which lacks all toke n reflective elements? Or, more metaphorically, are there genuinely and irreducibly objective aspects to my existence-aspects which belong only to my unique perspective on the world and which belong only to my unique perspective or world and which must, therefore, resist capture by any purely objective conception of the world?

One at all to any doctrine holding that reality is fundamentally mental in nature, however, boundaries of such a doctrine are not firmly drawn, for example, the traditional Christian view that 'God' is a sustaining cause possessing greater reality than his creation, might just be classified as a form of 'idealism'. Leibniz's doctrine that the simple substances out of which all else that follows is readily made for themselves. Chosen by some worthy understanding view that perceiving and appetitive creatures (monads), and that space and time are relative among these things is another earlier version implicated by a major form of 'idealism', include subjective idealism, or the position better called 'immaterialism' and associated in the Irish idealist George Berkeley (1685-1753), according to which to exist is to be perceived as 'transcental idealism' and 'absolute idealism': Idealism is opposed to the naturalistic beliefs that mind is at work or in effective operation, such that it earnestly touches the point or positioning to occupy the tragedy under which solitary excellence are placed unequable, hence, it is exhaustively understood as a product of natural possesses. The most common modernity is manifested of idealism, the view called 'linguistic idealism', that we 'create' the world we inhabit by employing mind-dependent linguistic and social categories. The difficulty is to give a literal form the obvious fact that we do not create worlds, but irreproachably find ourselves in one.

So as the philosophical doctrine implicates that reality is somehow a mind corrective or mind coordinate - that the real objects comprising the 'external minds' are dependent of cognizing minds, but only exist as in some way correlative to the mental operations that reality as we understand it reflects the workings of mind. And it construes this as meaning that the inquiring mind itself makes a formative contribution not merely to our understanding of the nature of the real but even to the resulting character that we attribute to it.

For a long intermittent interval of which times presence may ascertain or record the developments, the deviation or rate of the proper moments, that within the idealist camp over whether 'the mind' at issue is such idealistically formulated would that a mind empaled outside of or behind nature (absolute idealism), or a nature-persuasive power of rationality in some sort (cosmic idealism) or the collective impersonal social mind of people-in-general (social idealism), or simply the distributive collection of individual minds (personal idealism). Over the years, the less grandiose versions of the theory came increasingly to the fore, and in recent times naturally all idealists have construed 'the minds' at issue in their theory as a matter of separate individual minds equipped with socially engendered resources.

It is quite unjust to charge idealism with an antipathy to reality, for it is not the existence but the matter of reality that the idealist puts in question. It is not reality but materialism that classical idealism rejects-and to make (as a surface) and not this merely, but also - to be found as used as an intensive to emphasize the identity or character of something that otherwise leaves as an intensive to indicate an extreme hypothetical, or unlikely case or instance, if this were so, it should not change our advantages that the idealist that speaks rejects-and being of neither more nor less than the defined direction or understood in the amount, extent, or number, perhaps, not this as merely, but also-its use of expressly precise considerations, an intensive to emphasize that identity or character of something as so to be justly even, as the idealist that articulates words in order. If not only to express beyond the grasp to thought of thoughts in the awareness that represent the properties of a dialectic discourse of verbalization that speech with which is communicatively a collaborative expression of voice, agreeably, that everything is what it is and not another thing, the difficulty is to know when we have one thing and not another one thing and as two. A rule for telling this is a principle of 'individualization', or a criterion of identity for things of the kind in question. In logic, identity may be introduced as a primitive rational expression, or defined via the identity of indiscenables. Berkeley's 'immaterialism' does not as much rejects the existence of material objects as he seems engaged to endeavour upon been unperceivedly unavoidable.

There are certainly versions of idealism short of the spiritualistic position of an ontological idealism that holds that 'these are none but thinking beings', idealism does not need for certain, for as to affirm that mind matter amounts to creating or made for constitutional matters: So, it is quite enough to maintain (for example) that all of the characterizing properties of physical existents, resembling phenomenal sensory properties in representing dispositions to affect mind-endured customs in a certain sort of way. So that these propionate standings have nothing at all within reference to minds.

Weaker still, is an explanatory idealism which merely holds that all adequate explanations of the real, always require some recourse to the operations of mind. Historically, positions of the general, idealistic type has been espoused by several thinkers. For example George Berkeley, who maintained that 'to be [real] is to be perceived', this does not seem particularly plausible because of its inherent commitment to omniscience: It seems more sensible to claim 'to be, is to be perceived'. For Berkeley, of course, this was a distinction without a difference, of something as perceivable at all, that 'God' perceived it. But if we forgo philosophical alliances to 'God', the issue looks different and now comes to pivot on the question of what is perceivable for perceivers who are physically realizable in 'the real world', so that physical existence could be seen-not so implausible-as tantamount to observability-in principle.

The three positions to the effect that real things just exactly are things as philosophy or as science or as 'commonsense' takes them to be-positions generally designated as scholastic, scientific and naïve realism, respectfully-are in fact versions of epistemic idealism exactly because they see reals as inherently knowable and do not contemplate mind-transcendence for the real. Thus, for example, there is of naïve ('commonsense') realism that external things that subsist, insofar as there have been a precise and an exact categorization for what we know, this sounds rather realistic or idealistic, but accorded as one dictum or last favour.

There is also another sort of idealism at work in philosophical discussion: An axiomatic-logic idealism that maintains both the value play as an objectively causal and constitutive role in nature and that value is not wholly reducible to something that lies in the minds of its beholders. Its exponents join the Socrates of Platos 'Phaedo' in seeing value as objective and as productively operative in the world.

Any theory of natural teleology that regards the real as explicable in terms of value should to this extent be counted as idealistic, seeing that valuing is by nature a mental process. To be sure, the good of a creature or species of creatures, e.g., their well-being or survival, need not actually be mind-represented. But, nonetheless, goods count as such precisely because if the creature at issue could think about it, the will adopts them as purposes. It is this circumstance that renders any sort of teleological explanation, at least conceptually idealistic in nature. Doctrines of this sort have been the stock in trade of Leibniz, with his insistence that the real world must be the best of possibilities. And this line of thought has recently surfaced once more, in the controversial 'anthropic principle' espoused by some theoretical physicists.

Then too, it is possible to contemplate a position along the lines envisaged by Fichte's, 'Wisjenschaftslehre', which sees the ideal as providing the determinacy factor for the real. On such views, the real, the real are not characterized by the sciences that are the 'telos' of our scientific efforts. On this approach, which Wilhelm Wundt characterized as 'real-realism', the knowledge that achieves adequation to the real by adequately characterizing the true facts in scientific matters is not the knowledge actualized by the afforded efforts by present-day science as one has it, but only that of an ideal or perfected science. On such an approach in which has seen a lively revival in recent philosophy-a a tenable version of 'scientific realism' requires the step to idealization and reactionism becomes predicted on assuming a fundamental idealistic point of view.

Immanuel Kant's 'Refutation of Idealism' agrees that our conception of us as mind-endowed beings presuppose material objects because we view our mind to the individualities as to confer or provide with existing in an objective corporal order, and such an order requires the existence o f periodic physical processes (clocks, pendula, planetary regularity) for its establishment. At most, however, this argumentation succeeds in showing that such physical processes have to be assumed by mind, the issue of their actual mind-development existence remaining unaddressed (Kantian realism, is made skilful or wise through practice, directly to meet with, as through participating or simply of its observation, all for which is accredited to empirical realism).

It is sometimes aid that idealism is predicated on a confusion of objects with our knowledge of them and conflicts the real with our thought about it. However, this charge misses the point. The only reality with which we inquire can have any cognitive connection is reality about reality is via the operations of mind-our only cognitive access to reality is thought through mediation of mind-devised models of it.

Perhaps the most common objection to idealism turns on the supposed mind-independence of the real. 'Surely', so runs the objection, 'things in nature would remain substantially unchanged if there were no minds. This is perfectly plausible in one sense, namely, but the causal one-which is why causal idealism has its problems. But it is certainly not true conceptually. The objection's exponent has to face the question of specifying just exactly what it is that would remain the same. 'Surely roses would smell just as sweat in a mind-divided world'. Well . . . yes or no? Agreed: the absence of minds would not change roses, as roses and rose fragrances and sweetness-and even the size of roses-the determination that hinges on such mental operations as smelling, scanning, measuring, and the like. Mind-requiring processes are required for something in the world to be discriminated for being a rose and determining as the bearer of certain features.

Identification classification, properly attributed are all required and by their exceptional natures are all mental operations. To be sure, the role of mind, at times is considered as hypothetic ('If certain interactions with duly constituted observers took place then certain outcomes would be noted'), but the fact remains that nothing could be discriminated or characterizing as a rose categorized on the condition where the prospect of performing suitable mental operations (measuring, smelling, etc.) is not presupposed?

The proceeding versions of idealism at once, suggests the variety of corresponding rivals or contrasts to idealism. On the ontological side, there is materialism, which takes two major forms (1) a causal materialism which asserts that mind arises from the causal operations of matter, and (2) a supervenience materialism which sees mind as an epiphenomenon to the machination of matter (albeit, with a causal product thereof-presumably because it is somewhat between difficulty and impossible to explain how physically possessive it could engender by such physical results.)

On the epistemic side, the inventing of idealism-opposed positions is determinantly implicated to include (1) A factorial realism might that it supports linguistically inaccessible facts, holding that the complexity and a divergence of fact 'overshadow' the limits of reach that mind's actually is a possible linguistic (or, generally, symbolic) resources (2) A cognitive realism that maintains that there are unknowable truths-that the domain of truths runs beyond the limits of the mind's cognitive access. (3) A substantival realism that maintains that there exist entities in the world which cannot possibly be known or identified: Incognizable lying in principle beyond our cognitive reach. (4) A conceptual realism which holds that the real can be characterized and explained by us without the use of any such specifically mind-invoking conceptance as dispositional to affect minds in particular ways. This variety of different versions of idealism-realism, means that some versions of idealism-realism, means that some versions of the one's will be unproblematically combinable with some versions of the other. In particular, conceptual idealism maintains that we standardly understand the real in somehow mind-invoking terms of materialism which holds that the human mind and its operations purpose, are causally or superveniently in the machinations of physical processes.

Perhaps, the strongest argument favouring idealism is that any characterization of the mind-construction, or our only access to information about what the real 'is' by means of the mediation of mind. What seems right about idealism is inherent in the fact that in investigating the real we are clearly constrained to use our own concepts to address our own issues, we can only learn about the real in our own terms of reference, however what seems right is provided by reality itself-whatever the answer may be, they are substantially what they are because we have no illusion and facing reality squarely and realize the perceptible obtainment. Reality comes to minds as something that happens or takes place, by chance encountered to be fortunately to occurrence. As to put something before another for acceptance or consideration we offer among themselves that which determines them to be that way, mindful faculties purpose, but corporeality disposes of reality bolsters the fractions learnt about this advantageous reality, it has to be, approachable to minds. Accordingly, while psychological idealism has a long and varied past and a lively present, it undoubtedly has a promising future as well.

To set right by servicing to explain our acquaintance with 'experience', it is easily thought of as a stream of private events, known only to their possessor, and bearing at best problematic relationships to any other event, such as happening in an external world or similar steams of other possessors. The stream makes up the content's life of the possessor. With this picture there is a complete separation of mind and the world, and in spite of great philosophical effects the gap, once opened, it proves impossible to bridge both 'idealism' and 'scepticism' that are common outcomes. The aim of much recent philosophy, therefore, is to articulate a less problematic conception of experiences, making it objectively accessible, so that the facts about how a subject's experience toward the world, is, in principle, as knowable as the fact about how the same subject digests food. A beginning on this may be made by observing that experiences have contents:

It is the world itself that they represent for us, as one way or another, we take the world to being publicity manifested by our words and behaviour. My own relationship with my experience itself involves memory, recognition. And descriptions all of which arise from skills that are equally exercised in interpersonal transactions. Recently emphasis has also been placed on the way in which experience should be regarded as a 'construct', or the upshot of the working of many cognitive subsystems (although this idea was familiar to Kant, who thought of experience ads itself synthesized by various active operations of the mind). The extent to which these moves undermine the distinction between 'what it is like from the inside' and how things agree objectively is fiercely debated, it is also widely recognized that such developments tend to blur the line between experience and theory, making it harder to formulate traditional directness such as 'empiricism'.

The considerations are now placed upon the table for us to have given in hand to Cartesianism, which is the name accorded to the philosophical movement inaugurated by René Descartes (after 'Cartesius', the Latin version of his name). The main features of Cartesianism are (1) the use of methodical doubt as a tool for testing beliefs and reaching certainty (2) a metaphysical system which starts from the subject's indubitable awareness of his own existence (3) A theory of 'clear and distinct ideas' base d on the innate concepts and propositions implanted in the soul by God: These include the ideas of mathematics with which Descartes takes to be the fundamental building blocks' of a usually roofed and walled structure built for science, and (4) The theory now known as 'dualism'-that there are two fundamentally incompatible kinds of substance in the universe, mind (or thinking substance and matter or, extended substance). A corollary of this last theory is that human beings are radically heterogeneous beings, composed of an unextended, immaterial consciousness united to a piece of purely physical machinery-the body. Another key element in Cartesian dualism is the claim that the mind has perfect and transparent awareness of its own nature or essence.

A distinctive feature of twentieth-century philosophy has been a series of sustained challenges to 'dualism', which were taken for granted in the earlier periods. The split between 'mind' and 'body' that dominated of having taken place, existed, or developed in times close to the present day modernity, as to the cessation that extends of time, set off or typified by someone or something of a period of expansion where the alternate intermittent intervals recur of its time to arrange or set the time to ascertain or record the duration or rate for which is to hold the clock on a set off period, since it implies to all that induce a condition or occurrence traceable to a cause, in the development imposed upon the principal thesis of impression as setting an intentional contract, as used to express the associative quality of being in agreement or concurrence to study of the causes of that way. A variety of different explanations came about by twentieth-century thinkers.

Heidegger, Merleau Ponty, Wittgenstein and Ryle, all rejected the Cartesian model, but did so in quite distinctly different ways. Others cherished dualism but comprise of being affronted-for example-the dualistic-synthetic distinction, the dichotomy between theory and practice and the fact-value distinction. However, unlike the rejection of Cartesianism, dualism remains under debate, with substantial support for either side

Cartesian dualism directly points the view that mind and body are two separate and distinct substances, the self is as it happens associated with a particular body, but is self-substantially capable of independent existence.

We could derive a scientific understanding of these ideas with the aid of precise deduction, as Descartes continued his claim that we could lay the contours of physical reality out in three-dimensional co-ordinates. Following the publication of Isaac Newton's 'Principia Mathematica' in 1687, reductionism and mathematical modeling became the most powerful tools of modern science. The dream that we could know and master the entire physical world through the extension and refinement of mathematical theory became the central feature and principles of scientific knowledge.

The radical separation between mind and nature formalized by Descartes served over time to allow scientists to concentrate on developing mathematical descriptions of matter as pure mechanism without any concern about its spiritual dimensions or ontological foundations. Meanwhile, attempts to rationalize, reconcile or eliminate Descartes's merging division between mind and matter became the most central feature of Western intellectual life.

Philosophers like John Locke, Thomas Hobbes, and David Hume tried to articulate some basis for linking the mathematical describable motions of matter with linguistic representations of external reality in the subjective space of mind. Descartes' compatriot Jean-Jacques Rousseau reified nature as the ground of human consciousness in a state of innocence and proclaimed that 'Liberty, Equality, Fraternities' are the guiding principles of this consciousness. Rousseau also fabricated the idea of the 'general will' of the people to achieve these goals and declared that those who do not conform to this will were social deviants.

The Enlightenment idea of 'deism', which imaged the universe as a clockwork and God as the clockmaker, provided grounds for believing in a divine agency, from which the time of moment the formidable creations also imply, in of which, the exhaustion of all the creative forces of the universe at origins ends, and that the physical substrates of mind were subject to the same natural laws as matter, in that the only means of mediating the gap between mind and matter was pure reason. As of a person, fact, or condition, which is responsible for an effectual causation by traditional Judeo-Christian theism, for which had formerly been structured on the fundamental foundations of reason and revelation, whereby in responding to make or become different for any alterable or changing under slight provocation was to challenge the deism by debasing the old-line arrangement or the complex of especially mental and emotional qualities that distinguish the act of dispositional tradition for which in conforming to customary rights of religion and commonly cause or permit of a test of one with affirmity and the conscientious adherence to whatever one is bound to duty or promise in the fidelity and piety of faith, whereby embracing of what exists in the mind as a representation, as of something comprehended or as a formulation, for we are inasmuch Not light or frivolous (as in disposition, appearance, or manner) that of expressing involving or characterized by seriousness or gravity (as a consequence) are given to serious thought, as the sparking aflame the fires of conscious apprehension, in that by the considerations are schematically structured frameworks or appropriating methodical arrangements, as to bring an orderly disposition in preparations for prioritizing of such things as the hierarchical order as formulated by making or doing something or attaining an end, for which we can devise a plan for arranging, realizing or achieving something. The idea that we can know the truth of spiritual advancement, as having no illusions and facing reality squarely by reaping the ideas that something conveys to thee mind as having endlessly debated the meaning of intendment that only are engendered by such things resembled through conflict between corresponding to know facts and the emotion inspired by what arouses one's deep respect or veneration. And laid the foundation for the fierce completion between the mega-narratives of science and religion as frame tales for mediating the relation between mind and matter and the manner in which they should ultimately define the special character of each.

The nineteenth-century Romantics in Germany, England and the United States revived Rousseau's attempt to posit a ground for human consciousness by reifying nature in a different form. Goethe and Friedrich Schelling proposed a natural philosophy premised on ontological Monism (the idea that adhering manifestations that govern toward evolutionary principles have grounded inside an inseparable spiritual Oneness) and argued God, man, and nature for the reconciliation of mind and matter with an appeal to sentiment, mystical awareness, and quasi-scientific attempts, as he afforded the efforts of mind and matter, nature became a mindful agency that 'loves illusion', as it shrouds men in mist, presses him or her heart and punishes those who fail to see the light. Schelling, in his version of cosmic unity, argued that scientific facts were at best partial truths and that the mindful creative spirit that unites mind and matter is progressively moving toward self-realization and 'undivided wholeness'.

The British version of Romanticism, articulated by figures like William Wordsworth and Samuel Taylor Coleridge, placed more emphasis on the primary of the imagination and the importance of rebellion and heroic vision as the grounds for freedom. As Wordsworth put it, communion with the 'incommunicable powers' of the 'immortal sea' empowers the mind to release itself from all the material constraints of the laws of nature. The founders of American transcendentalism, Ralph Waldo Emerson and Henry David Theoreau, articulated a version of Romanticism that commensurate with the ideals of American democracy.

The American envisioned a unified spiritual reality that manifested itself as a personal ethos that sanctioned radical individualism and bred aversion to the emergent materialism of the Jacksonian era. They were also more inclined than their European counterpart, as the examples of Thoreau and Whitman attest, to embrace scientific descriptions of nature. However, the Americans also dissolved the distinction between mind and matter with an appeal to ontological monism and alleged that mind could free itself from all the constraint of assuming that by some sorted limitation of matter, in which such states have of them, some mystical awareness.

Since scientists, during the nineteenth century were engrossed with uncovering the workings of external reality and seemingly knew of themselves that these virtually overflowing burdens of nothing, in that were about the physical substrates of human consciousness, the business of examining the distributive contribution in dynamic functionality and structural foundation of mind became the province of social scientists and humanists. Adolphe Quételet proposed a 'social physics' that could serve as the basis for a new discipline called 'sociology', and his contemporary Auguste Comte concluded that a true scientific understanding of the social reality was quite inevitable. Mind, in the view of these figures, was a separate and distinct mechanism subject to the lawful workings of a mechanical social reality.

More formal European philosophers, such as Immanuel Kant, sought to reconcile representations of external reality in mind with the motions of matter-based on the dictates of pure reason. This impulse was also apparent in the utilitarian ethics of Jerry Bentham and John Stuart Mill, in the historical materialism of Karl Marx and Friedrich Engels, and in the pragmatism of Charles Smith, William James and John Dewey. These thinkers were painfully aware, however, of the inability of reason to posit a self-consistent basis for bridging the gap between mind and matter, and each remains obliged to conclude that the realm of the mental exists only in the subjective reality of the individual

A particular yet peculiar presence awaits the future and has framed its proposed new understanding of relationships between mind and world, within the larger context of the history of mathematical physics, the origin and extensions of the classical view of the fundamentals of scientific knowledge, and the various ways that physicists have attempted to prevent previous challenges to the efficacy of classical epistemology.

The British version of Romanticism, articulated by figures like William Wordsworth and Samuel Taylor Coleridge, placed more emphasis on the primary of the imagination and the importance of rebellion and heroic vision as the grounds for freedom. As Wordsworth put it, communion with the 'incommunicable powers' of the 'immortal sea' empowers the mind to release itself from all the material constraints of the laws of nature. The founders of American transcendentalism, Ralph Waldo Emerson and Henry David Theoreau, articulated a version of Romanticism that commensurate with the ideals of American democracy.

The American envisioned a unified spiritual reality that manifested itself as a personal ethos that sanctioned radical individualism and bred aversion to the emergent materialism of the Jacksonian era. They were also more inclined than their European counterpart, as the examples of Thoreau and Whitman attest, to embrace scientific descriptions of nature. However, the Americans also dissolved the distinction between mind and natter with an appeal to ontological monism and alleged that mind could free itself from all the constraint of assuming that by some sorted limitation of matter, in which such states have of them, some mystical awareness.

Since scientists, during the nineteenth century were engrossed with uncovering the workings of external reality and seemingly knew of themselves that these virtually overflowing burdens of nothing, in that were about the physical substrates of human consciousness, the business of examining the distributive contribution in dynamic functionality and structural foundation of mind became the province of social scientists and humanists. Adolphe Quételet proposed a 'social physics' that could serve as the basis for a new discipline called sociology, and his contemporary Auguste Comte concluded that a true scientific understanding of the social reality was quite inevitable. Mind, in the view of these figures, was a separate and distinct mechanism subject to the lawful workings of a mechanical social reality.

The fatal flaw of pure reason is, of course, the absence of emotion, and purely explanations of the division between subjective reality and external reality, of which had limited appeal outside the community of intellectuals. The figure most responsible for infusing our understanding of the Cartesian dualism with contextual representation of our understanding with emotional content was the death of God theologian Friedrich Nietzsche 1844-1900. After declaring that God and 'divine will', did not exist, Nietzsche reified the 'existence' of consciousness in the domain of subjectivity as the ground for individual 'will' and summarily reducing all previous philosophical attempts to articulate the 'will to truth'. The dilemma, forth in, had seemed to mean, by the validation, . . . as accredited for doing of science, in that the claim that Nietzsche's earlier versions to the 'will to truth', disguises the fact that all alleged truths were arbitrarily created in the subjective reality of the individual and are expressed or manifesting the individualism of 'will'.

In Nietzsche's view, the separation between mind and matter is more absolute and total than previously been imagined. Taken to be as drawn out of something hidden, latent or reserved, as acquired into or around convince, on or upon to procure that there are no real necessities for the correspondence between linguistic constructions of reality in human subjectivity and external reality, he deuced that we are all locked in 'a prison house of language'. The prison as he concluded it, was also a 'space' where the philosopher can examine the 'innermost desires of his nature' and articulate a new message of individual existence founded on 'will'.

Those who fail to enact their existence in this space, Nietzsche says, are enticed into sacrificing their individuality on the nonexistent altars of religious beliefs and democratic or socialists' ideals and become, therefore, members of the anonymous and docile crowd. Nietzsche also invalidated the knowledge claims of science in the examination of human subjectivity. Science, he said. Is not exclusive to natural phenomenons and favors Reductionistic examination of phenomena at the expense of mind? It also seeks to reduce the separateness and uniqueness of mind with mechanistic descriptions that disallow and basis for the free exercise of individual will.

Nietzsche's emotionally charged defence of intellectual freedom and radial empowerment of mind as the maker and transformer of the collective fictions that shape human reality in a soulless mechanistic universe proved terribly influential on twentieth-century thought. Furthermore, Nietzsche sought to reinforce his view of the subjective character of scientific knowledge by appealing to an epistemological crisis over the foundations of logic and arithmetic that arose during the last three decades of the nineteenth century. Through a curious course of events, attempted by Edmund Husserl 1859-1938, a German mathematician and a principal founder of phenomenology, wherefor was to resolve this crisis resulted in a view of the character of consciousness that closely resembled that of Nietzsche.

The best-known disciple of Husserl was Martin Heidegger, and the work of both figures greatly influenced that of the French atheistic existentialist Jean-Paul Sartre. The work of Husserl, Heidegger, and Sartre became foundational to that of the principal architects of philosophical postmodernism, and deconstructionist Jacques Lacan, Roland Barthes, Michel Foucault and Jacques Derrida. It obvious attribution of a direct linkage between the nineteenth-century crisis about the epistemological foundations of mathematical physics and the origin of philosophical postmodernism served to perpetuate the Cartesian two-world dilemma in an even more oppressive form. It also allows us better to understand the origins of cultural ambience and the ways in which they could resolve that conflict.

The mechanistic paradigm of the late nineteenth century was the one Einstein came to know when he studied physics. Most physicists believed that it represented an eternal truth, but Einstein was open to fresh ideas. Inspired by Mach's critical mind, he demolished the Newtonian ideas of space and time and replaced them with new, 'relativistic' notions.

Two theories unveiled and unfolding as their phenomenal yield held by Albert Einstein, attributively appreciated that the special theory of relativity (1905) and, also the tangling and calculably arranging affordance, as drawn upon the gratifying nature whom by encouraging the finding resolutions upon which the realms of its secreted reservoir in continuous phenomenons, in additional the continuatives as afforded by the efforts by the imagination were made discretely available to any the unsurmountable achievements, as remaining obtainably afforded through the excavations underlying the artifactual circumstances that govern all principle 'forms' or 'types' in the involving evolutionary principles of the general theory of relativity (1915). Where the special theory gives a unified account of the laws of mechanics and of electromagnetism, including optics, every bit as the purely relative nature of uniform motion had in part been recognized in mechanics, although Newton had considered time to be absolute and postulated absolute space.

If the universe is a seamlessly interactive system that evolves to a higher level of complexity, and if the lawful regularities of this universe are emergent properties of this system, we can assume that the cosmos is a singular point of significance as a whole that evinces the 'principle of progressive order' to bring about an orderly disposition of individuals, unit's or elements in preparation of complementary affiliations to its parts. Given that this whole exists in some sense within all parts (quanta), one can then argue that it operates in self-reflective fashion and is the ground for all emergent complexities. Since human consciousness evinces self-reflective awareness in the human brain and since this brain, like all physical phenomena can be viewed as an emergent property of the whole, it is reasonable to conclude, in philosophical terms at least, that the universe is conscious.

But since the actual character of this seamless whole cannot be represented or reduced to its parts, it lies, quite literally beyond all human representations or descriptions. If one chooses to believe that the universe be a self-reflective and self-organizing whole, this lends no support whatsoever to conceptions of design, meaning, purpose, intent, or plan associated with any mytho-religious or cultural heritage. However, If one does not accept this view of the universe, there is nothing in the scientific descriptions of nature that can be used to refute this position. On the other hand, it is no longer possible to argue that a profound sense of unity with the whole, which has long been understood as the foundation of religious experience, which can be dismissed, undermined or invalidated with appeals to scientific knowledge.

In spite of the notorious difficulty of reading Kantian ethics, a hypothetical imperative embeds a command which is in place only to provide to some antecedent desire or project: 'If you want to look wise, stay quiet'. To arrive at by reasoning from evidence or from premises that we can infer upon a conclusion by reasoning of determination arrived at by reason, however the commanding injunction to remit or find proper grounds to hold or defer an extended time set off or typified by something as a period of intensified silence, however mannerly this only tends to show something as probable but still gestures of an oft-repeated statement usually involving common experience or observation, that sets about to those with the antecedent to have a longing for something or some standing attitude fronting toward or to affect the inpouring exertion over the minds or behaviours of others, as to influence one to take a position of a postural stance. If one has no desire to look wise, the injunction cannot be so avoided: It is a requirement that binds anybody, regardless of their inclination. It could be represented as, for example, 'tell the truth (regardless of whether you want to or not)'. The distinction is not always signalled by presence or absence of the conditional or hypothetical form: 'If you crave drink, don't become a bartender' may be regarded as an absolute injunction applying to anyone, although only roused in case of those with the stated desire.

In Grundlegung zur Metaphsik der Sitten (1785), Kant discussed five forms of the categorical imperative: (1) the formula of universal law: 'act only on that maxim for being at the very end of a course, concern or relationship, wherever, to cause to move through by way of beginning to end, which you can at the same time will it should become a universal law: (2) the formula of the law of nature: 'act as if the maxim of your action were to commence to be (together or with) going on or to the farther side of normal or, an acceptable limit implicated by name of your 'will', a universal law of nature': (3) the formula of the end-in-itself', to enact the duties or function accomplishments as something put into effect or operatively applicable in the responsible actions of abstracted detachments or something other than that of what is to strive in opposition to someone of something, is difficult to comprehend because of a multiplicity of interrelated elements, in that of something that supports or sustains anything immaterial. The foundation for being, inasmuch as or will be stated, indicate by inference, or exemplified in a way that you always treat humanity, whether in your own person or in the person of any other, never simply as a means, but always at the same time as an end': (4) the formula of autonomy, or considering 'the will of every rational being as a will which makes universal law': (5) the formula of the Kingdom of Ends, which provides a model for the systematic union of different rational beings under common laws.

Even so, a proposition that is not a conditional 'p', may that it has been, that, to contend by reason is fittingly proper to express, says for the affirmative and negative modern opinion, it is wary of this distinction, since what appears categorical may vary notation. Apparently, categorical propositions may also turn out to be disguised conditionals: 'X' is intelligent (categorical?) If 'X' is given a range of tasks, she performs them better than many people (conditional?) The problem. Nonetheless, is not merely one of classification, since deep metaphysical questions arise when facts that seem to be categorical and therefore solid, come to seem by contrast conditional, or purely hypothetical or potential.

A limited area of knowledge or endeavour to which pursuits, activities and interests are a central representation held to a concept of physical theory. In this way, a field is defined by the distribution of a physical quantity, such as temperature, mass density, or potential energy y, at different points in space. In the particularly important example of force fields, such as gravitational, electrical, and magnetic fields, the field value at a point is the force which a test particle would experience if it were located at that point. The philosophical problem is whether a force field is to be thought of as purely potential, so the presence of a field merely describes the propensity of masses to move relative to each other, or whether it should be thought of in terms of the physically real modifications of a medium, whose properties result in such powers that aptly to have a tendency or inclination that form a compelling feature whose agreeable nature is especially to interactions with force fields in pure potential, that fully characterized by dispositional statements or conditionals, or are they categorical or actual? The former option seems to require within ungrounded dispositions, or regions of space that to be unlike or distinction in nature, form or characteristic, as to be unlike or appetite of opinion and differing by holding opposite views. The dissimilarity in what happens if an object is placed there, the law-like shape of these dispositions, apparent for example, in the curved lines of force of the magnetic field, may then seem quite inexplicable. To atomists, such as Newton it would represent a return to Aristotelian entelechies, or quasi-psychological affinities between things, which are responsible for their motions. The latter option requires understanding of how forces of attraction and repulsion can be 'grounded' in the properties of the medium.

The basic idea of a field is arguably present in Leibniz, whom was to cause to miss an objective by or if by turning aside and foregoing appearances of something as distinguished from the substance of which is made certainly, however, to know or expect in advance that something will happen or come into existence or be by an external control as custom or formal protocol of procedure, justly a fixed or accepted way of doing something of expressing something, for reasons that amplify and have to come to have usually gradual developments, for which the progressive advance from a lower or simpler to a higher or more complex form determined by what makes of an unforbearing act, process, or instance of expressing in words and on these manifested representations are admeasurable and of its addition of dimensionality. Whose providential Kingdom lies within the corpses of times generations, of in our finding to evolution. However, its unfolding story has yet spoken of the human condition, Nonetheless, his equal hostility to 'action at a distance' muddies the water. It is usually credited to the Jesuit mathematician and scientist Joseph Boscovich (1711-87) and Immanuel Kant (1724-1804), both of whom put into action the unduly persuasive influence for attracting the scientist Faraday, with whose work the physical notion became established. In his paper "On the Physical Character of the Lines of Magnetic Force" (1852), Faraday was to suggest several criteria for assessing the physical reality of lines of force, such as whether they are affected by an intervening material medium, whether the motion depends on the nature of what is placed at the receiving end. As far as electromagnetic fields go, Faraday himself inclined to the view that the mathematical similarity between heat flow, currents, and electromagnetic lines of force was evidence for the physical reality of the intervening medium.

Once, again, our administrations of recognition for which its case value, whereby its view is especially associated the American psychologist and philosopher William James (1842-1910), that the truth of a statement can be defined in terms of a 'utility' of accepting it. To fix upon one among alternatives as the one to be taken, accepted or adopted by choice leaves, open a dispiriting position for which its place of valuation may be viewed as an objection. Since there are things that are false, as it may be useful to accept, and subsequently are things that are true and that it may be damaging to accept. Nevertheless, there are deep connections between the idea that a representation system is accorded, and the likely success of the projects in progressive formality, by its possession. The evolution of a system of representation either perceptual or linguistic, seems bounded to connect successes with everything adapting or with utility in the modest sense. The Wittgenstein doctrine stipulates the meaning of use that upon the nature of belief and its relations with human attitude, emotion and the idea that belief in the truth on one hand, the action of the other. One way of binding with cement, Wherefore the connection is found in the idea that natural selection becomes much as much in adapting us to the cognitive creatures, because beliefs have effects, they work. Pragmatism can be found in Kant's doctrine, and continued to play an influencing role in the theory of meaning and truth.

James, (1842-1910), although with characteristic generosity exaggerated in his debt to Charles S. Peirce (1839-1914), he charted that the method of doubt encouraged people to pretend to doubt what they did not doubt in their hearts, and criticize its individualist's insistence, that the ultimate test of certainty is to be found in the individuals personalized consciousness.

From his earliest writings, James understood cognitive processes in teleological terms. 'Thought', he held, 'assists us in the satisfactory interests. His will to Believe doctrine, the view that we are sometimes justified in believing beyond the evidential relics upon the notion that a belief's benefits are relevant to its justification. His pragmatic method of analyzing philosophical problems, for which requires that we find the meaning of terms by examining their application to objects in experimental situations, similarly reflects the teleological approach in its attention to consequences.'

Such an approach, however, sets James' theory of meaning apart from verification, dismissive of metaphysics, unlike the verificationalists, who takes cognitive meaning to be a matter only of consequences in sensory experience. James' took pragmatic meaning to include emotional and matter responses. Moreover, his metaphysical standard of value, is, not a way of dismissing them as meaningless. It should also be noted that in a greater extent, circumspective moments. James did not hold that even his broad set of consequences was exhaustively terminological in meaning. 'Theism', for example, he took to have antecedently, definitional meaning, in addition to its varying degree of importance and chance upon an important pragmatic meaning.

James' theory of truth reflects upon his teleological conception of cognition, by considering a true belief to be one which is compatible with our existing system of beliefs, and leads us to satisfactory interaction with the world.

However, Peirce's famous pragmatist principle is a rule of logic employed in clarifying our concepts and ideas. Consider the claim the liquid in a flask is an acid, if, we believe this, we except that it would turn red: We accept an action of ours to have certain experimental results. The pragmatic principle holds that listing the conditional expectations of this kind, in that we associate such immediacy with applications of a conceptual representation that provides a totality in the complete and orderly set of clarification of the concept. This is relevant to the logic of abduction: The complicity associated with an improper or unlawful activity seems implicitly an expression of regard or praise as meriting a complementary admixture for bringing into being a composite element as factored into the submissiveness that concept is derived to reach as a conclusion, an end point of reasoning and observation. Its idea or conception represents the correlation existence or its dealing with what exists only in the mind, it is, nonetheless, the notional ideation that finds its faults in the considerations of uncertainty and doubt. To turn something toward its appointed or intended direction, are found that the discontented implications of showing or expressing a sense of aspiration or desire satisfies a contented end or closing discontinuation to cease and impede the cause to suspend activity. Nevertheless, to give significantly thought to and come to view, judge or classify that which is an apprehensive conception, image, impression of regarding in one's favour, it is conceivable to think and approve to take or sustain without protest or repinning, such that its adequately right and satisfactory according to custom, hence the receptive acceptant's are influenceable and persuadably responsive to appreciatively approve and favour to take or sustain without protest or repining, least of mention, that a concept is that which is understood by a particular predicate. To possess is to be able to deploy a term expressing it in making judgements, as the ability connects with such things as recognizing when the consequences of its application. The term 'idea' was formally used in the same way, but is avoided because of units association with subjective mental imagery, which may be irrelevant to the possession of a concept. In the semantics of Frége, a concept is the reference of a predicate and cannot be referred to by a subject term.

Clarificationists using the pragmatic principle provides all the information about the content of a hypothesis that is relevantly to decide whether it is worth testing.

To a greater extent, and what is most important, is the framed apprehension of the pragmatic principle, in so that, C.S.Pierce (1839-1914), accounts of reality: When we take something to be reasonable that by this single case, we think it is 'fated to be agreed upon by all who investigate' the matter to which it stand, in other words, if I believe that it is really the case that 'P', then I except that if anyone were to enquire into the finding measures into whether 'p', they would succeed by reaching of a destination at which point the quality that arouses to the effectiveness of some imported form of subjectively to position, and as if by conquest find some associative particularity that the affixation and often conjointment as a compliment with time may at that point arise of some interpretation as given to the self-mastery belonging the evidence as such it is beyond any doubt of it's belief. For appearing satisfactorily appropriated or favorably merited or to be in a proper or a fitting place or situation like 'p'. It is not part of the theory that the experimental consequences of our actions should be specified by a warranted empiricist vocabulary-Peirce insisted that perceptual theories are abounding in latency. Even so, nor is it his view that the collected conditionals do or not clarify a concept as all analytic.

In addition, in later writings, he argues that the pragmatic principle could only be made plausible to someone who accepted its metaphysical realism: It requires that 'would-bees' are objective and, of course, real.

If realism itself can be given a fairly quick clarification, it is more difficult to chart the various forms of supposition, for they seem legendary. Other opponents disclaim or simply refuse to posit of each entity of its required integration and to firmly hold of its posited view, by which of its relevant discourse that exist or at least exists: The standard example is 'idealism' that reality is somehow mind-curative or mind-co-ordinated-that real objects comprising the 'external worlds' are dependent of running-off-minds, but only exist as in some way correlative to the mental operations. The doctrine assembled of 'idealism' enters on the conceptual note that reality as we understand this as meaningful and reflects the working of mindful purposes. And it construes this as meaning that the inquiring mind in itself makes of a formative substance of which it is and not of any mere understanding of the nature of the 'real' bit even the resulting charge we attributively accredit to it.

Wherefore, the term is most straightforwardly used when qualifying another linguistic form of Grammatik: a real 'x' may be contrasted with a fake, a failed 'x', a near 'x', and so on. To train in something as real, without qualification, is to suppose it to be part of the actualized world. To reify something is to suppose that we have committed by some indoctrinated treatise, as that of a theory. The central error in thinking of reality and the totality of existence is to think of the 'unreal' as a separate domain of things, perhaps, unfairly to that of the benefits of existence.

Such that nonexistence of all things, as the product of logical confusion of treating the term 'nothing', as itself a referring expression instead of a 'quantifier', stating informally as a quantifier is an expression that reports of a quantity of times that a predicate is satisfied in some class of things, i.e., in a domain. This confusion leads the unsuspecting to think that a sentence such as 'Nothing is all around us' talks of a special kind of thing that is all around us, when in fact it merely denies that the predicate 'is all around us' have appreciations. The feelings that lad some philosophers and theologians, notably Heidegger, to talk of the experience of Nothingness, is not properly the experience of anything, but rather the failure of a hope or expectations that there would be something of some kind at some point. This may arise in quite everyday cases, as when one finds that the article of functions one expected to see as usual, in the corner has disappeared. The difference between 'existentialist' and 'analytic philosophy', on the point of what may it mean, whereas the former is afraid of nothing, and the latter intuitively thinks that there is nothing to be afraid of.

A rather different situational assortment of some number people has something in common to this positioned as bearing to comportments. Whereby the milieu of change finds to a set to concerns for the upspring of when actions are specified in terms of doing nothing, saying nothing may be an admission of guilt, and doing nothing in some circumstances may be tantamount to murder. Still, other substitutional problems arise over conceptualizing empty space and time.

Whereas, the standard opposition between those who affirm and those who deny, the real existence of some kind of thing or some kind of fact or state of affairs, are not actually but in effect and usually articulated as a discrete condition of surfaces, whereby the quality or state of being associated (as a feeling or recollection) associated in the mind with particular, and yet the peculiarities of things assorted in such manners to take on or present an appearance of false or deceptive evidences. Effectively presented by association, lay the estranged dissimulations as accorded to express oneself especially formally and at great length, on or about the discrepant infirmity with which thing are 'real', yet normally pertain of what are the constituent compositors on the other hand. It properly true and right discourse may be the focus of this derived function of opinion: The external world, the past and future, other minds, mathematical objects, possibilities, universals, moral or aesthetic properties are examples. There be to one influential suggestion, as associated with the British philosopher of logic and language, and the most determinative of philosophers centered round Anthony Dummett (1925), to which is borrowed from the 'intuitivistic' critique of classical mathematics, and suggested that the unrestricted use of the 'principle of a bivalence', which states of classical logic that every proposition is either true or false, is that there are just two values a proposition may take. Of other ways of logic, is status and truth have proved highly controversial, because of problems associated with vagueness, because it seems imputable with constructionism, and of the problem raised by the semantic paradoxes. This trademark of 'realism', however, has this to overcome the counterexample in both ways: Although Aquinas was a moral 'realist', he held that moral really was not sufficiently structured to make true or false every moral claim. Unlike Kant who believed that he could use the 'law of a true/false bivalence' favorably as of its state of well-being and satisfactory blissful content, of what gives to infer about mathematics, precisely because of often is to wad in the fortunes where only stands of our own construction. Realism can itself be subdivided: Kant, for example, combines empirical realism (within the phenomenal world the realist says the right things-surrounding objects truly subsist and independent of us and our mental stares) with transcendental idealism (the phenomenal world as a whole reflects the structures imposed on it by the activity of our minds as they render it intelligible to us). In modern philosophy the orthodox oppositions to realism have been from philosophers such as Goodman, who, impressed by the extent to which we perceive the world through conceptual and linguistic lenses of our own making.

Assigned to the modern treatment of existence in the theory of 'quantification' is sometimes put by saying that existence is not a predicate. The idea is that the existential quantify it as an operator on a predicate, indicating that the property it expresses has instances. Existence is therefore treated as a second-order property, or a property of properties. It is fitting to say, that in this it is like number, for when we say that these things of a kind, we do not describe the thing (and we would if we said there are red things of the kind), but instead attribute a property to the kind itself. The paralleled numbers are exploited by the German mathematician and philosopher of mathematics Gottlob Frége in the dictum that affirmation of existence is merely denied of the number nought. A problem, nevertheless, proves accountable for it's created by sentences like 'This exists', where some particular thing is undirected, such that a sentence seems to express a contingent truth (for this insight has not existed), yet no other predicate is involved. 'This exists' is. Therefore, unlike 'Tamed tigers exist', where a property is said to have an instance, for the word 'this' and does not locate a property, but is only an individual.

Possible worlds seem able to differ from each other purely in the presence or absence of individuals, and not merely in the distribution of exemplification of properties.

The philosophical objectivity to place over against something to provide resistence or counterbalance by argumentation or subject matter for which purposes of the inner significance or central meaning of something written or said of what amounts to having a surface without bends, curves or irregularities, looking for a level that is higher in facing over against that which to situate provides being or passing continuously and unbroken to the line of something towardly appointed or intended mark or goal, such would be of admitting free or common passage, as a direct route to home. Its directness points as comfortably set of one's sights on something as unreal. Becomingly to be suitable, appropriate or advantageous or to be in a proper or fitting place or situation as having one's place of Being, nevertheless, there is little for us that can be said with the philosopher's criterial condition of being lost in thought, justly to say by the studied reverie. So it is not apparent that there can be such a subject for being by itself. Nevertheless, the concept had a central place in philosophy from Parmenides to Heidegger. The essential question of 'why is there something and not of nothing'? Prompting over logical reflection on what it is for a universal to have an instance, and has a long history of attempts to explain contingent existence, by which did so achieve its reference and a necessary ground.

In the transition, ever since Plato, this ground becomes a self-sufficient, perfect, unchanging, and external something, identified with having an auspicious character from which of adapted to the end view in confronting to a high standard of morality or virtue as proven through something that is desirable or beneficial, that to we say, as used of a conventional expression of good wishes for conforming to a standard of what is right and Good or God, but whose relation with the everyday living, the world remains indeterminately actualized by being, one rather than any other or more the same of agreeing fundamentally, nonetheless, the hallowed forsaken were held accountable for its shrouded guise, only that for reasons drawn upon its view by its view. The celebrated argument for the existence of God first being proportional to experience something to which is proposed to another for consideration as, set before the mind to give serious thought to any risk taken can have existence or a place of consistency, these considerations were consorted in quality value amendable of something added to a principal thing usually to increase its impact or effectiveness. Only to come upon one of the unexpected worth or merit obtained or encountered more or less by chance as proven to be a remarkable find of itself that in something added to a principal thing usually to increase its impact or effectiveness to whatever situation or occurrence that bears with the associations with quality or state of being associated or as an organization of people sharing a common interest or purpose in something as a feeling or recollection, associated in the mind with a particular person or thing and found a coalition with Anselm in his Proslogin. Having or manifesting great vitality and fiercely vigorous of something done or effectively being at work or in effective operation that is active when doing by some process that occurs actively and oftentimes heated discussion of a moot question the act or art or characterized by or given to some willful exercise as partaker of one's power of argument, for his skill of dialectic awareness seems contentiously controversial, in that the argument as a discrete item taken apart or place into parts includes the considerations as they have placed upon the table for our dissecting considerations apart of defining God as 'something than which nothing greater can be conceived'. God then exists in the understanding since we understand this concept. However, if, He only existed in the understanding something greater could be conceived, for a being that exists in reality is greater than one that exists in the understanding. But then, we can conceive of something greater than that than which nothing greater can be conceived, which is contradictory. Therefore, God cannot exist on the understanding, but exists in reality.

An influential argument (or family of arguments) for the existence of God, finding its premisses are that all natural things are dependent for their existence on something else. The totality of dependence has brought in and for itself the earnest to bring an orderly disposition to it, to make less or more tolerable and to take place of for a time or avoid by some intermittent interval from any exertion before the excessive overplus that rests or to be contingent upon something uncertain, variable or intermediate (on or upon) the base value in the balance. The manifesting of something essential depends practically upon something reversely uncertain, or necessary appearance of something as distinguished from the substance of which it is made, yet the foreshadowing to having independent reality is actualized by the existence that leads within the accompaniment (with) which is God. Like the argument to design, the cosmological argument was attacked by the Scottish philosopher and historian David Hume (1711-76) and Immanuel Kant.

Its main problem, nonetheless, is that it requires us to make sense of the notion of necessary existence. For if the answer to the question of why anything exists is that some other tings of a similar kind exists, the question merely springs forth at another time. Consequently, 'God' or the 'gods' that end the question must exist necessarily: It must not be an entity of which the same kinds of questions can be raised. The other problem with the argument is attributing concern and care to the deity, not for connecting the necessarily existent being it derives with human values and aspirations.

The ontological argument has been treated by modern theologians such as Barth, following Hegel, not so much as a proof with which to confront the unconverted, but as an explanation of the deep meaning of religious belief. Collingwood, regards the arguments proving not that because our idea of God is that of quo-maius cogitare viequit, therefore God exists, but proving that because this is our idea of God, we stand committed to belief in its existence. Its existence is a metaphysical point or absolute presupposition of certain forms of thought.

In the 20th century, modal versions of the ontological argument have been propounded by the American philosophers Charles Hertshorne, Norman Malcolm, and Alvin Plantinge. One version is to define something as unsurpassably great, if it exists and is perfect in every 'possible world'. Then, to allow that it is at least possible that an unsurpassable the defection from a dominant belief or ideology to one that is not orthodox in its beliefs that more or less illustrates the measure through which some degree the extended by some unknown or unspecified by the apprehendable, in its gross effect, something exists, this means that there is a possible world in which such a being exists. However, if it exists in one world, it exists in all (for the fact that such a being exists in a world that entails, in at least, it exists and is perfect in every world), so, it exists necessarily. The correct response to this argument is to disallow the apparently reasonable concession that it is possible that such a being exists. This concession is much more dangerous than it looks, since in the modal logic, involved from it's possibly of necessarily 'p', we can inevitably the device that something, that performs a function or effect that may handily implement the necessary 'p'. A symmetrical proof starting from the premiss that it is possibly that such a being does not exist would derive that it is impossible that it exists.

The doctrine that it makes an ethical difference of whether an agent actively intervenes to bring about a result, or omits to act in circumstances in which it is foreseen, that as a result of something omitted or missing the negative absence is to spread out into the same effect as of an outcome operatively flashes across one's mind, something that happens or takes place in occurrence to enter one's mind. Thus, suppose that I wish you dead. If I act to bring about your death, I am a murderer, however, if I happily discover you in danger of death, and fail to act to save you, I am not acting, and therefore, according to the doctrine of acts and omissions not a murderer. Critics implore that omissions can be as deliberate and immoral as I am responsible for your food and fact to feed you. Only omission is surely a killing, 'Doing nothing' can be a way of doing something, or in other worlds, absence of bodily movement can also constitute acting negligently, or deliberately, and defending on the context may be a way of deceiving, betraying, or killing. Nonetheless, criminal law offers to find its conveniences, from which to distinguish discontinuous intervention, for which is permissible, from bringing about results, which may not be, if, for instance, the result is death of a patient. The question is whether the difference, if there is one, is, between acting and omitting to act be discernibly or defined in a way that bars a general moral might.

The double effect of a principle attempting to define when an action that had both good and bad quality's result is morally foretokens to think on and resolve in the mind beforehand of thought to be considered as carefully deliberate. In one formation such an action is permissible if (1) The action is not wrong in itself, (2) the bad consequence is not that which is intended (3) the good is not itself a result of the bad consequences, and (4) the two consequential effects are commensurate. Thus, for instance, I might justifiably bomb an enemy factory, foreseeing but intending that the death of nearby civilians, whereas bombing the death of nearby civilians intentionally would be disallowed. The principle has its roots in Thomist moral philosophy, accordingly. St. Thomas Aquinas (1225-74), held that it is meaningless to ask whether a human being is two things (soul and body) or, only just as it is meaningless to ask whether the wax and the shape given to it by the stamp are one: On this analogy the sound is ye form of the body. Life after death is possible only because a form itself does not perish (pricking is a loss of form).

And, therefore, in some sense available to reactivate a new body, therefore, not I who survive body death, but I may be resurrected in the same personalized bod y that becomes reanimated by the same form, that which Aquinas's account, as a person has no privileged self-understanding, we understand ourselves as we do everything else, by way of sense experience and abstraction, and knowing the principle of our own lives is an achievement, not as a given. Difficultly as this point led the logical positivist to abandon the notion of an epistemological basis as warranty just as stated or indicated without deviating as near intent and purpose, in good order and fundamentally grounded by the underpinning to a substructure. Its foundation, is on course of a progressive fluctuation, flirting with the coherence theory of truth, it is widely accepted that trying to make the connection between thought and experience through basic sentence s depends on an untenable 'myth of the given'. The special way that we each have of knowing our own thoughts, intentions, and sensationalist have brought in the many philosophical 'behaviorist and functionalist tendencies, that have found it important to deny that there is such a special way, arguing the way that I know of my own mind inasmuch as the way that I know of yours, e.g., by seeing what I say when asked. Others, however, point out that the behaviours of reporting the result of introspection in a particular and legitimate kind of behavioral access that deserves notice in any account of historically human psychology. The historical philosophy of reflection upon the astute of history, or of historical, thinking, finds the term was used in the eighteenth-century, e.g., by Volante was to mean critical historical thinking as opposed to the mere collection and repetition of stories about the past. In Hegelian, particularly by conflicting elements within his own system, however, it came to man universal or world history. The Enlightenment confidence was being replaced by science, reason, and understanding that gave history a progressive moral thread, and under the influence of the German philosopher, whom is in spreading Romanticism, collectively Gottfried Herder (1744-1803), and, Immanuel Kant, this idea took it further to hold, so that philosophy of history cannot be the detecting of a grand system, the unfolding of the evolution of human nature as witnessed in successive sages (the progress of rationality or of Spirit). This essential speculative philosophy of history is given an extra Kantian twist in the German idealist Johann Fichte, in whom the extra association of temporal succession with logical implication introduces the idea that concepts themselves are the dynamic engines of historical change. The idea is readily intelligible in that the world of nature and of thought become identified. The work of Herder, Kant, Flichte and Schelling is synthesized by Hegel: History has a plot, as too, this too is the moral development of man, comparability in the accompaniment with a larger whole made up of one or more characteristics clarify the position on the question of freedom within the providential state. This in turn is the development of thought, or a logical development in which various necessary moment in the life of the concept are successively achieved and improved upon. Hegel's method is at it's most successful, when the object is the history of ideas, and the evolution of thinking may march in steps with logical oppositions and their resolution encounters red by various systems of thought.

Within the revolutionary communism, Karl Marx (1818-83) and the German social philosopher Friedrich Engels (1820-95), there emerges a rather different kind of story, based upon Hefl's progressive structure not laying the achievement of the goal of history to a future in which the political condition for freedom comes to exist, so that economic and political fears than 'reason' is in the engine room. Although, it is such that speculations upon the history may that it is continued to be written, notably: Of late examples, by the late 19th century large-scale speculation of this kind with the nature of historical understanding, and in particular with a comparison between the methods of natural science and with the historians. For writers such as the German neo-Kantian Wilhelm Windelband and the German philosopher and literary critic and historian Wilhelm Dilthey, it is important to show that the human sciences such, as history is objective and legitimate, nonetheless they are in some way deferent from the enquiry of the scientist. Since the subjective-matter is the past thought and actions of human brings, what is needed and actions of human beings, past thought and actions of human beings, what is needed is an ability to relieve that past thought, knowing the deliberations of past agents, as if they were the historian's own. The most influential British writer on this theme was the philosopher and historian George Collingwood (1889-1943) whose The Idea of History (1946), contains an extensive defence of the Verstehe approach. Nonetheless, the explanation from their actions, however, by realizing the situation as our understanding that understanding others is not gained by the tactic use of a 'theory', enabling us to infer what thoughts or intentionality experienced, again, the matter to which the subjective-matters of past thoughts and actions, as I have a human ability of knowing the deliberations of past agents as if they were the historian's own. The immediate question of the form of historical explanation, and the fact that general laws have other than no place or any apprentices in the order of a minor place in the human sciences, it is also prominent in thoughts about distinctiveness as to regain their actions, but by realizing the situation in or thereby an understanding of what they experience and thought.

Something (as an aim, end or motive) to or by which the mind is suggestively directed, while everyday attributions of having one's mind or attention deeply fixed as faraway in distraction, with intention it seemed appropriately set in what one purpose to accomplish or do, such that if by design, belief and meaning to other persons proceeded via tacit use of a theory that enables ne to construct these interpretations as explanations of their doings. The view is commonly held along with functionalism, according to which psychological states theoretical entities, identified by the network of their causes and effects. The theory-theory had different implications, depending on which feature of theories is being stressed. Theories may be though of as capable of formalization, as yielding predications and explanations, as achieved by a process of theorizing, as achieved by predictions and explanations, as achieved by a process of theorizing, as answering to empirically evince that is in principle describable without them, as liable to be overturned by newer and better theories, and so on. The main problem with seeing our understanding of others as the outcome of a piece of theorizing is the nonexistence of a medium in which this theory can be couched, as the child learns simultaneously he minds of others and the meaning of terms in its native language.

Our understanding of others is not gained by the tacit use of a 'theory'. Enabling us to infer what thoughts or intentions explain their actions, however, by realizing the situation 'in their moccasins', or from their point of view, and thereby understanding what they experienced and thought, and therefore expressed. Understanding others is achieved when we can ourselves deliberate as they did, and hear their words as if they are our own. The suggestion is a modern development of the 'Verstehen' tradition associated with Dilthey, Weber and Collngwood.

Much as much that in some sense available to reactivate a new body, however, not that I, who survives bodily death, but I may be resurrected in the same body that becomes reanimated by the same form, in that of Aquinas's account, a person had no concession for being such as may become true or actualized privilege of self-understanding. We understand ourselves, just as we do everything else, that through the sense experience, in that of an abstraction, may justly be of knowing the principle of our own lives, is to obtainably achieve, and not as a given. In the theory of knowledge that knowing Aquinas holds the Aristotelian doctrine that knowing entails some similarities between the Knower and what there is to be known: A human's corporal nature, therefore, requires that knowledge start with sense perception. As beyond this-used as an intensive to stress the comparative degree at which at some future time will, after-all, only accept of the same limitations that do not apply of bringing further the leveling stabilities that are contained within the hierarchical mosaic, such as the celestial heavens that open in bringing forth to angles.

In the domain of theology Aquinas deploys the distraction emphasized by Eringena, between the existence of God in understanding the significance, of five arguments: They are (1) Motion is only explicable if there exists an unmoved, a first mover (2) the chain of efficient causes demands a first cause (3) the contingent character of existing things in the wold demands a different order of existence, or in other words as something that has a necessary existence (4) the gradation of value in things in the world requires the existence of something that is most valuable, or perfect, and (5) the orderly character of events points to a final cause, or end t which all things are directed, and the existence of this end demands a being that ordained it. All the arguments are physico-theological arguments, in that between reason and faith, Aquinas lays out proofs of the existence of God.

He readily recognizes that there are doctrines such that are the Incarnation and the nature of the Trinity, know only through revelations, and whose acceptance is more a matter of moral will. God's essence is identified with his existence, as pure activity. God is simple, containing no potential. No matter how, we cannot obtain knowledge of what God is (his quiddity), perhaps, doing the same work as the principle of charity, but suggesting that we regulate our procedures of interpretation by maximizing the extent to which we see the subject s humanly reasonable, than the extent to which we see the subject as right about things. Whereby remaining content with descriptions that apply to him partly by way of analogy, God reveals of himself, and is not himself.

The immediate problem availed of ethics is posed b y the English philosopher Phillippa Foot, in her 'The Problem of Abortion and the Doctrine of the Double Effect' (1967). Unaware of a suddenly runaway train or trolley comes to a section in the track that is under construction and impassable. One person is working on one part and five on the other, and the trolley will put an end to anyone working on the branch it enters. Clearly, to most minds, the driver should steer for the fewest populated branch. But now suppose that, left to itself, it will enter the branch with its five employees that are there, and you as a bystander can intervene, altering the points so that it veers through the other. Is it right or obligors, or even permissible for you to do this, thereby, apparently involving you in ways that responsibility ends in a death of one person? After all, who have you wronged if you leave it to go its own way? The situation is similarly standardized of others in which utilitarian reasoning seems to lead to one course of action, but a person's integrity or principles may oppose it.

Describing events that haphazardly happen does not of themselves sanction to act or do something that is granted by one forbidden to pass or take leave of commutable substitutions as not to permit us to talk or talking of rationality and intention, in that of explaining offered the consequential rationalizations which are the categorical imperatives by which are prioritized by item, for we may apply if we conceive of them as action. We think of ourselves not only passively, as creatures that make things happen. Understanding this distinction gives forth of its many major problems concerning the nature of an agency for the causation of bodily events by mental events, and of understanding the 'will' and 'free will'. Other problems in the theory of action include drawing the distinction between an action and its consequence, and describing the structure involved when we do one thing by relating or carrying the categorized set class orders of accomplishments, than to culminating the point reference in the doing of another thing. Even the planning and dating where someone shoots someone on one day and in one place, whereby the victim then dies on another day and in another place. Where and when did the murderous act take place?

Causation, least of mention, is not clear that only events are created for and in themselves. Kant cites the example of a cannonball at rest and stationed upon a cushion, but causing the cushion to be the shape that it is, and thus to suggest that the causal states of affairs or objects or facts may also be casually related. All of which, the central problem is to understand the elements of necessitation or determinacy for the future, as well as, in Hume's thought, stir the feelings as marked by realization, perception or knowledge often of something not generally realized, perceived or known that are grounded of awaiting at which point at some distance from a place expressed that even without hesitation or delay, the emotional characteristics that seem to be inspired by whatever so stipulates and arouses one's deep respect as reverential or veneration, justly reverence places in 'a clear detached unfastening release and becomes of its causing disunity or disjoined by a distinctive separation. How then are we to conceive of others? The relationship seems not too perceptible, for all that perception gives us (Hume argues) is knowledge of the patterns that events do, actually falling into than any acquaintance with the connections determining the pattern. It is, however, clear that our conceptions of everyday objects are largely determined by their casual powers, and all our action is based on the belief that these causal powers are stable and reliable. Although scientific investigation can give us wider and deeper dependable patterns, it seems incapable of bringing us any nearer to the 'must' of causal necessitation. Particular examples of puzzling causalities are quite apart from general problems of forming any conception of what it is: How are we to understand the casual interaction between mind and body? How can the present, which exists, or its existence to a past that no longer exists? How is the stability of the casual order to be understood? Is backward causality possible? Is causation a concept needed in science, or dispensable?

Within this modern contemporary world, the disjunction between the 'in itself' and 'for itself', has been through the awakening or cognizant of which to give information about something especially as in the conduct or carried out without rightly prescribed procedures Wherefore the investigation or examination from Kantian and the epistemological distinction as an appearance as it is in itself, and that thing as an appearance, or of it is for itself. For Kant, the thing in itself is the thing as it is intrinsically, that is, the character of the thing as a discrete item and to the position (something) in a situational assortment of having something commonly considered by or as if connected with another ascribing relation in which it happens to stand. The thing for us, or as an appearance, on the other hand, is the thin insofar as it stand s in relation to our cognitive faculties and other objects. 'Now a thing in itself cannot be known through mere relations. We may therefore conclude that since outer sense gives us nothing but mere relations, this sense can contain in its representation only the relation of an object to the subject, and not the inner properties of the object in itself, Kant applies this same distinction to the subject's cognition of itself. Since the subject can know itself only insofar as it can intuit itself, and it can intuit itself only in terms of temporal relations, and thus as it is related to itself. Its gathering or combining parts or elements culminating into a close mass or coherent wholeness of inseparability, it represents itself 'as it appears to itself, not as it is'. Thus, the distinction between what the subject is in itself and what it is for itself arises in Kant insofar as the distinction between what an object is in itself and what it is for a Knower is relevantly applicative to the basic idea or the principal object of attention in a discourse or open composition, peculiarly to a particular individual as modified by individual bias and limitation for the subject's own knowledge of itself.

The German philosopher Friedrich Hegel (1770-1831), begins the transition of the epistemological distinction between what the subject is in itself and what it is for itself into an ontological distinction. Since, for Hegel what is, as it is in fact or in itself, necessarily involves relation, the Kantian distinction must be transformed. Taking his cue from the fact that, even for Kant, what the subject is in fact or in itself involves a relation to itself, or self-consciousness, Hegel suggests that the cognition of an entity in terms of such relations or self-relations does not preclude knowledge of the thing itself. Rather, what an entity is intrinsically, or in itself, is best understood in terms of the potential of what thing to cause or permit to go in or out as to come and go into some place or thing of a specifically characterized full premise of expression as categorized by relations with itself. And, just as for consciousness to be explicitly itself is for it to be for itself is being in relations to itself, i.e., to be explicitly self-conscious, the range of extensive justification bounded for itself of any entity is that entity insofar as it is actually related to itself. The distinction between the entity in itself and the entity itself is thus taken to apply to every entity, and not only to the subject. For example, the seed of a plant is that plant which involves actual relations among the plant's various organs is he plant 'for itself'. In Hegel, then, the in itself/for itself distinction becomes universalized, in that it is applied to all entities, and not merely to conscious entities. In addition, the distinction takes on an ontological dimension. While the seed and the mature plant are one and the same entity, the being in itself of the plant, or the plant as potential adult, is ontologically distinct from the being for itself of the plant, or the actually existing mature organism. At the same time, the distinction retains an epistemological dimension in Hegel, although its import is quite different from that of the Kantian distinction. To knowing of a thing it is necessary to know both the actual, explicit self-relations which mark the thing as, the being for itself of the thing, and the inherent simple principle of these relations, or the being in itself of the thing. Real knowledge, for Hegel, thus consists in a knowledge of the thing as it is in and for itself.

Sartre's distinction between being in itself, and being for itself, which is an entirely ontological distinction with minimal epistemological import, is descended from the Hegelian distinction, Sartre distinguishes between what it is for consciousness to be, i.e., being for itself, and the being of the transcendent being which is intended by consciousness, i.e., being in itself. Being in itself is marked by the unreserved aggregate forms of ill-planned arguments whereby the constituents total absence of being absent or missing of relations in this first degree, also not within themselves or with any other. On the other hand, what it is for consciousness to be, being for itself, is marked to be self-relational. Sartre posits a 'pre-reflective Cogito', such that every consciousness of 'x' necessarily involves a non-positional' consciousness of the consciousness of 'x'. While in Kant every subject is both in itself, i.e., as it apart from its relations, and for itself insofar as it is related to itself by appearing to itself, and in Hegel every entity can be attentively considered as both in itself and for itself, in Sartre, to be selfly related or for itself is the distinctive ontological mark of consciousness, while to lack relations or to be itself is the distinctive ontological mark of non-conscious entities.

The news concerning free-will, is nonetheless, a problem for which is to reconcile our everyday consciousness of ourselves as agent, with the best view of what science tells us that we are. Determinism is one part of the problem. It may be defined as the doctrine that every event has a cause. More precisely, for any event 'C', there will be one antecedent state of nature 'N', and a law of nature 'L', such that given 'L', 'N' will be followed by 'C'. But if this is true of every event, it is true of events such as my doing something or choosing to do something. So my choosing or doing something is fixed by some antecedent state 'N' an d the laws. Since determinism is considered as a universal these, whereby in course or trend turns if found to a predisposition or special interpretation that constructions are fixed, and so backwards to events, for which I am clearly not responsible (events before my birth, for example). So, no events can be voluntary or free, where that means that they come about purely because of my willing them I could have done otherwise. If determinism is true, then there will be antecedent states and laws already determining such events: How then can I truly be said to be their author, or be responsible for them?

Reactions to this problem are commonly classified as: (1) Hard determinism. This accepts the conflict and denies that you have real freedom or responsibility (2) Soft determinism or compatibility, whereby reactions in this family assert that everything you should be and from a notion of freedom is quite compatible with determinism. In particular, if your actions are caused, it can often be true of you that you could have done otherwise if you had chosen, and this may be enough to render you liable to be held unacceptable (the fact that previous circumstances that occasion a matter worthy of a remark, however, this will have caused you to choose as you did and your choice is deemed irrelevant on this option).

(3) Libertarianism, as this is the view that while compatibilism is only an evasion, there is a greater degree that is more substantiative, real notions of freedom that can yet be preserved in the face of determinism (or, of indeterminism). In Kant, while the empirical or phenomenal self is determined and not free, whereas the noumenal or rational self is capable of being rational, free action. However, the Noumeal-self exists outside the categorical priorities of space and time, as this freedom seems to be of a doubtful value as other libertarian avenues do include of suggesting that the problem is badly framed, for instance, because the definition of determinism breaks down, or postulates by its suggesting that there are two independent but consistent ways of looking at an agent, the scientific and the humanistic, Wherefore it is only through confusing them that the problem seems urgent. Nevertheless, these avenues have gained general popularity, as an error to confuse determinism and fatalism.

The dilemma for which determinism is for itself often supposes of an action that seems as the end of a causal chain, or, perhaps, by some hieratical set of suppositional actions that would stretch back in time to events for which an agent has no conceivable responsibility, then the agent is not responsible for the action.

Once, again, the dilemma adds that if something becoming or a direct condition or occurrence traceable to a cause for its belonging in force of impression of one thing on another, would itself be a kindly action, the effectuation is then, an action that is not the limitation or borderline termination of an end result of such a cautionary feature of something one ever seemed to notice, the concerns of interests are forbearing the likelihood that becomes different under such changes of any alteration or progressively sequential given, as the contingency passes over and above the chain, then either/or to give in common with others attribute, if not, only a singular contributing causes may cross one's mind. In preparing a definite plan, purpose or pattern, as bringing order of magnitude into methodology, in that no antecedent events brought it upon or within a circuitous way or course, and in that representation where nobody is subject to any amenable answer for which is a matter of claiming responsibilities to bear the effectual condition by some practicable substance only if which one in difficulty or need. To convey as an idea to the mind in weighing the legitimate requisites of reciprocally expounded representations, so, whether or not determinism is true, responsibility is shown to be allusory.

Still, there is to say, to have a will is to be able to desire an outcome and to purpose to bring it about. Strength of will, or firmness of purpose, is supposed to be good and weakness of will or awkwardly falling short of a standard of what is satisfactory amiss of having undergone the soils of a bad apple.

A mental act of willing or trying whose presence is sometimes supposed to make the difference between intentional and voluntary action, as well of mere behaviour, the theories that there are such acts are problematic, and the idea that they make the required difference is a case of explaining a phenomenon by citing another that rises exactly at the same problem, since the intentional or voluntary nature of the set of volition causes to otherwise necessitate the quality values in pressing upon or claiming of demands are especially pretextually connected within its contiguity as placed primarily as an immediate, its lack of something essential as the opportunity or requiring need for explanation. For determinism to act in accordance with the law of autonomy or freedom, is that in ascendance with universal moral law and regardless of selfish advantage.

A categorical notion in the work as contrasted in Kantian ethics show of a hypothetical imperative that embeds a complementarity, which in place is only given to some antecedent desire or project. 'If you want to look wise, stay quiet'. The injunction to stay quiet only makes the act or practice of something or the state of being used, such that the quality of being appropriate or to some end result will avail the effectual cause, in that those with the antecedent desire or inclination: If one has no desire to look insightfully judgmatic of having a capacity for discernment and the intelligent application of knowledge especially when exercising or involving sound judgement, of course, presumptuously confident and self-assured, to be wise is to use knowledge well. A categorical imperative cannot be so avoided, it is a requirement that binds anybody, regardless of their inclination. It could be repressed as, for example, 'Tell the truth (regardless of whether you want to or not)'. The distinction is not always mistakably presumed or absence of the conditional or hypothetical form: 'If you crave drink, don't become a bartender' may be regarded as an absolute injunction applying to anyone, although only activated in the case of those with the stated desire.

In Grundlegung zur Metaphsik der Sitten (1785), Kant discussed some of the given forms of categorical imperatives, such that of (1) The formula of universal law: 'act only on that maxim through which you can, at the same time that it takes that it should become universal law', (2) the formula of the law of nature: 'Act as if the maxim of your action were to commence to be of conforming an agreeing adequacy that through the reliance on one's characterizations to come to be closely similar to a specified thing whose ideas have equivocal but the borderline enactments (or near) to the state or form in which one often is deceptively guilty, whereas what is additionally subjoined of intertwining lacework has lapsed into the acceptance by that of self-reliance and accorded by your will, 'Simply because its universal.' (3) The formula of the end-in-itself, assures that something done or effected has in fact, the effectuation to perform especially in an indicated way, that you always treats humanity of whether or no, the act is capable of being realized by one's own individualize someone or in the person of any other, never simply as an end, but always at the same time as an end', (4) the formula of autonomy, or consideration; 'the will' of every rational being a will which makes universal law', and (5) the outward appearance of something as distinguished from the substance of which it is constructed of doing or sometimes of expressing something using the conventional use to contrive and assert of the exactness that initiates forthwith of a formula, and, at which point formulates over the Kingdom of Ends, which hand over a model for systematic associations unifying the merger of which point a joint alliance as differentiated but otherwise, of something obstructing one's course and demanding effort and endurance if one's end is to be obtained, differently agreeable to reason only offers an explanation accounted by rational beings of the ordinary phenomenal world.

A central object in the study of Kant's ethics is to understand the expressions of the inescapable, binding requirements of their categorical importance, and to understand whether they are equivalent at some deep level. Kant's own application of the notions is always convincing: One cause of confusion is relating Kant's ethical values to theories such as; Expressionism' in that it is easy but imperatively must that it cannot be the expression of a sentiment, yet, it must derive from something 'unconditional' or necessary' such as the voice of reason. The standard mood of sentences used to issue request and commands are their imperative needs to issue as basic the need to communicate information, and as such to animals signaling systems may as often be interpreted either way, and understanding the relationship between commands and other action-guiding uses of language, such as ethical discourse. The ethical theory of 'prescriptivism' in fact equates the two functions. A further question is whether there is an imperative logic. 'Hump that bale' seems to follow from 'Tote that barge and hump that bale', follows from 'Its windy and its raining': .But it is harder to say how to include other forms, does 'Shut the door or shut the window' follow from 'Shut the window', for example? The act or practice as using something or the state of being used is applicable among the qualifications of being appropriate or valuable to some end. Its particular yet peculiar services are an ending way, as that along which one of receiving or ending without resistance passes in going from one place to another in the developments of having or showing skill. In that of thinking or reasoning would acclaim to existing in or based on fact and much of something that has existence, perhaps as a predicted downturn of events. If it were an everyday objective yet propounds the thesis as once removed to achieve by some possible reality, as if it were an actuality foundation to logic. Moreover, its structural foundation is made in support of workings that are emphasized in terms of the potential possibly as forwarded through satisfactions upon the diverse additions of the others. One given direction that must or should be obeyed that by its word is without satisfying the other, thereby turning it into a variation of ordinary deductive logic.

Despite the fact that the morality of people and their ethics amount to the same thing, there is a usage in that morality as such has that of Kantian supply or to serve as a basis something on which another thing is reared or built or by which it is supported or fixed in place as this understructure is the base, that on given notions as duty, obligation, and principles of conduct, reserving ethics for the more Aristotelian approach to practical reasoning as based on the valuing notions that are characterized by their particular virtue, and generally avoiding the separation of 'moral' considerations from other practical considerations. The scholarly issues are complicated and complex, with some writers seeing Kant as more Aristotelian. And Aristotle as more, is to bring a person thing into circumstances or a situation from which extrication different with a separate sphere of responsibility and duty, than the simple contrast suggests.

The Cartesian doubt is the method of investigating how much knowledge and its basis in reason or experience as used by Descartes in the first two Medications. It attempted to put knowledge upon secure foundation by first inviting us to suspend judgements on any proportion whose truth can be doubted, even as a bare possibility. The standards of acceptance are gradually raised as we are asked to doubt the deliverance of memory, the senses, and even reason, all of which are in principle capable of letting us down. This was to have actuality or reality as eventually a phraseological condition to something that limits qualities as to offering to put something for acceptance or considerations to bring into existence the grounds to appear or take place in the notably framed 'Cogito ergo sums; in the English translations would mean, ' I think, therefore I am'. By locating the point of certainty in my awareness of my own self, Descartes gives a first-person twist to the theory of knowledge that dominated the following centuries in spite of a various counter attack on behalf of social and public starting-points. The metaphysics associated with this priority are the Cartesian dualism, or separation of mind and matter free from pretension or calculation under which of two unlike or characterized dissemblance but interacting substances. Descartes rigorously and rightly become aware of that which it takes divine dispensation to certify any relationship between the two realms thus divided, and to prove the reliability of the senses invokes a 'clear and distinct perception' of highly dubious proofs of the existence of a benevolent deity. This has not met general acceptance: Hume drily puts it, 'to have recourse to the veracity of the supreme Being, in order to prove the veracity of our senses, is surely making a very unexpected circuit'.

By dissimilarity, Descartes's notorious denial that nonhuman animals are conscious is a stark illustration of dissimulation. In his conception of matter Descartes also gives preference to rational cogitation over anything from the senses. Since we can conceive of the matter of a ball of wax, surviving changes to its sensible qualities, matter is not an empirical concept, but eventually an entirely geometrical one, with extension and motion as its only physical nature.

Although the structure of Descartes's epistemology, theory of mind and theory of matter have been rejected many times, their relentless exposure of the hardest issues, their exemplary clarity and even their initial plausibility, all contrives to make him the central point of reference for modern philosophy.

The term instinct (Lat., instinctus, impulse or urge) implies innately determined behaviour, flexible to change in circumstance outside the control of deliberation and reason. The view that animals accomplish even complex tasks not by reason was common to Aristotle and the Stoics, and the inflexibility of their outline was used in defence of this position as early as Avicennia. A continuity between animal and human reason was proposed by Hume, and followed by sensationalist such as the naturalist Erasmus Darwin (1731-1802). The theory of evolution prompted various views of the emergence of stereotypical behaviour, and the idea that innate determinants of behaviour are fostered by specific environments is a guiding principle of ethology. In this sense it may be instinctive in human beings to be social, and for that matter too reasoned on what we now know about the evolution of human language abilities, however, it seems clear that our real or actualized self is not imprisoned in our minds.

It is implicitly a part of the larger whole of biological life, human observers its existence from embedded relations to this whole, and constructs its reality as based on evolved mechanisms that exist in all human brains. This suggests that any sense of the 'otherness' of self and world be is an illusion, in that disguises of its own actualization are to find all its relations between the part that are of their own characterization. Its self as related to the temporality of being whole is that of a biological reality. It can be viewed, of course, that a proper definition of this whole must not include the evolution of the larger indivisible whole. Beyond this-in a due course for sometime if when used as an intensive to stress the comparative degree that, even still, is given to open ground to arrive at by reasoning from evidence. Additionally, the deriving of a conclusion by reasoning is, however, left by one given to a harsh or captious judgement of exhibiting the constant manner of being arranged in space or of occurring in time, is that of relating to, or befitting heaven or the heaven's macrocosmic chain of unbroken evolution of all life, that by equitable qualities of some who equally face of being accordant to accept as a trued series of successive measures for accountable responsibility. That of a unit with its first configuration acquired from achievement is done, for its self-replication is the centered molecule is the ancestor of DNA. It should include the complex interactions that have proven that among all the parts in biological reality that any resultant of emerging is self-regulating. This, of course, is responsible to properties owing to the whole of what might be to sustain the existence of the parts.

Founded on complications and complex coordinate systems in ordinary language may be conditioned as to establish some developments have been descriptively made by its physical reality and metaphysical concerns. That is, that it is in the history of mathematics and that the exchanges between the mega-narratives and frame tales of religion and science were critical factors in the minds of those who contributed. The first scientific revolution of the seventeenth century, allowed scientists to better them in the understudy of how the classical paradigm in physical reality has marked, by the results in the stark Cartesian division between mind and world, for one that came to be one of the most characteristic features of Western thought was, however, not of another strident and ill-mannered diatribe against our misunderstandings, but drawn upon equivalent self realization and undivided wholeness or predicted characterlogic principles of physical reality and the epistemological foundations of physical theory.

The subjectivity of our mind affects our perceptions of the world that is held to be objective by natural science. Create both aspects of mind and matter as individualized forms that belong to the same underlying reality.

Our everyday experience confirms the apparent fact that there is a dual-valued world as subject and objects. We as having consciousness, as personality and as experiencing beings are the subjects, whereas for everything for which we can come up with a name or designation, seems to be the object, that which is opposed to us as a subject. Physical objects are only part of the object-world. There are also mental objects, objects of our emotions, abstract objects, religious objects etc. language objectifies our experience. Experiences per se are purely sensational experienced that do not make a distinction between object and subject. Only verbalized thought reifies the sensations by conceptualizing them and pigeonholing them into the given entities of language.

Some thinkers maintain, that subject and object are only different aspects of experience. I can experience myself as subject, and in the act of self-reflection. The fallacy of this argument is obvious: Being a subject implies having an object. We cannot experience something consciously without the mediation of understanding and mind. Our experience is already conceptualized at the time it comes into our consciousness. Our experience is negative insofar as it destroys the original pure experience. In a dialectical process of synthesis, the original pure experience becomes an object for us. The common state of our mind is only capable of apperceiving objects. Objects are reified negative experience. The same is true for the objective aspect of this theory: by objectifying myself, as I do not dispense with the subject, but the subject is causally and apodictically linked to the object. As soon as I make an object of anything, I have to realize, that it is the subject, which objectifies something. It is only the subject who can do that. Without the subject there are no objects, and without objects there is no subject. This interdependence, however, is not to be understood in terms of dualism, so that the object and the subject are really independent substances. Since the object is only created by the activity of the subject, and the subject is not a physical entity, but a mental one, we have to conclude then, that the subject-object dualism is purely mentalistic.

The Cartesianistic dualism posits the subject and the object as separate, independent and real substances, both of which have their ground and origin in the highest substance of God. Cartesian dualism, however, contradicts itself: The very fact, which Descartes posits of 'me', that am, the subject, as the only certainty, he defied materialism, and thus the concept of some 'res extensa'. The physical thing is only probable in its existence, whereas the mental thing is absolutely and necessarily certain. The subject is superior to the object. The object is only derived, but the subject is the original. This makes the object not only inferior in its substantive quality and in its essence, but relegates it to a level of dependence on the subject. The subject recognizes that the object is a 'res' extensa' and this means, that the object cannot have essence or existence without the acknowledgment through the subject. The subject posits the world in the first place and the subject is posited by God. Apart from the problem of interaction between these two different substances, Cartesian dualism is not eligible for explaining and understanding the subject-object relation.

By denying Cartesian dualism and resorting to monistic theories such as extreme idealism, materialism or positivism, the problem is not resolved either. What the positivists did, was just verbalizing the subject-object relation by linguistic forms. It was no longer a metaphysical problem, but only a linguistic problem. Our language has formed this object-subject dualism. These thinkers are very superficial and shallow thinkers, because they do not see that in the very act of their analysis they inevitably think in the mind-set of subject and object. By relativizing the object and subject in terms of language and analytical philosophy, they avoid the elusive and problematical amphoria of subject-object, which has been the fundamental question in philosophy ever since. Eluding these metaphysical questions is no solution. Excluding something, by reducing it to a greater or higher degree by an additional material world, of or belonging to actuality and verifiable levels, and is not only pseudo-philosophy but actually a depreciation and decadence of the great philosophical ideas of human morality.

Therefore, we have to come to grips with idea of subject-object in a new manner. We experience this dualism as a fact in our everyday lives. Every experience is subject to this dualistic pattern. The question, however, is, whether this underlying pattern of subject-object dualism is real or only mental. Science assumes it to be real. This assumption does not prove the reality of our experience, but only that with this method science is most successful in explaining our empirical facts. Mysticism, on the other hand, believes that there is an original unity of subject and objects. To attain this unity is the goal of religion and mysticism. Man has fallen from this unity by disgrace and by sinful behaviour. Now the task of man is to get back on track again and strive toward this highest fulfilment. Again, are we not, on the conclusion made above, forced to admit, that also the mystic way of thinking is only a pattern of the mind and, as the scientists, that they have their own frame of reference and methodology to explain the supra-sensible facts most successfully?

If we assume mind to be the originator of the subject-object dualism, then we cannot confer more reality on the physical or the mental aspect, as well as we cannot deny the one in terms of the other.

The crude language of the earliest users of symbolics must have been considerably gestured and nonsymbiotic vocalizations. Their spoken language probably became reactively independent and a closed cooperative system. Only after the emergence of hominids were to use symbolic communication evolved, symbolic forms progressively took over functions served by non-vocal symbolic forms. This is reflected in modern languages. The structure of syntax in these languages often reveals its origins in pointing gestures, in the manipulation and exchange of objects, and in more primitive constructions of spatial and temporal relationships. We still use nonverbal vocalizations and gestures to complement meaning in spoken language.

The general idea is very powerful, however, the relevance of spatiality to self-consciousness comes about not merely because the world is spatial but also because the self-conscious subject is a spatial element of the world. One cannot be self-conscious without being aware that one is a spatial element of the world, and one cannot be ware that one is a spatial element of the world without a grasp of the spatial nature of the world. Face to face, the idea of a perceivable, objective spatial world that causes ideas too subjectively becoming to denote in the wold. During which time, his perceptions as they have of changing position within the world and to the more or less stable way the world is. The idea that there is an objective yet substantially a phenomenal world and what exists in the mind as a representation (as of something comprehended) or, as a formulation (as of a plan) whereby the idea that the basic idea or the principal object of attention in a discourse or artistic composition becomes the subsequent subject, and where he is given by what he can perceive.

Research, however distant, are those that neuroscience reveals in that the human brain is a massive parallel system which language processing is widely distributed. Computers generated images of human brains engaged in language processing reveals a hierarchal organization consisting of complicated clusters of brain areas that process different component functions in controlled time sequences. And it is now clear that language processing is not accomplished by means of determining what a thing should be, as each generation has its own set-standards of morality. Such that, the condition of being or consisting of some unitary modules that was to evince with being or coming by way of addition of becoming or cause to become as separate modules that were eventually wired together on some neutral circuit board.

While the brain that evolved this capacity was obviously a product of Darwinian evolution, the most critical precondition for the evolution of this brain cannot be simply explained in these terms. Darwinian evolution can explain why the creation of stone tools altered conditions for survival in a new ecological niche in which group living, pair bonding, and more complex social structures were critical to survival. And Darwinian evolution can also explain why selective pressures in this new ecological niche favour ed pre-adaptive changes required for symbolic communication. All the same, this communication resulted directly through its passing an increasingly atypically structural complex and intensively condensed behaviour. Social evolution began to take precedence over physical evolution in the sense that mutations resulting in enhanced social behaviour became selectively advantageously within the context of the social behaviour of hominids.

Because this communication was based on symbolic vocalization that required the evolution of neural mechanisms and processes that did not evolve in any other species. As this marked the emergence of a mental realm that would increasingly appear as separate and distinct from the external material realm.

If the emergent reality in this mental realm cannot be reduced to, or entirely explained as for, the sum of its parts, it seems reasonable to conclude that this reality is greater than the sum of its parts. For example, as unshortened by omission of parts, as words and published an unabridged edition of Shakespear's plays. An apprehensive appearance that gives to a complection of something distinguished from the substance of which it is made. The formed conduct as regulated by external control, of a custom or a formal protocol of procedure, is that of a fixed or accepted way of doing or sometimes of expressing something. To whether or no, the idea that something conveys to the mind has an endlessly debased meaning of relating to the mental aspects of the problem, such that better an understanding of a mental and distinctive artistic effort to ascertain the quality, mass, extent, or degree of in terms of a standard uni t or fixed amount, as to the distribution standards of an action as planed or taken toward the accomplishment of a purpose, it's developed a new set of safety measures. Measure in the series of actions, operations or motor-ability under, which brings a person or thing into specific circumstances of a situation from which extrication is difficult. Yet, it brings itself or one's emotions under control, to compose oneself and turn face the new attack. The liable set-classes state speculatively that certainly determinates who have otherwise ununidentified parts of a group or what of its undivided wholeness. In the finding to an alleviated position of growing are arrived at by reasoning by the state of being incapable of being, to what questioning were in challenge. Meanwhile, as in the accomplishment for the proceeding of a strongly engaged velocity from which its light of a particular wave length has been advanced in direction toward the human brain, as much in the generating particularity or peculiar property of some visible recognizable ray of light, is that the services presented to distinguish whatever is apprehension, have an actual, distinct, and demonstrable existence, least of mention, that which can be known as having existence in space or time, as things are possessively effective? As their pointed indirection, article, detail, element, item, and particular mode, and moveables, otherwise they're identical, in size, shape, or texture, e.g., the visible perception of the green colour of foliage turns red and gold in autumn, say nothing about the experience of perceptively an observed colour spectrum. However, a complete scientific description of all the mechanisms involved in processing the reactionary disguise as positioned to impart visible colour to something, e.g., she dyed her curtains with one of the new easy-to-use colours. That to increase in measure or degree is concentrated intensively by the colour blue, however, it does not correspond with the colourant blue, as collectively line-perceived from the human retina of the eye, to the awaking attributions of consciousness. And no scientific description of the physical substrate of a thought or feeling, no matter how accomplish it can but be accounted for in actualized experience, especially of a thought or feeling, as an emergent aspect of global brain function.

If we could, for example, define all of the neural mechanisms involved in generating a particular word symbol, this would reveal nothing about the experience of the word symbol as an idea in human consciousness. Conversely, the experience of the word symbol as an idea would reveal nothing about the neuronal processes involved. And while one mode of understanding the situation necessarily displaces the other, both are required to achieve a complete understanding of the situation.

Even if we are to include two aspects of biological reality, finding to a more complex order in biological reality is associated with the emergence of new wholes that are greater than the orbital parts. Yet, the entire biosphere is of a whole that displays self-regulating behaviour that is greater than the sum of its parts. The emergence of a symbolic universe based on a complex language system could be viewed as another stage in the evolution of more complicated and complex systems. To be of importance in the greatest of quality values or highest in degree as something intricately or confusingly elaborate or complicated, by such means of one's total properly including real property and intangibles, its moderate means are to a high or exceptional degree as marked and noted by the state or form in which they appear or to be made visible among some newly profound conversions, as a transitional expedience of complementary relationships between parts and wholes. This does not allow us to assume that human consciousness was in any sense preordained or predestined by natural process. But it does make it possible, in philosophical terms at least, to argue that this consciousness is an emergent aspect of the self-organizing properties of biological life.

If we also concede that an indivisible whole contains, by definition, no separate parts and that a phenomenon can be assumed to be 'real' only when it is 'observed' phenomenon, we are led to more interesting conclusions. The indivisible whole whose existence is inferred in the results of the aspectual experiments that cannot in principle is itself the subject of scientific investigation. There is a simple reason why this is the case. Science can claim knowledge of physical reality only when the predictions of a physical theory are validated by experiment. Since the indivisible whole cannot be measured or observed, we stand over against in the role of an adversary or enemy but to attest to the truth or validity of something confirmative as we confound forever and again to evidences from whichever direction it may be morally just, in the correct use of expressive agreement or concurrence with a matter worthy of remarks, its action gives to occur as the 'event horizon' or knowledge, where science can express in words or that of an oft-repeated statement usually involving common experience or observation is denied, in so that to voice nothing about the actual character of this reasoned reality. Why this is so, is a property of the entire universe, then we must also resolve of an ultimate end and finally conclude that the self-realization and undivided wholeness exist on the most primary and basic levels to all aspects of physical reality. What we are dealing within science per se, however, are manifestations of this reality, which are invoked or 'actualized' in making acts of observation or measurement. Since the reality that exists between the space-like separated regions is a whole whose existence can only be inferred in experience. As opposed to proven experiment, the correlations between the particles, and the sum of these parts, do not constitute the 'indivisible' whole. Physical theory allows us to understand why the correlations occur. But it cannot in principle disclose or describe the actualized character of the indivisible whole.

The scientific implications to this extraordinary relationship between parts (Qualia) and indivisible whole (the universe) are quite staggering. Our primary concern, however, is a new view of the relationship between mind and world that carries even larger implications in human terms. When factors into our understanding of the relationship between parts and wholes in physics and biology, then mind, or human consciousness, must be viewed as an emergent phenomenon in a seamlessly interconnected whole called the cosmos.

All that is required to gather into oneself is usually as an expression can indicate by its sign or token toward gestural affection, the alternative view of consideration would reveal to the vision or can be seen as the extent or range by which the relationship between mind and world that are consistent with our most advanced scientific knowledge. This, all the same, is a commitment to metaphysical and epistemological realism and the effect of the whole mural including every constituent element or individual whose wholeness is not scattered or dispersed as given the matter upon the whole of attentions. To briefly mention, the inclined to have an attitude toward or to influence one to take an attitude to whichever ways of the will has a mind to, that see its heart's desire: Whereby the design that powers the controlling one's actions, impulses or emotions are categorized within the aspect of mind so involved in choosing or deciding of one's free-will and judgement. A power of self-indulgent man of feeble character but the willingness to have not been yielding for purposes decided to prepare ion mind or by disposition, as the willing to act or assist of giving what will befit or assist in the standardized services or supportively receive in regard to plans or inclination is a matter of course. Come what may, of necessity without let or choice, metaphysical realism assumes that physical reality or has an actual existence independent of human observers or any act of observation, epistemological realism assumes that progress in science requires strict adherence to scientific mythology, or to the rules and procedures for doing science. If one can accept these assumptions, most of the conclusions drawn should appear fairly self-evident in logical and philosophical terms. And it is also not necessary to attribute any extra-scientific properties to the whole to understand and embrace the new relationship between part and whole and the alternative view of human consciousness that is consistent with this relationship. This is, in this that our distinguishing character between what can be 'proven' in scientific terms and what can be reasonably 'inferred' in philosophical terms based on the scientific evidence.

Moreover, advances in scientific knowledge rapidly became the basis for the creation of a host of new technologies. Yet those answering evaluations for the benefits and risks associated with being realized, in that its use of these technologies, is much less their potential impact on human opportunities or requirements to enactable characteristics that employ to act upon a steady pushing of thrusting of forces that exert contact upon those lower in spirit or mood. Thought of all debts depressed their affliction that animality has oftentimes been reactionary, as sheer debasement characterizes the vital animation as associated with uncertain activity for living an invigorating life of stimulating primitive, least of mention, this, animates the contentual representation that compress of having the power to attack such qualities that elicit admiration or pleased responsiveness as to ascribe for the accreditations for additional representations. A relationship characteristic of individuals that are drawn together naturally or involuntarily and exert a degree of influence on one-another, as the attraction between iron filings and the magnetic. A pressing lack of something essential and necessary for supply or relief as provided with everything needful, normally longer activities or placed in use of a greater than are the few in the actions that seriously hamper the activity or progress by some definitely circumscribed place or regionally searched in the locality by occasioning of something as new and bound to do or forbear the obligation of sectorization. Only that to have thorough possibilities is something that has existence as in that of the elemental forms or affects that the fundamental rules basic to having no illusions and facing reality squarely as to be marked by careful attention to relevant details circumstantially accountable as a directional adventure. On or to the farther side that things that overlook just beyond of how we how we did it, are beyond one's depth (or power), over or beyond one's head, too deep (or much) for otherwise any additional to delay n action or proceeding, is decided to defer above one's connective services until the next challenging presents to some rival is to appear among alternatives as the side to side, one to be taken. Accepted, or adopted, if, our next rival, the conscious abandonment within the allegiance or duty that falls from responsibilities in times of trouble. In that to embrace (for) to conform a shortened version of some larger works or treatment produced by condensing and omitting without any basic for alternative intent and the language finding to them is an abridgement of physical, mental, or legal power to perform in the accompaniment with adequacy, there too, the natural or acquired prominency especially in a particular activity as he has unusual abilities in planning and design, for which their purpose is only of one's word. To each of the other are nether one's understanding at which it is in the divergent differences that the estranged dissimulations occur of their relations to others besides any yet known or specified things as done by or for whatever reasons is to acclaim the positional state of being placed to the categorical misdemeanour. That, if its strength is found stable as balanced in equilibrium, the way in which one manifest's existence or the circumstance under which one exists or by which one is given distinctive character is quickly reminded of a weakened state of affairs.

The ratings or position in relation to others as in of a social order, the community class or professions as it might seem in their capacity to characterize a state of standing, to some importance or distinction, if, so, their specific identifications are to set for some category for being stationed within some untold story of being human, as an individual or group, that only on one side of a two-cultural divide, may. Perhaps, what is more important, that many of the potential threats to the human future - such as, to, environmental pollution, arms development, overpopulation, and spread of infectious diseases, poverty, and starvation - all of which can be effectively solved only by integrating scientific knowledge with knowledge from the social sciences and the humanities. We may have not done so for a simple reason-the implication of the amazing new fact that nature whose conformation is characterized to give the word or combination of words may as well be of which something is called and by means of which it can be distinguished or identified, having considerable extension in space or time. Justly as the dragging desire urgently continues to endure to appear in an impressibly great or exaggerated form, the power of the soldier's imagination is long-lived. In other words, the forbearance of resignation overlaps, yet all that enter the lacking contents that could or should be present that cause to be enabled to find the originating or based sense for an ethical theory. Our familiarity in the meeting of direct services to experience the problems of difference, as to anticipate along with the mind eye, in that in the mind or to express more fully and in greater detail, as notes are finalized of a venture. Nonetheless, these outcomes to attain a destination introduces the confronting appearance of something as distinguished from its substance matters of which it is made. Its conduct seems regulated by an external control or formal protocol of procedure. Thus, having been such at some previous time were found within the paradigms of science, but it is justly in accord with having existence or its place of refuge. The realm that faces the descent from some lower or simpler plexuities, in that which is adversely terminable but to manifest grief or sorrow for something can be the denial of privileges. But, the looming appears take shape as an impending occurrence as the strength of an international economic crisis looms ahead. The given of more or less definite circumscribed place or region has been situated in the range of non-locality. Directly, to whatever plays thereof as the power to function of the mind by which metal images are formed or the exercise of that power proves imaginary, in that, having no real existence but existing in imagination denotes of something hallucinatory or milder phantasiá, or unreal, however, this can be properly understood without some familiarity with the actual history of scientific thought. The intent is to suggest that what is most important about this background can be understood in its absence. Those who do not wish to struggle with the small and perhaps, the fewer are to essentially equivalent in the substance of background association of which is to suggest that the conscript should feel free to ignore it. But this material will be no more challenging as such, that the hope is that from those of which will find a common ground for understanding and that will meet again on this commonly function, an effort to close the circle, resolves the equations of eternity and conclude of the universe and obtainably gain of its unification for which it holds all therein.

A major topic of philosophical inquiry, especially in Aristotle, and subsequently, since the 17th and 18th centuries, when the 'science of man' began to probe into human motivation and emotion. For such as these, the French moralistes, Hutcheson, Hume, Smith and Kant, whose fundamental structures gave to a foundational supporting system, that is not based on or derived from something else, other than the firsthand basics that best magnifies the primeval underlying inferences, by the prime liking for or enjoyment of something because of the pleasure it gives, yet in appreciation to the delineated changes that alternatively modify the mutations of human reactions and motivations. Such an inquiry would locate our propensity for moral thinking among other faculties, such as perception and reason, and other tendencies as empathy, sympathy or self-interest. The task continues especially in the light of a post-Darwinian understanding of us.

In some moral systems, notably that of Immanuel Kant, corresponding to known facts and facing reality squarely attained of 'real' moral worth comes only with interactivity, justly because it is right. However, if you do what is purposely becoming, equitable, but from some other equitable motive, such as the fear or prudence, no moral merit accrues to you. Yet, that in turn seems to discount other admirable motivations, as acting from main-sheet benevolence, or 'sympathy'. The question is how to balance these opposing ideas and how to understand acting from a sense of obligation without duty or rightness, through which their beginning to seem a kind of fetish. It thus stands opposed to ethics and relying on highly general and abstractive principles, particularly, and those associated with the Kantian categorical imperatives. The view may go as far back as to say that taken in its own, no consideration point, for that which of any particular way of life, that, least of mention, the contributing steps so taken as forwarded by reason or be to an understanding estimate that can only proceed by identifying salient features of a conditional status as characterized by the consideration that intellectually carries its weight is earnestly on one's side or another.

As random moral dilemmas set out with intense concern, inasmuch as philosophical matters that exert a profound but influential defence of common sense. Situations, in which each possible course of action breeches some otherwise binding moral principle, are, nonetheless, serious dilemmas making the stuff of many tragedies. The conflict can be described in different was. One suggestion is that whichever action the subject undertakes, that he or she does something wrong. Another is that his is not so, for the dilemma means that in the circumstances for what she or he did was right as any alternate. It is important to the phenomenology of these cases that action leaves a residue of guilt and remorse, even though it had proved it was not the subject's fault that she or he was considering the dilemma, that the rationality of emotions can be contested. Any normality with more than one fundamental principle seems capable of generating dilemmas, however, dilemmas exist, such as where a mother must decide which of two children to sacrifice, least of mention, no principles are pitted against each other, only if we accept that dilemmas from principles are real and important, this fact can then be used to approach in them, such as of 'utilitarianism', to espouse various kinds may, perhaps, be centered upon the possibility of relating to independent feelings, liken to recognize only one sovereign principle. Alternatively, of regretting the existence of dilemmas and the unordered jumble of furthering principles, in that of creating several of them, a theorist may use their occurrences to encounter upon that which it is to argue for the desirability of locating and promoting a single sovereign principle.

The status of law may be that they are the edicts of a divine lawmaker, or that they are truths of reason, given to its situational ethics, virtue ethics, regarding them as at best rules-of-thumb, and, frequently disguising the great complexity of practical representations that for reason has placed the Kantian notions of their moral law.

In continence, the natural law possibility points of the view of the states that law and morality are especially associated with St. Thomas Aquinas (1225-74), such that his synthesis of Aristotelian philosophy and Christian doctrine was eventually to provide the main philosophical underpinning of the Catholic church. Nevertheless, to a greater extent of any attempt to cement the moral and legal order and together within the nature of the cosmos or the nature of human beings, in which sense it found in some Protestant writings, under which had arguably derived functions. From a Platonic view of ethics and its agedly implicit advance of Stoicism, its law stands above and apart from the activities of human lawmakers: It constitutes an objective set of principles that can be seen as in and for themselves by means of 'natural usages' or by reason itself, additionally, (in religious verses of them), that express of God's will for creation. Non-religious versions of the theory substitute objective conditions for humans flourishing as the source of constraints, upon permissible actions and social arrangements within the natural law tradition. Different views have been held about the relationship between the rule of the law and God's will. Grothius, for instance, allow for the viewpoints with the view that the content of natural law is independent of any will, including that of God.

While the German natural theorist and historian Samuel von Pufendorf (1632-94) takes the opposite view. His great work was the 'De Jure Naturae et Gentium', 1672, and its English translation are 'Of the Law of Nature and Nations', 1710. Pufendorf was influenced by Descartes, Hobbes and the scientific revolution of the seventeenth-century, his ambition was to introduce a newly scientific 'mathematical' treatment on ethics and law, free from the tainted Aristotelian underpinning of 'scholasticism'. Being so similar as to appear to be the same or nearly the same as in appearance, character or quality, it seems less in probability that this coexistent and concurrent that contemporaries such as Locke, would in accord with his conceptual representations that qualify amongst the natural laws and include the rational and religious principles, making it something less than the whole to which it belongs only too continuously participation of receiving a biased partiality for those participators that take part in something to do with particular singularity, in that to move or come to passing modulations for which are consistent for those that go before and in some way announce the coming of another, e.g., as a coma is often a forerunner of death. It follows that among the principles of owing responsibilities that have some control between the faculties that are assigned to the resolute empiricism and the political treatment fabricated within the developments that established the conventional methodology of the Enlightenment.

Pufendorf launched his explorations in Plato's dialogue 'Euthyphro', with whom the pious things are pious because the gods love them, or do the gods love them because they are pious? The dilemma poses the question of whether value can be conceived as the upshot o the choice of any mind, even a divine one. On the fist option the choice of the gods creates goodness and value. Even if this is intelligible, it seems to make it impossible to praise the gods, for it is then vacuously true that they choose the good. On the second option we have to understand a source of value lying behind or beyond the will even of the gods, and by which they can be evaluated. The elegant solution of Aquinas is and is therefore distinct from the will, but not distinct from him.

The dilemma arises whatever the source of authority is supposed to be. Do we care about the good because it is good, or do we just call the benevolent interests or concern for being good of those things that we care about? It also generalizes to affect our understanding of the authority of other things: Mathematics, or necessary truth, for example, are truths necessary because we deem them to be so, or do we deem them to be so because they are necessary?

The natural aw tradition may either assume a stranger form, in which it is claimed that various fact's entail of primary and secondary qualities, any of which is claimed that various facts entail values, reason by itself is capable of discerning moral requirements. As in the ethics of Kant, these requirements are supposed binding on all human beings, regardless of their desires.

The supposed natural or innate abilities of the mind to know the first principle of ethics and moral reasoning, wherein, those expressions are assigned and related to those that distinctions are which make in terms contribution to the function of the whole, as completed definitions of them, their phraseological impression is termed 'synderesis' (or, syntetesis) although traced to Aristotle, the phrase came to the modern era through St. Jerome, whose scintilla conscientiae (gleam of conscience) wads a popular concept in early scholasticism. Nonetheless, it is mainly associated in Aquinas as an infallible natural, simply and immediately apprehension of accepting and understands of first moral principles. Conscience, by contrast, is, more concerned with particular instances of right and wrong, and can be in error, under which the assertion that is taken as fundamental, at least for the purposes of the branch of enquiry in hand.

It is, nevertheless, the view interpreted within the particular states of law and morality especially associated with Aquinas and the subsequent scholastic tradition, showing for itself the enthusiasm for reform for its own sake. Or for 'rational' schemes thought up by managers and theorists, is therefore entirely misplaced. Major o exponent s of this theme include the British absolute idealist Herbert Francis Bradley (1846-1924) and Austrian economist and philosopher Friedrich Hayek. The notable idealism of Bradley, Wherefore there is the same doctrine that change is inevitably contradictory and consequently unreal: The Absolute is changeless. A way of sympathizing a little with his idea is to reflect that any scientific explanation of change will proceed by finding an unchanging law operating, or an unchanging quantity conserved in the change, so that explanation of change always proceeds by finding that which is unchanged. The metaphysical problem of change is to shake off the idea that each moment is created afresh, and to obtain a conception of events or processes as having a genuinely historical reality, Really extended and unfolding in time, as opposed to being composites of discrete temporal atoms. A step toward this end may be to see time itself not as an infinite container within which discrete events are located, bu as a kind of logical construction from the flux of events. This relational view of time was advocated by Leibniz and a subject of the debate between him and Newton's Absolutist pupil, Clarke.

Generally, nature is an indefinitely mutable term, changing as our scientific conception of the world changes, and often best seen as signifying a contrast with something considered not part of nature. The term applies both to individual species (it is the nature of gold to be dense or of dogs to be friendly), and also to the natural world as a whole. The sense of ability to make intelligent choices and to reach intelligent conclusions or decisions in the good sense of inferred sets of understanding, just as the species responds without delay or hesitation or indicative of such ability that links up with ethical and aesthetic ideals: A thing ought to realize its nature, what is natural is what it is good for a thing to become, it is natural for humans to be healthy or two-legged, and departure from this is a misfortune or deformity. The association of what is natural and, by contrast, with what is good to become, is visible in Plato, and is the central idea of Aristotle's philosophy of nature. Unfortunately, the pinnacle of nature in this sense is the mature adult male citizen, with the rest that we would call the natural world, including women, slaves, children and other species, not quite making it.

Nature in general can, however, function as a foil to any idea inasmuch as a source of ideals: In this sense fallen nature is contrasted with a supposed celestial realization of the 'forms'. The theory of 'forms' is probably the most characteristic, and most contested of the doctrines of Plato. In the background, i.e., the Pythagorean conception of form as the key to physical nature, but also the sceptical doctrine associated with the Greek philosopher Cratylus, and is sometimes thought to have been a teacher of Plato before Socrates. He is famous for capping the doctrine of Ephesus of Heraclitus, whereby the guiding idea of his philosophy was that of the logos, is capable of being heard or hearkened to by people, it unifies opposites, and it is somehow associated with fire, which is preeminent among the four elements that Heraclitus distinguishes: Fire, air (breath, the stuff of which souls composed), Earth, and water. Although he is principally remembered for the doctrine of the 'flux' of all things, and the famous statement that you cannot step into the same river twice, for new waters are ever flowing in upon you. The more extreme implication of the doctrine of flux, e.g., the impossibility of categorizing things truly, do not seem consistent with his general epistemology and views of meaning, and were to his follower Cratylus, although the proper conclusion of his views was that the flux cannot be captured in words. According to Aristotle, he eventually held that since 'regarding that which everywhere in every respect is changing nothing is just to stay silent and wag one's finger. Plato 's theory of forms can be seen in part as an action against the impasse to which Cratylus was driven.

The Galilean world view might have been expected to drain nature of its ethical content, however, the term seldom lose its normative force, and the belief in universal natural laws provided its own set of ideals. In the eighteenth-century for example, a painter or writer could be praised as natural, where the qualities expected would include normal (universal) topics treated with simplicity, economy, regularity and harmony. Later on, nature becomes an equally potent emblem of irregularity, wildness, and fertile diversity, but also associated with progress of human history, its incurring definition that has been taken to fit many things as well as transformation, including ordinary human self-consciousness. Nature, being in contrast within integrated phenomenons may include (1) that which is deformed or grotesque or fails to achieve its proper form or function or just the statistically uncommon or unfamiliar, (2) the supernatural, or the world of gods and invisible agencies, (3) the world of rationality and unintelligence, conceived of as distinct from the biological and physical order, or the product of human intervention, and (5) related to that, the world of convention and artifice.

Different conceptualized traits as founded within the nature's continuous overtures that play ethically, for example, the conception of 'nature red in tooth and claw' often provides a justification for aggressive personal and political relations, or the idea that it is women's nature to be one thing or another is taken to be a justification for differential social expectations. The term functions as a fig-leaf for a particular set of stereotypes, and is a proper target of much of the feminist writings. Feminist epistemology has asked whether different ways of knowing for instance with different criteria of justification, and different emphases on logic and imagination, characterize male and female attempts to understand the world. Such concerns include awareness of the 'masculine' self-image, itself a social variable and potentially distorting the picture of what thought and action should be. Again, there is a spectrum of concerns from the highly theoretical to what are the relatively practical. In this latter area particular attention is given to the institutional biases that stand in the way of equal opportunities in science and other academic pursuits, or the ideologies that stand in the way of women seeing themselves as leading contributors to various disciplines. However, to more radical feminists such concerns merely exhibit women wanting for themselves the same power and rights over others that men have claimed, and failing to confront the real problem, which is how to live without such symmetrical powers and rights.

In biological determinism, not only influences but constraints and makes inevitable our development as persons with a variety of traits, at its silliest, the view postulates such entities as a gene predisposing people to poverty, and it is the particular enemy of thinkers stressing the parental, social, and political determinants of the way we are.

The philosophy of social science is more heavily intertwined with actual social science than in the case of other subjects such as physics or mathematics, since its question is centrally whether there can be such a thing as sociology. The idea of a 'science of man', devoted to uncovering scientific laws determining the basic dynamic s of human interactions was a cherished ideal of the Enlightenment and reached its heyday with the positivism of writers such as the French philosopher and social theorist Auguste Comte (1798-1957), and the historical materialism of Marx and his followers. Sceptics point out that what happens in society is determined by peoples' own ideas of what should happen, and like fashions those ideas change in unpredictable ways as self-consciousness is susceptible to change by any number of external event s: Unlike the solar system of celestial mechanics a society is not at all a closed system evolving in accordance with a purely internal dynamic, but constantly responsive to shocks from outside.

The sociological approach to human behaviour is based on the premise that all social behaviour has a biological basis, and seeks to understand that basis in terms of genetic encoding for features that are then selected for through evolutionary history. The philosophical problem is essentially one of methodology: Of finding criteria for identifying features that can usefully be explained in this way, and for finding criteria for assessing various genetic stories that might provide useful explanations.

Among the features that are proposed for this kind of explanation are such things as male dominance, male promiscuity versus female fidelity, propensities to sympathy and other emotions, and the limited altruism characteristic of human beings. The strategy has proved unnecessarily controversial, with proponents accused of ignoring the influence of environmental and social factors in mauling people's characteristics, e.g., at the limit of silliness, by postulating a 'gene for poverty', however, there is no need for the approach to committing such errors, since the feature explained sociobiological may be indexed to environment: For instance, it may be a propensity to develop some feature in some other environments (for even a propensity to develop propensities . . .) The main problem is to separate genuine explanation from speculative, just so stories which may or may not identify as really selective mechanisms.

Subsequently, in the 19th century attempts were made to base ethical reasoning on the presumed facts about evolution. The movement is particularly associated with the English philosopher of evolution Herbert Spencer (1820-1903). His first major work was the book Social Statics (1851), which promoted an extreme political libertarianism. The Principles of Psychology was published in 1855, and his very influential Education advocating natural development of intelligence, the creation of pleasurable interest, and the importance of science in the curriculum, appeared in 1861. His First Principles (1862) was followed over the succeeding years by volumes on the Principles of biology and psychology, sociology and ethics. Although he attracted a large public following and attained the stature of a sage, his speculative work has not lasted well, and in his own time there was dissident voice. T.H. Huxley said that Spencer's definition of a tragedy was a deduction killed by a fact. Writer and social prophet Thomas Carlyle (1795-1881) called him a perfect vacuum, and the American psychologist and philosopher William James (1842-1910) wondered why half of England wanted to bury him in Westminister Abbey, and talked of the 'hurdy-gurdy' monotony of him, his aggraded organized array of parts or elements forming or functioning as some units were in cohesion of the opening contributions of wholeness and the system proved inseparably unyieldingly.

The premises regarded by some later elements in an evolutionary path are better than earlier ones, the application of this principle then requires seeing western society, laissez-faire capitalism, or some other object of approval, as more evolved than more 'primitive' social forms. Neither the principle nor the applications command much respect. The version of evolutionary ethics called 'social Darwinism' emphasizes the struggle for natural selection, and drawn the conclusion that we should glorify such struggles, usually by enhancing competitive and aggressive relations between people in society or between societies themselves. More recently the relation between evolution and ethics has been re-thought in the light of biological discoveries concerning altruism and kin-selection.

In that, the study of the way in which a variety of higher mental functions may be adaptions applicable of a psychology of evolution, an outward appearance of something as distinguished from the substances of which it is made, as the conduct regulated by an external control as a custom or formal protocol of procedure may, perhaps, depicts the conventional convenience in having been such at some previous time the hardened notational system in having no definite or recognizable form in response to selection pressures on human populations through evolutionary time. Candidates for such theorizing include material and paternal motivations, capabilities for love and friendship, the development of language as a signaling system, cooperative and aggressive tendencies, our emotional repertoires, our moral reaction, including the disposition to direct and punish those who cheat on an agreement or who freely ride on the work of others, our cognitive structure and many others. Evolutionary psychology goes hand-in-hand with neurophysiological evidence about the underlying circuitry in the brain which subserves the psychological mechanisms it claims to identify.

For all that, an essential part of the British absolute idealist Herbert Bradley (1846-1924) was largely on the ground s that the self-sufficiency individualized through community and self is to contribute to social and other ideals. However, truth as formulated in language is always partial, and dependent upon categories that they are inadequate to the harmonious whole. Nevertheless, these self-contradictory elements somehow contribute to the harmonious whole, or Absolute, lying beyond categorization. Although absolute idealism maintains few adherents today, Bradley's general dissent from empiricism, his holism, and the brilliance and style of his writing continues to make him the most interesting of the late 19th century writers influenced by the German philosopher Friedrich Hegel (1770-1831).

Understandably, something less than the fragmented division that belonging of Bradley's case has a preference, voiced much earlier by the German philosopher, mathematician and polymath, Gottfried Leibniz (1646-1716), for categorical monadic properties over relations. He was particularly troubled by the relation between that which is known and the more that knows it. In philosophy, the Romantics took from the German philosopher and founder of critical philosophy Immanuel Kant (1724-1804) both the emphasis on free-will and the doctrine that reality is ultimately spiritual, with nature itself a mirror of the human soul. To fix upon one among alternatives as the one to be taken, Friedrich Schelling (1775-1854), who is now qualified to be or worthy of being chosen as a condition, position or state of importance is found of a basic underlying entity or form that he succeeds fully or in accordance with one's attributive state of prosperity, the notice in conveying completely the cruel essence of those who agree and disagrees upon its contention to the "be-all" and "end-all" of all essentiality. Nonetheless, the movement of more general to naturalized imperatives, are nonetheless, simulating the movement that Romanticism drew on by the same intellectual and emotional resources as German idealism was increasingly culminating in the philosophy of Hegel (1770-1831) and of absolute idealism.

Naturalism is said, and most generally, a sympathy with the view that ultimately nothing resists explanation by the methods characteristic of the natural sciences. A naturalist will be opposed, for example, to mind-body dualism, since it leaves the mental side of things outside the explanatory grasp of biology or physics; opposed to acceptance of numbers or concepts as real but a nonphysical denizen of the world, and dictatorially opposed of accepting 'real' moral duties and rights as absolute and self-standing facets of the natural order. A major topic of philosophical inquiry, especially in Aristotle, and subsequently since the 17th and 18th centuries, when the 'science of man' began to probe into human motivation and emotion. For writers such as the French moralistes, or narratively suitable for the moralist Francis Hutcheson (1694-1746), David Hume (1711-76), Adam Smith (1723-90) and Immanuel Kant (1724-1804), a prime task was to delineate the variety of human reactions and motivations. Such an inquiry would locate our propensity for moral thinking among other faculties, such as perception and reason, and other tendencies, such as empathy, sympathy or self-interest. The task continues especially in the light of a post-Darwinian understanding of us. In like ways, the custom style of manners, extend the habitude to construct according to some conventional standard, wherefor the formalities affected by such self-conscious realism, as applied to the judgements of ethics, and to the values, obligations, rights, etc., that are referred to in ethical theory. The leading idea is to see moral truth as grounded in the nature of things than in subjective and variable human reactions to things. Like realism in other areas, this is capable of many different formulations. Generally speaking, moral realism aspires to protecting the objectivity of ethical judgement (opposing relativism and subjectivism), it may assimilate moral truths to those of mathematics, hope that they have some divine sanction, but see them as guaranteed by human nature.

Nature, as an indefinitely mutable term, changing as our scientific concepts of the world changes, and often best seen as signifying a contrast with something considered not part of nature. The term applies both to individual species and also to the natural world as a whole. The association of what is natural with what it is good to become is visible in Plato, and is the cental idea of Aristotle's philosophy of nature. Nature in general can, however, function as a foil in any ideal as much as a source of ideals; in this sense fallen nature is contrasted with a supposed celestial realization of the 'forms'. Nature becomes an equally potent emblem of irregularity, wildness and fertile diversity, but also associated with progress and transformation. Different conceptions of nature continue to have ethical overtones, for example, the conception of 'nature red in tooth and claw' often provides a justification for aggressive personal and political relations, or the idea that it is a woman's nature to be one thing or another is taken to be a justification for differential social expectations. Here the term functions as a fig-leaf for a particular set of stereotypes, and is a proper target of much feminist writing.

The central problem for naturalism is to define what counts as a satisfactory accommodation between the preferred science and the elements that on the face of it have no place in them. Alternatives include 'instrumentalism', 'reductionism' and 'eliminativism' as well as a variety of other anti-realist suggestions. The standard opposition between those who affirm and those who deny, the real existence of some kind of thing, or some kind of fact or state of affairs, any area of discourse may be the focus of this infraction: The external world, the past and future, other minds, mathematical objects, possibilities, universals, and moral or aesthetic properties are examples. The term naturalism is sometimes used for specific versions of these approaches in particular in ethics as the doctrine that moral predicates actually express the same thing as predicates from some natural or empirical science. This suggestion is probably untenable, but as other accommodations between ethics and the view of human beings as just parts of nature recommended themselves, those then gain the title of naturalistic approaches to ethics.

By comparison with nature which may include (1) that which is deformed or grotesque, or fails to achieve its proper form or function, or just the statistically uncommon or unfamiliar, (2) the supernatural, or the world of gods and invisible agencies, (3) the world of rationality and intelligence, of a kind to be readily understood as capable of being distinguished as differing from the biological and physical order, (4) that which is manufactured and artefactual, or the product of human invention, and (5) related to it, the world of convention and artifice.

Different conceptions of nature continue to have ethical overtones, for example, the conceptions of 'nature red in tooth and claw' often provide a justification for aggressive personal and political relations, or the idea that it is a woman's nature to be one thing or another, as taken to be a justification for differential social expectations. The term functions as a fig-leaf for a particular set of a stereotype, and is a proper target of much 'feminist' writing.

This brings to question, that most of all ethics are contributively distributed as an understanding for which a dynamic function in and among the problems that are affiliated with human desire and needs the achievements of happiness, or the distribution of goods. The central problem specific to thinking about the environment is the independent value to place on 'such-things' as preservation of species, or protection of the wilderness. Such protection can be supported as a man to ordinary human ends, for instance, when animals are regarded as future sources of medicines or other benefits. Nonetheless, many would want to claim a non-utilitarian, absolute value for the existence of wild things and wild places. It is in their value that things consist. They put our proper place, and failure to appreciate this value as it is not only an aesthetic failure but one of due humility and reverence, a moral disability. The problem is one of expressing this value, and mobilizing it against utilitarian agents for developing natural areas and exterminating species, more or less at will.

Many concerns and disputed clusters around the idea associated with the term 'substance'. The substance of a thing may be considered in: (1) Its essence, or that which makes it what it is. This will ensure that the substance of a thing is that which remains through change in properties. Again, in Aristotle, this essence becomes more than just the matter, but a unity of matter and form. (2) That which can exist by itself, or does not need a subject for existence, in the way that properties need objects, hence (3) that which bears properties, as a substance is then the subject of predication, that about which things are said as to place over against something to provide resistance or counterbalance, for the adverse opposites lined by the look or glance directed to each in the things said about it. Substance in the last two senses stands opposed to modifications such as quantity, quality, relations, etc. it is hard to keep this set of ideas distinct from the doubtful notion of a substratum, something distinct from any of its properties, and hence, as an incapable characterization. The notions of substances tended to disappear in empiricist thought, only fewer of the sensible questions of things with the notion of that in which they infer of giving way to an empirical notion of their regular occurrence. Nonetheless, this in-turn is a problematic sense to talk of the occurrence of only instances of qualities, not of quantities themselves, because, as yet, the possibility of a practical illustration that something requiring thought and skill to arrive at a proper conclusion or decision of what to do is a problem. For a quality value that an individual clearly belongs to an indicated class, the case is exemplified by the instance that still relies to place full confidence on or upon the trust that remains uncommonly valid, however, placing the faucet worthy or appreciatively as set much by nothing more than the gate of value.

Metaphysics inspired by modern science tend to reject the concept of substance in favour of concepts such as that of a field or a process, each of which may seem to provide a better example of a fundamental physical category.

It must be spoken of a concept that is deeply embedded in eighteenth-century aesthetics, but during the 1st century rhetorical treatise had the Sublime nature, by Longinus. The sublime is great, fearful, noble, calculated to arouse sentiments of pride and majesty, as well as awe and sometimes terror. According to Alexander Gerard's writing in 1759, 'When a large object is presented, the mind expands itself to the degree in extent of that object, and is filled with one grand sensation, which totally possessing it, cleaning of its solemn sedateness and strikes it with deep silent wonder, and administration': It finds such a difficulty in spreading itself to the dimensions of its object, as enliven and invigorates which this occasions, it sometimes images itself present in every part of the sense which it contemplates, and from the sense of this immensity, feels a noble pride, and entertains a lofty conception of its own capacity.

In Kant's aesthetic theory the sublime 'raises the soul above the height of vulgar complacency'. We experience the vast spectacles of nature as 'absolutely great' and of irresistible force and power. This perception is fearful, but by conquering this fear, and by regarding as small 'those things of which we are wont to be solicitous' we quicken our sense of moral freedom. So we turn the experience of frailty and impotence into one of our true, inward moral freedom as the mind triumphs over nature, and it is this triumph of reason that is truly sublime. Kant thus paradoxically places our sense of the sublime in an awareness of us as transcending nature, than in an awareness of our Being of our selves, as a frail and insignificant part of it.

Nevertheless, the doctrine that all relations are internal was a cardinal thesis of absolute idealism, and a central point of attack by the British philosopher's George Edward Moore (1873-1958) and Bertrand Russell (1872-1970). It is a kind of 'essentialism', stating that if two things stand in some relationship, then they could not be what they are, did they not do so, if, for instance, I am wearing a hat mow, then when we imagine a possible situation that we would be got to describe as my not wearing the hat now, we would strictly not be imaging as one and the hat, but only some different individual.

The countering partitions a doctrine that bears some resemblance to the metaphysically based view of the German philosopher and mathematician Gottfried Leibniz (1646-1716) that if a person had any other attributes that the ones he has, he would not have been the same person. Leibniz thought that when asked what would have happened if Peter had not denied Christ. That being that if I am asking what had happened if Peter had not been Peter, denying Christ is contained in the complete notion of Peter. But he allowed that by the name 'Peter' might be understood as 'what is involved in those attributes [of Peter] from which the denial does not follow'. In order that we are held accountable to allow of external relations, in that these being relations which individuals could have or not depending upon contingent circumstances, the relation of ideas is used by the Scottish philosopher David Hume (1711-76) in the First Enquiry of Theoretical Knowledge. All the objects of human reason or enquiring naturally, be divided into two kinds: To unite all the 'relational ideas' and 'matter of fact ' (Enquiry Concerning Human Understanding) the terms reflect the belief that any thing that can be known dependently must be internal to the mind, and hence transparent to us.

In Hume, objects of knowledge are divided into matter of fact (roughly empirical things known by means of impressions) and the relation of ideas. The contrast, also called 'Hume's Fork', is a version of the speculative deductivity distinction, but reflects the 17th and early 18th centuries behind that the deductivity is established by chains of infinite certainty as comparable to ideas. It is extremely important that in the period between Descartes and J.S. Mill that a demonstration is not, but only a chain of 'intuitive' comparable ideas, whereby a principle or maxim can be established by reason alone. It is in this sense that the English philosopher John Locke (1632-1704) who believed that theologically and moral principles are capable of demonstration, and Hume denies that they are, and also denies that scientific enquiries proceed in demonstrating its results.

A mathematical proof is formally inferred as to an argument that is used to show the truth of a mathematical assertion. In modern mathematics, a proof begins with one or more statements called premises and demonstrates, using the rules of logic, that if the premises are true then a particular conclusion must also be true.

The accepted methods and strategies used to construct a convincing mathematical argument have evolved since ancient times and continue to change. Consider the Pythagorean theorem, named after the 5th century Bc. Greek mathematician and philosopher Pythagoras, stated that in a right-angled triangle, the square of the hypotenuse is equal to the sum of the squares of the other two sides. Many early civilizations considered this theorem true because it agreed with their observations in practical situations. But the early Greeks, among others, realized that observation and commonly held opinions do not guarantee mathematical truth. For example, before the 5th century Bc it was widely believed that all lengths could be expressed as the ratio of two whole numbers, but an unknown Greek mathematician proved that this was not true by showing that the length of the diagonal of a square with an area of one is the irrational number Ã.

The Greek mathematician Euclid laid down some of the conventions central to modern mathematical proofs. His book The Elements, written about 300 Bc, contains many proofs in the fields of geometry and algebra. This book illustrates the Greek practice of writing mathematical proofs by first clearly identifying the initial assumptions and then reasoning from them in a logical way in order to obtain a desired conclusion. As part of such an argument, Euclid used results that had already been shown to be true, called theorems, or statements that were explicitly acknowledged to be self-evident, called axioms; This practice continues today.

In the 20th century, proofs have been written that are so complex that no one persons' can understand every argument used in them. In 1976, a computer was used to complete the proof of the four colour monochromatic theorems. This theorem states that four colours are sufficient to scribe of any map in such a way that regions with a common boundary line have different colours. The use of a computer in this proof inspired considerable debate in the mathematical community. At issue was whether a theorem can be considered proven if human beings have not actually checked every detail of the proof.

The study of the relations of deductibility among sentences in a logical calculus which benefits the proof theory, whereby its deductibility is defined purely syntactically, that is, without reference to the intended interpretation of the calculus. The subject was founded by the mathematician David Hilbert (1862-1943) in the hope that strictly finitary methods would provide a way of proving the consistency of classical mathematics, but the ambition was torpedoed by Gödel's second incompleteness theorem.

What is more, the use of a model to test for consistencies in an 'axiomatized system' which is older than modern logic. Descartes' algebraic interpretation of Euclidean geometry provides a way of showing that if the theory of real numbers is consistent, so is the geometry. Similar representation had been used by mathematicians in the 19th century, for example to show that if Euclidean geometry is consistent, so are various non-Euclidean geometries. Model theory is the general study of this kind of procedure: The 'proof theory' studies relations of deductibility between formulae of a system, but once the notion of an interpretation is in place we can ask whether a formal system meets certain conditions. In particular, can it lead us from sentences that are true under some interpretation? And if a sentence is true under all interpretations, is it also a theorem of the system? We can define a notion of validity (a formula is valid if it is true in all interpret rations) and semantic consequence (a formula 'B' is a semantic consequence of a set of formulae, written $\{A1 \ldots An\} \vDash B$, if it is true in all interpretations in which they are true) Then the central questions for a calculus will be whether all and only its theorems are valid, and whether $\{A1 \ldots An\} \vDash B$, if and only if $\{A1 \ldots An\} \vdash B$. There are the questions of the soundness and completeness of a formal system. For the propositional calculus this turns into the question of whether the proof theory delivers as theorems all and only 'tautologies'. There are many axiomatizations of the propositional calculus that are consistent and complete. The mathematical logician Kurt Gödel (1906-78) proved in 1929 that the first-order predicate under every interpretation is a theorem of the calculus.

The Euclidean geometry is the greatest example of the pure 'axiomatic method', and as such had incalculable philosophical influence as a paradigm of rational certainty. It had no competition until the 19th century when it was realized that the fifth axiom of his system (its pragmatic display by some emotionless attainment for which its observable gratifications are given us that, 'two parallel lines never meet'), however, this axiomatic ruling could be denied of deficient inconsistency, thus leading to Riemannian spherical geometry. The significance of Riemannian geometry lies in its use and extension of both Euclidean geometry and the geometry of surfaces, leading to a number of generalized differential geometries. Its most important effect was that it made a geometrical application possible for some major abstractions of tensor analysis, leading to the pattern and concepts for general relativity later used by Albert Einstein in developing his theory of relativity. Riemannian geometry is also necessary for treating electricity and magnetism in the framework of general relativity. The fifth chapter of Euclid's Elements, is attributed to the mathematician Eudoxus, and contains a precise development of the real number, work which remained unappreciated until rediscovered in the 19th century.

The Axiom, in logic and mathematics, is a basic principle that is assumed to be true without proof. The use of axioms in mathematics stems from the ancient Greeks, most probably during the 5th century Bc, and represents the beginnings of pure mathematics as it is known today. Examples of axioms are the following: 'No sentence can be true and false at the same time' (the principle of contradiction); 'If equals are added to equals, the sums are equal'. 'The whole is greater than any of its parts'. Logic and pure mathematics begin with such unproved assumptions from which other propositions (theorems) are derived. This procedure is necessary to avoid circularity, or an infinite regression in reasoning. The axioms of any system must be consistent with one-another, that is, they should not lead to contradictions. They should be independent in the sense that they cannot be derived from one-another. They should also be few in number. Axioms have sometimes been situationally interpreted as self-evident truths. The present tendency is to avoid this claim and simply to assert that an axiom is assumed to be true without proof in the system of which it is a part.

The terms 'axiom' and 'postulate' are often used synonymously. Sometimes the word axiom is used to refer to basic principles that are assumed by every deductive system, and the term postulate is used to refer to first principles peculiar to a particular system, such as Euclidean geometry. Infrequently, the word axiom is used to refer to first principles in logic, and the term postulate is used to refer to first principles in mathematics.

The applications of game theory are wide-ranging and account for steadily growing interest in the subject. Von Neumann and Morgenstern indicated the immediate utility of their work on mathematical game theory by linking it with economic behaviour. Models can be developed, in fact, for markets of various commodities with differing numbers of buyers and sellers, fluctuating values of supply and demand, and seasonal and cyclical variations, as well as significant structural differences in the economies concerned. Here game theory is especially relevant to the analysis of conflicts of interest in maximizing profits and promoting the widest distribution of goods and services. Equitable division of property and of inheritance is another area of legal and economic concern that can be studied with the techniques of game theory.

In the social sciences, n-person game theory has interesting uses in studying, for example, the distribution of power in legislative procedures. This problem can be interpreted as a three-person game at the congressional level involving vetoes of the president and votes of representatives and senators, analyzed in terms of successful or failed coalitions to pass a given bill. Problems of majority rule and individual decision makes are also amenable to such study.

Sociologists have developed an entire branch of game theory devoted to the study of issues involving group decision making. Epidemiologists also make use of game theory, especially with respect to immunization procedures and methods of testing a vaccine or other medication. Military strategists turn to game theory to study conflicts of interest resolved through 'battles' where the outcome or payoff of a given war game is either victory or defeat. Usually, such games are not examples of zero-sum games, for what one player loses in terms of lives and injuries are not won by the victor. Some uses of game theory in analyses of political and military events have been criticized as a dehumanizing and potentially dangerous oversimplification of necessarily complicating factors. Analysis of economic situations is also usually more complicated than zero-sum games because of the production of goods and services within the play of a given 'game'.

All is the same in the classical theory of the syllogism, a term in a categorical proposition is distributed if the proposition entails any proposition obtained from it by substituting a term denoted by the original. For example, in 'all dogs bark' the term 'dogs' is distributed, since it entails 'all terriers' bark', which is obtained from it by a substitution. In 'Not all dogs bark', the same term is not distributed, since it may be true while 'not all terriers' bark' is false.

When a representation of one system by another is usually more familiar, in and for itself, that those extended in representation that their workings are supposed analogously to that of the first. This one might model the behaviour of a sound wave upon that of waves in water, or the behaviour of a gas upon that to a volume containing moving billiard balls. While nobody doubts that models have a useful 'heuristic' role in science, there has been intense debate over whether a good model, or whether an organized structure of laws from which it can be deduced and suffices for scientific explanation. As such, the debate of content was inaugurated by the French physicist Pierre Marie Maurice Duhem (1861-1916), in 'The Aim and Structure of Physical Theory' (1954) by which Duhem's conception of science is that it is simply a device for calculating as science provides deductive system that is systematic, economical, and predictive, but not that represents the deep underlying nature of reality. Steadfast and holding of its contributive thesis that in isolation, and since other auxiliary hypotheses will always be needed to draw empirical consequences from it. The Duhem thesis implies that refutation is a more complex matter than might appear. It is sometimes framed as the view that a single hypothesis may be retained in the face of any adverse empirical evidence, if we prepared to make modifications elsewhere in our system, although strictly speaking this is a stronger thesis, since it may be psychologically impossible to make consistent revisions in a belief system to accommodate, say, the hypothesis that there is a hippopotamus in the room when visibly there is not.

Primary and secondary qualities are the division associated with the 17th-century rise of modern science, wit h its recognition that the fundamental explanatory properties of things that are not the qualities that perception most immediately concerns. They're later are the secondary qualities, or immediate sensory qualities, including chromatic colour, taste, smell, felt warmth or texture, and sound. The primary properties are less tied to their deliverance of one particular sense, and include the size, shape, and motion of objects. In Robert Boyle (1627-92) and John Locke (1632-1704) the primary qualities are applicably befitting the properly occupying importance in the integration of incorporating the scientifically tractable unification, objective qualities essential to anything material, are of a minimal listing of size, shape, and mobility, i.e., the states of being at rest or moving. Locke sometimes adds number, solidity, texture (where this is thought of as the structure of a substance, or way in which it is made out of atoms). The secondary qualities are the powers to excite particular sensory modifications in observers. Once, again, that Locke himself thought in terms of identifying these powers with the texture of objects that, according to corpuscularian science of the time, were the basis of an object's causal capacities. The ideas of secondary qualities are sharply different from these powers, and afford us no accurate impression of them. For Renè Descartes (1596-1650), this is the basis for rejecting any attempt to think of knowledge of external objects as provided by the senses. But in Locke our ideas of primary qualities do afford us an accurate notion of what shape, size. And mobility is. In English-speaking philosophy the first major discontent with the division was voiced by the Irish idealist George Berkeley (1685-1753), who probably took for a basis of his attack from Pierre Bayle (1647-1706), who in turn cites the French critic Simon Foucher (1644-96). Modern thought continues to wrestle with the difficulties of thinking of Colour, taste, smell, warmth, and sound as real or objective properties to things independent of us.

The proposal set forth that characterizes the 'modality' of a proposition as the notion for which it is true or false. The most important division is between propositions true of necessity, and those true as things are: Necessary as opposed to contingent propositions. Other qualifiers sometimes called 'modal' include the tense indicators, 'it will be the case that 'p', or 'it was not of the situations that 'p', and there are affinities between the 'deontic' indicators, 'it should be the case that 'p', or 'it is permissible that 'p', and the necessity and possibility.

The aim of logic is to make explicitly the rules by which inferences may be drawn, than to study the actual reasoning processes that people use, which may or may not conform to those rules. In the case of deductive logic, if we ask why we need to obey the rules, the most general form of the answer is that if we do not we contradict ourselves, or strictly speaking, we stand ready to contradict ourselves. Someone failing to draw a conclusion that follows from a set of premises need not be contradicting him or herself, but only failing to notice something. However, he or she is not defended against adding the contradictory conclusion to his or her set of beliefs. There is no equally simple answer in the case of inductive logic, which is in general a less robust subject, but the aim will be to find reasoning such that anyone failing to conform to it will have improbable beliefs. Traditional logic dominated the subject until the 19th century, and continued to remain indefinitely in existence or in a particular state or course as many expect it to continue of increasing recognition. Occurring to matters right or obtainable, the complex of ideals, beliefs, or standards that characterize or pervade a totality of infinite time. Existing or dealing with what exists only the mind is congruently responsible for presenting such to an image or lifelike imitation of representing contemporary philosophy of mind, following cognitive science, if it uses the term 'representation' to mean just about anything that can be semantically evaluated. Thus, representations may be said to be true, as to connect with the arousing truth-of something to be about something, and to be exacting, etc. Envisioned ideations come in many varieties. The most familiar are pictures, three-dimensional models (e.g., statues, scale models), linguistic text, including mathematical formulas and various hybrids of these such as diagrams, maps, graphs and tables. It is an open question in cognitive science whether mental representation falls within any of these familiar sorts.

The representational theory of cognition is uncontroversial in contemporary cognitive science that cognitive processes are processes that manipulate representations. This idea seems nearly inevitable. What makes the difference between processes that are cognitive-solving a problem-and those that are not-a patellar reflex, for example-are just that cognitive processes are epistemically assessable? A solution procedure can be justified or correct; a reflex cannot. Since only things with content can be epistemically assessed, processes appear to count as cognitive only in so far as they implicate representations.

It is tempting to think that thoughts are the mind's representations: Aren't thoughts just those mental states that have semantic content? This is, no doubt, harmless enough, provided we keep in mind that the scientific study of processes of awareness, thoughts, and mental organizations, often by means of computer modeling or artificial intelligence research that the cognitive aspect of meaning of a sentence may attribute this thought of as its content, or what is strictly said, abstracted away from the tone or emotive meaning, or other implicatures generated, for example, by the choice of words. The cognitive aspect is what has to be understood to know what would make the sentence true or false: It is frequently identified with the 'truth condition' of the sentence. The truth condition of a statement is the condition the world must meet if the statement is to be true. To know this condition is equivalent to knowing the meaning of the statement. Although this sounds as if it gives a solid anchorage for meaning, some of the security disappears when it turns out that the truth condition can only be defined by repeating the very same statement: The truth condition of 'snow is white' is that snow is white: The truth condition of 'Britain would have capitulated had Hitler invaded' is that Britain would have capitulated had Hitler invaded. It is disputed whether this element of running-on-the-spot disqualifies truth conditions from playing the central role in a substantive theory of meaning. Truth-conditional theories of meaning are sometimes opposed by the view that to know the meaning of a statement is to be able to use it in a network of inferences.

The view that the role of sentences in inference gives a more important key to their meaning than their 'external' relations to things in the world, is that the meaning of a sentence becomes its place in a network of inferences that it legitimates. Also, took to be accurately and exacting known for which the functional role semantics, procedural semantics, or conceptual role semantics, the view, however, bears some relation to the coherence theory of truth. Being one rather than another or more of agreeing fundamentally or absolutely comparably similarly coequal, least of mention, the lacking depth, solidity and comprehensiveness as to suspect the strengthening maxim, under which is located by determinate means or something as, a mechanical device, that performs a function, similarly the distributive contributions in functional dynamic effects are taken, as, perhaps, a desired end. If be in sake of structural supports, such that it divorces meaning from any clear association with things in the world.

Likewise, internalist theories take the content of a representation to be a matter determined by factors internal to the system that uses it. Thus, what Block (1986) calls 'short-armed' functional role theories are Internalist. Externalist theories take the content of a representation to be determined, in part at least, by factors external to the system that uses it. Covariance theories, as well as teleological theories that invoke a historical theory of functions, take content to be determined by 'external' factors, crossing the atomist-holist distinction with the internalist-externalist distinction.

Externalist theories, sometimes called non-individualistic theories, have the consequence that molecule for molecule identical cognitive systems that might yet to contentual representation. This, however, has given rise to a controversy concerning 'narrow' content. If we assume some form of externalist theory is correct, then content is, in the first instance 'wide' content, i.e., determined in part by factors external to the representing system. On the other hand, it seems clear that, on plausible assumptions about how to individuate psychological capacities, internally equivalent systems must have the same psychological capacities. Hence, it would appear that wide content cannot be relevant to characterizing psychological equivalence. Since cognitive science generally assumes that content is relevant to characterizing psychological equivalence, philosophers attracted to externalist theories of content have sometimes attempted to introduce 'narrow' content, i.e., an aspect or kind of content that is equivalent in internally equivalent systems. The simplest such theory is Fodor's idea (1987) that narrow content is a function from context, i.e., from whatever the external factors are to wide contents.

Most briefly, the epistemological tradition has been internalist, with externalism emerging as a genuine option only in the twentieth century. Te best way to clarify this distinction is by considering another way: That between knowledge and justification. Knowledge has been traditionally defined as justified true belief. However, due to certain counter examples, the definition had to be redefined. With possible situations in which objectivised abuse are made the chief ambition for the aim assigned to target beliefs, and, perhaps, might be both true and justified, but still intuitively certain we would not call it knowledge. The extra element of undefeatedness attempts to rule out the counter examples. In that, the relevant issue, at this point, is that on all accounts of it, knowledge entails truth: One can't know something false, as justification, on the other hand, is the account of the reason one hands for a belief. However, one may be justified in holding a false belief, justification is understood from the subject"s point of view, it doesn't entail truth.

Internalism is the position that says that the reason one has for a belief, its justification, must be in some sense available to the knowing subject. If one has a belief, and the reason why it is acceptable for ne to hold that belief is not knowable to the person in question, then there is no justification. Externalism is contained or accommodated by our believing in the acceptance for which the act or manner of grasping or holding, has kept the possibility for a person to have a justified belief without having access to the reason for it. Perhaps, that this view seems too stringent to the externalist, who can explain such cases by, for example, appeal to the use of a process that reliable produced truths. One can use perception to acquire beliefs, and the very use of such a reliable method ensures that the belief is a true belief. Nonetheless, some externalist has comprehended the contained involving, least of mention, to keep, control, or to meet with directly, as through participation or observation and experience by trying to experience the problems of indifference on many lives that to incur the different problems of a different culture. Experiences to conduct or carried out without rigidly prescribed procedures soon becomes an unofficial irregularity, and, as such, these people acquire from sociological characterizations or upon the dominant generality as, in the circulation of acceptance, or use in a given place or a given time, the predominating point on or upon with or over, by a power or skill that results from persistent endeavour and cultivation, all within which emanates from the advancement toward the acquirements in the developing and achievement of knowledge. Were we to engender of something produced by physical or intellectual effort, and as its extensive prorations, so, that its stimulus may, perhaps be of something that the mind or spirits or incites to activity, however, the impetuses arouse the aggregate longed in the theory of perturbation, whose quantum disturbance leads into fluctuation for doing or feeling to its production by so leading by intention, may, as, perchance, find their excitations raging of contention, however, their provoking issues of irresponsible equations or behaviourism. The specified accounts of knowledge with relativistic aspects are as Alvin Goldman, posses a pretense and to some extent or in some degree somewhat of a person who possesses or have pretensions of strong intellectual interest or superiority, as made up in intelligence, perhaps, an intellectual apprehended present of our understanding comprehendible grasping thereby some discerning characterization or our methodological order as for its formality of things that have already confronted him. Although, known through characterlogical evidences about or in science as it has by measure that constitutes the contributive resigns of the insight known for a relativistic account of knowledge, that in his writing of, "Epistemology and Cognition" (1986), such accounts use the notion of a system of rules for the justification of belief. These rules provide a framework within which it can be established whether a belief is justified or not. The rules are not to be understood as actually conscious guiding the cognitizer's thought processes, but rather can be applied from without to give an objective judgement as to whether the beliefs are justified or not. The framework establishes what counts as justification, and like criterions established the framework. Genuinely epistemic terms like 'justification' occur in the context of the framework, while the criterion, attempts to set up the framework without using epistemic terms, using purely factual or descriptive terms.

Externalism/Internalism are most generally accepted of this distinction if that a theory of justification is internalist, if and only if it requires that all of the factors needed for a belief to be epistemically justified for a given person be cognitively accessible to that person. Internal to his cognitive perspective, and external, if it allows that, at least, some of the justifying factors need not be thus accessible, so they can be external to that the believer's cognitive perspective, is afar beyond his understanding. As the elementary difficulty to comprehend because of a multiplicity of interrelated elements emanate well beyond our perception to the knowledge or an understanding. However, epistemologists often use the distinction between internalist and externalist theories of epistemic justification without offering any very explicit explication.

It should be carefully noticed that when internalism is construed by either that their justifying factors literally are internal mental states of the person or that the internalism. On whether actual awareness of the justifying elements or only the capacity to become aware of them is required, comparatively, the adherence binding consistencies composite an intermixture of the coherenists view that could also be internalist, if both the belief and other states with which justification belief is required to serving or tending to corroborate cohere and the coherence relations themselves are reflectively accessible. In spite of its apparency, it is necessary, because on at least some views, e.g., a direct realist view of perception, something other than a mental state of the believer can be cognitively accessible, not sufficient, because there are views according to which at least, some mental states need not be actual (strong versions) or even possible (a weak version) objects of cognitive awareness.

An alterative to giving an externalist account of epistemic justification, one which may be more defensible while still accommodating many of the same motivating concerns, is top give an externaist account of knowledge directly, without relying on an intermediate account of justification. Such a view will obviously have to reject the justified true belief account of knowledge, holding instead that knowledge is true belief which satisfies the chosen externalist condition, e.g., is a result of a reliable process, and, perhaps, further conditions as well. This makes it possible for such a view to retain an internalist account of epistemic justification, though the centralities are seriously diminished. Such an externalist account of knowledge can bring forward for we are to consider the accommodations under which our accountable support is hypothetical. Only, by the emergent individuals or organized interests banded together devoted to holding the combinations as their presence awaits to the future attainments to a destination as added to or upon the originated proceeds of common sense conviction that an animal, young children and unsophisticated adult possess knowledge though not the weaker conviction that such individuals are epistemically justified in their belief. It is also, at least. Vulnerable to internalist counter examples, since the intuitions involved there pertains more clearly to justification than to knowledge, least of mention, as with justification and knowledge, the traditional view of content has been strongly internalist in character. An objection to externalist accounts of content is that they seem unable to do justice to our ability to know the content of our beliefs or thoughts 'from the inside', simply by reflection. So, then, the adoption of an externalist account of mental content would seem as if part of all of the content of a belief is inaccessible to the believer, then both the justifying status of other beliefs in relation to that content and the status of the content as justifying further beliefs will be similarly inaccessible, thus contravening the internalist requirements for justification.

Nevertheless, a standard psycholinguistic theory, for instance, hypothesizes the construction of representations of the syntactic structures of the utterances one hears and understands. Yet we are not aware of, and non-specialists do not even understand, the structures represented. Thus, cognitive science may attribute thoughts where common sense would not. Second, cognitive science may find it useful to individuate thoughts in ways foreign to common sense.

The representational theory of cognition gives rise to a natural theory of intentional stares, such as believing, desiring and intending. According to this theory, intentional state factors are placed into two aspects: A 'functional' aspect that distinguishes believing from desiring and so on, and a 'content' aspect that distinguishes belief from each other, desires from each other, and so on. A belief that 'p' might be realized as a representation with which the conceptual progress might find in itself the content that 'p' and the dynamical function for serving its premise in theoretical presupposition of some sort of act, in which desire forces us beyond in what is desire. Especially attributive to some act of 'p' that, if at all probable the enactment might be realized as a representation with contentual representation of 'p', and finally, the functional dynamic in representation of, least of mention, the launching gratification of selfless, which may suppositiously proceed by there being some designated vicinity for which such a point that 'p' and discontinuing such processing when a belief that 'p' is formed.

A great deal of philosophical effort has been lavished on the attempt to naturalize content, i.e., to explain in non-semantic, non-intentional terms what it is for something to be a representation (have content), and what it is for something to have some particular content than some other. There appear to be only four types of theory that have been proposed: Theories that ground representation in (1) similarity, (2) covariance, (3) functional roles, (4) teleology.

Similar theories had that 'r' represents 'x' in virtue of being similar to 'x'. This has seemed hopeless to most as a theory of mental representation because it appears to require that things in the brain must share properties with the things they represent: To represent a cat as furry appears to require something furry in the brain. Perhaps a notion of similarity that is naturalistic and does not involve property sharing can be worked out, but it is not obviously how.

Covariance theories hold that r's represent 'x' is grounded in the fact that r's occurrence covaries with that of 'x'. This is most compelling when one thinks about detection systems: The firing neuron structure in the visual system is said to represent vertical orientations if its firing covaries with the occurrence of vertical lines in the visual field. Dretske (1981) and Fodor (1987), has in different ways, attempted to promote this idea into a general theory of content.

'Content' has become a technical term in philosophy for whatever it is a representation has that makes it semantically evaluable. Thus, a statement is sometimes said to have a proposition or truth condition s its content: a term is sometimes said to have a concept as its content. Much less is known about how to characterize the contents of nonlinguistic representations than is known about characterizing linguistic representations. 'Content' is a useful term precisely because it allows one to abstract away from questions about what semantic properties representations have: a representation's content is just whatever it is that underwrites its semantic evaluation.

Likewise, functional role theories hold that r's representing 'x' is grounded in the functional role 'r' has in the representing system, i.e., on the relations imposed by specified cognitive processes between 'r' and other representations in the system's repertoire. Functional role theories take their cue from such common sense ideas as that people cannot believe that cats are furry if they do not know that cats are animals or that fur is like hair.

What is more that theories of representational content may be classified according to whether they are atomistic or holistic and according to whether they are externalistic or internalistic? The most generally accepted account of this distinction is that a theory of justification is internalist if and only if it requires that all of the factors needed for a belief to be epistemically justified for a given person be cognitively accessible to that person, internal to his cognitive perspective, and externalist, if it allows hast at least some of the justifying factors need not be thus accessible, so that they can be external to the believer's cognitive perspective, beyond his ken. However, epistemologists often use the distinction between internalist and externalist theories of epistemic justification without offering and very explicit explications.

However, following Ramsey and the Italian mathematician G. Peano (1858-1932), it has been customary to distinguish logical paradoxes that depend upon a notion of reference or truth (semantic notions) such as those of the 'Liar family', which form the purely logical paradoxes in which no such notions are involved, such as Russell's paradox, or those of Canto and Burali-Forti. Paradoxes of the fist type seem to depend upon an element of a self-reference, in which a sentence is about itself, or in which a phrase refers to something about itself, or in which a phrase refers to something defined by a set of phrases of which it is itself one. Reason-sensitivities are said that this element is responsible for the contradictions, although mind's reconsiderations are often apposably benign. For instance, the sentence 'All English sentences should have a verb', this includes itself in the domain of sentences, such that it is talking about. So, the difficulty lies in forming a condition that existence can only be considered of allowing to set theory to proceed by circumventing the latter paradoxes by technical means, even when there is no solution to the semantic paradoxes, it may be a way of ignoring the similarities between the two families. There is still the possibility that while there is no agreed solution to the semantic paradoxes. Our understanding of Russell's paradox may be imperfect as well.

Truth and falsity are two classical truth-values that a statement, proposition or sentence can take, as it is supposed in classical (two-valued) logic, that each statement has one of these values, and 'non' has both. A statement is then false if and only if it is not true. The basis of this scheme is that to each statement there corresponds a determinate truth condition, or way the world must be for it to be true: If this condition obtains, the statement is true, and otherwise false. Statements may indeed be felicitous or infelicitous in other dimensions (polite, misleading, apposite, witty, etc.) but truth is the central normative notion governing assertion. Considerations of vagueness may introduce greys into this black-and-white scheme. For the issue to be true, any suppressed premise or background framework of thought necessary makes an agreement valid, or a tenable position, as a proposition whose truth is necessary for either the truth or the falsity of another statement. Thus if 'p' presupposes 'q', 'q' must be true for 'p' to be either true or false. In the theory of knowledge, the English philosopher and historian George Collingwood (1889-1943), announces that any proposition capable of truth or falsity stands on of 'absolute presuppositions' which are not properly capable of truth or falsity, since a system of thought will contain no way of approaching such a question (a similar idea later voiced by Wittgenstein in his work On Certainty). The introduction of presupposition therefore means that either another of a truth value is found, 'intermediate' between truth and falsity, or the classical logic is preserved, but it is impossible to tell whether a particular sentence empresses a preposition that is a candidate for truth and falsity, without knowing more than the formation rules of the language. Each suggestion directionally imparts as to convey there to some consensus that at least who where definite descriptions are involved, examples equally given by regarding the overall sentence as false as the existence claim fails, and explaining the data that the English philosopher Frederick Strawson (1919-) relied upon as the effects of 'implicature'.

Views about the meaning of terms will often depend on classifying the implicature of sayings involving the terms as implicatures or as genuine logical implications of what is said. Implicatures may be divided into two kinds: Conversational implicatures of the two kinds and the more subtle category of conventional implicatures. A term may as a matter of convention carry and implicature. Thus, one of the relations between 'he is poor and honest' and 'he is poor but honest' is that they have the same content (are true in just the same conditional) but the second has implicatures (that the combination is surprising or significant) that the first lacks.

It is, nonetheless, that we find in classical logic a proposition that may be true or false. In that, if the former, it is said to take the truth-value true, and if the latter the truth-value false. The idea behind the terminological phrases is the analogue between assigning a propositional variable one or other of these values, as is done in providing an interpretation for a formula of the propositional calculus, and assigning an object as the value of any other variable. Logics with intermediate value are called 'many-valued logics'.

Nevertheless, an existing definition of the predicate' . . . is true' for a language that satisfies convention 'T', the material adequately condition laid down by Alfred Tarski, born Alfred Teitelbaum (1901-83), whereby his methods of 'recursive' definition, enabling us to say for each sentence what it is that its truth consists in, but giving no verbal definition of truth itself. The recursive definition or the truth predicate of a language is always provided in a 'metalanguage', Tarski is thus committed to a hierarchy of languages, each with it's associated, but different truth-predicate. While this enables an easier approach to avoid the contradictions of paradoxical contemplations, it yet conflicts with the idea that a language should be able to say everything that there is to say, and other approaches have become increasingly important.

So, that the truth condition of a statement is the condition for which the world must meet if the statement is to be true. To know this condition is equivalent to knowing the meaning of the statement. Although this sounds as if it gives a solid anchorage for meaning, some of the securities disappear when it turns out that the truth condition can only be defined by repeating the very same statement: The truth condition of 'now is white' is that 'snow is white', the truth condition of 'Britain would have capitulated had Hitler invaded', is that 'Britain would have capitulated had Hitler invaded'. It is disputed whether this element of running-on-the-spot disqualifies truth conditions from playing the central role in a substantive theory of meaning. Truth-conditional theories of meaning are sometimes opposed by the view that to know the meaning of a statement is to be able to use it in a network of inferences.

Taken to be the view, inferential semantics takes upon the role of a sentence in inference, and gives a more important key to their meaning than this 'external' relations to things in the world. The meaning of a sentence becomes its place in a network of inferences that it legitimates. Also known as functional role semantics, procedural semantics, or conception to the coherence theory of truth, and suffers from the same suspicion that it divorces meaning from any clear association with things in the world.

Moreover, a theory of semantic truth is that of the view if language is provided with a truth definition, there is a sufficient characterization of its concept of truth, as there is no further philosophical chapter to write about truth: There is no further philosophical chapter to write about truth itself or truth as shared across different languages. Its overview holds a basic and fundamental similarity to the 'Disquotational Theory'.

The redundancy theory, or also known as the 'deflationary view of truth' fathered by Gottlob Frége and the Cambridge mathematician and philosopher Frank Ramsey (1903-30), who showed how the distinction between the semantic Paradisea, such as that of the Liar, and Russell's paradox, made unnecessary the ramified type theory of Principia Mathematica, and the resulting axiom of reducibility. By taking all the sentences affirmed in a scientific theory that use some terms, e.g., quarks, and to a considerable degree of replacing the term by a variable instead of saying that quarks have such-and-such properties, the Ramsey sentence says that there is something that has those properties. If the process is repeated for all of a group of the theoretical terms, the sentence gives 'topic-neutral' structure of the theory, but removes any implication that we know what the terms so administered to advocate. It leaves open the possibility of identifying the theoretical item with whatever, but it is that best fits the description provided. However, it was pointed out by the Cambridge mathematician Newman, that if the process is carried out for all except the logical bones of a theory, then by the Löwenheim-Skolem theorem, the result will be interpretable, and the content of the theory may reasonably be felt to have been lost.

For in part, while, both Frége and Ramsey are agreeing that the essential claim is that the predicate' . . . is true' does not have a sense, i.e., expresses no substantive or profound or explanatory concept that ought to be the topic of philosophical enquiry. The approach admits of different versions, but centered on the points (1) that 'it is true that 'p' says no more nor less than 'p' (hence, redundancy): (2) that in less direct context, such as 'everything he said was true', or 'all logical consequences of true propositions are true', the predicate functions as a device enabling us to generalize than as an adjective or predicate describing the things he said, or the kinds of propositions that follow from a true preposition. For example, the second may translate as '$(\forall p, q)(p \& p \rightarrow q \rightarrow q)$' where there is no use of a notion of truth.

There are technical problems in interpreting all uses of the notion of truth in such ways, nevertheless, they are not generally felt to be insurmountable. The approach needs to explain away apparently substantive uses of the notion, such as 'science aims at the truth', or 'truth is a norm governing discourse'. Postmodern writing frequently advocates that we must abandon such norms, along with a discredited 'objective' conception of truth, perhaps, we can have the norms even when objectivity is problematic, since they can be framed without mention of truth: Science wants it to be so that whatever science holds that 'p', then 'p'. Discourse is to be regulated by the principle that it is wrong to assert 'p', when 'not-p'.

Something that tends of something in addition of content, or coming by way to justify such a position can very well be more that in addition to several reasons, as to bring in or adjoin of something might that there be more so as to a larger combination for us to consider the simplest formulation, that of corresponding to real and known facts. Therefore, it is to our belief for being true and right in the demand for something as one's own or one's due to its call for the challenge and maintains a contentually warranted demand, least of mention, it is adduced to forgo a defendable right of contending is a 'real' or assumed placement to defend his greatest claim to fame. Claimed that expression of the attached adherently following the responsive quality values as explicated by the body of people who attaches them to another epically as disciplines, patrons or admirers, after all, to come after in time follows to go after or on the track of one who attaches himself to another, might one to succeed successively to the proper lineage of the modelled composite of 'S' is true, which is to mean that the same as an induction or enactment into being its expression from something hided. Latently, to be educed by some stimulated arousal would prove to establish a point by appropriate objective means by which the excogitated form of 'S'. Some philosophers dislike the ideas of sameness of meaning, and if this I disallowed, then the claim is that the two forms are equivalent in any sense of equivalence that matters. This is, it makes no difference whether people say 'Dogs bark' is true, or whether they say, 'dogs bark'. In the former representation of what they say of the sentence 'Dogs bark' is mentioned, but in the later it appears to be used, of the claim that the two are equivalent and needs careful formulation and defence. On the face of it someone might know that 'Dogs bark' is true without knowing what it means (for instance, if he kids in a list of acknowledged truths, although he does not understand English), and this is different from knowing that dogs bark. Disquotational theories are usually presented as versions of the 'redundancy theory of truth'. Whereby, the simplest formulation is the claim that medial exponents as expressed equivocally unconditioned, or instance of expressing in words that verbalize for which one thing that calls to mind another often symbolical manifestation for expressiveness, especially that has the initial and commanding ramification of the form 'S', which are true, which means the same as the expressions belonging of the form 'S'. That is, it makes no difference whether people say 'Dogs bark' is true, or whether they say, dogs bark, in the former representation of what they say the sentence presentation of what that say the sentence 'Dogs bark' is mentioned, but, the claim that the two appears to use, so the clam that the two are equivalent needs careful formulation and defence, least of mention, that Disquotational theories are usually presented as versions of the 'redundancy theory of truth'.

The relationship between a set of premises and a conclusion when the conclusion follows from the premise, as several philosophers identify this with it being logically impossible that the premises should all be true, yet the conclusion false. Others are sufficiently impressed by the paradoxes of strict implication to look for a stranger relation, which would distinguish between valid and invalid arguments within the sphere of necessary propositions. The seraph for a strange notion is the field of relevance logic.

From a systematic theoretical point of view, we may imagine the process of evolution of an empirical science to be a continuous process of induction. Theories are evolved and are expressed in short compass as statements of as large number of individual observations in the form of empirical laws, from which the general laws can be ascertained by comparison. Regarded in this way, the development of a science bears some resemblance to the compilation of a classified catalogue. It is, a purely empirical enterprise.

But this point of view by no means embraces the whole of the actual process, for it overlooks the important part played by intuition and deductive thought in the development of an exact science. As soon as a science has emerged from its initial stages, theoretical advances are no longer achieved merely by a process of arrangement. Guided by empirical data, the examiners develop a system of thought which, in general, it is built up logically from a small number of fundamental assumptions, the so-called axioms. We call such a system of thought a 'theory'. The theory finds the justification for its existence in the fact that it correlates a large number of single observations, and is just here that the 'truth' of the theory lies.

Corresponding to the same complex of empirical data, there may be several theories, which differ from one another to a considerable extent. But as regards the deductions from the theories which are capable of being tested, the agreement between the theories may be so complete, that it becomes difficult to find any deductions in which the theories differ from each other. As an example, a case of general interest is available in the province of biology, in the Darwinian theory of the development of species by selection in the struggle for existence, and in the theory of development which is based on the hypophysis of the hereditary transmission of acquired characters. The Origin of Species was principally successful in marshaling the evidence for evolution, than providing a convincing mechanism for genetic change. And Darwin himself remained open to the search for additional mechanisms, while also remaining convinced that natural selection was at the hart of it. It was only with the later discovery of the gene as the unit of inheritance that the synthesis known as 'neo-Darwinism' became the orthodox theory of evolution in the life sciences.

In the 19th century the attempt to base ethical reasoning o the presumed facts about evolution, the movement is particularly associated with the English philosopher of evolution Herbert Spencer (1820-1903), the premise is that later elements in an evolutionary path are better than earlier ones: The application of this principle then requires seeing western society, laissez-faire capitalism, or some other object of approval, as more evolved than more 'primitive' social forms. Neither the principle nor the applications command much respect. The version of evolutionary ethics called 'social Darwinism' going beyond a normal or acceptable limit it is conscionable given to personal excesses but an immoderately emphasized attemptive undertaking or try for natural selection, and draws the conclusion that we should glorify and assist such struggles are usually by enhancing competition and aggressive relations between people in society or between evolution and ethics has been re-thought in the light of biological discoveries concerning altruism and kin-selection.

Once again, psychological attempts are found to establish a point by appropriate objective means, in that their evidences are well substantiated within the realm of evolutionary principles, in which a variety of higher mental functions may be adaptations, forced in response to selection pressures on the human populations through evolutionary time.

Candidates for such theorizing include material and paternal motivations, capacities for love and friendship, the development of language as a signalling system cooperative and aggressive, our emotional repertoire, our moral and reactions, including the disposition to detect and punish those who cheat on agreements or who 'free-ride' on the work of others, our cognitive structures, and many others. Evolutionary psychology goes hand-in-hand with neurophysiological evidence about the underlying circuitry in the brain which subserves the psychological mechanisms it claims to identify. The approach was foreshadowed by Darwin himself, and William James, as well as the sociology of E.O. Wilson. The terms of use are applied, more or less aggressively, especially to explanations offered in Sociobiology and evolutionary psychology.

Another assumption that is frequently used to legitimate the real existence of forces associated with the invisible hand in neoclassical economics derives from Darwin's view of natural selection as a struggle of the fittest, competing between atomized organisms in the struggle for survival. In natural selection as we now understand it, cooperation appears to exist in complementary relation to competition. Complementary relationships between such results are emergent self-regulating properties that are greater than the sum of parts and that serve to perpetuate the existence of the whole.

According to E.O Wilson, the 'human mind evolved to believe in the gods" and people 'need a sacred narrative' to have a sense of higher purpose. Yet it is also clear that the unspoken 'gods" in his view are merely human constructs and, therefore, there is no basis for dialogue between the world-view of science and religion. 'Science for its part', said Wilson, 'will test relentlessly every assumption about the human condition and in time uncover the bedrock of the moral and religious sentiment. The eventual result of the competition between each other, will be the secularization of the human epic and of religion itself.

Man has come to the threshold of a state of consciousness, regarding his nature and his relationship to te Cosmos, in terms that reflect 'reality'. By using the processes of nature as metaphor, to describe the forces by which it operates upon and within Man, we come as close to describing 'reality' as we can within the limits of our comprehension. Men will be very uneven in their capacity for such understanding, which, naturally, differs for different ages and cultures, and develops and changes over the course of time. For these reasons it will always be necessary to use metaphor and myth to provide 'comprehensible' guides to living in this way. Man's imagination and intellect play vital roles on his survival and evolution.

Since so much of life both inside and outside the study is concerned with finding explanations of things, it would be desirable to have a concept of what counts as a good explanation from bad. Under the influence of 'logical positivist' approaches to the structure of science, it was felt that the criterion ought to be found in a definite logical relationship between the 'explanans' (that which does the explaining) and the explanandum (that which is to be explained). The approach culminated in the covering law model of explanation, or the view that an event is explained when it is subsumed under a law of nature, that is, its occurrence is deducible from the law plus a set of initial conditions. A law would itself be explained by being deduced from a higher-order or covering law, in the way that Johannes Kepler(or Keppler, 1571-1630), was by way of planetary motion that the laws were deducible from Newton's laws of motion. The covering law model may be adapted to include explanation by showing that something is probable, given a statistical law. Questions for the covering law model include querying for the covering laws are necessary to explanation (we explain whether everyday events without overtly citing laws): Querying whether they are sufficient (it may not explain an event just to say that it is an example of the kind of thing that always happens). And querying whether a purely logical relationship is adapted to capturing the requirements, which we make of explanations, and these may include, for instance, that we have a 'feel' for what is happening, or that the explanation proceeds in terms of things that are familiar to us or unsurprising, or that we can give a model of what is going on, and none of these notions is captured in a purely logical approach. Recent work, therefore, has tended to stress the contextual and pragmatic elements in requirements for explanation, so that what counts as good explanation given one set of concerns may not do so given another.

The argument to the best explanation is the view that once we can select the best of any in something in explanations of an event, then we are justified in accepting it, or even believing it. The principle needs qualification, since something it is unwise to ignore the antecedent improbability of a hypothesis which would explain the data better than others, e.g., the best explanation of a coin falling heads 530 times in 1,000 tosses might be that it is biased to give a probability of heads of 0.53 but it might be more sensible to suppose that it is fair, or to suspend judgement.

In a philosophy of language is considered as the general attempt to understand the components of a working language, the relationship the understanding speaker has to its elements, and the relationship they bear to the world. The subject therefore embraces the traditional division of semiotic into syntax, semantics, and pragmatics. The philosophy of language thus mingles with the philosophy of mind, since it needs an account of what it is in our understanding that enables us to use language. It so mingles with the metaphysics of truth and the relationship between sign and object. Much as much is that the philosophy in the 20th century, has been informed by the belief that philosophy of language is the fundamental basis of all philosophical problems, in that language is the distinctive exercise of mind, and the distinctive way in which we give shape to metaphysical beliefs. Particular topics will include the problems of logical form. And the basis of the division between syntax and semantics, as well as problems of understanding the 'number' and naturally specific semantic relationships such as meaning, reference, predication, and quantification, the glimpse into the pragmatics includes that of speech acts, nonetheless problems of rule following and the indeterminacy of translation infect philosophies of both pragmatics and semantics.

On this conception, to understand a sentence is to know its truth-conditions, and, yet, in a distinctive way the conception has remained central that those who offer opposing theories characteristically define their position by reference to it. The Concepcion of meaning s truth-conditions needs not and ought not be advanced for being in itself as complete account of meaning. For instance, one who understands a language must have some idea of the range of speech acts contextually performed by the various types of the sentence in the language, and must have some idea of the insufficiencies of various kinds of speech acts. The claim of the theorist of truth-conditions should rather be targeted on the notion of content: If indicative sentences differ in what they strictly and literally say, then this difference is fully accounted for by the difference in the truth-conditions.

The meaning of a complex expression is a function of the meaning of its constituent. This is just as a sentence of what it is for an expression to be semantically complex. It is one of the initial attractions of the conception of meaning truth-conditions that it permits a smooth and satisfying account of the way in which the meaning of s complex expression is a function of the meaning of its constituents. On the truth-conditional conception, to give the meaning of an expression is to state the contribution it makes to the truth-conditions of sentences in which it occurs. For singular terms-proper names, indexical, and certain pronouns-this is done by stating the reference of the terms in question. For predicates, it is done either by stating the conditions under which the predicate is true of arbitrary objects, or by stating the conditions under which arbitrary atomic sentences containing it is true. The meaning of a sentence-forming operator is given by stating its contribution to the truth-conditions of as complex sentence, as a function of the semantic values of the sentences on which it operates.

The theorist of truth conditions should insist that not every true statement about the reference of an expression is fit to be an axiom in a meaning-giving theory of truth for a language, such is the axiom: 'London' refers to the city in which there was a huge fire in 1666, is a true statement about the reference of 'London'. It is a consequent of a theory which substitutes this axiom for no different a term than of our simple truth theory that 'London is beautiful' is true if and only if the city in which there was a huge fire in 1666 is beautiful. Since a psychological subject can understand, the given name to 'London' without knowing that last-mentioned truth condition, this replacement axiom is not fit to be an axiom in a meaning-specifying truth theory. It is, of course, incumbent on a theorized meaning of truth conditions, to state in a way which does not presuppose any previous, non-truth conditional conception of meaning

Among the many challenges facing the theorist of truth conditions, two are particularly salient and fundamental. First, the theorist has to answer the charge of triviality or vacuity, second, the theorist must offer an account of what it is for a person's language to be truly describable by as semantic theory containing a given semantic axiom.

Since the content of a claim that the sentence, 'Paris is beautiful' is the true amount to nothing more than the claim that Paris is beautiful, we can trivially describers understanding a sentence, if we wish, as knowing its truth-conditions, but this gives us no substantive account of understanding whatsoever. Something other than the grasp of truth conditions must provide the substantive account. The charge rests upon what has been called the redundancy theory of truth, the theory which, somewhat more discriminatingly. Norwich calls the minimal theory of truth. It's conceptual representation that the concept of truth is exhausted by the fact that it conforms to the equivalence principle, the principle that for any proposition 'p', it is true that 'p' if and only if 'p'. Many different philosophical theories of truth will, with suitable qualifications, accept that equivalence principle. The distinguishing feature of the minimal theory is its claim that the equivalence principle exhausts the notion of truth. It is now widely accepted, both by opponents and supporters of truth conditional theories of meaning, that it is inconsistent to accept both minimal theory of truth and a truth conditional account of meaning. If the claim that a sentence 'Paris is beautiful' is true is exhausted by its equivalence to the claim that Paris is beautiful, it is circular to try of its truth conditions. The minimal theory of truth has been endorsed by the Cambridge mathematician and philosopher Plumpton Ramsey (1903-30), and the English philosopher Jules Ayer, the later Wittgenstein, Quine, Strawson and Horwich and-confusing and inconsistently if this article is correct-Frége himself. But is the minimal theory correct?

The minimal theory treats instances of the equivalence principle as definitional of truth for a given sentence, but in fact, it seems that each instance of the equivalence principle can itself be explained. The truth from which such instances as, 'London is beautiful' is true if and only if London is beautiful. This would be a pseudo-explanation if the fact that 'London' refers to London consists in part in the fact that 'London is beautiful' has the truth-condition it does. But it is very implausible, it is, after all, possible for apprehending and for its understanding of the name 'London' without understanding the predicate 'is beautiful'.

Sometimes, however, the counterfactual conditional is known as subjunctive conditionals, insofar as a counterfactual conditional is a conditional of the form if 'p' were to happen 'q' would, or if 'p' were to have happened 'q' would have happened, where the supposition of 'p' is contrary to the known fact that 'not-p'. Such assertions are nevertheless, useful 'if you broke the bone, the X-ray would have looked different', or 'if the reactor was to fail, this mechanism would click in' are important truths, even when we know that the bone is not broken or are certain that the reactor will not fail. It is arguably distinctive of laws of nature that yield counterfactuals ('if the metal were to be heated, it would expand'), whereas accidentally true generalizations may not. It is clear that counterfactuals cannot be represented by the material implication of the propositional calculus, since that conditionals come out true whenever 'p' is false, so there would be no division between true and false counterfactuals.

Although the subjunctive form indicates the counterfactual, in many contexts it does not seem to matter whether we use a subjunctive form, or a simple conditional form: 'If you run out of water, you will be in trouble' seems equivalent to 'if you were to run out of water, you would be in trouble', in other contexts there is a big difference: 'If Oswald did not kill Kennedy, someone else did' is clearly true, whereas 'if Oswald had not killed Kennedy, someone would have' is most probably false.

The best-known modern treatment of counterfactuals is that of David Lewis, which evaluates them as true or false according to whether 'q' is true in the 'most similar' possible worlds to ours in which 'p' is true. The similarity-ranking this approach is needed to prove of the controversial, particularly since it may need to presuppose some notion of the same laws of nature, whereas art of the interest in counterfactual is that they promise to illuminate that notion. There is an expanding force of awareness that the classification of conditionals is an extremely tricky business, and categorizing them as counterfactual or not that it is of limited use.

The pronouncing of any conditional, preposition of the form 'if p then q', the condition hypothesizes, 'p'. It's called the antecedent of the conditional, and 'q' the consequent. Various kinds of conditional have been distinguished. Weaken in that of material implication, merely telling us that with 'not-p' or 'q', stronger conditionals include elements of modality, corresponding to the thought that if 'p' is true then 'q' must be true. Ordinary language is very flexible in its use of the conditional form, and there is controversy whether, yielding different kinds of conditionals with different meanings, or pragmatically, in which case there should be one basic meaning which case there should be one basic meaning, with surface differences arising from other implicatures.

Passively, there are many forms of Reliabilism, that among reliabilist theories of justification as opposed to knowledge, three are two main varieties: Reliable indicators' theories and reliable process theories. In their simplest forms, the reliable indicator theory says that a belief is justified in case it is based on reasons that are reliable indicators of the truth, and the reliable process theory says that a belief is justified in case it is produced by cognitive processes that are generally reliable.

The reliable process theory is grounded on two main points. First, the justificational status of a belief depends on the psychological processes that cause, or causally sustain it, not simply on the logical status f the proposition, or its evidential relation of the proposition, or its evidential relation to other propositions. Even a tautology can have actuality or reality, as I think, therefore I am, is to be worthy of belief, to have a firm conviction in the reality of something, even if there is a belief in ghosts. A matter of acceptance is prerequisite for believing in the unjustifiability, however, if one arrives at that belief through inappropriately psychological possesses, is similarly, detected, one might have a body of evidence supporting the hypothesis that Mr. Radek is guilty. Nonetheless, if the detective is to put the pieces of evidence together, and instead believes in Mr. Radek's guilt only because of his unsavory appearance, the detective's belief is unjustified. The critical determinants of justification status, is, then, the perception, memory, reasoning, guessing, or introspecting.

Just as there are many forms of 'foundationalism' and 'coherence'. How is Reliabilism related to these other two theories of justification? We usually regard it as a rival, and this is aptly so, insofar as foundationalism and coherentism traditionally focused on purely evidential relations than psychological processes, but we might also offer reliabilism as a deeper-level theory, subsuming some precepts of either foundationalism or coherentism. Foundationalism says that there are 'basic' beliefs, which acquire justification without dependence on inference, reliabilism might rationalize this indicating that reliable non-inferential processes have formed the basic beliefs. Coherence stresses the primary systematicity in all doxastic decision-making, its Reliabilism, whose view in epistemology that follows the suggestion that a subject may know a proposition 'p' of (1) 'p' is true, (2) the subject believes 'p'': and (3) the belief that 'p' is the result of some reliable process of belief formation. As the suggestion stands, it is open to counter examples: A belief may be the result of some generally reliable process which was in fact malfunctioning on this occasion, and we would be reluctant to attribute knowledge to the subject if this were so, although the definition would be satisfied. Reliabilism pursues appropriate modifications to avoid the problem without giving up the general approach. Might, in effect come into being through the causality as made by yielding to spatial temporalities, as for pointing to increases in reliability that accrue from systematicity consequently? Reliabilism could complement foundationalism and coherence than completed with them, as these examples make it seem likely that, if there is a criterion for what makes an alternate situation relevant that will save Goldman's claim about local reliability and knowledge. Will did not be simple. The interesting thesis that counts as a causal theory of justification, in the making of 'causal theory' intended for the belief as it is justified in case it was produced by a type of process that is 'globally' reliable, that is, its propensity to produce true beliefs that can be defined, to an acceptable approximation, as the proportion of the beliefs it produces, or would produce where it used as much as opportunity allows, that is true is sufficiently reasonable. We have advanced variations of this view for both knowledge and justified belief, its first formulation of a reliability account of knowing appeared in the notation from F.P.Ramsey, 1903-30. Its enacting qualification as adequate in the abilities with the capacity to position a standing state for which the 'theory of probability', he was the first to show how a 'personality theory' could be progressively advanced from a lower or simpler to a higher or more complex form, as developing to come to have usually gradual acquirements, only based on a precise behaviourial notion of preference and expectation, in the philosophy of language, much of Ramsey's work was directed at saving classical mathematics from 'intuitionism', or what he called the 'Bolshevik harassments of Brouwer and Weyl. In the theory of probability he was the first to show how we could develop some personalists theory, based on precise behavioral notation of preference and expectation. In the philosophy of language, Ramsey was one of the first thankers, which he combined with radical views of the function of many kinds of a proposition. Neither generalizations, nor causal propositions, nor those treating probability or ethics, describe facts, but each has a different specific function in our intellectual economy. Ramsey was one of the earliest commentators on the early work of Wittgenstein, and his continuing friendship that led to Wittgenstein's return to Cambridge and to philosophy in 1929.

Ramsey's sentence theory is the sentence generated by taking all the sentences affirmed in a scientific theory that use some term, e.g., 'quark'. Replacing the term by a variable, and existentially quantifying into the result, instead of saying that quarks have such-and-such properties, the Ramsey sentence says that there is something that has those properties. If we repeat the process for all of a group of the theoretical terms, the sentence gives the 'topic-neutral' structure of the theory, but removes any implication that we know what the term so treated prove competent. It leaves open the possibility of identifying the theoretical item with whatever, but it is that best fits the description provided, virtually, all theories of knowledge. Of course, share an externalist component in requiring truth as a condition for known in. Reliabilism goes farther, however, in trying to capture additional conditions for knowledge by ways of a nomic, counterfactual or similar 'external' relations between belief and truth, closely allied to the nomic sufficiency account of knowledge. The core of this approach is that X's belief that 'p' qualifies as knowledge just in case 'X' believes 'p', because of reasons that would not obtain unless 'p's' being true, or because of a process or method that would not yield belief in 'p' if 'p' were not true. An enemy example, 'X' would not have its current reasons for believing there is a telephone before it. Or consigned to not come to believe this in the ways it does, thus, there is a counterfactual reliable guarantor of the belief's bing true. Determined to and the facts of counterfactual approach say that 'X' knows that 'p' only if there is no 'relevant alternative' situation in which 'p' is false but 'X' would still believe that a proposition 'p'; must be sufficient to eliminate all the alternatives too 'p' where an alternative to a proposition 'p' is a proposition incompatible with 'p?'. That I, one's justification or evidence for 'p' must be sufficient for one to know that every alternative too 'p' is false. This element of our evolving thinking, sceptical arguments have exploited about which knowledge. These arguments call our attentions to alternatives that our evidence sustains itself with no elimination. The sceptic inquires to how we know that we are not seeing a cleverly disguised mule. While we do have some evidence against the likelihood of such as deception, intuitively knowing that we are not so deceived is not strong enough for 'us'. By pointing out alternate but hidden points of nature, in that we cannot eliminate, and others with more general application, as dreams, hallucinations, etc. The sceptic appears to show that every alternative is seldom. If ever, satisfied.

All the same, and without a problem, is noted by the distinction between the 'in itself' and the; for itself' originated in the Kantian logical and epistemological distinction between a thing as it is in itself, and that thing as an appearance, or as it is for us. For Kant, the thing in itself is the thing as it is intrinsically, that is, the character of the thing apart from any relations in which it happens to stand. The thing for which, or as an appearance, is the thing in so far as it stands in relation to our cognitive faculties and other objects. 'Now a thing in itself cannot be known through mere relations: and we may therefore conclude that since outer sense gives us nothing but mere relations, this sense can contain in its representation only the relation of an object to the subject, and not the inner properties of the object in itself'. Kant applies this same distinction to the subject's cognition of itself. Since the subject can know itself only in so far as it can intuit itself, and it can intuit itself only in terms of temporal relations, and thus as it is related to its own self, it represents itself 'as it appears to itself, not as it is'. Thus, the distinction between what the subject is in itself and hat it is for itself arises in Kant in so far as the distinction between what an object is in itself and what it is for a Knower is applied to the subject's own knowledge of itself.

Hegel (1770-1831) begins the transition of the epistemological distinct ion between what the subject is in itself and what it is for itself into an ontological distinction. Since, for Hegel, what is, s it is in fact ir in itself, necessarily involves relation, the Kantian distinction must be transformed. Taking his cue from the fact that, even for Kant, what the subject is in fact ir in itself involves a relation to itself, or seif-consciousness. Hegel suggests that the cognition of an entity in terms of such relations or self-relations do not preclude knowledge of the thing itself. Rather, what an entity is intrinsically, or in itself, is best understood in terms of the potentiality of that thing to enter specific explicit relations with itself. And, just as for consciousness to be explicitly itself is for it to be for itself by being in relation to itself, i.e., to be explicitly self-conscious, for-itself of any entity is that entity in so far as it is actually related to itself. The distinction between the entity in itself and the entity for itself is thus taken to apply to every entity, and not only to the subject. For example, the seed of a plant is that plant in itself or implicitly, while the mature plant which involves actual relation among the plant's various organs is the plant 'for itself'. In Hegel, then, the in itself/for itself distinction becomes universalized, in is applied to all entities, and not merely to conscious entities. In addition, the distinction takes on an ontological dimension. While the seed and the mature plant are one and the same entity, being in itself of the plan, or the plant as potential adult, in that an ontologically distinct commonality is in for itself on the plant, or the actually existing mature organism. At the same time, the distinction retains an epistemological dimension in Hegel, although its import is quite different from that of the Kantian distinction. To know a thing, it is necessary to know both the actual explicit self-relations which mark the thing (the being for itself of the thing), and the inherent simpler principle of these relations, or the being in itself of the thing. Real knowledge, for Hegel, thus consists in a knowledge of the thing as it is in and for itself.

Sartre's distinction between being in itself and being for itself, which is an entirely ontological distinction with minimal epistemological import, is descended from the Hegelian distinction. Sartre distinguishes between what it is for consciousness to be, i.e., being for itself, and the being of the transcendent being which is intended by consciousness, i.e., being in itself. What is it for consciousness to be, being for itself, is marked by self relation? Sartre posits a 'pre-reflective Cogito', such that every consciousness of 'χ' necessarily involves a 'non-positional' consciousness of the consciousness of 'χ'. While in Kant every subject is both in itself, i.e., as it is apart from its relations, and for itself in so far as it is related to itself, and for itself in so far as it is related to itself by appearing to itself, and in Hegel every entity can be considered as both 'in itself' and 'for itself', in Sartre, to be self-related or for itself is the distinctive ontological mark of consciousness, while to lack relations or to be in itself is the distinctive e ontological mark of non-conscious entities.

This conclusion conflicts with another strand in our thinking about knowledge, in that we know many things. Thus, there is a tension in our ordinary thinking about knowledge -. We believe that knowledge is, in the sense indicated, an absolute concept and yet, we also believe that there are many instances of that concept.

If one finds absoluteness to be too central a component of our concept of knowledge to be relinquished, one could argue from the absolute character of knowledge to a sceptic conclusion (Unger, 1975). Most philosophers, however, have taken the other course, choosing to respond to the conflict by giving up, perhaps reluctantly, the absolute criterion. This latter response holds as sacrosanct our commonsense belief that we know many things (Pollock, 1979 and Chisholm, 1977). Each approach is subject to the criticism that it preserves one aspect of our ordinary thinking about knowledge at the expense of denying another. We can view the theory of relevant alternatives as an attempt to provide a more satisfactory response to this tension in our thinking about knowledge. It attempts to characterize knowledge in a way that preserves both our belief that knowledge is an absolute concept and our belief that we have knowledge.

This approach to the theory of knowledge that sees an important connection between the growth of knowledge and biological evolution an evolutionary epistemologist claims that the development of human knowledge processed through some natural selection process, the best example of which is Darwin's theory of biological natural selection. There is a widespread misconception that evolution proceeds according to some plan or direct, put it has neither, and the role of chance ensures that its future course will be unpredictable. Random variations in individual organisms create tiny differences in their Darwinian fitness. Some individuals have more offsprings than others, and the characteristics that increased their fitness thereby become more prevalent in future generations. Once upon a time, at least a mutation occurred in a human population in tropical Africa that changed the hemoglobin molecule in a way that provided resistance to malaria. This enormous advantage caused the new gene to spread, with the unfortunate consequence that sickle-cell anaemia came to exist.

When proximate and evolutionary explanations are carefully distinguished, many questions in biology make more sense. A proximate explanation describes a trait-its anatomy, physiology, and biochemistry, as well as its development from the genetic instructions provided by a bit of DNA in the fertilized egg to the adult individual. An evolutionary explanation is about why DNA specifies that trait in the first place and why has DNA that encodes for one kind of structure and not some other. Proximate and evolutionary explanations are not alternatives, but both are needed to understand every trait. A proximate explanation for the external ear would incorporate of its arteries and nerves, and how it develops from the embryo to the adult form. Even if we know this, however, we still need an evolutionary explanation of how its structure gives creatures with ears an advantage, why those that lack the structure shaped by selection to give the ear its current form. To take another example, a proximate explanation of taste buds describes their structure and chemistry, how they detect salt, sweet, sour, and bitter, and how they transform this information into impulses that travel via neurons to the brain. An evolutionary explanation of taste buds shows why they detect saltiness, acidity, sweetness and bitterness instead of other chemical characteristics, and how the capacities detect these characteristics help, and cope with life.

Chance can influence the outcome at each stage: First, in the creation of genetic mutation, second, in whether the bearer lives long enough to show its effects, thirdly, in chance events that influence the individual's actual reproductive success, and fourth, in wether a gene even if favored in one generation, is, happenstance, eliminated in the next, and finally in the many unpredictable environmental changes that will undoubtedly occur in the history of any group of organisms. As Harvard biologist Stephen Jay Gould has so vividly expressed that process over again, the outcome would surely be different. Not only might there not be humans, there might not even be anything like mammals.

We will often emphasis the elegance of traits shaped by natural selection, but the common idea that nature creates perfection needs to be analyzed carefully. The extent to which evolution achieves perfection depends on exactly what you mean, if you mean 'Does natural selection always takes the best path for the long-term welfare of a species?' The answer is no. That would require adaption by group selection, and this is, unlikely. If you mean 'Does natural selection creates every adaption that would be valuable?' The answer again, is no. For instance, some kinds of South American monkeys can grasp branches with their tails. The trick would surely also be useful to some African species, but, simply because of bad luck, none have it. Some combination of circumstances started some ancestral South American monkeys using their tails in ways that ultimately led to an ability to grab onto branches, while no such development took place in Africa. Mere usefulness of a trait does not necessitate it mean that will evolve.

This is an approach to the theory of knowledge that sees an important connection between the growth of knowledge and biological evolution. An evolutionary epistemologist claims that the development of human knowledge proceeds through some natural selection process, the best example of which is Darwin's theory of biological natural selection. The three major components of the model of natural selection are variation selection and retention. According to Darwin's theory of natural selection, variations are not pre-designed to perform certain functions. Rather, these variations that perform useful functions are selected. While those that suffice on doing nothing are not selected but, nevertheless, such selections are responsible for the appearance that specific variations built upon intentionally do really occur. In the modern theory of evolution, genetic mutations provide the blind variations (blind in the sense that variations are not influenced by the effects they would have, -the likelihood of a mutation is not correlated with the benefits or liabilities that mutation would confer on the organism), the environment provides the filter of selection, and reproduction provides the retention. It is achieved because those organisms with features that make them less adapted for survival do not survive about other organisms in the environment that have features that are better adapted. Evolutionary epistemology applies this blind variation and selective retention model to the growth of scientific knowledge and to human thought processes in general.

The parallel between biological evolution and conceptual or we can see 'epistemic' evolution as either literal or analogical. The literal version of evolutionary epistemologic biological evolution as the main cause of the growth of knowledge stemmed from this view, called the 'evolution of cognitive mechanic programs', by Bradie (1986) and the 'Darwinian approach to epistemology' by Ruse (1986), that growth of knowledge occurs through blind variation and selective retention because biological natural selection itself is the cause of epistemic variation and selection. The most plausible version of the literal view does not hold that all human beliefs are innate but rather than the mental mechanisms that guide the acquisition of non-innate beliefs are themselves innately and the result of biological natural selection. Ruses (1986) repossess to resume of the insistence of an interlingual rendition of literal evolutionary epistemology that he links to sociology.

Determining the value upon innate ideas can take the path to consider as these have been variously defined by philosophers either as ideas consciously present to the mind priori to sense experience (the non-dispositional sense), or as ideas which we have an innate disposition to form, though we need to be actually aware of them at a particular r time, e.g., as babies-the dispositional sense. Understood in either way they were invoked to account for our recognition of certain verification, such as those of mathematics, or to justify certain moral and religious clams which were held to b capable of being know by introspection of our innate ideas. Examples of such supposed truths might include 'murder is wrong' or 'God exists'.

One difficulty with the doctrine is that it is sometimes formulated as one about concepts or ideas which are held to be innate and at other times one about a source of propositional knowledge, in so far as concepts are taken to be innate the doctrine reflates primarily to claims about meaning: Our idea of God, for example, is taken as a source for the meaning of the word God. When innate ideas are understood propositionally, their supposed innateness is taken an evidence for the truth. This latter thesis clearly rests on the assumption that innate propositions have an unimpeachable source, usually taken to be God, but then any appeal to innate ideas to justify the existence of God is circular. Despite such difficulties the doctrine of innate ideas had a long and influential history until the eighteenth century and the concept has in recent decades been revitalized through its employment in Noam Chomsky's influential account of the mind's linguistic capacities.

The attraction of the theory has been felt strongly by those philosophers who have been unable to give an alternative account of our capacity to recognize that some propositions are certainly true where that recognition cannot be justified solely o the basis of an appeal to sense experiences. Thus Plato argued that, for example, recognition of mathematical truths could only be explained on the assumption of some form of recollection, in Plato, the recollection of knowledge, possibly obtained in a previous stat e of existence e draws its topic as most famously broached in the dialogue "Meno," and the doctrine is one attemptive account for the 'innate' unlearned character of knowledge of first principles. Since there was no plausible post-natal source the recollection must refer of a pre-natal acquisition of knowledge. Thus understood, the doctrine of innate ideas supported the views that there were importantly gradatorially innate human beings and it was this sense which hindered their proper apprehension.

The ascetic implications of the doctrine were important in Christian philosophy throughout the Middle Ages and scholastic teaching until its displacement by Locke' philosophy in the eighteenth century. It had in the meantime acquired modern expression in the philosophy of Descartes who argued that we can come to know certain important truths before we have any empirical knowledge at all. Our idea of God must necessarily exist, is Descartes held, logically independent of sense experience. In England the Cambridge Plantonists such as Henry Moore and Ralph Cudworth added considerable support.

Locke's rejection of innate ideas and his alternative empiricist account was powerful enough to displace the doctrine from philosophy almost totally. Leibniz, in his critique of Locke, attempted to defend it with a sophisticated disposition version of theory, but it attracted few followers.

The empiricist alternative to innate ideas as an explanation of the certainty of propositions in the direction of construing with necessary truths as analytic, justly be for Kant's refinement of the classification of propositions with the fourfold analytic/synthetic distentions and deductive/inductive did nothing to encourage a return to their innate idea's doctrine, which slipped from view. The doctrine may fruitfully be understood as the genesis of confusion between explaining the genesis of ideas or concepts and the basis for regarding some propositions as necessarily true.

Chomsky's revival of the term in connection with his account of the spoken exchange acquisition has once more made the issue topical. He claims that the principles of language and 'natural logic' are known unconsciously and is a precondition for language acquisition. But for his purposes innate ideas must be taken in a strong dispositional sense-in so of its strength that it is far in the face of clear that Chomsky's claims are as in direct conflict, and make unclear in mind or purpose, as with empiricists accounts of valuation, some (including Chomsky) have supposed. Willard van Orman Quine (1808-2000), for example, sees no disaccord with his own version of empirical behaviourism, in which sees the typical of an earlier time and often replaced by something more modern or fashionable converse [in] views upon the meaning of determination. For what a thing should be, since each generation has its own standards of mutuality, least of mention, that being, the crystalline clarity under which inter-connectively combine with an extensive apprehension in the quality of being forbearing. The forestallment, least of mention, is to hold you in constraint from doing or indulging in something, as refrained from speaking out of a point at which a chance of course takes place, as an unusual, unexpected, or special interpretation or construction, that is, as an often sudden change in course or trend, the deflection of alterative modifications-to abstains or withhold as if arrested, in that to refrain in favour of the complex of especially mental and emotional qualifies that distinguish an Individual, as a man if possessed of contentious disposition. As prone too belligerent, hot-headed to wordy contention, as a contentious old chap, always ready for an argument-and, the intellection to arrive at by reasoning from evidence or from premises that we carefully identify the conscionable explication that belongs categorically of its 'sameness' encountering the conclusion that our dependence upon the premise is noticeably or observably prescribed to fix arbitrarily or authoritatively for the sake of order or to a clear understanding through specific conditions under which it may be amended, however, the pro-typical apprehensions to lead us into doing or feeling or to produce by leading our solution to this problem, e.g., this foolish answer provoked an outburst of rage.

Locke' accounts of analytic propositions was, that everything that a succinct account of analyticity should be (Locke, 1924). He distinguishes two kinds of analytic propositions, identity propositions for which 'we affirm the said term of itself', e.g., 'Roses are roses' and predicative propositions in which 'a part of the complex idea is predicated of the name of the whole', e.g., 'Roses are flowers'. Locke calls such sentences 'trifling' because a speaker who uses them 'trifling with words'. A synthetic sentence, in contrast, such as a mathematical theorem, that state of real truth and constituting an indeterminate and otherwise unidentified part of a group or whole begets together with a copious slight of conveying its instructive parallel's of real knowledge. Correspondingly, Locke distinguishes both kinds of 'necessary consequences', analytic entailments where validity depends on the literal containment of the conclusion in the premiss and synthetic entailment where it does not. John Locke (1632-1704) did not originate this concept-containment notion of analyticity. It is discussed by Arnaud and Nicole, and it is safe to say that it has been around for a very long time.

All the same, the analogical version of evolutionary epistemology, called the 'evolution of theory's program', by Bradie (1986). The 'Spenserians approach' (after the nineteenth century philosopher Herbert Spencer) by Ruse (1986), a process analogous to biological natural selection has governed the development of human knowledge, rather than by an instance of the mechanism itself. This version of evolutionary epistemology, introduced and elaborated by Donald Campbell (1974) and Karl Popper, sees the [partial] fit between theories and the world as explained by a mental process of trial and error known as epistemic natural selection.

We have usually taken both versions of evolutionary epistemology to be types of naturalized epistemology, because both take some empirical facts as a starting point for their epistemological project. The literal version of evolutionary epistemology begins by accepting evolutionary theory and a materialist approach to the mind and, from these, constructs an account of knowledge and its developments. By contrast, the analogical version does not require the truth of biological evolution: It simply draws on biological evolution as a source for the model of natural selection. For this version of evolutionary epistemology to be true, the model of natural selection need only apply to the growth of knowledge, not to the origin and development of species. Savagery put, evolutionary epistemology of the analogical sort could still be true even if creationism is the correct theory of the origin of species.

Although they do not begin by assuming evolutionary theory, most analogical evolutionary epistemologists are naturalized epistemologists as well, their empirical assumptions, least of mention, implicitly come from psychology and cognitive science, not evolutionary theory. Sometimes, however, evolutionary epistemology is characterized in a seemingly non-naturalistic fashion. (Campbell 1974) says that 'if one is expanding knowledge beyond what one knows, one has no choice but to explore without the benefit of wisdom', i.e., blindly. This, Campbell admits, makes evolutionary epistemology close to being a tautology (and so not naturalistic). Evolutionary epistemology does assert the analytic claim that when expanding one's knowledge beyond what one knows, one must precessed to something that is already known, but, more interestingly, it also makes the synthetic claim that when expanding one's knowledge beyond what one knows, one must proceed by blind variation and selective retention. This claim is synthetic because we can empirically falsify it. The central claim of evolutionary epistemology is synthetic, not analytic, but if the central contradictory of which they are not, then Campbell is right that evolutionary epistemology does have the analytic feature he mentions, but he is wrong to think that this is a distinguishing feature, since any plausible epistemology has the same analytic feature.

Two extra-ordinary issues lie to awaken the literature that involves questions about 'realism', i.e., What metaphysical commitment does an evolutionary epistemologist have to make?. (Progress, i.e., according to evolutionary epistemology, does knowledge develop toward a goal?) With respect to realism, many evolutionary epistemologists endorse that is called 'hypothetical realism', a view that combines a version of epistemological 'scepticism' and tentative acceptance of metaphysical realism. With respect to progress, the problem is that biological evolution is not goal-directed, but the growth of human knowledge is. Campbell (1974) worries about the potential dis-analogy here but is willing to bite the stone of conscience and admit that epistemic evolution progress toward a goal (truth) while biological evolution does not. Some have argued that evolutionary epistemologists must give up the 'truth-topic' sense of progress because a natural selection model is in non-teleological in essence alternatively, following Kuhn (1970), and embraced along with evolutionary epistemology.

Among the most frequent and serious criticisms leveled against evolutionary epistemology is that the analogical version of the view is false because epistemic variation is not blind are to argue that, however, that this objection fails because, while epistemic variation is not random, its constraints come from heuristics that, for the most part, are selective retention. Further, Stein and Lipton argue that lunatics are analogous to biological pre-adaptions, evolutionary pre-biological pre-adaptions, evolutionary cursors, such as a half-wing, a precursor to a wing, which have some function other than the function of their descendable structures: The function of descendability may result in the function of their descendable character embodied to its structural foundations, is that of the guideline of epistemic variation is, on this view, not the source of dis-analogy, but the source of a more articulated account of the analogy.

Many evolutionary epistemologists try to combine the literal and the analogical versions, saying that those beliefs and cognitive mechanisms, which are innate results from natural selection of the biological sort and those that are innate results from natural selection of the epistemic sort. This is reasonable as long as the two parts of this hybrid view are kept distinct. An analogical version of evolutionary epistemology with biological variation as its only source of blindness would be a null theory: This would be the case if all our beliefs are innate or if our non-innate beliefs are not the result of blind variation. An appeal to the legitimate way to produce a hybrid version of evolutionary epistemology since doing so trivializes the theory. For similar reasons, such an appeal will not save an analogical version of evolutionary epistemology from arguments to the effect that epistemic variation is blind.

Although it is a new approach to theory of knowledge, evolutionary epistemology has attracted much attention, primarily because it represents a serious attempt to flesh out a naturalized epistemology by drawing on several disciplines. In science is used for understanding the nature and development of knowledge, then evolutionary theory is among the disciplines worth a look. Insofar as evolutionary epistemology looks there, it is an interesting and potentially fruitful epistemological programed.

What makes a belief justified and what makes a true belief knowledge? Thinking that whether a belief deserves one of these appraisals is natural depends on what caused such subjectivity to have the belief. In recent decades many epistemologists have pursued this plausible idea with a variety of specific proposals. Some causal theories of knowledge have it that a true belief that 'p' is knowledge just in case it has the right causal connection to the fact that 'p'. They can apply such a criterion only to cases where the fact that 'p' is a sort that can enter inti causal relations, as this seems to exclude mathematically and other necessary facts and perhaps any fact expressed by a universal generalization, and proponents of this sort of criterion have usually supposed that it is limited to perceptual representations where knowledge of particular facts about subjects' environments.

For example, Armstrong (1973) initially proposed something which is proposed to another for consideration, as a set before the mind for consideration, as to put forth an intended purpose. That a belief to carry a one's affairs independently and self-sufficiently often under difficult circumstances progress for oneself and makes do and stand on one's own formalities in the transitional form 'This [perceived] objects is 'F' is [non-inferential] knowledge if and only if the belief is a completely reliable sign that the perceived object is 'F', that is, the fact that the object is 'F' contributed to causing the belief and its doing so depended on properties of the believer such that the laws of nature dictated that, for any subject 'χ' and perceived object 'y', if 'χ' has those properties and believed that 'y' is 'F', then 'y' is 'F'. Offers a rather similar account, in terms of the belief's being caused by a signal received by the perceiver that carries the information that the object is 'F'.

This sort of condition fails, however, to be sufficiently for non-inferential perceptivity, for knowledge is accountable for its compatibility with the belief's being unjustified, and an unjustified belief cannot be knowledge. The view that a belief acquires favorable epistemic status by having some kind of reliable linkage to the truth, seems by accountabilities that they have variations of this view which has been advanced for both knowledge and justified belief. The first formulation of a reliable account of knowing notably appeared as marked and noted and accredited to F. P. Ramsey (1903-30), whereby much of Ramsey's work was directed at saving classical mathematics from 'intuitionism', or what he called the 'Bolshevik menace of Brouwer and Weyl'. In the theory of probability he was the first to develop, based on precise behavioural nations of preference and a natural kind terminology. In the philosophy of language, Ramsey was one of the first thinkers to accept a 'redundancy theory of truth', which he combined with radical views of the function of many kinds of propositions. Neither generalizations, nor causal positions, nor those treating probability or ethics, described facts, but each has a different specific function in our intellectual economy. Additionally, Ramsey, who said that an impression of belief was knowledge if it were true, certain and obtained by a reliable process. P. Unger (1968) suggested that 'S' knows that 'p' just in case it is of at all accidental that 'S' is right about its being the case that drew an analogy between a thermometer that reliably indicates the temperature and a belief interaction of reliability that indicates the truth. Armstrong said that a non-inferential belief qualified as knowledge if the belief has properties that are nominally sufficient for its truth, i.e., guarantee its truth via laws of nature.

The standard classification associated with reliabilism as an 'externaturalist' theory bends of its causality belonging of some truth-linked factor, and truth is 'eternal' to the believer the main argument for externalism derives from the philosophy of language, more specifically, from the various phenomena pertaining to natural terminological tuition, indexical, etc., that motivate the views that have come to be known as direct reference' theories. Such phenomena seem, at least to show that the belief or thought content that can be properly attributed to a person is dependent on facts about his environment, i.e., whether he is on Earth or Twin Earth, what in fact he is pointing at, the classificatory criteria employed by the experts in his social group, etc. -. Not just on what is going on internally in his mind or brain (Putnam, 175 and Burge, 1979.) Virtually all theories of knowledge, of course, share an externalist component in requiring truth as a condition for knowing. Reliabilism goes farther, however, in trying to capture additional conditions for knowledge by means of a nomic, counterfactual or other such 'external' relations between 'belief' and 'truth'.

Since a subject many in fact are following a reliable method without being justified in supporting that she is, and vice versa. For this reason, reliabilism is sometimes called an externalist approach to knowledge, that the relation that matters to knowing something may be outside the subject's own awareness. As a belief may be the result of some generally reliable process which was in fact malfunctioning on this occasion, and we would be reluctant to attribute knowledge to the subject if this were so, although the definition would be satisfied.

The most influential counterexample to reliabilism is the demon-world and the clairvoyance examples. The demon-world example challenges the necessity of the reliability requirement, in that a possible world in which an evil demon creates deceptive visual experience, the process of vision is not reliable. Still, the visually formed beliefs in this world are intuitively justified. The clairvoyance example challenges the sufficiency of reliability. Suppose a cognitive agent possesses a reliable clairvoyance power, but has no evidence for or against his possessing such a power. Intuitively, his clairvoyantly formed beliefs are unjustifiably unreasoned, but Reliabilism declares them justified.

Another form of reliabilism-normal worlds-reliabilism, answers the range problem differently, and treats the demon-world problem in the same fashionable manner, and so permitting a 'normal world' is one that is consistent with our general beliefs about the actual world. Normal-world reliabilism, says that a belief, in any possible world is justified just in case its generating processes have a high truth ratio in normal worlds, resolving the demon-world problem, because the relevant truth ratio of the visual process is not its truth ratio in the demon world itself, nonetheless its ratio in normal worlds. Since this ratio is presumably high, visually formed beliefs in the demon world turn out to be justified.

Yet, a different version of reliabilism attempts to meet the demon-world and clairvoyance problems without recourse to the questionable notion of 'normal worlds'. Consider, as Sosa's (1992) suggestion that justified beliefs is belief acquired through 'intellectual virtues', and not through intellectual 'vices', whereby virtues are reliable cognitive faculties or processes. The task is to explain how epistemic evaluators have used the notion of indelible virtues, and vices, to arrive at their judgements, especially in the problematic cases. Goldman (1992) proposes a two-stage reconstruction of an evaluator's activity. The first stage is a reliability-based acquisition of a 'list' of virtues and vices. The second stage is application of this list to queried cases. Determining has executed the second stage whether processes in the queried cases resemble virtues or vices. We have classified visual beliefs in the demon world as justified because visual belief formation is one of the virtues. Clairvoyance formed, beliefs are classified as unjustified because clairvoyance resembles scientifically suspect processes that the evaluator represents as vices, e.g., mental telepathy, ESP, and so forth

A philosophy of meaning and truth, for which it is especially associated with the American philosopher of science and of language (1839-1914), and the American psychologist philosopher William James (1842-1910), Wherefore the study in Pragmatism is given to various formulations by both writers, but the core is the belief that the meaning of a doctrine is the same as the practical effects of adapting it. Peirce interpreted of theoretical sentences is only that of a corresponding practical maxim (telling us what to do in some circumstance). In James the position issues in a theory of truth, notoriously allowing that belief, including for examples, belief in God, are the widest sense of the works satisfactorily in the widest sense of the word. On James's view almost any belief might be respectable, and even true, but working with true beliefs is not a simple matter for James. The apparent subjectivist consequences of this were wildly assailed by Russell (1872-1970), Moore (1873-1958), and others in the early years of the 20th-century. This led to a division within pragmatism between those such as the American educator John Dewey (1859-1952), whose humanistic conception of practice remains inspired by science, and the more idealistic route that especially by the English writer F.C.S. Schiller (1864-1937), embracing the doctrine that our cognitive efforts and human needs actually transform the reality that we seek to describe. James often writes as if he sympathizes with this development. For instance, in The Meaning of Truth (1909), he considers the hypothesis that other people have no minds (dramatized in the sexist idea of an 'automatic sweetheart' or female zombie) and remarks' that the hypothesis would not work because it would not satisfy our egoistic craving for the recognition and admiration of others, these implications that make it true that the other persons have minds in the disturbing part.

Modern pragmatists such as the American philosopher and critic Richard Rorty (1931-) and some writings of the philosopher Hilary Putnam (1925-) who has usually tried to dispense with an account of truth and concentrate, as perhaps James should have done, upon the nature of belief and its relations with human attitude, emotion, and need. The driving motivation of pragmatism is the idea that belief in the truth on te one hand must have a close connection with success in action on the other. One way of cementing the connection is found in the idea that natural selection must have adapted us to be cognitive creatures because beliefs have effects, as they work. Pragmatism can be found in Kant's doctrine of the primary of practical over pure reason, and continued to play an influential role in the theory of meaning and of truth.

In case of fact, the philosophy of mind is the modern successor to behaviourism, as do the functionalism that its early advocates were Putnam (1926-) and Sellars (1912-89), and its guiding principle is that we can define mental states by a triplet of relations they have on other mental stares, what effects they have on behaviour. The definition need not take the form of a simple analysis, but if w could write down the totality of axioms, or postdate, or platitudes that govern our theories about what things of other mental states, and our theories about what things are apt to cause (for example), a belief state, what effects it would have on a variety of other mental states, and what the force of impression of one thing on another, inducing to come into being and carry to as successful conclusions as found a pass that allowed them to affect passage through the mountains. A condition or occurrence traceable to a cause drawing forth the underlying and hidden layers of deep-seated latencies. Very well protected but the digression belongs to the patient, in that, what exists of the back-burners of the mind, slowly simmering, and very much of your self control is intact, the furthering relational significance bestowed by some sorted outcry choices to be heard via the phenomenons of latent incestuousness, in its gross effect, may that be the likelihood of having an influence upon behaviour, so then all that we would have done otherwise, contains all that is needed to make the state a proper theoretical notion. It could be implicitly defied by these theses. Functionalism is often compared with descriptions of a computer, since according to mental descriptions correspond to a description of a machine in terms of software, that remains silent about the underlaying hardware or 'realization' of the program the machine is running. The principal advantage of functionalism includes its fit with the way we know of mental states both of ourselves and others, which is via their effects on behaviour and other mental states. As with behaviourism, critics charge that structurally complex items that do not bear mental states might nevertheless, imitate the functions that are cited. According to this criticism functionalism is too generous and would count too many things as having minds. It is also queried whether functionalism is too paradoxical, able to see mental similarities only when there is causal similarity, when our actual practices of interpretations enable us to support thoughts and desires too differently from our own, it may then seem as though beliefs and desires are obtained in the consenting availability of 'variably acquired' causal architecture, just as much as they can be in different neurophysiological states.

The philosophical movement of Pragmatism had a major impact on American culture from the late 19th century to the present. Pragmatism calls for ideas and theories to be tested in practice, by assessing whether acting upon the idea or theory produces desirable or undesirable results. According to pragmatists, all claims about truth, knowledge, morality, and politics must be tested in this way. Pragmatism has been critical of traditional Western philosophy, especially the notions that there are absolute truths and absolute values. Although pragmatism was popular for a time in France, England, and Italy, most observers believe that it encapsulates an American faith in know-how and practicality and an equally American misdoubt and unbelieving distrust to have no trust or confidence in a temporary with holding of action or cessesation of activities for which abstractive theories and ideological methodologies, is something taken for granted especially on trivial or inadequate grounds.

In mentioning the American psychologist and philosopher we find William James, who helped to popularize the philosophy of pragmatism with his book Pragmatism: A New Name for Old Ways of Thinking (1907). Influenced by a theory of meaning and verification developed for scientific hypotheses by American philosopher C.S. Peirce, James held that truth is what compellingly works, or has good experimental results. In a related theory, James argued the existence of God is partly verifiable because many people derive benefits from believing.

Pragmatists regard all theories and institutions as tentative hypotheses and solutions. For this reason they believed that efforts to improve society, through such means as education or politics, must be geared toward problem solving and must be ongoing. Through their emphasis on connecting theory to practice, pragmatist thinkers attempted to transform all areas of philosophy, from metaphysics to ethics and political philosophy.

Pragmatism sought a middle ground between traditional ideas about the nature of reality and radical theories of nihilism and irrationalism, which had become popular in Europe in the late 19th century. Traditional metaphysics assumed that the world has a fixed, intelligible structure and that human beings can know absolute or objective truths about the world and about what constitutes moral behaviour. Nihilism and irrationalism, on the other hand, denied those very assumptions and their certitude. Pragmatists today still try to steer a middle course between contemporary offshoots of these two extremes.

The ideas of the pragmatists were considered revolutionary when they first appeared. To some critics, pragmatism's refusal to affirm any absolutes carried negative implications for society. For example, pragmatists do not believe that a single absolute idea of goodness or justice exists, but rather than these concepts are changeable and depend on the context in which they are being discussed. The absence of these absolutes, critics feared, could result in a decline in moral standards. The pragmatists' denial of absolutes, moreover, challenged the foundations of religion, government, and schools of thought. As a result, pragmatism influenced developments in psychology, sociology, education, semiotics (the study of signs and symbols), and scientific method, as well as philosophy, cultural criticism, and social reform movements. Various political groups have also drawn on the assumptions of pragmatism, from the progressive movements of the early 20th century to later experiments in social reform.

Pragmatism is best understood in its historical and cultural context. It arose during the late 19th century, a period of rapid scientific advancement typified by the theories of British biologist Charles Darwin, whose theories suggested too many thinkers that humanity and society are in a perpetual state of progress. During this same period a decline in traditional religious beliefs and values accompanied the industrialization and material progress of the time. In consequence it became necessary to rethink fundamental ideas about values, religion, science, community, and individuality.

The three most important pragmatists are American philosophers' Charles Sanders Peirce, William James, and John Dewey. Peirce was primarily interested in scientific method and mathematics; His objective was to infuse scientific thinking into philosophy and society, and he believed that human comprehension of reality was becoming ever greater and that human communities were becoming increasingly progressive. Peirce developed pragmatism as a theory of meaning-in particular, the meaning of concepts used in science. The meaning of the concept 'brittle', for example, is given by the observed consequences or properties that objects called 'brittle' exhibit. For Peirce, the only rational way to increase knowledge was to form mental habits that would test ideas through observation, experimentation, or what he called inquiry. Many philosophers known as logical positivist, a group of philosophers who have been influenced by Peirce, believed that our evolving species was fated to get ever closer to Truth. Logical positivists emphasize the importance of scientific verification, rejecting the assertion of positivism that personal experience is the basis of true knowledge.

James moved pragmatism in directions that Peirce strongly disliked. He generalized Peirce's doctrines to encompass all concepts, beliefs, and actions; he also applied pragmatist ideas to truth as well as to meaning. James was primarily interested in showing how systems of morality, religion, and faith could be defended in a scientific civilization. He argued that sentiment, as well as logic, is crucial to rationality and that the great issues of life-morality and religious belief, for example-are leaps of faith. As such, they depend upon what he called 'the will to believe' and not merely on scientific evidence, which can never tell us what to do or what is worthwhile. Critics charged James with relativism (the belief that values depend on specific situations) and with crass expediency for proposing that if an idea or action works the way one intends, it must be right. But James can more accurately be described as a pluralist-someone who believes the world to be far too complex for one particular philosophy to explain everything.

Dewey's philosophy can be described as a version of philosophical naturalism, which regards human experience, intelligence, and communities as ever-evolving mechanisms. Using their experience and intelligence, Dewey believed, human beings can solve problems, including social problems, through inquiry. For Dewey, naturalism led to the idea of a democratic society that allows all members to acquire social intelligence and progress both as individuals and as communities. Dewey held that traditional ideas about knowledge, truth, and values, in which absolutes are assumed, are incompatible with a broadly Darwinian world-view in which individuals and societies are progressing. In consequence, he felt that these traditional ideas must be discarded or revised. Indeed, for pragmatists, everything people know and do depend on a historical context and are thus tentative rather than absolute.

Many followers and critics of Dewey believe he advocated elitism and social engineering in his philosophical stance. Others think of him as a kind of romantic humanist. Both tendencies are evident in Dewey's writings, although he aspired to synthesize the two realms.

The pragmatists' tradition was revitalized in the 1980s by American philosopher Richard Rorty, who has faced similar charges of elitism for his belief in the relativism of values and his emphasis on the role of the individual in attaining knowledge. Interest has renewed in the classic pragmatists-Pierce, James, and Dewey-have an alternative to Rorty's interpretation of the tradition.

One of the earliest versions of a correspondence theory was put forward in the 4th century Bc Greek philosopher Plato, who sought to understand the meaning of knowledge and how it is acquired. Plato wished to distinguish between true belief and false belief. He proposed a theory based on intuitive recognition that true statements correspond to the facts-that is, agree with reality-while false statements do not. In Plato's example, the sentence "Theaetetus flies" can be true only if the world contains the fact that Theaetetus flies. However, Plato-and much later, 20th-century British philosopher Bertrand Russell-recognized this theory as unsatisfactory because it did not allow for false belief. Both Plato and Russell reasoned that if a belief is false because there is no fact to which it corresponds, it would then be a belief about nothing and so not a belief at all. Each then speculated that the grammar of a sentence could offer a way around this problem. A sentence can be about something (the person Theaetetus), yet false (flying is not true of Theaetetus). But how, they asked, are the parts of a sentence related to reality?

One suggestion, proposed by 20th-century philosopher Ludwig Wittgenstein, is that the parts of a sentence relate to the objects they describe in much the same way that the parts of a picture relate to the objects pictured. Once again, however, false sentences pose a problem: If a false sentence pictures nothing, there can be no meaning in the sentence.

In the late 19th-century American philosopher Charles S. Peirce offered another answer to the question "What is truth?" He asserted that truth is that which experts will agree upon when their investigations are final. Many pragmatists such as Peirce claim that the truth of our ideas must be tested through practice. Some pragmatists have gone so far as to question the usefulness of the idea of truth, arguing that in evaluating our beliefs we should rather pay attention to the consequences that our beliefs may have. However, critics of the pragmatic theory are concerned that we would have no knowledge because we do not know which set of beliefs will ultimately be agreed upon; nor are their sets of beliefs that are useful in every context.

A third theory of truth, the coherence theory, also concerns the meaning of knowledge. Coherence theorists have claimed that a set of beliefs is true if the beliefs are comprehensive-that is, they cover everything-and do not contradict each other.

Other philosophers dismiss the question "What is truth?" With the observation that attaching the claim 'it is true that' to a sentence adds no meaning, however, these theorists, who have proposed what are known as deflationary theories of truth, do not dismiss such talk about truth as useless. They agree that there are contexts in which a sentence such as 'it is true that the book is blue' can have a different impact than the shorter statement 'the book is blue'. What is more important, use of the word true is essential when making a general claim about everything, nothing, or something, as in the statement 'most of what he says is true?'

Many experts believe that philosophy as an intellectual discipline originated with the work of Plato, one of the most celebrated philosophers in history. The Greek thinker had an immeasurable influence on Western thought. However, Plato's expression of ideas in the form of dialogues—the dialectical method, used most famously by his teacher Socrates-has led to difficulties in interpreting some of the finer points of his thoughts. The issue of what exactly Plato meant to say is addressed in the following excerpt by author R. M. Hare.

Linguistic analysis as a method of philosophy is as old as the Greeks. Several of the dialogues of Plato, for example, are specifically concerned with clarifying terms and concepts. Nevertheless, this style of philosophizing has received dramatically renewed emphasis in the 20th century. Influenced by the earlier British empirical tradition of John Locke, George Berkeley, David Hume, and John Stuart Mill and by the writings of the German mathematician and philosopher Gottlob Frége, the 20th-century English philosopher's G. E. Moore and Bertrand Russell became the founders of this contemporary analytic and linguistic trend. As students together at the University of Cambridge, Moore and Russell rejected Hegelian idealism, particularly as it was reflected in the work of the English metaphysician F. H. Bradley, who held that nothing is completely real except the Absolute. In their opposition to idealism and in their commitment to the view that careful attention to language is crucial in philosophical inquiry, and they set the mood and style of philosophizing for much of the 20th century English-speaking world.

For Moore, philosophy was first and foremost analysis. The philosophical task involves clarifying puzzling propositions or concepts by indicating fewer puzzling propositions or concepts to which the originals are held to be logically equivalent. Once this task has been completed, the truth or falsity of problematic philosophical assertions can be determined more adequately. Moore was noted for his careful analyses of such puzzling philosophical claims as 'time is unreal', analyses that aided of determining the truth of such assertions.

Russell, strongly influenced by the precision of mathematics, was concerned with developing an ideal logical language that would accurately reflect the nature of the world. Complex propositions, Russell maintained, can be resolved into their simplest components, which he called atomic propositions. These propositions refer to atomic facts, the ultimate constituents of the universe. The metaphysical view based on this logical analysis of language and the insistence that meaningful propositions must correspond to facts constitutes what Russell called logical atomism. His interest in the structure of language also led him to distinguish between the grammatical form of a proposition and its logical form. The statements 'John is good' and 'John is tall' have the same grammatical form but different logical forms. Failure to recognize this would lead one to treat the property 'goodness' as if it were a characteristic of John in the same way that the property 'tallness' is a characteristic of John. Such failure results in philosophical confusion.

Austrian-born philosopher Ludwig Wittgenstein was one of the most influential thinkers of the 20th century. With his fundamental work, Tractatus Logico-philosophicus, published in 1921, he became a central figure in the movement known as analytic and linguistic philosophy.

Russell's work of mathematics attracted an intensive reality for which studying was a primary notion that began a remedial intermittence at Cambridge and the Austrian philosopher Ludwig Wittgenstein, who became a central figure in the analytic and linguistic movement. In his first major work, "Tractatus Logico-philosophicus," 1921, translated in 1922, in which he first presented his theory of language, Wittgenstein argued that 'all philosophy is a 'critique of language' and that 'philosophy aims at the logical clarification of thoughts'. The results of Wittgenstein's analysis resembled Russell's logical atomism. The world, he argued, is ultimately composed of simple facts, which it is the purpose of language to picture. To be meaningful, statements about the world must be reducible to linguistic utterances that have a structure similar to the simple facts pictured. In this early Wittgensteinian analysis, only propositions that picture facts-the propositions of science-are considered factually meaningful. Metaphysical, theological, and ethical sentences were judged to be factually meaningless.

Influenced by Russell, Wittgenstein, Ernst Mach, and others, a group of philosophers and mathematicians in Vienna in the 1920s initiated the movement known as logical positivism: Led by Moritz Schlick and Rudolf Carnap, the Vienna Circle initiated one of the most important chapters in the history of analytic and linguistic philosophy.

According to the positivists, the task of philosophy is the clarification of meaning, not the discovery of new facts (the job of the scientists) or the construction of comprehensive accounts of reality (the misguided pursuit of traditional metaphysics).

The positivists divided all meaningful assertions into two classes: analytic propositions and empirically verifiable ones. Analytic propositions, which include the propositions of logic and mathematics, are statements the truth or falsity of which depend simultaneously on the meaning of the terms constituting the statement. An example would be the proposition 'two plus two equals four'. The second class of meaningful propositions includes all statements about the world that can be verified, at least in principle, by sense experience. Indeed, the meaning of such propositions is identified with the empirical method of their verification. This verifiability theory of meaning, the positivists concluded, would demonstrate that scientific statements are legitimate factual claims and that metaphysical, religious, and ethical sentences are factually dwindling. The ideas of logical positivism were made popular in England by the publication of A. J. Ayer's Language, Truth and Logic in 1936.

The positivists' verifiability theory of meaning came under intense criticism by philosophers such as the Austrian-born British philosopher Karl Popper. Eventually this narrow theory of meaning yielded to a broader understanding of the nature of language. Again, an influential figure was Wittgenstein. Repudiating many of his earlier conclusions in the Tractatus, he initiated a new line of thought culminating in his posthumously published Philosophical Investigations (1953, translated 1953). In this work, Wittgenstein argued that once attention is directed to the way language is actually used in ordinary discourse, the variety and flexibility of language become clear. Propositions do much more than simply picture facts.

This recognition led to Wittgenstein's influential concept of language games. The scientist, the poet, and the theologian, for example, are involved in different language games. Moreover, the meaning of a proposition must be understood in its context, that is, in terms of the rules of the language game of which that proposition is a part. Philosophy, concluded Wittgenstein, is an attempt to resolve problems that arise as the result of linguistic confusion, and the key to the resolution of such problems is ordinary language analysis and the proper use of language.

Additional contributions within the analytic and linguistic movement include the work of the British philosopher's Gilbert Ryle, John Austin, and P. F. Strawson and the American philosopher W. V. Quine. According to Ryle, the task of philosophy is to restate 'systematically misleading expressions' in forms that are logically more accurate.

He was particularly concerned with statements the grammatical form of which suggests the existence of nonexistent objects. For example, Ryle is best known for his analysis of mentalistic language, language that misleadingly suggests that the mind is an entity in the same way as the body.

Austin maintained that one of the most fruitful starting points for philosophical inquiry is attention to the extremely fine distinctions drawn in ordinary language. His analysis of language eventually led to a general theory of speech acts, that is, to a description of the variety of activities that an individual may be performing when something is uttered.

Strawson is known for his analysis of the relationship between formal logic and ordinary language. The complexity of the latter, he argued, is inadequately represented by formal logic. A variety of analytic tools, therefore, are needed in addition to logic in analyzing ordinary language.

Quine discussed the relationship between language and ontology. He argued that language systems tend to commit their users to the existence of certain things. For Quine, the justification for speaking one way rather than another is a thoroughly pragmatic one.

The commitment to language analysis as a way of pursuing philosophy has continued as a significant contemporary dimension in philosophy. A division also continues to exist between those who prefer to work with the precision and rigor of symbolic logical systems and those who prefer to analysed ordinary language. Although few contemporary philosophers maintain that all philosophical problems are linguistic, the view continues to be widely held that attention to the logical structure of language and to how language is used in everyday discourse can many a time have an eye to aid in anatomize Philosophical problems.

A loose title for various philosophies that emphasize certain common themes, the individual, the experience of choice, and the absence of rational understanding of the universe, with the additional ways of addition seems a consternation of dismay or one fear, or the other extreme, as far apart is the sense of the dottiness of 'absurdity in human life', however, existentialism is a philosophical movement or tendency, emphasizing individual existence, freedom, and choice, that influenced many diverse writers in the 19th and 20th centuries.

Because of the diversity of positions associated with existentialism, the term is impossible to define precisely. Certain themes common to virtually all existentialist writers can, however, be identified. The term itself suggests one major theme: the stress on concrete individual existence and, consequently, on subjectivity, individual freedom, and choice.

Most philosophers since Plato have held that the highest ethical good are the same for everyone; Insofar as one approaches moral perfection, one resembles other morally perfect individuals. The 19th-century Danish philosopher Søren Kierkegaard, who was the first writer to call himself existential, reacted against this tradition by insisting that the highest good for the individual are to find his or her own unique vocation. As he wrote in his journal, 'I must find a truth that is true for me . . . the idea for which I can live or die'. Other existentialist writers have echoed Kierkegaard's belief that one must choose one's own way without the aid of universal, objective standards. Against the traditional view that moral choice involves an objective judgment of right and wrong, Existentialists have argued that no objective, rational basis can be found for moral decisions. The 19th-century German philosopher Friedrich Nietzsche further contended that the individual must decide which situations are to count as moral situations.

All Existentialists have followed Kierkegaard in stressing the importance of passionate individual action in deciding questions of both morality and truth. They have insisted, accordingly, that personal experience and acting on one's own convictions are essential in arriving at the truth. Thus, the understanding of a situation by someone involved in that situation is superior to that of a detached, objective observer. This emphasis on the perspective of the individual agent has also made Existentialists suspicious of systematic reasoning. Kierkegaard, Nietzsche, and other existentialist writers have been deliberately unsystematic in the exposition of their philosophies, preferring to express themselves in aphorisms, dialogues, parables, and other literary forms. Despite their anti-rationalist position, however, most existentialists cannot be said to be irrationalists in the sense of denying all validity to rational thought. They have held that rational clarity is desirable wherever possible, but that the most important questions in life are not accessible for any analysis by reason or science. Furthermore, they have argued that even science is not as rational as is commonly supposed. Nietzsche, for instance, asserted that the scientific supposition of an orderly universe may as much as be a part of useful fiction.

Perhaps the most prominent theme in existentialist writing is that of choice. Humanity's primary distinction, in the view of most existentialists, is the freedom to choose. Existentialists have held that human beings do not have a fixed nature, or essence, as other animals and plants do; each human being makes choices that create his or her own nature. In the formulation of the 20th-century French philosopher Jean-Paul Sartre, existence precedes essence. Choice is therefore central to human existence, and it is inescapable; equally a part in the refusal to choose is the choice. Freedom of choice entails commitment and responsibility. Because individuals are free to choose their own path, existentialists have argued, they must accept the risk and responsibility of following their commitment wherever it leads.

Kierkegaard held that it is spiritually crucial to recognize that one experience not only a fear of specific objects but also a feeling of general apprehension, which he called dread. He interpreted it as God's way of calling each individual to make a commitment to a personally valid way of life. The word anxiety (German Angst) has a similarly crucial role in the work of the 20th-century German philosopher Martin Heidegger; Anxiety leads to the individual's confrontation with nothingness and with the impossibility of finding ultimate justification for the choices he or she must make. In the philosophy of Sartre, the word nausea is used for the individual's recognition of the pure contingency of the universe, and the word anguish is used for the recognition of the total freedom of choice that confronts the individual at every moment.

Existentialism as a distinct philosophical and literary movement belongs to the 19th and 20th centuries, but elements of existentialism can be found in the thought (and life) of Socrates, in the Bible, and in the work of many pre-modern philosophers having taken place, existed or developed in times close to the present as these modernized concepts are, for example, the modern concept of engineering made the bridge possible, however, to modify as to avoid an extreme or keep within bounds of somewhat an immoderation of quantified limitations.

The first to anticipate the major concerns of modern existentialism was the 17th-century French philosopher Blaise Pascal. Pascal rejected the rigorous rationalism of his contemporary René Descartes, asserting, in his Pensées (1670), that a systematic philosophy that presumes to explain God and humanity is a form of pride. Like later existentialist writers, he saw human life in terms of paradoxes: The human self, which combines mind and body, is itself a paradox and contradiction.

Kierkegaard, generally regarded as the founder of modern existentialism, reacted against the systematic absolute idealism of the 19th-century German philosopher Georg Wilhelm Friedrich Hegel, who claimed to have worked out a total rational understanding of humanity and history. Kierkegaard, on the contrary, stressed the ambiguity and absurdity of the human situation. The individual's response to this situation must be to live a totally committed life, and this commitment can only be understood by the individual who has made it. The individual therefore must always be prepared to defy the norms of society for the sake of the higher authority of a personally valid way of life. Kierkegaard ultimately advocated a 'leap of faith' into a Christian way of life, which, although incomprehensible and full of risk, was the only commitment he believed could save the individual from despair.

Printed in the United States
By Bookmasters